South America

PANAMA

Maracaibo

Caracas

TRINIDAD

Medellín

VENEZUELA

Georgetown
Paramaribo

GUYANA

Cayenne

Bogotá
(Santa Fé)

GUIANA HIGHLANDS

SURINAME

French
Guiana

Cali

COLOMBIA

Orinoco

Branco

Marajó I.

Quito

ECUADOR

Negro

Japur

Belém

uayaquil

Marañón

Juruá

Manaus

Amazon

Fortaleza

Ucayali

Purus

Madeira

Tapajós

Xingu

São Francisco

Recife
(Pernambuco)

Lima

PERU

A
N
D
E
S

BOLIVIA

Tocantins

B R A Z I L

Salvador
(Bahia)

La Paz

Brasília

Sucre

BRAZILIAN HIGHLANDS

Belo Horizonte

PARAGUAY

Paraguay

Paraná

São Paulo

Rio de Janeiro

Asunción

Pacific

Paraná

Pôrto Alegre

Ocean

Córdoba

Uruguay

Valparaíso

Rosario

URUGUAY

Santiago

Buenos Aires

Montevideo

Atlantic

Concepción

ARGENTINA

Ocean

Bahía Blanca

**FOR REFERENCE
ONLY**

P
A
T
A
G
O
N
I
A

Falkland Islands
(Islas Malvinas)

Punta Arenas

Tierra del Fuego

500 miles

805 kilometers

ENCYCLOPEDIA OF

LATIN AMERICAN HISTORY AND CULTURE

ADVISORY BOARD

ENCYCLOPEDIA OF

LATIN AMERICAN HISTORY AND CULTURE

BARBARA A. TENENBAUM

EDITOR IN CHIEF

Georgette Magassy Dorn
Mary Karasch
John Jay TePaske
Ralph Lee Woodward, Jr.
ASSOCIATE EDITORS

VOLUME 5

Charles Scribner's Sons

MACMILLAN LIBRARY REFERENCE USA

SIMON & SCHUSTER MACMILLAN

NEW YORK

SIMON & SCHUSTER AND PRENTICE HALL INTERNATIONAL

LONDON   MEXICO CITY   NEW DELHI   SINGAPORE   SYDNEY   TORONTO

Copyright © 1996 Charles Scribner's Sons

An imprint of Simon & Schuster Macmillan
866 Third Ave.
New York, NY 10022

Library of Congress Cataloging-in-Publication Data

Encyclopedia of Latin American history and culture / Barbara A.
    Tenenbaum, editor in chief ; associate editors, Georgette M. Dorn
    . . . [et al.].
        p.   cm.
        Includes bibliographical references and index.
        ISBN 0-684-19253-5 (set : alk. paper). — ISBN 0-684-19752-9 (v. 1
    : alk. paper). — ISBN 0-684-19753-7 (v. 2 : alk. paper). — ISBN
    0-684-19754-5 (v. 3 : alk. paper). — ISBN 0-684-19755-3 (v. 4 :
    alk. paper). — ISBN 0-684-80480-8 (v. 5 : alk. paper).
        1. Latin America—Encyclopedias.   I. Tenenbaum, Barbara A.
    F1406.E53   1996   95–31042
    980'.003—dc20   CIP

            5   7   9   11   13   15   17   19   V/C   20   18   16   14   12   10   8   6
                        PRINTED IN THE UNITED STATES OF AMERICA

The paper used in this publication meets the minimum requirements of American National Standard for Information Sciences—Permanence of Paper for Printed Library Materials. ANSI Z3948-1984.

USING THE ENCYCLOPEDIA

This encyclopedia contains nearly 5,300 separate articles. Most topics appear in English alphabetical order, according to the word-by-word system (e.g., Casa Rosada before Casals). Persons and places generally precede things (Roosevelt, Theodore, before Roosevelt Corollary). Certain subjects are clustered together in composite entries, which may comprise several regions, periods, or genres. For example, the "Slavery" and "Mining" entries contain separate articles for Brazil and Spanish America. "Art" embraces separately signed essays on pre-Columbian, colonial, nineteenth-century, and modern art, as well as folk art.

NATIONAL TOPICS are frequently clustered by country, under one or more of the following subheadings:

> *Constitutions*
> *Organizations* (administrative, cultural, economic, labor, etc.)
> *Political Parties* (listed under the English name and including former revolutionary movements that have entered the political system)
> *Revolutionary Movements*
> *Revolutions*

Note that an event with a distinctive name will be found under that term, whereas a generic name will appear under the appropriate country. Thus, the Chibata Revolt appears under *C* and the Pastry War under *P*, but the Revolution of 1964 appears under "Brazil: Revolutions."

MEASUREMENTS appear in the English system according to United States usage. Following are approximate metric equivalents for the most common units:

> 1 foot = 30 centimeters
> 1 mile = 1.6 kilometers
> 1 acre = 0.4 hectares
> 1 square mile = 2.6 square kilometers
> 1 pound = 0.45 kilograms
> 1 gallon = 3.8 liters

BIOGRAPHICAL ENTRIES (numbering nearly 3,000) are listed separately in an appendix in volume 5, where a rough classification is offered according to sex and field(s) of activity.

CROSS-REFERENCES appear in two forms: SMALL CAPITALS in the text highlight significant persons, concepts, and institutions that are treated in their own entries in the encyclopedia. *See also* references at the end of an entry call attention to articles of more general relevance. Cross-referencing is selective: obvious sources of information (such as most country, state, and city entries) are not highlighted. For full cross-referencing consult the index in volume 5.

ENCYCLOPEDIA OF

LATIN
AMERICAN
HISTORY
AND CULTURE

S

SÁ, ESTÁCIO DE (*b.* ca. 1520; *d.* 20 February 1567), nephew of Mem de Sá, Brazil's third governor-general, who had initially expelled French intruders from Guanabara Bay. In January 1565, Estácio sailed from Bahia de Todos os Santos to Guanabara Bay, where he found that the French had returned and were too strongly entrenched to be dislodged by his forces. Accordingly, he withdrew to Santos to await reinforcements. Upon his return to Guanabara Bay in March 1565, he founded a fortified outpost near the base of Sugar Loaf Hill, the nucleus of the future city of Rio de Janeiro. A year later Sá was wounded while leading his forces on Glória Hill. He died of his wounds just as Mem de Sá was refounding the city on Castle Hill, opposite the island of Villegaignon.

LUIS NORTON, *A dinastia dos Sás no Brasil* (1953); HERBERT EWALDO WETZEL, *Mem de Sá: Terceiro governador geral (1557–1572)* (1972).

DAURIL ALDEN

SÁ, MEM DE (*b. ca.* 1500; *d.* 1572), Brazilian high magistrate. Nominated third governor-general of Brazil, he arrived in Salvador, Bahia, on 28 December 1557. During his administration he fought the usury of merchants who sold SLAVES on credit with a gain of 100 percent a year, controlled the excessive enslavement of the Indians by the Portuguese colonists, and expanded the number of JESUIT *aldeias* (villages) from two or three to around eleven. Mem de Sá helped the chief-captain of Espirito Santo, Vasco Fernandes Coutinho, and the settlers of the captaincy of São Vicente in wars with the Indians. He attacked the French of the so-called ANTARCTIC FRANCE who had built the Coligny fort on an island in Rio de Janeiro Bay. The fortress was taken in 1560, but the French took shelter in some Indian villages around the bay. As Sá lacked men to occupy the fort, it was abandoned, and a second attack on the French survivors was led by Sá's nephew, Estácio de Sá (ca. 1526–1567), who established a military base at the foot of Sugarloaf Mountain in 1565. The primitive settlement was transferred to its current site in 1567 by Mem de Sá, who, in a letter to the king, considered himself the true founder of Rio de Janeiro. In 1569 he asked to be replaced as governor-general; he died in Salvador.

HERBERT EWALDO WETZEL, *Mem de Sá: Terceiro governador geral, 1557–1572* (1972); FRANCISCO ADOLFO DE VARNHAGEN, *História geral do Brasil*, 9th ed. (1975).

MARIA BEATRIZ NIZZA DA SILVA

SÁ E BENAVIDES, SALVADOR CORREIA DE (*b.* 1602; *d.* 1 January 1681), one of the most important figures in the seventeenth-century Portuguese South Atlantic Empire. Born in Cádiz, Spain, Salvador Correia de Sá e Benavides was the son of Martim de Sá, governor of Rio de Janeiro in 1602–1608 and 1623–1632.

In 1615 Salvador sailed with his father to Brazil for the first time. Back in the Iberian Peninsula by early 1618, he was again in Brazil with his father by the end of the year, searching for minerals in Bahia and Rio de Janeiro. Salvador returned to Portugal about 1623 and sailed to Brazil for the third time in 1624 to help defend it against the Dutch in Espírito Santo and Bahia.

Sá returned to Europe and in 1627 received the title of Admiral of the Southern Coast and Rio de la Plata. He was back in Rio de Janeiro by 1628. In the early 1630s, Sá pacified Payaguá and Guaicurú Indians in the Paraguayan Chaco and Calchaquis Indians in Tucumán Province in Argentina. Sá returned to Portugal and in 1637 was appointed governor and *capitão-mor* of Rio de Janeiro, where he fought attempts by the colonists to expel the JESUITS. Two years later he succeeded his grandfather as administrator of the mines of São Paulo and Santos. Sá returned to Portugal in 1643 and the next year was appointed to the OVERSEAS COUNCIL. In 1645 he began leading convoys to and from Portuguese America.

Named governor and captain-general of ANGOLA in 1647, Sá was given the task of driving the Dutch from that captaincy. In November 1647 Sá sailed from Lisbon. After picking up additional men and supplies in Rio de Janeiro, he arrived off the coast of Angola in July 1648. Dutch authorities in Luanda surrendered to him on 21 August 1648 and Benguela fell soon after. To contemporaries, his successes in Angola were Sá's greatest achievements.

In 1652 Sá left Luanda for Brazil but soon returned to Portugal. He was put in charge of the defense of the port of Lisbon in 1654. In September 1658 he was named governor and captain general of the Repartição do Sul–Rio de Janeiro and the captaincies to the south plus Espírito Santo to the north. Sá put down a revolt in 1661 but was relieved of his governorship in 1662 for his harshness in doing so. Returning to Portugal, Sá fell in and out of favor with the crown between 1663 and 1669, until he finally was restored to the good graces of the court in the latter year.

The best biography to date in any language is CHARLES R. BOXER, *Salvador de Sá and the Struggle for Brazil and Angola, 1602–1686* (1952). Also useful are LUIS FERRAND DE ALMEIDA, ''A data da morte de Salvador Correia de Sá,'' in *Revista Portuguesa de História* 8 (1959): 327–330; CHARLES R. BOXER, *Dicionário de História de Portugal*, vol. 3 (n.d.), pp. 702–703; MANOEL CARDOZO, ''Notes for a Biography of Salvador Correia de Sá e Benavides, 1594–1688,'' in *The Americas* 7, no. 2 (1950): 135–170. Three useful Portuguese accounts, the latter two of which include a number of documents on Sá's life and career, are CLADO RIBEIRO DE LESSA, *Salvador Correia de Sá e Benavides: Vida e feitos, principalmente no Brasil* (1940); BERTHA LEITE, ''Salvador de Sá e Benavides,'' in *Anais do IV Congresso de História Nacio-*

nal, 1949, vol. 12 (1951), pp. 261–559; LUIS NORTON, *A dinastia dos Sás no Brasil, 1558–1662*, 2d ed. (1965).

FRANCIS A. DUTRA

See also **Explorers.**

SAAVEDRA, CORNELIO DE (*b.* 15 September 1759; *d.* 29 March 1829), landowner and merchant who played a leading role in the first phase of Argentine independence. Born in Potosí of creole parents, Saavedra moved with his family to Buenos Aires, where he was educated at the Real Colegio de San Carlos. Alongside his merchant career he gained experience in public office, serving on the CABILDO and as grain administrator during the last decade of Spanish rule. He also demonstrated military leadership when he organized a creole militia unit, the Patricios, and commanded them in action against the British invaders in 1807. From his military power base Saavedra intervened decisively in the events of May 1810, voted for a change of government, and became president of the patriotic JUNTA which prepared the way for full independence. Saavedra led the conservative wing of the movement, favoring gradual change and representation of the provinces, against Mariano MORENO and the radical reformists who wanted to im-

Cornelio de Saavedra. ARCHIVO GENERAL DE LA NACIÓN, BUENOS AIRES.

pose instant revolution and sought a unified as well as an independent Argentina.

The conservatives ousted the radicals in April 1811 but were themselves weakened by internal opposition and military defeat in Upper Peru. Saavedra went personally to reorganize the Army of the North, but while absent from Buenos Aires (September 1811) he was ousted from government and deprived of his army command. He then suffered political persecution and periods of exile, until in 1818 the national Congress cleared his name and the Supreme Director, Juan Martín de PUEYRREDÓN, restored his military rank and appointed him chief of staff. He spent the year of anarchy (1820) in Montevideo but returned to Buenos Aires during the government of Martín Rodríguez. He retired to private life and died in Buenos Aires.

ENRIQUE RUÍZ GUIÑAZÚ, *El Presidente Saavedra y el pueblo soberano de 1810* (1960); JOHN LYNCH, *The Spanish American Revolutions 1808–1826*, 2d ed. (1986).

JOHN LYNCH

SAAVEDRA LAMAS, CARLOS (*b.* 1 November 1878; *d.* 5 May 1959), statesman and Nobel Prize–winning Argentine diplomat. Born in Buenos Aires, Saavedra Lamas received a law degree from the University of Buenos Aires in 1903. He began his career as a professor, but he turned to politics in 1912. As a national deputy he authored the tariff law that protected Argentina's SUGAR INDUSTRY in Salta Province. In 1915, he served as President Victorino de la Plaza's (1914–1916) minister of the interior and as minister of justice and public instruction.

It was as a member of the CONCORDANCIA that he achieved international prominence. Between 1932 and 1938 he served under President Agustín P. JUSTO (1932–1938) as minister of foreign affairs. Conservative and nationalistic, he represented Argentina at numerous international conferences. In particular, he challenged efforts to establish the hegemony of the United States in hemispheric affairs. He was instrumental in obtaining Latin American support for the Anti-War Pact (1933). His efforts to find a negotiated settlement to the CHACO WAR (1932–1935) between Bolivia and Paraguay earned him the Nobel Peace Prize in 1936. Although he remained active in national affairs, Saavedra Lamas retired from public service after 1938. He returned to teaching and became the rector of the University of Buenos Aires in 1941.

HAROLD F. PETERSON, *Argentina and the United States, 1810–1960* (1964); ALBERTO A. CONIL PAZ and GUSTAVO FERRARI, *Argentina's Foreign Policy, 1930–1962* (1966).

DANIEL LEWIS

SAAVEDRA MALLEA, BAUTISTA (*b.* 30 August 1870; *d.* 1 March 1939), president of Bolivia (January 1921–September 1925). Born in Sorata, La Paz Province,

Saavedra was a lawyer, journalist, and author. Following a peaceful palace revolt that ended several decades of government by the Liberal Party and installed the Republican Party, which appealed more to the literate, lower middle class, Saavedra became head of a governing junta in July 1920. In January 1921 he was elected president. He is considered one of the strongest civilian presidents of Bolivia, having captured the leadership of his party from the venerable Daniel SALAMANCA.

Although Saavedra's presidency was stormy, it also boasted solid achievements, including the first social and labor legislation and construction of direct rail links to Argentina. Saavedra left office in September 1925, turning it over to the president of the Senate, Felipe Segundo Guzmán. A year later, annoyed at postelection statements by the president-elect, Gabino Villanueva, Saavedra had the election annulled on a technicality and imposed Hernando Siles Reyes as his successor in the presidency. Saavedra died in Santiago, Chile.

PORFIRIO DÍAZ MACHICAO, *Saavedra, 1920–1925* (1954).

CHARLES W. ARNADE

See also **Bolivia: Political Parties.**

SABAT ERCASTY, CARLOS (*b.* 1887; *d.* 1982), Uruguayan poet, literary critic, and educator. Before teaching literature and mathematics in Montevideo and serving as administrator of the Young Women's Teachers College, he worked as a reporter for *El Día* and *La Razón*, both in Montevideo. Sabat Ercasty's prolific poetic production includes more than forty published collections. Early verses—such as the eight volumes of *Poemas del hombre* (1921–1958)—were characterized by Wagnerian thematic shifts from sensuality to mysticism, with traces of pantheistic musings. Later poetry, dramatic and fluid, treated philosophical issues and Oriental myths; at times a sense of abstract and conceptual stoicism predominated.

Works by Sabat Ercasty that were inspired by historical themes include *El charrúa* (1957) and *Himno a Artigas e Himno de mayo* (1964). His major works of poetry are *Sonetos de las agonías y los extásis* (1977), *Parábolas* (1978), *Cánticos a Euridice* (2 vols., 1978–1980), and *Antología* (2 vols., 1982). His major works of literary criticism are *Retratos del fuego: José Zorrilla de San Martín* (1958), *Retratos del fuego: Carlos Vaz Ferreira* (1958), and *Retratos del fuego: María Eugenia Vaz Ferreira* (1953).

SARAH BOLLO, *Literatura uruguaya, 1807–1965*, vol. 2 (1965); GARY LEWIS HAWS, *El Prometeo uruguayo: Carlos Sabat Ercasty* (1968); ISABEL SESTO GILARDONI, *Memoria y sed de Dios en la poesía de Carlos Sabat Ercasty* (1983).

WILLIAM H. KATRA

SÁBATO, ERNESTO (*b.* 24 June 1911), Argentine novelist, essayist, and thinker. The years during which Sábato studied at the University of La Plata, where he received a Ph.D. in physics, were crucial in the political life of Argentina. Since he felt great concern for the social problems of his country, Sábato embraced communism for five years, and as a spokesman for the party he suffered personal persecution. In 1934 he traveled secretly to Europe as a representative of the Argentine Communist Youth Organization to attend an antifascist congress in Brussels. However, after suffering a spiritual and ideological crisis, he severed his relationship with the party, refusing a trip to Moscow for indoctrination. In 1938, on a fellowship at the Joliot-Curie Laboratory in Paris, he became acquainted with the surrealists and began writing. This was a turning point in his life since, at that moment, Sábato understood his deeply felt interest in and aptitude for literature.

After a stay at MIT (1939), he taught at the University of La Plata and in Buenos Aires, and contributed to the newspaper *La Nación* and the literary journal *Sur*. At the end of 1945, with the Perón government securely in power, Sábato was fired from both of his teaching jobs because he was an enemy of the dictatorship and dared to proclaim this publicly. This precipitated a second crisis that ended his career in the sciences. Thus was born Sábato-the-writer and his public persona. For the next ten years he earned his livelihood with articles and conferences and as a consultant for the publishing houses Raigal, Codex, and Emecé. In 1947 he worked for two months as an assistant officer of the executive committee of UNESCO in Paris and Rome. In 1955, after Perón's fall and with a de facto government in power, Sábato showed his idealistic nature by accepting the directorship of the important weekly *Mundo Argentino*. But the relationship was short-lived when he resigned for not acquiescing to press censorship. Between 1958 and 1959 he served as director of cultural relations at the Foreign Ministry.

Sábato's scientific education together with his literary passion created an Apollonian and Dionysian personality. Like Sartre, Sábato is a thinker who uses fiction to fully express his ideas. To him, today's novel is closer to metaphysics than to literature. His novels and essays revolve around obsessive ideas that have conditioned his works and his social conduct: a deep existential preoccupation with humanity, literary creation, and his country. In some essays, Sábato emphasized that a writer should be at the service of truth and freedom. Of his three novels, the first, *El túnel* (1948; *The Tunnel*, 1988), could be considered a psychological, existential thriller. The second, *Sobre héroes y tumbas* (1961; *On Heroes and Tombs*, 1981), remains a veritable fresco of modern Argentina, a synthesis of his surrealistic imagination and speculative thinking. The third, *Abaddón, el Exterminador* (1974; *The Angel of Darkness*, 1991), is a "gnostic eschatology" showing that the prophecies of Apocalypse 9:11 are about to become a reality: our materialistic civilization will end and the human race will be renewed on the basis of a new principle that will reestablish the divine order.

The ideas that are the foundation of Sábato's fiction are expressed in five books of essays that must be read to fully understand him. He has also written numerous articles and has presided over the compilation of one of the most heinous texts in the letters of his country and of the world: *Nunca más* (1984), which was the report, based on the testimony of survivors and relatives, of the commission that he chaired to investigate the tragedy of the Argentine *desaparecidos* ("disappeared" persons). Sábato's texts are full of antidogmatic, testimonial, and denunciatory passages, which have revitalized Argentine letters. He has received numerous international awards and honors. At home Sábato was given the prestigious Prize of National Consecration for making the greatest contribution to the enrichment of Argentina's cultural heritage.

ANGELA B. DELLEPIANE, *Sábato: Un análisis de su narrativa* (1970); H. D. OBERHELMAN, *Ernesto Sábato* (1970); WILLIAM KENNEDY, "Sábato's *Tombs and Heroes*," in *Review* 29 (1981): 6–9; EARL M. ALDRICH, JR., "Esthetic, Moral, and Philosophic Concerns in *Sobre héroes y tumbas*," in *Romance Literary Studies, Homage to Harvey L. Johnson,* edited by Marie A. Wellington and Martha O'Nan (1983), pp. 3–14.

ANGELA B. DELLEPIANE

SABINADA REVOLT, the rebellion that led to the seizure of Brazil's second-largest city, Salvador (capital of the northeastern province of Bahia), from 17 November 1837 to 16 March 1838. Occurring during the tumultuous and experimental years of Brazil's Regency period (1834–1840), the Sabinada was initiated by radical liberals and republicans, the most famous of whom, Francisco Sabino Álvares da Rocha Vieira (or Sabino), gave the rebellion its name.

The movement began with the revolt of the soldiers of the Third Artillery Battalion, garrisoned in the Fort of São Pedro. Leading them were several civilians, including Sabino, a doctor and editor of the radical *Novo Diário*. Within hours, the city's Third Infantry Battalion had joined; ultimately, only the marines and part of the National Guard would remain loyal to the government. Soldiers and civilian adherents soon occupied the city and declared the province's independence from the central government in Rio de Janeiro.

At the onset of the Sabinada, many civilians, especially Portuguese merchants whose privileged position with the Rio government rendered them the source of widespread antipathy, fled to the Recôncavo (the nearby sugar-producing region), where large property owners had begun to organize the resistance forces known as the Restorationist Army. By the end of November, they had 1,900 men, mostly National Guardsmen, on the outskirts of Salvador. With land routes already cut off, the arrival of warships from Rio assured that the capital would also be without water-borne cargoes. By December, Salvador felt the first pangs of hunger resulting from the blockade.

Reinforcements from neighboring provinces swelled the Restoration Army to nearly 5,000, and on 12 March the siege to retake Salvador began. In what was easily one of the most violent periods in the city's history, hundreds of rebels and innocent bystanders were massacred within two days after the battle began. Surrender came quickly, on 16 March. A week later the government captured Sabino, and after lengthy court hearings, exiled him to remote Goiás. Thousands of others were condemned to hard labor on the island of Fernando de Noronha.

Scholars have interpreted the Sabinada in a number of ways: as the result of battles between liberal separatists and conservatives who supported greater centralization within Brazil's monarchy; as a reaction to the narrow scope of political options that followed independence in 1822; or as a conflict fueled by discontent within the army and the militia over a series of military reforms in the early 1830s.

Most recently scholars have explored the rebellion in social terms, highlighting the ways in which questions of race and class challenged the dominant political arrangements from "below." As the Sabinada ran its course, the goals of its poor mulatto and black adherents became far more radical than those of the men who initiated the rebellion. The latter group, for example, supported the monarchy and only grudgingly freed Brazilian-born slaves (on 19 February 1838) after vast numbers of them escaped bondage by joining the rebel army. Given this comparatively conservative stance, the lower classes had no choice but to take matters into their own hands: this they did by burning the houses of their enemies. As a result, mulatto and black rebels suffered the harshest punishments once the rebellion was over, and more vigorous government surveillance of the lower groups ensued. It would be decades before federalist and republican sentiments were so boldly expressed, and individual rather than collective acts would characterize the resistance of the poor to a system that continued to discriminate on the basis of skin color and to maintain humans in bondage.

PAULO CESAR SOUZA, *A Sabinada: A revolta separatista da Bahia* (*1837*) (1987), and HENDRIK KRAAY, " 'As Terrifying as Unexpected': The Bahian Sabinada, 1837–1838," in *Hispanic America Historical Review* 72, no. 4 (1992): 501–527.

JUDITH L. ALLEN

See also **Brazil: Regency.**

SABOGAL, JOSÉ (*b.* 11 March 1888; *d.* 15 December 1956), Peruvian artist. A native of Cajabamba, Sabogal was a prominent member of the Generation of 1919. He began to use indigenous people as subjects of his paintings while he was studying and teaching in Argentina. In Cuzco, he produced paintings with indigenous themes. Because he was heavily influenced by the famed Mexican revolutionary muralists, Sabogal soon attracted

The Indian Mayor of Chincheros: Varayoc. Oil on canvas by José Sabogal, 1925. MUSEO DE ARTE DE LIMA.

many students. José Carlos MARIÁTEGUI, who called him the first truly Peruvian painter, became a close friend. Sabogal suggested the name AMAUTA for Mariátegui's new journal. The name referred to the thinkers of the Incan Empire. Therefore, it won favor for conveying the idea of a uniquely Peruvian form of socialism linked to the nation's original Inca culture. Sabogal also taught at the Escuela de Bellas Artes in Lima. He died in Lima. *Del arte en el Perú y otros ensayos* (1975), a collection of his writings, was published posthumously.

THOMAS M. DAVIES, JR., *Indian Integration in Peru: A Half Century of Experience, 1900–1948* (1974); JESÚS CHAVARRÍA, *José Carlos Mariátegui and the Rise of Modern Peru, 1890–1930* (1979).

VINCENT PELOSO

SACASA, JUAN BAUTISTA (*b.* 21 December 1874; *d.* 17 April 1946), president of Nicaragua (1933–1936). Born in León, Sacasa rose to prominence in the volatile politics of Nicaragua as a leading member of the Liberal Party during the early twentieth century. He served as vice president in Carlos SOLORZANO's shaky coalition government in 1926 but was ousted after a coup by discontented Conservatives led by Emilano CHAMORRO VARGAS. Sacasa became the leader of Liberal opposition and along with General José María MONCADA led subsequent Liberal uprisings. The U.S. government opposed Sacasa's claim to the Nicaraguan presidency because of his ties with the Liberal Party and his support from Mexican president Plutarco ELÍAS CALLES. The United States placed Adolfo DÍAZ, a Conservative, in the presidency and backed him up with marines. After successfully splitting the Liberal forces of Sacasa and Moncada, the United States supervised the 1928 elections. Moncada became president and Sacasa served as Nicaraguan minister to Washington, D.C. Sacasa ultimately came to power in 1932, in the midst of guerrilla commander Augusto César SANDINO's war against the U.S. Marines. During this period, the United States established the Nicaraguan National Guard and placed Anastasio SOMOZA GARCÍA in its command. Sacasa attempted to negotiate a peace accord with Sandino in good faith, but Sandino was assassinated by the National Guard, leaving Sacasa locked in a power struggle with Somoza (his nephew-in-law). The increasing power and influence of Somoza and his National Guard soon decreased the de facto power of the president. Somoza forced Sacasa to resign from the presidency in June 1936, at which time he went into exile in the United States. He died in Los Angeles.

RICHARD MILLET, *Guardians of the Dynasty* (1977); EDUARDO D. CRAWLEY, *Dictators Never Die* (1979); THOMAS WALKER, *Nicaragua: The Land of Sandino* (1986); DAVID CLOSE, *Nicaragua: Politics, Economics, and Society* (1988).

HEATHER K. THIESSEN

SACO, JOSÉ ANTONIO (*b.* 7 May 1797; *d.* 26 September 1879), Cuban writer, editor, and statesman. Born in Bayamo, Cuba, Saco studied philosophy and politics and became a professor of philosophy at the San Carlos Seminary in Havana. In 1828 he traveled to New York, where he founded the *Mensajero Quincenal* (Quarterly Messenger), a liberal publication that stressed the evils of slavery. Four years later, back in Havana, Saco founded a similar publication, the *Revista Bimestre Cubana* (Cuban Bimonthly Review). In 1830 Saco wrote *Memoria sobre la vagancia* (On Vagrancy), a subtle attack on many aspects of Cuban government and society, which was still under Spanish colonial rule. In 1834 Saco was exiled to Trinidad for writing *Justa defensa de la Academia Cubana de literatura*, a piece that marked his emergence as one of the leading spokespersons for the progressive Cuban creoles. Two years later Saco returned from exile and was named the Cuban representative in the Spanish Cortes. He traveled throughout Europe and while in Paris published an article arguing

for U.S. annexation of Cuba. His greatest literary work was his monumental *Historia de la esclavitud* (History of Slavery) (2 vols., 1875–1879). Saco died in Barcelona, Spain.

RICHARD B. KIMBALL, *Cuba, and the Cubans* (1850); JOSÉ ANTONIO SACO, *Historia de la esclavitud de la raza africana* (1938); ROBERT M. LEVINE, comp., *Cuba in the 1850s: Through the Lens of Charles DeForest Fredericks* (1990).

MICHAEL POWELSON

SACRAMENTO, COLÔNIA DO, settlement on the north bank of the RÍO DE LA PLATA that was the focus of a territorial dispute between Portugal and Spain until the end of the eighteenth century. According to the Treaty of TORDESILLAS (1494), the region in question was Spanish, and while Portugal and Spain were united in one kingdom (1580–1640), a profitable commercial activity in meat, leather, and SILVER from Potosí in Upper Peru developed there. The king of Portugal, trying to find a substitute for the declining sugar trade by preserving the advantages of the period prior to the political separation from Buenos Aires, planned to establish a settlement on the north bank of the Río de la Plata. He influenced the Catholic church to include this area in the bishopric of Rio de Janeiro, created in 1676, and sent two expeditions to take possession of it. The first set sail in 1679 but failed. Its commander, Jorge Soares de Macedo, was imprisoned by the governor after a shipwreck. The second, led by Manuel Lobo, was partly successful. In January 1680 the Portuguese fortification and colony of Sacramento was settled. Soon, however, José de GARRO, governor of Buenos Aires, ordered an attack by 250 soldiers and 3,000 Indians. Lobo and his colonists surrendered later that year.

The hostilities were accompanied by intense diplomatic negotiations. The Treaty of Lisbon (1700) specified that the colony, occupied again in 1683, belonged to the Portuguese kingdom. Four years later the colony reverted to Spain, but the Treaty of Utrecht (1715) returned it to Portugal. The Treaty of MADRID (1750) once again restored it to Spain. Finally the Treaty of SAN ILDEFONSO (1777) fixed Lagoa Mirim, and not Río de la Plata, as the southern border of Brazil. Sacramento is the Uruguayan city of Colonia.

LUÍS FERRAND DE ALMEIDA, *A diplomacia portuguesa e os limites meridionais do Brasil* (1957); HÉLIO VIANNA, *História diplomática do Brasil* (1958); LUÍS FERRAND DE ALMEIDA, *A Colônia do Sacramento na época da sucessão de Espanha* (1973).

ELIANA MARIA REA GOLDSCHMIDT

SACRISTAN, QUESTION OF THE, a complex legal case that grew into a highly contentious political issue in 1856 in Chile. It began in January 1856 with the dismissal of a servant by the senior sacristan of Santiago cathedral. Two canons of the cathedral, seeking to overturn this action, appealed to the secular Supreme Court, a procedure disliked by many ecclesiastics, who felt that matters of ecclesiastical discipline should be dealt with by the church alone. The combative archbishop of Santiago, Rafael Valentín Valdivieso (1804–1878), denied the supreme court's competence in the affair. Backed by the government of President Manual MONTT (1809–1880), the court eventually ruled in favor of the two canons, and later threatened the archbishop with exile.

Deep passions were aroused by the issue. With fears of a political upheaval (which was almost certainly being plotted), the principals reached a compromise. The aftereffects of the "question" were serious: the powerful proclerical wing of the ruling Conservative Party, alienated by Montt's Erastian attitude, was prompted to defect and join forces with the Liberal opposition in the Liberal-Conservative Fusion (1858). This effectively undermined the Conservative hegemony in Chile and opened the way to greater political competition.

SIMON COLLIER

SACSAHUAMAN, the hill overlooking the city of Cuzco, Peru, from the northwest. An important HUACA in Inca times, Sacsahuaman, which in Quechua means "hill of the hawk," was believed to represent the head of the PUMA that was reproduced in the ground plan of Inca Cuzco. Elaborate construction projects, probably beginning in the time of PACHACUTI, transformed Sacsahuaman into the largest megalithic structure in the ancient Americas. The most impressive portion of the ruins that still stand is composed of three walls of zigzag design laid in Inca polygonal stonework. Some of the individual stones in this wall have been calculated to weigh as much as 60 tons. Above these walls, on the crest of the hill, originally stood three towers that were razed by the Spanish during the Conquest. The function of Sacsahuaman has never been definitely established. Probably it served multiple functions including religious, military, and royal residence.

Sources on Sacsahuaman include GRAZIANO GASPARINI and LUISE MARGOLIES, *Inca Architecture* (1980); and VINCENT R. LEE, "The Building of Sacsahuaman," in *Nawpa Pacha* 24 (1986): 49–56.

GORDON F. McEWAN

See also **Archaeology; Incas.**

SÁENZ, JAIME (b. 8 October 1921; d. 1986), Bolivian poet and novelist. Sáenz is one of the most original poets of contemporary Bolivia. Oblivious to common sense, his works reject the construction of clear and well-defined meanings. Syllogistic, closer to concept than to image, Sáenz's poetry is made up of syntactic torsions, paradoxes, and tautologies. From *El escalpelo* (1955), *Muerte por el tacto* (1957), *Aniversario de una visión* (1960), and *Visitante profundo* (1963) to *El frío* (1967), *Recorrer esta distancia* (1973), and *Bruckner: Las tinieblas* (1978), this poetic universe follows a spiral movement, in search of the unity of being. This search, which places Sáenz within the tradition of German romanticism, is markedly subjective. For Sáenz, the human body, the corporeal, is merely an "instrument of living" with little influence on the routines of everyday life. This eccentric view of the world is also present in his novel, *Felipe Delgado* (1979), a challenging exploration of the modern grotesque.

The most comprehensive analysis of Sáenz's poetry is BLANCA WIETHÜCHTER, "Las estructuras de lo imaginario en la obra poética de Jaime Sáenz," in *Obra poética de Jaime Sáenz* (1975). Two other major contributions are LUIS H. ANTEZANA, "Hacer y cuidar" in *Ensayos y lecturas* (1986), and EDUARDO MITRE, *El árbol y la piedra: Poetas contemporáneos de Bolivia* (1988). In English, see JAVIER SANJINÉS C., "Jaime Sáenz," in *Dictionary of Literary Biography: Modern Latin American Fiction Writers*, edited by William Luis and Ann González (1993).

JAVIER SANJINÉS C.

SÁENZ, MOISÉS (b. 1888; d. 1941), Mexican educator. Sáenz was born in Monterrey and studied at a Presbyterian preparatory school in Coyoacán. He received his teaching degree from the Escuela Normal of Jalapa, studied at the Sorbonne, and completed his graduate studies at Columbia Teachers College in New York, where he became a disciple of John Dewey. He was influential in Mexican revolutionary education when, as undersecretary of education in the Plutarco Elías CALLES government (1924–1928), he fleshed out a program of rural education based on Dewey's notions of action education. The Casa del Pueblo, as the rural school was called by the then *secretaría de educación pública*, was designed to teach farming, hygiene, horticulture, apiculture, aviculture, and civics through student-operated gardens, beehives, orchards, chicken coops, and producer and consumer cooperatives. Sáenz was a strong advocate of indigenous and rural integration into a modernizing, Western society.

Sáenz was known for promoting North American ideas in Mexican education and was singled out by some Catholics as a propagandist for Protestantism. Nonetheless, after José VASCONCELOS, no other Mexican has had as much influence on rural education. Sáenz was also influential in the creation of Mexico's system of secondary schools and the Casa de Estudiante Indígena. He held many educational posts in Mexico, organized the Primer Congreso Indigenista Interamericano, and served as Mexican ambassador to Denmark, Ecuador, and Peru, where he died in 1941. He was the author of several books, including *Sobre el indio peruano y su incorporación al medio nacional* (Mexico, 1933); *Carapán: Bosquejo de una experiencia* (Lima, 1936); *México íntegro* (Lima, 1939); and, with Herbert J. Priestley, *Some Mexican Problems* (Chicago, 1926).

RAMÓN EDUARDO RUÍZ, *Mexico: The Challenge of Poverty and Illiteracy* (1963); JOHN BRITTON, ''Moisés Sáenz, nacionalista mexicano,'' in *Historia Mexicana* 22 (July–September 1972): 77–98; MARY KAY VAUGHAN, *The State, Education, and Social Class in Mexico, 1880–1928* (1982).

MARY KAY VAUGHAN

SÁENZ DE THORNE, MANUELA (*b.* 1797; *d.* 23 November 1856), best known as the lover of Simón BOLÍVAR, but also a political figure in her own right. Though she was of illegitimate birth, her parents belonged to the upper class of late colonial Quito. At age twenty she was given in an arranged marriage to an English merchant, James Thorne. However, the enduring passion of her life was for Bolívar, whom she met in 1822, when he first came to Ecuador.

Abandoning her husband, Sáenz followed Bolívar to Peru. She was with him on campaign and subsequently in Lima, where she assumed a prominent role in social and political life. But her most controversial role was in Bogotá, where she arrived in late 1827. There she showed uninhibited vigor in defending Bolívar against his opponents, especially the faction of Vice President Francisco de Paula SANTANDER, at one point having Santander shot in effigy. When an attempt was made on Bolívar's life in September 1828, she was in the palace with him and helped him escape.

Sáenz remained in Bogotá after the final departure of Bolívar in 1830. She continued to be active in politics on behalf of the Bolivarian party and was implicated in a conspiracy against her old enemy Santander after he became president of New Granada. Exiled in 1833, she eventually settled in Paita, on the Peruvian coast, where she lived until her death.

ALFONSO RUMAZO GONZÁLEZ, *Manuela Sáenz, la libertadora del Libertador* (1944); VICTOR W. VON HAGEN and CHRISTINE VON HAGEN, *The Four Seasons of Manuela: A Biography* (1952).

DAVID BUSHNELL

SÁENZ GARZA, AARÓN (*b.* 1 June 1891; *d.* 26 February 1983), Mexican politician and entrepreneur. A native of Monterrey, Nuevo León, Sáenz was trained as a lawyer at the National University. He joined the revolutionary army of General Álvaro OBREGÓN in 1913 and thereafter steadily rose in national politics. He was minister of foreign relations from 1924 to 1927, manager of Obregón's successful presidential campaign in 1928, a founder of the National Revolutionary Party in 1928–1929, and minister of public education in 1930. A powerful ally of Obregón (who was assassinated after his election in 1928), Sáenz was a prime contender for the presidential nomination of the National Revolutionary Party in 1929 but lost it to Pascual ORTIZ RUBIO. Although he remained active in politics, Sáenz focused on his business ventures, particularly a multimillion-dollar system of sugar mills. With the help of his sons he expanded the family business interests into paper manufacturing and aviation during the 1950s and 1960s to become one of the nation's leading entrepreneurs.

JAMES C. HEFLEY, *Aarón Sáenz: Mexico's Revolutionary Capitalist* (1970), is a laudatory biography. AARÓN SÁENZ, *La política internacional de la Revolución: Estudios y documentos* (1961), covers the author's work in diplomacy in the 1920s.

JOHN A. BRITTON

SÁENZ PEÑA, LUIS (*b.* 2 April 1822; *d.* 4 December 1907), Argentine politician. Born and raised in Buenos Aires, Sáenz Peña received his law degree from the University of Buenos Aires in 1845. He entered politics in 1860 as a deputy to the Constitutional Convention, thereafter serving in both Buenos Aires provincial assemblies and the national assembly. He also held posts in the provincial Supreme Court, the Provincial Bank, and the General Council on Education. In the wake of the 1890 uprising of the Civic Union and the stock market crash, Sáenz Peña became the compromise candidate for president in 1892. In that post he served the interests of the National Autonomist Party of Julio A. ROCA and Carlos PELLEGRINI, but he never succeeded in emerging from their shadows. Afflicted by ill health and an indecisive temper, Sáenz Peña served a two-year term marred by strong opposition in Congress, an uprising by the new Radical Civic Union led by Leandro ALEM and future president Hipólito YRIGOYEN, and a worsening economic situation after the BARING BROTHERS crisis. He submitted his resignation in January 1895 and was replaced by the equally ill-fated José Evaristo URIBURU. Argentine politics did not settle down until Roca reassumed the presidency in 1898. Sáenz Peña's son, ROQUE, followed in his father's footsteps. Elected in 1910, he was best known for the electoral reform law of 1912.

NATALIO BOTANA, *El orden conservador: La política argentina entre 1880 y 1916* (1985); EZEQUIEL GALLO, ''Argentina: Society and Politics, 1880–1916,'' translated by Richard Southern, in *The Cambridge History of Latin America*, edited by Leslie Bethell, vol. 5 (1986), pp. 359–391; PAULA ALONSO, ''Politics and Elections in Buenos Aires, 1890–1898: The Performance of the Radical Party,'' in *Journal of Latin American Studies* 25 (October 1993): 465–487.

JEREMY ADELMAN

SÁENZ PEÑA, ROQUE (*b.* 19 March 1851; *d.* 9 August 1914), president of Argentina (1910–1914) who in 1912 initiated an electoral reform law that made voting compulsory and provided for the secret ballot and minority political representation in Congress. The law is known as the SÁENZ PEÑA LAW. Sáenz Peña belonged to the Argentine upper class. His father, Luis, was president of Argentina (1892–1895). Roque Sáenz Peña studied law at the University of Buenos Aires, but in 1874 he discontinued his studies for a brief period to join the forces that were suppressing a rebellion led by former President Bartolomé MITRE. He graduated in 1875 and a year later was elected to the Buenos Aires legislature representing the Partido Autonomista Nacional. When the WAR OF THE PACIFIC broke out in 1879, Sáenz Peña moved to Lima and joined the alliance of Peru and Bolivia against Chile. He became known for his bravery and participated in the battles of San Francisco and Tarapacá and also in the heroic defense of Arica, where he was taken prisoner in 1880.

After his return to Argentina, he was named undersecretary of the Ministry of Foreign Relations. In August 1887 he was appointed special envoy and minister plenipotentiary to Uruguay. In 1888 he served as a member of the delegation representing Argentina at the South American Conference of Private International Law held in Montevideo. A year later, he participated in the PAN-AMERICAN CONFERENCE in Washington, D. C. In 1890, he served briefly as minister of foreign relations, having to resign as a consequence of the revolution of 26 July 1890. In 1891, Sáenz Peña became a presidential candidate but withdrew when Julio A. ROCA and Bartolomé Mitre engineered his own father's candidacy. He resigned from the Senate in December 1892 to avoid a confrontation with his father and retired for three years to an *estancia* in the province of Entre Ríos. He returned to Buenos Aires in 1895 after his father's resignation. From that moment on he began attacking the corrupt, personalistic political system. The Reformista faction of the Partido Autonomista Nacional, headed by Carlos PELLEGRINI until his death in 1906, supported Sáenz Peña in the congressional elections of 1906 and 1908. In 1910, he was elected president.

FERMÍN VICENTE ARENAS LUQUE, *Roque Sáenz Peña: El presidente del sufragio libre* (1951); FELIPE BARREDA Y LAOS, *Roque Sáenz Peña* (1954); MIGUEL ANGEL CÁRCANO, *Sáenz Peña: La revolución por los comicios*, 2d ed. (1977).

JUAN MANUEL PÉREZ

SÁENZ PEÑA LAW, measure initiated by Argentine President Roque SÁENZ PEÑA, also known as the Law of 1912, which provided for the secret ballot and minority party representation in Congress. It also made voting compulsory for all native and naturalized Argentine men over the age of 18. The electoral roll was to be based on the military's conscription lists. The military was also given policing duties during electoral periods to ensure a peaceful and orderly process. The law, which altered the political process, was passed after a protracted congressional debate stemming from Conservative opposition to it.

The minority representation was to be established through the incomplete list, a process by which it was possible to give one-third of the seats available in each electoral district to the party with the second-highest number of votes.

This law radically changed Argentine politics. For ex-

ample, voter turnout in the elections increased to between 70 and 80 percent of eligible voters, while before its passage, about a third of eligible voters turned out. As a result of the law, the number of eligible voters increased to 1 million in 1912. Also as a result of these changes, the Unión Cívica Radical, part of the opposition since the late nineteenth century, won the presidential election of 1916, and its leader, Hipólito YRIGOYEN, became the first president who did not come from the traditional ruling class. The Radicals remained in control until they were overthrown by a military coup in 1930.

MIGUEL ANGEL CÁRCANO, *Sáenz Peña: La revolución por los comicios*, 2d ed. (1977); HONORIO ALBERTO DIAZ, *Ley Sáenz Peña: Pro y contra* (1983); DAVID ROCK, *Argentina, 1516–1982* (1985).

JUAN MANUEL PÉREZ

SAGRA, RAMÓN DE LA (*b.* 1798; *d.* 1871), Spanish naturalist and economist. De la Sagra studied agriculture in Madrid until 1820; subsequently he was appointed director of the botanical gardens in Havana, where he arrived in 1823. While there he also served as professor of agricultural botany at the university and studied the plant life of the island to assess its potential productivity. In 1828 he began to contribute to the new journal *Anales de la ciencia* and kept in close touch with academics abroad. In 1831 he published *Historia económica, política y estadística de la Isla de Cuba*. De la Sagra relocated to Paris in 1835 and there published an expanded version as *Histoire physique, politique et naturelle de l'Île de Cuba* (1842–1857). The latter, considered his masterwork, describes all aspects of the lives of the Cuban people and their environment. In his later years de la Sagra fell under the influence of the French socialist Pierre-Joseph Proudhon and wrote on social and economic issues.

FERMÍN PERAZA SARAUZA, *Diccionario biográfico cubano* (1951–); DAWN ADES, *Art in Latin America: The Modern Era, 1820–1980* (1989).

KAREN RACINE

SAHAGÚN, BERNARDINO DE (*b.* 1499/1500; *d.* 1590), a FRANCISCAN friar who went to New Spain in 1529 and quickly became one of the key interpreters of the NAHUATL language and NAHUA culture of all time. Born Bernardino de Ribeira in Sahagrin, Spain, he was a pioneer ethnographer and devoted messenger of the Gospel, studying Aztec culture with the goal of deepening the indigenous people's conversion to Christianity. He understood that the best pedagogy required an exchange and that a two-way encounter demanded serious language study. It was Franciscan policy to teach both Latin and Nahuatl to the elite indigenous boys of Mexico who would later, ideally, instruct their parents and future generations. The Royal College or Colegio of Santa Cruz, in Tlatelolco, was established for this purpose, and Sahagún and Fray Andrés de Olmos, another renowned *nahuatlato*, were among the instructors.

While teaching at the Colegio (1536–1540), Sahagún began collaborating with some of his best students in producing Nahuatl manuscripts. They started with Christian sermons but shifted to the philosophy and oratory of the Nahua elders, indigenous versions of the Spanish conquest, native religious beliefs and practices, calendar, social and political organization, economic production and exchange, daily life, and environment as Sahagún compiled in his magnum opus of twelve parts, the *Historia general de las cosas de Nueva España*, or FLORENTINE CODEX (so called for the locale where it was preserved). Based on testimony and *códices* (paintings/writings) made by people born and raised prior to European contact, this spectacular work has immense value for ethnohistorians trained to detect what might be the Nahua voice and what has been filtered by the priest-interpreter.

BERNARDINO DE SAHAGÚN, *Florentine Codex: General History of the Things of New Spain*, no. 14, 13 pts., rev. ed. translated and edited by Arthur J. O. Anderson and Charles E. Dibble (1950–1982); LUIS NICOLAU D'OLWER, *Fray Bernardino de Sahagún (1499–1590)*, translated by Mauricio J. Mixco (1987); J. JORGE KLOR DE ALVA, H. B. NICHOLSON, and ELOISE QUIÑONES KEBER, *The Work of Bernardino de Sahagún: Pioneer Ethnographer of Sixteenth-Century Aztec Mexico* (1988).

STEPHANIE WOOD

SAINT AUGUSTINE, Spanish capital of FLORIDA and East Florida. Saint Augustine, the earliest permanent city of European origin in the United States, was an afterthought. Pedro MENÉNDEZ DE AVILÉS, charged by PHILIP II in 1565 with cleansing the Florida coast of French interlopers, hurried across the Atlantic to destroy Fort Caroline, a French fort in the mouth of the Saint Johns River, only to find it reinforced by a fleet under Jean Ribault. Menéndez fell back to the nearest harbor and took possession of it in the king's name, commandeering and fortifying an Indian village. In honor of the patron saint of Avilés, he named the camp Saint Augustine. From there, he marched on during a hurricane and took Fort Caroline. Ribault's ships were wrecked in the storm, and the castaways received short shrift as pirates. Having cleared the land of intruders, Menéndez moved to strengthen Spain's hold on the Southeast by founding forts and settlements at every deep water port and far into the interior. But this expansion was premature. Famines, mutinies, and Indian warfare gradually reduced the Spanish presence to Saint Augustine and the capital of Santa Elena, on Parris Island.

Sir Francis DRAKE stopped by Saint Augustine in 1586 to burn the houses and cut down the fruit trees. Governor Pedro Menéndez Márquez reacted by abandoning Santa Elena to consolidate his forces. In 1599 the city was again devastated, this time by a fire and a hurricane. After some debate over whether to abandon the flood-prone port, with its shallow bar and sandy soil, the Spanish rebuilt Saint Augustine where it was.

As Florida's one Spanish municipality, formally titled "the noble and loyal city," Saint Augustine was the seat of all branches of government. The two officials of the royal treasury were also *regidores* (governors) of the *cabildo*. The royal governor doubled as captain-general. Florida was a presidial colony, with officers, warehouses, and quarters for convicts and slaves. Of the 300 to 350 soldiers stationed there, a portion was always on detachment at secondary garrisons or on coast guard and supply vessels. A creole elite of *floridanos* drew pay as reserve officers while tending to their personal trading ventures and ranches in the provinces. Indian chiefs stalked through town, delivering Spanish-imposed labor levies and burdened with food and other products from the provinces.

Saint Augustine was also a religious center. The parish priest exercised a monopoly on sacramental services for non-Indians and supervised the confraternities. The friary, headquarters of the Franciscan province of Santa Elena, which took in both Florida and Cuba and at full strength numbered seventy missionaries, provided the community with a grammar school and a locus for political opposition.

In 1668 Jamaican privateers raided Saint Augustine in the dead of night, killing sixty people in the streets. Their captain, Robert Searles, allowed his Spanish prisoners to be ransomed but kept all the Indians, free blacks, and mestizos to sell as slaves. This raid, followed by the founding of Charleston in 1670, persuaded the COUNCIL OF THE INDIES to grant Florida a larger share of the defense budget. The Castillo de San Marcos, begun in 1672 and completed in 1695, fortified the center of the settlement at the expense of the peripheries. Provincial defenses were neglected and food reserves fell to dangerous lows as extra laborers and maize were channeled toward the capital.

The *castillo* quickly proved its worth as a place of refuge from pirates. Later governors added a seawall to protect the city from storms. The Christian Indians, however, were left exposed not only to pirates but also to their native enemies equipped with firearms to take slaves for the English. The demoralized provinces collapsed during Queen Anne's War, and by 1706, Saint Augustine had lost its hinterland.

Twice in the eighteenth century English invaders besieged the *castillo* without success. After 1702, when they watched Colonel James Moore of Carolina destroy their homes, the fifteen hundred or so inhabitants rebuilt Saint Augustine as a walled city, with earthworks and a fort, Mose, to defend the only road out of town. In 1740, when General James Oglethorpe of Georgia came to lay siege, the city was saved. However, the Indian refugees living in pueblos outside the walls were not as fortunate. When the Spanish refused to come to their aid during Colonel William Palmer's attack in 1728, many of them left Florida for good. The last remnants of the

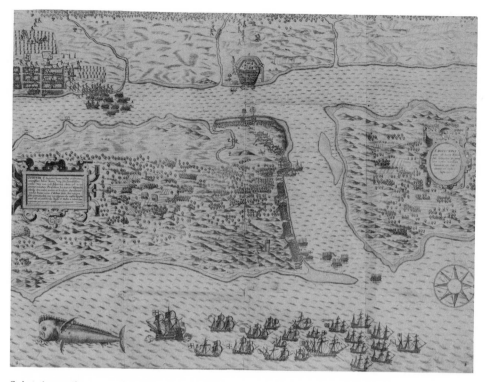

Saint Augustine. COURTESY OF THE JOHN CARTER BROWN LIBRARY AT BROWN UNIVERSITY.

missions were secularized and the FRANCISCANS, bereft of purpose, split into factions.

As military expenditures escalated during the wars for empire, Saint Augustine's presidio and population grew, and with them opportunities for illicit trade and smuggling. Florida's newly appointed auxiliary bishop reported English ships in the harbor and English traders walking about town. Southeastern Indians were demanding—and getting—English goods as gifts from a Spanish governor. It was time again to consolidate. In 1763, after the SEVEN YEARS' WAR, Spain exchanged Florida for British-held Havana. Approximately three thousand soldiers, friars, *floridanos*, and slaves, in company with eighty-three Indians, pulled up stakes and left, mostly for Cuba.

Twenty years later the British returned Florida to Spain. From 1784 to 1821, Saint Augustine was the capital of EAST FLORIDA, a colony much changed in character. Few of the expatriates returned. The populace was a cosmopolitan mixture of Minorcans and others from the Mediterranean, assorted Europeans, Canary Islanders, Scots, English, Americans, and Africans. The soldiers of several companies from Cuba were mulattoes or free blacks and the Hibernian Regiment was Irish, as were two of the governors. A distinctive style of domestic architecture developed featuring two-story houses of coquina with a loggia, an outside stairway, and a balcony facing the street. The public buildings erected included a parish church, a school, a hospital, and barracks.

Plans for further progress were interrupted when the Napoleonic invasion of Spain created a vacuum in metropolitan government. To commemorate Spain's Constitution of 1812 local liberals erected a monument on the plaza that stood there undisturbed through royal reversals, distant wars for independence, transient republics, and Jacksonian invasions. By the time the United States annexed East Florida in 1821, Saint Augustine was Spanish chiefly in name.

CHARLES W. ARNADE, *The Siege of St. Augustine in 1702* (1959); ALBERT C. MANUCY, *The Houses of St. Augustine, 1565–1821* (1962; repr. 1992); LUIS RAFAEL ARANA and ALBERT MANUCY, *The Building of Castillo de San Marcos* (1977); AMY TURNER BUSHNELL, *The King's Coffer: Proprietors of the Spanish Florida Treasury, 1565–1702* (1981); KATHLEEN DEAGAN, *Spanish St. Augustine: The Archaeology of a Colonial Creole Community* (1983); JEAN PARKER WATERBURY, ed., *The Oldest City: St. Augustine, Saga of Survival* (1983).

AMY TURNER BUSHNELL

SAINT BARTHÉLEMY (also Saint Barts). In 1493 Christopher COLUMBUS named the island after his brother Bartolomeo. Now part of the French department of GUADELOUPE, French West Indies, it encompasses 8.3 square miles and has 3,500 inhabitants, almost all white, the descendants of fishermen from Brittany, Normandy, and Poitou. Strategically located between the Dutch and English LEEWARD ISLANDS, the daily language is English. It was held by Sweden from 1784 to 1877, then was bought back by France.

French from Saint Kitts (Leeward Islands) settled before 1648, and the Knights of Malta assumed ownership in 1656. The CARIBS forced them to leave, only to have the French reoccupy Saint Barts in 1674 and establish a fishing economy. The knights were evacuated to reinforce the French at Saint Kitts in 1689, but a remnant returned to their devastated island after the Treaty of Ryswick (1697).

Saint Barts was briefly occupied by Great Britain during the SEVEN YEARS' WAR (1756–1763). The French traded the island to the Swedes in return for concessions on the Baltic island of Gotland. The Swedish renamed the port of Saint Barts Gustavia, and its free trade status rivaled that of nearby Danish Saint Thomas during the remaining Caribbean wars.

After 1877, the French maintained Gustavia's free port status. Swedish/French architecture and Swedish/French road signs attest to the island's mixed heritage. MANIOC, COTTON, pineapple, and cattle and goat herding complement fishing. A controlled and exclusive tourism is based on its isolated beaches, French cuisine, and "unspoiled" rustic atmosphere.

SIR ALAN BURNS, *History of the British West Indies* (1965); ROBERT L. BREEDAN, ed., *Isles of the Caribbean* (1980); FRANKLIN W. KNIGHT, *The Caribbean* (1990).

PAT KONRAD

See also **French in Latin America.**

SAINT CHRISTOPHER (SAINT KITTS), an island in the Lesser Antilles that was of strategic importance in colonial times. Saint Christopher is a Caribbean island just west and a bit north of Antigua, and east and slightly south of Puerto Rico. It represented the earliest nucleus of French and English colonization in the area. Thomas Warner, an Englishman, first settled the island in 1623.

Having stopped off there briefly in 1620, Warner went to England, secured capital, returned to Saint Christopher with forty to fifty companions, and quickly commenced planting tobacco. Difficulties arose with the native Carib tribe, however, and in order to secure assistance Warner agreed to the division of the island with some French settlers who had arrived shortly after he had. According to the terms of the agreement, the French would occupy the northern and southern extremities, and the English, the middle coastal strips.

In 1625, Warner obtained from the crown its letters patent, meaning that the English government officially recognized his settlement. Later, however, while in England, Warner received the news that on 7 September 1629 a Spanish fleet had taken Saint Christopher and expelled most of the French and English inhabitants. Nevertheless, after the Spanish departed some fugitives reestablished a provisional government and Warner returned.

A serious depression resulting from an oversupply of tobacco, and the growing conversion to sugar cultivation after 1630 led some colonists from Saint Kitts to move to Tortuga Island and numerous others to become BUCCANEERS. Saint Christopher became an important buccaneering base during this era.

Although French Bourbons briefly conquered Saint Christopher early in 1782, the Treaty of Versailles later that year returned the island to Great Britain. Slave trading was abolished in 1807, and the Emancipation Act followed in 1833; Saint Christopher, however, remained predominantly a SUGAR producer until well into the twentieth century.

By the mid-twentieth century, many British West Indian colonies were clamoring for autonomy, and in the early 1960s these efforts accelerated. Thus, in May 1962 the British Parliament dissolved the Federation of the West Indies. In August of that year Jamaica and Trinidad and Tobago achieved independence. The eight remaining states of the federation, including Saint Christopher, entered into negotiations with the United Kingdom to form a smaller federation within the empire. By 1965 the negotiations had proved fruitless, and Barbados declared independence in 1966.

Trinidad and Tobago offered the remaining seven countries statehood, but they instead chose to pursue new negotiations with Great Britain. They wanted to be self-governing while maintaining their eligibility for financial assistance from their mother country. In the course of the discussions, it was agreed in 1966 that each of the seven states would enter into a free, voluntary association with Britain. Each island-state would be fully self-governing internally, and either side could terminate the agreement at any time. Thus, in 1961, when Saint Christopher joined this association, it simultaneously became fully self-governing internally for the first time in its history.

By 1974 Saint Christopher averaged 439 people per square mile. In 1982 its population was 100,000, and its gross national product was $750 per capita. Its economic growth rate decreased severely in the 1970s and early 1980s, however, with the annual economic growth rate from 1960 to 1982 being a mere 1.1 percent. Penury existed throughout the island.

N. M. CROUSE, *The French Struggle for the West Indies, 1665–1713* (1943); G. C. MERRILL, *The Historical Geography of St. Kitts and Nevis* (1958); J. H. PARRY et al., *A Short History of the West Indies*, 4th ed. (1987); W. T. BROWNE, *From Commoner to King: Robert L. Bradshaw, Crusader for Dignity and Justice in the Caribbean* (1992).

BLAKE D. PATRIDGE

See also **Piracy; Slave Trade.**

SAINT LUCIA, one of the Windward Islands in the Lesser Antilles. Castries is the major city and capital of the 238-square-mile island.

Saint Lucia's earliest known inhabitants were Arawak

and CARIB Amerindians. Although Spanish explorers first reached the island around 1500, the Caribs repelled European settlers until the mid-seventeenth century, when the French established a permanent colony. French sovereignty was challenged repeatedly by the British. In fact, the island passed between the two European powers fourteen times. From 1803 until independence on 22 February 1979, Saint Lucia was controlled by the British.

In the 1990s the British monarch remains the nominal head of government, but executive power is vested in the island's prime minister and cabinet. There is a bicameral parliament: the Senate with eleven members and the House of Assembly with seventeen representatives.

Although the population has increased from 17,485 in 1820 to 145,000 in 1989, the ethnic composition has remained nearly the same. In the 1990s, about 87 percent of the population are of African descent and 1.3 percent of European descent. When slavery was abolished in 1834, 10,328 slaves were freed. Indentured servants were then brought to Saint Lucia from India. Today, 2.6 percent of the population is of Asian Indian descent.

English is the official language, but a French patois is also spoken. The predominant religion is Roman Catholicism. AGRICULTURE is the island's leading industry. The main crops are bananas, coconuts, fruits and vegetables, and cocoa. TOURISM is another important industry. In 1985, the per capita income was U.S. $1,320.

FRANKLIN W. KNIGHT, *The Caribbean: The Genesis of a Fragmented Nationalism*, 2d ed. (1990); BONHAM C. RICHARDSON, *The Caribbean in the Wider World, 1492–1992: A Regional Geography* (1992); *Worldmark Encyclopedia of the Nations*, 7th ed. (1988), vol. 3.

STEPHEN E. HILL

See also **Caribbean Sea: Commonwealth States.**

SAINT VINCENT, one of the Windward Islands in the Lesser Antilles. Kingstown is its major city and capital. The self-governing state of Saint Vincent, with a total area of 150 square miles, comprises the island of Saint Vincent and dozens of the northern GRENADINE islands (including Union and Bequia).

In 1989, the population of Saint Vincent and the Grenadines numbered 145,000. About 75 percent of the population are of African descent, 20 percent of mixed origin, 3 percent of European descent, and 2 percent of Asian descent. Although English is the official language, French and a French patois are still spoken. About 36 percent of the population are Anglicans, another 40 percent are affiliated with other Protestant churches, and 19 percent are Roman Catholics.

The first known inhabitants were Arawak and CARIB Amerindians. Although Christopher Columbus reached the island on 22 January 1498, Saint Vincent was not settled by Europeans for another two and a half centu-

ries. Without European interference, the native population prospered. In addition, runaway and shipwrecked African slaves intermarried with the native population, creating a distinct ethnic group known as Black Caribs. Except when France governed the island from 1779–1783, the British occupied Saint Vincent from 1762 until independence on 27 October 1979.

In the 1990s the British monarch remains the nominal head of government. But executive power is vested in the island's prime minister and cabinet. There is a nineteen-seat unicameral legislature.

AGRICULTURE is the mainstay of the island's economy, producing bananas, vegetables, coconuts, spices, and sugar. TOURISM is another important industry. In 1985, the per capita income on the island was U.S. $960.

FRANKLIN W. KNIGHT, *The Caribbean: The Genesis of a Fragmented Nationalism*, 2d ed. (1990); BONHAM C. RICHARDSON, *The Caribbean in the Wider World, 1492–1992: A Regional Geography* (1992).

STEPHEN E. HILL

See also **Caribbean Sea: Commonwealth States.**

SAINTES, BATTLE OF THE, a Franco-British engagement of 12 April 1782. Admiral François Joseph Paul, Comte de Grasse, brought a large French fleet into the Caribbean early in 1781. He won several minor victories against British naval forces but failed to take full advantage of his numerical strength over the British forces commanded by Admiral George Rodney. Instead, de Grasse sailed north to Chesapeake Bay, where his presence contributed to General Charles Cornwallis's surrender at Yorktown, ending the AMERICAN REVOLUTION. De Grasse then returned to the Caribbean with the intention of attacking Jamaica, but Rodney inflicted a major defeat at the Isles des Saintes (between Dominica and Guadeloupe) on 12 April 1782. Although much of de Grasse's fleet escaped destruction, Rodney's victory restored British maritime supremacy in the Caribbean.

ALFRED T. MAHAN, *The Influence of Seapower upon History* (1890), pp. 317–355; MICHAEL CALVERT and PETER YOUNG, *A Dictionary of Battles* (1979), pp. 177–178.

PHILIPPE L. SEILER

SÁINZ, GUSTAVO (*b*. 13 July 1940), Mexican fiction writer and critic. Born in Mexico City, Sáinz is known as a writer of Mexican "urban picaresque." *Gazapo* (1965), *Obsesivos días circulares* (1969), *La princesa del Palacio de Hierro* (1974), and *Compadre Lobo* (1977) are his best-known novels. Other works include *Fantasmas aztecas* (1982), *Paseo en trapecio* (1985), and *Muchacho en llamas* (1988). Together with José AGUSTÍN, Sáinz is associated with the generation of "La Onda," a group of young Mexican writers who published in the 1960s and 1970s and whose literature was characterized by attention to an urban adolescent subculture, the use of colloquial language and the oral quality of the text, and the characters' self-centered, nonconformist attitudes toward established social codes. In Sáinz's fiction Mexico City is a constant, autobiographically based reference, a voracious space intimately experienced by his characters, where language acts, in his words, "as the major protagonist of history."

LAURA GARCÍA-MORENO

SALADERO, a slaughterhouse and meat-salting plant. During much of the colonial era, gauchos slaughtered wild cattle on the pampa for their hides and tallow. During the eighteenth century, dried meat, exported to feed slaves in Cuba and Brazil, became another important product. During the late eighteenth and early nineteenth centuries, the slaughtering and meat-drying operations were moved from the ESTANCIA to the *saladero*. Quick, substantial profits attracted many investors, including young Juan Manuel de ROSAS, who later gained infamy as a ruthless despot.

These primitive factories depended more on manpower than on technology. Discarded meat, bones, and blood drew scavengers, emitted a stench, and created health hazards, including water pollution. Despite such primitive methods, *saladeros* south of Buenos Aires were processing some 250,000 cattle per year by about 1850. In Uruguay and the Brazilian state of Rio Grande do Sul, the traditional *saladeros* remained important livestock markets into the twentieth century. Buenos Aires, however, modernized its cattle-processing industry, and FRIGORÍFICOS (cold-storage plants) largely supplanted *saladeros* in the late nineteenth century.

ALFREDO MONTOYA, *Historia de los saladeros argentinos* (1956; repr. 1970); JONATHAN C. BROWN, *A Socioeconomic History of Argentina, 1776–1860* (1979), pp. 109–114.

RICHARD W. SLATTA

SALADO RIVER, also known as Río Salado del Norte to differentiate it from the Río Salado that flows south of San Luis and the Río Salado that serves as boundary to the province of Buenos Aires in Argentina. The river springs from the Nevado del Acay (near Salta) and after 1,200 miles empties into the PARANÁ RIVER at SANTA FE. Discovered in 1573 by Juan de GARAY, it was an active border between the southern Chaco and the province of Córdoba during colonial times. On its banks the Army of the North commanded by Manuel BELGRANO swore allegiance to the confederation of the UNITED PROVINCES OF THE RÍO DE LA PLATA IN 1813.

CÉSAR N. CAVIEDES

SALAMANCA, DANIEL (*b.* 8 July 1868; *d.* 17 July 1935), president of Bolivia (1931–1934). Blamed for Bo-

livia's defeat by Paraguay in the CHACO WAR (1932–1935), Salamanca may be the most controversial figure of twentieth-century Bolivian history. A wealthy Cochabamba landowner and eloquent congressional deputy and senator for thirty years, he served as secretary of treasury in the cabinet of President José Manuel PANDO (1899–1904). In 1914 he broke with the conservative Liberal Party and helped found the Republican Party, only to break away again in 1921 to form the Genuine Republican Party. Hailed as the "new messiah" and *hombre símbolo* (human symbol) because of his fierce nationalism and scrupulous integrity in an era of political corruption, Salamanca was the establishment's popular choice for president in March 1931. However, his economic austerity, political repression of the opposition (particularly leftists and Communists), and failed Chaco policy soon left him one of the most unpopular of Bolivian presidents. In November 1934, while he was visiting the Chaco command in Villa Montes, the military seized and deposed him.

JULIO DÍAZ ARGUEDAS, *Como fue derrocado el hombre símbolo, Salamanca* (1957); DAVID ALVÉSTEGUI, *Salamanca, su gravitación sobre el destino de Bolivia,* 4 vols. (1962); HERBERT S. KLEIN, *Parties and Political Change in Bolivia, 1880–1952* (1969); AUGUSTO CÉSPEDES, *Salamanca: O el metafísico del fracaso* (1973).

WALTRAUD QUEISER MORALES

SALARRUÉ. *See* **Salazar Arrué, Salvador Efraín.**

SALAS, MANUEL DE (*b.* 19 June 1754; *d.* 28 November 1841), Chilean reformer and patriot, and one of the best-loved Chileans of his time. From a rich creole family, Salas studied law at the University of San Marcos, Lima, from which he graduated in 1774. In the later 1770s he paid a long visit to Spain, taking great interest in economic reforms and education. Superintendent of public works under the governorship of Ambrosio O'HIGGINS, he was named a member of the newly founded *consulado* (merchant guild) of Santiago in 1795. The following year he wrote a classic report on the economy and society of Chile for the Spanish finance minister. In 1798 he founded the Academia de San Luis, a college which aimed to introduce stronger technical education in Chile. He also played an active part in introducing vaccination into the colony in 1806.

Salas's early hopes for reform rested in the Spanish crown, but from 1810 onward he was a patriot, a member of the first national congress (1811), and, briefly, foreign minister (1812–1813). He was exiled to Juan Fernández (an island prison for exiled political prisoners) during the Spanish reconquest (1814–1817). The first director of Chile's National Library, Salas retained a strong interest in educational matters, often visiting schools and advising them.

MIGUEL LUIS AMUNÁTEGUI, *Don Manuel de Salas*, 3 vols. (1895); *Escritos de don Manuel de Salas y documentos relativos a él y a su familia*, 3 vols. (1910–1914).

SIMON COLLIER

SALAVARRIETA, POLICARPA (*b.* 26 January 1795; *d.* 14 November 1817), heroine of Colombian independence. Born into a respectable creole family, Policarpa Salavarrieta ("La Pola") grew up in Guaduas, a way station between Bogotá and the Magdalena River. When the independence movement started, she became a strong sympathizer, and the flow of traffic through her town kept her well informed. With the Spanish reconquest of New Granada in 1816, Salavarrieta began providing information and other assistance to the patriot underground, first in Guaduas and then in Bogotá, where it was easier for her to remain inconspicuous. Nevertheless, her key role in the urban network of the resistance was discovered, and she was condemned to death. She went to her execution shouting a tirade against Spanish oppression. Salavarrieta's place in the pantheon of patriot martyrs is indicated by the fact that she was the first Latin American woman commemorated on a postage stamp, one of Colombia's 1910 independence-centennial issue.

OSWALDO DÍAZ DÍAZ, *Los Almeydas: Episodios de la resistencia patriota contra el ejército pacificador de Tierra Firme* (1962); JAMES D. HENDERSON and LINDA RODDY HENDERSON, *Ten Notable Women of Latin America* (1978), chap. 5.

DAVID BUSHNELL

SALAVERRY, FELIPE SANTIAGO (*b.* 6 March 1805; *d.* 18 February 1836), Conservative caudillo who became president of Peru (1835–1836). A participant in the final battles against the Spanish in 1824, Salaverry, a native of Lima, was promoted to general by President Luis José Orbegoso in 1834. In February 1835, however, the twenty-nine-year-old Salaverry denounced the government of the Liberal Orbegoso and took power in Lima. By the middle of the year, he had allied with Agustín GAMARRA against General Andrés de SANTA CRUZ and Orbegoso, who still claimed the presidency. Salaverry imposed an authoritarian government that gained broad support in Lima and along the coast. In February 1836, his forces finally squared off against those of Santa Cruz. Salaverry was taken prisoner in the battle of Socabaya and, in an unusual action for the period, was executed at Arequipa, setting the stage for the PERU-BOLIVIA CONFEDERATION.

MANUEL BILBAO, *Historia del General Salaverry*, 3d ed. (1936); FREDRICK B. PIKE, *The Modern History of Peru* (1967), pp. 76–81; JORGE BASADRE, *Historia de la República del Perú*, 7th ed., vol. 2, (1983), pp. 27–51.

CHARLES F. WALKER

SALAZAR, MATÍAS (*b.* 1828; *d.* 17 May 1872), Venezuelan caudillo. Salazar participated in the FEDERAL WAR (1859–1863) as a military chief of the central region. After the Federalist triumph he fought in several local armed controversies. When President Juan Crisóstomo FALCÓN was deposed in 1868, Salazar joined the April Revolution of 1870 led by Antonio GUZMÁN BLANCO, becoming an important military leader for Yellow Liberalism, second only to Guzmán. When Guzmán took control of the government, Salazar was named second appointee to the presidency of the republic and later president of the state of Carabobo. He gradually distanced himself from Guzmán and organized a conspiracy against the government but was discovered and expelled from the country. From abroad Salazar instigated a new armed movement in 1872. He was defeated, tried by the War Council, convicted of treason, and sentenced to death by firing squad.

FELIPE LARRAZÁBAL, *Asesinato del General Salazar* (1873), and JOSÉ CARRILLO MORENO, *Matías Salazar, historia venezolana* (1954).

INÉS QUINTERO

SALAZAR ARRUÉ, SALVADOR EFRAÍN (SALARRUÉ); (*b.* 22 October 1899; *d.* 27 November 1975), Salvadoran writer and painter who used the pseudonym Salarrué. A native of Sonsonate, he became the most popular literary figure of mid-twentieth-century El Salvador. After education in San Salvador and at the Corcoran Art Academy in Washington, D.C. (1917–1919), Salazar produced short stories, novels, poems, and paintings that reflected the Salvadoran common people; helped to preserve Salvadoran folk culture; and awakened a social consciousness in the country. In the late 1920s he was an important contributor to Alberto MASFERRER's *Patria*, and he continued to be an influential writer and intellectual force in El Salvador until his death in 1975. Rural Salvadoran themes dominate Salazar's major novel, *El señor de la burbuja* (1927), and his classic collection of stories, *Cuentos de barro* (1933).

LUIS GALLEGOS VALDÉS, *Panorama de la literatura salvadoreña del período precolombino a 1980* (1987), esp. pp. 239–258; RAMÓN L. ACEVEDO, "Salvador (Salarrué) Salazar Arrué," in *Latin American Writers*, edited by Carlos A. Solé and Maria Isabel Abren, vol. 2 (1989), pp. 875–879; JOHN BEVERLEY and MARC ZIMMERMAN, *Literature and Politics in the Central American Revolutions* (1990), p. 119.

RALPH LEE WOODWARD, JR.

SALAZAR BONDY, SEBASTIÁN (*b.* 4 February 1924; *d.* 4 July 1965), Peruvian writer and journalist. Salazar Bondy, born in Lima, began publishing his poetry while studying literature at San Marcos University. His artistic interest led him to work in Buenos Aires (1948–1951) and study in Paris (1956–1957). Twice he received the Peruvian national prize for theater (1948, 1952) and once the national prize for journalism (1958). Although he earned his living as a newspaperman, briefly directed the Institute of National Art, and participated in politics as an activist member of the Movimiento Social Progresista (Social Progressionist Movement) he had helped to found, Salazar Bondy devoted most of his time to creative writing, purportedly divested of social and ideological content. He is remembered for his strong opposition to pro-Indianist literary trends and advocacy of art for art's sake. His play *Amor, gran laberinto* (1948), his short stories *Pobre gente de París* (1958), and his essay *Lima la horrible* (1964) are among his best books. In collaboration with other writers, he edited *La poesía contemporánea del Perú* (1946), *Antología general de la poesía peruana* (1957), and *Cuentos infantiles peruanos* (1958).

MANUEL SALAZAR BONDY, *Obras* (1967); LUIS ALBERTO SÁNCHEZ, *La literatura peruana*, vol. 5 (1975), pp. 1580–1581, 1607–1609; MAURILIO ARRIOLA GRANDE, *Diccionario literario del Perú*, vol. 2 (1982), pp. 256–259; PEDRO SHIMOSE, *Diccionario de autores hispanoamericanos* (1982), p. 385.

EUGENIO CHANG-RODRÍGUEZ

SALDANHA DA GAMA, LUÍS FELIPE DE (*b*. 7 April 1846; *d*. 24 June 1895), Brazilian admiral and principal figure in a revolt of the fleet during the civil war of 1893. Gama had been the navy's chief representative in the court of Dom PEDRO I because he was cultured, brave, well traveled, and of noble ancestry. Although a monarchist by preference, he acknowledged the republic as an accomplished fact.

Gama and two other Brazilian admirals, Custódio José de MELO and Eduardo Wandenkolk, became unhappy over the way that the new government had placed the army over the navy in terms of prestige and material benefits. Wandenkolk wasted his prestige in aborted political adventures. Melo, having successfully led a naval revolt against President Deodoro da FONSECA, then tried the same maneuver against Vice President Floriano PEIXOTO, but without success. Gama opposed Melo's revolt and declared his neutrality. Then head of the Naval Academy, Gamma was offered the vacated position of minister of the navy, which he refused. He felt that once the fighting was over his mission would be to rebuild the navy using the Naval Academy. His position of neutrality eventually became unbearable since he could not declare loyalty to Peixoto. Finally, despite the evidence that the Federalist and naval revolts would fail, Gama joined the losing cause, and, along with Federalist leader Gaspar da Silveira Martins, called for a plebiscite on the issue of the restoration of the monarchy. That stand ensured their defeat, since the pro-Republican forces by then were strong enough to win the war. Gama was killed in fighting while trying to reach neutral territory (Uruguay).

RAUL OLIVERIA RODRIGUES, *Um militar contra o militarismo: A vida de Saldanha da Gama* (1959); JOSÉ MARIA BELLO, *A History of Modern Brazil*, translated by James L. Taylor (1966), pp. 119–129, 134–145; JUNE E. HAHNER, *Civilian-Military Relations in Brazil, 1889–1898* (1969), pp. 63–66, 71–72.

ROBERT A. HAYES

SALES, EUGÊNIO DE ARAÚJO (*b*. 8 November 1920), archbishop and cardinal of Rio de Janeiro. For decades, Sales has been one of the most important and visible leaders of the Brazilian Catholic church. Ordained as a priest in 1942, Sales became bishop of Natal, Rio Grande do Norte, in 1954. In the 1950s and 1960s, he was known as a leader of the moderately progressive faction within the Brazilian church. As archbishop of Natal, he promoted radio schools as a means of working with the poor, and he supported the creation of the Basic Education Movement in 1958 and of rural Catholic unions in the late 1950s and early 1960s. Both initiatives became important within the Brazilian church and in national politics.

After the coup in 1964, Sales was less critical of the military government and more willing to work with it than most other prominent church leaders. For this reason, he became identified as a leader of the moderately conservative faction of the Brazilian hierarchy. He was named archbishop of Salvador in 1968 and of Rio de Janeiro in 1971. As archbishop of Rio, convinced that the church needed to focus on religious issues, he became one of Brazil's most prominent critics of LIBERATION THEOLOGY. His theological and ecclesiastical positions made him a favorite of Pope John Paul II after 1978.

SCOTT MAINWARING

See also **Catholic Church.**

SALESIANS. The Society of Saint Francis de Sales is a male religious order of the Roman Catholic church founded in 1859 in Turin, Italy, by Giovanni Bosco (1815–1888), who was canonized as a saint in 1934. An innovative educator, Don Bosco began his charitable works in 1841 by helping poor and abandoned youngsters. The Vatican formally approved the constitution of the Pious Society of Saint Francis de Sales in 1874. The order's purpose was to educate the poor and the lower classes by establishing vocational education programs, day and boarding schools, and orphanages. The order also fostered adult education and the formation of groups of families who needed help (the Salesian "family" remains a goal in the 1990s). More than other religious orders of the time, the Salesians relied on "coadjutors," or religious brothers, who were not ordained priests. These lay brothers were craftsmen and teachers whose role was to educate youngsters and assist in missionary activities. A parallel order of female religious, the Salesians Figlie di Maria Ausiliatrice (Daughters of Mary, Help of Christians), was established to complement the order and to help support the education of the poor.

The Salesians looked beyond Europe and undertook ambitious programs of missionary activities in other lands. Argentina attracted Don Bosco's attention because of its burgeoning Italian population. Italian Giovanni Cagliero (1838–1926), the first Salesian priest who became a bishop and later a cardinal, and a group of his brethren arrived in Argentina in 1875. They established schools and parishes for Italian immigrants in the slums of Barracas, Boca, and Avellaneda near Buenos Aires. The Salesians founded industrial and agricultural schools, teacher training schools, and business colleges, many of which provided subsistence for boarders. Many of these schools still function today.

In 1875 intrepid Salesian missionaries set out to evangelize the Amerindians from the vast territory of Patagonia to the far reaches of Tierra del Fuego. Santiago Costamagna, a Salesian priest, accompanied General Julio A. Roca's campaign of 1879 to subdue the Amerindian populations of southern Argentina. Ceferino NAMUNCURÁ, revered as a saint by the Roman Catholic church since 1905, was a product of Salesian schools. Salesians played a prominent role in incorporating the Amerindians of Patagonia into national life. They established agricultural and technical schools for settlers and Amerindians in the northwestern region of Argentina, and they trained people to work in Mendoza. By the end of the century, their institutions were present throughout Argentina.

The Salesian missions and schools in Chile were mainly geared toward the southern part of the country. The first Salesian schools were established in Concepción, Punta Arenas, and Talca, all in 1887. Bishop Cagliero then sent Father Santiago Costamagna to establish missions and schools in the Andean highlands of Peru, Bolivia, and Ecuador from 1888 to 1890. Technical schools, secondary institutes, orphanages, and parishes were established in the *altiplano* and in the lowlands of the Beni in Bolivia.

Salesians worked with Amerindians throughout Latin America teaching and converting them to Christianity, forming communities, and often recording and documenting their ways of life, which were being lost to industrialization and urbanization. The Salesians working in the Paraguayan Chaco and in Ecuador are good examples. In Ecuador, Salesian Father Juan Bottasso established the Ediciones Abya-Yala and the Latin American Center of Indigenist Documentation in Quito, which preserves invaluable ethnographic records of the SHUAR and other tribes. The Salesians also made an impact on the educational and social systems in Brazil. In 1988 there were 123 Salesian institutions in Brazil, 47 in Mexico, 33 in Venezuela, 36 in Colombia, 14 in Bolivia, 11 in Paraguay, 25 in Chile, 24 in Uruguay, and 114 in Argentina. The Salesians' hands-on activities, their technical schools, and their printing presses helped shape infrastructures throughout Latin America. Salesians also trained many political and professional leaders.

RAÚL A. ENTRAIGAS, *Los Salesianos en la Argentina*, 5 vols. (1918–1989); JOSÉ DE ALARCÓN Y CANEDO and RICARDO PITTINI, *El chaco paraguayo y sus tribus* (1924); LORENZO MASSA, *Monografía de Magallanes: 60 años de acción Salesiana en el sur, 1886–1946* (1946); PASCUAL PAESA, *El Patiru Domingo: La cruz en el ocaso Mapuche* (1964); LORENZO MASSA, *Historia de las misiones Salesianas de la Pampa* (1968); OSVALDO VENTURUZZO, *Bandeirantes, atuais* (1969); ALBERTO ARAMAYO, *Los Salesianos en Bolivia*, 2 vols. (1976–1988); JUAN ESTEBAN BELZA, *La expedición al desierto y los Salesianos, 1879* (1979); RIOLANDO AZZI, *Os Salesianos no Rio de Janeiro*, 4 vols. (1982–1984); JUAN BOTTASSO, *Los Shuar y las misiones: Entre la hostilidad y el diálogo* (1982); ERNESTO SZANTO, *Los Salesianos en el país de los Césares* (1982); RIOLANDO AZZI, *Os Salesianos no Brasil: A luz da historia* (1983); SIMÓN KUZMANICH BUVINIC, *Presencia Salesiana en Chile: 100 años en Chile. Los inicios* (1987); CARLOS VALVERDE ROMERO, ed., *Presencia Salesiana en el Ecuador* (1987); CAYETANO BRUNO, *Los Salesianos y las Hijas de María Auxiliadora en la Argentina*, 4 vols. (1989).

GEORGETTE MAGASSY DORN

SALGADO, PLINIO (*b.* 22 January 1895; *d.* 7 December 1975), Brazilian politician and journalist. Salgado was born in São Bento de Sapucaí, São Paulo and died in São Paulo. As a youth, he began his long and prolific career as a writer when he founded the hometown paper *O Correio de São Bento*. After moving to the state capital, Salgado began contributing regularly to nationwide newspapers and magazines. In 1931, he launched an integralist campaign and made himself the movement's supreme authority. One year later, the writer and politician founded the Ação Integralista Brasileira. On May 10, 1937, a group of anti-Vargas and integralist demonstrators attacked the presidential palace in Rio de Janeiro. The attack was repulsed and Salgado was exiled to Portugal until 1945. After returning to Brazil, he founded the Partido de Representação Popular (PRP) and became its presidential candidate in 1955. From 1958 to 1966, he served as a federal deputy representing the PRP and, later, the ARENA party from 1966 to 1974.

Salgado was a member of the Academia Paulista de Letras and authored numerous political, fictional, and poetic works such as *Tabor, O estrangeiro, O cavaleiro de Itararé, Literatura e política, A psicologia da revolução, O que é integralismo, Cartas aos camisas-verdes, A doutrina do sigma, O conceito cristão da democracia, Extremismo e democracia, Direitos e Deveres do homem,* and *Espírito de burguesia.* His integralist movement (or *camisas verdes*—green shirts) envisaged an integral state under a single authoritarian head of government patterned after European corporatist movements. Using the motto "God, country, and family," the movement sought to enlist the middle classes who feared communism.

IÊDA SIQUEIRA WIARDA

See also **Vargas, Getúlio.**

SALGADO, SEBASTIÃO (*b.* 8 February 1944), Brazilian photographer. Born in Minas Gerais, Salgado was the only son among eight children of the owners of a large cattle farm. In 1963, he began studying law, and later switched to economics. Around this time, he married the architect Lélia Deluiz Wanick; they had two children. In 1968, Salgado obtained two master's degrees in economics: one from São Paulo University, and one from Vanderbilt University; in 1971, he received a doctorate in agricultural economy from the Sorbonne. Immediately thereafter he went to work in Africa for the London-based International Coffee Organization. In 1973, Salgado changed careers once again and became a freelance photojournalist documenting the drought in the Sahel region of Africa for the World Council of Churches. The following year he joined the Paris-based Sygma agency and covered the coup in Portugal and the revolutions in its colonies of Mozambique and Angola. In 1975, he switched to the Gamma agency, covering stories in Africa, Europe, and Latin America. He began the work on peasants that was featured in his 1986 book *Other Americas* started around this time. Three years later, Salgado joined Magnum, a cooperative agency founded in 1947 by Henri Cartier-Bresson, Robert Capa, and others. In 1982 he received the W. Eugene Smith grant in humanistic photography and an award from the French Ministry of Culture to continue his work in Latin America. Working with a French humanitarian aid group, Médecins sans Frontières, he returned to the Sahel to photograph the calamitous effects of famine in 1984. After the publication of his book *Sahel: L'homme en détresse*, Salgado was internationally recognized as a leading photojournalist. His most ambitious project, on workers and the end of manual labor, was completed in 1992 and published as *Workers: An Archeology of the Industrial Age* (1993). Salgado's work has gone beyond the printed page and onto the walls of galleries and museums. Controversy has arisen over the alleged "beautification of tragedy" in his work, and in an attempt to understand it, critics have variously labeled it "lyric documents," "mannerist documents," or "documentary photography."

Collections of Salgado's photographs also include *An Uncertain Grace*, with essays by EDUARDO GALEANO and FRED RITCHIN (1990). Articles on Salgado include LIBA TAYLOR, "Sebastião Salgado," in *British Journal of Photography*, 12 November 1987; INGRID SISCHY, "Good Intentions," in *The New Yorker*, 9 September 1991; and HENRY ALLEN, "Of Beatitudes and Burdens," in *The Washington Post*, 19 January 1992.

FERNANDO CASTRO

See also **Photography.**

SALGAR, EUSTORGIO (*b.* 1 November 1831; *d.* 25 November 1885), president of Colombia (1870–1872). Scion of prominent Santander families, he was born in Bogotá, where he received his law doctorate in 1851. Salgar's talents and Liberal affiliation brought him responsible posts in Cundinamarca. He went on to govern portions of Santander (1853–1855, 1856–1857), was elected a senator (1858–1859), was governor of Cundinamarca (1859), and was a delegate to the Rionegro Convention (1863). He served as Colombian minister in Washington, D.C., (1865–1866) and was elected president in 1870 (nominated in part to attract votes away from General Tomás CIPRIANO MOSQUERA). A devout Catholic and friend of Archbishop Vincente Arbeláez, Salgar won easily. His administration sponsored educational expansion at the primary and secondary levels and established normal schools. Other notable achievements during Salgar's presidency were the chartering of the Banco de Bogotá, Colombia's first successful bank (1870); a reduction of the army by 29 percent; and the construction of roads and of asylums for the insane and leprous. Salgar's elegant personal style and courtesy won him plaudits from both parties. After his term as president, he was governor of Cundinamarca (1874–1876), minister of war (1876), minister of foreign affairs (1878), and minister of the interior (1884). Salgar died in Bogotá.

ANTONIO PÉREZ AGUIRRE, *Los radicales y la regeneración* (1941), pp. 87–97; HELEN DELPAR, *Red Against Blue* (1981), pp. 67ff.; ARIZMENDI IGNACIO POSADA, *Presidentes de Colombia, 1810–1990* (1989), pp. 137–141.

J. LEÓN HELGUERA

See also **Colombia: Political Parties; Parra, Aquileo.**

SALINAS DE GORTARI, CARLOS (*b.* 3 April 1948), president of Mexico (1988–1994). After taking office in 1988, Carlos Salinas established himself as a major figure in contemporary Mexican presidential history. Elected in the most disputed presidential campaign since the government party's (PRI) formation in 1929, Salinas came into office with barely a simple majority of the officially tallied vote, the lowest figure ever in a successful presidential campaign. With little legitimacy, outside of and within his own party, he took charge of the presidency in a dynamic, decisive manner. The major leitmotif of his ideology was economic liberalization and political modernization. Building on the legacy of his predecessor, Miguel de la MADRID, in whose administration Salinas himself played a major role as secretary of budgeting and planning, Salinas sought to engineer a reversal of the growing role of the state in Mexican economic life. His administration sold off hundreds of state-owned enterprises, allowed North American firms to participate in the exploration of oil for the first time since 1938, significantly denationalized the banking industry, and advocated the establishment of a regional free trade block among Mexico, the United States, and Canada, thereby significantly reducing many of Mexico's traditional trade barriers. He continued to renegotiate the debt, while keeping up payments, and implemented policies to attract large amounts of foreign capital. As of 1994, those policies had yet to succeed in bringing economic benefits to the working and lower middle classes, who saw their standard of living decline markedly after 1980.

Salinas's promises of political modernization were not fulfilled. Although some structural reforms were implemented during the 1990 PRI convention, and the government successfully legislated political reform through Congress in 1989, elections were characterized by excessive fraud and poliltical violence. The government pursued a political strategy of co-opting the traditional right, represented by the National Action Party (PAN), and implementing an uncompromising, repressive policy toward the new middle left, represented by Cuauhtémoc CÁRDENAS and the Democratic Revolutionary Party (PRD). This strategy was reflected in the 1989 and 1990 state and local elections, in which the National Action Party won its first gubernatorial race since 1929, but in which the PRD fared badly in every contest. This failure of political reform was a factor in the sudden emergence of a revolutionary peasant movement (the Zapatista Army of National Liberation) in Chiapas at the start of 1994. That uprising, together with a series of political assassinations (including that of the PRI's presidential candidate, Luis Donaldo COLOSIO), dominated the troubled close of the Salinas administration. When economic collapse ensued in December 1994 and Salinas's own brother, Raúl, was implicated in one of the assassinations, Carlos Salinas left Mexico with his reputation in considerable disarray.

Salinas also adopted a controversial policy toward the Catholic church, appointing an official representative to the Vatican, consulting the hierarchy on numerous matters, inviting clergy to his inauguration, and welcoming Pope John Paul II to Mexico in 1990. Human rights organizations, including Americas Watch and Amnesty International, severely criticized his administration for the increase in human rights violations and abuses. In response, the government established a new Human Rights Commission in the summer of 1990, but its impact remains to be seen. On other bilateral fronts, especially in drug eradication, Salinas increased cooperation with the United States and took a hard-nosed approach toward this problem within Mexico.

Born in Mexico City, the son of Raúl Salinas Lozano, a former cabinet secretary, and Margarita de Gortari Carvajal, a teacher, Salinas pursued an economics degree at the National University. After graduating in 1971, he earned three degrees from Harvard, two M.A.'s in public administration and political economy, and a Ph.D. in political economy and government (1978). In 1966 he began his political career in the PRI under Gonzalo Martínez Corbalá, but quickly entered the public financial sector on completion of his first master's degree. After serving in several posts in the 1970s, Salinas became director general of social and economic policy under Miguel de la MADRID in the secretariat of planning and budgeting (1979–1981). When de la Madrid was selected as the PRI presidential candidate,

he asked Salinas to serve as director of the PRI's Institute of Political, Economic, and Social Studies during the campaign of 1981–1982. He also served as de la Madrid's secretary of budgeting and planning, following in his mentor's footsteps, until his own designation as the PRI candidate for president in 1987. His designation, and the economic policies he represented, helped provoke a split within his party, in which Cuauhtémoc Cárdenas and Porfirio MUÑOZ LEDO bolted the organization to form their own political movement in support of political reforms and more populist economic policies. Another group of reformers, calling themselves the "Critical Current," remained within the party, adopting a new structure in 1990, in hopes of exerting further pressure favoring internal reforms.

WAYNE A. CORNELIUS, et al., eds., *Mexico's Alternative Political Futures* (1989); RODERIC AI CAMP, "Camarillas in Mexican Politics, the Case of the Salinas Cabinet," in *Journal of Mexican Studies* 6, no. 1 (1990): 85–107; CENTRO DE INVESTIGACIÓN PARA EL DESARROLLO (CIDAC), *Reforma del sistema político mexicano* (1990); SIDNEY WEINTRAUB, *A Marriage of Convenience: Relations between Mexico and the United States* (1990).

RODERIC AI CAMP

See also **Mexico: Political Parties.**

SALNAVE, SYLVAIN (*b.* 1827; *d.* 15 January 1870), president of Haiti (1867–1869). Sylvain Salnave's presidency was marked by civil unrest that threatened to tear the country apart and tempted foreign powers to intervene, once again, in Haitian affairs. Tensions produced in part by the collapse of cotton exports to the United States contributed to the problems Salnave faced. Yet, Salnave's seizure of power through a military rebellion backed by U.S. and Dominican elements also provoked angry reactions from other Haitian leaders. Salnave faced a general uprising in the countryside as various chieftains from the provinces refused to recognize his regime. This led to a state of chronic civil war in which the country became divided into the northern, southern, and central regions. While Salnave faced opposition from armed peasants in the North, the CACOS, and peasant bands in the South, the *piquets*, most of his support came from the center, especially the capital. Salnave became quite popular among the black urban masses, who appreciated his populist economic policies, including the establishment of state-run food stores where basic goods could be bought at low prices. Because of this black support and despite his status as a mulatto, he has been viewed as a founder of Haiti's National Party, which has claimed to speak for the interests of the ordinary black Haitian.

FRANK MOYA PONS, "Haiti and Santo Domingo, 1790–ca. 1870," in *The Cambridge History of Latin America*, vol. 3, edited by Leslie Bethell (1985), pp. 237–275; MICHEL-ROLPH TROUILLOT, *Haiti: State Against Nation* (1990).

PAMELA MURRAY

SALOMON, LOUIS ÉTIENNE LYSIUS FÉLICITÉ

(*b.* 1820; *d.* 1888), Haitian president (1879–1888) and polemicist. He was born to an elite black landowning family in Les Cayes, and after a brief period in the army, turned while still young to politics. He became known as a *noiriste*, an advocate of black dominance, and an opponent of the mulatto elite.

Salomon served as minister of finance and commerce under Faustin SOULOUQUE (1785–1867) and tried to emphasize state ownership of coffee exports. When Fabre Nicolas GEFFRARD (1806–1878) overthrew Soulouque, Salomon left for Jamaica, and from there he bitterly opposed Geffrard.

After his election to the presidency in 1879, many Liberals were exiled or fled. In 1880 Salomon founded the National Bank with foreign capitalization. Some have argued that he thus opened the way for foreign interference and, perhaps, the nineteen-year U.S. occupation that began in 1915. He gave some state land to the peasantry, but he was permissive toward foreign ownership. He was overthrown by a northern coalition in 1888, and he died soon after in exile.

MURDO J. MACLEOD

SALOMÓN–LOZANO TREATY (1922),

a controversial agreement that settled a border dispute between Peru and Colombia. The treaty ceded Colombia a narrow corridor of land between the Putumayo and Amazon rivers (and thus granted it long-desired access to the Amazon River) that included the port of Leticia. In return, Peru received land south of the Putamayo River that Colombia had received from Ecuador in 1916. The latter served Peru's interest by undermining Ecuadorian claims in the Oriente. The treaty was strongly criticized by the Ecuadorian government, which suddenly found itself confronting an antagonist where it had previously had an ally (Colombia).

RONALD BRUCE ST. JOHN, *The Foreign Policy of Peru* (1992).

PETER F. KLARÉN

SALT TRADE

Andean Region

The pre-Columbian agricultural peoples of the Andes and the adjacent coastal valleys considered salt an essential component of their cuisine. In the northern Andes of Ecuador and Colombia, where salt was relatively scarce, its production and trade granted economic power to the tribes that controlled access to it. Northern Andean salt was traded for gold, emeralds, cotton, hot pepper, and dried fish from the coast. Relatively abundant in the southern and central Andes and the adjacent coast, salt constituted a fundamental product to which the states maintained access.

Andean peoples preferred cooked salt loaves, processed at salt springs by full-time specialists, typically women. In Ecuador, this preference had a medicinal basis—salt loaves contained the iodine needed to prevent goiter and cretinism. However, salt was also gathered from salt outcrops and dried salt lake beds—the latter abundant in the Andes of Bolivia, Chile, and Argentina.

Sea salt was produced by solar evaporation in the populated coastal valleys of Peru and at PUNÁ ISLAND (Ecuador) and the mouth of the MAGDALENA RIVER (Colombia). Sea salt from Puná Island and Paita (Peru) was transported long distances north along the coasts of Ecuador and Colombia and reached much of the Ecuadorian highlands.

In the northern Andes, commoners and trade specialists (*mindalaes*) participated in the distribution of salt within and between tribes. In Inca areas, salt specialists (*cachicamayoc*) from diverse ethnic groups shared the saline waters at the major sites, each providing for the salt needs of her or his group.

During colonial times, Spanish entrepreneurs and holders of crown grants took control over much of the native salt production, often to the detriment of native peoples. Mule teams replaced human carriers in the northern Andes, facilitating Spanish trade there. The production of salt loaves continued during colonial times but was eclipsed by that of sea salt and lake bed salt, which were abundant and easily obtained.

A good primary source for the sixteenth century is MARCOS JIMÉNEZ DE LA ESPADA, ed., *Relaciones geográficas de Indias* (1965). Brief overviews of salt trade and production are MARIANNE CARDALE-SCHRIMPFF, "Salt Production in the Eastern Cordillera of Colombia Before and After the Spanish Conquest—A Preliminary Survey," in *Actas del XLI Congreso internacional de americanistas*, vol. 2 (1976), pp. 419–428; and CHERYL POMEROY, "The Salt of Highland Ecuador: Precious Product of a Female Domain," in *Ethnohistory* 35, no. 2 (1988): 131–160.

CHERYL POMEROY

Brazil

The salt trade in Brazil lasted from 1631 to 1801, during which time the Portuguese crown kept salt as a royal monopoly, forbidding colonists to develop it locally or to sell it freely. Salt was shipped to Brazil from Portugal and distributed by those who had purchased monopoly contracts (usually for three years) in Lisbon. Because of its fundamental dietary importance for humans and domesticated animals, and its use as a food preservative, salt was one of the most prominent and controversial monopolies in colonial Brazil. Although the salt trade furnished lucrative revenues for the crown, it created artificially high prices and intermittent shortages for colonists, producing widespread complaints and periodic riots over its imposition.

MYRIAM ELLIS, *O monopólio do sal no estado do Brasil (1631–1801)* (1955); JOEL SERRÃO, ed., *Dicionário de história de Portugal*, 6 vols. (1979).

WILLIAM DONOVAN

Mesoamerica

Salt sources are found throughout MESOAMERICA, though their uneven distribution, coupled with high levels of dietary demand, have made salt a strategic trade commodity. The largest production areas are located in the Central Highlands of Mexico and along the north coast of the Yucatán peninsula. Other production areas include the highlands and Pacific coasts of El Salvador, Guatemala, Chiapas and Oaxaca states in Mexico, and Mexico's west coast. Traditional native production techniques vary. Coastal salt is obtained by solar evaporation (*sal solar*) or by the cooking of saline estuarine waters, sometimes leached through salt-impregnated soils (*sal cocida*); most highland salt is produced by the cooking of salt from wells that tap underground brine springs, or by a process that combines soil leaching and the cooking of the resulting saline residue.

At the beginning of the Late Formative period (ca. 300 B.C.), trade networks originating in the main production areas supplied most of Mesoamerica with salt. The trade was a prominent part of the economy of pre-Hispanic Classic (first millennium A.D.) and Postclassic (ca. 1000 to the Conquest) states of Central Mexico and the Valley of Oaxaca; salt from northern Yucatán was exported throughout the Maya lowlands, and was a key economic factor in the growth of political complexity in the north. The trade of salt continued under Spanish control during the colonial period, and demand increased with its use in the cattle, tanning, and silver mining industries. Today, most table salt is manufactured by large coastal solar producers; it is heavily used in the food preparation and chemical industries.

MIGUEL OTHON DE MENDIZÁBAL, *Influencia de la sal en la distribución geográfica de los grupos indígenas de México* (1929, 1944); RAÚL LOZANO GARCÍA, *Estudio tecnológico de la industria de la sal en México* (1946); ANTHONY P. ANDREWS, *Maya Salt Production and Trade* (1983); URSULA EWALD, *The Mexican Salt Industry, 1560–1980: A Study in Change* (1985); Anthony P. Andrews, "Las salinas de El Salvador: Bosquejo histórico, etnográfico y arqueológico," in *Mesoamérica* 21 (1991): 71–93.

ANTHONY P. ANDREWS

Río de la Plata

Increasing exports of hides and dried beef from the RÍO DE LA PLATA after 1770 required large quantities of salt. Shipments of those commodities, first from the BANDA ORIENTAL and later from Buenos Aires, relied mainly on salt carried overland from the Salinas Grandes (large salt flats), located approximately 240 miles southwest of Buenos Aires, in the unsettled PAMPAS. Large escorted caravans (*tropas*), consisting of hundreds of carts drawn by thousands of oxen, made annual trips to the *salinas* to obtain sufficient supplies of salt for the hide processors and *frigoríficos* (packing houses) of Buenos Aires. The *cabildo* of Buenos Aires organized this trade, reserving for itself the exclusive right to market the salt brought back.

Pampas Indian groups extracted tariffs from the *tropas*. The many different caciques demanded constant negotiations and repeated payments in *aguardiente*, tobacco, yerba maté, bread, and meat. By 1809, in an effort to alleviate recurrent shortages and inconvenient negotiations, many in Buenos Aires called for agreements with the PEHUENCHE and RANQUELE Indians to mine salt and supply the city's *tropas*. Periodic shortages of salt forced suppliers to turn to alternative sources, which included the Río Negro, the Bahía de San Julián, imports from La Rioja and Tucumán, and occasional shipments from Cádiz. Despite the difficulties of bringing enough salt to Buenos Aires, the export of hides and beef continued to grow during the viceregal era and made the Río de la Plata an important region of Bourbon Spain's empire.

ALFREDO J. MONTOYA, *Historia de los saladeros argentinos* (1956); PEDRO ANDRÉS GARCÍA, *Viajes a Salinas Grandes* (1969); JONATHAN C. BROWN, *A Socioeconomic History of Argentina* (1979).

JEREMY STAHL

See also **Hides Industry.**

SALTA, capital of the province of the same name in northwestern Argentina, located at an elevation of 3,893 feet and 140 miles north of Tucumán (1980 population of 260,750). Founded at its present site in 1582 by Hernando de Lerma, it was intended, along with other settlements in northwestern Argentina, to secure the presence of the Spaniards in RÍO DE LA PLATA against territorial claims of advancing conquerors from Peru. During colonial times it gained notoriety for blending Spanish and Indian traditions in its religious art and as the site of the Intendancy of Salta. However, constant attacks from Calchaquí Indians and devastating earthquakes halted an otherwise sustained development based on agriculture (maize, wheat, alfalfa) and the export of mules for the silver mines of Potosí in Bolivia. Near Salta, General Manuel BELGRANO defeated the Spanish royalists in 1813 and brought this conservative province over to the independents. Today the city is an active center of communications; railway lines lead to Antofagasta (Chile) and to La Paz (Bolivia) via La Quiaca, and there is a motorway to Potosí, Oruro, and La Paz. The city's industries are restricted to cement factories and ironworks in the Chachapoyas district.

GRACIELA M. VINUALES, *La ciudad de Salta y su región* (Buenos Aires, 1983); and JAMES R. SCOBIE, *Secondary Cities of Argentina:*

Church of San Francisco, Salta, Argentina. C. FADIGATI / STOCK FOCUS FOTOGRÁFICO.

The Social History of Corrientes, Salta, and Mendoza, 1850–1910 (1988).

CÉSAR N. CAVIEDES

SALTO, capital of the department of the same name in Uruguay on the eastern margins of the URUGUAY RIVER, 260 miles from Montevideo, and second-largest individual city of Uruguay, with 80,823 inhabitants (1985). One of the oldest settlements in the country, Salto was founded in 1756 as a military post not far from the noted Salto Grande waterfalls and rapids, which made upstream navigation impossible. It was originally meant to be a mission, but the foundation of Paysandú in 1772 diminished its significance as a center of evangelism. The proper city was founded in 1817, and the department of the same name in 1837. Mainly a service hub for the numerous sheep ranches of the region, it is the most important administrative center of Uruguay's Littoral.

ELZEAR GIUFFRA, *La República del Uruguay* (Montevideo, 1935).

CÉSAR N. CAVIEDES

SALVACIONISMO, movement by Brazilian military officers to "redeem" their home states from control by local oligarchies (1910–1914). When the 1910 election divided the dominant state parties of São Paulo and Minas Gerais, Rio Grande do Sul's Republican Party and the army emerged as the dominant political forces, and Marshal Hermes Rodrigues da FONSECA became the first soldier to attain the presidency in sixteen years. In these circumstances, officers sought to overthrow oligarchies in state governments through military force and "clean" elections. Localized anarchy followed, as garrisons used cannon to achieve power. By 1912 army officers had taken the governorships in four northeastern states—Ceará, Alagoas, Pernambuco, and Sergipe—in contests marked by military intervention.

By 1914 *salvacionismo* was spent, because of compromises with local elites, military dissension, a new Minas–São Paulo alliance, and lack of support from Hermes, who was dominated by Riograndense Senator José Gomes PINHEIRO MACHADO. The *salvacionistas* broke with Pinheiro, who consequently helped local oligarchs overthrow Ceará's *salvacionista* governor.

Pinheiro was assassinated in 1915, but *salvacionismo* had already dissipated when a new president, supported by Mineiros and Paulistas, took office in 1914. Nonetheless, the myth of military "redemption" remained alive, influencing the TENENTES (lieutenants) a decade later.

EMYGDIO DANTAS BARRETO, *Conspirações* (1917); FERNANDO SETEMBRINO DE CARVALHO, *Memórias: Dados para a história do Brasil* (1950), pp. 87–126; EDGARD CARONE, *A república velha (evolução política)* (1971), pp. 255–296; JOSEPH L. LOVE, *Rio Grande do Sul and Brazilian Regionalism, 1882–1930* (1971), chap. 6.

JOSEPH L. LOVE

See also **Armed Forces.**

SALVADOR, capital of BAHIA State, Brazil, with an estimated population of more than 2 million in 1993. Located on a hilly promontory overlooking the large Bay of All Saints, the city of Salvador (also known during much of its history as Bahia) was founded in 1549 by Tomé de SOUSA, the first governor-general of Brazil, near the site of an earlier Portuguese settlement destroyed by Indian attacks in 1545. Serving from its foundation as the seat of royal government in Brazil, the city housed, after 1609, the colony's first high court. After the 1763 transfer of the viceregal government to RIO DE JANEIRO, the city remained the capital of the captaincy (later province and, after 1889, state) of Bahia. Made the seat of Brazil's first bishopric in 1551, the city became an archepiscopal see in 1676.

Salvador ranked, throughout the colonial period, as one of the wealthiest and largest cities in Brazil, claiming perhaps 15,000 inhabitants by the 1680s and more than 50,000 by the start of the nineteenth century. Visitors were impressed not only by its spectacular location straddling a high bluff along the bay, but also by its dozens of churches and chapels, several convents and monasteries, and public buildings. Although it lost its Jesuit college after 1759, the city gained a public library in 1811, a theater in 1812, and Brazil's second medical school in 1813.

Salvador owed its colonial prosperity to the rich slave-based agricultural export economy of the RECÔNCAVO, the city's immediate hinterland, which early on had emerged as a major sugar-producing region and, from the start of the seventeenth century, also as the chief center of tobacco production in colonial Brazil. The demand for slave labor in sugar and tobacco production in turn made Salvador a principal port in the transatlantic SLAVE TRADE and helped establish strong and lasting cultural links between the city and West Africa. Moreover, throughout Salvador's history, the population of African descent has always outnumbered by a wide margin its white inhabitants. Even in the early nineteenth century, slaves made up somewhere between one-third and two-fifths of the city's population.

Salvador, Brazil. Reproduced from Kaspar van Baerle, *Rerum per Octennium in Brasilia* (Amsterdam, 1647). BY PERMISSION OF THE HOUGHTON LIBRARY, HARVARD UNIVERSITY.

Social and political turmoil, beginning with the IN-CONFIDÊNCIA DOS ALFAIATES (1798), an early and quickly crushed independence movement, characterized Salvador's history in the first decades of the nineteenth century. Held by forces loyal to the Portuguese crown, the city suffered a nine-month siege in 1822–1823 during Brazil's brief war for independence. After 1823 Salvador witnessed revolts, numerous anti-Portuguese riots, and barracks uprisings, culminating in 1837–1838 in the SABINADA, a federalist rebellion, during which the city again was besieged. The city and the neighboring Recôncavo also experienced a spectacular series of SLAVE REVOLTS between 1809 and 1835, including the 1835 Malê revolt, led by Muslim urban slaves and freed slaves of West African origin, which was perhaps the best-planned slave rising in Brazilian history.

In the late nineteenth and early twentieth centuries, Salvador continued to grow (reaching a population of 283,422 by 1920) but suffered with the decline in sugar production in the Recôncavo and the stagnation of the Bahian export economy. Petroleum production in the city's hinterland and the later development of a petrochemical industry gave the city new dynamism from the 1960s onward. Today, Salvador ranks as a major industrial and commercial center and also carries enormous weight in cultural matters—contributing disproportionately to innovative trends in popular music and serving as the country's principal center of Afro-Brazilian culture.

PIERRE VERGER, *Flux et reflux de la traite des nègres entre le Golfe de Bénin et Bahia de Todos os Santos, du dix-septième au dix-neuvième siècle* (1968); THALES DE AZEVEDO, *Povoamento da cidade do Salvador* (1969); KATIA M. DE QUEIRÓS MATTOSO, *Bahia: A cidade do Salvador e seu mercado* (1978); STUART B. SCHWARTZ, *Sugar Plantations in the Formation of Brazilian Society: Bahia, 1550–1835* (1985), and *Bahia, século XIX: Uma província no Império* (1992); JOÃO JOSÉ REIS, *Slave Rebellion in Brazil: The Muslim Uprising of 1835 in Bahia* (1993).

B. J. BARICKMAN

SALVADOR, VICENTE DO (*b.* 1564; *d.* 1639), Portuguese historian and member of the FRANCISCAN order. At the age of sixty-three he wrote a *History of Brazil* that was more concerned with human events than with Brazilian fauna and flora as had been the case with his sixteenth-century predecessors. The first chapter was still devoted to nature and to Brazil's original inhabitants, but all the others narrated the main events of Portuguese colonization in America from 1500 until 1627. In his dedication to the Portuguese scholar Manuel Severim de Faria, the author wrote that he expected his work to be printed at this patron's expense. However, his *History* remained unpublished until the nineteenth century, and some chapters were lost.

Written in Bahia, Salvador's opus is a general history, rather than a local one. The Franciscan does not reveal his sources, but João Capistrano de ABREU, the nineteenth-century historian, proved that Frei Vicente had read Simão Estácio da Silveira's *Relação sumária das cousas do Maranhão* (1624) and Pero de Magalhaes GANDAVO's *História da Província de Santa Cruz* (1576). Wars against the Indians, the French pirate attacks, and the Dutch invasions are narrated. Military actions of governors-general attract his attention more than the colonists and their agricultural and mercantile activities.

JOÃO CAPISTRANO DE ABREU, *Ensaios e estuados: Crítica e história* (2d ser. 1976); JOSÉ HONÓRIO RODRIGUES, *História da história do Brasil*, vol. 1, *Historiografia colonial* (1979).

MARIA BEATRIZ NIZZA DA SILVA

SALVATIERRA, CONDE DE. *See* **Sarmiento de Sotomayor, García.**

SALVATIONISM. *See* **Salvacionismo.**

SAM, JEAN VILBRUN GUILLAUME (*d.* 28 July 1915), president of Haiti (March–July 1915). Sam's brief presidency was marked by mounting chaos and violence that resulted in the occupation of the country by U.S. Marines. While responding to U.S. pressures to arrange a customs receivership similar to the one the Americans had created for the Dominican Republic, Sam spent most of his time fighting his political enemies, who were led by the virulently anti-American Rosalvo BOBO. Sam ordered the execution of 167 prisoners, many of them Bobo's supporters. In retaliation, on 28 July 1915, he was lynched and butchered by a mob in Port-au-Prince. Shortly thereafter, the U.S. Marines occupied Haiti.

RAYFORD W. LOGAN, *Haiti and the Dominican Republic* (1968); LESTER D. LANGLEY, *The Banana Wars: United States Intervention in the Caribbean, 1898–1934*, rev. ed. (1988); MICHEL-ROLPH TROUILLOT, *Haiti: State Against Nation* (1990).

PAMELA MURRAY

SAM, TIRÉSIAS AUGUSTIN SIMON (dates unknown), president of Haiti (31 March 1896–12 May 1902). Military potentate of his native North, minister of war and marine under the presidency of Lysius SALOMON (1879–1888), Sam had strong ties within the then dominant dark-skinned faction of the oligarchy. He offered the Haitian elites the combination of force and compromise they expected. With limited formal training, he used his contacts to bring competence to the service of government. He encouraged the construction of railroads around Cap Haïtien and Port-au-Prince. Financial scandals, factionalism, and the renewed bullying of Haiti by foreign powers, notably Germany, France, and the United States, distracted him from an already loose agenda. Forced out of power when he tried to prolong his constitutional mandate, he predicted an endless civil war: "I am the last president of Haiti."

BRENDA G. PLUMMER, *Haiti and the Great Powers, 1902–1915* (1988).

MICHEL-ROLPH TROUILLOT

SAMANÁ BAY, harbor on the Samaná Peninsula, at the northeasternmost point of the Dominican Republic. Facing the Mona Passage, the key exit channel of the Caribbean for warships, oil tankers, and civilian passenger vessels, Samaná Bay is the Caribbean's best natural harbor. During the second half of the nineteenth century, U.S. presidents Ulysses Grant, James Buchanan, and Andrew Johnson, Dominican presidents Buenaventura BÁEZ and Pedro SANTANA, naval strategists, and diplomats all made efforts to purchase or lease Samaná Bay and the peninsula on which it is located. At the same time, the United States was eager to keep the area out of the control of its European rivals, England, France, and Germany.

FRANK MOYA PONS, *Manual de historia dominicana,* 7th ed. (1983), esp. pp. 376–377, 380; MICHAEL J. KRYZANEK and HOWARD J. WIARDA, *The Politics of External Influence in the Dominican Republic* (1988), esp. pp. 5, 27, 29–30, 153.

KAI P. SCHOENHALS

SAMANEZ OCAMPO, DAVID (*b.* 1866; *d.* 1947), landowner, provincial leader of Nicolás de PIÉROLA's Democratic Party, and president of a provisional government in Peru between March and December 1931. Born in Huambo, Samanez Ocampo was elected deputy of the province of Antabamba, Apurímac. In 1909 he rebelled against the first government of Augusto B. LEGUÍA and later supported President Guillermo BILLINGHURST (1912–1914). In political retirement by the time Colonel Luis M. SÁNCHEZ CERRO was forced to resign as de facto president in March 1931, Samanez Ocampo was selected to head a transitional government that held presidential and congressional elections in October 1931. Samanez Ocampo's government partially adopted some of adviser Edwin W. KEMMERER's economic recommendations. Samanez Ocampo retired again from national politics when Sánchez Cerro assumed power after the contested elections of 1931.

STEVE STEIN, *Populism in Peru: The Emergence of the Masses and the Politics of Social Control* (1980).

ALFONSO W. QUIROZ

SAMAYOA CHINCHILLA, CARLOS (*b.* 10 December 1898; *d.* 14 February 1973), Guatemalan writer. A member of the same generation as Miguel Ángel ASTURIAS and Luis CARDOZA Y ARAGÓN, he is especially famous for his nativist short stories collected in *Madre Milpa* (1934).

Born in Guatemala City, the son of wealthy landowners, Samayoa traveled extensively throughout Europe in the 1920s. Forced to return to his native country after the stock market crash of 1929, he served as a minor bureaucrat in the Jorge UBICO administration (1931–1944). While traveling with the dictator throughout the country, he developed his ideas for *Madre Milpa.* The Ubico dictatorship collapsed in 1944, and Samayoa published a book of memoirs about his experience working with the most feared man in the country, *El dictador y yo* (1945). During the 1940s he was director of the National Library and was active in founding several museums. As the new democratic administration became more liberal, Monterroso became a bitter critic of its progressive tendencies and joined in red-baiting the Arbenz government (1951–1954). In his later years he published books of short stories, but none were as accomplished as his original success. Other books by Samayoa are *Cuatro suertes* (1936); *Estampas de la costa grande* (1954); *El quetzal no es rojo* (1956); and *Chapines de ayer* (1957).

FRANCISCO ALBIZÚREZ PALMA and CATALINA BARRIOS Y BARRIOS, *Historia de la literatura guatemalteca,* vol. 3 (1987), pp. 38–52.

ARTURO ARIAS

SAMBA, the most famous Brazilian musical form and dance. Musically, samba is characterized by a 2/4 meter with the heaviest accent on the second beat and features pronounced syncopation, a stanza-and-refrain structure, responsorial singing, and many interlocking rhythmic parts. Samba has African roots, but its exact origins are unknown. Samba's true parent may have been the *lundu* song and circle dance, featuring the *umbigada* navel-touching movement, which came to Brazil from Angola. A primitive type of samba may have developed in Bahia from African musical elements and then brought to Rio de Janeiro by slaves and former slaves in the late 1800s.

Samba began to crystallize into its modern form in the early 1900s at the homes of Bahian matriarchs such as Tia Ciata, who lived near Rio's Praça Onze. There, musicians like PIXINGUINHA, Donga, João da Baiana, and SINHÔ developed the budding form and added influences from the *maxixe* and *marcha* styles. The first recorded samba was "Pelo telefone" (On the Phone), composed by several musicians (but registered to Donga) and performed by the Banda Odeon in 1917.

Near Praça Onze was Estácio, the neighborhood of the sambistas Ismael Silva, Nilton Bastos, and Armando Marçal, who added longer notes, two-bar phrasing, and a slower tempo to samba, and solidified what would be samba's standard form for decades (later called, in the 1950s, *samba de morro*). It was they who also founded Deixa Falar, the first *escola de samba* (samba school), in 1928. Later important samba composers include: Noel Rosa, Caninha, Heitor dos Prazeres, Ataulfo Alves, Assis Valente, Geraldo Pereira, Lamartine Babo, Ary Barroso, Braguinha, Dorival CAYMMI, Martinho da Vila, and Paulinho da Viola.

Samba's primary rhythm and its cross-rhythms can be carried by drum and percussion playing (the *batucada*) involving numerous instruments such as *surdo* (three different sizes), *caixa, repique, tamborim, pandeiro, prato, cuíca, frigideira, agogô, reco-reco,* and *chocalho*. Samba is also typically accompanied by guitar, four-string *cavaquinho,* and—less frequently—brass instruments.

Different styles of samba include *samba-canção* (a slower, more sophisticated style with more emphasis on melody and harmony than on the rhythm); *samba de breque* (a samba that features a "break" in which the singer dramatizes the story told in the lyrics); *samba de gafieira* (a dance-hall type of samba, usually instrumental, with horn arrangements influenced by American big-band jazz); *samba de roda* (a circle-dance samba, accompanied by hand clapping and *batucada*); *samba-enredo* (a "theme" samba, performed by samba schools during Carnaval in Rio); *pagode samba* (a "street"-type of samba popularized in the 1980s by composers from Rio's Ramos neighborhood, who added *tan-tan* and banjo to the instrumentation); and *samba-reggae*. In addition, bossa nova mixed simplified samba rhythms with harmonies influenced by American West Coast "cool" jazz and classical music.

SERGIO CABRAL, *As escolas de samba* (1974); RITA CAURIO, ed., *Brasil musical* (1988); JOÃO MAXIMO and CARLOS DIDIER, *Noel Rosa: Uma biografia* (1990); and CHRIS MC GOWAN and RICARDO PESSANHA, *The Brazilian Sound: Samba, Bossa Nova, and the Popular Music of Brazil* (1991).

CHRIS MCGOWAN

SAMBA SCHOOLS, Brazilian organizations (*escolas de samba*) that plan and stage samba parades during Carnaval. Based for the most part in Rio de Janeiro, they often perform other social functions and may serve as community centers in poorer neighborhoods. For decades they have served as a source of pride, identity, and creativity for working-class Brazilian blacks and mulattoes, who make up the majority of members of each samba school.

As of 1990, there were fifty-six officially registered *escolas de samba* in Rio and dozens more in other cities throughout Brazil. The bigger ones, such as Mangueira, typically parade with four to five thousand singers and dancers, and three hundred-member percussion section. Every *escola*'s parade has a theme, an *enredo,* for that year's performance, which often focuses on Brazilian culture, history, or politics. This theme is explored in the lyrics of a *samba-enredo* chosen for that year, and these songs are often written by some of Brazil's top samba composers. The *enredo* is also illustrated in the ornamented floats and the lavish costumes of the participants, who are divided into several dozen different wings (*alas*), each of which features a distinct costume. The *carnavalesco* is the art director who coordinates the visual aspects of the floats (*carros alegóricos*) and the *alas*

in order to elaborate upon the theme. The *puxador* is the lead singer of the *escola,* and the *mestre de bateria* is the percussion director who conducts the musicians playing a dozen or more different drum and percussion instruments. The latter typically include the *surdo* (three different sizes), *caixa, repique, tamborim, pandeiro, prato, cuíca, frigideira, agogô, reco-reco,* and *chocalho*.

The first *escola,* Deixa Falar, was founded on 12 August 1928 in Rio's Estácio neighborhood by the famed samba musicians Ismael Silva, Bide, Armando Marçal, and Nilton Bastos. Deixa Falar was defunct by 1933, but other schools rose up to take its place, such as Mangueira (founded in 1929) and Portela (1935). At the beginning, the government repressed manifestations of Afro-Brazilian culture and discouraged blacks and mulattoes from parading. But, with official recognition by the Getúlio VARGAS administration in 1935, the festivities moved to the wide avenues of downtown Rio and then in 1984 to the Passarela do Samba (or Sambódromo), designed by architect Oscar NIEMEYER. From the 1960s on, the *escola de samba* parades have been broadcast live on national television, which has firmly established their importance and also made them into a major tourist attraction.

By the 1970s there were complaints that the *escolas* and the parade had become too large and overly commercialized; many poorer members had to save all year to pay for their parade costumes, and the huge budgets of certain schools were often bankrolled by drug dealers or the *bicheiros* who ran illegal lotteries. Many musicians left the larger *escolas* and formed smaller groups independent of the televised festivities in the Sambodromo. One example was Quilombo, founded in 1975 by samba singer-songwriter Paulinho da Viola and composer Candeia.

Among Rio's biggest and most important *escolas* in the 1980s were the aforementioned Mangueira and Portela, as well as Império Serrano, Salgueiro, Imperatriz Leopoldinense, Império da Tijuca, Unidos do Cabaçu, Beija-Flor, Mocidade Independente de Padre Miguel, and Vila Isabel.

SÉRGIO CABRAL, *As Escolas de Samba* (1974); RITA CAURIO, ed., *Brasil musical* (1988); CHRIS MC GOWAN and RICARDO PESSANHA, *The Brazilian Sound: Samba, Bossa Nova, and the Popular Music of Brazil* (1991).

CHRIS MCGOWAN

SAMBAQUI, word of Tupi origin (tãba'ki) designating shell mounds, archaeological sites found in Brazilian seashore paleo-environments near rivers, lagoons, and mangroves. These shell mounds consist mainly of large accumulations of mollusk shells, remains of crustaceans, and fish bones from seasonal campsites of small prehistoric groups of coastal fishermen and collectors. In spite of the similar sources of subsistence of these groups, adaptive variations characterize the *sambaqui*. Different types resulted from successive or simultaneous phases of intense collecting of mollusks and phases of intense gathering of crustaceans and/or catching of fish, followed by hunting as well as fruit collecting. The term *sambaqui* has synonyms: in São Paulo and Santa Catarina shell mounds are *casqueiro*, *concheira*, or *ostreira*; in Pará, *cernambi* or *sarnambi*; in other places, *samauqui*, *caieira*, or *caleira* and even "island of shell."

LINA MARIA KNEIP et al., *Pesquisas arqueológicas no litoral de Itaipú* (1981), and *Coletores e pescadores pré-históricos de Guaratiba* (1985).

CHARLOTTE EMMERICH

SAMBUCETTI, LUIS (NICOLÁS) (*b.* 29 July 1860; *d.* 7 September 1926), Uruguayan composer, conductor, violinist, and teacher. Born in Montevideo, Sambucetti first studied with his father, a musician, and later with Luigi Preti, who instructed him in violin, and José Strigelli, in counterpoint. He enrolled at the National Conservatory in Paris in 1885, where he studied violin with Hubert Léonard, harmony with Théodore Dubois, and composition under Ernest Guiraud, Jules Massenet, and Léo Delibes for three years. For two years he was the concertmaster of the Chatelet Théâtre Orchestra under the baton of Édouard Colonne. In 1890 he returned to Montevideo, where he founded the Instituto Verdi, one of the major conservatories of Uruguay. He also started three chamber groups: the Cuarteto Sambucetti (1891), a second Cuarteto Sambucetti (1900), and the Sociedad de Conciertos (1911). As founder, organizer, and conductor of the Orquesta Nacional (1908), he introduced to Montevideo the contemporary symphonic repertoire, especially that of the French impressionists.

As a composer Sambucetti is considered the master of early Uruguayan symphonism. Besides his lyric poem, *San Francesco d'Assisi,* winner of a first prize and gold medal at the Milan International Fair Competition (1906), his *Suite d'orchestre*—a symphonic triptych performed at the TEATRO SOLÍS on 29 September 1899—has unique shades of orchestral color, particularly in the use of woodwind instruments. It is considered the best Uruguayan symphonic work of the nineteenth century. As a teacher and educator Sambucetti guided a whole generation of Uruguayan composers in the early twentieth century. He also wrote three operettas, orchestral and chamber music, and works for voice and piano and for violin. With his wife, the pianist María Verninck, he translated Reber-Dubois's *Harmony Treatise* and other didactic music books into Spanish. He died in Montevideo.

LAURO AYESTARÁN, *Luis Sambucetti: Vida y obra* (1956); *Composers of the Americas,* vol. 14 (1968), pp. 140–146; SUSANA SALGADO, *Breve historia de la música culta en el Uruguay,* 2d ed. (1980).

SUSANA SALGADO

SAMPER, JOSÉ MARÍA (*b.* 31 March 1828; *d.* 22 July 1888), Colombian writer. Samper came from a mercantile family of Honda, Tolima. He received his law doctorate in Bogotá, in 1846, and plunged into politics. In his early years a Liberal with romantic socialist ideas, he began, after his second marriage (1855), to move toward more traditional political views, culminating in his return to Catholicism in 1865. Samper's abandonment of his earlier principles (added to a difficult personality) resulted in his effective exclusion from major political office until a decade before his death. It also meant that he had to earn a living by writing. His production was enormous. Poetry, drama, essays, editorials, novels, travel accounts, history, and legal treatises flowed from his pen. His autobiography, *Historia de un alma . . . 1834 a 1881* (1881), remains a classic; so does his play *Un alcalde a la antigua y dos primos a la moderna* (1856). His reportage, *El sitio de Cartagena de 1885* (1885), and his *Ensayos sobre las revoluciones políticas de las repúblicas colombianas* (1861) are Colombian literary treasures. Samper represented Colombia in the Netherlands and Belgium (1858–1863) and in Argentina (1884). He also served several terms as a congressman. He died in Anapaima, Cundinamarca.

FRANK M. DUFFEY, *The Early Cuadro de Costumbres in Colombia* (1956), pp. 102–106; HAROLD E. HINDS, JR., "José María Samper: The Thought of a Nineteenth-Century New Granadan During His Radical-Liberal Years (1845–1865)" (Ph.D. diss., Vanderbilt University, 1976); HELEN DELPAR, *Red Against Blue* (1981), pp. 47–48, 59–60, 62–63.

J. LEÓN HELGUERA

See also **Literature; López, José Hilario.**

SAMPER AGUDELO, MIGUEL (*b.* 24 October 1825; *d.* 16 March 1899), Colombian Liberal economist and politician. Samper's devotion to liberal economic principles distinguishes him as one of Colombia's leading nineteenth-century Liberals. Born to a modest family in Guaduas, Cundinamarca, Samper was trained as a lawyer at San Bartolomé College in Bogotá. He dedicated his energies to business rather than politics and invested profitably in tobacco production and trade in the Magdalena Valley during the 1850s. His brothers, José María, Silvestre, Antonio, and Manuel, were also active in politics and commerce. Samper's liberalism is apparent in his noted social commentary *La miseria en Bogotá* (1867), his fervent support of lower tariff rates (1880), and his staunch opposition to the monetary policies of the Regeneration. Despite his economic beliefs, his social conservatism is evident in his increased devotion to Catholicism later in his life. Samper's political roles included positions in the national congress, minister of finance under two administrations, and the Liberal presidential candidate in 1897.

MIGUEL SAMPER, *Escritos político-económicos*, 4 vols. (1925–1927), and *La miseria en Bogotá y otros escritos* (1969); JAIME JARAMILLO URIBE, *El pensamiento colombiano en el siglo XIX* (1969).

DAVID SOWELL

SAMUDIO, JUAN A. (*b.* 21 April 1879; *d.* 1936), Paraguayan artist. Often considered the finest Paraguayan painter of the twentieth century, Samudio was a native-born Asunceño. Though he received his early education in the capital city, he was irresistibly drawn to painting—an interest that he could little hope to pursue if he stayed in Paraguay. Thanks to a scholarship, he went to Rome in 1903 for five years of study.

In Italy, Samudio developed a painting style characterized by a careful interplay of shadows. He limited himself to traditional subjects and avoided the avant garde, but his work nonetheless received a measure of acclaim. He was already winning prizes while still a student in Rome. In 1910 he exhibited two canvases at the International Exposition of Art in Buenos Aires. One of these, entitled *Noche de luna*, brought the artist a bronze medal and was later acquired by the National Museum in Asunción.

After his return to Paraguay, Samudio dedicated himself as much to teaching and to artistic theory as to painting. He became director of the Paraguayan Academy of Fine Arts, a position he held throughout the 1920s. He also cooperated with the municipal government of Asunción in the design of public parks and gardens.

WILLIAM BELMONT PARKER, *Paraguayans of To-Day* (1921), pp. 134–136; RAFAEL ELADIO VELÁZQUEZ, *Breve historia de la cultura en el Paraguay* (1984), p. 246.

THOMAS L. WHIGHAM

SAN AGUSTÍN, archaeological region located at the headwaters of the Magdalena River in southern Colombia. Containing evidence of statuary and artifical mounds, San Agustín and neighboring areas have been the focus of intensive archaeological research. Human occupation of the area probably dates back to before 1000 B.C., but evidence is still scarce. In the Valle de la Plata, to the south of where the construction of the most impressive statues and mounds took place, archaeological research has allowed the reconstruction of three periods of pre-Columbian development. Since ceramic materials found in La Plata and in San Agustín are similar, and chronological periodization is comparable, results from La Plata help to reconstruct patterns of social evolution in the Upper Magdalena in general.

By the Early Period (1000 B.C.–A.D. 1) the population

San Agustín, Colombia. ANTHRO-PHOTO.

was concentrated in areas of fertile soil where conditions favored agriculture with simple technologies. The population density was low. Little is known in terms of social organization and trade activities. During the Middle Period (A.D. 1–850) there was strong population growth; the total number of people in the area doubled. Two concentrations of population correspond to areas where monumental sculpture and barrows were found, suggesting increasing political centralization. This period also marks the peak of sculpture in San Agustín. Pollen analysis indicates that maize, potato, sweet potato, quinoa, and beans were cultivated at this time. There is also evidence of gold trade, and probably of gold adornments production, but at a small scale when compared with other southern Colombian societies such as CALIMA.

The Late Period (A.D. 850–1530) represents a continuation of population growth. At one of the large sites that emerged during the previous period, funerary monuments were found. The monuments investigated are less impressive than those of the Middle Period, inasmuch as the tombs are now deep narrow shafts. Pottery and goldwork of this time are simpler than that of previous periods. At the time of the Spanish Conquest, populations of the region are described as small chiefdoms with little political centralization compared with other societies in northern South America, such as the MUISCA. As of yet, it is not clear if processes of social change implied the decadence of regional elites before the Conquest. It is just as possible that chiefly status in the region was displayed by means other than the construction of splendid monuments.

LUIS DUQUE and JULIO CÉSAR CUBILLOS, *Arqueología de San Agustín: Alto de Lavapatas* (1988). Also see GERARDO REICHEL-DOLMATOFF, *San Agustín: A Culture of Colombia* (1972). For research conducted in the Valle de la Plata see ROBERT DRENNAN, "Regional Dynamics of Chiefdoms in the Valle de la Plata," in *Journal of Field Archaeology* (1991).

CARL HENRIK LANGEBAEK R.

See also **Archaeology**.

SAN ANDRÉS (Campana San Andrés), the primary regional center for the Zapotitán Valley in central El Salvador during the Late Classic period (A.D. 650–900). The site is located west of San Salvador, in the eastern part of the Zapotitán Valley, along the upper Río Sucio drainage. San Andrés covers approximately 6 square miles and includes about sixty mounds. Over 200 mounds are clustered around the site center.

San Andrés was first settled in the Preclassic period (400 B.C.–A.D. 250). Little is known about this initial occupation. The Ilopango volcano, just east of San Salvador, erupted violently about A.D. 250, depositing a thick layer of ash over the site that rendered the area uninhabitable.

During the Late Classic, San Andrés was reoccupied and reached its zenith in size and power. Stylistically it is most strongly associated with the major Maya center of COPÁN, in southwestern Honduras, and with TAZUMAL, in the Chalchuapa region of western El Salvador. Artifacts such as Copador polychrome ceramics, pyrite mirrors, and finely carved jadeite suggest connections with these major Maya centers. The architectural plan of San Andrés is comparable to that of Copán, especially in its plaza-acropolis arrangement. The balustraded stairways at San Andrés are reminiscent of those at Tazumal and Copán.

Mound construction is of two types: adobe block cores, with wall facings and floors covered with mortar, as at Tazumal, and talpetate masonry walls covered with mortar. San Andrés structures included terraced pyramidal temples, residences, and walled courts. The majority of construction took place during the Late Classic period.

Postclassic (A.D. 900–1400) occupation of San Andrés, evinced by artifacts such as Nicoya polychrome ceramics, was sparse. Thus, it appears that San Andrés was heavily occupied for only the brief span of the Late Classic period, then was largely abandoned.

MAURICE RIES, "First Season's Archaeological Work at Campana–San Andrés, El Salvador," in *American Anthropologist* 42 (1940):712–713; JOHN M. DIMICK, "Notes on Excavations at Campana–San Andrés, El Salvador," in *Carnegie Institution of Washington Yearbook* 40 (1941):298–300; STANLEY H. BOGGS, "Notas sobre las excavaciones en la hacienda 'San Andres,' departamento de La Libertad," in *Tzumpame* 3, no. 1 (1943):104–126; JOHN M. LONGYEAR III, "Archaeological Survey of El Salvador," in *Handbook of Middle American Indians*, Vol. 4, *Archaeological Frontiers and External Connections*, edited by Gordon Ekholm and Gordon Willey (1966).

KATHRYN SAMPECK

SAN ANDRÉS ISLAND, one of six islands comprising the Colombian intendancy of San Andrés, which also includes the islands of PROVIDENCIA, Santa Catalina, San Bernardo, El Rosario, and Isla Fuerte. San Andrés, the largest and most populous of these islands, is slightly more than 100 miles east of Nicaragua and about 400 miles northwest of Cartagena, Colombia.

Although the islands had been discovered by COLUMBUS or other early Spanish navigators, English loggers, buccaneers, privateers, and pirates intermittently occupied them in the seventeenth century. There was no permanent colonization of San Andrés until the eighteenth century, when settlers arrived from Jamaica, closely connecting the island to other British settlements on the Mosquito shore of Nicaragua. When the Convention of London recognized Spanish claims to the islands in 1786, some of the British left, but a strong African-English cultural and economic influence remains in the 1990s. In the early nineteenth century cotton and contraband characterized the San Andrés economy. Later coconuts, tortoiseshell, and other tropical products became important. Colombia claimed the islands in 1810 and successfully resisted Central American, Nicaraguan, British, and Spanish claims.

Creation of San Andrés as a free port in 1953 greatly increased its economic activity, and with the addition of an airport in 1955, its population grew rapidly through the arrival of many Colombians and foreigners. Its population had grown slowly from about 1,000 in 1800 to about 3,000 in 1900 and approximately 4,000 by 1950; by 1990 it had reached nearly 35,000.

JAMES J. PARSONS, *San Andrés and Providencia: English-speaking Islands in the Western Caribbean* (1956).

RALPH LEE WOODWARD, JR.

SAN ANTONIO, a presidio–mission-town complex founded in 1718, as a way station between Spanish settlements on the Río Grande and the recently founded Spanish outpost on the French Louisiana frontier. Originally composed of Presidio San Antonio de Béxar and Misión San Antonio de Valero (now the ALAMO), the settlement was enlarged in 1720 with the addition of a second Franciscan mission, San José y San Miguel de Aguayo, and in 1731 by the relocation of three other missions, Nuestra Señora de la Purísima Concepción, San Juan Capistrano, and San Francisco de la Espada. That same year Canary Islands colonists, holding a royal charter, founded Villa San Fernando de Béxar adjacent to the presidio and Misión San Antonio.

San Antonio grew slowly through the 1760s because of chronic Indian warfare, an absence of mineral wealth, and remoteness from colonial population centers. Throughout the colonial and Mexican periods the economy depended on cattle ranching, subsistence agriculture, and the furnishing of services to the presidio. In the 1770s, as part of a reform of New Spain's frontier defenses, the garrison was strengthened and the population augmented by the resettlement of settlers from the extinguished East Texas presidio of Los Adaes. In 1773 San Antonio became the capital of Texas, a position it maintained until its status was reduced to departmental seat of government following the union of Texas with Coahuila under the Mexican constitution of 1824.

During the Mexican War of Independence the city experienced outbreaks of violence and brief insurrectionary governments in 1811 and 1813. In the 1820s secularization of the missions, which had begun in 1793, was completed. The presidio went out of existence in the spring of 1836, following the successful Texan revolt against Mexico, but the town survived as the largest Texas city for much of the nineteenth century.

CARLOS E. CASTAÑEDA, *Our Catholic Heritage in Texas,* 7 vols. (1936–1958); JESÚS F. DE LA TEJA, *San Antonio de Béxar: A Community on New Spain's Frontier* (1995).

JESÚS F. DE LA TEJA

SAN CARLOS DE GUATEMALA, UNIVERSITY OF. This regionally important colonial Hispanic American university was begun with a legacy left by Francisco Marroquín, first bishop of Guatemala, who endowed the College of Saint Thomas, attached to the Dominican convent in Guatemala City. The town council at once tried to raise the college to the status of a university, but encountered financial problems and bureaucratic delays. In 1622, the JESUITS secured the right to confer degrees in their own college, further complicating the town council's efforts. It was only in 1676 that a combination of a fortunate legacy and patient maneuvering finally induced the crown to authorize a public university, named for the then reigning Charles II.

The new foundation followed the pattern used at the University of Salamanca by confiding governance to the body of doctors and masters in residence (called the Cloister) led by a rector elected annually from its members. Both were subject to crown authority through the captain-general. Faculty positions were filled by *oposiciones,* contests of specimen lectures, given before a body of judges. Winners of the *oposiciones* filled junior chairs for a term of years, and senior (proprietary) posts were held for life. The faculty consisted of nine to twelve professors at a time. Between 1625 and 1821 2,006 students received bachelor's degrees and 504 earned advanced degrees.

The university's economic base was always fragile. Guatemala was a poor area, and the crown adamantly resisted using any of its monies for education. In addition, relations between the University and the Jesuits remained delicate. Until their expulsion in 1767, the Jesuits continued to grant degrees and enjoyed a high reputation for their instruction.

San Carlos, like other Hispanic UNIVERSITIES, exemplified and exalted the neoscholastic learning of sixteenth-century Spain. But again in common with others, the curriculum had become stale and routine by the first decades of the eighteenth century, and demands for reform emerged.

In 1784 a Dominican professor, newly arrived from Spain, officially accused his colleagues of laxity and backwardness. The responses to these charges showed that quiet changes had been going on for a decade or more. For example, the Franciscan José Antonio Goicoechea had taught experimental physics since about 1770. Goicoechea and others submitted plans of reform, and over the next three decades there was a ferment of new projects and ideas. These included incorporating mathematics and up-to-date geography and cosmography in the curriculum, introducing experimental (Newtonian) physics, and shifting the theology curriculum to emphasize scripture study, dogmatic theology, and moral philosophy at the expense of speculative scholasticism. A strong regalist impulse was imposed on law studies, with great emphasis on the power and authority of the crown and the importance of Spanish law. Finally, the study of medicine was made current by new texts, anatomical studies, and training in botany and chemistry.

These reforms in the university were encouraged and paralleled by the actions of a coterie of government officials, professors, clerics, students, and prominent citizens who clustered around the SOCIEDAD ECONÓMICA DE AMIGOS DEL PAÍS and wrote in the GAZETA DE GUATEMALA. They clearly had access to new books and benefited from contact with two visiting scientific expeditions. The *Gazeta* discussed such questions as the wisdom of replacing Latin with Spanish as the language of the schools, advocated sensationalist psychology, and considered various plans to improve the lot of the Indians as well as numerous other economic questions.

The political and intellectual significance of the university and the impact of the intellectual changes made after 1780 is best indicated by the fact that nine of the thirteen signers of the 1821 declaration of Guatemalan independence were graduates of San Carlos.

The definitive study is JOHN TATE LANNING's twin volumes, *The University in the Kingdom of Guatemala* (1955) and *The Eighteenth-Century Enlightenment in the University of San Carlos de Guatemala* (1956). Lanning's *Academic Culture in the Spanish Colonies* (1940) provides a general comparative picture.

GEORGE M. ADDY

See also **Dominicans; Enlightenment, The.**

SAN CRISTÓBAL DE LAS CASAS, the preeminent city (1990 population of 90,000) of the central highlands of the southernmost Mexican state of CHIAPAS. Founded in 1524 by Luis Marín, it was originally called La Chiapa de los Indios and renamed Ciudad Real de Chiapa in 1527. As the provincial capital of isolated Chiapas, Ciudad Real fell within the jurisdiction of the Kingdom of Guatemala of the Viceroyalty of NEW SPAIN. It served as the diocesan center of Chiapas until 1744 despite the fact that its Spanish population never exceeded 250 during the seventeenth century.

When Chiapas joined the Mexican federation in 1824, this city became the state capital. During the nineteenth century its name changed from San Cristóbal (1829) to San Cristóbal de las Casas (1844), in honor of Chiapas' first bishop, Bartolomé de LAS CASAS. During the mid-nineteenth-century struggle between Liberals and Conservatives, San Cristóbal was the bastion of provincial Conservatives. As a delayed consequence of Liberal ascendancy in Chiapas, the powers of the state government were transferred definitively to Tuxtla Gutiérrez in 1892. Cristobalense malcontents attempted without success to exploit the national revolution of 1910–1911 by initiating a rebellion against the government in Tuxtla Gutiérrez in order to reestablish San Cristóbal as the state capital.

The political and economic marginalization of the city in the twentieth century has contributed to the preservation of the city's numerous colonial-era architectural monuments. Its colonial and Indian ambience has made it a popular tourist attraction in recent decades. In January 1994 the city was briefly seized by the Ejército Zapatista de Liberación Nacional during a regional uprising of Indians and peasants.

JAN DE VOS, *San Cristóbal ciudad colonial* (1986); ANDRÉS AUBRY, *San Cristóbal de las Casas: Su historia urbana, demográfica y monumental, 1528–1990* (1991).

THOMAS BENJAMIN
VIRGINIA GARRARD-BURNETT

SAN DOMINGO IMPROVEMENT COMPANY, a group of U.S. investors (including many high government officials) who, in 1893, bought up the Dominican interests of the bankrupt Westendorp Company of Amsterdam. Beginning in 1888, Westendorp had made several large loans to Dominican President Ulises Heureaux (1882–1899). The San Domingo Improvement Company assumed the financial interests of Westendorp in the Dominican Republic at a time when Heureaux was secretly negotiating with Washington over the leasing of the Samaná Peninsula to the United States. In return for being permitted to assume the Westendorp interests, the San Domingo Improvement Company loaned Heureaux U.S. $1,250,000 and £2,035,000 to enable him to cover the internal debt of the country. Like Westendorp, the San Domingo Improvement Company took control of the Dominican Republic's customhouse in order to ensure that the loans would be repaid. The activities of the San Domingo Improvement Company symbolized the increasing power of U.S. interests in the economic and political spheres of the Dominican Republic and the simultaneous decline of European influence, which had been paramount at Santo Domingo during the nineteenth century.

FRANK MOYA PONS, *Manual de historia dominicana*, 7th ed. (1983), esp. pp. 416–427, 429–431, 436.

KAI P. SCHOENHALS

SAN FERNANDO DEL VALLE DE CATAMARCA. *See* **Catamarca.**

SAN GIL, a town in northeastern Colombia, 186 miles northeast of Bogotá, 1990 estimated population 40,000. Site of an Indian parish from the 1620s, San Gil was founded as a town in 1689, becoming the seat for a large, initially desolate region south of the Río Chicamocha. The growth of other towns in the jurisdiction, especially the artisanal and commercial center of SOCORRO, gave rise to endless struggles for municipal status, culminating in the separation of Socorro in 1776 and of Barichara in 1803. Bitterness produced by these losses may have inspired the San Gil elite's opposition to the COMUNERO REVOLT of 1781, and indifference to the Independence struggle, both movements which had their epicenter in the northeast. In the early republican period, San Gil achieved relative prosperity as an educational, bureaucratic, and urban artisanal center. Its merchant-landholder elite combined economic liberalism and social conservatism, the tensions of which led them to switch from Liberal to Conservative affiliation in the 1850s, making the town a Conservative redoubt for the rest of the nineteenth century. In the twentieth century San Gil retained its regional economic supremacy, particularly as a road transportation center, but its political importance declined.

RITO RUEDA, *Presencia de un pueblo* (1968); JOHN L. PHELAN, *The People and the King* (1978); ISAÍAS ARDILA DÍAZ, *Historia de San Gil en sus 300 años* (1990).

RICHARD J. STOLLER

SAN ILDEFONSO, TREATY OF (1777), one in a series of agreements aimed at settling territorial disputes between Portugal and Spain regarding the interior of South America. On 1 October 1777 the Treaty of San Ildefonso ended fifteen years of irregular open fighting. The Portuguese regained Santa Catarina, seized by Spain in 1777, and the coastal Rio Grande area but acknowledged Spanish control of Colônia do Sacramento, a center of Portuguese contraband trade and an access to the silver mines of Potosí; the Seven Missions territory, occupied by seven Jesuit missions and thirty thousand Guaraní Indians; and the Banda Oriental (now Uruguay). Although neither power achieved its objective of complete control of what was known as the Debatable Lands, secret treaty provisions provided Spanish access to the Portuguese islands of Principe and São Tomé for the purpose of purchasing African slaves. Thus the Spanish gained direct access to the African slave market and circumvented the necessity of relying on foreign middlemen.

The Treaty of San Ildefonso was significant because it satisfactorily implemented the practical solution of recognizing that possession is the legal basis of territorial settlement (*uti possidetis*). This principle was originally agreed upon in the Treaty of MADRID (1750), but practical implementation of territorial allocation had been ignored since that treaty was nullified by the Treaty of El Pardo (1761).

In 1776 a Spanish expedition crossed the Río de la Plata and forcibly claimed a portion of what now is the southernmost territory of Brazil. The Treaty of San Ildefonso then recognized Spanish claims based on *uti possidetis* and inadvertently confirmed Portuguese claims to the Amazon basin, which was accepted as Brazilian territory because the Portuguese had explored, charted, and established permanent outposts there. The Spanish invasion of Portugal in 1801 prompted the Brazilian reconquest of portions of the contested area and reestablished the Chui River as Brazil's southern boundary. This was confirmed by the Treaty of Badajoz (1801), but the remainder of Brazil's territorial boundaries would not be settled until the twentieth century.

RICHARD PARES, *War and Trade in the West Indies, 1739–1763* (1936); DAURIL ALDEN, *Royal Government in Colonial Brazil* (1968), pp. 262–267, 474; GEOFFREY J. WALKER, *Spanish Politics and Imperial Trade, 1700–1789* (1979); E. BRADFORD BURNS, *A History of Brazil* (1980), pp. 70–72, 107, 146; PEGGY K. LISS, *Atlantic Empires: The Network of Trade and Revolution, 1713–1826* (1983); *The Cambridge History of Latin America,* edited by Leslie Bethell, vol. 1 (1984), pp. 401, 473.

SUZANNE HILES BURKHOLDER
LESLEY R. LUSTER

SAN JACINTO, BATTLE OF (21 April 1836), the final military action of the TEXAS REVOLUTION. On 13 March 1836 the Texan forces under General Sam HOUSTON began a retreat eastward to Louisiana, joined by hundreds of families dispossessed by the advancing Mexican army. The retreat continued until 17 April, when General Houston ordered a movement to meet the enemy. Two days later, the Texans arrived at Buffalo Bayou, where the Mexican army under President Antonio López de SANTA ANNA intended to pass en route to the coast. On 20 April the Texan cavalry fought a brief skirmish with Santa Anna's advance guard, while the main body of the Mexican army encamped on the plains between Buffalo Bayou and San Jacinto Bay. On the morning of 21 April the Mexican army was reinforced, and General Houston ordered the destruction of Vince's Bridge, preventing the further reinforcement or retreat of either army. That afternoon, while the Mexicans were taking their siesta, the Texans attacked. The conflict lasted only eighteen minutes but resulted in the decimation of the Mexican force and the capture of Santa Anna. Moreover, the battle secured Texas independence and nearly a million square miles of territory.

FRANK X. TOLBERT, *The Day of San Jacinto* (1959); JAMES W. POHL, *The Battle of San Jacinto* (1989).

MICHAEL R. GREEN

SAN JOSÉ, COSTA RICA, capital city of Costa Rica. The most populous city in San José Province, it is the governmental, educational, business, banking, and manufacturing center of the country.

San José was first settled during the second quarter of the eighteenth century, principally by immigrants from Cartago. It takes its name from Saint Joseph, the patron saint of the first parish established in the Asserí Valley. For some time the settlement was referred to as Villa Nueva to distinguish it from the earlier settlement at Villa Vieja (present-day Heredia).

The village grew more rapidly than Cartago for the rest of the colonial period and by the time of independence, San José challenged the colonial capital for hegemony in the sparsely populated new nation. San José had prospered in the second half of the eighteenth century as a commercial center from a significant amount of contraband trade as well as from legitimate tobacco production.

The final shift in power from Cartago to San José came in 1823 in a short, violent clash in which armed bands from the four centers of population in the central valley fought to determine whether Costa Rica would be part of Agustín ITURBIDE's Mexican empire (Cartago and Heredia's position) or would join the Central American Federation (San José and Alajuela's position). San José's victory marked the beginning of its ascension as the great city of Costa Rica. San José defeated a combined force from the other three cities in 1835 (The War of the League) to assure its position. Throughout the rest of the nineteenth century and into the early twentieth century the city grew more rapidly than its rivals.

With the rapid modernization that has taken place since 1940, San José has grown prodigiously and has become ever more dominant in power and population. Its growth has been so dynamic that the distinctions among the four cities of the central valley have been blurred in functional terms as they begin to blend into one great central megapolis that embraces almost one-half of the nation's population (over one million inhabitants). San José is the unquestioned hub of politics, business, culture, education, transportation, and industry; San José province remains a major agricultural producer.

CAROLYN HALL, *Costa Rica: A Geographical Interpretation in Historical Perspective* (1985); and CARLOS MONGE ALFARO, "The Development of the Central Valley," in *The Costa Rica Reader*, edited by MARC EDELMAN AND JOANNE KENEN (1989), pp. 1–9.

JOHN PATRICK BELL

SAN JOSÉ CONFERENCE OF 1906. As stipulated in the 20 July 1906 MARBLEHEAD PACT, representatives of El Salvador, Guatemala, and Honduras met in September 1906 in San José, Costa Rica. Nicaragua was invited to attend the conference, but President José Santos ZELAYA declined the invitation. Most observers agreed that Zelaya's refusal was a protest against what he considered to be the excessive interference of the United States in isthmian affairs. The Conference produced an impressive series of treaties and conventions designed to promote isthmian peace and stability. The promise of the San José accords, however, was not immediately fulfilled, for within a matter of months a new round of hostilities erupted in Central America that led to the 1907 WASHINGTON CONFERENCE.

Papers Relating to the Foreign Relations of the United States, 1906 (1909), esp. pp. 853–866; DANA G. MUNRO, *Intervention and Dollar Diplomacy in the Caribbean, 1900–1921* (1964), esp. pp. 146–147.

RICHARD. V. SALISBURY

SAN JUAN, ARGENTINA, capital city (119,399 inhabitants in 1991) of the province of the same name in western Argentina (population 475,000). The city of San Juan

de la Frontera was founded in 1562 by Captain Juan de Jofré under orders from Francisco de VILLAGRA, governor of Chile, and moved to its present location in 1593 to avoid the floods caused by the high waters of the San Juan River. In 1776 it passed to the Viceroyalty of Río de la Plata, and in 1813 it joined Mendoza and San Luis in the intendancy of Cuyo. After the repulsion of the British invasions of Buenos Aires in 1806 and 1807, English prisoners were interned in San Juan, and several decided to settle there. The city is known as the birthplace of political leader Domingo Faustino SARMIENTO. After the passage of laws encouraging foreign immigration in 1860, there was a great influx of Italian and German families, who planted vineyards in the area. The city was destroyed by several earthquakes, the most damaging being those of 1894 and 1944. Clean, hospitable, and progressive, San Juan is a showcase of the agricultural development achieved by western Argentina under European colonization.

CÉSAR N. CAVIEDES

SAN JUAN, PUERTO RICO, capital (1990 pop. 420,000). Christopher COLUMBUS discovered the island of Puerto Rico on 19 November 1493 during his second transatlantic voyage. As with the majority of islands in the Caribbean, there was a preexisting indigenous culture. A permanent Spanish foothold, however, was not established until 1509, when Juan PONCE DE LEÓN, leading some settlers from Hispaniola, founded the town of Caparra near the present capital, San Juan.

After initial peaceful contacts with the native population, a rebellion occurred in 1511. It was promptly quelled by Ponce de León. Against his approval, the city was transferred to San Juan's present location in 1521. The new city, located on the islet of an open and spacious bay, was called Puerto Rico, the name later given to the island itself.

Efforts were made to fortify the port during the early years with the construction of a bulwark in 1522 and a defensive house (Casa Blanca) in 1530; however, these efforts were relatively futile and prompted some early emigration. In 1540 an ill-situated fort was completed and another fortress was constructed in the 1540s at the harbor's entrance. Over the years these edifices were further fortified. These forts afforded protection against the Spaniards' three main enemies: Caribs, the French, and the English. In 1765, the city was further fortified with plans drawn up by Field Marshal Alejandro O'REILLY and military engineer Tomás O'Daly. While the city continued to be fortified, the island itself was defenseless and often fell prey to French privateers.

In 1536, the island's political control reverted back to the throne, and Puerto Rico was incorporated into the traditional Spanish colonial system. One of the island's two CABILDOS was located in San Juan. The new town, although underpopulated, was also home to a strong religious community which over time included convents of FRANCISCANS, DOMINICANS, and CARMELITES. The church also played an important role in the island's education and health needs. For the next two centuries, San Juan would maintain its status as the island's only legal port. In the mid-eighteenth century trade with the non-Hispanic world was still forbidden.

In 1796 Spain and France declared war on Great Britain. The English quickly captured the island of Trinidad and set their sights on Puerto Rico as both islands were considered strategically important. With sixty vessels and 10,000 men, the English prepared to attack the now well-fortified city of San Juan. In 1797 the Spanish withstood the assault and after two weeks, English forces withdrew.

On 25 July 1898, U.S. troops landed at the bay of Guánica. Initially, San Juan resisted the invasion; however, within months the Americans effectuated a peaceful transfer of power. Over the next several decades Puerto Rican dependence on U.S. capital increased. Notwithstanding, San Juan benefited from the relationship and by the 1950s, a burgeoning middle class emerged in the city's suburbs.

ADOLFO DE HOSTOS, *Historia de San Juan: Ciudad Murada* (1966); F. M. ZENO, *Historia de la capital de Puerto Rico* (1981); ARTURO MORALES CARRIÓN, ed., *Puerto Rico: A Political and Cultural History* (1983).

ALLAN S. R. SUMNALL

SAN JUAN DE ULÚA, a fortress on La Gallega Island, a coral key facing the Mexican port of VERACRUZ. Juan de GRIJALVA gave it this name on his first expedition in 1518. Cortés landed there in 1519. Until the beginning of the seventeenth century, it was the port where the Spanish fleets moored and from where silver and gold were shipped. In the late 1500s, Juan Bautista Antonelli began its fortification, which was completed by Jaime Franck in 1692. John Hawkins and Francis Drake attacked San Juan de Ulúa in 1568. In 1683 it was taken by Lorencillo (Lorenzo Jácome), who also captured and sacked Veracruz. It was the last stronghold of the Spanish on the continent and resisted a siege from 1821 until 1825. Occupied by French troops in 1838 and American forces in 1847, the fortress was the presidential residence of Benito Juárez (1859–1860) during the war of the Reform and of Carranza in the Revolution (1915). That same year it ceased being used as a prison. Its narrow cells, made dank by the sea, were known as *las tinajas* (large earthen jugs). The Jesuits expelled in 1767 were imprisoned there, as were supporters of independence and some opponents of Porfirio Díaz.

When the modern port of Veracruz was completed in 1902, the key on which the fortress stands was connected to the mainland by a breakwater. All but abandoned for many years, San Juan de Ulúa was restored in 1991. It is preserved as a historic monument, the site of much Mexican and American history throughout four centuries.

FRANCISCO SANTIAGO CRUZ, *San Juan de Ulúa: Biografía de un presidio* (1966); LEONARDO PASQUEL, *San Juan de Ulúa: Fortaleza, presidio, residencia presidencial* (1969); BERNARDO GARCÍA DÍAZ, *Puerto de Veracruz* (1992).

J. E. PACHECO

SAN JUAN DEL NORTE. *See* **Greytown.**

SAN LORENZO, the earliest center of archaeological OLMEC culture. San Lorenzo is not one but three archaeological sites, the largest of which, San Lorenzo, is located on an artificially heightened plateau near the banks of the Coatzacoalcos River below the city of Minatitlán, Veracruz, Mexico. Radiocarbon dates obtained during excavations by Yale University between 1966 and 1968 demonstrate that the site was inhabited by 1500 B.C. and reached its apogee between 1150 and 900 B.C. The plateau on which the main site of San Lorenzo is located had at least sixty-five stone monuments, including ten colossal stone heads. The plateau supported several platform mounds, a series of artificially constructed ponds, and at least one stone fountain carved in the shape of a duck. The water level in these ponds and in the fountain was controlled by an intricate series of drainage lines, the sections of which were of basalt. The majority of the monuments from San Lorenzo are displayed in the archaeological museum of the University of Veracruz in Jalapa. Recent excavations have uncovered several more monuments, a workshop for the reworking of older monuments into new sculptures, and a large structure, possibly the residence of the San Lorenzo ruler.

MICHAEL D. COE and RICHARD A. DIEHL, *In the Land of the Olmec*, 2 vols. (1980); RICHARD A. DIEHL, "Olmec Architecture: A Comparison of San Lorenzo and La Venta," in *The Olmec and Their Neighbors: Essays in Memory of Matthew W. Stirling*, edited by Elizabeth P. Benson (1981), pp. 69–81; GARETH W. LOWE, "The Heartland Olmec: Evolution of Material Culture," in *Regional Perspectives on the Olmec*, edited by Robert J. Sharer and David C. Grove (1989), pp. 33–67.

F. KENT REILLY III

SAN LORENZO, BATTLE OF, fought on 3 February 1813 between Spanish loyalists ascending the Paraná River and Argentine revolutionaries led by José de SAN MARTÍN. This was the first engagement in which San Martín commanded the patriot forces following his return to Argentina from Spain in 1812. The site was a monastery not far from Rosario, on the west bank of the Paraná. Troops from a Spanish flotilla landed and began to move inland, only to be surprised and routed by the mounted grenadiers whom San Martín had concealed behind the building. Though few men were involved, the victory helped secure the river for the patriots and gave an important boost to morale.

J. C. J. METFORD, *San Martín the Liberator* (1950), pp. 36–38; RICARDO ROJAS, *San Martín, Knight of the Andes*, translated by Herschel Brickell and Carlos Videla (1967), pp. 31–35.

DAVID BUSHNELL

See also **Wars of Independence.**

SAN LUIS, capital city (121,146 inhabitants in 1991) of the homonymous province (1991 population 286,334) in western Argentina. San Luis was founded in 1594 near Punta de los Venados by Spanish forces from Chile commanded by Juan de Jofré. The natives of San Luis are still referred to as *puntanos*. Rebuilt in 1596, after its destruction by Indians, the city was continually attacked by Indians throughout colonial times as it developed into a prosperous cattle-raising center. In 1711 and 1750 punitive action was taken against the TEHUELCHE Indians. In 1776 the city became part of the Viceroyalty of RÍO DE LA PLATA, and in 1782 it was incorporated into the Intendancy of Córdoba. Finally, in 1813, it returned to the Intendancy of Mendoza, as part of the Cuyo region. Cattle and durum wheat are the main products of the province. Since the 1940s the region has been progressively losing inhabitants to the dynamic and prosperous city of Mendoza.

CÉSAR N. CAVIEDES

SAN LUIS POTOSÍ, north-central Mexican state and its capital city, historically connected to the revolutionary Plan of SAN LUIS POTOSÍ (1910) of Francisco I. MADERO. In the sixteenth century, the region was settled by Spaniards seeking to protect ZACATECAS from Indian attacks. The town of San Luis Potosí, named after Upper Peru's POTOSÍ, was founded in 1591 or 1592 in the wake of silver strikes. MINING remained an important part of the colonial economy, invigorated by the discovery of the rich Catorce veins in 1778. In the arid lands surrounding the mines, there were stock-raising estates and, to the east, some agricultural properties, on which lived much of the working rural population.

During the independence struggle, leaders of San Luis city and rural village residents supported Miguel HIDALGO, while estate owners and their workers were loyalists; a militia drawn from this latter group was largely responsible for Hidalgo's shattering defeat at Aculco in 1811. Following independence, the new state of San Luis Potosí's mining economy was disrupted, not recovering until late in the century. Stock raising and agriculture improved, sparked by the advent of rail service, but deteriorating conditions for the rural majority led to a number of uprisings. Dissatisfaction with the Porfirio DÍAZ regime in San Luis city led to the formation of Ricardo Flores Magón's radical Mexican Liberal Party (Partido Liberal Mexicano) in 1900, and after Francisco MADERO's call for revolution, the countryside erupted under the leadership of a Zapata-like figure, Saturnino

CEDILLO MARTÍNEZ. San Luis weathered the storm of revolution, and its importance as a communications, industrial, and agricultural center was enhanced.

The rural history and revolutionary connections of San Luis Potosí are featured in JAN BAZANT, *Cinco haciendas mexicanas: Tres siglos de vida rural en San Luis Potosí (1600–1910)* (1975); Bazant also has some information on sixteenth-century San Luis and the development of mining there. DUDLEY ANKERSON, *Agrarian Warlord: Saturnino Cedillo and the Mexican Revolution in San Luis Potosí* (1984); and JOHN TUTINO, *From Insurrection to Revolution in Mexico: Social Bases of Agrarian Violence, 1750–1940* (1986). Scattered information is provided in DAVID A. BRADING, *Miners and Merchants in Bourbon Mexico, 1763–1810* (1971).

ROBERT HASKETT

SAN MARCOS, UNIVERSITY OF, premier university of colonial South America. Because Spanish colonists in Peru wanted their sons to be eligible for positions that required a university education, the city council of Lima petitioned for a university. Authorized in 1551 by Charles V, the Royal and Pontifical University of San Marcos finally became an endowed secular institution with sixteen academic chairs in the 1570s.

Modeled on the University of Salamanca, the University of San Marcos boasted the five faculties necessary to be a major university: arts (philosophy), theology, medicine, civil law, and canon law. In addition, it initially offered instruction in Quechua, and in 1678 it added a chair of mathematics. The religious orders also sponsored chairs offering instruction in the writings of their most venerated theologians—for example, St. Thomas Aquinas and St. Augustine. At its peak, San Marcos had about thirty-five academic chairs. Although religious institutions in Lima offered college-level instruction, only San Marcos was authorized to confer baccalaureate, master's, licentiate, and doctoral degrees.

The faculty of San Marcos long used prescribed texts employed throughout the Hispanic world. In the late eighteenth century, however, some more contemporary authors' works were incorporated into the curriculum as the university sought to regain its former glory after suffering a period of decline.

The intellectual elite of colonial Lima passed through the halls of San Marcos and often taught there. As a focus of intellectual life for much of the viceregal era, the university fulfilled its charge of educating men for service in the clergy or bureaucracy.

JOHN TATE LANNING, *Academic Culture in the Spanish Colonies* (1940), chap. 1.

MARK A. BURKHOLDER

See also **Universities.**

SAN MARTÍN, JOSÉ FRANCISCO DE (*b.* 25 February 1778; *d.* 17 August 1850), the liberator of three South American countries who aspired to create the United

States of South America. San Martín was born in Yapeyú, in the province of Corrientes, Argentina. His Spanish parents took him to Spain in 1784, where he studied at the Seminary of Nobles in Madrid. In 1789 he joined the Murcia Regiment as a cadet, and later participated in military campaigns in Africa, the Iberian Peninsula, and France. His first combat experience was at Oran (25 June 1791), where he fought the Moors. In 1793 he served under General Ricardos, the tactician who had led his troops across the Pyrenees to attack the French enemies of Louis XVI. At Bailén he fought under General Castaños and later was an aide to the Marquess of Coupigny.

In 1811, San Martín retired from the army without a pension, and although authorized to go to Lima, he sailed instead for London. Before leaving Spain, however, San Martín was initiated into the Caballeros Racionales No. 3, which sought the independence of South America. He later joined a similarly inspired secret organization, the Great American Assembly of Francisco de MIRANDA in London, where he met the Venezuelan Andrés BELLO and the Argentines Manuel Moreno and Tomás GUIDO. Bello was the teacher of General Simón BOLÍVAR, and Moreno and Guido were the brother and secretary, respectively, of Mariano MORENO, a prominent leader of the independence movement in Buenos Aires. In January 1812, San Martín sailed for Buenos Aires aboard the British frigate *George Canning,* with fellow passengers Carlos de ALVEAR and his young wife, José Zapiola, and Francisco Chilavert.

In Buenos Aires, Alvear introduced San Martín to the most influential members of PORTEÑO society. The ruling triumvirate recognized his Spanish military grade of lieutenant colonel and asked him to organize the Regimiento de Granaderos a Caballo (Mounted Grenadier Regiment). Alvear was second in command. Its personnel eventually consisted of veteran officers of the revolutionary war, young men drawn from the leading families of the city of Buenos Aires, and the provinces of La Rioja, Córdoba, Banda Oriental del Uruguay, and the Guaraní of Corrientes. San Martín taught them military tactics and the use of different weapons. The grenadiers became a model for other regiments.

On 12 September 1812, with Alvear and his wife, María del Carmen Quintanilla, as witnesses, San Martín married fifteen-year-old María de los Remedios de Escalada de la Quintana, daughter of a wealthy Spanish merchant. On 8 October, he and his regiment participated in the military movement that replaced the existing triumvirate with another. This revolution bolstered the independence movement. Four months later he commanded the troops that repulsed superior Spanish numbers seeking to land at San Lorenzo.

In December 1813, San Martín replaced Manuel BELGRANO as commander of the Expeditionary Force to liberate Upper Peru at Posta de Yatasto. In March 1814 he proposed that the best way to win independence was to take Lima by way of Chile, not Bolivia, believing that a small, well trained army invading Chile from Mendoza would prevail in ending Spanish rule on the continent. At his request Supreme Director Gervasio Antonio de POSADAS appointed him intendant governor of the province of Cuyo (14 August 1814), with an annual salary of 300 pesos and instructions to prepare the defenses of Mendoza against any possible Spanish invasion. San Martín established himself at Plumerillo, outside Mendoza, and took steps to provide smallpox vaccinations for all the inhabitants of Cuyo, to help Chilean émigrés arriving after Rancagua, and to persuade those not in militia units to join one or be called traitors to the fatherland. Among the Chilean émigrés were Bernardo O'HIGGINS and the CARRERA brothers. In February 1815 he declined promotion to major colonel in the Armies of the United Provinces of the Río de la Plata, saying that he expected to withdraw from military service once independence was won, and the order relieving him of his command was revoked at the request of the local *cabildo.*

In 1816, San Martín informed the Supreme Director that he needed an army of 4,000 to invade Chile, and with the aid of the Cuyo deputies, and especially of Tomás GODOY CRUZ, he obtained from the TUCUMÁN CONGRESS a declaration of the independence of the United Provinces of South America. On 21 July 1816 he and the new Supreme Director Juan Martín de PUEYRREDÓN, met in Córdoba, completing arrangements for the liberation of Chile. Pueyrredón agreed to send him more men, armaments, and supplies, and he appointed San Martín commanding general of the Army of the Andes. The army then took an oath to defend the independence of the United Provinces of South America. San Martín now trained his troops and the local militia in basic military tactics and maneuvers, personally instructed the officers in military subjects, and invited neutral foreigners to join him. One of his students was José María PAZ, later a prominent leader in Argentine civil wars. The local people freed their slaves on the condition that they enlist in the army. They supplied San Martín with provisions and transported military goods without charge. The labor guilds took up voluntary contributions, and women offered their jewels. San Martín levied forced loans on the royalists and extracted extraordinary contributions from wealthy natives. The Army of the Andes made its own armaments, ammunition, guns, gunpowder, saddles, bayonets, cannons, and cannonballs. The provincial women sewed military uniforms without charge.

San Martín was named captain-general so that he could have both military and political authority, but he delegated the political functions to Colonel Toribio Luzuriaga, who was ably assisted by the lieutenant governors of San Juan and San Luis. The commander of the general staff was Brigadier General Miguel Estanislao Soler, and the battalion commanders were Juan Gregorio de LAS HERAS, Rudecindo Alvarado, Pedro Conde, and Ambrosio Crámer. The five squadrons of the Granaderos a Caballo were under Mariano Necochea, and among its officers were Juan LAVALLE, Federico de Brandzen, Manuel Medina y Escalada, and Domingo Arcos. The Patriotic Legion of the South was formed primarily by Chilean émigrés who supported O'Higgins. Another Chilean émigré, José Ignacio Zenteno, was the military secretary.

San Martín inaugurated the so-called *guerra de zapa* by placing spies in the enemy camps, spreading false rumors, sending secret emissaries to collect information throughout Chile, and encouraging uprisings. Field Marshal Francisco Marcó del Pont, in charge of the Chilean government, reacted by increasing political repression and stationing his forces at possible invasion points along the Andes. Replying to his request for military and political guidance, Supreme Director Pueyrredón sent San Martín his instructions on 24 December 1816, setting forth in fifty-nine articles how he was to conduct the war, deal with political parties and governments, and pay all expenses of the expeditionary force. The sole purpose of the campaign, he emphasized, was to secure American independence and the glory of the United Provinces. San Martín was to avoid favoring any of the political groups dividing Chile, to seek to improve the condition of the people, and to negotiate a perpetual alliance between the two nations.

Once the Army of the Andes was fully organized and trained, San Martín named the Virgin of Carmen del Cuyo as its patron and gave it a flag that his wife and other patriots embroidered. He also provided it with a printing press, which was to spread revolutionary ideas and publish battle bulletins. At San Martín's suggestion Brigadier O'Higgins was to become the temporary governor of Chile once Santiago was free.

The Army of the Andes that moved out of Mendoza on 18–19 January 1817 consisted of 4,000 soldiers, over 1,000 militiamen to transport munitions and a twenty-day supply of provisions, muleteers, and laborers to repair the roads. The Andean passes had been surveyed in advance by the engineer Álvarez Condarco. The bulk of the army, under San Martín, used Los Patos pass to cross the Andes to the valley of Putaendo, in the province of Aconcagua. An army division under General Soler formed the vanguard; O'Higgins commanded the reserve division. A column of 800 men under Las Heras used the USPALLATA PASS to Chile. It had the ammunition train, the dismounted artillery, and the arsenal, with workers armed with long poles and ropes so that they could suspend the cannons on litters. Once across the peak of the Andes, they defeated the royalists at Guardia Vieja and took Santa Rosa de los Andes. A northern column under Commandant Cabot, crossing the Andes in fourteen days, defeated the royalists at Salala, and took the province of Coquimbo, while a detachment from La Rioja took Copiapó. A southern column under the Chilean Captain Freyre used the Planchón pass to cross the Andes, defeated the royalists at Vega del Campeo, and entered Talca. All the soldiers were mounted on mules, and moved slowly according to the availability of pasture, water, and wood.

The entire army reached San Felipe, from which it dominated the valley of Aconcagua, and its forward units made contact with the royalists at CHACABUCO. The Spanish army of 2,500 under Brigadier Rafael Maroto occupied advantageous positions on the hill of Chacabuco, which blocked the road to Santiago. When his army was assembled, San Martín attacked in two corps: the one on the left, under O'Higgins, was to distract the enemy until the corps on the right, under Soler, could attack the enemy from the rear. O'Higgins advanced without waiting for Soler to complete his maneuver, but reinforced by cavalry troops under Zapiola and Necochea, he was able to destroy the royalist squadrons. The retreating Spaniards were routed by Soler. The patriots captured all the enemy artillery, its ammunition train, and 600 prisoners. The battle of Chacabuco (12 February) marked the beginning of the patriot offensive.

On 14 February, the patriot army entered Santiago. An assembly convoked by San Martín elected him governor of Chile, a position he declined, and it then named O'Higgins. Marcó del Pont and other Spanish leaders were captured and sent to San Luis. On 10 March, the Santiago *cabildo* presented San Martín with 10,000 gold pesos, which he donated for the establishment of the national library. An overjoyed directorate in Buenos Aires rewarded him the title of brigadier general of the Armies of the Fatherland (26 February 1817), which he did not accept. San Martín went to Buenos Aires with his aide, John T. O'Brien, to settle military problems and to obtain the resources needed to organize the expedition to Peru. He entered the city disguised, hoping to avoid a public demonstration, but he was detected, and the *cabildo* honored him on 9 April 1817. San Martín discussed the forthcoming campaign to liberate Peru with Pueyrredón, and then left for Santiago.

On 20 June, O'Higgins appointed San Martín commanding general of the Chilean army, and on 12 February 1818, he and San Martín proclaimed the independence of Chile. Meanwhile, the Spanish forces under Colonel José ORDÓÑEZ, which had not been involved in any battle, gathered in the plaza of Talcahuano. Las Heras and O'Higgins unsuccessfully attacked the town fortifications. General Mariano Osorio then arrived with 3,000 men, stationing them in the town of Talca. San Martín went to help O'Higgins, and while he was repositioning the troops, he was attacked on 19 March at Cancha Rayada by Ordóñez, and was forced to retreat. Las Heras alone kept his division intact. The patriots regrouped and, 5,000 strong, attacked and defeated the royalists under Osorio at MAIPÚ (5 April). San Martín was compelled to use his reserves in the battle. Osorio and his escort abandoned the battlefield, leaving Ordóñez to negotiate surrender. One thousand Spaniards were killed and 3,000 taken prisoners. Victory established the independence of Chile, and pro-

Portrait of José Francisco de San Martín. Oil on canvas by José Gil de Castro, 1818. ARCHIVO GENERAL DE LA NACIÓN, BUENOS AIRES.

vided for Argentina's security by giving it a base of operations on the Pacific. Argentina and Chile concluded an alliance to liberate Peru, while San Martín asked Great Britain to persuade Spain to grant independence to South America.

With the Spaniards now on the defensive, San Martín left for Buenos Aires to obtain the support needed for invading Peru. On 4 May, Congress congratulated O'Higgins, awarded a prize to San Martín and the army, and authorized a loan of 500,000 pesos to finance the expedition to Peru and the formation of a naval unit. It also ordered the erection of a statue to commemorate Chacabuco and Maipú and recognized the officers and soldiers of the Army of the Andes as "heroic defenders of the nation." San Martín asked Congress to prevent Pueyrredón from promoting him, saying that the army alone deserved praise for the victories. On 14 May, Congress appointed him Brigadier of the Armies of the Fatherland. Three days later Congress celebrated in extraordinary session the victories of Chacabuco and Maipú. After Congress authorized a personal coat of arms for him on 20 October, San Martín left for Santiago

de Chile. The Buenos Aires government later informed him that it was unable to fulfill its promise of aid.

At the end of 1818, Commandant Manuel BLANCO ENCALADA, an Argentine serving Chile, doubled the size of the Chilean navy by capturing first a Spanish frigate in the Bay of Talcahuano and then five Spanish transports with 700 men bound for the city with abundant military supplies. He relinquished command of the fleet to Lord Thomas Alexander COCHRANE, who had signed a contract in London with the agents of O'Higgins and San Martín. In January 1819, Cochrane attacked the Spanish fleet in Callao, but he was unable to destroy it. Early in 1820, San Martín refused the request of Director José RONDEAU to concentrate his troops in Buenos Aires in order to fight the CAUDILLOS. However, he did send a division to Mendoza and San Juan, but he soon withdrew half of it for his campaign to liberate Peru. San Martín went to Mendoza to recover his health, returning to Chile in a litter in January, still expecting to unite Argentina, Chile, and Peru as one nation. On 20 August 1820 the liberating expedition of 2,300 Argentines and 2,100 Chileans sailed from Valparaiso. Most of the officers were Argentines. The fleet consisted of eight warships and sixteen troop transports with a crew of 1,600 men under Cochrane. The cargo of the transports consisted of rifles, swords, cannons, ammunition, artillery shells, grenades, gunpowder, and horses with their feed. San Martín commanded the expedition as captaingeneral, and he informed the *cabildo* of Buenos Aires of his departure for Peru.

The royal armies San Martín faced consisted of 23,000 men in Upper and Lower Peru. San Martín disembarked in the port of Paracas and established his headquarters at Pisco. His aim was to avoid battle and to provoke rebellions among the people and desertions in the Spanish troops by spreading revolutionary propaganda. Desertions among Spanish commanders and officers did increase, and an entire battalion surrendered. He moved to Ancón, then to Huaura, and finally to Huamanga, from which he could dominate the valley of Huancayo. He negotiated an armistice of short duration with Viceroy Pezuela at Miraflores (26 September). He assured the success of the expedition when he defeated Brigadier Alejandro o'REILLY at Cerro de Pasco (6 December 1820), and captured both O'Reilly and Mayor Andrés de SANTA CRUZ. On 2 June 1821, San Martín met Viceroy Pezuela at Punchauca and asked him to recognize Peru as a sovereign nation, to approve a junta which would write a temporary constitution, and to join him in naming a commission that would ask FERDINAND VII to select a son to become king of Peru after accepting a constitution. The vacillating viceroy agreed only to another armistice. On 19 July, San Martín entered Lima and called a council of notables, which voted for independence. Peruvian independence was declared on 28 July.

San Martín assumed political and military command of the new nation as "protector of a free Peru." He thus prevented Simón Bolívar from seizing Peru. Then, through his secretary, Dr. Bernardo MONTEAGUDO, he abolished the personal service of the Indians (the tributes, the MITAS, and ENCOMIENDAS); declared the freedom of the newborn children of slaves; established a free press and the sanctity of the home; and ended torture in judicial proceedings. He fought gambling and maintained security and order in town. On 21 November, Lima awarded 500,000 pesos to the officers and commissioned officers of the liberating army. The reward was distributed by lot among the twenty officers named by San Martín. The officers who were ignored probably participated in the conspiracy that led to the downfall of San Martín.

With the bulk of the royalist army, Canterac was in the valley of Jauja, controlling the sierra and suppressing Indian revolts supporting the revolution. Bolívar sent General Antonio José de SUCRE with a division to liberate Quito Province. This inadequate force sought reinforcements from San Martín, who sent Santa Cruz with 1,000 men. The war ended when the Argentine granaderos under Lavalle destroyed the Spanish cavalry at Riobamba and Sucre and the Argentine Manuel de Olazábal defeated the royalists at Pichincha (24 May 1822). By that time the port of Guayaquil had declared its independence, and Peru wanted to annex it. On 13 July, Bolívar placed the port under the protection of Colombia.

San Martín landed at Guayaquil on 25 July, and held three interviews with Bolívar. What transpired at these meetings is still disputed, but the two men evidently discussed the form of government the new nations should have and the military operations required to end the war. San Martín favored a constitutional monarchy for South America, Bolívar a republic. Both men sought the formation of something like the United States of America, a goal which would be reached by first uniting the former viceroyalties, now republics, in a South American Confederation and then fusing them in a federation, the United States of South America. With too meager a force to end the war alone, San Martín asked for help and reminded Bolívar of the aid he had given to Sucre. Bolívar declined to place a substantial Colombian force under his command, and refused San Martín's offer to serve under him. San Martín returned to Lima, and at the meeting of the Constituent Congress on 20 September 1822 he resigned as Protector. He then sailed for Chile, where he was no longer popular, and crossed the Andes to his small farm in Mendoza. In late 1823 he learned that his ailing wife had died on 3 August.

San Martín enjoyed the support of the federalists and the provincial governors, especially that of Governor Estanislao LÓPEZ of Santa Fe, but Bernardino RIVADAVIA was his enemy. He left for Buenos Aires in November to see Rivadavia, who already had negotiated a preliminary peace treaty with Spain (4 July 1823). On 7 February he sailed with his daughter Mercedes for Le Havre and from there to Southampton, England, finally settling in Brussels. In 1828 San Martín briefly returned to Buenos Aires, but he never landed and instead stayed for two months in Montevideo. He declined an invitation from Juan Lavalle to assume command of the government and army of Buenos Aires. He returned to Brussels. In 1834 the wealthy Spaniard Alejandro Aguado helped San Martín purchase a house in Grand Bourges. In 1838, when France was blockading Buenos Aires, San Martín offered his services to Juan Manuel de ROSAS, who declined. Attacks against him appeared in the Buenos Aires press, but Domingo F. SARMIENTO and later Bartolomé MITRE rose to his defense. He was restored to his former rank of captain-general, and Chile awarded him a lifelong pension in 1842.

San Martín died in Boulogne-sur-Mer. He bequeathed his sword to Rosas. At the suggestion of Sarmiento a statue in his honor was erected in Buenos Aires in 1862. In 1880 his remains were moved from the cemetery in Brunoy to the cathedral in Buenos Aires.

BARTOLOMÉ MITRE, *Historia de San Martín y de la emancipación sudamericana*, 3 vols. (1887–1888); MUSEO MITRE, *Documentos del Archivo de San Martín*, 12 vols. (1910–1911); JOSÉ PACÍFICO OTERO, *Historia del Libertador don José de San Martín*, 4 vols. (1932); JACINTO R. YABEN, *Biografías argentinas y sudamericanas*, vol. 5 (1940), pp. 507–528; RICARDO ROJAS, *San Martín, Knight of the Andes*, translated by Herschel Brickell and Carlos Videla (1945); JOSÉ LUIS BUSANICHE, *San Martín vivo* (1950), J. C. J. METFORD, *San Martín the Liberator* (1950); INSTITUTO NACIONAL SANMARTINIANO, *Documentos para la historia del libertador general San Martín*, 12 vols. (1953–); RICARDO PICCIRILLI, *San Martín y la polítca de los pueblos* (1957); JOSÉ LUIS ROMERO, *A History of Argentine Political Thought*, translated by Thomas F. McGann (1963); HAROLD F. PETERSON, *Argentina and the United States, 1810–1960* (1964); ENRIQUE DE GANDÍA, *San Martín: Su pensamiento político* (1964); CRISTIÁN GARCÍA-GODOY, ed., *The San Martín Papers*, translated by Barbara Huntley and Pilar Liria (1988).

JOSEPH T. CRISCENTI

See also **Wars of Independence.**

SAN NICOLÁS, ACUERDO DE (1852), an agreement reached on 31 May 1852 by representatives of the UNITED PROVINCES OF THE RÍO DE LA PLATA at a small town on the Arroyo del Medio, the brook that forms the boundary between the provinces of Buenos Aires and Sante Fe. The three provinces whose governors arrived late—Salto, Jujuy, and Córdoba—later approved the accord. Justo José de URQUIZA, representing Entre Ríos and Catamarca, called the meeting to organize the nation. The governor of Buenos Aires was authorized by the provincial legislature only to attend the meetings, while the others received instructions from their provincial legislatures. The accord declared that the Treaty of the Littoral (1831)—an alliance between the provinces of Buenos Aires, Corrientes, Entre Ríos, and Santa Fe—was the fundamental law of the nation, and asked each province to send two deputies without restrictions to a constituent congress. A majority vote would suffice to approve a constitution. Urquiza was appointed temporary director of the ARGENTINE CONFEDERATION. Free trade was approved and transit duties abolished. Each province was to contribute to the administrative expenses in proportion to its customhouse revenues. The provincial legislature of Buenos Aires rejected the accord.

DAVID ROCK, *Argentina, 1516–1987: From Spanish Colonization to Alfonsín*, rev. ed. (1987); JOSEPH T. CRISCENTI, ed., *Sarmiento and His Argentina* (1993).

JOSEPH T. CRISCENTI

SAN RAFAEL, city of 158,410 inhabitants (1991) located 125 miles south of Mendoza in Argentina. The settlement emerged at the northern margin of the Diamante River as a trading place for cattle drivers taking their herds across the Andes to Chile. A fort was built in 1770 to keep Indians at bay, and in 1777 punitive actions against the raiders were taken from this stronghold. In 1805 commander Teles Meneses founded the fort of San Rafael, as well as a permanent settlement, to establish a Spanish presence in the region. As a well-irrigated oasis, San Rafael attracted French and Italian families who from 1870 to 1890 began to cultivate grapes in well-irrigated vineyards. San Rafael produces one of the finest white wines of Argentina. Situated in the agrarian province of Mendoza, it is the last major city on the border of the desert south of the Atuel River.

CÉSAR N. CAVIEDES

SAN SALVADOR, name given in the colonial period to both the approximate territory of present-day El Salvador and the city that historically presided over it. The territory was an *alcaldía mayor* until 1785, when it became an *intendencia*. During the Central American Federation (1824–1839) it was one of the five constituent states. When the state left the federation and was renamed El Salvador, the name San Salvador was reserved for one of its subdivisions. Today it is one of fourteen departments of the country (1990 est. pop., 1,417,953). It is located in the central region with an area of 354 square miles. Its most prominent geographical features are the San Salvador volcano and Lake Ilopango.

The city (1990 est. pop., 553,162), now capital of El Salvador, was founded in 1525, probably by Diego de Alvarado. Twenty years later it moved to its present location, a valley 2,200 feet above sea level, 19.3 miles north of the Pacific coast. The valley is called "Valley of the Hammocks" because of the frequency of earthquakes. San Salvador is linked with the other major cities of the country and the capitals of Central America by the PAN-AMERICAN HIGHWAY, and has easy access to an international airport located on the coast.

Historically the city has been the uncontested administrative, economic, cultural, and educational center of the country. In 1811, San Salvador's city notables, a group of creole INDIGO producers, led the first stage of Central American independence and thereafter played a prominent role in the movement. Francisco MORAZÁN made it capital of the Central American Federation from 1834 until 1839. After an EARTHQUAKE in 1854 the capital was moved east to Cojutepeque until 1859, when it returned to San Salvador. The most recent earthquake was in 1986, when important buildings, including the largest children's hospital and the American embassy, were seriously damaged and about a thousand people died. The city witnessed some of the most dramatic moments of the 1979–1992 civil war, including the murders of Archbishop Oscar Arnulfo ROMERO in 1980 and of six Jesuit priests nine years later, and the emotional celebration of the end of the civil war in January 1992.

Thanks to its central location, good communications, and access to government and financial services, San Salvador and its metropolitan area have become the heart of the industrial sector. According to the 1979 industrial census, almost half of the manufactures of the country were produced in the area. Migration from the countryside increased in the 1960s and accelerated after the outbreak of the civil war, when thousands of peasants abandoned their land and sought refuge in the capital. More than one-fifth of the total population of the country lives within San Salvador's metropolitan area (1990 est. pop., 1,256,259).

For the early history of the city, see RODOLFO BARÓN CASTRO, *La población de El Salvador* (1942) and *Reseña histórica de la villa de San Salvador* (1950). For recent population and economic data, see REPÚBLICA DE EL SALVADOR, *Indicadores económicos y sociales, 1987–1989* (1989).

HÉCTOR LINDO-FUENTES

SAN SIMÓN. *See* **Maximón.**

SANABRIA MARTÍNEZ, VÍCTOR M. (*b.* 17 January 1898; *d.* 8 June 1952), archbishop of San José, Costa Rica (1940–1952).

Archbishop Sanabria's advocacy of social justice and his political role in the 1940s make him the most famous, popular, and controversial twentieth-century Costa Rican prelate. He rose from humble beginnings to become a well-educated, "people's" priest who addressed the issues that moved his nation during the tumultuous decade 1940–1950. As the established leader of the Costa Rican church, he committed his institution to the social reforms called for in the papal encyclical *Rerum Novarum*. He studied civil and canon law in Rome and returned to San José with an earned doctorate in canon law.

Sanabria wrote extensively on church history. He also produced a multivolume genealogy of Cartago that elicited almost as much controversy as his social activism because it brought to light so many details that the residents of that patriarchal city wished to maintain in obscurity.

Sanabria was appointed the second archbishop of San José in March 1940, the same year in which his friend Dr. Rafael Ángel CALDERÓN GUARDIA (1940–1944) was inaugurated. These two young leaders shared the deep conviction that their nation needed profound social change based on church teachings in order to ensure social justice and progress. Somewhat the older, Sanabria came to political prominence as a mentor to the president. Together they worked to pass a sweeping program of legislation that culminated in the amendment of the constitution to include social guarantees, such as social security insurance, an eight-hour workday, minimum wage, the right to organize trade unions and to form cooperatives, and the basic right to human dignity.

Sanabria publicly advocated the government's reform program and indirectly sanctioned its political alliance with the Popular Vanguard Party (PVP), a communist party. Sanabria was criticized by conservative Catholics at home, and he was denied entry to Guatemala because of his political orientation. He played an active role in organizing Catholic labor unions to rival those organized by the communists.

Sanabria tried valiantly but in vain to mediate the political crisis following the 1948 election. He helped protect president-elect Otilio ULATE BLANCO (1949–1953) and he participated in the mediations that led to the cessation of the armed conflict.

His active role in a time of change and conflict made Sanabria a towering but controversial personage. His accomplishments were recognized after his death, when he was named Benemérito de la Patria by the national congress in 1959.

RICARDO BLANCO SEGURA, *Monseñor Sanabria* (1962); FRANKLIN D. PARKER, *The Central American Republics* (1964); JOHN PATRICK BELL, *Crisis in Costa Rica* (1971); RICHARD BIESANZ, KAREN ZUBRIS BIESANZ, and MAVIS HILTUNEN BIESANZ, *The Costa Ricans* (1982; rev. ed. 1988).

JOHN PATRICK BELL

See also **Costa Rica: Political Parties.**

SÁNCHEZ, FLORENCIO (*b.* 17 January 1875; *d.* 2 November 1910), Uruguayan playwright. Born in Montevideo and raised in the interior, Sánchez, one of eleven children, left high school to help support his family. He worked as a clerk, wrote theater reviews and articles for small-town newspapers, and acted in amateur plays. He fought with the caudillo Aparicio SARAVIA against President Juan Idiarte Borda, an experience that inspired his work *El caudillaje criminal en Sudamérica* (Criminal Caudillo Rule in South America [1914]). Disillusioned with traditional politics, Sánchez became interested in the anarchist movement; his earliest plays were presented in anarchist recreation centers.

Working for newspapers such as *La República* in Rosario, Argentina, Sánchez attained recognition with his muckraking play *El canillita* (The Newspaperboy), which was performed on 2 October 1904. He lost his job as a result of his anarchist activities. In ill health, he accepted a friend's invitation to spend time in the Argentine countryside. The sojourn inspired Sánchez's famous rural plays *La gringa* (The Immigrant Girl [1904]), *M'hijo el dotor* (My Son the Lawyer [1903]), and *Barranca abajo* (Down the Gully [1905]). He then moved to Buenos Aires, where he worked feverishly on a succession of plays and married, but he continued his bohemian life of much drinking and little sleep.

With a sharp ear for dialogue, Sánchez's plays depicted racial antagonism between the native *criollos* and the immigrants. A social activist, Sánchez used theater as vehicle to educate the public about poverty and the plight of people in urban tenements. His play, *Nuestros hijos* (Our Children [1907]), influenced progressive legislation enacted in Uruguay. On the verge of bankruptcy and struggling with depression and tuberculosis, Sánchez received a grant from the Uruguayan government to survey Italian theater. He died in Milan shortly after his arrival.

ROBERTO FERNANDO GIUSTI, *Florencio Sánchez: Su vida y su obra* (1920); RUTH RICHARDSON, *Florencio Sánchez and the Argentine Theater* (1933); KARL EASTMAN SHEDD, *Florencio Sánchez's Debt to Eugène Brieux* (1936); FERNANDO GARCÍA ESTEBAN, *Vida de Florencio Sánchez: Con cartas inéditas del insigne dramaturgo*

Florencio Sánchez. MUSEO HISTÓRICO NACIONAL, MONTEVIDEO, URUGUAY.

(1939); FLORENCIO SÁNCHEZ, *Representative Plays of Florencio Sánchez*, translated by Willis Knapp Jones (1961); WALTER RELA, *Florencio Sánchez: Persona y teatro* (1967); VLADIMIRIO MUÑOZ, *Florencio Sánchez: A Chronology*, translated by Scott Jacobesen (1980).

                                  GEORGETTE MAGASSY DORN

See also **Anarchists.**

SÁNCHEZ, LUIS ALBERTO (*b.* 12 October 1900; *d.* 6 February 1994), Peruvian literary historian and politician. Sánchez received doctorates in literature (1922) and law (1925) from the University of San Marcos, where he taught Latin American LITERATURE for forty years and served three times as president (1946–1949, 1961–1963, 1966–1969). After joining the Peruvian Aprista Party in 1931, he was elected to two Constituent Assemblies (1932, 1978–1979), the Chamber of Deputies (1945–1948), the Senate (1963–1968, 1980–1992), and the vice presidency of the Republic (1985–1990), and served as acting president of the country on several occasions from 1985 to 1990. During two decades as a political exile, Sánchez was literary editor of *Ercilla* in Chile and visiting professor in several universities, including Columbia and the Sorbonne. In 1980 he was elected a member of the Peruvian Academy of the Spanish Language and corresponding member of the Spanish Royal Academy. Sánchez, one of the most prolific Peruvian writers of his time, wrote more than sixty books, including *La literatura peruana* (5 vols., 1982), *Historia comparada de las literaturas americanas* (4 vols., 1973–1976), and *Perú: Nuevo retrato de un país adolescente* (Lima, 1981). He died in Lima.

EUGENIO CHANG-RODRÍGUEZ, "¿Tuvimos maestros en nuestra América?" in *Hispania* 40 (1957): 251–253; *Homenaje a Luis Alberto Sánchez* (1960); DONALD C. HENDERSON and GRACE R. PÉREZ, eds., *Literature and Politics in Latin America* (1982); *Homenaje a Luis Alberto Sánchez* (1983).

                                  EUGENIO CHANG-RODRÍGUEZ

SÁNCHEZ, LUIS RAFAEL (*b.* 1936), Puerto Rican playwright, story writer, essayist, and novelist. Born in Humacao and educated at the University of Puerto Rico (B.A., 1960), Columbia University (M.A., 1963), and the Central University of Mexico (Ph.D., 1966), Sánchez was recognized as a talented young actor and playwright in the late 1950s and early 1960s. He emerged shortly thereafter, the first major voice of a new literary generation, as an equally inventive and critically probing fictional observer of contemporary Puerto Rican life and experience. Beginning with *La espera* (1958; The Wait), *Los ángeles se han fatigado* (1960; The Angels Have Become Weary), *La hiel nuestra de cada día* (1962; Our Daily Bile), and more recently, with *Quintuples* (1985), he examines the insular and more broadly Hispanic American predicament of a dependent society confronted by an often fraudulent and lethal "modernity" as well as the delusions, poses, moral complicity, and uncertain personas assumed by different participants in a poignant national drama. His most widely celebrated play, *La pasión según Antigona Pérez: Crónica americana en dos actos* (1968), reimagines the classical Greek heroine as a twenty-five-year-old mestiza condemned to death by the dictator of a paradigmatic Latin American republic for her dissenting ideas and identification with "those of us growing up in a harsh America, a bitter America, a captured America." (*La pasión según Antigona Pérez* [1973], p. 14)

Sánchez's first collection of stories, *En cuerpo de camisa* (1966), demonstrates his singularly keen ear and eye for the various inflections and social and psychological textures of island life. He especially captures the furtive, taboo worlds of the delinquent, socially alienated, sexually outcast, misfit, and derelict that are produced by a still-colonial society, its failed social policies, clash of classes, prudishness, crude machismo, and pretentious mimicry. *La guaracha del Macho Camacho* (1976) and *La importancia de llamarse Daniel Santos* (1989), his only published novels to date, confirm their author's analytical acuity, thematic daring, and linguistic and formal virtuosity. Powerful repositories of his characters' universe of meaning and an irrepressible popular ethos, language and music ultimately emerge as organizing metaphors for a miscegenated, culturally syncretic creole sensibility of stubborn ubiquity and resilience, despite both internal and external assault. Empathetic recognition of this defining resilience in the "commuting" experience and shifting spaces of Puerto Rican (im)migrants to (and from) the United States is more evident in his later than in his earlier essays and short fiction.

A member of the faculty of the University of Puerto Rico and the most celebrated Puerto Rican writer of his generation, Sánchez has produced many other works, including the plays *Farsa del amor compradito* (1960), *Sol 13, interior* (1961), and *O casi el alma* (1969); the popular short story "La guagua aérea," (1983) (made into an equally popular film in the early 1990s); *Ventana interior*, an unpublished book of verse; the monograph *Fabulación e ideología en la cuentística de Emilio S. Belaval* (1979); and a collection of selected essays, commentaries, and reviews also entitled *La guagua aérea* (1994).

EFRAÍN BARRADAS, *Para leer en puertorriqueño: Acercamiento a la obra de Luis Rafael Sánchez* (1981); ELISEO R. COLÓN ZAYAS, *El teatro de Luis Rafael Sánchez* (1985).

                                  ROBERTO MÁRQUEZ

SÁNCHEZ, PRISCILIANO (*b.* 4 January 1783; *d.* 30 December 1826), Mexican federalist leader and first governor of Jalisco. Born in the village of Ahuacatlán, Nueva Galicia province, Sánchez's parents died when he was young. After largely educating himself, Sánchez entered Guadalajara's Conciliary Seminary (1804). He briefly took the Franciscan habit, later studying law.

During Hidalgo's revolution (1810), Sánchez served in various municipal positions in Compostela, where he was known to sympathize with the insurgent cause.

After independence Sánchez helped make Jalisco a federalist center. He served in the first Mexican congress (Iturbide period) and in 1823 published his influential Federal Pact (Pacto Federal de Anáhuac). In the Constitutional Congress (1823–1824) and as Jalisco's governor (1826), Sánchez helped frame federalist measures, notably Article 7, which made Catholicism the state religion, and the personal contribution tax.

LUIS PEREZ VERDÍA, Biografías: Fray Antonio Alcalde, Priscilliano Sánchez (1981).

STANLEY GREEN

SÁNCHEZ CERRO, LUIS MANUEL (b. 1889; d. 1933), military officer and president of Peru (1930–1931, 1931–1933). The politically ambitious Sánchez Cerro, who was born in Piura, participated in three military uprisings between 1914 and 1931. The first ousted President Guillermo BILLINGHURST. The second, in 1922, was an unsuccessful rebellion against President Augusto LEGUÍA in Cuzco. Imprisoned for his participation, Sánchez Cerro later was allowed to serve in the Ministry of War and to advance his training in Spain. Finally, Lieutenant Colonel Sánchez Cerro led the military putsch that ousted Leguía in August 1930. Opposition within the armed forces, however, forced Sánchez Cerro to resign in March 1931. Back from exile and embracing the support of the fascist Revolutionary Union, he claimed victory after the general elections of October 1931. As constitutional president he unleashed a harsh political and military repression of the opposition Aprista Party led by Víctor Raúl HAYA DE LA TORRE. Aprista members conspired to assassinate Sánchez Cerro, failing in 1932 and succeeding in Lima in 1933.

CARLOS MIRÓ QUESADA LAOS, Sánchez Cerro y su tiempo (1947); DANIEL MASTERSON, Militarism and Politics in Latin America: Peru from Sánchez Cerro to "Sendero Luminoso" (1991).

ALFONSO W. QUIROZ

SÁNCHEZ DE BUSTAMANTE Y SIRVEN, ANTONIO (b. 13 April 1865; d. 24 August 1951), Cuban jurist and politician. A professor of international law at the University of Havana, Bustamante achieved widespread prestige and distinction as an orator and the author of numerous scholarly books that were translated into many languages, including Turkish and modern Greek. Upon the inauguration of the Cuban republic in 1902, he was elected to the Cuban Senate, serving several terms. In 1922 he was chosen as one of the first eleven justices who sat on the Permanent Court of International Justice established at The Hague, and in 1929 he was chosen for a second term. His most celebrated contribution to international law, however, was the Code of

International Private Law (known as the Bustamante Code), approved by the Sixth International Conference of American States that met in Havana in 1928 and subsequently ratified by fifteen member states. Accused of supporting the MACHADO dictatorship (1925–1933), he was exonerated and continued to teach international law until his death.

For a short biography of Bustamante see JOSÉ I. LASAGA, Cuban Lives: Pages from Cuban History, vol. 2 (1988), pp. 397–409; also, OTTO SCHOENRICH, "Dr. Antonio Sánchez de Bustamante," in The American Journal of International Law 45 (1951): 746–749.

JOSÉ W. HERNÁNDEZ

See also **Pan-American Conferences: Havana Conference.**

SÁNCHEZ DE LOZADA BUSTAMANTE, GONZALO (b. 1930), president of Bolivia (1993–). Born in La Paz, Sánchez de Lozada studied at the University of Chicago, receiving a bachelor's degree in philosophy in 1951. Wealthy from mining interests, he rapidly established himself as a promising political leader, first as an outspoken leader of the opposition in the Chamber of Deputies, later as president of the Senate, and then as minister of planning and coordination in the PAZ ESTENSSORO government. He was one of the principal architects of that government's economic stabilization and reactivation programs. A strong believer in privatization, his views prevailed, and he received the support necessary to turn the economic system away from state capitalism.

Sánchez de Lozada was chosen as the Nationalist Revolutionary Movement (MNR) candidate for the May 1989 elections and won a small plurality with 23.07 percent of the vote. It was presumed that he would be named president in the congressional runoff, but he and the MNR failed to work out a satisfactory arrangement with the Nationalist Democratic Action (ADN). Bitterly disappointed, he became the outspoken head of the opposition. He charged the government with undermining the New Economic Policy and was critical of the natural gas agreements with Argentina.

Sánchez de Lozada was elected party chief at the MNR's national convention in August 1990, and went on to win the 1993 presidential election.

EDUARDO A. GAMARRA, "Crafting Political Support for Stabilization: Political Pacts and the New Economic Policy in Brazil," in Democracy, Markets, and Structural Reform in Latin America, edited by William C. Smith, Carlos H. Acuña, and Eduardo A. Gamarra (1994), and "Market-Oriented Reforms and Democratization in Bolivia," in A Precarious Balance, edited by Joan M. Nelson, vol. 2 (1994).

EDUARDO A. GAMARRA

See also **Bolivia: Political Parties.**

SÁNCHEZ DE TAGLE, FRANCISCO MANUEL (*b.* 11 January 1782; *d.* 17 December 1847), a politician. In 1794 Sánchez, a native of Valladolid, entered the Colegio de San Juan de Letrán in Mexico City. He received a bachelor's degree in philosophy and theology and was appointed to the chair of philosophy in 1803. He was active in politics, becoming *regidor perpetuo* of the Ayuntamiento of Mexico from 1805 to 1812 and from 1815 to 1820. Because of his autonomist leanings, Sánchez became a member of the secret society Los GUADALUPES, and he participated in the elections resulting from the Constitution of Cádiz; he was elected constitutional *regidor* in 1813 and in 1820. In 1821 he signed the Declaration of Independence, and he was a member of the Provisional Governing Junta. Sánchez remained active in politics after independence; he was elected deputy on various occasions as well as senator, vice governor of the state of Mexico, governor of the state of Michoacán, and secretary of the Supreme Conservative Power. In addition, he was one of the best-known members of the *escocés* (Scottish rite Masons) party. At his death, he was director of the national pawnbrokerage.

JOSE MARÍA MIGUEL I VERGÉS, *Diccionario de insurgentes* (1969), pp. 537–538; *Diccionario Porrúa de historia, geografía y biografía de México*, 5th ed. (1986), vol. 3, p. 2,642; and VIRGINIA GUEDEA, *En busca de un gobierno alterno: Los Guadalupes de México* (1992).

VIRGINIA GUEDEA

SÁNCHEZ DE THOMPSON, MARÍA (*b.* 1 November 1786; *d.* 23 October 1868), author, social reformer. "Mariquita" Sánchez de Thompson was born in Buenos Aires, the daughter of a prominent local merchant. As a young woman she showed herself to be headstrong and independent, going as far as marrying the man of her choice, Martín J. Thompson y López Cárdenas, over parental objections in 1805. Thompson, a career naval officer, died in 1817, while returning from a diplomatic mission to the United States. A widow with five small children, Mariquita soon remarried (1820); her second husband was the young French consul in Buenos Aires, Jean-Baptiste Washington de Mendeville.

Her position in society secure, Mariquita then formed a salon that served as a meeting place for liberal politicians, poets, and other literary figures such as her friends Bernardino RIVADAVIA, Juan María Gutiérrez, Esteban ECHEVERRÍA, and Juan Bautista ALBERDI. A leading member of *porteño* society, Mariquita took a commanding role in the founding of the Sociedad de Beneficencia, and served as the organization's secretary and president. She pressed for elementary education for girls, founding schools in Buenos Aires and the surrounding towns.

Although her second husband was forced from his diplomatic post by Juan Manuel de ROSAS and returned to France in 1835, Mariquita continued to live in Buenos Aires, serving as a magnet for the defeated *unitarios*. An outspoken foe of her childhood friend Rosas, Mariquita was alternately forced into exile in Montevideo and allowed to return to Buenos Aires between 1836 and 1852. After Rosas's downfall, Mariquita once again established herself in Buenos Aires, befriending a new generation of reformers, such as Domingo SARMIENTO. She died in Buenos Aires just short of her eighty-second birthday.

Throughout her life Mariquita had been an avid letter writer, and her published letters, *Cartas de Mariquita Sánchez* (1952), provide an interesting view of daily life, politics, and society under Rosas. Her reminiscences of life in preindependence Buenos Aires, *Recuerdos de Buenos Aires virreynal* (1953), give a valuable albeit pointed view of late colonial society.

JORGE A. ZAVALÍA LAGOS, *Mariquita Sánchez y su tiempo* (1986).

SUSAN M. SOCOLOW

SÁNCHEZ HERNÁNDEZ, FIDEL (*b.* 1917), president of El Salvador (1967–1972). Born in San Miguel, Sánchez Hernández graduated from the National Military Academy. He was minister of the interior when he was tapped by outgoing president Julio A. RIVERA (1962–1967), to be the candidate of the military-backed National Conciliation Party (PCN) in 1967. Although winning easily nationwide, the PCN won only 41 percent of the votes in San Salvador. As a result, Sánchez Hernández felt pressed to continue the mild reformism of his predecessor, pushing through a rural minimum-wage law.

Falling coffee and cotton prices in 1968 stimulated trade union militancy and the congressional elections brought the opposition parties within two seats of the PCN. However, success in fighting in the 1969 "FOOTBALL WAR" with Honduras (a conflict over borders, trade relations, and immigration policy triggered by the actions of unruly fans at two preliminary World Cup soccer matches held in Tegucigalpa and San Salvador in June 1969) restored the popularity of the government.

THOMAS P. ANDERSON, *The War of the Dispossessed: Honduras and El Salvador, 1969* (1981); KENNETH L. JOHNSON, "Parties, Union and the State: An Historical-Structural Interpretation of the Salvadoran Crisis, 1948–1982."(M.A. thesis, Tulane University, 1988).

ROLAND H. EBEL

SÁNCHEZ MANDULEY, CELIA (*b.* 1920; *d.* 11 January 1980), Cuban revolutionary and adviser to Fidel CASTRO. A dentist's daughter born in Oriente Province, Celia Sánchez Manduley was a leader of the TWENTY-SIXTH OF JULY MOVEMENT. She helped to organize the shipment of arms and matériel to the forces fighting against Fulgencio BATISTA in the Sierra Maestra. At El Uvero (a battle fought on 28 May 1957), she became the first woman combatant in the revolutionary army; subsequently she formed the Mariana Granjales Platoon for women. She held the position of secretary of the Council of State, and she was a member of both the Communist Party Central Committee and the National Assembly. Her most influential position was as secretary and lifelong companion to Fidel Castro. After her death from cancer, she was given a state funeral and buried in the Mausoleum of the Revolutionary Armed Forces.

HUGH THOMAS, *Cuba: The Pursuit of Freedom* (1971); CARLOS FRANQUI, *Diary of the Cuban Revolution*, translated by Georgette Felix, et al. (1980); "Celia Sánchez Manduley," in *Cuba Update* 1, no. 1 (1980): 6–7; TAD SZULC, *Fidel: A Critical Portrait* (1986).

DANIEL P. DWYER, O.F.M.

SÁNCHEZ VILELLA, ROBERTO (*b.* 19 February 1913), governor of Puerto Rico (1965–1969). Born in Ponce, Sánchez Vilella studied civil engineering at Ohio State University, graduating in 1934. He was one of the founders of the Partido Democrático Popular (PDP). From 1940 on, he occupied important posts in the public administration of Puerto Rico. Sánchez became governor in 1965 and interpreted his victory as a mandate for change. Because of his governing style, however, he soon ran into problems with the old guard of the party. Although for personal reasons he announced that he would retire from politics upon completing his term as governor in 1969, he nevertheless sought reelection in 1968. When he was unsuccessful, however, he left the PDP and joined the Partido del Pueblo (PP). Because of the PP's inability to become a registered party, Sánchez failed to be elected a member of the legislature in 1972.

OSCAR G. PELÁEZ ALMENGOR

See also **Puerto Rico: Political Parties.**

SANCHO DE HOZ, PEDRO (also Pero; *d.* December 1547), Spanish conquistador, secretary to Francisco PIZARRO, and author (at Pizarro's request) of a valuable account of the first phase of the conquest of Peru. He secured from Emperor Charles V the right to conquer territory south of the Strait of Magellan, which conflicted with the claim to Chile then being made by Pedro de VALDIVIA. At Cuzco, in December 1539, Pizarro persuaded the two men to jointly undertake the conquest of Chile. Sancho de Hoz, frustrated in an effort to assassinate Valdivia in the Atacama Desert, was permitted to remain with the expedition, with the Cuzco agreement rescinded. A plot to seize control of the newly established Chilean colony (1547) was also treated leniently. A third plot, soon thereafter, when Valdivia had left Santiago for Peru, caused Valdivia's lieutenant, Francisco de VILLAGRA, to have Sancho de Hoz beheaded without trial.

H. R. S. POCOCK, *The Conquest of Chile* (1967).

SIMON COLLIER

SANDI, LUIS (*b.* 22 February 1905), Mexican composer, music teacher, administrator, and critic. When Carlos CHÁVEZ was appointed director of the National Conservatory in 1929, he named Sandi head of choral activities. Sandi also assisted Chávez in reforming public music education within the department of fine arts of the Ministry of Public Education in 1933. He was later chief music administrator in the Ministry of Public Education (1946–1951) and the National Institute of Fine Arts (1959–1963). His *Yaqui Music* for Mexican orchestra, performed at the Museum of Modern Art in New York in 1940, brought him international attention. Other works include the opera *Carlotta*, about the wife of Emperor Maximilian; the Mayan ballet *Bonampak*; and a number of didactic and critical writings.

GÉRARD BÉHAGUE, *Music in Latin America: An Introduction* (1979).

ROBERT L. PARKER

SANDINISTAS. *See* **Nicaragua: Political Parties.**

SANDINO, AUGUSTO CÉSAR (*b.* 18 May 1895; *d.* 21 February 1934), general of guerrilla liberation army and Nicaraguan hero. Sandino was the illegitimate son of Gregorio Sandino, a small businessman, and Margarita Calderón, a coffee picker, in the town of Niquinohomo. From an early age he was exposed to bitter human experiences and poverty. At the age of ten, he witnessed his mother's miscarriage while she was imprisoned for debt. He also toiled in the coffee fields with his mother before returning to live with his father in Niquinohomo in 1906. However, his life was not much better with his father. His half brother Socrates received all the attention and benefits while Augusto worked and ate with the servants. He began to question the fairness of society, life, and God. In school, he learned the principles of capitalism and the meaning of exploitation. His education ended in 1910, when he was forced to work in his father's grain business.

In 1916, Sandino left Nicaragua to work as a mechanic in Costa Rica, then returned three years later to start his own grain business. Despite some success, he had to abandon the enterprise after shooting a man during an argument. Between 1920 and 1923, he worked odd jobs until he found employment as a mechanic with the Southern Pennsylvania Oil Company in Tampico, Mexico. There he acquired an eclectic political and spiritual philosophy and an understanding of social revolution.

POLITICAL THOUGHT AND LIBERAL REVOLT
In Mexico, Sandino absorbed a wide range of political ideologies in the midst of revolutionary change. Anarchism, socialism, and communism competed in the workers' unions in the oil fields of Tampico and Veracruz. Sandino grasped the unconditional opposition of government, church, and capitalist institutions ad-

Augusto César Sandino (center). ARCHIVO GENERAL DE LA NACIÓN, MÉXICO.

vanced by the anarchists; he learned the importance of strategies of social change from the socialists; and he endorsed the Communists' demand for proletarian revolution. In addition, Sandino immersed himself in theological doctrines that attempted to explain the human relationship to God. Mexican Freemasonry and spiritualism penetrated his thinking by 1926, when he returned to Nicaragua to join the Liberal opposition to the Conservative government. Sandino's expectations upon his arrival on the Atlantic coast, to join the constitutionalist army of General José María MONCADA, are conjecture. Moncada espoused classical liberal values of law, property, and limited government.

At the behest of the U.S. government, Emiliano CHAMORRO yielded the presidency to his Conservative colleague Adolfo DÍAZ at the end of 1926. Concurrently, the Liberals formed a provisional government in Puerto Cabezas. Sandino continued to press Moncada for stronger and faster action. Moncada rejected Sandino's request for arms in their only face-to-face meeting in late December. When U.S. Marines landed at the Pacific coast port of Corinto in January 1927, Sandino decided to go to San Juan del Norte in the northern mountains and establish his own military command.

The Liberal-Conservative conflict continued until May 1927, when U.S. envoy Henry Stimson arranged a truce between Moncada and Díaz. Both agreed that Díaz would serve until the 1928 election. The Liberal troops voluntarily disarmed, and the U.S. Marine Corps took control of the Nicaraguan National Guard on 16 May

1927. Moncada sent a telegram to Sandino, asking him to give up the fight. Sandino responded bluntly: "Now I want you to come and disarm me. . . . You will not make me cede by any other means. I am not for sale. I do not give up. You will have to defeat me" (Ramírez, p. 85).

In September 1927, in the village of El Chipote, Sandino promulgated the Articles of Incorporation of the Defending Army of the National Sovereignty of Nicaragua. The Chilean poet Gabriela Mistral later called Sandino's guerrilla band "the crazy little army." The army launched attacks against the marines and the Conservative government, each time retreating to El Chipote. Gradually, the general achieved a mystical quality in Latin America, the United States, and Europe. The marines constantly searched for El Chipote, often interrogating uncooperative peasants in the dense jungle of Las Segovias. The secret camp was discovered in January 1928 by air reconnaissance. Intense bombings began immediately, and the marines entered El Chipote on 3 February, to find only stuffed "soldiers."

Over the next few years, Sandino rejected compromises with the Liberal government that came to power in 1928. His army achieved many small victories, such as downing a U.S. bomber. Carleton Beals of *The Nation* provided an inside look at Sandino's life for the North American public. However, a review of recent literature does not reveal a consensus on Sandino's political thought and revolutionary intentions. The eclectic mix of socialism, nationalism, and theosophy has created disagreement about Sandino's intelligence and ability to apply abstract ideas to the Nicaraguan reality. He insisted on social justice for workers and peasants, often using deeply philosophical and sometimes confusing language to explain his motivation.

TRUCE AND DEATH

In 1932, political conditions in the United States and Nicaragua changed. Franklin D. ROOSEVELT succeeded the conservative Herbert Hoover. Roosevelt promulgated the Good Neighbor Policy, which redirected resources away from U.S. political adventures abroad. And Liberal candidate Juan Batista SACASA triumphed over Adolfo Díaz in the 1932 presidential election. Thus, the U.S. Department of State laid the groundwork for the withdrawal of the marines and the installation of the National Guard with Anastasio SOMOZA GARCÍA as chief. One of Sacasa's first actions was to send a peace delegation to San Rafael del Norte, to negotiate a truce with Sandino. On 23 January 1933, an agreement was reached that facilitated the departure of the marines on 1 February. Three weeks later, the Defending Army was disarmed.

From this point Sandino's life took a severe turn for the worse. In June 1933 his wife, Blanca, died giving birth to their daughter; in August the National Guard attacked Sandinistas in Las Segovias, which prompted Sandino to request that President Sacasa declare the Guard unconstitutional. Sacasa invited Sandino to come to Managua in late February 1934. Sandino met with Sacasa and Somoza on the evening of 21 February. Upon leaving the presidential house, apparently satisfied with the result, Sandino, his brother Socrates, and two Sandinista generals were kidnapped by the National Guard. They were murdered in an open field. Sandino's remains have never been found.

NEILL MACAULAY, *The Sandino Affair* (1967); GREGORIO SELSER, *Sandino: General de los hombres libres* (1979); MIGUEL JESÚS BLANDÓN, *Entre Sandino y Fonseca Amador* (1980); CARLOS FONSECA, *Ideario político de Augusto César Sandino* (1984); DAVID NOLAN, *The Ideology of the Sandinistas and the Nicaraguan Revolution* (1984); SERGIO RAMÍREZ, *El pensamiento vivo de Sandino*, 5th ed. (1979); DONALD HODGES, *The Intellectual Foundations of the Nicaraguan Revolution* (1986); STEVEN PALMER, ''Carlos Fonseca and the Construction of Sandinismo in Nicaragua,'' in *Latin American Research Review* 23, no. 1 (1989): 91–109; WAYNE G. BRAGG, trans., *Sandino in the Streets* (1991).

MARK EVERINGHAM

See also **Communism; Nicaragua: Political Parties; United States–Latin American Relations.**

SANDOVAL, JOSÉ LEÓN (*b*. 1789, *d*. October 1854), supreme director (chief of state) of Nicaragua (4 April 1845–24 July 1846). A MESTIZO descendant of the conquistador Gonzalo de Sandoval, Sandoval was a justice of the peace at the close of the colonial period in his native Granada, but he also worked in transporting goods on Lake Nicaragua and the Río San Juan. Resentful of the privileges of Spanish officials and wealthier CREOLES, Sandoval supported independence from Spain and then opposed Nicaraguan incorporation into ITURBIDE's Mexican Empire. In 1825 he became *jefe político* of Granada and later served in other government positions while rising in military rank.

A fervent unionist, he also served Francisco MORAZÁN's federal government in San Salvador. He was supreme director of Nicaragua during the violent struggles among the CAUDILLOS Francisco MALESPÍN, José María Valle, José Trinidad MUÑOZ, and Bernabé Somoza. Although a liberal, Sandoval remained loyal to the elected governments, and under the conservative Fruto CHAMORRO, he directed Granada's defense against the siege begun in May 1854 by Máximo JÉREZ. Brigadier General Sandoval died in this defense and was buried in Granada.

EMILIO ÁLVAREZ, *Ensayo biográfico del prócer José León Sandoval* (1947).

RALPH LEE WOODWARD, JR.

SANDOVAL VALLARTA, MANUEL (*b*. 11 February 1899; *d*. 18 April 1977), Mexican physicist and educator. A graduate of the Massachusetts Institute of Technology in 1921, Sandoval Vallarta later became a disciple of Albert Einstein and other scientists of that time, as well as a costudent and collaborator of Robert Oppenheimer. He received a Guggenheim fellowship to study in Berlin in 1927–1928 and was an exchange professor at Louvain University, Belgium. He began teaching at MIT in 1926 and left his position in 1943 to return to Mexico, where he became director of the National Polytechnic Institute in 1944 and assistant secretary of education in 1953. An internationally recognized physicist, he produced many students who formed the next generation of important Mexican scientists, including Carlos GRAEF FERNÁNDEZ. The Mexican government selected him as one of the original members of the National College and awarded him its National Prize in Sciences in 1959.

MANUEL SANDOVAL VALLARTA, ''Reminiscencias,'' in *Naturaleza* 4 (1973): 178; *Proceso*, 23 April 1977, 28.

RODERIC AI CAMP

SANFUENTES ANDONAEGUI, JUAN LUIS (*b*. 27 December 1858; *d*. 1930), president of Chile (1915–1920). The younger brother of Enrique Sanfuentes (whom President José Manuel BALMACEDA FERNÁNDEZ had tapped as his successor in 1891), Juan Luis Sanfuentes was a supporter of Balmaceda in the civil war of 1891 and later led the Liberal Democratic Party, which nominally espoused Balmaceda's principles. Sanfuentes held several ministerial posts and was a prominent figure during the "parliamentary republic" period in Chile. His main achievement was to uphold Chile's neutrality in World War I. His administration marked the end of the oligarchic era in Chilean politics.

SIMON COLLIER

SANGUINETTI, JULIO MARÍA (*b.* 1936), president of Uruguay (1985–1989). Sanguinetti was the first president to be elected following the 1973 coup. A forty-eight-year-old lawyer at the time of his election, he had thirty years of experience in the Colorado Party. He was elected to the Chamber of Deputies in 1962 and reelected in 1966 and 1971. He served as minister of education and culture under President Juan María BORDABERRY in 1972 but resigned in early 1973 in protest over the increasing political role of the military. An erudite speaker and skilled negotiator, Sanguinetti was general secretary of the Colorado Party during the negotiations in 1983 and 1984 that led to the Pact of the NAVAL CLUB, which paved the way for the November 1984 elections. Building on the success of his newspaper, *Correo de los Viernes*, Sanguinetti ran a skillful campaign for president, putting several young newcomers on his ticket and making effective use of television. His party received 41 percent of the vote to 35 percent for the Blancos (National Party).

Sanguinetti inherited a country mired in recession and still traumatized by the repression and torture that were the hallmarks of military rule. He immediately released the remaining political prisoners and restored all constitutional rights. He made the economist and diplomat Enrique Iglesias his minister of foreign affairs and gave him the leeway to develop an active trade policy. The years 1986 and 1987 were a period of economic recovery but growing political controversy. The stated refusal of the military to participate in any civilian trials concerning human-rights abuses led the government to sponsor and pass an amnesty law. This law was challenged in 1989 by a plebiscite that divided the country. Although the vote ultimately upheld the amnesty for the military, it cost the government much political goodwill.

A stagnant economy in the last two years of his administration and a bitter struggle for the presidential nomination of the Batllist wing of the party, with Jorge Batlle prevailing over Sanguinetti's choice, vice president Enrique Tarigo, led to a Colorado defeat in the November 1989 elections. Sanguinetti, who could not succeed himself, was eligible to run for president in future elections. Head of the Colorado faction known as the Batllist Forum and the major Colorado presidential candidate, Sanguinetti won the election of 1994.

MARTIN WEINSTEIN, *Uruguay: Democracy at the Crossroads* (1988); CHARLES GILLESPIE, *Negotiating Democracy: Politicians and Generals in Uruguay* (1991).

MARTIN WEINSTEIN

SANJUANISTAS, a group of individuals gathered at the Hermitage of San Juan Bautista in Mérida, Yucatán, to discuss religious and social questions, particularly the conditions of Indian servitude. They were under the direction of the hermitage's chaplain, Father Vicente María Velázquez. The imperial crisis of 1808 turned their discussions to political issues. Avowed autonomists, the Sanjuanistas supported the liberal reforms introduced by the Cortes and were determined partisans of the Constitution of 1812. When the first printing press was brought to Mérida in 1813, the Sanjuanistas battled the *rutineros,* the partisans of absolutism, through newspapers and pamphlets.

The Sanjuanistas included Lorenzo de ZAVALA, José Matías Quintana—father of Andrés QUINTANA ROO—and Francisco Bates. When the constitutional system was abolished in 1814, the Sanjuanistas were persecuted and some of them were imprisoned. Zavala, Quintana, and Bates were sent to San Juan de Ulúa, where they remained imprisoned until 1817. Encouraged by Zavala, the former Sanjuanistas reorganized the society when the constitution was restored in 1820, and numerous Masons joined the new organization. The Junta de San Juan ultimately changed its name to the Confederación Patriótica, which managed to force the swearing in of the constitution once again, even though the authorities opposed it. Shortly afterward the group deposed both the governor and the captain-general of Yucatán.

IGNACIO RUBIO MAÑÉ, "Los sanjuanistas de Yucatán I. Manuel Jiménez Solís, el padre Justis," in *Boletín del Archivo general de la nación*, 2nd ser., 8, nos. 3–4 (1967): 1,211–1,234, 9, nos. 1–2 (1968): 193–243, and nos. 3–4 (1968): 401–508, 10, nos. 1–2 (1969): 127–252; and VIRGINIA GUEDEA, "Las sociedades secretas durante el movimiento de independencia," in *The Independence of Mexico and the Creation of the New Nation,* edited by Jaime E. Rodríguez O. (1989), pp. 45–62.

VIRGINIA GUEDEA

SANTA ANNA, ANTONIO LÓPEZ DE (*b.* 21 February 1794; *d.* 21 June 1876), president of Mexico (nine times, 1833–1855). Santa Anna was the most important political figure in Mexico between 1821 and 1855. He was in many ways a quintessential CAUDILLO, one of the regional military leaders who played such important roles in nineteenth-century Latin America. With a strong base in the Veracruz region in eastern Mexico, Santa Anna was consistently able to recruit and finance an army, which brought him to national power nine times. He never remained in the capital long, however, and often abdicated his authority soon after gaining executive office, only to return. Over the course of his career, Santa Anna became increasingly conservative. His first ascension to the presidency was as an ostensible federalist, his last as an ostentatious dictator. He was known as an untrustworthy but sometimes necessary political ally and a military tactician with an uncanny knack for survival.

Santa Anna was born in Jalapa, Veracruz, and began his military career in 1810 with the Fixed Infantry Regiment of Veracruz. During most of the WAR OF INDEPENDENCE, he was involved in royalist counterinsurgency. However, in March 1821, the young lieutenant colonel switched sides in support of Agustín de ITURBIDE's plan to achieve independence. Upon Iturbide's victory, Santa Anna was awarded a political-military position in his native region.

Santa Anna, whose relationship with Iturbide quickly soured, was instrumental in overthrowing the infant monarchy in 1823. For the rest of the decade, he played an intermittent role in national politics from his Veracruz stronghold, but it was not until the very end of the decade that the first of several military engagements with foreign troops greatly elevated his national stature.

In 1829 Spanish troops made an ill-fated attempt to reconquer Mexico. Santa Anna's victory against the invasion force at Tampico earned him popular approval and a certain cachet as a nationalist and military strategist. He would capitalize on this reputation often in the following twenty-five years.

Santa Anna gained the presidency for the first time on 1 April 1833, in a coalition with federalists who needed his military support to oust a conservative regime. However, he quickly turned the government over to his vice president, the ardent reformer Valentín GÓMEZ FARÍAS. At this point in his career, Santa Anna's political affiliations turned away from the federalist-liberal camp. Conservative leaders convinced him to oust Gómez

Farías, whose proposed reforms were deemed a threat to both the Catholic church and the military. Santa Anna thus began his next presidential term in April 1834 on the opposite end of the political spectrum from his first.

In the last half of the 1830s, Santa Anna's career was almost ended, and then resurrected, by international conflicts. He chose to lead the Mexican army sent to squelch the TEXAS REVOLUTION. In 1836, after a number of early victories, including the infamous battle at the ALAMO, Santa Anna was captured. He conceded Texas independence and then retired in defeat from public life. However, in 1838, French troops invaded Mexico to collect indemnities from the government. Santa Anna lost a leg in battle against the French and was once again proclaimed a hero. His role in national politics resumed when he was declared president in March 1839, and in the early 1840s his now familiar oscillation between power (1841, 1843, 1844) and exile was repeated.

Santa Anna's conduct during the MEXICAN-AMERICAN WAR formed another controversial episode in the general's life. Although in exile when the war broke out in 1846, he managed to slip through a U.S. naval blockade, an act that spurred accusations he had secretly agreed to peace terms with the United States. Once back in Mexico, however, Santa Anna took up arms, was appointed president by the congress in December 1846, and for a time bravely led his troops before experiencing defeat and exile once again.

The war with the United States brought Mexico to the

Invasion at Tampico. Santa Anna at center. Oil on canvas by Carlos Paris, 1835. LAURIE PLATT WINFREY, BRADLEY SMITH.

brink of disintegration. The political situation in the late 1840s and early 1850s was more chaotic than ever. Santa Anna was in and out of office in 1847. Finally, in 1853 a fragile conservative coalition formed to bring him back to Mexico, and he was granted extraordinary powers in the hope that he might somehow hold the nation together. From 1853 to 1855, as a military dictator he ruled imperiously, the coalition that had brought him to power disintegrated, and he was forced yet again into exile by the liberal leaders of the Revolution of Ayutla. From 1855 until his death in 1876, Santa Anna played only a marginal role in Mexican politics.

What are we to make of the "age of Santa Anna's revolutions"? The traditional view of Mexican history portrays his greed and fickleness as one of the main causes of the nation's instability. However, Santa Anna's role must be placed within the broader context of Mexican society during this era. He was an important military leader at a time when military power was the key to political control in Mexico. His unique asset was his ability to present himself as a necessary ally to extraordinarily different political factions. Ultimately, though, his career was more a symptom of Mexico's deeper political, social, and economic problems than the cause of them.

A truly satisfying biography of Santa Anna remains to be written, though several have been attempted in English. Two dramatic portraits were produced in the 1930s: WILFRID HARDY CALLCOTT, *Santa Anna: The Story of an Enigma Who Once Was Mexico* (1936), and FRANK C. HANIGHEN, *Santa Anna: The Napoleon of the West* (1934). A third biography is OAKAH L. JONES, *Santa Anna* (1968). Santa Anna's autobiography is an interesting attempt by the general himself to justify his checkered career and answer his critics: ANTONIO LÓPEZ DE SANTA ANNA, *The Eagle: The Autobiography of Santa Anna*, translated and edited by Ann Fears Crawford (1988). An influential study of *caudillismo* that compares Santa Anna and Juan Álvarez is FERNANDO DÍAZ DÍAZ, *Caudillos y caciques: Antonio López de Santa Anna y Juan Álvarez* (1972). Two recent attempts to reevaluate Santa Anna are CHRISTON I. ARCHER, "The Young Antonio López de Santa Anna: Veracruz Counterinsurgent and Incipient Caudillo," in *The Human Tradition in Latin America: Nineteenth Century*, edited by William Beezley and Judith Ewell (1989), which examines Santa Anna's emergence as a political actor during the Independence wars; and CARMEN VÁZQUEZ MANTECÓN, *Santa Anna y la encrucijada del estado: La dictadura (1853–55)* (1986), a fine analysis of Santa Anna's last years as ruler of Mexico.

RICHARD WARREN

SANTA CATARINA, state in southern Brazil bordered on the east by the Atlantic Ocean, on the west by Argentina, and along the south by the Pelotas and Uruguay rivers. The interior region of Santa Catarina lagged significantly behind the coast in population and economic development until the twentieth century, even as Santa Catarina as a whole was overshadowed by states in Brazil such as São Paulo and Rio Grande do Sul. Lages, the largest city in its interior, was founded in 1770 by cattle ranchers who gradually expanded land development west and north toward Paraná.

Until the expansion of the Brazil Railway Company into Santa Catarina after 1906, and its subsequent lumbering, sawmill, and colonization enterprises, landowners largely depended upon sharecropping to attract workers to the interior. One of Santa Catarina's most famous historical figures was José Maria, whose millenarian movement within the CONTESTADO called for a restoration of the monarchy in opposition to the capitalist transformations of the beginning of the twentieth century. The railroad expansion and subsequent land boom had led to a convergence of national, international, and private interests in the removal of subsistence peasants or "squatters." To defeat the 15,000 peasant followers of José Maria after his death, the Brazilian army utilized nearly half its forces and $250,000 from 1912 to 1916.

In 1991 the population of Santa Catarina was 4,085,847 with an area of 37,060 square miles. Since 1823 its capital city has been FLORIANÓPOLIS (originally Destêrro; renamed for President Floriano PEIXOTO in 1893). At present Santa Catarina's economy depends on cattle raising, coal mining, food processing, textiles, and petrochemical production.

ALEXANDER LENARD, *The Valley of the Latin Bear* (1965); WALTER F. PIAZZA, *Santa Catarina: Sua historia* (1983); TODD A. DIACON, "Peasants, Prophets, and the Power of a Millenarian Vision in Twentieth-Century Brazil," in *Comparative Studies in Society and History* 32 (1990): 488–514.

CAROLYN E. VIEIRA

SANTA CRUZ, ANDRÉS DE (*b.* 30 November 1792; *d.* 25 September 1865), president of Peru (1827), president of Bolivia (1829–1836), and president of the PERU-BOLIVIA CONFEDERATION (1836–1839).

A royalist officer who switched to the patriot side in 1820, Santa Cruz distinguished himself in the WARS OF INDEPENDENCE and later became one of the longest lasting and most able presidents of Bolivia. His reorganization of governmental institutions on the Napoleonic model provided the basis for republican government for over a century. However, his attempt in 1836 to reunite Peru and Bolivia engendered a Chilean invasion that led to his downfall in 1839.

The son of a minor Spanish colonial official and the wealthy heiress of an Indian chieftainship, Santa Cruz was born in La Paz to wealth and received a good education in Cuzco, though he left school before graduating. He first joined his father's regiment in 1811, and in 1817 fought against the invading Argentine armies. Taken prisoner the same year, Santa Cruz was sent to a prison close to Buenos Aires but managed to escape and return to Peru. Recaptured in 1820, he decided to become a patriot. In 1822, Santa Cruz distinguished himself in the battle of PICHINCHA, Ecuador, under Antonio José de SUCRE, achieving the rank of brigadier general in

Andrés Santa Cruz. PHOTOGRAPHIE BULLOZ.

both the Colombian and Peruvian patriot armies. Despite a victory in Zepita over the Spanish army (for which he was promoted to grand marshal), Santa Cruz was unable to liberate his home territory.

After Peru and Bolivia achieved independence, Santa Cruz briefly became president of Peru in 1827 under the auspices of Simón BOLÍVAR. Voted out in the anti-Bolivarian reactions of 1827, Santa Cruz went to Chile on a diplomatic mission. Wanting to reunite Peru and Bolivia, Santa Cruz was convinced that Antonio José de Sucre should be ousted from the Bolivian presidency because his presence made the reunification impossible. In 1828, in the wake of Agustín GAMARRA's invasion of Bolivia, Sucre resigned and Santa Cruz was elected president. He took power in 1829.

Santa Cruz was a mercantilist and favored domestic industries, particularly textiles, over foreign products. Nevertheless, he developed the port of Cobija on the Pacific coast by building a road and providing import tax relief as a way of achieving sovereignty over this sparsely populated desert region.

Santa Cruz also lowered MINING taxes, but this action did not stimulate silver mining sufficiently to provide enough government revenues. In 1830 he resorted to minting debased silver currency as a way of covering the fiscal deficit, thereby setting a pattern that would continue into the 1860s and provide a relatively high indirect tariff that protected domestic production from foreign competition.

Recognizing the lack of government revenue and for-ever a pragmatist, Santa Cruz formally reinstituted the payment of Indian tribute in return for which the state guaranteed the Indians' possession of community lands for ten years. Although this went against the president's otherwise Bolivarian ideas (Bolívar had abolished tribute payments in 1824 and 1825), Santa Cruz recognized the crucial economic role of the Indian communities' economies and the benefits of a regular and substantial income for the fiscally strapped government.

This legislation also provided resources and a stable home base for his other projects, most notably the reunification of Peru and Bolivia. In 1836, Santa Cruz briefly tried to take advantage of the political chaos in Argentina and attempted unsuccessfully to annex Jujuy to Bolivia. More successful, at least temporarily, were Santa Cruz's expansionist plans toward Peru. In 1835 he moved against the divided Peruvian leadership and was able to defeat his rival, Agustín Gamarra, and by 1836 the Peruvian president, Felipe Santiago SALAVERRY.

Once Santa Cruz had conquered Peru, he reorganized the two states into three units, Northern Peru, Southern Peru, and Bolivia. Each unit elected its own president, and Santa Cruz named himself the confederation's protector. As a result, Santa Cruz dropped his efforts at developing the port of Cobija and encouraged trade between the more easily accessible southern Peruvian ports of Arica and Tacna.

Both Chile and Argentina feared a powerful northern neighbor and did everything in their power to eliminate the confederation. While Argentina was suffering from its own internal problems, Chile actively aided Peruvian dissidents, finally invading the confederation in 1838. In 1839 the Chileans won a major battle outside Lima, and Santa Cruz fled into exile in Ecuador. However, in 1841 pro–Santa Cruz forces overthrew the Bolivian president, General José Miguel de VELASCO, precipitating the invasion of Peruvian General Agustín Gamarra. When it became clear that Gamarra intended to annex parts of Bolivia to Peru, Bolivian forces united under the anti–Santa Cruz General José BALLIVIÁN and, in the battle of Ingaví in 1841, defeated the Peruvian army and killed the Peruvian leader. As a result, Santa Cruz was prevented from returning to Bolivia. More important, the battle of Ingaví signaled the end of overt Peruvian and Bolivian intervention into each other's affairs and the end of Bolivia's dominance as a regional power. Santa Cruz was exiled for life and died in Nantes, France.

A standard popular biography is ALFONSO CRESPO RODAS, *Santa Cruz, el cóndor indio* (1944). The best recent work is PHILIP PARKERSON, *Andrés de Santa Cruz y la Confederación Perú-Boliviana 1835–1839* (1984), a Spanish translation of his Ph.D. dissertation, "Sub-Regional Integration in Nineteenth Century South America: Andrés de Santa Cruz and the Peru-Bolivia Confederation, 1835–39" (Univ. of Florida, 1979). A good brief summary of the Santa Cruz period is contained in HERBERT S. KLEIN, *Bolivia: The Evolution of a Multi-Ethnic Society* (1982), pp. 112–119.

ERICK D. LANGER

SANTA CRUZ, region in Bolivia's eastern tropics, and its capital city. The region was once a part of the Audiencia of CHARCAS. Shortly after the Spanish conquest, this legendary, remote jungle area attracted Spanish explorers whose expeditions, vulnerable to the hostile environment and attacks by ferocious CHIRIGUANO INDIANS, rarely succeeded. Conflicts of interest between Paraguayans and Peruvians also hampered efforts to penetrate and settle the area. The Paraguayans sought to open the region to exploit its resources and establish a trade route via the Paraguay and La Plata river systems to the Atlantic Ocean and Europe. But nervous *charqueños*, threatened by Paraguayan expansionism, saw the region as their defense zone against the Chiriguanos, to be settled and incorporated into the Audiencia of Charcas.

By the 1540s, Paraguayan explorers had established permanent outposts in the MOJOS and Chiquitos territories. In 1559, the Paraguayan Ñulfo de Cháves founded Nueva Asunción on the eastern banks of the Río Guapay (Grande). It was not until 1561 that Cháves, despite the destruction of his outposts by the Chiriguanos and clashes with the Peruvian-sponsored explorer Andrés Manso (who was soon killed), founded the city of Santa Cruz de la Sierra in Chiquitos territory east of the Río Guapay. Cháves continued to push deeper into the region, prompting Peruvian authorities to incorporate both the Mojos and Santa Cruz into the Audiencia of Charcas in 1563. Yet the ambitious Cháves remained in control of the entire region until his murder. He brought in people from Asunción and planned to relocate residents from Buenos Aires to the area. He initiated cattle and horse protection, followed by the cultivation of sugarcane, corn, and cotton. Soon *cruzeños* demanded permits to send their Indians to the highland mines.

By now Santa Cruz was drawn into the POTOSÍ market and exported cotton cloth, sugar, fruits, and jams to the highlands in exchange for imported Spanish textiles, agricultural equipment, wine, and wheat flour. But the region's entrepreneurs still had their eyes on the eastern gateway and a promising European market. Hopes dissipated in 1591, when the city of Santa Cruz de la Sierra was twice relocated for defense as well as political reasons to a less vulnerable zone on the western banks of the Río Guapay. Although a bishopric was established in Santa Cruz in 1605, the region remained isolated, depopulated, and imbued with the rugged hostile frontier image established from the onset.

Over time, the local elite assumed control of the region beyond the grasp of the remote and distant government. By the late eighteenth century, Santa Cruz continued to demonstrate economic promise and became an intendancy that included the province of Cochabamba. Yet the region remained relatively untapped until the rubber and oil booms of the late nineteenth and early twentieth centuries. It endured the disastrous CHACO WAR (1932–1935), in which the Paraguayans invaded Santa Cruz. Finally, as a result of Bolivia's 1952 revolution, a vast plan for regional development was initiated, ultimately involving heavy government investment. Santa Cruz's development today is best seen in its diversified economy (including hydrocarbon exploitation), population growth, paved highways, international airport, and recognition as a bastion of economic and political power.

JOSEP M. BARNADAS, *Charcas: Orígenes históricos de una sociedad colonial* (1973), pp. 25–26, 56–57, 61–65, 277, 293, 359, 398, 459; ENRIQUE FINOT, *Historia de la conquista del Oriente boliviano*, 2d ed. (1978), pp. 245–249; HERBERT S. KLEIN, *Bolivia: The Evolution of a Multi-Ethnic Society* (1982), pp. 35, 193, 235, 251–257, 268; HUMBERTO VÁZQUEZ MACHICADO, JOSÉ DE MESA Y TERESA GISBERT, *Manual de historia de Bolivia* 2d ed. (1983), pp. 135–136; BROOKE LARSON, *Colonialism and Agrarian Transformation in Bolivia: Cochabamba, 1550–1900* (1988), pp. 119–120, 174, 243.

LOLITA GUTIÉRREZ BROCKINGTON

SANTA CRUZ, FORTALEZA DE, a fort at the northeastern lip of Guanabara Bay's narrow mouth, which since the sixteenth century functioned as the first line of land-based defense against enemy naval attack on the city of Rio de Janeiro. The fortifications constructed over the centuries on this site, christened Santa Cruz in 1632, command an enviable artillery position. In the colonial period the fort easily repelled several pirating expeditions, allowing Rio de Janeiro to develop in relative peace. The fort's cold gray granite environs also surrounded one of Brazil's largest and oldest prisons. It held both military and civilian convicts, including such notable figures as TIRADENTES, Plínio SALGADO, and Juarez TÁVORA. The prison's conditions were harsh, some cells being so small and crowded that inmates had to squat once inside. These cruel conditions encouraged rebellions.

The revolt in 1892 of Sergeant Silvino Honório de Macedo, a promonarchist noncommissioned officer, threatened to topple President Floriano PEIXOTO's republican government. Silvino plotted a successful mutiny in Santa Cruz, armed the prisoners there, and subverted other garrisons around the bay. It required a full-scale army assault on Santa Cruz finally to overwhelm the insurgent inmates. No longer a prison but still an army barracks, Santa Cruz now also serves as a historical museum.

Sources on Santa Cruz's history are sparse, even in Portuguese. AUGUSTO FAUSTO DE SOUZA provides a brief history of the fort in "Fortificações no Brazil," in *Revista do Instituto Histórico, Geográphico e Ethnográphico do Brazil* 48 (1885): 5–140. GENERAL DERMEVAL PEIXOTO provides a description of conditions in Santa Cruz at the turn of the century in *Memórias de um velho soldado* (1960).

PETER M. BEATTIE

SANTA CRUZ PACHACUTI YAMQUI SALCAMAYGUA, JOAN DE, writer. Not much is known about the life of Santa Cruz Pachacuti other than that he lived in the first part of the seventeenth century in the region between Cuzco and Lake Titicaca in Peru. But his importance grows day by day because of the information contained in his work *Relación de la antigüedades de este reyno del Pirú* (1613; An Account of the Antiquities of Peru), one of the most interesting views of the INCA world. The text includes several drawings that have served as clues to the interpretation of the QUECHUA cosmological view of the world. At the time, Spanish culture, which emphasized writing as its privileged system of recording and as the mark of civilization, coexisted with Quechua culture, based on oral and visual systems of signification. Santa Cruz Pachacuti attempts to explain his native religion in the framework of the Christianity brought by the Spaniards, and in doing so he discovers that language is limited and must employ visual images. From this tension emerges the force of the *Relación.* Together with the works of El Inca GARCILASO DE LA VEGA and Felipe GUAMÁN POMA DE AYALA, that of Santa Cruz Pachacuti is one of the most important indigenous sources of Inca society as well as of the conflicts of acculturation during the colonial period in the Andean region.

GARY URTON, *At the Crossroads of the Earth and the Sky: An Andean Cosmology* (1981); REGINA HARRISON, "Modes of Discourse: *Relación de antigüedades de este reyno del Pirú* by Joan Santa Cruz Pachacuti Yamqui Salcamaygua," in *From Oral to Written Expression: Native Andean Chronicles of the Early Colonial Period,* edited by Rolena Adorno (1982), pp. 65–100; REGINA HARRISON, "Script and Sketch: A Semiotics of Knowledge in Santa Cruz Pachacuti Yamqui's *Relación,*" in her *Signs, Songs, and Memory in the Andes* (1989), pp. 55–84.

LEONARDO GARCÍA PABÓN

SANTA CRUZ Y ESPEJO, FRANCISCO JAVIER EUGENIO DE (*b.* 21 February 1747; *d.* 27 December 1795), Ecuadorian writer. Born in Quito to a Quechua father and a mulatto mother, Espejo rose from humble origins to become one of Ecuador's leading intellects. Although mostly self-taught through first-hand observation at a women's hospital, he received the degree of doctor of medicine in July 1767 from the Colegio de San Fernando, and later obtained degrees in civil and canon law.

Espejo became most widely known for his diverse writings on economics, medicine, pedagogy, politics, sociology, and theology. In a frequently satirical tone he criticized the clergy and Ecuador's backwardness. His most famous works are *El nuevo Luciano o despertador de ingenios* (1779), which aimed at educational reform, and *Reflexiones . . . acerca de un método seguro para preservar a los pueblos de las viruelas* (1785), which proposed ways to prevent smallpox and received international recognition.

In 1788 Espejo successfully defended himself in Bogotá against charges of having written and circulated *El retrato de Golilla,* which ridiculed both CHARLES III and José de GÁLVEZ, minister of the Indies. While in Bogotá, Espejo met such New Granadan firebrands as Antonio NARIÑO and Francisco Antonio Zea, who radicalized his

thought. Upon returning to Quito, he helped establish the Sociedad Patriótica de Amigos del País de Quito on 30 November 1791. He also edited the society's newspaper, Ecuador's first, the short-lived *Primicias de la Cultura de Quito* in 1792. At the same time he became director of Ecuador's first public library and was founder of the National Library.

Espejo was tried and imprisoned on charges of sedition in January 1795. He became ill while in jail and died shortly after being released.

FRANCISCO JAVIER EUGENIO SANTA CRUZ Y ESPEJO, *Escritos del doctor Francisco Javier Eugenio Santa Cruz y Espejo,* edited by Federico González Suárez (1912); PHILIP L. ASTUTO, "Eugenio Espejo: A Man of the Enlightenment in Ecuador," in *Revista de historia de América* (1957): 369–391.

PHILIPPE L. SEILER

SANTA ELENA, city in Spanish colonial Florida, founded in 1566 by Pedro MENÉNDEZ DE AVILÉS on Parris Island in present-day South Carolina. Its garrison manned three successive forts. In 1569, 193 settlers came to Santa Elena, bringing with them many of the trades, crafts, and professions of Spain. Secondary to SAINT AUGUSTINE until 1571, Santa Elena became the capital of Florida in that year when Menéndez moved his wife and household there. Menéndez hoped to establish his royal land grant in the upland piedmont, at Guatari, near present-day Charlotte, North Carolina. He imported many rich household goods, and began the fur trade with the Native Americans. Other economic enterprises included the raising of corn and hogs, the export of sassafras root and lumber, and the building of two small ships. Jesuit and Franciscan missionaries came to Santa Elena but failed to make many converts among the Native Americans. After Menéndez's death at Santander, Spain, in 1574, relations with the Indians deteriorated, and a confederation of neighboring CACIQUES forced the Spaniards to evacuate Santa Elena in 1576. The city was rebuilt the following year and was finally abandoned in 1587.

EUGENE LYON, *Santa Elena: A Brief History of the Colony, 1566–1587* (1984); STANLEY SOUTH, RUSSELL K. SKOWRONEK, and RICHARD E. JOHNSON, with contributions by EUGENE LYON, RICHARD POLHEMUS, WILLIAM RADISCH, and CARL STEEN, *Spanish Artifacts from Santa Elena* (1988).

EUGENE LYON

SANTA FE, ARGENTINA, administrative province and historical region of Argentina significant for its size (with 2,765,678 inhabitants in 1989, it has the second-largest provincial population) and for its economic output. The region around the city of Sante Fe was pioneered by Juan de GARAY in 1573 and comprised within its jurisdiction the present provinces of Santa Fe, Entre Ríos, and northern Buenos Aires. Sante Fe was an important port on the fluvial route to Asunción. It exported salted meat, hides, and wood products, as well as yerba maté and wheat.

As an active supporter of the federalists struggling in the wake of independence against the centralism of Buenos Aires, Santa Fe paid dearly as it became a theater of action for federalist and unitarian warlords. The wars continued until the fall of Manuel de ROSAS in 1852. Right after approval of the federalist constitution, signed in Santa Fe, the first attempts were made at establishing farming colonies with foreign immigrants in Argentina. Thus Esperanza was founded in 1854, and other agricultural colonies multiplied in the northern part of the PAMPA, growing grain and raising cattle. Today Santa Fe province produces 35 percent of Argentina's wheat as well as more than half of the country's sunflower seeds. Other agricultural commodities include flax, lentils, soybeans, and potatoes. The main population centers in the province are Greater Rosario, Santa Fe, Esperanza, La Paz, Villa Federal, and San Lorenzo.

LEONCIO GIANELLO, *Historia de Sante Fe* (Buenos Aires, 1978); and EZEQUIEL GALLO, *La Pampa gringa: La colonización agrícola de Santa Fé (1870–1895)* (Buenos Aires, 1983).

CÉSAR N. CAVIEDES

SANTA FE, NEW MEXICO, capital of New Mexico founded about 1609 by governor Pedro de PERALTA (*ca.* 1584–1666). The villa stood close to the banks of the upper Rio Grande at the southernmost tip of the Sangre de Cristo mountains; to the east were the plains; to the west, the pueblos. To the southwest were the river communities and the Camino Real (Royal Road) that tied New Mexico to the rest of New Spain and the world beyond.

Santa Fe played a crucial role in the PUEBLO REBELLION of 1680. In August the pueblos, briefly united in their hatred of the injustices of the colonial system, laid siege to the capital and forced the Spaniards to flee, first to Isleta, some 70 miles to the south, and then to El Paso. Thirteen years later, Diego de Vargas (*d.* 1704) led a recolonizing force into New Mexico. In the Battle of Santa Fe (29 December 1693), he retook the capital with the help of Pecos Pueblo auxiliaries who had grown disillusioned with pueblo rule. This was the last major battle in Santa Fe history, and by 1697 Vargas had subdued the last of the rebellious pueblos and completed the reconquest of New Mexico.

Santa Fe developed into a unique Hispanic frontier community in the eighteenth century. Although a presidio town that lived under the constant threat of attack from NAVAJO and Ute Indians, Santa Fe was not walled and its settlement pattern was notably decentralized. It hardly resembled other fortified presidios nor did it have the strict gridlike pattern of most other Hispanic cities. Santa Fe was an agricultural community of 2,542 people in 1790. Other than the occasional trade caravan that came up the Royal Road from Chihuahua with lux-

ury items, New Mexico and its capital lived in isolation and became nearly self-sufficient.

New Mexico's role in the fight for independence from Spain was small; of more importance to the isolated community was the end of the Spaniards' monopoly on trade. In 1821 William Becknell brought a small trade caravan from Missouri to Santa Fe and found a ready market for his goods. The opening of the Santa Fe Trail that tied New Mexico to the United States affected the frontier community immediately. Calicos and gingham fabrics were found in most houses; American styles and furniture became commonplace on the streets and in homes. The duties collected from the traders supplemented the town's meager income.

In the New Mexico Revolution of 1837, the rebels from the northern communities held Santa Fe for a short time until the capital was retaken by former and future governor Manuel ARMIJO. And in 1846 General Stephen W. KEARNY marched into the town without bloodshed and established U.S. rule. Santa Fe remained the capital when New Mexico became a U.S. Territory in 1850 and when statehood was achieved in 1912.

JOSIAH GREGG, *Commerce of the Prairies*, edited by Max L. Moorehead (1954); MARC SIMMONS, *Yesterday in Santa Fe: Episodes in a Turbulent History* (1969); PAUL HORGAN, *The Centuries of Santa Fe* (1976); SUSAN HAZEN-HAMMOND, *A Short History of Santa Fe* (1988); DAVID GRANT NOBLE, ed. *Santa Fe: History of an Ancient City* (1989).

AARON PAINE MAHR

SANTA FE DE BOGOTÁ. *See* **Bogotá.**

SANTA LUISA, a major archaeological site with one of the longest culture chronologies in coastal Mexico, dating from about 6,000 B.C. to the present. Covering a 6.2-square-mile area of alluvial terraces between the modern towns of Gutiérrez Zamora and Tecolutla, in the state of Veracruz, this significant ancient site along the Tecolutla River has extremely abundant cultural remains. Its strategic location at the convergence of diverse riverine, estuarine, forest, and savannah zones with plentiful food resources made it attractive for long-term human occupation. At nearby La Conchita, a small, closely related site, there are remains of extinct Pleistocene fauna as well as later campsites radiocarbon-dated to 5,600 B.C.

The population peak at Santa Luisa, which corresponds with the construction of numerous temple structures and extensive irrigated field systems for intensive agriculture, occurred during the Classic period (about A.D. 300–900) and the locally defined Epi-Classic period (about A.D. 900–1100). At that time the site was dominated by and heavily reflected the regional culture, whose major expression was the city of EL TAJÍN, some 21 miles distant.

Extensive explorations of Santa Luisa were undertaken between 1968 and 1979 by this writer in the effort to define a workable culture chronology for the north-central region of Veracruz. The resulting nearly continuous evidence of human presence, currently divided into seventeen archaeological phases, has been most useful for interpreting the processes of cultural evolution throughout the region since the time of Early Archaic hunter-gatherers. One of the unanticipated conclusions of these excavations was that, in this traditional Totonac area, the oldest identifiable ethnic evidence appears to be Huastec.

Other important discoveries at Santa Luisa include evidence of preceramic villages on deltaic islands, early ceramics, Olmec-inspired artifacts, vestiges of various forms of intensive agriculture, rare in situ examples of ritual BALL-GAME sculptures called yokes and *palmas*, painted stucco fragments, and architectural remains.

S. JEFFREY K. WILKERSON, *Ethnogenesis of the Huastecs and Totonacs* (1973); "Pre-Agricultural Village Life: The Late Preceramic Period in Veracruz," in *Contributions of the University of California Archaeological Research Facility*, edited by John A. Graham, no. 27 (1975):111–122; "Man's Eighty Centuries in Veracruz," in *National Geographic Magazine* 158, no. 2 (August 1980):202–231; "The Northern Olmec and Pre-Olmec Frontier on the Gulf Coast," in *The Olmec and Their Neighbors: Essays in Memory of Matthew W. Sterling*, edited by Michael D. Coe and David Grove (1981), pp. 181–194.

S. JEFFREY K. WILKERSON

See also **Huasteca; Totonacs.**

SANTA MARÍA, ANDRÉS DE (*b.* 10 December 1860; *d.* 29 April 1945), Colombian artist. Born to a wealthy family that left Colombia for Europe during the civil war of 1862, Santa María spent most of his life in Europe. In 1882 he studied at the École des Beaux Arts in Paris and in 1887 his work *Seine Laundresses* was exhibited at the Salon des Artistes Français and the Salon des Tuileries. He returned to Bogotá in 1893 and was appointed professor of landscape painting at the School of Fine Arts the following year. He went back to Europe in 1901, but returned to Colombia in 1904 and was appointed director of the School of Fine Arts. He generally painted landscapes and scenes of daily life in an impressionist style. His work was shown at the School of Fine Arts, the TEATRO COLÓN (1906), and the Exposición del Centenario (1910). Criticism of his work at the School of Fine Arts prompted his return to Brussels, where he lived for the rest of his life.

His paintings were shown in Paris, Brussels, and Bogotá. In 1923 the French government made him a chevalier of the Legion of Honor and in 1930 he was named academic correspondent of the Academy of San Fernando in Madrid. His later work had richer colors as well as chiaroscuro. Santa María had retrospective exhibitions in Bogotá (1931), Brussels (1936), and London (1937). In 1971 the Museum of Modern Art in Bogotá

honored him with a posthumous exhibition of 126 works.

GABRIEL GIRALDO JARAMILLO, *La miniatura, la pintura y el grabado en Colombia* (1980); EDUARDO SERRANO, *Andres de Santa María* (1988).

BÉLGICA RODRÍGUEZ

SANTA MARÍA GONZÁLEZ, DOMINGO (*b.* 4 August 1825; *d.* 18 July 1889), president of Chile (1881–1886). The early political activities of this attorney, professor, and civil servant twice forced him into exile. Following his second return to Chile in 1862, he served numerous terms in both houses of the legislature and as a justice of the Supreme Court, a cabinet minister, and a diplomat. Elected president in 1881, he led the nation to triumph over Peru and Bolivia in the WAR OF THE PACIFIC.

Apparently a haughty, if not arrogant, man, Santa María launched his own *Kulturkampf*, forcing the legislature to remove the cemeteries from the control of the Roman Catholic church, make marriage a civil contract, and have the state—not the church—keep the civil registry. Violently anticlerical, Santa María supposedly improved the political environment by limiting the power of provincial officials, increasing individual freedoms, and extending suffrage by ceasing to demand that voters possess property. Paradoxically, he shamelessly manipulated the 1882 congressional and 1886 presidential elections.

Ending the War of the Pacific constituted Santa María's greatest achievement. Chile had to withstand pressure from the United States to abandon its demands for territorial concessions and wage a prolonged guerrilla war before forcing Peru to cede to Chile the province of Tarapacá. The following year, in 1884, Bolivia agreed to an armistice.

Santa María concluded his term by pacifying the ARAUCANIAN INDIANS in the south. By 1886, when he left office, Chile had increased its size by approximately a third, controlled the world's supply of nitrates, and dominated the Southern Hemisphere's Pacific coast.

LUIS GALDAMES, *A History of Chile* (1941), pp. 336–340; WILLIAM F. SATER, *Chile and the War of the Pacific* (1986), pp. 60–61, 184–189, 192–195, 206–207, 211–222.

WILLIAM F. SATER

SANTA MARTA, a city and province in northern New Granada (Audiencia of Santa Fe de Bogotá and, in the eighteenth century, the Viceroyalty of the New Kingdom of Granada). Founded by Rodrigo de BASTIDAS in 1525, twenty-five years after Spanish mariners first sighted its location, the town of Santa Marta played an important role in the history of New Granada during the Conquest. For a short time it was the capital of Tierra Firme and the port of call for the galleons. It was also the first bishopric see established in present-day

Colombia (1531) and the location from which Gonzalo JIMÉNEZ DE QUESADA launched his conquest of the Chibcha Indians.

The prominence of the port faded with the founding of Cartagena de Indias in 1533. Political, commercial, ecclesiastical, and military focus shifted westward, leaving Santa Marta relatively undeveloped and thus more susceptible to political corruption, repeated foreign attacks, and Indian hostilities throughout the eighteenth century. Santa Marta province extended from the Magdalena River to the Sierra de Perijá and from the Caribbean southward to Ocaña.

A straightforward history of Santa Marta can be found in ERNESTO RESTREPO TIRADO, *Historia de la Provincia de Santa Marta*, 2 vols. (1953). A useful, though biased, contemporary description of the region is ANTONIO JULIÁN, *La perla de la América: Provincia de Santa Marta* (1951). For the military and architectural history of the port of Santa Marta see JUAN MANUEL ZAPATERO, *Historia de las fortalezas de Santa Marta y estudio asesor para su restauración* (1980). For an overview of the province see also JAMES R. KROGZEMIS, *A Historical Geography of the Santa Marta Area, Colombia* (1967).

LANCE R. GRAHN

SANTAMARÍA, HAYDÉE (*b.* 1927; *d.* 26 July 1980), Cuban revolutionary and cultural director. Haydée Santamaría was one of two women who participated in the 1953 attack on Cuba's Moncada army barracks in Santiago. Arrested and imprisoned, she was released on 20 February 1954. She met with Fidel CASTRO in Mexico, and then returned to Cuba to organize resistance to the BATISTA government in Santiago. Santamaría was a founding member of the national directorate of the TWENTY-SIXTH OF JULY MOVEMENT. She was a member of the Central Committee of the Cuban Communist Party, and the director of the CASA DE LAS AMÉRICAS, an institution for the study of popular culture. Santamaría was married to Minister of Education Armando Hart. She died from a self-inflicted gunshot wound.

CARLOS FRANQUI, *Diary of the Cuban Revolution*, translated by Georgette Felix, et al. (1980); "Haydée Santamaría, Director of Casa de las Américas Dies," in *Cuba Update* 1, no. 3 (1980):16; TAD SZULC, *Fidel: A Critical Portrait* (1986); ERNESTO GUEVARA, *Che Guevara and the Cuban Revolution: Writings and Speeches of Ernesto Che Guevara*, edited by David Deutschmann (1987).

DANIEL P. DWYER, O.F.M.

SANTANA, PEDRO (*b.* 29 June 1801; *d.* 14 June 1864), cattle rancher, general, and president of the Dominican Republic (1844–1848, 1853–1856, and 1857–1861). Santana was a wealthy landowner from the eastern part of Hispaniola known as El Seibo, where he organized the armed forces at the time of the Dominican Republic's declaration of independence from Haiti on 27 February 1844. Heading the victorious Dominican troops during the battle of 19 March 1844 at Azua, he emerged as one of the heroes of the war of liberation against Haiti as well as the commander in chief of the liberation forces.

After becoming the first president of the Dominican Republic, Santana ruled as a caudillo with an iron hand, suppressing all opposition and exiling many of his former associates, including the "father of the Dominican Republic," Juan Pablo DUARTE. Santana executed many Dominican patriots, including María Trinidad Sánchez, who had sewn the first Dominican flag; the brothers José Joaquín and Gabiño Puello, who had distinguished themselves in the war against Haiti; General Antonio Duvergé, victor of many battles against the Haitians; and the national hero, Francisco del Rosario Sánchez, who along with Duarte and Ramón Matias MELLA is regarded as one of the three founding fathers of the Dominican Republic.

Throughout his terms as president, Santana faced Haitian invasions that were organized by the Haitian ruler Faustin SOULOUQUE. In the battles of Santomé (1845), Las Carreras (1845), Cambronal (1855), and Sabana Larga (1856), Santana nullified all Haitian attempts to reconquer the Dominican Republic. However, the frequent Haitian incursions convinced Santana that his country should be annexed by a larger nation. His efforts to persuade France or the United States to annex the Dominican Republic proved futile.

Pedro Santana. BENSON LATIN AMERICAN COLLECTION, UNIVERSITY OF TEXAS AT AUSTIN.

In 1861, Santana made arrangements with the government of Queen Isabel II for the reannexation of the Dominican Republic by Spain and was rewarded with the title of Marqués de Las Carreras. The majority of Dominicans opposed the renewal of Spanish control and fought the successful War of Restoration (1863–1865) against Spain. By the time Santana died at Santo Domingo in 1864, he was no longer regarded by most Dominicans as the hero of the fight against Haiti but as the traitor in the War of Restoration against Spain. His reburial in the Pantheon of Dominican Heroes by order of President Joaquín Balaguer stirred up the controversy over Santana's ambivalent role in the history of his country.

EMILIO RODRÍGUEZ DEMORIZI, *El General Pedro Santana* (1982).

KAI P. SCHOENHALS

SANTANDER, FRANCISCO DE PAULA (*b.* 2 April 1792; *d.* 6 May 1840), vice president of GRAN COLOMBIA and later president of NEW GRANADA. Born at Cúcuta, on the New Granada-Venezuela border, to a locally prominent family of cacao planters, Santander was sent at age thirteen to Bogotá to complete his education. He studied for a law degree, but after the independence movement began, he enlisted in the armed forces of the revolution without completing his studies.

In the civil warfare that soon broke out between centralists in Bogotá and the federalist United Provinces of New Granada, Santander, a junior officer, sided with the latter and in 1813 joined the patriot army defending northeastern New Granada against the royalists. Victory alternated with defeat until the patriots suffered a crushing setback at the battle of Cachirí in February 1816. Santander was among the survivors who made their way to relative safety on the eastern llanos, the lowland plains stretching from the foothills of the Andes to the Orinoco Basin.

Santander helped defend the llanos against royalist incursions, ultimately winning promotion to general. It was also in the llanos that he first displayed his talents as an administrator by organizing the province of Casanare as a base of patriot resistance. His success in this effort was one reason Simón BOLÍVAR decided in 1819 to strike westward from the llanos of Venezuela into the heart of New Granada. He picked Santander to lead the vanguard of his army as he invaded the Andean highlands and won the decisive battle of BOYACÁ on 7 August.

Although Santander played an important part in that victory, Boyacá was the last battle he fought, for Bolívar placed him in charge of organizing all the liberated territories of New Granada. Santander put government on a sound footing and raised troops and supplies for the armies still fighting. When, in 1821, Gran Colombia was formally constituted by the Congress of CÚCUTA, Santander was elected vice president. Since the president, Bolívar, was still leading the military struggle

Portrait of Francisco de Paula Santander. Oil on canvas by José María Espinosa, 1853. MUSEO NACIONAL DE COLOMBIA.

against Spain, Santander became acting chief executive and as such again provided an effective administrator. He also endeavored to implement the liberal reforms adopted by the Congress of Cúcuta and subsequent legislatures, which ranged from a free-birth law to tax reforms and various measures curbing the traditional wealth and power of the church.

The government of Santander faced growing disaffection especially in Venezuela, which resented subordination to authorities in Bogotá. These feelings came to a head with the revolt of José Antonio PÁEZ in 1826, just as Bolívar prepared to return home from Peru. Santander was disappointed when Bolívar proceeded to pardon Páez and to work towards revamping the new nation's institutions as a way of preventing future upheavals. Bolívar wanted a moratorium on liberal reform and strengthening of the national executive, policies that, combined with personal and factional rivalry, produced an open split with Santander. Following an unsuccessful attempt at constitutional reform, Bolívar assumed dictatorial powers and stripped Santander of the vice presidency. When liberal supporters of the latter attempted to assassinate Bolívar in September 1828, Santander himself was charged with complicity. Although the charge was never substantiated, the former vice president was exiled.

From 1829 to 1832 Santander traveled in Europe and the United States. He was still in exile at the final breakup of Gran Colombia and the reorganization of its central core as the Republic of New Granada. He returned in 1832 to become the first elected president of New Granada, a position he held until 1837. Once again exercising his administrative talents, he consolidated public order and even produced a balanced budget. Now more cautious than before, he did not push for sweeping reforms, although he did work hard to expand public education.

Santander was succeeded as president by José Ignacio de MÁRQUEZ, a one-time collaborator of Santander who had forged an alliance with his main political adversaries, the former supporters of Bolívar. As ex-president, Santander won election to the Chamber of Representatives, where he was a leader of congressional opposition to Márquez until his death in 1840.

Santander has been revered as "Man of Laws" and "Civil Founder of the Republic" in token of his lasting commitment to constitutional government. He received special honor from members of Colombia's Liberal Party, whose principal founders had been among his strongest supporters. Proclerical conservatives were less enthusiastic, and in recent years they have been joined by new detractors on the left who depict Santander as a spokesman for creole oligarchs and friend to the United States. Nevertheless, among the founders of the Colombian nation he has no close rival apart from Bolívar himself.

DAVID BUSHNELL, *The Santander Regime in Gran Colombia* (1954; repr. 1970); JOSÉ MANUEL RESTREPO, *Diario político y militar*, 4 vols. (1954); INDALECIO LIÉVANO AGUIRRE, *Razones socioeconómicas de la conspiración de septiembre contra el Libertador* (1968); GILBERTO SALAZAR PARADA, *El pensamiento político de Santander* (1969); EUGENE R. HUCK, "Economic Experimentation in a Newly Independent Nation: Colombia Under Francisco de Paula Santander, 1821–1840," *The Americas* 29, no. 1 (1972):17–29; HORACIO RODRÍGUEZ PLATA, *Santander en el exilio* (1976); PILAR MORENO DE ÁNGEL, *Santander* (1989).

DAVID BUSHNELL

SANTARÉM, third largest city in the Brazilian Amazon (1990 population 265,000). It is located halfway between Belém and Manaus on the southern bank of the Amazon River where it meets the Tapajós River in the state of Pará. It was founded in 1661 as a Jesuit ALDEIA (large MISSION settlement), in which many Indians were enslaved and exposed to Portuguese diseases to which they had no immunities. On 9 January 1799, Governor Sousa Coutinho officially declared it an assembly town, where Indians were collected for redistribution as a labor supply. Although Indians and CABOCLOS captured Santarém during the CABANAGEM rebellion in the 1830s, the government reclaimed it with the help of Munduruku warriors, who had been pacified in the eighteenth century. In the 1850s, RUBBER gatherers began extracting latex from the Tapajós River region, which they exported on steamships that serviced Santarém from 1853.

After the collapse of the rubber boom, Santarém experienced a slump. Subsequently, it has begun to thrive as a jumping-off point for GOLD prospectors and miners. Commercial Santarém fishermen extract sizable catches from the Amazon; Santarém also has a large timber and bauxite industry. The town, with its white, sandy beaches and Indian artifacts, also attracts some tourists. The advanced pottery of a pre-Columbian civilization was discovered in its streets in 1922 and was named for the town.

JOHN HEMMING, *Red Gold: The Conquest of the Brazilian Indians, 1500–1760* (1978); and his *Amazon Frontier: The Defeat of the Brazilian Indians* (1987).

CAROLYN JOSTOCK

SANTARÉM CULTURE, an archaeological complex culture of the AMAZON, circa A.D. 1000–1550. East of the Andes there is an elaborate, late prehistoric pottery culture known as the incised and punctate horizon. Santarém in the Brazilian Amazon is the most elaborate culture of the horizon, but whether or not Santarém was the center of the horizon is not certain because there are few radiocarbon dates for the horizon. The few Santarém radiocarbon dates suggest that the culture existed there by 500 years before the European conquest of the Amazon and died out soon after the Conquest. The culture is distinguished by elaborate pottery decorated with modeled animal and human images and incised or polychrome geometric designs. (A related but bolder

Santarém lamp. PULSAR IMAGENS E EDITORA / ROSA GAUDITANO.

pottery style in the area is called Kondurí.) There are vessels with scenes from creation myths that survive among South American lowland Indians. Also found are terra-cotta sculptures of nude humans (mostly female) with long, slit earlobes. In addition to the pottery, carved jade pendants, stone sceptors, ground rock mace heads, and projectile points have been found. The sceptors depict alter ego figures of humans or animals with animals on their shoulders. Archaeological sites are numerous and varied, indicating a complex settlement system. Santarém city, with many acres of low archaeological mounds containing ritual caches, hearths, and middens, may have been the capital. In a cave occupation of the period, dry MAIZE cobs were recovered.

Conquest documents mention a warlike chiefdom called Tapajó, a ranked society with a paramount chief over lower chiefs, some of whom were women. The chief was said to be descended from the sun and from a woman culture hero, in whose name maize tribute was given for beer for ceremonies. Cultivation and fishing furnished subsistence, and there was extensive trade. Large war parties with poisoned arrows resisted the Europeans, but eventually they were defeated and the Tapajó merged into the racially mixed population of the region.

HELEN CONSTANCE PALMATARY, *The Archaeology of the Lower Tapajos Valley, Brazil* (1960); REGINA MAC DONALD, *The Order of Things: An Analysis of the Ceramics of Santarém* (1972).

ANNA CURTENIUS ROOSEVELT

SANTERÍA, the Spanish name for a system of religious practices of African origin brought to Cuba in the late eighteenth and early nineteenth centuries. In that period hundreds of thousands of Africans were enslaved to work in the thriving sugar industries of the island. A plurality of these arrivals shared a similar culture and language called Yoruba by English ethnographers and Lucumí in Cuba. Since they came in such large numbers in such a short period of time, the Lucumí were able to maintain and adapt many of their cultural institutions, not the least of which were the complex theology and liturgies for a pantheon of spirits called *orishas* (ORIXÁS). The Lucumí found correspondences between their *orishas* and the saints of popular Cuban Catholic piety, often masking their secret and suppressed traditions with the public faces of the saints. Thus, the tradition came to be known as *Santería,* the way of the saints.

The name *Santería* is not always acceptable to many present-day practitioners, since it has so long borne, like the North American use of "voodoo," the misrepresentations of outsiders. By its reference to the Catholic saints, the name also implies an admixture of Catholic elements to African traditions that present-day practitioners would argue are purely African. Alternatives such as *la regla de ocha* (the order of the *orishas*), *la religión Lucumí,* or simply "Lucumí" or "Orisha" are used.

The core of the Cuban *orisha* tradition is the development of an intimate relationship between a human being and his or her patron spirit, or *orisha.* The relationship often begins when an individual is so troubled by problems such as ill health or lack of money that he or she will consult a priest or priestess of the *orishas.* The priest and priestess will have been trained as diviners and, depending on their rank, they will utilize a variety of means to determine the spiritual source of and solutions to the seeker's problem. All priests and priestesses are empowered to divine solutions with sixteen cowrie shells called *dilogun.* The heads-or-tails patterns that result from the fall of the shells reveal the path of action for the seeker to take to resolve his or her problem. A related but more complex system of divination called *ifa* is reserved for a special male priest called the *babalawo,* the "father of the mystery." In either system the diagnosis of the problem will lie in the seeker's neglect of his or her patron *orisha.* The divination will tentatively determine the *orisha's* identity, and a resolution of the problem will be found in a series of ritual actions culminating in a sacrifice to the *orisha.*

This opening sacrifice leads toward a growing, reciprocal relationship with the *orisha* as a human being offers respect, praise, and ritual food while the *orisha* reciprocates with gifts of power, blessings, and wisdom. As the relationship matures, divination will determine that the *orisha* seeks a permanent relationship, a kind of marriage in which the human being will become an *iyawo,* a bride to the spirit. In a lengthy and costly series of ceremonies, the initiate will have the *orisha* "seated" in his or her "head," thus marking the permanent presence of the spirit within the consciousness of the human being. This *asiento* (seating) initiation marks the entry of the individual into the *orisha* priesthood, and he or she is to be called a *babalorisha* (father in the *orisha*) or *iyalorisha* (mother in the *orisha*). Often enough the Spanish terms *santero* and *santera* are applied to this level of priesthood.

The most dramatic encounters with the *orishas* are found in communal drum and dance ceremonies called *bembés.* Here, amid elaborate polyrhythms and complex choreography, certain *orishas* are called to "mount" the heads of their initiates so that they lose consciousness while the *orishas* use their bodies to join in the ceremony. Manifested in the bodies of their "horses," the *orishas* sing and dance with the community, offer advice and warnings, and gladden the hearts of their devotees.

Since the Cuban Revolution of 1959, nearly 1 million Cubans have left the island to form communities, primarily on the U.S. mainland and in Puerto Rico and Venezuela. Carried by Cuban *babalorishas* and *iyalorishas,* the *orisha* tradition has undergone a second diaspora, adapting itself to these new environments. Just as it is likely that there are more *orisha* devotees in the New World than in the Old, so there are probably more in the Cuban diaspora than in Cuba itself. Since every community is autonomous, it is impossible to determine the numbers of practitioners of the tradition. It has grown well beyond its original Cuban community to include Latin Americans of all nationalities and ethnicities, as well as North American blacks and whites.

WILLIAM R. BASCOM, "The Focus of Cuban Santería," in *Southwestern Journal of Anthropology* 6, no. 1 (1950): 64–68; FERNANDO ORTÍZ, *Los bailes y el teatro de los negros en el folklore de Cuba* (1951); MERCEDES CROS SANDOVAL, *La religión afrocubana* (1975); JULIO SÁNCHEZ, *La religión de los orichas* (Hato Rey, Puerto Rico: Colección Estudios Afrocaribeños, 1978); LYDIA CABRERA, *Koeko iyawó, aprende novicia: pequeño tratado de regla Lucumí* (1980); JOSEPH M. MURPHY, *Santería: An African Religion in America* (1988); MIGENE GONZÁLEZ-WIPPLER, *Santería: The Religion* (1989); GEORGE BRANDON, *Santería from Africa to the New World: The Dead Sell Memories* (1993).

JOSEPH M. MURPHY

See also **African–Latin American Religions; Syncretism.**

SANTIAGO, CHILE, capital of Chile and major center of the metropolitan region (385,481 inhabitants in 1991), located in a closed basin between the ANDES and the Coastal Range (Cordillera de la Costa). The only natural openings are the Maipo River valley and the narrow passage of the Angostura de Paine that leads into the Central Valley. Founded in February of 1541 by Pedro de VALDIVIA, who had been appointed *adelantado* (governor) of Chile by Francisco PIZARRO, governor of Peru, it developed at the site of a small Indian settlement located between the southern bank of the MAPOCHO RIVER and the Santa Lucía hill. During colonial times it was only one of several Spanish administrative and cultural centers. Its position was contested by the outpost of Concepción, where much of the military was amassed against the ARAUCANIAN Indians and pirates, and by the center of commerce and communications of LA SERENA. An inland town, Santiago needed a port, which was provided by VALPARAÍSO, 85 miles to the west. During the early years of independence, La Serena and CONCEPCIÓN continued to challenge Santiago's primacy over the emerging country, but the colonial, cultural, and elite power of Santiago prevailed and established the strongly centralized tradition of government that characterizes Chile.

The basin of Santiago stretches out at the foot of the Andes, which serve as a majestic backdrop to the eastern segment of the city. Well ventilated by the mountain winds, this area—the Barrio Alto—is the preferred place of residence of the wealthy: among numerous parks and traversed by wide avenues are located the boroughs of Providencia, Vitacura, Valdivia, Los Leones, Los Condes, and La Reina. Here also are the largest malls, the residences of diplomats, the military academy, and the medical school. The original site of Santiago, be-

Plaza de Armas, Santiago. The statue represents Pedro de Valdivia. HELEN HUGHES.

tween the Mapocho River and the Avenida de las Delicias, is still the core of the city and lodges ministries, corporate agencies, major banks, embassies, large department stores, theaters, and cultural institutions. Facing the old Avenida de las Delicias (today Alameda Bernardo O'Higgins) and the Barrio Cívico—a complex of ministries constructed in the 1930s—is the presidential palace, Casa de la Moneda (the colonial Mint House).

To the north of the city, at the feet of the lofty San Cristóbal hill, spread the popular neighborhoods of El Salto, Conchali, and Huechuraba. Also to the north lie the plains of Colina and Pudahuel, where the international airport of Santiago was built. To the west are found more popular boroughs interspersed with industrial establishments—Renca, Quinta Normal, Los Pajaritos, and Maipú. Nearby lies the industrial park at Los Cerrillos at the former site of the international airport of Santiago. Toward the south, and readily accessible by a modern subway and the wide southern segment of the Pan-American Highway, are found middle-class boroughs, such as San Miguel and San Bernardo, and extensive poorer neighborhoods, such as La Cisterna, Espejo, and Cardenal Caro. Slums are located in the southwest: it was in La Florida that the *pobladores* and the forces of General Augusto PINOCHET clashed during his rule (1973–1989). Santiago is the final station of a major railway to the south of the country and of another from the port city of Valparaíso—now only 70 miles from Santiago. The city is also the connecting point of the northern and southern segments of the Pan-American Highway.

Enhancing the centralized character of the capital city was the decision of past administrations to bolster the industrial clout of Santiago by allowing the establishment of manufacturing plants in the capital, which account for nearly 55 percent of the country's total. In addition, the leading papers, television stations, the stock exchange, three major universities (Universidad de Chile, Universidad Católica de Chile, and the technical school Universidad de Santiago), the Air Force Academy, and the Officers School of Carabineros (the national police) are established in Santiago. Notwithstanding its attractive site, the excessive motorization, the concentration of industries, and dangerous chemical discharges into the Mapocho River have compounded the pollution problems of Greater Santiago and accelerated the exodus of the affluent toward the slopes of the Andes, thus accentuating socioeconomic differences in the city's layout.

For a historical account of colonial times the classic work is BENJAMÍN VICUÑA-MACKENNA, *Historia de Santiago* (Santiago, 1938). Contemporary sources include HUGO BODINI, "Tendencias recientes en el desarrollo de Santiago de Chile," in *Revista Geográfica* (Mexico), 110 (1989): 267–281; CENTRO DE ESTUDIOS DEL DESARROLLO, *Santiago: Dos ciudades* (1990); and JOSEPH L. SCARPACI, *Primary Medical Care in Chile* (1988).

CÉSAR N. CAVIEDES

SANTIAGO DE COMPOSTELA, famous medieval shrine of the apostle Saint James. Santiago de Compostela was the shrine of Saint James the Apostle who, according to tradition, was the first to preach the gospel in Spain. The legend suggests that Saint James's remains were miraculously transported by ship from the Holy Land to a remote Galician coastal town (Iria Flavia, today Padrón) and then taken inland to a Roman burial ground in A.D. 44. The site, discovered by a shepherd in the early ninth century, was made the seat of a bishopric and the first cathedral was completed in A.D. 874. (The present cathedral dates from the eleventh century.) Under the banner of Saint James, the patron saint of Spain, the Christians reconquered the peninsula from the Moors. Soldiers reported seeing the saint on a white horse leading them into battle and slaying Moors by the thousands. Thus, he also became known as Saint James the Moorslayer (Santiago de Matamoros). The discovery of the burial site enabled the Spanish church to claim apostolic origins and the shrine at Compostela rivaled Rome and Jerusalem as a focus for pilgrimages.

CLAUDIO SÁNCHEZ-ALBORNOZ, *España, un enigma histórico,* translated by Colette Joly Dees and David Sven Reher (1975), esp. pp. 265–299; JAMES A. MICHENER, *Iberia: Spanish Travels and Reflections* (1968), esp. pp. 712–795; AMÉRICO CASTRO, *The Spaniards: An Introduction to Their History,* translated by Willard F. King and Selma Margaretten (1971), esp. pp. 420–470.

SUZANNE HILES BURKHOLDER

SANTIAGO DE CUBA, the second city of Cuba from colonial through modern times and capital of Oriente Province. With a 1981 population of 403,604, it is located on the southeastern side of the island. Founded in 1514 by Diego de VELÁZQUEZ, it quickly became an ecclesiastical and administrative center as well as an active international port. Following the British seizure of nearby Jamaica in 1655 and an influx of refugees and contraband, Santiago's economy flourished—a situation similar to that of the French planters during the Haitian Revolution in the 1790s. The harbor and region around Santiago were sites of numerous military engagements between Spain and its rivals in the eighteenth century, of considerable anticolonial activities during the TEN YEARS' WAR (1868–1878), of a decisive naval battle between the United States and Spain in 1898, and of early revolutionary operations involving Fidel CASTRO. The city has long been an industrial and commercial center; the original home of Bacardi rum, it boasts the oldest chamber of commerce in Cuba (1885).

EMILIO BACARDÍ MOREAU, *Crónicas de Santiago de Cuba,* 10 vols. (1972–1973); VICENTE BÁEZ, ed., *La Enciclopedia de Cuba: Municipios, Oriente,* vol. 12 (1974); LEVÍ MARRERO, *Cuba: economía y sociedad,* 15 vols. (1974–1992).

LINDA K. SALVUCCI

SANTIAGO DE LOS CABALLEROS, the second largest city in the Dominican Republic (after Santo Domingo) with a population of 400,000 in 1992 and the most Spanish city in the province of Santiago. The city gets its name from the thirty Spanish gentlemen who settled there in 1504; in Dominican history it is the city of earthquakes and uprisings. Santiago is the economic center and historical rival of Santo Domingo, the political center, less than 85 miles to the southeast. It is 23 miles from the main port on the north coast, Puerto Plata. The city lies in the rich Cibao Valley, the country's breadbasket.

Santiago is the home of a prosperous, enlightened conservative elite. These *cibaeños* are the landed aristocracy, the best educated and most cosmopolitan and cultured citizens. A score of related families have dominated business, and their wealth is based on land, cattle, sugar and rum, tobacco, coffee, cacao, and rice. An example of the enlightened business community is that it, along with the Conference of Dominican Bishops, established the UNIVERSIDAD CATÓLICA MADRE Y MAESTRA in 1962 as an alternative to the politicized (leftist) and overcrowded UNIVERSIDAD AUTÓNOMA DE SANTO DOMINGO. It was modeled after the U.S. style of university in terms of curriculum, pedagogy, and organization.

JOHN BARTLOW MARTIN, *Overtaken by Events: The Dominican Crisis from the Fall of Trujillo to the Civil War* (1966), chap. 6; FRANK MOYA PONS, *El pasado dominicano* (1986); HOWARD J. WIARDA and MICHAEL J. KRYZANEK, *The Dominican Republic: A Caribbean Crucible*, 2d ed. (1992).

LARMAN C. WILSON

SANTO, SANTA, a term that may refer to a saint or holy person in Roman Catholicism or, by extension, to a representation of such a person in sculpted or flat format. The term is the basis for *santero*, a maker of religious images, and SANTERÍA, a folk religion of African origin. Historical records also refer to a holy image as *imagen*, but the modern use of the term may emphasize material form over spiritual content. *Santo* often referred to a smaller domestic representation while *imagen* was used for a larger, church sculpture defined as *de talla* if carved or *de bulto* if also dressed in clothing.

In popular Catholicism and Caribbean *santería*, folk religious images of Puerto Rico, the Dominican Republic, Venezuela, and New Mexico are known as *santos*. In the United States, many non-Hispanic dealers and collectors use the term to promote the artistic and monetary value of *santos* while *Hispano* and CHICANO artisans use the term to enforce the ethnic and cultural identity of the images and themselves.

E. BOYD, *Popular Arts of Spanish New Mexico* (1974); YVONNE LANGE, " 'Santos': The Household Saints of Puerto Rico" (Ph.D. diss., University of Pennsylvania, 1975); WILLIAM WROTH,

Santo image of Saint Joseph. ALAN MOSS GALLERY.

Christian Images in Hispanic New Mexico (1982); TEODORO VIDAL, *Los espada: Escultores sangermeños* (1994).

RICHARD E. AHLBORN

SANTO DOMINGO, capital of the Dominican Republic, situated on the southern shore of the island of Hispaniola along the Ozama River. Since earliest Spanish colonial times, Santo Domingo has been the largest and most important urban settlement in the Dominican Republic. Its role as administrative, trade, and industrial center helped to make it the largest urban agglomeration of the entire Caribbean. Almost a quarter of the country's population of about 7.3 million resides in the 60 square miles of this city, which is home to 47 percent of the urban population, 55 percent of all industrial workers, and 63 percent of all white-collar workers of the Dominican Republic. The population can be divided into four major social groups: (1) the largest group, constituting 48 to 50 percent of all households, consists of poor and marginal slum dwellers who reside in some of the worst barrios of the Caribbean; (2) the second largest group (30–35 percent) consists of those who have overcome extreme poverty and live in relatively stable

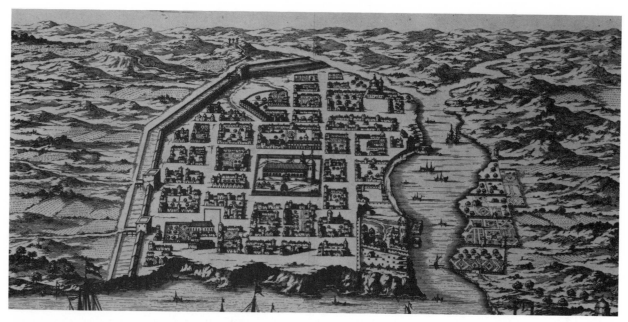

Urbs Domingo in Hispaniola (Santo Domingo, Dominican Republic). Engraving in Montanus, *De Niewe en Onbekende Weerld* (1671). LIBRARY OF CONGRESS.

economic conditions; (3) a heterogeneous middle class constitutes 12 to 15 percent of the population; and (4) a very wealthy elite makes up 2 percent of the populace.

The city of Santo Domingo was founded on 4 August 1496 by Bartolomé Colón, brother of Christopher Columbus. It became the capital of the Spanish colonial realm in the Americas, and it was from here that Spanish conquistadores (Hernán Cortés, Diego de Velásquez, Juan Ponce de León) launched their conquests of other parts of the Americas. The city's buildings were originally made of wood, but after a violent hurricane in 1502, many stone buildings were erected, among them the first cathedral (Catedral Primada de India), first university, first hospital, and first paved street in the Americas. In 1586 the city was pillaged and partially destroyed by Francis Drake.

With the rapid expansion of Spanish colonial rule in the Americas and the discovery of gold in Mexico and Peru, Santo Domingo, along with the rest of the country, became a backwater of the Spanish colonial empire. Natural catastrophes, Haitian invasions, and civil wars prevented the growth and expansion of the city during the next three centuries. The census of 1908 registered a mere 19,000 inhabitants.

After a devastating hurricane destroyed most of the capital in September 1930, Santo Domingo had to be reconstructed. The only buildings that withstood the storm were the stone buildings dating from colonial times. It was not until the reign of dictator Rafael Leónidas Trujillo Molina (1930–1961) that Santo Domingo—named Ciudad Trujillo from 1936 to 1961—underwent a large public building program consisting of massive neoclassical edifices such as the Presidential Palace, the Palace of Fine Arts, and buildings at "La Feria" (the fair).

JOAQUÍN BALAGUER, *Guía emocional de la ciudad romántica* (1969).

KAI P. SCHOENHALS

SANTO DOMINGO, AUDIENCIA OF, the first appeals court in the New World, it heard civil and criminal appeals from Spain's Caribbean colonies and had original jurisdiction over matters involving the royal treasury (including auditing the accounts). From its creation in 1511 until 1799 it was convened in the city of Santo Domingo, Hispaniola, and from 1799 to 1861 in Puerto Príncipe, Cuba. The AUDENCIA returned to Santo Domingo in 1861 when the Dominican Republic was again made part of the Spanish Empire. That episode, and the audiencia's existence, ended in 1865.

A royal decree of 5 October 1511 created this three-judge appeals court, ostensibly to save litigants the delay and expense of appeals to courts in Spain. The unstated purpose was to limit the judicial and administrative powers that Diego COLÓN, son and heir of Christopher COLUMBUS, had won in his lawsuit against the crown over the validity of the privileges granted to his father in the CAPITULATION OF SANTA FE (1492) and later reaffirmed by royal decrees of 1493 and 1497. According to the judgment, Colón had the right as governor to appoint the judges of first instance (*justicias*) and the district judges (*justicias mayores*, so named to distinguish them from royally appointed ALCALDES MAYORES, even though their duties were the same) on Hispaniola, Puerto Rico, and Jamaica. As viceroy and governor of

Hispaniola, he had extensive administrative powers there and in Puerto Rico.

The audiencia's area of jurisdiction included all of the Spanish conquests until 1527, when NEW SPAIN was given its own audiencia with a district that ran from the Cape of Honduras to Cape Sable, Florida. In subsequent decades, the on-going conquest temporarily added parts of Central America, NEW GRANADA (Colombia), and Venezuela and (in theory) Peru, Ecuador, and even Chile to the Santo Domingo district. Central America, Colombia, Peru, and all Spanish territories along the Pacific coast were transferred to the new Audiencia of Panama (created in 1538) when it began operation in 1540 and then to other audiencias as they were created. This left the Audiencia of Santo Domingo with jurisdiction over Maracaibo, Venezuela, Cumaná, Margarita, Guiana, and the Caribbean islands. The conquest of Florida in 1565 added that area to the district. The district remained stable except for the addition of Trinidad and the loss of the Lesser Antilles, Haiti, and Jamaica during the seventeenth century.

In the eighteenth century, the audiencia's district underwent many changes. Florida was transferred to the British for a time (1763–1783) and Louisiana was added (1763), although most of Louisiana's appeals went to a special court at Havana. The provinces of the northern coast of South America from Maracaibo east were withdrawn from the district in 1717–1723 and again in 1739–1777 and assigned to the Audiencia of Santa Fe de BOGOTÁ as part of the creation of the Viceroyalty of New Granada. The province of Venezuela was returned to Santo Domingo's jurisdiction in 1742 and the others in 1777. These territories were again withdrawn in 1786 when the Audiencia of CARACAS was founded. Finally, the Spanish part of Hispaniola was ceded to France in 1795, and the audiencia moved to Puerto Príncipe, Cuba, in 1799. Thereafter, its jurisdiction was confined to Cuba, Hispaniola (until the Haitian conquest of 1821), Puerto Rico, Florida (to 1821), and Louisiana (to 1803).

The Audiencia of Santo Domingo played its greatest historical role during the first thirty or so years of its existence. Not only did it help reduce Colón's power, it also attempted to mediate the early CONQUISTADORES' conflicts over territory, for example, those between Hernán CORTÉS and Diego de VELÁZQUEZ over New Spain (1520) and among the various claimers of Honduras. The court also helped formulate and implement policies of various kinds because its original mandate included instructions to meet with Colón and the royal treasury officials for a meeting called the *real acuerdo* to open royal letters and formulate policies for implementing orders. This function grew during the 1520s, becoming the characteristic political advisory role later exercised by other audiencias, especially those in the viceregal capitals. The audiencia was not active in the protection of the Indians. The private interests of its early judges in the trade in Indian slaves and in *encomiendas* caused them to make common cause with other Span-

iards in the Caribbean, at least until the 1540s, when the disappearance of Indians on the islands and the NEW LAWS changed attitudes.

After Colón's final return to Spain in 1523, the Audiencia of Santo Domingo assumed the additional duties of governor of the island. The arrival of the first president of the tribunal, Bishop Sebastián Ramírez de Fuenleal, in 1529 began a pattern of conflict between the judges and the president, each claiming the right to govern as well as administer justice. In theory, they were to govern the island jointly. This conflict was never fully resolved, although in 1583 the crown borrowed from the practice in other audiencias and added the title of governor to those held by the president and spelled out his duties as chief administrative officer. During the 1530s the president began to exercise the military functions of a captain-general, an office formally added to his titles in 1577.

During the second half of the sixteenth century, the audiencia judges became notorious for their inspection tours of the northern and western districts of Hispaniola. The public purposes were to gather current information about the districts and to see that royal laws were being enforced. The latter especially meant arresting smugglers and confiscating their goods. However, many contemporaries charged that the judges used the tours to enrich themselves and the staff that accompanied them by claiming shares of the confiscated goods and by charging high per-diem fees, which the residents of the visited areas had to pay. In 1605 the crown ordered the northern and western coasts depopulated because of smuggling and evidence that Protestants had given Spanish Bibles to the residents. Baltasar López de Castro, an official from Santo Domingo, was a key figure in lobbying for this action. Judicial visits continued to the remaining districts of the island.

With the reduction of the audiencia's district as other audiencias were created, and the gradual decline of the economy of Hispaniola, the audiencia's prestige and influence also declined. By 1600 it serviced mostly Hispaniola, Puerto Rico, and the Venezuelan settlements. As often as not, Cuban appeals went to Spain because that journey was no more difficult than the one to Santo Domingo. This declining area of effective jurisdiction and the general decline of Santo Domingo meant that by the last quarter of the sixteenth century the Audiencia of Santo Domingo was considered the lowest ranking of the audiencias, the normal point of entrance for jurists hoping to work their way up the ladder of appointments to the more prestigious audiencias of Lima and, especially, Mexico City. The rank and prestige of the court were further diminished in 1786 when it lost jurisdiction over the northern coast of South America and was reduced from four judges to three, and again in 1861, when it returned to Santo Domingo, where it became a territorial audiencia like all those in Spain's other provinces.

There is no comprehensive study of this audiencia, but parts of its history can be found in CLARENCE H. HARING, *The Spanish*

Empire in America (1947), esp. pp. 84–86; FERNANDO MURO ROMERO, *Las presidencias-gobernaciones en Indias (siglo XVI)* (1975), pp. 73–84; and JAVIER MALAGÓN BARCELO, *El distrito de la Audiencia de Santo Domingo en los siglos XV a XIX*, 2d ed. (1977). Information on the judges and *fiscales* who served on the court from 1687 to 1808 is in MARK A. BURKHOLDER and D. S. CHANDLER, *From Impotence to Authority: The Spanish Crown and the American Audiencias, 1687–1808* (1977). FRANK MOYA PONS, *Historia colonial de Santo Domingo* (1974), provides general context. Details of particular periods are in AMÉRICO LUGO, *Historia de Santo Domingo desde el 1556 hasta el 1608* (1952); MARÍA ROSARIO SEVILLA SOLER, *Santo Domingo: Tierra de frontera, 1750–1800* (1980); and JUANA GIL-BERMEJO GARCÍA, *La española: Anotaciones históricas, 1600–1650* (1983).

PAUL E. HOFFMAN

SANTO TOMÁS. *See* **Belgian Colonization Company.**

SANTO TORIBIO. *See* **Mogrovejo, Toribio Alfonso de.**

SANTORO, CLAUDIO (*b.* 23 November 1919; *d.* 27 March 1989), Brazilian composer, conductor, violinist, and teacher. Santoro studied composition with Hans Joachim KOELLREUTTER, a pupil of Paul Hindemith. Through his studies with Koellreutter, he was introduced to serial compositional techniques, which, according to Santoro, were the most significant single influence on the works he produced between 1939–1947. His *Impressions of a Steel Mill* (1943), an orchestral composition, won a competition sponsored by the Orquestra Sinfônica Brasileira, and his First String Quartet won the Chamber Music Guild Award, Washington, D.C.

From 1950 to 1960 Santoro focused on national subjects for his compositions. The period after 1960 represents a return to serialism and the beginnings of electro-acoustical writing. In 1962 Santoro became director of the department of music of the University of Brasília, a post he held until 1964, when political changes in the government resulted in resignations at the university. Following his departure from Brasília, Santoro went to Germany, where he did research in Heidelberg on electronic music and experiments in aleatoric sketches combining painting and aleatoric sound.

Santoro returned to Brazil in 1978 as professor of composition at the University of Brasília. He founded the Orquestra Sinfônica do Teatro Nacional and worked tirelessly to establish a national center for theater. Santoro's final Symphony no. 14, first performed eight months after his death, is one of his best works.

The New Grove Dictionary of Music and Musicians (1980); DAVID P. APPLEBY, *The Music of Brazil* (1983).

DAVID P. APPLEBY

SANTOS, one of the most important of Brazil's deep-water ports. First in Brazil in exports and second only to Rio de Janeiro in imports, Santos is the world's largest coffee-exporting port. The neighboring countries of Bolivia and Paraguay have free ports at Santos.

Located in the state of São Paulo, Santos is approximately 30 miles southeast of São Paulo, Brazil's largest city, and 200 miles southwest of Rio de Janeiro. The city itself is 3 miles from the Atlantic Ocean on São Vicente Island, in a tidal inlet called the Santos River. Its modern dock and warehouse facilities, the largest in Latin America, now handle over 40 percent (by value) of Brazil's imports and over half its exports, which include bananas, beef, oranges, and hides, in addition to coffee. The suburb Guarujá is one of Brazil's principal seaside resorts.

Modern-day Santos stands near the site of Brazil's first permanent European settlement, SÃO VICENTE, which was founded in 1532. The city of Santos itself was settled between 1543 and 1546. Linked to the city of São Paulo by railroad, Santos became the fastest-growing port in Brazil by the late nineteenth century as coffee cultivation developed in the interior of the state of São Paulo. Its population grew from 30,000 in 1900 to 295,000 in 1960 and to 429,000 in 1990.

Just outside Santos is one of Brazil's major industrial areas that houses oil refineries, chemical plants, and the hydroelectric plant at Cubatão. Severe pollution resulted in the area being called "Valley of Death" by the local populace. However, a loan from the World Bank facilitated the reduction of pollution from petrochemical and fertilizer plants to a fraction of their previous levels.

ROLLIE E. POPPINO, *Brazil: The Land and People* (1968); E. BRADFORD BURNS, *A History of Brazil* (1970).

MARY JO MILES

SANTOS, EDUARDO (*b.* 28 August 1888; *d.* 27 March 1974), president of Colombia (1938–1942). A lawyer by training, Santos entered Liberal politics through journalism; in the 1920s he built Bogotá's *El Tiempo*, which he owned and directed, into one of the continent's most important newspapers and a force in the Liberal Party. In 1938 he succeeded Alfonso LÓPEZ PUMAREJO in the presidency, abandoning his predecessor's vocal reformism but laying the institutional basis for much of Colombia's modern economic structure. The Industrial Development Institute, the Municipal Development Institute, and the Territorial Credit Institute, among others, were created during his regime. Santos was among the most pro–United States leaders of Latin America, for which he was attacked by the pro-Axis Conservative leader Laureano GÓMEZ. During his administration the Conservatives returned to Congress after four years' absence, and political life was relatively normal. Santos's battles to publish *El Tiempo* during the military regime of the mid-1950s attracted world attention.

DAVID BUSHNELL, *Eduardo Santos and the Good Neighbor, 1938–1942* (1967); IGNACIO ARIZMENDI POSADA, *Presidentes de Colombia, 1810–1990* (1990), pp. 237–240.

RICHARD J. STOLLER

SANTOS, JUAN. *See* **Atahualpa (Juan Santos).**

SANTOS, MARQUESA DE (Domitila de Castro Canto e Melo; *b.* March 1797; *d.* 13 November 1867), Emperor Pedro I's Brazilian mistress. Domitila was Pedro I's lover from 1822 to 1831. She was one of many Castro women who were chosen to be the mistresses of PEDRO I of Castile and PEDRO II of Portugal. A striking beauty with ivory skin and dark hair, the marquesa was married at age fourteen. She bore three children during her first marriage. Unknown to her spouse, they were actually Pedro's. Eventually, her deranged and jealous husband drove her out of their home. Pedro I arranged an ecclesiastical divorce for his lover. Domitila and the emperor had four children during this often stormy love affair. After Pedro left Brazil, the marquesa married for a second time. She was one of the richest women in Brazil when she died, leaving a fortune of over 1 million *milréis*, the equivalent of $1 million U.S.

SERGIO CORREA DA COSTA, *Every Inch a King: A Biography of Dom Pedro I, First Emperor of Brazil* (1950); ALBERTO RANGEL, *Dom Pedro I e a Marquesa de Santos á vista de cartas íntimas e de outros documentos públicos e particulares,* 3d ed. (1969), and *Marginados: Anotações e as cartas de D Pedro I a D Domitila* (1974); EUL-SOO PANG, *In Pursuit of Honor and Power: Noblemen of the Southern Cross in Nineteenth-Century Brazil* (1988).

EUL-SOO PANG

SANTOS, SÍLVIO (Senhor Abravanel; *b.* 1931), Brazilian television variety show host, network owner, and 1989 presidential candidate, represents one of the major rags-to-riches stories of Brazil. He started as a street peddler (*camelô*) and developed a Sunday afternoon television variety show that is still one of the most popular in Brazil, featuring games, amateur performances, music, and sensational interviews, such as an adaptation of *Queen for a Day,* in which poor women vie to tell the most pathetic life story. In 1976, he purchased TV Record (São Paulo), and in 1978, TV Rio. In 1981, Santos was awarded four licenses for Rio de Janeiro, São Paulo, Belém, and Pôrto Alegre that belonged to TV Tupi, the earliest Brazilian network, which had gone bankrupt. Within two years, his SBT/TVS network had twenty-one affiliates and roughly 25 percent of the audience, ranking second after TV Globo, which often had 60–80 percent of the audience. The network followed the pattern of Santos's own programs, emphasizing four or five live variety shows, lowbrow comedies, imported series and films from the United States, and TELENOVELAS and comedies from Mexico. Santos's programming aimed at a "popular" (lower-middle-class to lower-class) audience and was very successful. He briefly tried to compete for a broader audience with more news and his own *telenovelas,* but returned to "popular" programming. In 1989, after creating an empire of over forty businesses, including some in agriculture, real estate, and sales, Santos made a late entry into the 1989 Brazilian presidential race. His personal popularity put him high in polls, but the party that nominated him was found to be improperly registered and his candidacy was quickly canceled.

JOSEPH STRAUBHAAR, "Brazilian Television Variety Shows," in *Studies of Latin American Popular Culture* 2 (1983): 71–78.

JOSEPH STRAUBHAAR

SANTOS-DUMONT, ALBERTO (*b.* 20 July 1873; *d.* 23 July 1932), pioneer aviator, inventor, and engineer. Known internationally as the "father of aviation," Santos-Dumont was born on his family's coffee plantation in Palmira (now Santos Dumont), Minas Gerais, Brazil. His engineer father encouraged the young man's passion for mechanics and interest in flying machines, and supported his move in 1891 to Paris, where Santos-Dumont joined an international coterie of aviators experimenting with all manner of aircraft.

During the next three decades Santos-Dumont won international renown for his achievements. He was the first person to turn the internal combustion engine to practical use for aviation (1897). In 1901, flying a dirigible of his own design, he won the coveted Deutsch Prize for being the first to navigate a set-time course, from Saint-Cloud, around the Eiffel Tower, and back. He subsequently turned his attention to the development of heavier-than-air machines and in 1906 piloted his *14-Bis* to claim the Archdeacon Award. The European press proclaimed him the first man to conquer the air, a title immediately disputed by the Wright Brothers, who were conducting their experiments in secrecy in North Carolina. Santos-Dumont, who believed that his designs belonged to the world, began work on a new model. In 1908 he constructed a waterplane, the *Santos Dumont 18,* that is regarded as the precursor of the hydroplane. His *Demoiselle,* completed in 1909, became the world's first successful monoplane, the prototype of the modern airplane.

Santos-Dumont's interests and inventions were broad. He designed the model from which the French jeweler Cartier constructed the first wristwatch, and he wrote three books: *A Conquista do ar* (1901), *Os meus balões* (1903), and *O que eu vi o que nós veremos* (1918). At the outbreak of World War I, he denounced the employment of aircraft for the purposes of war. The Allied governments accused him of espionage, and the French government stripped him of the Legion of Honor it had awarded him in 1909. In poor health, he returned to São Paulo in 1928. During the 1932 CONSTITUTIONAL REVOLT, the federal government of Brazil sent planes to bomb the city of São Paulo. Horrified that bombs were being dropped by Brazilians on their fellow countrymen, Santos-Dumont committed suicide.

ALEXANDRE BRIGOLE, *Santos-Dumont: The Air Pioneer* (1943); *Santos-Dumont: Cinquecentenario de primero vôo do mais pesado que o ar* (1956); PETER WYKEHAM, *Santos-Dumont: A Study in*

Alberto Santos-Dumont with an electric car and a dirigible balloon, two of his creations. ICONOGRAPHIA.

Obsession (1962); FRANCESCA MILLER, "Alberto Santos-Dumont," in *Biographical Dictionary of Modern Peace Leaders,* edited by Harold Josephson (1984).

FRANCESCA MILLER

See also **Aviation.**

SÃO FRANCISCO RIVER, waterway that rises in the Brazilian highlands and flows north and east through the semiarid backlands of the Northeast of Brazil for approximately 1,988 miles. About 44 percent of the population of Brazil (as of 1990) lives in the São Francisco River region.

Known as "the river of national unity," the São Francisco River is famed for the political, social, and economic union of northeastern and southern Brazil. André João Antonil spoke in 1711 of over five hundred large ranches in the vicinity of the São Francisco River. Since then the river has provided the water necessary for pastures and irrigated farmlands as well as a transportation system for the cattle ranches that dot the river region. It is also a major source of hydroelectric power in the Northeast. In its lower reaches the river drops abruptly over the Itapárica and Paulo Afonso falls. In 1955 the Paulo Afonso power plant, with a generating capacity of more than 1 million kilowatts, was constructed. Another large dam was built far inland at Três Marias in 1960.

ROBERT M. LEVINE, *Historical Dictionary of Brazil* (1979), pp. 192–193; CHRISTOPHER RICHARD, *Brazil* (1991), p. 20.

ORLANDO R. ARAGONA

SÃO LUÍS, capital of the state of MARANHÃO, Brazil (population 781,346 as of 1990), and island on which the city is located (originally called *Upaon-açu* [Big Island] by the native Tupinambá). The Frenchman Daniel de La Touche founded the city on 8 September 1612, naming it in honor of King Louis XIII. The Portuguese drove out the French in 1615; the Dutch occupied the city from 1641 to 1644, when they, too, were expelled.

São Luís became the capital of the vast colonial state of Maranhão in 1626. With the growth of Maranhão's slave-based economy in the seventeenth and eighteenth centuries, significant quantities of sugar, cotton, and rice were exported through São Luís. The city maintained direct relations with the Court in Lisbon. Sons of the elite, educated in Coimbra, held key court positions and received noble titles. São Luís was known as the "Athens of Brazil" owing to the remarkable number of its authors, poets, playwrights, scientists, journalists, and politicians who were nationally known during the 1800s. Modern writers, including Josué Montello and Ferreira Gullar, continue to give Maranhão national literary prominence.

São Luís was the first city in northern Brazil to feature public gas illumination, a trolley system, and public fountains with piped water. More than 4,000 buildings still remain from the seventeenth, eighteenth, and nineteenth centuries, many with facades of colorful tiles brought as ballast from Portugal, along with the cobblestones that pave the narrow streets of the historical district. Brazilian independence and the abolition of slavery, followed by declining markets for agricultural exports, initiated a period of economic decline that continued through the early 1990s, despite the metallurgical industries and port facilities that were built in the 1980s.

CÉSAR AUGUSTO MARQUES, *Dicionário histórico-geográfico da Provincia do Maranhão,* 2d ed. (1970); IVAN SARNEY COSTA, *São*

Luís: Nature's Island of Loveliness (1989); JOMAR DA SILVA MO-RAES, Guia de São Luís do Maranhão (1989).

GAYLE WAGGONER LOPES

SÃO PAULO (CITY). Located on a plateau over the sierra about 30 miles from the coastal port of Santos, the city of São Paulo was founded in 1554 by a group of Jesuit priests who decided to build a school to proselytize among Indians who lived in the region. Through most of the colonial period São Paulo remained an isolated, impoverished town with no more than a few thousand inhabitants. It was the base from which the famous BANDEIRAS—slave-hunting expeditions into the unexplored interior—were launched during the seventeenth century. During the eighteenth century the city lived off the gold trade of MINAS GERAIS. With the decline of mining, São Paulo became a modest commercial entrepôt for trade in mules, cotton cloth, and SUGAR.

In the nineteenth century São Paulo underwent a dramatic transformation as it became the center of the world's largest COFFEE exporting economy. Early in the century, with a population approaching 20,000, its primary product was tea, won with great effort from the infertile land surrounding the city. At mid-century it was a thriving if modest city of 25,000, with a prominent law school and a number of colleges. By the 1860s proliferating coffee plantations in the northwest of the state were fueling the growth of São Paulo, as all export shipments had to pass through the city on their way to the port at Santos. This relationship was strengthened in the 1870s and 1880s as coffee surpassed sugar and cotton in Brazil's export portfolio and as railroads were built to transport coffee from the hinterland to São Paulo and then on to Santos.

After mid-century São Paulo's importance also grew in other ways. The law school, founded in 1827, was by the 1870s a cynosure of intellectual and political thought, and turned out a substantial number of BACHA-RÉIS, many of whom were destined for careers in politics or the government bureaucracy. With an eye turned toward European political currents, PAULISTANO landowners founded a republican party in the early 1870s that espoused the end of monarchic rule. By the 1880s the city was the headquarters of the São Paulo State Republican Party, the largest and most important republican organization in Brazil.

Also in the 1870s, a new group of professionals and military officers began to discuss the ideas of POSITIV-ISM, a doctrine of "progress" in human affairs derived from the writings of the Frenchman Auguste Comte (1798–1857). São Paulo also became a center of the abolitionist movement in the 1880s. By the late 1880s *paulistano* abolitionists were able to persuade the Republican Party to condemn slavery outright, which it had been unwilling to do initially because so many Republicans were themselves slave owners. When slavery was abolished in 1888 and the Republic was declared in 1889, members of the *Paulista* coffee elite, many of whom lived in the city of São Paulo, were poised to take

View of São Paulo. PULSAR IMAGENS E EDITORA / DELFIM MARTINS.

control of the nation's political apparatus. They established a political alliance with their wealthy counterparts in Minas Gerais. Their shared dominion lasted for the next forty years, during which time São Paulo underwent yet another remarkable transformation.

The character of the city changed dramatically in the three decades after the turn of the century. Between 1890 and 1920 its population mushroomed from 65,000 to nearly 600,000. Much of this growth was due to the arrival of immigrants from Italy, Portugal, Spain, Japan, and the Middle East. Industry made enormous strides during the period, financed by coffee magnates who were willing to invest because of a continuing price-production crisis in COFFEE. The growth of industry created a true urban working class, which in 1917–1920 launched a series of general strikes that were brutally repressed by the government, and a population of non-manual employees who formed the embryo of a salaried, white-collar middle class.

After the Revolution of 1930, which removed the *paulista* oligarchy from power, economic momentum in São Paulo passed from coffee to industry. Between 1920 and 1940 the number of industrial firms increased from 4,000 to over 11,500. The city's population exploded from roughly 600,000 to nearly 2 million. In the 1950s the pace of change accelerated even further, and São Paulo became the engine of Brazil's modernizing economy, producing textiles, shoes, furniture, chemicals, pharmaceuticals, automobiles, and electrical equipment. As a part of this process, São Paulo industrialists became a political force unto themselves, industrial workers organized into powerful unions, and a salaried middle class was incorporated into political life and enjoyed the benefits of a consumer economy.

In the years after 1960 São Paulo attained the status of a megalopolis. In 1991 it was the third most populous metropolitan area in the world, with a population approaching 19 million. Population growth in the last two decades has been the result primarily of rural–urban migration that has made São Paulo a focus of the country's social and economic ills.

RICHARD MORSE, *From Community to Metropolis: A Biography of São Paulo, Brazil* (1974), is a standard work on the growth of the city and the culture of urbanization. The collection of essays *Manchester and São Paulo: Problems of Rapid Urban Growth* (1978), edited by JOHN D. WIRTH and ROBERT L. JONES, provides a comparative perspective. WARREN DEAN, *The Industrialization of São Paulo, 1880–1945* (1969), is the standard text on the early period of industrialization. See also JOSEPH LOVE, *São Paulo in the Brazilian Federation, 1889–1937* (1980), for a study of regional politics. A very personal vision of São Paulo's poorest can be had from CAROLINA MARIA DE JESUS, *Child of the Dark*, translated by David St. Clair (1962).

BRIAN OWENSBY

See also **Brazil: Political Parties; Brazil: Revolutions; Immigration; Mining; Slavery.**

SÃO PAULO (STATE). The first settlement in what is toady the south-central state of São Paulo was established at the coastal island of SÃO VICENTE in 1532 by the explorer Martim Afonso de SOUSA. Until mid-century settlements hugged the coast, producing a thriving enclave based on exports of sugar, brazilwood, and agricultural products second in prosperity only to the captaincy of Pernambuco in Northeastern Brazil. The interior was officially settled in 1554, when Jesuit priests climbed the steep sierra to the inland plateau and founded São Paulo do Campo de Piratininga as a base for proselytizing among the Indians. For the remainder of the sixteenth century, the captaincy was subject to attacks by TAMÓIO Indians in league with the FRENCH from "Antarctic France" (today Rio de Janeiro) and by foreign raiders along the coast.

In the first half of the seventeenth century, explorers from the town of São Paulo made expeditions, known as BANDEIRAS, into the unexplored interior, drawn by the chance to enslave Indians and by persistent rumors of gold deposits. The Jesuits of São Paulo condemned slave-hunting raids against the TUPI-GUARANÍ Indians of the Jesuit missions in the southwest (today Paraguay), and were forced to leave the São Vicente captaincy by a citizen uprising in 1640.

The discovery of gold in what became MINAS GERAIS resulted in a frantic GOLD RUSH, led by longtime São Vicente residents, who abandoned the sugar mills along the coast, and swelled by European fortune seekers who flocked to Brazil. PAULISTAS lost control of the gold fields to Portuguese foreigners in the War of the Emboabas (1708–1709). Now displaced, *paulistas* pushed deeper into the interior, opening up new areas for exploration. Mining and population growth led the government to create the captaincy of São Paulo and Minas Gerais in 1710. Gold exports during this period shored up Portugal's sagging economy and contributed to Great Britain's industrialization. Mining declined through the eighteenth century, however, and the captaincy of São Paulo was thrown back on commerce in mules, cotton cloth, and sugar.

The modern chapter of the state's history dates from the early nineteenth century, as COFFEE cultivation gradually replaced SUGAR cultivation. After mid-century, coffee wealth and republican sentiment grew in tandem, such that São Paulo's upper class led the opposition to the emperor. By the 1880s São Paulo had the strongest Republican Party in Brazil. With the advent of the Republic in 1890, the *paulistas* formed the "coffee with cream" political alliance with Minas Gerais (so called because of São Paulo's coffee and Minas's dairy products) that dominated Brazilian politics until 1930. The *paulista* oligarchy was ousted from national power by the Revolution of 1930, though it still retained considerable political clout.

The period after 1930 was defined by continued coffee exports, greater agricultural diversification, and the coffee-financed industrialization that had begun around 1900. Together these made the state of São Paulo the dynamo of Brazil's modernizing economy until the present day.

The importance of the state of São Paulo in Brazilian history cannot be underestimated. The *bandeirantes* expanded Portuguese territorial claims well beyond the line separating Portuguese from Spanish America (established by the TREATY OF TORDESILLAS in 1494), and were the basis of the Brazilian myth of rugged individualism that lives on to this day. The rise of *paulista* republicanism, colored by patriarchy and exclusionary political practices, was at the center of Brazilian politics between the mid-nineteenth century and 1930. Finally, São Paulo has been a driving economic force in the twentieth century.

A good background is available from RICHARD MORSE, *From Community to Metropolis: A Biography of São Paulo, Brazil* (1974). Morse also has a useful book on the *bandeirantes, The Bandeirantes: The Historical Rule of the Brazilian Pathfinders* (1965). CLODOMIR VIANNA MOOG has an interesting comparative study of the United States and Brazil in *Bandeirantes and Pioneers* (1964), focusing on Brazilian and U.S. national character. JOSEPH LOVE, *São Paulo in the Brazilian Federation, 1889–1937* (1980), is the standard study of regional political history. WARREN DEAN, *Rio Claro: A Brazilian Plantation System, 1820–1920* (1976), usefully details a São Paulo coffee community and its incorporation into an export economy.

BRIAN OWENSBY

See also **Brazil: Political Parties; Brazil: Revolutions; Mining.**

SÃO TOMÉ, an island with a population of 132,000 (1994 estimate), 190 miles off the west coast of Africa. São Tomé was uninhabited when the first Portuguese navigators arrived in the early 1470s. It became a base for trade with the adjacent coast of west and central Africa and a plantation colony. Its original colonists were convicts and exiled Jews from Portugal as well as enslaved Africans. By the mid-sixteenth century it had become a leading producer of sugar. The hostile climate of the island made it difficult for Europeans to settle there, and the sugar planters were largely the racially mixed offspring of Portuguese settlers and African women (mestizos) and free Africans, some of noble birth and others who had obtained freedom and become prominent. São Tomé was unusual in the Portuguese Empire in that local official positions were not subject to a color bar. However, it did experience a major slave revolt at the end of the sixteenth century and the establishment of a maroon community (the Angolars) in the mountains.

Although its role as a sugar producer was soon surpassed by Brazil, the island remained an important base for Portuguese activities in Africa, especially the SLAVE TRADE. Its economic functions were revived in the late nineteenth century when cacao planting became prominent, utilizing British capital and contract labor, especially from Nigeria and Angola.

Although the island did not develop a major dissident movement in the 1960s, the republic of São Tomé and Príncipe achieved independence in 1975 as a result of Portugal's disengagement from Africa.

JOHN THORNTON

See also **Portuguese Empire.**

SÃO VICENTE, Portugal's first permanent settlement in Brazil. São Vicente was founded by Martim Afonso de SOUSA in 1532 as was the much larger captaincy of the same name which dominated the settlement of southern Brazil. The settlement of São Vicente survived while other settlements failed because of the good relations the Portuguese established with nearby Indians. The JESUIT ORDER played an important role in São Vicente by building missions, churches, and schools for the Indians and by opposing the widespread use of Indian slavery. By the second half of the sixteenth century the sugar mills of Bahia and Pernambuco had rapidly overshadowed those of São Vicente, so that in the seventeenth century, the colonists of São Vicente turned inward, toward the wilderness. Claiming large tracts of virgin land, they created wheat farms and ranches worked by Indian slaves brought by the BANDEIRAS to the major towns, such as São Paulo.

In the early eighteenth century, after the discovery of gold in the interior, the captaincy of São Vicente reverted to the crown. It was renamed "São Paulo and the Mines of Gold," after its largest and most prosperous town. Thereafter, the name São Vicente referred only to the small coastal town, site of Brazil's first settlement.

ALIDA C. METCALF, *Family and Frontier in Colonial Brazil* (1992).

ALIDA C. METCALF

See also **Slavery.**

SÃO VICENTE, JOSÉ ANTÔNIO PIMENTA BUENO, MARQUÊS DE (*b.* 4 December 1803; *d.* 19 February 1878), Brazilian jurist and statesman. Born in São Paulo, São Vicente earned a doctorate from the São Paulo faculty of law and went on to judicial appointments in that province. He represented São Paulo in the Chamber of Deputies (after 1845), the Senate (after 1853), and served on the Council of State (after 1859). There, with José Tomás Nabuco de Araújo (1813–1878), he shared the task imposed by PEDRO II of researching and writing (1866–1868) a legislative project to effect the gradual abolition of slavery. His political career included portfolios for foreign affairs and justice in the Liberal cabinets of 1847 and 1848 and the provincial presidencies of Mato Grosso (1836) and Rio Grande do Sul (1850); he also dabbled in Paraguayan diplomacy in the 1840s. His most important position, however, was as prime minister of a moderate Conservative cabinet in 1870, when he tried, and failed, to marshal the political support for the abolitionist legislation he had helped author in the Council of State; it was the visconde do RIO BRANCO (1819–1880), a consummate politician, who realized the project instead in 1871. São Vicente's greatest legacy is his widely read discussion of the monarchy's charter: *Direito publico brazileiro e analise da Constituição do Império* (1857).

JOAQUIM NABUCO, *Um estadisto do império*, vol. 3 (1899).

JEFFREY D. NEEDELL

See also **Brazil: Political Parties; Paulistas; Slave Trade.**

SAQUAREMAS. *See* **Brazil: Political Parties: Conservative Party.**

SARAIVA, JOSÉ ANTÔNIO (*b.* 1 March 1823; *d.* 23 July 1895), prime minister of Brazil (1880–1882, 1885). After beginning his political career in the judiciary and the provincial legislature of his native Bahia, Saraiva quickly rose to national prominence in the Liberal Party. Between 1850 and 1858 he served as president of the provinces of Piauí, Alagoas, São Paulo, and Pernambuco. In the first of these he ordered the construction of a new capital city, Teresina. In the same years he won election to the national Chamber of Deputies. His success continued in the Congress; in 1857 and in 1865 he held cabinet posts in Liberal ministries.

Saraiva's greatest fame came during his tenure as prime minister. Showing tremendous political skills, he oversaw the passage of important reform laws in both of his administrations. In 1880 he proposed an electoral reform bill that became known as the Saraiva Law after its passage the following year. By mandating direct elections for the two houses of Congress and easing income criteria for voters, this law ostensibly expanded suffrage. Its provisions dealing with how voters were to prove their qualifications were, however, restrictive. In practice, the law ensured that the wealthy and politically powerful would retain control of Brazil's electoral politics.

When Saraiva became prime minister in 1885, after the fall of the Manuel DANTAS regime, he once more proposed a key reform bill. This bill was a more conservative version of Dantas's proposal to free all slaves over sixty years of age and to increase the effectiveness of the system of buying slaves' emancipation. In Saraiva's legislation, only slaves aged sixty-five or over would receive freedom immediately; those between sixty and sixty-five would have to continue in their masters' service for up to three more years. By making such concessions to slaveholding interests, Saraiva managed to have his bill passed by the Chamber of Deputies. In the partisan confusion that this reform provoked, approval by the Senate seemed in doubt. In response, Saraiva dissolved his cabinet, thus clearing the way for the Conservative Cotegipe ministry to achieve final passage of the bill, now known as the Saraiva–Cotegipe Law (SEXAGENARIAN LAW), in the Senate.

After the advent of the republic in 1889, Saraiva withdrew from politics for two years. He was elected to the new regime's first Senate in 1891, but soon resigned from office.

ROBERT E. CONRAD, *The Destruction of Brazilian Slavery, 1850–1888* (1972); *José Antônio Saraiva: Discursos parlamentares,* edited by Álvaro Valle (1978); RICHARD GRAHAM, *Patronage and Politics in Nineteenth-Century Brazil* (1990).

ROGER A. KITTLESON

See also **Slavery, Abolition of.**

SARAIVA-COTEGIPE LAW. *See* **Sexagenarian Law.**

SARAVIA, APARICIO (*b.* 1856; *d.* 1 September 1904), leader of the last of Uruguay's many uprisings of mounted insurgents. Born near Santa Clara de Olimar in northern Uruguay, the son of a Brazilian-born landowner, Saravia was not a member of the country's traditional ruling groups. Most Brazilian-born landowning families in northern Uruguay maintained social and political contacts in Brazil, which explains the Saravias' involvement in the Brazilian civil war of 1893–1895. Aparicio's oldest brother, Gumercindo Saravia, rose to the rank of general during the fighting, and Aparicio won fame leading the charges of his brother's horsemen. At Gumercindo's death in 1894, Aparicio inherited his army. Meanwhile, the Blancos (National Party) of Uruguay had begun to reorganize after many years of proscription. When Saravia returned from the Brazilian war with the rank of general, many young Blancos saw in him the leader they awaited. An "armed demonstration" led by Saravia in 1896 galvanized Blancos all over the country to rebel in 1897, and Saravia was acclaimed the party's new CAUDILLO. Unable to subdue the rebels, the government made some power-sharing concessions to the Blancos, and Saravia emerged from the war a symbol of Blanco unity and pride. Within a few years, the Colorado government tried to withdraw the concessions, and Saravia mobilized the Blanco militia again in 1903 and 1904. Though bloodier and on a larger scale, this second period of fighting might have resulted in another standoff if not for Saravia's death in Masoller.

ENRIQUE MENA SEGARRA, *Aparicio Saravia: Las últimas patriadas* (1981).

JOHN CHARLES CHASTEEN

SARDÁ, JOSÉ (*d.* 22 October 1834), Colombian military officer and conspirator. Born in Catalonia (or possibly

Navarra), José Sardá fought in the Napoleonic wars in Europe and later joined the 1817 expedition of Francisco Javier MINA in the fight for Mexican independence. Escaping from capture, he eventually joined the patriots in Gran Colombia, where he was a strong supporter of Simón BOLÍVAR and of the short dictatorship of Rafael URDANETA. With the latter's fall in 1831, liberal supporters of Francisco de Paula SANTANDER purged Sardá from the army. After Santander became president of New Granada in 1832, Sardá and other malcontents turned to plotting against him, but they were discovered and Sardá, along with other ringleaders, was condemned to death. He again escaped but was tracked down and killed by loyal officers, whose alleged "assassination" of Sardá gave rise to bitter criticism of Santander.

MARCO AURELIO VILA, *Josep Sardá, un general catalá en le independéncia d'América* (1980); PILAR MORENO DE ÁNGEL, *Santander* (1989), pp. 585–608.

DAVID BUSHNELL

SARDANETA Y LLORENTE, JOSÉ MARIANO DE

(Second Marqués de San Juan de Rayas; *b.* 1761; *d.* 1835), a politician. Sardaneta was a rich miner and landowner from Guanajuato, who served as *regidor* (alderman), magistrate, and administrator in Guanajuato, as well as administrator of mining in Mexico City. In 1808 he favored the establishment of a governing junta in New Spain. After the coup d'état of that year, Sardaneta, who was a friend of the deposed viceroy José de ITURRIGARAY, tried to vindicate him. A well-known autonomist, he was denounced in 1809 as disaffected with the colonial regime, but nothing was proved against him. In 1811 he was accused of corresponding with the insurgent leader Ignacio ALLENDE, and he was listed as an accomplice of the conspiracy in April of that year. As a member of the secret society of Los GUADALUPES, Sardaneta corresponded with José María MORELOS and with Carlos María de BUSTAMANTE and participated in the arrangements to buy a printing press for Morelos. In 1813 he was elected to the Cortes, although he did not occupy his seat. That same year he voted for Morelos as generalísimo in the insurgent elections. Imprisoned by the authorities in February 1816, Sardaneta was sentenced to be deported to Spain, but after reaching Veracruz, he was able to remain. He was one of the signers of the Declaration of Independence in 1821 and a member of the Provisional Governing Junta. He was elected to the Constituent Congress in 1822, and became a member of the Junta Nacional Instituyente during 1822 and 1823. Sardaneta died in Guanajuato.

WILBERT H. TIMMONS, "Los Guadalupes: A Secret Society in the Mexican Revolution for Independence," in *Hispanic American Historical Review* 30, no. 4 (Nov. 1950): 453–479; DORIS LADD, *The Mexican Nobility at Independence, 1780–1826* (1976); ERNESTO DE LA TORRE VILLAR, *Los Guadalupes y la independencia, con una selección de documentos inéditos* (1985); and VIRGINIA

GUEDEA, *En busca de un gobierno alterno: Los Guadalupes de México* (1992).

VIRGINIA GUEDEA

SARDUY, SEVERO

(*b.* 25 February 1937; *d.* 8 June 1993), Cuban novelist, poet, and essayist. Sarduy was born in Camagüey. In 1956 he moved to Havana, where he came in contact with the vital community of writers associated with the literary magazine *Ciclón* and where he began to publish poetry. He studied medicine for two years at the University of Havana, but left to concentrate on writing. After the Cuban Revolution of 1959, he became a contributor to *Lunes de Revolución*, a literary weekly edited by Guillermo Cabrera Infante.

In 1960 Sarduy left for France to study art history at the École du Louvre. From 1964 to 1967 he continued his studies in Paris and became a member of two influential literary groups associated with the publications *Mundo Nuevo*, edited by the critic Emir Rodríguez Monegal, and *Tel quel*, the most influential French publication of the 1960s and 1970s, where he collaborated with Roland Barthes. As editor of the Latin American collection of Éditions du Seuil since 1966, Sarduy has been responsible for launching the writers Gabriel GARCÍA MÁRQUEZ, José LEZAMA LIMA, Jorge Luis BORGES, and Guillermo CABRERA INFANTE into the French arena. In 1971 he was awarded the Prix Paul Gilson for his radio play *La playa* (The Beach). The following year his novel *Cobra* received the prestigious Prix Médici, and another radio play, *Relato*, won the Prix Italia.

Sarduy's work has received enormous critical acclaim, as he is one of the most innovative of Latin American writers. An aesthetic heir of Cuban master José Lezama Lima, for whom he professes great admiration, he uses a rich, elaborately baroque style to combine such seemingly disparate elements as Cuban folklore and music and the art, philosophy, and religion of the Far East. His work has been translated into many languages.

Sarduy's best-known works are *De dónde son los cantantes* (From Cuba with a Song [novel, 1967]), *La playa* (play, 1971), *Cobra* (novel, 1972), *Relato* (play, 1972), and *Maitreya* (novel, 1980; trans. 1987). He died of AIDS in Paris.

JULIA ALEXIS KUSHIGIAN deals extensively with Sarduy in *Orientalism in the Hispanic Literary Tradition* (1991). The most authoritative source on Sarduy's work is ROBERTO GONZÁLEZ ECHEVARRÍA, *La ruta de Severo Sarduy* (1986).

See also JORGE AGUILAR MORA, *Severo Sarduy* (1976); ADRIANA MÉNDEZ RÓDENAS, *Severo Sarduy: El neobarroco de la transgresión* (1983); OSCAR MONTERO, *The Name Game: The Semiotic Intertext of "De dónde son los cantantes"* (1988).

ROBERTO VALERO

SARMIENTO, DOMINGO FAUSTINO

(*b.* 15 February 1811; *d.* 11 September 1888), writer, educator, journalist, historian, linguist, and president of Argentina (1868–1874). According to Mary Peabody Mann, Sarmiento was "not a man but a nation." Born in the frontier city of San Juan, near the Andes, he was the son of a soldier who fought in the wars of independence and a mother who supported the family by weaving. An early intellectual influence was a maternal uncle and private tutor, the priest José de Oro. Steeped in the classics, the Bible, Latin, and French, Sarmiento began teaching elementary school in his teens. Post-Independence chaos and anarchy awakened his interest in orderly government. By 1829 he fought with the unitarists against caudillo rule. When the federalists gained control of San Juan, he fled to Chile to the town of Los Andes, where he taught school and worked in a store. Upon returning to San Juan in 1836, he started the newspaper, *El Zonda*, in which he expounded his ideas about education, agriculture, and modernization. Ahead of his time, Sarmiento advocated educating women. In 1839 he founded a secondary school for girls in San Juan (Colegio de Santa Rosa de América), for which he wrote the by-laws. Facing jail because of political activities against tyrant Juan Manuel de ROSAS, Sarmiento fled to Chile in 1840.

In contrast to Argentina, Chile was developing peacefully under a government framework organized by

Domingo Faustino Sarmiento. Reproduced from *Américas* (August 1971). ORGANIZATION OF AMERICAN STATES.

Diego PORTALES. In Santiago, Sarmiento rose to a position of prestige and influence; he befriended educator and writer Andrés BELLO, director of education (and later president of Chile) Manuel MONTT, historian José Victorino LASTARRIA, and political activist Francisco BILBAO. Sarmiento pursued his twin interests—education and journalism—and he contributed articles to the influential newspapers *El Mercurio, El Nacional,* and *El Progreso.* He believed that Argentina's problems were "rooted in barbarism," and he said that he "only dreamed of founding schools and teaching the masses to read." For him, universal education was the key to defeating backwardness, and he thought he could transform the GAUCHO. In 1845 he serialized and also published in book form the work for which he is best known: *Civilización i barbarie: Vida de Juan Facundo Quiroga. I aspecto físico, costumbres, i ámbitos de la República Argentina* (translated by Mary Mann as *Life in the Argentine Republic in the Days of the Tyrants; or, Civilization and Barbarism* [1868]). In this work, also known as *Facundo,* Sarmiento expounded penetrating observations about the Argentine countryside and gaucho life and about the depredations caused by caudillo warfare, and he described the career of the federalist caudillo Juan Facundo QUIROGA. The book represented a passionate indictment of Rosas, which the tyrant perceived as a threat.

In Santiago, Sarmiento served as the head of a new normal school (teacher training institute). He prepared textbooks, school programs, and curricula. Many of his progressive ideas were adopted in Chilean elementary and secondary education. Following the lead of preeminent thinker and educator Andrés Bello, Sarmiento tried to simplify Spanish orthography and render it more phonetic. He published *Memoria sobre ortografía americana* (Compendium of American Orthography [1843]), and all his writings used the new phonetic spelling. He tirelessly advocated universal education—the cornerstone of a true democracy—believing that an educated electorate is the best antidote to anarchy and tyranny.

Rosas dispatched a diplomatic mission to Chile to secure the extradition of the man who wrote *Facundo.* Coincidentally, the Chilean government sent Sarmiento to Europe and the United States to survey various educational methods. Disappointed in the rigid social class system, the lack of democratic governments, and the stultifying educational methods he saw in Spain, France, Germany, Holland, and Switzerland, Sarmiento did not think the fledgling American republics should emulate European models. In England, Sarmiento chanced upon a report written by Horace Mann to the Massachusetts Board of Education. During his stay in the United States, he met in Boston with educators Horace Mann and Mary Peabody Mann, who influenced his ideas about public education. His visit to the Boston area and other parts of the United States convinced Sarmiento of the importance of strong, representative, local government for a meaningful democracy on the national level. He also visited public libraries; elementary, secondary, and normal schools; and universities.

Upon returning to Chile he married his common-law wife Benita Martínez (1848), and he wrote *Viajes en Europa, Africa, i América, 1845–1847* (2 vols., 1849–1851). The portion relating to the United States was translated by Michael Rockland as *Sarmiento's Travels in the United States in 1847* (1970). Like Alexis de Tocqueville before him, Sarmiento perceptively analyzed life in the United States. His *Travels* remains a timeless classic. In addition to his two popular works, *Facundo* and *Travels*, Sarmiento also produced the romantic prose masterpiece *Recuerdos de provincia* (Provincial recollections [1850]); *De la educación popular* (About public education [1849]), which was revised as *Memoria sobre educación común* (Report on public education [1856]); and *Las escuelas: Base de prosperidad i de la república en los Estados Unidos* (Schools as the basis of prosperity and republican government in the United States [1866]).

When General Justo José de URQUIZA successfully rallied the remaining caudillos against Rosas in 1851, Sarmiento traveled to Montevideo to join the armed struggle. After the defeat of Rosas at the Battle of CASEROS (1852), and as a result of disagreements with Urquiza, Sarmiento returned to Chile. He moved permanently to Argentina in 1855, where he became the director of the department of education in Buenos Aires Province and threw himself into reforming education with his accustomed energy. Juana Manso de Noronha, an Argentine educator, became his closest assistant and confidante. He founded the journal *Anales de la educación común* (Annals of public education) in 1858; he wrote for the newspaper *El Nacional;* and he continued to promulgate ideas about universal public education with a modern curriculum that included science, practical learning, and gymnastics for both men and women. The proposed reforms met the stiff resistance of the SOCIEDAD DE LA BENEFICIENCIA (Society for Charity), which had been in charge of women's education since the 1820s. Sarmiento was prevented from reforming women's education. Between 1856 and 1861 Sarmiento founded thirty-four new schools, and he ordered the publication of new textbooks.

Following national unification in 1882, Sarmiento played an important role in bringing peace and order to the provinces. He served as senator and later as governor of San Juan Province (1862–1864), where he tried to implement programs of education reforms and economic development; he also continued writing for newspapers. His projects for land reform were relentlessly opposed by the caudillo Angel Vicente PEÑALOZA (El Chacho). Federal forces defeated El Chacho on 12 November 1863, and his severed head was displayed on a pike, as was the custom of the times.

By 1862 Sarmiento had separated from his wife Benita and was engaged in a long-term liaison with Aurelia Vélez. In 1864 he became minister plenipotentiary first to Peru, then to the United States. Finding Washington provincial, Sarmiento settled in New York, where he saw greater opportunities to learn about educational innovations and business practices. He reacquainted himself with Mary Mann (Horace Mann died in 1859) and other educators and intellectuals he had met during his previous trip. He visited teachers' colleges and universities in Boston, New York, and Chicago, always helped by Mary Mann. He lectured on North and South America to the Rhode Island Historical Society (1865). The talk was translated into English by the young Bartolomé MITRE, the Argentine president's son. In 1866 Sarmiento's only son, twenty-year-old Dominguito, was killed in the Battle of CURUPAITÍ in the WAR OF THE TRIPLE ALLIANCE.

In 1868 Sarmiento was elected the second president of a newly unified Argentina. His presidency was the culmination of his tireless struggle to transform Argentina into a modern nation. As president he vigorously promoted economic, social, and cultural development. Following the ideas of Juan Bautista ALBERDI and Bartolomé Mitre, Sarmiento fostered European immigration and encouraged the establishment of agricultural colonies. He worked to expand railways and roads; he promoted shipping, commerce, and advances in public health; and he modernized and beautified the city of Buenos Aires. To further educational reforms, he established public libraries throughout the country, and he recruited North American schoolteachers. More than eighty-eight teachers came to Argentina between 1867 and 1889. In 1869 he mandated the establishment of a normal-school network. He introduced advanced teaching techniques, added foreign languages to curricula, and founded kindergartens. Many of the educational reforms were implemented by Sarmiento's successor, President Nicolás AVELLANEDA. As a result of their efforts, Argentine schools became the best in Latin America. Sarmiento ordered the first national census of Argentina in 1869; he founded the COLEGIO MILITAR (National Military Academy), the first astronomical observatory, and trade and technical schools; he fostered the modernization of agriculture, mining, and industry; and he established the SOCIEDAD RURAL to improve livestock breeds.

After leaving the presidency, Sarmiento served in the Senate (1875–1880), held the office of interior minister, visited Chile, was once again superintendent of education of Buenos Aires Province (1879–1882), and founded the journal *La educación común* (Public Education) in 1876 and the newspaper *El Censor* in 1885. Quite ill during the last three years of his life, he died in Asunción, Paraguay.

Political and historical writings of Sarmiento include: *Comentarios de la constitución de la Confederación Argentina* (1853), *Arjirópolis: O la capital de los estados confederados del Río de la Plata* (1850), *Discursos parlamentarios* (2 vols. [1933]), *Emigración alemana al Río de la Plata* (1851), *Condición del extranjero en América* (The Foreigner's Condition in the Americas [1888]), and studies about the War of the Triple Alliance.

Published correspondence includes: *Sarmiento-Mitre: Correspondencia, 1846–1868* (1911), *Epistolario íntimo* (1963), and Julia Ottolenghi's *Sarmiento a través de un epistolario* (Sarmiento Through His Correspondence [1940]). Sarmiento's last publication was *La vida de Dominguito* (1886), which mourned his son Domingo Fidel. Posterity harshly criticized him for the 1883 book *Conflicto y armonías de las razas* (Conflict and Harmony in the Races), in which he largely repeats the prevalent theories about race mixing and racial purity. His *Obras completas* in fifty-three volumes were published in 1888.

During his presidency, Sarmiento dealt with the last of the caudillos. Despite his lifelong opposition to caudillo rule, Sarmiento governed as a personalist and strengthened the power of the executive. As president he used the central government's power to crush political opposition in the interior provinces, and he imposed sieges to quell uprisings. When the law seemed inadequate, he ruled by decree. Viewed by some of his contemporaries as an egotist ("don Yo" or "Mr. Me"), Sarmiento nevertheless looms as a protean figure: a visionary, an educator, a writer, and a seminal nation-builder.

WATT STEWART and WILLIAM M. FRENCH, "Influence of Horace Mann on the Educational Ideas of Domingo Faustino Sarmiento," in *Hispanic American Historical Review* 20 (1940):12–31; RICARDO ROJAS, *El profeta de la pampa* (1945); ALLISON WILLIAMS BUNKLEY, *The Life of Sarmiento* (1952; repr. 1969); ALBERTO PALCOS, *Sarmiento: La vida, la obra, las ideas, el genio,* 4th ed. (1962), and "La presidencia de Sarmiento," in *Historia argentina contemporaranea,* vol. 1, ed. Academia Nacional de Historia (1963), pp. 89–148; PAUL VERDEVOYE, *Domingo Faustino Sarmiento: Educateur et publiciste, 1839–1852* (1964); EZEQUIEL MARTÍNEZ ESTRADA, *Meditaciones sarmientinas* (1968); FRANCES G. CROWLEY, *Domingo Faustino Sarmiento* (1972); ELDA CLAYTON PATTON, *Sarmiento in the United States* (1976); ANÍBAL PONCE, *Sarmiento: Constructor de la nueva Argentina* (1976); MANUEL GÁLVEZ, *Vida de Sarmiento* (1979); NOÉ JITRIK, *Muerte y resurrección del Facundo* (1983); NATALIO BOTANA, *Alberdi, Sarmiento, y las ideas políticas de su tiempo* (1984); GABRIEL BRIZUELA, *Bibliografía sarmientina* (1989); DARDOS PÉREZ GUILHOU, *Sarmiento y la constitución: Sus ideas políticas* (1989); JOSEPH T. CRISCENTI, ed., *Sarmiento and His Argentina* (1993).

GEORGETTE MAGASSY DORN

SARMIENTO DE GAMBOA, PEDRO (*b.* ca. 1530; *d.* 1608), Spanish admiral and chronicler of South America. Born in Pontevedra, in northwestern Spain, Sarmiento served in the navy of Philip II, reaching the rank of admiral. Combining his maritime profession with the writing of history, he researched the history of the INCAS before the Conquest, pursuing his work on *Historia índica* (History of the Incas, 1572) while Viceroy Francisco de TOLEDO ruled Peru. He voyaged to the Strait of Magellan, becoming the first to enter from the

west, and attempted to found a colony there. Lacking the enthusiastic backing of the king, the colony failed and its inhabitants perished while Sarmiento was imprisoned in Europe. He described his experience in *Derrotero al Estrecho de Magallanes* (Voyage to the Straits of Magellan, 1580).

Among the chroniclers of sixteenth-century Peru, Sarmiento stands out for these two works. The *Historia* is an example of the efforts of Viceroy Toledo and those around him to establish a historiographic record that would confirm the justification for Spanish dominance of the Andean peoples. Arguing against the claims of native Andeans to self-government, chroniclers such as Sarmiento promoted a providentialist view of Spain's role as Christianizer of the New World.

CLEMENTS R. MARKHAM translated the *Narratives of the Voyages of Pedro Sarmiento de Gamboa to the Straits of Magellan* into English (1895). A biography in Spanish is that by ERNESTO MORALES, *Sarmiento de Gamboa, un navegante español del siglo XVI* (1932).

KATHLEEN ROSS

SARMIENTO DE SOTOMAYOR, GARCÍA (count of Salvatierra), viceroy of Peru (1648–1654). Faced with the continuing decline in crown revenues, Salvatierra initiated various policies to increase state income. Citing weaknesses in the official trade system of the CONSULADO (merchant guild), Salvatierra proposed altering that system to reduce smuggling and collect more taxes. Salvatierra wanted to increase Indian tribute payments as well, but his inconsistent policies, including initiating and then suspending a census of the Indian community, failed. Although not as effective as his predecessor, the marquis of Mancera, Salvatierra did raise some crown revenues through *composiciones de tierras,* the practice of declaring Indian lands depopulated or abandoned and thus the property of the crown, subject to sale to private investors. His efforts to tighten control over the regional treasuries were less successful.

KENNETH J. ANDRIEN, *Crisis and Decline: The Viceroyalty of Peru in the Seventeenth Century* (1985); ANN M. WIGHTMAN, *Indigenous Migration and Social Change: The Forasteros of Cuzco, 1570–1720* (1990).

ANN M. WIGHTMAN

SARMIENTOS DE LEÓN, JORGE ALVARO (*b.* 1933), Guatemalan composer, conductor, and percussionist. Born in San Antonio Suchitepéquez, Sarmientos began his training at the National Conservatory of Music in Guatemala City under Ricardo Castillo, José Arévalo Guerra, and other distinguished Guatemalan musicians. He continued his studies in Paris and later at the Instituto Torcuato di Tella in Buenos Aires. Sarmientos returned to Guatemala, where he taught at the National

Conservatory and served as musical and artistic director of the National Symphony Orchestra. He has composed over sixty works, among them film scores, chamber music, orchestral works, and a ballet. His music often features indigenous themes, as in his *Las estampas del Popol Vuh*.

RONALD R. SIDER, "Central America and Its Composers," in *Inter-American Music Bulletin*, no. 77 (May 1970): 10–16; ENRIQUE ANLEU DÍAZ, *Esbozo histórico-social de la música en Guatemala* (1978), pp. 107–108.

STEVEN S. GILLICK

SARNEY, JOSÉ (*b.* 24 April 1930), president of Brazil (1985–1990) and writer. José Ribamar Ferreira Araújo Costa was born in Pinheiro, Maranhão, and received a law degree in 1953. From childhood he was referred to as Zé do Sarney. For electoral purposes, in 1958 he adopted the name José Sarney and legally changed his name to José Sarney da Costa in 1965.

Sarney began his political career in 1954 as an alternate federal deputy from the National Democratic Union (UDN) and assumed the deputy position in 1956. He was reelected in 1958 and 1962, and in 1965 he became the governor of his home state on the Arena ticket, the same party that brought him to the federal senate in 1970 and 1978. He was a founder of the Social Democratic Party (PDS) and twice its president. Asked by President FIGUEIREDO to coordinate the presidential succession with the goal of finding a national union candidate within the PDS, Sarney failed and renounced the party presidency at that time. Subsequently he ran for vice president on the Democratic Alliance ticket of the PMDB–PFL (Brazilian Democratic Movement Party–Liberal Front Party) in the indirect elections won by Tancredo NEVES in January 1985.

When Neves fell ill on the eve of his inauguration in March 1985, Sarney became interim president and reaffirmed the ministerial choices made by Neves. With the death of Neves in April, Sarney was sworn in as president and governed until March 1990. He helped to lead the country toward direct elections and a new constitution in 1988. In November 1990 he was elected senator from Amapá on the PMDB ticket. His attempts to become a presidential candidate in 1994 were frustrated even though polls indicated he still retained a small but solid following.

Sarney became a member of the Brazilian Academy of Letters in 1980. He has written several books, including *Norte das águas* (1969), *Marimbondos de fogo* (1980), *Brejaldos guajas* (1985), and *Sentimento do mundo* (1985).

Enciclopedia Mirador Internacional, vol. 18 (1991), p. 10,252.

IÊDA SIQUEIRA WIARDA

SARRATEA, MANUEL DE (*b.* 13 August 1774; *d.* 21 September 1849), Argentine statesman of the independence and early national periods. Born in Buenos Aires into a distinguished family that eventually included Santiago de LINIERS Y BREMOND as his brother-in-law, Sarratea spent much of his early life in Spain but returned in time to take part in the independence movement. Though Sarratea received important government positions (such as president of the First Triumvirate in 1811 and captain-general and governor of Buenos Aires Province in 1820), he seldom retained any post for long. Some authors have focused on these career changes and his friendship with British merchants to dismiss him as an intriguer, yet he made numerous contributions during three decades of public service. During the second regime of Juan Manuel de ROSAS, for example, Sarratea was named special envoy and minister plenipotentiary to Brazil (in 1838) and France (in 1841). He died in Limoges and his remains were transported to Buenos Aires in 1850.

JACINTO R. YABEN, *Biografías argentinas y sudamericanas* vol. 5 (1938–1940), pp. 591–593; ORESTE CARLOS ALES, *D. Manuel de Sarratea: ensayo histórico* (1975).

FIDEL IGLESIAS

SAS, ANDRÉS (*b.* 6 April 1900; *d.* 26 August 1967), Peruvian musicologist and composer. Born in Paris, Sas grew up in Brussels, where from 1918 to 1923 he studied at the Royal Conservatory under Fernand Bauvais (theory), Alfred Marchot (violin), Paul Miry (chamber music), and Ernest Closson (music history). He took private lessons in fugue and counterpoint with Maurice Imbert. In 1920 he began studies in harmony at the Anderlecht Academy in Brussels. Soon afterward he started a teaching career as a violin instructor at the Forest Music School in Brussels. In 1924 the Peruvian government invited him to direct violin classes and chamber music concerts at the National Academy of Music in Lima. The following year he was appointed an instructor in music history at the academy. He returned to Belgium, where he founded and directed the Municipal School of Music in Ninove (1928–1929). Again in Lima, he established the Sas-Rosay Academy with his wife, the pianist Lily Rosay, in 1930. With María Wiesse de Sabogal, he started the *Antara/Revista Musical* (1935). Sas was director of Lima's Bach Institute (1931–1933) and vice president of the Lima Orchestral Society (1932).

Sas was known for his studies of pre-Columbian instruments such as the clay syrinx of the Nazca tribe; his numerous writings on the music of the Nazca and other indigenous groups made him a leading authority on the history of Peruvian music. In addition to his research, Sas was active as an editor of music magazines, lecturer, conductor, recitalist, and teacher. Sas composed symphonic pieces (*Recuerdos* for violin or piano and orchestra [1927]) and choral works (the triptych *Ollantai* [1933]), ballets (*Sueño de Zamba* [1943]), music for the stage, chamber music (*Cuarteto de cuerdas* [1938]) and songs (*Seis canciones indias del Perú* [1946]). Although some of his songs used French texts, most of his works were inspired by Indian themes and display the pentatonic melodies of the Andean region, but were written with an almost impressionist technique. He died in Lima.

Composers of the Americas, vol. 2 (1956), pp. 116–125; "Andrés Sas (1900–1967)" in *Revista Musical Chilena*, no. 101 (1967): 123–125; *New Grove Dictionary of Music and Musicians*, vol. 16 (1980).

SUSANA SALGADO

SAYAÑA, a plot of land in the Bolivian altiplano and in the valleys to which the holder and his family have exclusive access. A *sayaña* may consist of a single plot, but it is often fragmented because of inheritance patterns and additional land acquired by the *sayañero*. *Sayañas* range in size from less than 2.5 acres to 75 acres or more. *Sayañas* probably existed during pre-Columbian times, and on the northern altiplano present-day house plots may still correspond to their boundaries.

Prior to the agrarian reform of 1953, both the free peasant and the peon on the hacienda had *sayañas* that they could cultivate as they desired. However, the *colono* had to work (as much as five days weekly) without pay on hacienda lands in exchange for usufruct rights on the *sayaña*.

The agrarian reform did not drastically change land categories. It gave legal titles to all peasants for the land they had previously occupied and worked for their own benefit. It did not break up large *sayañas* but increased the number of *sayañas* by converting some *aynokas* (large sections of land cultivated in a strict pattern of rotation).

WILLIAM E. CARTER, *Aymara Communities and the Bolivian Agrarian Reform* (1964); DWIGHT B. HEATH, CHARLES J. ERASMUS, and HANS C. BUECHLER, *Land Reform and Social Revolution in Bolivia* (1969).

MARIA LUISE WAGNER

SAYIL, an ancient Maya city located in what has been called the "breadbasket" of Yucatán that flourished in the Terminal Classic period (A.D. 800–1000). Sayil rose to prominence in the hilly Puuc region following the collapse of the southern dynastic centers of the MAYA in the Petén during the ninth century. At its height Sayil covered more than 1.5 square miles and housed from eight to ten thousand people. Research has shown that this thriving urban center might best be described as having been a "garden" city where urban and agricultural space were mixed in a pattern well adapted to the food needs of the people and to the health of a forested environment.

Picking up the fallen standard of Classic Maya civilization, Sayil and other Terminal Classic centers of the Puuc represent some of the finest examples of monumental architecture anywhere in the ancient world. The elaborate decorative motifs of the Puuc style, which dominate the façade of the three-story palace at Sayil, commemorate the major Maya deities, including the peculiar "diving god," who ruled over honey and beekeeping, as well as curly-nosed Chac, the god of rain. Ancient Sayileños did well to honor Chac, for surface streams are nonexistent and water was at a premium in this dry, karstic landscape. To assure a good supply of drinking water, the Maya of Sayil excavated water cisterns (*chultunes*) in the soft, limestone substrate. Around the *chultunes* they piled rubble into large platforms upon which they erected massive cut-stone buildings that survive to this day in the Yucatán forest. Recently completed maps of this site represent one of the most detailed records available for any ancient urban center in the Maya world and provide a blueprint for research in the years to come.

HARRY E. D. POLLOCK, *The Puuc: An Architectural Survey of the Hill Country of Yucatán and Northern Campeche, Mexico* (1980); THOMAS W. KILLION ET AL., "Intensive Surface Collection of Residential Clusters at Terminal Classic Sayil, Yucatán, Mexico," in *Journal of Field Archaeology* 16 (1989): 273–294; JEREMY A. SABLOFF and GAIR TOURTELLOT, *The Ancient Maya City of Sayil: The Mapping of a Puuc Region Center* (1991).

THOMAS W. KILLION

See also **Mesoamerica.**

SCALABRINI ORTIZ, RAÚL (*b.* 14 April 1898; *d.* 30 May 1959), Argentine nationalist writer and historian. Although trained in the physical sciences, Scalabrini early showed literary talent in his collection of short stories, *La manga* (1923). In 1931 he published a famous analysis of the Argentine mind-set *El hombre que está solo y espera*, from which emerge two key ideas. First, echoing nationalist thinkers from Johann Gottfried von Herder to Charles Maurras, Scalabrini holds that authentic Argentines uncontaminated by foreign ideas find their real identity in "the spirit of the land." Second, he argues that nineteenth-century Argentine liberalism, by failing to understand the country's true spirit, had built a country at cross-purposes with its true destiny. Scalabrini's increasing nationalist militance eventually produced two famous revisionist studies, *Política británica en el Río de la Plata* (1940) and *Historia de los ferrocarriles argentinos* (1940), which argue that British imperialists in cahoots with Argentine liberals had dispossessed Argentines of their rightful patrimony. Distrusting the British, Scalabrini supported Argentine neutrality during World War II, a position that led to charges of pro-Nazi sympathies. While he never became a Peronist functionary, his rhetoric and ideas became staples of Peronist thinking. Scalabrini's sympathy for Peronism emerges most powerfully in his book of poetry, *Tierra sin nada, tierra de profetas* (1946). His other writings include *Historia del primer empréstito* (1939), *Cuatro verdades sobre nuestras crisis* (1948; 2d ed. 1985), and *Bases para la reconstrucción nacional* (1965). After Juan PERÓN's ouster in 1955, Scalabrini fought until his death for the president's return and vindication.

VICENTE C. TRIPOLI, *Raúl Scalabrini Ortiz* (1943); NORBERTO GALASSO, *Scalabrini Ortiz* (1975); RENÉ ORSI, *Jauretche y Scalabrini Ortiz* (1985).

NICOLAS SHUMWAY

SCHAERER, EDUARDO (*b.* 2 December 1873; *d.* 12 November 1941), Paraguayan statesman and president (1912–1916). Schaerer was related to German colonists who came to Paraguay in the wake of the disastrous WAR OF THE TRIPLE ALLIANCE. Though he was born in Caazapá, a small hamlet in the Paraguayan interior, Schaerer displayed distinctly urban ambitions and efficiency, which stood him in good stead at the Colegio Nacional and ultimately in his business affairs.

Politically, Schaerer was a Liberal, and after the Liberal Party came to power after the 1904 revolution, he held a variety of important government posts, including director general of the Customs House, mayor of Asunción, and interior minister. Schaerer's business acumen had already made him a wealthy man, and he used his money to promote his candidacy for president. During his administration, considerable progress was made in the modernization of Asunción, an undertaking highlighted by the inauguration of a tramway system. In foreign relations, he kept Paraguay neutral during World War I.

Schaerer remained influential in Liberal circles after his term of office had expired. For a time he was a national senator and eventually became president of the Senate. He provided financial backing for various Liberal newspapers and remained an important force in the party into the 1930s.

WILLIAM BELMONT PARKER, *Paraguayans of To-Day* (1921), pp. 161–162; HARRIS GAYLORD WARREN, *Rebirth of the Paraguayan Republic: The First Colorado Era, 1878–1904* (1985), pp. 125–126.

THOMAS L. WHIGHAM

SCHENDEL, MIRA (*b.* 1919; *d.* 1988), graphic artist, painter, and sculptor. Swiss born, Schendel lived in Italy until age thirty, when she emigrated to Brazil. Abstract art with minimalist overtone dominated her repertory until the 1960s, when her work took on constructivist influences, with a monumentality of void characterizing her graphic works. In one piece, simply entitled *Drawing*, for example, linguistic and mathematical signs and scratches are drawn on inked glass and are then transferred onto delicate Japanese paper. The visual result recalls Chinese painting. In 1964 Schendel represented Brazil in the Second Biennial of American Art of Córdoba, Argentina, She had solo exhibitions at the Museum of Modern Art in São Paulo in 1964, at a London gallery in 1965, and in 1971 at the Brazilian-American Cultural Institute in Washington, D.C. In 1975 she was one of twelve artists selected to participate in a nationally sponsored traveling exhibition and discussion series.

FUNDAÇÃO NACIONAL DE ARTE, *Pinacoteca do Estado—São Paulo* (1982), p. 174; DAWN ADES, *Art in Latin America: The Modern Era, 1820–1980* (1989), pp. 275–276.

CAREN A. MEGHREBLIAN

SCHICK GUTIÉRREZ, RENÉ (*b.* 1909; *d.* 1966), president of Nicaragua from 1963 to 1966. A close associate of the Somoza family, Schick served as Anastasio SOMOZA GARCÍA's personal secretary and was named minister of education and of foreign relations during the presidency of Luis SOMOZA DEBAYLE. Long portrayed as a quiet "yes-man" and Somoza puppet, Schick proved to be more independent. His term in office was relatively peaceful and he followed Luis Somoza's lead in liberalizing Nicaragua. The Nicaraguan state and economy boomed as government expenditure and entrepreneurial activity increased. Schick, who died in office, was succeeded by Vice President Lorenzo Guerrero Gutiérrez.

EDUARDO CRAWLEY, *Dictators Never Die* (1979); CLARIBEL ALEGRÍA and D. J. FLAKOLL, *Nicaragua: La revolución Sandinista, una crónica política, 1855–1979* (1982); THOMAS WALKER, *Nicaragua: The Land of Sandino* (1986).

HEATHER K. THIESSEN

SCHNEIDER, RENÉ (*b.* 31 December 1913; *d.* 22 October 1970), Chilean military officer. A graduate of the Chilean military school, Schneider became the army's top-ranking officer in 1968. Appointed by Eduardo FREI to end unrest in the army, Schneider quickly restored discipline and reinforced the principle of civilian supremacy over the armed forces. He also indicated that, regardless of its outcome, the military would not intervene in the 1970 election. This promise became known as the Schneider Doctrine. Forces hostile to the Popular Unity Party (*Unidad Popular*) wanted the army to launch a preventive coup to prevent Salvador ALLENDE from taking office. When it became clear that Schneider would neither countenance nor cooperate with a putsch, the anti-Allende forces, under the leadership of an ex-general, tried to neutralize Schneider by kidnapping him. The conspirators, however, bungled the attempt, in the process mortally wounding Schneider, who put up unexpected resistance. Schneider's death precluded future military participation in an anti-Allende movement, thus ensuring that Allende would take office.

U.S. SENATE SELECT COMMITTEE TO STUDY GOVERNMENTAL OPERATIONS WITH RESPECT TO INTELLIGENCE ACTIVITIES, *Alleged Assassination Plots Involving Foreign Leaders* (1976), pp. 225–254; PAUL E. SIGMUND, *The Overthrow of Allende and the Politics of Chile, 1964–1976* (1977), pp. 99, 114–115, 120–121, 123.

WILLIAM F. SATER

SCHWARZ-BART, SIMONE (*b.* 8 January 1938), Guadeloupean novelist and dramatist. Schwarz-Bart was born in Charente-Maritime, where her father was serving in the army. Her mother returned to Guadeloupe with her daughter, whose early schooling took place in Trois-Rivières. Schwarz-Bart began the lycée in Point-à-Pitre and finished in Paris. Married in Paris, Simone and André Schwarz-Bart spent a year in Dakar, and then settled in Switzerland, where Simone began writing short stories. Returning to Guadeloupe, she was instrumental in editing the encyclopedic *Hommage à la femme noire*, 6 vols. (1988–1989).

Schwarz-Bart has been compared with writers as diverse as Antonine Maillet and Toni Morrison. Through her presentation of various insular experiences (a Haitian sugarcane worker, an elderly Martinican woman in a French hospice) she would seem to be in the process of creating a Caribbean mythology in her dramatic and fictional writing. In 1973, she won the Grand Prize of the magazine *Elle* for her novel *Pluie et vent sur Télumée-Miracle* (1972)/*The Bridge of Beyond* (1982). All of her individually authored works have appeared in English.

Un plat de porc aux bananes vertes (novel, with Andre Schwarz-Bart, 1967); *Ti-Jean l'horizon* (novel, 1979), translated as *Between Two Worlds* (1981); and *Ton beau capitaine* (theater, 1987), translated as *Your Handsome Captain* (1989).

See also RONNIE SCHARFMAN, "Mirroring and Mothering in Simone Schwarz-Bart's *Pluie et vent sur Télumée-Miracle* and Jean Rhys' *Wide Sargasso Sea*," in *Yale French Studies* 62 (1981): 88–106; FANTA TOUREH, *L'imaginaire dans l'oeuvre de Simone Schwarz-Bart: Approche d'une mythologie antillaise* (1986); ELIZABETH MUDIMBE-BOYI, "*Pluie et vent sur Télumée-Miracle*," in *Continental, Latin American, and Francophone Women Writers*, edited by GINETTE ADAMSON et al., vol. 2 (1987), pp. 155–164; MONIQUE BOUCHARD, *Une lecture de "Pluie et vent sur Télumée-Miracle . . ."* (1990); MARIE-DENIS SHELTON, "Literature Extracted: A Poetic of Daily Life," in *Callaloo* 15, no. 1 (1992): 167–178.

CARROL F. COATES

SCIENCE

THE COLONIAL ERA

Beginning with Christopher COLUMBUS's terse descriptions of Caribbean natural history, Latin America was a source of scientific information diffused through the new print technology and was evaluated by Europeans in the context of the received view of the natural world, highly colored by the works of classical antiquity. Thus Columbus's discovery stimulated the comparative study of Old World and New World nature. Works like Gonzalo Fernández de OVIEDO Y VALDÉS's *Historia general de las Indias* (1535), itself conceptually dependent on ancient authors like Pliny, made available data that eventually led to the overthrow of classical authority in science, thus feeding directly into the scientific revolution. The Spanish crown in particular was eager to learn of the economically useful natural products, especially minerals and plants, of the new hemisphere and dispatched an expedition led by Francisco HERNÁNDEZ in 1570–1577, mainly to investigate the flora of New Spain. Hernández built upon the codification of Aztec materia medica and its translation into Spanish in works like the Badianus Codex of 1552, compiled by Indian physicians in both Latin and Nahuatl versions.

The scientific revolution of the seventeenth century largely bypassed the Spanish Empire. But Galileo's astronomical writings were read and appreciated by Diego Rodríguez and Carlos SIGÜENZA Y GÓNGORA in New Spain, although they failed to push Galileo's critique of classical cosmology to its ultimate limits. New World naturalists of Galileo's generation and later shared Europe's passion for observing comets; indeed, the Spanish crown stimulated such research by collecting observational data from various sites in its empire.

The eighteenth century saw a fully developed colonial science system characterized by militarization and centralization. Like their French cousins, the Spanish Bourbons believed that investment in science was both a way of associating the crown with a prestigious activity and a largely utilitarian pursuit that promised economic benefits to the entire empire. As early as the 1750s, the crown was devoting around 0.5 percent of its annual budget to scientific activities, a very large investment in science among European nations of the day. The real science budget was even larger because numerous scientific activities were hidden in the military budget. The preponderance of scientists gravitated toward military careers: the navy in particular cultivated officers attracted to the new Newtonian science and gave them commissions that exploited their interest in cosmology while they carried out strategically important "hydrographical" activities, such as the mapping of the coastlines of Latin America and service on numerous boundary commissions. The navy procured the best scientific instruments produced in London and Paris, and made them available to colonial men of science, in contrast with the restrictive practices of the British in their American colonies. The American team on the joint Spanish–American commission to establish the boundary of Florida in 1796 used instruments loaned them by Spanish officers. The problem with the militarization of science was that its net effect was to delay the emergence of science as a profession and to discourage the open discussion or publication of scientific results, which were frequently viewed as state secrets. Thus a concomitant of militarization was a scientific system that was highly centralized. All results were communicated to the relevant officials in Madrid rather than published directly by the scientist. A botanist of independent mind, like José Celestino MUTIS, incurred the wrath of his superiors in Madrid when he corresponded directly with Carl Linnaeus.

The two areas that most attracted those who wished to associate themselves with modern science were Newtonian physics and Linnaean taxonomy. In an intellectual world that had officially rejected the views of Copernicus, heliocentrism was diffused and accepted in the eighteenth century through the circulation of books popularizing Newtonian physics. Newton's work was studied in the intellectual centers of the empire: in Lima, Cosme Bueno diffused Newtonian ideas from his chair of Galenic medicine (which he used as a platform to attack outmoded Galenic concepts), and theses on Newtonian subjects were produced at the University of San Marcos. In Bogotá, Mutis lectured on Newton at the Colegio Mayor de Nuestra Señora del Rosario and prepared a partial translation of the *Principia,* the first in Spanish. In these capitals and in Mexico City roughly the same proportion of Newtonian works circulated in relation to population as in any European center. The notion of the empire as a scientific backwater must be rejected, or at least carefully qualified.

Among the numerous botanists working in colonial Latin America, the acceptance of Linnaean taxonomy allowed the naturalist to be a participant in a vast international network of botanical information gathered by disciples dispatched to various parts of the world by Linnaeus himself or by institutions that adopted his system. Linnaeus's man in Latin America was to have been Pehr Loefling, whom he sent first to Madrid in 1751 and to New Granada in 1754, where he died. Mutis, who began to correspond with Linnaeus in 1764, believed he had inherited Loefling's mantle. Mutis was not an uncritical Linnaean, however, offering a number of refinements to the system. All botanists who were subjects of the crown worked as dependents of the Madrid Botanical Garden, which had become a Linnaean stronghold in the 1770s. Because of this tight centralization, budding nationalists in New Spain, led by José Antonio de ALZATE Y RAMÍREZ, rejected the Linnaean system while attempting to revive Aztec taxonomy, essentially for nationalistic reasons. When the Linnaeans of the Malaspina expedition arrived in New Spain in 1791, they became embroiled in a dispute over taxonomy with botanists influenced by Alzate. At this time, there were so many naturalists working in New Spain in official capacities that one of them complained to the crown that botanists were tripping over each other in the jungle.

The two most characteristic forms of centralized scientific institutions in the eighteenth century were the botanical expedition and the boundary commission. The first important expedition of the century, the La Condamine expedition (1735–1745), was a geophysical enterprise, although botanists were included. Although the expedition was French-led, two Spanish military officers, Jorge JUAN Y SANTACILIA and Antonio de ULLOA, were attached to it. The purposes of the expedition were to establish a value for an arc of the meridian in equatorial South America and to corroborate Newton's prediction regarding the flattening of the Earth's poles and consequent shortening of the degree of longitude near the equator. Thus Spain entered Enlightenment science in Newtonian guise: for their efforts, Ulloa was elected a Fellow of the Royal Society, and Juan a member of the French Academy of Sciences, whereas in Spain their careers were wholly military.

The three great botanical expeditions were to New Granada, Peru, and New Spain. Only the first, conducted in 1782–1810, was established in the colonies rather than by Madrid directly; it also became, under Mutis's direction, a full-fledged scientific institution, establishing an astronomical observatory (1803), and conducting research in zoology and mineralogy as well as botany. The Peruvian expedition (1777–1788), led by Hipólito Ruiz and José Antonio Pavón, was more narrowly botanical, its major focus being the species of quinine-producing cinchona. The expedition to New Spain (1787–1804), led by the Spaniard Martín de Sessé and the creole José Mociño, made a systematic study of Mexican flora and established a botanical garden in Mexico City. The greatest and most productive expedition of the period was that led by the Italian Alessandro di Malaspina (1789–1794). The expedition was influenced in its style by Captain James Cook's second voyage, the first voyage of discovery that had mainly scientific objectives. The Malaspina expedition collected data and natural history specimens from Uruguay up the Pacific coast of South and North America as far as Alaska, as well as from the Philippines, New Zealand, and Australia. The last expedition of the colonial period, the royal vaccination expedition (1803–1806), led by Francisco Balmis, was a public health venture designed to inoculate as many subjects of the empire as possible with the Jenner smallpox vaccine.

Enlightenment naturalists were concerned to defend the environment and biota of the New World against Europeans, like Georges Buffon, who held that both were degenerate and inferior with respect to their European counterparts. In this "dispute of the New World," Hipólito UNANUE in Peru and Alzate in Mexico (and Thomas Jefferson in the United States) presented data to demonstrate the falsity of the original proposition. This kind of polemic provided a scientific contribution to a creole ideology already building justifications for independence. In Bogotá, Francisco José de CALDAS, in whose work resentment of creole dependence on European science was a constant theme, asserted that America was not in need of any second discovery by foreign expeditions.

In the area of technology and technical education, two first-class institutions emerged in eighteenth-century Mexico City. One was the Colegio de Minería, where mining engineers were trained by a gifted staff using the advanced European science and technology. The mineralogy professor, Andrés de Río, discovered vanadium and produced the first translation of Lavoisier in the New World. The other institution was the Casa de Moneda (mint), which became an important center for technological, particularly mechanical, innovation. Thus, by the end of the colonial period a foundation had been laid for scientific as well as political independence, a promise that the dislocation of the wars of independence completely frustrated.

The fate of science in colonial Brazil was largely determined by the absence of universities there. There were a few individual naturalists of high quality, such as the botanist José Mariano de Conceição Vellozo, a Linnaean, whose *Flora fluminensis,* a description of the flora of Rio de Janeiro province completed in 1790 (published in 1825), is considered the best representative of Enlightenment science in Brazil. An attempt to found a Brazilian university is associated with José Bonifácio ANDRADA E SILVA, a native of Santos who studied chemistry and mineralogy in Paris and Freiburg in the 1790s. His conception of science was highly utilitarian, for its core was the study of the mineral wealth of the vast nation.

THE INDEPENDENCE PERIOD

The keynote of the history of science in Latin American countries since independence is rebuilding. In the former countries of the Spanish Empire, science had been integrated into a tightly centralized institutional and economic system in which scientific communication within the empire was not encouraged and all information flowed to and from Madrid. This meant that when Madrid's patronage and tutelage were removed, the infrastructure that had supported scientific achievement in Mexico, Colombia, and Peru disappeared. So did many of the practitioners of Enlightenment science—either killed in the revolutionary upheaval (as in Colombia) or co-opted by the new state bureaucracies (as in Peru). Brazil was spared such an upheaval but began from a lower level of science. In the eighteenth century, science there had been as much (or even more) centered on the mother country than had that of its neighbors.

Then, too, creole elites, which before independence had seen science as a symbol of intellectual and political freedom, set their sights on the more pressing problem of maintaining and consolidating power in the new nations. If the military was the surest road to success, then parents would not encourage their children to take up scholarly careers. Medicine, military engineering, surveying, and a few other fields for which there was constant demand, constituted exceptions.

Science, therefore, may be pictured as having taken refuge in the most proximate fields available in these years of severe deinstitutionalization: during the first half of the nineteenth century, biology was cultivated by medical doctors; mathematics and physics, by military engineers.

The fate of colonial scientific institutions is exemplified by the Royal College of Mining in Mexico City and the Astronomical Observatory of Bogotá: both lingered on in impoverished conditions after independence. The former was officially abolished in 1833 and reorganized as a general science faculty; the latter suffered long periods of inactivity, notably between 1851 and 1858, after the death of the director, F. J. Matiz, the last survivor of Mutis's expedition. Brazil fared better than the Spanish viceroyalties during the first half of the nineteenth century owing to the foundation in 1810 of a central technical institution, the Royal Military Academy, which had a rigorous four-year course of mathematics that preceded military training.

The second half of the century was marked by the introduction of positivist philosophy and a general movement of institutionalization, particularly of applied sciences. POSITIVISM describes the followers of Auguste Comte and Herbert Spencer who developed philosophies of "positive" (that is, objective) knowledge that was supposed to replace outmoded forms of human thought, notably religion. In Europe, positivism was developed as a kind of philosophical synthesis of scientific method, based on secure knowledge and appreciation of the success of the scientific revolution. But Latin America was virtually untouched by the scientific revolution, so positivism there tended to be programmatic, and in Brazil, radical Comteans actually created a positivist religion. Important scientific institutions were founded in most Latin American countries in the second half of the century: in Brazil, the Polytechnic School was founded in 1874 in open imitation of the French engineering school of the same name; the following year the Mining School of Ouro Preto was established to train technicians to develop the country's ample mineral resources. Toward the end of the century, the Brazilian Ministry of Agriculture became a center of practical positivist programs in technology and applied sciences, including the Geological and Mineralogical Service and the Experimental Fuel and Mineral Station (1921); it even ran the old Imperial Observatory (created in 1827, active from 1845), which had an important meteorological section.

In Mexico, a number of important institutions were organized under the banner of positivism, including the National Preparatory School (1868), the Mexican Society of Natural History (1868), the Geographical and Exploring Commission (established in 1877 by the Darwinian industry minister, Vicente RIVA PALACIO), the Geological Commission, and the National Medical Institute (both in 1888). In Uruguay, under the regime of the positivist Lorenzo LATORRE, the entire educational system was controlled by positivists who overhauled the educational establishment from the primary grades through university, promoting positivist norms of science education.

Latin American science was noted for highly visible participation of foreigners, particularly Americans, in scientific enterprises, especially in geology. Thus in Brazil, the Imperial Geological Commission (1875–1877) was headed by Charles F. Hartt. His disciple Orville A. Derby was director of the Geographical and Geological Commission of the state of São Paulo from 1886 to 1906, when he resigned to head the making of the geological map of the state of Bahia. Derby was head of the Brazilian Geological and Mineralogical Service in 1906–1915 and trained a generation of Brazilian geologists. In Brazil, Peru, Chile, and elsewhere, the U.S. Geological Service provided a model for professional geology from the late nineteenth century well into the twentieth, particularly in the design and execution of geological maps and surveys of mineral resources.

As the practice of science revived, Latin Americans sought training abroad, with different disciplinary groups showing partiality for distinctive European traditions: thus, Brazilian engineers preferred to study in Belgium, Mexican chemists in Germany, Argentine mathematicians in Italy, and Mexicans in the United States.

Besides positivism, a number of important European scientific ideas had powerful repercussions in Latin America. Darwinism was widely debated in virtually all Latin American countries (Paraguay being the most prominent exception). In general, Comtean positivists opposed Darwinism, occasionally forming tenuous alliances with Catholics to defeat evolutionary ideas, while Spencerians supported it. However, in those countries where Comteans were strong (Brazil, Mexico, Venezuela), later generations of Spencerians introduced Darwin's ideas once the Comteans had left the educational stage. Thus in Brazil, the Polytechnic School, which had been a Comtean stronghold, became a focus of Darwinian discussion in the 1880s. In Mexico, Gabino BARREDA, the Comtean founder of the Preparatory School, was anti-Darwinian, whereas the next generation of positivists, led by Porfirio Parra, was evolutionist.

In some countries Darwinism became elevated to the rank of national ideology: in Brazil, Republican medical doctors, almost universally Darwinian, elaborated a Darwinian worldview mixed with polygenism, the notion that mankind emerged from several ancestral racial lines, a doctrine designed to support racial stratification. Argentine governments, for nationalist reasons, supported paleontologist Florentino AMEGHINO's claim that *Homo sapiens* had emerged in Argentina, making it the cradle of the human race. In Venezuela at the turn of the century, the positivist dictator Cipriano Castro financed the Darwinian anatomist Luis Razetti's materialist account of the nature of life as a way of supporting anti-Catholic policies.

In Uruguay, even cattlemen discussed Darwinism in the 1870s and 1880s. They divided into two factions who debated whether and how to improve the herds of creole cattle (the descendants of cattle brought by the Spanish in the sixteenth century). One group, comprising the wealthier cattlemen, wanted to cross creole cows with expensive Durham bulls imported from England. The other group, citing Darwin, claimed that natural selection had already acted on the creole herd, adapting it admirably to the local pastures.

Another European scientific idea with tremendous transcendence in late nineteenth-century Latin America was the germ theory of Louis Pasteur. In Paris, Pasteur had founded an institute where he imparted his views of epidemiology as well as the techniques according to which preventive serum could be produced. Numerous Latin Americans studied there, including the Brazilian Oswaldo CRUZ, who later founded a Pasteur-type institute at Manguinhos, near Rio de Janeiro, that developed into the premier biomedical research institute in Latin America during the first half of the twentieth century (OSWALDO CRUZ INSTITUTE). There Carlos CHAGAS solved the riddle of American sleeping sickness (trypanosomiasis) now called "Chagas' disease," and made it one of the most studied pathologies in the history of medicine. Other Pasteur-style institutes were founded in São Paulo, Caracas, Maracaibo, and Asunción, all before 1900.

Around 1900, yellow fever was the most urgent medical problem. As early as 1881 a Cuban, Carlos FINLAY, had identified the vector of disease, the mosquito *Aedes aegypti*, but the hypothesis was not confirmed until after the Spanish–American War of 1898, when the U.S. Public Health Service effectively wiped out the disease both in Cuba and in Panama. When the Rockefeller Foundation (RF) was established in 1913, it made the eradication of yellow fever a high priority, going so far as to have the Peruvian government name an RF doctor director of public health in 1919–1922.

Almost from its inception, the RF assumed an active role in the promotion of science in Latin America. It was opposed to what it called "didactic" science—that is, university science instruction that was limited to classroom lectures and textbooks and lacked a laboratory component. The RF also favored full-time teaching or research positions rather than the part-time positions standard in all Latin American universities, which had the effect of forcing scientists to support themselves with multiple jobs. Finally, the RF, seeking to "make the peaks higher," tried to identify the best scientific minds in the region and to support those persons. With these objectives in mind, the RF surveyed medical education in virtually all Latin American countries between 1916 and the late 1920s. Out of these reports emerged a roster of biomedical scientists that the RF supported over the next several decades, including the Argentine physiologist Bernardo HOUSSAY, who won the Nobel Prize in 1947 for research on the role of the pituitary gland in the metabolism of carbohydrates. Latin America's second

Nobel Prize was won in 1970 by a disciple of Houssay's, Luis LELOIR, for work on the biochemistry of carbohydrates. Thus the region's first two Nobel prizes were in part the result of the RF's support for research. In Peru, another group of physiologists led by Carlos Monge built a successful research program that concentrated on problems related to the high altitudes of the Andean region.

Classical genetics had an early introduction in Argentina where the rediscovery of Mendel's theories was recognized as early as 1908 by the biologist Angel Gallardo. At the University of La Plata, German-trained Miguel Hernández began teaching Mendelian genetics in 1915. Hernández trained Salomón Horovitz and Francisco Alberto Sáez, whose research centered on plant genetics and cytogenetics, respectively. Sáez was coauthor of a general cytology textbook that was widely adopted in the English-speaking world. Population genetics was introduced in Brazil by Theodosius Dobzhansky, a Russian-born biologist trained in the United States by Thomas Hunt Morgan. Dobzhansky had studied wild populations of the fruit fly *Drosophila* in temperate climates and came to Brazil to study a tropical population. In the fifteen years that Dobzhansky pursued Brazilian research (intermittently in 1943–1958), he trained a generation of geneticists in seminars held at the University of São Paulo (USP). This research was not only backed in large part by the RF; USP had been founded in part to meet RF specifications regarding full-time research and teaching appointments. Dobzhansky's group discovered that tropical populations of *Drosophila* display considerably more variation and genetic plasticity than their temperate cousins do, in response to the greater variety of ecological niches available in the tropics. The second generation of Dobzhansky's Brazilian students founded a strong group in human genetics that worked mainly with models derived from population genetics.

The third major scientific discipline in Latin America was physics. In the nineteenth century mathematics and physics throughout Latin America were as much as a century behind Europe. In order to raise the level of discipline quickly, the Argentine government contracted with a number of German professors to found a modern Institute of Physics at the University of La Plata in 1909. The institute's long-time director, Richard Gans, trained the first generations of Argentine physicists, including a group of relativists who worked with Albert Einstein during his Latin American visit in 1925. In Latin America, Einstein was viewed as a symbol of modernization, or rather the will to modernize, because, it was said, a country could not hope to modernize if its mathematicians and physicists could not master the theory of relativity. Inasmuch as Maxwellian physics had been scantily diffused in Argentina (and the other countries of the region), there was no entrenched scientific resistance to Einstein anywhere, except for a small group of Comtean mathematicians in Brazil. Einstein's trip stimulated an outpouring of books on relativity and a general public debate on the role of science in modern society, in the three countries—Argentina, Uruguay, and Brazil—he visited. In Argentina, two physicists trained at La Plata, Ramón Enrique Gaviola and Enrique Lodel, published papers on relativity in the 1920s.

In Brazil, Einstein's visit caused a debate in the Brazilian Academy of Sciences between relativists, led by the mathematician Manoel Amoroso Costa and the engineer Roberto MARINHO, and the Comtean mathematician Vicente Licínio Cardoso. An older generation of Comteans who rejected most of modern mathematics and physics still controlled the Academy; but the younger generation, with relativity as their battle cry, used Einstein's trip as the occasion to overthrow the positivists and take control.

Brazil became a leader in experimental physics after the arrival, in the 1930s, of the German Jewish refugee Bernard Gross and the Italo-Russian Gleb Wataghin. Gross's group, in Rio de Janeiro, and Wataghin's, in São Paulo, performed research on cosmic rays. Gross measured the intensity of cosmic rays in an ionization chamber, and his student Joaquim Costa Ribeiro discovered the thermodielectric effect in 1944. Wataghin's group studied cosmic ray showers and two of his disciples, Marcello Damy de Souza and Paulus Aulus Pompéia, discovered the penetrating or "hard" component of cosmic radiation. A third disciple, Mário Shenberg, collaborated with George Gamow on the neutrino theory of stellar collapse, and a fourth, Cesare Lattes was part of an international team that discovered the pi-meson (pion) at the Bolivian astrophysical laboratory at Chacaltaya in 1947.

Nuclear physics was introduced after World War II. In Brazil, Richard Feynman collaborated with José Leite Lopes on weak particle interactions, and the São Paulo group under Damy de Souza acquired a particle accelerator and worked on elementary particles. Argentine physics had a parallel history: first, cosmic radiation studies and then atomic physics. In 1949 Juan PERÓN hired a German physical chemist named Ronald Richter to perform experiments on nuclear fusion. Richter proved to be a charlatan who was able to fool Perón's generals by exploding hydrogen in a voltaic arc; but even though he was exposed, his laboratory at Bariloche became the center of advanced nuclear physics research, and cyclotrons purchased to support his group were used to train a new generation of physicists.

In Mexico, MIT-trained Manuel SANDOVAL VALLARTA (one of Feynman's professors, incidentally) introduced cosmic radiation studies, especially the effect of the Earth's magnetic field on the rays. Sandoval and some of his students also did research in theoretical physics and were especially interested in George Birkhoff's notion of gravitation in flat space-time, a relativistic model that avoided certain difficulties related to the curvilinear nature of Einstein's general theory.

By the 1940s there was sufficient scientific activity in Argentina, Brazil, Venezuela, Mexico, Uruguay, and a few other nations to stimulate scientists to organize themselves into self-consciously national scientific communities. Thus in 1948 the Brazilian Association for the Progress of Science was organized, in 1950 a similar association in Venezuela, and so forth. These societies viewed their roles as both professional and political. They wanted to stimulate a positive climate of public and governmental interest in science and pressed for the formation of national research councils, which were established in most Latin American countries between 1958 and 1979. These institutions all had similar objectives and helped channel government money into scientific projects. In spite of these efforts the scientifically advanced countries experienced severe "brain drains" from the 1950s through the 1970s. The 1966 Onganía coup in Argentina decimated the Faculty of Exact Sciences at the University of Buenos Aires, which lost 215 members. Entire research groups emigrated at the same time, mainly to Chile, Venezuela, and the United States. Mexico was one of the few Latin American countries that did not lose scientists in the 1960s because of the capacity of the National Autonomous University (UNAM) to absorb them.

The period since the late 1960s has also witnessed a general debate over the role of science in Latin American society. Of particular concern has been the issue of whether a developing country can afford to invest money in "pure" (that is, basic) science when it is desperately in need of utilitarian, practical projects that will aid in the country's modernization and improve its standard of living. According to DEPENDENCY THEORY, national science communities should concentrate on the specific social and economic needs of their country. Moreover, if the elites are content to import technology, then why have scientists at all? This mentality lay behind much of the impetus for scientists to emigrate. In fact, however, the debate was an oversimplification. Applied scientists soon discovered, or admitted, that they were unable to pursue complex projects without the aid of basic science. It was also realized that science, being international in nature (because of the way ideas circulate), cannot truly restrict itself to the national level, if it is to continue to be inventive and original.

Since the time of Perón, science and scientists have repeatedly fallen victim to the whims of authoritarian repressive regimens. In Brazil, soon after the military regime came to power in 1964, threats were directed at the Oswaldo Cruz Institute. Finally in 1970 ten researchers were fired by the government and the institute's research program severely compromised. In Argentina in 1978, a provincial governor attempted to outlaw the "new math," finding set theory to be subversive of Western values, at the same time that the generals in Buenos Aires were denouncing Freud and Einstein, along with Marx.

In spite of these problems, the scientific establishments continue to grow both in quality and quantity, not only in Brazil, Argentina, and Mexico but also in Colombia, Venezuela, Bolivia, Peru, and other countries that had lagged until midcentury. As economies improve and educational standards rise, the integration of Latin American science into the international science system is likely to accelerate.

On colonial science, see ARTHUR R. STEELE, *Flowers for the King: The Expedition of Ruiz and Pavón and the Flora of Peru* (1964); IRIS H. W. ENGSTRAND, *Spanish Scientists in the New World: The Eighteenth-Century Expeditions* (1981); ANTONELLO GERBI, *Nature in the New World from Christopher Columbus to Gonzalo Fernández de Oviedo* (1985); VIRGINIA GONZÁLEZ CLAVERÁN, *La expedición científica de Malaspina en Nueva España, 1789–1794* (1988); MANUEL SELLÉS, JOSÉ LUIS PESET, and ANTONIO LAFUENTE, eds., *Carlos III y la ciencia de la ilustración* (1988); JOSÉ LUIS PESET, ed., *Ciencia, vida y espacio en Iberoamérica* (1989); MARÍA PILAR DE SAN PÍO ALADRÉN, ed., *Mutis and the Royal Botanical Expedition of the Nuevo Reyno de Granada* (1992).

For a survey of science in twentieth-century Latin America, see THOMAS F. GLICK, "Science and Society in Twentieth-Century Latin America," in *The Cambridge History of Latin America*, vol. 6, pt. 1 (1993), 463–535. Single-country studies include SIMON SCHWARTZMAN, *A Space for Science: The Development of the Scientific Community in Brazil* (1991); JOSÉ BABINI, *Historia de la ciencia en la Argentina* (1986); COLCIENCIAS, *Historia social de la ciencia en Colombia*, 9 vols. (1993); ELI DE GORTARI, *La ciencia en la historia de México* (1963); ERNESTO YEPES, ed., *Estudios de historia de la ciencia en el Perú*, 2 vols. (1986); HEBE M. C. VESSURI, ed., *La ciencia académica en la Venezuela moderna* (1984).

THOMAS F. GLICK

See also **Astronomy; Diseases; Technology.**

SCLIAR, MOACYR (*b.* 23 March 1937), Brazilian author. Born in Pôrto Alegre, Rio Grande do Sul, Scliar studied medicine and has worked in the public health field for most of his life. As a fiction writer, he has published more than twenty books, including novels, collections of short stories, and chronicles. Many of his works have been translated into English and other languages. He has also written stories for children and short novels for young adults. A descendant of Russian JEWS, Scliar is internationally recognized as having raised Jewish consciousness in Latin American fiction, focusing on the Jewish immigrant in Brazil. Scliar's writings are characterized by a subtle irony; his short stories have been widely anthologized. He has received prestigious prizes for his fiction in Brazil and elsewhere, and is known as a gifted lecturer. Scliar's works include *O carnaval dos animais* (1968; *The Carnival of Animals*, 1985); *A guerra do Bom Fim* (1972); *O exército de um homem só* (1973); *Os deuses de Raquel* (1975; *The Gods of Raquel*, 1986); *O ciclo das águas* (1977); *Mês de cães danados* (1977); *O centauro no jardim* (1980; *The Centaur in the Garden*, 1985); *A estranha nação de Rafael Mendes* (1983; *The Strange Nation of Rafael Mendes*, 1988); and *Cenas da vida minúscula* (1991).

NORA GLICKMAN, "Os Voluntários: A Jewish-Brazilian Pilgrimage," in *Modern Jewish Studies* Annual 4 (1982); NELSON VIEIRA, "Judaic Fiction in Brazil: To Be and Not to Be Jewish," in *Latin American Literary Review* 14, no. 28 (July–December 1986): 31–45; ROBERT DI ANTONIO, "The Brazilianization of the Yiddishkeit Tradition," in *Latin American Literary Review* 17, no. 34 (July–December 1989): 40–51; GILDA SALEM SZKLO, *O bom fim do shtetl: Moacyr Scliar* (1990).

REGINA IGEL

SCOTT, WINFIELD (*b*. 13 June 1786; *d*. 29 May 1866),

U.S. army general who led the invasion and occupation of central Mexico in 1847. Scott ordered the largest amphibious landing yet attempted south of Veracruz on 9 March 1847. His troops thus avoided the fortress of San Juan de Ulúa guarding the harbor. Scott ordered his artillery to surround and bombard the city, ignoring the pleas of foreign diplomats to allow women, children, and other noncombatants to escape. He would accept no truce without unconditional surrender. By the time the city surrendered on 27 March, there were twice as many civilian as military casualties.

After Scott's army outmaneuvered General SANTA ANNA's troops at CERRO GORDO, the city of Puebla surrendered without opposition. The defense of Mexico City was poorly coordinated, but soldiers under Pedro María ANAYA at Churubusco and young cadets defending Chapultepec fought valiantly. During the occupation of Mexico City, civilians threw stones and sniped at U.S. troops until Scott threatened to turn his artillery on the city. Word of the destruction of Veracruz was so widespread that the disturbances stopped. The Duke of Wellington considered Scott's campaign against Mexico City the most brilliant in modern warfare.

The Whig Party, which had opposed the war with Mexico, chose Scott as its candidate for president in the election of 1852, but he lost to the Democratic candidate, Franklin Pierce. Scott was later general-in-chief under President Abraham Lincoln. He is buried at West Point.

CHARLES L. DUFOUR, *The Mexican War: A Compact History* (1968); K. JACK BAUER, *The Mexican War, 1846–1848* (1974); JOHN S. D. EISENHOWER, *So Far from God: The U.S. War with Mexico, 1846–1848* (1989).

D. F. STEVENS

See also **Mexican–American War.**

SEBASTIAN (SEBASTIÃO) OF PORTUGAL (*b*. 20

January 1554; *d*. 4 August 1578), king of Portugal. CAMÕES called him "the well-born hope" of the Portuguese; his nation remembers him as "O Desejado," the Desired One; yet Sebastian also became a symbol of the disgrace the Portuguese dreaded most: loss of their independence.

Sebastian succeeded his grandfather, Dom JOÃO III of Portugal, in 1557, and assumed his powers as ruler in 1568. Educated by the Jesuits, Sebastian had acquired a taste for religion; had developed the belief that he was to be Christ's soldier; and had dedicated himself to the goal of leading a crusade to rid North Africa of the Muslims. A succession dispute in Morocco that pitted Abd-al-Malik against his nephew Sultan Al-Mutawakki provided Sebastian with the pretext for launching his crusade. After collecting a force of Portuguese, Spanish, German, and Italian mercenaries, Sebastian invaded North Africa in June 1578. On 4 August, at Al-Ksar-al-Kabir in Morocco, in what became known as the Battle of the Three Kings, Sebastian's army was crushed by a vastly superior Moroccan force. During this battle, three "kings" lost their lives: Al-Mutawakki, Abd-al-Malik, and Sebastian. Sebastian was childless; after his death the Portuguese crown passed to his aged great-uncle, Cardinal Henry, the last monarch of the house of Aviz. After Henry died in 1580, the crown passed to PHILIP II OF SPAIN, who was acclaimed king of Portugal in 1581; Portugal did not regain its independence until 1640.

The death of King Sebastian left a vacuum in the Portuguese soul that was filled by the illusion that the king was not really dead and that he would return to claim his throne and initiate a new golden age. "Sebastianismo" is the longing for the return of King Sebastian, a longing that crossed the ocean to Brazil and became part of that country's popular culture.

JOSÉ MARIA DE QUEIRÓS VELOSO, *D. Sebastiao, 1554–1578* (1945); JOSÉ TIMÓTEO MONTALVÃO MACHADO, *Causas da morte dos reis portugueses* (1974); JOAQUIM VERISSIMO SERRÃO, *História de Portugal*, 12 vols. (1978–1990); A. H. DE OLIVEIRA MARQUES, *História de Portugal*, 3 vols. (1981–1983); M. EL FASI, "Morocco," in *Africa from the Sixteenth to the Eighteenth Century*, edited by B. A. Ogot, vol. 5 of the *UNESCO General History of Africa* (1992).

TOMÉ N. MBUIA JOÃO

See also **Sebastianismo.**

SEBASTIANISMO, the popular beliefs surrounding the figure of the Portuguese king Sebastian (1557–1578). Even before his birth, Sebastian was heralded as *o Encoberto*, "the hidden-one," the mythical ruler who was to establish a powerful Portuguese empire. The popular reinterpretation of an apocalyptic poem, the "Trovas do Bandarra," confirmed his divine commission. The dismal outcome of his reign—his untimely death in battle, the failure of his troops to recover his body, and the loss of the Portuguese throne to the Spanish in 1580—gave rise to Sebastianist legends in Portugal and later Brazil. While some claimed that he had merely vanished to perform penances for his failures, and others that he had died but would be resurrected, supporters agreed that Sebastian would yet inaugurate the *Quinto Império*, or Fifth Empire.

Reports of his return began soon after his death, and at least four claimants appeared between 1580 and 1610. Portuguese folktales still eulogize their lost leader. Brazilian Sebastianists connected the legends with their New World experiences, and three messianic movements, in 1817, the 1830s, and the 1890s, linked their rebellions to the long-awaited king. Predictions of his return (in the year 2000) still recur in songs and popular publications.

JOÃO LÚCIO DE AZEVEDO, *A evolução do sebastianismo*, 2d ed. (1947); MARY ELIZABETH BROOKS, *A King for Portugal* (1964); ANTÓNIO MACHADO PIRES, *D. Sebastião e o Encoberto* (1971); CAROLE A. MYSCOFSKI, "Messianic Themes in Portuguese and Brazilian Literature in the Sixteenth and Seventeenth Centuries," in *Luso-Brazilian Review* 28 (1991): 77–94.

CAROLE A. MYSCOFSKI

See also **Messianic Movements: Brazil.**

SECHÍN ALTO, a large complex of sites located in the Casma Valley on the north-central coast of Peru. The complex, probably once the center of a larger polity, covers 4.2 square miles and consists of four sites: Sechín Alto proper, Sechín Bajo, Taukachi-Konkán, and Cerro Sechín. The group of sites dates between 1900 B.C. and 1200 B.C. All construction at the sites is stone set in mud mortar.

The main mound at Sechín Alto is the largest monumental construction for its time period in the New World, measuring 990 feet by 825 feet by 145 feet tall. Off its front face is a series of four rectangular plazas that extend 4,620 feet to the northeast. Within these rectangular plazas are three sunken circular courts. The mound and its associated plazas and courts were probably used for a variety of public ceremonial activities.

Sechín Bajo and Taukachi-Konkán contain numerous mounds, plazas, and circular courts. Some of these structures may have been used as warehouses to store commodities or as administrative buildings to monitor the movement of goods in and out of the complex. This would be a situation similar to that documented for the site of PAMPA DE LAS LLAMAS-MOXEKE, located only a few miles to the south.

Cerro Sechín is the best known of the four sites that comprise the Sechín Alto complex. Extensive excavation there has revealed a moderate-sized square building, some 175 feet on a side, that is decorated on all four exterior faces with carved stones set in mud mortar. The stones, carved in a simple, realistic style, depict the results of a military engagement in which warrior figures, holding large clubs or axes, stand triumphantly over victims who have been decapitated or whose bodies have been cut into various pieces.

SHELIA POZORSKI and THOMAS POZORSKI, *Early Settlement and Subsistence in the Casma Valley, Peru* (1987); SHELIA POZORSKI, "Theocracy vs. Militarism: The Significance of the Casma Valley in Understanding Early State Formation," in *The Origins and Development of the Andean State,* edited by Jonathan Haas et al. (1987), pp. 15–30.

SHELIA POZORSKI
THOMAS POZORSKI

SEDEÑO, ANTONIO DE (*d.* 1539), conquistador of Tierra Firme, *adelantado* of Trinidad. In 1531 Sedeño, a *contador* of San Juan, Puerto Rico, was granted the title of ADELANTADO for the island of Trinidad. Sedeño's original assault of the island with eighty men was repulsed by hostile ARAWAKS. In spite of the tenacity of the island's native population, a second attempt by Sedeño to conquer the island proved successful. Drawn to the wealth of the South American mainland, Sedeño proceeded to the Gulf of Paria, where he competed with Jerónimo de Alderete and Martín Nieto for conquest of the coastal region in open rebellion of the legitimate governor, Jerónimo de Ortal. The Audiencia of Santo Domingo sent its *fiscal* Juan de Frías to bring Sedeño to trial, but Sedeño captured the royal official and proceeded inland along the Orinoco River. During his escape, Sedeño was poisoned by one of his own men.

PIERRE G. L. BORDE, *The History of Trinidad Under Spanish Government,* vol. 1, translated by James Alva Bain (1982), esp. pp. 92–124; MICHAEL ANTHONY, *First in Trinidad* (1985), pp. 5–7; JOSÉ DE OVIEDO Y BAÑOS, *The Conquest and Settlement of Venezuela,* translated by Jeannette Johnson Varner (1987), esp. pp. 59–60.

MICHAEL A. POLUSHIN

SEGALL, LASAR (*b.* 1891; *d.* 2 August 1957), Brazilian painter considered the pioneer of expressionism in Brazil. Born in Vilna, Lithuania, Segall moved to Berlin at the age of fifteen and studied at the Imperial Academy of Fine Arts from 1907 to 1909, the year he was expelled for participating in the Freie Sezession, an exhibition by artists opposed to official aesthetics. In 1910 he moved to Dresden to study at the Meisterschüle (Art Academy). A year later he joined the German expressionist movement, and in 1912 made his first trip to Brazil.

In Brazil from 1912 to 1914, Segall prompted controversy over expressionism when his work was displayed in 1913 at solo exhibitions in São Paulo and Campinas. In 1923 he returned to Brazil and became a citizen. His paintings of Brazilian themes (1923–1926) were exhibited in 1926 in Dresden, Stuttgart, and Berlin. From 1928 to 1932 he lived in Paris. Segall returned once again to Brazil in 1932, when he cofounded the São Paulo Society of Modern Art.

In 1935, Segall completed a series of Campos de Jordão landscape paintings of Brazil and his *Portraits of Lucy* series. From 1936 to 1950, he produced paintings like *Concentration Camp* (1945) that focused on such social themes as the suffering and plight of Jews in Europe. He also participated in the Brazilian People's Graphics Workshop, a collective work center for artists founded first in Mexico in 1937, producing a series of linocut and woodcut prints published in an album entitled *Mangue* (1944), in which he depicted the theme of prostitution. In 1938, he represented Brazil at the International Congress of Independent Arts (Paris) and had a solo exhibition at the Renou et Colle Gallery in Paris. In the 1940s, his work was exhibited in New York and Rio de Janeiro, and in 1951 and 1953, he had special exhibitions at the São Paulo Biennial. He died in São Paulo.

PIETRO MARIA BARDI, *Lasar Segall* (1959); LEOPOLDO CASTEDO, *A History of Latin American Art and Architecture* (1969); GILBERT CHASE, *Contemporary Art in Latin America* (1970); CARLOS LEMOS, *The Art of Brazil* (1983); DAWN ADES, *Art in Latin America* (1989).

MARY JO MILES

SEGUÍN, JUAN JOSÉ MARÍA ERASMO (*b.* 26 May 1782; *d.* 30 October 1857), TEXAS political figure. A merchant, farmer, and rancher, Seguín served as San Antonio postmaster and held other municipal posts in the 1810s and 1820s. During the Mexican War of Independence he apparently remained loyal to Spain.

Seguín undertook special assignments for the government. In 1821 the governor of Texas sent him to inform Moses AUSTIN of approval of the latter's colonization plan. Elected Texas representative to the Constituent Congress of 1823–1824, Seguín spent much time in Mexico City advocating Anglo immigration to Texas.

Closely identified with the Anglos, Seguín was removed from government office at the outbreak of the Texas rebellion in 1835. Following the war he served briefly as county judge. He soon retired to rebuild his farm and ranch, where he died.

JESÚS F. DE LA TEJA, ed., *A Revolution Remembered: The Memoirs and Selected Correspondence of Juan N. Seguín* (1991).

JESÚS F. DE LA TEJA

SEGUÍN, JUAN NEPOMUCENO (*b.* 27 October 1806; *d.* 27 August 1890), TEXAS political and military figure. Son of the politically prominent Erasmo Seguín, he served in a number of political posts between 1829 and 1835, including *alcalde* and interim *jefe político* in 1834. Like his father, he was a strong supporter of Anglo settlement.

Seguín, a federalist, involved himself in the 1834–1835 dispute with the centralists over control of the state government. At the outbreak of the Texas revolt, he was commissioned a captain of the Texas forces, and he led the only Mexican-Texan company at the Battle of SAN JACINTO, 21 April 1836. In the late 1830s Seguín served as senator from Bexar County in the Texas Congress and as mayor of San Antonio.

Compromised by political enemies in early 1842, Seguín was forced to flee to Mexico, where he apparently was given a choice of joining the army or going to prison. He participated in General Adrián Woll's invasion of Texas later that year and remained in the Mexican service through the end of the MEXICAN-AMERICAN WAR. He subsequently returned to San Antonio, and again entered politics in the 1850s, serving as a justice of the peace and as one of the founders of the Bexar County Democratic Party. Increasingly alienated by conditions in Texas, Seguín took his family to Nuevo Laredo, Mexico, where he lived with one of his sons until his death.

IDA VERNON, "Activities of the Seguíns in Early Texas History," in *West Texas Historical Association Year Book* 25 (1949): 11–38; JESÚS F. DE LA TEJA, ed., *A Revolution Remembered: The Memoirs and Selected Correspondence of Juan N. Seguín* (1991).

JESÚS F. DE LA TEJA

SEIBAL, Maya archaeological site located at the great bend of the Pasión River, near the southwestern corner of Guatemala's Petén rain forest. Extensive investigations by Harvard University archaeologists from 1964 to 1968 revealed an occupation history of approximately 2,000 years, considerably older and longer than that of most Maya sites. The site's initial occupation during the Xe phase (900–600 B.C.) of the early Middle Preclassic period is represented by distinctive ceramics and the remains of simple houses. The emergence of an incipient sociopolitical hierarchy (600–300 B.C.), reflected in the construction of small public works, was followed during the Late Preclassic (300 B.C.–A.D. 150) by dramatic population increases and the construction of imposing public structures, when the Seibal people developed many of the hallmarks of Maya civilization (monumental architecture, hieroglyphic inscriptions, elaborate pottery). This era of florescence was interrupted by an abrupt 150-year "hiatus" (A.D. 450–600), when the site was largely abandoned.

During the Late Classic period (A.D. 600–771) Seibal reemerged as a powerful political center, a process halted in November 735, when Ruler 3 of the PETEXBATÚN polity, centered at the nearby site of DOS PILAS, captured the Seibal ruler Yich'ak Balam, or "Jaguar Paw," and killed him. When the Petexbatún polity broke apart during the mid-eighth century, the newly independent Seibal enjoyed unprecedented prosperity. Between A.D. 771 and 950, after Maya civilization collapsed and most Maya centers were abandoned, Seibal thrived under the rulership of probable outsiders, sometimes identified as Putun Maya invaders, whose presence is marked by fine paste pottery, an art style not fully in the Classic Maya tradition, and by distinctive skeletal attributes. Yet the Maya collapse isolated Seibal politically and economically, and sometime in the late eleventh century the site was abandoned.

RICHARD E. W. ADAMS, "Maya Collapse: Transformation and Termination in the Ceramic Sequence at Altar de Sacrificios," in *The Classic Maya Collapse,* edited by T. Patrick Culbert (1973), pp. 133–163; JEREMY A. SABLOFF, *Excavations at Seibal, Department of Petén, Guatemala: Ceramics* (Memoirs of the Peabody Museum, Harvard University, 1975) vol. 13, no. 2; GORDON R. WILLEY, "The Rise of Classic Maya Civilization: A Pasión Valley Perspective," in *The Origins of Maya Civilization,* edited by Richard E. W. Adams (1977), pp. 133–157; GORDON R. WILLEY, ed., "General Summary and Conclusions," *Excavations at Seibal, Department of Petén, Guatemala* (Memoirs of the Peabody Museum, Harvard University, 1990), vol. 17, no. 4, pp. 175–276.

KEVIN JOHNSTON

See also **Achaeology; Mayas.**

SELK'NAMS (also referred to as ONAS), indigenous inhabitants of the northern and eastern regions of Tierra del Fuego. The first recorded sightings of the Selk'nams indicate that they occupied the northern steppes and southern forests of the island of Tierra del Fuego, surviving on the fruits of the hunt for GUANACO, rodents, and other small mammals, as well as wild fruits, mushrooms, and mollusks gathered along the coasts. The archeological record leads anthropologists to suggest that Selk'nam occupation of Tierra del Fuego predates the separation of the island from the continent more than 11,000 years ago.

Terrestrial hunters and gatherers arrived in the Patagonian region by land during the Paleoindian phase (ca. 9000 B.C.), when the climactic conditions of the last Pleistocene glaciation permitted. They hunted the now extinct American horse and mylodon, as well as guanaco, puma, fox, rodents, and nandu (rhea). Between 8,500 and 6,000 years ago, during the temperate Altithermal epoch, they began to employ more specialized tools, including spears and *boleadoras,* as well as the bow and arrow.

About 5,000 to 4,500 years ago, when the Altithermal period ended and the Neoglacial period began, less favorable climatic conditions precipitated cultural changes. The wider demographic distribution and more numerous groups of hunters in the region encouraged more intensive exploitation of specific ecological zones to hunt and gather the different species available. Around A.D. 1000, the separation, both geographically as well as culturally, of the Selk'nams from the TEHUELCHES was complete.

The Selk'nams subsisted on hunting (by foot) and gathering (exclusive of maritime navigation), although they did take advantage of sources of coastal shellfish and the bounty provided by beached whales and other large sea creatures. The Selk'nams in the northern regions of the island specialized in the hunt of guanaco and rodents; those in the southeast hunted marine animals off the rocky coast; and those in the south hunted guanaco. Organized in small family groups with defined territorial limits, the northern Selk'nams found shelter around fires in lean-tos constructed from posts and skins, while their relatives in the colder southern regions lived in conical huts reinforced with earth as protection from the bitingly cold winds. Each local group claimed specific hunting territories and respected the rights of others.

Early European expeditioners commented on the notable lack of protective clothing, apart from occasional skin mantles (constructed to leave the right shoulder free) with the fur on the outside. While some anthropologists note a similarity between Selk'nam ceremonial and familial structures and those of the maritime Fuegian peoples (ALAKALUFS or YAMANAS), their exclusively terrestrial orientation as well as linguistic similarity support a stronger relationship to the Tehuelches or PATAGONES of continental Patagonia.

When colonization of Tierra del Fuego began in the late nineteenth century, the Selk'nams numbered around 4,000; as of 1990 fewer than 50—some say only 2—of their descendants remained as a result of massive deportations, sport hunting, massacres, diseases, and other little-studied factors.

OSVALDO SILVA G., *Culturas y pueblos de Chile prehispano* (1980); ANNE CHAPMAN, *Drama and Power in a Hunting Society: The Selk'nam of Tierra del Fuego* (1982) and *Los Selk'nam: La vida de los Ona* (1986); MUSEO CHILENO DE ARTE PRECOLOMBINO, *Hombres del sur: Aonikenk, Selknam, Yamana, Kaweshkar* (1987).

KRISTINE L. JONES

SELVA (ECUADOR), the forest regions of Ecuador. The *selva* of the coast has long been of great economic importance to Ecuador. In the early national period the *selvas* were open public zones in which mixed-blood freemen, known in Ecuador as *montuvios* (part Indian, African, and European), collected a variety of wild plants: *tagua* (vegetable ivory), *paja* (straw, used for weaving "Panama hats"), rubber, quinine, and cinnamon. In the late nineteenth century, great CACAO estates appeared on the open lands. The labor force gravitated to cacao production, and the export of wild forest products all but ceased.

Details on Ecuador's geography can be found in PRESTON JAMES, *Latin America* (1986). For information on the natives of Ecuador's *selvas,* see *Handbook of South American Indians,* vol. 2, *The Andean Civilizations,* edited by Julian H. Steward (1963).

RONN F. PINEO

SELVA (PERU), one of the three principal geographic regions of Peru, with the costa and sierra. The selva, or tropical rain forest, is located east of the Andes in an area that comprises fully two thirds of the country's total landmass, but contains only 11 percent of the population. Most of its cultivatable land and population is located in the *ceja de montaña* (eyebrow of the jungle), a subregion of broad tropical valleys along the eastern Andean foot-

Selva in Peru. INSTITUTO AUDIO-VISUAL INKA, CUZCO.

hills. Although sparsely populated, mostly by Amerindians, the selva has long loomed large in the imagination of policymakers, who historically envisioned its resources and vast space as a potential panacea for resolving the nation's chronic underdevelopment.

PETER F. KLARÉN

SEMANA DE ARTE MODERNA. *See* **Modern Art Week.**

SEMANA ROJA, a riot which swept Santiago, Chile, from 22 to 25 October 1905. Upset by the high price of food, a mass of Santiago's poorer urban residents demonstrated to demand that the government rescind an import tax on Argentine meat. Some of the protestors, who had initially behaved peacefully, became unruly. When various demonstrators began to loot, the local authorities overreacted by opening fire and charging the crowds. It soon became clear that the police could not calm the situation. With the army away on maneuvers, Santiago's officials created a ''white guard,'' consisting of members of the upper class and some of the foreign community, who brutally repressed the demonstrators until the army could return and restore order. Although this riot should have forced the upper class to recognize that it had to address the needs of the lower classes, the elites instead tended to blame the demonstration on foreigners, anarchists, and unspecified troublemakers. Conversely, the riot galvanized the working class and encouraged the formation of unions.

GONZALO IZQUIERDO, ''Octubre de 1905: Un episodio en la historia chilena,'' in *Historia* 13 (1976): 55–96; PETER DE SHAZO, *Urban Workers and Labor Unions in Chile 1902–1927* (1983), pp. 124–126.

WILLIAM F. SATER

SEMANA TRÁGICA, a period of labor unrest that shook Argentina in early January 1919. The Semana Trágica (Tragic Week) was the result of a conflict that had been brewing for quite some time. Since the Radicals had come to power in 1916, they had been courting labor for its support. This courtship created resentment among conservative and business circles. Employers were allied against the Radicals' labor policies and in 1918 even created a strikebreaking body called the Asociación Nacional de Trabajo. Discontent among workers increased in part also as a result of the poor economic situation after World War I.

The problems began outside the metallurgical plant of Talleres Metalúrgicos Pedro Vasena, where workers had been on strike since 2 December 1918. At 4:00 P.M. on 7 January, as a truck under armed guard made its way into the plant, shots were fired, and a confrontation took place between security forces and strikers. Two hours later four people were dead, and thirty were wounded. Two days later a general strike was called by FORA IX (Federación Obrera Regional Argentina) in solidarity with the metallurgical workers. The workers took to the streets very early, and clashes with security forces soon ensued, such as the one that began in a cemetery at the burial of one of the victims of the fight-

Streets of Buenos Aires during "Tragic Week," 7–14 January 1919. ARCHIVO GENERAL DE LA NACIÓN, BUENOS AIRES.

ing on 7 January. Many were killed. In desperation, President Hipólito YRIGOYEN called in the army to restore order, perhaps the first time the army had been used to quell social unrest. Thousands were arrested. After the strike was crushed, civilian vigilante groups patrolled the streets for several days in a sort of witch hunt against those suspected of having instigated the strike. Among their targets were Russian Jews, who were accused of planning a Communist uprising. There are no definite figures as to the casualties. Government sources put the figures at about forty dead and several hundred wounded. On the other hand, labor sources put the death toll at over 100. The strike reflected the long-standing antagonism between labor and business.

JULIO GODIO, *La Semana Trágica de enero de 1919* (1972); EDGARDO J. BILSKY, *La Semana Trágica* (1981); ENRIQUE DÍAZ ARAUJO, *La Semana Trágica de 1919: Precedida de un estudio de los antecedentes de la inmigración y la rebelión social*, 2 vols. (1988).

JUAN MANUEL PÉREZ

SENADO DA CÂMARA, town council. In colonial Brazil municipal government was in the hands of the *senado da câmara*. Elected by the propertied men of status (*homens bons*), it was the smallest and most independent unit of local self-government. Similar to the Spanish *cabildo*, it was an arena where local elites fought with the Portuguese-born royal officials for control of local affairs. The first town councillors (*vereadores*) were chosen by the governor rather than elected by the people. Even when elected, the number of electors was restricted to local propertied elites and landowners. The town council was composed of the following: a president or presiding judge, an ordinary judge or a crown judge, two justices of the peace (*juiz de paz*), three aldermen (*verea-*

dores*), and one procurator (*procurador*). The ordinary judge (*juiz ordinário*) was elected by the other councillors, but the crown judge (*juiz de fora*) was sent by the crown. The justices of the peace, aldermen, and procurators were elected once every three years by an indirect system of election, whereby local electors composed of propertied men drew up names of qualified candidates.

The town council was in charge of local justice, land disputes, and implementation of royal laws and collection of municipal taxes. The *senado da câmara* had its seat in a town or city but exercised jurisdiction over the county. The town council met in session twice weekly every Wednesday and Saturday. It had its own source of revenue and patrimony independent of public funds or the royal treasury. Rent on land and local taxes were its chief sources of income.

In important cities like São Luís de Maranhão, Rio de Janeiro, and Salvador, the town councils challenged the governor's power and succeeded in having him removed from office. During the colonial period, the town councils increased their power and independence. In emergencies the *senado da câmara* was responsible for calling upon the people to meet together to draw up local bylaws and rule on cases of petty theft, land disputes, verbal abuse, and disputes over rights of way. The crown judges meddled in municipal affairs by confirming appointments to the local *senado da câmara*. The crown judge decided who was eligible for local office, and attended council meetings and special sessions. The governors also intervened in municipal affairs by controlling nominations to government office, extending terms of office, and initiating public works.

The town councils acted as local executive agents of the government by enforcing royal laws, thus functioning as an agency of the central government. Although the governors held the town councillors responsible for the execution of their written orders, the town council was also responsible to the local elite interests for transmitting their complaints to the higher authorities. Municipal government survived the colonial period and was actively involved in the independence movement.

CHARLES R. BOXER, *Portuguese Society in the Tropics: The Municipal Councils of Goa, Macao, Bahia, and Luanda, 1510–1800* (1965); CAIO PRADO, JR., *The Colonial Background of Modern Brazil* (1971).

PATRICIA MULVEY

SENDERO LUMINOSO. *See* **Peru: Revolutionary Movements: Shining Path.**

SENDIC, RAÚL (*b.* 1925; *d.* 28 April 1989), Uruguayan politician and guerrilla leader. As a prominent young socialist, Sendic worked as a legal adviser for rural labor unions in the northern region of Uruguay during the late 1950s. In 1961, he participated in the foundation of the sugarcane workers' union. Due to the lack of response from political institutions to the workers' request for land distribution, Sendic became disappointed with legal procedures as a means to achieve social justice. Starting in 1962, Sendic and other members of the Uruguayan left formed the National Liberation Movement, TUPAMAROS, one of Latin America's most important urban guerrilla organizations. As a Tupamaro leader, Sendic was captured in December 1964, released, and captured again in 1970. In September 1971 he escaped in a massive jail break. In September 1972, Sendic was shot in the face and captured and the Tupamaros were destroyed by the armed forces. For twelve years Sendic was imprisoned and tortured at various military units. In 1985 Sendic and other Tupamaro leaders were freed by an amnesty granted by the new democratic government. After 1985, Sendic remained a leader of the Tupamaros, as they reentered the political arena on peaceful and legal terms. As a consequence of his torture, Sendic became sick with Charcot's disease and died in France in 1989. While in prison he wrote *Cartes desde la prisión* (1984) and *Reflexiones sobre política económica: Apuntes desde la prisión* (1984).

ARTURO C. PORZECANSKI, *Uruguay's Tupamaros: The Urban Guerrilla* (1973); and LUIS COSTA BONINO, *Crisis de los partidos tradicionales y movimiento revolucionario en el Uruguay* (1985).

ASTRID ARRARÁ

See also **Guerrilla Movements.**

SENZALA, the slave quarters on Brazilian plantations during the colonial period and the Empire. Typically a long, one-story building, the *senzala* was divided into a series of separate units, each housing four or five indi-

vidual slaves or an entire slave family. The *senzala* frequently formed one side of a rectangular compound of buildings that included workshops, a waterwheel or mill, storage sheds, and even the CASA GRANDE of the plantation owner. In this way, the planter or his foreman could readily observe slaves and their daily comings and goings; proximity made clandestine activity or flight more difficult. On large plantations on which a single *senzala* could not house all the slaves, additional slave quarters were built outside but near the central compound. Some descriptions indicate that many slaves were housed dormitory-style, with single women and men separately housed in two large rooms. One practical nineteenth-century coffee planter urged building a veranda the length of the *senzala* so that slaves could visit one another in rainy weather without getting soaked and risking illness.

FRANCISCO PEIXOTO DE LACERDA WERNECK, *Memória sobre a fundação de uma fazenda na província do Rio de Janeiro*, edited by Eduardo Silva (1847; 1985); STUART B. SCHWARTZ, *Sugar Plantations in the Formation of Brazilian Society: Bahia, 1550–1835* (1985), esp. pp. 135–136; STANLEY J. STEIN, *Vassouras: A Brazilian Coffee Country, 1850–1900* (1985).

SANDRA LAUDERDALE GRAHAM

SEOANE, MANUEL (*b.* 1900; *d.* 10 September 1963), Peruvian journalist, author, and politician, one of the most conspicuous leaders of the Aprista Party. Born in Lima, Seoane was educated in a Jesuit school and at San Marcos University. In 1922 he was elected vice president of the Student Federation led by Víctor Raúl HAYA DE LA TORRE. In 1924, President Augusto B. LEGUÍA deported Seoane to Buenos Aires, where he engaged in journalism. After the fall of Leguía, Seoane returned to Lima to found the newspaper *La Tribuna* and to activate the Aprista political campaign for the 1931 elections. Elected deputy for the Constituent Assembly, he was forced into exile by President Luis M. SÁNCHEZ CERRO in 1932.

Seoane lived mostly in exile until 1945, when he was elected senator for Lima and vice president of the Chamber of Senators. General Manuel ODRÍA exiled him again after the 1948 coup against President BUSTAMANTE Y RIVERO, who had governed with initial Aprista support. Although Seoane criticized Haya on several ideological and political points in 1954 and 1957, he participated once more as first vice-presidential candidate in the nullified elections of 1962. Retired from politics, he died in Washington, D.C., while working for the ALLIANCE FOR PROGRESS.

MANUEL SEOANE, *Nuestros fines* (1931); FREDERICK PIKE, *The Politics of the Miraculous in Peru: Haya de la Torre and the Spiritualist Tradition* (1986).

ALFONSO W. QUIROZ

See also **Peru: Political Parties.**

SEPP, ANTON (*b*. 21 November 1655; *d*. 13 January 1733), Tyrolean-born Jesuit active in the MISSIONS of Paraguay. Of noble birth, Sepp dedicated himself early to various scholarly pursuits. For a time, he taught rhetoric at Augsburg. Then, in 1674, he entered the Society of Jesus, hoping to be sent to missionary fields in South America. Being a non-Spaniard, however, Sepp encountered many obstacles in securing permission to travel in the New World. Only in 1690 was permission finally granted.

A cloud of unwarranted suspicion followed Sepp throughout his labors. He spent forty-one years in the JESUIT *reducciones* of Paraguay, yet he never held high office, nor was his ordination as priest ever confirmed. Still, he had a claim on being the most important cleric in the lives of thousands of GUARANI Indians. His talent and energy seemed boundless. He founded one major mission, San Juan Bautista, in 1698. He designed buildings for several more missions, and organized workshops for the manufacture of musical instruments. He wrote poetry, sermons, and musical compositions that became well known in the region. The schools that he operated at Yapeyú gave the Indians access to many aspects of Western culture. The Indians, in turn, made the Jesuit missions so prosperous and so famous that Voltaire later described them as a sort of Utopia in his classic, *Candide.*

Sepp's own role in giving life to this image was revealed in a series of copious letters he wrote to European relatives. These were published in two volumes between 1696 and 1709, and still constitute a key source for historians studying the Jesuit missions. Sepp died at San José, in what later became the Argentine Misiones.

EFRAÍM CARDOZO, *Historiografía paraguaya* (1959), pp. 263–270; PHILIP CARAMAN, *The Lost Paradise* (1976), pp. 120–122, 134–136, 140–143, 150–155, and *passim.*

THOMAS L. WHIGHAM

SEPÚLVEDA, JUAN GINÉS DE (*b.* ca. 1490; *d.* 1573), Spanish humanist. "The most strident champion of Spanish imperialism," to quote Anthony Pagden, Sepúlveda translated Aristotle, supported the idea of universal monarchy, and wrote a number of works, including *Democrates alter* (or *secundus*, published 1780), which strongly defended the rights of the Castilian crown in the New World. He is best known for his opposition to the Dominican friar Bartolomé de LAS CASAS in "the Spanish struggle for justice" in the mid-sixteenth century. In contrast with Las Casas and the theologians of Salamanca, Sepúlveda believed that the Aristotelian doctrine of natural aristocracy and natural servitude justified the Spanish conquest of the Indies and wars against the native populations. He also believed that the conquest of the natives was an act of charity, for it brought them the benefits of civilization, religion, and trade with Spain. The colonists' exploitation of native labor, thus, was justified. Not surprisingly, the conquistadores and early settlers considered Sepúlveda their champion.

LEWIS HANKE, *All Mankind Is One: A Study of the Disputation Between Bartolomé de Las Casas and Juan Ginés de Sepúlveda in 1550 on the Intellectual and Religious Capacity of the American Indians* (1974); ANTHONY PAGDEN, *Spanish Imperialism and the Political Imagination: Studies in European and Spanish-American Social and Political Theory 1513–1830* (1990).

MARK A. BURKHOLDER

See also **Slavery.**

SEREBRIER, JOSÉ (*b.* 3 December 1938), Uruguayan composer and conductor. Of Russian and Polish descent, Serebrier was born in Montevideo, where he studied violin with Juan Fabbri. At Montevideo's Municipal School of Music his instructors were Miguel Pritsch (violin) and Vicente Ascone (harmony). He also took lessons in composition, fugue, and counterpoint with Guido Santórsola, and piano with Sarah Bourdillon. After attending counterpoint and composition classes at the National Conservatory with Carlos ESTRADA, he moved to the United States to enter the Curtis Institute in Philadelphia (1956), where he studied composition under Vittorio Giannini. He has resided in the United States ever since. Serebrier attended Aaron Copland's classes at Tanglewood, and Antal Dorati and Pierre Monteux coached him in conducting. Leopold Stokowski chose him, when he was only seventeen, to be associate conductor of the American Symphony Orchestra (1962–1967). He received scholarships and grants from the Organization of American States, and the Guggenheim, Rockefeller, and Koussevitsky foundations. Serebrier served as conductor of the Utica Symphony (1960–1962) and composer-in-residence with the Cleveland Orchestra (1968–1971). At eighteen Serebrier composed his *Leyenda de Fausto Overture*, which won the Uruguayan National Award. He experimented with mixed media, adding lighting to his works, as in *Colores mágicos*, premiered by him at the Fifth Inter-American Music Festival in Washington, D.C., in 1971. In his later works, he explored more advanced composition techniques.

Since 1989 Serebrier has conducted the Scottish Chamber Orchestra and frequently has been guest conductor of the Royal Philharmonic. Many of his compositions have been performed, among them Concerto for Violin and Orchestra (Winter), which premiered March 1994 in New York and which he later recorded with the Royal Philharmonic. In addition to his recordings, Serebrier also has numerous film scores to his credit. In 1984 he founded the Miami Music Festival. He is the recipient of the Alice Ditson Award for his achievements in contemporary music. He conducts and records frequently in the United States and London.

JOHN VINTON, ed., *Dictionary of Contemporary Music* (1974); *New Grove Dictionary of Music and Musicians* (1980); SUSAN SAL-

GADO, *Breve historia de la música culta en el Uruguay,* 2d ed. (1980).

SUSANA SALGADO

SEREGNI, LÍBER (*b.* 3 December 1917), Uruguayan military leader and politician. The son of an anarchist father, Seregni opted paradoxically for a military career and achieved the rank of general. Toward the end of his military career, he was known to be sympathetic to progressive elements in the Colorado Party. By 1971 he had distanced himself from this position to become a founding member and presidential candidate of the FRENTE AMPLIO, receiving 18 percent of the national vote. With the coup d'état of 1973, the leftist coalition and its political leaders were outlawed. Seregni was imprisoned until 1984.

Both in freedom and from prison, Seregni was a central proponent of democratization. He defended the blank ballot in the internal elections of 1982, which left the Frente outlawed. He later promoted and supported the strategy of negotiation that led to the legalization of many of the Frente's political forces and from which came the final formula for the democratic movement. Prevented from running for president in the November 1984 elections, Seregni assumed the presidency of the Frente Amplio. He did run for president of Uruguay again in 1989 and received 21 percent of the vote.

MIGUEL AGUIRRE, *El Frente Amplio* (1985); ALVARO BARROS LEMES, *Seregni* (1989).

FERNANDO FILGUEIRA

SERGIPE (formerly Sergipe Rei), one of Brazil's easternmost states, whose capital is ARACAJU. With an area of 8,490 square miles, roughly half of which is classified as CAATINGA, Sergipe is the smallest Brazilian state. Approximately 75 percent of its 1,140,121 people (1980) are of mixed racial origin. About 50 percent of the total population are urban dwellers, but agricultural products (including tobacco, cotton, rice, sugar, beans, coconut, and livestock), nevertheless, dominate the economy. The state possesses some mineral and oil reserves.

Indigenous peoples occupied the region that is now Sergipe until well beyond the mid-1500s, but the Portuguese, plagued by a risky sea route and by a strong French presence along the Brazilian coast, needed a secure hold over the Rio São Francisco and the surrounding area. Portuguese conquest commenced in 1589 when the crown, temporarily abrogating a 1587 law forbidding attacks on Indian populations, granted permission to wage a "just" war. By early 1590, the Portuguese controlled most of the territory.

In the 1700s, Bahian cattle ranchers and sugar planters settled the region. Originally a dependency of Bahia, Sergipe became an independent captaincy in 1821, a province of the empire (provincial capital São Cristovão) in 1824, and a state of the republic in 1889. The state continues to fall under Bahia's influence politically and economically.

LUIZ R. B. MOTT, *Sergipe del Rey: População, economia e sociedade* (1986).

CARA SHELLY

SERINGAL. A *seringal,* or RUBBER estate, is a large tract of Amazonian rain forest usually located on a river to facilitate the transport of rubber to market. Although land titles were easy to come by after the rubber boom began in the 1840s, they were often ill-defined, and battles were often fought over ownership of the *seringal.* The owner, or *seringalista,* often lived in Manaus, while agents or lessees (usually in debt to the rubber baron) ran their vast estates. Rubber barons kept gatherers on their *seringais* through a system of debt peonage. After World War II, the large rubber estates began to break up, and many *seringalistas* abandoned or sold their estates. Many rubber gatherers have remained on the land and continue to collect rubber from the trees.

BARBARA WEINSTEIN, *The Amazon Rubber Boom, 1850–1920* (1983); AUSTIN COATES, *The Commerce in Rubber: The First 250 Years* (1987); WARREN DEAN, *Brazil and the Struggle for Rubber* (1987).

CAROLYN JOSTOCK

SERINGUEIROS, Brazilian rubber gatherers. These workers were extracting latex from Amazonian RUBBER trees by the sixteenth century, when Indians collected rubber to make items such as water bags or syringes, from which the name *seringueiro* evolved. After the rubber boom began in the 1840s, *seringueiros* collected rubber to sell in towns. SERINGALISTAS (rubber estate owners) soon took over the rubber-rich rain forest. They exploited CABOCLOS, Indians, and workers imported from the poverty-stricken Northeast for their labor force. The workers were assigned an area where they would live and tend up to 200 trees. To extract rubber, the gatherer made a shallow incision in the bark of the rubber tree, allowing the latex to flow into a cup attached below it. Many *seringueiros* lived under the DEBT PEONAGE system, and they were often forced to stay on the estate until they paid off their endless debts.

In 1910, the Brazilian rubber market collapsed, and *seringalistas* allowed workers to leave the rubber estates. When the demand for rubber rebounded during World War II, recruits from the Northeast once more filled the ranks. Brazilian and U.S. authorities promised these "rubber soldiers" (*soldados da borracha*) military pensions and repatriation for their labor, but they failed to keep their word. Although many estates broke up after the war, most *seringueiros* stayed and continued to extract rubber from the deserted rain forest.

Barbara Weinstein, *The Amazon Rubber Boom, 1850–1920* (1983); Austin Coates, *The Commerce in Rubber: The First 250 Years* (1987); Warren Dean, *Brazil and the Struggle for Rubber* (1987).

Carolyn Jostock

SERRA, JUNÍPERO (*b.* 24 November 1713; *d.* 28 August 1784), Franciscan missionary in New Spain. The founder of Mission San Diego de Alcalá, Serra was born in Petra, on the Spanish island of Mallorca, to Antonio and Margarita Ferrer de Serra. Christened Miguel José, he attended a Franciscan primary school in Petra until age fifteen, when he traveled to Palma, the capital of Mallorca, to study theology. Serra took the name Junípero upon joining the Order of Friars Minor (FRANCISCANS) in 1730; he was ordained a priest in 1738. Serra received a doctorate in theology in 1742 and served as a professor of philosophy at Palma's Lullian University until 1749, when he decided to leave Spain and become a missionary among the Indians in the Americas.

Serra began his new career in 1750, working among the natives in the Sierra Gorda region north of Mexico City until 1758. He then returned to the Mexican capital and, although suffering at times from asthma and a painful leg injury, assumed the duties of a traveling missionary priest. In 1768 Serra was placed in charge of former Jesuit missions in Baja (Lower) California, and from there helped plan the occupation of Alta (Upper) California.

Serra, at age fifty-six, accompanied a Spanish overland expedition led by Gaspar de PORTOLÁ that reached San Diego in the summer of 1769 and founded the first mission there on 16 July. His second mission, San Carlos Borromeo, founded at Monterey on 3 June 1770, served, with the adjoining presidio, as capital of California. The Franciscans, under Serra's direction as father president for the next fourteen years, founded nine missions; taught the Indians Christian doctrine, agricultural techniques, pottery making, and other useful arts; and helped in the settlement of California.

Serra served and protected the Indians until his death at Mission San Carlos Borromeo, by then located on the Carmel River. Because of his accomplishments and exemplary life, he is known as "the Apostle of California." He was declared venerable by Pope John Paul II in May 1986, beatified in Rome on 25 September 1988, and is under consideration for canonization as a saint.

Serra's treatment of his Indian charges is a topic that has aroused much debate. Native Americans claim that he enslaved their ancestors. It must be admitted that the mission system did at times result in harsh treatment of Native Americans. Attracted to the missions with offerings of food and gifts, they were given religious instruction, but they also were often pressed into arduous work in the fields. Unmarried Indians were housed separately by sex and punished for attempting to leave the mission or for other infractions. Punishments included whipping and shackling—common disciplinary measures in the eighteenth century. European diseases spread through the confined areas and killed many Native Americans. The natural hunting-and-gathering economy and loose social organization of the Indians were replaced by a more structured, paternalistic administration. Serra's defenders claim that despite its failings, the Spanish mission system was humanitarian in its intent and sought to prepare Indians to live a settled, church-oriented, European way of life. Serra followed the teachings of his order and the goals of Catholic Spain. The California missions prospered and paved the way for a lasting agricultural economy on the Pacific Coast.

Francisco Palóu, O.F.M., *Palóu's Life of Fray Junípero Serra,* translated and edited by Maynard J. Geiger, O.F.M. (1945); Junípero Serra, O.F.M., *Writings,* 4 vols. edited by Antonine Tibesar, O.F.M. (1955–1966); Maynard Geiger, O.F.M., *The Life and Times of Fray Junípero Serra,* 2 vols. (1959); Francis J. Weber, "California's Serrana Literature," in *Southern California Quarterly* 51 (1969): 325–342; Iris H. W. Engstrand, *Serra's San Diego* (1982); Don De Nevi and Noel Francis Moholy, O.F.M., *Junípero Serra* (1985); Martin J. Morgado, *Junípero Serra: A Pictorial Biography* (1991).

Iris H. W. Engstrand

See also **Missions.**

Junípero Serra, from a painting preserved at Mission Santa Barbara. Copied by Rev. José Mosqueda from a now-unknown original. BENSON LATIN AMERICAN COLLECTION, UNIVERSITY OF TEXAS AT AUSTIN.

SERRA DO MAR, a thousand-mile escarpment that runs from northern Río Grande do Sul into Espírito Santo. In many places the Serra do Mar rises straight from the sea, itself forming the coastline. The sharpness of its peaks and the dense rain forest combine to form an almost impenetrable barrier from the Brazilian plateau to the sea. During the early colonial period it was a great obstacle to trade and commerce between the coast and São Paulo. The highest peak is the Pedra do Sino, which reaches 7,323 feet. The greatest rainfall in the country occurs on the escarpment near São Paulo.

Indians had long known about passages through the Serra do Mar and taught the European colonists about them. In 1790 a stone road was built across the Serra, but it was not kept in repair and eventually deteriorated until unsafe for use. A franchise was granted in 1840 to Thomas COCHRANE, an Englishman, to build a railroad across the escarpment, but difficulties in financing and engineering delayed completion of the project until 1863. The abundant waters along the Serra do Mar contributed to the industrialization of Rio de Janeiro and São Paulo during the late nineteenth century.

SERGIO BUARQUE DE HOLANDA, *História geral da civilização brasileira* (1967).

SHEILA L. HOOKER

SERRANO, JOSÉ (*b.* 1634; *d.* 1713), Spanish missionary and translator. Serrano, born in Andalusia, entered the Society of Jesus and arrived in the Río de la Plata in 1658. In order to be appointed parish priest in the reductions, he had to take an examination in the Guaraní language. He passed the examination, and began mission work in 1665. Serrano is credited with the translation of two Spanish books into the Guaraní language: *De la diferencia entre lo temporal y eternal,* by Jesuit Juan Eusebio Nieremberg, and *Flos sanctorum.* The former was subsequently published and printed with illustrations in 1705, the first book printed in Argentina. Serrano was the rector of the Jesuit college in Buenos Aires in 1696. He died in the Guaraní mission town of Loreto.

NICHOLAS P. CUSHNER

See also **Jesuits; Missions.**

SERRANO ELÍAS, JORGE ANTONIO (*b.* 26 April 1945), president of Guatemala (1991–1993), the first active Protestant to be elected president of a Latin American nation. Born in Guatemala City and educated at the University of San Carlos and at Stanford, Serrano became an evangelical Protestant in 1975. He served as president of the Council of State under the administration of General Efraín RÍOS MONTT (1982–1983). Serrano then formed the Solidary Action Movement (MAS) and placed third among eight candidates in the 1985 presidential election. In 1990, after the Court of Constitution-

ality ruled Ríos Montt ineligible for another term, most of his electoral support switched to Serrano. This propelled Serrano into the January 1991 runoff election in which he defeated National Center Union (UCN) candidate Jorge CARPIO in a landslide. Serrano's administration was neoliberal and private-sector oriented. With army support, he suspended the Constitution on 25 May 1993 to quell rising social unrest. In the face of widespread domestic and international pressure, however, the military removed Serrano on 1 June 1993 and allowed the Congress to elect a successor, Ramiro de León Carpio.

For a more detailed biographical sketch of Serrano, see the entry by RALPH LEE WOODWARD, JR., in the *Encyclopedia of World Biography*, vol. 18, edited by David Eggenberger (1994). For a detailed overview of recent Guatemalan political history, see JAMES DUNKERLEY, *Power in the Isthmus: A Political History of Modern Central America* (1988). Details of Serrano's presidential administration may be found in HOWARD H. LENTNER, *State Formation in Central America: The Struggle for Autonomy, Development, and Democracy* (1993). For an excellent summary and analysis of Serrano's religious background, see DAVID STOLL, "Guatemala Elects a Born-Again President," in *Christian Century* 108, no. 6 (20 February 1991):189–190. For a perceptive interpretation of Guatemalan society and politics prior to and during the administration of Serrano, see VÍCTOR PERERA, *Unfinished Conquest: The Guatemalan Tragedy* (1993).

RALPH LEE WOODWARD, JR.

SERTANISTA (backwoodsman), a specialist in the ways of the SERTÃO (undeveloped interior) of Portuguese America. Often MAMELUCOS (mixed bloods), these hardy backwoodsmen were fluent in the *língua geral* (vulgar TUPI-GUARANI), well versed in indigenous forest lore, and indispensable to Portuguese military, slaving, and prospecting expeditions. During the seventeenth century, *sertanistas* from São Paulo gained significant notoriety for their frequent slave raids on Indian villages, as royal authorities, sugar planters, and cattle ranchers in the Northeast recruited them to combat recalcitrant tribes and runaway slave communities. In the northern colonies of Maranhão and Pará, *sertanistas* plied the Amazon region for Indian slaves and forest products throughout the seventeenth and eighteenth centuries.

JOHN HEMMING, *Red Gold* (1978), describes the *sertanistas'* activities in detail. Specifically on the backwoodsmen of São Paulo, RICHARD MORSE, ed., *The Bandeirantes* (1965), provides an excellent introduction. A beautifully written Brazilian account is SERGIO BUARQUE DE HOLANDA, *Caminhos e fronteiras* (1957).

JOHN M. MONTEIRO

SERTÃO, SERTANEJO. Except during periodic droughts, average annual rainfall in the *sertão*—the semiarid region of Brazil extending from the interior of Minas Gerais and Bahia to the interior of Piauí and

Inhabitants of the Sertão. PULSAR IMAGENS E EDITORA / JUCA MARTINS.

Maranhão—differs little from that of other areas; but rain tends to come in violent downpours punctuating prolonged dry spells. *Sertanejos* (inhabitants of the *sertão*), predominantly people of mixed European, Indian, and African ancestry, live as subsistence farmers, cotton sharecroppers, or ranch hands. In some contexts, *sertanejo* connotes uncouthness.

During the 1600s, the decline of coastal Indian populations and rumors of riches in the interior fueled exploration of the *sertão* by BANDEIRAS (armed expeditions privately organized by coastal settlements) and other *sertanistas* (backlands explorers). Cattle ranchers spearheaded settlement of the backlands in the late seventeenth and eighteenth centuries, and in the 1800s, cotton became a significant *sertão* crop.

Fazendeiros (owners of great estates) exercised broad economic, social, and political power over the majority of *sertanejos*. Among some *sertanejos*, such domination—together with poverty and weak policing mechanisms—fostered a tradition of banditry (*cangaço*) lasting until the late 1930s, when federal troops subdued the CANGACEIROS. Occasionally, rebellions or movements superseded banditry, notably the followers of Antônio CONSELHEIRO (suppressed at Canudos in 1896–1897) and the movement (ca. 1891–1934) headed by Padre Cícero Romão BATISTA of Joaseiro in Ceará.

In the twentieth century, leftist appeals seemed potential sparks of popular unrest; but despite the PRESTES COLUMN (1924–1927), popular-front propaganda, and the example of the Cuban Revolution, Communism failed to attract a large following in the Brazilian hinterlands.

In normal years, the *sertanejos* raise livestock and crops sufficient to feed themselves. Drought, however, leads quickly to hunger, driving tens of thousands of *flagelados* (literally, "the flagellated") or *retirantes* from the *sertão* to commercial and industrial centers and to the Amazon Basin. Government efforts to improve conditions in the *sertão* by encouraging industrial development, undertaking irrigation projects, and providing medical, educational, and other services progress slowly.

EUCLIDES DA CUNHA, *Os Sertões* (1902), translated by Samuel Putnam as *Rebellion in the Backlands* (1944); JOÃO CAPISTRANO DE ABREU, *Caminhos Antigos e o Povoamento do Brasil* (1930); ALLEN W. JOHNSON, *Sharecroppers of the Sertão: Economics and Dependence on a Brazilian Plantation* (1971); JOSEPH A. PAGE, *The Revolution That Never Was: Northeast Brazil, 1955–1964* (1972); EDINALDO G. BASTOS, *Farming in the Brazilian Sertão: Social Organization and Economic Behavior* (1980); THOMAS E. SKIDMORE, *The Politics of Military Rule in Brazil, 1964–85* (1988).

CARA SHELLY

See also **Messianic Movements: Brazil.**

SERVICE FOR PEACE AND JUSTICE (SERPAJ), international organization dedicated to promoting justice through active nonviolence. Founded in 1974 in Buenos Aires, by a group of Catholic activists, the goals of the

Servicio de Paz y Justicia include education in nonviolent strategies to promote human rights, disarmament and demilitarization, alternative modes of economic development, effective political participation for all, and communal approaches to societal problems. Strongly influenced by the examples of Mohandas Gandhi and Martin Luther King, Jr., Serpaj emerged in a period of increasing violence by both the Right and the Left in Latin America.

Seeking to bring together groups experimenting with nonviolence and to increase knowledge of such strategies, the organization emphasized popular education, training, and networking. Serpaj spread throughout Latin America in the 1970s with an international headquarters established in 1974 in Buenos Aires under the direction of Adolfo PÉREZ ESQUIVEL, a sculptor and peace activist.

National units of international bodies tend to reflect the particular needs of specific countries and hence there is some variety in their programmatic emphases. In Uruguay, Serpaj emerged as the principal human rights organization engaged in the documentation and denunciation of civil and political violations, particularly during the 1973–1985 military regime; in Ecuador and Paraguay the emphasis was on organizing for greater economic self-sufficiency among the rural poor. Serpaj also works closely with CHRISTIAN BASE COMMUNITIES to promote socioeconomic justice. In 1980 its general coordinator, Pérez Esquivel, was awarded the Nobel Peace Prize.

LAWRENCE WESCHLER, *A Miracle, A Universe: Settling Accounts with Torturers* (1990); SERVICIO PAZ Y JUSTICIA, URUGUAY, *Uruguay, Nunca Más: Human Rights Violations, 1972–1985* (1992).

MARGARET E. CRAHAN

SERVICE SECTOR, a term used in economics to describe the output of sectors outside agriculture and industry that produce goods. Service sectors such as education, health, finance, government, transportation, and trade provide intangible outputs that satisfy human needs. Since Independence, services have been at least as vital in reflecting and shaping the historical evolution of Latin America as either agriculture or industry. Often they have generated more income and employment than either or both of these sectors.

Based on the United Nations, *International Standard Industrial Classification of All Economic Activities,* 3d revision (1990), service activities include: (1) wholesale and retail trade; repair of motor vehicles, motorcycles, and personal and household goods; (2) hotels and restaurants; (3) transport, storage, and communications; (4) financial intermediation; (5) real estate, renting, and business activities; (6) public administration and defense; compulsory social security; (7) education; (8) health and social work; and (9) other community, social, and personal-service activities.

Services are classified as private, semipublic, or collective, depending on whom they serve. Private (or rival) services satisfy individual needs and are consumed by one person only. They are produced by private or state-owned enterprises for sale in a market. Examples include transportation (taxi rides), financial intermediation (lending), housing (renting), and retail trade (selling fruit in a supermarket).

Semipublic (partly rival or excludable) services satisfy semipublic needs and are consumed by one or more persons. For example, attendance of a class lecture by one student does not preclude attendance (that is, consumption of the educational service) by other students. Semipublic services are produced by nonprofit institutions, the state, and private enterprise. Education, health, and welfare are semipublic services.

Collective (or public) services satisfy public needs and are said to be nonrival and nonexcludable in consumption. That is, consumption by one person does not reduce their availability to, or consumption by, someone else. Once the service is provided, the additional cost of its consumption by another person is zero. Public administration and defense are typical collective services. Collective services can be provided by the state or private enterprise.

THE YEARS 1820 TO 1930
Private services grew rapidly in Latin America between 1820, the beginning of Independence, and 1930, the start of the Great Depression. Their expansion largely reflected the powerful market forces unleashed by the entrance of Latin America into the international trading system (see FOREIGN TRADE). Phenomenal increases in exports and imports created an unprecedented demand for trade, transport, storage, communications, and financial services. Prosperous trading houses were established throughout Latin America. Railroads linked rural agricultural regions and distant mining centers with ports and major urban centers. Foreign (British, German, French, Italian, and U.S.) and national banks, which served the needs of producers, governments, and consumers, proliferated. Money and capital markets grew rapidly and became closely integrated with those of Europe, especially London, and New York City. These services provided vital income components for the composite commodities being traded. In many instances, as much as 50 percent of the price of exports and imports reflected value added (markups) by trade, transport, finance, insurance, and related service activities. The agricultural (staples) bonanzas of Argentina, Uruguay, Brazil, and Colombia, and the mineral wealth of Chile, Venezuela, Peru, Bolivia, and Mexico, gave rise to corresponding production booms in private business, personal, and social services. Demand for private services gained an additional momentum as a consequence of rising domestic incomes, urbanization, and industrialization.

In response to these rapid rises in demand by producers, households, and governments, Latin America experienced sharp supply increases, modernization, and turmoil in all private service activities. Service output increased through domestic production, being supplemented, whenever shortages arose, by imported services. Financial, transport, trade, insurance, and other services were predominantly produced locally by private (national and foreign) enterprises and banks. Output increases, including output through import substitution (i.e., domestic production of previously imported services) were largely natural (i.e., a result of free market forces). Although often cyclical and precarious, prosperity in service activities was widespread in Argentina, Uruguay, Brazil, Mexico, Chile, and most urban and export centers in the rest of Latin America. Foreigners and immigrants made significant contributions to the development of modern, private services as entrepreneurs, capitalists, managers, professionals, and skilled workers. In few countries, however, did foreigners and immigrants play as important a role as in Argentina and Uruguay—the countries of new settlement.

Incomes in these modern, rapidly growing service activities often matched or even exceeded those of their European and North American counterparts. Socioeconomic inequality inherited from the colonial period was reinforced in much of Latin America as foreigners, immigrants, and skilled nationals earned incomes that greatly exceeded those of indigenous and other populations with limited skills and political power. The parallel existence of very rich, middle-class, poor, and indigent workers and households resulted from plural (i.e., highly differentiated in terms of income and productivity) labor markets in service activities. In Argentina and Uruguay almost all socioeconomic groups benefited from the agricultural, industrial, and service prosperity between Independence and the Great Depression. In Brazil, Mexico, Peru, Chile, Guatemala, Bolivia, and Honduras, however, the benefits from the expansion of services, industry, agriculture, and mining accrued primarily to the upper socioeconomic groups.

The semipublic services of education, health, and welfare also experienced significant growth between Independence and the Great Depression. The degree of illiteracy declined, especially in the cities, as primary education gradually became compulsory. Secondary education also improved, with immigrants and foreigners creating first-rate secondary schools for their children. Furthermore, almost all Latin American countries had established internationally recognized universities by 1930. In many countries, universities, which often received disproportionate shares of governmental expenditures on education, catered almost exclusively to the middle- and upper-income strata. In Brazil, Mexico, Peru, Bolivia, Ecuador, Central America, and Paraguay, indigenous populations, women, and the poor frequently had no access to public education. Furthermore, even though health services improved significantly, mortality rates, especially of infants, remained especially high in rural areas and among the urban poor and the indigenous populations. Welfare services also grew but they covered almost exclusively organized labor, the politically powerful middle classes, and the rich. In Argentina and Uruguay, governments, to use modern terminology, invested heavily in human capital by providing educational, health, nutrition, and other services to all population segments, although not always to the same degree. In much of the rest of Latin America, semipublic services offered by the state to the poor, indigenous, and rural populations, especially women, were minimal—often nonexistent. Almost everywhere in Latin America, the relative distribution of government (and privately) produced semipublic educational, health, and welfare services suffered from extreme inequality. The 40 to 60 percent of households experiencing severe underinvestment in human capital—poor health, inadequate nutrition, illiteracy—neither contributed to nor shared much in the fruits of semipublic service development.

The collective services of law, order, justice, equality, and freedom, which were produced by public administration and defense agencies, also improved significantly, but by no means sufficiently, between 1820 and 1930. Democratic governments, such as those of Chile and Costa Rica, were the exception rather than the rule. The bundle of political, economic, human, and social rights delivered by governments before 1930 was, in most countries, grossly inadequate. Far too often vast governmental incomes and riches created by the guano, wheat, coffee, tin, copper, and other agricultural and mineral export bonanzas were not invested in either physical (buildings, roads, ports) or human (education, health) capital to the extent necessary to achieve sustainable growth, reduce inequality, and remove poverty.

During the period 1820 to 1930, services may have created as much as 50 percent of income in some countries and employed between 20 and 30 percent of the labor force.

THE YEARS 1930 TO 1973

Total services continued to grow after 1930. Employment in services increased both in absolute and relative terms. At least in part, service employment growth reflected the inability of manufacturing to absorb the increments in the labor force caused by the post-1940 population explosion and persistent migration of labor from rural agriculture to urban areas. Unlike past experiences, labor released by agriculture moved directly into services, as industrial employment growth was slow. In some activities, such as finance, government, health, and education, labor found employment in average- and high-paying service jobs. To a large extent, however, service employment increases materialized in low-paying, often marginally productive, informal activities in transportation (driving taxis, minibuses), trade (selling retail), and personal services (working as household servants or in repair shops). Especially in urban areas, much poverty and deprivation have been associated with the expansion of informal employment in services. The rural poor and destitute who migrated into the cities often joined the ranks of the urban poor and destitute in informal services.

As early as 1950, more than half of total income, or gross domestic product (GDP), was being generated in services in Chile (52.2 percent) and Uruguay (57.5 percent). By 1965, services were also creating more than half of income in Brazil (54.6 percent), the Dominican Republic (51.9 percent), El Salvador (50.6 percent), Guatemala (51.1 percent), Mexico (54.0 percent), and Panama (51.9 percent). Services also played an important role as an employer. By 1965, they employed more than 40 percent of the labor force in Argentina (48.7 percent), Chile (41.3 percent), Uruguay (52.6 percent), and Venezuela (46.7 percent). Sharp increases in service employment, in relative terms, occurred in all Latin American countries.

Services displayed some new features from 1930 to 1973. Increasingly, private services in transportation, finance, storage, and trade were provided by STATE CORPORATIONS that often competed with or replaced national or foreign enterprises. Furthermore, as a result of protectionism and nationalism, previously imported services were now produced locally. At least in part, therefore, the growth of services during this period was "artificial," that is, it was determined by policies of government intervention rather than free market forces. Services also acted as a sector of employment of last resort, absorbing labor that was unable to enter the state- or privately-owned formal economy.

In some activities, government intervention and protectionism reduced, at least temporarily, employment growth while permitting rapid expansion of income. Such a pattern, which coincided with high income but low employment shares, characterized trade and banking services, whose contribution to total income (GDP) by 1965 exceeded 20 percent—in Argentina (20.8 percent), Brazil (22.0 percent), Chile (25.1 percent), El Salvador (28.3 percent), Guatemala (30.2 percent), Mexico (32.5 percent), and Paraguay (22.6 percent). In contrast, trade and banking services absorbed less than 10 percent of employment in all countries in 1965 except Argentina (15.5 percent), Peru (10.0 percent), and Venezuela (13.6 percent).

Employment in government services in 1950–1965 was 3 percent or less of total employment in Brazil, Colombia, Costa Rica, El Salvador, Guatemala, Haiti, Honduras, Nicaragua, and Paraguay. It exceeded 5 percent in Argentina (10.3 percent in 1960), Chile (5.6 percent in 1965), and Peru (6.0 percent in 1965). Income generated by government services, which consisted of wages and salaries of government employees, regularly exceeded 5 percent of GDP in all of Latin America except Colombia, Guatemala, Honduras, Nicaragua, Panama, and Paraguay.

Personal services, which played a key role as a sector of employment of last resort, experienced a growth in employment that exceeded income growth. By 1965 personal services absorbed at least 15 percent of total employment in Argentina, Chile, Colombia, Costa Rica, and Panama. In Panama personal services created at least 25 percent of total income from 1950 to 1965. Elsewhere, their income share was below their employment share, suggesting low income and productivity, poverty, and possibly indigence.

The transportation sector was also significant in Latin America, employing more than 5 percent of the labor force in Argentina (6.7 percent in 1960), Chile (6.0 percent in 1965), and Venezuela (6.0 percent in 1965). Its income share in 1950–1965 was above 5 percent of GDP in Argentina, Bolivia, Chile, Guatemala (1965), Honduras, Nicaragua (1965), Panama (1960, 1965), and Venezuela (1950). Production and private ownership of automobiles also increased the supply of transport services by households. Use of private automobiles manifested itself in large household expenditures on transportation, including the purchase of automobiles. These, however, do not form part of the statistics of employment and income generated by the transportation sector and enterprises.

According to the World Bank, as early as 1965, 50 percent of the regional GDP originated in service activities. By 1990, services generated 54 percent of the GDP, much the same as in the whole world. Thus, at least since 1965, Latin America can be characterized as a service region. Service production, as measured by the percentage contribution of service activities to GDP, was equal to or exceeded agricultural, industrial, and their combined "goods" production. Statistics of the percentage of income generated in services in Latin America and the Caribbean in 1970 and 1992 are presented in Table 1.

Service activities clearly dominated all regional economies by generating a larger share of GDP than agriculture, industry, and all goods sectors combined. The increase in regional relative income generated by services coincided with a decrease in relative income generated by agriculture, which was offset only partially (one third) by an increase in relative income generated by industry.

According to the figures of the percentage distribution of the labor force in Latin America and the Caribbean in 1965 and 1981 presented in Table 2, the size of the total service sector, as measured by its share in the labor force, differed significantly between countries of the region, was generally larger in richer than in poorer countries, and, with rare exceptions, increased, often significantly, between 1965 and 1981. In the larger and richer countries, services were by far the largest and most rapidly growing economic activity, in terms of labor-force share. In 1981 they accounted for more than half of the labor force in Venezuela, Uruguay, Chile, and Colombia. By 1993 probably at least half of the region's labor force was employed in service activities. Thus, Latin America can be described as a service region, and the largest and medium-size countries as service economies, whether the criterion used is contribution to income (GDP) or share in the labor force.

TABLE 1   Percentage of income generated in services in Latin America and the Caribbean, 1970, 1992[a]

	Distribution of Gross Domestic Product (%)	
	---	---
	1970	1992
Argentina	47	63
Bolivia[b]	48	—
Brazil	49	52
Chile[b]	52	—
Colombia	47	49
Costa Rica[b]	53	55
Dominican Republic[b]	51	56
Ecuador[b]	51	48
El Salvador[b]	48	66
Guatemala[b]	—	55
Honduras	45	49
Jamaica[b]	51	51
Mexico[b]	59	63
Nicaragua[b]	49	50
Panama[b]	66	76
Paraguay[b]	47	52
Peru[c]	50	—
Puerto Rico[b]	62	58
Trinidad and Tobago	51	61
Uruguay[b]	53	61
Venezuela[b]	54	53
Latin America & Caribbean	52[c]	—
World	54[c]	—

[a] Services includes value added in all branches of economic activities outside agriculture and industry (mining; manufacturing; construction; and electricity, water, and gas). It includes imputed bank service charges, import duties, any statistical discrepancies noted by national compilers, and unallocated items.
[b] The service component is at purchaser values.
[c] Weighted average.

SOURCE: World Bank, *World Development Report 1994: Infrastructure for Development* (1994), table 3, pp. 166–167.

As the provision of educational services improved, most Latin American countries experienced large increases in the levels of educational attainment of the population. Schooling levels have been lower, however, in rural areas, in poorer regions, and among the 30 million indigenous peoples. Improvements in health services have led to significant increases in life expectancy and declines in mortality rates, especially of infants. Welfare services also improved, but rarely have they adequately covered the poorest 40 percent of households operating in the informal economy. Collective services were guided in 1930–1973 by philosophies of intervention, protectionism, redistribution, central planning, and pervasive distrust of private ownership, free markets, and open trade.

By the 1960s, Latin America had started displaying symptoms of acute fatigue with government interven-

tion in the production of private and semipublic services and goods. State ownership and intervention in the financial sector, which had created a privileged class of bank employees, had contributed to a sharp decline in financial services and private saving, acceleration of inflation, disintegration of money and capital markets, capital flight, and speculation. International and interregional trade had been victimized by excessive protectionism. Rarely did governments assign priority in delivering collective services that promoted universal respect of basic human, political, social, and economic rights and freedoms.

THE YEARS SINCE 1973

Responding to this fatigue with state interventionism, attitudes toward and delivery of services experienced phenomenal, almost revolutionary, changes, beginning with

TABLE 2   Percentage of labor force in services in Latin America and the Caribbean, 1965, 1981

	Percentage of Labor Force in Services	
	1965	1981
Argentina	48	59
Bolivia	22	26
Brazil	34	46
Chile	53	62
Colombia	35	53
Costa Rica	33	48
Cuba	41	46
Dominican Republic	23	33
Ecuador	25	31
El Salvador	23	28
Guatemala	20	24
Haiti	16	19
Honduras	20	17
Jamaica	41	47
Mexico	29	38
Nicaragua	27	47
Panama	39	49
Paraguay	26	32
Peru	31	41
Trinidad and Tobago	42	51
Uruguay	52	57
Venezuela	46	55

SOURCE: World Bank, *World Development Report 1985, International Capital and Economic Development* (1985), table 21, pp. 214–215.

Chile in 1973. Collective services began actively to promote free markets, private ownership, and trade liberalization. Governments in Chile, Argentina, Mexico, Peru, Colombia, Venezuela, and elsewhere withdrew from the production of private services and goods through privatization of banks, airlines, railroads, telephone companies, and other state-owned enterprises. The quantity and quality of private services in finance, transport, storage, communications, and trade improved. Public-sector deficits were reduced or eliminated. Price stability was largely restored, except in Brazil. Money and capital markets gained impressive dynamism. Financial capital returned. Both international and interregional trade recovered some of their dynamism as barriers to trade were reduced or eliminated. Because of improved (liberalized) trade services, exports originating in manufacturing increased rapidly, especially in Mexico and Brazil.

Major changes also affected the semipublic services of education, health, and welfare. A consensus emerged that the intractable problems of poverty and inequality could not be solved unless people, in particular the rural poor, women, and indigenous populations, were "put first." Increased emphasis was placed on investment in human capital (education, health, nutrition, and welfare) for the needy. However, even though health, education, nutrition, and welfare standards have improved markedly, according to World Bank statistics, in 1989, 130.9 million people, or 31.0 percent of Latin America's population, lived in poverty. Inequality has also persisted. In the 1970s the poorest 20 percent of households received only 4.0 percent of income. A minor reduction in inequality in income distribution may have occurred in the 1990s. The need for change in public policy was increasingly documented by international organizations, academia, and even Latin American governments themselves.

It has been increasingly recognized that public expenditures on services do not by themselves reveal whether the beneficiaries have been the rich, the middle classes, or the poor. Recent studies have offered ample evidence that throughout the post-Independence period, public expenditures on services, which have often been both absolutely and relatively high, have benefited primarily, if not exclusively, the high- and middle-income groups. The evidence for recent years on this matter, which is presented below, has been obtained from the World Bank's *Poverty Reduction Handbook* (1993).

According to a 1988 World Bank analysis of the incidence of major social-service expenditures in Brazil (which include social security, education, health, nutrition, housing, water, sanitation, and other urban services), "19 percent of the population, with per capita annual income below U.S. $180, benefits from 6 percent of social expenditures: whereas the top 16 percent receive 34 percent of social expenditures" (p. 59). In Bolivia, as a consequence of the urban concentration of public services and infrastructure, the very poor have had little or no access in the 1980s to health care, education, and training, thus deriving few benefits from public expenditures. Similarly, in Guatemala in the late 1980s, the urban areas and the nonpoor benefited disproportionately from spending on health and education. In Honduras most social programs in 1988 benefited primarily the middle- and upper-income groups through spending on curative hospital care, pension benefits, and university education. In Venezuela, Peru, Paraguay, Ecuador, Central America, and Chile, the poorest 40 percent of households received limited or few benefits from social spending by government. With few exceptions, social-services spending by governments in Latin America has been characterized by inequality involving neglect and ostracism of the poorest households. A major effort is underway in much of the region to establish a more equitable distribution of semipublic and collective services.

Household expenditures on private medical, education, transport, and communication services, the structure of which is presented in Table 3, have also been significant. Expenditures on transport, including automobiles, have been the largest in most countries.

It is increasingly recognized that achievement of sustained growth, reduction of poverty and inequality, environmental protection, and stable democracy require continued quantitative expansion, qualitative improvement, and a fair distribution of private, semipublic, and collective services.

Comprehensive statistics on income and employment are in MARKOS MAMALAKIS, "Urbanization and Sectoral Transformation in Latin America, 1950–65," in *Actas y Memorias del XXXIX Congreso Internacional de Americanistas Lima*, vol. 2 (1972), and "Urbanización y transformaciones sectoriales en Latinoamérica (1950–1970). Antecedentes e implicaciones para una reforma urbana," in *Asentamientos urbanos y organización socioproductiva en la historia de América Latina*, compiled by J. E. Hardoy and R. P. Schaedel (1977).

A comprehensive discussion of health services is in WORLD BANK, *World Development Report 1993: Investing in Health, World Development Indicators* (1993). The annual *World Development Reports* contain statistics related to the percentage contribution of overall services to GDP in selected Latin American countries.

One of the earliest and most comprehensive analyses of services is MARKOS MAMALAKIS, *The Growth and Structure of the Chilean Economy: From Independence to Allende* (1976), especially chaps. 1 and 9.

TABLE 3 Structure of consumption of services in Latin America and the Caribbean

	Percentage Share of Total Household Consumption		
	Medical Care	Education	Transport and Communication
Argentina	4	6	13
Bolivia	5	7	12
Brazil	6	5	8
Chile	5	6	11
Colombia	7	6	13
Costa Rica	7	8	8
Dominican Republic	8	3	4
Ecuador	5	6[b]	12[c]
El Salvador	8	5	10
Guatemala	13	4	3
Honduras	8	5[b]	3
Jamaica	5	5	16
Mexico	5	5	12
Panama	8	9	7
Paraguay	2	3	10
Peru	4	6	10
Trinidad and Tobago	8	8	12
Uruguay	6	4	13
Venezuela	8	5[b]	11

[a] Data refer to either 1980 or 1985.

[b] Refers to government expenditure.

[c] Includes fuel.

SOURCE: World Bank, *World Development Report 1993: Investing in Health* (1993), table 10, pp. 256–257.

The evolution of financial systems in Latin America in recent decades is described in detail in WORLD BANK, *World Development Report 1989: Financial Systems and Development, World Development Indicators* (1989). A theory of financial services is in MARKOS MAMALAKIS, "The Treatment of Interest and Financial Intermediaries in the National Accounts: The Old 'Bundle' Versus the New 'Unbundle' Approach," in *The Review of Income and Wealth*, ser. 33, no. 2 (June 1987). A comprehensive examination of financial services in Chile from Independence until 1985 is in MARKOS MAMALAKIS, *Historical Statistics of Chile: Money, Prices, and Credit Services*, vol. 4 (1983), and *Historical Statistics of Chile: Money, Banking, and Financial Services*, vol. 5 (1985).

A comprehensive analysis of social-security services in Latin America is in CARMELO MESA-LAGO, *Social Security in Latin America: Pressure Groups, Stratification, and Inequality* (1978), and *Social Security and Prospects for Equity in Latin America* (1991). The latter volume contains an extensive bibliography on social-security services throughout Latin America.

A general discussion of the role of education, health, and other services in economic development is in WORLD BANK, *World Development Report 1991: The Challenge of Development* (1991), esp. chap. 3. A theory of services is in MARKOS MAMALAKIS, *Historical Statistics of Chile: Government Services and Public Sector and a Theory of Services*, vol. 6 (1989), chap. 15, which also contains an analysis of the historical evolution of governmental services in Chile since Independence.

MARKOS J. MAMALAKIS

SERVICIO DE PAZ Y JUSTICIA. *See* **Service for Peace and Justice.**

SESMARIA, plot of land of varied size granted to petitioners in colonial Brazil by the Portuguese monarchy in recognition of service to the crown. The *sesmaria* was the principal form of land distribution implemented by Portuguese colonizers, although purchase and inheritance were also legitimate forms of land acquisition.

Land was the domain of the crown and the personal patrimony of the king or queen. Personal contacts at court often influenced the granting of land in Brazil to persons of "quality." In keeping with the objectives of colonization, crown grants were subject to strict, selective regulation, defined by law and aimed at assuring effective settlement and exploration as well. The laws governing the granting of *sesmarias* restricted the amount of land assigned to any one grantee, regulated the exploration of the land, and did not confer private ownership of the *sesmaria*. By the eighteenth century it was necessary to confirm *sesmarias* in Lisbon.

Despite numerous abuses, including the sale and exchange of grants, the distribution of land in this form permitted the crown control over the effective settlement of Brazil and fixed on that country an archaic, long-lasting system of LAND TENURE dominated by powerful sugar and coffee planters and cattle ranchers.

When Brazil became independent in 1822, the granting of *sesmarias* was suspended. Henceforth, they were officially recognized, but until 1850 effective occupation was the only form of legal acquisition of public lands.

Until passage of the LAND LAW OF 1850 there was unregulated occupancy of both small holdings and vast expanses of unclaimed public lands.

WARREN DEAN, *Rio Claro: A Brazilian Plantation System, 1820–1920* (1975); JACOB GORENDER, *O escravismo colonial* (1980); EMÍLIA VIOTTI DA COSTA, *The Brazilian Empire: Myths and Histories* (1985).

NANCY PRISCILLA SMITH NARO

SEVEN CITIES OF CÍBOLA, the first name given to New Mexico. The reference to Cíbola dates back to the medieval legend of the seven bishops who fled the Iberian Peninsula and founded the Seven Cities of Cíbola, noted for their gold, on the island of Antillia in 734, after Don Rodrigo of Spain lost his kingdom to the Moors in A.D. 714. In 1539 Fray Marcos de Niza set out from Mexico City to seek the Seven Cities in the northern territories that CABEZA DE VACA had visited. Estevanico, the African slave in Cabeza de Vaca's party, led the expedition and was instructed to send back crosses whose size would indicate the significance of the towns. Estevanico was killed when he insisted on entering the Zuni village of Hawikuh. On his return, Fray Marcos described a kingdom that exceeded Mexico and Peru in size and wealth. This news prompted Viceroy Antonio de MENDOZA to send Francisco Vásquez de CORONADO to conquer Cíbola in April 1540.

CARL O. SAUER, *The Road to Cibola* (1932); STEPHEN CLISSOLD, *The Seven Cities of Cibola* (1962); JOHN UPTON TERRELL, *Estevanico the Black* (1968); and MAUREEN AHERN, "The Cross and the Gourd: The Appropriation of Ritual Signs in the *Relaciones* of Alvar Núñez and Fray Marcos de Niza," in *Early Images of the Americas: Transfer and Invention*, edited by Jerry M. Williams and Robert E. Lewis (1993).

JOSÉ RABASA

SEVEN YEARS' WAR, conflict (1756–1763) also known in North America as the French and Indian War. The Seven Years' War aligned Prussia and England against France, Austria, and Russia in Europe and England against France in North America. It began when Frederick II the Great (1712–1786) of Prussia invaded Saxony and then Austria and ended after Great Britain, with the strongest navy, conquered all of Canada and took the French sugar islands. The final settlement, the Peace of Paris (10 February 1763) was favorable to Great Britain, which received all of Canada and land east of the Mississippi. Although unprepared to challenge British naval power, Spain entered the war after making the third (Bourbon) Family Compact with France on 15 August 1761. Britain captured Havana in 1762, but returned the port to Spain in 1763. Spain ceded Florida and all Spanish territory in North America to Great Britain. Spain's only victory in the war was taking COLÔNIA DO SACRAMENTO from Portugal, Britain's ally, but the peace terms required that Spain return the RÍO DE LA PLATA colony. The war exposed Spain's colonial vulnerability and subsequently CHARLES III (1716–1788) instituted a variety of reforms to strengthen the ties between the colonies and Spain and improve military defense.

RICHARD PARES, *War and Trade in the West Indies, 1739–1763* (1963); MAX SAVELLE, *Empires to Nations: Expansion in America, 1713–1824* (1974).

SUZANNE HILES BURKHOLDER

SEXAGENARIAN LAW, or the Saraiva–Cotegipe Law (named for its principal sponsors), an 1885 decree that freed all Brazilian slaves when they reached age sixty. Proponents recognized that planters who had lied about the ages of African-born slaves—listing them as older than they were in order to subvert the 1831 law that prohibited the importation of African slaves into Brazil after that date—were now caught with slaves who would be eligible for freedom even though they were actually younger than sixty. The law stipulated that slaves thus freed would continue to work for an additional three years or until age sixty-five (whichever came first) as compensation to their owners. The ambiguously "freed" slaves, moreover, were to perform their work in the countries in which they were freed; elsewhere they would be regarded as vagabonds, arrested, and put to work on state projects. Unless they found work they would be imprisoned. In these ways planters could keep tight rein on former slaves, who they feared would become troublesome drifters. If the law largely favored planters, at least one provision satisfied abolitionists: not only did the law abolish the trading of slaves across provincial boundaries, but to penalize their owners, it also declared such slaves freed.

ROBERT CONRAD, *The Destruction of Brazilian Slavery, 1850–1888* (1972), esp. pp. 210–237.

SANDRA LAUDERDALE GRAHAM

See also **Free Birth Law; Golden Law; Queiróz Law; Slave Trade.**

SHARP, BARTHOLOMEW (late 1600s), one of the last of the buccaneers. In 1679, Captain Bartholomew Sharp and other BUCCANEERS from Jamaica raided the Caribbean ports of Honduras, plundering royal storehouses and carrying off some 500 chests of INDIGO, as well as cocoa, COCHINEAL, tortoiseshell, money, and silver plate.

Later that year the same buccaneers, including Sharp and Captain John Coxon, set out upon a plan of much larger design. Six captains met at Point Morant, Jamaica, and on 7 January 1680, set sail for PORTO BELLO. They entered the town on 17 February. Meeting little resistance, they pillaged it, took prisoners and booty, and departed just after the arrival of Spanish troops. Then they captured two Spanish vessels headed for the port and divided their large haul of plunder. Finally, Sharp and the other buccaneers marched across the Isthmus of Darién to the coasts of Panama and the Pacific, wreaking havoc as they went.

In May 1680, Lord Charles Carlisle, governor of Jamaica, put out a warrant for the apprehension of Sharp and his associates. On 1 July, Henry MORGAN issued a similar arrest order. Sharp eventually returned to England, where he was charged with committing piracy on the South Seas, but he was acquitted because of a reported lack of evidence.

A. D. EXQUEMELIN, *The Buccaneers of America* (1678, repr. 1972); PHILIP AYRES, *The Voyages and Adventures of Captain Barth. Sharp and Others* (1684); C. H. HARING, *The Buccaneers in the West Indies in the XVII Century* (1910); N. M. CROUSE, *The French Struggle for the West Indies, 1665–1713* (1943).

BLAKE D. PATTRIDGE

See also **Piracy.**

SHEEP. *See* **Livestock.**

SHIMOSE, PEDRO (*b.* 1940), Bolivian poet. Shimose also sketches and composes popular music. Born in Riberalta del Beni, Bolivia, to Japanese immigrants, Shimose received a degree in communication sciences from the Universidad Complutense in Madrid. He worked as columnist and editor for the daily *Presencia* of La Paz and later taught literature at the Universidad Mayor de San Andrés in La Paz. In the early 1990s he was working at the Institute of Spanish-American Cooperation in Madrid. His poetry has received various prizes: Bolivia's National Poetry Prize in 1960 and 1966, Cuba's House of the Americas Prize in 1972, and Spain's Olive Prize in 1974 and Leopoldo Panero Prize in 1975.

Shimose's early poetry (*Triludio del exilio* [1961], *Sardonia* [1967], *Poemas para un pueblo* [1968], and *Quiero escribir, pero me sale espuma* [1972]) is characterized by a humanist social commitment of a mythico-religious nature, which evolves into a definitive denunciation of those who perpetuate the conditions causing misery and pain in Latin America. In *Caducidad del fuego* (1975), *Al pie de la letra* (1976), *Reflexiones maquiavélicas* (1980), and *Poemas* (1988), the tone changes. The violence is transformed into a bitter irony mixed with tenderness and humor. Shimose also published a book of stories, *El Coco se llama Drilo* (1976), and *Diccionario de autores iberoamericanos* (1982).

JOSÉ ORTEGA, *Letras bolivianas de hoy: Renato Prada y Pedro Shimose* (1973).

SILVIA M. NAGY

SHINING PATH. *See* **Peru: Revolutionary Movements.**

SHUAR, indigenous people of the Ecuadorian Amazon. The Shuar people, known historically as Jívaro (a derogatory term no longer used), live in wet, mountainous *montaña*, where they practice shifting cultivation and hunt. Their unstratified and kin-ordered social organization was based on autonomous households, constantly engaged in feuding, shifting alliances, and trade. Heads taken in warfare were preserved as *tsantas*, the well-known shrunken-head trophies. Informal leadership roles were assumed by outstanding warriors and superior shamans. The first Spanish penetration of Shuar territory in 1549 was followed by the founding of two major communities, Logroño and Sevilla del Oro, occupied by colonists and soldiers, who exploited rich placer gold deposits. The Shuar's resentment of domination and exactions of tribute in gold dust led, in 1599, to the only successful Indian revolt against the Spanish Empire, which was never able to reconquer their territory. Not until the mid-nineteenth century were trading relationships reestablished, followed eventually by missionary posts. With increasing pressure on their territory from colonists as the twentieth century advanced, the Shuar organized themselves into the Federación de Centros Shuaras, which has been functioning since 1964. As one of the oldest and most successful organizations of indigenous resistance, this body attracts foreign assistance and serves as a model to other indigenous peoples of the Amazon.

MICHAEL J. HARNER, *The Jívaro* (1972); HENNING SIVERTS, "Jivaro Headhunters in a Headless Time," in *Western Expansion and Indigenous People*, edited by Elias Sevilla-Casas (1977); ERNESTO SALAZAR, "The Federación Shuar and the Colonization Frontier," in *Cultural Transformations and Ethnicity in Modern Ecuador*, edited by Norman E. Whitten, Jr. (1981); JANET HENDRICKS, "Symbolic Counterhegemony Among the Ecuadorian Shuar," in *Nation-States and Indians in Latin America*, edited by Greg Urban and Joel Sherzer (1991).

MADELINE BARBARA LEONS

See also **Indianismo, Indian Policy, Indians.**

Maria Kunkumas with typical Shuar basket made from *Caludovica palmata* (the Panama hat palm). DR. BRADLEY C. BENNETT.

SICÁN, indigenous name in the Muchik language for an area in the lower La Leche Valley (the Poma district of BATÁN GRANDE) on the north coast of Peru. Literally, it means the house or temple of the moon. The term "Sicán" has been adopted to refer to the archaeological culture that emerged in the Batán Grande region following the demise of the MOCHE culture around A.D. 700–750.

The chronology of the ancient Sicán culture is divided into three periods: Early Sicán lasted from A.D. 700–750 to A.D. 900 but is still poorly known. By A.D. 900, the florescent middle period begins. The Middle Sicán often has been confused with the protohistoric CHIMÚ Kingdom. Sicán was centered on the northern north coast and largely antecedent to the Chimú. The name "Lambayeque" is also sometimes applied to Middle Sicán. Usage of Lambayeque has been problematical as it was defined on the basis of looted ceramics (as a style) and its broader cultural significance built on a literal reading of the legend of Naymlap and his descendants, recorded early in the colonial era.

Middle Sicán cultural characteristics include: (1) a distinct religious art featuring the Sicán Deity and Sicán Lord, who represent the parallel natural and supernatural universes; (2) a powerful theocracy centered at the capital of Sicán, with its dozen monumental temples and rigid, hierarchical society; (3) production and use of arsenical copper (a type of bronze) and gold alloys on an unprecedented scale; and (4) control of an extensive trade in exotic luxury goods (such as gold nuggets, tropical shells, and emeralds) that reached as far as southern Colombia, the upper Amazon, and the Peru-Chile border area. Overall, the economic wealth, political clout, and religious prestige of the Middle Sicán culture were clearly unrivaled in Peru for its period and in some respects unprecedented within Andean civilization. Diffusion of its influence represented a major cultural horizon.

The culture's preeminence came to an end around A.D. 1050. Temples at the capital of Sicán were burned and a new capital was established farther west at El Purgatorio, near Túcume, marking the onset of the Late Sicán (A.D. 1100 to 1375). Around A.D. 1375, the Chimú Kingdom began its northward expansion toward Ecuador, conquering the Sicán people on its way. Within a hundred years, the expanding Inca defeated the Chimú, its coastal rival, and some seventy years later was in turn conquered by the Spaniards.

IZUMI SHIMADA, "Cultural Continuities and Discontinuities on the Northern North Coast, Middle-Late Horizons," in *The Northern Dynasties: Kingship and Statecraft in Chimor,* edited by Michael E. Moseley and Alana Cordy-Collins (1990), pp. 297–392; IZUMI SHIMADA and JOHN F. MERKEL, "Copper-Alloy Metallurgy in Ancient Peru," in *Scientific American* 265, no. 1 (1991): 80–86; IZUMI SHIMADA, "The Regional States of the Coast during Late Intermediate Period: Archaeological Evidence, Ethnohistorical Record and Art Outline (in Italian), in *I Regni Preincaici e Il Mondo Inca* (Pre-Inca regional states and Inca empire), edited by Laura Laurencich-Minelli (1992), pp. 49–64, 97–110; IZUMI SHIMADA and JO ANN GRIFFIN, "Precious Metal Objects of the Middle Sicán," in *Scientific American* 270, no. 4 (1994): 82–89.

IZUMI SHIMADA

SICARIO. *See* **Drugs and Drug Trade.**

SIERRA, STELLA (*b.* 5 July 1917), Panamanian poet. Sierra was born in Aguadulce, Panama. In 1936, she graduated from the Colegio Internacional de María Inmaculada, and in 1954 she received a degree in education with specialization in Spanish from the University of Panama.

Her first two books, *Sinfonía jubilosa en doce sonetos* (1942; Joyful Symphony in Twelve Sonnets) and *Canciones de mar y luna* (1944; Songs of Sea and Moon), confirmed her place in Panamanian letters. Her later publications, *Libre y cautiva* (1947; Free and Captive), *Cinco poemas* (1949; Five Poems), *Poesía* (1962; Poetry), and *Presencia del recuerdo* (1965; Presence of Memory) revealed her control over her poetic resources and the universality of her poetry.

Sierra has won many awards for both her poetry and her fiction. Among them the Demetrio H. Brid Prize for her short story *Con los pies descalzos* (1944; Barefooted), the Miró Prize for *Sinfonía jubilosa,* and a first prize from the Chancellery of Uruguay for her *Himno para la glorificación de Franklin D. Roosevelt* (1946; Hymn in Homage of Franklin D. Roosevelt). She has contributed to the weekly *Semanario Mundo Gráfico,* to *Correo Literario,* and to such literary magazines as *Poesía de América, Cultura,* and *Épocas.* Sierra has taught at the National Institute of Panama and at the University of Panama and has been a delegate at various international conferences.

ENRIQUE JARAMILLO LEVI, *Poesía erótica de Panamá* (1982); GLORIA GUARDIA, *Aproximación a Libre y Cautiva obra escogida de Stella Sierra* (1990); DIANE E. MARTING, ed., *Women Writers of Spanish America* (1987); DAVID FOSTER, comp. *Handbook of Latin American Literature,* 2d ed. (1992), p. 461.

ELBA D. BIRMINGHAM-POKORNY

SIERRA (ECUADOR) the mountain region, covering about 27,500 square miles, or about one quarter of the nation. Despite its location along the equator, the elevation of the sierra (often 9,000 feet and above) gives the region a temperate climate, what *serranos* call eternal springtime. Made up of two parallel branches of the ANDES (375 miles north to south), the sierra has ten major basins, each formed by mountain spurs that connect the two main branches of the mountains. These verdant zones produce barley, CORN, POTATOES, wheat, fruit, and vegetables. Most Ecuadorian cities are set in these valleys, including Ibarra, QUITO, Ambato, RIOBAMBA, and Cuenca. Thickly populated by sedentary farming Indians, the sierra was the focus of Spanish colonizing efforts. In 1800 as much as 90 percent of the population of Ecuador lived in the sierra. By 1992 only about half did, as people fled overcrowding and exploitation by whites. Transportation difficulties have made the sierra a relatively isolated and culturally more traditional zone in Ecuador. The sierra corridor is sometimes known as the "Avenue of the Volcanoes," a name given by nineteenth-century naturalist Baron Alexander von HUMBOLDT.

Details on Ecuador's geography can be found in PRESTON JAMES, *Latin America* (1986). For information on the natives of Ecuador's sierra, see *Handbook of South American Indians,* vol. 2, *The Andean Civilizations,* edited by Julian H. Steward (1963).

RONN F. PINEO

SIERRA (PERU), the Andean highland region where approximately half of the country's population lived in 1990. It is formed by three ranges of mountains with fertile river valleys, high plains, and deep canyons. The western Andean slopes lead to the desertic coastal region, while the easternmost slopes—the *ceja de selva* (jungle's eyebrow)—start the region of the Amazonian rain forest. By the time of the Spanish Conquest, the Andean people had developed a sophisticated system of vertical control that allowed access to a rich variety of crops at different altitudes as well as agrarian techniques such as terracing and irrigation. Under Spanish rule the Sierra became a highly productive mineral region.

JAVIER PULGAR VIDAL, *Geografía del Perú: Las ocho regiones naturales del Perú* (1972).

ALFONSO W. QUIROZ

SIERRA MADRE, the principal mountain system of Mexico. It consists of the Sierra Madre Oriental, Sierra Madre Occidental, Sierra Madre del Sur, Sierra Madre de Oaxaca, and the Sierra Madre de Chiapas. The first four groups form the dissected edges of the vast central plateau of Mexico, while the Chiapas range lies east of the Isthmus of Tehuantepec. Extending the length of Mexico, from the United States to Guatemala, the mountains form a broad northwest-southeast arc. The average elevation of the range is 6,000 to 13,000 feet. Metals such as silver, gold, zinc, and iron first attracted Spanish settlers

Sierra valley, Peru. INSTITUTO AUDIO-VISUAL INKA, CUZCO.

to the Sierra Madre, especially in the northern ranges. Although mining remained important, the exploitation of forest reserves and hydroelectric sites drew developers during the twentieth century. Throughout the Sierra Madre, isolated sections remain a refuge for small Indian groups maintaining their traditional ways of life.

The Occidental and Oriental mountains define the western and eastern edges of the central plateau and are similar in height. The Occidental range is volcanic and parallels the western coast of Mexico for 1,000 miles through the states of Chihuahua, Sonora, Sinaloa, Durango, and Nayarit. Vegetation on the steep lower slopes is poor, but the higher elevations contain some of the most important coniferous forest stands in the country. The deep canyons along the western slope support half a dozen major dams that provide water to the irrigated fields of Sonora and Sinaloa. Some agriculture exists within the intermontane valleys, but mining, especially of silver, has been the principal motive for settlement in the Sierra Madre Occidental.

The Sierra Madre Oriental is a series of elongated limestone ranges that parallel the Gulf of Mexico, crossing through Coahuila, Nuevo León, Tamaulipas, and San Luis Potosí states. From the central plateau, the Oriental range appears as a small lip, but from the Gulf, the peaks form an impressive escarpment. During the

colonial era, the Veracruz-Jalapa road that crossed the sierra was the principal artery between the coast and the central plateau. The southern tip of the 700-mile-long chain is crowned by 18,760-foot Mount Orizaba (Citlaltépetl), the highest mountain in Mexico.

The Sierra Madre del Sur extends from Mount Orizaba toward the Pacific coast, ending at the Isthmus of Tehuantepec. This highly dissected upland area contains knife-edged ridges and steep valleys that cover Guerrero and Oaxaca states. Formed by ancient crystalline rock, the southern highlands average 7,000 feet in height and contain a few peaks over 10,000 feet. The eastern portion of this uplifted area is called the Sierra Madre de Oaxaca. Before the Conquest this area was inhabited by several important Indian groups, notably the ZAPOTECS and MIXTECS. Twentieth-century economic activities throughout the area have been limited to mining, forestry, coffee production, and subsistence farming.

The smaller Sierra Madre de Chiapas begins east of the Isthmus of Tehuantepec, crosses the state of Chipas, and reaches into western Guatemala. It is mostly crystalline rock with some volcanic activity. This area does not seem to have been very populated during pre-Hispanic times and is still sparsely populated. Forestry and coffee are the most important activities in this isolated area.

DAVID HENDERSON, "Land, Man, and Time," in *Six Faces of Mexico,* edited by Russell C. Ewing (1966), pp. 103–160; JORGE L. TAMAYO, *Geografía moderna de México,* 9th ed. (1980); D. J. FOX, "Mexico," in *Latin America: Geographical Perspectives,* 2d ed., edited by Harold Blakemore and Clifford Smith (1983), pp. 25–76; ROBERT C. WEST and JOHN P. AUGELLI, *Middle America: Its Lands and Peoples,* 3d ed. (1989), pp. 24–31.

MARIE D. PRICE

SIERRA MAESTRA, the coastal mountain chain in Cuba's southeast Oriente Province. Coastal swampland gives way to an inaccessible, rugged spine dividing the island. The Sierra Maestra is the highest Cuban range, with such local branches as Sierra Norte and Sierra Trinidad. It was the refuge of Cuba's rebels: runaway slaves, independence leaders José MARTÍ and Máximo GÓMEZ Y BÁEZ, Fidel CASTRO, and finally anti-Castro guerrillas in the 1960s.

In the Sierras, during the TEN YEARS' WAR (1868–1878), Carlos Manuel de CÉSPEDES and Máximo Gómez y Báez developed a guerrilla strategy later used by Castro: using *guajiro* (mountain peasant) guerrillas in hit-and-run tactics, burning cane fields, and courting dissatisfied planters. In the War for Independence (1895–1899), Cuban literary figure and patriot José Martí died in a Sierras ambush.

In December 1956, Fidel Castro, a native of Oriente, repeated Martí's return from exile to a Sierra-based campaign. The climax was the BATISTA offensive "Fin de Fidel," from May to August 1958. The decisive battles were for the Sierra ridge, at Santo Domingo; and for Castro's headquarters, at El Jigüe.

The Sierra Maestra Manifesto and the agrarian reform law (Revolutionary Law 1) were symbolic measures to win middle-class support. However, Castro reached a secret alliance with the Communist Party, and Sierra "liberated zones" foreshadowed social revolution. Anti-Castro guerrillas were effectively eliminated from the Sierras only in the late 1960s.

TAD SZULC, *Fidel: A Critical Portrait* (1986).

PAT KONRAD

SIERRA MÉNDEZ, JUSTO (*b.* 26 January 1848; *d.* 13 September 1912), Mexican writer, political thinker, historian, and educational leader. Sierra was born in Campeche, the son of prominent Yucatecan politician, writer, and jurist Justo SIERRA O'REILLY, and after 1861 lived and was educated in Mexico City, receiving a law degree in 1871 from the Escuela de Derecho. A protégé of Ignacio M. ALTAMIRANO, in 1868 Sierra began to write poetry, short stories, plays, and a novel. His career as a political journalist and thinker began in 1874 and reached a climax in the important newspaper *La Libertad* (1878–1884), which he directed until 1880, and which was an exponent of a "new" or transformed liberalism that called for a strong government and economic development. Of several histories, his most important was *Evolución política del pueblo mexicano,* first published under another title in 1900–1902. He was a deputy to Congress from 1880 until 1894, when he was appointed to

Sierra Madre. © KAL MULLER / WOODFIN CAMP & ASSOCIATES.

the Supreme Court. As an educator, he taught at the National Preparatory School after 1877 and led the First and Second National Congresses of Public Instruction in 1889 and 1891, which established the principle of free obligatory primary education and reaffirmed the positivist preparatory curriculum. In 1901 he became subsecretary of public instruction, and then secretary from 1905 to 1911. He founded the NATIONAL AUTONOMOUS UNIVERSITY OF MEXICO (UNAM) in 1910. In 1912 he was appointed minister to Spain, where he died.

Sierra was the major Mexican intellectual of his era. His political and educational thought was characterized by a continuing tension between classic liberal principles, including French spiritualism, and POSITIVISM. Though an adherent of the regime of Porfirio DÍAZ (1877–1880, 1884–1911), Sierra led the effort (1892–1893) by the CIENTÍFICOS to limit presidential authority.

Sierra's *Obras completas*, 15 vols. (1948), includes a biography by editor Agustín Yáñez. See also C. A. HALE, *The Transformation of Liberalism in Late Nineteenth-Century Mexico* (1989).

CHARLES A. HALE

SIERRA O'REILLY, JUSTO (*b.* 24 September 1814; *d.* 15 January 1861); Yucatecan jurist, journalist, novelist, and historian. The illegitimate son of a parish priest, Sierra grew up in Mérida and was educated first at the local seminary. Later he studied law in Mexico City (1838). After graduation he returned to Yucatán and practiced as a lawyer before turning to politics (serving as judge, ambassador, and congressman) and literary pursuits. He founded newspapers and wrote books on history and literature. He also composed fiction, his most famous novel probably being *La hija del judío* (The Jew's Daughter), a romance. He is the author of the Mexican republic's civil code (1860) and the father of Justo SIERRA MÉNDEZ (1847–1912).

MARY WILHELMINE WILLIAMS, "Secessionist Diplomacy of Yucatán," in *Hispanic American Historical Review* 9, no. 2 (1929): 132–143; *Enciclopedia yucatanense* (1944), vol. 5, pp. 623–631, and vol. 7, pp. 205–244.

ROBERT W. PATCH

SIETE DE MARZO (1849), a divisive Colombian presidential selection. The tumultuous presidential selection of José Hilario LÓPEZ on the siete de marzo (7 March) signaled the Colombian Liberal Party's domination of the central government that lasted until 1885. The nascent Conservative Party, seriously divided by the reformist administration of the nominally conservative Tomás Cipriano de MOSQUERA, fielded several candidates in the 1848 contest. Splitting the vote in this manner enabled López to gain a plurality (López, 725; José Joaquín Gori, 384; Rufino Cuervo, 304; Mariano Ospina Rodríguez, 81; Joaquín María Barriga, 74; Florentino González, 71; and Eusebio Borrero, 52). The Congress,

following its constitutional mandate to select the president, chose the Liberal López on 7 March 1849 in the face of severe intimidation by student and artisan militants in the congressional gallery. Conservatives claimed that crowd pressures had made the selection process illegitimate. The López regime (1849–1853) initiated sweeping liberal reforms, which heightened the symbolism of the pivotal event.

JOSÉ MANUEL RESTREPO, *Historia de la Nueva Granada: 1845–54*, vol. 2 (1963), pp. 103–106; HELEN DELPAR, *Red Against Blue: The Liberal Party in Colombian Politics, 1863–1899* (1981), pp. 5–6; DAVID BUSHNELL and NEILL MACAULAY, *The Emergence of Latin America in the Nineteenth Century* (1988), pp. 209–220.

DAVID SOWELL

See also **Colombia: Political Parties.**

SIETE PARTIDAS, Castilian legal code influenced by principles of Roman law. The *Siete Partidas* (Seven Divisions of Law) (1265) was the greatest achievement of Alfonso X of Castile and León. Produced by jurists well-versed in Roman law, the compendium was meant to provide the Castilian monarch with a universal system of royal justice and absolute authority that would replace the jurisdictional privileges of the towns and noble estates of the realm. Because of strong opposition, the law was never put into effect and the *Siete Partidas*, written in the Castilian vernacular, merely served as a textbook or legal reference work to supplement previously existing laws.

EVELYN STEFANOS PROCTER, *Alfonso X of Castile: Patron of Literature and Learning* (1951); JOSÉ ANTONIO MARAVALL, *Estudios de historia del pensamiento español* (1967); COLIN M. MAC LACHLAN, *Criminal Justice in Eighteenth-Century Mexico* (1974).

SUZANNE HILES BURKHOLDER

SIGAUD, EUGENIO DE PROENÇA (*b.* 1889; *d.* 1979) Brazilian architectural engineer and painter. Born in the interior of the state of Rio de Janeiro, Sigaud moved to Rio in the early 1920s to study architecture at the National School of Fine Arts. While there, the artist Modesto Brocos helped perfect Sigaud's drawing skills. In 1931 Sigaud joined Edson Mota, João Rescala, José Pancetti, Milton Dacosta, and other young artists to form the Núcleo Bernardelli, a group that sought to counter the aesthetic traditionalism of the National School of Fine Arts. The Núcleo came to represent a moderate wing of the Brazilian modernist movement.

Sigaud's career consisted of two parallel aspects: he owned an architectural engineering and construction company, and he achieved prominence as a painter of social themes. His canvases and murals depict urban construction workers on scaffolding as well as rural coffee pickers. His most celebrated works include a painting entitled *Work Accident*, an architectural and interior design project for the church of São Jorge, and mural paintings for the cathedral of Jacarèzinho. He also dabbled in printing and book illustration.

Arte no Brasil, vol. 2 (1979), pp. 763–765.

CAREN A. MEGHREBLIAN

SIGÜENZA Y GÓNGORA, CARLOS DE (*b.* 20 August 1645; *d.* 22 August 1700), premier intellectual of seventeenth-century Mexico. Born in Mexico City, Sigüenza y Góngora was the son of a former tutor to the Spanish royal family; on his mother's side, he was distantly related to the poet Luís de Góngora. As a youth, he entered the JESUIT order, but curfew violations led to his expulsion in 1668. He then resumed theological and secular studies at the University of Mexico, where, in 1672, he gained the chair of mathematics and astrology. Over time, he accumulated several other important positions, including those of royal cosmographer of New Spain, chaplain of the Amor de Dios Hospital, and almoner to the archbishop of Mexico.

This talented polymath wrote extensively on a wide variety of subjects, but most of his works were not published. Despite his official capacity as an astrologer, Sigüenza y Góngora roundly belabored contemporary "superstitions." His scientific endeavors reached their summit with the *Libra astronómica y filosófica* (1690), an astronomical treatise in which he argued that comets were a natural phenomenon rather than an omen of divine displeasure; the work also attacked Aristotelian orthodoxy and upheld the validity of Mexican scholarship. In a more journalistic vein, Sigüenza y Góngora chronicled the triumph of Spanish arms in New Mexico and the Caribbean and wrote the finest eyewitness account of the Mexico City riot of 1692.

Sigüenza y Góngora devoted much scholarly energy to the study of Mexico's pre-Hispanic past. More important, he acquired and preserved the magnificent Ixtlilxochitl collection of codices and manuscripts. However, while he glorified the Aztec Empire, even claiming it as Mexico's version of classical antiquity, he despised the Indian masses of his own day. This contradiction ultimately proved fatal to his studies of indigenous peoples, which (along with a projected Indian museum) he abandoned after the 1692 riot.

His intellectual activities were further curtailed after 1694, when failing health forced him to resign his university post. Assailed by numerous ailments, he died in Mexico City. In retrospect, Sigüenza y Góngora appears as a precursor of both the Mexican Enlightenment and Mexican nationalism. Throughout his writings, he sought to delineate, praise, and defend the emerging creole *patria,* particularly as exemplified in its greatest center, Mexico City.

IRVING A. LEONARD, *Don Carlos de Sigüenza y Góngora: A Mexican Savant of the Seventeenth Century* (1929); ELÍAS TRABULSE, *Ciencia y religión en el siglo xvii* (1974); ANTHONY PAGDEN, *Spanish Imperialism and the Political Imagination* (1990), pp. 90–116; D. A. BRADING, *The First America: The Spanish Monarchy, Creole Patriots, and the Liberal State, 1492–1867* (1991), pp. 363–371.

R. DOUGLAS COPE

SILES ZUAZO, HERNÁN (*b.* 21 March 1914), president of Bolivia (1956–1960, 1982–1985). Born in La Paz, the son of Hernando Siles Reyes, president of Bolivia (1926–1930), Siles Zuazo studied there at the American Institute and the National University. One of the founders of the Nationalist Revolutionary Movement (MNR) in 1941, he personally commanded the MNR forces in the April 1952 revolution. That year Siles became vice president of Bolivia, and in 1956 he was elected president. His principal task in office was to control the high inflation rate set off by the revolutionary process. Confronting organized labor, a faction of which supported the MNR, he was responsible for the implementation of an International Monetary Fund stabilization program. In 1960 he stepped down and was named Bolivian ambassador to Uruguay.

When the military overthrew the MNR in 1964, Siles became the consummate opponent of the authoritarian rulers, searching for ways to restore civilian rule. Unlike other founders of the MNR, Siles never allied himself with any faction of the military; instead he suffered imprisonment on several occasions and exile in Uruguay. In 1972 Siles founded a leftist offshoot of the MNR, which he called the MNR de Izquierda (MNRI). When the military convoked elections in the late 1970s, Siles led his MNRI into a coalition dubbed the Popular and Democratic Union (Unidad Democrática y Popular—UDP) that included the Communist Party and the young Movimiento de Izquierda Revolucionaria (MIR). As the UDP's presidential candidate, Siles won three consecutive elections in 1978, 1979, and 1980; each time he was denied victory either because his coalition did not achieve the 50 percent plus required or because the military prevented him from taking power.

In October 1982, Siles Zuazo was elected president of Bolivia by the Congress. Over the next three years, he presided over one of the most difficult periods in Bolivian history. His government faced the impossible task of both resolving the country's worst economic crisis, caused by years of military mismanagement, and responding to the pent-up demands of social groups. At the same time, Siles faced extreme pressure from international financial institutions to implement harsh austerity measures and from the United States to combat the booming cocaine industry. Governing Bolivia under these circumstances proved to be a daunting task. By late 1984, the economy had fallen to a historic low, reaching a yearly hyperinflation rate of 26,000 percent. Faced with tremendous pressure from every sector of Bolivian society, Siles was forced to convoke elections for July 1985 and step down one year before his term expired.

Siles retired from politics in 1985 and returned to

Uruguay, where he has lived ever since. Siles was largely responsible for launching Bolivia on the route to democracy.

JAMES M. MALLOY and EDUARDO A. GAMARRA, *Revolution and Reaction: Bolivia, 1964–1985* (1988); LUIS ANTEZA ERGUETA, *Hernán Siles Zuazo: El estrategy y la contrarevolución* (1979).

EDUARDO A. GAMARRA

See also **Bolivia: Political Parties; Drugs and Drug Trade.**

SILK INDUSTRY AND TRADE. Brazil never assumed an importance comparable to that of Mexico within the context of colonial trade with Asia. Nevertheless, by the mid-seventeenth century, Portuguese East India merchantmen were calling at major Brazilian ports on their return voyages, in spite of official restraints regarding direct trade with the American colony. Silk ranked high among the products "illicitly" sold in Brazil, and studies based on estate inventories have demonstrated that fine textiles, including silk, were an important component of the possessions of wealthy Brazilians, as they were in Mexico. The discovery of gold in Minas Gerais led to an intensification of this direct trade in Asian goods during the eighteenth century. During the phase of Pombaline monopoly trade companies (1755–1777), silkworms and the cultivation of mulberry trees were successfully introduced to Maranhão, and Brazilian silk was actually exported to Lisbon. However, the experience was apparently short-lived. In the second quarter of the nineteenth century the provincial government of Minas Gerais attempted to promote silk production there, but these efforts resulted in failure. Similar efforts had been made in the province of Rio de Janeiro since 1811, and government subsidies were to prove vital to the success of a silk enterprise established at Itaguaí in the 1840s. Cloth produced by the Imperial Companhia Serapédica de Itaguahy figured at the Paris Exposition of 1851, but this vertically integrated "factory" did not survive beyond the last decade of the nineteenth century. Silk production was not taken up again until the 1920s, when a factory was established at Campinas in the state of São Paulo. The key to the success of this PAULISTA enterprise was the availability of Japanese immigrants who were familiar with the various phases of production. This immigrant element explains the near total concentration of the present-day Brazilian silk industry in São Paulo.

The silk trade is dealt with in C. R. BOXER, *The Portuguese Seaborne Empire, 1415–1825* (1973). For a brief account of silk production in Brazil see ANDRÉE MANSUY-DINIZ SILVA, "Imperial Re-organization, 1750–1808," in *Colonial Brazil*, edited by Leslie Bethell (1987), p. 268.

DOUGLAS COLE LIBBY

See also **Textile Industry.**

SILVA, BARTOLOMEU BUENO DA. See **Bandeiras.**

SILVA, BENEDITA DA (Benedita Souza da Silva; *b.* 11 March 1942), first Afro-Brazilian woman to be elected to Brazil's congress. Da Silva, known as Bené, was one of thirteen children born to a poor Rio de Janeiro family. Married at sixteen, she had five children in rapid succession, of whom only two survived. She was an early member of the newly formed Worker's Party (Partido dos Trabalhadores—PT), and in 1982 successfully ran on the PT ticket for Rio's city council. In 1986, having campaigned largely in Rio's FAVELAS (slums), she was elected as a federal deputy to the Chamber of Deputies, Brazil's lower house, becoming one of only nine blacks and twenty-five women in Brazil's 559-member Congress. Reelected in 1990, she continues to live in Chapéu da Mangueira, the Rio *favela* that is her home.

An energetic supporter of the rights of the oppressed, da Silva describes herself as "three times a minority," stating: "As a black, a woman, and a *favelada* [slum dweller], I have a special responsibility to speak out on the subjects that I know about—against racial discrimination, against the unequal rights of women, and against the injustices suffered by the poor." An evangelical Christian, da Silva is a member of Brazil's rapidly growing Assembly of God Church. She ran unsuccessfully for mayor of Rio de Janeiro in 1992. In 1994 she was elected senator from Rio de Janeiro, becoming the first black woman to serve in the Senate.

ALAN RIDING, "One Woman's Mission: To Make Brasília Sensitive," *New York Times*, 19 February 1987, 4; HAL LANGFUR, "From Slums of Rio to Halls of Power," *Christian Science Monitor*, 24 September 1987, 1; JOHN MARCOM, JR., "The Fire Down South," *Forbes*, 15 October 1990, 56; JOANN MCFARLANE-TAYLOR, "Benedita da Silva Fighting for the Favelas," *Essence*, June 1991, 36.

DAPHNE PATAI

See slso **Brazil: Political Parties; Women.**

SILVA, CLARA (*b.* 1907; *d.* 1976), Uruguayan poet, novelist, and critic. Silva was born in Montevideo and began writing poetry early on. Her first book, *La cabellera oscura* (The Dark Mane, 1945), showed a mature writer. It was followed by *Memoria de la nada* (1948). A second phase in her work began with *Los delirios* (1954), a collection of sonnets on human and divine love. *Las bodas* (The Wedding, 1960) is a collection of poems that deal with religion, a preoccupation that continued in *Preludio indiano y otros poemas* (1960) and more pointedly in *Guitarra en sombra* (1964). *Juicio final* (1971) is her last book of poems. Her fiction included *El alma y los perros* (The Soul and the Dogs, 1962), *Aviso a la población* (Warning to the Population, 1964), *Habitación testigo* (A Room as Witness, 1967), *Prohibido pasar* (1969), a collection of short stories, and *Las furias del sueño* (The Furies of Dreaming, 1975).

An active participant in the cultural and literary life of Montevideo, she was married to Alberto ZUM FELDE, a prominent critic and writer. She wrote two books on the life and work of the modernist Uruguayan poet Delmira AGUSTINI and elaborated an idealist vision of America through three universal themes: nature, love, and death. In 1976 she received the Grand National Prize of Literature of Uruguay. Silva died in Montevideo.

The Archive of Hispanic Literature on Tape: A Descriptive Guide, compiled by FRANCISCO AGUILERA and edited by GEORGETTE MAGASSY DORN (1974); SARAH BOLLO, *Literatura uruguaya, 1807–1975* (1976); and *Diccionario de literatura uruguaya* (1987).

MAGDALENA GARCÍA PINTO

SILVA, FRANCISCO MANUEL DA (*b.* 21 February 1795; *d.* 18 December 1865), Brazilian conductor, cellist, teacher, and composer. Silva studied at the music school in which Padre José Maurício Nunes GARCIA taught children who were unable to pay for musical instruction. At the age of ten he began to study cello and shortly thereafter was accepted as a boy soprano in the Royal Chapel Choir. He studied counterpoint and composition with Sigismund Neukomm, the Austrian composer who had been lured to Brazil by the promises of Dom JOÃO VI, the reigning monarch intent on establishing a school of fine arts. Although Silva wrote considerable sacred music, several art songs, and some instrumental and piano music, he is remembered principally for his patriotic songs and especially for composing the Brazilian national anthem.

AYRES DE ANDRADE, *Francisco Manuel da Silva e seu tempo, 1808–1865,* 2 vols. (1967); GÉRARD BÉHAGUE, *Music in Latin America* (1979).

DAVID P. APPLEBY

SILVA, JOSÉ ANTÔNIO DA (*b.* 1909), Brazilian painter. Born in the interior of the state of São Paulo, Silva gave up his life as a rural agricultural laborer and at the age of thirty-seven, moved to São José do Rio Prêto, where he taught himself painting. Iconoclastic, with a contempt for art critics, Silva did a painting entitled *Hanging the Critics.* For his first three compositions, he won the first prize at a local exhibition whose jury, ironically, was composed of several important art critics.

While early works such as *Houses in the Rain* have an impressionistic look, later paintings were more radical and expressionistic. Examples of these latter include *Roundup, Crucifixion, Swimmers,* and *Demon Stampeding the Herd.* In his best-known work, *The Cotton Harvest,* for instance, painted in 1949, Silva attained dramatic effects by his unconventional use of color and bold composition. His paintings document his own life as well as that of the history of Brazil. He participated in a number of São Paulo biennials and exhibited his works outside of Brazil, including the 1954 Hispano-American Biennial in Havana and two Venice bienalles. In 1967 he founded a musuem in São José do Rio Prêto in which he housed old baroque artwork from the local area, paintings of other artists, and those of his own. Silva is the author of *The Romance of My Life* (1949) and two novels, *Alice* and *Maria Clara.*

SELDEN RODMAN, *Genius in the Backlands: Popular Artists of Brazil* (1977), pp. 54–73; *Arte no Brasil,* vol. 2 (1979), pp. 828–829; FUNDAÇÃO NACIONAL DE ARTE, *Pinacoteca do Estado—São Paulo* (1982), pp. 138–139.

CAREN A. MEGHREBLIAN

SILVA, JOSÉ ASUNCIÓN (*b.* 26 November 1865; *d.* 24 May 1896), Colombian poet and important precursor of Spanish modernism. Silva was born into wealth, but left school early due to difficulties with his fellow students. He continued to read the classics (French, English, and Spanish) with other young literati and traveled extensively in Europe (1884–1886), where he met Oscar Wilde and Stéphane Mallarmé. His family's ruin in the 1885 civil war forced his return. He attempted to establish a business career, but failed. His lack of success and his sister's death forced him to work as secretary of the Colombian Legation in Venezuela (1894). He lost his manuscripts in a shipwreck on his return trip to Colombia and committed suicide upon failing to rebuild his career a second time. Silva's works are the posthumous *De sobremesa* (1925), a partly autobiographical novel, and *Poesías* (1910). Despite their brevity, both are revolutionary in theme and technique. His poems rate among the most musical and rhythmic in the Spanish language. Most notable are "Nocturno III," on the death of his sister Elvira, "Día de difuntos," "Los maderos de San Juan," and "Vejeces."

Diccionario de la literatura latinoamericana: Colombia (1959); BETTY TYREE OSIEK, *José Asunción Silva: Estudio estilístico de su poesía* (1968); HÉCTOR H. ORJUELA, *"De sobremesa" y otros estudios sobre José Asunción Silva* (1976); BETTY TYREE OSIEK, *José Asunción Silva* (1978); SONYA A. INGWERSEN, *Light and Longing: Silva and Darío: Modernism and Religious Heterodoxy* (1986).

MARÍA A. SALGADO

SILVA, JOSÉ BARBOSA DA. *See* **Sinhô.**

SILVA, LINDOLFO (*b.* 25 November 1924), rural labor spokesman of the Brazilian Communist Party (PCB). Born on a farm in Rio de Janeiro State, he worked as a tailor until hired by the PCB in 1952. In 1954, he helped found the semiclandestine Union of Farmers and Agricultural Laborers of Brazil (ULTAB), becoming its first secretary. He traveled the nation to address farm workers, published regularly on rural labor matters, and led delegations of workers to lobby officials and attend Soviet-bloc conferences on peasants. Silva's 1963 election as president of the government-sanctioned National Confederation of Agricultural Laborers demonstrated PCB strength in the countryside and in national politics. With the coup d'état of 1964, the military suppressed the PCB, and Silva went into hiding. He did, however, remain a party bureaucrat into the 1990s.

NEALE J. PEARSON, *Small Farmer and Rural Worker Pressure Groups in Brazil* (1967); CLODOMIR MORAES, "Peasant Leagues in Brazil," in *Agrarian Problems and Peasant Movements in Latin America,* edited by Rodolfo Stavenhagen (1970).

CLIFF WELCH

SILVA, LUÍS INÁCIO LULA DA (b. 6 October 1945), Brazilian politician. Luís Inácio Lula da Silva (popularly known as Lula) was born in Garanhuns, Pernambuco, the son of Aristides Inácio da Silva and Euridice Ferreira de Melo. A lathe operator, he became a prominent labor leader of the *novo sindicalismo* labor movement that emerged after the Getúlio Vargas era.

From 1979 to 1981, he was president of the São Bernardo do Campo Metallurgical Workers Union of São Paulo and led several strikes in the São Paulo industrial area. In 1986, he received the most votes in the parliamentary elections of the state of São Paulo and was elected federal deputy. In that capacity, he was a participant in the *constituinte* (constitutional convention) that drafted the 1988 constitution. During this constitutional convention, he voted in favor of nationalization of the country's mineral reserves, agrarian reform, protection of national enterprises, and a forty-hour work week. He continued to serve in the federal congress until 1990.

After founding the Partido dos Trabalhadores (Workers' Party, or PT) in 1980, he ran for the presidency of the republic in 1989 and again in 1994. In the runoff elections, Lula lost to Fernando COLLOR DE MELLO and to Fernando Henrique CARDOVA, respectively. He remains a major political figure in Brazil and frequently travels and lectures abroad where he is a well-known socialist labor leader.

For further reading, see Lula's biography: EMIR SADER, *Without Fear of Being Happy* (1991).

IÊDA SIQUEIRA WIARDA

SILVA, ORLANDO (Orlando Garcia da Silva; *b.* 3 October 1915; *d.* 1978), Brazilian singer and songwriter. As a youngster, Silva loved to sing, carrying leaflets of popular songs with him everywhere. Despite his lack of formal training either in music or voice, Silva received an invitation from Francisco ALVES to sing in his program on Rádio Cajuti in 1934. That same year, Silva starred in radio shows under the pseudonym Orlando Navarro and made his first recordings, "Olha a baiana" (Look at the Girl of Bahia) and "Ondas curtas" (Short Waves). Throughout his career, Silva appeared in various films, including *Cidade-mulher* (City Woman, 1934), *Banana da terra* (Banana of the Earth, 1938), and *Segura*

essa mulher (Hold That Woman, 1946). In 1936 he participated in the inauguration of Rádio Nacional, where he became the first singer to have his own show. The following year he recorded one of his greatest hits, "Lábios que beijei" (Lips That I Kissed). Silva was the first singer to interpret PIXINGUINHA's famous "Carinhoso" (Darling). In 1939, four of his productions received prizes: "A jardineira" (The Gardener), "Meu consolo é você" (You Are My Solace), "História antiga" (Ancient History), and "O homem sem mulher não vale nada" (A Man Is Worthless Without a Woman). In 1954, while broadcasting his midday radio program Doze Badaladas, which boasted a huge audience, Silva was awarded the title *rei do rádio* (king of radio). A few years later, he released the record *Carinhoso*, a recording of his greatest hits.

MARCOS ANTÔNIO MARCONDES, ed., *Enciclopédia da música brasileira: Erudita folclórica popular* (1977).

LISA MARIĆ

SILVA, XICA DA (*b.* ca. 1745; *d.* ca. 1796), mulatto mistress of the fantastically rich João Fernandes de Oliveira the younger, a diamond contractor in Minas Gerais from 1759 to 1771. Oliveira was so deeply in love with the slave Francisca (her baptismal name) that he convinced her owner to set her free. The story of Xica da Silva is a mixture of fact and legend. Apparently, Oliveira lavished a fortune on her, including building an artificial lake complete with sailing vessels.

Xica da Silva, the daughter of a Portuguese man and an African slave, has assumed an enduring place in the history of Brazil as a personification of the slave woman whose beauty and charms permit her to gain power over her master and lover. For some, her stature is a reflection of the cult of *mulata* beauty. For others, she represents a nationalist anti-imperialist statement. This latter perspective is evident in the film *Xica da Silva* (directed by Carlos Diegues, 1976; released in the United States, 1982), in which Xica da Silva uses her wiles to combat the Portuguese imperial authorities.

JOAQUIM FELICIO DOS SANTOS, *Memórias do distrito diamantino,* 3d ed. (1956); CHARLES R. BOXER, *The Golden Age of Brazil: 1695–1750* (1964).

DONALD RAMOS

SILVA HENRÍQUEZ, RAÚL (*b.* 27 September 1907), archbishop of Santiago, Chile (1961–1983), during a period of intensifying political struggle between the Left, Right, and Center, which culminated in the 1973 right-wing military coup that brought General Augusto PINOCHET to power.

Unlike the majority of Chilean bishops, Silva was a member of the Salesians, a religious order dedicated primarily to missionary and educational work. Trained as a lawyer at the Catholic University in Santiago, Silva studied philosophy and theology in Italy, where he was ordained in 1938. Upon his return to Chile, he served as a professor and administrator in the Salesian major seminary and secondary schools. In the 1950s he became the director of Cáritas, a church-sponsored social welfare agency that focused on the urban and rural poor.

Silva was appointed to the archbishopric of Santiago in 1961 as a compromise between ostensibly more liberal and conservative candidates. The prelate soon became identified with the progressive sector and was particularly active in promoting workers' rights and agrarian reform, in part through divestment of some of the Catholic church's own properties. He was made a cardinal in 1962.

Silva maintained courteous relations with the Socialist government of Salvador ALLENDE (1970–1973), repeatedly serving as a mediator between it and the centrist Christian Democratic opposition. Eventually he came to accept military intervention as necessary in view of escalating public chaos and a deepening economic crisis. After the coup that ousted Allende, as the extent of assassinations, torture, and disappearances, as well as generalized repression became apparent, Silva helped organize the ecumenical Committee of Cooperation for Peace. When Pinochet forced that institution to close in 1975, the prelate created the VICARIATE OF SOLIDARITY to provide legal, medical, and social services to victims of the Pinochet regime. He also supported the creation of the Academy of Christian Humanism to analyze public policy issues and assess government responses. By the time of his retirement in 1983, he had become one of the most outspoken critics of the military government.

HANNAH W. STEWART-GAMBINO, *The Church and Politics in the Chilean Countryside* (1992).

MARGARET E. CRAHAN

SILVA HERZOG, JESÚS (*b.* 14 November 1892; *d.* 14 March 1985), leading Mexican economist, author, intellectual, and public figure. Born in San Luis Potosí, he was the son of a German immigrant mother and Mexican engineer. Silva Herzog began his career as a teacher at the National Teachers School in 1919 and rose to prominence in the Secretariat of Education. After serving as ambassador to the Soviet Union, he managed Pemex, the national petroleum concern, for Lázaro Cárdenas in 1939. He served many years as a professor of economics at the National University, where he trained many disciples, and founded and directed *Cuadernos Americanos*, a leading interdisciplinary, intellectual journal. A recipient of the National Prize in Arts and Sciences (1962), Silva Herzog died in Mexico City.

JESÚS SILVA HERZOG, *Una vida en la vida de México* (1972) and *Mis últimas andanzas, 1947–1972* (1973).

RODERIC AI CAMP

SILVA LISBOA, JOSÉ DA (Visconde de Cairú; *b.* 16 July 1756; *d.* 20 August 1835), Brazilian political economist and politician. Born in Brazil of a Portuguese father and Bahian mother, Silva Lisboa, completed his education at the University of Coimbra in Portugal, then taught Greek, Hebrew, and moral philosophy at Coimbra and in Bahia. Influenced especially by Adam Smith, he published *Princípios de direito mercantil* (1798, 1801) and *Princípios de economia política* (1804), the first major works in Portuguese about liberal political economic theory.

When the Portuguese court, fleeing Napoleon's invasion of the Iberian Peninsula, arrived in Bahia in 1808, Silva Lisboa inspired Emperor João VI's first decree in Brazil, which opened Brazilian ports to direct commerce with foreign nations. Serving as government spokesman, he argued in *Observações sobre o comércio franco do Brasil* (1808) that his free-trade measure would increase government revenues and revive Portuguese manufacturing by forcing it to compete with other nations' industries. Although it did not remove all monopolies and special privileges, the decree that opened Brazil's ports represented a major shift away from mercantilist colonial policies.

In the last years before independence, Silva Lisboa defended the idea of constitutional monarchy and opposed the reimposition of mercantilism but did not call for Brazil's separation from Portugal. After that separation came to pass, his loyalty to the first emperor of independent Brazil marked him as a political conservative. Through his career, Silva Lisboa held high political offices, including member of the 1823 Constituent Assembly and senator from Bahia (1826–1835).

JOÃO SOARES DUTRA, *Cairú* (1943, 1964); PINTO DE AGUIAR, *A abertura dos portos: Cairú e os ingleses* (1960); EMÍLIA VIOTTI DA COSTA, "The Political Emancipation of Brazil," in *From Colony to Nation: Essays on the Independence of Brazil*, edited by A. J. R. Russell-Wood (1975), pp. 43–88.

ROGER A. KITTLESON

SILVA XAVIER, JOAQUIM JOSÉ DA (Tirandentes; *b.* 1746; *d.* 21 April 1792), a participant in the INCONFIDÊNCIA MINEIRA. Silva Xavier was born near São João del Rei, Minas Gerais, Brazil. His father was a Portuguese-born gold miner important enough to be elected to the town council of São João del Rei; his mother was a native of Minas Gerais. Orphaned at an early age, Silva Xavier was raised by his brother, a priest. It is probable that his godfather, a dentist, provided Silva Xavier with the skills of what became his occasional trade and thus was the source of his nickname, Tiradentes (Toothpuller).

After an unsuccessful career as a muleteer and gold miner, Silva Xavier joined the royal dragoons as an *alferes* (ensign). He became the commander of the troops guarding a crucial portion of the Caminho Novo, the road between the mining district and Rio de Janeiro—an important post because gold and diamonds were shipped over this road.

Joaquim José da Silva Xavier. COLLECTION OF VICENTE GESUALDO.

Silva Xavier became involved in plotting independence after meeting José Álvares Maciel, newly returned from Portugal and England and imbued with the ideas of the French Enlightenment. The serious planning took shape in late 1788. Silva Xavier's motives for participating were probably a mixture of personal frustration at repeatedly being passed over for promotion and ideological commitment to ending Portuguese domination. Of the central group of plotters, Silva Xavier was the least important socially but perhaps was the most active in spreading their ideas. Under questioning he was unique in assuming sole responsibility for the plot. He was the only plotter to be executed by the state.

Silva Xavier has become one of the major heroic figures of Brazil's past—a symbol of opposition to Portuguese imperialism and of advocacy of Brazilian independence. While his role in the Inconfidência Mineira has often been controversial, he now is a significant symbol of Brazilian nationalism, reflecting the need for a national hero with strong republican roots.

KENNETH R. MAXWELL, *Conflicts and Conspiracies: Brazil and Portugal, 1750–1808* (1973).

DONALD RAMOS

SILVER MINING. *See* **Mining: Colonial Spanish America.**

SIMON, ANTOINE (*b.* ca. 1844; *d.* ca. 1923), president of Haiti (1908–1911). Simon overthrew Pierre NORD-

ALEXIS and became the first black since Lysius SALOMON to occupy the president's chair. From southern Haiti, uneducated, and with real sympathy for common folk and folk culture, Simon exhibited populist qualities. But overwhelming problems isolated him from those whom he might have served well.

Growing U.S. capitalist interests burdened his administration. The City Bank of New York extended its interests in the Bank Nationale d'Haiti and financed the McDonald contract—based on grants to James P. McDonald to build a railroad from Port-au-Prince to Cap Haitien. The McDonald contract especially irked rural *cacos* of northern Haiti, who envisioned the confiscation of their small farms to build the hated American railroad. German and French capitalists also were active in the Haitian economy.

Simon's oppression of mulattoes, arbitrary arrests of protesting schoolteachers, and mass slaughter of a *caco* town in northeastern Haiti focused foreign scorn on him. In August 1911 he went into exile.

JAMES LEYBURN, *The Haitian People* (1941); DAVID NICHOLLS, *From Dessalines to Duvalier: Race, Colour, and National Independence in Haiti* (1979); BRENDA GAYLE PLUMMER, *Haiti and the Great Powers, 1902–1915* (1988).

THOMAS O. OTT

SIMONSEN, MÁRIO HENRIQUE (*b.* 19 February 1935), Brazilian minister of finance (1974–1979) and of planning (1979). Economist, professor, public official, and business administrator, Simonsen served as Brazil's principal economic minister following the high-growth period known as the ECONOMIC MIRACLE (1968–1974). Relatively orthodox in his economic thinking, Simonsen joined the faculty of the Instituto Brasileiro de Economia of the FUNDAÇÃO GETÚLIO VARGAS in Rio de Janeiro in 1961, acted as director of the Graduate School of Economics (1965–1974), and became vice president of the institute (1979). In the mid-1960s, as a staff member in the planning ministry led by Roberto CAMPOS, he designed the wage policy formula and participated in the creation of the housing finance system. In addition to his term as minister, he served as the president of the Brazilian Literacy Movement Foundation (Fundação Movimento Brasileiro de Alfabetização—MOBRAL) from 1970 to 1974 and as director of Citicorp (since 1979) and of other companies.

As minister of finance, Simonsen organized Brazil's response to the increase in world oil prices in 1973 and the adjustment to its spectacular growth in manufacturing capacity during the Economic Miracle. His program, reflected in the Second National Development Plan (II Plano Nacional de Desenvolvimento), attempted to reduce dependence on external energy and other imports through large public investment projects in basic industry and infrastructure, including transportation and communications. Brazilian private and state companies as well as foreign firms participated in the program, which was financed in part with petrodollars. At the same time, to control inflation and to deal with recurring problems in Brazil's balance of payments and foreign reserves, Simonsen often resorted to restrictive macroeconomic policies in spite of their recessionary impact, although growth during the period was still substantial. In 1979, he resigned as planning minister in the new president's cabinet, owing to public resistance to the prospect of even harsher macroeconomic policies in response to rising inflation; he was replaced by Antônio DELFIM NETO.

ISRAEL BELOCH and ALZIRA ALVES DE ABREU, eds., *Dicionário histórico-biográfico brasileiro, 1930–1983,* vol. 4 (1984); WERNER BAER, *The Brazilian Economy: Growth and Development,* 3d ed. (1989).

RUSSELL E. SMITH

See also **Economic Development.**

SIMONSEN, ROBERTO COCHRANE (*b.* 18 February 1889; *d.* 25 May 1948), Brazilian economist and industrialist. Raised in the port city of Santos, Simonsen studied engineering at São Paulo's Escola Politécnica. He graduated in 1909. In the 1910s, as director of a construction company in Santos, Simonsen experimented with methods of scientific management as well as with new forms of labor negotiation.

In the 1920s and 1930s, Simonsen became Brazil's most prominent advocate of industrialization, and emerged as the leading spokesman for São Paulo's powerful industrialist federation. In 1933 he founded the Escola Livre de Sociologia e Política; his appointment as professor of economic history at this institution for advanced study in the social sciences led him to compose his most famous work, *História econômica do Brasil, 1500–1820* (1937).

By the late 1930s Simonsen had become a supporter of the authoritarian regime of Getúlio VARGAS, participating in several national economic commissions in which he called for protective tariffs, state intervention, and economic planning to promote industrial development. Simonsen energetically defended this position at the end of World War II, when Brazil faced intensified foreign competition and U.S. pressure for a return to liberal trade policies.

With the transition to electoral politics, Simonsen successfully ran for the federal senate in 1947. As senator he continued to promote the interests of industry, calling for the suppression of the newly legalized Communist Party, which he considered the chief threat to "social peace." Simonsen died while delivering an address to the Brazilian Academy of Letters, to which he had been elected in 1946.

The best collection of Simonsen's writings is *Evolução industrial do Brasil e outros estudos* (1973). A brief biography emphasizing Simonsen's professional accomplishments can be found in HEITOR FERREIRA LIMA, *Três industrialistas brasileiros* (1976),

especially pp. 141–185. On Simonsen's role in promoting industrialization, see WARREN DEAN, *The Industrialization of São Paulo, 1880–1945* (1969), and MARISA SAENZ LEME, *A ideologia dos industriais brasileiros, 1919–1945* (1979).

BARBARA WEINSTEIN

SINALOA, a state in northwestern Mexico. Sinaloa's elongated coastal plain, centrally located on the Mexican Pacific coast, fostered first commerce, and later fishing and tourism. Its numerous rivers, fed from the Sierra Madre Occidental, comprise more than a quarter of the country's usable surface water. Through extensive modern irrigation techniques and transportation infrastructure, Sinaloa has become one of Mexico's leading agricultural producers in the twentieth century.

During almost the entirety of the colonial period, Hispanic settlement was limited to a few communities eking out a meager existence. Sinaloa was largely isolated from the rest of the Viceroyalty of New Spain; and the tribes in the north and in the mountains to the east that resisted conquest in the sixteenth century were pacified by and subordinated to the JESUITS thereafter. The decisive intervention of the Bourbon crown after 1765 led the transformation of the region. There was an intense rural colonization in northern and central Sinaloa, while mining activities became significant. Culiacán and Rosario emerged as commercial centers.

The colonial union of Sinaloa and Sonora was continued briefly after independence in the state of Occidente. The rise of the port of Mazatlán in the south as commercial entrepôt for western Mexico, combined with the decline of mining and the stagnation of commercial agriculture, left the economy and politics of the new state of Sinaloa (1830) concentrated in the hands of the foreign merchants who quickly came to dominate Mazatlán and the notables of Culiacán. From 1830 to 1880, their commercial rivalry became increasingly intertwined with national political currents. Then, under the political clique headed by Francisco CAÑEDO, as subordinate allies of the Porfirio DÍAZ regime, the state experienced profound changes. The Mazatlán-Culiacán rivalry was mitigated politically and directed economically toward more diversified activities within the state. The tenuous balance in the north and center between villagers and small-to-middling estate owners gave way to the rise of large commercialized haciendas, many owned by immigrants. The Revolution of 1910, along with completion of railroads connecting the state with the United States and the coast with the interior, accelerated this commercialization of agriculture. Sinaloa's revolutionary leaders were part of the Sonoran-led faction that dominated the national government from 1920 to 1934. Northern Sinaloa, aided by government-built dams and subsidies, became one of the nation's major centers of large-scale irrigated agriculture. Mazatlán became a major tourist center.

EUSTAQUIO BUELNA, *Apuntes para la historia de Sinaloa* (1924); JOSÉ MENA CASTILLO, *Historia compendiada del Estado de Sinaloa,*

2 vols. (1942); THOMAS A. ROBERTSON, *A Southwestern Utopia* (1947); AMADO GONZÁLEZ DÁVILA, *Diccionario geográfico, histórico y estadístico del Estado de Sinaloa* (1959); JOSÉ C. VALADÉS, *Mis confesiones* (1966); STUART F. VOSS, *On the Periphery of Northwest Mexico: Sonora and Sinaloa, 1810–1877* (1982); ANTONIO NAKAYAMA, *Sinaloa: Un bosquejo de su historia* (1983).

STUART F. VOSS

SINÁN, ROGELIO (Bernardo Domínguez Alba; *b.* 25 April 1902; *d.* 1993), Panamanian writer and diplomat. Sinán was born on the island of Taboga in the Gulf of Panama. After graduating from the National Institute of Panama in 1923, he attended the Pedagogical Institute in Santiago, Chile, the University of Rome, and was awarded a degree in dramatic arts from the National University of Mexico.

With the appearance, in 1929, of his first book, *Onda* (Wave), Sinán became known as the initiator of the vanguard movement in Panama. *Plenilunio* (1947; Full Moon), *A la orilla de las estatuas maduras* (1946; At the Edge of the Aged Statues), *La boina roja* (1954; The Red Beret), *La isla mágica* (1979; The Magic Island), *La cucarachita Mandinga* (1937; Mandinga, the Little Cockroach), and *Chiquilinga* established his impact on the renewal of the short story, the novel, and theater in Panama, and earned him the title of "Sinán the Magician." He received various literary prizes: first prize in the Inter-American short-story competition sponsored by the Mexican newspaper *El Nacional* (1953) for *La boina roja,* and the 1943, 1949, and 1977 Miró Prize for *Plenilunio* (novel), *Semana Santa en la niebla* (poetry), and *La isla mágica* (novel).

He taught Spanish literature at the National Institute of Panama. He was also director of the department of fine arts and professor of theater at the University of Panama and a member of the Panamanian Academy of the Spanish Language, as well as consul for Panama in India.

ENRIQUE JARAMILLO LEVI, *Homenaje a Rogelio Sinán* (*poesía y cuento*) (1982); DAVID FOSTER, comp., *Handbook of Latin American Literature*, 2d ed. (1992), pp. 459–464; ENRIQUE JARAMILLO LEVI et al., *El mago de la isla: Reflexiones críticas en torno a la obra literaria de Rogelio Sinán* (1992).

ELBA D. BIRMINGHAM-POKORNY

SINARQUISMO, a movement of conservative, lay Mexican Catholics that originated in opposition to radical and liberal tendencies during the presidency of Lázaro CÁRDENAS (1934–1940). The term *sinarquismo* literally means "with order," the opposite of anarchism, but its advocates intended to counter not that ideology (peripheral in the 1930s) but both communism and capitalism by appeals to a traditional, hierarchical, Hispanic, corporate social order.

Allegedly founded at a clandestine meeting in León, Guanajuato, in May 1937, the National Sinarquist Union's (Unión Nacional Sinarquista) penchant for secrecy makes historical documentation difficult. The use of obscure gestures, code words, and a quasi-military structure has led some observers to overstate its ties with European fascism during World War II. The Sinarquistas claimed 900,000 members in 1944, but in view of its rapid decline soon thereafter, this figure seems inflated. Members were largely peasants from Guanajuato, Jalisco, and neighboring states where the CRISTEROS had arisen in the 1920s. Often left out of land reform and other government programs, these peasants turned to Sinarquismo as a form of political protest. After 1950 Sinarquistas maintained a marginal but outspoken opposition to the dominant National Revolutionary Party (by 1950 named the Institutional Revolutionary Party).

The historical and political context is explored in DONALD J. MABRY, *Mexico's Acción Nacional: A Catholic Alternative to Revolution* (1973), esp. pp. 16–31, 43–44, 52–53, 193–194; and JEAN MEYER, *El Sinarquismo: ¿Un fascismo mexicano?*, translated by Aurelio Garzón del Camino (1979). NATHAN L. WHETTEN exaggerates Sinarquista influence in the 1940s but includes translations from several Sinarquista publications of that period in his *Rural Mexico* (1948), esp. pp. 454–522.

JOHN A. BRITTON

SINCLAIR, ALFREDO (*b.* 8 December 1914), Panamanian painter. After working as a neon sign technician, Sinclair studied under Humberto IVALDI in Panama and then at the Escuela Superior de Bellas Artes E. de la Cárcova in Buenos Aires until 1950. Upon his return to Panama, he became an art professor at the Escuela Nacional de Artes Plásticas and later at the National University.

Initially a figurative painter, in the 1950s Sinclair was influenced by abstract expressionism, which led to the development of a personal style dominated by color and light. His paintings fluctuate from a semi-abstraction with references to the real world, as exemplified by his numerous collages and cityscapes like *La Ciudad* (1962), to a complete lyrical abstraction, as in his series *Movimientos de un río* (1981).

GILBERT CHASE, *Contemporary Art in Latin America* (1970); P. CORREA, "Sinclair o los mundos olvidados," in *Estrella de Panamá* (6 March 1975); MÓNICA KUPFER, "Los cincuenta años de pintura de Alfredo Sinclair," in *Sinclair: el camino de un maestro* (1991).

MONICA E. KUPFER

SINHÔ (José Barbosa da Silva; *b.* 18 September 1888; *d.* 4 August 1930), Brazilian songwriter. Born on Rua do Riachuelo, Rio de Janeiro, Sinhô was encouraged to study the flute by his father, who revered *chôro* performers. Sinhô (his family nickname) eventually abandoned the flute in favor of the piano and guitar. To earn a living, Sinhô played the piano at the society balls and in the dance clubs of Cidade Nova. At twenty-six, he was well regarded as a professional pianist.

His samba "Quem são eles?" (Who Are They?)

of 1918 won immediate attention for its innovative rhythm and sparked a musical debate about the samba that soon became tradition in Rio de Janeiro. Organizing a group by the same name, Sinhô and his Quem São Eles? provoked traditional *sambistas*, who were devoted to their folkloric roots and resented Sinhô's urban melodies. He won tremendous success at CARNIVAL in 1920 with "Fala, meu louro" (Speak, My Parrot), a parody of Rui BARBOSA, and "O pé de anjo" (Angel's Foot). Persecuted by the police for his political satire, such as in "Fala baixo" (Speak Softly), a title alluding to government censorship, Sinhô was temporarily forced into hiding. He was named the *rei do samba* (king of the samba) in 1927 and reached the height of his popularity in 1928 with "Jura" (Promise) and "Gosto que me enrosco" (I Like to Swing), the latter coauthored by Heitor dos Prazeres. Although diagnosed with tuberculosis, Sinhô continued to write music intensively until his death in 1930. Numbering almost 150 published compositions, of which more than 100 have been recorded, Sinhô's music is remembered for its urban character, providing a chronicle of daily life and customs.

MARCOS ANTÔNIO MARCONDES, ed., *Enciclopédia da música brasileira: Erudita folclórica popular* (1977).

LISA MARIĆ

SIPÁN, Peruvian archaeological site (ca. 200–1200) that derives its name from a modern-day village of approximately 1,500 inhabitants located in the central LAMBAYEQUE Valley, 12 miles southeast of the city of Chiclayo on the north coast of Peru. Sipán is one of a number of ancient truncated pyramid complexes and associated cemeteries known from this area, which today is dedicated primarily to sugarcane cultivation.

The site of Sipán consists of two large truncated pyramidal mounds constructed of mud bricks, and a smaller, earlier mud brick platform on their east side. It was the smaller platform that drew attention to the site when a high-status MOCHE tomb was discovered and plundered by looters in early 1987. Salvage excavations resulted in the discovery and subsequent scientific excavation of several large chamber tombs and a series of smaller tombs of very high-status Moche individuals. The first of these tombs, whose principal occupant became known as the "Lord of Sipán," focused worldwide attention on the Moche culture. Previous looting of the site, and the rapid appearance of Sipán objects on the international art market, also focused renewed attention on the issue of looting and international trafficking of archaeological artifacts, and led to the passage of a U.S. law specifically prohibiting the importation of archaeological objects from Sipán.

Principal figures in the chamber tombs at Sipán were flanked by retainers, along with sacrificed animals, *Spondylus* and other marine shells, and ceramic offerings. The Sipán tombs are most distinctive, however, for the quantity and quality of metalwork buried with the principal figures in the tombs. These objects include masks; beads; nose, ear, and headdress ornaments; as well as bells, rattles, and other paraphernalia constructed of gold, gilded copper, and silver. Radiocarbon determinations and the iconography of the Sipán metalwork suggest that the platform was used as a funerary structure during the early to middle phases of the Moche kingdom (ca. A.D. 200–300).

WALTER ALVA, "Discovering the New World's Richest Unlooted Tomb," in *National Geographic*, 174, no. 4 (1988): 510–549, and "The Moche of Ancient Peru: New Tomb of Royal Splendor," in *National Geographic*, 177, no. 6 (1990): 2–15; WALTER ALVA and CHRISTOPHER B. DONNAN, *Royal Tombs of Sipán* (1993).

JOHN W. VERANO

SIQUEIROS, DAVID ALFARO. *See* **Alfaro Siqueiros, David.**

SITIO. *See* **Land Tenure: Brazil.**

SKÁRMETA, ANTONIO (*b.* 7 November 1940), Chilean novelist and short story writer. The relevant literary figure of a generation of Chileans who lived under the military dictatorship of 1973–1990, Skármeta went into voluntary exile in 1975. He lived in Argentina and Germany and returned to Chile in 1989. Skármeta is the author of the short story collections *El entusiasmo* (1967), *Desnudo en el tejado* (1969), *Tiro libre* (1973), and *Novios y solitarios* (1975). His novel *Soñé que la nieve ardía* (1975) (*I Dreamt the Snow Was Burning* [1985]) attests to the social and political aspirations and frustrations of the Salvador ALLENDE years. *No pasó nada* (1980) is a short novel of the experience of exile, and *Insurrección* (1982) (*The Insurrection* [1983]), describes the eve of the Sandinista revolution in Nicaragua. *Ardiente paciencia* (1986) (*Burning Patience* [1987]), a humorous novel portraying Pablo NERUDA as matchmaker, was also presented as a drama and a video-film, and *Match Ball* (1989) is a satirical novel of the world of tennis. Skármeta's narrative style mixes the nostalgia of a young generation's dream of social revolution with the experience of exile, parodying many literary genres from poetry to popular fiction to drama to journalism. Skármeta has also written a number of dramatic scripts besides *Ardiente paciencia*, among them *Si viviéramos juntos* (If We Lived Together) and *Permiso de residencia* (Residence Permit).

RAÚL SILVA CÁCERES, ed., *Del cuerpo a las palabras: La narrativa de Antonio Skármeta* (1983); GRÍNOR ROJO, *Crítica del exilio* (1989); MONIQUE LEMAITRE, *Una narrativa de la liberación* (1991).

CEDOMIL GOIC

SKINNER, GEORGE URE (*b.* 18 March 1804; *d.* 9 January 1867), British merchant in Guatemala. The son of a Scottish Episcopal minister and great-grandson of an ecclesiastical historian of Scotland, Skinner worked in London and in Leeds before going to Guatemala in 1831. The company he formed with Charles Klée, a German merchant, linked Guatemalan commerce closely with Great Britain, via Belize, and became a major creditor of the Guatemalan government. In addition to building a large estate based on INDIGO and COCHINEAL exports from Guatemala, Skinner became a noted naturalist; he was interested in insects, birds, and orchids, and shipped many of the latter to England. He died in Panama of yellow fever as he was returning from England.

''The Late Mr. G. Ure Skinner,'' *Gardeners' Chronicle*, no. 8 (1867); MERLE A. REINIKKA, *A History of the Orchid* (1972), pp. 169–173; RALPH LEE WOODWARD, JR., *Rafael Carrera and the Emergence of the Republic of Guatemala, 1821–1871* (1993).

RALPH LEE WOODWARD, JR.

SLAVE REVOLTS

Brazil

Slave uprisings and the formation and defense of runaway slave communities (called QUILOMBOS or *mocambos* in Brazil) were common facts of Brazilian slavery. But whereas *quilombos* occurred throughout the history of slavery and throughout the vast territory of Brazil, slave revolts occurred primarily in certain areas and in certain periods. Over one hundred *quilombos* have been identified in the rich mining region of Minas Gerais in the seventeenth and eighteenth centuries, but there is no record of a slave uprising there except for three abortive conspiracies in 1711, 1719, and 1729. Most slave revolts happened in the plantation areas of the Northeast during the first half of the nineteenth century. Some of these were linked to or benefited from divisions that flourished among the free classes after the independence of Brazil in 1822. During the second half of the nineteenth century, the majority of the slave population was concentrated in the prosperous coffee regions to the south. There small but numerous rebellions took place independently of or in combination with the white-dominated abolitionist movement in the last decades of slavery, which was finally abolished in 1888.

The colonial era, however, did see one big slave movement: the large and long-lived Palmares *quilombo*, founded ca. 1630. Finally defeated in 1694 after having repelled many attacks, Palmares was a runaway community with the stature of an organized, independent state. Nothing like it would ever be allowed to happen again in Brazil.

Often, however, the history of smaller-scale *quilombos* and that of insurrection merged. Although many *quilombos* were begun peacefully by small groups of individual fugitives, there were cases in which they developed from slave insurrections. In 1838 in the parish of Pati do Alferes, in the province of Rio de Janeiro, more than 100 slave men and women, the majority from a large coffee plantation, rose and ran away under the leadership of Manuel Congo. Most of these slaves were southern and central Africans from Angola, Mozambique, and the Congo, but a few creoles also joined the movement. Possessing firearms and other weapons, they immediately tried to organize a *quilombo* in a nearby mountain range but were quickly dispersed, with seven killed and twenty-two arrested on the spot. Manuel Congo was sentenced to be hanged. Although most runaways later were returned to their masters, some managed to escape into the woods.

If there were insurrections that became *quilombos*, there were also *quilombos* behind insurrections. Some of the famous nineteenth-century Bahian revolts were initiated by groups of runaway slaves. In 1809 fugitives from the city of Salvador, Bahia's capital, and from plantations in the neighboring sugar zone, the Recôncavo, formed a *quilombo* on the banks of a river. From there they attacked and nearly took control of the village of Nazaré, a food-producing area. They were defeated by local militias and troops sent from the capital; many died, and eighty-three men and twelve women were arrested. The rebels were Hausa, jeje (Aja-Fon), and Nagô (Yoruba) slaves, some of whom escaped in small groups to live as highwaymen and raiders in the Recôncavo. Five years later, in 1814, a *quilombo* near Salvador was also involved in an insurrection of captives, mostly Hausas, who worked in whaling warehouses. It was a bloody affair in which perhaps fifty people were killed by the rebels, who were defeated with heavy losses, but only when they were already marching toward the plantation districts. Finally, there was the rebellion of the Urubu (Vulture) *quilombo* in 1826, which was strengthened by many new escapees in an attempt to occupy Salvador on Christmas eve. But the rebels were denounced and then overcome by militia and regular troops before they were able to begin acting on their plan. During the battle a valiant woman named Zeferina led the warriors, mainly Yoruba slaves.

Bahia was by far the region experiencing the greatest number and the most serious slave revolts. There were more than twenty slave uprisings and conspiracies in Bahia between 1809 and 1835. Most of them were local affairs in the sugar plantation area of the Recôncavo, carried on by slaves protesting against local working or living conditions. At least two of the uprisings were led by Muslim slaves, the one in 1814 mentioned above and a more serious episode in 1835, often called the Malê revolt (from Imale, meaning Muslim in Yoruba). The latter occurred in Salvador. The result of long planning, it was led by Muslim religious preachers. The revolt was intended to begin on 25 January 1835, a Catholic holiday that fell at the end of the Muslim Ramadan. The police heard of the plot only hours before, which was time enough, however, to give them an advantage. But the uprising started anyway. For close to four hours, some 500 rebels fought in the streets and door-to-door, more than 70 dying before the uprising was defeated. The rebels were mostly Yoruba and Hausa slaves and freedmen, who later received punishments that varied from the death penalty (applied to four of them), whippings, prison with work, and deportation to Africa (for the freedmen).

As in other areas of the New World, slave revolts in Brazil, especially those in Bahia, have been explained by the high concentration of slaves in the population and by the fact that the majority were African-born and had common ethnic backgrounds. Thus, the revolts were in part ethnic rebellions. In the case of Bahia, scholars have added the role of Islam as a revolutionary religious ideology. Slave revolts may have been spurred by other ideological elements, such as the influence of the Haitian revolution (*haitianismo*), the liberal discourse peculiar to a time of decolonization, and after the mid-nineteenth century, abolitionist ideas. The creoles, however, were more in tune with these influences than the Africans.

In Bahia and other northern provinces, for instance, creole slaves joined several revolutionary movements of the free between 1823 and 1840. The movement known as the Balaiada exploded between 1838 and 1841 in the province of Maranhão. It mobilized thousands of poor country people under the leadership of liberal and federalist rebels who, like other rebels in this period, did not seek abolition. Slaves, however, took advantage of the rebellion to carry on their own movement guided by an extraordinary leader, Cosme Bento das Chagas, a black freedman who sought the destruction of slavery and the establishment of a color-blind republic. Faced with defeat, radical liberals eventually had to accept an alliance with slave forces that counted on hundreds of fugitives (*quilombolas*). But the very presence of slaves in the Balaiada pushed white supporters away. Thus weakened, both slave and free rebels became easy prey for the many troops sent from Rio de Janeiro to put down the rebellion. Chagas was captured and hanged, accused of murder and of leading a slave rebellion.

The 1870s and 1880s, especially the last years before abolition in 1888, saw a significant increase of tensions between slaves and masters, especially in the coffee-growing regions and suburbs of Rio de Janeiro and São Paulo. Recent studies have shown that individual flights and violent crimes against masters and overseers grew in the police statistics of this period, mostly accounted for by African slaves and captives imported from the declining sugar areas of the Northeast. The increasing unrest became a strong argument used by white politicians and ideologues in the abolitionist movement. As abolition approached, small slave uprisings, collective flights, and the formation of suburban *quilombos* multiplied by many times. Between 1885 and 1888, São Paulo alone witnessed more than two-dozen uprisings, although most were either small, localized, and hastily improvised or only potentially serious conspiracies that never materialized. In the same period, fires on several occasions destroyed plantations in the sugar districts of Campos in Rio de Janeiro. The radicalization of the slave movement radicalized the abolitionist movement, which often supported the former. The last country in the New World to abolish slavery, Brazil would surely have prolonged the system even longer had it not been for the struggle of the slaves themselves.

RAYMOND KENT, "African Revolt in Bahia: 24–25 January 1835," *Journal of Social History* 3, no. 4 (1970): 334–356; CLOVIS MOURA, *Rebeliões da senzala* (1972); LANA LAGE GAMA LIMA, *Rebeldia negra e abolicionismo* (1981); MARIA JANUÁRIA VILELA DOS SANTOS, *A balaiada e a insurreição de escravos no Maranhão* (1983); JULIO PINTO VALLEJOS, "Slave Control and Slave Resistance in Colonial Minas Gerais, 1700–1750," *Journal of Latin American Studies* 17 (1985): 1–34; STUART B. SCHWARTZ, *Sugar Plantations in the Formation of Brazilian Society: Bahia, 1550–1835* (1985), pp. 468–488; JOÃO LUIZ PINAUD et al, *Insurreição negra e justiça* (1987); LUIZ R. B. MOTT, "Rebeliões escravas em Sergipe," *Estudos Econômicos* 17 (1987): 111–130; JOÃO JOSÉ REIS, *Slave Rebellion in Brazil: The Muslim Uprising of 1835 in Bahia* (1993).

JOÃO JOSÉ REIS

Spanish America

Spanish America experienced many slave revolts during the more than three centuries of colonial rule and in some mainland countries during the first decades after Independence. Because the NEW LAWS OF 1542 forbade the enslavement of Indians except under narrow conditions, slave revolts in Spanish America quickly became the almost exclusive accomplishment of Africans and those of African descent. Some revolts displayed impressive size, intensity, and organization, and although sporadic and usually short-lived, they erupted with sufficient frequency to place rational masters in recurrent fear of what Simón Bolívar called "the volcano at their feet."

INCIDENCE OF REVOLT
Probably the first serious slave revolt by African slaves in the Americas broke out in 1522 in southeastern Hispaniola on a sugar estate owned by the son of Christopher Columbus. The revolt involved about forty slaves, most of them Wolofs from Senegambia in West Africa. Most of the principal slave revolts and conspiracies in Spanish America emerged from concentrations of slaves in plantation agriculture, mines, and urban services. For decades after the 1522 revolt, bands of runaway slaves preyed on Santo Domingo's sugar region. Although MAROON activity continued there for centuries, not until the end of the eighteenth century did planters witness slave revolts or conspiracies of any significance. The most violent revolt began near the city of Santo Domingo in 1796 on a large sugar estate called Boca Nigua.

Puerto Rico experienced few slave revolts or conspiracies before the expansion of sugar cultivation during the first half of the nineteenth century in the coastal districts of Ponce in the south and Vega Baja and Toa Baja in the north. Most instances occurred from 1820 to 1848 and were minor; the majority never reached the stage of open rebellion.

Cuba's first slave revolt seems to have been the 1533

rising of a few slave gold miners. In 1731 copper mines in roughly the same area of eastern Cuba gave rise to a larger revolt that embraced scores of slaves. During its nineteenth-century sugar boom western Cuba experienced one of the most intense periods of collective slave resistance in the history of Spanish America. The conspiracies of Aponte (1812) and LA ESCALERA (1843–1844) involved extensive networks of people of color, slave and free, rural and urban, and rank among the largest slave resistance movements in the history of the Americas. The most destructive slave revolt in Cuban history occurred in 1825, when hundreds of slaves killed fifteen whites and ravaged more than twenty coffee and sugar estates in the western province of Matanzas.

In Spanish Louisiana the same district of tobacco and indigo plantations up-river from New Orleans served as a base for a preempted ethnic revolt of MINA slaves in 1791 and for a more broadly based and revolutionary conspiracy four years later that stands as one of the largest acts of collective slave resistance in the history of colonial North America.

Mexico developed sugar plantations and sizable slave holdings around the port of Veracruz soon after the Spanish conquest. By the end of the sixteenth century, maroon raiders had created a battle zone comparable to that around the city of Santo Domingo a few decades earlier. In 1609, shortly after a slave conspiracy was wildly rumored in Mexico City, Spanish authorities decided to launch a military campaign against a mountain settlement of rebellious slaves led by an African named Yanga. An extraordinary sequence of five bloody slave rebellions afflicted the sugar heartland of Veracruz Province from 1725 to 1768; the largest, in 1735, lasted months and may have embraced 2,000 slaves. Mexico City suffered no large-scale slave revolts even though it had the largest slave population in New Spain, but extensive conspiracies were allegedly found in 1537, 1608, and 1612.

The seaboard provinces of Venezuela had slave revolts and conspiracies more serious than those of any other region in Spanish South America. A LADINO slave named Miguel, who ran away from the Buria gold mines near the Yaracuy River, became king of a large maroon enclave. In 1555 Spanish forces crushed his effort to unite Indians and slaves into an anti-Spanish rebellion. In the early 1730s a ZAMBO slave called ANDRESOTE proved more successful. With Dutch help, he joined Indians and people of color from the cacao-producing region of the Yaracuy River Valley in a great insurgency in which a slave rebellion conjoined with a popular outburst against the CARACAS COMPANY. Andresote's rebellion lasted several years and eventually took a government force of 1,500 men to put down. In 1795 a free *zambo*, José Leonardo CHIRINO, headed a destructive and bloody rebellion of slaves and free people of color in the western province of Coro. Slaves also combined with free people of color to hatch ambitious conspiracies in Caracas (1749) and Maracaibo (1799).

Conspicuous slave resistance in Colombia began with the razing by Africans of the Caribbean port of Santa Marta in 1529, four years after its founding. By the end of the sixteenth century gold mining had pulled thousands of African slaves into the region drained by the Cauca River. Several small revolts surfaced near the town of POPAYÁN around mid-century; these paled by comparison to the great rising in 1598 by perhaps several thousand slaves from the gold mines near Zaragoza. An uprising of about forty slaves at a gold mine near the town of Tadó in 1728 quickly spread to other mines. Troops sent by the governor of Popayán finally drowned the threat in blood.

Cartagena, the central port through which slaves passed to the mines, seems to have had a number of slave conspiracies—in 1619, 1693, and 1799, for example—but no serious slave revolts. Neither did colonial Lima, although several haciendas in coastal Peru gave rise to minor slave revolts during the second half of the eighteenth century. Two larger, violent revolts, among the last in Spanish America, broke out in 1851 on sugar plantations in Peru's Chicama and Cañete valleys. The most notable act of collective slave resistance in colonial Argentina appears to have been some loose plotting in Buenos Aires in 1795 that was inspired by the French and St. Domingue revolutions.

CONTRIBUTING FACTORS

Conditions that favored slave revolt included high concentrations of slaves, master absenteeism, sharp reversals in working conditions, real or perceived weakening in the forces of control, divisions within the master class or between elite social groups, favorable terrain for establishing lines of communication and conducting subversive activity, and sufficient space within the slave system for the creation of a viable slave leadership. A strong tradition of resistance also mattered, whether carried from Africa by enslaved members of warrior societies or inherited in Spanish America by successive generations of unruly CREOLE slaves.

Few of Spanish America's revolts and conspiracies lacked privileged slaves in leadership roles. Drivers, for example, figure conspicuously as leaders in most of nineteenth-century Cuba's great acts of collective slave resistance. Domestic slaves appear centrally in plot after plot in Spanish American cities. The conspiracies of Aponte and La Escalera and the rebellions of Andresote and Coro attest to the complex relations and chains of command developed by slaves as arrangements were made and deals were struck between rural and urban slaves, mulatto and black slaves, African and creole slaves, and privileged and unprivileged slaves.

GOALS

The specific goals of collective resistance, whether expressed as personal liberation, extermination of whites, access to land, or the creation of a new society, could differ markedly from one rebel group to another or from the leadership to the soldiery. Ethnic tensions surfaced among African rebels, and intimacies existed with whites. Differences among slaves help to account for so many betrayed and failed revolts. In numerous cases slave rebels formed ties with other oppressed people or with foreign powers. Free people of color participated in and even led a number of the larger movements of slave resistance; Indians participated in some of the larger movements, particularly those on the mainland. Yet members of both groups also acted with whites as agents of repression.

Over time, patterns of slave resistance changed. The 1791 slave revolution in Saint Domingue was a turning point, for it marked the integration of American revolts into the Age of Democratic Revolution, a decisive shift away from restorationist revolts directed at withdrawal from the prevailing social arrangements to resistance directed at liberal-democratic restructuring of society. Evidence for this shift can be found after 1791 in slave conspiracies and revolts throughout Spanish America, especially those in Venezuela, Cuba, and Puerto Rico.

JOSÉ ANTONIO SACO, *História de la esclavitud de la raza africana* (1879); CARLOS FEDERICO GUILLOT, *Negros rebeldes y negros cimarrones* (1961); LESLIE B. ROUT, JR., *The African Experience in Spanish America* (1976), chap. 4; EUGENE D. GENOVESE, *From Rebellion to Revolution* (1979); GUILLERMO A. BARALT, *Esclavos rebeldes* (1982); ROBERT L. PAQUETTE, *Sugar Is Made with Blood* (1988).

ROBERT L. PAQUETTE

See also **Slavery.**

SLAVE TRADE. Latin America, including the Caribbean region, received more than 85 percent of the 10 million or so Africans brought to the New World between 1494 and sometime in the 1860s. Brazil took about 35 percent of the total, the Caribbean (including the British islands) somewhat more, and the mainland colonies of Spain only about 10 percent.

The leading slavers of the fifteenth and sixteenth centuries were the Portuguese. The Dutch joined them during the seventeenth century, and the British and French transported the majority of the captive humans taken across the Atlantic in the 1700s. Among the Americans, only Brazilians at Rio de Janeiro and Salvador became prominent as slavers, accounting for a major part of the trade to those ports in the eighteenth century. As the British withdrew from slaving starting in 1807, Brazilians and Portuguese became the major nineteenth-century purveyors, with the Spaniards joined by a few North Americans and, intermittently, the French in providing African labor to Cuba (see accompanying table).

OUTLINE HISTORY

The slave trade began as a minor component in Portugal's fifteenth-century attempts to buy gold and commodities in West Africa. Africans at first tended to sell products, not people. But droughts there threw the region into violent conflict. Warlords seized captives and thrived on selling them to other Africans and to Europeans. Also, in western Africa there was an older trans-Saharan trade to Muslim lands with which European Atlantic traders competed.

New African mercantile sectors arose to broker this trade in labor and to import textiles and commodity currencies (particularly shells, copper rods, iron bars, and beads), along with smaller quantities of spirits and wines, firearms, and consumer luxuries. The growing cohort of Africans committed to selling refugees from drought and captives taken in wars thrived on the Europeans' willingness to pay higher and higher prices for labor.

Gradually, the dominant African political interests in

Some Estimates of Numbers of Slaves Transported to Latin America, by Destination

Period	Exports from Africa (1)	Imports in Americas (2)	Brazil (3)	Caribbean (4)	Spanish Main (5)
1450–1600	367,000	293,400	50,000	(??)	483,900
1601–1700	1,868,000	1,494,500	560,000	463,500	
1701–1800	6,133,000	5,737,600	1,891,400	2,939,700	(??)
1811–1867*		2,294,400	1,478,200	789,300	8,700
Total**	11,863,000	9.6–10.8 million			

* 1811–1867 from DAVID ELTIS, "The Nineteenth-Century Transatlantic Slave Trade: An Annual Time Series of Imports into the Americas Broken Down by Region," in *Hispanic American Historical Review* 67, 1 (1987): 109–138.

** Total from PAUL E. LOVEJOY, "The Impact of the Atlantic Slave Trade on Africa: A Review of the Literature," in *Journal of African History* 30 (1989): 368; not modified by new Dutch figures from JOHANNES MENNE POSTMA, *The Dutch in the Atlantic Slave Trade, 1600–1815* (1990). Columns do not add to the revised totals given in this line.

SOURCES: Columns (1) and (2): PAUL E. LOVEJOY, "The Volume of the Atlantic Slave Trade: A Synthesis," in *Journal of African History* 23, 4 (1982): 473–501, Tables 1, 9; Column (3): PHILIP D. CURTIN, *The Atlantic Slave Trade: A Census* (1969); Column (4): Interpolated from PHILIP D. CURTIN, *The Atlantic Slave Trade: A Census* (1969).

the most densely inhabited portions of the continent became dependent on selling slaves. Most came from the Lower Guinea Coast between modern Ghana and Cameroon or from Angola, a vaguely defined region along the west-central shores of Africa on either side of the mouth of the Zaire River (see accompanying map).

Demand for African slaves arose out of long-term shortages in American colonies. There, low-cost virgin lands and accessible deposits of precious metal ores—principally silver in Mexico and Peru and gold in Minas Gerais, Brazil—generated rapid economic growth. Already sparse Native American populations declined under the onslaught of European diseases, while an expanding economy in Europe absorbed the local working population there. With the demographic stage thus set, American specie, multiplied by early modern banking techniques, financed merchants in buying the refugees and captives of Africa to fill the labor deficit. American land, African labor, and European capital formed an economic triangle that generated lethally explosive growth.

Slavers delivered human cargoes in large numbers, first to the expanding sugar captaincies of the Brazilian Northeast at the end of the sixteenth century through Recife, in Pernambuco, and Salvador da Bahia. The Dutch then invested in and supplied labor for English cane plantations in the Caribbean, the main magnet for slavers about 1640. By 1700, the English West Indies, principally Jamaica, and French Saint Domingue drove the West Africa–Caribbean branch of the trade, with Bahian sugar and tobacco planters adding a second major, southern Atlantic, sector. Gold and diamonds in south-central Brazil propelled the trade from Angola to Rio de Janeiro until about 1760. Thereafter, diversifying exports of sugar, cotton, and coffee led Brazilian economic expansion into the nineteenth century. The African slaves headed to the New World thus formed one leg of an Atlantic commercial triangle completed by European manufactured goods sent to Africa and American minerals and agricultural commodities headed for Europe.

War in Europe from 1793 and British efforts at suppressing Atlantic slaving from 1807 gradually ended the trade from West Africa, with the Bahians among the last to give up there in the 1840s. Cuba, with Havana the main entry point, became the principal nineteenth-century Caribbean importer of African labor, increasingly from central Africa, to support the island's emergence as a major producer of sugar and, later, coffee. In southern Brazil, Rio slavers intensified their exploitation of Angola and expanded into Indian Ocean markets, particularly Mozambique. Brazil suppressed these last currents of slaving after 1850, and the Cuban trade finally died out in the 1860s. Thereafter, free immigrants from Europe replaced enslaved Africans in Brazil and Argentina, and indentured Asians supplemented French and British needs in the Caribbean region and the Guianas.

GOVERNMENT PARTICIPATION

The Spanish and Portuguese monarchies attempted to regulate and tax the trade in slaves to their American colonies, with decreasing success. Spain's famous ASIENTO contracts, begun in 1518, licensed royally favored Seville merchants to hire foreign traders to carry slaves to its mainland colonies, mostly through Cartagena and Buenos Aires, until the middle of the eighteenth century. These foreigners—Italians; then Portuguese; and eventually Dutch, French, and English, in a succession that reflected the rise of commercial bourgeoisies in Europe—exploited the privilege of delivering slaves by smuggling manufactured goods into the Spanish preserves and selling them there for silver.

The Portuguese concentrated their regulatory efforts on the Angolan coast, which they treated as a trading monopoly centered on a small colony at Luanda. They levied export taxes on slaves leaving the port and until 1769 subcontracted these duties out to Lisbon merchant interests, who dominated the trade financially. In Angola a community of resident colonials who intermarried with their African suppliers, along with exiled Portuguese criminals, Jews, and Gypsies, brought the slaves down to the coast, often owning them on through the point of sale in Brazil.

Brazil-based Portuguese merchants, who had married into American planting families, became the dominant shippers of slaves and supplied the sugarcane brandies that lubricated Angolan slaving and the sweetened tobacco that gave Bahians a secure niche in a separate "Mina" trade (named for a Portuguese post in Africa) between northeastern Brazil and the West African Lower Guinea coast. These varying commercial structures allowed Portuguese merchants to limit their involvement to the low-risk financial aspects of the trade until the late 1700s. Iberian merchants left the hazards of owning and carrying the slaves to foreigners within the Spanish sphere and, in Portugal's domains, to colonials.

COMMERCIAL ORGANIZATION

Private commercial interests gradually took over slaving, as early government-sponsored trade receded before the rising tides of mercantilism and, later, of liberal "free trade." In northern Europe only a few early ventures enjoyed royal patronage or participation. The precocious DUTCH WEST INDIA COMPANY led Netherlands merchants in their assault on Iberian slaving beginning in the 1620s. By the 1670s and 1680s, companies of private merchants, though still aided by royal charters and grants of monopoly trading privileges, had emerged everywhere, even to buy up Spain's asiento—notably the Royal African Company and the South Sea Company in England, the Compagnie des Indes in France, and the Companhia da Guiné in Portugal. By 1700, smaller free traders that were intruding as smugglers or interlopers quickly overwhelmed the unwieldy corporate behemoths. The Brazilians in the southern Atlantic, British shipping interests from Bristol and Liverpool, French

Spanish and Portuguese Atlantic Slaving and Commodity Flows

ca. 1520–1860

Maps include slaves delivered by British ships to Spanish and Portuguese territories in the New World but do not indicate British sources of exports to Africa or commodity returns from the New World. Nor do they include separate, and significantly larger, British, Dutch, and French shipments of slaves to the West Indies and North America, or the manufactures and commodity flows supporting and generated from northern European slaving.

Portuguese flows

Spanish flows

Widths of arrows in the map at right represent relative volumes of movements of slaves, but are greatly magnified in relation to scales of arrows showing European exports and American commodities and specie in the maps below.

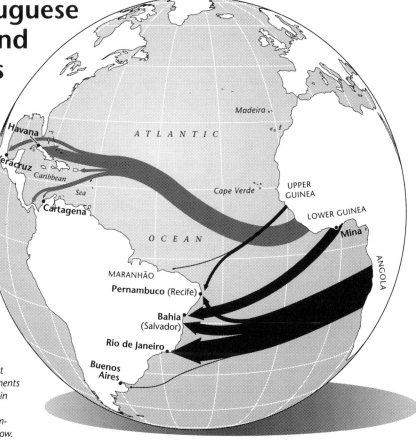

Slaves

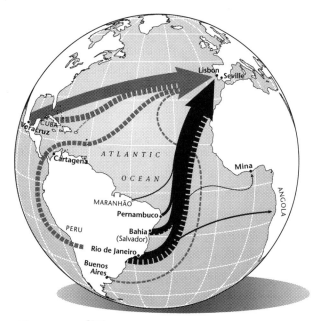

Commodities (solid lines): Sugar, gold, cotton, coffee
Specie (dashed lines): Silver, gold, diamonds

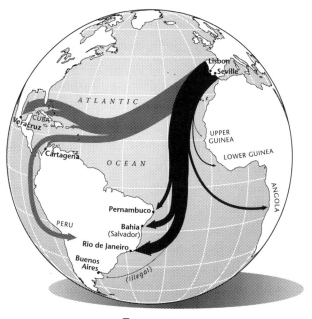

Exports
Manufactured goods

traders in Nantes and small Breton ports, private merchants in Holland, and Rhode Islanders from North America then pushed the trade to its eighteenth-century heights.

Portugal, which had lost the slave trade in its own empire to the colonials in Angola and Brazil, went against this tide of private entrepreneurship by floating two old-fashioned chartered companies of national merchants, active in the 1750s and 1760s. These commercial anachronisms, the Maranhão and Pernambuco companies, quickly failed. Spain finally loosened its antiquated restrictions on private trade in the empire during the 1780s, but too late. Its merchants had too small a market for slaves, too little capital, and only a toehold in Africa on the equatorial island of Fernando Po and so did not consolidate a Spanish slaving industry before American independence movements ended the mainland trade after 1810.

The nineteenth-century slave trade to Cuba and Brazil depended on colonial capital in Havana, Rio de Janeiro, and Bahia, supplemented by emigrant Portuguese merchants resident in Brazil. British manufacturers and merchants, though forbidden by Parliament from investing directly in slaving, drew profits from captive humans by financing the trade of the Iberians, safely protected by contracts from its primary risk—mortality. North Americans provided ships for the illegal trade of the 1840s. Thus, although the trade has sometimes been termed a "triangular" one because of the European goods, African slaves, and American commodities flowing clockwise with the winds of the North Atlantic, few individual ships or shippers completed all three of its legs. The institutions of slaving thus reflected the broad outlines of economic growth throughout the Atlantic economy, in Europe, America, and Africa.

Historians have inquired also into the economic contribution that slave trading may have made to the growth and transformation of the European economy, some claiming that it directly financed industrialization in Britain. Though exceptionally profitable voyages inspired many hopes, average returns did not exceed those common in other sectors of the economy. Slaving was a small component of all international trade flows and was minor in relation to domestic economies everywhere—including Africa and Brazil—except in the specialized sugar islands of the Caribbean.

On the other hand, slaving allowed new and still-fragile munitions and other manufacturing sectors in England and France to reach captive colonial and some African markets for their early, crude products. In Brazil the Africa trade sustained indebted planters unable otherwise to support the burden of Portuguese mercantilist taxes and monopolies. It restored the fortunes of a few of the Portuguese exiled and condemned to Angola and enabled even weak Portuguese merchants to compete with British-backed competitors in Brazil. For Portugal, too, it delayed the decline of national munitions and textile makers, as the country's economy fell steadily behind that of the rest of the continent. It animated commerce in the outports of northern Europe at a time when Amsterdam, London, Paris, and Rouen were moving ahead in finance and in continental trade. As trans-Atlantic economic diversification and specialization accelerated, Europe's weaker economic sectors, and disadvantaged colonial subjects, found markets in Africa and used the slaves acquired there to buy the American gold, silver, sugar, cotton, and coffee that they would otherwise have had to concede to stronger competitors.

DEMOGRAPHY

Slavers purchased enslaved Africans in ratios of about two males to each female, although sex ratios varied somewhat from one part of the African coast to another. American planters and miners may have preferred males because they found the costs of raising slave children—including high infant and child mortality—high so long as the price of African labor remained low. On the other hand, Africans may have preferred to retain women for themselves, to bear replacements for the people they lost to drought, war, disease, and enslaved exile abroad. Women worked in the fields on both continents, alone in Africa but alongside male slaves on American plantations. The high cost of raising children to an age of productivity reduced the number of youngsters in the trade to a small fraction. Slave prices rose steadily into the 1790s, however, and the differential between buying and training youngsters decreased so that the average age of the slaves carried across the Atlantic tended to fall through time. By the nineteenth century, the typical enslaved individual was an adolescent boy.

The European slavers refined their techniques over the centuries so that more slaves survived, at lower transport cost, though without significantly relieving the extreme discomfort of their captives. The earliest human cargoes rode in the holds of ships built for carrying commodities rather than people, with no special accommodation. Provision for food and, in particular, water while at sea was minimal. Slaves died in numbers averaging as much as 25 percent during crossings that ranged from 40 or 50 days in the South Atlantic upward toward 80 to 120 days between West Africa and the Caribbean. By the early eighteenth century, slavers had developed specialized vessels carrying 300 to 400 passengers, though smaller operators, particularly Americans, still used general cargo vessels of lesser capacity.

On African coasts, slavers established commercial contacts that reduced the highly lethal time spent loading slaves, and they could estimate the water and food requirements of their captives closely enough that mortality at sea dropped toward 10 percent. Captains under pressure from their employers, or novice sailors, still sometimes dangerously overloaded their ships. Calms or storms at sea, pirates, war, equipment failure, or other accidents could always strike the slaves with cat-

Sections of a slave ship. © BRITISH LIBRARY.

astrophic losses. However, on balance slaving in the high-volume decades of the 1700s tended toward business as usual, risky but bearable—for the slavers.

As the British navy gradually drove the slavers from the seas after 1811, the traders dispersed to remote and concealed ports in both Africa and the Americas. Although abolition raised the costs and risks of slaving, African and European traders survived the challenge. Africans held slaves safely near the coast and Europeans loaded ships in shorter periods of time when they arrived. The ships themselves became faster, some of them adding copper plating on their hulls. The slaves, packed more closely than ever below decks, bore the burden of other cost efficiencies, such as reduced rations of water and food, but gross neglect was less common in the furtive, highly professional, last, illegal years of slaving. As a result mortality among the slaves dropped further toward 5 percent on average, and catastrophes occurred less often.

Medical conditions, though always deadly, moderated over time. Throughout the long years of the trade, most slaves entered the holds of the ships in marginal nutritional condition. Many boarded after weeks and months of forced and underfed marches over long distances to the coast and after lengthy confinement with inadequate food or water in overcrowded shoreside barracoons. Spoiled foodstuffs, contaminated water, and illnesses acquired in unfamiliar disease environments left many with uncontrollable diarrheas. The stench added horribly to the miseries of those confined below decks, and ships carrying slaves trailed their malodorous stigma for hundreds of meters downwind.

Slaves from the higher African elevations also suffered from fevers picked up on the low-lying coast, particularly malaria. Contagious afflictions, especially smallpox, surged through some vessels in waves that, from Angola at least, rose after extended periods of drought in Africa. Emotional trauma was severe. Slaves experienced the loss of family and home, extreme isolation and dependency, and utter terror at an experience many believed had delivered them into the hands of red cannibals from beyond unending waters of death. Diarrheas, the nausea of seasickness, and profuse sweating in the holds must have depleted the body fluids faster than scarce supplies of drinking water could replace them. Slaves appeared to grow despondent and die, and these morbid melancholies, or *banzos*, may have been symptoms of terminal dehydration and mineral imbalances as well as of the profound psychological shock of captivity. The multiple afflictions of the slaves are almost impossible to translate into precise modern medical diagnoses.

Slavers gradually stumbled into remedies for starvation, dehydration, and salt depletion. From the early eighteenth century, the British occasionally inoculated slaves against smallpox, and slavers in the nineteenth century sometimes used Jennerian vaccine to prevent epidemic outbreaks of the disease in Africa from coming on board the slave ships. However, European medical technology never became widely efficacious under the extreme conditions of the trade. Better care for slaves before they boarded the ships, faster crossings, and adequate water and food probably contributed more to the falling death rates over the long history of the trade.

Most slave males spent the passage crammed below

decks, lying beneath low ceilings on rough planks in darkness, chained to hull, deck, or bulkhead, so close to companions that they could not move. Some captains brought small, heavily guarded groups of their captive passengers onto the deck once or twice a day to get a breath of fresh air, exercise a bit, and eat a ration of manioc or rice or other starchy porridge flavored with small quantities of cooking oil, peppers, or dried meat or fish. On some ships, women, some with infants, occupied cabins, where the crew surely subjected many to sexual assault.

In a tragic irony, the slaves' human frailty, their very susceptibility to death, gave them their principal—albeit passive—influence over the organization and history of the trade. Monetary investments in people led the slavers to adopt technological and financial refinements that gradually enhanced the chances of their human cargoes for survival. The presence of hundreds of resentful captives bound below decks, ill and weakened as they were, frightened crews into designing specialized slaving ships for security, with heavy bars and barriers, chains and irons. Some slaves somehow occasionally overcame these obstacles to seize or scuttle ships, though recorded instances of revolt at sea number only in the dozens out of tens of thousands of voyages.

For bibliographic information, see the bibliography supplements in the historical journal *Slavery and Abolition* (1983–) and JOSEPH C. MILLER, *Slavery: A Worldwide Bibliography, 1900–1982* (1985).

See also ERIC WILLIAMS, *Capitalism and Slavery* (1944); PHILIP D. CURTIN, *The Atlantic Slave Trade: A Census* (1969); ROBERT LOUIS STEIN, *The French Slave Trade in the Eighteenth Century: An Old Regime Business* (1979); EDWARD REYNOLDS, *Stand the Storm: A History of the Atlantic Slave Trade* (1985); HERBERT S. KLEIN, *African Slavery in Latin America and the Caribbean* (1986); DAVID ELTIS, *Economic Growth and the Ending of the Transatlantic Slave Trade* (1987); BARBARA L. SOLOW and STANLEY L. ENGERMAN, *British Capitalism and Caribbean Slavery: The Legacy of Eric Williams* (1987); JOSEPH C. MILLER, *Way of Death: Merchant Capitalism and the Angolan Slave Trade, 1730–1830* (1988); PAUL E. LOVEJOY, "The Impact of the Atlantic Slave Trade on Africa: A Review of the Literature," in *Journal of African History* 30 (1989): 365–394; PHILIP D. CURTAIN, *The Rise and Fall of the Plantation Complex: Essays in Atlantic History* (1990); PATRICK MANNING, *Slavery and African Life: Oriental, Occidental, and African Slave Trades* (1990); and JOHANNES MENNE POSTMA, *The Dutch in the Atlantic Slave Trade, 1600–1815* (1990).

JOSEPH C. MILLER

SLAVE TRADE, ABOLITION OF

In Brazil

The struggle to end the Brazilian slave trade lasted more than forty years and was essentially a conflict between Britain on the one hand and Portugal and Brazil on the other. For hundreds of years prior to the nineteenth century, transporting the enslaved blacks from Africa to Brazil was considered essential in the Luso-Brazilian world because of the great importance of slave labor to the Brazilian economy and the inability of the slave population in that country to increase or even maintain itself through natural reproduction. The essentiality of the Brazilian slave trade is revealed by its long duration and the huge numbers of slaves involved. No precise figures exist, but it is certain that the volume of this forced migration was much larger than that to any other American colony or country, including the United States. According to recent estimates, perhaps 100,000 slaves arrived in Brazil from Africa in the sixteenth century, 2 million in the seventeenth, another 2 million in the eighteenth, and about 1.5 million in the last fifty years of the slave trade, which finally ended in 1852. This total of well over 5 million persons does not include the hundreds of thousands who died en route.

In the early years of the nineteenth century, when the British campaign against the Brazilian slave trade began, the demand for slaves in Brazil was as large as it had ever been, so it is not surprising that Portuguese governments in Rio de Janeiro (and later those of independent Brazil) resisted British interference in this basic enterprise. However, for many complex economic and humanitarian reasons, including the cost advantage that the slave trade gave Brazilian producers over British competitors in the world sugar markets, British governments persisted in their crusade for nearly half a century, forcing the rulers of Brazil outwardly to restrict, then outlaw, the traffic while in fact they continued to tolerate and even encourage it on a vast scale.

The following key events in this long struggle suggest the high level of determination on both sides. In 1810, following the transfer of the Portuguese royal government from Lisbon to Rio de Janeiro, the prince regent of Portugal, Dom João, reluctantly agreed to ban participation by Portuguese subjects in slave trading in the non-Portuguese territories of Africa. In two agreements reached in 1815 and 1817, Portugal yielded to British demands to outlaw Portuguese slave trading north of the equator and to establish measures to enforce certain restrictions. These included the British right to board and search Portuguese ships at sea, to detain vessels involved in illegal trafficking, and to deliver those ships to special tribunals or "mixed commissions" in Brazil and Africa. Finally, in 1826, four years after Brazil became independent, the imperial government grudgingly agreed to a total ban on the slave trade, to take effect three years from the date of the treaty's ratification, such trading in slaves henceforth to be "deemed and treated as piracy." Thus, after nearly twenty years of unrelenting British effort and almost equally adamant Luso-Brazilian resistance, the Brazilian slave trade became illegal on 13 March 1830. Less than two years later, on 7 November 1831, a Liberal government in Rio de Janeiro confirmed this commitment with legislation declaring the freedom of slaves entering the country from that day forth.

These extraordinary British efforts did not, however, end the slave trade. For seven years after the legal prohibition, Liberal governments made serious efforts to enforce the law, and the number of Africans entering Brazil, therefore, remained comparatively small. In 1837, however, with the rise to power of a proslavery Conservative government, attempts to prevent slave landings or otherwise to control the traffic all but ceased, and an illegal slave trade involving ships and citizens of many countries developed on a large scale that continued for another fifteen years. During those years the energies of Brazilian governments were in fact more often directed toward deceiving British diplomats and protecting slave importers and their illegal property than toward complying with treaties and enforcing laws. To cite one of the most egregious examples, under the first article of the anti-slave-trade law of 7 November 1831, the many hundreds of thousands of slaves who entered Brazil after that date were legally free, but most were in fact condemned along with their children to live out their lives in a state of de facto SLAVERY.

In the 1840s, Britain persisted in its efforts to end the slave trade, seizing hundreds of ships at sea and on the African coast, and even encouraging a wave of public opposition within Brazil in the late 1840s. However, it was not until 1850, when the British government forcefully extended its naval campaign to the Brazilian coast itself, that the imperial government was at last persuaded to adopt more serious measures. Humiliated by British seizures of slave ships in Brazilian harbors and territorial waters, and fearing a British blockade of legitimate shipping and even war, the Brazilian government legislated the QUEIRÓS LAW of 4 September 1850, which provided severe penalties for slave traders and permitted Brazilian authorities to seize ships known to be involved in the traffic, even when no slaves were found on board. Even then, however, Brazilian efforts were piecemeal and selective, and all but nonexistent at the port of Bahia. Thus another British threat to send warships into Brazilian territorial waters was made in January 1851. From then on, the Brazilian campaign against the slave trade was serious and effective, all but suppressing it by 1852.

The ending of the African slave trade generated an unprecedented internal commerce in slaves between the northern and southern provinces and a rapid decline of the slave population in the country as a whole, both of which were significant causes of outright abolition of slavery in 1888, less than forty years later.

EMÍLIA VIOTTI DA COSTA, *Da senzala à colônia* (1966); PHILIP D. CURTIN, *The Atlantic Slave Trade: A Census* (1970); STANLEY J. STEIN, *Vassouras, a Brazilian Coffee Country, 1850–1900* (1970); LESLIE BETHELL, *The Abolition of the Brazilian Slave Trade* (1976); JOAQUIM NABUCO, *Abolitionism: The Brazilian Antislavery Struggle*, edited and translated by Robert Edgar Conrad (1977); JACOB GORENDER, *O escravismo colonial* (1978); ROBERT EDGAR CONRAD, *Children of God's Fire: A Documentary History of Black Slavery in Brazil* (1983), and *World of Sorrow: The African Slave Trade to Brazil* (1986); MARY C. KARASCH, *Slave Life in Rio de Janeiro, 1808–1850* (1987); JOSEPH CALDER MILLER, *Way of Death: Merchant Capitalism and the Angolan Slave Trade, 1730–1830* (1988).

ROBERT EDGAR CONRAD

Spanish America

The ending of the slave trade to the Spanish Americas is replete with paradoxes. More African slaves arrived in the region during the abolition era than in the long preceding period when the transatlantic traffic in people was never questioned. Indeed, many of the factors that explain the ending of the traffic are also vital to understanding its last rapid expansion. To make sense of these developments it is first necessary to look beyond Latin America.

Before the mid-nineteenth century, transatlantic migrants—whatever the labor regime under which they traveled—went in largest numbers to those areas that had the strongest export-based economies. After the early boom in gold and silver, Spanish America lagged behind the rest of European America in producing commodities that would sell in world markets. Thus in 1770, despite a nascent sugar and tobacco economy, the Spanish Caribbean accounted for less than 3 percent of all Caribbean exports. The English, French, and Portuguese colonies accounted for almost all slaves and free migrants that left the Old World between 1650 and 1800. During this period the natural advantages of Cuba and Puerto Rico in the growing and processing of a range of plantation products were held in check by the restrictive polices of the Spanish crown and premodern attitudes on private ownership of land.

Three factors transformed Spanish America in the century after 1770 and, at the same time, ensured in the long run that the slave trade would end. The first was a policy shift by the Spanish crown that liberalized colonial trade and encouraged the development of plantation agriculture. But while the tension this liberalization created was not immediately apparent, the so-called BOURBON REFORMS of CHARLES III also drew on a worldview—espoused by Adam Smith and the philosophes, and certainly mistaken—that saw slavery as inefficient. The second was the impact of industrialization in the North Atlantic. This greatly increased the demand for commodities of all types, and at the same time increased production and facilitated technological changes in transportation, agriculture, and primary processing that greatly cheapened their production. Industrialization also reinforced the ideological commitment to free labor—especially in Great Britain and the United States. The third factor was the disappearance of competitors to the Spanish plantation system. Between 1791, when the Saint-Domingue slave revolt broke out, and 1865, the end of the Civil War in the United States, the British, French, Dutch, Brazilians, and Americans all saw the ending of either the slave trade or slavery itself in their territories. Only in Cuba and Puerto Rico was the slave trade and slavery allowed to continue virtually unchecked. But the other countries that were in the vanguard of abolition (also erstwhile competitors) were not likely to allow this situation to continue. British and U.S. diplomatic pressure against an open transatlantic slave trade escalated steadily throughout this period.

There was thus a pattern of an expanding system of coercion and increasing efforts to suppress that system, the contradiction lying in the fact that the same forces drove both. The Spanish had never been major slave traders, preferring to buy from other Europeans. But as the British and Americans withdrew from direct participation after 1807, the Spanish filled the void at least in the branch of the trade to Cuba and Puerto Rico. British capital, or at least credit, however, remained very important. So too did British goods used to obtain slaves and insurance. Americans supplied ships and a flag that the British navy would be hesitant to challenge in peacetime. Attempts to suppress the traffic at sea foundered on the rights of merchants to sail without interference from other nationals. Slave trading never became piracy, and while the British probably had the naval power to suppress most of the traffic, they could have done so only by ignoring international law. When the British obtained the right to challenge a flag, the slave trader simply changed registration. Thus the Anglo-Spanish conventions of 1817 and 1835, which gave the British some legal rights over those carrying slaves to the Spanish Americas, were largely ineffective.

On the surface, the key initiatives were within the Spanish rather than the British domain. The 1845 Spanish penal law and efforts by Spanish governors of the early 1860s, such as Francisco Serrano y Domínguez, had the effect of raising the costs of slave traders after they had run the British gauntlet at sea. The new Spanish law of 1867, which greatly increased penalties and widened the definition of slave trading, was probably unnecessary, yet the important point is that all these internal moves were taken at the behest of the British, and after 1861, the Americans. In a very real sense early Spanish attempts to restrict the slave trade and slavery must be seen as attempts to win time for the institution of coerced labor. By conceding something to international pressures, the ending of the institution itself could be delayed until an alternative source of labor, such as Chinese contract labor or free migration from Spain and the Canary Islands, became available. In this, the Spanish were very successful. At the very least, however, these developments cannot be understood without the international backdrop.

By 1850 Cuba and Puerto Rico, which together in 1770 had accounted for 3 percent of Caribbean export output by value, now generated close to 60 percent. Yet the system that made this possible—slavery and the slave trade—was subject to strangulation at the very time that this hegemony was being established. Nearly three-quarters of a million Africans arrived in the Spanish Caribbean and the Rio de la Plata after 1800. The last slaves from Africa landed in Puerto Rico in the mid-1840s (other than victims of shipwrecks) and in Cuba in 1867. Like slavery itself shortly afterwards, the slave trade was suppressed. It did not die a "natural" economic death.

DAVID MURRAY, Odious Commerce: Britain, Spain, and the Abolition of the Cuban Slave Trade (1980); DAVID ELTIS, Economic Growth and the Ending of the Transatlantic Slave Trade (1987).

DAVID ELTIS

SLAVERY. [Covered here are **Brazil; Spanish America; Indian Slavery and Forced Labor;** and **Abolition.** See above for related articles on **Slave Revolts** and the **Slave Trade.**]

Brazil

The enslavement of Africans in Brazil had begun by 1550. The first enslaved Africans were introduced to Pernambuco and São Vicente, in the modern state of São Paulo. The centers of African slavery evolved not in colonial São Paulo, however, but in the Northeast of Brazil in the sixteenth and seventeenth centuries and in Minas Gerais, Goiás, and Mato Grosso in the eighteenth century. Only in the nineteenth century did African slavery supplant Indian slavery in São Paulo. African slavery also existed in the far north in Amazonia, as well as in the far south in Rio Grande do Sul. How many Africans were imported to be enslaved in Brazil over a little more than three centuries is uncertain; some estimates are 3.5 to 4 million. Nor do we know how many Africans served in Brazil, except for specific areas in which censuses were taken in the eighteenth and nineteenth centuries. Several censuses reveal that black and PARDO slaves comprised 40 percent or more of the total population.

The Africans who journeyed to Brazil on the slave ships came from many parts of West and west-central Africa. Those traded from the Costa da Mina of what is now Ghana were known as Minas in Brazil, and by extension MINA often defined a person from West Africa, also known as GUINEA. The second major region of export was the modern country of Angola, hence many Africans were known in Brazil as "Angolans," or "Congos" for the old kingdom of Kongo in northern Angola (and by extension all those exported from the mouth of the Congo River). A minority of Africans originated in East Africa, principally Mozambique.

African slavery was the foundation of the coastal Brazilian export economy until its abolition in 1888. The Africans provided the labor to produce the wealth based on plantation agriculture and gold mining. Those who aspired to wealth and status owned slaves, and slave ownership was dispersed among all strata of society throughout Brazil.

The conquest and settlement of coastal Brazil was a

joint Luso-African project in the colonial period. The Portuguese first brought their African slaves from Portugal to assist them in the conquest of Brazil. Lacking enough Portuguese soldiers, the Portuguese employed soldier-slaves to protect themselves from Indian and French attacks or to wage offensive wars against the coastal Indians. Black troops termed "Henriques," in honor of Henrique DIAS, the black hero in the Dutch wars of the seventeenth century, were essential thereafter to the defense of colonial Brazil.

Also introduced to Brazil in the sixteenth century was the sugar plantation (the ENGENHO), which was worked by African slaves, and most of the Africans in Brazil labored as slaves on the *engenhos* in the sixteenth and seventeenth centuries or in support positions, such as food production, cattle raising, and transportation of sugar to the port cities, such as Salvador and Olinda. The first *engenhos* were established in São Vicente and Pernambuco in the 1530s and 1540s, and by 1570 an estimated 2,000 to 3,000 blacks lived in Brazil. As sugar became the dominant export, Africans grew in number, replacing Indian slaves who died or fled the plantations. In the last decades of the sixteenth century, Bahia and Pernambuco imported 30,000 Africans from the Guinea coast, but the dominant era of sugar cultivation was the seventeenth century, when a half million Africans were imported, mostly before 1640. They were forced to plant and harvest sugarcane for the great *senhores de engenho*, who owned large plantations, hundreds of slaves, and the sugar mills; or for the LAVRADORES DE CANA, who owned or rented smaller plots of land, employed fewer slaves, and sent their cane to a nearby mill for processing. Because of the extraordinary labor demands of the sugar harvest, slave

mortality was high, leading to the importation of more Africans.

Africans also labored in other areas of agriculture, such as the production of staple crops, TOBACCO, COTTON, RICE, and COFFEE. Small farmers, often free people of color, employed their slaves in raising tropical fruits, BEANS, corn, MANIOC, and small animals for sale in nearby towns, while others worked patches of land near great plantations. Others cultivated tobacco in Bahia for export to Europe and Africa. Further inland, especially in the backlands of the Northeast and Goiás, slaves raised cotton, spun it into thread, and wove cloth on wooden looms and made lace. Africans also labored on rice plantations, utilizing methods familiar to them in West Africa.

Experiments with coffee plantations in the early nineteenth century soon led to the rapid expansion of coffee plantations worked by African slaves, first in the Paraíba Valley of Rio de Janeiro, with subsequent expansion into São Paulo, Minas Gerais, and Goiás. While slavery was being abolished elsewhere in Latin America, African slavery actually expanded on the coffee plantations of the southeast in the nineteenth century. By the time of abolition in 1888, the majority of slaves labored in the coffee regions.

Although plantation labor dominated African lives in Brazil, some Africans escaped the harsh labor demands of plantations in pastoral activities, such as raising cattle, horses, and goats. Africans, familiar with such animals in their homelands, quickly took to animal husbandry in the Northeast, central Brazil, and the far south. From the interior, black and mulatto cowboys drove cattle for slaughter to the coastal cities to be converted into dried beef on *charqueadas*, especially in Rio

Coffee Harvest. Reproduced from Johann Moritz Rugendas, *Malerische Reise in Brasilian* (Paris, 1835). BY PERMISSION OF THE HOUGHTON LIBRARY, HARVARD UNIVERSITY.

Grande do Sul. As muleteers and drivers, slaves also conducted mule teams and oxcarts between cities and plantations.

African fishermen also transferred their skills to Brazil and went deep-sea FISHING using rafts with triangular sails. They were also the whalers of colonial Rio and Bahia, returning to warehouses to cut up and process the whales, extracting whale oil. Their familiarity with the sea meant that many Africans were also put to work as slave sailors, boatmen, and oarsmen, who were essential to the coastal and river trade of Brazil.

The African tradition of head porterage was also important in Brazil, and slaves moved heavy loads on their heads, including jars of water from wells and rivers. They were also the stevedores in port cities and loaded Brazil's exports of sugar, tobacco, and coffee and imports of Asian textiles and English manufactures on and off ships in the harbors. In addition, slaves had to carry their owners in sedan chairs or in hammocks. In the absence of large animals, enslaved Africans served as "beasts of burden," being particularly important in the transportation infrastructure.

African slavery was also essential to the MINING sector of the Brazilian economy, especially in the eighteenth century in the mining captaincies of Minas Gerais, Goiás, and Mato Grosso. Miners who aimed to strike it rich purchased young Africans in Rio and Bahia and led them to the gold-rush camps to work as *garimpeiros*, who panned for gold and diamonds in the rivers. Young women worked as the cooks of the mining gangs or as domestic servants as the camps evolved into towns. Although a few black women mined gold, most acquired gold through retail trades. With what they earned from the trade in foodstuffs, they purchased their freedom or that of their children.

The retail trades and domestic service were closely linked in Brazil, and female slaves usually did both. Not only did they care for customers, serving them food or drink, but they also prepared the meals for the household, did the cleaning, and took the laundry to wash in nearby rivers. In larger households there was more labor specialization, with ladies in waiting known as *mucamas*, a housekeeper, an *ama de leite* to nurse the children, cooks, buyers, seamstresses, and laundresses. Male slaves served as coachmen, footmen, uniformed sedan-chair porters, and stablemen. Additional slaves attached to large urban households were sent into the streets as *negros de ganho* (blacks for hire) to earn wages for their owners as tailors, shoemakers, carpenters, and street vendors.

Most African slaves, however, did not serve in luxurious houses as elegantly dressed domestic servants or as skilled craftsmen in the towns and cities. The vast majority of enslaved Africans, including the women, were forced to work in the fields or at hard menial labor as porters. They were the indispensable labor force of the Brazilian economy without which Brazil would not have developed as quickly as it did between 1532 and 1888. Most of this labor was not done willingly; it had to be coerced, and only fearful punishments forced the Africans to work against their wills, although some slaveowners used the promise of MANUMISSION to "persuade" their unwilling captives to labor for them. Thus, just as hard labor was one aspect of the history of African slavery in Brazil, the other side was implacable resistance to escape the slave status, symbolized by the great seventeenth-century QUILOMBO of PALMARES.

GILBERTO FREYRE, *The Masters and the Slaves*, translated by Samuel Putnam (1946); STANLEY J. STEIN, *Vassouras: A Brazilian Coffee County, 1850–1900* (1957); WARREN DEAN, *Rio Claro: A Brazilian Plantation System, 1820–1920* (1976); GERALD CARDOSO, *Negro Slavery in the Sugar Plantations of Veracruz and Pernambuco, 1550–1680: A Comparative Study* (1983); ROBERT E. CONRAD, *Children of God's Fire* (1983); STUART B. SCHWARTZ, *Sugar Plantations in the Formation of Brazilian Society: Bahia, 1550–1835* (1985); MARY C. KARASCH, "Suppliers, Sellers, Servants, and Slaves," in *Cities & Society in Colonial Latin America*, edited by Louisa Schell Hoberman and Susan Migden Socolow (1986), and *Slave Life in Rio de Janeiro, 1808–1850* (1987); KATIA M. DE QUEIRÓS MATTOSO, *To Be a Slave in Brazil, 1550–1888*, translated by Arthur Goldhammer (1986).

MARY KARASCH

See also **Senzala; Slave Revolts; Brazil; Slavery, Indian; Slave Trade.**

Spanish America

Spain enjoys the dubious distinction of having introduced the institution of African slavery to the Americas. In 1501 the Catholic monarchs, Ferdinand and Isabella, granted permission to Nicolás de OVANDO, the governor of Hispaniola, to import Africans as slaves to that island. The first slaves arrived from Spain in 1502, thereby inaugurating a trade in human beings that would last until about 1870. Africans and their progeny helped change the human landscape of the Americas and contributed their energies to the making of the colonial societies.

Slavery was a feature of Spanish society prior to the colonization of the Americas. Black Africans, however, formed only one of several groups from which slaves were drawn. Spanish slaves also included Jews, Muslims, and other Spaniards. When the indigenous population of the Caribbean islands declined as a consequence of mistreatment and disease, the Iberian colonists introduced a form of labor exploitation with which they were already familiar. Although Indians were subjected to enslavement in the early years, slavery was increasingly confined to the peoples of African descent. Past practice, economic necessity, cultural chauvinism, and racist ideology all combined to legitimize slavery for Africans in the Spanish colonies.

Once slavery was established in Hispaniola, it soon spread to the other Spanish Caribbean colonies of Cuba, Puerto Rico, and Jamaica. Shortly after the defeat of the

A Rebel Negro Armed and on His Guard. Reproduced from J. G. Stedman, *Narrative of a Five Years' Expedition Against the Revolted Negroes of Surinam* (London, 1796). TOZZER LIBRARY, HARVARD UNIVERSITY.

liable census data. It is certain, nonetheless, that the life expectancy of the slave population everywhere was short. Most fell victim to overwork, poor diet, and disease. Consequently, the slaves in all of the societies generally experienced an annual rate of natural decrease.

Slavery was recognized in Spanish law, and slaves were accorded certain rights by the SIETE PARTIDAS, the body of laws that constituted the basis of Spanish jurisprudence. Drawing its inspiration from the law of ancient Rome, Spanish law granted slaves the right to marry, have a family, and be manumitted. Slaves were also protected from mistreatment by their masters. They could appeal to the authorities for redress of their grievances. Modern research has shown that in Spanish America, these rights were not always upheld. In fact, the laws that were enacted by the colonists themselves frequently contradicted the liberal spirit of the Siete Partidas. The colonists developed an extensive body of legislation that circumscribed the movement of the slaves, imposed harsh punishments for infractions, and regulated their public and private behavior.

Spanish American slaveowners used their human property in a variety of ways. Since slaves were acquired to help create wealth for the master class, it is not surprising that they constituted a significant share of the labor force in the silver mines of Mexico and Peru. Others were employed on the sugarcane plantations of Cuba, Puerto Rico, Mexico, and Peru. Some worked on cattle ranches in several societies, planted ginger in Puerto Rico and Hispaniola, coffee and tobacco in Cuba, and cacao in Venezuela. In the urban centers, particularly those of Mexico and Peru, they labored in the textile factories (*obrajes*) under very difficult physical conditions. Slaves who had specialized skills worked as carpenters, shoemakers, bakers and in a range of other trades. Many were domestic workers. There was not much gender differentiation in the assignment of tasks, although men tended to predominate in the artisanal trades, the mining industry, and the processing of sugar. The majority of the domestic workers were women; other women worked on the plantations.

There can be no doubt that slaves in Spanish America, in common with their peers elsewhere, experienced severe and sustained assaults on their personhood. Lacking liberty and occupying a subordinate place in society, African slaves and their progeny struggled to carve out a place for themselves in all of the societies of the Americas. It is impossible to measure their degree of success, but they were able, whenever and wherever their demographic structure permitted, to sustain families, practice their religions, and retain important aspects of their variegated African heritages.

While it is difficult to generalize about the content of the slaves' religious beliefs, one can say with some assurance that religion played a significant role in their lives. The Catholic church made some attempt to catechize the slaves, but the results varied from colony to colony. Much depended on the size of the slave popu-

Aztecs, the colonists introduced the institution to Mexico. In time, African slaves served in Peru, Bolivia, Venezuela, Colombia, and Argentina; indeed they were present in all of the colonies. Their number varied, to be sure. Cuba, which experienced its heyday as a slave society during the nineteenth century, imported the largest number of Africans, probably around 700,000. Since Cuba lacked an indigenous population, the colonists came to depend on black slaves to perform a wide range of labor services. Mexico received about 200,000 slaves, Venezuela 121,000, Peru 95,000, and Puerto Rico about 80,000. The rest were divided among the remaining colonies, depending on the nature of their economies and the size of their native populations. Taken together, the Spanish colonies received from about 1.5 million to 2 million slaves. The aforementioned number does not include those who were born in the Americas and inherited their mother's slave status.

We will never know exactly how many Africans were actually enslaved, given the absence of regular and relation, the energy of the priests, and the ratio of priests to slaves. Some Africans embraced aspects of Catholic dogma, went to confession, and received the sacraments of baptism, matrimony, and the Holy Eucharist. Many adopted the Catholic saints with a high degree of enthusiasm. But often these saints were Africanized and became symbolic representations of African deities. In fact, and in a larger sense, blacks Africanized Catholicism and imposed their own flavor upon its rituals and practices. African religious beliefs and practices were not usually abandoned, as slaves inhabited several spiritual worlds at once. In Mexico and Peru, the Holy Office of the Inquisition tried to ferret out and destroy surviving African religious beliefs, but to no avail.

The COFRADÍA, or religious brotherhood, was one of the institutions that attracted Christianized slaves. Essentially charitable and mutual aid organizations, the brotherhoods sponsored recreational activities and offered financial assistance to their members in times of difficulty. *Cofradías* appear to have been most prevalent in urban centers such as Lima, Mexico City, Caracas, and Havana, where slaves had greater opportunities for social interaction. Only a small minority of the black population, however, belonged to these organizations. They were the preserve of the elite slaves and to some extent reflected class and ethnic differences among the slave population.

Slaves also sought to establish some degree of family life. Yet their family life, it must be said, was precarious everywhere. Although slave marriages were protected by the Siete Partidas, in practice such unions could be broken up with impunity by the masters. The imbalance in the sex ratio that favored men almost everywhere complicated the difficulty of finding partners. Miscegenation became a characteristic feature of these societies as Africans, Spaniards, and Indians produced a variety of racially mixed children.

Slaves who applied for marriage licenses generally chose their partners from their own ethnic group. Similarly, creole slaves—those born in the Americas—tended to choose other creoles as their spouses. This should not be particularly surprising, since a shared ethnic heritage generally plays a role in spouse selection. The absence of a large number of formal Christian marriages, however, should not lead to the conclusion that family units did not exist or that men and women failed to establish enduring bonds. Slaves, as people, fell in love, reared children, and often created long-term unions without the sanction of the church or the state. They had to develop kinship ties and function as normally as they could within the boundaries set by those who owned them.

One of the important features of Spanish American slavery was the real possibility that slaves could be freed before death intervened. The Siete Partidas encouraged the manumission of slaves, since it held that the institution was contrary to natural law and that there should be no legislation that would impede their inexorable march to freedom. Accordingly, Spanish laws and traditions had the effect of creating a climate favorable to manumission. Most slaves, to be sure, were never manumitted, and those who were so privileged consisted primarily of women and children, elderly slaves, and those whose freedom was purchased by themselves, a relative, or some other benefactor. The emergence of a significant free black population was due, in part, to the absence of laws prohibiting manumission. Panama, for example, boasted 33,000 free persons of African descent in 1778 to 3,500 slaves. Peru had 41,000 free persons in 1792 and 40,000 slaves. And in 1861 Cuba had 232,000 free persons and 371,000 slaves.

Many slaves rejected their condition by engaging in various forms of resistance. As early as 1522, the slaves in Hispaniola rose in rebellion, setting a precedent for their peers in other parts of Spain's empire. Thus Mexico, Peru, Cuba, Venezuela, and other colonies experi-

Slaves at work in a field. BRITISH LIBRARY.

enced challenges to the institution. Unlike their peers on the French island of Saint Domingue, however, Spanish American slaves were never able to achieve a successful revolution.

Some slaves, in spite of the obstacles they confronted, succeeded in claiming their freedom even while the institution continued to exist. These were the individuals who escaped and established sanctuaries, usually in very inaccessible parts of the colonies. Mexico, Cuba, Colombia, and Venezuela were topographically conducive to flight, and slaves were quick to exploit the advantages that the physical environment offered them. Known as *cimarrones* (MAROONS), the runaways were a thorn in the side of the colonists because of their frequent assaults on Hispanic settlements. They established their own settlements (PALENQUES) in several colonies and defended them against the frequent attacks of the masters and the authorities.

One of the most famous *palenques* existed in the area between Mount Orizaba and Veracruz, Mexico, in the early seventeenth century. Led by Ỹanga, an Angolan who had managed to maintain his freedom for thirty years, the community numbered about 500 inhabitants in 1608. After holding off the assaults of the Spaniards for some time, Ỹanga and his people eventually signed a truce recognizing their freedom and awarding them land upon which to build a pueblo. The town of San Lorenzo de los Negros was built by these *cimarrones* and received its charter in 1617. Runaway slaves signed similar treaties with the authorities elsewhere in the Americas, thereby demonstrating their extraordinary success in claiming and sustaining their freedom.

The institution of slavery ended at different times in the Spanish colonies. Many countries freed their slaves in the aftermath of their wars for independence. Only Chile, however, freed the slaves unconditionally and almost immediately after it won its independence. In the other societies, slavery ended gradually. By 1860, only Cuba and Puerto Rico held Africans in bondage. Puerto Rico freed all her slaves in 1873, and Cuba followed suit in 1886 after a period of gradual emancipation.

Africans and their children served as slaves in Spanish America for almost four centuries (1502–1886). They played important roles in building the economies of these New World societies and in helping shape their cultural life and institutions. In none of these societies were blacks accorded much personal worth. They had, perforce, to struggle to define themselves as human beings and to order their lives as best they could under the most difficult of circumstances.

FRANKLIN W. KNIGHT, *Slave Society in Cuba During the Nineteenth Century* (1970); JOHN V. LOMBARDI, *The Decline and Abolition of Negro Slavery in Venezuela, 1820–1954* (1971); FREDERICK P. BOWSER, *The African Slave in Colonial Peru, 1524–1650* (1974); COLIN A. PALMER, *Slaves of the White Gold: Blacks in Mexico, 1570–1650* (1976); LESLIE B. ROUT, JR., *The African Experience in Spanish America, 1502 to the Present Day* (1976); GEORGE REID ANDREWS, *The Afro-Argentines of Buenos Aires, 1800–1900* (1980); and HERBERT S. KLEIN, *African Slavery in Latin America and the Caribbean* (1986).

COLIN A. PALMER

See also **African–Latin American Religions; Africans in Hispanic America.**

Indian Slavery and Forced Labor

During the colonial period in Brazil (1500–1822), Indian labor provided a fundamental source of manpower for Portuguese enterprises, particularly in areas peripheral to the Atlantic export economy. Early on, with the development of the SUGAR INDUSTRY along the coast, settlers turned to the indigenous population in their search for labor. Though they attempted alternative forms of labor appropriation, the colonists ultimately favored native bondage. In a strictly legal sense, however, Indian slavery failed to unfold on a large scale, since protective Portuguese legislation and Jesuit opposition to illegal slaving practices constrained its development. According to the law of 20 March 1570, slaves could be acquired legitimately only through the prosecution of "just wars" against tribes who had refused or renounced Christianity, or through the "ransom" of captives destined to be sacrificed in cannibalistic rituals. Colonists found many ways to circumvent legal restrictions, forging pretexts for "just wars," often with the collusion of corrupt authorities, and declaring that every captive taken had been "ransomed."

While native labor gradually was replaced by African slavery in the sugar zones, Indian slavery reached massive proportions in the southern colony of São Paulo and in the northern state of Maranhão, where the local economies revolved around the services of Indian agricultural laborers and porters. In seventeenth-century São Paulo, the colonists focused their attentions on the southern GUARANI INDIANS, organizing several large-scale expeditions to assault Guarani villages and Jesuit missions, bringing thousands of Indians back to the Portuguese settlements. Though treating the Indians as captives and disposing of them as property, the colonists did not consider them formally as slaves, always referring to them as *forros* (freedmen).

Claiming rights to the labor of the Indians they had extracted from the wilderness at great personal expense—feeding them, clothing them, and giving them Christian instruction—the colonists developed a parallel system of personal administration. In effect, though, the expansion and reproduction of this system depended less on its institutional contours than on objective demographic and economic variables. Subject to periodic epidemics and negative natural growth rates, the captive population had to be replenished by new expeditions. As a result, Indian slavery flourished as long as the flow of new captives continued.

In Maranhão and Pará, the colonists also developed a labor-recruitment scheme based on slaving expeditions,

Civilized Indian Soldiers from the Province of Coritiba Bringing Back Prisoner Savages, from Jean-Baptiste Debret, *Voyage pittoresque et historique au Brésil*, vol. 1 (Paris, 1834). BY PERMISSION OF THE HOUGHTON LIBRARY, HARVARD UNIVERSITY.

though with peculiar regional characteristics. Throughout the seventeenth and eighteenth centuries, the basic organizational form was the *tropa de* RESGATE (ransom expedition), canoe convoys that penetrated the many navigable rivers of the Amazon Valley in search of slaves and forest products. Though frequently contested by the Jesuits, many captives taken were judged legal slaves, even as late as the 1740s.

Though the POMBALINE REFORMS eradicated all forms of forced native labor in 1755, legal Indian slavery reemerged briefly after 1808, when the crown permitted the temporary bondage of war captives, especially among the Kaingang of São Paulo and the Botocudo of Minas Gerais and Espírito Santo. The province of Goiás and the cattle frontier of southern Maranhão also witnessed the reintroduction of Indian slavery during this period. Indian slavery was proscribed once again in 1831, though other forms of native forced labor, such as debt servitude in the Amazon, persisted into the twentieth century.

On early labor relations see ALEXANDER MARCHANT, *From Barter to Slavery* (1942), which remains an important source. STUART SCHWARTZ, *Sugar Plantations in the Formation of Brazilian Society* (1985), provides an illuminating discussion of Indian labor in the northeast. JOHN MONTEIRO, "From Indian to Slave," in *Slavery and Abolition* 9, no. 2 (1988): 105–127, examines the development of Indian slavery in São Paulo. MATHIAS KIEMEN, *The Indian Policy of Portugal in the Amazon Region* (1954), deals with the legal dimensions of native labor in Maranhão, while DAURIL ALDEN, "Indian versus Black Slavery in the State of Maranhão During the Seventeenth and Eighteenth Century," in *Bibliotheca Americana* 1 (1983): 91–142, offers a cogent summary of demographic and economic aspects. For a general

treatment see JOHN HEMMING, *Red Gold* (1978) and *Amazon Frontier* (1987). For indigenous history, see MANUELA CARNEIRO DA CUNHA, ed., *Historia dos índios no Brasil* (1992).

JOHN M. MONTEIRO

See also **Mita; Slavery: Brazil; Slavery: Hispanic America.**

Abolition

The abolition of slavery in the Americas occurred in fits and starts, some of them convulsive, between the outbreak of the Haitian Revolution in 1791 and the promulgation of the GOLDEN LAW of Brazil in 1888. Slavery was an institution entrenched both in economic life and in the social fabric of essentially hierarchical societies. The commodities produced by slave labor, particularly sugar, cotton, and coffee, were crucial to the expanding network of transatlantic trade. In Brazil and Cuba slaveholding was also widespread in the cities and in some food-producing regions. Thus while the ideological transformations accompanying the growth of capitalism in Great Britain set the stage for a general critique of chattel slavery and championing of "free labor," it took more than a changing intellectual climate to dislodge the institution. Abolitionism took on its greatest force when it coincided with economic change and domestic social upheaval, and particularly when it became an element in the defining of new nations or new colonial relationships.

It was often slaves themselves who forced the question to the center of the stage, threatening or carrying out revolt, and offering or withholding support for republican challenges to colonialism. Slaves seized upon moments of division within the free population to expand or redefine their customary rights, advance new claims, flee their owners, or join in the warfare that might finally bring slavery to an end. At times they found allies among free people of color, whose civil rights were in continual danger as long as slavery was recognized in law and in social practice.

Over the past decades scholars have moved from a chronicling of the political process of formal abolition to an examination of the dynamics of emancipation as a social and economic process, one intertwined with the politics of abolitionism but not simply derivative of it. While different studies vary in the weight given to slave initiatives and economic necessity, external pressures and internal conflicts, elite ideology and popular resistance, there is no necessary contradiction involved in recognizing the importance of each of these. As Robin Blackburn has argued, the key turning points in the campaign against slavery generally occurred when some combination of class conflict, war, and pressure for new forms of government brought into question the rights of property and encouraged a widening of the concepts of citizenship and national interest. Internal and external forces were thus inextricable.

In Latin America, the ending of slavery took place in three successive stages. The first was marked by emancipation in the context of and as a consequence of war. The Haitian Revolution opened the age of emancipation and helped to place abolition on the agenda when anticolonial rebellions erupted in Spanish America. This emancipationist phase was consolidated in Haiti, remained incomplete in most of the Spanish American republics, and was thwarted in Brazil and Cuba. The second stage was a more gradual one, marked by the slow breakdown and elimination of slavery through the nineteenth century in the mainland republics. But concurrent with this phase was the expansion of what one scholar has termed the "second slavery"—vigorous export economies based on slave labor in Cuba, Brazil, and the United States. The third and final phase of emancipation was initiated by the Civil War in the United States, the Liberal Revolution of 1868 in Spain, and the definitive suppression of the transatlantic slave trade. Nominal abolitionism finally became part of the Liberal creed in Spain, while a more militant opposition to slavery became central to Cuban anticolonial struggles. In Brazil a cautious abolitionism emerged as an element in the public moral stance of the imperial state. But in both cases the pace and character of emancipation were shaped by slave initiatives, including participation in insurgency in Cuba and widespread flight from plantations in Brazil.

EMANCIPATION IN THE CONTEXT OF WAR
The French colony of Saint Domingue (the western part of Hispaniola) was between 1791 and 1804 the site of the first successful large-scale slave revolt in the Amer-

icas, which established the second independent state in the hemisphere—one founded on a repudiation of slavery. The mobilization of rebellion rested on a longstanding tradition of slave resistance, combined with the cultural creations of a new, shared language (Creole, or Kreyol) and a vigorous popular religion (Vodun), as well as brilliant military leadership under Toussaint L'OUVERTURE and Jean Jacques DESSALINES. The opening for revolt was provided by an unparalleled international conjuncture, marked by the ideological innovations and ambiguities of the French Revolution, the fragmentation of colonial authority during that upheaval, and the military and political divisions with France itself. At the same time, events in Haiti illustrated the ambiguous role of free populations of color, torn between an isolated struggle for group privilege, allegiance to established authority in defense of property and order, or allegiance to slaves in revindication of broader rights. The insurgents were eventually able to achieve independence from France and establish the new nation of Haiti, while continuing to resist multiple efforts by both the French and British to recolonize them. Under Toussaint L'Ouverture's leadership, the insurgents were also able to take over Spanish Santo Domingo (the eastern part of Hispaniola) and abolish slavery there in 1801, but this accomplishment was reversed one year later by a French military expedition.

The Haitian Revolution frightened slaveholders throughout the Americas and had an important direct effect on the course of the Spanish American wars of independence. After being thwarted in his initial revolutionary efforts, the "Liberator" Simón BOLÍVAR went in 1815 to Jamaica and then to Haiti to seek assistance. President Alexandre PÉTION of Haiti insisted on a commitment to emancipation as a condition for support, and Bolívar made such a commitment. Opposition to slavery became an element in a new Spanish American ideal of citizenship, expanding the possibility of recruiting among slaves and others opposed to the power of slaveholders. Material and strategic support from Pétion gave Bolívar's cause new life, but many of the leaders of the independence movement continued to temporize when faced with the choice between forthright abolitionism and the mobilization of slaves and free people of color on the one hand, and the continued protection of property rights as a means for obtaining or retaining elite support on the other.

It was thus not surprising that antislavery commitments were ratified by some of the early republican congresses, such as that of the Republic of Gran Colombia at Cúcuta in 1821, but encumbered with conditions and timetables that stalled the actual process of emancipation. The republicans of Peru were even more cautious, putting property rights and social stability first and not declaring emancipation, even as they sought to recruit among slaves and free people of color. In what was later to become the Dominican Republic, however, nationalists were overtaken by events, as Haitian forces under President Jean-Pierre BOYER invaded in 1822, declaring the freedom of all slaves for a second time, promising land to the freedmen, and enforcing these policies through a military occupation.

THE BREAKDOWN OF SLAVERY IN THE MAINLAND REPUBLICS

In the newly established mainland Spanish American republics, the question of slavery continued to be a contested one. Chile, where slaves were few in number and largely engaged in domestic service, was the first to make a definitive abolition of slavery, through a Senate decree in 1823. Abolition was declared in Central America in 1824. In Mexico, slavery, already in decline, was suppressed by decree during the presidency of Vicente GUERRERO in 1829. In most of South America, however, there was sparring over the mode and timetable for conforming to this element of the republican credo. Estate owners and other slaveholding elites generally stalled, while some leaders, including Bolívar, argued for abolition as a matter of moral authority and nation building. Weak manumission laws and "free womb" legislation (declaring free the children of slave mothers) initiated very gradual processes of abolition, but final emancipation was delayed for decades in Venezuela, Colombia, Paraguay, and Argentina.

Around mid-century, as much of Latin America moved into a new and more externally oriented political economy, the aging slave populations of the remaining republics finally achieved juridical freedom. Slavery was legally abolished in Uruguay in 1846; in Colombia in 1850; in the Argentine Republic in 1853; in Venezuela and Peru in 1854; and, finally, in Paraguay in 1870. In each case formal abolition was essentially a coda to a longer process of gradual emancipation. The development of new economic sectors largely rested on modes of labor in which workers were nominally free—though the exaction of their labor might contain significant elements of coercion. Chattel slavery, the holding of property rights in men and women, had become a relic.

Symbolically and to some extent juridically, emancipation in the Spanish American republics can be seen as an outgrowth of the independence struggles, in which many slaves and free people participated. The ideology of those struggles and the mobilization of so many persons of color during them made a full reimposition of slavery nearly impossible. In that sense, the independence movement brought the ending of slavery. In practical terms, however, slavery died a more lingering death. Juridically, drastic inequalities of power within the nation and within the slaveholding household blocked full revindication of the rights of slaves and their freeborn children, keeping gradual abolition to a slow pace and minimizing its social consequences. Economically, free labor gradually supplanted slave labor and diminished the vested interests of slaveholders in the institution.

EMANCIPATION IN CUBA AND BRAZIL

Resisting the tide of emancipation and republicanism, the elites of colonial Cuba and imperial Brazil constructed vigorous slave-based export economies in sugar and coffee. They purchased new slaves from Africa, oversaw the opening of new lands on the frontier, and developed new and expanded overseas markets. In Cuba, the most prosperous planters also purchased modern processing equipment, hired technicians from overseas, and established massive sugar factories. Into the 1870s, the work of Cuban sugar plantations continued to be done by slave men and women, as well as indentured Chinese immigrants and small numbers of free workers. In Brazil, the internal trade in slaves from north to south enabled coffee plantations to expand on the basis of slave labor, despite the attacks on the transatlantic trade.

Scholars differ in their opinions of the viability of this "second slavery." On one level, it was a great success for the planters, yielding numerous fortunes for Brazilian coffee "barons" and Cuban sugar "aristocrats." On another level, it was increasingly vulnerable, as the British campaign against the slave trade threatened its labor supply and increased labor costs. Some historians have argued that slave-based prosperity was founded on a central contradiction, and that rising slave prices, and a necessarily uneducated work force, would block the full modernization of the plantation complex. Slavery was a rapacious form of economic development, exploitative of those who labored and of the land they worked. Whether such rapaciousness had truly led to crisis, however, remains in dispute. One view is that slavery was essentially incompatible with the development of capitalism and that the resulting decline in profitability was leading unavoidably to abolition. Others argue, however, that planters were highly adaptable capitalists, preferring a gradual substitution of free laborers to taking substantive steps toward full emancipation.

Wherever one stands on the question of "internal contradictions," it is clear that by the late 1860s the slave economies of both Cuba and Brazil faced major challenges. The victory of the Union Forces in the Civil War in the United States was a major ideological blow to modernizing slaveholders in Cuba and Brazil. It cast doubt on the compatibility of slavery and sustained economic progress and removed a key example that pro-slavery apologists had cited in debates with proponents of free labor. Equally important, the transatlantic slave trade was definitively abolished by the 1860s. Since the slave populations of Cuba and Brazil did not, overall, sustain their numbers through natural reproduction, planters would have to find some alternative sources of labor. And many feared—correctly—that free immigrants would shun societies based on coerced labor.

In Cuba, these latent contradictions became an open crisis when the question of abolition was taken up by anticolonial insurgents. Spain, the colonial power, was placed on the defensive by the Cuban rebels who rose up in 1868. To try to undercut the appeal of the rebellion, and to bring Spain into belated conformity with liberal principles, a cautious law of gradual abolition, the Moret Law, freeing children and the elderly, was approved by the Spanish Cortes in 1870. It was enforced even more cautiously by the colonial authorities in Cuba. (In Puerto Rico, where the stakes were lower, it was followed by abolition in 1873.) By 1879, however, continued nationalist rebellion in the eastern end of Cuba, and resistance to work on the part of slaves, forced the issue. The Spanish Cortes declared all Cuban slaves free in 1880, though it imposed upon them an eight-year "apprenticeship" to their former masters. This apprenticeship was drastically undermined by multiple initiatives on the part of the apprentices, many of whom achieved their own freedom through flight, self-purchase, and legal challenge, hastening the arrival of formal emancipation, finally declared in 1886.

In Brazil, the balance of forces within the elite was changing, particularly with the growth of urban professional sectors. Moreover, many believed that the future of agriculture lay with the attraction of immigrant labor. But Brazilian slaveholders remained very powerful and were able to help shape and control the cautious responses to abolitionist pressure. Although abolition was formally carried out through a series of parliamentary and executive maneuvers, much of the driving force came from slaves themselves. Legal abolition began with the Law of the Free Womb (FREE BIRTH LAW) in 1871, followed by municipal and provincial legislation in selected areas of the Northeast. In the final phase, slave initiatives accelerated what was intended to be a controlled process, and flights from the estates became widespread in the period just prior to the proclamation of final abolition in the *Lei Aurea,* or Golden Law, of 1888.

By 1888, almost a century after the Haitian Revolution, formal chattel slavery was gone from Latin America. In some areas, particularly Mexico and Argentina, the descendants of former slaves were absorbed, at least in theory, by a larger process of *mestizaje,* though death and social denial also figured in their apparent disappearance. In Colombia, the descendants of slaves remained regionally isolated, their presence viewed as anomalous within a nation defined by its elite as European and mestizo. In Cuba and Brazil, where the descendants of slaves constituted a large fraction of the population, class divisions continued to be marked by distinctions of "race." Though legal freedom made new forms of struggle possible, people of African descent generally faced discrimination and lack of access to productive resources, which together undermined the juridical equality that was the legacy of abolition.

EMÍLIA VIOTTI DA COSTA, *Da senzala à colônia* (1966); ROBERT CONRAD, *The Destruction of Brazilian Slavery, 1850–1888* (1972); ROBERT BRENT TOPLIN, *The Abolition of Slavery in Brazil* (1975); MANUEL MORENO FRAGINALS, *El ingenio: Complejo económico social cubano del azúcar* (1978); GEORGE REID ANDREWS, *The Afro-Argentines of Buenos Aires, 1800–1900* (1980); LESLIE BETHELL, ed., *The Cambridge History of Latin America,* vol. 3 (1985), pp. 299–346; REBECCA J. SCOTT, *Slave Emancipation in Cuba: The Transition to Free Labor, 1860–1899* (1985); HERBERT S. KLEIN, *African Slavery in Latin America and the Caribbean* (1986); ROBIN BLACKBURN, *The Overthrow of Colonial Slavery, 1776–1848* (1988); REBECCA J. SCOTT et al., *The Abolition of Slavery and the Aftermath of Emancipation in Brazil* (1988); DALE W. TOMICH, "The 'Second Slavery': Bonded Labor and the Transformation of the Nineteenth Century World Economy," in *Rethinking the Nineteenth Century: Movements and Contradictions,* edited by Francisco O. Ramirez (1988); PETER WADE, *Blackness and Race Mixture: The Dynamics of Racial Identity in Colombia* (1993).

REBECCA J. SCOTT

SLOTH, slow-moving edentate mammal found in Central and South America. The sloth's slow movements help protect it from its principal enemy, the jaguar, and the blue-green algae that grow on the sloth's hair allow the animal to blend well with the tree foliage where it spends its time hanging upside down.

The five species of sloths are strictly Neotropical in their range. The three species of three-toed sloths (family Bradypodidae) are found throughout much of Central America and the northern two-thirds of South America. Two-toed sloths (family Choloepidae) have a far more limited range, covering most of Central America but only a small part of northwestern South America. Although no species is considered threatened or endangered, sloths face the same pressures as other animals in the face of humanity's extensive assault on the world's FORESTS.

BERNARD GRZIMEK, *Grzimek's Encyclopedia of Mammals* (1990).

SHEILA L. HOOKER

SMALLPOX. *See* **Diseases.**

SMUGGLING. *See* **Contraband.**

SOBREMONTE, RAFAEL DE (b. 27 November 1745; d. 14 January 1827), intendant of Córdoba (1783–1797), viceroy of Río de la Plata (1804–1807). Born in Seville to a noble family, Sobremonte trained for a military career. After service in Ceuta and Puerto Rico, he arrived in Buenos Aires in 1779 as viceregal secretary under Viceroy VÉRTIZ. Three years later he married Juana María de Larrazábal, the daughter of a prominent local family. With Vértiz's patronage, he secured the post of intendant of Córdoba (1783), where he served as a dynamic, model administrator. In 1797 Sobremonte was promoted to subinspector general of the military within the viceroyalty, and seven years later was named viceroy.

Although he was well-known and respected throughout the region, Sobremonte's tenure as viceroy proved to be deeply disappointing. He is best remembered for his ignominious flight to Córdoba (ostensibly to raise fresh troops) during the English invasion of 1806, leaving the city of Buenos Aires to defend itself as best it could. Sobremonte was deposed by the Buenos Aires *cabildo* in 1807 and arrested shortly thereafter. He was allowed to return to Spain in 1809. Exonerated of any wrongdoing in 1813, he was allowed to continue his military career. Named to the Council of the Indies in 1814, he retired the next year, dying in Cádiz after a long illness.

ENRIQUE UDAONDO, *Diccionario biográfico colonial argentino* (1945), pp. 845–847; JOHN LYNCH, *Spanish Colonial Administration, 1782–1810: The Intendant System in the Viceroyalty of the Río de la Plata* (1969).

SUSAN M. SOCOLOW

SOCCER. *See* **Sports.**

SOCCER WAR. *See* **Football War.**

SOCONUSCO, a rich agricultural region on the narrow, Pacific coastal plain of Chiapas, Mexico. The area was famous in prehistoric and colonial times for its high-quality cacao and later for its coffee. Today agriculture and ranching are major economic activities. In late prehistoric times (and probably much earlier) the native population of Soconusco spoke a Mixe-Zoquean language, but today residents speak Spanish and are culturally LADINO.

Archaeologists have uncovered evidence of human occupation in Soconusco as early as 3000 B.C., when small groups living in the estuaries subsisted primarily on shellfish. Pottery, some of the earliest in Mesoamerica, was used by ancient Soconuscans by around 2000 B.C. IZAPA, an archaeological site near Tapachula, is well known for its more than 250 carved stone monuments erected between ca. 300 B.C. and 50 B.C. In the late 1490s Soconusco came under Aztec control.

In 1524 Soconusco was conquered by the Spanish, and for most of the colonial period it was part of the Audiencia of Guatemala. The introduction of Old World diseases reduced its Indian population by over 90 percent in the first fifty years after contact. Spanish presence in the area consisted largely of merchants involved in the cacao trade. Throughout the colonial period the cacao plantations were controlled primarily by the native population.

Following Mexican independence, Soconusco declared itself an independent state (1824), but by 1842 it was annexed by Mexico. In the late nineteenth century,

foreign investors and colonists became active in Soconusco, and large coffee, rubber, and banana plantations were established.

Following the Mexican Revolution many of the large plantations were broken up and became part of the *ejido* system. Today much of the population has access to land and engages in subsistence agriculture, but increasingly larger portions live in urban settings or work as wage laborers on large plantations and ranches.

PETER GERHARD, *The Southeast Frontier of New Spain*, rev. ed. (1991), esp. pp. 165–172; GARETH W. LOWE, THOMAS A. LEE, JR., and EDUARDO MARTÍNEZ ESPINOSA, *Izapa: An Introduction to the Ruins and Monuments* (1982); DANIELA SPENSER, "Soconusco: The Formation of a Coffee Economy in Chiapas," in *Other Mexicos: Essays on Regional Mexican History, 1876–1911*, edited by Thomas Benjamin and William McNellie (1984); BARBARA VOORHIES, ed., *Ancient Trade and Tribute: Economies of the Soconusco Region of Mesoamerica* (1989).

JANINE GASCO

SOCORRO, a town in northeastern Colombia, 172 miles north-northeast of Bogotá, 1990 estimated population 25,000. Settled in the mid-1600s and formally founded in 1683, Socorro became an important commercial and textile-producing center by 1750, a status it partially lost over the nineteenth century. The town led the COMUNERO REVOLT against colonial taxation in 1781, and played an active role on the patriot side in the Independence struggle, for which it suffered the rigors of the Spanish *reconquista* of 1816–1819. From 1821 to 1857 Socorro was capital of a province of the same name (1851 population 157,000), and from 1862 to 1885 it was capital of the much larger state of SANTANDER. Socorro has historically been a Liberal Party bastion; in the nineteenth century it produced such notable political figures as Vicente AZUERO (1787–1844) and Gonzalo A. Távera. Since the late 1800s the town has been surpassed in size and economic importance by its perennial rival SAN GIL, fourteen miles to the northeast.

HORACIO RODRÍGUEZ PLATA, *La antigua provincia del Socorro y la independencia* (1963); JOHN L. PHELAN, *The People and the King* (1978).

RICHARD J. STOLLER

SODRÉ, NELSON WERNECK (*b.* 27 April 1911), retired Brazilian army officer, historian, and intellectual. Son of a lawyer-businessman, Sodré, a native of Rio de Janeiro, attended the Colegio Militar (1924–1930) and the Escola Militar in Rio de Janeiro (1931–1934). He was a career army officer until his retirement in 1961. He was a professor of military history at the Escola do Estado Maior do Exército (Army General Staff School) from 1948 to 1950. In 1955 and 1956 Sodré was editorial editor

139

at the center-left Rio newspaper *Última Hora*. In 1954 he became chairman of the history department at the Instituto Superior de Estudos Brasileiros (ISEB), a position he held until the military government closed the ISEB in the immediate aftermath of the coup in 1964. Since 1964 he has lived in Rio de Janeiro, devoting himself to intellectual pursuits.

Sodré participated in the Brazilian nationalist movement of the 1950s and early 1960s. During the 1950s he was influential in the Military Club, a group that generally sought to represent the interests of army officers, and played a role in the successful campaign to nationalize Brazilian oil. He also participated in ISEB's efforts to articulate a ''national-developmentalist'' ideology, which sought to overcome Brazil's colonial economic structure through national capitalist development.

Though never a political militant, Sodré has been a lifelong Marxist, and in addition to his other works, he has written texts on Marxist theory. He was imprisoned for several months after the coup of 1964 and for a time thereafter was prohibited from public speaking and writing in the press.

Sodré's works include *Formação da sociedade brasileira* (1944); *História da burguesia brasileira* (1964); *História militar do Brasil* (1965); *História da imprensa no Brasil* (1966); *Memorias de um soldado* (1967); *Memorias de um escritor* (1970); *Síntese de história da cultura brasileira* (1970); *Que se dove ler para conhecer o Brasil* (1973); *Formação histórica do Brasil*, 9th ed. (1976); *História da história nova* (1986), a history of ISEB. See also E. BRADFORD BURNS, *Nationalism in Brazil: A Historical Survey* (1968); and SIMON SCHWARTZMAN, ed., *O pensamento nacionalista e os ''Cadernos de Nosso Tempo''* (1981).

BRIAN OWENSBY

See also **Brazil: Organizations: Advanced Institute of Brazilian Studies; Nationalism.**

SOJO, FELIPE (*d.* 1869), Mexican sculptor. At the Academy of San Carlos in Mexico City, Sojo was a part of the first generation of students to leave behind the colonial technique of sculpture in wood and color, replacing it with white marble. In 1853 students under the Catalán master Manuel VILAR presented a biennial exhibition of their work. Sojo's contributions, a relief entitled *La degollación de San Juan Bautista* and the portrait *Señorita Barreiro*, are representative of two of the most common forms of sculpture at the time: the religious theme and the portrait. Sojo later took up another theme in sculpture: allegory. After the death of Manuel Vilar in 1860, Sojo was named director of sculpture at the academy.

The variety of patrons with whom Sojo became connected is notable. In 1853 he sculpted an industrial allegory for the Spanish architect Don Lorenzo de la Hidalga's private residence. As director at the academy during the reign of MAXIMILIAN, he undertook two projects commissioned by the emperor himself: a sar-

cophagus for the emperor Agustín de Iturbide, which was never completed, and whose plaster model was destroyed by the new republican regime after its triumph over the French, and a portrait in marble of Maximilian, which resides at the Mexican Museum of National History.

FAUSTO RAMÍREZ, *La plástica del siglo de la independencia* (1985); ELOÍSA URIBE, ed., *Y todo . . . por una nación: Historia social de la producción plástica de la Ciudad de México, 1781–1910*, 2d ed. (1987).

ESTHER ACEVEDO

SOLANO, FRANCISCO (*b.* March 1549; *d.* 14 July 1610), Franciscan missionary. Born in Montilla, Spain, Solano studied at the Jesuit college in that country, took minor orders, and was professed as a FRANCISCAN in 1570. For twenty years he worked in Spain as a preacher and a novice master. In 1589 he arrived in America, where he worked principally with the Calchaquí Indians of central Argentina. Solano was the superior of all Franciscan houses and missions in the area and established houses and missions throughout Tucumán. He was noted for his compassion, patience, and love of the Indians. Solano died in Lima and was buried in the Franciscan church there. He was beatified in 1675 and canonized in 1726.

CLAUDE MAIMBOURG, *The Lives of St. Thomas of Villanova, Archbishop of Valentia, and Augustinian Friar; and of St. Francis Solano, Apostle of Peru, of the Order of St. Francis* (1847); JOSÉ PACÍFICO OTERO, *Dos heroes de la conquista, la Orden franciscana en el Tucumán y en el Plata* (1905); LUIS JULIÁN PLANDOLIT, *El apóstol de América, San Francisco solano* (1963).

NICHOLAS P. CUSHNER

SOLDADERAS, women warriors, camp followers, also known as ''Juanas,'' ''Adelitas,'' *viejas* (old ladies), *galletas* (cookies), *cucarachas* (cockroaches), *soldadas, capitanas,* and *coronelas. Soldaderas* are Mexican women who served in armies as camp followers and soldiers during wars. The custom of women fighting in wars, defending their tribes, or accompanying warriors also goes back to Mesoamerican practices. The Spanish origin of the word is *soldada,* which means ''the pay of the soldier.'' A *soldadera* is a female servant who takes the *soldada* of the soldier and buys him food and other essentials.

Soldaderas functioned as foragers, cooks, nurses, laundresses, baggage carriers, sentinels, spys, gunrunners, prostitutes, and front-line soldiers. Because of the variety of roles and their semiofficial acceptance in the military until 1925, the *soldaderas* have an ambivalent position in Mexican society and popular culture. They are considered variously as silent bystanders, self-abnegating patriots, loose women, or valiant fighters for justice.

Soldaderas, 1912. LA FOTOTECA DEL INAH.

A comprehensive study is ELIZABETH SALAS, *Soldaderas in the Mexican Military: Myth and History* (1990). See also MARÍA DE LOS ÁNGELES MENDIETA ALATORRE, *La mujer en la revolución mexicana* (1961).

ELIZABETH SALAS

SOLDADOS DE CUERA, leather-armored cavalrymen of late-eighteenth-century presidios in northern New Spain. The *Regulation and Instruction for the Presidios of New Spain* of 1772 established a fortified line of fifteen forts, approximately 100 miles apart, from the Gulf of California to the Gulf of Mexico. To man these isolated posts with minimal troops, "flying companies" (*compañías volantes*) of cavalry patrolling between forts were formed to defend against possible foreign encroachment and hostile Indians. Armed with lances, short swords, muskets, and shields of two or three thicknesses of bullhide, the men wore knee-length, sleeveless leather coats, which gave them their name, cloth trousers, and high cowhide boots. As protection against attack and the thorny brush, horses wore leather "armor."

SIDNEY B. BRINCKERHOFF and ODIE B. FAULK, *Lancers for the King* (1965); ODIE B. FAULK, *The Leather Jacket Soldier* (1971).

W. MICHAEL MATHES

SOLDI, RAÚL (*b.* 27 March 1905; *d.* 21 April 1994), Argentine painter, printmaker, and muralist. Soldi was born in Buenos Aires and studied there, at the National Academy of Fine Arts, as well as at the Brera Royal Academy in Milan. He had a strict figurative training in drawing; later, in contact with the school of light devotees (Chiaristi), he developed his own technique and style. In 1938–1939 he worked in theater design and on numerous films. In 1953 he began painting murals in the chapel of Santa Ana in Glew, a small village in the province of Buenos Aires. Working there only in the summer, he finished in 1976. He painted the dome of the TEATRO COLÓN in Buenos Aires in 1966 and a mural at the basilica of the Annunciation in Nazareth, Israel, in 1968. Soldi received numerous awards, including the Palanza Prize from the National Academy of Fine Arts (1952). In 1993 he had a retrospective of his work at the Salas Nacionales de Exposición.

VICENTE GESUALDO, ALDO BIGLIONE, and RODOLFO SANTOS, *Diccionario de artistas plásticos en la Argentina* (1988).

AMALIA CORTINA ARAVENA

SOLER, ANDRÉS, DOMINGO, AND FERNANDO (*b.* 1899, 1902, 24 May 1900; *d.* 1969, 1961, 25 October 1979), Mexican film and stage actors. Three pillars of Mexican theater, altogether, the Soler brothers starred in over 200 films. They were key players in the "golden age" of Mexican cinema. Andrés and Domingo Soler served as character and secondary actors in such films

141

as *Doña Bárbara* (1943), *Historia de un gran amor* (1942), *La barraca* (1944), and *Si yo fuera diputado* (1951). Fernando Soler had leading roles in the films *Rosenda* (1948), *La oveja negra* (1949), *México de mis recuerdos* (1943), *Una familia de tantas* (1948), and *Sensualidad* (1950), and received the Ariel from the Mexican film academy in 1951 for best performance by an actor. The Solers constitute one of the few family dynasties of Mexican cinema.

LUIS REYES DE LA MAZA, *El cine sonoro en México* (1973); E. BRADFORD BURNS, *Latin American Cinema: Film and History* (1975); CARL J. MORA, *Mexican Cinema: Reflections of a Society: 1896–1980* (1982); and JOHN KING, *Magical Reels: A History of Cinema in Latin America* (1990).

DAVID MACIEL

SOLÍS, JUAN DÍAZ DE (*b.* mid-1400s; *d.* 1516), navigator who explored the RÍO DE LA PLATA estuary. The birthplace of Díaz is unclear. Some think it was Lebrija (Seville); others argue that his family migrated from Asturias to Portugal, where he was born. He voyaged to India for Portugal several times, served French corsairs, then moved to Spain in late 1505. He met Juan de la Cosa and Amerigo VESPUCCI at a conference summoned by King Ferdinand in Burgos in 1508, and was commissioned on 23 March 1508 to search for a passage to the Orient along with Vicente Yáñez PINZÓN. The exact itinerary is debated; it seems there was a coastal reconnaissance from central America north to the Yucatán, then Mexico's central Gulf coast.

Díaz de Solís returned to Spain and was serving in the CASA DE CONTRATACIÓN in Seville in the late summer of 1509. When Amerigo Vespucci died (22 February 1512), Díaz de Solís was named *piloto mayor* (chief pilot) and commissioned to head two voyages, both of which came to naught. He was encharged with another expedition, which left Sanlúcar on 8 October 1515. This group explored the Río de la Plata estuary in early 1516. When Solís and his party disembarked to take possession of the left bank of the estuary, at a place before the confluence of the Uruguay and Paraná rivers, they were attacked. Indians wielding bows and arrows killed Solís and several companions.

JUAN MANZANO MANZANO, *Los Pinzones y el descubrimiento de América* (1988).

NOBLE DAVID COOK

SOLÍS FOLCH DE CARDONA, JOSÉ (*b.* 4 February 1716; *d.* 27 April 1770), viceroy of the New Kingdom of Granada (1753–1761). Born in Madrid into a prestigious and noble family, Solís arrived in New Granada as one of the youngest American viceroys yet appointed. He was accused by contemporaries and modern historians of having a youthful and dissipate moral character, as evidenced by the notorious Marichuela liaison, which created a scandal in Bogotá. But his political administration has generally been judged one of the best in the eighteenth century. Solís is especially known for his promotion of transportation improvements throughout the viceroyalty.

As with his predecessors, complaints of poor health led him in 1757 to request a replacement. Two years later Ferdinand VI tapped Pedro MESSÍA DE LA CERDA (1761–1772) as the next viceroy. Surprisingly, after he stepped down, Solís entered the Franciscan order and gave much of his personal fortune to the church. He remained in a Santa Fe de Bogotá monastery until his death.

Solís is the subject of a biography by DANIEL SAMPER ORTEGA, *Don José Solís, virrey del Nuevo Reino de Granada* (1953). See also the discussion in SERGIO ELÍAS ORTIZ, *Nuevo Reino de Granada: El virreynato*, pt. 2: *1753–1810*, in *Historia extensa de Colombia*, vol. 4 (1970); and Solís's own report of his administration in GERMÁN COLMENARES, ed., *Relaciones e informes de los gobernantes de la Nueva Granada*, vol. 1 (1989).

LANCE R. GRAHN

SOLOGUREN, JAVIER (*b.* 19 January 1921), Peruvian poet, publisher, and essayist. His father was the cousin of the poets Ricardo and Enrique Peña Barrenechea. Javier Sologuren studied literature and humanities in Peru, Mexico, and Belgium. He began publishing in the 1940s. In the 1950s, he lived in Sweden for seven years. Upon returning to Peru, Sologuren undertook the publication of his Ediciones de La Rama Florida, printing Peruvian and foreign literatures on a manual press. In 1960, he received the National Poetry Award. Later, Sologuren organized his poetry architectonically under the title *Vida continua* (1944, 1971, 1980, 1989, 1992).

Sologuren's essays on pre-Columbian and contemporary Peruvian arts, crafts, and literature, reformulating national Andean tradition, link him to such writers as Emilio Adolfo Westphalen, José María Arguedas, and Jorge Eduardo Eielson, and to the painter Fernando de Szyszlo. He also worked with European and Asian literatures, translating Swedish, French, Italian, and Brazilian poetry into Spanish and collaborating in the translation of classical Japanese works.

ANNA SONCINI, ed., *Javier Sologuren, Vita continua: Poesie (1947–1987)* (Italian translation, 1988, pp. 9–14); ANA MARÍA GAZZOLO, "Javier Sologuren: Poesía, razón de vida," in *Lienzo* 9 (1989): 219–278.

LUIS REBAZA-SORALUZ

SOLÓRZANO, CARLOS (*b.* 1 May 1922), Mexican playwright, director, professor, critic, historian, and governmental impresario. Born in Guatemala City, Solórzano moved to Mexico in 1939 to pursue studies in architecture and literature. In 1948 he received a degree from the National Autonomous University of Mexico. He studied dramatic art in Paris until 1951. Solórzano's exposure to French existentialism resulted in a successful three-act play, *Las manos de Dios* (1956), in which the protagonist chooses personal freedom and metaphorically the freedom of humanity over the repressive forces of church and state. Two earlier full-length plays and several one-acters deal with similar issues. Solórzano was the first critic to deal with twentieth-century Latin American theater on a hemispheric scale; his two books present overviews of major currents and comparative views by country. For years Solórzano was artistic director of the University Theater, taught classes, and wrote reviews and criticism; during the presidency of José López Portillo, he promoted theater under a project called Teatro de la Nación (1977–1981). He is married to Beatriz Caso de Solórzano, a sculptor and artist.

El teatro hispanoamericano del siglo XX (1961 and 1964); DOUGLAS RADCLIFF-UMSTEAD, "Solórzano's Tormented Puppets," in *Latin American Theatre Review* 4, no. 2 (Spring 1971): 5–11; JOHN ROSENBERG, "The Ritual of Solórzano's *Las manos de Dios*," in *Latin American Theatre Review* 17, no. 2 (Spring 1984): 39–48; and WILMA FELICIANO, "Myth and Theatricality in Three Plays by Carlos Solórzano," in *Latin American Theatre Review* 25, no. 1 (Fall 1991): 123–133.

GEORGE WOODYARD

SOLÓRZANO PEREIRA, JUAN DE (*b.* 1575; *d.* 1655), Spanish jurist and author. Solórzano studied civil and canon law at the University of Salamanca and taught there before being named OIDOR of the Audiencia of Lima in 1609. In Peru he oversaw the rehabilitation of the HUANCAVELICA mercury mine, married a creole woman from Cuzco, and mastered legislation related to the Indies. By the time he returned from what he considered exile in the New World as *fiscal* of the COUNCIL OF THE INDIES in 1627, he was the foremost authority on the laws of the Indies. He published *De Indiarum iure* from 1629 to 1639 and, in 1647, a modified five-volume version, *Política indiana*, for readers of Spanish. Solórzano also was a major contributor, in 1636, to the final draft of the *Recopilación de leyes de los reynos de las Indias*, which was finally published in 1681. Unlike many of his contemporaries, Solórzano considered public office to be a public trust rather than a piece of property.

D. A. BRADING, *The First America: The Spanish Monarchy, Creole Patriots, and the Liberal State 1492–1867* (1991), chap. 10; JOHN LEDDY PHELAN, *The Kingdom of Quito in the Seventeenth Century: Bureaucratic Politics in the Spanish Empire* (1967).

MARK A. BURKHOLDER

SOMERS, ARMONÍA (Armonía Etchepare de Henestrosa; *b.* 1914; *d.* 1994), Uruguayan writer, educator, and critic. Born in Montevideo, Somers taught elementary school for many years and served in various capacities in the Montevideo school system. She has written on subjects related to the education of adolescents. Her

literary career began in 1950 with the publication of her first novel, *La mujer desnuda*.

From the beginning, Somers has been considered one of the major fiction writers of Uruguay, together with Juan Carlos ONETTI and Felisberto HERNÁNDEZ. She is known for the innovative narrative style that she incorporates in her novels, considered by many as a fundamental break with the Uruguayan novel of the 1950s. In 1953 she published her first collection of short stories, in which a nightmarish and erotic atmosphere becomes almost unbearable to the alienated characters. *La calle del viento norte y otros cuentos* (The North Wind Street and Other Stories, 1963), her second collection of short stories, shows a more mature writer in style and depth, one who works slowly and patiently on the margins of literary circles.

Two novels followed, *De miedo en miedo* (From Fear to Fear, 1965) and *Un retrato para Dickens* (1969). *Todos los cuentos* (1967) included the two earlier collections of stories plus two unpublished ones. In these works Somers continued to elaborate the fictional world created in her previous works, emphasizing cruelty and loneliness as central elements that shape the lives of her protagonists.

After a silence of nine years, Somers published a second edition of her short stories. By that time her work had begun to be noticed by critics and readers in several countries. In 1986 she published *Viaje al corazón del dia* and *Sólo los elefantes encuentran mandrágora* (Only Elephants Encounter Mandragora), the latter being her most ambitious and difficult text. She also published two additional anthologies of her work, *Muerte por alacrán* (1979; Death by Scorpion) and *La rebelión de la flor* (1988).

Armonía Somers: Papeles críticos. Cuarenta años de literatura, edited by R. Cosse (1990); ANA MARÍA RODRÍGUEZ-VILLAML, *Elementos fantásticos en la narrativa de Armonía Somers* (1990).

MAGDALENA GARCÍA PINTO

SOMOZA DEBAYLE, ANASTASIO (*b.* 5 December 1925; *d.* 17 September 1980), president and dictator of Nicaragua (1967–1979). "Tachito" Somoza was the younger son of Anastasio SOMOZA GARCÍA. Unlike his older brother, Luis, Tachito rose to power through the Nicaraguan military. A graduate of West Point (1948), he returned to Nicaragua to take on a number of high-ranking positions in the National Guard. His father, while president, made him commander of the Guard. Like his father, Tachito believed the National Guard was the only reliable constituency of support for the Somoza family. While Luis, as president, implemented liberal policies and moderate social reform, Anastasio provided the muscle to maintain control over Nicaraguan society. He used the National Guard to quell minor outbreaks of social unrest. During his brother's presidency (1956–1963), Tachito increasingly came into conflict with Luis on the issue of his own presidential ambitions. His brother's death in 1967 removed a restraining influence over Tachito, who engineered his temporary resignation from the National Guard to be eligible constitutionally to run for president. In 1967, the third Somoza was "elected" to the presidency of Nicaragua.

Tachito proved to be much more his father's son than did his older brother. He has been characterized as greedy, cruel, repressive, and inhuman. He continued his father's methods in maintaining Conservative compliance by raising the party's congressional seat allocation to 40 percent. He continued the pro-U.S. policy of his father and brother (his father had allowed the CIA to use the Managua airport in 1954 for bombing raids against the Arbenz government in Guatemala) and even offered Nicaraguan troops for Vietnam. Strict and repressive control kept him in power, and the stable economy initially kept discontent in check. The middle sectors of Nicaraguan society were weak and divided, and Somoza still represented order in a country where a small guerrilla group, the Sandinista National Liberation Front (FSLN), was beginning to cause political concern.

On 23 December 1972 a massive earthquake hit Managua and Somoza reclaimed the presidency under the auspices of a state of emergency. The corruption that characterized this period included the diversion of in-

ternational relief funds and the private access to relief supplies of Somoza, his cronies, and the National Guard. Such behavior alienated the Nicaraguan upper classes and resulted in the formation of a broad opposition front, which was formed to challenge Somoza in the 1974 elections and led by *La Prensa* editor Pedro Joaquín CHAMORRO CARDENAL. Increasing numbers of young Nicaraguans from all classes were joining the FSLN in its struggle against the Somoza dictatorship. As the success of FSLN attacks increased, Somoza used the National Guard to repress violently any form of perceived opposition. The human-rights abuses caused U.S. President Jimmy Carter to cool relations with the once favorite son.

In 1977 Somoza suffered a heart attack but did not relinquish power. In 1978 Chamorro was assassinated. Somoza and the guard were blamed, and Somoza's violent repression of the ensuing demonstrations solidified opposition forces on the left and the right. Washington attempted to negotiate, offering "Somocismo without Somoza," but with Somoza's own intransigence and the opposition's strength, the mediation was rejected. An Organization of American States resolution demanded his resignation, and Tachito was forced to leave Nicaragua on 17 July 1979.

On the invitation of President General Alfredo STROESSNER, Somoza ultimately went into exile to Paraguay. On 17 September 1980 he was killed in Asunción when a

President Anastasio Somoza Debayle (second from left) opening new session of the National Congress, June 1973. SUSAN MEISELAS / MAGNUM PHOTOS INC.

bomb exploded in the car he was driving. An Argentine guerrilla organization was initially held responsible, but subsequently the FSLN military was connected to the assassination.

RICHARD MILLET, *Guardians of the Dynasty* (1977); EDUARDO CRAWLEY, *Dictators Never Die* (1979); ANASTASIO SOMOZA DE-BAYLE and JACK COX, *Nicaragua Betrayed* (1980); BERNARD DIEDRICH, *Somoza and the Legacy of U.S. Involvement in Central America* (1981) and *Somoza* (1982); THOMAS WALKER, *Nicaragua: The Land of Sandino* (1986); DAVID CLOSE, *Nicaragua: Politics, Economics, and Society* (1988); DENNIS GILBERT, *Sandinistas* (1988); ANTHONY LAKE, *Somoza Falling* (1989).

HEATHER K. THIESSEN

See also **Nicaragua: Political Parties.**

SOMOZA DEBAYLE, LUIS (*b.* 18 November 1922; *d.* 13 April 1967), president of Nicaragua (1956–1963). Son of Nicaraguan dictator Anastasio SOMOZA GARCÍA, Luis Somoza was the elder and more liberal brother of Anastasio SOMOZA DEBAYLE. He attended a number of universities in the United States and returned to Nicaragua to sit as a member of the Nationalist Liberal Party (PLN) in Congress while his father was president. Although Luis had an officer's commission in the National Guard, he chose the path of politics and became the president of the PLN, the president of Congress, and the first designate to the Nicaraguan presidency. Upon his father's assassination, Luis assumed the presidency. He served out his father's term and then was elected to the presidency in his own right.

Luis Somoza is best known for relaxing the political repression that characterized his father's time in power. Social reforms of his term included housing development, social-security legislation, limited land reform, and university autonomy. He allowed some measure of freedom of the press and released political detainees, measures that were aimed at improving the regime's image. His liberal social policy notwithstanding, four out of his seven years in office were conducted under martial law, and a number of abortive uprisings were repressed. His goal in liberalizing Nicaragua's political environment was the removal of the Somoza family from obvious political power, making them less vulnerable to attack and opposition. It has been suggested that Luis Somoza envisioned a role for the PLN based on the corporate political model of Mexico. Moreover, he sought a way for his family to exercise "discreet control" through the PLN, a plan that brought him into direct conflict with his younger brother, Anastasio ("Tachito"), who had assumed control of the National Guard under their father's last term in office. Luis's moderate approach was rejected by Tachito, who, like his father, felt control could be maintained only through the National Guard and a hard-line military style. Luis restored the constitutional articles banning the immediate reelection or succession to the presidency by any

relative of the incumbent or by the incumbent himself. He reinforced this legislation by stepping down at the end of his term. Luis did not intend to remove the Somozas from power, however, and engineered the selection and election of PLN candidate René SCHICK GUTIÉRREZ, a close Somoza associate, in 1963.

During his time in office, Luis attempted to reestablish friendly relations with Nicaragua's neighbors and supported the establishment of the CENTRAL AMERICAN COMMON MARKET (CACM). Despite the variance in political style, Luis maintained the strong pro–United States stance of his father, allowing the ill-fated BAY OF PIGS INVASION to be launched from Nicaragua's eastern coast. His last years were spent in conflict with his younger brother over the latter's aspirations to the presidency. Luis's death from a heart attack in 1967 removed a moderating influence from the Somoza family.

RICHARD MILLET, *Guardians of the Dynasty* (1977); EDUARDO CRAWLEY, *Dictators Never Die* (1979); BERNARD DIEDRICH, *Somoza and the Legacy of U.S. Involvement in Central America* (1981), and *Somoza* (1982); THOMAS WALKER, *Nicaragua: The Land of Sandino* (1986); DAVID CLOSE, *Nicaragua: Politics, Economics, and Society* (1988); ANTHONY LAKE, *Somoza Falling* (1989); DENNIS GILBERT, *Sandinistas* (1990).

HEATHER K. THIESSEN

SOMOZA GARCÍA, ANASTASIO (*b.* 1 February 1896; *d.* 29 September 1956), Nicaraguan dictator (1936–1956) and patriarch of the Somoza dynasty. Born in San Marcos, "Tacho" Somoza dominated Nicaragua from 1930 to 1956. Born in Carazo, department of San Marcos, Tacho was the grandnephew of Bernabé Somoza, Nicaragua's most notorious outlaw. He attended school in Philadelphia, where he gained an excellent command of English. Upon returning to Nicaragua, Somoza embarked upon a military career that would result, with the support of the U.S. representatives in Nicaragua, in his meteoric and violent rise to the presidency. He married Salvadora Debayle, the niece of leading Liberal and President Juan Bautista SACASA, and gained entrance to the upper circles of Nicaraguan society and politics. During the 1927–1933 U.S. military occupation of Nicaragua, Somoza came to the attention of U.S. Secretary of State Henry Stimson. Based on his command of English and charismatic enthusiasm for the United States, he was named Stimson's envoy and also nicknamed "el yanqui." In 1927 the United States gave him command of the newly created National Guard. The guard was created to maintain order in the violent world of Nicaraguan politics, thus allowing the withdrawal of the U.S. Marines.

Under Somoza's tutelage, the guard became increasingly powerful, placing him in a position to challenge and surpass even the political and legal authority of the Nicaraguan president. Not surprisingly, he became embroiled in a struggle for political power with President Sacasa, his uncle-in-law, and increasingly used the

Anastasio Somoza García (left) and U.S. President Franklin D. Roosevelt. ORGANIZATION OF AMERICAN STATES.

guard to exert his influence and control over Nicaragua. In 1934, after Sacasa had completed peace negotiations with the guerrilla commander Augusto César SANDINO, Somoza arranged for Sandino's murder. It has been suggested that he was forced into the plot to maintain his control over the guard. Somoza's authorization for the murder, however, was representative of his methods. Using the guard as a power base, Somoza ousted Sacasa from the presidency in 1936.

Backed by the guard, Somoza came to the presidency with more personal power than any other president in Nicaraguan history. Despite legal blocks to his becoming president—he was barred from the position as a relation of Sacasa and as commander of the National Guard—Somoza was "elected" to the presidency in December 1936. Although described as charming, astute, and ambitious, Tacho Somoza used guile, opportunism, and ruthlessness to maintain and build a political and economic dynasty. As president he maintained supreme command of the National Guard. He reestablished the Nationalist Liberal Party as a personal political machine, dusted off at election time to ensure his candidacy. The Conservative opposition was bought off with the 1948 and 1950 political pacts that guaranteed them one-third of congressional seats and a place on the Supreme Court while ensuring their compliance with Somoza's domination of Nicaragua.

His economic control of the country increased steadily. He came to power with the proverbial "ruined coffee finca," and died leaving personal wealth esti-

mated between $100 and $150 million. His attitude toward Nicaragua was summed up in a single line, "Nicaragua es mi finca" (Nicaragua is my farm). His exploitation of foreign aid and technical assistance (a substantial amount due to his very pro-U.S. stance) and his opportunism during World War II increased his private holdings dramatically. Under the pretext of combating Nazism, he confiscated German and Italian-owned properties. By 1944 Somoza was the largest private landowner and the leading producer of sugar in the country. His holdings soon expanded to include meat and mining companies, cement works, textile mills, milk processing, and state transport facilities, many of which were monopolies. There were also the "dirty" businesses of gambling, brothels, racketeering, illegal alcohol production, and monopoly control of export-import licensing, much of which occurred with National Guard participation.

Somoza's ability to stay in power stemmed from his control over the National Guard but also from political astuteness. When the winds of political change began to favor prodemocracy movements and rising discontent resulted in democratically elected governments in Guatemala and El Salvador in the 1940s, Somoza enacted a new labor code in 1944 and an income tax law in 1952, and established a development institute in 1953. This "social progress" coincided with an economic boom from the expansion of the cotton industry. Somoza's support was also bolstered by Washington. His pro-U.S. line brought funding for infrastructure development.

146

Despite increasing discontent with his economic and political domination and repressive tactics, the United States saw him as a staunch ally in a region that was fast becoming a concern for U.S. policy. His heavy-handed methods were cause for President Franklin D. ROOSEVELT's famous description of Somoza as "a son of a bitch, but our son of a bitch." Other Central American leaders became increasingly concerned with his power. In 1954 the ORGANIZATION OF AMERICAN STATES (OAS) had to intervene to prevent Somoza from supporting Costa Rican exiles in launching a coup attempt on President José FIGUERES FERRER from Nicaraguan soil.

Ultimately, the repressive nature of Somoza's economic, political, and military dictatorship resulted in his assassination. On 21 September 1956, a young Nicaraguan poet, Rigoberto López Pérez, shot Somoza in León. Somoza had been in the city to receive the presidential nomination from the Nationalist Liberal Party. U.S. Ambassador Thomas Wheaton, with support from President Dwight D. Eisenhower, airlifted Somoza to the American military hospital in Panama, where he died. He was survived by his wife, a daughter, and three sons (one illegitimate). Two of his sons, Luis and Anastasio, would continue the dynasty for another twenty-three years.

RICHARD MILLET, *Guardians of the Dynasty* (1977); EDUARDO CRAWLEY, *Dictators Never Die* (1979); ANASTASIO SOMOZA and JACK COX, *Nicaragua Betrayed* (1980); BERNARD DIEDRICH, *Somoza and the Legacy of U.S. Involvement in Central America* (1981) and *Somoza* (1982); THOMAS WALKER, *Nicaragua: The Land of Sandino* (1986); DAVID CLOSE, *Nicaragua: Politics, Economics, and Society* (1988); ANTHONY LAKE, *Somoza Falling (1989).*

HEATHER K. THIESSEN

SONORA, a state in northwest Mexico covering 110,000 square miles. Located between 108 degrees and 115 degrees west longitude and 26 degrees and 32 degrees north latitude, Sonora borders Arizona, the Gulf of California, Chihuahua, and Sinaloa. The Yaqui, Mayo, Sonora, and Concepción drainages constitute its principal river systems, flowing westward from the highlands to the Gulf of California. The Santa Cruz River flows northward to the Gila River; the Colorado River forms the boundary between Sonora and Baja California.

The Sierra Madre Occidental and the Sonoran Desert define its geographic features. Characteristic desert vegetation includes mesquite, paloverde, *palofierro* (ironwood), *gobernadora* (creosote), saguaro, *pitahaya* (a cactus), jojoba, and chollas. The mountains bear varieties of agaves, *encina,* and pine forests. Native fauna include bear, coyote, deer, mountain lion, wild boar, wild turkey, and the protected species of *bura* deer and long-horned sheep.

Firm archaeological evidence of human presence in Sonora can be dated from 10,000 to 15,000 years ago. Nomadic bands of lithic toolmakers hunted mammoths, mastodons, bison, and some animals that have survived to the present. These people left enduring remains in geoglyphs, petroglyphs, and stone artifacts, including the highly crafted Clovis point. Sedentary villagers have practiced agriculture in Sonora at least since the beginning of the Christian era. Lowland cultivation dependent on flows in ephemeral arroyos specialized in drought-resistant plants like cotton, *quelites* (wild greens), calabashes, and beans. More abundant rainfall and permanent streams sustained several varieties of maize, beans, squash, and gourds in the highlands, where agriculturalists developed irrigation systems and built permanent settlements.

On the eve of the Spanish conquest, Sonoran peoples comprised many tribes and dialects grouped in two major linguistic families: Hokan and Uto-Aztecan. Highland villagers traveled long-distance trade routes extending from Mesoamerica to the Rio Grande pueblos. European exploration of Sonora began in the 1530s, but no permanent settlements were established until after 1610, when Jesuit missionaries brought riverine farmers under Spanish rule. Missions and presidios formed the nuclei of Sonoran rural towns, which have endured to the present. Mining strikes attracted private settlers to Sonora by the mid-seventeenth century. The mature colonial society of the late eighteenth century relied on a mining and ranching economy that was integrated into regional marketing networks, even as the BOURBON REFORMS joined the separate provinces of Sinaloa, Ostimuri, and Sonora in the Intendancy of Arizpe.

The frontier quality of life persisted after Mexican independence, as Sonoran ranchers and townsmen fought against Apache bands who roamed the sierra and raided both white and Indian settlements. Moreover, Yaqui and Mayo villagers tenaciously defended their fertile lands against expanding private landholdings. The market economy grew: by the mid-nineteenth century Sonorans exported wheat to California and received increasing European trade through the port of Guaymas. The state capital moved from Arizpe to Ures and Hermosillo, as the leading landed and commercial families established their power base along the Hermosillo-Guaymas axis.

The U.S. invasion of Mexico (1846–1848) and the Treaty of Mesillas (1854), followed by the War of the Reform (1857–1860) and the FRENCH INTERVENTION (1864–1867) were important political events for Sonora that redrew its territorial boundaries and redefined its relations with the central government. After 1880, the politics stemming from the presidency of Porfírio DÍAZ brought a new elite to power in the state and accelerated capitalist development through commercial agriculture and industrial mining. Sonoran leaders played a major role in the Revolution of 1910 and with their military strength brought the Constitutionalists to power. During the 1920s, Sonorans dominated the presidency, reshaping Mexico's political structures.

PETER GERHARD, *The North Frontier of New Spain* (1982), provides a masterful overview of history and political geography for northern colonial Mexico. ARMANDO HOPKINS DURAZO, gen. coord., *Historia general de Sonora,* 5 vols. (1985), is a summary of geographic, anthropological, and historical research to date. Principal published sources include ANDRÉS PÉREZ DE RIBAS, *Los Triunfos de nuestra Santa Fé,* 3 vols. (1645; published in Mexico, 1944, 1985); JUAN NENTVIG, *Descripción geográfica, natural, y curiosa de la Provincia de Sonora,* edited by Germán Viveros (1971), also in English as *Rudo Ensayo, A Description of Sonora and Arizona in 1764,* edited by Alberto Francisco Pradeau (1980); IGNAZ PFEFFERKORN, *Beschreibung der Landschaft Sonora* (1795), also in English as *Sonora: A Description of the Province,* edited by Theodore Treutlein (1949). The Documentary Relations of the Southwest, University of Arizona, has compiled a computerized index to microfilmed documents in various archives and has published a number of annotated texts in translation, with introductions. Outstanding examples include CHARLES W. POLZER, *Rules and Precepts of the Jesuit Missions of Northwestern New Spain* (1976); THOMAS H. NAYLOR and CHARLES W. POLZER, eds., *The Presidio and Militia on the Northern Frontier of New Spain: A Documentary History, 1570–1700* (1986); and *Pedro de Rivera and the Military Regulations for Northern New Spain, 1724–1729* (1988). EDWARD H. SPICER, *Cycles of Conquest* (1962) and *The Yaquis: A Cultural History* (1980), are classic ethnohistorical works. STUART F. VOSS, *On the Periphery of Nineteenth-Century Mexico: Sonora and Sinaloa, 1810–1877* (1982); and EVELYN HU-DEHART, *Yaqui Resistance and Survival: The Struggle for Land and Autonomy, 1821–1910* (1984), are two outstanding histories of nineteenth-century Sonora. STEVEN E. SANDERSON, *Agrarian Populism and the Mexican State: The Struggle for Land in Sonora* (1981) provides an analysis of twentieth-century Sonora.

CYNTHIA RADDING

See also **Gadsden Purchase; Mexican-American War.**

SONSONATE, one of fourteen departments of El Salvador (1990 estimated pop. 397,552). It was part of the territory of the colonial region of Izalcos, which later became the *alcaldía mayor* of Sonsonate, a colonial subdivision incorporated into the state of San Salvador in 1824. Economic activities include port services (at Acajutla), oil refining, and production of dairy products, cereals, COFFEE, COTTON, and SUGAR. The capital city of the department, also named Sonsonate (1983 est. pop. 73,294), is 37.8 miles west of San Salvador. Founded in 1552 with the name of Santísima Trinidad de Sonsonate, it was one of the first Spanish settlements in present-day El Salvador. It owed its early prosperity to the production of CACAO and to the proximity of the Pacific port of Acajutla.

RODOLFO BARÓN CASTRO, *La población de El Salvador* (1942); INSTITUTO SALVADOREÑO DE ADMINISTRACIÓN MUNICIPAL, *Prontuario municipal, departamento de Sonsonate* (1987).

HÉCTOR LINDO-FUENTES

SONTHONAX, LÉGER FÉLICITÉ (*b.* 17 March 1763; *d.* 28 July 1813), French politician and lawyer. Sonthonax, a native of Oyonnax, France, was a controversial figure whose actions led to profoundly important but unintended results. Appointed commissioner of Saint-Domingue by Louis XVI in June 1792, with the mandate to halt revolutionary activity in the French colony, he implemented the 1792 decree that gave civil rights to coloreds (persons of mixed black and white heritage) and outlawed slavery. The decree had been designed to quell the frustration of blacks and win their support against the British. Instead, revolutionary momentum continued to increase. In 1794 irate white landowners and the revolutionary leader Toussaint L'OUVERTURE forced Sonthonax out of Saint-Domingue and into the hands of the British. He returned to France but two years later was sent back to Haiti, where he undertook an unsuccessful campaign to eradicate voodoo (VODUN) culture. Sonthonax retired to France in 1797 and died at Oyonnax.

GÉRARD MENTOR LAURENT, *Le commissaire Sonthonax à Saint-Domingue,* 4 vols. (1965–1974); ROBERT LOUIS STEIN, *Léger Félicité Sonthonax: The Lost Sentinel of the Republic* (1985); MICHEL LAGUERRE, *Voodoo and Politics in Haiti* (1989).

ANNE GREENE

SORBONNE GROUP, Brazilian reformist-nationalist army officers trained by the French Military Mission of 1919–1940. Instructed by battle-tested veterans under Chief of Mission General Maurice Gamelin (1919–1925), these junior officers, called *Tenentes* (literally, "lieutenants"), graduated from the General Staff School, the Advanced Officers Training School, and their Realengo Military Academy better trained than their superiors. Some Tenentes led a series of mutinies during the 1920s; others joined the Getúlio VARGAS Revolution of 1930; and many fought in Italy in 1944–1945 with the BRAZILIAN EXPEDITIONARY FORCE (*Força Expedicionária Brasileira—FEB*).

In 1949 these Tenentes and the World War II veterans known as Febianos took the lead in founding the ESCOLA SUPERIOR DA GUERRA (ESG), or Superior War College. Since the staff of this school, Brazil's highest-ranking military institution, either had been French-trained or had undertaken advanced studies in Paris, civilian politicians tended to view the ESG with suspicion, scornfully dubbing it the SORBONNE GROUP. Not without reason did they distrust this group. As Tenentes ESG generals Oswaldo Cordeiro de Farias and Juarez Távora had called for a temporary military dictatorship to initiate social, economic, and political reforms. Febiano general Humberto de CASTELLO BRANCO served as Távora's assistant. The Sorbonne Group, made up of Tenentes and Febianos, took the lead in overthrowing President João GOULART in 1964. Many members of the group served in subsequent military administrations.

NELSON WERNECK SODRÉ, *História militar do Brasil* (1965); JOHN W. F. DULLES, *Unrest in Brazil: Political-Military Crises, 1955–1964* (1970); RAYMOND ESTEP, *The Military in Brazilian Politics, 1821–1970* (1971); LEWIS A. TAMBS, "Five Times Against the System," in *Perspectives on Armed Politics in Brazil,* edited by Henry H. Keith and Robert A. Hayes (1976), pp. 177–206.

LEWIS A. TAMBS

See also **Tenentismo.**

SORIANO, JUAN (*b.* 18 August 1920), Mexican painter and sculptor. Born in Guadalajara, Jalisco, Mexico, he studied with Roberto MONTENEGRO and Jesús (Chucho) Reyes Ferreira. In 1934, Soriano participated in the first one-person show of his paintings in the Guadalajara Museum. He left Guadalajara for Mexico City in 1935 and became affiliated with the Primary School of Art, where he later taught, and the Group of Revolutionary Writers and Artists (LEAR). In the 1950s, Soriano was at the forefront of the Mexican avant-garde movement. He lived for several periods in Rome: 1951–1952, 1956, and 1970–1974. Beginning in 1975 he lived in both Paris and Mexico City.

While Soriano has, throughout his career, associated with all of the great Latin American artists of his time, he has never been identified as a member of a particular group or school. His lyrical and idiosyncratic style does not lend itself easily to classification. He possesses a distinct quality of "Mexican-ness," which is graphically reflected in his works of the 1940s. Since the 1950s his work has reflected a more international scope. With Rufino TAMAYO, Soriano has had a major impact on the internationalization of Mexican art, and his own work has been exhibited internationally since the 1970s. In 1991, the Museum of Modern Art in Mexico City presented a major retrospective exhibition of his work.

CARLOS FUENTES and TERESA DEL CONDE, *Juan Soriano y su obra* (1984); ERIKA BILLETER, ed., *Images of Mexico* (1988); OCTAVIO PAZ and EDWARD J. SULLIVAN, *Juan Soriano: Retratos y esculturas* (1991).

CLAYTON KIRKING

SORIANO, OSVALDO (*b.* 1943), Argentine writer. Born in Mar del Plata, Soriano is perhaps best known for the film adaptations of several of his novels, especially *No habrá más penas ni olvido* (1980; *A Funny Dirty Little War,* 1986), which uses the microcosm of a small town in the province of Buenos Aires as the arena for the bloody internal conflicts within the Peronist Party during its brief return to power (1973–1976). The events described in the novel become an allegory of Argentine sociopolitical violence and the irrational yet deadly forces it unleashes. *Cuarteles de invierno* (1982)—the film version starred the actor, psychiatrist, and dramatist Eduardo Pavlovsky, whose own works constitute a prominent entry in contemporary Argentine culture—focuses on the arbitrary exercise of violent power as yet another microcosmic example (it too takes place in a small town on the pampas) of a constant in Argentine history and life.

Soriano, as a significant example of the generation of writers in Argentina to emerge during the neofascist tyranny of the 1976–1983 period, has shown a particular talent for using a narrative voice colored by an intense black humor to describe common men (his narrative world is resolutely sexist) enmeshed in a horrendously violent political process. In his first novel, *Triste, solitario y final* (1976), an acerbic attack on U.S. culture is an oblique condemnation of Argentine cultural dependency.

NORA CATELLI, "Ni penas ni olvido: Entrevista con Osvaldo Soriano," in *Quimera,* no. 29 (1983): 26–31; LOIS BAER BARR, "*Cuarteles de invierno:* The Reign of the Unrighteous," in *Revista de Estudios Hispánicos* 19, no. 3 (1985): 49–59; CORINA S. MATHIEU, "La realidad tragicómica de Osvaldo Soriano," in *Chasqui* 17, no. 1 (1988): 85–91; MARTA GIACOMIMO, "Espacios de soledad: Entrevista con Osvaldo Soriano," in *Quimera,* no. 89 (1989): 45–51.

DAVID WILLIAM FOSTER

SOROCHE, the South American word for the "mountain sickness" experienced by people entering high altitude regions such as the Andes or the Sierra Madre in Mexico. The Spanish conquistadores were the first in the New World to write about it. Symptoms include fatigue, headache, forgetfulness, extreme thirst, nausea, and a propensity to frostbite and respiratory infection. Although the percentage of oxygen in the air remains constant, air pressure decreases at high altitudes; thus there is decreased pressure driving oxygen from the lungs into the bloodstream, resulting in hypoxia, or a deficient level of oxygen. Indigenous peoples have adapted with increased lung capacity and higher numbers of red blood cells; and newcomers can successfully adapt over time. Some scholars believe *soroche* has had a historical impact, in that, for example, it decreases fertility and may have helped slow the increase of the European population in the Andes.

PAUL T. BAKER and MICHAEL A. LITTLE, eds., *Man in the Andes* (1976).

CAMILLA TOWNSEND

SOSÚA, a Jewish agricultural settlement founded in 1940 on the north coast of the Dominican Republic. At the invitation of President Rafael Leonidas Trujillo, approximately one thousand European JEWS, mostly Germans and Austrians, fled to the Dominican Republic to escape Nazi persecution. Trujillo hoped their presence would counteract the Haitian influence in his country and improve relations with the United States. The colony at Sosúa received funding from the U.S.-based Dominican Republic Settlement Association (DORSA) and became famous for the manufacture of cheese. However, the Jewish colonists failed to integrate successfully into Dominican life, and Sosúa has suffered from the emigration of second- and third-generation inhabitants to the

United States. As of 1990 their numbers had dwindled to 25 families from a high of 125 in 1947.

JOSEF DAVID EICHEN, *Sosúa: Una colonia hebrea en la República Dominicana* (1980); JUDITH LAIKIN ELKIN, *Jews of the Latin American Republics* (1980); FRANCES HENRY, "Strangers in Paradise: The Jewish Enclave at Sosúa," and KAI P. SCHOENHALS, "An Extraordinary Migration: Jews in the Dominican Republic," in *Caribbean Review* 14, no. 4 (Fall 1985).

KAREN RACINE

SOTO, HERNANDO DE (*b.* ca. 1496/1497; *d.* 21 May 1542), Spanish explorer and conquistador. Born in Villanveva de Barcarrota, Soto came to America in 1514 as a member of the Pedro Arias de ÁVILA expedition to DARIÉN. By 1520, Soto had acquired substantial wealth from the SLAVE TRADE in Central America. In 1532, he joined Francisco PIZARRO in the conquest of Peru, and after accumulating significant wealth from the spoliation of Peru, returned to Spain in 1536. Soto had been present at the capture of ATAHUALPA at CAJAMARCA and afterward had taken Cuzco. Although Soto was at this time one of the richest conquistadores, on his return he sought the governorship of Florida. His expedition landed in Florida near modern Tampa in May 1539. Soto's search for a kingdom as wealthy as Tenochtitlán and Cuzco led his group from Tampa Bay to the modern states of Tennessee and Arkansas. The armada then moved to northwest Texas, and after traveling east to modern Georgia, marched west again to the Mississippi River, reaching Pánuco after crossing the Gulf of Mexico in makeshift boats. Soto died in Guachoya in present-day Louisiana. His corpse was thrown into the Mississippi River to keep the Indians from learning that he had died. Only his cruelty toward Indians compares with his foolhardy pursuit of the mirage of a flourishing city in the hinterland.

The major Soto narratives are available in English: *Narratives of the Career of Hernando de Soto in the Conquest of Florida*, edited by Edward Gaylord Bourne, 2 vols. (1922); GARCILASO DE LA VEGA's masterpiece, *La Florida del Inca* (1605) also in English as *The Florida of the Inca*, translated and edited by John Grier Varner and Jeannette Johnson Varner (1951); and *The Soto Chronicles: The Expedition of Hernando de Soto to North America in 1539–1543*, edited by Lawrence A. Clayton, Vernon James Knight, Jr., and Edward C. Moore (1993). For romanticized profiles of Soto, see ROBERT B. CUNNINGHAME GRAHAM, *Hernando de Soto* (1912); and MIGUEL ALBORNOZ, *Hernando de Soto: Knight of the Americas*, translated by Bruce Boeglin (1986). On Soto's violence see "Hernando de Soto: Scourge of the Southeast," special section of *Archaeology* 42, no. 3 (May/June 1989): 26–39.

JOSÉ RABASA

SOTO, JESÚS RAFAEL (*b.* 5 June 1923), Venezuelan artist. Born in Ciudad Bolívar to a peasant family living on the edge of the Orinoco River, Soto spent his youth in the countryside with Indian companions. He began his career by painting posters for the local movie house.

At age nineteen he won a scholarship to study at the Cristóbal Rojas School of Fine and Applied Arts in Caracas, where he met Alejandro OTERO and Carlos CRUZ DIEZ. He became interested in synthetic and geometric forms in the manner of Cézanne and the cubists. In 1947 he was named director of the School of Fine Arts in Maracaibo and held his first exhibition two years later at the Taller Libre de Arte in Caracas. In 1950 he traveled to Paris, where he became friendly with Vasarely, Duchamp, and Calder and exhibited at the Salon des Réalités Nouvelles in 1951 and 1954. In 1955 his relief *Spiral* (composed of a sheet of plexiglass separated from the background, which by repeating the same thumb-like fingerprint pattern produced visual movement) was included in the exhibition The Movement, which officially launched the kinetic art movement. In 1958 he launched his *Vibration* series (formed by a black and white thin-striped surface in which twisted wires or squares were hung in front, producing a visual vibration whenever the viewer moved in front of them). That same year he created two kinetic murals for the Venezuelan Pavilion at the Brussels International Exposition.

In 1963 Soto's work in the São Paulo Bienal was awarded the Grand Wolf Prize. The following year he won the David Bright Prize at the Venice Biennale and the second place at the American Bienal in Córdoba, Argentina. In 1965 he received the first prize at the first Salón Pan-Americano of Painting in Cali, Colombia. He had major retrospectives at the Stedelijk Museum, Amsterdam (1968), and at the Museum of Modern Art of Paris, where he presented his *Penetrable* (1969), an environment constructed out of plastic wires in which the viewer could play.

In 1969 the Venezuelan government created the Jesús Soto Foundation. Four years later the Museum of Modern Art Jesús Soto opened in Ciudad Bolívar filled with Soto's own private collection, which he had donated to his native city. Soto has also completed many public commissions, including kinetic murals for UNESCO in Paris (1970), and the *Esfera Virtual* for the Hilton Hotel in Caracas and the Olympic Sculpture Park in Seoul, South Korea (1988).

BÉLGICA RODRÍGUEZ, *La pintura abstracta en Venezuela, 1945–1965* (1980); MUSEO DE ARTE CONTEMPORÁNEO DE CARACAS, *Soto: Cuarenta años de creación* (1983).

BÉLGICA RODRÍGUEZ

SOTO, MARCO AURELIO (*b.* 13 November 1846; *d.* 25 February 1908), president of Honduras (1876–1883). Born in Tegucigalpa, the son of Máximo Soto and Francisca Martínez, Soto studied at universities in Honduras and Guatemala. Soto represented the best of the second generation of Liberal politicians who governed in Central America beginning in the 1870s. The Soto administration was characterized by an emphasis on scientific progress, education, foreign investment, and infrastructural development typical of the positivist governments that came to power after overthrowing Conservative regimes.

Soto had very strong connections to the Liberal Guatemalan government of Justo Rufino BARRIOS, whom he served at the cabinet level as minister of foreign affairs in the mid-1870s. In addition, he and Ramón ROSA had studied together with Barrios at the University of San Carlos in Guatemala. It was natural for Barrios to support Soto in his efforts to remove Ponciano Leiva and José María Medina as contenders for the presidency of Honduras, and at the second Conference of Chingo on 17 February 1876, Barrios and Andrés Valle of El Salvador signed a pact to do so. Meanwhile, Medina defeated Leiva at the Battle of El Naranjo on 22 February 1876, and on 8 June 1876 Medina and Soto signed the Convenio de Cedros, agreeing to name General Marcelino Mejía interim president. (Mejía served as president one week.) Soto followed as provisional president on 27 August 1876 and became constitutional president on 30 May 1877. He remained in power until 9 May 1883, when he resigned because of differences with Barrios.

Soto's administration dedicated itself to the economic progress and developmental goals espoused by Comtian POSITIVISM. The political and philosophical strength of the Liberal regime was sufficient to allow Soto to be relatively lenient with his former Conservative enemies. He was politically tolerant as a statesman, yet he did not apply this tolerance to people belonging to the lower sector of society, whom he considered lazy and without motivation. He did open a national library and initiate free public education, which had been previously decreed several times but never implemented. At the same time, Soto lamented the military interventionism in Central American civilian governments and institutionalized the armed forces on 21 December 1876 in an effort to check the military's power while defining its social and political role. These and other policies culminated in a new Liberal constitution in 1880 and the establishment of Liberal Tegucigalpa as the permanent national capital the same year.

There was also substantial economic progress during Soto's presidency. He personally helped revive the declining silver-mining industry of Tegucigalpa, particularly the El Rosario mine (Rosario Mining Co.). The government also founded a mint (Casa de la Moneda), which acted as a central bank. Soto opened up the country to foreign investment as a matter of policy, a liberal practice that paved the way for the banana boom of the early twentieth century. Infrastructural improvements accompanied economic reforms, and Soto's regime created a national postal service and a national telegraph service that provided relatively rapid and often instant communication in a country known for its regional isolation. Soto resigned in 1883, having asserted both Tegucigalpa's primacy over Comayagua and the Liberal Party's agenda as national policy. His chosen successor, Luis Bográn Baraona, continued to support Liberal oligarchical interests.

RÓMULO E. DURÓN Y GAMERO, *Biografía del Doctor Marco Aurelio Soto* (1944); CHARLES ABBEY BRAND, *The Background of Capitalist Underdevelopment: Honduras to 1913* (1972); KENNETH V. FINNEY, *Precious Metal Mining and the Modernization of Honduras: In Quest of El Dorado, 1880–1900* (1973); GENE S. YEAGER, *The Honduran Foreign Debt, 1825–1953* (1975); LUIS MARIÑAS OTERO, *Honduras* (1983).

JEFFREY D. SAMUELS

SOTO, PEDRO JUAN (*b.* 11 July 1928), Puerto Rican short-story writer, playwright, novelist, and essayist. After finishing grade and secondary schools in Puerto Rico, Soto went to New York City, where, in 1950, he received a B.A. degree in English literature and language from Long Island University, and a master's degree in art from Columbia University in 1953. He divided his life between Puerto Rico and New York City, and his works show the clash between Puerto Rico and North American cultures through his characters, humble Puerto Ricans, as they struggle with life in New York City. He published articles in *El Diario de Nueva York, Temas,* and *Ecos de Nueva York*. He was a member of a group of writers who from the 1940s on renovated the short story through new techniques and styles, such as the use of stream of consciousness, interior monologues, and a boldness in the treatment of sexual topics. Faulkner, Hemingway, Joyce, and other modern writers inspired him to break away in his own narratives from the mere depiction of rural life and customs of the Puerto Rican man of the times. Among his most known works are *Spiks* (1956), a collection of short stories, *Usmaíl* (1959), and *Las máscaras* (1958), a three-act play.

LUZ MARÍA UMPIERRE, *Ideología y novela en Puerto Rico* (1983).

MAYRA FELICIANO

SOTO ALFARO, BERNARDO (*b.* 12 February 1854; *d.* 28 January 1931), president of Costa Rica (1885–1889). As first designate, Soto assumed the presidency in 1885 following the death of Próspero Fernández, and a year later he was elected to a full four-year term. Continuing the liberal policies of his two immediate predecessors, Fernández and Tomás Guardia, Soto emphasized educational and social reforms. His Fundamental Law of Public Instruction (1886) committed the nation to free, compulsory, and secular education. The education budget was tripled during his administration. Other notable achievements included the construction of the National Library and the Asilo Chapuí mental hospital. Soto demanded complete separation of church and state, which resulted in the closing of the Jesuit University of Santo Tomás.

DANA G. MUNRO, *The Five Republics of Central America* (1918); CHESTER LLOYD JONES, *Costa Rica and Civilization in the Caribbean* (1935; 2d ed., 1941); JOHN HALE ET AL., *Costa Rica en el siglo XIX* (1972).

THOMAS M. LEONARD

SOUBLETTE, CARLOS (*b.* 15 December 1789; *d.* 11 February 1870), president of Venezuela (1837–1839, 1843–1847). Between 1810 and 1869, Soublette served Venezuelan governments as a soldier and a civilian. Perhaps no other military officer of his generation equaled his reputation for honesty and efficiency. Soublette served twice as president, between 1837 and 1839, following the resignation of José María VARGAS, and between 1843 and 1847. A staunch ally of José Antonio PÁEZ and a Conservative oligarch, he earned a reputation as a cautious but able administrator. His career as a politician included other important positions: vice president (1821, 1836–1837, 1839–1841), minister of war and marine (1825–1827, 1841–1842), and minister plenipotentiary to Europe (1835–1836). Forced into exile in 1848 as a result of the collapse of the Páez faction, Soublette returned in 1858, after the downfall of the Monagas regime, and served in various capacities as a military officer and as a senator, deputy, and minister between 1859 and 1869.

FRANCISCO GONZÁLEZ GUINÁN, *Historia contemporánea de Venezuela*, vol. 3 (1954); JUAN BAUTISTA QUERALES D., comp., *Estudios sobre el General Carlos Soublette* (1977) and *Soublette y la prensa de su época* (1980); LIGIA DELGADO and MAGALY BURGUERA, comps., *Carlos Soublette, correspondencia*, 3 vols. (1981).

WINTHROP R. WRIGHT

SOULOUQUE, FAUSTIN ÉLIE (*b.* 1785; *d.* 1867) President of Haiti (1 March 1847–28 August 1849), emperor of Haiti (29 August 1849–15 January 1859). Faustin Soulouque was the fourth president selected to govern by the Haitian army between 1844 and 1859. Faustin, an illiterate, conducted an extremely incompetent administration. In 1847 he was elected by the Assembly to succeed President Jean-Baptiste Riché because he was perceived as being docile, and thus easily manipulated. Once in power, however, he began a twelve-year regime of terror conducted by his secret police.

A plot to eliminate him in his first year in office failed. Following the example of DESSALINES, in his second year in office, Soulouque named himself Emperor Faustin I and created a peerage drawn from black generals that included 4 princes, 59 dukes, 90 counts, 215 barons and 30 knights. These men had no governmental or bureaucratic functions to perform; they were merely reflections of Soulouque's desire for grandeur.

To legitimize his empire, in 1849 Soulouque created his own constitution. Under Soulouque, the Haitian economy was completely destroyed. He lived like an over-indulgent aristocrat, defaulting on the national debt and increasing the deficit of the Haitian government. Soulouque's desire for more power motivated him to lead costly wars against the Dominican Republic, which resulted in the intermittent occupation of Dominican territory. During his reign, Soulouque openly practiced and encouraged voodoo (VODUN). It was the first time in Haitian history that voodoo flourished openly,

Faustin Soulouque. LIBRARY OF CONGRESS.

with official approval. Nevertheless, his unpopularity and the opposition to his regime increased until the end of 1858. In January 1859 he fled Haiti to escape the forces of General Nicholas GEFFRARD, who became his successor.

SELDEN RODMAN, *Haiti: The Black Republic* (1955); CYRIL L. R. JAMES, *The Black Jacobins*, 2d ed. (1963); JAMES G. LEYBURN, *The Haitian People* (1966). A more recent work is MICHEL-ROLPH TROUILLOT, *Haiti: State Against Nation* (1990).

DARIÉN DAVIS

SOUSA, GABRIEL SOARES DE (*b.* ca. 1540s; *d.* 1592), Brazilian colonist. Nineteenth-century historian Francisco Adolfo de VARNHAGEN (1816–1878) determined that Sousa was the author of the seminal work *Tratado descriptivo do Brasil em 1587*. The original manuscript was lost, but with more than twenty copies, Varnhagen was able to establish the text and the identity of its author. In 1569, Sousa went to Bahia, where he acquired ownership of a sugar mill as well as several other rural estates. He lived in Brazil for seventeen years, during which he took note of everything he thought worth remembering. While in Madrid in March 1587, Sousa offered his work to Cristóvão de Moura. This manuscript was known in Portugal as early as 1589, when Pedro de Mariz (*d.* 1615) quoted it in the second edition of his *Diálogos de varia historia*.

Sousa's treatise is divided into two parts. In the first one, *Roteiro geral da costa brasílica,* he describes the Brazilian coast from the Amazon to the Río de la Plata; in the second part, *Memorial e declaração das grandezas da Bahia,* he analyzes the Government General in Salvador. This second part, the most frequently quoted by historians, documents the establishment of the colonial government by Tomé de SOUSA, describes the city of Salvador, and enumerates all the SUGAR mills located in the Bahian Reconcavo.

FRANCISCO ADOLFO DE VARNHAGEN, *Historia geral do Brasil,* 5 vols. 8th ed. (1975); MASSAUD MOISÉS, *História da literatura brasileira,* vol. 1, *Origens, barroco, arcadismo* (1983).

MARIA BEATRIZ NIZZA DA SILVA

SOUSA, IRINEU EVANGELISTA DE. *See* **Mauá, Visconde de.**

SOUSA, MARTIM AFONSO DE (*b.* 1500; *d.* 1564), Portuguese navigator and explorer. In 1531 he was the commander in chief of a naval and military expedition to Brazil whose purpose was fighting the French who were trying to settle along the Brazilian coast. Sousa also intended to explore the rivers and the hinterland and to create Portuguese settlements. He was given full jurisdiction: power to appoint governors, to choose notaries and justice officials, and to grant land under the Portuguese formula of SESMARIAS. He left Lisbon with five ships and approximately five hundred men (sailors, troops, and settlers). He fought the French on the Pernambuco coast and, sailing south, stayed three months in Rio de Janeiro Bay in order to acquire food supplies and two more ships. The expedition went as far as Río de la Plata. Pero de Sousa (ca. 1500–ca. 1539), Martim's brother, went up this river with thirty men to take possession of the territory for the Portuguese crown.

Returning to São Vicente, Pero de Sousa was sent to Portugal with news for King JOÃO III. Martim Afonso returned to Portugal later in July or August 1533, after having created the first *vila* of São Vicente, where the SUGAR enterprise was begun. Sousa received a donation from the king of one hundred leagues on the Brazilian coast.

CARLOS MALHEIRO DIAS, ed., *História da colonização portuguesa no Brasil* (1921–1924); LESLIE BETHELL, ed., *Colonial Brazil* (1987).

MARIA BEATRIZ NIZZA DA SILVA

SOUSA, OTÁVIO TARQÜÍNIO DE (*b.* 7 September 1889; *d.* 22 December 1959), Brazilian historian. Born in Rio de Janeiro, Sousa graduated from Rio's Faculdade de Ciências Jurídicas e Sociais in 1907. He held high positions in public bureaucracies from the 1910s to 1932, after which he turned earlier interests into a career in literary journalism, publishing, and historiography, achieving his reputation in the latter two. He succeeded Gilberto de Melo FREYRE and preceded Afonso Arinos de MELO FRANCO in the direction (1939–1959) of the Coleção Documentos Brasileiros, the pivotal nationalist series published by José Olympio. He also edited the *Revista do Brasil* (1938–1943).

Sousa's own works, devoted to the key statesmen of the era from 1822 to 1850, suggest the preoccupation with the nation-state common to the period. During his Coleção stewardship over ninety volumes were published by such figures as Freyre, Jõao Camilo de Oliveira Torres, Cassiano Ricardo, Luís Viana Filho, Nelson Werneck SODRÉ, Luís da Câmara Cascudo, Afonso de E. TAUNAY, Afonso Arinos de Melo Franco, and Sérgio Buarque de HOLANDA. Sousa's role in the nationalist milieu was central to the reconstruction and rehabilitation of Brazilian studies from the 1930s through the 1950s.

OTÁVIO TARQÜÍNIO DE SOUSA'S works include *Bernardo Pereira de Vasconcellos e seu tempo* (1933), *Evaristo da Veiga* (1939), *História de dois golpes de estado* (1939), *Diogo Antônio Feijó* (1942), *José Bonifacio, 1763–1838* (1945), *A vida de D. Pedro I,* 3 vols. (1952), and *História dos fundadores do império do Brasil,* 10 vols. (1957–1958). Another helpful source is JOSÉ HONÓRIO RODRIGUES, "Otávio Tarqüínio de Sousa," in *Hispanic American Historical Review* 40, no. 3 (August 1960): 431–434.

JEFFREY D. NEEDELL

SOUSA, PAULINO JOSÉ SOARES DE. *See* **Uruguai, Visconde do.**

SOUSA, TOMÉ DE (*b.* ca. 1502; *d.* 1579) first governor-general of Brazil. Of noble birth, Sousa was the illegitimate son of a prior. A descendant of King Afonso III, he spent his youth at the royal court under the patronage of his cousin, the count of Castenheira, Antônio de Ataíde. As a soldier he fought in Morocco and participated in the spice trade with India. Appointed the first governor-general of Brazil, he arrived in Brazil in 1549 with six ships and one thousand settlers, including sailors, soldiers, six Jesuit missionaries, artisans, carpenters, stone masons, and criminals. His job was to centralize royal control over Brazil, defend the territory from French pirates, and pacify and Christianize the Indians. The Portuguese settler CARAMURÚ met the new governor and promised an Indian alliance.

Sousa purchased land from the heirs of Francisco Pereira Coutinho, the DONATÁRIO of Bahia for the seat of a new capital and center of royal government in Brazil. Salvador, the new capital, was built on a location more suitable for defense. The governor provided a good example by helping personally with the construction. He then sent the chief justice and treasurer to the other captaincies to check on abuses and regularize administration, but he also went on an inspection tour of all the captaincies except Pernambuco. The new governor made land grants to settlers and expelled hostile Indians to make the settlement more attractive for European colonization. Livestock was introduced from the Atlantic islands, while *engenhos* (sugar mills) were built and fortified. Market days were established to facilitate trade with the Indians. A customhouse was erected in Salvador. Sousa fortified unprotected towns and patrolled the coastal waters to keep them free of foreign interlopers.

Tomé de Sousa had a close relationship with Manuel da NÓBREGA and the Jesuits. He relied on Jesuit reports for information and sent Jesuits on inspection tours of the captaincies. During his governorship, forts and courts were established, new towns were laid out, and missions, churches, and schools were founded.

PEDRO DE AZEVEDO, "Documentos para a história do Brasil—Thomé de Sousa e sua familia," *Revista de historia* 3–4 (1914–1915): 68–81; RUTH LAPHAN BUTLER, "Thomé de Sousa, First Governor General of Brazil, 1549–1553," *Mid-America* 24, no. 4 (1942): 229–251; E. BRADFORD BURNS, *A History of Brazil* (1980); BAILEY W. DIFFIE, *A History of Colonial Brazil, 1500–1792* (1987).

PATRICIA MULVEY

SOUSA, WASHINGTON LUÍS PEREIRA DE. *See* **Luís Pereira de Sousa, Washington.**

SOUTH AMERICA: PRE-COLOMBIAN HISTORY

Amazonia

Covering well over 2 million square miles, the humid tropical forests of the Amazon and Orinoco basins remain relatively unstudied from the standpoint of scientific archaeology. Complete cultural sequences are few and widely scattered. Perhaps because of the paucity of data, Amazonian prehistory has been the subject of much debate. The region has been seen as an immense and uniform tract of tropical forest cleaved by mighty rivers but otherwise only occasionally broken by the small clearings of native agricultural fields. It has been characterized as a stable and unchanging environment—the largest remaining vestige of a forest primeval, a virginal land largely untouched by human endeavor until the coming of Europeans. In the eyes of some nineteenth-century naturalists, it was portrayed as an incredibly rich land with unlimited agricultural potential and teeming with fish and game. Under the gaze of twentieth-century anthropologists, this charitable view has been challenged. From a Paradise Lost, Amazonia has been recast as a counterfeit paradise, one beset by environmental limiting factors such as poor soils that constrain agriculture or by scant and dispersed faunal resources that limit protein intake. These polar verdicts, whether leaning toward the paradisiacal or toward the bleak view of a reluctantly giving nature, are imported caricatures and, as such, are unlikely to be correct.

As the custodian of the long stretches of time during which Amazonian societies diversified and evolved, archaeology has a privileged role in evaluating the mercurial vogues that have been brought to bear on the nature of Amazonia as a stage for cultural development. Although archaeological work in the lowland tropics is scant in comparison with most other parts of the world, it constitutes a large and growing body of evidence that forces this overview to be selective and to focus on three central issues: (1) the existence and nature of a preceramic and perhaps preagricultural or foraging way of life; (2) the development of pottery and agriculture; and (3) the emergence of complex societies.

FORAGING IN THE FOREST
A current debate centers on the feasibility of subsisting in the tropical forest through hunting and gathering (foraging) alone. Some see the tropical forest as a poor environment for foragers. Game tends to be dispersed, nocturnal, or arboreal, and wild flora is often deficient in energy-yielding carbohydrate. In support of this argument, it is pointed out that most recent foraging populations in the tropical forest have regularized exchange relations with nearby farmers. It does not follow, however, that because recent foragers have links with farmers, an independent foraging way of life was impossible in the past.

Archaeological discoveries indicate that there *were* preagricultural foragers in greater Amazonia. On the middle Orinoco, an area where tropical forest and savanna interface, a long preceramic sequence beginning by at least 7000 B.C. has been identified. Early artifacts include pitted stones (presumably for the cracking of palm nuts), ground stone axes, scrapers made of local quartz, and stemmed points made from nonlocal chert. Certainly these stone artifacts are but the durable part of a more complex material culture based on perishable wood and other organic materials. Twelve hundred miles to the south, on the upper Madeira, the beginnings of a long archaeological sequence have been dated to the tenth millennium B.C. in deposits buried deep beneath later pottery-bearing occupations. On the lower Amazon, near Santarém, stone tools at the base of a stratified rock shelter date as early as 9000 B.C. On the basis of this evidence, it would seem that the time depth of Amazonian culture history is fully in line with that known for other parts of the Americas, namely a terminal Pleistocene occupation by Paleo-Indians that reached from the Arctic to Tierra del Fuego. Although the nature of these pioneering adaptations to diverse habitats spanning two continents remains poorly understood, archaeological fact clearly indicates that Amazonia was hardly a no-man's land avoided by early foragers.

POTTERY AND PLANTS
To outsiders, the archaeologist's apparent infatuation with pottery may seem mysterious; however, there are good reasons for this obsession. Pottery is a relatively

nonbiodegradable, and therefore abundant, residue of human behavior. As plastic art, it solidifies decorative and formal information that can reveal much about the past. From a technological perspective, pottery represents a breakthrough that facilitated the boiling of foods. Boiling, in turn, is an effective means of detoxifying many plant foods and opens up the new culinary possibilities of stews, porridges, and, perhaps above all, beer. Beer, brewed from manioc, maize, or other plants, is an ancient staple and social lubricant in much of Amazonia.

With respect to pottery, Amazonia is precocious. Seven thousand-year-old ceramics have been reported from the TAPERINHA shell midden at Santarém. If confirmed by further research, the Taperinha finds represent the oldest pottery yet identified in the Americas. At the mouth of the Amazon, pottery of the MINA style is dated to the fourth millennium B.C. In northwestern South America, in environments that some have viewed as Amazonian extensions, several cases of fourth millennium B.C. ceramics are well documented. In terms of pottery, lowland South America, including the Amazon, has a decided jump on the rest of the Americas. These Amazonian data also bring into question the long-held notion that pottery and agriculture necessarily go together. In some areas of Amazonia such as the upper Madeira, agriculture would appear to have preceded pottery, whereas the Santarém evidence suggests the opposite. Or perhaps our notions of what constitutes "agriculture," based as they are on temperate-latitude models, need to be rethought to be applicable to the tropical forest, where the arboriculture of useful palms and other species is a widespread and presumably ancient practice. The peach palm (*Guiliema gasipaes*) is a case in point. It produces a biannual harvest of nutritious fruit, an edible heart, and an extremely hard wood widely used in house construction and for clubs and bows. The peach palm qualifies as a cultigen. Supposed wild specimens are probably feral, and a cluster of useful palms, anywhere in Amazonia, often marks the former presence of meddlesome humans.

In terms of the more familiar cultigens that fueled the American Neolithic, Amazonia would also seem to play a pivotal role. Maize is attested for the Ecuadorian and Colombian Amazon by the fourth millennium B.C., and a suite of cultivated plants including achira, soursop, canavalia beans, and manioc had a variable presence along the Peruvian and Ecuadorian coasts by 2000 B.C. On botanical grounds, many of these plants are likely to have a prior history of cultivation in the humid lowlands east of the Andes. Although sparse, these data suggest that Amazonia was a participant in the emergence of early agriculture.

COURSES TOWARD COMPLEXITY

Far-flung similarities in pottery styles indicate that Amazonia constituted a vast network of interacting societies at least by the first millennium B.C. This network was based on canoe travel along riverine highways that connected local farming and fishing economies on the fertile floodplains of major waterways. In the first millennium of our era, complex societal configurations that anthropologists call chiefdoms emerged throughout Amazonia. Recent research indicates that MARAJOARA culture at the mouth of the Amazon, long renowned for its fancy polychrome ceramics, mortuary elaboration, and monumental earthworks, was indeed an autochthonous development with local roots extending back to the first centuries of our era. It can no longer be viewed as an import from the Andes that, over time, withered away under the rigors of an inhospitable environment.

Marajoara is not unique in the scale of its earthern monuments. At the fringes of Amazonia, where gallery forests penetrate seasonally flooded savannas, extensive networks of raised agricultural fields, causeways, and house mounds were erected by pre-Colombian populations. Ethnohistorically these sophisticated systems of hydraulic engineering were associated with complex chiefdoms such as the Mojos; archaeological work indicates that their construction began in the first millennium A.D. in both Bolivian and Venezuelan lowlands. In the upper Amazon abutting the Ecuadorian Andes, the site of Sangay provides another impressive case of prehistoric construction. This site contains dozens of earthen mounds, some arranged in geoglyphic patterns. Midden is deep over an area about 0.5 square mile. Although the radiocarbon dates span several millennia, most of the ceramic debris at Sangay appear to date after 500 B.C.

In the 1540s, the expedition led by Francisco de ORELLANA reported extensive and expansive polities stretching along the Napo and Amazon. Settlements were large; subsistence entailed intensive agriculture and the tending of river turtles in artificial corrals; and chiefs were able to mobilize sizable forces to defend their territories. The archaeological record testifies that these polities were the culmination of a long in-place development, one rather abruptly truncated under the assault of European colonial expansion and introduced diseases.

Basic introductions are DONALD LATHRAP, *The Upper Amazon* (1970) and BETTY MEGGERS, *Amazonia: Man and Culture in a Counterfeit Paradise* (1971). Overviews of more recent work include J. SCOTT RAYMOND, "A View from the Tropical Forest," in *Peruvian Prehistory*, edited by Richard Keatinge (1988); and ANNA C. ROOSEVELT, "Resource Management in Amazonia Before the Conquest: Beyond Ethnographic Projection," in *Resource Management in Amazonia*, edited by D. Posey and W. Balée (1989). On the foraging debate, see the special issue "Human Foragers in Tropical Rain Forests," *Human Ecology* 19, no. 2 (1991). Also consult WILLIAM BARSE, "Preceramic Occupations in the Orinoco River Valley," *Science*, 250 (1990): 1388–1390; EURICO MILLER et al., *Archeology in the Hydroelectric Projects of Eletronorte* (1992). The issue of early ceramics is covered in JOHN W. HOOPES, "Ford Revisited: A Critical Review of the Chronology and Relationships of the Earliest Ceramic Complexes in the New World, 6000–1500 B.C.," in *Journal of World Prehistory* 8, no. 1 (1994): 1–49. On the historiography of complex societies in prehistoric Amazonia, see THOMAS MYERS, "Agricultural Limitations on the Amazon in Theory and Practice," in *World Archaeology* 24, no. 1 (1992): 82–97. For Marajoara, check ANNA C. ROOSEVELT, *Moundbuilders of the Amazon* (1991); and the review by BETTY MEGGERS in *Journal of Field Archaeology* 19, no. 3 (1992): 399–404. An accessible introduction to Sangay is PEDRO PORRAS, "Investigations at the Sangay Mound Complex, Eastern Ecuador," in *National Geographic Research* 5, no. 3 (1989): 374–381.

WARREN DeBOER

See also **Archaeology.**

Andean Region

The history of the Andean region before the Spanish Conquest is long, complex, and poorly understood. In the absence of indigenous writing systems, most information on the subject comes from archaeology, and in many regions little, if any, archaeological research has been conducted. Descriptive chronicles, government administrative records, and other written evidence left by the sixteenth- and seventeenth-century Spanish regimes shed some light on the centuries immediately prior to the Iberian invasion, but have limited value for understanding the many millennia that preceded it.

Unlike Mesoamerica, the Andes never constituted a single area of cultural development. In a comprehensive archaeological synthesis by Gordon Willey, four archaeological culture areas were recognized in South America: the Intermediate (or northern Andean) area, which includes much of the present-day Venezuela, Colombia, and Ecuador; the Peruvian (or central Andean) area, which consists of the Andean portions of present-day Peru and northernmost Bolivia; the South Andean area, which includes portions of Bolivia, northern Chile, and northwest Argentina; and the Fuegian area, which encompasses southern Chile. Until the fifteenth century, contact was limited between the different Andean archaeological areas, and even less communication occurred with areas outside the South American continent.

The situation changed dramatically when the INCAS of CUZCO created an empire that grew well beyond their homeland in the southern Peruvian highlands and expanded to incorporate portions of what are now Bolivia, Ecuador, Argentina, and Chile. With the Inca military and administrative expansion came the introduction of an imperial language (Quechua) and cultural elements native to the central Andes. However, the veneer of similarity left by the short-lived Inca presence never fully obscured the fundamental cultural diversity that characterized the pre-Columbian Andes.

THE SETTLEMENT OF SOUTH AMERICA
South America remained unoccupied by human populations before the arrival of small bands of hunters and gatherers during the late Pleistocene. These groups en-

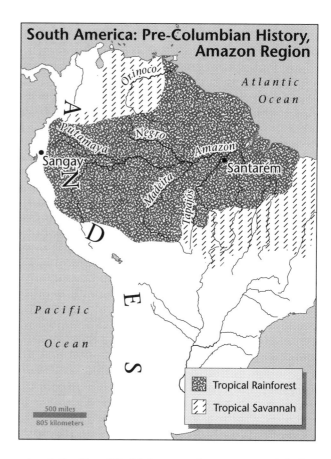

South America: Pre-Columbian History, Amazon Region

Tropical Rainforest
Tropical Savannah
500 miles
805 kilometers

tered the New World from northeasternmost Asia by crossing a now largely submerged landmass known as Beringia. Small nomadic groups following animal herds moved into the rich hunting lands of Alaska and eventually down through North America into the Andes. There is little consensus concerning the exact timing of entry either into North or South America, but groups already had dispersed into a variety of Andean habitats by 12,000 years ago.

Due to the limitations of preservation in the archaeological record, most of these groups are known mainly through their stone tools. By 10,000 years ago there was already considerable diversity in the unifacial and bifacial lithic assemblages that they employed. One striking exception to the widespread variability was the production of bifacial tools known as "fishtail points" because of their characteristic shape. Fishtail points have been found at sites in Panama, Ecuador, Peru, Uruguay, and Chile in early contexts, and the frequent presence of fluting on these points, as well as their early date, has led some to see a relation between them and the famous Clovis points of North America.

Evidence of the perishable structures in which these early Andean peoples lived is rare. However, at Monte Verde in Chile, excavations unearthed a settlement of small rectangular huts built of wood and skin; the dwellings are dated to around 11,000 B.C. While there is evidence that early Andean peoples occasionally hunted large mammals like mastodon, smaller animals and a variety of wild plant species comprised the core of the daily diet.

With the end of the Pleistocene, the variety of utilizable habitats increased sharply, and many environments that had been glaciated became available for occupation. Human populations expanded both numerically and geographically. Groups focused on a broad range of resources from the rich marine stocks of the Pacific to the high plains of the central Andes. Over the subsequent millennia, subsistence strategies increasingly focused on stable localized resources. For example, at rock shelters like Uchkumachay in Peru there was a shift from a generalized strategy of hunting to a more specialized pattern of wild camelid exploitation, and ultimately by 3500 B.C., to the development of llama herding. During this time, many groups began to manipulate flora to enhance the qualities or the environmental range of food or industrial plants; this process ultimately resulted in domesticated crops such as POTATOES, sweet potatoes, quinoa, peanuts, squash, COTTON, and coca that made pre-Columbian civilizations possible and which remain one of the most enduring contributions of the ancient Andes to the modern world. While these plants initially supplemented the core of gathered foods and hunted game, they steadily increased in importance and eventually made possible the shift to a sedentary lifestyle.

A well-documented expression of differing preceramic cultural patterns exists in the sphere of mortuary ritual. The oldest example of New World mummification

Frozen remains of Inca boy sacrificed to the sun on peak of El Plomo, Chile. LOREN MC INTYRE.

was developed by the Chinchorro Tradition in what is now northern Chile and southernmost Peru. Between 5500 B.C. and 2000 B.C. these coastal peoples introduced artificial treatment of the dead that included desiccation, evisceration, and reconstitution of the body through the use of fillers, clay modeling, and wigs. These elaborate practices contrasted with those of other areas, such as the simple pit-burials placed beneath the floors of houses in the early Peruvian coastal village of Paloma or the carefully arranged secondary burials of disarticulated human bones by the LAS VEGAS culture of southern Ecuador.

SEDENTARY LIFE AND THE BEGINNINGS OF ANDEAN CIVILIZATION

In the Andes, as in the rest of the world, the adoption of a sedentary lifestyle resulted in population increases, and these demographic pressures ultimately reinforced a dependence on the raising of food crops and, where appropriate, on the breeding of livestock or the exploitation of year-round maritime resources. Sedentary farming villages appeared first in the northern Andes of Ecuador and Colombia sometime before 3000 B.C. At sites like VALDIVIA and PUERTO HORMIGA these early agriculturists introduced the first ceramic vessels for the preparation and storage of the new dietary staples.

Along the coast of the central Andes, at roughly the same time, large shoreline settlements focused on the rich fishing and shellfish resources of the HUMBOLDT CURRENT. This maritime emphasis was made possible by the cultivation of cotton for fishing line and bottle gourds for floats. Some domesticated food plants also were consumed and there were strong ties between the fisherfolk and the inland valley farmers. Communal activity was central to group subsistence and identity, and these coastal cultures were responsible for erecting some of the oldest monumental architecture in the New World. At shoreline sites like ASPERO and Bandurria and inland sites like EL PARAÍSO and Chupacigarro, stepped pyramids were built as settings for public ceremonies and religious rituals and as the focus for community life.

In the adjacent highlands in the third millennium B.C., dispersed farming populations began to construct public buildings with central hearths for the presentation of burnt offerings. While these ceremonial structures were small, their repeated burial and re-creation at higher levels gradually resulted in the growth of large pyramid-platforms at sites like KOTOSH on the eastern Andean slopes and LA GALGADA in the entrenched western Andean valleys.

Agricultural expansion and intensification characterize the second millennium B.C. in much of the central Andes. Through the creation of gravity canals, the cultivable lands of the Peruvian coastal desert were greatly expanded and new centers with monumental architecture were established throughout the central and northern coast. Some find it a paradox that while this period produced some of the largest public constructions in Andean history, like SECHÍN ALTO in Casma and GARAGAY in Rímac, there is only limited evidence for sharp differences in economic and political power; hence the suggestion that the scale of these constructions may be a function of communal solidarity and cultural continuity rather than an expression of coercive political power by an overbearing elite.

Near the end of the first millennium B.C., most of these coastal centers were abandoned, while coeval settlements in the adjacent highlands continued to flourish. One of these highland centers, CHAVÍN DE HUÁNTAR, achieved special prominence by 500 B.C. because of the pan-regional importance of its temple, as well as its role in an expanding sphere of long-distance exchange. Its ceremonial center became the focus of pilgrims from distant areas, while branches of the center's religious cult were established elsewhere in the highlands and coast. Distinctive coastal cultures like PARACAS on the south coast and CUPISNIQUE on the north coast were drawn into this sphere of interaction but maintained their independence and cultural distinctiveness.

It is within this context that we find the first indisputable evidence for sharp hierarchical differences in socioeconomic status. Elaborate elite burials have been found at sites like Kuntur Wasi and Chongoyape. Innovations in textile manufacture and metallurgy were used to represent the symbols of the Chavín cult, in some cases on clothing or jewelry worn by elites. Although *Spondylus* and *Strombus* shells from the shores of Ecuador were imported for use in the central Andes, northern Andean agricultural villages of the first millennia B.C., such as COTOCOLLAO near Quito, appear largely free of influence from the central Andes and do not show a degree of social complexity or cultural accomplishment comparable to that of the Cupisnique or Chavín cultures.

With the collapse of the Chavín sphere of interaction at the end of the first millennium B.C., local identity reasserted itself in the form of distinctive local styles. Nevertheless, the existence of social inequality remained as a legacy of the preceding period. For example, on Peru's south coast the large Paracas mummy bundles from Cerro Colorado contained many layers of multicolored cloth mantles embroidered with highland alpaca wool, and dozens of other objects, while burials at a nearby coeval cemetery had few, if any, grave goods. Defensive architecture became widespread in the central Andes for the first time as small-scale political units and short-lived confederations engaged in fluctuating cycles of warfare and alliance.

In the lands surrounding Lake Titicaca, a trajectory of local development toward more complex societies occurred during the first millennium B.C. With an economy focusing on camelid herding, lacustrine resources, and high altitude agriculture, large sedentary populations developed and began to produce major centers for civic and ceremonial activities. At centers like CHIRIPÁ in northern Bolivia, highland populations erected public architecture decorated with distinctive stone sculpture in what has been called the Yaya Mama Religious Tradition. By the end of the first millennium B.C., PUCARÁ culture and the other heirs to the Yaya Mama Tradition flourished and became increasingly involved with the groups and resources at lower elevations of the Chilean western slopes and coast.

CONQUEST STATES AND URBANISM

Over the next five centuries, there were repeated attempts by small polities to expand into neighboring territories and establish multivalley states. One of the first attempts was by the GALLINAZO culture (A.D. 100–300), which expanded from the Viru Valley on Peru's north coast into several of the adjacent valleys, including MOCHE. The capital of this short-lived state was the GALLINAZO GROUP, an urban center that covered 1.5 to 2 square miles. Between A.D. 300 and 500, the center of power shifted to the neighboring valley of MOCHE, where a capital was established at Cerro Blanco. Large adobe pyramids were built for religious and civic activities, and substantial residential populations, including specialized artisans, were present. The naturalistic ceramics of the Moche give a vivid picture of a warlike people whose leaders identified with the mythical supernaturals of their cosmology. In 1987 intact tombs of Moche elite dressed in the costume of mythical figures and buried with enormous qualities of fine gold and silver artifacts were discovered at SIPÁN in the LAMBAYEQUE drainage. The Moche culture stretched over 250 miles from the Huarmey to Lambayeque, and materials of the Moche culture have been found still farther north alongside GUANGALA materials from southern Ecuador and local cultural materials known as VICÚS.

The emergence of elites in the northern Andean area can be traced through the presence of elaborate shaft tombs, like those of La Florida near Quito and Las Cruces in southern Colombia. The presence of elites are also suggested by the growth of large public centers, such as La Tolita and COCHASQUÍ, and the artistic sophistication of the ceramics of northern Andean cultures like the JAMA-COAQUE, the fine goldwork of the QUIMBAYA and TAIRONA, and the stone tomb sculptures at SAN AGUSTÍN. Nevertheless, none of these northern Andean cultures seems to have established a multivalley state comparable to that of the Gallinazo or Moche. Unlike their neighbors to the south, these northern Andean societies appear to have remained small in scale, non-urban in character, and politically balkanized.

Yet even in the central Andes, some well-known contemporaries of the Moche, like the NASCA culture of the Peruvian south coast, apparently lacked urban centers. Investigations at Cahuachi, the largest known Nasca site, failed to reveal evidence of large resident populations. The ceremonial center at Cahuachi along with the nearby geometric and figurative geoglyphs, known as the NASCA LINES, apparently provided the religious focus for an otherwise decentralized agrarian society.

PRE-HISPANIC ANDEAN EMPIRES
AND THEIR COLLAPSE

The earliest large highland state apparently developed out of the cultural tradition represented by Pucara and the older Yaya Mama Religious Tradition. Its capital was located in highland Bolivia at the site of TIWANAKU. Large constructions were under way there by A.D. 100 and the center reached its apogee by A.D. 600, when it covered over 3.5 square miles. Tiwanaku controlled much of the land surrounding Lake Titicaca, and its authority extended into neighboring valleys to the east and west. Vast tracts of ridged fields were created on the high plains, and government centers were built to administer these lands. Long-distance exchange linked the Tiwanaku heartland to distant resource areas like the desert coast of northern Chile and the tropical montane forests of Bolivia.

In southern Peru, an equally formidable urban center developed in AYACUCHO during the sixth century. Drawing upon elements of the same religious tradition as Tiwanaku, HUARI developed its own distinctive architectural and artistic style. From its urban core of roughly 1.5 square miles, the Huari state expanded into neighboring highland and coastal lands, subjugating other cultures and constructing distinctive rectangular multistory administrative structures. Huari expansion eventually reached into the northern and southern highlands of the central Andes. Moreover, burials of the Huari administrators and Huari religious offerings have been found in centers on the south and central coasts of Peru. The Huari Empire provides a clear antecedent for the later Inca Empire in its unification of diverse coastal and highland cultures under the control of a highland center. It also foreshadowed the Inca in many respects, including its maintenance of road systems, its standardization of government architecture and dress, its emphasis on terracing and maize agriculture, and its use of QUIPUS (coded cords that served as accounting devices).

In most areas, the collapse of the Huari Empire around A.D. 800 and of the Tiwanaku state around A.D. 1000 led to increased political fragmentation and the reemergence of extreme cultural diversity. On the north coast of Peru, legends tell of the arrival by sea of a cultural hero who established a new dynasty. Archaeologists have tried to link this legend to the appearance of a new culture, known as SICÁN, and to equate CHOTUNA, one of its early centers, with the founding settlement mentioned in the myth. BATÁN GRANDE is the largest center of this culture, and it contains vast cemeteries and over a dozen adobe pyramids. By A.D. 1100, the center of power on the north coast shifted again to the Moche Valley where the urban center of CHAN CHAN gained ascendency as the capital of the Chimor Empire, a conquest state that spanned all of Peru's north coast and part of its central coast. A host of other distinctive cultures, such as CHANCAY on the central coast and ICA on the south coast, coexisted with Chimor, and some of

these societies had centers, like La Centinela in Chincha, that were very impressive.

In the fifteenth century, the INCA, a small and rather undistinguished highland ethnic group, successfully resisted defeat by larger cultures to the north and south. Under the leadership of a remarkable king known as PACHACUTI, they began a succession of conquests and alliances that ultimately united much of the Andes. Few aspects of Inca culture were innovative, and indeed their success was made possible by the millennia of Andean cultural achievements that preceded their rise. The Inca built hundreds of state administrative centers throughout their empire. Among the most impressive of these is SACSAHUAMAN, a temple-fortress that overlooks the Inca capital of Cuzco, and MACHU PICCHU, a royal estate built within the montane forests of the eastern Andean slopes. An effort was made to transform the Andes into a coherent political unit through a multitude of cultural, social, and economic strategies. Yet, like the preceding empires and states, this attempt was short-lived, lasting less than a century. In 1532, weakened by European diseases, civil war, and internal rebellions by defeated ethnic groups, the empire of the Incas crumbled before a tiny invading force led by Francisco PIZARRO.

General surveys include GORDON WILLEY, *An Introduction to American Archaeology*, vol. 2, *South America* (1971); LUIS LUMBRERAS, *Arqueología de la américa andina* (1981); ROGGER RAVINES, *Panorama de la arqueología andina* (1982); JUAN SCHOBINGER, *Prehistoria de Sudamérica* (1988); RICHARD L. BURGER, *Chavin and the Origins of Andean Civilization* (1992); MICHAEL MOSELEY, *The Incas and Their Ancestors* (1992); and KAREN BRUHNS, *Ancient South America* (1994).

More detailed studies on the northern and southern Andean areas include GERARDO REICHEL-DOLMATOFF, *Colombia* (1965), and *Arqueología de Colombia: Un texto introductorio* (1986); BETTY MEGGERS, *Ecuador* (1966); ENRIQUE AYALA MORA, *Nueva historia del Ecuador*, vols. 1–2, *Época aborigen* (1983); and JORGE HIDALGO, ed., *Culturas de Chile: Prehistoria desde sus orígenes hasta los albores de la conquista* (1989).

RICHARD L. BURGER

SOUTHERN CONE, a term applied to the three southernmost nations of Latin America: Argentina, Chile, and Uruguay. The expression "Southern Cone" has its source in the appearance of the southern tip of Latin America as seen on a map, but the bond between the three nations that comprise this region extends beyond cartography. Argentina, Chile, and Uruguay share similarly temperate climates and geographic features, as well as a rich supply of natural resources. These features, along with the presence of a population that was unique among the Latin American nations in being almost completely of European origin, contributed to the emergence of the Southern Cone nations as social and economic powers in the late nineteenth century.

For the first half of this century, the Southern Cone countries consistently led the turbulent continent of Latin America in economic growth and democratic development. The United States and the European powers viewed Argentina, Chile, and Uruguay as their most profitable and reliable economic and political allies, and other Latin American nations envied the level of modernization of these three nations.

This condition changed abruptly, however, with the onset of economic difficulties after World War II and particularly with the violent upheavals of the 1970s, which brought to power repressive and undemocratic regimes. Growing nationalism and political volatility isolated the Southern Cone culturally, politically, and economically from its traditional partners. Despite recent political reforms, the Southern Cone nations, brought together in adversity as well as success, continue to struggle to regain their leadership status in Latin America.

ARTHUR PRESTON WHITAKER, *The United States and the Southern Cone: Argentina, Chile, and Uruguay.* (1976); WILLIAM F. SATER, *The Southern Cone Nations* (1984).

JOHN DUDLEY

SOUTHERN PERU COPPER CORPORATION, a joint venture of the American Smelting and Refining Company, Cerro de Pasco, and other U.S. corporations that commenced mining operations in Peru in 1952. Over the next two decades Southern gained rights to and developed three great COPPER mines: Quellaveco, Toquepala, and Cuajone. Located in the southern departments of Moquegua and Tacna, these mines made Southern one of the largest and most profitable mining and smelting firms in the world.

Southern financial's gains evoked considerable nationalist resentment in Peru. In the 1960s and 1970s the civilian government of Fernando BELAÚNDE TERRY and the revolutionary military government of Juan VELASCO ALVARADO criticized the company for its repatriation of profits, investment policy, and low tax rate. By reaching an accord with the Velasco regime, Southern, unlike other foreign mining firms in Peru, avoided expropriation.

CHARLES T. GOODSELL, *American Corporations and Peruvian Politics* (1974); DAVID G. BECKER, *The New Bourgeoisie and the Limits of Dependency: Mining, Class, and Power in "Revolutionary" Peru* (1983); ELIZABETH DORE, *The Peruvian Mining Industry: Growth, Stagnation, and Crisis* (1988).

STEVEN J. HIRSCH

SOUTHEY, ROBERT (*b.* 12 August 1774; *d.* 21 March 1843), British poet laureate, epic poet, playwright, and historian who wrote a three-volume *History of Brazil.*

Southey was born in Bristol, England, to a family of farmers and tradesmen and educated at Oxford. In 1800, he spent the first of two extended visits with his uncle, the Reverend Herbert Hill, in Portugal. Hill had begun to amass a collection of manuscripts and notes on Portugal and her colonies. Southey became interested in writing a

history of Brazil as part of a set of historical volumes on Portugal, Spain, the Portuguese Empire in Asia, the JESUITS in Japan, and monasticism. Begun in 1807, the *History of Brazil* was the only work completed in the set.

Detailing Brazilian history from 1500 to 1808, the three volumes of the *History of Brazil* were published in 1810, 1817, and 1819. Criticized for incorporating too much detail and too little interpretation, Southey was nonetheless recognized for the tremendous scope of his work by the queen of Portugal, who honored him in 1839 by naming him knight of the Order of the Tower and Sword.

GEOFFREY CARNALL, *Robert Southey* (1964); JACK SIMMONS, *Southey* (1968); ROBERT SOUTHEY, *The History of Brazil,* 3 vols., edited by Herbert Cahn (1971); LIONEL MADDEN, *Robert Southey: The Critical Heritage* (1972); KENNETH CURRY, *Southey* (1975).

MARY JO MILES

SOUZA, LUIZA ERUNDINA DE (*b.* 30 November 1934), Brazilian political figure and first woman mayor of South America's largest city, SÃO PAULO, which has a population of 12 million (1989) and provides one-third of Brazil's GNP. Born in the small town of Uiraúna, in the backlands of the northeastern state of Paraíba, Erundina, as she is known, was one of ten children. An unmarried Catholic who considered becoming a nun, she trained as a social worker and in 1971 moved to São Paulo (which, despite its location in the southeast of Brazil, has the largest concentration of Northeasterners of any Brazilian city, the result of migration due to drought and unemployment in the Northeast). Politically active first in the struggle to unionize social workers, in 1979 she became a founding member of the opposition Worker's Party (Partido dos Trabalhadores—PT), which she later represented on the São Paulo City Council and then as a state assemblywoman. A self-proclaimed Marxist who has described capitalism as "unjust and inhuman by nature," Erundina successfully ran for mayor of São Paulo in 1988 on a platform defending the rights of the landless, the working class, and the poor. She held office until 1992, when she served briefly in the cabinet of President Itamar FRANCO but experienced constant conflict with her own party, the PT. Always outspoken, she denounced corruption within the government. In 1994 she ran for a Senate seat, once again without proper support of her party, and was not elected.

MAC MARGOLIS, "Brazilians Turning Out Ruling Party's Mayors," *Washington Post,* 17 November 1988, A27; RICHARD HOUSE, "São Paulo's Marxist Mayor Adjusts Her Tactics," *Washington Post,* 10 January 1989, A20; ALAN RIDING, "A Mayor Bent on Inverting Priorities," *New York Times,* 18 March 1989, 4; JOSÉ NÊUMANNE, *Erundina: A mulher que veio com a chuva* (1989).

DAPHNE PATAI

See also **Brazil: Political Parties.**

SOUZA, MÁRCIO GONÇALVES BENTES (*b*. March 1946), Brazilian writer. A native of the state of Amazonas, Souza has been one of the most influential Brazilian writers since 1977, when his best-selling *Galvez, imperador do Acre* (*The Emperor of the Amazon*, 1980) was first published. Before then he had been a movie critic in his hometown of Manaus (early 1960s), a journalist in São Paulo (1965–1973), and a filmmaker, theater director, and playwright again in Manaus in the mid-1970s. A highly politicized author, Souza belongs to the generation of Brazilian artists who struggled under the constraints imposed by the military dictatorship between 1964 and the early 1980s. Although his reputation is due mostly to the sarcastic tone of his novels of Amazonian inspiration, including *Mad Maria* (1980; Eng. transl. 1985) and *A resistível ascensão do Boto Tucuxi* (1982), the core of his ideological and aesthetic beliefs can be found in *A expressão amazonense: Do colonialismo ao neocolonialismo* (1978). In this history of the literature of his native state, Souza develops the concept of cultural extractivism, according to which Amazonia has always been exploited aesthetically by authors in search of the exotic for its own sake, without any commitment to the region's social or political realities.

PEDRO MALIGO, "Márcio Souza and His Predecessors," in *Tropical Paths: Essays on Modern Brazilian Literature,* edited by Randall Johnson (1993), pp. 53–75.

PEDRO MALIGO

SOVIET–LATIN AMERICAN RELATIONS often commanded the world's attention during the cold war because of the competitive relationship between the United States and the Soviet Union. From the 1960s until the 1980s the Soviet Union expanded its diplomatic, political, and military presence in Latin America in spite of the huge distance that separated the two regions and the limited common interests throughout their histories.

Tsarist Russia's relations with Latin America began through the visits to the region of famous writers and scientists, including G. I. Langsdorf and F. P. Vrangel, when there were no official relations. Russia did not establish diplomatic relations with Latin America until late in the nineteenth century, and then only with Argentina (1885), Uruguay (1887), and Mexico (1890). Russia's principal emigration into Latin America was to Argentina and Brazil.

After the Russian Revolution only two states recognized the USSR before World War II: Mexico and Uruguay, and only Mexico exchanged diplomatic representatives with the USSR (from 1924 to 1930). From the beginning, Soviet governments capitalized on two political issues in the region: capitalist exploitation and foreign domination. Soviet-sponsored Communist parties attempted to mobilize industrial and agricultural workers against the "exploitation" imposed by the "ruling classes," and they rallied support against "foreign domination," usually by the United States.

The USSR's most important relations with Latin America in the interwar period were through the Communist International (Comintern), which was dissolved in 1943 as a concession to Stalin's Western allies in World War II. During the Comintern's lifetime Soviet leaders made the unconvincing argument that it was an independent international organization although it was, in fact, run by the executive organs of the Communist Party of the Soviet Union (CPSU). By the late 1930s, Communist parties, which had been established in most countries in Latin America, controlled trade unions in Chile, Cuba, and a few other countries but had limited electoral support, usually far less than 15 percent. Following Moscow's lead, the local parties sometimes favored overthrowing local governments, but mostly they participated in elections. The latter strategy was most prominent during the Popular Front period in the late 1930s in Chile and a little later in Cuba. Soviet foreign policies and the foreign policies of the Communist parties were virtually identical.

Toward the end of World War II most governments in the region recognized the USSR for the first time. At that time Argentina and Uruguay established relations, and Mexico resumed them; these three countries alone maintained relations during the cold war that began in the late 1940s. Although the Comintern no longer existed, Moscow and the Latin American Communist parties continued to maintain close ties. They included contacts with the radical nationalist revolution in Guatemala (1954), in which the Communists participated as a minority force, that was put down with U.S. support.

The Cuban Revolution of 1959 was a watershed in Soviet relations with Latin America. Fidel CASTRO was competing with the local Communist Party, most of whose members did not support him in his successful overthrow of Fulgencio Batista. When the United States imposed economic sanctions on the Cuban revolutionary regime, Moscow purchased Cuban sugar and provided oil and arms to Castro in 1960, permitting him to survive. Castro and the USSR disagreed over Cuban domestic policy and revolutionary tactics in Latin America, but by early 1970 Castro had adopted the Soviet political model and consistently backed Soviet foreign policy with regard to China and armed interventions in Africa, and through Cuba's leadership of the nonaligned movement. Soviet assistance mounted to billions of rubles in subsidies for Cuban sugar and nickel and provision of Soviet oil, trade-deficit financing, and technical assistance, as well as almost all of Cuba's military equipment and arms.

The Soviet effort to establish medium-range nuclear missiles in Cuba created the threat of a global nuclear war in October 1962. As became public only many years later, the Soviet commanding general had authority to use tactical nuclear weapons in the event of a U.S. invasion. President John F. Kennedy forced Soviet chairman Nikita Khrushchev to remove the missiles under threat of military action in exchange for a U.S. commitment not to invade Cuba.

Perhaps the Communists' greatest electoral success in Latin America was in Chile; in 1970, the party helped elect Salvador Allende Gossens, a socialist, to the presidency and was the second party in the government. The USSR gave strong moral support to Allende but was unwilling to provide the hard-currency grants he needed to survive. Fearful of a coup, the Chilean Communists tried to restrain Allende's most radical followers. The latter's leftist policies alienated the large Chilean middle class and facilitated the military's takeover and Allende's death in 1973.

In 1979 the Sandinistas, a radical nationalist revolutionary movement, overthrew the dictatorial Somoza regime in Nicaragua while the Nicaraguan Communists stood by and watched. Soviet General Secretary Leonid Brezhnev agilely shifted support to the Sandinistas. When the latter's relations with the United States deteriorated and civil conflict fueled by the Reagan administration began, Moscow provided economic and military assistance of more than $1 billion a year, an important sum but far less than Cuba received.

Moscow also backed the Farabundo Martí Front for National Liberation (FMLN), a radical political movement in El Salvador whose main foreign support came from Cuba and other leftist third-world governments. The Communist Party joined the Front late, as one of five guerrilla formations in an inconclusive armed struggle that continued into the early 1990s.

Radical nationalists took over the island of Grenada in 1979. They wooed Moscow ardently and won material support for their Marxist-oriented party, the New Jewel Movement, as well as arms, presumably to defend the movement from domestic or foreign enemies. After the popular leader Maurice Bishop was assassinated (1983) and some of his authoritarian lieutenants took over, President Ronald Reagan ordered an invasion of the island, which ended the New Jewel Movement and its relations with the Soviet Union.

Soviet trade with Latin America was minuscule before the 1960s. Prior to that time most Soviet interest was expressed in attempts to develop trade with the Río de la Plata countries (Argentina, Paraguay, and Uruguay) and Brazil, seeking to purchase grain, coffee, cocoa, wool, hides, and the like. When many Latin American nations established diplomatic relations with Moscow beginning in the late 1960s, Soviet buyers began to show interest in nonferrous metals from Peru and Bolivia. The difficulty was that none of the Latin American countries, except Cuba and Nicaragua, where trade was subsidized, were interested in Soviet exports. The USSR has never been able to develop a consistently favorable trade balance with Latin America. Most Soviet trade with the area's market economies has consisted of Soviet purchases.

Moscow's political efforts have had limited results. Its one triumph was the establishment of a Marxist-Leninist regime in Cuba, unexpectedly achieved through the July 26 Movement, not the Cuban Communists. That victory

Fidel Castro in Moscow with Nikita Khrushchev, 1963. AP / WIDE WORLD.

was achieved and maintained at huge cost to the Soviet economy.

The establishment of a network of Communist parties throughout the Western hemisphere is an unprecedented achievement, but no Communist party has seized control of a Latin American government by force. The revolutionary parties that have taken power have been radical nationalist, not Marxist-Leninist, in their origins, and except in Cuba, all have been swept away. Linked closely and publicly to Moscow, most Communist parties have never been able to shake the image that they were serving Moscow's interests rather than those of their own country.

Soviet priorities changed rapidly after 1985. *Perestroika* and domestic problems meant that less attention could be devoted to low-priority areas like Latin America, and the USSR could not afford to continue its assistance at the former high levels. The December 1990 agreement with Cuba reduced Soviet aid and sought to put commercial relations on a business basis. The Cuban economy, cut off from its natural partners in the West, had been unable to stand firmly on its feet even with Soviet economic assistance. These developments portended a grim future for the Cuban economy and the Castro regime.

The emphasis on self-determination in Eastern Europe and inside the Soviet Union itself, which accelerated after the failed coup of August 1991, made the formerly Moscow-dominated Communist parties in Latin America an anachronism. Moreover, the Soviet Union, usually perceived as the main enemy of the United States in Latin America, sought arms agreements, closer commercial arrangements, and aid from the United States. Such arrangements were inconsistent with the support of national Communist parties, which the United States regarded as anti-American and destabilizing. In any case, Moscow set these parties loose. As a result, many were split by factionalism, and domestic and world events caused them to lose much of their popular support.

As the cold war ended in Latin America, and the political geography of Eastern Europe and the Soviet Union was being redrawn, there were new trends in Soviet relations with Latin America: Soviet aid to Cuba was rapidly ending; Soviet support for Communist parties, revolutionary movements, and radical governments was disappearing; Soviet trade, always low with most of the area, declined even more, due partly to economic turmoil in the USSR; and normal, often friendly diplomatic relations were being conducted with many governments.

The most convenient sources of information on this subject are RUSSELL H. BARTLEY, ed., *Soviet Historians on Latin America: Recent Scholarly Contributions* (1978); COLE BLASIER, *The Giant's Rival: The USSR and Latin America*, rev. ed. (1987), pp. 91ff.; AUGUSTO VARAS, *Soviet–Latin American Relations in the 1980's* (1987); NICOLA MILLER, *Soviet Relations with Latin America, 1959–1987* (1989), pp. 226ff.; EUSEBIO MUJAL-LEÓN, ed., *The USSR and Latin America* (1989); and the biannual *Latinskaia Amerika v Sovetskoi pechati*.

COLE BLASIER

See also **Communism; Cuban Missile Crisis.**

SOYBEANS, one of the most important commercial crops in Argentina and Brazil. These two nations not only satisfied domestic demand for soybeans, but in 1989 they also supplied nearly two-thirds the total exports of world soybean meal. From the 1960s both countries pursued policies favorable to soybean agriculture and were rewarded with ever-rising output. Brazil ranks second to the United States in world soybean production. Only a few other Latin American countries, including Bolivia, Colombia, Paraguay, and Uruguay have a history of producing significant soybean surpluses.

Soybeans originated in Asia and many, therefore, credit Japanese immigrants with introducing the beans to Latin America. But in 1882, before many Asians arrived in South America, the botanist Gustave Dutra reported experimenting with soybean crops in the state of Bahia, Brazil. Experiments were also conducted in Argentina before World War I. Scientists noted the special properties of the legume: one of the richest foods known, soybeans contain 38 percent protein and 18 percent oils and fats. They can be cooked and eaten in hundreds of different ways, used industrially to make everything from soaps to glue, and ground into a meal to make an excellent feed for hogs and chickens. Nevertheless, demand for soybeans did not begin to grow in the West until after World War II, and the great expansion of soybean agriculture came to Argentina and Brazil only after 1970. Between 1970 and 1980, Argentine production increased more than 140 times, from 29,700 to 4.3 million short tons.

Government policy has figured prominently in the growth of soybean agriculture in Latin America. In Brazil in the 1950s, the state encouraged wheat cultivation in the grasslands of the southernmost state of Rio Grande do Sul. When climatic conditions weakened crop yields, growers started to rotate soybeans with wheat. Much the same pattern developed in the state of Paraná in the early 1960s, when the government sponsored the eradication of coffee trees and the planting of soybeans and wheat. By the 1980s these two states yielded more than two-thirds the national total. State-sponsored experimentation produced soybean strains that would grow in the tropical, central plateau of Brazil. By 1990 soybeans were grown in twelve of Brazil's twenty-six states. In order to work the 500- to 2,500-acre fields of this highly mechanized crop, landowners and tenants relied on substantial government credit.

As an especially nutritious food, the soybean has been seen as a means for ending starvation in Latin America. Most production, however, is geared toward export surpluses, cooking oil, derivatives for industrial use, and animal feed. Not only are fattened pig and poultry too expensive for the poor, critics note, but the expansion of soybean farming has come at the expense of land once devoted to black beans, a traditional source of cheap protein in South America. Thus, rather than alleviate nutritional problems, soybean agriculture has tended to aggravate them. Supporters, however, point to the tremendous foreign exchange earned by soybean exports and the thousands of jobs created by the soybean processing industry.

DAN MORGAN, *Merchants of Grain* (1979); K. HINSON and E. E. HARTWIG, *Soybean Production in the Tropics* (1982); M. A. C. MIRANDA et al., ''Soybean Situation in Brazil,'' in *Proceedings of the International Symposium on Soybean in the Tropics and Subtropics, September 26–October 1, 1983* (1984), pp. 1–10; ANTHONY B. SOSKIN, *Nontraditional Agriculture and Economic Development: The Brazilian Soybean Expansion, 1964–1982* (1988).

CLIFF WELCH

See also **Beans.**

SPAIN. Contemporary Spain occupies approximately 195,000 square miles of the Iberian Peninsula. Its land connection to continental Europe is in the northeast quadrant, where the Pyrenees span the border with France. The Mediterranean Sea forms its eastern and southern boundaries, extending to the Strait of Gibraltar. Most of its western boundary is shared with Portugal, and the remainder is bounded by the Atlantic Ocean (Bay of Biscay). Mountains dominate the Spanish landscape, and there are few navigable rivers.

From the voyages of Columbus to the nineteenth century, Spain was committed to the exploration, settlement, development, administration, defense, and exploitation of its colonies in the Americas. It emerged as a major European power in the 1490s, declined in the seventeenth century, reemerged in the eighteenth century, and then fell to the rank of a minor power in the nineteenth century.

In the mid-fifteenth century, ''Spain'' did not exist as a political entity. The term simply referred to the Iberian Peninsula and included several kingdoms. The marriage of ISABELLA I OF CASTILE and FERDINAND II OF ARAGON in 1469 and the couple's succession to their respective thrones in 1474 and 1479 brought about a union of crowns, but each realm retained its distinctive institutions, language, customs barriers, and other pre-union features. Each considered itself in a separate, patrimonial relationship to the monarch rather than part of a political entity known as Spain.

When CHARLES I (1516–1556), who later became Holy Roman Emperor Charles V (1519–1556), ascended the throne in 1516, Spain had a population of just under five million. Castilian society was stratified, with relatively few titled nobles who controlled most of the land, a larger group of untitled nobles, a few professionals, some merchants, and a large overtaxed peasantry.

New World bullion, which began to arrive in significant quantities late in Charles's reign, provided substantial revenues to his successor, PHILIP II (1556–1598), in some years furnishing as much as a quarter of the crown's income. Military expenses, especially in the Low Countries following the revolt of the Netherlands in 1566, however, constantly drained state finances. The government was always in debt and periodically, beginning in 1557, was forced into bankruptcy. Although the population rose in the sixteenth century, inflation adversely affected the economy and trade.

The following Hapsburg monarchs—PHILIP III (1598–1621), PHILIP IV (1621–1665), and CHARLES II (1665–1700)—struggled against a decline in population, a weak economy, an ongoing fiscal crisis, and, by the 1620s, a trade system with the New World colonies that was rapidly disintegrating as a result of extensive contraband trade. The revolt of Catalonia and Portugal that began in 1640 further strained the crown's coffers, and military defeat at the hands of the French in 1643 put a definitive end to Spain's era of glory. Fiscal crisis followed fiscal crisis until a deflationary policy implemented in the mid-1680s provided a base that made subsequent economic recovery possible.

Charles II's designation of Philip, duke of Anjou and a grandson of Louis XIV, as his heir provoked the War of the Spanish Succession. In the end, the Bourbon PHILIP V (1700–1746) gained the Spanish throne. Philip strengthened royal administration in Spain. Population rose in the eighteenth century and the economy improved. Philip's successors—FERDINAND VI (1746–1759), CHARLES III (1759–1788), and CHARLES IV (1788–1808), paid increased attention to reestablishing control over the colonies and securing for Spain the economic benefits of empire. Efforts at reform, especially during the reign of Charles III, paid dividends. Registered bullion production from Mexico, Peru, and Upper Peru almost quadrupled during the eighteenth century, and significant amounts entered the royal treasury. Trading restrictions were loosened and legal trade expanded rapidly between the late 1770s and the mid-1790s.

The outbreak of the French Revolution and Spain's almost constant involvement in European wars beginning in 1793 ended an era of relative prosperity. After Napoleon forced the abdications of Charles IV and Ferdinand VII (1808, 1814–1833), Spain was occupied by French troops and was the site of the bloody Peninsular War. The constitutional crisis provoked by the abdications led both Spaniards and Americans to proclaim that sovereignty had reverted to the people and they, through their juntas, would exercise it until Ferdinand returned. The crisis, war on the peninsula, the promulgation of a liberal constitution in 1812 that established constitutional monarchy, and the emergence of autonomist and independence movements on the American mainlands presaged the end of empire. By 1826 all of the mainland colonies were independent and Spain was left with only Cuba, Puerto Rico, and the Philippines.

Political stability was gone as well, both in Spain and in its erstwhile colonies.

SPANISH MONARCHS FROM 1474

Isabella I of Castile, 1474–1504

Ferdinand II of Aragon, 1479–1516

Charles I, 1516–1556 (Holy Roman Emperor as
    Charles V, 1519–1556)

Philip II, 1556–1598

Philip III, 1598–1621

Philip IV, 1621–1665

Charles II, 1665–1700

Philip V, 1700–1746

Ferdinand VI, 1746–1759

Charles III, 1759–1788

Charles IV, 1788–1808

Ferdinand VII, 1808, 1814–1833

Isabella II, 1833–1868

Alfonso XII, 1874–1885

María de las Mercedes, 1885–1886

Alfonso XIII, 1886–1931

María Cristina, queen regent, 1885–1902

Juan Carlos I, 1975–present

JOHN HUXTABLE ELLIOTT, *Imperial Spain 1469–1716* (1964); JOHN LYNCH, *Bourbon Spain 1700–1808* (1989); HENRY KAMEN, *Spain 1469–1714: A Society of Conflict*, 2d ed. (1991); JOHN LYNCH, *Spain 1516–1598: From Nation State to World Empire* (1991) and *The Hispanic World in Crisis and Change 1598–1700* (1992).

SUZANNE HILES BURKHOLDER

SPAIN: CONSTITUTION OF 1812. The Political Constitution of the Spanish Monarchy, promulgated on 18 March 1812 by the CORTES OF CÁDIZ, defined Spanish and Spanish-American liberalism for the early nineteenth century. It was a response to the constitutional crisis caused by the forced abdication and exile of Spain's legitimate monarch, FERDINAND VII, in 1808. Spanish liberals hoped to regenerate Spain through the adoption of a modern constitution influenced by Enlightenment principles and concepts stemming from the French and American revolutions. Although liberals dominated the Cortes, the resulting constitution was a blend of modern and traditional elements. Its controversial restriction of aristocratic and clerical privileges encouraged and strengthened liberal political arguments and emphasized the function and rights of local and provincial governments in making decisions for themselves, opposing traditional elites. The central idea behind the constitution was that sovereignty resided in the nation, which alone had the right to establish fundamental laws. Its makers hoped to correct the abuses of absolute monarchy without rejecting traditional features of Spanish law. Five American delegates sat on the committee in charge of drafting the document for debate.

The Constitution of 1812 essentially established a constitutional monarchy. Although it retained Roman Catholicism as the established church, it abolished the INQUISITION, aristocratic privileges, feudal obligations, and seignorial levies. It provided for elections of deputies to future Cortes, representation without class distinctions, and the abolition of entailed estates. The Cortes were to convene on 1 March each year, for three months. Deputies were chosen every two years and sat for two consecutive sessions. Although not rejecting the monarchy, the constitution did moderate the power of the crown to ensure constitutional government. The crown retained only those functions that the Cortes could not exert, royal control over the administration was subjugated to an elected, unicameral assembly that met annually. A council of state watched over the crown's actions, although its members were chosen by the crown from a list compiled by the Cortes. Such restrictions on the monarch's powers, not surprisingly, caused great friction when Ferdinand VII returned to the Spanish throne in 1814.

The Constitution of 1812 extended universal suffrage to all free males under a deliberately indirect representative electoral system. Colonial representation in the Cortes provided political definition and substance to the demands of the creole liberal delegates. Although the American colonies gained full political rights within a unified Spanish empire, the Constitution did not allow the American dominions full self-rule. On the issue of free trade, for which the colonial delegates pressed, the constitution encouraged freer trade, but not to the full extent the colonies wished.

The document also provided for elected city councils and for representative provincial bodies (*diputaciones provinciales*). It proclaimed freedom of the press and threatened traditional FUEROS and monopolies. To encourage agrarian production, the constitution established clear and absolute property rights. True to liberal principles, individual property rights took precedence over corporate or collective rights. The constitution assured the individual's right to enclose, sell, or rent his land, paving the way for alienation of indigenous communal lands in some areas of Spanish America.

Although the conservatives tried to present the constitution of 1812 as the work of a radical minority—"a criminal conspiracy of a handful of *facciosos* [agitators]"—in reality the constitution had widespread support. Even the most radical of the clauses passed without effective opposition in the Cortes. What opposition to the constitution did exist was presented by the ecclesiastical orders and institutions whose petitions and privileges had been curtailed by the liberal clauses. The attack on church privilege, however, excited greater disapproval of the document outside the Cortes. In general, the Constitution of 1812 provided for a division of governmental powers, consolidated and updated the Spanish legal system, ensured civil equality, and curtailed corporate privilege.

Its restriction of monarchical power, however, led to open conflict upon Ferdinand VII's return to power. The king dissolved the Cortes and abrogated the constitution on 4 May 1814, restoring the unrestricted monarchy that had existed prior to 1808. Liberal opposition to Ferdinand's repressive power and to the war in the colonies led to the Riego Revolt of 1 January 1820, which reestablished the Constitution of 1812. In 1823, however, with the assistance of Bourbon troops from France, Ferdinand recovered his full authority and once more suppressed the constitution. The Constitution of 1812, however, both in Spain and in Spanish America, served as the initial model for the early nineteenth-century liberals. It is reflected strongly, for example, in the Mexican constitutions of 1814 (Apatzingán) and 1824, the CENTRAL AMERICAN CONSTITUTION OF 1824, and several early South American Republican constitutions.

The Constitution of 1812 was published as *Constitución política de la monarquía española, promulgada en Cádiz a 19 de marzo de 1812* (1820). Secondary works dealing with the constitution and its influence include LUIS ALAYZA PAZ SOLDÁN, *La Constitución de Cádiz, 1812: El egregio limeño Morales y Duárez* (1946); RAFAEL DE ALBA and MANUEL PUGA Y ACAL, eds., *La Constitución de 1812 en la Nueva España* (1912); CESAREO DE ARMELLADA, *La causa indígena americana en las Cortes de Cádiz* (1959); NETTIE LEE BENSON, ed., *Mexico and the Spanish Cortes, 1810–1822* (1966); RAYMOND CARR, *Spain 1808–1978* (1982); MARÍA TERESA BERRUEZO, *La participación americana en las Cortes de Cádiz, 1810–1814*

(1986); JORGE MARIO GARCÍA LA GUARDIA, *La Constitución de Cádiz y su influencia en América: Años 1812–1987* (1987); DANIEL A. MORENO, *Las Cortes de Cádiz y la Constitución de 1812* (1964); and MARIO RODRÍGUEZ, *The Cádiz Experiment in Central America, 1808 to 1826* (1978).

HEATHER THIESSEN

See also **Mexico: Constitutions of.**

SPANISH–AMERICAN WAR, a short and decisive conflict fought in 1898 that assured the final expulsion of Spain from the New World and the emergence of the United States as the dominant Caribbean power. Public opinion and the media in the United States had been urging intervention since the beginning of the Cuban rebellion against Spain in 1895. Many of the Cuban landowning elite had also been calling for U.S. intervention to restore order to the island. The pretext for the U.S. to enter the war was provided on 15 February 1898, when the U.S.S MAINE, sent to Havana harbor to protect U.S. citizens, exploded and sank, killing 260 officers and enlisted men. No agreement was reached as to the cause of the explosion, but the United States concluded that it had been perpetrated from outside the ship. Since no accord for reparations was reached with Spain, the U.S. Congress declared war against Spain on 25 April. In the

U.S. forces landing at Daiquiri. Photograph by James Burton. Reproduced from *Harper's Pictorial History of the War with Spain* (New York, 1899). COURTESY OF THE HARVARD COLLEGE LIBRARY.

TELLER AMENDMENT to the war declaration, the United States asserted that it would make no attempt to establish control over the island.

The first battle of the war was fought in the Philippine islands, where the U.S. Navy destroyed the Spanish fleet in Manila Bay on 1 May 1898. The Spanish quickly surrendered possession of the Philippines to the U.S. In June, 17,000 troops landed at Siboney and Daiquirí, east of Santiago de Cuba. On 3 July the U.S. Navy destroyed the Spanish fleet, and subsequent land victories by Cuban and U.S. forces prompted the final surrender of the Spanish troops on 12 August.

The Cuban struggle for independence played a key role in Spain's defeat. The conflict had been consuming the crown's resources for several decades. From the outset of the rebellion in 1895, the Cuban Army of Liberation had controlled the rural areas, although not Havana or Santiago, the major cities. By the end of 1897, Cuban victory was all but complete. Yet although the war was fought between Cuban revolutionaries, the Spanish army, and the U.S. forces, Cuba was excluded from the peace negotiations that resulted in the Treaty of Paris. The independence movement of 1895–1898 had lost its most vital, younger leaders in the struggle, leaving older men and a weary liberation army to accept the compromise of its independence that was demanded by the U.S.

The Treaty of Paris, signed on 10 December 1898, involved more than just Spain's withdrawal from Cuba. In addition Spain lost Puerto Rico, the Philippine islands, and other islands in the Pacific and the West Indies. It terminated Spain's overseas empire. On 1 January 1899, when Spanish government officials retired from Cuba, General John R. Brooke established the U.S. military occupation of the island. Advocates of Manifest Destiny were vindicated by a relatively easy and inexpensive war. The United States assumed formal possession of Cuba and the right to supervise its national government by claiming responsibility for ending Spanish colonial government and unilaterally negotiating the peace terms.

FRENCH E. CHADWICK, *The Relations of the United States and Spain: The Spanish-American War*, 2 vols. (1911); WALTER MILLIS, *The Martial Spirit* (1931); JOSEPH E. WISAN, *The Cuban Crisis as Reflected in the New York Press, 1895–1898* (1934); JULIUS W. PRATT, *Expansionists of 1898: The Acquisition of Hawaii and the Spanish Islands* (1936); COSME DE LA TORRIENTE Y PERAZA, *Fin de la dominación de España en Cuba* (1948), and *Calixto García: Cooperó con las fuerzas armadas de los Estados Unidos en 1898, cumpliendo órdenes del gobernio cubano* (1950); RAMIRO GUERRA Y SÁNCHEZ, et al., eds., *Historia de la nación cubana*, 10 vols. (1952); FRANK FREIDEL, *The Splendid Little War* (1958); HUGH THOMAS, *Cuba; or, the Pursuit of Freedom* (1971); JAMES D. RUDOLPH, *Cuba: A Country Study* (1985); LOUIS A. PÉREZ, JR., *Cuba: Between Reform and Revolution* (1988).

DAVID CAREY, JR.

See also **Cuba: War of Independence.**

SPANISH EMPIRE. The Spanish empire unofficially began in 1402 when French explorer Jean de Béthencourt claimed the CANARY ISLANDS for Henry III of Castile. In 1462 the Crown of Castile took Gibraltar as part of its war against the Moors. Spain was accorded official possession of the Canary Islands by the Treaty of Alcaçovas in 1479, although it did not conquer the three major islands of Grand Canary (1478–1483), La Palma (1492–1493), and Tenerife (1494–1496) until the end of the century. Christopher COLUMBUS used the Canaries as a fueling stop on his way to what would come to be known as the New World. While he was sailing in 1497, the Spanish seized the North African town of Melilla. After Columbus's initial coasting among the Caribbean islands, Spanish explorers began sailing along the coasts of North and South America in pursuit of the mythical Strait of Anián that would lead across the mainland. By the early 1500s, Spaniards had established themselves in Hispaniola, Puerto Rico, and Cuba, venturing out from there to new destinations. Their voyages led them to Florida in 1513, the estuary of the RÍO DE LA PLATA in 1515–1516 and, by the early 1530s, as far north as Nova Scotia. Unsuccessful expeditions beginning about 1500 on the northern coast of Venezuela (Tierra Firme) and to Panama were followed by Vasco Núñez de BALBOA's crossing the Isthmus of Panama and sighting the Pacific (South Sea) in 1513. The fall of TENOCHTITLÁN in 1521 opened Mexico up for exploration, conquest, and settlement; the capture of ATAHUALPA in 1533 did the same for Peru.

The lure of finding "another Mexico" or "another Peru" stimulated rapid exploration of what became the viceroyalties of New Spain and Peru. The discovery of silver, notably in Potosí (Bolivia) and Zacatecas (Mexico); the presence of readily available native labor; and administrative and commercial needs determined the principal settlements of the Spanish Empire. Outlying regions lacking significant mineral wealth grew more slowly, but defensive needs and the development of nonmineral exports such as hides, cacao, tobacco, dyes, and sugar brought permanent settlement and expansion over a vast territory. At its apogee, the Spanish Empire stretched from the Pacific Northwest and California to Florida and from the northern border of the Louisiana Territory south through Central America. In South America it encompassed roughly present-day Venezuela, Colombia, Ecuador, Peru, Bolivia, Chile, Argentina, Uruguay, and Paraguay. Island holding in the Caribbean rounded out the New World possessions. Far west in the Pacific lay the Philippine Islands, a valuable entrepôt for the East Asian trade and an integral part of the Viceroyalty of New Spain, as well as the Caroline, Marshall, and Mariana Islands (including Guam) in Micronesia.

Spain's extensive territorial claims first suffered erosion in the seventeenth century, when English, Dutch, and French settled on a number of Caribbean islands, including Jamaica. Portuguese expansion extended the

Expansion of Spanish America

Zacatecas
Tenochtitlán (México)
Havana
Gulf of Mexico
Atlantic Ocean
Santo Domingo
Caribbean Sea
Cartagena
Pacific Ocean
Bogotá
Quito
Lima
Cuzco
Potosí
Asunción
Santiago
Buenos Aires
Río de la Plata
Atlantic Ocean
Falkland Islands (Islas Malvinas)
Treaty of Tordesillas, 1494

750 mi
1205 km

1 Bahamas: Partially occupied by the English in the latter half of the 17th century.
2 Belize: Partially occupied by the English in the latter half of the 17th century.
3 Jamaica: Under English control by 1660.
4 Saint Dominique (Haiti): Ceded to the French in 1697.
5 Mosquito Coast: Partially occupied by the English in the latter half of the 17th century.
6 Windward and Leeward Islands: Settled by northern Europeans in the early half of the 17th century.
7 Settled by northern Europeans in the early half of the 17th century.

Spanish Occupation
- 1565
- 1700
- 1800
- Disputed Territory

boundary of Brazil far beyond the line established by the Treaty of TORDESILLAS in 1494, but the border conflict was not resolved until 1777 with the Treaty of SAN ILDEFONSO, when Spain recognized the Portuguese claim to the Côlonia do Sacramento (present-day Uruguay) in exchange for the area now known as the Republic of Equatorial Guinea. In the meantime Spain gained the Mediterranean port of Ceuta from the Portuguese in the Treaty of Lisbon in 1668, but lost Gibraltar to Great Britain in 1704 as part of the WAR OF SPANISH SUCCESSION. By the Treaty of San Lorenzo del Escorial (Pinckney's Treaty) of 1795, Spain bowed to U.S. claims to the Ohio Valley and land below the Yazoo River. In 1800 it agreed to return the Louisiana Territory to France. In 1803 the United States purchased Louisiana and in 1819 gained Florida by treaty. The WARS OF INDEPENDENCE (1810–1826) ended Spain's mainland empire in Latin America; at their conclusion the once

great imperial presence was reduced to Cuba and Puerto Rico in North America; the Philippines and Micronesian islands in Asia, and Melilla and Ceuta in North Africa.

However, in 1860 Spain gained control over the Atlantic coast town of Ifni, 200 miles southwest of Marrakech and declared it a protectorate in 1884. The Cuban wars for independence began in 1868 and continued sporadically until 1898 when the United States intervened and defeated Spain. The empire lost its North American holdings as well as Guam and Puerto Rico and it sold the remaining Mariana and the Marshall islands to Germany the following year. As the twentieth century began, the Spanish empire consisted solely of its few African possessions. The Treaty of Paris of 1898 recognized Spanish claims to Equatorial Guinea and the Franco-Spanish Convention in 1912 formalized Spain's claims to Spanish Morocco, divided into Northern (south of Larache on the Atlantic coast to the Moulouya River and north to the Mediterranean) and Southern Zones (from the northern boundary of Spanish Sahara to the Qued Draa and 150 miles into the African mainland). In 1934 Ifni and the Northern Zone began to be governed with Spanish Sahara; in 1946 this arrangement incorporated the Southern Zone and was renamed Western Sahara. The Northern Zone was given to Morocco in 1956, the Southern Zone in 1958, and Ifni in 1969. Spanish Equatorial Guinea achieved independence as the Republic of Equatorial Guinea in 1968 and in 1975 Spanish Sahara was divided between Morocco and Mauritania. After that time all that remained of the empire was Ceuta, Melilla, and Spanish claims to Gibraltar.

DAVRIL ALDEN, *Royal Government in Colonial Brazil* (1968); JOHN HORACE PARRY, *The Discovery of South America* (1979); JAMES S. OLSON, ed., *Historical Dictionary of the Spanish Empire, 1402–1975* (1992); DAVID J. WEBER, *The Spanish Frontier in North America* (1992).

MARK A. BURKHOLDER

See also **Spanish-American War.**

SPICES AND HERBS. Native populations in America used plants for flavoring their foods before the arrival of Europeans, but the importance and varieties of these plants are poorly known. The most popular species that originated in present-day Latin America are discussed below.

Vanilla comes from the cured seedpod of an orchid vine that grows in tropical forests. In pre-Columbian times, the Aztec nobility used vanilla to flavor their chocolate drinks; several South American tribes considered it a desirable body perfume, wearing the pods in strings around the neck; medicinal properties were also attributed to it. The pod arrived in Spain aboard the first ships returning from America; it was used by priests and nuns to flavor their chocolate beverages. The aristocracy followed, then the French court in the seventeenth century. In colonial Latin America, vanilla was favored by the elites as an addition to chocolate drinks and sweet confections. During the seventeenth and eighteenth centuries, the Dutch, French, and British tried to start large-scale production of vanilla in their colonies in Africa and Asia; frequently they smuggled plants from the Spanish and Portuguese colonies in America for that purpose, but plants never produced seedpods outside their native habitats. It was not known then that a small bee found only in the American tropics is needed to pollinate the flowers. In the 1840s a former French slave developed a technique of hand-pollination; it proved so effective that later Mexico adopted it for large-scale production. Today vanilla is produced in tropical America, some Pacific islands, and Asia.

Chili peppers Many varieties of chili peppers were widely cultivated throughout Mesoamerica and South America, and some of their ancient names are still in use: *chile* (Mexico), *ají* (the Caribbean), *huayka* (Peru, Bolivia). CHILIES were so important in the diets of South American tribes that going without them was considered similar to fasting. Employed in initiations of young men and for protection in war, they were also used as medicines and insect repellents; the hottest varieties, macerated and mixed with water, served occasionally as weapons against the Spaniards. The Portuguese took hot peppers from Brazil around the world in the early 1600s; by the end of the century several varieties were grown in Africa, India, China, and some of the Pacific Islands, becoming important ingredients in their CUISINES. The Ottoman Turkish armies brought hot peppers with them from India to Hungary, where it became established as paprika. Chilies entered colonial Anglo-America with the African slaves. Today chilies lend their fiery grace to foods from all over the world. All Latin American countries use hot peppers in their cuisine to a greater or lesser extent, either in sauces or as condiments for various dishes.

Achiote (annato) is a seed that serves as both a red colorant and a spice. Native populations painted their bodies with *achiote* for ceremonial occasions and war. In Nicaragua it was added to chocolate to give the beverage a bloodlike color. Spanish colonists accepted it as a substitute for saffron. Today it flavors and colors dishes like *pollo pibil* (Yucatán), *corvina a la chorrillana* (Peru), and the ever-prevalent *arroz con pollo*.

Allspice This Caribbean seed, used also by the Aztecs, was exported to Europe in 1601 as a substitute for cardamom and became popular in German, Italian, and Scandinavian sausages and other dishes. Most of the world's production comes from Jamaica, Honduras, Guatemala, and Mexico.

Between the twelfth and seventeenth centuries, the spice trade had enormous economic importance in Europe, comparable to that of oil today; in fact, it was in search of a spice route that Europeans first reached America. However, once established as a colonial power, Spain abandoned its interest in the spice trade: the exploitation of American precious stones and metals prevailed. Portugal, and later the Netherlands, France, and Britain, monopolized the spice trade in fierce competition. Oriental spices favored in Europe were traded with the colonies; black pepper, cinnamon and cloves, still popular in Latin America today, are often imported. Some herbaceous spices of Asian origin that rooted well in American soil have been staple flavorings since early colonial times: the ever-popular cilantro, mostly as an herb; cumin seeds, for *sofrito* and *guisado* preparations; gingerroot, for drinks and as medicine; anise, to flavor alcoholic beverages like *aguardiente*; and cardamom. The last, once more valuable than gold to Arabs, is cultivated today in Central America, Guatemala being the world's first producer. Plants of European origin like onion, garlic, parsley, and oregano, also introduced in the sixteenth century, are today essential flavorings in Latin American cooking.

A scholarly and well-documented ethnobotanical history of equatorial America and Central America is VICTOR MANUEL PATIÑO, *Plantas cultivadas y animales domésticos en América equinoccial* vols. 2 (*Plantas alimenticias*) and 4 (*Plantas introducidas*) (1962). Good information on the origin and present situation of individual spices is KENNETH FARRELL, *Spices, Condiments, and Seasonings* (1990). A fascinating introduction to the general history of spices is WOLFGANG SCHIVELBUSH, *Tastes of Paradise: A Social History of Spices, Stimulants, and Intoxicants,* translated by David Jacobson (1992), chap. 1. Also useful are introductory chapters of Latin American cookbooks such as BARBARA KAROFF, *South American Cooking* (1989) and ELIZABETH LAMBERT DE ORTÍZ, *The Book of Latin American Cooking* (1979). See also AMAL NAJ, *Peppers: A Story of Hot Pursuits* (1992); and LARRY LUXNER, "A Spicy Tale," in *Américas* 44, no. 1 (1992): 2–3, on cardamom.

CARMENZA OLAYA FONSTAD

SPIRITISM. In everyday Spanish and Portuguese, the word *espiritismo* refers to a wide range of beliefs—including African, Native American, and Western—that have to do with spirits and mediums (people who claim they can communicate with spirits). However, for people more versed in the distinctions among the various spirit-oriented religious and philosophical systems in Latin America, "spiritism" usually refers to the movement founded by the French educator Allan Kardec (born Hippolyte Léon Denizard Rivail).

In the 1850s, Kardec began to attend sittings with mediums, and eventually he codified the spirits' teachings into a multivolume spiritist doctrine that began with his *Le livre des esprits* (1857; first translated into English as *Spiritualist Philosophy; The Spirits' Book*). In addition to supporting the idea of communication with the dead via mediums, Kardec also argued in favor of spiritual illnesses, reincarnation, and the existence of a spiritual body (perispirit). He saw spiritism not as a religion but as a philosophy rooted in observation and having moral implications. Kardec embraced Christian morality, but he did not accept key Christian dogmas such as the Trinity and the reality of heaven and hell.

The spiritist movement grew rapidly in France in the mid-nineteenth century, as did its nonreincarnationist sibling spiritualism in the English-speaking countries, and both were propagated in Latin America as well. In Europe and North America, spiritism and spiritualism soon faded into minor sects, whereas in Latin America they encountered a warm reception that was due in large part to the affinities between spiritism and African, Native American, and Iberian folk Catholic magic and religion. The result was, in many places, a SYNCRETISM, or blending of spiritist beliefs and practices with those of the local religions, such as the African religions of the Caribbean and coastal Brazil.

There are many today who follow Kardec's spiritism in a fairly pure form, especially in Brazil, where the spiritist population was estimated at 7 million in 1990. At one extreme of this diverse movement are the intellectuals: doctors, engineers, and lawyers who are more interested in psychical research and alternative medicine. At the other extreme are those who regard Kardec's doctrine as one element in a syncretic religious and healing system. In between are a large number of spiritists who have a frankly evangelical style; they tend to study closely Kardec's *The Gospel According to Spiritism,* and many view themselves as Christians.

In most countries, there are spiritist magazines and books, and in Brazil there is a huge network of bookstores to support the spiritist press. Spiritist publications include "psychographed" books, that is, texts that the spirits write via mediums in trance states. In Brazil, some of the medium-authors, such as Francisco Cãndido ("Chico") Xavier, have best-seller status.

Spiritists meet in spiritist centers, where they study the works of Kardec and other spiritists, develop their skills as mediums (although not all spiritists are mediums), and provide charitable services. In Brazil, spiritists run outpatient clinics, dental services, psychiatric hospitals, orphanages, pharmacies (sometimes homeopathic), and a number of other free services to the poor.

Spiritist centers also offer spiritual healing, which most frequently involves "passes" (roughly, the laying on of hands) and a type of exorcism known as "disobsession." Spiritists believe that one cause of illness is affliction from earthbound spirits, which attach themselves to people and cause them mental distress and physical illness.

Some mediums have also been known to practice "psychic" or "spirit surgery." One type involves pantomime-like operations over the body of the patient; spiritists operate on the spiritual body without actually touching the patient. Another type involves cutting into the skin with a scalpel or other instrument, usually to remove minor tumors such as lipomas. The latter type is extremely controversial, and in Brazil the practice has been condemned by an association of spiritists who are also practicing medical doctors. They prefer conventional "passes" and "disobsession," as well as alternative psychotherapies such as "past-lives" therapy and neurolinguistic programming.

Spiritists occupy a position of mediation in the religious and class structure (between Roman Catholicism and Native American/African religions), but it is difficult to generalize about their politics and political ideology. Historically, they have suffered persecution by church and state, such as in Puerto Rico before the American occupation and in Brazil during the Getúlio VARGAS years. Spiritists defend freedom of religion, rights for religious healers, and various other sorts of liberal freedoms. Spiritist doctrine also maintains that spirits have no sex and that the sex (and sexuality) of "incarnate" humans is a result of the karmic processes of past lives. Because at the spiritual level there are no sexual differences (and the same would apply to race or other biological differences), spiritists believe in human equality.

However, in practice spiritism tends to reveal the patriarchical and Eurocentric values of Latin American elite culture. Most of the positions of high prestige (psychographer mediums and organizational presidencies) are occupied by men, although women occasionally rise to power and prominence as well. In Brazil, spiritist mediums tend not to receive the *pretos velhos* (old black slave) and CABOCLO (Native American) spirits of the more syncretic UMBANDA centers, and while spiritists support birth control, they are often adamantly opposed to abortion. However, while older spiritists are often quite conservative, younger and university-educated spiritists tend to be more progressive. Thus, any discussion of spiritism should always keep in mind its tremendous variation across cultures and social strata, as well as its ongoing historical development.

For Brazil, see DAVID J. HESS, *Spirits and Scientists* (1991). For Puerto Rico, see ALAN HARWOOD, *Rx: Spiritist as Needed* (1977); VIVIAN GARRISON, "The Puerto Rican Syndrome in Psychiatry and *Espiritismo*," in *Case Studies in Spirit Possession*, edited by Vincent Crapanzano and Vivian Garrison (1977), pp. 383–449; and appendix 3 of DAVID J. HESS, *Spirits and Scientists* (1991). For Mexico, see JUNE MACKLIN, "Belief, Ritual, and Healing: New England Spiritualism and Mexican-American Spiritism Compared," in *Religious Movements in Contemporary America*, edited by Irving Zaretsky and Mark P. Leone (1974), pp. 383–417. On the spiritualist movement in Mexico, see KAJA FINKLER, *Spiritualist Healers in Mexico* (1985).

DAVID J. HESS

See also **African-Brazilian Religions; Candomblé; Syncretism; Vodun.**

SPOONER ACT, a decree that authorized the president of the United States to conduct negotiations for the PANAMA CANAL route. In early 1902, when the U.S. government appeared ready to select a transisthmian route in Nicaragua, the French-owned New Panama Canal Company lowered the asking price for its Panamanian rights to $40 million, an act that persuaded the Interoceanic Canal Commission (popularly known as the Walker Commission) to reverse its original recommendation and favor the Panama route. This action prompted the Senate to amend the Hepburn Bill, which had authorized the Nicaraguan site, with a proposal made by John C. Spooner (Republican of Wisconsin) that directed President Theodore Roosevelt to first pursue the Panamanian option. Roosevelt signed the revised bill on 28 June 1902.

DWIGHT CARROLL MINER, *The Fight for the Panama Route: The Story of the Spooner Act and the Hay–Herrán Treaty* (1940); CHARLES D. AMERINGER, "The Panama Canal Lobby of Philippe Bunau-Varilla and William Nelson Cromwell," in *American Historical Review* 68 (1963): 346–363; DAVID MC CULLOUGH, *The Path Between the Seas: The Creation of the Panama Canal, 1870–1914* (1977).

THOMAS M. LEONARD

SPORTS. The history of sports in Latin America (including recreation and physical education) has been marked by great variety, both socially and geographically, and a recognition that sports are an integral part of society and an interactive dimension of larger historical processes. After the Conquest the Spanish, and less vigorously the Portuguese, sought to suppress indigenous games and sports as part of their pursuit of political and cultural domination and religious purification. Few Europeans participated in the remnants of Mesoamerican BALL GAMES, *chueca* (resembling field hockey and played by indigenous groups in Argentina and Chile), or other athletic activities surviving in isolated communities.

Simultaneously, the colonial era saw the emergence of various competitive and recreational physical activities derived mainly from older Iberian traditions, often linked to rural equestrian practices or other animal sports, and of numerous games of chance. Whites and mixed ethnic groups derived pleasure from hunting, BULLFIGHTING, horse racing (straight line), cockfighting, and card games. Also important were work-related festivals and competitions that evolved into the "cowboy" cultures of the Mexican CHARRO, Argentine GAUCHO, Chilean huaso, and Venezuelan llanero.

By the mid-1800s sport was increasingly tied to the spread of so-called modern, European culture and its evolving recreational practices. These practices came to Latin America mainly with British, French, and, later and mostly around the Caribbean, North American businessmen, missionaries, teachers, soldiers, sailors, and others, as well as with Latin Americans who studied on either side of the North Atlantic. They became part of the schools and the social and athletic clubs opened by foreigners and of similar institutions built by progressive locals who gradually displaced the foreigners as leaders of the sporting community. These newer, imported sports spread from capital cities and major ports into secondary cities and eventually rural areas. Consequently, most popular sports in Latin America today have little connection with traditional or colonial society, and even less with pre-Columbian civilizations.

Modernization altered the recreational landscape: *patolli* (a Mexican indigenous board game similar to Parcheesi), PATO (an Argentine gaucho sport best described as basketball on horseback), cockfighting, *tejo* (stones are tossed underhand to explode blasting caps set on a target at the end of a measured path—played mostly in Colombia), *sortija* (riders on horseback try to place a thin needle through a hanging ring—seen today in Argentina), and other pre-industrial games and sports either disappeared or survived regionally in modified forms. *Patolli* is today virtually nonexistent; *tejo*, often accompanied by heavy drinking, is a game of lower-class mestizos; *pato* has moved from the rural pampa to enclaves of upper-class urban whites.

The British amateur ideal did not prevail for long in Latin America, as the desire to improve performance led to longer practice sessions, salaries, and the acceptance of lower-class and darker-skinned players. Also, the increase in free time allowed workers to become recreational athletes and spectators, and paid admission, souvenir sales, and broadcasting rights boosted profits. Soccer, for example, allowed partial salaries for about three decades before embracing full professionalization in the early 1930s. Today soccer and auto racing are highly professional, baseball and cycling are both amateur and professional, basketball and tennis are slightly professional, and volleyball and swimming remain entirely amateur. Yet even amateur sports require structure and capital investment and carry with them the concomitant features of modern sports: rationalization, standardization, specialization, bureaucratization, and internationalization. They also enhance the sales of equipment.

Professionalization also encouraged unionization, codification of contract law, and welfare legislation for players. In truth, despite higher selective player incomes, at least in soccer, baseball, and boxing, such efforts protect few athletes from exploitation, and confrontations such as the Argentina soccer strike of 1948 and the Mexican baseball players' protest of the early 1980s normally end in failure for the athletes.

By the twentieth century, soccer (Spanish: *fútbol;* Portuguese: *futebol*) had become the preferred participant and spectator sport, a reflection of its intrinsic sportive qualities and its ties with British society and the values that it represented. As Cubans have done with baseball and West Indians with cricket, some Latin Americans adapted soccer, a sport of white foreigners, turning it into an anticolonial force to establish their dominion, if only symbolic, over those who previously dominated them. Through 1994, Latin Americans have won the World Cup eight times: Uruguay (1930, 1950), Brazil (1958, 1962, 1970, 1994), Argentina (1978, 1986). Brazil is the only country to have played in all fifteen Cups between 1930 and 1994. In addition, Latin Americans support regional tournaments such as the Copa América (played since 1917) for national teams and the Copa Libertadores de América (created in 1960) for club champions, the winner of which each year plays the European club champion in Tokyo's Toyota Cup. They also participate in world and inter-American competitions for youth teams. Success in soccer enhances, however briefly, national pride and identification. Unfortunately, soccer has not escaped the illegal narcotics scourge, as half of Colombia's clubs are reported to be owned by persons with drug connections, drug money is laundered through soccer deals and salaries, and individuals such as Argentina's heralded soccer hero of the 1986 World Cup, Diego Maradona, have fallen victim to drug usage.

Playing baseball at El Morro, San Juan, Puerto Rico. © PETER MENZEL / STOCK, BOSTON.

Soccer's popularity is not unchallenged, however. In the Spanish-speaking circum-Caribbean, including Mexico's Yucatán, baseball (*béisbol*) has been the "king of sports" for almost a century due to its leisurely pace, low cost, and association with more powerful societies. As early as the 1870s, baseball had numerous Cuban enthusiasts who joined North Americans in spreading the diamond game among their neighbors. Eventually, Puerto Rico, the Dominican Republic, Mexico, Nicaragua, Venezuela, Panama, and Colombia became at least partial supporters of the Yankee pastime, all of them leaping into international competitions and exporting stars to northern professional leagues. Cuba, the Dominican Republic, Nicaragua, and Venezuela have each won the world series of amateur baseball at least once. After 1959, Puerto Rico, the Dominican Republic, and Venezuela replaced Cuba as the primary sources of Latin American talent in the majors. San Pedro de Macorís, on the southeastern coast of the Dominican Republic, have supplied more players per capita to the major leagues than any city in the world. Because of its own legal code, Mexico has not exported a substantial number of players.

Latin America has produced numerous world champions in boxing, especially in the lighter weight divisions. The best known include Carlos Monzón and Pascual Pérez (Argentina), Alexis Argüello (Nicaragua), Luis Ibarra and Roberto Durán (Panama), Juan Guzmán (Dominican Republic), Vicente Rondón (Venezuela), and Julio César Chávez (Mexico), who in 1994 was knocked out and defeated, both for the first time, after ninety fights and three world titles. Today Cuba rules the amateur sphere at the Pan-American Games, Olympics, world boxing tournaments, and binational competitions with the United States. Individually best known has been heavyweight Teófilo Stevenson, who dominated the Olympics in the 1970s and later successfully coached his national team.

Basketball spread initially via teachers and students, although in recent years it has benefited from the televising of National Basketball Association games and high-level international competitions. Goodwill tours by such U.S. stars as Earvin (Magic) Johnson have raised interest and skills. In most countries basketball is an important part of the school physical education and recreation programs, and Brazil and Cuba have developed strong national teams. Uruguay has a limited professional league. Argentina hosted and won basketball's first world championship in 1950. Volleyball, carried worldwide by YMCA workers, has gained less acceptance, although Brazil and Cuba have done well internationally, as have the Peruvian women, and beach varieties of the game have won adherents in some places.

Bullfighting and other Iberian sports remain most viable in countries where the European colonial presence was strongest and later immigration did less to alter the inherited traditions. Thus, Mexico, Colombia, Peru, and Venezuela have the leading taurine establishments;

Mexico, some Andean countries, and Cuba have long promoted jai alai and related ball games.

Latin American tennis stars have increasingly populated world rankings since the late 1950s and early 1960s, the glory days of Anita Linzana (Chile), Pancho Segura (Ecuador), Pancho González (Mexico), and Maria Bueno (Brazil). Since the 1970s such stars as Guillermo Vilas (Argentina), Alex Olmedo (Peru), Andrés Gómez (Ecuador), and Gabriela Sabatini (Argentina) have emerged, and their success has promoted tennis as a recreational activity for a limited middle class in their home countries.

Perhaps because of their early industrialization, Argentina and Brazil embraced auto racing, both track and open-road, and produced international champions such as Argentina's Juan Manuel Fangio and Oscar Gálvez and Brazil's Emerson Fittipaldi, Nelson Piquet, and Ayrton Senna. Colombia's Roberto Guerrero joined the Indianapolis car circuit in the 1980s. Cycling, an early import from Europe because of its ties with technology, exercise, and French leisure, has been more prominent in mountainous countries like Colombia, Costa Rica, and Mexico.

Latin Americans also support track and field, horse racing (in areas under British influence, the horses run clockwise on grass), field hockey, swimming, handball and related court ball games (many derived from various old Basque sports [including jai alai] and collectively labeled *pelota vasca*), chess (which is considered a sport in the region and was led for years by the Cuban grandmaster José Raul CAPABLANCA). More recently, recreational activities such as hiking, camping, jogging, survivalism, boating, and sport fishing have become popular.

American football has gained greater spectator interest with the spread of satellite television, but only in Mexico (and in the old Panama Canal Zone) has it recruited a noticeable number of scholastic participants, beginning as early as the 1930s. Professional wrestling (*lucha libre*) has achieved popularity among Mexico's working classes.

Participants and spectators alike have been increasingly influenced by forces directed by private and public agencies seeking to use sport and recreation, including physical culture and education, for larger economic and political objectives: to teach constructive values, improve health and morality, increase labor productivity, reduce vice and crime, develop a sense of community and cooperation, promote patriotism and nationalism, attract foreign investment, and improve a nation's image abroad—objectives often aimed at social control as much as social development. These goals have been pursued by (1) the establishment of domestic physical education programs, sports competitions, and permanent institutions necessary to oversee athletic programs; (2) the preparation of individuals and teams capable of competing successfully at the international level; and (3) the hosting of international sporting events.

Some examples of the overt use or abuse of sports for political reasons include the Guatemalan government's promotion of the Sixth Central American and Caribbean Games (1950) to enhance its revolutionary program, the attempt by the ruling Brazilian military in 1970 to exploit the country's third soccer World Cup victory to strengthen its authoritarian rule, and in Chile the efforts of the Augusto Pinochet dictatorship after September 1973 to suppress all sports clubs and events that might give voice to suspected critics and protesters.

All Latin American countries have, however ineffective and poorly funded, some version of an integrated national sports federation (such as Chile's Digeder, Colombia's Coldeportes, Cuba's Inder, and Mexico's Conade), national associations for most sports, Olympic organizing committees, a physical education institute, and periodic "national games" at different age levels.

Overlapping these are expanding linkages to international networks. Latin Americans began to join Olympic competitions in 1900 and FIFA, soccer's governing body founded in 1904, in 1913. In 1922, on the centenary of its independence, Brazil organized the now defunct South American Games; in 1926, encouraged by the Olympic leadership in Paris in 1924, Mexico hosted the first Central American and Caribbean Games; the more limited Central American Games started in Guatemala in 1973; in 1938, on the 400th anniversary of the founding of its capital, Colombia initiated the Bolivarian Games. In 1951 Juan Perón's Argentina inaugurated the Pan-American Games, a competition likewise encouraged by the Olympic leadership as early as the 1932 Los Angeles Olympics and originally scheduled for Buenos Aires in 1942. A smaller winter version of the Pan-American Games was launched in 1990.

Uruguay hosted and won the first soccer World Cup (Mundial) in 1930, after winning the previous two Olympic gold medals in that sport. Brazil (1950), Chile (1962), Mexico (1970, 1986), and Argentina (1978) have also hosted the World Cup, which is the largest sporting event in the world other than the Olympics. Mexico was the first third world country to sponsor the Summer Olympics (1968), an event marred by domestic political violence and the death and disappearance of numerous students and workers shortly before the torch arrived, but which the government cited as proof of Mexico's progress and international acceptance.

In addition to the competitive encounters and organizational ties, the growing internationalization of sports has generated increased migration of players and coaches within Latin America and to and from Europe and North America, as well as sales of foreign sporting equipment and televised sporting events. Building on a tradition that dates back to the 1930s, for example, over 400 Argentine soccer players were estimated to be playing in other countries in 1992.

Prior to 1959, Cuba had won numerous Olympic medals (the first in 1900), produced skilled professional boxers such as Kid Tunero and Kid Chocolate, and sent more baseball players to the U.S. major leagues than any foreign country. But critics contend that the Cuban sports structure, like that of other Latin American countries, was elitist, sexist, and too respondent to external monetary pressures. Following the revolution, Cuba eliminated open professionalism, increased its Olympic medal count (to thirty-one at Barcelona in 1992, for example) and built a balanced program of mass physical culture superior to any other in Latin America. However, some forty Cuban athletes defected during the Central American and Caribbean Games in Puerto Rico in 1993, suggesting that dissatisfaction runs high even among the privileged, a conviction reaffirmed by the similar flight of an increasing number of players from Cuba's Pan-American, world amateur, and Olympic championship baseball team, several of whom signed professional contracts in North America.

Before Barcelona, probably Cuba's greatest international sporting achievement occurred at the Eleventh Pan-American Games (1991), which it hosted. Under severe economic and political difficulties, the Cubans provided the facilities for 4,519 athletes from thirty-nine countries and won ten more gold medals than did the United States (140–130), although the total medal count favored the United States (352–265).

Cuba has been nearly as successful in developing women champions as men, although critics of the Castro system still identify sexist qualities in the Cuban sports system. Women from other Latin American countries have achieved far less than the Cubans, in part because their societies value women athletes less and provide less support. There are notable exceptions, of course, such as Neomí Simonetto (long jump, Argentina), Marlene Ahrens (javelin throw, Chile), and Silvia Poll (swimming, Costa Rica), and the tennis stars cited above. The 1988 Olympic Games displayed the continuing prowess of the Peruvian women's volleyball team, which took the silver medal.

Sport's importance in Latin American society is reflected in the use of sport jargon in the ordinary language and of sport themes in artistic expressions. Politicians often "move pieces on the board" in hopes of "getting to the head of the pack" in order to "score more goals," while great writers such as Argentina's Julio CORTÁZAR (boxing), and Chile's Antonio SKÁRMETA (cycling and soccer), have long used play and game settings to convey their ideas. Increasingly authors depict sport as physical activity rather than spectacle, thus providing a means to represent social and psychological conflicts among literary characters. This is evident in the boxing plays of Eduardo Pavlosky (Argentina) and Vicente LEÑERO (Mexico) and the novels of Isaac GOLDEMBERG (soccer, Peru) and José AGUSTÍN (baseball, Mexico).

While originally the language of many sports was built on the Latinized pronunciation of imported, usually English terms ("golf," "round," "football"), more recently Spanish and Portuguese linguistic inventions have replaced many foreign words (*boxeo* for "boxing," *gol* for "goal," *arquero* for "goalie") and reasonable translations have been identified (*fuera de lugar* for "offside," *lanzador* for "pitcher," *árbitro* for "referee"). The importance of games and sports in the lives of Latin Americans is further evident in the success of sports periodicals of the quality of *El Gráfico* (Argentina) and *Placar* (Brazil).

EDUARDO GALEANO, ed., *Su majestad, el fútbol* (1968); JUAN JOSÉ SEBRELI, *Fútbol y masas* (1981); JANET LEVER, *Soccer Madness* (1983); WILLIAM H. BEEZLEY, *Judas at the Jockey Club and Other Episodes of Porfirian Mexico* (1987); JOSEPH L. ARBENA, ed., *Sport and Society in Latin America: Diffusion, Dependency, and the Rise of Mass Culture* (1988); JOSEPH L. ARBENA, comp., *An Annotated Bibliography of Latin American Sport: Pre-Conquest to the Present* (1989); LILIANA MORELLI, *Mujeres deportistas* (1990); ALAN M. KLEIN, *Sugarball: The American Game, the Dominican Dream* (1991); ROB RUCK, *The Tropic of Baseball: Baseball in the Dominican Republic* (1991); JOSEPH L. ARBENA, "Sports, Development, and Mexican Nationalism, 1920–1970," in *Journal of Sport History* 18, no. 3 (1991): 350–364; MICHAEL M. and MARY ADAMS OLEKSAK, *Béisbol: Latin Americans and the Grand Old Game* (1991); JOSEPH L. ARBENA and DAVID LA FRANCE, eds., *Studies in Latin American Popular Culture* 13 (1994), a special issue devoted to Latin American sport.

JOSEPH L. ARBENA

SQUIER, EPHRAIM GEORGE (*b.* 17 June 1821; *d.* 17 April 1888), U.S. diplomat and writer. Squier was one of the most important diplomats to represent the United States in Central America in the nineteenth century. Appointed in 1849, Squier was in Central America only one year. In that short period he energetically assisted agents of Cornelius Vanderbilt in negotiating a contract to build a transisthmian canal, signed a treaty with Nicaragua guaranteeing U.S. protection of the canal route, and persuaded Honduran authorities to cede territory in the Gulf of Fonseca to the United States. These actions, which exceeded his instructions, provoked a dispute with Great Britain that led to the negotiation of the CLAYTON–BULWER TREATY. The treaty declared that neither country would attempt to colonize Central America or control any isthmian transportation facility. Although Squier thought that the treaty signaled a defeat for the United States, in reality it marked the beginning of the replacement of British influence in Central America with that of the United States.

The brief visit to Central America turned Squier into a publicist for Central America and an entrepreneur. He wrote extensively about Central American topics, ranging from archaeology to contemporary foreign relations, and was recognized in mid-century as the leading authority on the region. As an entrepreneur he was unsuccessful in his attempts to build a railway across Honduras.

The following studies by CHARLES L. STANSIFER cover differing aspects of Squier's career: "The Central American Writings of E. George Squier," in *Inter-American Review of Bibliography* 16, no. 2 (1966): 144–160; "E. George Squier and the Honduras Interoceanic Railroad Project," in *Hispanic American Historical Review* 46, no. 1 (1966): 1–27; *E. George Squier: Diversos aspectos de su carrera en Centro América* (1968).

CHARLES L. STANSIFER

STADEN, HANS (*b.* ca. 1525; *d.* ca. 1576), a German who wrote a first-hand account of his captivity by the TUPINAMBÁ Indians in Brazil.

Staden was born in Bad Homburg, Hesse. Employed as a gunner by the Portuguese to oversee the artillery defenses at Fort Bertioga on the island of Santo Amaro, near the port of Santos, Brazil, Staden was captured by TUPI warriors in 1552 while hunting wild game. He survived his experience among the Tupi Indians and subsequently wrote of his captivity. In his account, *Warhafig Historia* (1557), which remains a principal source on sixteenth-century coastal Indians of Brazil, Staden described how the Tupi paraded him naked through their village at Ubatuba as a prelude to eating him. He stayed alive because a toothache left him unable to eat much and he became too thin to be eaten. He also made lucky predictions that came true.

Having witnessed the murder and dismemberment of some of his comrades, Staden described in detail the religious rituals and ceremonies of the Tupi, who, as Staden explained, regarded CANNIBALISM as a form of revenge and a deterrent against other warring tribes who also ate captured enemies. He returned to Europe in 1554.

HANS STADEN, *Hans Staden: The True History of his Captivity*, translated by Malcolm Letts (1929); JOHN HEMMING, *Red Gold: The Conquest of the Brazilian Indians* (1978); JOHN HORACE PARRY, *The Discovery of South America* (1979).

MARY JO MILES

STANDARD FRUIT AND STEAMSHIP COMPANY, a firm that grew out of VACCARO BROTHERS and Company. The conversion of the latter to a public corporation—Standard Fruit and Steamship Company—in 1925, plus consistently high profits, provided sufficient capital for the firm to expand beyond Honduras, and to grow fruit or buy from producers in much of tropical America, including Mexico, Nicaragua, Guatemala, Costa Rica, Panama, Haiti, Cuba, and Ecuador. Most of its banana production was sold in the United States.

Honduras, the company's most reliable producer, originally lacked the infrastructure to support Standard's growth. Hence Standard pioneered in many related businesses, such as the manufacturing of paper, boxes, and beer; as Vaccaro Brothers, it built the first railroad, bank, and hospital in the land.

Although it was a public corporation, Standard continued to be managed by the Vaccaro and D'Antoni families until 1964. Family representatives always made their home in La Ceiba, Honduras, close to the banana farms; this personal stake meant that the company regularly directed much money and energy into research, seeking better soils and varieties of fruit, and new methods of combating the omnipresent and destructive Panama and Sigatoka diseases. Standard accomplished its greatest gain on the competition in the 1960s with the invention of a cardboard carton that could protect and keep cool a new variety of disease-resistant but easily bruised banana. This simple development thrust Standard into a position of marketing leadership and in time saved the entire industry from having to leave Central America.

From time to time Standard has owned and operated a fleet of banana freighters capable of carrying passengers on cruises. Since the 1960s economic conditions have dictated the leasing of ships and an end to the cruise business.

Standard has attempted to avoid involvement with local factions. Management has found it profitable to stay out of political affairs rather than attempt to manipulate them for the company's benefit.

The most serious business mistakes were the expensive and repeated efforts to grow bananas in the unsuitable soil found in much of Nicaragua; attempting to do business as usual in Mexico following the 1917 revolution; and battling (unsuccessfully) Haiti's preposterously small landholding patterns, thereby wiping out one of that nation's few viable industries.

Heirs of the Vaccaro and D'Antoni families eventually lost interest in the banana business; the last family chairman of the board, Joseph D'Antoni, was a physician who wanted to return to medical research and teaching. In 1964 the company was sold to Castle & Cooke, vast landowners in Hawaii and distributors of the best-selling brand of pineapple. Castle & Cooke poured millions into the merger and placed the Dole label on Standard's products.

New Orleans Daily Picayune (1899–1913); CLAUDE W. WARD-LAW and LAURENCE P. MC GUIRE, *Panama Disease of Bananas* (1929); CHARLES D. KEPNER, JR., and JAY H. SOOTHILL, *The Banana Empire* (1935), esp. pp. 102, 112; STANDARD FRUIT AND STEAMSHIP COMPANY, *Annual Reports*; THOMAS L. KARNES, *Tropical Enterprise: The Standard Fruit and Steamship Company in Latin America* (1978); TOM BARRY and DEB PREUSCH, *The Central American Fact Book* (1986), pp. 148–152.

THOMAS L. KARNES

See also **Banana Industry.**

STATE CORPORATIONS, business entities also known as public enterprises, government enterprises, or state-owned enterprises (SOEs) that are devoted to economic development under state patronage.

ORIGINS

The etiology of state interventionism in a nation's economy frequently has been identified with Keynesianism. However, it was the prevailing local political culture that led to the different forms of state interventionism practiced by Asian and Latin American states. In the newly industrialized countries (NICs) of Asia, the state intervened with infusions of capital designed to help private-sector business grow and expand. In Latin America, however, the state spent its money to create companies that were financed, owned, and operated by the state. As a result, whereas the NICs of Asia have fewer government enterprises and are comparatively less burdened with financial woes, the opposite is the case in Latin America.

Latin America's oldest state corporation still in operation, the Bank of Brazil, goes back to 1808, but Latin America began to establish state corporations only after the dawn of the continent's populist age, around 1930. And the proliferation of today's major state-owned enterprises occurred only after World War II. By the 1960s and 1970s, nationalized foreign corporations became state enterprises. Finally, after Latin America's external-debt crisis crested in 1982, more state-owned enterprises were created. That same year, for example, Mexico nationalized its banking system. Throughout Latin America, except in Chile, the state added failed private enterprises to its traditional list of government corporations to preserve jobs. By the mid-1980s the state in Latin America was a significant owner of resources, companies, banks, utilities, heavy manufacturing industries, airlines and shippers, land transportation systems, hotels, resorts, farms, bakeries, bookstores, and even beauty shops. Excessive proliferation led to overinvestment and heavy borrowing. By mid-decade, the Latin American state typically became insolvent and was forced to divest itself of many of its enterprises by privatizing them.

Soon after the Great Depression, the statist and social democratic approach to economic growth and development that had been pioneered in Italy, France, Austria, and the Scandinavian countries came to appeal to Latin America as a viable alternative. As a response to failed liberal democracy and market capitalism, no Latin American state was prepared to adopt communism, but many were in favor of instituting structural reforms that would allow greater flexibility in and nationalist control over economic growth, social justice, and equitable access to political power. The rural landholding elite and their allies in export trade fell from power. The social discontent, political instability, and economic depression of the era brought into power a new urban-based alliance of industrialists, businessmen, state bureaucrats, the military, organized labor, and liberal professionals. The new elite, or populist rulers, introduced a series of measures to stabilize society, rekindle economic growth, and launch new development projects with the state as the locomotive of economic reform and growth. In this schema, state corporations played a pivotal role.

The prototype of Latin America's state corporation is Italy's Institute of Industrial Reconstruction (IRI), founded in 1922. IRI first served as the government's financing agency to rescue failing businesses and industries, but once it proved successful, the Mussolini government extended its life indefinitely. By the 1930s it had acquired the role of a development bank. IRI has since grown to be Italy's largest holding company, administering more than 500 state corporations. Latin America also drew inspiration from other western European countries, so that the continent's state corporations are a patchwork reflecting European models, a domestic desire to meet social and economic needs, and the political aims of the continent's populist movements.

VARIETIES

There are three functional types of state-owned enterprises currently in operation throughout Latin America: production-oriented SOEs, service-providing SOEs, and financial and banking SOEs. Before populism took firm root in the region's domestic politics in the 1930s, many countries restricted their public corporations to the fields of banking, land, sea, and riverine transportation, and such utilities as those for electricity, gas, potable water, and hydrocarbon resources. Because the state was responsible for financing many of these industries, it became the owner and operator of these service companies. In 1922, Argentina became the first Latin American country to claim public control of petroleum resources when it established the Yacimientos Petrolíferos Fiscales. Also, railroads and shipping lines, formerly owned by foreign investors, were bought up by the states. Mexico, Chile, Brazil, and Peru had state-operated railway systems before 1930. The motivation for setting up these companies was the desire to provide public services accessible to all. The cost of building and maintaining such infrastructure was so exorbitant that private investors were not interested. The liberal state of the time did not see its role in the national economy as that of planner, financier, producer of raw materials, manufacturer, and distributor of goods and services. Rather, it saw its primary function in the economy as that of guaranteeing a stable environment in which business, industry, and agriculture could function normally. Only in emergencies was the state forced to intervene.

Populist politicians established state-owned enterprises in areas formerly dominated by the private sector and turned them into an integral part of the state development agency. In Argentina, for instance, the populist age began with the advent of Juan Domingo PERÓN in 1943. There the Fabricaciones Militares (founded 1943) manufactured weapons, munitions, and other military equipment to meet internal needs during the height of World War II, when Argentina had nowhere else to turn for supplies and matériel. However, by defining military needs broadly, Fabricaciones Militares was able to branch out into other nonmilitary enterprises such as mining and real estate. In Brazil, the first Getúlio VARGAS administration (1930–1945) brought

state intervention into agriculture through subsidies for such state corporations as the Institute of Sugar and Alcohol and the National Council of Coffee, into steel through the National Steel Company (CNS) in Volta Redonda, into iron ore mining through the Companhia Vale do Rio Doce (CVRD), into petroleum through Petróleo Brasil (Petrobrás), into electric power through Centrais Eléctricas Brasileiras (Electrobrás), and into investment banking through the Banco Nacional de Desenvolvimento Econômico (later BNDES), among other economic activities.

In Mexico, Lázaro CÁRDENAS (1934–1940) expropriated and nationalized foreign-held petroleum companies and transferred the properties and facilities to the country's oil monopoly, Pemex (Petróleos Mexicanos). Today Pemex is one of the world's largest oil companies and Latin America's second largest. In Chile, in 1939 the government established an economic development bank called Corfo (Corporación de Fomento de la Producción–Chile), which weathered both scheduled and unscheduled changes of governments of such leftist and rightist philosophical persuasions as the Salvador ALLENDE government and the Augusto PINOCHET regime. Corfo was responsible for the state's expansion into electric power, a hotel chain, steel, petroleum, telecommunications, and copper mining. By the mid-1980s Corfo had become the first Latin American state financing corporation to launch an ambitious privatization program for the very corporations whose establishment it had financed decades earlier. The move toward nationalizing the economy was equally popular in small countries.

NUMBERS AND DECLINE

It is difficult to count prescisely how many state corporations have existed in Latin America. However, in the early 1980s there were more than 3,000 state-owned enterprises in Argentina, Brazil, Chile, Mexico, and Venezuela alone. Collectively, they have represented more than two-thirds of Latin America's gross domestic product (GDP). Mexico had more than 1,200 in its heyday of populist state capitalism, before it was largely dismantled by the Carlos SALINAS DE GORTARI government. In Brazil the military created at least 500 public corporations of federal, state, and municipal ownership and management during its twenty-year rule from 1964 to 1985. At its peak, Argentina had 746 corporations, while in 1973 Chile had more than 500. These myriad companies operated in all aspects of economic life. Brazil's state-owned enterprises produced at least two-thirds of the country's GDP. In Argentina, more than 80 percent of the government's deficit was attributed to the mismanagement of its state-owned enterprises. In Venezuela, one such enterprise alone, Petróleos de Venezuela, S.A. (PDVSA), has generated some 80 percent of all foreign trade revenues. And in Nicaragua, the Sandinistas created more than 180 state-owned enterprises, including such nonessential businesses as beauty shops, nightclubs, and hotels—all properties expropriated from Somoza supporters.

The history of Latin America's state corporations is complex, but it is clear that they were originally intended to operate in those sectors that had no access to national private capital and technology and were barred by the state from using international capital. Over time, state corporations diverged from their mandated role and began to expand into areas about which they knew little and for which they had little technical competence.

There are significant reasons for the current privatization movements throughout the continent. State corporations overexpanded during times of easy international credit and the flourishing global trade of the 1960s and 1970s. Many SOEs became economic and financial behemoths that often consumed more money than they produced. The deficits were often made up by infusions of funds from the public treasury. Inefficiency, mismanagement, and outright corruption became their hallmarks. Spawning innumerable subsidiaries and often branching into nonessential businesses, Latin America's state corporations became ripe targets of public criticism, refuges for hard-to-place retired military officers, and growing nests of political nepotism. And savvy private businessmen learned to live off of major state companies as contractors and suppliers who regularly overcharged for their goods and services, by socializing the cost while privatizing the profits.

JUDITH TENDLER, *Electric Power in Brazil: Entrepreneurship in the Public Sector* (1968); SÉRGIO HENRIQUE ABRANCHES ET AL., *A empresa pública no Brasil: Uma abordagem multidisciplinar* (1980); JANET KELLY ESCOBAR, "Comparing State Enterprises Across International Boundaries: The Corporación Venezolana de Guayana and the Companhia Vale do Rio Doce," in *Public Enterprise in Less-Developed Countries*, edited by Leroy P. Jones (1982), pp. 103–127; PAULO RABELLO DE CASTRO ET AL., *A crise do "bom patrão"* (1984); ANA SOJO, *Estado empresario y lucha política en Costa Rica* (1984); ALBERTO J. UGALDE, *Las empresas públicas en la Argentina* (1984); MARIAN RADETZKI, *State Mineral Enterprises* (1985); YAIR AHARONI, *The Evolution and Management of State Owned Enterprises* (1986); WILLIAM P. GLADE, ed., *State Shrinking: A Comparative Inquiry into Privatization* (1986); ROGÉRIO L. F. WERNECK, *Empresas estatais e política macroeconômica* (1987); RAYMOND VERNON, ed., *The Promise of Privatization* (1988); SINDICATURA GENERAL DE EMPRESAS PÚBLICAS (SIGEP), *Estado de situación empresaria. Cuarto trimestre 1989* (Dec. 1989); WILLIAM P. GLADE, ed., *Privatization of Public Enterprises in Latin America* (1991).

EUL-SOO PANG

See also **Informal Economy; Privatization; Public Sector;** and individual industries and corporations.

STATE OF SIEGE, a situation in which constitutional guarantees in a country are suspended and emergency powers of government are granted to the president. The provision of *estado de sitio* (*estado do sítio* in Portuguese) is put into action to deal with emergencies caused by invasion by a foreign power or major social disturbance. Usually such situations are declared by the legislature. Most Latin American constitutions contain the provision for the implementation of state of siege, usually with some restrictions. The president is granted the authority for all executive and legislative powers and can suspend judicial prerogative.

In most cases, a state of siege has been implemented for domestic crises. Abuse of the condition has been common in the region as dictators and military governments have used it as a legal pretext to act against political opponents or against perceived opposition. Indeed, such governments often keep the country under state of siege long after the initial crisis has subsided. Attempts to limit or restrict the implementation of state of siege have been successful only in those countries that have been able to attain some level of political stability or legislative strength.

HEATHER K. THIESSEN

STEFANICH, JUAN (*b.* 3 May 1889; *d.* 1975), Paraguayan politician. Born in Asunción, Stefanich first came to public notice during the 1910s, when, as a brilliant law student, he won a series of prizes in literature and philosophy. Awarded a doctorate in law in 1920, he had already become a well-known professor, author, and political commentator.

In 1928 Stefanich helped found the National Independence League, a radical pressure group that offered a strong nationalist response to Bolivian incursions in the Gran CHACO region. After full-fledged war with Bolivia became a reality in 1932, Stefanich pushed for the strongest possible territorial gains for Paraguay, becoming disappointed when his country had to settle for less.

The fall of the Liberal government in 1936 gave Stefanich an opportunity to try to transform these attitudes into reality. Allying himself with Colonel Rafael Franco and the military insurgents who had seized power, he became the main spokesman for their quasi-authoritarian ideology of *febrerismo*. In this, he drew his inspiration from an eclectic mix of Italian and Spanish fascism, German nazism, Soviet communism, and individualist democracy. He argued that the new Paraguay presented the chance for a new kind of democracy (*democracia solidarista*) in which all class conflicts would cease and be replaced by a dynamic sense of community. Some elements of *febrerista* thinking, especially those that stressed firm executive power, found their way into the 1940 constitution.

Stefanich himself became foreign minister in the FRANCO government, but when the latter regime was overthrown in 1937, he fled into exile. He continued to participate in party politics and publish *febrerista* tracts and philosophical works from exile, and periodically reappeared in Asunción. He later came to repudiate his earlier extremism, however, in favor of a social-democratic model.

WILLIAM BELMONT PARKER, *Paraguayans of To-Day* (1921), pp. 81–82; PAUL H. LEWIS, *The Politics of Exile* (1965), *passim*.

THOMAS L. WHIGHAM

See also **Paraguay: Political Parties.**

STEIMBERG, ALICIA (*b.* 1933), Argentine fiction writer, born in Buenos Aires. Her first novel, *Músicos y relojeros* (Musicians and Watchmakers, 1971), was a finalist in two major literary contests. Her second novel, *La loca 101* (Insane Prisoner 101, 1973), won the Satiricón de Oro Award from Argentina. In the 1980s she published several novels and a collection of short stories. The short stories are in *Como todas las mañanas* (1983), and the novels are *Su espíritu inocente* (1981), which is set in the Buenos Aires of the 1940s, *El árbol del placer* (1986; The Tree of Pleasures), and *Amatista* (1989), a humorous erotic novel that portrays the apprenticeship of a serious gentleman in the practice of erotic games. This book came out in the series La Sonrisa Vertical by Tusquets of Barcelona as the result of winning an award as the best erotic novel of the year. That same year she also published *Salirse de madre*. In 1991 she published a "gastronomic novel" for adolescents, *El mundo no es polenta* (The World Is Not Humor).

The humor and wit of the female protagonists is an important feature of Steimberg's fiction. Her novel *Cuando digo Magdalena* (1992; When I Pronounce Magdalena) won the distinguished Premio Planeta Biblioteca del Sur for 1992. It describes the daily life of a group of people confined on a ranch while practicing "mental control," a technique that became popular in Argentina in the 1990s.

SAÚL SOSNOWSKI, "Alicia Steimberg: Enhebrando pequeñas historias," in *Folio: Essays on Foreign Languages and Literatures*, (1987); MONICA FLORI, "Alicia Steimberg and Cecilia Absatz: Dos narradores argentinas" in *Chasqui* 17 (November 1988): 2, 83–92.

MAGDALENA GARCÍA PINTO

STEPHENS, JOHN LLOYD (*b.* 28 November 1805; *d.* 12 October 1852), U.S. diplomat, author, and president of the PANAMA RAILROAD Company (1849–1852). Stephens served as U.S. minister to Central America in 1839 and 1840. His diplomatic mission—to renew a treaty of commerce and seek trans-isthmian railroad and canal routes—failed due to the collapse of the Central American Federation. Stephens proved more interested in archaeology than diplomacy. He visited a number of Maya ruins during his first and second (1841) trips to Central America and Mexico. Stephens's *Incidents of Travel in Central America, Chiapas, and Yucatán* (1841) is probably the most interesting and useful nineteenth-century traveler's account of Central America.

Stephens played a pivotal role in building the first trans-isthmian railroad. He helped William H. Aspinwall secure a concession for the Panama route from the Colombian government in 1848 and later became president of Aspinwall's Panama Railroad Company. Stephens spent a great deal of time in Panama during the railway's construction. He contracted a fever there and died in New York City before the railroad began operation in 1855.

JOHN LLOYD STEPHENS, *Incidents of Travel in Central America, Chiapas, and Yucatán* (1841); JOHN HASKELL KEMBLE, *The Panama Route, 1848–1869* (1943); JOSEPH L. SCHOTT, *Rails Across Panama: The Story of the Building of the Panama Railroad, 1849–1855* (1967); VICTOR WOLFGANG VON HAGEN, *Search for the Maya: The Story of Stephens and Catherwood* (1973).

STEVEN S. GILLICK

Temple at Tuloom from Catherwood, *Views of Ancient Monuments* (London, 1844). John Lloyd Stephens (left) pulls one end of a measuring tape; Catherwood holds other end. ARCHIVO GENERAL DE LA NACIÓN, MÉXICO.

STORM, RICARDO (b. 14 March 1930), Uruguayan composer. Storm was born in Montevideo and began his musical education while very young. He studied piano under Wilhelm Kolischer and composition with the Spanish composer Enrique Casal Chapí, who was living in Montevideo at that time. Storm's initial works, dating from the early 1950s, already showed the composer's preferred style: vocal pieces in the form of songs, lieder and opera. His compositions for piano include a suite (1949), *Fantasía* (1950), several fugues (1950–1951), and a Sonata (1963). *Introducción y allegro*, Storm's first orchestral work, was premiered in 1954 by the OSSODRE (national public broadcast symphony orchestra) under Juan Protasi. His opera *El regreso* is an intensive work, substantial in scope, based on Aeschylus's *Choephoroi*, with a libretto written by the composer. It premiered at the SODRE theater on 17 April 1958. The music is in universalist style, sober in its musical language but distinctly Italian in its dramatic vocal treatment. Among Storm's vocal and choral productions is *Tres canciones para mezzosoprano y orquesta*, on texts by the Nicaraguan poet Rubén DARÍO, performed by Matilde Siano and the OSSODRE under Antonio Pereira Arias in February 1963. Other works of his include *Música para cuerdas, piano y timbales* (1959) and a symphony (1989), both premiered by the OSSODRE.

Composers of the Americas, vol. 16 (1970), pp. 149–153; SUSANA SALGADO, *Breve historia de la música culta en el Uruguay*, 2d ed. (1980); *Diccionario de la música española e hispanoamericana* (1993).

SUSANA SALGADO

STORNI, ALFONSINA (b. 29 May 1892; d. 25 October 1938), Argentine poet, teacher, and journalist. Born in Switzerland, Storni emigrated to Argentina with her prosperous Italian Swiss family when she was four. Losing most of their possessions shortly thereafter owing to bad management, they lived in San Juan Province until 1901, when they moved to Rosario, in Santa Fe Province. Storni went to work when she was ten, washing dishes and serving tables in a short-lived family restaurant, helping her mother with sewing, and taking care of her youngest brother. Her father died young in 1906, and his death changed the family's fate. Storni began to work in a factory and became interested in anarchist ideas. This background gave her the knowledge and motivation for her later work as a journalist and a feminist.

Storni joined a theatrical company that performed around the country and then taught in a rural school for two years. In 1910 she completed her degree and began a new teaching career in Rosario. She also began to write steadily. In Rosario she met a married man with whom she had a child in April 1912. She remained a single mother for the rest of her life, thus confronting the code of moral behavior of her time.

In 1912 Storni arrived in Buenos Aires, then a city of 1.5 million people. It was a booming city built after the image of Paris. At first she held small jobs and had to compete with male workers until she found a teaching position. In 1916 she published her first collection of poems, *La inquietud del rosal* (The Disquiet of the Rosebush). She also began to write articles for the magazine *Caras y Caretas*. Being a single woman, the self-supporting mother of a child, and a published poet made Storni a symbol of the rebel, the revolutionary, the feminist, and the fighter against a male-dominated society. She published *El dulce daño* (Sweet Harm) in 1918 and *Irremediablemente* the following year.

Storni began writing articles for the daily *La Nación* with the pen name of Tao-Lao. *Languidez* (1920; Languor) was received with great acclaim and won two important literary awards. That same year she was invited to Montevideo to speak about the Uruguayan poet Delmira AGUSTINI. She published *Ocre*, her major collection of poems, in 1925, and the following year *Poemas de amor* appeared in the journal *Nosotros*. She also wrote for children's theater and the play *El amo del mundo* (1927).

In 1930 Storni traveled to Europe where she met many writers, including Federico García Lorca and Ramón Gómez de la Serna. She underwent surgery for breast cancer in 1935, from which she recovered only partially. In 1938 she was honored in a ceremony along with Gabriela MISTRAL of Chile and Juana de IBARBOUROU of Uruguay. That fateful year she published her last book of poems, *Mascarilla y trébol*, and she took her life in Mar del Plata.

CONRADO NALÉ ROXLO, *Genio y figura de Alfonsina Storni* (1964); RACHEL PHILLIPS, *Alfonsina Storni: From Poetess to Poet* (1975); ISABEL CUCHÍ COLL, *La poetisa de los tristes destinos* (1979); MIRIAM FIGUERAS, *Alfonsina Storni, análisis de poemas y antología* (1979); SONIA JONES, *Alfonsina Storni* (1979); GABRIELLA VERNA, *Alfonsina* (1985); JOSEFINA DELGADO, *Alfonsina Storni: una biografía* (1990).

MAGDALENA GARCÍA PINTO

STRANGFORD TREATIES (1810), a series of agreements between Portugal and Great Britain that granted the British special commercial privileges in exchange for their defense of Portugal and its colonies during the Napoleonic War. Earlier, in 1807, Britain had threatened to destroy Portuguese naval forces and merchant fleets and to seize Portugal's colonies if Portugal acceded to Napoleon's demand and closed its ports to British ships. At that time, the Portuguese royal family agreed to British demands in exchange for protection during a forced retreat resulting in an imminent invasion by the French army. The English envoy to Lisbon, Percy Clinton Sydney Smythe, Viscount Strangford, negotiated the evacuation of the Portuguese royal family and followed them to Brazil, where in 1810 he negotiated the Treaty of Commerce and Navigation and the Treaty of Alliance and Friendship. These agreements, known as the Strangford Treaties, set preferential tariffs of 15 percent on British goods imported into Brazil and effectively undermined Brazilian industrialization. British merchants were granted the right to live in Brazil while they sold British products in both wholesale and retail establishments, but they were subject only to British-appointed magistrates when accused of wrongdoing. Portugal also agreed to restrict the importation of African slaves and to consider the abolition of such trade.

Brazilians were angered over the preferential treatment the Strangford Treaties gave to the British and considered them another example of Portuguese interests taking priority over colonial concerns. For example, British duties on Brazilian sugar and coffee imports were not reduced. Furthermore, Great Britain established itself as a major economic force in Brazil, and the British navy patrolled the coastal waters as a protective force for British commerce and a deterrent to the African SLAVE TRADE.

RICHARD GRAHAM, *Britain and the Onset of Modernization in Brazil, 1850–1914* (1968); E. BRADFORD BURNS, *A History of Brazil* (1980), pp. 146–147; LESLIE BETHELL, ed., *The Cambridge History of Latin America*, vol. 2 (1984), pp. 168–174, 177, 203–204; RON SECKINGER, *The Brazilian Monarchy and the South American Republics, 1822–1831: Diplomacy and State Building* (1984); GERVASE CLARENCE-SMITH, *The Third Portuguese Empire, 1825–1975: A Study in Economic Imperialism* (1985); RODERICK J. BARMAN, *Brazil: The Forging of a Nation, 1798–1852* (1988), pp. 44–65, 146–149; JOSEPH CALDER MILLER, *Way of Death: Merchant Capitalism and the Angolan Slave Trade, 1730–1830* (1988).

LESLEY R. LUSTER

See also **Commercial Policy: Colonial Brazil; Trade: Colonial Brazil.**

STROESSNER, ALFREDO (*b.* 3 November 1912), president of Paraguay (1954–1989). Alfredo Stroessner ruled Paraguay for thirty-five years, becoming thereby the most durable dictator in Latin America's history. The secret of his success was not to be found in any personal charisma, for he had none, nor in the support of a mass revolutionary movement, because he ruled in favor of the status quo. Nevertheless, he was more than a mere army strongman. Stroessner's longevity in power was due to an extraordinary capacity for work, an attention to detail, and a genius for organization. Behind a dull, plodding appearance he created a system of rule that approached totalitarian thoroughness, reaching into every corner of the republic and tying every significant social group to his political machine.

Little is known of his early life except that he was born in Encarnación, a southern border town on the Paraná River, to a German immigrant father and a Paraguayan mother. In 1929, at the age of sixteen he entered the Military Academy in Asunción. Three years later the CHACO WAR broke out and, even though his

studies were not completed, Stroessner was sent to the front. Decorated for bravery at the battle of Boquerón (1932), he was awarded his commission as a second lieutenant and given an artillery command. He won a second medal after the battle of El Carmen (1934). By the end of the war (1935) he was a first lieutenant.

After the war Stroessner continued to receive favorable notice from his commanding officers, rising to captain in 1936 and major in 1940. In October 1940 he was selected as one of a group of junior officers to go to Brazil for special artillery training. After returning to Paraguay, Stroessner continued to rise in the military hierarchy. President Higínio MORÍNIGO rewarded him for staying loyal during an abortive coup in 1943 by sending him to the Superior War School; upon graduating he was appointed commander of Paraguay's main artillery unit. In 1946 Stroessner was assigned to the army's General Staff Headquarters.

The civil war of 1947 brought Stroessner to real prominence because he was one of the few officers who remained loyal to the government. Morínigo ordered him to use his artillery to smash a revolt by the navy, which had taken over the Asunción shipyards in the name of the rebel cause. Next, Stroessner took command of the southern front and successfully prevented two heavily armed rebel gunboats from ascending the Paraguay River to bombard the capital. When the rebels were finally defeated, in August 1947, he was one of a handful of officers heading a purged and reorganized army.

Post-civil war Paraguay was dominated by the Colorado Party, one of Paraguay's two traditional parties, which had provided mass support for Morínigo. With their rivals eliminated, the Colorados had a clear political field, which they took advantage of by removing Morínigo in 1948 and seizing power for themselves. Soon afterward, however, the Colorados divided into factions whose leaders struggled for the presidency. From the end of the civil war until May 1954, Paraguay had five different presidents. Stroessner was deeply involved in all the plotting. On 25 October 1948 he backed the wrong side in a coup and had to escape the country hidden in the trunk of a car; three months later he slipped back into Paraguay and rallied his artillery regiment to support the winning side in a new coup. After that he rose rapidly to the top, becoming army commander in chief in April 1951. In May 1954 he ousted the Colorados' Federico CHAVES, who still headed a faction-ridden administration, and seized the presidency for himself.

Stroessner based his government on two pillars: the army and the Colorado Party. As a much-decorated veteran of two wars he enjoyed great prestige among the soldiers. The few officers who opposed him were soon eliminated, with major purges taking place in February 1955 and June 1959. Those coincided with upheavals inside the Colorado Party, for Stroessner encouraged party bickering that allowed him to play the factions off against each other. By mid-1959 factional purges had eliminated all independent spirits among the Colora-

Alfredo Stroessner during Independence Day ceremonies, 15 May 1986. REUTERS / BETTMANN.

dos, leaving Stroessner with a docile organization that he could dominate.

The control of a political party with a mass following made Stroessner's right-wing military dictatorship unique. By manipulating party symbols and patronage he was able to generate mass demonstrations in support of his policies. Businessmen, professionals, youth, women, veterans, and peasants were tied to the regime through the Colorados' ancillary organizations, and party cells (*seccionales*) reached into every village and every city block. Though his economic policies tended to favor large landowners and foreign investors, Stroessner was able to reward his followers through public works projects that generated jobs and contracts. Up to about 1981 steady economic growth and material improvements made the regime popular. Stroessner also permitted widespread smuggling and racketeering among top military and Colorado Party officials, with benefits trickling down through the clientele system. Those who refused to conform, however, such as the opposition Liberal and Febrerista parties and the CATHOLIC CHURCH, were ruthlessly persecuted.

Stroessner's regime began to crumble during the 1980s. Inflation became unmanageable, capital dried up for new public works projects, and the emergence of a new middle class—the fruit of previous economic growth—challenged the regime's rigid structure. Above all, Stroessner was aging, and those around him began jockeying over the question of succession. Some of his cabinet ministers and presidential aides, calling themselves "the militants," wanted to name Stroessner's son,

Gustavo, as his successor; but opposing them were the Colorado "traditionalists," who saw their chance to regain the party's independence. The feud split the military as well. When Stroessner backed the "militants" and plotted to remove General Andrés RODRÍGUEZ as army commander, the latter struck first. During the night of 2 February 1989 Rodríguez's tanks forced Stroessner to relinquish power and leave the country for Brazilian exile.

RICHARD BOURNE, *Political Leaders of Latin America* (1969); PAUL H. LEWIS, *Paraguay Under Stroessner* (1980); PAUL H. LEWIS, *Socialism, Liberalism, and Dictatorship in Paraguay* (1982); CARLOS MIRANDA, *The Stroessner Era* (1990).

PAUL H. LEWIS

SUÁREZ, INÉS DE (*b.* 1512?; *d.* 1580?), Spanish woman who played a forceful and colorful part in the conquest of Chile. In her twenties she went to America, where she became the mistress of Pedro de VALDIVIA (1500–1553). She accompanied him on his expedition to Chile in 1540, and was well liked by the conquistadores. In September 1541, during Valdivia's temporary absence, the newly founded settlement at Santiago was attacked by large numbers of natives. With the inadequate Spanish force facing total defeat, Inés de Suárez suggested the murder of seven captive caciques (chiefs) as a means of instilling terror among the natives. It is generally accepted that she did (or helped with) the killing herself. After the heads (or possibly the corpses) of the dead caciques were thrown into the crowd of attackers, Suárez donned a coat of mail and led the fighting during the remainder of the battle. The only Spanish woman in the settlement, she devoted herself to caring for the wounded and supervising food supplies.

In recognition of her contributions, Valdivia granted her an *encomienda*. When the king's representative in Lima, Pedro de la GASCA, heard charges against Valdivia in November 1548, he advised him to terminate his liaison with Suárez. (Valdivia's wife, who was in Spain, traveled to Chile soon afterward, but arrived there only after his death.) Valdivia complied with La Gasca's suggestion, and married Suárez off to one of his most trusted lieutenants, Rodrigo de Quiroga, who himself later became governor of Chile (1565–1567 and 1575–1580). As an act of penitence, Suárez maintained a small church on the Cerro Blanco in Santiago. In 1553 she and Quiroga presented it to the Dominican order. The present church near the site dates from the 1830s.

STELLA (BURKE) MAY, *The Conqueror's Lady* (1930).

SIMON COLLIER

SUÁREZ, MARCO FIDEL (*b.* 23 April 1855; *d.* 3 April 1927), Colombian man of letters and president (1918–1921). Suárez was born out of wedlock in Hatoviejo (now Bello), Antioquia. Although his mother, a washerwoman, was very poor, a visiting priest recognized his intellectual ability and secured his admission to the seminary in Medellín. Suárez left the seminary in 1877 before ordination and found employment as a teacher in Antioquia and Bogotá. He first gained notice in 1881, when he won a contest sponsored by the Colombian Academy to commemorate the centenary of the birth of philologist Andrés Bello. His winning essay, *Ensayo sobre la "Gramática castellana de D. Andrés Bello,"* was published, and he became a member of the academy in 1883.

In the 1880s and 1890s Suárez held increasingly important government positions and was an articulate spokesman for the Nationalist wing of the Conservative Party. As a cabinet member under President Manuel A. Sanclemente, he protested the latter's removal on 31 July 1900. Returning to public life in 1910, Suárez defeated two other candidates in the presidential election of 1917. Critics charged that his victory was fraudulent, and he had to contend with bitter opposition during his administration.

In 1919 workers who erroneously believed that the government planned to buy army uniforms abroad staged a demonstration in Bogotá. When the crowd prevented Suárez from speaking, there was an outbreak of violence in which seven persons were killed. There was also controversy over ratification of the Thomson–Urrutia Treaty, which aimed at restoring harmonious relations between Colombia and the United States. On 26 October 1921 Laureano GÓMEZ, then a Conservative deputy, directed a vitriolic attack at Suárez, accusing him of various financial improprieties. Suárez denied any misconduct but resigned the following month. He spent his remaining years writing his memoirs in dialogue form. These were published in twelve volumes as *Sueños de Luciano Pulgar* (1925–1940).

FERNANDO GALVIS SALAZAR, *Don Marco Fidel Suárez* (1974); CHARLES W. BERGQUIST, *Coffee and Conflict in Colombia, 1886–1910* (1978).

HELEN DELPAR

SUASSUNA, ARIANO VILAR (*b.* 16 June 1927), poet, playwright, and novelist from João Pessoa, Paraíba, in northeastern Brazil. Suassuna received an informal education during the years he lived in the SERTÃO among ballad singers, puppeteers, and storytellers whose themes, poetic forms, and language would be the substance of his writing. In 1946 Suassuna enrolled at the university in Recife, Pernambuco. With Hermilo Borba Filho and others, he founded in 1948 the Teatro do Estudante de Pernambuco, whose purpose was to bring literature to the masses through theater. Performances were given in parks, factories, churches, and squares. The same year, Suassuna received the prestigious Carlo Magno Prize for *Uma mulher vestida de sol*, a play written in 1947.

His next important work for the theater was *O auto da compadecida* (1957). No other Brazilian play has become as nationally and internationally well known as *The Rogue's Trial,* first presented in Recife. Its novelty was in the revelation of Northeastern Brazil's harsh reality, with its social problems and cultural values. The author incorporates this reality into the traditions of European theater, medieval liturgical drama, and the religious theater of the Golden Age. Suassuna was inspired by the *romanceiro popular do nordeste,* as he called the literature of the CORDEL.

Suassuna dedicated himself to the theater until 1971. Not only *O auto da compadecida* but *O casamento suspeitoso, O santo e a porca,* and *A pena e a lei* were awarded prizes in Brazil and abroad. From 1971 to 1977 he wrote a novel in two parts, *Romance d'a pedra do reino,* based on ten years of historical and literary research and announced as the first volume of a trilogy. Enthusiastically received, it is an extremely ambitious work in which Suassuna, through a main character representing earlier real or fictional heroes, attempts to create an epic according to armorial or formulaic patterns. After 1977, Suassuna abandoned the theater and the novel, and returned to writing poetry. He also took up painting, illustrating *A pedra do reino,* and taught at the Federal University of Pernambuco.

RICHARD A. MAZZARA, "Poetic Humor and Universality of Ariano Suassuna's *Compadecida,*" in *Ball State University Forum* 10 (1969): 25–30.

RICHARD A. MAZZARA

See also **Literature: Brazil.**

SUAZO CÓRDOVA, ROBERTO (*b.* 17 March 1927), president of Honduras (1982–1986). Suazo was born in the small town of La Paz, where he practiced medicine for twenty-five years. Active in the Liberal Party for a number of years, Suazo succeeded Modesto RODAS ALVARADO in 1979 as general coordinator of the Liberal Party and leader of its conservative Rodista wing. After the military rulers agreed in 1980 to restore civilian government, Suazo was elected president in November 1981 and took office on 27 January 1982. He promoted the democratic process and moderate economic reform while cooperating with a U.S. military buildup in response to the Sandinista rise in Nicaragua, which included a substantial increase in the Honduran military as well as support of the Nicaraguan contras in Honduras. In collaboration with U.S. ambassador John Negroponte, the Honduran military, led by Colonel Gustavo ÁLVAREZ MARTÍNEZ, retained much power, thereby creating considerable anti-Americanism and internal criticism of Suazo. Suazo, however, successfully reasserted civilian authority when he dismissed Álvarez in March 1984 and replaced him with Air Force General Walter López Reyes as commander in chief of the armed forces. The FBI arrested Álvarez in Miami in November 1984 in connection with a plot to murder Suazo. Despite this shakeup in the military, there was no reversal of the trend toward greater militarization of Honduras.

JAMES A. MORRIS, *Honduras: Caudillo Politics and Military Rulers* (1984); RALPH LEE WOODWARD, JR., "Suazo Córdova," in *Encyclopedia of World Biography*, vol. 15 (1987), pp. 378–379.

RALPH LEE WOODWARD, JR.

SUB-COMANDANTE MARCOS. *See* **Mexico: Revolution.**

SUBERO, EFRAÍN (*b.* 16 October 1931), Venezuelan scholar, critic, and poet. Professor of literature at the Universidad Católica Andrés Bello and the Universidad Simón Bolívar, Subero has been a prolific writer and an important scholar in the fields of literary history and criticism, cultural criticism, and folklore. His poetry, most of which was published between 1956 and 1974, reflects his interest in popular expression and his concern for accessibility even when his writing is of private or intimate content. *Matarile* (1968) is a charming collection of poetry, stories, and one Christmas play for children. *La décima popular en Venezuela* (1977; 2d ed. 1991) is a major contribution to folklore scholarship, an extensive study and presentation of texts of this ancient traditional Hispanic form. He is also noted for his editions and bibliographical work on such figures as Rómulo GALLEGOS, Miguel Otero Silva, Arturo USLAR PIETRI, Teresa de la PARRA, Aquiles Nazoa, Andrés Eloy BLANCO, and Manuel Vicente Romero García.

Collections of notes and essays are *Norte franco* (1961) and *La vida perdurable*, 2 vols. (1989). Representative books of poetry are *Todavía la noche* (1963), *En estos parajes* (1965), and *Razones* (1969). Other contributions in folklore and popular culture include *Poesía infantil venezolana* (1967), *Orígen y expansión de la quema de Judas* (1974), and *La navidad en la literatura venezolana* (1977).

MICHAEL J. DOUDOROFF

SUBIRANA, MANUEL DE JESÚS (*b.* 1807; *d.* 27 November 1864), Spanish missionary in Cuba and Honduras. Born in Manresa and educated in the seminary in nearby Vich, Subirana was ordained in 1834. He left Spain in 1850 for Cuba, where he worked in El Cobre. In 1856 he was sent to Christianize the Indians of Honduras. Finding them exploited, he struggled to alleviate their misery while catechizing them. He won land and ownership titles for the Jicaque Indians of Yoro and the Paya Indians of Olancho. Subirana's protests to the central government succeeded in mitigating the widespread practices of DEBT PEONAGE and forced labor. He ended the practice of paying lower prices to Indians for their sarsaparilla than was paid to ladinos. Such efforts won the trust of the Indians, enabling Subirana to baptize thousands. After his death his work passed on to less zealous priests, and past abuses were soon revived.

ERNESTO ALVARADO GARCÍA, *El misionero español Manuel Subirana* (1964); JOSÉ MARÍA TOJEIRA, *Panorama histórico de la iglesia en Honduras* (1986), pp. 173–177; William V. Davidson, "El Padre Subirana y las tierras concedidas a los indios, hondureños en el siglo XIX," in *América Indígena* 44, no. 3 (1984): 447–459. DONNA WHITSON BRETT and EDWARD T. BRETT, *Murdered in Central America: The Stories of Eleven U.S. Missionaries* (1988), pp. 6–7.

EDWARD T. BRETT

SUCRE. Called La Plata or Chuquisaca during the colonial period, the city was the seat of the important colonial court, the Audiencia of CHARCAS, and after independence the capital of Bolivia. Chuquisaca is also the name of the surrounding department, whose capital is Sucre. Closely tied to the silver-MINING centers of Potosí, Sucre was the residence of many silver-mine owners throughout its history.

Sucre was founded in 1538 or 1539 by Pedro de Anzures, lieutenant of Gonzalo PIZARRO, on a site inhabited by the Yampara ethnic group. It quickly became the administrative center of the vast territories of the southern Andean region. With the discovery of the rich silver deposits of Potosí, many Spaniards moved to the mining boomtown. Nevertheless, La Plata (as it was called then) remained politically important, for it was the legal residence of the *encomenderos*, who lorded over the Indian population of the region. Moreover, La Plata's temperate climate at 8,500 feet of altitude was much more agreeable than the cold city of Potosí, at 15,000 feet. The region around the city also became an important producer of foodstuffs for the mining centers, and many of the first HACIENDAS grew up on the outskirts of the city.

The importance of the southern Bolivian region was such that in 1552, La Plata became the new episcopal seat; even today the city is the religious capital of the nation. In 1559 La Plata became the seat of the Audiencia of Charcas, the highest colonial judicial body in the vast region south of Lake Titicaca to Paraguay and Argentina. This jurisdiction, with subsequent modifications, later became the basis for the territorial claims of the Republic of Bolivia.

The city reached its apogee during the seventeenth century, when most prosperous Potosí silver-mine owners took up residence there. Pedro Ramírez del Águila's seventeenth-century description of the city reveals an urban center intent on the celebration of ostentatious religious rituals and other such luxuries. This wealth was not restricted to the city alone. Indeed, in the eighteenth century one traveler compared the sumptuous haciendas of the nearby Cachimayo Valley to the aristocratic manors of Spanish Cantabria. Farther south, the Cinti region provided mine owners with warm valleys where they could send their families and grow wine and fruit for consumption in Potosí. A typical example was the important seventeenth-century mine owner Antonio López de QUIROGA, who owned several vast estates in Cinti.

However, only a few hundred kilometers farther east of Cinti was the dangerous Indian frontier. In the sixteenth century the CHIRIGUANO Indians had reached Tacopaya (Zudáñez) in an effort to conquer the Potosí mines. Later, after Viceroy Francisco TOLEDO failed in his punitive expedition in 1574 against the Chiriguanos, the Spanish set up a series of fortress-towns in the Tomina jurisdiction to the east to keep them at bay. Until the 1780s, warfare kept the Chuquisaca frontier with the Chiriguanos in constant flux. Only in the last decades of the eighteenth century were the Spanish able to push the Chiriguanos permanently out of some of their lands in the Sauces (Monteagudo) and Pomabamba districts.

La Plata was the first city in colonial Spanish America to experience political unrest as a result of Napoleon's capture of the Spanish king and the invasion of Spain. This was not surprising, for La Plata was an important cultural center, with one of the oldest universities in the colonies. When on 25 May 1809 the president of the AUDIENCIA imprisoned Jaime Zudáñez, a radical in favor of independence, a popular revolt took place and the president and the archbishop had to flee for their lives. However, Spanish troops sent from Buenos Aires suppressed the revolution by December 1809.

The various invasions of patriot Argentine and Spanish forces during the more than sixteen years of the WARS OF INDEPENDENCE destroyed the countryside around La Plata. In particular, the guerrilla warfare between Spanish troops and patriot forces led by Manuel Ascencio Padilla and his wife Juana Azurduy de Padilla left much of the rural areas in ruins. The patriots even allied themselves with Cumbay, the most important Chiriguano chief of the region. Spanish forces were only able to suppress the guerrillas in 1818.

The Sucre area, with the rest of Bolivia, became independent as a result of the invasion of the Colombian army under Antonio José de SUCRE in 1825. La Plata (later changed to Sucre, in honor of the independence hero and first president) became the capital of the new Republic of Bolivia. Despite its status as the capital, few Bolivian presidents stayed in town for long, as they administered the country (and put down revolts) while moving from city to city.

Many mine owners remained in Sucre, but only an infusion of fresh capital and entrepreneurship from merchants-turned-miners helped revive the silver-mining industry in the 1860s. By the 1870s the Sucre mining elite had gathered much financial and political power, which they used in the aftermath of the WAR OF THE PACIFIC (1879–1884) to take direct power through the Conservative Party. Through the Conservative Party they dominated national politics and promoted their own economic agenda during the last two decades of the nineteenth century. Thus, the last four decades of the nineteenth century constituted the region's second boom period, during which the Sucre elites remodeled

their houses to imitate Parisian styles and built ostentatious hacienda houses, especially in the nearby Cachimayo River valley. Prosperity was a double-edged sword for some: while the wine-producing Cinti area also thrived, the Indian communities in the area surrounding Sucre lost their lands to the miners. In turn, the demand for cattle heightened by the silver boom brought about a period of intense frontier expansion to the east, against which the Chiriguanos actively resisted. Finally, after numerous wars and revolts, they lost their independence.

The declining price of silver put an end to the boom in the late 1890s. In the wake of this loss of economic clout, the Conservative Party lost the FEDERALIST WAR (1898–1899), and La Paz became the de facto capital, with Sucre keeping only the Supreme Court. Since then, the Sucre economy has stagnated. A brief petroleum rush and an attempt by Sucre elites to form new mining companies in the early twentieth century failed due to a lack of capital. The last refuge of the Sucre elites, their HACIENDAS (many of which they had purchased when silver mining turned unprofitable), were confiscated and divided among the estate's workers after the agrarian reform of 1953.

Today, Sucre and the surrounding region is one of the poorest areas in the country. The city is mainly service-oriented and survives in great part on the income brought by the many students who come to study. The only other regular source of income is that from oil wells in the former Chiriguano territory.

An overview is provided in GUNNAR MENDOZA ET AL., Monografía de Bolivia, vol 1 (1975). For the colonial period, see INGE WOLFF, Regierung and Verwaltung der kolonialspanischen Städte in Hochperu, 1538–1650 (1970); JOSEP BARNADAS, Charcas: Orígenes históricos de una socieded colonial (1973); and ROBERTO QUEREJAZU CALVO, Chuquisaca: 1539–1825 (1987). For the republican period, see ERICK D. LANGER, Economic Change and Rural Resistance in Southern Bolivia: 1880–1930 (1989).

ERICK D. LANGER

SUCRE ALCALÁ, ANTONIO JOSÉ DE (*b.* 3 February 1795; *d.* 4 June 1830), Venezuelan military officer in the WARS OF INDEPENDENCE, Simón BOLÍVAR's trusted lieutenant, statesman, and the first constitutionally elected president of Bolivia. Sucre's parents were descended from well-to-do Europeans established in the coastal town of Cumaná. When news of the Napoleonic invasion of Spain reached Venezuela, Sucre was studying military engineering in Caracas. In July 1810 he joined the patriotic militia in Cumaná, launching a distinguished military career that culminated in the 9 December 1824 final victory of patriot forces over the Spanish at the battle of AYACUCHO (Peru).

Sucre saw active service under the first and second Venezuelan republics but was forced to flee to the Antilles in 1814. After a brief effort to join patriot forces in NEW GRANADA (Colombia) at the end of 1815, he again went into exile. Aligning himself with Bolívar, who by 1816 was beginning to succeed in his campaign against loyalists in Venezuela, Sucre undertook a number of successful military assignments for the Liberator and by late 1820 had become his chief of staff. As such, Sucre undertook a delicate mission as head of an expeditionary force sent to Guayaquil (Ecuador) to aid local patriots following their October 1819 uprising against royal authority. Success in Guayaquil was followed by an expedition to liberate Quito, aided by auxiliary forces sent from Peru, which culminated in a patriot victory at the pivotal battle of PICHINCHA (24 May 1822) on the outskirts of Quito.

With virtually all of Gran Colombia liberated, Bolívar and Sucre turned their attention southward to Peru, where the army of José de SAN MARTÍN and its Peruvian allies were engaged in a bitter struggle against the Spanish army and royalists for possession of Lima and the once-rich viceroyalty. After Bolívar's arrival in Lima, Sucre took charge of the military campaign in the Andean highlands, achieving a crucial victory at the battle of JUNÍN (6 August 1824) and final victory at Ayacucho in December. Sucre was the author of a brilliant strategy that led to the humiliating defeat of the royalist forces, and dictated generous, humanitarian terms of surrender.

After Ayacucho the only serious obstacle to the liberation of Spanish South America was the ragtag army of royalist General Pedro de Olañeta in Upper Peru (today Bolivia). With Sucre in hot pursuit, Olañeta's forces melted away early in 1825, leaving the twenty-five-year-old Venezuelan with the responsibility for creating a republican form of government in the former Audiencia of CHARCAS. Two days after his triumphant arrival in La Paz, Upper Peru's largest and economically most important city, Sucre issued a decree (9 February 1825) convoking a constituent assembly of delegates from the audiencia's five former *intendencias* to decide whether they wished to ally themselves with the former viceroyalty of the Río de la Plata, with that of Lima, or to become an independent nation. Sucre, without explicit authorization from Bolívar (who had returned to Lima after the victory at Junín) pledged to respect the wishes of the Upper Peruvian delegates.

The assembly, which met during July and August 1825 in Chuquisaca (renamed Sucre in honor of the victor of Ayacucho), voted overwhelmingly to create an independent state. Anticipating Bolívar's unhappiness, the delegates also voted to call the new nation the "Republic of Bolívar" and to name the Liberator its first constitutional president. Reluctantly accepting this fait accompli, during his visit to Upper Peru (July–December 1825) Bolívar acted as president of the infant nation, but most of the routine details of government were left to Sucre. Sucre's presidency ended when he was seriously wounded in a barracks revolt in the Bolivian capital and was forced to delegate his powers (April 1828). He left Bolivia in August of the same year

for Quito, to join the woman to whom he had been married by proxy while still in Chuquisaca, Mariana Carcelén y Larrea, the Marquesa de Solanda, one of the wealthiest women in the former Audiencia of Quito.

Sucre's tenure as president of Bolivia (December 1825–April 1828) was marked by a revolutionary effort to impose economic and social reform upon a racially divided, geographically dispersed, and economically weak society led by a traditionalist elite that was jealous of its prerogatives and in time became very resentful of outside political and military influence. This effort included a wholesale reform of the Upper Peruvian church and the liquidation of most of its assets in favor of public education. Sucre created and funded a network of public secondary schools, for which he dictated a modern curriculum, recruited teachers, and provided books and supplies. New primary schools, orphanages, and asylums for the destitute were part of this reform, as were efforts to provide the principal cities with better water supplies, new public markets, street lighting, and public cemeteries. Sucre created a new port for the infant nation at Cobija, on the Atacama coast, in territory that would eventually become part of Chile. He tried to revive silver mining, the traditional mainstay of the Upper Peruvian economy, by attracting European investment, employing new technology, and reforming colonial institutions. Finally, Sucre tried to impose a revolutionary new experiment in public financing, eliminating the Indian tribute and the tithe and creating in their stead a system of taxes on wealth and income, and a universal head tax. Financially, the experiment was a dismal failure. The negative reaction toward this radical reform effort and toward the continued presence in Bolivia of large numbers of Colombian troops, along with growing hostility from Peru, eventually provoked Sucre's downfall.

Returning to Quito in September 1828, Sucre hoped to dedicate himself to family life and the administration of his wife's estate. But with the outbreak of hostilities between Peru and Gran Colombia, his military services were again needed. In February 1829 an army under his command defeated Peruvian invaders at the battle of Tarqui, in what is today southern Ecuador. Fresh from the victory at Tarqui, in 1830 Sucre served as president of the Congreso Admirable meeting in Bogotá, a last-ditch effort to preserve Gran Colombian unity. The Congreso failed, despite Sucre's prestige, and Bolívar's creation broke up into three independent republics. On his way back to Quito, Sucre was killed at Berruecos, near Pasto. The identity of the assassins remains the object of historical speculation.

LAUREANO VILLANUEVA, *Vida de don Antonio José de Sucre, Gran Mariscal de Ayacucho* (1945); GUILLERMO A. SHERWELL, *Antonio José de Sucre (Gran Mariscal de Ayacucho), Hero and Martyr of American Independence: A Sketch of His Life* (1924); CHARLES W. ARNADE, *The Emergence of the Republic of Bolivia* (1957); ALFONSO RUMAZO GONZÁLEZ, *Sucre, Gran Mariscal de Ayacucho* (1963); WILLIAM LOFSTROM, *La presidencia de Sucre en Bolivia* (1987);

THOMAS MILLINGTON, *Debt Politics after Independence: The Funding Conflict in Bolivia* (1992).

WILLIAM LOFSTROM

SUGAR INDUSTRY. Carried to the New World from the Spanish Canary Islands by COLUMBUS on his second voyage in 1493, sugar was first grown in the New World in Spanish Santo Domingo and was exported to Europe beginning around 1516. Santo Domingo's incipient sugar industry was worked by African slaves who were imported soon after the sugarcane itself. Thus, Spain pioneered growing sugarcane, making sugar, using African slaves as labor, and establishing the plantation form in the Americas.

Within the New World, however, the early achievements in Santo Domingo and the rest of the Caribbean were surpassed by developments on the mainland. By 1526 Brazil was shipping sugar to Lisbon in commercial quantities. In Mexico, Paraguay, the Pacific coast of South America, and in fertile valleys everywhere, sugarcane thrived. In the other Greater Antilles—Cuba, Puerto Rico, and Jamaica—Spanish settlers eventually imported sugarcane plants, the methods for their cultivation, the technology of water and animal-powered mills, enslaved labor, and the processes of grinding, boiling, and fabricating sugars, creating molasses from extracted sugar juice, and distilling rum from the molasses.

Portuguese planters in Brazil, with the assistance of Dutch capital and merchants, enormously expanded sugarcane cultivation throughout the Northeast. A typical plantation consisted of fifteen or twenty Portuguese workers and more than one hundred African and Indian slaves, a chapel, workshops, a processing plant, a *casa grande* (big house) for the owner and his family, and a SENZALA (slave quarters). The entire enterprise depended on its ENGENHO (mill), a water- or oxen-powered grinder that used a three-roller mechanism to extract the cane's juices. By 1618 the larger mills could produce between 192,000 and 320,000 pounds of sugar annually (85.7 and 143 tons), of which they exported some 384 million pounds to Europe.

The productive capacity of Brazilian sugar plantations drew foreign invaders to Brazil: first the French fruitlessly tried to found their own colonies there, then the Dutch succeeded in capturing Brazil from 1630 to 1654. In the meantime the British and the French were themselves trying to establish a presence on other Caribbean islands and turn them into sugar factories as well. By the time the Brazilians under Mem da SÁ finally drove the Dutch out of Brazil in 1654, they had lost their predominance over world markets to competition from a series of new Caribbean producers and the erection of tariff barriers in Europe, notably in France and England. Nevertheless, the lust for sugar profits resulted in the continuous populating of other Caribbean islands with masters and slaves and helped spur the settlement of areas of the present-day United States, like South Carolina.

Within a century the French and, even more so, the British became the New World's great sugar makers and exporters. Inseparably linked to this development was the emergence of the triangular trade and mercantilism in the latter half of the seventeenth century. Finished European goods were sold in Africa, where African slaves were bought and transported to the Americas for sale, and then the profits from the first two parts of the journey were used to buy American tropical commodities (especially sugar) to market in the mother country and her importing neighbors. In the eighteenth century, as the imperial relationship solidified between mother country and colony, the French and British slave-based plantations of the Caribbean reached their apogee.

The late eighteenth and early nineteenth centuries brought dramatic changes to the Caribbean sugar colonies. First, revolution destroyed France's most lucrative and profitable slave-based sugar economy, Haiti. Subsequently, the British moved to limit and then abolish the SLAVE TRADE and SLAVERY (1834–1838). In the wake of these developments, European demand for other sugar sources increased significantly in the early decades of the nineteenth century.

Although sugarcane was planted there in the sixteenth century, Cuba was the last Caribbean island to develop its industry. By the beginning of the nineteenth century, sugar had become Cuba's main export. In the late 1820s about 1,000 sugar plantations covered some 500,000 acres, largely in the western region of the island. Investments in sugar, including the mechanization of the industry, led to spectacular increases in production and the construction of a railroad system. Before the TEN YEARS' WAR for independence (1868–1878), owners grew their own cane and milled it in their own mills. Massive destruction of property throughout the island coupled with the emancipation of the slaves, upon whom the industry had depended, led to bankruptcies and purchases by foreign investors, largely from the United States. After the war, the number of mills declined to 500 and the cultivation of sugarcane fell increasingly into the hands of COLONOS, renters, or sharecroppers who depended on the mill. Some scholars have speculated that this investment played a role in U.S. involvement in Cuba's second war for independence (1895–1898) with Spain, which became the SPANISH-AMERICAN WAR. Furthermore, the production of beet sugar in Europe and the United States forced sugar prices down on the global market.

Technological innovations developed during the twentieth century led to even further mechanization and concentration within the industry: by the 1920s there were fewer than 200 mills working on the island, of which 40 to 50 percent were controlled by U.S. investors. During World War I, when Cuban sugar had to make up for losses of European beet sugar, cultivation expanded and prices skyrocketed. From the end of the war until 1920, a time known in Cuba as the DANCE OF THE MILLIONS, sugar reigned supreme. But then average prices per pound dropped from a high of 22.5 cents in May 1920 to a mere 3.75 cents by the end of the year, causing industry collapse and opening the door to greater U.S. takeover. Yet, the sugar industry continued to dominate Cuba throughout the first half of the twentieth century and affected all segments of its economy. By 1958, for example, it is estimated that the sugar industry alone generated one-quarter of national GNP.

After the success of the CUBAN REVOLUTION in 1959, Fidel CASTRO believed that agrarian reform measures would finally end the island's dependence on sugar cultivation. Yet, despite efforts to diversify agriculture and industrialize, Cuba soon found itself desperately trying to harvest 10 million metric tons of sugar in 1970. Meanwhile, international agricultural conglomerates rapidly developed sugar substitutes for use in food processing and as sweeteners for the diet-conscious, thus cutting the need for sugarcane even further. Cuba, more than any other economy in the Western Hemisphere, has dramatically demonstrated the risks and rewards that come from dependency on a monocultural crop like sugar.

FRANKLIN W. KNIGHT, *Slave Society in Cuba During the Nineteenth Century* (1970); ERIC EUSTACE WILLIAMS, *From Columbus to Castro: The History of the Caribbean, 1492–1969* (1970); MANUEL MORENO FRAGINALS, *El ingenio. El complejo económico social cubano del azúcar*, 3 vols. (1978); LESLIE BETHELL, ed., *Cambridge History of Latin America*, vols. 1 and 2 (1984); SIDNEY W. MINTZ, *Sweetness and Power: The Place of Sugar in Modern History* (1985); STUART B. SCHWARTZ, *Sugar Plantations in the Formation of Brazilian Society* (1985); FRANKLIN W. KNIGHT and COLIN A. PALMER, eds., *The Modern Caribbean* (1989); LOUIS A. PÉREZ, *Cuba: Between Reform and Revolution* (1989); LESLIE BETHELL, *Cuba: A Short History* (1993).

WADE A. KIT

See also **Economic Development.**

SUMAC, YMA (*b*. 10 September 1927), Peruvian-born singer, noted for the extraordinary range of her voice and her exotic stage presence. Sumac was born in Ichocan, a small mountain village in Peru. Her parents named her Emperatriz Chavarri, but she chose a variation of her mother's name when she began her singing career.

When she was little more than a child she was heard singing in a local festival by an official from Lima. He persuaded her parents to bring her to the capital, where she could be presented in concert while continuing her education at a convent school. In Lima Sumac met her husband, Moises Vivanco, a composer, musician, and the director of the Peruvian National Board of Broadcasting. He cast her as the star of his musical group, the Compania Peruana de Arte. After a successful career in Latin America, in 1946 Sumac and Vivanco moved to the United States. Sumac became a naturalized U.S. citizen in 1955.

Sumac struggled to advance her career in the United States. With the 1950 release of her first album for Capitol Records, *Voice of Xtabay* (a nonsense word coined by the recording company to underscore Sumac's Incan roots), she caught the public's attention. Her popularity reached its climax in the early 1950s. Her records sold over a million copies. She appeared on television, in a minor Broadway musical, and appeared in the films *Secret of the Incas* (1954) and *Omar Khayyam* (1957).

Sumac's music, much of it written by her husband, was based on ancient Peruvian folk music. It was adapted to showcase her remarkable four-octave voice, and her ability to evoke the sounds of jaguars and Andean birds. Sumac also performed in opera houses in Europe and South America, singing roles in *The Magic Flute*, *Lakmé*, and *La Traviata*. After a hiatus of several years, Sumac returned to American music clubs in the 1970s and 1980s. She received good reviews and a modest popularity that did not match her earlier acclaim.

SHEILA HOOKER

SUMAPAZ, REPUBLIC OF, Colombian peasant squatter colony located in portions of Cundinamarca, Tolima, Huila, Caquetá, and Meta departments. The site of numerous peasant–landlord conflicts since 1870, Sumapaz developed peasant leaders in Erasmo Valencia and Juan de la Cruz Varela in the 1920s and 1930s. Autonomous in many ways, the squatters' colony represented some 6,000 peasants. Liberal governments' efforts to mediate agrarian conflicts there in the later 1930s and early 1940s failed. After 1948, officially sponsored violence by the Conservative regimes of Mariano OSPINA PÉREZ and Laureano GÓMEZ CASTRO triggered the creation of the Communist-led Republic of Sumapaz in the later 1940s. The region was the site of three military campaigns (1948–1953, 1954–1957, 1958–1965) that, together with counterviolence, left its agricultural base in ruins. They also ended (by 1958) the Sumapaz Republic. With coffee growing partly replaced by cattle, the population has been beggared and dispersed.

CATHERINE LE GRAND, *Frontier Expansion and Peasant Protest in Colombia, 1830–1936* (1986), pp. 110ff.; ELSY MARULANDA, *Colonización y conflicto: Las lecciones del Sumapaz* (1991).

J. LEÓN HELGUERA

See also **Colombia: Revolutionary Movements; Violencia, La.**

SUR, prestigious and influential cultural review published in Buenos Aires. Following the advice of the Spanish philosopher José Ortega y Gasset, and with his support as well as that of the American writer Waldo Frank and the Argentine novelist Eduardo MALLEA, Victoria OCAMPO founded *Sur* in 1931. It was financed out of Ocampo's personal fortune. *Sur* contained fiction, poetry, philosophy, criticism, and history. Distinguished men of letters, including Jorge Luis BORGES, Pedro HENRÍQUEZ UREÑA, and Ortega y Gasset, served on the editorial board. Writer José BIANCO was head of the editorial staff between 1938 and 1961, the most prosperous years for the journal. Highly controversial, *Sur* was considered elitist and Europeanized by nationalist and leftist writers, such as Pablo NERUDA. Writers were not excluded for ideological reasons, however; literary excellence was the requisite for inclusion. Ocampo, a woman of strong opinions, did refuse to publish people she did not like. The journal became the best-known literary magazine in Latin America and served to introduce many foreign writers in translation, including T. S. Eliot, Ezra Pound, Henry Miller, Jacques Maritain, Aldous Huxley, André Gide, and Nathalie Sarraute.

Politically, *Sur* staunchly opposed every form of totalitarianism, both of the Right and the Left. It was published every month or two until 1971. Since then, special issues have appeared occasionally.

VICTORIA OCAMPO, "Vida de la revista *Sur*: 35 años de una labor," in *Sur*, no. 303–305 (November 1966–April 1967): 1–36 (this issue also contains an index for issues 1–302); H. R. LAFLEUR et al., *Las revistas literarias argentinas, 1893–1967* (1968); JOHN KING, *Sur: A Study of the Argentine Literary Journal and Its Role in the Development of a Culture* (1986).

ROLANDO COSTA PICAZO

SURINAME AND THE DUTCH IN THE CARIBBEAN.

Suriname, which obtained its independence in 1975, became a Dutch colony in 1667 when the Dutch acquired it from the English. In 1954 it became an autonomous territory, as did the Netherlands Antilles, within the Kingdom of the Netherlands. Suriname has an area of 63,251 square miles and a population of 404,000 (1992 estimate). Dutch is the official language but Sranan, which is the Creole language based on English, Dutch, and African dialects, is also widely spoken. Furthermore, East Indians and other Asians as well as the amerindians often use their own languages.

Two self-governing island countries, the Netherlands Antilles and ARUBA, which left the Netherlands Antilles federation in 1986, form today the Caribbean possessions taken by the Dutch in the seventeenth century. The islands of Curaçao and Bonaire off the coast of Venezuela and three small islands of the northern Lesser Antilles, St. Martin, St. Eustatius, and Saba, sometimes referred to as the Dutch Windward Islands, comprise the federation of the Netherlands Antilles. Each island government has a significant degree of autonomy. The total area of this federation is 308 square miles and its population is 196,000 (1994). Aruba has an area of 75 square miles and a population of 69,000 (1994). The official language of the federation is Dutch, but in Curaçao, Bonaire, and Aruba the people speak mainly Papiamento, a language de-

rived primarily from Portuguese and heavily influenced by Spanish, Dutch, and African languages. On the northern Windward Islands, English dominates.

In its early years, Suriname was a typical plantation colony, but by the mid-nineteenth century sugar cultivation became less profitable. The abolition of slavery in 1863 caused a scarcity of labor. To solve this, contract labor was attracted, at first from China and Madeira, then from India (1873–1916), and finally from Indonesia (1890–1939). Nevertheless, attempts to keep sugar production profitable failed, and by the 1930s it had become insignificant. BAUXITE was discovered in Suriname in 1915, and the next year the United States Alcoa Company began exploring for it. Today the mining of bauxite forms the basis of the Suriname economy.

Past immigration policies have given modern Suriname a very segmented population structure. The East Indians are the largest population group, followed by creoles (people of African and African-European descent), and by Javanese Indonesians. Small groups of Amerindians, Europeans, and Chinese form the rest of the population.

During the eighteenth century the Dutch islands of Curaçao and St. Eustatius were two of the most important trade centers in the Caribbean. The latter was nicknamed the "Golden Rock" because of its wealthy merchants. Because it was an important source for supplies for the thirteen colonies during the American Revolution, the British sacked Oranjestad, its only town, in 1781. The island never recovered economically and is one of the poorest of the Dutch Caribbean islands. Curaçao is no longer the rich center it once was.

Few immigrants went to the six Dutch Caribbean islands in the nineteenth century due to the weak economy. In the early twentieth century, however, the British-Dutch Shell Oil Company established refineries in Curaçao for its crude oil from Venezuela, and Standard Oil Company of the United States did the same in Aruba. Soon these two islands had among the highest standards of living in the Caribbean. In the 1980s the oil companies abandoned both Curaçao and Aruba, aggravating the already serious unemployment situation. Tourism, which had been important for all of the islands, also declined, although it improved in the late 1980s, especially in St. Martin and Aruba.

When Suriname gained self-government, a multiparty system developed based on ethnicity. The Suriname National Party (NPS) is mainly creole; the Progressive Reform Party (VHP) is East Indian; and the Indonesian Party (KTPI) is Indonesian. Henck Arron of the NPS led the country to independence in 1975. His government, accused of being corrupt, was overthrown in 1980 by a group of soldiers led by Desi (Desire) Bouterse, and supreme power passed to the National Military Council (NMR), which he dominated.

The deteriorating economy forced Bouterse, in the latter part of the 1980s, to ask the leaders of the traditional parties to assist him in forming a new government, and in 1988 a new civilian government took office. A new constitution was adopted, replacing the one of 1975, and the new National Assembly was controlled by an alliance of the traditional parties known as the Front for Democracy and Development (FDO), which won forty of the fifty-one seats, while Bouterse's National Democratic Party (NDP) captured only three seats. The Netherlands resumed sending aid, and the new Surinamese government, in an attempt to stop the guerrilla war in the interior started by the Bush Creoles—descendants of African slaves who escaped to the jungle and established communities there—opened up negotiations with the Surinamese Liberation Army (SLA). A military coup in December 1990, however, forced the civilian government out of office. Again the Netherlands suspended its aid. The National Assembly was dissolved and new elections were held in May 1991. This time the FDO, now called the New Front for Democracy (NF), won thirty seats. In September 1991, Ronald R. Venetiaan became president. His vice president, Jules R. Ajodhia, also became prime minister.

The party system in the Netherlands Antilles developed along island lines, as the political allegiance of the people is primarily to their home island. In 1954, when full self-government was acquired, the People's National Party (PNP) of Curaçao was already well-established, as was the Democratic Party (DP). The latter attempted to become a regional party, but with little success. Among the many other parties then existing on the islands, one of the most important was the Aruban People's Party.

The strikes of the oil workers and the riots that followed in 1969 indicated that there was much dissatisfaction among the poorer population in Curaçao. As a consequence of these disturbances, more labor-oriented parties came into existence: the Workers Liberation Front (FOL), led by Wilson (Papa) Godett, and New Antilles Movement (MAN), led by Dominico (Don) Martina. In 1971 the Electoral Movement of the People (MEP) was formed on Aruba, led by Gilberto (Betico) Croes. The MEP felt that Curaçao was dominating the federation and ignoring Aruba's problems. Croes and his party demanded that Aruba be allowed to leave the federation and become a separate country within the kingdom. This was realized in 1986, but with the proviso that Aruba would become independent in 1996 while retaining commonwealth status within the kingdom.

Each island government continues to seek more autonomy. That this would cause the federation to collapse does not seem to bother many of the leaders. P. Claude Wathey, chairman of the Democratic Party of St. Martin, has indicated that independence for his island and for Saba and St. Eustatius might be the best solution. Critics feel, however, that further decentralization would increase administrative costs and hamper economic recovery. In 1994 Miguel Pourier became prime minister of the Netherlands Antilles. J. M. A. Eman became prime minister of Aruba that same year.

H. HOETINK, *Het patroon van de oude Curacaose samenleving: Een sociologische studie* (1958); JOHN Y. KEUR, *Windward Children: A Study in Human Ecology of the Three Dutch Windward Islands in the Caribbean* (1960); ALBERT GASTMANN, *The Politics of Surinam and the Netherlands Antilles* (1968); VERA M. GREEN, *Migrants in Aruba: Interethnic Integration* (1974); CORNELIUS GOSLINGA, *A Short History of the Netherlands Antilles and Surinam* (1979); RENE A. RÖMER, *Curaçao* (1981); ANKE KLOMP, *Politics on Bonaire* (1986); "Caribbean Politics: The Case of Suriname," in Paul B. Goodwin et al., eds., *The Caribbean After Grenada* (1988), pp. 127–137; ROBERTICO CROES, "The Dutch Caribbean Islands," in *Latin America and Caribbean Contemporary Record, 1987–88*, vol. 7 (1990), pp. B415–B432; TONY THORNDIKE, "Netherlands Dependencies," in *South America, Central America, and the Caribbean, 1991* (1990), pp. 429–443.

ALBERT GASTMANN

SYNCRETISM, a process of assimilating different religious beliefs into a system different from its component parts. Strictly, this process does not include the retention of old beliefs or forms under a veneer of new ones, especially if the latter are imposed by force or represent merely the adoption of certain alien rituals. More widely, however, the term is used to signify the borrowing of beliefs and ritual of one religious system by another. In this latter sense, syncretism is as old as religion itself. Syncretic elements appear in the Bible, derived from Canaanite, Babylonian, and Greek sources. Almost from its origins, Christianity has incorporated features of other religions. The first part of the Roman Catholic Mass is based on the first-century Jewish synagogue service. Pagan feasts were freely borrowed, such as that of Sol Invictus (the Unconquered Sun), a Syrian solar god whose anniversary on 25 December, at the winter solstice, gives the date of modern Christmas, or the pagan seasonal celebrations that became the Ember Days. The bold experiment of the Jesuits in sixteenth-century China in adapting Catholicism to native customs and rites was eventually condemned by the papacy because it seemed to involve genuine syncretism.

Though Spanish Catholicism of the sixteenth century was often a folk religion mingled with superstition, the process of syncretism with pre-Christian elements had been so thorough that it is difficult to separate these syncretic elements from orthodox Catholicism. The syncretic process is seen more easily in the religion of the *conversos* (Jewish converts to Catholicism), who often retained Judaic practices that still can be found in New Mexico among present-day descendants of *conversos* who moved north from New Spain in the colonial period.

In pre-conquest America, religious syncretism seems to have been common. The Mexica (AZTECS) commonly adopted the gods of conquered or tributary peoples, thus adding greatly to the complexity of their myths and deities. The southward movement of Mexican, or Toltec, influences from the central plateau had a strong impact on Maya religion of the post-Classical Period.

Tarahumara Easter celebration. Procession to village cemetery and funeral service for straw "body" representing Jesus are performed in honor of the Crucifixion. ANTHRO-PHOTO FILE.

Prominent among these was the acceptance of QUETZALCOATL under the name Kukulcan and the increased emphasis on human sacrifice. Because of the lack of clear evidence, it is difficult to draw definitive conclusions about pre-Conquest syncretism in Latin America.

The open-minded attitude of the Mexicas found difficulty with the exclusive demands of the Christian God preached by the early Spanish friars. There seems, however, to have been little active resistance, in part because of the wholesale disappearance of the native priesthood and temples during and after the Spanish Conquest. In the sixteenth century, cases were reported of relapses into idolatry and even of secret human sacrifice. More common were passive/aggressive techniques that involved external compliance without substantially altering the pre-Conquest religious viewpoint. In seventeenth-century Peru the church launched a major campaign against residual idolatry and syncretism.

Late twentieth-century research emphasized the subtle role played by the translation of religious concepts from one language to another. Europeans and Native Americans were separated by a vast cognitive and psychological gap. Basic Christian concepts, such as the afterlife as reward or punishment, hell, personal sin, and redemption, did not exist in the pre-Conquest New World. Translating these concepts and making them intelligible and acceptable to the Indians was one of the most daunting challenges faced by the early missionaries. The translation of western European religious terms into the native languages added nuances and were received by the Indians in terms of their own religious mentality and worldview. In Mexico this process has been called the "nahuatilization" of Christianity. The assertion that the early friars deliberately substituted Christian devotions or saints for pre-Conquest deities lacks any firm evidence. Most missionary friars were strongly opposed to any form of syncretism, which they regarded as neo- or crypto-idolatry.

The retention of native beliefs or their mingling with Christianity seems to have been strongest among Native Americans in those areas that were farthest from Spanish influence or those who held most tenaciously to traditional ways. The MAYAS, in a special way, were resistant to change. In 1585, Pedro de Feria, the bishop of Chiapas, complained that Christianity was only a veneer among the Maya Indians of his diocese. The same thing was encountered among the Yaqui of northern Mexico, the Hopis of Arizona, and among the various Maya groups of Guatemala. In South America the old ways were reinforced by geographical isolation.

In the twentieth century some missionaries grew more tolerant and even accepting of syncretism, which they used as a missionary tool. The mingling of Christian and pre-Christian elements is regarded as inevitable and not subject to immediate change.

CHARLES GIBSON, *The Aztecs Under Spanish Rule* (1964); CHARLES E. DIBBLE, "The Nahuatilization of Christianity," in *Sixteenth Century Mexico: The Work of Sahagún*, edited by Munro S. Edmonson (1974), pp. 225–233; MIRCEA ELIADE, *A History of Religious Ideas*, 3 vols. (1978–1985); JOHN M. INGHAM, *Mary, Michael, and Lucifer: Folk Catholicism in Central Mexico* (1986); MURIEL THAYER PAINTER, *With Good Heart: Yaqui Beliefs and Ceremonies in Pascua Village*, edited by Edward H. Spicer and Wilma Kaemlein (1986); LOUISE BURKHART, *The Slippery Earth: Nahua-Christian Moral Dialogue in Sixteenth-Century Mexico* (1989).

STAFFORD POOLE, C.M.

SYPHILIS. *See* **Diseases.**

191

SZYSZLO, FERNANDO DE (*b.* 1925), Peruvian artist. Szyszlo was born in Lima. His father was a Polish geographer, his mother a native Peruvian of Spanish-Indian descent. He studied at the school of fine arts at Lima's Catholic University with Austrian artist Adolfo Winternitz (1944–1946). Soon after, he joined *Espacio* (Space), a group of painters and architects who addressed nativism—indigenous cultures—and sought renewal in their disciplines. His early paintings were figurative; after his first trip to Europe in 1949, he turned to abstraction. Szyszlo studied the lore, language, and arts of Peruvian pre-Conquest cultures. He experimented with plastic symbols derived from these cultures as they appear in architecture, ceramics, and textiles. He traveled to the United States in 1953 and remained in Washington, D.C., to serve as a visual arts unit consultant to the ORGANIZATION OF AMERICAN STATES (1957–1960). He eventually settled permanently in Lima in 1970.

In the 1960s, Szyszlo worked on a series of thirteen paintings inspired by a QUECHUA elegy on the death of ATAHUALPA, the last ruling Inca. Each painting was inspired by an image or a phrase in the elegy. By the late 1960s, Szyszlo had created a personal style called "abstract nativism." He was artist in residence at Cornell University in 1962 and a visiting lecturer at Yale University in 1966. He received several Guggenheim Fellowships and won the first national prize for painting at the Esson Salon of Young Artists in Lima in 1964. He began to incorporate shapes suggestive of knives, ceremonial tables, and mummies wrapped in sacred gowns in his abstract paintings of the 1970s. In the 1980s he painted totemic forms in closed three-dimensional spaces that suggest chambers. Szyszlo has had a powerful influence on Peruvian painting.

GILBERT CHASE, *Contemporary Art in Latin America* (1970), pp. 105–107; MARTA TRABA, *Museum of Modern Art of Latin America: Selections from the Permanent Collection* (1985), p. 86; FÉLIX ANGEL, "The Latin American Presence," in *The Latin American Spirit: Art and Artists in the United States, 1920–1970* by Luis Cancel et al. (1988), pp. 243–244.

MARTA GARSD

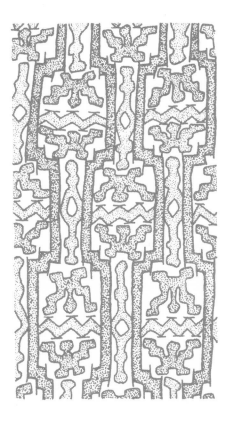

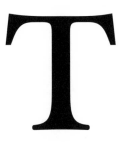

TÁBARA, ENRIQUE (*b.* 1930), Ecuadorian artist. Tábara studied painting at the School of Fine Arts in Guayaquil, his native city, and began to paint abstract compositions in 1954. With the aid of a fellowship from the Ecuadorian House of Culture the following year, he moved to Barcelona, where he studied at the School of Fine Arts and participated in the city's Hispanic-American Biennial (1955). He was influenced by Spanish informalism, from which he derived heavy impastos and textures, applying them to a repertoire of pre–Conquest-inspired themes: Ecuadorian Indian traditions, including rattlesnakes, mirrors, feathers, hieroglyphics, pyramids, and other motifs.

Returning to Ecuador in 1964, Tábara founded VAN, an Ecuadorian artists' movement against figurative indigenist art (1968). In the early 1970s he turned to a new figuration, often depicting human limbs across his canvases. He won a gold medal at the First Salon of Drawing, Watercolor, and Tempera at the House of Culture in Quito (1970).

MARTA TRABA, *Museum of Modern Art of Latin America: Selections from the Permanent Collection* (1985), pp. 114–115. FÉLIX ANGEL, ''The Latin American Presence,'' in *The Latin American Spirit: Art and Artists in the United States, 1920–1970,* by Luis R. Cancel et al. (1988), pp. 244–246.

MARTA GARSD

TABLADA, JOSÉ JUAN (*b.* 3 April 1871; *d.* 2 August 1945), Mexican writer. Born in Mexico City, José Juan de Aguilar Acuña Tablada y Osuna first published in *El Universal* in 1892; by the time of his death, more than 10,000 of his poems, essays, chronicles, novels, works of literary criticism, memoirs, and diaries had appeared under more than fifteen pseudonyms. Founder of *La Revista Moderna,* Tablada was strongly influenced by the French poet Charles Baudelaire. A trip to Japan in 1900 led to his introduction of the Japanese haiku into Spanish, influencing Ezra Pound and the Anglo-American imagist group, as well as poets in his own language. From 1911 to 1912 Tablada lived in Paris. When he returned to Mexico he became a supporter of Victoriano HUERTA, for which he was forced into exile in New York in 1914.

Tablada was the first to publish ideographic poems in Spanish; his book *Li-Po y otros poemas: Poemas ideográficos* appeared in 1920, following closely upon Guillaume Apollinaire's *Calligrammes.* Mexican president Venustiano CARRANZA named Tablada a member of the diplomatic service in Colombia and Venezuela, but Tablada soon resigned and returned to New York in 1920. He went back to Mexico in 1935, but spent his last years in New York, where he died. His inventive, often ingenious imagery, anticipating vanguard tendencies, gave new life to widely varied but common poetic themes, including Mexican landscapes, natural elements, and travel impressions. Tablada's reputation was solidly re-established in the mid-twentieth century by a new generation of Mexican writers and critics, including Octavio PAZ.

EDUARDO MITRE, "Los ideogramas de José Juan Tablada," in *Revista Iberoamericana* 40, no. 89 (October–December 1974): 675–679; MARK CRAMER, "José Juan Tablada and the Haiku Tradition," in *Romance Notes* 16 (1975):530–535; ALLEN W. PHILLIPS, "Cuatro poetas hispanoamericanos entre el modernismo y la vanguardia," in *Revista Iberoamericana* 55, nos. 146–147 (January–June 1989): 427–449.

KEITH McDUFFIE

TACNA, southernmost department in Peru. Forming part of the country's Pacific littoral, Tacna is bordered by the Peruvian departments of Moquegua and Puno on the north, Bolivia on the east, and Chile on the south. It is divided into two provinces, Tacna and Tarata; the capital city of the department, also called Tacna, has a population of approximately 150,000. Copper mining, cattle raising, and irrigated agriculture, including cotton and alfalfa, are the major economic activities.

Tacna, along with the former Peruvian province of ARICA, has a significant position in the history of Latin American international relations. Chile occupied the two provinces during the WAR OF THE PACIFIC (1879–1883), and then, under the provisions of the Treaty of ANCÓN, was to retain possession of them for ten years, after which a plebiscite would determine whether the inhabitants wished to be citizens of Chile or Peru. The plebiscite was not held, however, and from 1893 to 1929 the Tacna-Arica controversy strained relations between the two countries as Chile continued to occupy the disputed territory. As a last resort, Chile and Peru asked the United States to mediate the dispute. The two nations could never settle on a protocol for the plebiscite, however, and by treaty in 1929 the countries agreed to divide the provinces; Peru reincorporated Tacna, and Chile annexed Arica.

The controversy surrounding the Chilean occupation of Tacna and Arica, and the surrender of Arica to Chile, continues to affect relations between the countries. The city of Tacna has become a powerful national symbol for Peru and is called "the heroic city" to honor the patriotism exhibited by its citizens during the war and throughout the Chilean occupation.

WILLIAM JEFFERSON DENNIS, *Tacna and Arica* (1931), is dated but useful. In the *Colección Documental de la Independencia del Perú*, see vol. 23 (1971) for Tacna.

WILLIAM E. SKUBAN

TACNA–ARICA DISPUTE, a diplomatic confrontation between Chile and Peru arising out of the WAR OF THE PACIFIC (1879–1884). The Treaty of ANCÓN (1883) spec-

ified that Chile could occupy the provinces of Tacna and Arica until 1894, when a plebiscite would determine their status. The winner would retain the two provinces; the loser would receive a monetary indemnity. Unfortunately, the treaty did not specify the conditions under which the two nations would conduct the plebiscite. The government in Santiago, hoping to retain sovereignty over the disputed territory, utilized this issue to refuse to hold the election, infuriating Peru, which felt despoiled. Peru repeatedly sought the intervention of others in the Pan-American movement, a strategy Chile successfully defeated. When the Pan-American Union could not force Santiago to cooperate, Peru contemplated using force. Meanwhile, Chile attempted to convert the Peruvian population to its own cause. Failing in its attempt to win over the Peruvians, Chile then tried to populate the disputed territory with Chilean citizens while simultaneously attempting to repress its Peruvian residents. In 1929, during the Carlos IBÁÑEZ administration, Chile and Peru signed the Treaty of LIMA and finally settled the dispute: Chile retained Arica, while Peru won Tacna. The resolution of this dispute ended the animus between Santiago and Lima but infuriated Bolivia, which remained without a seacoast.

WILLIAM J. DENNIS, *Tacna and Arica: An Account of the Chile-Peru Boundary Dispute and the Arbitrations by the United States* (1931); WILLIAM F. SATER, *Chile and the United States: Empires in Conflict* (1990), pp. 76–78, 94, 96–97, 101.

WILLIAM F. SATER

TACUARÍ, BATTLE OF (9 March 1811), a major engagement in the Paraguayan struggle for independence. The January 1811 defeat of a *porteño* invasion force near the town of Paraguarí brought a sense of great pride to the defending Paraguayan militiamen. Led by colonels Juan Manuel Gamarra and Manuel Antanacio Cavañas, these men were normally more accustomed to subsistence farming than to fighting professional soldiers. Once victorious, however, they were more willing to see themselves as masters of their own destiny, even to the point of questioning the instructions of their *peninsular* governor, Bernardo Velazco, as they pursued the *porteños* southward beyond the Río Tebicuary. Despite orders to the contrary from Velazco, they started to fraternize with their *porteño* opponents. General Manuel Belgrano, chief of the invasion force, sent gifts to Cavañas and Gamarra, as well as political missives outlining the goals of the patriots' cause, while his troops took up defensive positions along the shallow Río Tacuarí in the extreme south of Paraguay.

In the end, prodded by Velazco, Cavañas ordered a general assault against the *porteño* position on 9 March 1811, after which Belgrano immediately sued for peace. In turn, he received generous terms from Cavañas and was allowed to depart Paraguay with his army intact. Velazco arrived at the Tacuarí ten days later expecting to preside over Belgrano's surrender and was much abashed to learn of Colonel Cavañas's actions. The majority of Paraguayans, however, knew better. The militia's resistance to Belgrano was less an act of servility to Spanish authority than it was an affirmation of localism. Two months after the victory at Tacuarí, this sentiment was reenacted in a *cuartelazo* (barracks revolt) that brought national independence to Paraguay.

HARRIS GAYLORD WARREN, *Paraguay: An Informal History* (1949), pp. 145–147; JOHN HOYT WILLIAMS, *Rise and Fall of the Paraguayan Republic, 1800–1870* (1979), pp. 24–27.

THOMAS L. WHIGHAM

See also **Paraguarí, Battle of.**

TAFT AGREEMENT (1904), a concession made by the administration of President Theodore ROOSEVELT to the republic of Panama. Under the HAY–BUNAU-VARILLA TREATY (1903), Panama granted the United States the right to "act as if it were sovereign" in the newly created Canal Zone. Roosevelt issued an executive order establishing U.S. customhouses in the Canal Zone. Panamanian businessmen, fearing competition from rival commercial enterprises, protested. Roosevelt dispatched Secretary of War William Howard Taft to Panama to settle the matter. The resulting Taft Agreement provided that the PANAMA CANAL Zone would be permitted to import only those materials deemed necessary for the construction of the canal, the use of its employees, or sale to transiting ships. Canal Zone commissasaries would not be open to the general public, though enforcement of this rule was sometimes lax. the Taft Agreement expired in 1924.

GUSTAVE ANGUIZOLA, *The Panama Canal: Isthmian Political Instability* (1977); WALTER LA FEBER, *The Panama Canal: The Crisis in Historical Perspective* (1978).

LESTER D. LANGLEY

See also **United States–Latin American Relations.**

TAHUANTINSUYU, the name given by the INCAS to their empire. Meaning "Land of the Four Quarters," it derives from the Quechua words for "four" (*tawa*) and "quarter" (*suyu*). The empire of Tahuantinsuyu stretched in the north from the Ancasmayo River, on the modern border between Ecuador and Colombia, to the Maule River in the south, just below the modern city of Santiago, Chile, a distance of 2,500 miles. The *suyus* were the four main administrative units of the empire, and each was named for a province within it: Chinchasuyu, the northwestern quarter; Antisuyu, the northeastern quarter; Contisuyu, the southwestern quarter; and Collasuyu, the southeastern quarter. The *suyus* were originally conceived as four equal units, with the city of Cuzco located at the central point where they all came

together. Over time, however, the expansion of the empire increased the territory of the *suyus* unequally.

JOHN H. ROWE, "Inca Culture at the Time of the Spanish Conquest," in *Handbook of South American Indians*, vol. 2 (1946), p. 262.

GORDON F. McEWAN

TAILORS' CONSPIRACY. *See* **Inconfidência dos Alfaiates.**

TAÍNOS, name given Indian group Columbus encountered at first landfall in the Caribbean. Also known as Island Arawak, they are believed to have migrated from South America between 200 B.C. and A.D. 1200, and shared the islands of the Caribbean with the Ciboney and CARIB Indians at the time of the Spanish incursion. Mainly agriculturalists, some aided the Spanish in procuring food and shelter. Their numbers were decimated within a century by illness, malnutrition, overwork, and social collapse precipitated by Spanish colonization of their islands. Knowledge of this group is from the early Spanish chronicles, archaeologists, and linguists.

LOUIS A. PÉREZ, *Cuba: Between Reform and Revolution* (1988), esp. pp. 16–20; ANTONIO M. STEVENS ARROYO, *Cave of the Jagua: The Mythological World of the Taínos* (1988); FRANKLIN W. KNIGHT, *The Caribbean, The Genesis of a Fragmented Nationalism*, 2d ed. (1990), esp. pp. 7–23; SAMUEL M. WILSON, *Hispaniola: Caribbean Chiefdoms in the Age of Columbus* (1990).

JOYCE E. NAYLON

TAIRONA refers to a diverse archaeological complex distributed on the northern and northwestern faces of the Sierra Nevada de Santa Marta, Colombia. The term is also used to refer to an ancient indigenous ethnic group from a territory (*provincia*) located near the upper Don Diego and Buritaca rivers. Tairona also refers to a cultural area (*cultura Tairona*) characterized by a style of prehispanic gold, pottery, and architectural remains dating from A.D. 1000 until the Spanish conquest. Three periods of development are recognized for the archaeological complex.

The Early Tairona period is divided into two phases. The first phase dates from 500 B.C. to A.D. 600 and is characterized by small fishing and farming populations that lived in independent hamlets on the coast. An archaeological site example is Puerto Gaira. The second phase dates between A.D. 600 and A.D. 900 and is characterized by the development of inland settlements with more emphasis on agricultural production and larger populations that led to the colonization of the Sierra Nevada de Santa Marta. A chiefdom society developed, accompanied by the use of stone in construction of dwellings and pathways connecting the town of the chief with the neighboring hamlets. More variation in the burial practices within and between regions is ob-

Bat-Man pendant. Tairona gold, 10th–16th centuries. THE METROPOLITAN MUSEUM OF ART / JAN MITCHELL AND SONS COLLECTION. PARTIAL GIFT OF AND PROMISED GIFT OF JAN MITCHELL. 1991. (1991.419.31).

served in this period. Burial offerings include gold, pottery, staffs, beads, and other artifacts of stone. Archaeological site examples of this phase are Mamorón, Nahuanjue, and Cinto.

The second period is the Middle, or Classic, Tairona (1000–1501). This period is characterized by the consolidation of the colonized regions, the development of towns, stone road systems, irrigation and agricultural terrace systems, complex chiefdom hierarchies, strong microvertical trade, and an increase in the regional specialization of food and artifact production (pottery, gold, beads, axes, and other lithic artifacts). Examples of urban sites are Ciudad Perdida and Pueblito. The political divisions of these chiefdoms were mainly religious in character, with a chief and/or priest as a head. The principal chiefdoms that controlled relatively large areas during this period were referred to by the Spanish as the Bondas, Posigueicas, Betomas, and Taironas.

The last period is the Conquest (1501–1600). This period is characterized by a decline in population through disease and intensive warfare with the Spanish; collapse of chiefdom societies; abandonment of villages, towns, and road systems; and creation by the survivors of highland refuge areas. A small number of descendants of the chiefdoms that formed the Tairona complex live today in the highlands of the Sierra Nevada and are known as the Kogy (Kogi) or Kaggaba (Kágaba) Indians.

For illustrations of the material culture as well as a general review, see HENNING BISCHOF, "Tairona Archaeology," in *Arte de la Tierra: Taironas* (1991). For a synthesis of the development of Ciudad Perdida and Pueblito, see JACQUES APRILE-GNISET, *La ciudad colombiana*, vol. 1, *Prehispánica, de conquista e indiana* (1991). For a perspective on the descendants of the Tairona chiefdoms, see AUGUSTO OYUELA-CAYCEDO, "Ideology and Structure of Gender Spaces: The Kaggaba Indians," in *The Ar-*

chaeology of Gender, edited by D. Walde and N. D. Willows (1991), pp. 327–335.

AUGUSTO OYUELA-CAYCEDO

TAJES, MÁXIMO (*b.* 23 November 1852; *d.* 21 November 1912), military leader and president of Uruguay (1886–1890). Tajes began his military career as a distinguished soldier in the army while it was at war with Paraguay. He rose rapidly to the rank of captain (1875) and lieutenant colonel (1880), became minister of war and the navy in 1882, and assumed the presidency in 1886. Tajes pursued the course that had moved Colonel Lorenzo LATORRE, who became dictator in 1876, and General Máximo Santos (president, 1882–1886), two men who implanted what has come to be known in Uruguayan history as "militarism." After the resignation of Santos in 1886, however, Tajes followed the advice of Dr. Julio HERRERA Y OBES and offered himself as constitutionally elected president in order to manage peacefully the transition from militarism to "civilism," a task he fulfilled satisfactorily. His administration took place during the "era of Reus," named after Emilio Reus, a young Spanish financier widely known at the time.

ENRIQUE MÉNDEZ VIVES, *El Uruguay de la modernización* (1976); WASHINGTON REYES ABADIE and ANDRÉS VÁZQUEZ ROMERO, *Crónica general del Uruguay*, vol. 3 (1984); GONZALO AGUIRRE RAMÍREZ, *La revolución del Quebracho y la conciliación: De Ellauria a Tajes, 1873–1886* (1989).

JOSÉ DE TORRES WILSON

TALAMANTES, MELCHOR DE (*b.* 10 January 1765; *d.* 3 May 1809), Mercedarian friar, precursor of Mexican independence. Born in Lima, Talamantes earned his doctorate in theology at the University of San Marcos. In 1807, Viceroy José de ITURRIGARAY (1742–1815) charged him with establishing the boundaries of Texas. He gained prestige and influence with important people in the capital. In 1808 he supported the proposal of the *ayuntamiento* (city council) to establish a junta of authorities and submitted a plan to form a national congress. He was imprisoned during the 1808 coup; among his papers was found a plan for independence. He died in San Juan de Ulúa, while on his way to Spain, the victim of yellow fever.

MELCHOR DE TALAMANTES, *Biografía y escritos póstumos* (1909); JOSÉ MARÍA MIQUEL I VERGÉS, *Diccionario de insurgentes* (1969), p. 560; *Diccionario Porrúa de historia, geografía y biografía de México*, vol. 3 (1986), p. 2822.

VIRGINIA GUEDEA

TALAMBO AFFAIR, a local incident in northern Peru in 1863 that had international repercussions. Because of the strained diplomatic relations between Spain and some of its former colonies, an isolated altercation resulted in an armed confrontation between a Spanish fleet and allied forces of four South American republics (Bolivia, Chile, Ecuador, and Peru) in 1866.

In 1860 the owner of the Talambo estate in Chiclayo had contracted through an agent to hire approximately 175 Basque immigrants to work in the estate's cotton fields. In August 1863 two Basque farmers quarreled with the estate's owner and his men. In the ensuing fight two immigrants were killed and several imprisoned. This incident led to a diplomatic complaint by the Spanish embassy and government.

The commander of the Spanish fleet, allegedly performing a scientific expedition off the Peruvian coast at the time, pressed the Peruvian government of Juan Antonio PEZET to apologize and pay past debts to Spanish nationals. The Spaniards seized the GUANO-producing islands of Chincha and threatened to bomb the port of Callao in 1865. Pezet tried to find a peaceful solution by supporting the Vivanco-Pareja Treaty. Other military leaders and the public, however, considered Pezet's actions a form of capitulation and ousted him.

JORGE BASADRE, *Historia de la República del Peru,* vol. 3 (1963); DAVID WERLICH, *Peru: A Short History* (1976).

ALFONSO W. QUIROZ

TALAVERA, MANUEL (*b.* 8 December 1875; *d.* 27 July 1950), Paraguayan politician and businessman. Talavera was a dynamic member of the Colorado Party after the 1947 civil war where the Colorados emerged victorious. A member of the right-wing *Guion rojo* (Red Banner), Talavera led his faction to victory in the aftermath of the Colorado Party convention in November 1947. The Guionists had actually lost the internal election by two votes, but Talavera's friend and presidential candidate, Natalicio González, also a *Guion rojo,* took control of the Colorado Party by force. After winning the February 1948 elections without opposition, González was sworn in as president on 15 August 1948. In February 1949 a group of dissenters in the party, led by Felipe Molas López, succeeded in overthrowing Gonzalez. Talavera's political career ended after the coup.

OSVALDO KALLSEN, *Asunción y sus calles* (1974); PAUL LEWIS, *Paraguay Under Stroessner* (1980).

MIGUEL A. GATTI

See also **Paraguay: Political Parties.**

TALAVERA, NATALÍCIO (*b.* 1839; *d.* 14 October 1867), Paraguayan poet and journalist. Born in Villarrica, Talavera became independent Paraguay's first published poet. He studied in his native town and in Asunción, where he came to the attention of Ildefonso Bermejo, a Spanish publicist who had been contracted by the Carlos Antonio LÓPEZ government to launch a new state newspaper and other cultural projects. Under Bermejo's tutelage, Talavera became a first-rate writer. He contributed poems and literary essays to Asunción's cultural journal, *La Aurora,* and translated Lamartine's poem *Graciela* from the French.

It was in the field of journalism, however, that Talavera most distinguished himself, regularly producing articles and essays for the state newspaper, *El Semanario de Avisos y Conocimientos Utiles.* More important, after the beginning of the WAR OF THE TRIPLE ALLIANCE (1864–1870), Talavera was chosen to edit *Cabichuí,* a satirical newspaper written mostly in the GUARANI Indian language. His own contributions to this periodical included biting accounts of Allied cowardice as well as clever ditties attacking the character of Emperor Dom PEDRO II and his consort. Paraguayan soldiers, it was said, set these verses to music and sang them in the trenches to taunt the enemy, who lay just beyond gunshot range.

Talavera wrote a series of chronicles from the battlefield that were serialized in *El Semanario* and much later published as a book, *La guerra del Paraguay.* He himself did not survive the war, becoming ill with what was probably pneumonia as a result of hard campaigning, and died at the Paraguayan army camp of Paso Pucu.

NATALÍCIO TALAVERA, *La guerra del Paraguay* (1958); CARLOS ZUBIZARRETA, *Cien vidas paraguayas,* 2d ed. (1985), pp. 179–181.

THOMAS L. WHIGHAM

TALLER DE GRÁFICA POPULAR (TGP), Mexican artists' collaborative. Founded in 1937 by Leopoldo Méndez, Luis Arenal, and Pablo O'HIGGINS, this popular graphics workshop is a center for the collective production of art with sociopolitical content. Sharing the post-Revolutionary idealism of the Mexican muralists, the TGP aimed to reach as broad an audience as possible, primarily through the dissemination of inexpensive wood- and linoleum-block prints. Although still extant, the collaborative was most prominent in the 1930s and 1940s, an era when populist struggles reached their apogee worldwide. In this period it published over 45,000 prints, including posters, broadsheets, and portfolios; these works became known internationally through exhibitions. The TGP, which attracted such artists as Mexicans Raúl Anguiano, Alberto Beltrán, José CHÁVEZ MORADO, and Alfredo Zalce, and Americans Elizabeth Catlett and Mariana Yampolsky, became a center for preservation of Mexico's strong tradition in the graphic arts.

HANNES MEYER, ed., *El Taller de Gráfica Popular* (1949); JUDITH KELLER, *El Taller de Gráfica Popular* (1985); MUSEO DE PALACIO DE BELLAS ARTES, MUSEO NACIONAL DE LA ESTAMPA, and GALERÍA JOSE VELASCO, *50 años Taller de Gráfica Popular* (1987); DAWN ADES, "The Taller de Gráfica Popular," in *Art in Latin America: The Modern Era, 1820–1980* (1989).

ELIZABETH FERRER

TALLET, JOSÉ ZACARÍAS (*b.* 18 October 1893; *d.* 1985), Cuban journalist. Born in Matanzas, Cuba, Tallet moved to the United States with his family in 1912. He graduated with a bachelor's degree in accounting from the Heffly Institute of Commerce in New York City. Upon his return to Cuba in 1923, he participated in the Protesta de los Trece and the Grupo Minorista, both consisting of disenchanted intellectuals who called for change in Cuban letters and politics in the 1920s. He was instrumental in the formation of several leftist organizations, including the Falange de Acción Cubana, the Movimiento de Veteranos y Patriotas, and the Universidad Popular José Martí, of which he was first president. An ardent Marxist, Tallet expressed his ideas in such journals and newspapers as *Social, Alma Mater, Carteles,* and *Revista de La Habana.* In 1927–1928, he was editor of the journal *Revista de avance,* director of the magazine *El Mundo* from 1928 to 1933, and subdirector of the daily newspaper *Ahora* from 1933 to 1935.

For seventeen years Tallet taught world and Cuban history at the Escuela Profesional de Periodismo "Manuel Márquez Sterling," of which he was director (1959–1960). He is best known for his poetry, in which he treated both the social relevance and the aesthetic contribution of all sectors to Cuban culture. He received the Bonifacio Byrne Prize in Poetry (1944). His first book of poetry was *La semilla estéril* (1951) and his best-known poem is "La rumba."

After 1959 he became an enthusiastic supporter of the Castro revolution. He was a frequent contributor to *Bohemia,* one of Cuba's major journals, until his death.

LUIS E. AGUILAR, *Cuba 1933: Prologue to Revolution* (1972); HARRY SWAN, "The Nineteen Twenties: A Decade of Intellectual Change in Cuba," in *Revista interamericana* 8, no. 2 (1978); INSTITUTO DE LITERATURA Y LINGÜÍSTICA DE LA ACADEMIA DE CIENCIAS DE CUBA, *Diccionario de la literatura cubana,* vol. 2 (1984), pp. 997–998, with extensive bibliography; LESLIE WILSON, "Tallet," in *Dictionary of Twentieth-Century Cuban Literature,* edited by Julio A. Martínez (1990).

DARIÉN DAVIS

TAMANDARÉ, ALMIRANTE. *See* **Lisboa, Joaquim Marques.**

TAMARÓN Y ROMERAL, PEDRO (*b.* ca. 1695; *d.* 21 December 1768), bishop in colonial Mexico. Tamarón was born in Villa de la Guardia, in the archdiocese of Toledo, but nothing more is known of him until 1719, when he was in Caracas with Bishop Juan José de Escalona y Calatayud. In 1758 he became bishop of Durango in Mexico. Besides some religious tracts, he wrote a long description of his bishopric (1765), based on first-hand knowledge of practically every settlement of the diocese. Because of the amount of detailed information it contains, it is one of the principal sources for colonial NUEVA VIZCAYA. Tamarón died in Bamos, Sinaloa, while on the first leg of a general pastoral visit.

PEDRO TAMARÓN Y ROMERAL, *Demostración del vastísimo obispado de la Nueva Vizcaya* (1765; repr. 1937, 1958).

CLARA BARGELLINI

TAMAULIPAS, a Mexican state bordering Texas to the north, Nuevo León to the west, the Gulf of Mexico to the east, and the states of San Luis Potosí and Veracruz to the south. It consists of forty-three counties and its state capital is Ciudad Victoria. Tamaulipas covers an area of some 31,800 square miles (just over 4 percent of Mexico's territory) and has 1,924,484 inhabitants (1980) (2.9 percent of the national total).

Evidence of gathering and hunting activities was found at the Cueva del Diablo, the oldest archeological site in the area at about 8,000 years old. The area was occupied by Olmec, Chichimec, and Huastecan Indians and was conquered by Aztec ruler Motecuhzoma Inhuicamina around 1445–1466.

Américo Vespucci might have traveled the area around 1497–1502. By 1517 Francisco HERNÁNDEZ DE CÓRDOBA led the Spaniards to the Pánuco River but was defeated by the Huastecan Indians. Francisco de GARAY attempted the conquest in 1518, and the next year Juan de GRIJALVA, Alfonso ÁLVAREZ DE PINEDA, and Diego Camargo repeated the attempt. Finally Hernán Cortés's forces took Chila in 1522.

The area was not easily subdued, and evangelist Fray Andrés de Olmos failed in an attempt to settle the region around mid-century. Franciscan friars founded the missions of Tula, Jaumave, and Palmillas and introduced sheep and cattle in the area, displacing the Indians. By the 1730s Spanish authorities had promoted further colonization north of the Tamaulipas Sierra. In May 1748 the province of Nuevo Santander was founded by José de Escandón.

In 1810 independence sympathizers proclaimed their opposition to the Spanish government and, under the leadership of Albino García, were able to control the area in support of Father Miguel Hidalgo. By mid-1811 loyalists to the Spanish Crown, commanded by Joaquín de Arredondo, had taken Aguayo. In 1817 Spanish liberal Francisco Javier MINA Y LARREA landed in Soto la Marina, then took Santander and the Bajío area. In 1821 Zenón Fernández, commander of Río Verde, took up arms against the Spanish government in favor of the PLAN OF IGUALA. Antonio Fernández de Córdoba took up the insurgent cause in Aguayo and became governor of the area. After Agustín de ITURBIDE's empire fell, Felipe de la Garza moved the capital to Padilla, and the area joined the Mexican federation as the new state of Tamaulipas. The capital was moved to Ciudad Victoria. In 1829 the state was invaded by Spaniard Isidro Barradas, who with Spanish support took Tampico. Manuel MIER Y TERÁN and Antonio López de SANTA ANNA defended the area.

In 1830 local caudillo Francisco Vital Fernández supported the Plan of Jalapa against Vicente Guerrero. Joining the liberals two years later, he took Matamoros and Ciudad Victoria. During the centralist administration, the area became a department. In 1836 Tamaulipas sent forces against Texas. After Santa Anna's defeat, the area was in dispute between Texas and Mexico. Supporting federalism in 1838, area residents rebelled against President Anastacio Bustamante but were defeated. In 1846 U.S. general Zachary TAYLOR invaded the area, and after the MEXICAN-AMERICAN WAR (1846–1848) the territory between the Nueces River and the Rio Grande became part of Texas.

In 1854 José de la Garza led the region's liberal rebellion against Santa Anna in support of the PLAN OF AYUTLA. During the Revolution of Ayutla, or the REFORM, there was little conservative opposition to the liberals. In 1864, however, the conservative forces of Tomás MEJÍA took Matamoros, and Governor Juan Nepomuceno Cortina supported Maximilian's empire. In 1866 Tamaulipas was captured by liberal general Mariano ESCOBEDO, who took Matamoros and Tampico. In 1876 Porfirio DÍAZ took Matamoros and proclaimed the Plan of Palo Alto, which modified the PLAN OF TUXTEPEC. During the PORFIRIATO, Tamaulipas was governed by Servando Canales (1880–1884), Alejandro Prieto (1888–1896), Alejandro Mainero (1896–1901), Pedro Argüelles (1901–1908), and Juan B. Castelló (1908–1911).

During the MEXICAN REVOLUTION, the state was taken in 1914 by the forces of Pablo GONZALEZ, who defeated Carrancist general Lucio Blanco. In 1917 Francisco Gonzalez Villarreal became governor, and in 1920 Emilio PORTES GIL was appointed governor by the Obregonist followers of the Plan of Agua Prieta.

GABRIEL SALDÍVAR, *Historia compendiada de Tamaulipas* (1945); TORIBIO DE LA TORRE, *Historia general de Tamaulipas*, 2d ed. (1986); INSTITUTO NACIONAL DE ESTADÍSTICA, GEOGRAFÍA E INFORMÁTICA, *Estructura económica del estado de Tamaulipas: Sistema de cuentas nacionales de Mexico* (1987); and MARÍA DEL PILAR SÁNCHEZ GÓMEZ, *Catálogo de fuentes de la historia de Tamaulipas* (1987); GABRIEL SALDÍVAR, *Historia compendida de Tamaulipas* (1988).

CARMEN RAMOS-ESCANDÓN

TAMAYO, FRANZ (*b.* 29 February 1879; *d.* 29 July 1956), Bolivian poet and politician. Sophisticated and well educated (he spoke several languages and was an accomplished pianist), Tamayo is considered the dominant intellectual figure of the first half of the twentieth century in Bolivia. His ideas on education and the importance of the Indian culture in Bolivia, expressed in *Creación de la pedagogía nacional* (1910), are still relevant today. But it is his poetry that secured his place in Bolivian literature. Tamayo's work is the last major example of the poetic movement of *modernismo*. With his mix of musical verse, baroque erudition (mainly classical Greek and Roman literature), and German philosophy, he created a poetry strongly metaphysical in nature. Tamayo idealized the Indian, the Andes, and the poet as

transcendental entities. During the years of Bolivia's war with Paraguay (1932–1935), Tamayo was a strong supporter of Daniel SALAMANCA's government. In 1934 he was Salamanca's chosen candidate in the national election. Tamayo won the election but never became president because of a coup d'état at the war front.

NICOLÁS FERNÁNDEZ NARANJO, *Concepción del mundo e ideas filosóficas de Franz Tamayo* (1966); DORA GÓMEZ DE FERNÁNDEZ, *La poesía de Franz Tamayo* (1968); GUILLERMO FRANCOVICH, "Franz Tamayo," in his *Tres poetas modernistas* (1971); RAMIRO CONDARCO MORALES, *Franz Tamayo: El pensador* (1989).

LEONARDO GARCÍA PABÓN

TAMAYO, RUFINO (*b.* 26 August 1899; *d.* 24 June 1991), Mexican painter. Tamayo was born in Oaxaca, with its strong pre-Hispanic cultural heritage and Indian population. In 1907 his mother died and the family moved to a different neighborhood, where he began a very intense Catholic and musical education. In 1910–1911, Tamayo lived in Mexico City with his aunt. There he discovered a profound interest in drawing. He earned his living selling fruit. In 1917 he entered the National School of Fine Arts, which he abandoned because of its mediocrity and his lack of interest. Tamayo received almost no formal artistic training, but he acquired a fundamental education from drawing the pre-Hispanic objects and folk art in the Ethnographic Section of the National Museum of Archaeology.

His first solo show took place in 1926 in Mexico City. The twenty paintings and watercolors in that show already displayed his personal use of color and the peculiar images and iconography that characterized his future work. Immediately after, he moved to New York City and became acquainted with and lived near Marcel Duchamp, Stuart Davis, and Reginald Marsh. In October 1926 he opened an exhibition that was well received. In fact, Tamayo was first recognized in the United States and Europe, and only later in his own country. In 1928 he returned to Mexico and began to participate in group shows with Mexican artists. He taught painting at the National School of Fine Arts (1928–1930). Tamayo painted a series of still lifes, although in 1938 his themes centered on portraits and the feminine figure.

The 1930s were important in Tamayo's life. He painted his first mural, *The Music and the Song,* for the National School of Music (1933). In 1936 he again moved to New York, where he lived until 1944. He participated in a New York City project for the Works Progress Administration, which he never completed. At the end of the 1930s his painting began to be acclaimed because of its universal and Mexican meanings. He taught at the Dalton School in New York City and showed his paintings in several galleries. In 1949 he made his first trip to Europe, where he visited France, Spain, Holland, England, and Italy. He lived in Paris for several months. In the later decades of his life, Tamayo worked on his paintings, exploring the richness of the

Rufino Tamayo drawing on the lithographic stone for *Dos personajes atacados por perros.* COURTESY OF MIXOGRAFÍA WORKSHOP / REMBA GALLERY, PHOTO BY ISAIAS REMBA.

texture of canvas and working with sand, marble powder, and other material.

Rufino Tamayo: Myth and Magic (1979); *Rufino Tamayo* (1982).

BÉLGICA RODRÍGUEZ

TAMBOR DE MINA (or Mina) is a regional variant of the AFRICAN-BRAZILIAN religion in northern Brazil. Two cult houses founded in the first half of the nineteenth century in São Luís, Maranhão, are still in existence. The Casa das Minas, probably established by members of the royal family of Abomey, who were sold as slaves, is the rare case of a dominant Dahoman tradition in Brazil. Members worship a pantheon of *voduns* (deities) and *tôbôssi* (female child entities) organized in extended families, the most important of which are the Real (Dahoman) or Davice family, the Dambirá family, and the Quevioçô family.

The Casa de Nagô, originally a Yoruban cult house, formed strong ties with the nearby Casa das Minas. Its gods are called *voduns* (not *orishás*), and several *jeje* deities are worshipped. Six Mina cult houses were founded between 1910 and 1920. In the 1990s their number reached about 1,000 in São Luís, and dozens of others were established in the interior of Maranhão, as well as in Pará, Amazônas, and Piauí.

Tambor de Mina is distinguished by the integration of *caboclo* (Indian) deities, the *fidalgos* (Portuguese kings), and the *gentilheiros* (Turkish warriors), as well as by particular forms of ceremonies, dress, music, ritual language, and spirit possession.

OCTÁVIO DA COSTA EDUARDO, *The Negro in Northern Brazil: A Study in Acculturation* (1966); MANUEL NUNES PEREIRA, *A Casa das Minas: Culto dos voduns jeje no Maranhão*, 2d ed., enl. (1979); SÉRGIO FIGUEIRADO FERRETTI, *Querbentam de Zomadonu: Etnografia da Casa das Minas* (1985); MUNDICARMO FERRETTI, "Rei da Turquia, o Ferrobrás de Alexandria? A importância de um livro na mitologia de Tambor de Mina," in *Meu sinal está no teu corpo: Escritos sobre a religião dos orixás*, edited by Carlos Eugênio Marcondes de Moura (1989), pp. 202–219; SÉRGIO FIGUEI-RADO FERRETTI, "Voduns da Casa das Minas," in *Meu sinal está no teu corpo: Escritos sobre a religião dos orixás*, edited by Carlos Eugênio Marcondes da Moura (1989), pp. 176–201.

MATTHIAS RÖHRIG ASSUNÇÃO

TAMOIO, Tupi term for "forebear," adopted by the TUPINAMBÁ of southern Brazil. In the mid-sixteenth century, when the Portuguese colonists of coastal Brazil began to acquire Tupinambá captives through their Tupinikin and Tememinó allies, several Tupinambá groups near Guanabara Bay formed a military alliance which came to be known as the "Tamoio Confederation." While essentially an indigenous movement, the Tamoio revolt gained strength with the arrival of the FRENCH in Rio de Janeiro in 1555, who formed an alliance with the Tupinambá. Victimized by a brutal military campaign, especially under Governor Mem de SÁ (1557–1572), weakened by the 1563 smallpox pandemic, and stripped of their French allies when those colonists abandoned Brazil, the Rio de Janeiro Tamoio finally succumbed in 1567, though Tamoio groups in Cabo Frio continued to resist until the 1570s. Many survivors of the war were reduced to slavery or placed in Jesuit MISSIONS, but others retreated to the interior and reconstructed village society as far away from the Portuguese as possible. By the end of the sixteenth century, the Tamoio had ceased to exist as an independent society, though Tamoio slaves were to be found on farms and plantations throughout Brazil.

The most complete account in English is JOHN HEMMING, *Red Gold* (1978), ch. 6–7. On early Portuguese-Indian relations, see the still-useful work of ALEXANDER N. MARCHANT, *From Barter to Slavery* (1942). On the French in Rio de Janeiro, OLIVE P. DICKASON, *The Myth of the Savage* (1984), ch. 9.

JOHN M. MONTEIRO

TANGA, a Portuguese word of African origin; it comes from the Quimbundo term *ntanga*, which means "cloth covering tied to the waist." This clothing was characteristic of Africa. Slaves arrived in Brazil wearing a strip of cloth they called *tanga.* The term is also used in other former Portuguese territories to mean "little skirt." It came to designate a kind of apron used by some indigenous peoples in Brazil to cover the belly and thighs. Used mainly by women to cover their private parts, the tanga can be made of cords or woven with cotton thread and may contain seeds or glass beads. It is triangular and can vary in pattern and decoration.

CHARLOTTE EMMERICH

TANGO, Argentine dance and popular song. The tango first won international notoriety just before World War I. Its origins can be traced to the *arrabales* (poor outskirts) of Buenos Aires, some time around 1880. It was a spontaneous creation that fused the Spanish-Cuban *habanera,* the Argentine MILONGA, and the dance tradition of Buenos Aires's declining black communities. The tango's definitely lower-class background meant its immediate repudiation by Argentina's upper and middle classes, but this scarcely affected its rise in popularity. In 1913 ("the tango year," in H. G. Wells's phrase), it became the focus of an intense craze in Western Europe, from where it spread to North America. Its initially rather wild steps were gradually modified into an acceptable form for European and Argentine ballrooms. The version exhibited by Rudolph Valentino in *The Four*

The tango. PHOTO BY A. R. WILLIAMS.

Horsemen of the Apocalypse (1921) is singularly inauthentic.

The tango's musical tradition, one of the two or three richest in the Western Hemisphere, took shape between 1890 and 1920. The *bandoneon,* a German-made accordion variant, became the key instrument in the trios and quartets that played the music in the 1900s. The worldwide fame of the tango spelled an end to upper-class disapproval of it in Argentina, where the dance and especially the music entered a genuine golden age from approximately 1920 to 1950, much enhanced by phonograph records, radio programs, and (after 1933) Argentine sound films. The standard tango band, *orquesta típica,* of the 1920s and early 1930s was a sextet of two *bandoneons,* two violins, a piano, and a double bass.

In the early 1920s the tango also became a form of popular song, marvelously perfected by the legendary baritone Carlos GARDEL (1890–1935). The dance itself was revived strongly in the late 1930s. Tango bands then reached their fullest size, with upward of a dozen players. Perhaps the most brilliant star of this period was the great *bandoneon* player Aníbal Troilo (1914–1975).

After the early 1950s, tango music lost its supremacy in Argentina, though it retained its share of public affection. Smaller instrumental groups came to replace the magnificent bands of the 1940s, while an "avantgarde" outgrowth of the music developed under the leadership of Astor Piazzolla (1921–1992), who achieved considerable European renown in the 1970s and 1980s.

A musical form rather than a style, the tango should be referred to in English as "the tango," never just as "tango."

DEBORAH L. JAKUBS, "From Bawdyhouse to Cabaret: The Evolution of the Tango as an Expression of Argentine Popular Culture," in *Journal of Popular Culture* 18 (1984): 133–145; SIMON COLLIER, *The Life, Music and Times of Carlos Gardel* (1986); DONALD S. CASTRO, *The Argentine Tango as Social History, 1880–1955* (1990).

SIMON COLLIER

See also **Music.**

TANNENBAUM, FRANK (*b.* 4 March 1893; *d.* 1 June 1969), pioneering Latin Americanist in the United States. The son of Austrian immigrants who arrived in the United States in 1904, Tannenbaum did graduate work at the Brookings Institution, receiving his doctorate there in 1927. Subsequently, he was an internationally recognized historian at Columbia University from 1935 until his death. A versatile scholar in a time of narrow specialization, he wrote on topics ranging from prison reform to international relations to the history of slavery, arguing that Latin American slavery was more benign than slavery in the United States. His chosen area of concentration, however, was the Mexican Revolution and its consequences. His ground-breaking study of land reform, *The Mexican Agrarian Revolution* (1929), established the focus for his research: village Mexico and its struggle to adjust to the modern world.

Tannenbaum was highly skeptical of large organizations—whether governmental or private sector—and wrote provocative critiques of various theories and plans for large-scale industrialization in Latin America. Often in disagreement with other scholars, he was one of the few leftists to criticize Fidel CASTRO's government in Cuba in the early 1960s.

For Tannenbaum's early career see HELEN DELPAR, "Frank Tannenbaum: The Making of a Latin Americanist, 1914–1933," in *The Americas* 45 (1988): 153–171. Two of TANNENBAUM's many publications are *Peace by Revolution: An Interpretation of Mexico* (1933), and *Ten Keys to Latin America* (1962), which contains his critique of Castro's policies on pp. 201–237.

JOHN A. BRITTON

See also **Manumission.**

TAPAJÓS CHIEFDOM. *See* **Santarém.**

TAPAJÓS RIVER, a major tributary of the AMAZON in central Brazil. About 1,200 miles in length, the Tapajós is 8 to 10 miles wide at its mouth. Only 170 miles of the Tapajós is navigable for steamers due to the large number of cataracts throughout the river. At the mouth of the Tapajós is the city of SANTARÉM, the only major city on the river. In the pre-Columbian period the mouth of the Tapajós was a thriving area, with an estimated population of 86,000. The region is noted for the development of the SANTARÉM civilization, characterized by its high-quality pottery and powerful military, which included the women warriors who are credited with inspiring the myths about the Amazons. The Tapajós region resisted European encroachment until 1639, when it was subjugated by the Portuguese. Throughout most of the colonial period the Tapajós was used as a principal route to the gold-mining regions of MATO GROSSO. In 1956 gold was discovered in the Tapajós region just south of Santarém, an area that is still productive today.

JOHN HEMMING, *Red Gold: The Conquest of the Brazilian Indians, 1500–1760* (1978); *Rand McNally Encyclopedia of World Rivers* (1980); DAVID CLEARY, *Anatomy of the Amazon Gold Rush* (1990); EDWARD J. GOODMAN, *The Explorers of South America* (1992).

MICHAEL J. BROYLES

TAPERINHA, an archaeological culture of the Amazon, circa 7500–5000 B.P. The earliest pottery-age culture in the Americas, Taperinha was first discovered in the 1860s and 1870s by naturalists. The type site is a large shell-heap about 6 yards deep and several acres in area, overlooking the AMAZON floodplain just east of the city of SANTARÉM in Pará. Later archaeologists dismissed

such early pottery sites, as they thought that pottery had come into the basin from the Andes, where pottery is not more than about 4,000 years old. Recent excavations and geophysical surveys at Taperinha and other sites have revealed that they are ancient fishing villages. Whether horticulture was used at this time is not certain because there were few plant remains in the mound. The red-brown pottery was shaped into simple bowls with rare decoration of curved incised lines at the rim. The culture is dated by fifteen radiocarbon dates on pottery, charcoal, and shells and two thermoluminescence dates on the pottery from the type site and a nearby cave.

ANNA CURTENIUS ROOSEVELT et al., "Eighth Millennium Pottery from a Shell Midden in the Brazilian Amazon," in *Science* (1991).

ANNA CURTENIUS ROOSEVELT

TAPIR, mammal related to the horse and rhinoceros. There are three species in the Americas: *Tapirus terrestris* (Brazilian tapir), *Tapir pinchaque* (mountain tapir), and *Tapir Bairdii* (Baird's tapir). The tapir looks like a combination of its two closest relatives and a large pig: it is of short stature, with a heavy body, a thick neck, a prehensile upper lip forming a short, movable trunk, a short tail, and four toes on the front feet and three on the hind feet.

American tapirs, which have dark brown coats, were widely hunted by natives for their highly valued meat and their supposed supernatural healing powers. Their range is from Mexico to South America.

All are threatened with extinction due mainly to destruction of their sole habitat: tropical rain forests. All are legally protected.

ERWIN PATZELT, *Fauna del Ecuador* (1989), pp. 89–91; LUIGI BOITANI and STEFANIA BARTOLI, *Simon and Schuster's Guide to Mammals* (1982), p. 345; FRANCESCO B. SALVATORI, *Rare Animals of the World* (1990), pp. 90, 147.

RAÚL CUCALÓN

TAPUIA, a generic term used by Europeans in colonial Brazil to designate non-Tupi indigenous societies. In the sixteenth century the term applied mainly to Gê-speaking peoples living near the Atlantic coast, particularly the Aimoré south of Bahia, whose persistent opposition to colonial rule lent the Tapuia archetype negative overtones. Though often portrayed as a rude and barbarous people, Tapuia groups possessed an extraordinarily complex social organization and developed sophisticated political relations with the Europeans, particularly with the Dutch during their occupation of Pernambuco (1630–1654) and with the Portuguese during the Indian wars of the Northeast (1687–1720).

JOHN HEMMING, *Red Gold* (1978), esp. chaps. 14 and 16, includes detailed discussions of Tapuia-Dutch and Tapuia-

Portuguese relations during the seventeenth century. For anthropological treatment of Gê social organization, see DAVID MAYBURY-LEWIS, ed., *Dialectical Societies* (1979); and MANUELA CARNEIRO DA CUNHA, ed., *História dos índios no Brasil* (1992).

JOHN M. MONTEIRO

TARAPACÁ, northernmost region of Chile (1990 population 358,088), located almost completely in a desert environment. Only at isolated points along the coast did the availability of water allow the development of major settlements, such as ARICA (1990 population 177,330) and Iquique (1984 population 118,735), dedicated to trade, the shipping of minerals, and fisheries. In some river oases, such as NORTE GRANDE, the production of vegetables, olives, and citrus fruits has flourished. In the past, Iquique was the leading city of Tarapacá for its role as the primary port of export for the nitrate mined in the interior. With the demise of nitrate mining, Arica—only 13 miles from the border with Peru and connected with La Paz, Bolivia, by a narrow-gauge rail—eclipsed Iquique and became even more important in the 1950s and 1960s as a free-trade and duty-free industrial zone. Industry collapsed in the 1970s, but Arica maintained its regional leadership as a trading center with Peru and Bolivia and the site of fish-meal factories.

FEDERICO MARULL BERMÚDEZ, *Historia de la antigua provincia de Tarapacá* (Santiago, 1969); and SERGIO VILLALOBOS, *La economía de un desierto: Tarapacá durante la colonia* (Santiago, 1979).

CÉSAR N. CAVIEDES

TARASCANS (now also called Purépecha), the Native American linguistic and cultural group that in pre-Spanish times occupied most of the area of the present Mexican state of MICHOACÁN. The Tarascans dominated an empire that extended into regions of the present states of Guerrero, Guanajuato, and Jalisco but probably did not reach the Pacific coast. The expansionism of the Tarascans and the AZTECS brought them into conflict that cost many lives but did not give either side a decisive victory.

The Tarascan ruler, known as the *cazonci,* had his capital at Tzintzuntzan on Lake PÁTZCUARO in central Michoacán. The population of the Lake Pátzcuaro basin at the time of the Spanish Conquest was about 100,000. Tzintzuntzan was dominated by a platform on which there were five temple structures called *yácatas.* The principal deity was Curicaueri, a god of the sun and fire, to whom perpetual fires were kept burning. A major female deity, Cuerauáperi, was goddess of fertility in humans and the soil. Religious ceremonies included human sacrifice, particularly of war captives.

The first major Spanish expedition entered the region in 1522, under the leadership of Christóbal de OLID, but it withdrew after six months. The last *cazonci,* Tzintzicha

Tangaxoan, was executed by Nuño de GUZMÁN in 1530. FRANCISCAN missionaries arrived in 1525, followed by AUGUSTINIANS in 1537. The royal judge Vasco de QUIROGA, who became first bishop of Michoacán in 1538, is revered as the protector of the Tarascans.

In 1540–1541 one of the Franciscans, probably Jerónimo de Alcalá, wrote *Relación de las ceremonias y ritos y población y gobierno de los indios de la provincia de Michoacán,* the most informative description of the life and culture of the Tarascans. The missionaries also prepared grammars and dictionaries of the language, which is unrelated to other Mesoamerican tongues. The Tarascan grammar published by Maturino Gilberti in 1558 was the first grammar of an American Indian language to be printed.

During the colonial period the Tarascans maintained a mixed cultural identity at the village level, largely centered in their churches, hospitals, and confraternities. They have survived as an identifiable group in Michoacán, where the language is still spoken in a number of villages, and they are noted for craftsmanship in copper, wood, lacquer, textiles, and pottery.

MATURINO GILBERTI, *Arte de la lengua de Michuacán* (1558; 1987); GEORGE M. FOSTER, *Empire's Children: The People of Tzintzuntzan* (1948); JERÓNIMO DE ALCALÁ, *Relación de las ceremonias y ritos y población y gobierno de los indios de la provincia de Michoacán* (1956; 1977); J. BENEDICT WARREN, *Vasco de Quiroga and His Pueblo-Hospitals of Santa Fe* (1963); DELFINA E. LÓPEZ SARRELANGUE, *La nobleza indígena de Pátzcuaro en la época virreinal* (1965); JERÓNIMO DE ALCALÁ, *The Chronicles of Michoacán,* translated and edited by Eugene R. Crane and Reginald C. Reindorp (1970), a somewhat faulty translation; SHIRLEY GORENSTEIN and HELEN PERLSTEIN POLLARD, *The Tarascan Civilization: A Late Prehispanic Cultural System* (1983); J. BENEDICT WARREN, *The Conquest of Michoacán* (1985).

J. BENEDICT WARREN

TARIJA, a temperate, densely populated, subpuna valley in the southern Andean ranges of Bolivia as well as a city. The region was formerly in the Audiencia of CHARCAS. The "garden city" of Tarija—reminiscent of Seville—was founded in 1574 or 1575 by Luís de Fuentes and named after the first Spanish conqueror to enter the area, Francisco de Tarija. Tarija served as a fortress city against the violent CHIRIGUANO INDIANS, whose territories bordered the valley and whose hostilities continually threatened the stability of the entire *audiencia.* As a defense zone, Tarija (and other similar settlements) prevented Chiriguano expansion, thus fostering economic growth in the Charcas highlands and valleys.

Apart from defense, Tarija functioned as an important agricultural and livestock supplier to the growing POTOSÍ market, especially after the 1545 silver strike. Tarija became a livestock center soon after Hernando PIZARRO established livestock activities there in 1547. The valley also produced maize, wheat, fruits, vegetables, wine, and preserves for the highlands. Tarija, like other areas, was also designated to supply *mita* (draft labor) for the Potosí mines, a considerable burden on local Indians, many of whom, terrified by Chiriguano raids, had fled the area.

Located on the trade route between Tucumán (itself a supplier to the highlands) and Potosí, Tarija was always economically oriented to the highlands. After independence in 1825, Tarija resisted incorporation into Argentina's administrative orbit. Yet, in the 1920s, Bolivia's national railway system excluded Tarija, leaving it to cope with an inadequate transport system to truck products to the highlands. The CHACO WAR further isolated the region, and the 1952 revolution in Bolivia failed to bring Tarija into the mainstream. Continued economic stagnation has prompted many *tarijeños* to migrate to Argentina as seasonal labor, particularly to the Jujuy, Salta, and Tucumán regions. Today, the department of Tarija is the object of several government-sponsored development programs aimed at revitalizing this once-important region.

J. VALERIE FIFER, *Bolivia: Land, Location, and Politics Since 1825* (1972), pp. 7, 168, 186, 191, 224–225, 235; JOSEP M. BARNADAS, *Charcas: Orígenes históricos de una sociedad colonial* (1973), pp. 27, 32, 41, 48, 351, 378–380, 393, 470; HERBERT S. KLEIN, *Bolivia: The Evolution of a Multi-Ethnic Society* (1982); HUMBERTO VÁZQUEZ MACHICADO, JOSÉ DE MESA, and TERESA GISBERT, *Manual de historia de Bolivia*, 2d ed. (1983), p. 126; BROOKE LARSON, *Colonialism and Agrarian Transformation in Bolivia: Cochabamba, 1550–1900* (1988), pp. 60, 70; ENRIQUE FINOT, *Nueva historia de Bolivia* (1989), p. 98.

LOLITA GUTIÉRREZ BROCKINGTON

TARMA, province in the central highlands of Peru, department of Junín, and also the name of its provincial capital. The city of Tarma (1990 population 47,472) is situated at an altitude of 10,130 feet above sea level and only 30 miles east of La Oroya, the RAILWAY and HIGHWAY linkage point with Lima, the capital of Peru. The city was founded in 1538 only 4 miles away from the Incan city of Tarmatambo by orders from conquistador Francisco PIZARRO. Since precolonial times the area has served as a base for penetrating the eastern jungle. During the colonial period Tarma was a strategic commercial, missionary, and military post. It produced coarse TEXTILES. The millenarianist and anti-Spanish Indian rebellion led by Juan Santos ATAHUALPA caused social turmoil in the region between 1742 and 1753.

In modern times Tarma has been a gateway to jungle colonization and the development of the COFFEE-producing areas and the easternmost towns of San Ramón, La Merced, and Satipo. The province has a wide variety of agricultural produce including potatoes, wheat, barley, corn, and quinoa, as well as livestock. In the city of Tarma there are a few factories for producing cement and processing food and fruits. In the early 1950s, Tarma benefited from the regional policy of President Manuel A. ODRÍA, a native of the city of Tarma.

FLORENCIA MALLON, *The Defense of Community in Peru's Central Highlands: Peasant Struggle and Capitalist Transition, 1860–1940* (1983).

ALFONSO W. QUIROZ

TAUBATÉ CONVENTION, an agreement reached in 1906 by the Brazilian coffee-producing states of Minas Gerais, São Paulo, and Rio de Janeiro in the Paulista town of Taubaté. Faced with Brazil's largest bumper coffee crop, state officials and planters sought through federal financial aid and state intervention to control the supply of coffee and support coffee prices.

Coffee was Brazil's leading export product during the nineteenth century and production spread from the Paraíba Valley of São Paulo and Rio de Janeiro into the neighboring provinces of Minas Gerais and Espíritu Santo. The initial problems that beset the coffee economy were associated with the capitalist crises in overseas markets in the early 1870s, coupled with local problems related to deforestation, soil depletion, shortage of capital, and planter indebtedness in the initial coffee-producing areas. The emancipation of the slave labor force in 1888 without compensation to slave owners was followed a year later by the fall of the Brazilian monarchy and the onset of the First Republic. In the final decades of slavery and the monarchy, the dynamic center of the coffee economy shifted from Rio de Janeiro to the interior of São Paulo, where pro-monarchist sectors of the Paulista planter class became increasingly disenchanted with the Republican government's ineffective support measures. Between 1901 and 1903 mildly successful efforts were made to form a planters' political party and in 1902, monarchist coffee planters led a protest rebellion to unseat President CAMPOS SALES and the state government that had responded to the coffee crises of overproduction with a decree that prohibited further planting.

The election of Afonso PENA to the presidency in 1906 coincided with the onset of bureaucratic centralization and modernization under the São Paulo state governorship of Jorge Tibiriçá, and, sympathetic to the plight of Paulista planters, the federal government in 1908 approved the valorization measures outlined in the Taubaté treaty. The treaty called for a £15 million loan with a federal guarantee for the purchase of coffee to hold it off the market and maintain a price above the 1897–1905 international average of thirty-eight francs. All states were to follow São Paulo's example and levy a prohibitive tax on new coffee trees to reduce the supply of coffee. A Coffee Institute was established in São Paulo to regulate the production and commercialization of coffee. A public coffee exchange run by representatives of the planters was to replace the exporters who had been grading coffee, and campaigns to promote Brazilian coffee among foreign consumers were called for. Repayment of the loan would be financed through a three-franc-per-sack export surcharge on coffee and a Caixa de Conversão (Bureau of Exchange) would stabilize the exchange rate.

Many of the treaty's provisions were only implemented partially and some not at all. Financing and storage of coffee continued to be inadequate; the call for a coffee exchange was only fulfilled in 1916; the prohibition on planting new land in São Paulo ended in 1912; and two years later the Caixa de Conversão was terminated. Two additional federal government valorization initiatives rescued coffee producers in ad hoc reactions to crises in the world markets in 1918 and again in 1921.

STEPHEN C. TOPIK, *The Political Economy of the Brazilian State, 1889–1930* (1987); MAURICIO A. FONT, *Coffee, Contention, and Change in the Making of Modern Brazil* (1990).

NANCY PRISCILLA S. NARO

See also **Coffee, Valorization of (Brazil); Coffee Industry.**

TAUNAY, AFFONSO D'ESCRAGNOLLE (*b.* 11 July 1876; *d.* 20 March 1958), Brazilian historian and educator. Taunay's historical studies centered on his adopted city and state of SÃO PAULO. He wrote extensive multivolume works on the early history of that city, on São Paulo's *bandeirantes* (colonial explorers of Brazil's interior), and on the history of Brazilian coffee. He was the son of Alfredo d'Escragnolle Taunay, the Viscount Taunay, a distinguished novelist, historian, and statesman. Educated in Rio de Janeiro as an engineer, the younger Taunay settled in the city of São Paulo to teach science, but soon gravitated to history. He was the director of the Paulista Museum there from 1917 until his retirement in 1945. In 1934 he was named to the first chair of Brazilian history at the University of São Paulo. In addition to history, Taunay's writings include studies on philology and lexicography, and translations of history and literature. He was extremely prolific, authoring an estimated 1,500 books and articles. He also located and edited numerous descriptive works by foreign travelers on Brazil. Taunay's writing tended to be prolix and short on interpretation, but his research was distinguished by solid archival documentation, much of which he himself discovered and published. He pioneered in the history of the city and state of São Paulo and of coffee and is credited with establishing the exploits of the *bandeirantes* as part of the Brazilian historical consciousness.

JOSÉ HONÓRIO RODRIGUES, "Afonso d'Escragnolle Taunay, 1876–1958," in *Hispanic American Historical Review* 38, no. 3 (August 1958): 389–393; MYRIAM ELLIS, *Affonso d'Escragnolle Taunay no Centenário do seu Nascimento* (1977); ODILON NOGUEIRA DE MATOS, *Afonso de Taunay, Historiador de São Paulo e do Brasil* (1977).

EUGENE RIDINGS

TAUNAY, ALFREDO D'ESCRAGNOLLE, VICOMTE DE (*b.* 22 February 1843; *d.* 25 January 1899), Brazilian author and politician. Taunay, born in Rio de Janeiro, was the son of Félix Émile de Taunay, a French painter who came to Brazil in 1816 as a member of the FRENCH ARTISTIC MISSION, with Jean-Baptiste DEBRET. Taunay enlisted in the army in 1861, graduated from the Military Academy in 1864, and served in the WAR OF THE TRIPLE ALLIANCE (1864–1870), in particular at the heroic retreat from Laguna. Soon afterward he wrote an account of the latter, *La retraite de la Lagune* (1871), which was translated into Portuguese a year later by his son, Affonso d'Escragnolle TAUNAY. He published some seven novels, often under pseudonyms, and several travel books. As a deputy for Goiás (1872–1875) and a senator for Santa Catarina (1886–1889), Taunay was active in politics during the last years of the Brazilian Empire, particularly in the cause of immigration. He remained a monarchist during the first years of the Republic. He died in Rio de Janeiro.

The quality of Taunay's fiction varies. The only novel that has been republished, *Inocência* (1872), his second, is the story of an itinerant doctor who falls in love with the young daughter of a landowner in the distant interior of Mato Grosso and of their tragic death while being pursued by her jealous father. Its most notable quality is its realism: Taunay knew this remote area well, and his descriptions of it are much more authentic than those of his contemporary José Martiniano de ALENCAR. Two other novels are *A mocidade de Trajano* (1871), his first, which is set in the coffee-growing area of Campinas, São Paulo, and combines romantic plot and realistic setting, and *O encilhamento* (1893), a rather clumsy but interesting roman à clef about the scandal-ridden boom and bust of 1890–1891. His *Memórias*, up to 1870, published (according to his wishes) a century after his birth, in 1943, is one of the few valuable personal reminiscences written in nineteenth-century Brazil.

ANTÔNIO CÂNDIDO, *Formação da literatura brasileira*, vol., 2 pp. 307–315.

JOHN GLEDSON

TAURIELLO, ANTONIO (*b.* 20 March 1931), Argentine composer, pianist, and conductor. Born in Buenos Aires, he studied composition with Alberto GINASTERA at the National Conservatory and piano with Walter Gieseking in Tucumán. A resident conductor with the opera and ballet at the Teatro Colón, he worked extensively in the United States as assistant director and conductor of the New York City Opera, the American Opera Theater at the Juilliard School of Music, and the Chicago Lyric Opera. Tauriello has been a member of the Agrupación Música Viva (AMV) in Buenos Aires, a group founded by Gerardo GANDINI, Alcides LANZA, and Armando Krieger. The AMV ensemble presented premieres of his works, and with it Tauriello conducted performances of contemporary music in Argentina and New York. He has also appeared as conductor at the Inter-American Music Festivals in Washington, D.C. In 1968 his Piano Concerto was premiered there, a work in which Tauriello sought to explore freer relationships between the soloist and the orchestra, with the piano part existing as an independent entity. Except for some synchronization cues, the pianist can choose the speed and pacing of musical phrases and the duration of individual notes.

Other works by Antonio Tauriello: *Obertura Sinfónica* (1951); *Ricercari 1 à 6* (1963); *Transparencias* for six orchestral groups (1964); *Música* no. 3 for piano and orchestra (1965); *Canti* for violin and orchestra (1967); and *La mansión de Tlaloc* (1969), which premiered during the Third Festival of Music of the Americas and Spain in Madrid in 1970.

Among his chamber music compositions Tauriello has written *Ilynx* for clarinet, double bass, piano, and percussion (1968); *Diferencias* for flute and piano (1969); *Signos de los tiempos* for flute, violin, clarinet, violoncello, and piano (1969); Serenade no. 2 for eight instruments (1966), written to celebrate Alberto Ginastera's fiftieth birthday and *Diferencias* no. 2 for piano (1969).

RODOLFO ARIZAGA, *Enciclopedia de la música argentina* (1971), p. 295; JOHN VINTON, ed., *Dictionary of Contemporary Music* (1974), p. 731; GÉRARD BÉHAGUE, *Music in Latin America: An Introduction* (1979), p. 338; *New Grove Dictionary of Music and Musicians* (1980).

ALCIDES LANZA

TÁVARA Y ANDRADE, SANTIAGO (*b.* 1790; *d.* 28 January 1874), a major liberal intellectual and politician in the mid-nineteenth century. Távara, a native of Piura, received a degree from the Royal Medical College of San Fernando in 1819. He contributed two widely read works to the formation of a liberal outlook in Peru. *Historia de los partidos políticos* was a series of articles explaining the Peruvian political situation in 1851 that appeared in the Lima newspaper *El Comercio*. The articles were collected and edited in 1951 by Jorge BASADRE. Távara also wrote against slavery. His writings formed part of the campaign conducted by a small antislavery movement in Peru. A staunch supporter of Ramón CASTILLA, Távara penned the only coherent argument for the abolition of black slavery in Peru, *Abolición de la esclavitud en el Perú* (1855), which attacked those who argued that abolition would mean a great increase in crime. He won a seat in the National Convention, serving in 1855–1857, and in the national Chamber of Deputies, which he held from the mid-1860s until his defeat in the hotly contested election of 1868. Távara long had fought electoral corruption, but in this instance both he and his opponent were accused of fraud. After his defeat Távara retired from politics. He died in Piura.

HENRY F. DOBYNS and PAUL L. DOUGHTY, *Peru: A Cultural History* (1976); PETER BLANCHARD, *Slavery and Abolition in Early Republican Peru* (1992).

VINCENT PELOSO

See also **Slavery.**

TAVARES, ANTÔNIO RAPÔSO (*b.* 1598; *d.* 1658), backwoodsman of São Paulo, born in São Miguel de Beja, Portugal. In 1628, Tavares commanded a powerful military force of several hundred *paulistas* (residents of São Paulo) and about 2,000 Indians that crushed the Jesuit reductions of Guairá and transferred at least 30,000 GUARANÍ slaves to the farms and plantations of São Paulo. Tavares himself set up a wheat farm along the TIETÊ RIVER with over 100 of the Indian slaves. In search of new captives, he led another large expedition to the Tape missions along the Uruguay River in 1636, again capturing thousands of Guarani slaves.

In 1648, in his most ambitious adventure, Tavares set out from São Paulo in search of the Serranos (possibly Guarani) Indians of the Andean foothills. Repelled by Spanish and Jesuit forces in Paraguay and weakened by hunger and disease, the expedition disbanded, with Tavares and a few followers plunging forward through the heart of the Amazon, finally reaching the Portuguese fort of Gurupá in 1651. Though acclaimed subsequently by historians as a great exploratory venture that contributed to the territorial formation of modern Brazil, the expedition was a resounding failure in its time. After wandering aimlessly through the forests of South America for over three years in search of Indian slaves, Tavares returned to São Paulo, where he died a shattered and impoverished man.

RICHARD MORSE, ed., *The Bandeirantes* (1965), provides translations of contemporary descriptions of *paulista* raids on the missions and an article on Tavares's 1648 expedition. CHARLES RALPH BOXER, *Salvador de Sá and the Struggle for Brazil and Angola* (1952), provides an excellent context for Tavares's activities. See also the detailed account in JOHN HEMMING, *Red Gold* (1979), chaps. 12–13.

JOHN M. MONTEIRO

TAVARES BASTOS, AURELIANO CÂNDIDO (*b.* 20 April 1839; *d.* 3 December 1875), Brazilian legislator and publicist. Tavares Bastos was Brazil's leading exponent of the precepts of nineteenth-century LIBERALISM, promoting them in newspaper articles, books, and parliamentary speeches. Intellectually precocious, he received a doctorate in law at the age of twenty from the law school at São Paulo and was elected imperial deputy of his native province of Alagôas the following year. He served the Liberal Party in Parliament from 1861 until 1868. Tavares Bastos ascribed most of the problems of nineteenth-century Brazil to the heritage of Portuguese absolutism, which he said had bequeathed a deficiency of individual liberty and public spirit. His goal was the modernization of Brazil, based on the examples of the United States and Great Britain. He argued for individual liberty, the usefulness of competition, religious freedom, and administrative decentralization. Among the modernizing measures he advocated were the lessening of government restrictions on business enterprise, the lowering of tariffs, the gradual abolition of slavery, the encouragement of immigration (particularly from northern Europe), the reform of education at all levels, and the creation of competent statistical services. He also called for constitutional change in the form of an independent judiciary, direct elections, and a lessening of the power of the emperor. Based on familiarity with British and French liberal thought, Tavares Bastos's proposals for reform were characterized by thorough research and investigation. The most famous of the legislative measures he fostered was Brazil's opening of the Amazon river system to international commerce in 1866. Many other changes he advocated came to fruition after his premature death from pneumonia.

AURELIANO CÂNDIDO TAVARES BASTOS, *Cartas do Solitário*, 3d ed. (1938); CARLOS PONTES, *Tavares Bastos (Aureliano Cândido), 1839–1875* (1939); EVARISTO DE MORAES FILHO, *As Ideias Fundamentais de Tavares Bastos* (1987).

EUGENE RIDINGS

TÁVORA, JUAREZ (*b.* 14 January 1898; *d.* 18 July 1975), Brazilian military officer, *tenente* leader, and 1955 presidential candidate.

Fifteenth son of a politically active family in Ceará, Távora attended school in nearby towns and then went to Rio and Pôrto Alegre with his brothers to complete high school. In 1916 he began army officer training. After commissioning, he met other junior officers and cadets with whom he would later revolt.

After participating in the 1922 *tenente* rebellion, Távora helped capture São Paulo in 1924. Upon abandoning the city, he assumed greater responsibility for leading the rebels and joined forces with Luís Carlos PRESTES. He gained a lasting reputation for calm, courageous behavior. Captured in 1925, he was sent to prison and began writing a memoir about the revolt.

Escaping in 1927, Távora fled the country and resumed the conspiracy. Eventually he and most of the others joined the REVOLUTION OF 1930, which was organized by Getúlio VARGAS's supporters. Távora assumed command of the Northeast and managed to gain control of the entire region within days. Afterward, he was appointed "Viceroy of the North" to oversee security in that region and became active in the Club 3 de Outubro. He formulated vaguely socialist goals for the movement, some of which he pursued in various administrative posts, including minister of agriculture (1932–1934). When his party failed to win a majority in Ceará in 1934, he returned to active duty as road engineer in the south.

In 1945 Távora joined the National Democratic Union party to support fellow *tenente* Eduardo GOMES. Throughout the coming years Távora acted as senior statesman of the officer corps concerned with petroleum, electric power, steel, and national defense. Finally he ran for president in 1955 but came in second to Juscelino KUBITSCHEK. Mostly retired, Távora remained on the political sidelines until becoming congressman from Rio de Janeiro. His last post was minister of transport under Humberto de Alencar CASTELLO BRANCO (1964–1967).

NEILL MACAULAY, *The Prestes Column* (1974); ISRAEL BELOCH and ALZIRA ALVES DE ABREU, comps., *Dicionário histórico-biográfico brasileiro, 1930–1983* (1984); MARIA CECÍLIA SPINA FORJAZ, *Tenentismo e forças armadas na revolução de 30* (1989).

MICHAEL L. CONNIFF

See also **Tenentismo.**

TAXATION: SPANISH AMERICA. *See* **Public Sector.**

TAXCO, an important Mexican silver-MINING center in the state of GUERRERO, especially associated with the

The town of Taxco, ca. 1928. From Enrique A. Cervantes, *Tasco en el año mil novecientos veintiocho* (Mexico City, 1933). LATIN AMERICAN LIBRARY, TULANE UNIVERSITY.

eighteenth-century mine owner José de la Borda. Known as Tlachco ("place of the ball court") in pre-Hispanic times, it was a source of copper for the Mexica empire. Along with some iron ore, this copper was being worked by Indians under Spanish direction in the 1520s, soon after the triumph of Hernán CORTÉS. The first major silver strikes were made in the 1530s, and Taxco (the Spanish corruption of "Tlachco") became one of the more productive silver-mine towns (*reales de minas*) of New Spain. Since it was located in the indigenous heartland, Indian tribute workers could be used to augment slave and wage labor, something that was not possible in northern mining regions. Despite a series of booms and busts, Taxco remained productive into the twentieth century. It is now a popular tourist site and the source of fine silver products.

There is no scholarly English-language monograph about Taxco currently available. The standard account in Spanish remains MANUEL TOUSSAINT, *Tasco* (1931). Brief, comparative mention of Taxco can be found in PETER J. BAKEWELL, *Silver Mining and Society in Colonial Mexico: Zacatecas, 1546–1700* (1971); and DAVID A. BRADING, *Miners and Merchants in Bourbon Mexico, 1763–1810* (1971). Forced labor in colonial Taxco is discussed in ROBERT HASKETT, " 'Our Trouble with the Taxco Tribute': Involuntary Mine Labor and the Indians of Colonial Cuernavaca," in *Hispanic American Historical Review* 71 (August 1991): 447–475.

ROBERT HASKETT

TAYASAL, the last settled outpost of independent MAYA to be conquered by the Spanish. It is on the south shore of Lake Petén in the central lake region of the department of Petén, Guatemala. Yucatecan chronicles report that the Itzá Maya fled to the south following the fall of CHICHÉN ITZÁ and settled at Tayasal. CORTÉS passed through Tayasal on his cross-peninsular expedition of 1525. Canek, the local Maya ruler, promised Cortés and his twenty soldiers that the Indians would convert to Christianity. However, this had not occurred by 1618, when two Franciscans, dispatched from Mérida, also failed in efforts to convert the Indians to Christianity. (During their visit to Tayasal they smashed a stone idol of one of Cortes's horses, made by fearful Indians when the lame original, left behind in 1525, died.) In 1622 a small military expedition from Mérida was slaughtered before it could attain its goal of conquering Tayasal.

In 1696 and 1697, a 235-man Spanish expeditionary force from Mérida, under the direction of Martín de Ursua, governor of Yucatán, succeeded in reaching the lake. Within a month they built a galley from locally hewn timbers. For twelve days, peaceful efforts to effect the conquest were unsuccessful. Finally, after celebrating a mass at dawn, half the Spanish force rowed toward the town in the galley and defeated the numerous defending Tayasal war canoes with heavy musket fire. The Spaniards seized the town, smashed the Maya idols,

and completed the conquest of the Mayas on 13 March 1697.

In the course of modern archaeological research, questions have arisen about the endpoint of the Itzá migration from northern Yucatán (some evidence suggests nearby TOPOXTÉ rather than Tayasal), although the identification of Tayasal with the final conquest of the MAYA is not subject to doubt.

For an account of the conquest of Tayasal, see J. DE VILLAGUTIERRE SOTO-MAYOR, *Historia de la conquista de la Provincia de el Itzá* (Biblioteca Goathemala, Guatemala, 1933). For information on modern archaeological work in Tayasal, consult ARLEN F. CHASE, "A Contextual Consideration of the Tayasal-Paxcaman Zone, El Peten, Guatemala" (Ph.D. diss., University of Pennsylvania, 1983), "Con manos arriba: Tayasal and Archaeology," in *American Antiquity* 47, no. 1 (1982): 154–167, and "Archaeology in the Maya Heartland: The Tayasal-Paxcaman Zone, Lake Peten, Guatemala," in *Archaeology* 37, no. 5 (1985).

WALTER R. T. WITSCHEY

TAYLOR, ZACHARY (*b.* 24 November 1784; *d.* 9 July 1850), general during the MEXICAN WAR and twelfth president of the United States. Taylor, born in Montebello, Virginia, served in the War of 1812 and in various Indian wars in the Midwest and South. Promoted to brigadier general in the Seminole Wars, he was ordered to Texas in 1844 to provide military support for its annexation by the United States. President James POLK ordered him to the Rio Grande in early 1846 to enforce the U.S. claim to the disputed territory north of that river. On 8 and 9 May 1846, Taylor's troops fought skirmishes with the Mexican army commanded by General Mariano ARISTA. Polk later claimed that these hostilities were the result of a Mexican invasion of U.S. territory, and thus justified a declaration of war.

As commander of the Army of the Rio Grande, Taylor invaded Mexico, and fought and defeated a Mexican army commanded by General Antonio López de SANTA ANNA at Buena Vista, thus securing northern Mexico for the United States. In 1848 he was nominated and elected president. A member of the Whig Party, he opposed slavery in the newly acquired Mexican territories but supported it in the Old South. He died after a short time in office.

OLIVER O. HOWARD, *General Taylor* (1892); JUSTIN HARVEY SMITH, *The War with Mexico*, 2 vols. (1919); BRAINERD DYER, *Zachary Taylor* (1967); JACK K. BAUER, *Zachary Taylor: Soldier, Planter, Statesman of the Old Southwest* (1985).

RICHARD GRISWOLD DEL CASTILLO

TAZUMAL, the most complex architectural group within the Chalchuapa archaeological zone in western El Salvador. It was an important ceremonial and residential center for over a millennium, from the Late Preclassic to the Early Postclassic period (A.D. 1–1300). The largest Classic center in western El Salvador, Tazumal marks the boundary between the Maya to the west and north, and the non-Maya to the southeast.

The Chalchuapa archaeological zone is located in a broad, fertile basin that is ecologically and physiographically intermediate between the Pacific coastal plain and the Maya highlands. It is composed of a series of ceremonial and residential areas, of which Tazumal is the southernmost.

A massive pyramid temple atop a substructural platform dominates the site. A smaller platform, a ball court, and several house mounds complete the group. Construction of Tazumal probably began around A.D. 1. Construction of the pyramid foundation was interrupted about A.D. 250, when the Ilopango volcano erupted violently, blanketing the site with ash, which rendered the area uninhabitable. Construction resumed between A.D. 450 and 650. Basic construction materials were earthen fill, adobe brick or stone set in adobe, and lime-plaster facing painted white. The style of the pyramid is akin to the neighboring and contemporary Teotihuacán-influenced KAMINALJUYÚ.

The final, main period of architectural construction at Tazumal lasted from A.D. 650 to 1300 and witnessed the repeated expansion of the pyramid to its final, massive dimensions—over 23,544 cubic yards in volume. One of the last structures built at Tazumal was the smaller platform, constructed during the Postclassic period (A.D. 900–1400).

Several stone sculptures have been found at Tazumal, including a stela, known as the "Virgin of Tazumal," in the Late Classic Copán Maya tradition. Of the many freestanding sculptures, two were CHACMOOLS, Mexican sacrificial altars.

The contents of several tombs at Tazumal indicate Honduran and other Central American contact. Polychrome pottery from COPÁN and the Ulúa Valley, both in western Honduras, was found in tombs at Tazumal. One tomb contained copper-gold figurines from the Nicoya Peninsula of Costa Rica.

As a border area between the Maya and non-Maya, Tazumal never reached a size comparable to its early Classic ally, Kaminaljuyú, or its Late Classic ally, Copán; but neither did it suffer the devastating effects of shifting Classic Maya political fortunes.

Tazumal was probably abandoned during the late Postclassic period, around A.D. 1300. By the time of the Spanish conquest, Maya-speaking Pogomam lived in the Chalchuapa zone.

JOHN M. LONGYEAR III, "Archaeological Investigations in El Salvador," in *Memoirs of the Peabody Museum of Archaeology and Ethnology, Harvard University* 9, no. 2 (1944); STANLEY H. BOGGS, "Archaeological Excavations in El Salvador," in *For the Dean*, edited by Erik K. Reed and Dale S. King (1950); JOHN M. LONGYEAR III, "Archaeological Survey of El Salvador," in *Handbook of Middle American Indians*, vol. 4, *Archaeological Frontiers and External Connections*, edited by Gordon Ekholm and Gordon Willey (1966); ROBERT J. SHARER, ed., *The Prehistory of Chalchuapa, El Salvador*, 3 vols. (1978).

KATHRYN SAMPECK

TEATRO COLÓN, Argentina's principal opera house, located in Buenos Aires. The Teatro Colón opened on 25 May 1908 with Verdi's *Aïda* under the baton of Luigi Mancinelli; it succeeded an 1857 house of the same name. Seating approximately four thousand people, the Teatro Colón is the biggest and most prominent opera house in Latin America and one of the major houses of the world. Fifty-eight premieres of Argentine operas have been staged there, among them Héctor Panizza's *Aurora* (1908), Felipe BOERO's *El matrero* (1929), Juan José CASTRO's *Bodas de sangre* (1956) and the first Argentine performance of Castro's *Proserpina y el extranjero* (1960), Alberto GINASTERA's *Don Rodrigo* (1964), and Mario Perusso's *La voz del silencio* (1969) and *Escorial* (1989).

The Teatro Colón's repertory included works by Monteverdi and Cavalli, all the traditional Italian, French, and German operatic repertoire as well as contemporary works such as Berg's *Wozzeck* and *Lulu*, Stravinsky's *The Rake's Progress*, Janáček's *Jenůfa*, Dallapiccola's *Il prigioniero* and *Volo di notte*, Pizzetti's *La figlia di Jorio*,

The Teatro Colón. Buenos Aires. © PETER MENZEL / STOCK, BOSTON.

Schoenberg's *Erwartung* and *Moses and Aaron*, Milhaud's *Christophe Colomb*, and Poulenc's *Dialogues des Carmélites*. One of the Teatro Colón's most notable events was the world premiere of Ernesto Halffter's completed version of Manuel de Falla's *La Atlántida*, sung in Catalán (1963). Also noteworthy were the South American premieres of Mozart's *Idomeneo* and Berlioz's *Les Troyens* and *Benvenuto Cellini*. A very special event was the production in 1982 of the earliest Spanish opera preserved, *Celos aun del aire matan* (1660), by Juan Hidalgo with a libretto by Pedro Calderón de la Barca. The Teatro Colón also presents symphonic concerts, recitals, and ballet.

ROBERTO CAAMAÑO, *La historia del Teatro Colón* (1969); RODOLFO ARIZAGA, *Enciclopedia de la música argentina* (1971); *New Grove Dictionary of Opera*, vol. 1 (1992).

SUSANA SALGADO

TEATRO SOLÍS, Uruguay's principal opera house, located in Montevideo. Opened on 25 August 1856, the Teatro Solís seats twenty-eight hundred people and is the oldest opera house in the Americas. In 1888 Adelina Patti, the great nineteenth-century diva, sang in seven operas there. That same year Verdi's *Otello* was performed with the soprano Romilda Pantaleoni in the role of Desdemona, which she had created for the world premiere at Milan's La Scala the year before. The Solís's golden age began in 1903, when the 285-member opera company of La Scala arrived, led by the conductor Arturo Toscanini and with a roster of singers headed by Enrico Caruso. The Solís presented operatic masterpieces very soon after their world premieres. Puccini's *Madama Butterfly* was performed with both Rosina Storchio and maestro Toscanini, six months after its La Scala premiere. José Oxilia, Victor Damiani, and José Soler were among the world-renowned Uruguayan singers who performed at the Solís. During World War I and the postwar era the Solís hosted famous artists such as Artur Rubinstein and leading orchestras like the Vienna Philharmonic. Vaslav Nijinsky's last stage performance was at the Solís in October 1917. George Gershwin's *Porgy and Bess* was performed for the first time in Montevideo at the Solís in 1955, under the direction of Alexander Smallens, who conducted the Broadway premiere in 1935. The Teatro Solís maintains its commitment to the presentation of local and foreign artists in operatic, orchestral, dance, and dramatic performances.

SUSANA SALGADO, *Breve historia de la música culta en el Uruguay*, 2d ed. (1980), and *The Teatro Solís of Montevideo* (forthcoming); *New Grove Dictionary of Opera*, vol. 3 (1992), p. 453.

SUSANA SALGADO

TEBICUARY RIVER, stream approximately 300 miles long springing from the Sierra de Caapacú in the south-central highlands of Paraguay and draining the Cordillera of Caaguazú. In a wide but shallow basin around Villarrica, the soil lends itself to cotton and rice cultivation and serves as natural pastures for cattle. In the extended wetlands, ranching is also practiced, and hides are processed in the tanneries of Villarrica or other small settlements along the river, such as Borja, Iturbe, and Villa Florida. The Tebicuary River joins the PARAGUAY RIVER 9 miles north of Pilar after draining the Lago Venturoso swamps.

HUGO G. FERREIRA, *Geografía del Paraguay* (Asunción, 1975).

CÉSAR N. CAVIEDES

TECHNOLOGY. The Spaniards arrived in the New World to find advanced civilizations coexisting with less advanced tribal organizations. The archaeological sites of MACHU PICCHU, TEOTIHUACÁN, and TIKAL testify to the remarkable construction and architectural skills of pre-Columbian civilizations. Mayan knowledge of astronomy, the pre-Incan irrigation works (1300–1400 B.C.) in northern Peru, and the terraced agricultural system of the Incas are additional evidence of advanced Indian technology. Indians had bred a variety of lupine seed into a prolific bean and accomplished equally stunning advances with corn, potatoes, and many other plants. They also developed a method for predicting climate by observing astrological, atmospheric, and oceanic phenomena, as well as the behavior of flora and fauna. All of this existed side by side with slash-and-burn agriculture and the primitive hunting methods of other Indians.

Since the pre-Columbian period, Latin America has relied heavily on technology from abroad, yet the region has not been without its own important innovations. But despite the steady introduction of new technologies to advanced economic sectors, a vast segment of Latin America's population has not experienced the impact of new technologies. Moreover, the adoption of new techniques has often failed to produce sustained, domestic technological advance.

MINING, SUGAR, AND HENEQUEN

Indians mined silver, gold, copper, and lead, usually from shallow pits, long before the arrival of the Spaniards. During colonization the Spanish introduced deep-shaft mining techniques that significantly increased the amount of ore that was accessible, and a major technological breakthrough was achieved at the Purísima Grande mine in Pachuca, Mexico, in the mid-1550s when Bartolomé de Medina developed a new amalgamation process for silver, which used large amounts of mercury to extract prodigious amounts of silver from mines in such areas as Zacatecas, Mexico, and Pachuco, Peru. Although the basic technology remained in use for about three centuries, there were significant increases in productivity due to technological change. For example, improved furnaces for processing mercury were introduced in Peru in 1633 by Lope de Saavedra, and steam engines were used in mining from the early 1800s.

During the late nineteenth century, sugar from the Pernambuco region was Brazil's leading export. The Pernambuco sugar industry demonstrated an ability to absorb both superior species of cane and move efficient equipment. In the first part of the 1800s, creole sugar-cane was replaced by cayenne cane, which was larger, had more extensive branching, contained greater amounts of sugar, and more effectively withstood drought. After 1879 a disease afflicting the cayenne cane motivated the importation of species from Java and Mauritius. As for advances in sugar-processing technology, around the middle of the nineteenth century, sugar producers began shifting from vertical rollers for grinding cane to horizontal rollers that applied greater pressure, faster grinding, and better distribution of the cane on the rollers. Steam engines gradually replaced animal power, and vacuum pans were installed in the 1870s for evaporation.

The production and export of Yucatán henequen fiber expanded rapidly in the 1880s. Equipment for stripping the fiber was invented in the Yucatán, but interests from the United Kingdom and the United States took over most of the production. By 1880 replacement parts were being produced in the Yucatán, and by 1910 local shops built defibration machines and henequen presses. Innovators in the Yucatán were able to improve on designs and increase operating efficiency, and production reached a peak with World War I.

Mining in Latin America, Pernambucan sugar, and henequen fiber in the Yucatán all enjoyed a period of success and demonstrated an ability to adopt new production techniques. The mining and the henequen industries displayed a good deal of local technological mastery. Yet none of these activities launched sustained technological innovations that could spread to other sectors. Cheap land and labor blunted the incentive to modernize production techniques and held the rate of technology adoption far below optimum.

OTHER DISAPPOINTING EXPERIENCES
When considered as components of a productive system, imported technologies were not always unequivocally superior. The *chinampa* agricultural technique used by the Aztecs, and probably the Mayans, featured raised fields, intensive cultivation, and a variety of crops.

During the first half of the nineteenth century, SALADEROS (beef drying and salting plants) along the Río de la Plata began to operate for an export market. In the 1870s freezing and insulation technologies gave rise to the FRIGORÍFICOS (refrigeration ships) that began to replace the *saladeros*. Further advances in temperature control led to significant exports of beef and mutton to Great Britain beginning around 1900. Although Argentine entrepreneurs recognized a high profit opportunity, virtually all of the *frigoríficos* were operated by

foreign interests. The refrigeration technology itself posed no problem for national entrepreneurs, but the main difficulty lay in mastering the complex "soft technologies" involving the precise timing of receiving beef consignments and loading, unloading, and wholesaling the product with little room for error. Without these organizational, managerial, and marketing capacities, Argentine entrepreneurs faced high risks.

During 1944–1955 a Mexican monopoly, Syntex Company, gained complete dominance over European competitors in the production of steroid hormones. The firm's success was based on three discoveries. In 1949 barbasco was discovered in Mexico. This plant had much higher yields of steroids and was in greater supply than alternative sources. During the same year, two researchers at the Mayo Clinic in the United States found that cortisone was helpful in treating the symptoms of arthritis. And in 1951 the Upjohn Company discovered an inexpensive technique for altering the molecular structure of the steroid. This meant an increased demand for barbasco-derived progesterone that could now be used as an intermediate material for the production of cortisone. Syntex thrived during the 1960s, but by the mid-1970s, steroid hormone production was once again controlled by foreign enterprises and exports had shrunk from 545 pounds in 1969 to 260 pounds in 1976.

Technological breakthroughs outside the region have occasionally hurt Latin American development. A classic example was the drastic decline in Chile's nitrate exports due to the Haber process, a method of synthesizing ammonia from nitrogen and hydrogen, developed in the early 1900s by the German Fritz Haber.

ENCOURAGING EXPERIENCES
Mexican research led to the successful development and export of glass manufacturing equipment, technologies for deep drilling in petroleum extraction, and a method of producing paper from bagasse.

Brazil's production of ethanol from sugarcane and other vegetation is an impressive technological achievement, although it is controversial in terms of economic justification and environmental impact. In 1975 Brazil launched its huge research and development program to produce and substitute ethanol for gasoline. Brazilian researchers were able to upgrade older fermentation methods and achieve necessary technological changes in processing equipment, automobile engines, and sugar production. As of 1990 ethanol accounted for about 15 percent of Brazil's liquid fuel requirements. Brazil also has a thriving small- and medium-sized aircraft industry. Based largely on Brazilian design and technical innovations, the industry has been able to adjust rapidly to changing global technological and market conditions.

The first nuclear power in Latin America was produced at the Atucha I plant in Argentina in 1974, a year during which Brazil and Mexico began to install nuclear

Alcohol at the pumps in Rio de Janeiro. © ROBIN LAURANCE / PHOTO RESEARCHERS, INC.

power reactors. During the 1970s Colombia, Chile, Peru, and Venezuela had working nuclear centers, while Bolivia, Ecuador, Jamaica, and Uruguay announced intentions to establish their own centers. Cuba signed an agreement with the Soviet Union to install nuclear stations, but after a long series of difficulties, Cuba finally stopped construction in 1992. Chile and Peru have been in the forefront of experimental research to commercialize the extraction of copper through a process of microbial leaching. In Mexico, iron ores are transported by the most advanced, computer-driven pipeline system in the world. Iron slurry is piped from the mining sites of La Perla and Hercules to a steel plant in the city of Monclova and arrives at the end of the 135-mile system with the ores blended to achieve the proper mix of impurities. Studies indicate that many Latin American manufacturing firms have improved productivity by a constant stream of minor intraplant innovations.

RECENT TRENDS

During the late 1960s and early 1970s many of the larger nations of Latin America, including Chile, Colombia, Mexico, Peru, and Venezuela, established or significantly strengthened their national councils for science and technology. During the same period, Argentina,

Brazil, Mexico, and the Andean Pact established measures to regulate the importation of technology; this was meant to eliminate imperfections in the transfer of technology that Latin American countries felt put them at a disadvantage. At the same time there has been an increase in the importation of technology along with an emphasis on fostering internal technological capacity. There is evidence that Argentina, Brazil, and Mexico are achieving success. All three are exporting capital goods, consulting contracts, civil engineering contracts, and turnkey plant facilities, as well as making some foreign investments that involve technology transfers. While hardly significant by world standards, the small but growing export of technically sophisticated goods and services is a promising indicator of growing regional technological capabilities.

The economically advanced nations in Latin America seem determined to participate in the microelectronics and biotechnological revolutions. Argentina, Brazil, and Mexico have national policies that promote local production of computers and associated peripheral equipment, and the latter two countries have met with some success. They are also experiencing a rapid expansion of software production. Progress in biotechnology is illustrated by the propagation of potato cultivars through tissue-culture techniques in Argentina, a new strain of inoculums for soybeans developed in Brazil, and single-cell protein production in Mexico.

Despite encouraging bright spots, Latin American efforts to develop technology face a number of problems. There are wide fluctuations in national science and technology budgets, and little research and development is undertaken outside the largest metropolitan areas. A disproportionate emphasis is placed on pure research as opposed to more applied pursuits, resources are spread too thin to support individual research projects, there are inadequate linkages between research institutes and professions using technology, and there is a lack of appreciation in political and economic circles for the potential of technological advance for socioeconomic development. Outside Argentina, Brazil, and Mexico, Latin America's technological achievements have been modest at best.

MODESTO BARGALLÓ, *La minería y la metalurgía en América Española durante la época colonial (1955)*; PETER L. EISENBERG, *The Sugar Industry in Pernambuco: Modernization Without Change, 1840–1910* (1974), esp. pp. 32–62; M. B. A. CRESPI, "La energía nuclear en América Latina; Necesidades y Posibilidades," in *Interciencia* 4, no. 1 (1979): 22–29; DAVID FELIX, "On the Diffusion of Technology in Latin America," in *Technological Progress in Latin America: Prospects for Overcoming Dependency*, edited by James H. Street and Dilmus D. James (1979); ERIC N. BAKLANOFF and JEFFERY T. BRANNON, "Forward and Backward Linkages in a Plantation Economy: Immigrant Entrepreneurship and Industrial Development in Yucatán, Mexico," in *Journal of Developing Areas* 19, no. 1 (1984): 83–94; GARY GEREFFI, *The Pharmaceutical Industry and Dependency in the Third World* (1983), esp. pp. 53–163; CHRISTOPHER ROPER and JORGE SILVA, eds., *Science and Technology in Latin America* (1983); CARL J.

DAHLMAN and FRANCISCO C. SERCOVICH, "Exports of Technology from Semi-Industrial Economies and Local Technological Development," in *Journal of Development Economics* 16, nos. 1–2 (1984): 63–99; ARMAND PEREIRA, *Ethanol, Employment, and Development: Lessons from Brazil* (1966); JORGE M. KATZ, ed., *Technology Generation in Latin American Manufacturing Industries* (1987); INTER-AMERICAN DEVELOPMENT BANK, *Economic and Social Progress in Latin America, 1988 Report* (1988), esp. pp. 105–283); WILLIAM E. COLE, "Technology, Ceremonies, and Institutional Appropriateness: Historical Origins of Mexico's Agrarian Crisis," in *Progress Toward Development in Latin America: From Prebisch to Technological Autonomy*, edited by James L. Dietz and Dilmus D. James (1990).

DILMUS D. JAMES

See also **Agriculture; Energy; Gasohol Industry; Henequen Industry; Mining; Nuclear Industry; Sugar Industry.**

TECÚN-UMÁN (*d.* 20 February 1524), native-American leader of resistance to the Spanish conquest of Guatemala under Pedro de ALVARADO Y MESÍA. Son of the Quiché king Kicab Tanub, and a leader of the Quiché armies, Tecún-Umán has been identified by some writers as the war leader mentioned by Pedro de Alvarado in his first letter of *relación* (recounting) to Hernán CORTÉS. Alvarado speaks of the warrior as one of the four lords of Utatlán, the Quiché capital, and as general of the region. Alvarado says that Tecún-Umán was killed at the battle of Piñal. (The date is disputed, but many agree on 20 February 1524.)

Since then, especially in the twentieth century, there has been considerable accretion of myth and legend to the name of Tecún-Umán. He was proclaimed the national hero of Guatemala on 22 March 1960.

MURDO J. MACLEOD

TEGUCIGALPA, capital of Honduras. Although the site was probably occupied for millennia before the Spanish conquest, the municipality itself was founded upon the discovery of silver mines by Spanish explorers in the 1570s (according to local lore, "Tegucigalpa" means "hill of silver"). When reports of the rich lodes in and around Tegucigalpa reached the Spanish king, he designated the region an *alcaldía mayor*, raising it to municipal status and granting it limited autonomy from Comayagua. The *Real de Minas de San Miguel de Tegucigalpa* was probably formally established on 29 September 1578. By this act, Tegucigalpa became independent of the provincial capital and episcopal see at Comayagua, thus planting a seed of municipal rivalry between the two.

When the most accessible veins of silver played out a few years later, and the lack of adequate labor and transportation facilities, insufficient capital, inappropriate technology, and meager supplies of mercury severely reduced MINING activity, the town shrank in size but

did not disappear altogether. Cattle ranching, commerce, and political and ecclesiastical administration combined with residual silver mining to sustain Tegucigalpa as the largest and most prosperous town in colonial Honduras. Indeed, there was still sufficient mining activity to prompt CHARLES III to redesignate Tegucigalpa an official mining district (*real de minas*) in 1762. Although the *alcaldía mayor* was briefly suppressed in the waning days of the Spanish era, it was revived in 1812.

When Central America gained its independence from Spain, Tegucigalpa and Comayagua agreed, on 30 August 1824, at the Constituent Assembly meeting at Cedros, that the two towns would take turns serving as the capital of the Province of Honduras. This arrangement was continued informally after the breakup of the UNITED PROVINCES OF CENTRAL AMERICA after 1838. In 1880, however, President Marco Aurelio SOTO moved the seat of government permanently to Tegucigalpa, where it has remained ever since. In 1907, Bishop José María Martínez y Cabañas successfully negotiated the translation of the ecclesiastical see from Comayagua to Tegucigalpa; since then the seat has been raised to archbishopric. For historical and geographical reasons, the country was never able to link its new capital, Tegucigalpa, to a railroad, and, even today, the PAN-AMERICAN HIGHWAY passes some fifty miles to the south of the capital on its way down the isthmus from San Salvador to Managua. Despite both these bottlenecks, Tegucigalpa, with a population of more than 600,000, has experienced a massive influx of CAMPESINOS from the hinterland and is undergoing all the typical growing pains of rapid urbanization.

WILLIAM V. WELLS, *Explorations and Adventures in Honduras* (1857); RÓMULO ERNESTO DÚRON Y GAMERO, *La provincia de Tegucigalpa bajo el gobierno de Mallol* (1904); OSCAR ACOSTA, ed., *Antología elogio de Tegucigalpa* (1978); LESTER D. LANGLEY, "Down in Tegoose," in his *Central America: The Real Stakes— Understanding Central America Before It's Too Late* (1985).

KENNETH V. FINNEY

TEHUACÁN, a city and a valley, about 150 miles south of Mexico City at the southern edge of the state of Puebla. In this valley, corn (*Zea mays*) was first domesticated some 7,000 years ago. Early corncobs, less than an inch long, were uncovered in early levels of two rock shelters, Ajuereado and San Marcos; from the upper levels of these caves and others 26,000 specimens have been gathered that document corn's development from its wild ancestor to the present-day races. Paralleling the record of maize evolution in this stratified cave sequence are data showing the complete cultural development, starting with the early hunters of Ajuereado from 1500 to 900 B.C. In El Riego times (7000–5000 B.C.) they became foragers. These foragers then began to cultivate some plants—mixta squash, avocado, gourds, and CHILI peppers—in the incipient agricultural stage called

Coxcatlán (5000–3400 B.C.). During the Abejas phase (3400–2300 B.C.), the Tehuacán people grew increasing numbers of domesticated plants—moschata squash, black and white zapotes, common and tepary beans—but continued to be incipient agriculturalists, sometimes living in pit house villages.

Sedentary village life, characterized by corn agriculture and crude pottery, occurred in the poorly documented Purrón phase (2300–1500 B.C.). Subsequent stages of development were much like those in the rest of Mesoamerica: Formative—Ajalpán (1500–900 B.C.) and Santa María (900–200 B.C.); Classic—Palo Blanco (200 B.C.–A.D. 700); and Postclassic—Venta Salada (A.D. 700–1500, the time of the Spanish conquest).

Archaeological investigations in this valley over a twenty-five-year period (1960–1985) have documented one of the few complete and unbroken cultural sequences for Middle America. Even more significant, Tehuacán records not only the domestication of basic New World plants—corn, squash, and beans—but also the development of agriculture itself.

DOUGLAS S. BYERS, *Tehuacán: El primer horizonte de Mesoamérica* (1968): RICHARD S. MAC NEISH, ed., *The Prehistory of the Tehuacán Valley*, 5 vols. (1972).

RICHARD S. MacNEISH

TEHUANTEPEC, ISTHMUS OF. The Mexican Isthmus of Tehuantepec, 137 miles wide, is located between the Bay of Campeche on the north and the Gulf of Tehuantepec on the south. Described by Miguel Covarrubias as "a bottleneck of jungle and brush," the isthmus is the natural frontier between North and Central America. Its territory is shared almost equally by the states of Oaxaca and Veracruz, and it separates the southern states of Yucatán, Campeche, Tabasco, and Chiapas from the rest of Mexico. Its geography is extremely diverse, ranging from the isolated Chimalapa Mountains to the fertile plains and tropical grasslands on the Gulf coast, and to the arid Pacific lowlands. Its indigenous inhabitants (NAHUAS, Popolocas, Mixes, Zoques, Huaves, Chontales, and both valley and isthmus ZAPOTECS) have maintained a diverse linguistic and cultural heritage despite numerous conquests, colonizations, and intrusions from pre-Columbian to modern times. Despite that diversity, however, the region is known for its matriarchal society and distinctive female costumes and hairstyles, often worn and depicted by Mexican artist Frida KAHLO.

The geography and strategic location of the isthmus made it the favored site of numerous international schemes to construct interoceanic communication between the Gulf and the Pacific. Hernán CORTÉS first referred to that possibility in his fourth letter to King Charles V, and the first detailed survey was performed in 1771. Between 1842 and 1894 more than nine different foreign promoters were granted concessions and generous subsidies to complete the route, all of which failed.

President Porfirio DÍAZ inaugurated the Tehuantepec Railroad and the modern port facilities at COATZCOALCOS and Salina Cruz in 1907. The railway was immensely profitable until 1914, when the combination of

Tehuantepec women, Mexico City, 1986. Reproduced from *Juchitan de las mujeres* (Mexico, 1989). PHOTO BY GRACIELA ITURBIDE.

the Mexican Revolution, World War I, and the inauguration of the Panama Canal severely limited its usefulness. In recent decades, the Mexican government has invested substantially in local infrastructure to support the PETROLEUM and TOURISM industries, but the area remains underdeveloped.

CHARLES ÉTIENNE BRASSEUR DE BOURBOURG, *Voyage sur l'Isthme de Tehuantepec, dans l'état de Chiapas et de la République de Guatemala* (1861), translated into Spanish by Elisa Ramírez Castañeda as *Viaje al istmo de Tehuantepec* (1981); MIGUEL COVARRUBIAS, *Mexico South: The Isthmus of Tehuantepec* (1946); EDWARD B. GLICK, "The Tehuantepec Railroad: Mexico's White Elephant," in *Pacific Historical Review* 22 (1953): 373–382.

PAUL GARNER

TEHUELCHES (or Aonikenks, as they refer to themselves), indigenous inhabitants, also called PATAGONES, of the Patagonian steppes north of the Strait of Magellan. Anthropologists divide the group into those people who occupied the area from the strait north to the Santa Cruz River—the Tehuelche meridionals—and those who occupied the semiarid region east of the cordillera from the Santa Cruz River north to the Río Negro—the Tehuelche septentrionals. The word *tehuelche* means "people of the south" (*tehuel*, meaning "south," and *che*, "people") in Mapudungun (Mapuche) and came into common usage in the mid-colonial era as intercultural contacts between Mapuches, CREOLES, and pampas Indian groups intensified in the aboriginal homelands of the Aonikenks.

The hunt for GUANACO organized the movements of the Tehuelches, who followed the dispersed herds on foot through the arid Patagonian steppes in a seasonal cycle. Tehuelche subsistence on guanaco was supplemented by the rhea (nandu) and roots and seeds gathered seasonally. Known for their endurance in the desertlike environment of the Patagonian region south of the Río Negro, the Tehuelche meridionals maintained a footbound transhumant subsistence cycle well into the eighteenth century.

When neighboring groups to the north and west (MAPUCHES, PEHUENCHES, PAMPAS) acquired the horse in the sixteenth century, they expanded their barter and hunting excursions into the frontiers of the aboriginal territory of the Tehuelches. The northern Tehuelches, however, continued to maintain their traditional subsistence patterns on foot until the beginning of the eighteenth century, when they too adopted the horse, which facilitated a greater range for hunting and intensified inter-ethnic trading. This innovation led finally to a strong commercial exchange with Chilean colonists in Punta Arenas in the nineteenth century, by which time the Tehuelches had replaced the stone and bone tools used for millennia with tools of metal, glass, and other foreign elements.

It was not until the end of the nineteenth and early twentieth centuries that the Tehuelches lost their cultural autonomy, but the end came quickly when Argentine, Chilean, and European colonists effectively curtailed their movements through a combination of military operations, *matanzas* (slaughters), massive deportations, and the intensified exposure to contagious diseases.

JULIAN H. STEWARD, ed., *Handbook of South American Indians*, vol. 1 (1946), pp. 17–29; RODOLFO M. CASAMIQUELA, *Rectificaciones y ratificaciones hacia una interpretación definitiva del panorama etnológico de la Patagonia y area septentrional adyacente* (1965); MUSEO CHILENO DE ARTE PRECOLOMBINO, *Hombres del sur: Aonikenk, Selknam, Yamana, Kaweshkar* (1987).

KRISTINE L. JONES

TEIXEIRA, ANISIO ESPINOLA (*b.* 12 June 1900; *d.* 11 March 1971), rector of the University of Brasília (1963–1964) and one of Brazil's most influential educational reformers. In his career as educational administrator he took steps to expand, democratize, and secularize public education. He was born to a landowning family in Caetité, Bahia. After working in Bahia from 1924 to 1927, Teixeira, an admirer of John Dewey and aspects of the North American educational system, earned an M.A. in 1928 from Columbia University's Teachers' College. Moving in 1931 to Rio de Janeiro, Teixeira became a leader of a group known as the Pioneers of New Education. Accused of being a subversive, a populist, and an atheist by various conservative groups, he lost his administrative post in 1935 because of political purges and stayed out of government work, alternately managing a prosperous export business in Bahia and living in Europe, until the end of Getúlio VARGAS's Estado Novo in 1945. He then resumed work as a high-level educational administrator, running two national institutes—the Coordination of Training for Advanced Scholars (Coordenação de Aperfeiçoamento de Pessoa de Nivel Superior—CAPES) and the Instituto Nacional de Estudos Pedagógicos (INEP)—and earning the wrath of conservative political groups and the support of intellectuals.

In 1963 Teixeira became rector of the University of Brasília, only to be ousted by the military coup a year later. When the new government threatened to prosecute him for alleged administrative irregularities, a wave of protests from international academic circles came to his defense. Granted special permission to leave Brazil by President Humberto Castelo Branco, Teixeira traveled to the United States, where he accepted university teaching positions. He returned to Brazil in 1966.

Teixeira's personal archive is held by the Centro de Pesquisa e Documentação de História Contemporánea (CPDOC) of the Fundação Getúlio Vargas. A partial list of his publications includes *Educação para a democracia* (1936); *Educação progressiva* (1950); *Pequena introdução à filosofia da educação, a escola progressiva ou, a transformação da escola*, 7th ed. (1975); and *Educação e o mundo moderno*, 2d ed. (1977). Works about Teixeira include FERNANDO DE AZEVEDO, "Anisio Teixeira e a inteligéncia," in

Figuras de meu convívio (1960); HERMES LIMA, *Anisio Teixeira: Estadista da educação* (1978); *Dicionário histórico-biográfico brasileiro, 1930–1983,* vol. 4 (1984).

SUEANN CAULFIELD

TEJADA SORZANO, JOSÉ LUIS (*b.* 12 January 1882; *d.* 4 October 1938), president of Bolivia (27 November 1934–17 May 1936). A lawyer by profession, Tejada Sorzano was an expert in banking and a diplomat. He was a legislator from 1914 to 1918 and was minister of finance (Hacienda) during the government of José GUTIÉRREZ GUERRA. He was elected vice president in 1931 and assumed the presidency when President Daniel SALAMANCA was forced to resign.

The CHACO WAR with Paraguay was the main preoccupation of Tejada Sorzano. There were genuine attempts to secure peace for the beleaguered nation, but Tejada Sorzano had little support and was overthrown by frustrated military officers.

PORFIRIO DÍAZ MACHICAO, *Historia de Bolivia: Salamanca, Guerra de Chaco, Tejada Sorzano 1931–1936* (1955); DAVID H. ZOOK, JR., *The Conduct of the Chaco War* (1960).

CHARLES W. ARNADE

TEJEDA, LEONOR DE (*b.* 1574; *d.* ca. 1640), educator and nun. Born in Córdoba to a prominent conquistador family, Leonor de Tejeda was married to general Manuel de Fonseca y Contreras when she was twenty years old. While her husband was serving as lieutenant governor of Buenos Aires (1594–1598), Leonor began to see a need for an institution to harbor elite women with a religious vocation. When her husband returned to Córdoba, she began a school for gentlewomen in her home. The childless couple soon petitioned the crown to allow them to undertake the foundation of the first convent in Córdoba. Widowed in 1612, Tejeda continued to use her fortune and her influence with the bishop to press for the convent, which was finally created on the site of her home in 1613. Among the first group of sixteen women who entered the convent of Santa Catalina de Sena was Tejeda, who took the name of Mother Catalina de Sena and served as prioress until 1627. In 1628 she moved to the city's newly founded second convent, that of Santa Teresa de Jesús, where she served as prioress until 1637. She returned to the Sena convent sometime before her death.

ENRIQUE UDAONDO, *Diccionario biográfico colonial argentino* (1945), pp. 870–872.

SUSAN M. SOCOLOW

TEJEDA OLIVARES, ADALBERTO (*b.* 28 March 1883; *d.* 8 September 1960), military figure and governor of the state of Veracruz (1920–1924 and 1928–1932). Adalberto Tejeda Olivares was a well-known Mexican statesman of the 1920s who strove to implement the Constitution of 1917 through radical political, economic, social, and anticlerical reforms.

Tejeda grew up in the predominantly Indian canton of Chicontepec, Veracruz, and attended engineering school in Mexico City. With the outbreak of the MEXICAN REVOLUTION in 1910, he enlisted in the forces of Venustiano CARRANZA (1859–1920) and rose to the rank of colonel. While serving as state delegate to the Constitutional Convention of 1916–1917, he advocated strong anticlerical measures and stringent limits on foreign ownership of subsoil rights. The two-time governor of Veracruz championed the rights of the urban and rural lower classes by supporting their efforts to organize, strike, obtain land, and enter into politics. President Plutarco E. CALLES (1877–1945) appointed him to serve as minister of government from 1925–1928, during which time he pursued an active anticlerical policy against the Catholic rebels, the *cristeros.* In 1934 the ex-governor ran for the presidency as an independent socialist, defying the official revolutionary party. He was subsequently politically ostracized by his assignment to diplomatic posts in France (1935–1937), Spain (1937–1939), and Peru. In 1948 he became a brigadier general. He died in Mexico City.

HEATHER FOWLER SALAMINI, *Agrarian Radicalism in Veracruz, 1920–1938* (1978); ROMANA FALCÓN and SOLEDAD GARCÍA MORALES, *La semilla en el surco, Adalberto Tejeda y el radicalismo en Veracruz, 1883–1960* (1986); OLIVIA DOMÍNGUEZ PÉREZ, *Política y movimientos sociales en el tejedismo* (1986).

HEATHER FOWLER SALAMINI

TEJEDOR, CARLOS (*b.* 4 November 1817; *d.* 3 January 1903), Argentine educator, journalist, lawyer, and politician of the national period. Born in Buenos Aires, Tejedor studied law at its university and graduated in 1837. His academic and judicial pursuits included appointments as professor of criminal and mercantile law at his alma mater in 1856 and government counsel two years later. Tejedor also edited the local *El Nacional* (1852). His greatest contribution, however, was in politics. An opponent of Juan Manuel de ROSAS, the Federalist caudillo of Buenos Aires, Tejedor returned from Chilean exile after the dictator's overthrow in 1852. He later became a representative to the Buenos Aires provincial legislature (1853). Tejedor was also minister to Brazil (1875) and governor of Buenos Aires Province (1878–1880). As governor, he opposed federalization of the city of Buenos Aires, which was accomplished only after his defeat by General Julio Argentino ROCA in the presidential election of 1880 and in the civil war that accompanied it. Tejedor justified his role in that bloody conflict by writing *La defensa de Buenos Aires* (1881). He died in the capital and his statue was erected in Palermo in 1909.

JUAN SILVA RIESTRA, *Carlos Tejedor: Su influencia en la legislación penal argentina* (1935); RICARDO PICCIRILLI, et al., eds.,

Diccionario histórico argentino, vol. 6 (1953–1954), pp. 586–587; JOSÉ CAMPOBASSI, *Mitre y su época* (1980).

FIDEL IGLESIAS

TELA RAILROAD, a RAILROAD line built by the UNITED FRUIT COMPANY on the north coast of Honduras, radiating inland from Tela. United Fruit acquired the rights from Sam ZEMURRAY, owner of the rival CUYAMEL FRUIT COMPANY, in 1913. The Tela Railroad Company, a United Fruit subsidiary, constructed an ice plant, a water system, electrical generators, a hospital, and a 1,000-foot wharf at Tela. United also acquired rights to the Trujillo Railroad, which lay to the east of the holdings of VACARRO BROTHERS, a rival banana firm operating from La Ceiba. By 1921, Tela had moved ahead of La Ceiba as Honduras's chief banana port.

STACY MAY and GALO PLAZA, *The United Fruit Company in Latin America* (1958); THOMAS KARNES, *Tropical Enterprise: The Standard Fruit and Steamship Company in Latin America* (1978).

LESTER D. LANGLEY

TELENOVELAS, the most popular form of television in Latin America, are serial dramas that tend to run five to six nights a week in prime time for a limited duration of up to eight or nine months. They usually develop a specific main story, along with various subplots involving major and minor characters. The themes usually involve family dramas, romance, villains, urban settings, social mobility, and, increasingly, other social issues. They dominate prime-time viewing hours in almost all of Latin America and tend to receive the highest audience ratings of all programs.

Historically, *telenovelas* are related to soap operas and serial novels. They are derived from *radionovelas*, which were first produced in Cuba by Colgate-Palmolive to sell soap to housewives, following North American successes with the soap opera. The genre spread to other countries, often in the form of exported scripts that were reproduced locally. *Telenovelas* were first produced in Cuba by Colgate-Palmolive in the early 1950s, and again scripts, scriptwriters, directors, and producers flowed to other countries, particularly after the Cuban Revolution in 1959. Many scholars think that *telenovelas'* roots include French and English serial novels, which were imported and translated throughout Latin America.

The present-day *telenovela* has changed quite a bit from its roots in soap opera. Most popular culture scholars now consider it a distinct genre. The main differences are more varied themes, increasingly realistic production styles and values, and a very broad audience. While some *telenovelas* are still oriented to family dramas and romance, many have more realistic themes. Some are oriented to current social issues, such as Brazilian *telenovelas* like *Vale tudo*, about economic corruption, and *Pantanal*, about ecology. Other *telenovelas*,

particularly Brazilian, Colombian, and Venezuelan, are historically focused, such as the Brazilian *Escrava Isaura* or the Venezuelan *Doña Barbara*. Other *telenovelas* are based on well-known national novels, such as Jorge Amado's *Gabriela* and *Tieta*. While Mexico produces more traditional family dramas, it has also innovated in creating educational *telenovelas* with themes on health, family planning, and the need for education. The production style of *telenovelas* has become more similar to North American series and films, using more exterior shots, action sequences, and regional and historical settings.

The *telenovela* has a very strong relationship to its audience. *Telenovelas* loom large in many Latin American conversations, and popular ones are watched for months by almost everyone with a television set. Many are heavily influenced by audience feedback. Plots are changed, and characters accentuated or dropped over time. *Telenovelas* also play the primary commercial role in selling products to the audience, since they are the most widely viewed productions. In Brazil and some other countries, commercial product exposures, such as labels, use of visibly identified products, and discussions of products are worked into the visual design and dialogue of *telenovelas*, a practice that has caused considerable concern.

Most of the major Latin American countries produce *telenovelas*. Mexico and Brazil are the largest producers and export them. Colombia, Venezuela, Argentina, Puerto Rico, and the United States also produce quite a few and sometimes export them. Most other Latin American countries import them. By the 1970s, *telenovelas* had displaced imported North American programs from prime time in most of the smaller Latin American countries that are heavy importers of television programs.

CONRAD KOTTAK, *Prime Time Society* (1989); NIKO VINK, *The Telenovela and Emancipation* (1990); MICHELE MATTELART and ARMAND MATTELART, *The Carnival of Images*, translated by David Buxton (1991).

JOSEPH STRAUBHAAR

See also **Clair, Janete; Radio and Television.**

TELEVISION. *See* **Radio and Television.**

TELLER AMENDMENT, proposed by Senator Henry M. Teller in 1898 as an amendment to the U.S. declaration of war against Spain in Cuba. It asserted that the United States would make no attempt to establish permanent control over Cuba. The amendment specified that the United States "hereby disclaims any disposition of intention to exercise sovereignty, jurisdiction, or control over said island except for pacification thereof, and asserts its determination, when that is accomplished, to leave the government and control of the island to its people." But though the Teller Amendment restrained the United States from annexing Cuba after the war, when the Spanish forces surrendered in 1898, the United States established military occupation of Cuba, which ended in 1902.

JULIUS W. PRATT, *Expansionists of 1898: The Acquisition of Hawaii and the Spanish Islands* (1936); JAMES D. RUDOLPH, *Cuba: A Country Study* (1985); LOUIS A. PÉREZ, JR., *Cuba: Between Reform and Revolution* (1988); JAIME SUCHLICKI, *Cuba from Columbus to Castro* (1990).

DAVID CAREY, JR.

See also **Spanish–American War.**

TELLES, LYGIA FAGUNDES (*b*. 19 April 1923), Brazilian fiction writer. As a law student in São Paulo, Telles published a short story collection, *Praia viva* (Living Beach), in 1944. In 1949 her collection of short stories *O cacto vermelho* (The Red Cactus) received the Brazilian Academy of Letters prize for fiction, marking the beginning of a distinguished literary career that includes four novels, seven short-story collections, and eight prizes. Telles's fiction exhibits both modern literary techniques and knowledge of Brazilian life, with emphasis on the female psyche. Her most celebrated novel, *As meninas* (1973; *The Girl in the Photograph*, 1982), re-creates aspects of the 1964–1984 military regime. Telles's forte is the short story; she is known for her use of the fantastic. Her fiction reflects her era, attracting both readers and critics. Female readers recognize themselves in her strong characterizations of urban women. Her 1990 novel, *As horas nuas* (Naked Hours), follows previous directions in presenting an actress's existential concerns in present-day São Paulo. Politically outspoken, Telles participated in protests against the military regime. In 1985 she became the third woman elected to the Brazilian Academy of Letters.

Other works by Telles include *Histórias do desencontro* (1958); *Seminário dos ratos* (1977); *Mistérios* (1981); and *Tigrela and Other Stories* (1986). Critical interpretations of her fiction include RICHARD BURGIN, "Tigrela and Other Stories," in *New York Times Book Review* (4 May 1986); and JOHN M. TOLMAN, "New Fiction: Lygia Fagundes Telles," in *Review* no. 30 (1981): 65–70.

MARIA ANGÉLICA LOPES

TELLO, JULIO CÉSAR (*b*. 11 April 1880; *d*. 3 June 1947), Peruvian who played a central role in initiating the scientific study of Andean prehistory and establishing the institutional framework for protecting and conserving the Peruvian archaeological patrimony. A native Quechua speaker from Huarochirí, in the highlands east of Lima, Tello brought to his research an indigenous perspective and a passionate commitment to uncovering and elucidating the accomplishments of Andean cultures before the Spanish conquest.

Tello studied science and medicine at the Universidad Nacional Mayor de San Marcos and wrote his doctoral dissertation on the antiquity of syphilis in Peru. With support from the Peruvian government he subsequently attended Harvard, where he studied ARCHAEOLOGY and anthropology at the Peabody Museum and completed a master's degree in anthropology. Tello then studied at London University before returning to Peru as that nation's first professional archaeologist. He immediately became the director of archaeology at the Museo Histórico Nacional and launched a series of expeditions that made him world famous.

By 1924 Tello had been appointed director of both archaeological museums in Lima while introducing the teaching of archaeology and anthropology into the Peruvian university system. During a remarkable career that spanned four decades, Tello founded anthropological journals including *Chaski, Inca,* and *Wira-kocha,* as well as Peru's principal archaeological museum, the Museo Nacional de Antropología y Arqueología.

Concurrent with these academic activities, Tello carried on a political career dedicated to the defense of Peru's indigenous population. In 1917 he was elected as Haurochirí's representative to Congress, where he served for the next eleven years.

Tello's explorations and discoveries covered much of the Peruvian coast and highlands. He identified the CHAVÍN civilization as the matrix out of which later Peruvian cultures developed, and he considered the highland site of CHAVÍN DE HUÁNTAR as its center. Many of Tello's most important investigations—including those at PARACAS on the south coast; Ancón on the central coast; Cerro Sechín, Moxeke, and Cerro Blanco (Nepeña) on the north-central coast; and Kuntur Wasi and Cumbemayo in the northern highlands—demonstrated the existence, temporal priority, and panregional extent of what is now known as the Chavín horizon. By establishing that highland Chavín civilization preceded the better-known coastal cultures such as MOCHE and NASCA, Tello was able to demonstrate the autochthonous character of Andean civilization and disprove Max Uhle's hypothesis of Mesoamerican and Asian origins of Peruvian high culture. Tello's contention that the roots of Andean civilization lay in still earlier developments within the tropical forest, bolstered by his research at the site of KOTOSH, also proved to be influential. His contributions to later Peruvian prehistory include his excavations of the Inca occupation at PACHACAMAC. Tello's theoretical orientation differed significantly from the approach advocated by his North American colleagues, and in many respects his publications anticipated the ecological and structuralist approaches that became popular many decades later in U.S. and European archaeology.

Tello's publications include "Wira-Kocha," in *Inka,* 1, no. 1 (1923): 94–320, and 1, no. 3 (1923): 583–606; "Discovery of the Chavín Culture in Peru," in *American Antiquity,* 9, no. 1 (1942): 35–66; *Origen y desarrollo de las civilizaciones prehistóricas andinas* (1942); *Arqueología del Valle de Casma* (1956); *Paracas,* 2 vols. (1959–1979);

Chavín, cultura matriz de la civilización andina (1960); *Páginas escogidas* (1967).

A good source of biographical and bibliographical information is S. K. LOTHROP, "Julio C. Tello, 1880–1947," in *American Antiquity*, 14 (July 1948): 50–56.

RICHARD L. BURGER

TEMPLO MAYOR (main temple) refers generally to the chief ceremonial center of the Aztec capital of Mexico TENOCHTITLÁN or more specifically to its major pyramid temple. According to Fray Bernardino de SAHAGÚN, the precinct walls enclosed seventy-eight structures, including temples and shrines to various deities, the priests' residence and school, a ball court, and a skull rack. The main temple proper consisted of a base of four progressively smaller platforms crowned by twin shrines dedicated to the solar god of warfare and Mexican patron HUITZILOPOCHTLI and to the rain god TLALOC. The original fourteenth-century building was periodically enlarged by the superimposition of one structure atop the other, with the last major renovation completed in 1487. Of the final temple described by CORTÉS and others,

Templo Mayor. PHOTOGRAPH BY DAVID HISER WITH OVERLAY BY NED M. SEIDLER. © 1980 NATIONAL GEOGRAPHIC SOCIETY.

little remains. Extensive archaeological excavations of the site, directed by Eduardo Matos Moctezuma from 1978 through the 1980s, exposed numerous structures and unearthed thousands of sculptures, artifacts, and ritual items buried in offertory caches.

EDUARDO MATOS MOCTEZUMA, *The Great Temple of the Aztecs: Treasures of Tenochtitlán* (1988) and *Treasures of the Great Temple* (1990); LEONARDO LÓPEZ LUHAN, *The Offerings of the Templo Mayor of Tenochtitlán,* translated by Bernard R. Ortìz de Montellano and Thelma Ortìz de Montellano (1994).

ELOISE QUIÑONES KEBER

TEMUCO, city of 211,693 inhabitants (1990) on the northern bank of the Cautín River, the most important urban center of the Araucanía region of Chile (1980 population 692,500). Founded in 1881 by General Gregorio Urrutia after a pacification campaign conducted against the bellicose Araucanian Indians, it became an active colonization center and an outpost to keep the ARAUCANIANS at bay. Chilean, Swiss, and German families settled in Temuco, which by 1950 had grown into the fourth-largest urban center of the country. More than an industrial city, Temuco is a service and administrative center for wheat and dairy farmers and for the 185,000 Araucanians who still live in Temuco's environs.

CÉSAR N. CAVIEDES

TEN YEARS' WAR (1868–1878), the first major Cuban struggle for independence. It was also a manifestation of serious social, economic, and political grievances on the island. While it failed to win independence, it did begin the process of slave emancipation in Cuba.

By the 1850s, Cuba had become the world's leading sugar exporter, tied increasingly to the U.S. market. But many agrarian workers had been displaced in the shift from a more diversified agricultural economy to one dominated by slave-produced sugar at the same time that Cuba's population was growing rapidly, as Louis Pérez has asserted. Eastern Cuba was suffering especially in comparison to the newer sugar-producing regions of the west. Abolitionists demanded an end to SLAVERY. Many CREOLES wanted political and economic reform and some favored independence or annexation to the United States, which had showed repeated interest in acquiring Cuba. The liberal Spanish government of General Enrique O'Donnell (1858–1863) raised Cuban expectation of reform, but the subsequent conservative government pursued a repressive policy that alienated Cubans of many classes, especially in eastern Cuba.

Political turmoil in Spain, in fact, contributed to the breakdown of order in Cuba. On 18 September 1868 naval officers at Cádiz revolted and ten days later revolutionaries took Madrid, proclaiming a liberal republic. The new government's refusal to grant reforms, however, led an eastern Cuban creole planter, Carlos Manuel de CÉSPEDES, to proclaim Cuban independence on 10 October 1868 in what came to be known as the GRITO DE YARA. Calling for independence as well as gradual emancipation of slaves and universal male suffrage, he rallied support against Spain, and began a guerrilla war at Bayamo. On 20 April 1869, a constitutional convention organized a republican government at Guámairo, which supported annexation to the United States. Bitter guerrilla warfare followed, while Spain vacillated between monarchy and republic until the Bourbons were finally restored with the coronation of Alfonso XII in January 1875.

The slavery issue created a deep schism within the revolutionary movement and cost it support of some of the planters of western Cuba. Many of those fighting came from the colored classes, who favored complete and immediate abolition. The military leaders Máximo Gómez and Antonio MACEO represented that view, but the rebel government leaders, dominated by planters, repeatedly refused to allow them to carry the war into the west.

The United States, Britain, and France all were interested in Cuba but none intervened in the devastating conflict. The VIRGINIUS AFFAIR, in which Spanish naval forces on 31 October 1873 seized a filibustering ship flying the U.S. flag off Jamaica and executed more than fifty of her officers, crew, and passengers, seriously strained relations with the United States, but U.S. intervention was averted by the diplomatic pressure of England and France.

By 1878 the war had damaged the SUGAR INDUSTRY and cost 250,000 lives. At El Zanjón (11 February 1878), the Spanish agreed to some political reform, to freedom for all those slaves who had fought with the rebels, and gradual emancipation for the rest with compensation to the owners. This agreement with the creole leadership, however, fell far short of giving Cubans autonomy or the social reforms for which many had fought, so that the Pact of ZANJÓN itself became an issue for continued dissent in Cuba. Immediately after the pact was signed, General Maceo issued the "Protest of Baraguá" and continued to fight on for nearly three more months before finally succumbing to Spanish forces in May.

The war led to a major reorganization of the sugar industry in the 1880s, with major capital investment from the United States. But the Spanish failure to implement the reforms and the continued social and economic problems would contribute to a resumption of the CUBAN WAR FOR INDEPENDENCE in 1895.

Although it failed to achieve independence, the Ten Years' War spawned a number of important later Cuban leaders, including José MARTÍ, Fernando Figueredo, and Tomás ESTRADA PALMA.

FERNANDO FIGUEREDO, *La revolución de Yara* (1902; repr. 1969); HUGH THOMAS, *Cuba, the Pursuit of Freedom* (1971); MARÍA CRISTINA LLERENA, ed., *Sobre la guerra de los 10 años, 1868–1878* (1973); ALEIDA PLASENCIA, ed., *Bibliografía de la guerra de los diez años* (1968); VIDAL MORALES Y MORALES, *Iniciadores y primeros martires de la revolución cubana*, 3 vols. (1931); MAGDALENTA PANDO, *Cuba's Freedom Fighter, Antonio Maceo, 1845–1896* (1980); PHILIP FONER, *Antonio Maceo: The "Bronze Titan" of Cuba's Struggle for Independence* (1977); FLORENCIO GARCÍA CISNEROS, *¿Máximo Gómez, caudillo o dictador?* (1986), RAMIRO GUERRA Y SÁNCHEZ, *Guerra de los diez años, 1868–1878*, 2 vols. (1972); RICHARD H. BRADFORD, *The "Virginius" Affair* (1980); JAMES M. CALLAHAN, *Cuba and International Relations* (1899); ENRIQUE COLLAZO, *Desde Yara hasta Zanjón* (1893; 1967); JUAN ALMEIDA BOSQUE, *El general en jefe Máximo Gómez* (1986); LOUIS A. PÉREZ, *Cuba, Between Reform and Revolution* (1988); BENIGNO SOUZA Y RODRÍGUEZ, *Máximo Gómez, el generalisimo* (1986).

RALPH LEE WOODWARD, JR.

TENENTISMO, a 1920s Brazilian politico-military movement that, after joining forces with the 1930 Revolution, exercised great power in the early 1930s. The *tenentes* were young military officers and intellectuals who participated in conspiracies and revolts to protest against political corruption and to force government reforms, especially elimination of the extreme federalism of the period. They first rebelled on 5 July 1922 in Rio de Janeiro against the inauguration of President-elect Artur da Silva BERNARDES, who for them symbolized the iniquity of Brazilian politics and social structure. Most troops remained loyal and quickly put down the uprising, but eighteen rebels refused to surrender and marched down Copacabana beach, where they were fired upon and arrested. Two were martyred and the rest went to prison, among them Antônio de Siqueira Campos and Eduardo GOMES.

During the next two years several more *tenente* revolts erupted, culminating in the July 1924 capture of the city of São Paulo for a month under the leadership of Miguel Costa, of the state police. The brothers Juarez and Joaquim TÁVORA were among the masterminds of this victory. The *tenentes* escaped into the interior, where they joined with other groups, especially one commanded by Luís Carlos PRESTES, a captain in the engineering corps.

Led by Prestes and Costa, the revolutionaries (numbering several thousand) set out on a great march (the PRESTES COLUMN) through the backlands to publicize their demands for honest elections, political freedoms, amnesty for themselves, and strengthening of the national state. They covered some 15,000 miles in eleven states, mostly in the poor Northeast, using guerrilla tactics to avoid major engagements. Finally, with their ranks thinned and the army dogging their tracks, the *tenentes* crossed into Bolivia in February 1927 and dispersed.

From 1927 until 1930, the *tenentes* remained in exile or underground, hoping for pardons but continuing their criticism of the government and oligarchic society. Those in hiding often met in the Rio clinic of a sympathizer, Dr. Pedro Ernesto Batista. Their ideas ranged from fascist on the right to communist on the left, and no single person spoke for the group. Many took hope when presidential candidate Getúlio VARGAS promised them amnesty in the 1930 campaign; and most answered the call when Vargas's managers, Oswaldo Aranha and Góis MONTEIRO, recruited them for a revolt later in the year. *Tenente* leaders such as João Alberto Lins de Barros, Djalma Dutra, Oswaldo Cordeiro de Farias, and Juracy Magalhães, among the most experienced soldiers in the country, made up the high command of the revolutionary army.

In the months following Vargas's victory, the *tenentes* became convinced that they were being passed over. They wanted army reinstatement at the ranks they would have held, control over a majority of the troops, and influence in government policy. In order to achieve these goals, they formed the Club 3 de Outubro in early 1931 to pressure Vargas. They soon chose their ally Pedro Ernesto as president, partly because he had access to Vargas as the first family's physician.

Within several months Vargas came to depend on the club for political support—his hold on power was extremely tenuous—and in exchange he appointed them as state interventors, promoted them in the army, and consulted them on major decisions. The *tenentes* reached the pinnacle of their power in early 1932, serving as a praetorian guard for Vargas. They compiled an eclectic program of reforms, some socialist, others fascist, to be enacted by a corporatist regime. By mid-1932, however, the club had outlived its usefulness, having provoked a civil war in São Paulo. After his victory, Vargas decided

to democratize his government. Some *tenentes* went into civilian politics, while others returned to military life. The club symbols were invoked from time to time, but its leadership had disbanded. Several *tenentes* went on to prominence during the Vargas era and enjoyed heroic images, for example, Távora, Prestes, Gomes, José Américo de ALMEIDA, and Cordeiro de Farias; they did not work together, however, nor forge a common program.

Tenentismo was uniquely Brazilian; nothing like it occurred elsewhere in Latin America, despite frequent military intervention in politics.

JORDAN YOUNG, *The Brazilian Revolution of 1930 and the Aftermath* (1967); BORIS FAUSTO, *A revolução de 1930* (1970); NEILL MACAULAY, *The Prestes Column* (1974); MICHAEL L. CONNIFF, "The Tenentes in Power," in *Journal of Latin American Studies* 10, no. 1 (1977): 61–82; JOSÉ AUGUSTO DRUMMOND, *O movimento tenentista* (1986); MARIA CECÍLIA SPINA FORJAZ, *Tenentismo e forças armadas na revolução de 30* (1989).

MICHAEL L. CONNIFF

TENOCHTITLÁN, capital city of AZTEC Empire, center of present-day Mexico City. According to native histories, the Mexica founded Tenochtitlán in 1325. They were led by their god HUITZILOPOCHTLI to a spot where an eagle perched atop a prickly pear cactus, or *tenochtli*; Tenochtitlán means "By the Prickly Pear Fruits." This divinely ordained site was a marshy island in Lake Texcoco east of Chapultepec. The Mexica developed this

Model reconstructing the central square of Tenochtitlán. COURTESY OF DEPARTMENT LIBRARY SERVICES, AMERICAN MUSEUM OF NATURAL HISTORY.

marginal property by trading ducks, fish, and other edible lake products for wood and stone from the mainland. As the Mexica gained political power, eventually dominating what is now called the Aztec Empire, they were able to commandeer building supplies and labor and Tenochtitlán grew in size and population. At the time of the Spanish invasion it was the largest city in Mesoamerica, with a probable population of 125,000 or more.

A "Venice of the New World," Tenochtitlán was crisscrossed by canals that served for canoe transportation; moveable wooden bridges allowed for pedestrian passage. The basic layout of the city comprised four sectors, separated by major canals, surrounding the central political-ceremonial precinct (now the zócalo), where the rulers had their palaces and the major deities their temples—most notably the Great Temple of Huitzilopochtli and TLALOC. Within each residential sector lay a variable number of CALPULLI, or "big houses," neighborhood units tending toward endogamy and occupational specialization. These served as administrative units for taxation and military draft; each had its own temple and schools. Toward the city's outskirts, raised fields, or CHINAMPAS, provided a local source of fresh vegetables and flowers. Causeways to the west and the south linked the city to the mainland; an aqueduct brought fresh water from Chapultepec because the lake water was too saline for drinking. Flood control, another major problem, was partly solved by means of a system of dikes.

Just north of Tenochtitlán lay TLATELOLCO, originally an independent Mexica settlement but conquered by Tenochtitlán in 1473. The two islands were separated by a narrow waterway (today the site of the Lagunilla market). Tlatelolco boasted the principal market for the greater urban district. The two islands covered an area of about 3 square miles.

Although CORTÉS and his Spanish followers marveled at the beauty and orderliness of the island city, they and their native allies leveled most of it during the two-and-a-half month siege that led to Spanish control of the city and its transformation into the capital of New Spain.

JACQUES SOUSTELLE, *Daily Life of the Aztecs on the Eve of the Spanish Conquest* (1961); DIEGO DURÁN, *The Aztecs: The History of the Indies of New Spain,* translated by Doris Heyden and Fernando Horcasitas (1964); LUIS GONZÁLEZ APARICIO, *Plano reconstructivo de la región de Tenochtitlán* (1973); FRANCES BERDAN, *The Aztecs of Central Mexico: An Imperial Society* (1982); JOHANNA BRODA, DAVÍD CARRASCO, and EDUARDO MATOS MOCTEZUMA, *The Great Temple of Tenochtitlán* (1987).

LOUISE M. BURKHART

TEOTIHUACÁN, the preeminent center of religious, economic, and political power in central Mexico from approximately 100 B.C. to A.D. 750. The site of this ancient city is about 30 miles northeast of Mexico City, in the Valley of Mexico, a temperate, semiarid region in the central Mexican highlands. At its height (A.D. 500–600)

it was home to at least 125,000 inhabitants and covered 7 to 8 square miles. As the first "true city" in the New World, Teotihuacán represented an unprecedented social transformation and had a significant impact on all subsequent pre-Columbian civilizations in Mexico.

Teotihuacán was above all the seat of a vigorous religion whose most sacred precepts were played out in the construction of a monumental ceremonial center that was the setting for ritual performances and extravaganzas, often including human sacrifice. A wide, north–south thoroughfare, the Street of the Dead, bisected the center and provided the basic orientation (15°25' east of north) to which virtually all later ceremonial and residential construction conformed. Three immense pyramid complexes dominate its core: the Pyramid of the Moon, at the north end of the "Street of the Dead"; the Pyramid of the Sun, along its east side; and the CIUDADELA, the city's administrative center, on the southeast. Directly opposite the Ciudadela is an enormous enclosure that served as the central marketplace. Scores of smaller temple platforms lining the "Street of the Dead" and elsewhere are built in a style found only in Teotihuacán.

The city's population grew rapidly during the period of major pyramid construction. Its growth involved the massive, planned resettlement of most of the region's rural inhabitants within its limits and the immigration of many "foreign" residents, probably emissaries and merchants. Problems of housing and administering this diverse agglomeration of people were met through the construction of more than 2,000 stone-walled apartment compounds organized into barrios. Most of these single-story, windowless structures housed from 60 to 100 people and contained a number of separate apartments consisting of rooms and porticoes arranged around open patios.

At least two-thirds of the urban population were farmers who cultivated land around the city, utilizing the valley's permanent springs for irrigation. Staples such as corn and beans, along with a variety of wild plants, game, and domesticated dog and turkey, constituted the city's food supply. Another large segment of the population were full-time craftsmen involved in ceramic production and the working of obsidian, bone, and feathers. Others were plasterers, painters, warriors, merchants, or bureaucrats. At the apex of this highly stratified society were priest-rulers who governed in the name of the gods.

The Teotihuacán state exercised strong control over its economy, managing (to varying degrees) critical resources, production, and exchange both within the Valley of Mexico and beyond. For example, the distribution of green obsidian for the city's vital obsidian industry was regulated, and many workshops are thought to have been under direct state control. Even some items produced far outside of the city, such as the popular Thin Orange pottery, appear to have been marketed through the city. Although Teotihuacán's long-distance

Teotihuacán. PHOTO BY ENRIQUE FRANCO TORRIJOS.

trade and foreign relations are poorly understood, the impact of the city was felt as far away as the Maya area in Guatemala.

Sometime in the eighth century the ceremonial heart of Teotihuacán was systematically burned and destroyed; the citizens may have been involved. The population fell sharply, its great culture disintegrated, and the city never regained its former eminence.

RENÉ MILLÓN, R. BRUCE DREWITT, and GEORGE L. COWGILL, *Urbanization at Teotihuacán, Mexico.* Vol. 1, *The Teotihuacán Map* (1973), pts. 1 and 2; WILLIAM T. SANDERS, JEFFREY R. PARSONS, and ROBERT S. SANTLEY, *The Basin of Mexico: Ecological Processes in the Evolution of a Civilization* (1979); RENÉ MILLÓN, "Teotihuacán: City, State, and Civilization," in *Supplement to the Handbook of Middle American Indians.* Vol. 1, *Archaeology,* edited by Victoria R. Bricker and Jeremy A. Sabloff (1981), 198–243; GEORGE L. COWGILL, "Rulership and the Ciudadela: Political Inferences from Teotihuacán Architecture," in *Civilization in the Ancient Americas: Essays in Honor of Gordon R. Willey,* edited by Richard M. Leventhal and Alan L. Kolata (1983), pp. 313–343; RENÉ MILLÓN, "The Last Years of Teotihuacán Dominance," in *The Collapse of Ancient States and Civilizations,* edited by Norman Yoffee and George L. Cowgill (1988), pp. 102–164; RUBEN CABRERA CASTRO, SABURO SUGIYAMA, and GEORGE L. COWGILL, "The 'Templo de Quetzalcoatl' Project at Teotihuacán," in *Ancient Mesoamerica* 2, no. 1 (1991).

MARTHA L. SEMPOWSKI

TEPITO, a traditional, stable, working-class neighborhood, comprising approximately one square kilometer of downtown MEXICO CITY north of the Zócalo and roughly bounded by the following four streets: Cinco de Mayo, Lázaro Cárdenas, Rayón, and República de Argentina. The neighborhood has an intense community spirit as well as a barrio dialect and culture, and has been the neighborhood of origin for many of the country's best-known boxers. The "thieves' market" in

Tepito in the past had a reputation for smuggled and other goods of dubious origin.

Most of the population rent single rooms in converted and now derelict mansions and palaces long since vacated by the elite. Alternatively, they live in other *vecindades* (tenements) that were built for that purpose until rent control legislation in the 1940s made their construction unprofitable. The Casa Blanca *vecindad* was home to the Sánchez family in Oscar Lewis's classic text *The Children of Sánchez* (1964). The local economy is based on petty services, sweatshops, and small workshops that specialize in furniture and shoe manufacture.

GUSTAVO GARZA, "Ciudad de México: Dinámica industrial y perspectivas de decentralización," in *Decentralización y democracia en México,* compiled by Blanca Torres (1986); SUSAN ECKSTEIN, *The Poverty of Revolution: The State and the Urban Poor in Mexico* (1988); and RENÉ COULOMB, "Rental Housing and the Dynamics of Urban Growth in Mexico City," in *Housing and Land in Urban Mexico,* edited by Alan Gilbert (1989).

PETER M. WARD

TEQUESTA, a native American group in southeast Florida during the colonial period. The Tequesta were encountered in the Miami area by the Juan Ponce de León expedition in 1513. Archaeological evidence indicates the Tequesta and their pre-Columbian ancestors had inhabited the region for at least two thousand years. Their economy was centered on the collection of wild resources, especially fish. Early accounts refer to a chief called Tequesta, who at times was a vassal to the Calusa chief.

In 1566 Pedro Menéndez de Avilés installed a garrison with a Jesuit priest in the main town of Tequesta, but it was withdrawn the following year. In 1568 the Jesuit mission was reestablished, but lasted only to 1570. In 1743 Tequesta was the location of yet another attempt to establish a Jesuit mission and a fort. By then, only remnants of the Tequesta and other south Florida aborigines remained.

JOHN M. GOGGIN, "The Tekesta Indians of Southern Florida," in *Florida Historical Quarterly* 18 (1940): 274–284; FELIX ZUBILLAGA, ed., *Monumenta antiquae Floridae (1566–1572)* (1946); WILLIAM C. STURTEVANT, "The Last of the South Florida Aborigines," in *Tacachale: Essays on the Indians of Florida and Southeast Georgia During the Historic Period*, edited by Jerald T. Milanich and Samuel Proctor (1978); JERALD T. MILANICH and CHARLES FAIRBANKS, *Florida Archaeology* (1980), esp. pp. 232–237.

JERALD T. MILANICH

TERESA CRISTINA (*b.* 14 March 1822; *d.* 30 December 1889), empress of Brazil, youngest daughter of Francis I, king of Naples, and María Isabel, princess of Spain. Raised in a traditionalist court, Teresa Cristina was notable for her kindness but not for looks or intelligence. When her wedding to her cousin PEDRO II was arranged, she wrote promising to do everything to assure his happiness and to follow his counsels, a promise faithfully kept. They were married on 4 September 1843. Her patience and good humor overcame Pedro's initial disappointment and coldness, and the birth of children finally aroused affection on her husband's part. Closing her eyes to his subsequent infidelities, she kept as close to him as he would allow. She avoided all involvement in public affairs and devoted her time and income to charity. Sickness plagued her final years. Following the empire's overthrow, she could not adjust to her sudden exile from Brazil. She died in Pôrto, Portugal.

MARY WILHELMINE WILLIAMS, *Dom Pedro the Magnanimous* (1937).

RODERICK J. BARMAN

TERESINA (formerly Therezina, or Terezhina), capital of the state of PIAUÍ, Brazil. Teresina, the chief commercial center of the middle of the Parnaíba Valley, has a population of 533,678 (1989 est.). Founded in 1852 as a new state capital, Teresina stands at the confluence of the Parnaíba and Poti rivers and is linked by the former to the Atlantic port city of Parnaíba, 220 miles downstream. It exports livestock, hides, rice, cotton, carnauba wax, palm oil, and other agricultural products of the region. Local industries produce textiles, lumber, soap, sugar, and rum.

CARA SHELLY

TERRA, GABRIEL (*b.* 1873; *d.* 1942), president of Uruguay (1931–1938). Terra was a Colorado Party political leader who ostensibly considered himself a Batllist, that is, a follower of the great political leader and two-time Colorado president José BATLLE Y ORDÓÑEZ. By late 1932,

Terra had moved ideologically to the right and became increasingly frustrated with the fact that he had to share decision making with a National Council of Administration under the partially collegial executive structure established by the 1918 Constitution. Amid the economic turmoil brought on by the depression, Terra joined forces with the Blanco (National Party) leader, Luis Alberto de HERRERA, in a nonviolent coup on 13 March 1933, taking total control of the government. The regime drafted a new constitution that returned Uruguay to a full presidential system and left the Senate in total control of the procoup factions of the Colorados and Blancos. Terra repressed the labor movement and devalued the peso in an attempt to help exporters of livestock. He served a full term under the 1934 Constitution, turning the presidency over to his elected successor, his brother-in-law Alfredo BALDOMIR.

PHILIP B. TAYLOR, JR., *Government and Politics of Uruguay* (1960).

MARTIN WEINSTEIN

TERRAZAS, LUIS (*b.* 20 July 1829; *d.* 15 June 1923), governor of the state of Chihuahua, Mexico (1860–1873, 1879–1884, 1903–1904). A hero of the wars against the northern Indians and the FRENCH INTERVENTION (1861–1867), General Terrazas was the political boss and governor of Chihuahua for much of the period from 1860 to 1910. He and his family came to own more than 10 million acres of land in Chihuahua with a half million head of cattle. He was also one of Mexico's foremost bankers and industrialists.

During the French Intervention, Terrazas stood with President Benito JUÁREZ in Mexico's darkest hours, leading the forces that eventually pushed the French from the state. He maintained his alliance with Juárez, defending him against the revolt of La Noria, led by Porfirio DÍAZ, in 1872. Terrazas continued to oppose Díaz during the first decade of the latter's dictatorship. Díaz forced him out of power in Chihuahua from 1884 to 1892, but the overwhelming economic resources of the Terrazas family produced a stalemate. A reconciliation was achieved with the return of Terrazas to the governorship in 1903.

Because he and his sons and sons-in-law ran the state as a family fiefdom, occupying nearly all the important government posts, and used their positions to further their economic interests, they became the lightning rod for the discontent that erupted in the MEXICAN REVOLUTION of 1910. After Terrazas fled to the United States, Pancho VILLA confiscated his properties in 1913. The old general returned to Mexico in 1920 and two years later the federal government gave him 13 million pesos as compensation for the loss of his lands.

A critical examination of Terrazas's early career is found in FRANCISCO R. ALMADA, *Juárez y Terrazas: Aclaraciones históricas* (1958). Although commissioned by the Terrazas family, the best biography remains JOSÉ FUENTES MARES, *. . . Y México se* *refugió en el desierto: Luis Terrazas, su historia y destino* (1954). For a complete study of the Terrazas era in Chihuahua, see MARK WASSERMAN, *Capitalists, Caciques, and Revolution* (1984).

MARK WASSERMAN

TETZCOCO, the great capital of the Acolhuaque and one of the leading cities in the Basin of Mexico in the late pre-Hispanic period. Located near the eastern edge of Lake Tetzcoco, it was also the head of a powerful confederation of neighboring towns. Founded by the CHICHIMECS in the twelfth century, it was conquered by the Tepanecs in the early fifteenth century. Following the overthrow of the Tepanec Empire, Mexico Tenochtitlán, Tetzcoco, and Tlacopán (present-day Tacuba) established the succeeding Empire of the Triple Alliance by 1434. The mestizo chronicler Fernando de Alva Ixtlilxóchitl extolled his native city as the cultural and intellectual center of the basin, led by two outstanding rulers: the warrior, builder, seer, and poet NEZAHUALCOYOTL and his son NEZAHUALPILLI. Remains of Nezahualcoyotl's famed pleasure garden, Tetzcotzinco, survive on a hill outside the present-day city of Texcoco, although there has been little excavation of the ancient capital buried beneath the city.

NIGEL DAVIES, *The Aztecs* (1973); EDMUNDO O'GORMAN, ed., *Fernando de Alva Ixtlilxóchitl: Obras históricas*, 3d ed., 2 vols. (1975–1977).

ELOISE QUIÑONES KEBER

TEXAS, northeasternmost of the provinces of New Spain, and later of the Republic of Mexico. The name derives from the Spanish term for some of the Caddoan peoples of east Texas. Permanently occupied in 1716, following French incursions in the area, the province remained sparsely settled until after Mexican independence, when an effort was made to attract Anglo-American and European immigrants. In 1845, after having been a separate republic since 1836, Texas annexed itself to the United States.

The Texas coast was first explored by Alonso ÁLVAREZ DE PINEDA in 1519. Parts of the interior were later traversed by Alvar Núñez CABEZA DE VACA and three other survivors of the Pánfilo de NARVÁEZ expedition (1528–1536), by the Francisco Vázquez de CORONADO expedition (1540–1544), and by Luis Moscoso de Alvarado, successor to Hernando de SOTO, and his men (1542). Following these unsuccessful expeditions, the region was ignored until the late seventeenth century.

The establishment of a colony on the Texas coast in 1685 by René Robert Cavelier, Sieur de la Salle, brought a brief Spanish occupation of east Texas (1690–1693). Domingo Ramón led a colonizing expedition northward in 1716, following the arrival of a French trader at a Río Grande outpost, and established missions and a presidio near present-day Robeline, Louisiana. Governor

Martín de ALARCÓN led a reinforcing expedition in 1718 and founded the presidio-mission complex that became SAN ANTONIO. With the founding of another presidio-mission complex on Matagorda Bay four years later, the three centers of Euro-American settlement in colonial Texas had been established.

Throughout the colonial period, Texas remained an essentially military province. Along with a base from which to guard against the French (and later the Anglo-Americans) in Louisiana, Texas also provided a buffer against Indian penetration of interior New Spain. Aside from military service, the principal economic activities in the province consisted of maize farming and cattle driving. Smuggling seems also to have been important, particularly in east Texas. The province's population on the eve of the MEXICAN WAR OF INDEPENDENCE totaled approximately 4,500, not including un-Hispanicized Indians.

With the adoption of the Mexican constitution of 1824, Texas was united with the neighboring province of COAHUILA to form a single state. Anglo-American settlement, which had begun in 1821 under the auspices of Moses Austin, brought thousands of colonists from the United States but only a few from Mexico. Consequently, according to the conservative estimates of Juan N. Almonte, a Mexican government agent, the Texas population stood at 21,000 in 1834, including 15,000 Anglo-Americans, 2,000 slaves, and 4,000 Mexican Texans. Disputes over land distribution, import tariffs, tax exemptions, and future immigration from the United States combined with political upheavals in Mexico to produce an insurrection and a declaration of independence on 2 March 1836.

Soon after its separation from Mexico, Texas laid claim to all land north of the Río Grande from its source to its mouth, territory that had previously been part of the Mexican states of Tamaulipas, Coahuila, and Chihuahua, and New Mexico Territory. Mexican refusal to acknowledge Texas's annexation to the United States and its territorial claims resulted in the MEXICAN–AMERICAN WAR (1846–1848).

EUGENE C. BARKER, *The Life of Stephen F. Austin, Founder of Texas, 1793–1836* (repr. 1969); Carlos E. Castañeda, *Our Catholic Heritage in Texas, 1519–1936*, 7 vols. (repr. 1976); VITO ALESSIO ROBLES, *Coahuila y Texas desde la consumación de la Independencia hasta el Tratado de Paz de Guadalupe Hidalgo*, 2 vols., 2d ed. (1979); GERALD E. POYO and GILBERTO M. HINOJOSA, eds., *Tejano Origins in Eighteenth-Century San Antonio* (1991); ANDREAS V. REICHSTEIN, *Rise of the Lone Star: The Making of Texas* (1989); DONALD CHIPMAN, *Spanish Texas, 1519–1821* (1992).

JESÚS F. DE LA TEJA

TEXAS REVOLUTION, series of events and military battles that resulted in the independence of Texas. Unrest began with the Fredonian Rebellion (1826), when some Anglo settlers disputed with Mexican authorities over land claims. In 1832 Anglo-Mexican clashes were exacerbated by the end of the customs exemption (a seven-year dispensation from paying some tariffs or customs taxes on imports and exports to promote economic development of the region), the desire for more local government, and fears that SLAVERY might be abolished as well as by underlying ethnic and cultural differences. Despite creation of new municipalities in Texas, centralization of power in Mexico by President Antonio López de SANTA ANNA in 1834 and land speculation revived earlier issues and led to renewed conflict in 1835. Opposition to Santa Anna flared in several Mexican states. Texans rejected calls for the arrest of resistance leaders in the summer of 1835. In October they defended a cannon at Gonzales and then captured a small Mexican garrison at Goliad. Under Stephen Fuller AUSTIN, an army of Anglo and Mexican Texans besieged San Antonio later that month. Led by Edward Burleson (1793–1851) and Ben Milam (1788–1835), they captured the town from General Martín Perfecto de cos in December.

In November, the Texas Consultation government publicly took a federalist stand in favor of the Constitution of 1824, though many Anglo Texans urged independence. Governor Henry Smith (1788–1851) and a general council failed to cooperate or accomplish much during the winter. Meanwhile, Santa Anna gathered an army to put down the revolt. A few Texas troops held San Antonio while volunteers from the United States moved to the Goliad area for an advance on Matamoros. Santa Anna's army surrounded the Texans in San Antonio, commanded by William B. Travis during late February 1836 and stormed the ALAMO on March 6, while the Texas Convention of 1836 declared an independent republic on March 2. Later that month, near Goliad, a second Mexican force under José URREA defeated or captured four groups of Texans, the largest led by James W. Fannin, and executed the prisoners. Sam HOUSTON gathered another Texas army but retreated. The government of President David G. Burnet retreated as well. On April 21 at SAN JACINTO, Houston defeated a wing of the Mexican army led by Santa Anna. As a prisoner, Santa Anna signed the Velasco treaty, which granted Texas independence and ended the conflict.

The best summaries of the Texas Revolution are in DAVID J. WEBER, *The Mexican Frontier, 1821–1846* (1982); and PAUL D. LACK, *The Texas Revolutionary Experience: a Political and Social History, 1835–1836* (1992). ANDREAS V. REICHSTEIN, *Rise of the Lone Star: The Making of Texas* (1989), emphasizes land issues. An older account of some value is EUGENE C. BARKER, "Texas Revolution," in *The Handbook of Texas,* edited by Walter Prescott Webb and H. Bailey Carroll, vol. 2 (1952), pp. 757–758.

ALWYN BARR

See also **Mexico: Colonization of the Northern Frontier.**

TEXCOCO. *See* **Tetzcoco.**

TEXTILE INDUSTRY

The Colonial Era

Spanish America satisfied its clothing needs from a combination of household production, a commercialized colonial textile industry, and imports from Europe and Asia. At the time of the Conquest, there was already an appreciable degree of regional specialization in textile manufacturing. Cotton and woolen (vicuña and llama in the Andes) cloth formed an important part of Aztec and Inca imperial tribute. The Spanish endeavored to maintain the flow of tribute in cloth through the ENCOMIENDA system until a drastic decline in Indian population undermined this source of supply. From the 1570s, the REPARTIMIENTO system of trade through ALCALDES MAYORES attempted, but failed (in Mexico at least), to compensate for the decline of tribute in *manta* (ordinary cotton cloth). As a consequence, settlers and Indians were obliged to depend more upon domestic production, to use more leather and less cloth, and to develop a commercialized colonial textile industry. This third course, notably in woolens and silk, was under way within two decades of the conquest of Mexico. Silk enjoyed a brief flurry of growth in Mexico during the mid-sixteenth century until Asian imports and a shrinking Indian population also damaged this labor-intensive industry. Wool proved more successful.

WOOLENS

In response to the high prices of imported cloth, an abundance of wool in the depopulated valleys of central Mexico, and the growth in silver production in the mid-1530s, the OBRAJES of PUEBLA grew to supply fine WOOL cloth for the entire Mexican *tierradentro* and for the Peruvian market. From the late sixteenth century, Quito's *obrajes* supplied markets to the north in Santa Fe de Bogotá and as far south as Concepción de Chile, Tucumán, Córdoba, and Buenos Aires. By the 1630s, however, the golden age of Puebla's woolen industry had passed, as a result of the prohibition of New Spain's trade with Peru, the enforcement of regulations restricting access to Indian labor, and, above all, Mexico's mining depression. Because of the continued buoyancy of Peruvian silver production, Quito's *obrajes* maintained their prosperity until the early eighteenth century.

During the final century of colonial rule, although the manufacture of fine cloth all but ceased, Spanish America's woolen industry was far from stagnant. In the face of increasing European competition, production shifted from finer to more ordinary and cheaper cloth. Weaving also moved closer to the principal sources of wool supply; Puebla-Tlaxcala yielded to the Bajío and the *tierradentro*, and Quito yielded to Bogotá, Huamanga, Cuzco, La Paz, and Córdoba. Finally, production tended to devolve from the larger *obrajes* to smaller units (containing fewer than ten looms), known as *trapiches* in Mexico and *chorrillos* in the Andes. Where the larger *obrajes* did survive—Mexico City, Tlaxcala, Querétaro, San Miguel el

Grande, Huamanga, Quito, Cuzco, La Paz—they tended to be part of larger agricultural enterprises. Salvucci's work on *obraje* woolens rates their potential for transformation as uniformly low. The modernization of woolen spinning technology in Mexico during the 1830s and 1840s sounded the death knell of the *obraje* while granting the domestic weaver and the *trapiche* a new lease on life.

COTTONS

From the later seventeenth century, the resurgence of the Indian population prompted a growth in COTTON manufacturing. This took a variety of forms. At first there was a revival of Indian village production in areas that since pre-Hispanic times had specialized in cotton weaving (such as Villa Alta in Oaxaca), through REPARTIMIENTO or in response to local and regional market mechanisms, backed by direct mercantile investment (*habilitación*). More significant, however, was the growing specialization of non-Indians—creoles and mestizos—in cotton spinning and weaving in the cities of Mexico's central plateau. The application of the European spinning wheel and the Castilian treadle loom to an industry that still adhered to native technology reversed cotton's decline and set in motion one of the more important (and, until recently, little appreciated) developments in Spanish America's eighteenth century. Backed by merchants at every stage of production, responding to demographic and ecological pressures, affecting rural as well as urban areas, involving production for extraregional as much as for local markets, and inspiring some notable technological as well as organizational developments, Mexico's new creole-mestizo cotton industry resembled, in most respects, the "protoindustrialization" occurring contemporaneously in Europe.

Again, it was in the Puebla region that these developments first took root, with creoles and mestizos—members of the silk weavers' guild—engaging in cotton weaving from the 1670s. By the second half of the eighteenth century, large groups of non-Indian cotton weavers were in Antigua Guatemala, Puebla, Tlaxcala, Antequera de Oaxaca, Mexico City, Valladolid, Querétaro, and Guadalajara, as well as in numerous smaller towns and villages throughout central and southern Mexico. Similar developments occurred in the Andes, the only difference being that cotton weaving tended to be more of a rural, Indian, and female occupation than in Mesoamerica. Large numbers of cotton weavers could be found in the Socorro region of New Granada, the Cuenca region of Quito, and the Cochabamba region of Upper Peru, transforming cotton grown in Piura, Trujillo, and Arequipa on the Peruvian coast and producing cloth for extraregional markets. Brooke Larson shows that Cochabamba *tocuyo* (the Andean equivalent of the Mexican *manta*) reached the counters of Buenos Aires during the Napoleonic wars.

The potential for the transformation of the cotton industry proved to be considerably greater in Mexico than in the Andes. This was a result of the predominantly urban location of Mexico's cotton weaving, a larger internal market, the greater degree of mercantile involvement, and the more favorable disposition of the postcolonial state toward industrial protection. Against these advantages, Andean cotton weaving could count upon only "the tariff of distance," sufficient to sustain the traditional (unmechanized) industry at modest levels throughout the nineteenth century in parts of Colombia, Ecuador, Peru, and Bolivia.

OTHER TEXTILES

Official attempts in Mexico to encourage the cultivation and manufacture of linen and hemp during the later eighteenth century were unsuccessful. Calico printing experienced a short burst of activity during the Napoleonic Wars. Manufacture of felt and straw hats in households and small workshops (*obradores*) was a dynamic industry during the eighteenth and nineteenth centuries in both Mexico and the Andes. Fibers such as istle, sisal, and palm were used for manufacture of coarse cloth and matting throughout Mesoamerica.

For a review of the literature, see MANUEL MIÑO GRIJALVA, "La política textil en México y Perú en la época colonial. Nuevas consideraciones," in *Historia mexicana*, 38 (1988): 283–323; "La circulación de mercancias: Una referencia al caso textil latinoamericano (1750–1810)," in *Empresarios, indios y estado: Perfil de la la economía mexicana (siglo XVIII)* edited by Arij Ouweneel and Cristina Torales Pacheco (1988); and "¿Protoindustria colonial?" in *Historia mexicana*, 38 (1989): 793–818. New Spain's textile industry can now count two important monographs: RICHARD SALVUCCI, *Textiles and Capitalism in Mexico: An Economic History of the Obrajes, 1539–1840* (1987); and MANUEL MIÑO GRIJALVA, *Obrajes y tejedores de Nueva España, 1750–1810* (1990). For Puebla's silk, cotton, and woolen textiles, see JAN BAZANT, "Evolución de la industria textil poblana (1544–1845)," in *Historia mexicana*, 1 (1962): 473–516; GUY P. C. THOMSON, "The Cotton Textile Industry in Puebla During the Eighteenth and Early Nineteenth Centuries," in *The Economies of Mexico and Peru During the Late Colonial Period, 1760–1810*, edited by Nils Jacobsen and Hans-Jurgen Puhle (1986); and *Puebla de los Angeles: Industry and Society in a Mexican City, 1700–1850* (1989). For Mexican woolen manufactures, see RICHARD SALVUCCI, "Entrepreneurial Culture and the Textile Manufactories in Eighteenth-Century Mexico," in *Anuario de estudios americanos*, 39 (1982): 397–419. For late colonial calico printing in Mexico, see MANUEL MIÑO GRIJALVA, "El camino hacia la fábrica en Nueva España: El caso de la 'Fábrica de Indianillas' de Francisco de Iglesias, 1801–1810," in *Historia méxicana*, 34 (1984): 135–148. For New Granada, see ANTHONY MC FARLANE, *Colombia Before Independence* (1993). For Quito, see JAVIER ORTIZ DE LA TABLA, "Obrajes y obrajeros del Quito Colonial," in *Anuario de estudios americanos*, 39 (1982): 341–365; and JOHN LEDDY PHELAN, *The Kingdom of Quito in the Seventeenth Century* (1967). For Peru, see FERNANDO SILVA SANTIESTEBAN, *Los obrajes en el virreinato del Perú* (1964); MIRIAM SALAS DE COLOMA, "Evolución de la propiedad obrera en la Huamanga colonial," in *Anuario de estudios americanos*, 39 (1982): 367–395, and *De los obrajes de Canaria y Chincheros a las comunidades de Vilcashuamán, siglo XVI* (1979); MAGNUS MÖRNER, *Perfil de la sociedad rural del Cuzco a fines de la colonia* (1978). For

Alto Perú and Río de la Plata, see BROOKE LARSON, "The Cotton Textile Industry of Cochabamba, 1770–1810: The Opportunities and Limits of Growth," in *The Economies of Mexico and Peru During the Late Colonial Period, 1760–1810*, edited by Nils Jacobsen and Hans-Jurgen Puhle (1986); and CARLOS SEMPAT ASSADOURIAN, *El sistema de la economía colonial. El mercado interior: Regiones y espacio económico* (1983).

GUY P. C. THOMSON

Modern Textiles

The first line of manufactures in Latin America to be produced by the factory system was the COTTON textile industry. Throughout the nineteenth and early twentieth centuries, cotton textiles made up the greatest part of the industrial output of most Latin American countries. By the 1930s their relative importance had declined as other lines of manufacturing, such as paper, cement, and steel, adopted the factory system.

Cotton and wool goods were being spun and woven prior to the conquest of the Americas, and artisanal production of cloth continued throughout the colonial period. The two centers of colonial production were PUEBLA, Mexico, and MINAS GERAIS, Brazil. All production took place in the weaving sheds of independent cottage producers or in rudimentary manufactories that at times used coerced labor. The output of these operations was almost entirely coarse goods for the popular market, high-quality goods being beyond their technical abilities. Though the data are rough, wool goods were probably more important than cotton goods during this period, with the exception of Brazil, where cotton cloth production dominated.

EARLY FACTORIES

The first factories appeared in the 1830s, when Mexican entrepreneurs in the states of Puebla and México began to mechanize the spinning of cotton yarn. Most of the capital for the construction of these water-powered factories came from merchant activities, though the Mexican government provided some help as well through an industrial development bank, the BANCO DE AVÍO, founded in 1830. By the late 1830s, Mexico's textile industrialists had begun to move into mechanized weaving as well. In 1843 Mexico possessed 59 factories operating 125,362 spindles and 2,609 looms in the modern sector of the industry. Almost all of this output was in coarse, gray cloth called *manta*, because high-quality, fine-weave goods continued to be imported from Europe. By Western European or U.S. standards, Mexico's textile industry was extremely small, but it was the largest in Latin America. This relatively early start allowed Mexico to be the preeminent producer of cotton goods in Latin America until the turn of the century.

By the 1850s the factory system had slowly begun to spread to other countries in the region, and by the 1870s virtually every Latin American country was producing at least some cotton goods by machine. Mexico and Brazil, however, were clearly the two most important producers, because they possessed large markets, good lands for growing cotton, long traditions of artisanal cotton cloth production, and sources of water power near the population centers that consumed the output of their mills. By the early 1880s, the Mexican industry had grown to 99 factories running 249,334 spindles and 8,864 looms with a work force of roughly 11,500. An additional 9,000 spindles, 350 looms, and 700 workers were dedicated to wool production. The annual output of cotton cloth probably ran to 100 million meters. Brazil's industry was approximately one-third the size of Mexico's, with 43 factories running 80,420 spindles and 2,631 looms. Roughly 3,600 workers were employed in these firms, and annual output was in the area of 24 million meters.

EXPANSION

It was not until the 1890s that the textile industry began to grow at a rapid rate. The process of economic growth induced by the export boom of the last decades of the nineteenth century created conditions that were propitious for the industry's expansion. Incomes grew, markets were unified by the building of railroad networks, capital markets matured, and the wealth of the mercantile classes, the most important source of capital for the textile industry, grew rapidly. By 1920 the Mexican cotton goods industry included 120 mills operating 753,837 spindles and 27,301 looms and providing employment for 37,936 workers. Brazil's cotton industry had grown even larger, with 202 mills employing 78,911 workers and running nearly 1.6 million spindles and 52,254 looms. The total production of Brazil's mills was probably close to 500 million meters of cloth. By this point, domestically produced cotton cloth accounted for roughly 80 percent of the market in both countries. Other Latin American countries had viable, but significantly smaller, cotton industries by this time. Chile, for example, had but three mills employing less than 500 workers and running only 5,000 spindles and 400 looms, while Argentina and Colombia had cotton industries that were roughly three times that size.

LARGE FIRMS

What is particularly remarkable about the cotton industries in Brazil and Mexico was the size of the largest firms, which were gigantic even by U.S. standards. Mexico's largest firm, the Compañía Industrial de Orizaba (CIDOSA), founded in 1889, was by 1900 a four-mill operation employing 4,284 workers running 92,708 spindles and 3,899 looms. Had it been in the United States, it would have ranked among the twenty-five largest cotton textile enterprises. Brazil's largest producer, the Companhia América Fabril, was not far behind the CIDOSA operation; it controlled six mills employing 3,100 workers running 85,286 spindles and 2,170 looms. The predominance of a few large firms in both countries meant that the level of concentration was

Textile mill in Medellín, Colombia, ca. 1937. FRANCISCO MEJÍA, COLTEJER / CENTRO DE MEMORIA VISUAL FAES, MEDELLÍN, COLOMBIA.

significantly higher than that which prevailed in the United States; the percentage of the market controlled by the four largest Latin American firms in 1910 was 7.5 percent in the U.S., 16.8 percent in Brazil, and 28.7 percent in Mexico. A similar situation prevailed in the production of wool textiles, where a few firms controlled the lion's share of the market. In Mexico, for example, two firms, the Compañía Industrial de San Ildefonso and La Victoria, S.A., most likely accounted for better than one-third of all the machine-produced wool cloth.

CAPITAL
By the turn of the century, Brazil had overtaken Mexico as the region's premier textile producer, thanks in large part to the capital provided by the Rio de Janeiro stock exchange. Indeed, 28 percent of Brazil's cotton factories were financed through the sale of equity, compared to just 3 percent in Mexico.

As in the United States and Western Europe, merchants played the most important role in industrial finance throughout Latin America. One reason for their prominence was that only merchants possessed the kind of liquid capital necessary to undertake the sizable investment needed. Another was that merchants had more knowledge of the market than other entrepreneurs

and could dovetail their mercantile operations into their manufacturing operations. Indeed, the largest shareholders in the mills often were important cloth merchants who sold to their own wholesaling and retailing operations at a discount.

COMPETITIVENESS
Throughout its history the Latin American textile industry operated behind high tariff barriers and often received both direct and indirect government subsidies. This support was crucial for an industry that could not compete internationally against England and the United States. For this reason almost all of the production of most countries was consumed in the domestic market. Two factors prevented Latin America from developing internationally competitive textile industries. First, start-up costs were higher than those that prevailed in the advanced industrial countries. Lacking the ability to produce their own machinery, Latin American countries imported all of the necessary equipment from abroad and thus needed to set aside funds to cover the costs of transport and insurance in transit. They also needed to pay the salaries of the foreign technical personnel who set up the plant. These added expenses could push up the cost of erecting a mill by as much as 60 percent. Higher start-up costs were compounded by interest rates higher than those in the advanced industrial countries, due in part to a risk premium and less well-integrated financial markets. Second, the productivity of labor in Latin America was a good deal lower than that in the advanced industrial countries. Because workers resisted attempts to instill industrial discipline and routinize work, Latin America's mills typically employed from two to three times the number of workers per machine as did firms in the advanced industrial countries. Output per worker was therefore much lower as well; in 1925 labor productivity in Brazil, Mexico, and Argentina was roughly half that of the U.S. Northeast, one-sixth that of the U.S. South, and one-third that of Japan. Thus, even though wages for Latin American textile workers were from one-third to one-half of those prevailing abroad, these lower wages were offset by lower work intensity.

WORLD WAR I AND AFTER
Contrary to DEPENDENCY THEORY, Latin America's textile industry did not do well during World War I, since capital goods were hard to purchase and the domestic market was depressed because of the decline in the export sector. The industry did even worse during the Great Depression. It was not until World War II that the industry once again faced the kind of favorable conditions that it had experienced in 1890–1914. By this point, however, the industry was even further behind the rest of the world; decades of protectionism and the lack of new investment meant that most of the installed plant and equipment dated from the years prior to 1914. After 1945 the textile industry was thoroughly eclipsed in im-

portance by the newer, heavy industries that had begun to develop during the 1920s.

STANLEY J. STEIN, *The Brazilian Cotton Manufacture: Textile Enterprise in an Underdeveloped Area, 1850–1950* (1957); WARREN DEAN, *The Industrialization of São Paulo, 1880–1945* (1969); DAWN KEREMITIS, *La industria textil mexicana en el siglo XIX* (1973); RICHARD J. SALVUCCI, *Textiles and Capitalism in Mexico: An Economic History of the Obrajes, 1539–1840* (1987); STEPHEN H. HABER, *Industry and Underdevelopment: The Industrialization of Mexico, 1890–1940* (1989), and "Industrial Concentration and the Capital Markets: A Comparative Study of Brazil, Mexico, and the United States, 1830–1930," in *Journal of Economic History* 51, no. 3 (1991); GUY P. C. THOMPSON, *Puebla de los Angeles: Industry and Society in a Mexican City, 1700–1850* (1989); and DOUGLAS COLE LIBBY, "Proto-Industrialization in a Slave Society: The Case of Minas Gerais," in *Journal of Latin American Studies* 23 (1991), especially pp. 23–33.

STEPHEN H. HABER

See also **Cotton Industry; Wool Industry.**

TEXTILES, INDIGENOUS. The tradition of weaving is one of the earliest crafts known to the inhabitants of Latin America. Before the Conquest it was a major expression of culture. Pictorial motifs denoting rank, religion, and politics were a form of visual communication that allowed the weavings to be traded over very large areas, throughout the Andean region and from Mexico to Costa Rica.

Basic to most early cultures were the techniques of twining and, very early on, weaving. Twining, or twisting the fibers together to produce a long continuous rope, was the primary skill needed to provide a satisfactory alternative to vines and reeds, both used by hunters and basket makers. Twined flexible fibers such as grasses, cotton, and hair produced the first weaving threads. COTTON was one of the first cultivated crops in the warm coastal areas of the Americas. Used throughout the weaving cultures of the Americas was a loom based on a group of sticks using the body or stakes to provide tension. The backstrap loom was used by many indigenous groups and a variation of it can be seen in the stake loom of the Andes. These lightweight, wooden looms were economical and easily transported. Common also to the varied societies were the dynamic use of color with availability of an abundance of natural dyes. Although many indigenous groups wove, the craft as an art form was developed by the MAYA in Mesoamerica and the INCA in the Andes. A full range of techniques were developed, including gauze, brocading or secondary warp and weft threads, double-cloth, and tapestry weaving.

In Mesoamerica the culture of the early OLMEC evolved into the civilization known as the Maya (1500 B.C.–A.D. 1100). In the Mayan religion Ixchel was the goddess of weaving and women were the primary weavers. Despite the decline of the Mayan civilization in the eleventh century, weaving continued. In the AZTEC codices of the fif-

teenth century the tribute lists show the old Mayan area under Aztec control paid tribute in woven goods. The nobles, priests, and warriors wore mantles with brocaded motifs denoting their rank and status. Acid soil conditions have destroyed most of the native textiles and there are few left more than a century old. Motifs on pottery, murals, stelae, and codices depicting ceremonial figures dressed in court attire have been our best early evidence with the exception of textile fragments retrieved from the sacred Canada at the Toltec-Maya site of CHICHÉN ITZÁ. These were woven in a variety of complex patterns decorated with brocading and open-weave techniques.

In the pre-Conquest Andes the early culture of the CHAVÍN and other regional cultures evolved into the civilization of the Inca. These developing cultures supported and encouraged the weaving craft. And, fortunately, unlike Mesoamerica, the arid Paracas peninsula held its treasure of bodies wrapped in their layers of beautifully woven costumes: color coordinated, with matching motifs brocaded in complimentary hues. There is an abundance of materials sufficient to study the evolution of design elements in these materials, unlike their Mesoamerican counterparts.

Fibers used during the pre-Conquest period in Mesoamerica and eastern South America include a fine white cotton, a short-fiber brown cotton, bast fibers, rabbit hair, spider web, and feathers, all of these plus cameloid hair (llama, alpaca, and vicuña) were used in western South America as well. Dyes and mordants were found in plants, insects, marine creatures, and minerals. The fibers and dyes were found locally or were traded for at markets. Dyes commonly used today in the Andes are soot, leaves from the walnut tree, and COCHINEAL, while INDIGO is still used in Mesoamerica. Very early fragments show color added by stamping and painting. As the craft developed, additional color was added with designs brocaded into the fabric as it was woven. Appliqué and embroidery were also used. Common to most American weavers was the use of the piece goods as it comes off the loom. Prior to European influence, all clothing was contrived from these straight pieces: skirts, hip wraps, mantles, stoles, and a garment made with a place for the head in the center. Variations on these styles were worn by both men and women. Utilitarian pieces such as men's bags, as well as ceremonial burial robes for their rulers, were made in the same manner. The Andean weavers developed a technique to manipulate the warp and weft threads into shaped pieces. In addition to the backstrap looms, they also developed small string looms for weaving narrow bands that required no wooden parts. Finishes on woven pieces of circular tassels and figures were elaborate.

The European treadle loom introduced very shortly after the Conquest brought many changes to the textile tradition. Native men were taught to weave on the new treadle looms and women were excluded from a craft that had been dominated by women. Clothing and household goods and ceremonial items were no longer woven in traditional designs and qualities at home. Bulk yardage needed strong machine-spun threads. Hand-spun yarn gave way to factory produced threads. Wool was introduced and, to a limited degree, silk. Women were employed in households to make lace and embroideries in the European mode. These crafts were taught by the nuns in church schools.

Native dress has changed the least in women's attire. In Guatemala and Chiapas today the native design is seen in the huipil. A woman's top is woven in one, two, or three panels, with an opening for the head in the center and the sides usually sewn below an armhole. The number of panels, length of garment, design, and color are usually determined by the local town, as each is distinct. Huipils seem to be alike, but they vary by ability, arrangement of a common group of motifs and color. Skirts are rectangles but may no longer be dyed with indigo or cochineal. One can still see the Maya wearing huipils, skirts, vests, and carrying bags in the old style especially in areas of strong native church groups. But since 1970 in Guatemala there has been a drastic change in the number of women wearing their village huipil. Many young women favor a lighter commercial huipil or a pattern of their own design for everyday and keep the village huipil for church and celebrations. In the Andes the AYMARA still prefer bright colors and motifs from the native flora, while the Quechuas use animal motifs in harmonious patterns. But many of the early influences are more elusive. Natives on the coasts have turned to muslin cut in old styles such as tucked shirt fronts in Honduras or sailor collar shirts in Mexico. Old-style native dress cut from *manta* (muslin) are often embroidered in a running stitch, to look like brocading, or cross-stitched. In Chile a short woolen poncho was adapted by the indigenous horsemen.

New technology and style have also been added to the native textile art. Twentieth-century Cuna in Panama have evolved a women's blouse, *mola*, from body painting. The designs were worked in layers of solid-colored, European cotton fabric in a variety of techniques of layering and appliqué. Over the decades these designs have evolved into a cartoon of Cuna life and religion. Although a form of cross-knit looping was known prior to the Conquest, the indigenous people of Peru and Bolivia have made the craft of multiple-needle knitting into a native art form. Earflap caps, or *ch'ullus*, masks, armwarmers, and leggings have been incorporated into the native costume and ceremonies. Andean knitted products are now sold by commercial designers and alpaca knitting yarn is prized by knitters for its soft hand and lovely colors. In Guatemala the art of *ikat*, tie-dying threads into designs for both the warp and the weft before weaving, are now used in both the backstrap-loomed materials as well as the European-loomed yardage. This patterning was first used in women's skirts and is now produced and traded in such quantities as to be seen throughout the world and copied in India and China.

Major changes have evolved in indigenous textiles in the twentieth century. Air transportation and roads have opened up sheltered cultures to outside influences. Men have worked in factories and positions away from their village and in different climates. Progressive schools and institutions have tried to westernize the natives, diminishing the use of and need for native dress. Native style has been regulated by laws to make it conform to modern decorum. Colors and designs have changed to make textile goods more marketable and pleasing to tourists and wholesalers. Chemical dyes have changed the color from soft or faded natural color to vibrant hues. New fibers such as synthetic silk-like rayon and Orlon have been exchanged for wool and cotton or used as secondary fibers in weaving. In some communities there has been a deliberate attempt to develop new dyes to duplicate the hue of natural dyes and provide a more satisfactory spun thread. Where technology has been used to enhance the native textile culture, everyone has benefited; where it has been used to eliminate the culture by producing a poor, cheap substitute, all societies have suffered.

LILA M. O'NEALE, *Textiles of Highland Guatemala* (1945); LILLY DE JONGH OSBORNE, *Indian Crafts of Guatemala and El Salvador* (1965); DONALD CORDRY and DOROTHY CORDRY, *Mexican Indian Costumes* (1968); MARJORIE CASON and ADELE CAHLANDER, *The Art of Bolivian Highland Weaving* (1976); PATRICIA REIFF ANAWALT, *Indian Clothing Before Cortez* (1981); TAMMARA E. WASSERMAN and JONATHAN S. HILL, *Bolivian Indian Textiles: Traditional Designs and Costumes* (1981); LAURIE ADELSON and ARTHUR TRACHT, *Aymara Weavings: Ceremonial Textiles of Colonial and 19th Century Bolivia* (1983); ADELE CAHLANDER with Suzanne Baizerman, *Double-Woven Treasures from Old Peru* (1985); CYNTHIA GRAVELLE LE COUNT, *Andean Folk Knitting: Traditions and Techniques from Peru and Bolivia* (1990).

SUE DAWN MCGRADY

TEZCATLIPOCA, Aztec deity of rulership, destruction, the night, and the magic arts. The most important deity in AZTEC religion, Tezcatlipoca is a complex composite of shifting identities who, like his North American cousin Trickster, defies definition by being himself a principle of disorder. He incited immoral behavior and then punished or pardoned the wrongdoer. He was a shaman, a *nahualli* or shape-changer whose hidden self was the JAGUAR, though he had many disguises. As the Big Dipper he ruled the night sky, but lost his left foot to the crocodilian earth monster when the constellation's end star dropped below the horizon. The serpent-footed God K (Tahil) of the Classic MAYA is Tezcatlipoca's analogue.

The name Tezcatlipoca, "Smoking Mirror" or "The Mirror's Smoke," alludes to his practice of divination with torch-lit obsidian mirrors. His other names include Yohualli Ehecatl, "The Night, The Wind"; Titlacahuan, "We are His Slaves"; Necoc Yaotl, "Enemy on Both Sides"; Ipalnemohuani, "By Him One Lives"; and Tloque Nahuaque, "Possessor of the Near, Possessor of the Nigh."

Tezcatlipoca was at once one being and four: the Four Tezcatlipocas, lords of the directions, governed the creation and destruction of the earth and sun. In the east was the red Tezcatlipoca, Xipe Totec; in the south the blue HUITZILOPOCHTLI; white QUETZALCOATL in the west; in the north the Black Tezcatlipoca or Tezcatlipoca proper. He and Quetzalcoatl were paired in a cosmic conflict. Tezcatlipoca humiliated Quetzalcoatl and destroyed the mythic city Tollan (Tula). Placing these events in their historic past, the fatalistic Aztecs saw their own age as controlled by capricious Tezcatlipoca; rulers owed to him their tenuous hold on authority.

Spanish friars saw Tezcatlipoca as particularly demonic, and even identified him as Lucifer; therefore, he may appear more malevolent in colonial sources than he had been before contact.

BERNARDINO DE SAHAGÚN, *Florentine Codex,* translated by Arthur J. O. Anderson and Charles Dibble (1952–1983), esp. Books 3, 5, and 6; DIEGO DURÁN, *Book of the Gods and Rites and the Ancient Calendar,* translated and edited by Fernando Horcasitas and Doris Heyden (1971); LOUISE M. BURKHART, *The Slippery Earth: Nahua-Christian Moral Dialogue in Sixteenth-Century Mexico* (1989).

LOUISE M. BURKHART

THEATER. The history of the theater in Latin America is significantly longer than the period of the occupation by the Europeans. Before Columbus's arrival the great civilizations of the New World had developed drama and theatrical forms which satisfied ritual and aesthetic purposes. The Inca Garcilaso de la Vega refers to the comedies and tragedies of the Incas; the Aztecs had developed forms of dance and spectacle in a theatrical mode. Regrettably, none of these survived the conquest. The only extant pre-Columbian theater piece is the *Rabinal Achí,* a curiously repetitious Maya drama elaborated by the K'iche' (Quiché) of Guatemala. After centuries of oral transmission it was transcribed in 1850 as the *Dance of Tun* and later translated into French by the Abbé Étienne Brasseur de Bourbourg. The play recounts the capture, questioning, and death of the K'iche' warrior. Although the cast is large, there are only five speaking parts and the notable feature is the parallelism that marks the principal interaction between the two warriors.

Theater may have contributed little to the conquest of the Americas, but it was vital to their colonization. The Spanish cleverly adapted indigenous artistic forms to hasten the process of converting the Indians to Catholicism, one of the two major objectives of the Conquest. The earliest recorded theatrical forms in the New World are, in fact, short religious pieces (known as *autos, loas,* or *mojigangas*) developed by the clergy, who at times distorted indigenous concepts in order to convey the tenets of Christianity, primarily for the purpose of catechization. Little evidence remains because of the ephemeral nature of these plays and the severe ecclesi-astical censorship of the times. In sixteenth-century Brazil, Padre José de ANCHIETA wrote *autos sacramentales* incorporating the flora, fauna, and ethnology of the new land, in combinations of Spanish, Portuguese, Latin, and indigenous languages.

By the middle of the sixteenth century, a secular theater responding to the needs of the growing population began to flourish, especially in Lima and other major centers. In Mexico, Fernán GONZÁLEZ DE ESLAVA wrote both religious and secular pieces, some in honor of vice-regal celebrations and special events. The rapid growth and development in the theater in Spain during the golden age of Lope de Vega, Tirso de Molina, and others, provided impetus for writers in Latin America.

SEVENTEENTH CENTURY

In the seventeenth century the theater of Latin America continued to reflect the literary traditions of Europe, and there was regular interaction between the two continents. The celebrated Spanish playwright Pedro Calderón de la Barca visited the New World, whereas the Mexican-born Juan RUÍZ DE ALARCÓN established residency in Spain; his twenty-four plays, although claimed by Mexico as a national legacy, show little evidence of the New World in language or customs. Known as the moralist of his time, he valued human dignity, and his best plays, *Las paredes oyen* (1628) and *La verdad sospechosa,* (1634) are both didactic and entertaining.

The literary genius of the era is the Mexican nun Sor JUANA INÉS DE LA CRUZ, a prodigy whose superb gift for language combined with a powerful sense of social and sexual equality to produce works with lasting value. *El divino Narciso* (1690) is written as an *auto sacramental,* and *Los empeños de una casa* (1683) represents the American baroque in theater. In 1990 a play attributed to Sor Juana was discovered in the Mexican archives.

In Brazil the theater of the seventeenth century is marked by a decline of the activities of the Jesuits in presenting drama. In general the representations are linked to religious festivals or to other popular feasts or public occasions. Manuel Botelho de OLIVEIRA is known as one of the first Brazilians to publish his works, but they are Spanish in spirit, technique, themes, and even at times in language.

Throughout the Americas the theater movement reflected the tastes and interests of the privileged classes. The theatrical artists who toured in the New World with Spanish-based productions stimulated local activity, and writers and plays in the Americas tended to echo the themes and styles of European theater.

EIGHTEENTH CENTURY

Just as the eighteenth century in Spain failed to shine after the literary splendor of the baroque had passed, the New World currents also showed little originality. In Mexico, Eusebio de Vela (1688–1737) wrote *comedias* for his Coliseo de Mexico. In Lima in 1837, Father Antonio Valdez reportedly "discovered" an ancient Inca text, *Ollantay*, but its European structure led critics to conclude that he had written the text based on ancient themes and legends. In Brazil, "O Judeu" (the pen name of Antônio José da SILVA) wrote satirical works caricaturing both the nobility and the church, which led to his persecution and burning at the stake. The earliest theater pieces from Argentina are *Siripo* (1789), by Manuel José de Lavardén, and the anonymous *El amor de la estanciera* (ca. 1792), which is recognized as a humble precursor of the gaucho drama.

NINETEENTH CENTURY

The Wars of Independence that rumbled across Latin America between 1810 and about 1825 did little to break the cultural ties with Spain. Theater fare often consisted of adaptations or translations of European works, and the neoclassical tendencies of the period served didactic purposes, with an emphasis on reason rather than on emotion. In Buenos Aires the Sociedad de Buen Gusto was founded in 1817 to develop an autonomous theater in this fledgling provincial capital, but it survived only two years. As both playwright and actor, Luis Ambrosio Morante (1775–1837) was responsible for its first production, *Cornelia Bororquía* (1817), one of several plays that dealt with conflicts between civil and religious power. In Mexico the celebrated novelist José Joaquín Fernández de Lizardi (1776–1827) wrote didactic, neoclassical plays. In Brazil, King João VI ordered the construction of the Royal Theater after his flight from the Napoleonic invasion, in order to transplant his favorite Italian operas to Rio de Janeiro. The first play by a Brazilian with a national theme is *Antônio José, ou O Poeta e a Inquisição* (1838), by J. D. Gonçalves de MAGALHÃES, written as a classical tragedy to express his disgust with the new school of romanticism.

While romanticism was sweeping the European continent, its arrival in Spain and Latin America was arrested by political issues in both sites. In 1833 the Mexican expatriate Manuel Eduardo de Gorostiza (1789–1851) brought his masterpiece, *Contigo pan y cebolla*, back to Mexicoa as a satirical view of the excessive sentimentalism and idealization of the romantic mode. From the 1830s to the 1870s the theater was still nourished largely by European themes and techniques. There was a cleavage between exotic and chivalric revivals of European inspiration and incipient efforts to identity customs, deeds, and values of the Americas. The new political and literary freedom of the period generated polemical initiatives to use the stage for propaganda.

The most representative Mexican playwrights of the period reflected both tendencies: Fernando Calderón (1809–1845) generally escaped Mexican boundaries in a search for esoteric European fancies, while his compatriot Ignacio Rodríguez Galván (1816–1842) looked to the traditions and legends of the New World, as in *Muñoz, Visitador de México* (1838). The brutality of the Juan Manuel de ROSAS dictatorship in Argentina stifled a free theater development, but while in exile in Bolivia, Pedro Echagüe (1821–1889) staged his version of *Rosas* (1851), full of political invective and recrimination. At home the theater tended to be adulatory or to follow the sentimental, exotic, or satiric-regionalistic models of the romantic period.

Interior of Iturbide Theater. Reproduced from *México y sus alrededores*, (Mexico City, 1855/1856). COURTESY OF HARVARD COLLEGE LIBRARY.

The monarchy in Brazil created an entirely different political climate, and the Brazilian playwrights ranged from escapist theater to advocating the abolition of slavery. The most important was Martins Pena, who with wit and grace developed the comedy of manners, leaving a dramatic legacy that captured the essence of Brazilian customs and values in the mid-nineteenth century.

The disparities in the latter part of the century are even more pronounced throughout the Americas. Just as neoclassic modes survived into the romantic period, the romantic modes continued well into the period in which realism characterized the novel and a new psychological base, inspired by Sigmund Freud and Henrik Ibsen, underscored the Spanish theater known as the *alta comedia,* which tried to capture a realistic view of life. The Mexican playwrights José Peón Contreras (1843–1907) and Manuel José Othón (1858–1906) exemplified the period with facile verses and romantic excesses. In Brazil a new theater modeled on the Gymnase in Paris, where the repertoire of French realism triumphed, enjoyed a brief period of enthusiastic support for its thesis plays on important social issues of the time, but it was superseded by the success of the *revista* (review), a light and comical form popularized by the prolific Artur Azevedo (1855–1908), whose talent for spontaneity, improvisation, and popular psychology ensured success for his farces and satires about Brazilian customs and politics.

In the latter part of the century, in the Río de la Plata region, there developed the *sainete criollo* (creole burlesque or farce), a theatrical form driven by the moral values, social problems, and ethnic complications of an area rapidly settled by European immigrants, and derived from the indigenous and gaucho traditions. When Eduardo Gutiérrez's novel *Juan Moreira* was adapted for the circus by the Uruguayan clown José Podestá in 1884, the door was opened to a new combination of the Spanish picaresque traditions and local elements full of both life and sadness.

TWENTIETH CENTURY

The foregoing emphasis on Mexico, Brazil, and the Río de la Plata in no way is meant to suggest a lack of theatrical activity in other countries, all of which have their own rich histories, reflecting the strong influence of European models. It is only in the twentieth century that the theater of Latin America takes on a unique and original quality that allows it to stand with the best of world drama.

In much of Latin America the nineteenth-century traditions continued well into the new century. The exception is the Río de la Plata area, where the picturesqueness of the European migration fused with the national atmosphere to provide raw material for the modernized *sainete,* embodied in the plays of the Uruguayan Florencio SÁNCHEZ. In such dramas as *La gringa* (1904) and *Barranca abajo* (1905), he melded the concerns of people struggling with their ambience and their own shortcomings into dynamic models that set the standards for his generation. Roberto Payró (1867–1928), Gregorio Laferrère (1867–1913), and Ernesto Herrera (1886–1917) continued the *sainete* tradition.

The impetus for a modernized theater originated in Mexico in 1928 when Salvador Novo and Xavier Villaurrutia, with the patronage of Antonieta Rivas Mercado, launched the Teatro de Ulises, a vanguard theater that brought to Mexico the latest techniques in staging, lighting, and direction. Earlier efforts by the Grupo de los Siete Autores had made some progress, but had not succeeded in breaking the old traditions of the prompter's box or the domination by the primary actor or actress. The new experimental format required a small theater, electric lighting, memorized text, and coordination by the director of all elements of the performance. Other Mexican groups, such as Orientación, quickly followed suit in the effort to establish these universal phenomena in the national aesthetic consciousness.

During the 1930s and into the early 1940s, similar initiatives sprang up throughout the Latin American republics. In Argentina the work of Leónidas Barletta with the Teatro del Pueblo had the double objective of modernizing theater craft and delivering a social message. With this group Roberto ARLT, a major playwright long undervalued, staged such plays as *Saverio el cruel* (1936), which incorporates metatheatrical concepts with elements of class conflict.

The renovation occurred in Puerto Rico in 1938 when the Ateneo Puertorriqueño presented three plays selected by Emilio Belaval for their national themes. The national conscience of Puerto Rico was awakened by the desire for social reform for the displaced *jíbaro* (hillbilly) or the immigrant to New York. Belaval's short-lived group, Areyto, was soon followed by others with the same objectives.

The Brazilian theater was characterized during these years by reviews, farces, operettas, and burlesque, represented by authors continuing the traditions of Artur Azevedo. Although the Semana de Arte Moderna in 1922 revolutionized Brazilian letters, its impact was not felt in the theater. During the 1930s the theater of Joracy Camargo explored sociopolitical theories of class struggle. Change came through Os Comediantes's brilliant staging of Nelson RODRIGUES's multilevel *Vestido de noiva* (1943) by the Polish-emigré director Zbigniew Ziembinski, who had been trained in German Expressionism.

A curious aspect of the Chilean theater movement was that the renaissance occurred through the universities. In 1941 at the University of Chile and in 1943 at the Catholic University of Santiago, semiprofessional theater companies were established to bring to the Chilean stage the principles espoused by Margarita Xirgú with her touring productions of Federico García Lorca's plays.

All of these experimental and independent initiatives,

combined with those of other countries, laid the groundwork for the boom in Latin American theater that took form in the 1950s and 1960s. The play by the Argentine Carlos Gorostiza, *El puente*, which premiered in 1949, moved from the experimental stage to the commercial stage in 1950, marking the beginning of a new era. Throughout the Americas, conditions favored an expansion in the theater, and playwrights and directors responded to the challenge with exciting new plays in imaginative stagings. Their numbers are legion. Their objectives, however, were amazingly cohesive: to bring to the Latin American theater a new sense of its own identity, capturing the national and human spirit through believable characters who manifested the social, political, religious, and personal conflicts of individuals in modern societies.

Not all plays, naturally, were masterpieces, but the new generation included those who produced the contemporary canon: Emilio CARBALLIDO and Luisa Josefina HERNÁNDEZ (Mexico), Osvaldo de DRAGÚN and Griselda GAMBARO (Argentina), Jorge DÍAZ and Egon WOLFF (Chile), René MARQUÉS and Francisco ARRIVÍ (Puerto Rico), José TRIANA (Cuba), and a host of others. Their experiments with lights, music, sound, and movement were inspiring to a new generation of directors, including Jorge Lavelli and Jaime Kogan (Argentina), Julio Castillo and Juan Tovar (Mexico), Isaac Chocrón (Venezuela), José Lacomba (Puerto Rico), Orlando Rodríguez (Chile), Zbigniew Ziembinski, Luciano Salce, and José Celso (Brazil), and many others.

This expansion continued virtually unchecked into the 1960s, national differences duly noted, when Latin Americans began to seek inspiration not so much from the traditional European or American sources as from within Latin America itself, and to develop the *creación colectiva* (theater developed by the group). The year 1968 marks a critical juncture when theater festivals were organized in Lima, Peru; San José, Costa Rica; Mexico City, and Manizales, Colombia, the latter an event that has continued into the 1990s. These festivals developed a sense of solidarity within the Latin American theater community, providing groups with the opportunity to be seen and to see and to draw from the best of their counterparts.

At the same time, in contrast with the "well-made plays" of the 1950s and early 1960s, the theater again became more experimental, reacting against bourgeois standards in favor of a more egalitarian system. Directors assumed a less authoritarian role in order to allow actors to create their own works collectively, especially in those cases where groups felt that plays capable of expressing their sociopolitical aims were not available. Drawing on the models set by the Living Theatre and the Berliner Ensemble, the manifestations of the *creación colectiva* in Latin America are as varied as the groups that represented them, but some are exemplary. In Brazil, Augusto Boal established the Teatro de Arena in 1965 using the *teatro de coringa,* a form that allowed

great flexibility in putting actors into direct contact with the staging and the public. Boal, at times in exile, later developed a journalistic theater, an invisible theater, and an image theater under the broad rubric of "theater of the oppressed." Teatro Aleph (Chile), Libre Teatro Libre (Argentina), CLETA (Mexico), Yuyachkani and Cuatrotablas (Peru), and many others experimented with similar politically oriented theatrical forms. The most developed activity was in Colombia, where the TEC (Teatro Experimental de Cali) and La Candelaria (Bogotá) under the direction of Enrique Buenaventura and Santiago García, respectively, developed coherent methodological systems for inverting traditional bourgeois structures.

The Cuban theater followed the typical Latin American patterns until the Revolution of 1959 began to use the theater as an instrument for social change. Writers such as José Triana and Antón ARRUFAT fell from favor and were replaced by the collectives such as Teatro Escambray, a group formed in the mountains to address social issues at a popular level within the new government structure. With major funding, the theater movement has flourished in Cuba but always within approved ideological limits.

The politicization of the theater in Latin America throughout the 1970s did not replace other forms entirely. While the influence of Bertolt Brecht was ubiquitous, Artaudian strains of total theater were also common, as were occasional remnants of theater of the absurd. Some playwrights experimented with ritual and game-playing, and metatheatrical forms kept pace with a new insistence on documentary-style drama. A new generation of playwrights emerged, including Vicente LEÑERO, Oscar Liera, and Oscar VILLEGAS (Mexico); José Ignacio Cabrujas and Román Chalbaud (Venezuela), Eduardo Pavlovsky, Ricardo Talesnik, and Diana Raznovich (Argentina), Marco Antonio de la Parra (Chile), Roberto Ramos-Perea (Puerto Rico), Reynaldo Disla (Dominican Republic), Roberto Athayde, Naum Alves de Sousa, and María Adelaide Amaral (Brazil), and many others. The experiment with Teatro Abierto in Buenos Aires in 1981, a collaboration originally between twenty playwrights and twenty directors, gave new impetus to the Argentine theater. By the late 1980s, the restoration of democratic governments in most countries relieved some political problems in the theatrical arena, but the crushing economic issues brought on by inflation and the debt crisis, coupled with overpopulation, inadequate social programs, and the narcotics traffic, left Latin America in danger of falling hopelessly behind during the technological and industrial advances of the 1990s. The theater continues to make heroic efforts to respond to, or even to anticipate, the needs of the multiform societies represented in Latin America.

Documentation on theater has become increasingly sophisticated in recent years as critics and scholars respond to new challenges. A rash of new journals regularly publishes analytical and informational items: *Conjunto* and *Tablas* (Cuba), *Apuntes* (Chile), *Teatro* (Argentina), *Revista Teatro* (Colombia), *Tramoya* (Mexico), *Latin American Theatre Review* and *Gestos* (United States), and *La Escena Latinoamericana* (Canada), not to mention *Primer Acto,* which provides excellent coverage of Latin America.

The standard works in the field are eight companion volumes titled *Historia del teatro hispanoamericano;* see especially JOSÉ JUAN ARROM, *Época colonial* (1966); and FRANK DAUSTER, *Historia del teatro hispanoamericano (siglos XIX–XX),* 2d ed. (1973). LEON F. LYDAY and GEORGE WOODYARD edited a volume of essays on major playwrights, *Dramatists in Revolt: The New Latin American Theater* (1976).

The rate of growth in documentation is evident in several excellent publications: SEVERINO JOÃO ALBUQUERQUE, *Violent Acts: A Study of Contemporary Latin American Theatre* (1991); RONALD D. BURGESS, *The New Dramatists of Mexico, 1967–1985* (1991); GERARDO LUZURIAGA, *Introducción a las teorías latinoamericanas del teatro* (1990); and DIANA TAYLOR, *Theatre of Crisis: Drama and Politics in Latin America* (1991).

An indispensable 4-vol. overview of the field was published in Spain by the Centro de Documentación Teatral: MOISÉS PÉREZ COTERILLO, ed., *Escenarios de dos mundos: Inventario teatral de Iberoamérica* (1988).

GEORGE WOODYARD

See also **Literature.**

THIEL, BERNARDO AUGUSTO (*b.* 1 April 1850; *d.* 9 September 1901), bishop of Costa Rica (1880–1901). Thiel was born in Elberfeld, Germany, and was ordained in Paris in 1874. He became a seminary professor in Costa Rica in 1877. He was named to a politically controversial and vacant bishopric by the anticlerical Liberal president Tomás GUARDIA GUTIÉRREZ as a moderate candidate but was subsequently expelled, along with the JESUITS, by Liberal authorities in 1884. After his return in 1886, Thiel became involved in electoral politics, and in 1889 founded the Catholic Union Party, which campaigned actively against the Liberal regime in 1894. Thiel also made several doctrinal statements on labor's right to organize and to receive "just salaries" in the face of widespread recession during the crisis in world coffee prices, which reduced real wages by 50 percent from 1870 to 1930. He founded a clerical newspaper, *El Mensajero del Clero,* in 1897, and was extremely active in national cultural life. His classic work, "Monografía de la Poblacíon de Costa Rica en el Siglo XIX," in *Revista de Costa Rica en el siglo XIX* (1902), remains a standard source. Thiel died in San José, Costa Rica.

VICTOR MANUEL SANABRIA MARTÍNEZ, *Bernardo Augusto Thiel* (1941); OCTAVIO CASTRO SABORÍO, *Bernardo Augusto Thiel en la historia* (1959); CONSTANTINO LÁSCARIS COMNENO, *Desarrollo de las ideas en Costa Rica,* 2d ed. (1975); JAMES BACKER, *La iglesia y*

el sindicalismo en Costa Rica, 3d ed. (1978); RICARDO BLANCO SEGURA, *1884: La iglesia y las reformas liberales* (1984).

LOWELL GUDMUNDSON

THOMPSON, GEORGE (*b.* 1839; *d.* 1876), British military engineer active in Paraguay. Coming to Asunción in 1858 under a contractual agreement with the government of Carlos Antonio LÓPEZ, Thompson helped design and build the Paraguay Central Railroad. He remained in the country after the beginning of the WAR OF THE TRIPLE ALLIANCE in 1864, serving the regime of Field Marshal Francisco Solano LÓPEZ as colonel and commander of engineers. His preparation of trenches and defensive earthworks made a critical difference in the early stages of the conflict, particularly at CURUPAYTY (September 1866), where the Brazilians and Argentines were repulsed with extremely heavy losses.

Thompson's spirited defense at Angostura in December 1868 facilitated Solano López's escape northward with what remained of the Paraguayan army. After Lopéz's subsequent surrender to the Brazilians, Thompson was permitted to return to Britain, where he wrote *The War in Paraguay* (1869), a highly detailed account of his experiences that was also highly critical of López. After the war, Thompson returned to Asunción, married into the local elite, and became an important official in the Paraguay Central Railway. He died in Asunción.

JOSEFINA PLÁ, *The British in Paraguay* (1976); JOHN HOYT WILLIAMS, "Foreign Técnicos and the Modernization of Paraguay, 1840–1970," in *Journal of Interamerican Studies and World Affairs* 19, no. 2 (1977): 233–257.

THOMAS L. WHIGHAM

THOMSON PORTO MARIÑO, MANUEL TOMÁS (*b.* 1839; *d.* 1880), Chilean military leader. He entered the Chilean navy during the early 1850s. During the war against Spain (1865–1866) he commanded the captured Spanish warship *Covadonga* and served as its captain during the Battle of Abtao (7 February 1866), the only battle between opposing fleets. During the early days of the WAR OF THE PACIFIC (1879–1883), Thomson commanded the *Esmeralda, Abtao,* and *Amazonas.* In September 1879 the *Amazonas* was dispatched to the Atlantic to intercept the fast Peruvian transport *Oroya* but failed to find the enemy. On 22 December the *Amazonas* captured the Peruvian torpedo launch *Alay* at Ballenitas in northern Peru. In late January 1880 Thomson was given command of the former Peruvian seagoing monitor *Huáscar,* which had been captured at the battle of Angamos (8 October 1879). The *Huáscar* took part in the attack on Arica on 27 February 1880. While engaging the Peruvian coastal monitor *Manco Capac,* Thomson attempted to maneuver between the *Manco Capac* and the Peruvian shore batteries in order to deprive the enemy of its anchorage. At a critical moment the *Huáscar*'s engine failed, and the ship became an easy target. The *Huáscar* was hit by a large-caliber shell and Thomson was killed instantly.

RODRIGO FUENZALIDA BADE, *Marinos ilustres y destacados del pasado* (1985).

ROBERT SCHEINA

THOUSAND DAYS, WAR OF THE. *See* **War of the Thousand Days.**

THREE GUARANTEES, ARMY OF THE, a military unit based upon the three major planks of Agustín de ITURBIDE'S PLAN OF IGUALA (24 February 1821)—religion, independence, union. Following a decade of war, Iturbide called upon former insurgent and royalist military commanders to join a new army. Given the exhaustion of both sides, the call came at a most propitious moment. The renewal of the Spanish constitution in 1820 permitted Mexican towns and communities to cast off the intolerable burden of wartime taxation and service that had supported district and regional defenses. Realizing that the royalist army was crumbling, officers believed that Iturbide's offer would allow them to retain their positions and powers. Similarly, many insurgent commanders accepted Iturbide's offer of peace and patronage, leaving the few remaining royalist commanders without an effective fighting force. Following triumphant progress with only a few isolated skirmishes fought by the die-hard Spaniards, Iturbide led his victorious army to Mexico City and independence. Unfortunately, accelerated promotions within this army helped to create future problems for Mexican governments.

WILLIAM SPENCE ROBERTSON, *Iturbide of Mexico* (1968); CHRISTON I. ARCHER, "Where Did All the Royalists Go? New Light on the Military Collapse of New Spain, 1810–1822," in *The Mexican and Mexican American Experience,* edited by Jaime Rodríguez O. (1989), pp. 24–32; TIMOTHY E. ANNA, *The Mexican Republic of Iturbide* (1990).

CHRISTON I. ARCHER

TIAHUANACO. *See* **Tiwanaku.**

TIERRA DEL FUEGO, southernmost region of the South American continent and administrative territories of both Argentina and Chile: Argentine Tierra del Fuego counts 69,323 inhabitants (1991), while its Chilean counterpart has 9,257 (1980). The region comprises the island of Tierra del Fuego, south of the STRAIT OF MAGELLAN, and other large islands, such as Navarino, Hoste, and Staten Island (Isla de los Estados), as well as myriad small islands, channels, and fjords. The southernmost tip of Tierra del Fuego is the islet of Cape HORN, located at 57 degrees south latitude. Almost half of Tierra del Fuego consists of flat plains of glacial origin (among them, the plains of PATAGONIA), while the rest, the western segment, consists of the ice- and snow-covered summits of the southern ANDES and drowned valleys, fjords, and channels.

One of the major channels, and the southern boundary of the island of Tierra del Fuego, is BEAGLE CHANNEL, named after the ship on which Charles Darwin sailed through these islands in 1832. On the northern shore is located USHUAIA (1980 population 11,029), the southern-most town of Argentina, which caters to the sheep-raising ranches and to the activities of a duty-free port. On the southern shore of the channel, Puerto Williams—a Chilean outpost with nearly 2,500 inhabitants—is mainly a naval station, with a few ALAKALUF Indian descendants living nearby. The second-largest settlement in Argentine Tierra del Fuego is Río Grande (14,852 inhabitants in 1991) on the Atlantic coast. Por-

Tierra del Fuego. ARCHIVO GENERAL DE LA NACIÓN, BUENOS AIRES.

venir (1982 pop. 4,560) and Cerro Sombrero (the major oil-producing center of Chile, with 1,325 inhabitants in 1982) are the principal settlements in the Chilean part of Tierra del Fuego.

SAMUEL K. LOTHROP, *The Indians of Tierra del Fuego* (New York, 1928); JUAN H. LANZI, *Tierra del Fuego* (Buenos Aires, 1967); ERIC STRIPTON, *Tierra del Fuego: The Fatal Lodestone* (1973); and E. LUCAS BRIDGES, *Uttermost Part of the Earth: Indians of Tierra del Fuego* (1988).

CÉSAR N. CAVIEDES

TIETÊ RIVER, a waterway originating in the mountains on the Atlantic coast of Brazil and flowing westerly through the state of São Paulo until joining the Paraná River. Formerly called the Anhembi, the Tietê River's headwaters are the closest to the ocean of all Brazilian rivers. From the many falls and rapids that characterize its course, it got its name "Tietê," meaning "river of many waters."

Through its riparian connections, the Tietê afforded the *bandeirantes* access to the interior of much of Brazil. These explorers used the river to explore for mineral wealth and to capture and enslave the TUPI Indians who lived in the river valley. In the eighteenth century travelers journeyed from the port of Aritaguaba to the mines of Minas Gerais by way of the Tietê. After an 1838 typhoid epidemic decimated most of the boatmen and pilots who knew how to navigate the river, there were fewer water voyages. Eventually railways replaced the Tietê canoe route that had served the PAULISTAS for two hundred years.

In modern times the Tietê suffers from pollution originating from the city of São Paulo.

RICHARD M. MORSE, ed., *The Bandeirantes* (1965); E. BRADFORD BURNS, ed., *A Documentary History of Brazil* (1966).

SHEILA L. HOOKER

See also **Bandeiras.**

TIKAL, a major pre-Hispanic MAYA center located in the dense jungles of the northern department of Petén, Guatemala. Tikal is both the largest and the most thoroughly studied Maya site. The site core consists of several large areas of major temple-pyramid complexes on high rocky ground, linked by causeways (*sacbeob*) and surrounded by over 20 square miles of scattered residential remains and distant defensive fortifications. Nearby *bajos* (lowlands) were modified to trap rainwater. Major structures date from the Late Formative to the Late Classic Periods, and known monuments span 8.12.14.8.15 (A.D. 292) on Stela 29 to 10.2.0.0.0 (A.D. 869) on Stela 11.

Carved stelae, ceramics, and burial offerings show very close ties between Tikal, TEOTIHUACÁN, and KAMINALJUYÚ in the Early Classic Period (about A.D. 378). Stela 31 (dated A.D. 435) of ruler Stormy Sky depicts

Temple 1, Tikal, Guatemala. PHOTO BY IAN GRAHAM.

attendants in Teotihuacán military attire with Teotihuacano weapons. These ties vanish after A.D. 534, when a period of reduced construction and activity began. This Middle Classic hiatus, which corresponds to the decline of Teotihuacán, lasted until nearly A.D. 700, when renewed activity began the Late Classic Period at Tikal.

Tikal's Great Plaza of Late Classic structures is defined by two east-west facing temple-pyramids (I and II). Temple I (155 feet high) was the burial pyramid of ruler Ah Cacau, inaugurated A.D. 682. The adjacent north acropolis consists of large temple-pyramids built above tombs of the ruling elite. The burials include skeletons, painted inscriptions, inscribed bones, jade offerings, animal offerings, and ceramic vessels. To the south is a large elite residence. West of the plaza is the largest pyramid at Tikal (230 feet high) and the probable tomb of Yax Kin Caan Chac, son of Ah Cacau.

For two major epochs Tikal sat astride the headwaters of rivers flowing eastward to the Caribbean and westward to the Gulf of Mexico, dominating the cross-peninsular trade routes.

See the *Tikal Report, Nos. 1–11: Facsimile Reissue of Original Reports Published 1958–1961* (1986), edited by Edwin M. Shook; and WILLIAM R. COE, *Tikal: A Handbook of the Ancient Maya Ruins* (1967).

WALTER R. T. WITSCHEY

TIMERMAN, JACOBO (*b.* 6 January 1923) Argentine journalist, publisher, editor, and writer. Jacobo Timerman was born in Bar, Ukraine (then, the USSR). When he was five years old, his family emigrated to Argentina. He began his career in journalism in 1944. Timerman founded the newsweeklies *Primera Plana* (1962) and *Confirmado* (1969) and became a radio and television commentator. He was a political columnist at the Argentine daily *La Razón,* one of the most widely read papers in the nation during the late 1950s and the 1960s. From 1971 to 1977 he was editor and publisher of the influential Argentine daily *La Opinión.* He was imprisoned by the Argentine military dictatorship from 1977 to 1979. International pressures, as well as internal dissension among the military, gained his freedom. He left Argentina for Israel in 1979, and subsequently lived in Madrid and New York. The story of his imprisonment and torture by the military, *Prisoner Without a Name, Cell Without a Number* (1981), is a forceful account of repression and the violation of HUMAN RIGHTS in Argentina. The book became an international best-seller. In *The Longest War: Israel in Lebanon* (1982), Timerman expresses his anguish over actions taken by the Israeli armed forces in Lebanon. Upon his return to Argentina in 1984, Timerman became editor-in-chief of *La Razón* for a brief period. His book *Cuba: A Journey* (1990) is based upon a trip that he made to the island in 1987. He has written for the *New Yorker* magazine and in 1987 he published an account of Chile under General Pinochet, *Chile: Death in the South.*

RAMÓN JUAN ALBERTO CAMPS, *Caso Timerman: Punto final* (1982); *Timerman: The News from Argentina* (1984), a video recording available from PBS Video; *Jacobo Timerman: Prisoner Without a Name, Cell Without a Number* (television film, 1990).

DANUSIA L. MESON

TIMUCUA, a native people and Spanish mission province in north Florida. In the early 1500s the north half of peninsular Florida and the extreme southeast part of Georgia were the home of people who spoke dialects of Timucua. At least twenty-five separate groups, each consisting of from one or two to as many as forty villages, existed. At times chiefs established alliances with one another or one chief established military dominance over others, thereby forming larger political units. The Timucua in north Florida and the lower Saint John's River cultivated corn and other crops. These groups on the coast and in central Florida apparently were not farmers.

The Pánfilo de Narváez (1528) and Hernando de Soto (1539) expeditions traveled through the territories of various of the Timucua groups and severely impacted them. Beginning in the late 1500s and continuing into the seventeenth century, Spanish Franciscan missions, farms, and ranches were established among Timucua peoples. North and north-central Florida became known as Timucua Province. By 1650 disease epidemics had greatly reduced the population of Timucua, and native peoples from Georgia repopulated some of the missions. Only a handful of the Timucua survived past about 1730.

JERALD T. MILANICH and WILLIAM C. STURTEVANT, *Francisco Pareja's 1613 Confessionario: A Documentary Source for Timucuan Ethnography* (1972); KATHLEEN A. DEAGAN, "Cultures in Transition: Fusion and Assimilation Among the Eastern Timucua," and JERALD T. MILANICH, "The Western Timucua: Patterns of Acculturation and Change," in *Tacachale: Essays on the Indians of Florida and Southeastern Georgia During the Historic Period,* edited by Jerald T. Milanich and Samuel Proctor (1978).

JERALD T. MILANICH

TIN INDUSTRY. The tin industry in Latin America is largely concentrated in Bolivia, which, after Malaysia, has been the largest producer of tin in the world. For over eighty years (1900–1980), tin was Bolivia's largest export. The owners of the tin mines became some of the wealthiest men in the world and extremely powerful within Bolivia. The 1952 revolution of the National Revolutionary Movement (MNR) brought about the nationalization of the most important mines, providing jobs and income for the government. The tin industry also engendered one of the most powerful labor unions in Latin America.

Tin MINING became important at the beginning of the twentieth century just as SILVER mining, the previous economic mainstay of the country, became unprofitable. Nevertheless, the nineteenth-century silver-mining boom was important, for the silver miners built the RAILROADS that connected the highland mining areas

Workers in a tin mine. ORGANIZATION OF AMERICAN STATES.

239

with the Pacific coast and made feasible the transportation of a relatively inexpensive product like tin ore. Strikingly, few silver miners were able to make the transition from silver to tin. Only the ARAMAYO family from southern Potosí, with heavy infusions of European capital, was able to make the switch; they eventually controlled about one-fifth of the country's production. The change from silver to tin also shifted economic power from the Potosí-Sucre axis in the south to La Paz and Oruro in the north. The FEDERALIST WAR of 1898–1899, which pitted the Conservative government based in the south against the Liberal Party and La Paz Federalists, confirmed the new political and economic configuration of the country. After the Liberals won, La Paz became the permanent seat of the executive and legislative powers and the de facto capital of the country.

Tin mining required a much higher level of capital investment than silver, and for this reason successful tin miners quickly allied themselves with foreign capital. By the early twentieth century three major companies controlled tin mining. In addition to the Aramayo holdings, Mauricio HOCHSCHILD, a Bolivian Jew also backed by European companies, held about 20 percent of the market. The most important tin miner, Simón PATIÑO, a Cochabamba MESTIZO who produced about half of Bolivian output, worked with British and later U.S. companies. Despite heavy foreign financial participation, most of the tin industry remained in the hands of Bolivian nationals throughout the twentieth century.

The control the tin barons exerted over Bolivian politics from the early twentieth century to the 1952 revolution was deeply resented by many Bolivians. The Liberal Party and the Republicans were deeply influenced by Patiño and his colleagues. Patiño, however, left Bolivia in the 1920s, never to return. His company, incorporated in Delaware, was run in Bolivia by a series of administrators out of the central office in Paris, France. By this time Patiño's Bolivian mining holdings formed only a fraction of his business enterprises. His other interests included British and German tin smelteries, agro-industrial enterprises in Bolivia, and tin mines in Malaysia. Thus, although the country's largest tin miner was Bolivian, the mines themselves were run as a small portion of a multinational corporation. The mine owners, their subordinates, and their political allies were called LA ROSCA, a term that contained many negative connotations.

Despite the attempts at maintaining a paternalistic regime in the mine labor camps, various strikes by miners and their bloody repression by the Bolivian army led to greater labor militancy. The massacre at Uncía in 1923 and especially the CATAVI MASSACRE in 1942 helped create antipathy toward mine owners and made it possible for labor leaders to create alliances with leftist political parties such as the MNR. The alliance with mine labor helped bring about the MNR's opposition to the mine owners and its programmatic commitment to the nationalization of the Big Three's tin operations.

When the MNR finally triumphed in the bloody revolution of 1952, one of the new government's first administrative acts was to nationalize the mines and create the Corporación Minera de Bolivia, or COMIBOL. In fact, the tin miners were instrumental in the triumph of the revolution. They descended from the mines and helped rout the army and occupied the major Bolivian cities. Thereafter, the largely Trotskyist mine workers remained an important force in national politics and, until the late 1980s, the leaders of the Bolivian labor movement. Although mine owners were later compensated for their losses—the United States insisted on compensation before it would recognize the revolutionary regime—the power of la rosca had been broken.

When the military overthrew the MNR in 1964, the new president, René BARRIENTOS ORTUÑO, attempted to reform Comibol with U.S. advice. To make these reforms possible, Barrientos broke the power of the unions. He sent the army to occupy the mines and arrested labor leaders. This type of repression reoccurred under right-wing military dictators Hugo Banzer in 1971 and Luís GARCÍA MEZA in 1981.

Comibol remained the principal source of cash for the Bolivian government until the 1980s, when declining world tin prices led to the shutting down of most tin mines. The government offered to relocate the unemployed mine workers to the subtropical jungles of Bolivia. Some went to these zones, but poor infrastructure and lack of resources doomed this policy. Other former miners went to work in the coca fields of Cochabamba, and many more moved to the cities, creating a surge of urbanization in cities such as Sucre, Tarija, Cochabamba, and Santa Cruz.

There is no adequate monograph on the history of the Bolivian tin industry. Partial efforts include SERGIO ALMARAZ PAZ, *El poder y la caída: El estaño en la historia de Bolivia* (1967); JUAN ALBARRACÍN MILLÁN, *El poder minero en la administración liberal* (1972); WALTER GÓMEZ, *La minería en el desarrollo económico de Bolivia, 1900–1970* (1976). See also ALFONSO CRESPO, *Los Aramayo de Chichas: Tres generaciones de mineros bolivianos* (1981). A useful account of Bolivian tin miners is JUNE NASH, *We Eat the Mines and the Mines Eat Us: Dependency and Exploitation in Bolivian Tin Mines* (1979).

ERICK D. LANGER

TIN-TAN (Germán Valdés Castillo; *b.* 1915; *d.* 29 June 1973), Mexican comedian and film star. In 1943, Tin-Tan began a radio career in Ciudad Juárez. Turning to comedy, he performed in various border cities of Mexico and the United States. He made his film debut in 1945 with *El hijo desobediente*. He went on to star in thirty-eight films and acted in over 100 more. His unique style incorporated slapstick, satire, musical and dance numbers, and a peculiar manner of speech. Among his classic films are *Calabacitas tiernas* (1948), *El rey del barrio* (1949), *El revoltoso* (1951), and *El campeón ciclista* (1956). Tin-Tan was one of the greatest Mexican film comedians and remains one of the most popular entertainers of all time.

LUIS REYES DE LA MAZA, *El cine sonoro en México* (1973); E. BRADFORD BURNS, *Latin American Cinema: Film and History* (1975); CARL J. MORA, *Mexican Cinema: Reflections of a Society: 1896–1980* (1982); and JOHN KING, *Magical Reels: A History of Cinema in Latin America* (1990).

DAVID MACIEL

TINOCO GRANADOS, FEDERICO (*b.* 1870; *d.* 1931), the extraconstitutional president of Costa Rica (1917–1919) following the overthrow of President Alfredo GONZÁLEZ FLORES (1914–1917). As the last military figure to seize power in modern Costa Rica, Tinoco is still a controversial figure. He was minister of war and the navy, commandant of San José, and head of the police at the time of the coup against González. Faced with crushing economic difficulties as a consequence of World War I, González had attempted a series of progressive tax measures in the face of inflationary pressures. Both wealthy and popular interests welcomed his overthrow, but the popularity of the Tinoco regime, led by Federico and his brother José Joaquín, faded quickly. U.S. president Woodrow Wilson chose to make an example of Tinoco and refused to recognize his regime, both on principle and out of a partisan Democratic suspicion that Republican investors such as Minor KEITH (United Fruit) and Luis Valentine (Rosario Mining of Honduras) were in league with Tinoco, expecting to conduct oil exploration and to receive investment incentives. Once Costa Rica was isolated internationally, popular living standards suffered even more under Tinoco, and his occasionally bloody repression of would-be rebellions and exile invasions caused his regime's early popularity to evaporate. Just as he was turning power over to his successor, Vice President Juan Bautista Quirós Segura, on 10 August 1919, his brother Joaquín, the war minister, was assassinated in San José. Tinoco left power two days later. Elections were held later that year, and Julio ACOSTA GARCIA was elected president. Tinoco died in Paris.

FEDERICO TINOCO GRANADOS, *Páginas de ayer* (1928); CARLOS LUIS FALLAS MONGE, *Alfredo González Flores* (1976); HUGO MURILLO JIMÉNEZ, *Tinoco y los Estados Unidos: Génesis y caída de un régimen* (1981); MERCEDES MUÑOZ GUILLÉN, *El estado y la abolición del ejercito, 1914–1949* (1990).

LOWELL GUDMUNDSON

TIPITAPA AGREEMENTS, the settlement marking the end of Nicaragua's Constitutionalist War. United States envoy Henry L. STIMSON and José María MONCADA met on 4 May 1927 in the small town of Tipitapa, a few miles east of Managua, to negotiate an end to the Constitutionalist War in Nicaragua. After Emiliano CHAMORRO's unsuccessful coup d'état, fellow Conservative Adolfo DÍAZ regained the presidency in 1926, despite the claims

on the office by exiled former vice president Juan Bautista SACASA, a Liberal. Under Moncada's protection, Sacasa returned from Mexico and appointed Moncada his minister of war. While Moncada mounted his campaign against the Conservatives, Sacasa set up a "constitutional government" in Puerto Cabezas.

To resolve the crisis, U.S. President Calvin Coolidge sent Stimson as his personal representative. Stimson first held negotiations with the Conservatives, who agreed to the retention of Díaz as president until the 1928 elections and to a general amnesty for all rebels. Once Stimson had secured Conservative support, he then met with Moncada—Sacasa refused to leave Puerto Cabezas. Stimson, realizing that the Liberals would not accept Díaz as president, advised Moncada to accept the terms of the agreement or risk fighting the U.S. In addition to the retention of Díaz as president until the 1928 elections (to be supervised by the U.S., which had given its tacit support to Moncada), the Tipitapa Agreements, as negotiated by Stimson and Moncada, guaranteed the Liberals control of six departments in exchange for an end to hostilities. Finally, they called for the organization of a nonpolitical National Guard under the leadership of U.S. officers.

On 5 May, Moncada told his troops of the agreements; President Díaz declared a general amnesty and appointed a number of Moncada's generals to government positions. All but one of Moncada's generals accepted the Tipitapa Agreements on 12 May 1927 through a signed telegram. The sole exception was Augusto César SANDINO, who refused to lay down his arms.

RICHARD MILLETT, *Guardians of the Dynasty* (1977), esp. p. 55; NEILL MACAULAY, *The Sandino Affair* (1985), esp. pp. 31–47.

SHANNON BELLAMY

TIRADENTES. *See* **Silva Xavier, Joaquim José da.**

TITHE. *See* **Diezmo.**

TITICACA, LAKE, the highest navigable lake in the world, dominating the highlands of southern Peru and northern Bolivia. At an elevation of 12,467 feet, the lake, actually an inland sea, extends 122 miles in length and 45 miles in width. Its massive surface area of 3,200 square miles moderates the climate of surrounding areas. Several inhabitable islands, including the popular tourist attraction of Taquile, dot the lake.

The lake has had a dominating historical influence on the region. Its waters and shoreline have supported fishing and agricultural practices for millennia. Archaeological investigations reveal the existence of complex societies that long ago benefited from the resources and climatic influence of the lake. Technological changes, especially the advent of steam transportation in the late nineteenth century, contributed to the lake's role as a

View of Lake Titicaca, 1925. PHOTO BY MARTÍN CHAMBI. COURTESY OF JULIA CHAMBI.

link between southern Peru and northern Bolivia. With transportation and refrigeration, fish products have recently enhanced the regional economic significance of the lake.

EMILIO ROMERO, *Perú: Una nueva geografía*, 2 vols. (1973).

JOHN C. SUPER

TIWANAKU (Tiahuanaco), a pre-Columbian Andean empire whose most important ceremonial and political center was the city of the same name located on the ALTIPLANO (high plateau) in what is now Bolivia. Although there is some disagreement among scholars as to the exact dates of Tiwanaku culture, it is generally accepted to have been the dominant society in the basin of Lake TITICACA from at least 100 to approximately 1200.

At an altitude of 12,600 feet, the ancient city of Tiwanaku comprised a ceremonial-administrative center with monumental stone architecture surrounded by more humble residential areas. Radiocarbon dating indicates that the main temples, courtyards, and stelae were constructed between 100 and 725. Although the public precinct of Tiwanaku is relatively small, excavations by Carlos Ponce Sanginés have led him to conclude that the whole city covered about 420 hectares (approximately 1037 acres) and probably had a population of between 20,000 and 40,000.

The size of the city and other Tiwanaku urban administrative centers in the Titicaca basin (Lukurmata, Pajchiri, Oje), as well as the material evidence of different social classes found during excavations of city sites, indicate that Tiwanaku society was highly stratified. The social complexity was possible because an economic surplus was produced through the skillful use of the *altiplano* environment for extensive agricultural and

herding activities. The highland economy was also supplemented with products from other ecological zones that could not be raised on the high plateau. These items may have been acquired through trade or by means of an "archipelago" system in which groups of settlers were sent by the highland state to establish agricultural colonies in the lowlands.

After about 375, Tiwanaku material culture spread through wide areas of the Andes, including Bolivian inland valleys and coastal areas of Chile and Peru. In the sixth century another major center of Tiwanaku culture emerged at HUARI (Wari) in the central highlands of Peru. The origins of Huari and its connections with Bolivian Tiwanaku are not clear, but the site may have been established through conquest and then later have operated as an independent imperial capital. Huari culture declined in the ninth century, while Tiwanaku itself survived until about 1200.

LUIS G. LUMBRERAS, *The Peoples and Cultures of Ancient Peru* (1974), esp. pp. 139–145 and 151–177; CARLOS PONCE SANGINÉS, *Tiwanaku: Espacio, tiempo y cultura: Ensayo de síntesis arqueológica*, 4th ed. (1981); ALAN L. KOLATA, "The South Andes," in *Ancient South Americans*, edited by Jesse D. Jennings (1983); ELÍAS MÚJICA, "Altiplano–Coast Relationships in the South-Central Andes: From Indirect to Direct Complementarity," in

Tiwanaku girl at the Monolith, Bolivia, 1970. ORGANIZATION OF AMERICAN STATES.

Andean Ecology and Civilization: An Interdisciplinary Perspective on Andean Ecological Complementarity, edited by Shozo Masuda, Izumi Shimada, and Craig Morris (1985); ALAN L. KOLATA, ed., *La tecnología y organización de la producción agrícola en el estado de Tiwanaku* (1989).

ANN ZULAWSKI

TLALOC (He Who Has Earth), a major god of rain, fertility, and agriculture and one of the most ancient of the MESOAMERICAN supernaturals. He is easily identified by a distinctive face mask, formed by circular blue rings around his eyes, a moustachelike labial band, and prominent fangs. The object of widespread veneration, carved and painted images of Tlaloc survive at archaeological sites in central Mexico from Classic period TEOTIHUACÁN to Postclassic Mexico TENOCHTITLÁN. Chac of the Maya, Tajin of the Gulf Coast Totonacs, and Cocijo of the Zapotecs and Dzahui of the Mixtecs in Oaxaca are counterparts of Tlaloc in other areas. In Mexico Tenochtitlán one of the twin shrines atop the TEMPLO MAYOR (main temple) of the Aztecs was dedicated to him. Five of the eighteen annual *veintena* feasts (Atlcahualo-Cuahuitlehua, Tozoztontli, Etzalcualiztli, Tepeilhuitl, Hueypachtli, and Atemoztli) especially honored Tlaloc and his small assistants, called *tlaloques* (little Tlalocs), who were credited with producing rain, lightning, thunder, and hail. The greatest of all Tlaloc shrines was atop Mount Tlaloc, located between TETZCOCO and Huexotzinco, and elaborate ceremonies were staged there. People who died by drowning and other water-related deaths were believed to dwell in Tlalocán, the paradise of Tlaloc.

MARK MILLER and KARL TAUBE, *The Gods and Symbols of Ancient Mexico and the Maya* (1993).

ELOISE QUIÑONES KEBER

TLAPACOYA, an archaeological site in the eastern Valley of Mexico, on lower slopes of the east edge of a small volcanic hill. These slopes were once the shores of a huge extinct lake, Lago de Chalco, that covered much of what is now eastern Mexico City. The lake's beaches, as well as small caves up the slopes from them, were first occupied by early hunters between 10,000 and 40,000 years ago. Their cultural remains are meagerly documented by crude choppers, scrapers, and knives; a fine prismatic obsidian blade found in the lake deposits was dated by hydration at about 19,000 years old.

Just north of the Paleoindian remains, a series of deep trenches documented a sequence of Archaic occupation. Study of the meager lithic tools taken from these trenches has allowed us to divide the Archaic sequence into three phases: Playa 1, 5500–4500 B.C.; Playa 2, 4500–3500 B.C.; and Zohapilco, 3500–2000 B.C. During the first two phases the occupants were probably collectors,

while the Paleoindians of the third phase were sedentary agriculturists in preceramic times—although a single crude clay figurine was found.

Above these remains, probably not much earlier than 1300 B.C., were a series of strata with abundant ceramics, figurines, and grinding stones of the Formative period (1300–200 B.C.), during which people lived in definite villages and practiced agriculture full time. A study of the ceramics and figurines allows this sequence to be divided into a series of phases: Nevada (1300–1200 B.C.), Ayotla (1200–1000 B.C.), Manantial (1000–800 B.C.), Zacatenco (800–400 B.C.), and Ticomán (400–200 B.C.). The phases document the shift from a time of village agriculture to a period (Ayotla) when the pyramids were constructed and there was influence from the Veracruz coast OLMEC (Manantial). During Ticomán, the rise of the state began and laid the foundation for establishment of TEOTIHUACÁN.

PAUL TOLSTOY and LOUISE I. PARADIS, "Early and Middle Preclassic Culture in the Basin of Mexico," in *Science* 167 (1970): 344–351, and "Early and Middle Preclassic Culture in the Basin of Mexico," in *Observations on the Emergence of Civilization in Mesoamerica. Contributions of the University of California Archaeological Research Facility*, edited by Robert F. Heizer and John A. Graham (1971), pp. 7–28; CHRISTINE NIEDERBERGER, *Zohapilco, cinco milenios de ocupación humana en un sitio lacustre de la Cuenca de México* (1976); PAUL TOLSTOY, SUZANNE K. FISH, MARTIN W. BOKSENBAUM, KATHRYN B. VAUGHN, and C. EARLE SMITH, "Early Sedentary Communities of the Basin of Mexico," in *Journal of Field Archaeology* 4 (1977): 91–106; CHRISTINE NIEDERBERGER, "Early Sedentary Economy in the Basin of Mexico," in *Science* 203 (1979): 131–142; PIERRE BECQUELIN and CLAUDE F. BAUDEZ, *Toniná, une cité maya du Chiapas (Mexique)*, 3 vols. (1979–1982).

RICHARD S. MACNEISH

TLATELOLCO, the greatest late pre-Hispanic commercial center of the Basin of Mexico and site of its largest marketplace. The sister city and rival of Mexico TENOCHTITLÁN, Tlatelolco was inhabited by a fiercely independent branch of the Mexica who derived their dynasty from AZCAPOTZALCO. Like the Tenochca, another Mexica branch, they claimed HUITZILOPOCHTLI as their patron and their ceremonial precincts were also similarly constructed. Tlatelolco's autonomy ended in 1473 with its defeat by the Tenochca, who thereafter appointed its governors. In 1521 the final, devastating siege of the Spanish conquest took place within its ceremonial precinct. After the Conquest, Tlatelolco became the Indian sector of the colonial city of Mexico, and Franciscan missionaries established the College of Santa Cruz there to educate the sons of Aztec nobility. Tlatelolco's ancient ceremonial precinct is now the location of the Plaza of the Three Cultures, which is marked by the excavated ruins of its TEMPLO MAYOR, the adjoining colonial church, and surrounding modern structures.

JESÚS MONJARÁS-RUIZ, ELENA LIMÓN, and MARÍA DE LA CRUZ PAILLÉS H., eds., *Obras de Robert H. Barlow*, vol. 2, *Tlatelolco:*

Fuentes e historia (1989); PATRICIA GALEANA DE VALADÉS and FRANCISCO BLANCO FIGUEROA, eds., *Tlatelolco* (1990).

ELOISE QUIÑONES KEBER

TLATOANI, paramount ruler of the central Mesoamerican Nahua ALTEPETL (regional state or province). *Tlatoque* (plural) rulership was dynastic, but succession practices varied; the *tlatoani* of TENOCHTITLÁN was "elected" by a small body of elites, with brothers and nephews likely to succeed. The *tlatoani* had broad civil, military, and religious powers, and the *tlatocayotl* (rulership) brought many privileges, including the ability to keep multiple wives and rights to tribute and labor, to private property, and to the best material items available. After the Spanish conquest, *tlatoque* typically became the first governors of the reorganized indigenous communities. Their dominance faded as other elites successfully competed for access to this office.

There is an extensive literature dealing with the *tlatoani*. One of the best primary sources is BERNARDINO DE SAHAGÚN, *Florentine Codex.* Book 8, *Kings and Lords,* translated and edited by Arthur J. O. Anderson and Charles E. Dibble (1954). An excellent study is SUSAN D. GILLESPIE, *The Aztec Kings: The Construction of Rulership in Mexica History* (1989). The evolution of *tlatocayotl* in the colonial period is examined in CHARLES GIBSON, *The Aztecs Under Spanish Rule* (1964); ROBERT HASKETT, *Indigenous Rulers: An Ethnohistory of Town Government in Colonial Cuernavaca* (1991); SUSAN SCHROEDER, *Chimalpahin and the Kingdons of Chalco* (1991); and JAMES LOCKHART, *The Nahuas After the Conquest: A Social and Cultural History of the Indians of Central Mexico, Sixteenth through Eighteenth Centuries* (1992).

ROBERT HASKETT

TLAXCALA, an indigenous city-state in the highlands of Mexico, east of the capital. Prior to European contact, Tlaxcala was a vital pocket of independent Nahuatl, Otomí, and Pinome speakers who had resisted absorption into the surrounding Aztec Empire. For about two centuries the Tlaxcalans and the Mexica had enjoyed good relations; the former were important trade partners. But wealth accumulated by Tlaxcalan merchants became the envy of the imperialistic Mexica leaders, and a century of conflict began in the early fifteenth century. Wars between the neighboring rivals became frequent yet indecisive and took on a traditional, ceremonial aspect called *xochiyaoyotl,* literally "FLOWERY WAR," a heated contest not originally intended to incur battlefield deaths. Mexica soldiers used this to sharpen battle skills, to obtain honor, and to secure captives to sacrifice later to their gods.

The constant friction with Tlaxcala suited MOTECUHZOMA, but he did not foresee how it would push the Tlaxcalans into the arms of the Spaniards in their march against Mexico-Tenochtitlán. The Tlaxcalans had become impoverished because of cut trade lines and, constantly facing war, were anxious to throw off their adversaries completely. Still, in 1519 the Tlaxcalans first fought the Spaniards for two weeks, suffering considerable losses, before surrendering and siding with them to fight their traditional enemies. Thereafter, thousands of Tlaxcalans accompanied Spaniards in the battles of conquest all over Mexico and on distant frontiers, many never to return home, either because they died or because they settled with Spaniards, becoming their *naborías* (dependents), or formed model communities for them on the frontier, setting an example for nonsedentary indigenous peoples and helping hold new territorial acquisitions. One example is San Estéban de Nueva, founded next to Saltillo in 1591.

The Tlaxcalans set an example that was followed by other resisters of Aztec rule, but none became so renowned or so well rewarded, partly because of the tireless campaigns by Tlaxcalans to secure privileges as a result of their alliance with the Europeans. Tlaxcalan assistance proved to be a vital factor in tipping the scale in the lopsided battle between the few Spaniards and the large and powerful Aztec empire, and the victors were not allowed to forget their allies. Thus, Tlaxcalans were exempted from the usual pattern of having a Spanish city superimposed over theirs and having their people's labor and tributes divided among Spanish *encomenderos* (*encomienda* grant holders), a departure that makes their colonial history unique.

The best source on pre-Conquest Tlaxcala is DIEGO MUÑOZ CAMARGO, *Historia de Tlaxcala* (1892). CHARLES GIBSON, *Tlaxcala in the Sixteenth Century* (1952), provides good coverage of the Conquest era and after. Rich new sources in Nahuatl have afforded a more detailed description of Tlaxcalan life, clarifying, among other things, the complex four-part division of the province; see JAMES LOCKHART, FRANCES BERDAN, and ARTHUR J. O. ANDERSON, *The Tlaxcalan Actas: A Compendium of the Records of the Cabildo of Tlaxcala (1545–1627)* (1986). The reference to the Tlaxcalan community of the north comes from LESLIE SCOTT OFFUTT, "Urban and Rural Society in the Mexican North: Saltillo in the Late Colonial Period" (Ph.D. diss., University of California, Los Angeles, 1982), p. 9.

STEPHANIE WOOD

TLAXILACALLI, a territorial subdivision of the Nahua ALTEPETL (provincial unit) before and after the Spanish invasion. It was the main holder and distributor of land to its citizens, who paid tribute through *tlaxilacalli* officials. Often grouped in units of four, six, or eight within a single *altepetl,* the *tlaxilacalli* had its own religious structure and marketplace, and was itself subdivided into smaller districts. The term has a very similar meaning to the better-known and more-studied CALPULLI, and there seems to have been some regional variation in the application of the terms; a definitive conclusion about their exact relationship and usage awaits further research.

The meaning and structure of *tlaxilacalli* are discussed in several works, among them PEDRO CARRASCO, "Social Organization of Ancient Mexico," in *Archaeology of Northern*

Mesoamerica. Pt. 1, *Handbook of Middle American Indians*, vol. 10, edited by Gordon F. Ekholm and Ignacio Bernal (1971), pp. 363–368; EDWARD CALNEK, "The Internal Structure of Tenochtitlán," in *Ancient Mesoamerica*, edited by John A. Graham (1976), pp. 337–338; RUDOLF VAN ZANTWIJK, *The Aztec Arrangement: The Social History of Pre-Spanish Mexico* (1985), pp. 249ff.; SUSAN SCHROEDER, *Chimalpahin and the Kingdoms of Chalco* (1991); and JAMES LOCKHART, *The Nahuas After the Spanish Conquest: A Social and Cultural History of the Indians of Central Mexico, Sixteenth Through Eighteenth Centuries* (1992).

ROBERT HASKETT

TOBACCO INDUSTRY. The tobacco plant (any of the several species belonging to the genus *Nicotiana*, especially *N. tabacum*), is indigenous to the New World, where archaeological evidence indicates that it had been domesticated by 3500 B.C., if not earlier. Many pre-Columbian societies smoked tobacco, often as part of religious ceremonies or in the context of ritual healing—practices that have survived into the present not only among Indian groups but also in African Latin religions such as CANDOMBLÉ, UMBANDA, and SANTERÍA. Early European explorers commented on the strange habit of smoking leaves, and carried samples of tobacco back across the Atlantic. The commercial potential of the plant became apparent only from the end of the sixteenth century onward, when snuff and pipe smoking gained widespread popularity in Europe and then in Asia and Africa. Thereafter, tobacco quickly became a major staple in the colonial export trade.

One of the first New World colonies to export tobacco was Brazil, where, in the seventeenth century, the northeastern captaincy of Bahia emerged as the main center of production. Bahian farmers specialized in twist tobacco (tobacco tightly woven into ropelike cords, appropriate for both pipe smoking and chewing). The mixture of molasses and herbs that farmers brushed onto the finished twists gave them a distinctive and much appreciated flavor. There were two main markets for Bahian tobacco: Portugal took the better twists (often for reexport) while tobacco judged lower in quality was shipped to West Africa, where it soon became a highly prized trade good used in bartering for slaves. As the slave trade grew, so too did the volume of exports to West Africa. Tobacco was thus crucial to the development and growth of slave-based agriculture and mining in colonial Brazil.

The years following Brazil's independence (1822) brought a serious decline in the Bahian tobacco trade. Independence by itself weakened established links, through Portugal, to markets in northern and southern Europe. At the same time, British efforts to halt the importation of slaves hampered trade with West Africa. Changing fashions also contributed to the decline. European consumers increasingly preferred cigars (and later cigarettes) to snuff and pipe tobacco. The decline was reversed after 1840, when Bahian growers began to harvest varieties of leaf tobacco that could be used in manufacturing cigars.

A significant export trade in tobacco also developed in colonial Spanish America and most notably in Cuba, where the seventeenth-century surge in European demand encouraged increased production at first near and around Havana and then throughout the island. The real heyday of Cuban tobacco was, however, the nineteenth century, when, paradoxically, sugar had already displaced tobacco as the island's most profitable export. The rapid development of the SUGAR INDUSTRY in Cuba, from about 1760 on, had come at the expense of tobacco: in one district after another, *vegas* (tobacco farms) had been replanted with cane. Only in the western and eastern extremes of the island and at a few scattered points in between did tobacco hold its own. Yet from these regions (especially the famous Vuelta de Abajo in western Cuba) came leaf tobacco that was ideally suited for cigars. As early as the 1820s, English consumers eagerly sought out hand-rolled "Havanas." Cigar exports more than doubled between 1840 and 1855. Thereafter, sales of unprocessed leaf quickly outstripped the trade in finished cigars.

At various times, other regions in Latin America have also produced tobacco for export: colonial Venezuela on a small scale, Colombia and Paraguay in the nineteenth century, and, from the end of that century onward, Mexico, Puerto Rico, and the Dominican Republic.

Moreover, tobacco early on became an important commodity in local and regional commerce. By the eighteenth century, one third of the Bahian crop was sold within Brazil. Regional markets absorbed virtually all the tobacco grown in colonial Colombia and Paraguay. In the late eighteenth century, local production as well as imports from Cuba helped meet the enormous demand for tobacco in Mexico, the wealthiest and most populous of Spain's American colonies.

The tobacco sold in domestic and foreign markets frequently came from small and medium-size farms. Tobacco was in many ways an ideal cash crop for the small holder. Although labor intensive, it required neither great amounts of land nor any large outlay of capital. Yet, more often than is commonly acknowledged, tobacco production in Latin America depended on onerous sharecropping arrangements or on coerced labor. Slaves accounted for at least a third of the population in the tobacco districts of colonial and nineteenth-century Bahia, where well-to-do growers typically owned a dozen or more slaves (see also SLAVERY). As late as 1862, more than 17,000 slaves still worked on tobacco farms in Cuba. At the end of the nineteenth century, tobacco growers of Oaxaca, in Mexico, were notorious for relying on a particularly harsh form of debt peonage.

The tobacco trade has long been subject to various restrictions and controls. During the colonial period, many of those restrictions were linked to the creation of ESTANCOS (royal monopolies). The Portuguese *estanco*, established in 1659, handled the sale and distribution of

245

Brazilian tobacco in European markets. On its behalf, colonial authorities enforced numerous laws that governed warehousing, prices, and quality controls. The first Spanish *estanco* lasted only a few years (1717–1724), but a second *estanco,* organized in the 1760s and 1770s, became a major source of revenue for the crown. It monopolized both exports and sales of tobacco within the colonies. To keep prices high, the *estanco* attempted to limit output. The imposition of these controls met with resistance: merchants turned to smuggling, and growers rebelled in Cuba in 1717, 1720, and 1723, and in Colombia in 1781. After Independence, financial necessity led several Spanish American governments to reestablish state tobacco monopolies, which survived until the mid-nineteenth century. In the twentieth century, both Mexico and Cuba granted monopoly privileges to state-owned tobacco companies.

Tobacco also has links to the early history of manufacturing and industry in Latin America. In the 1790s, as many as 8,900 workers—more than half of them women—were employed by the Spanish *estanco* at its cigar and cigarette factory in Mexico City. By the 1850s, both slaves and wage workers manufactured cigars and other tobacco products at numerous workshops and factories in Bahia and Rio de Janeiro. Several hundred workshops competed with larger factories and domestic manufacturing in Cuba's nineteenth-century cigar industry. In the 1860s the Susini firm of Havana pioneered mechanization in the production of cigarettes. By 1900, the tobacco industry in both Cuba and Brazil had already begun to attract foreign investment. Today, large foreign firms dominate the sector in Latin America, where tobacco remains a widely cultivated cash crop.

FERNANDO ORTÍZ, *Cuban Counterpoint: Tobacco and Sugar* (1947); CATHERINE LUGAR, "The Portuguese Tobacco Trade and Tobacco Growers of Bahia in the Late Colonial Period," in *Essays Concerning the Socioeconomic History of Brazil and Portuguese India,* edited by Dauril Alden and Warren Dean (1977); ARTURO OBREGÓN M., *Las obreras tabacaleras de la ciudad de México (1764–1925)* (1982); JEAN STUBBS, *Tobacco on the Periphery: A Case Study in Cuban Labour History, 1860–1958* (1985); SUSAN DEANS-SMITH, *Bureaucrats, Planters, and Workers: The Making of the Tobacco Monopoly in Bourbon Mexico* (1992).

B. J. BARICKMAN

TOBACCO MONOPOLY. Tobacco has traditionally occupied a favored position in state taxation systems because of its popularity and high levels of consumption. Spain monopolized its domestic tobacco trade as early as 1636, and extended a government monopoly over the tobacco trade of its American possessions between 1717 and 1783. The organization and administration of the tobacco monopolies were virtually uniform throughout the empire, although the degree of state regulation varied. In Mexico, the state eventually took over all aspects of the domestic tobacco trade, from the cul-

tivation and purchase of leaf, to manufacture of cigars and cigarettes in state-managed factories, to marketing by government-licensed stores. In comparison, in Cuba and Venezuela the monopoly managed the cultivation and production only of the varieties of raw leaf tobacco that grew in these colonies and were exported to Spain for processing as cigars, cigarettes, and snuff.

The tobacco monopoly proved to be a critical source of government income both in Spain and throughout its empire. Revenues earned from the tobacco monopoly in Spain accounted for almost one-third of total domestic public revenues. Combined, the tobacco monopolies of Spanish America at their peak made significant contributions to crown revenues, representing the second greatest source of revenue after silver and gold. In addition, throughout the eighteenth century monopoly revenues played an increasingly important role in the financial and fiscal affairs of the colonies, which suffered from shortage of specie and lack of formal banks. Historians differ on the economic costs to the colonies of the tobacco monopolies: some argue that they resulted in capital exports and the reduction of capital stock, while others argue that monopoly restrictions redirected resources into other activities.

Recent research suggests that the political and social consequences of Spain's monopolization of the tobacco trade varied, as did the effectiveness of monopoly policy, the variations being explained by the strategies adopted to implement the monopoly, the structure of the local society and economy, and alternative sources of employment. Responses ranged from contraband in tobacco leaf and products, to riot and rebellion by disgruntled farmers and peasants. One of the most extreme examples of opposition to the imposition of a tobacco monopoly is the COMUNERO REVOLT in 1781 in New Granada (Colombia). The social dimensions of the monopoly have recently attracted the attention of historians who emphasize the tobacco monopoly's impact on labor and working conditions, gender roles in the workplace, and the changes engendered in rural society as a result of monopoly policy. Much more research, however, is needed in these areas.

After the colonies declared their political independence from Spain, restructuring of tobacco cultivation, manufacturing, and marketing occurred. Although monopolies were legally abolished, many continued to exist as penurious governments desperately sought revenues. The difficulties of re-creating the colonial-style monopolistic structure manifested itself in the cycles of abolition of a tobacco monopoly, by reestablishment, only to be succeeded by abolition throughout the nineteenth century, although in Colombia, for example, the monopoly facilitated the development and expansion of the tobacco export trade. A major influence on the structure of the tobacco trade and industry in the late nineteenth and twentieth centuries came from monopolies in Europe and the United States, such as the British-American Tobacco Company, a consequence of which was the consolidation of, and division of business between, tobacco-exporting and tobacco-manufacturing countries.

JOHN B. HARRISON, "The Colombian Tobacco Industry from Government Monopoly to Free Trade, 1778–1876" (Ph.D. diss., University of California, Berkeley, 1951); G. CÉSPEDES DEL CASTILLO, "La renta del tabaco en el virreinato de Perú," in *Revista histórica* 21 (1954); AGNES STAPFF, "La renta del tabaco en Chile de la época virreinal," in *Anuario de estudios americanos* 18 (1961): 1–63; JOSÉ RIVERO MUÑIZ, *Tabaco: Su historia en Cuba*, 2 vols. (1964–1965); CAM HARLAN WICKHAM, "Venezuela's Royal Tobacco Monopoly, 1799–1810: An Economic Analysis" (Ph.D. diss., University of Oregon, 1975); JUAN CARLOS ARIAS DIVITO, "Dificultades para establecer la renta de tabaco en Paraguay," in *Anuario de estudios americanos* 33 (1976): 1–17; JOHN LEDDY PHELAN, *The People and the King: The Comunero Revolution in Colombia, 1781* (1978); JESÚS JÁUREGUI ET AL., *Tabamex, un caso de integración vertical de la agricultura* (1980); JEAN STUBBS, *Tobacco on the Periphery: A Case Study in Cuban Labour History, 1860–1958* (1985); JESÚS ANTONIO BEJARANO and ORLANDO PULIDO, *El tabaco en una economía regional: Amablema, siglos XVIII y XIX* (1986); CHRISTINE HÜNEFELDT, "Etapa final del monopolio en el virreinato del Perú: El tabaco de Chachapoyas," in *The Economies of Mexico and Peru*, edited by Nils Jacobsen and Hans Jurgen Puhle (1986); JERRY W. COONEY, "La Dirección General de la Real Renta de Tabacos and the Decline of the Royal Tobacco Monopoly in Paraguay, 1779–1800," in *Colonial Latin American Historical Review* 1, no. 1 (1992): SUSAN DEANS-SMITH, *Bureaucrats, Planters, and Workers: The Making of the Monopoly in Bourbon Mexico* (1992).

SUSAN DEANS-SMITH

TOBAGO. *See* **Trinidad and Tobago.**

TOBAR DOCTRINE. In a 15 March 1907 letter to the Bolivian consul in Brussels, Carlos R. Tobar, a former Ecuadorian foreign minister, affirmed that "The American republics . . . ought to intervene indirectly in the internal dissensions of the republics of the continent. Such intervention might consist, at the least, in the denial of recognition to de factor governments springing from revolution against the constitutional order." In December 1907 representatives of the Central American nations, meeting in Washington, D.C., officially incorporated Tobar's de jure recognition policy into the 1907 WASHINGTON TREATIES. At the request of Costa Rica more stringent de jure recognition provisions were written into the 1923 Washington Treaties. A succession of isthmian recognition crises, however, convinced many Central Americans that strict adherence to the Tobar Doctrine was not in their best interests. In 1932 Costa Rica and El Salvador, dissatisfied with the existing recognition policy, denounced the 1923 Washington Treaties. Efforts to resurrent the Tobar Doctrine at the 1934 Central American Conference were unsuccessful.

LEÓNIDAS GARCÍA, "La doctrina Tobar," in *Revista de la Sociedad "Jurídico-Literaria"* (Quito) 1 (January–February 1913): 25–71; CHARLES L. STANSIFER, "Application of the Tobar Doctrine to Central America," in *Americas* 23, no. 3 (1967):251–272; RICHARD V. SALISBURY, "Domestic Politics and Foreign Policy: Costa Rica's Stand on Recognition, 1923–1934," in *Hispanic American Historical Review* 54, no. 3 (1974):453–478.

RICHARD V. SALISBURY

TOCANTINS, a Brazilian state created on 1 March 1989 from the portion of the state of GOIÁS that lay to the north of the thirteenth parallel. It consists of 79 municipalities covering an area of 110,698 square miles and with a population of 919,918 (1993 est.). The separation of Tocantins from the rest of the state of Goiás was a vindication for its inhabitants. For a very long time, they had complained that due to the great distances involved, the north received no benefits from the state governments for the development of their area. In 1822, after Brazil had won its independence, the north seceded from the south but was incapable of maintaining its autonomy. In 1956 the Movement for the Creation of the State of Tocantins was formed. The Constitution of 1988 finally made the creation of the state a reality.

CELIO COSTA, *Fundamentos para Criação do Estado de Tocantins* (1982) and *O Estado do Tocantins: Uma geopolítica de desenvolvimento* (1985).

LUIS PALACIN

TOCANTINS RIVER, a waterway in Brazil that rises from the central altiplano in the state of Goiás and flows about 1,500 miles north to empty into the bay of Marapatá across from the island of Marajó on the Atlantic coast near Belém. Its basin covers an area of 301,600 square miles in the Federal District and the states of Goiás, Tocantins, Mato Grosso, Maranhão, and Pará. Its entire course was once inhabited by indigenous tribes: Tocoiuna, Tocantin, Pacajá, Guaraju, Tupinambá, Inhaiguara, Bilreiro, Guaiase, Parissó, Apinage, and Cherente. The French explorers La Blanjartier (1610) and La Ravardière (1613) reached it by way of the Maranhão. During the seventeenth century, numerous raids and explorations out of São Paulo and Belém headed toward the Tocantins area in search of Indians to work on the religious settlements and farms.

When gold was discovered in the eighteenth century, settlements were established along the tributaries and affluents of the Tocantins. Once the gold was gone, the river became a trade route, despite its cataracts and the great distances it traversed, for towns in the north of Goiás and Pará, with a continuous series of cities: Palma, Porto Real, Pedro Afonso, Carolina, Boa Vista, Imperatriz, Marabá, Tucuruí, and Cametá. Since the 1960s, projects in agriculture, the raising of livestock, and mining have resulted in further settling of the Tocantins valley.

LYSIAS A. RODRIGUES, *O Rio dos Tocantins* (1945) and *Roteiro do Tocantins*, 3d ed. (1987); FRANCISCO AYRES DA SILVA, *Caminhos de outrora: Diário de viagens* (1972); DALÍSIA ELISABETH MARTINS DOLES, *As comunicações fluviais pelo Tocantins e Araguaia no século XIX* (1973).

LUIS PALACÍN

See also **Bandeirantes.**

TOCORNAL, JOAQUÍN (*b.* 1788; *d.* 1865), Chilean Conservative politician. Tocornal was the youngest man invited to the *cabildo abierto* (open town meeting) that elected Chile's first national junta on 18 September 1810. He became politically prominent with the Conservative rebellion of 1829–1830, serving as vice president of the Congress of Plenipotentiaries, the body that was chiefly instrumental in establishing the new Conservative regime. During the presidency of Joaquín PRIETO (1831–1841), he acted as minister of the interior (1832–1835) and as finance minister (1835–1841). He assumed the interior ministry again (1837–1840) following the murder of Diego PORTALES (1793–1837).

Tocornal played a key part in ensuring the continuity of government. Despite his ministerial eminence, however, he was unable to win Prieto's approval for his own presidential candidacy in 1841. Prieto preferred the war hero General Manuel BULNES (1799–1866): Tocornal did not obtain a single vote in the electoral college. He did retain his influence in the Conservative Party, however, and in January 1858 he helped negotiate the formation of the Liberal-Conservative Fusion. His son Manuel Antonio Tocornal (1817–1867) played a prominent part in politics in 1849–1850 and again in the 1860s as a Fusion leader. Had he not died prematurely, he might well have been the Fusion's presidential candidate in 1871.

SIMON COLLIER

TOLEDO, FRANCISCO (*b.* 7 July 1940), Mexican artist. Francisco Toledo was born in the Zapotec town of Juchitán, Oaxaca. From Zapotec folklore his paintings, drawings, prints, sculptures, and ceramics re-create the Zapotec world in which reptiles, amphibians, fish, insects, and human beings exude sexuality. Toledo studied five years in Europe, including some time in William Stanley Hayter's print workshop, and has lived in New York City and Mexico City.

TERESA DEL CONDE, *Francisco Toledo* (1981); LUIS CARDOZA Y ARAGÓN, *Toledo* (1987); ANDREW KLINE, "Francisco Toledo," in *Latin American Art* 3 (1991):35–37.

SHIFRA M. GOLDMAN

Francisco Toledo. From Guamán Poma de Ayala, *El primer nueva corónica y buen gobierno* (ca. 1615). ROYAL LIBRARY, COPENHAGEN.

TOLEDO Y FIGUEROA, FRANCISCO DE (*b.* 10 July 1515; *d.* 21 April 1582), viceroy of Peru (1569–1581). Don Francisco de Toledo, as he signed himself, was born in Oropesa, New Castile, the third son of the third Count of Oropesa. Through his mother he was closely related to the dukes of Alba and distantly to Emperor Charles V. In 1535 he became a member of the Order of Alcántara.

After many years in the crown's military and diplomatic service, Toledo was appointed viceroy of Peru in 1568. The journey to his new post took him from February to September of 1569. He left ship in the extreme north of Peru and traveled by land to Lima, the capital, inspecting settlements on the desert coast as he progressed.

Peru had a thirty-five-year history of interrupted government and rebellion. Toledo immediately showed himself to be suspicious of any group with power on whatever level: the AUDIENCIAS (courts) of Lima and La Plata, the secular and regular clergy, the *encomenderos,* the CABILDOS (town councils), and, of course, the independent Inca state of VILCABAMBA. After a critical examination of their actions during his administration, he attacked, and generally managed to reduce, their authority and autonomy.

Among his other duties, Toledo was ordered to make a *Visita General* (general inspection) of his viceroyalty. To visit the entire territory, from New Granada (now Colombia) to Chile, was clearly impossible. But in October 1570 Toledo began a tour of the heartland of his jurisdiction that lasted more than five years and took him through the major administrative, economic, and population centers of the Central Andes: Huamanga, Cuzco, Potosí, La Plata, and Arequipa. No other viceroy in the Spanish Empire ever knew his territory as intimately as Toledo came to know his through this exacting personal inspection.

During the *visita*, Toledo achieved the elimination of Inca resistance at Vilcabamba and the execution of the last independent Inca ruler, TÚPAC AMARU; the *reducción* (resettlement) of many native people in new towns for more efficient government, evangelization, and extraction of their labor; the final formulation of the MITA supplying workers to Spanish mercury and silver mines at Huancavelica and Potosí; and full adoption of a silver-refining process utilizing mercury (see also MINING). These last two measures stimulated a vast growth in silver production. Toledo also issued a multitude of regulations on other administrative, economic, and social matters.

Much of what is attributed to Toledo alone, such as the *reducción* program and the mining *mita,* had origins in earlier administrations, but he certainly gave final and legal form to such schemes. Many of his actions seemed, then and later, highly damaging to the native people. For them, he was, and still is, criticized. He was determined that Peru should submit to firm Spanish control and serve Spain's purposes. To those ends, he used whatever means seemed necessary, enforcing the rules with an intolerant and impatient authoritarianism. He enthusiastically praised the efforts of the first inquisitors in Peru, who had traveled with him to Lima. To justify his attacks on Vilcabamba, Túpac Amaru, and other descendants of Inca rulers and nobles, he gathered evidence designed to show that the Incas had been tyrants and that therefore Spaniards had been, and were, fully justified in destroying them.

The rigors of the *Visita General* left Toledo tired and ill. The final five years of his administration were far less active than its first half. Nevertheless, he laid a solid foundation for future Spanish administration of South America. His legislation became a model for governors throughout the empire. He was in a substantial sense the organizer of Spanish Peru, comparable to Viceroy Antonio de MENDOZA in Spanish Mexico.

ROBERTO LEVILLIER, *Don Francisco de Toledo, supremo organizador del Perú. Su vida, su obra (1515–1582)* (1935); ARTHUR FRANKLIN ZIMMERMAN, *Francisco de Toledo; Fifth Viceroy of Peru, 1569–1581* (1938); LEWIS HANKE, *The Spanish Struggle for Justice in the Conquest of America,* (1949: repr. 1965), esp. pp. 135–137, 165–172; JOHN HEMMING, *The Conquest of the Incas* (1970), esp. chaps. 20–23; LEWIS HANKE, ed., *Los virreyes españoles en América durante el gobierno de la casa de Austria: Perú* (1978); KAREN SPALDING, *Huarochirí: An Andean Society Under Inca and Spanish Rule* (1984), esp. pp. 156–168, 209–227; GUILLERMO LOHMANN VILLENA and MARÍA JUSTINA SARABIA VIEJO, eds., *Francisco de Toledo. Disposiciones gubernativas para el virreinato del Perú, 1569–1574,* 2 vols. (1986, 1989).

PETER BAKEWELL

TOLEDO Y LEYVA, PEDRO DE (Marqués de Mancera; *b.* 1585; *d.* 9 March 1654), viceroy of Peru (1639–1648). Designated the first marqués de Mancera in 1633, former governor of Galicia, and a member of PHILIP IV's Council of War, Mancera took office as viceroy of Peru in December 1639. He was a vigorous administrator with a mixed reputation. On the one hand he was known for his charity, piety, and Christian fervor. A special friend to the DOMINICANS, he established a chair of Thomistic theology at the University of San Marcos in Lima exclusively for a Dominican and supported construction of a Dominican church and the school of Santo Tomás. Also in Lima he helped to found a CARMELITE nunnery, a hospice and hermitage for the FRANCISCANS, and hospitals for Indians, blacks (San Bartolomé), and the poor. In addition he assisted Franciscan missions in Panataguas with public funds.

Mancera was an efficient but oftentimes arbitrary administrator. On one occasion he ordered the expulsion of all Portuguese Jews living in Peru—6,000 by one estimate—and on another the removal of Lima prostitutes to Valdivia, Chile, to stimulate population growth in that remote region. Imposing a highly unpopular tax on meat and wine to pay the costs, he strengthened fortifications at the port of Callao, where his son Antonio Sebastián was commandant, and built two new galleons for the Pacific fleet (*Armada del Sur*). He also suppressed sixteen holidays, opened new veins at the mercury mine of HUANCAVELICA, and revamped the tribute system. Anxious to immortalize himself, Mancera gave his name to the new fort at Valdivia and to the town of Pisco (San Clemente de Mancera). He stepped down as viceroy on 20 September 1648.

MANUEL DE MENDIBURU, ed., *Diccionario histórico-biográfico del Perú,* vol. 10 (1934); ROBERT R. MILLER, ed., *Chronicle of Colonial Lima: The Diary of Josephe and Francisco Mugaburu* (1975).

JOHN JAY TePASKE

TOLSÁ, MANUEL (*b.* 4 May 1757; *d.* 24 December 1816), sculptor and architect. Tolsá was trained in Valencia and at the Academia de San Fernando in Madrid. In 1791 he arrived in New Spain as director of sculpture at the ACADEMIA DE SAN CARLOS, bringing with him an important collection of plaster casts of classical works.

His activity in New Spain soon included architectural as well as sculptural projects. His best-known work is the equestrian statue of King CHARLES IV of Spain (1796, cast in bronze in 1803). Popularly known as the "Caballito," it was inspired by the Roman Capitol with its sculpture of Emperor Marcus Aurelius, and was the focal point of the 1796 renovation of the Plaza Mayor of Mexico City. Tolsá also worked on the completion of Mexico City's cathedral, on the baldachin (an ornamental structure over the central altar) of the cathedral of Puebla, on the house of the count of Buenavista (today Museo de San Carlos), and on the Palacio de Minería in Mexico City, as well as on many other projects. Because of his energetic participation in so many endeavors, Tolsá is considered largely responsible for the definitive entry of academic neoclassicism into New Spain.

MANUEL TOUSSAINT, *Colonial Art in Mexico* (1967); JOAQUÍN BÉRCHEZ, "Manuel Tolsá en la arquitectura española de su tiempo," in *Tolsá, Gimeno, Fabregat,* edited by Generalitat Valenciana (1989), pp. 13–64; ELOÍSA URIBE, *Tolsá, hombre de la ilustración* (1990).

CLARA BARGELLINI

See also **Architecture.**

TOLTECS, a people who dominated central Mexico in the years A.D. 950–1150/1200 and exerted influence over much of the territory of modern Mexico and Central America. Their capital Tula (Nahuatl: Tollan) occupied a ridge overlooking the Tula River in Hidalgo, 40 miles northwest of modern Mexico City. Spanish chroniclers recorded AZTEC legends and historical traditions about the Toltecs and QUETZALCOATL, their semilegendary ruler, whose identity and exploits became fused with those of the Feathered Serpent, his deified namesake. Unfortunately, contradictions are so abundant in these accounts that it is difficult to reconstruct a coherent Toltec history. Archaeological investigations at Tula and elsewhere add substantially to the corpus of data, but it is difficult to reconcile much of this information with the ethnohistoric accounts.

Ethnically and linguistically the Toltecs were an amalgam of small migrant groups who entered southern Hidalgo during Teotihuacán's last decades. They included the Nonoalca, refugees from TEOTIHUACÁN itself, and the CHICHIMECS, farmers fleeing south from the increasingly turbulent Mesoamerican frontier zone in north Mexico. There is good reason to believe that NAHUATL was the dominant language in Toltec society, although speakers of OTOMÍ and perhaps other Otomanguean languages were also present in significant numbers.

Agriculture was the basis of Toltec existence, and maize was the staple crop. Beans, squash, cactus fruits and juice, numerous minor plants, and the flesh of dogs, deer, and rabbits all supplemented the diet. Although irrigation was practiced where possible, adequate sub-sistence was a recurrent problem in this arid region and became a paramount concern as the population grew. The recorded legends suggest that famine, perhaps triggered by decreasing rainfall, led to civil war and, ultimately, Tula's abandonment in the twelfth century.

In addition to farming, the Toltec economy depended upon craft production and commerce. Pottery, stone tools, textiles, personal ornaments, and other products were manufactured in the city and exchanged in markets. Specialized merchants imported fancy pottery, marine shells, green stones, rare animal skins and feathers, cacao, exotic foods, and other luxury goods into Tula while distributing Toltec products far from their homeland.

The evidence suggests the existence of a Toltec "empire," but its extent and duration are unknown. Some archaeologists believe it included Pacific coastal Chiapas and Guatemala, the Yucatán peninsula with its Toltec-Maya center of CHICHÉN ITZÁ, and much of north and west Mexico, but others challenge this hypothesis.

The Aztecs proudly claimed Toltec ancestry and praised their putative forebears as warriors, master craftsmen, builders, and wise men. They exaggerated, perhaps intentionally, the justifiably impressive accomplishments of the Toltecs while creating a historical fiction designed to validate their own status. The Aztec embellishments notwithstanding, the Toltec legacy in modern Mexico remains considerable.

NIGEL DAVIES, *The Toltecs Until the Fall of Tula* (1977); WILLIAM T. SANDERS, JEFFREY R. PARSONS, and ROBERT S. SANTLEY, *The Basin of Mexico: The Ecological Processes in the Evolution of a Civilization* (1979); NIGEL DAVIES, *The Toltec Heritage* (1980); MURIEL PORTER WEAVER, *The Aztecs, Maya, and Their Predecessors: Archaeology of Mesoamerica,* 2d ed. (1981); RICHARD A. DIEHL, *Tula: The Toltec Capital of Ancient Mexico* (1983).

RICHARD A. DIEHL

See also **Archaeology; Mesoamerica.**

TOMEBAMBA, the principal INCA administrative center for the northern sector of the empire, located in the southern Ecuadorian highlands. The site was founded by Topa Inca Yupanqui during the military campaigns he led against the indigenous Cañari population between A.D. 1460 AND A.D. 1470. HUAYNA CAPAC, successor to Topa Inca and penultimate ruler of the empire, was born in Tomebamba and resided there for much of his life. Various ethnohistoric sources describe Tomebamba as a "second CUZCO," suggesting that the site was deliberately created in the image of the sacred capital of the Inca Empire. Indeed, certain features of the local landscape are reminiscent of the Cuzco Valley. This resemblance was not lost on the Inca, who sought to magnify the similarities through the imposition of Cuzqueño place-names upon the local topography. Many of these toponyms are still used today.

The site of Tomebamba was first excavated by Max

Uhle in the 1920s. Many of the ruins he described now lie beneath the modern city of Cuenca, Ecuador. The architectural remains Uhle encountered were vast in scale and included what he interpreted as religious structures, a central plaza, a palatial residence, guards' quarters, and a convent (*aqllawasi*). Elaborate waterworks, including pools, baths, and canals, as well as terraces and roads, were also recorded. The palatial sector, known as Puma Pungo, is believed to have been the royal residence of Huayna Capac. Substantial quantities of Inca pottery have been recovered from this portion of the site. Tomebamba was devastated by ATAHUALPA during the Inca civil war that ensued after the death of Huayna Capac in 1527. Though the site lay in ruins by the time the Spanish chronicler Pedro de CIEZA DE LEÓN passed through some twenty years later, it was nonetheless impressive enough for him to describe it as one of the most magnificent Inca sites in all the empire.

On the archaeology of Tomebamba, see MAX UHLE, *Las ruinas de Tomebamba* (1923); JAIME IDROVO, "Tomebamba: Primera fase de conquista Incasica en los Andes septentrionales," in *La frontera del estado Inca* (1988), Proceedings of the 45th Congreso Internacional de Americanistas, edited by Tom D. Dillehay and Patricia Netherly, BAR International Series, no. 442, pp. 87–104; and JOHN HYSLOP, *Inka Settlement Planning* (1990), pp. 140–142, 264–265. For the most detailed ethnohistoric account of the site, see MIGUEL CABELLO DE BALBOA, *Miscelánea Antártica* (1951; written in 1586), chaps. 21–22.

TAMARA L. BRAY

TOMIC, RADOMIRO (*b*. 7 May 1914), Chilean politician and former ambassador to the United States. Tomic, born in the Yugoslav enclave in Antofagasta, helped form the Partido Demócrata Cristiano (PDC). In 1968, after serving as ambassador to the United States, he returned to Chile, where he emerged as one of the leaders of the PDC's progressive wing. Selected as the Christian Democratic candidate for president in 1970, Tomic attempted to hold onto the Christian Democratic faithful while reaching out to the leftist vote by advocating more radical agrarian reform, nationalization of the copper mines, and massive state involvement in economic development. Tomic's tactics failed. Unable to retain the vote of those who had voted for Eduardo FREI six years earlier and often ridiculed for being bombastic, he came in a distant third, winning but 27 percent of the vote.

True to an earlier promise, Tomic endorsed the election of Salvador ALLENDE to the presidency. But the Christian Democrat did not abandon his party and even repudiated those who did leave to join the Movimiento de Acción Popular Unitaria (MAPU) or the Christian Left. Tomic, moreover, became increasingly discontented when it became clear that the Unidad Popular (UP) government would refuse to cooperate with the PDC and that it would not moderate its more radical policies. So much so, apparently, that Tomic, like Frei, supported the 1973 anti-Allende coup. He subsequently fled Chile, later returning to join the anti-PINOCHET movement and to act as an elder statesman of the Christian Democratic Party.

RADOMIRO TOMIC, *Fundamentos cristianos para una nueva política en Chile* (1945); PAUL E. SIGMUND, *The Overthrow of Allende and the Politics of Chile, 1964–1976* (1977), pp. 26, 36, 45, 68, 72, 80, 84, 94–95, 104, 106, 150–151; MICHAEL FLEET, *The Rise and Fall of Chilean Christian Democracy* (1985), pp. 44, 50, 114–116, 119–123.

WILLIAM F. SATER

See also **Chile: Political Parties.**

TOMOCHIC REBELLION, an uprising in Mexico's northwestern state of Chihuahua in 1891. Villagers of the mountain pueblo of Tomochic denied allegiance to the government and vowed to obey no one but a teenage folk saint, Teresa URREA, known as la Santa de Cabora, who, for more than a year, had been preaching social reform in the neighboring state of Sonora. Perhaps half of the 300 villagers did not concur with this millenarian vision and left town, but those who remained began to develop their utopian dream. In September 1892, after failed efforts to negotiate the faithful out of their intransigence, government troops sought to stamp out the movement but were routed by the outmanned, religiously inspired Tomochitecos.

The next month truly formidable army units from two states besieged the village. For a week the heroic defense held, but with the outcome inevitable, the Tomochitecos released their women and children to federal custody, then fought to the last man. Word of these events spread rapidly throughout the republic; Tomochic became a symbol of steadfast struggle by ordinary Mexicans against the oppressive dictatorship of Porfirio DÍAZ. Today that resistance is enshrined in literature and *corridos* (ballads) as well as school textbooks.

HERIBERTO FRÍAS, *Tomochic* (1989); PAUL J. VANDERWOOD, "None but the Justice of God," in *Patterns of Contention in Mexican History*, by Jaime E. Rodriguez O. (1992), pp. 227–241.

PAUL J. VANDERWOOD

TONINÁ, a large center of the MAYA Classic period (roughly A.D. 200–850). It may have been a provincial city in the PALENQUE sphere of influence or perhaps a capital in the southwest highlands of the Maya region in the state of Chiapas, Mexico. Although the art, architecture, and hieroglyphs of Toniná are similar to those of Palenque, its pottery types resemble those of Chiapa de Corzo, to the north and west. From these pottery types the site occupations can be classified into a series of distinctive cultural phases. Toniná also has sherds from Oaxaca and Mexico, even farther north, linking the Classic period of the Maya with the distinct cultural development of the highlands of Mexico.

Unique to Toniná are its fifteen sculptured stelae

(there is also one plain stela). The stelae are relatively short (less than 6 feet) and carved in the round. All have figures with large headdresses and elaborate clothing. Some of the stelae are crudely made or incomplete; some are of rough sandstone. Also unearthed at Toniná are a jade bead with a hieroglyph date incised, jade plaques with grotesque hands carved on both sides, and jade pendants with relief figures. Toniná also has monuments with distinctive glyphs, but little study of them has been undertaken. Although a sketch map has been made of the site, it has not yet been investigated intensively.

PIERRE BECQUELIN and CLAUDE F. BAUDEZ, *Toniná, une cité maya du Chiapas (Mexique)*, 3 vols. (1979–1982).

RICHARD S. MACNEISH

TONTON MACOUTES (properly Tonton-Makout or Tontonmakout, sing. and pl.), a Haitian term that describes an old folktale character (Uncle Knapsack) who snatches children into a knapsack or basket (*makout*) and often eats them alive. In the late 1950s, Haitians applied this term to the masked goons working for François DUVALIER's secret police, a largely middle-class organization set up to control urban opposition.

Although at first the regime denied the existence of the secret police, in 1962 it presented the Volontaires de la Sécurité Nationale (VSN), a new civil militia composed primarily of peasants, as the official version of the dreaded Tonton Macoutes. In fact, although most VSN leaders were members of the political police, most Tonton Macoutes did not formally join the militia as *milisyen*.

Nevertheless, the regime did its best to merge the identification of the two organizations, already linked by leadership. For more than ten years, the secret police operated away from public eyes, which were constantly distracted by a colorful militia whose main role was symbolic. Throughout the 1960s, unarmed *milisyen* showed their support in government-sponsored parades. Their uniform—blue denim shirt and pants, straw hat, and a red sash—evoked the traditional costume of the peasant god Zaka, the colors of the Haitian flag before Duvalier, and peasant armies of the nineteenth century.

The secret police grew behind this symbolic shield. So did the power and training of selected groups of *milisyen* who came to constitute a real counterpart to the traditional power of the Haitian army. The regime of Jean-Claude Duvalier (1971–1986) reinforced the links between the most active branches of the political police, the militia, and selected segments of the army devoted to the Duvalier family: the Leopards anti-insurgency corps, the Presidential Guard, the Port-au-Prince police. By the mid-1980s, the 9,000-strong VSN counted members of these various groups. Even some ministers of government wore the VSN uniform.

By the late 1980s, the name Tonton Macoutes applied to *milisyen*, informers, and torturers alike. After the 1987 overthrow of the dictatorship, the ambiguity of the name protected middle-class members of the secret police who had never worn the VSN uniform: summary justice was applied primarily to lower-class folk, at least some of whom had been *milisyen*.

BERNARD DIEDERICH and AL BURT, *Papa Doc: The Truth About Haiti Today* (1969); MICHEL-ROLPH TROUILLOT, *Haiti: State Against Nation. The Origins and Legacy of Duvalierism* (1990).

MICHEL-ROLPH TROUILLOT

President François Duvalier's forces parade in front of the National Palace in Port-au-Prince, 15 May 1963. WIDE WORLD.

TOPOXTÉ, a Late Postclassic (A.D. 1250–1500) ceremonial center located on an island of the same name in the southwestern part of Lake Yaxha, in the northeastern Petén, Guatemala. It is the most important site of a cluster of three contemporaneous island occupations that constitute a large and complex Late Postclassic Maya settlement: adjacent islands are Paxté, with an elite residential and ceremonial settlement, and the larger Cante, with over 100 primarily residential structures.

Topoxté, the eastern and largest island, has elite ceremonial architecture and ceramics. Its temple assemblage—a tall masonry temple, a perpendicular open hall, and two shrines within the plaza that are aligned with the main axis of the temple—stands on the highest point of the island. There are 100 house platforms on the island. The most notable ceramics are effigy censers, ritual pottery, and a red-on-cream decorated type.

This defensive island grouping is part of a network of occupations in the lacustrine environments of the central Petén prior to the Spanish conquest. The architectural data of Topoxté show striking similarities to a center site, Mayapán, in the Yucatán of Mexico; and ceramic censers are similar to contemporaneous pottery from the Yucatán. However, the archaeological culture of the site is also related to the elite culture of regional Petén centers. Topoxté and its neighboring islands form one of several defensive settlements in the lake region of the Petén, suggesting that there were competitive sociopolitical groups in the area prior to the Spanish conquest.

WILLIAM ROTCH BULLARD, JR., "Topoxté, a Postclassic Maya Site in Petén, Guatemala," in *Monographs and Papers in Maya Archaeology*, edited by William Rotch Bullard, Jr., Papers of the Peabody Museum of Archaeology and Ethnology, vol. 61 (1970); JAY K. JOHNSON, "Postclassic Maya Site Structure at Topoxté, El Petén, Guatemala," in *The Lowland Maya Postclassic*, edited by Arlen F. Chase and Prudence M. Rice (1985), pp. 151–165; and PRUDENCE M. RICE and DON S. RICE, "Topoxté, Manache, and the Central Petén Postclassic," in *The Lowland Maya Postclassic*, edited by Arlen F. Chase and Prudence M. Rice (1985), pp. 166–183.

EUGENIA F. ROBINSON

See also **Mayas; Mesoamerica.**

TOQUI, the term applied to ARAUCANIAN (MAPUCHE) military leaders during the warfare that followed the Spanish invasion of Chile in the 1540s. It seems likely that Europeans imposed their own categories of leadership and government on the Araucanian warriors who were most prominent in the wars. In traditional Araucanian society, the *toqui* was less a "generalissimo" or "paramount chief" then a temporary leader chosen by alliances of families to take charge of fighting against other alliances or to supervise communal economic tasks such as pine nut collection or fishing. LAUTARO (1535–1557), CAUPOLICÁN (*d.* 1558), and Colo Colo (1515–1561), celebrated *toquis* of the sixteenth century, may have had their true status magnified by such poets as Alonso de ERCILLA Y ZÚÑIGA (1533–1594). To what extent the pressure of the Spanish offensives caused greater concentration of authority among Araucanians is still debated. No centralized state with single leadership ever emerged in Araucania.

SIMON COLLIER

TORDESILLAS, TREATY OF (1494), agreement between Spain and Portugal that divided administration of their overseas territories. The Papal Donation of ALEXANDER VI in 1493 had conferred to the crown of Castile jurisdiction over newly discovered lands 100 leagues "to the west and south of the so-called AZORE and CAPE VERDE ISLANDS" that were not already under the control of a Christian prince. For reasons still disputed, the Portuguese protested what came to be known as the LINE OF DEMARCATION and demanded a meeting to discuss the issue. Negotiators convened at the small town of Tordesillas to the north of Medina del Campo in Spain and reached an agreement that extended Portuguese jurisdiction a full 270 leagues farther west (between 48° and 49° west of Greenwich). The treaty, enacted on 7 June 1494, provided the Portuguese with the legal claim to a large strip of the Brazilian coast, subsequently discovered during the expedition of Pedro Alvares CABRAL in 1500.

LYLE N. MC ALISTER, *Spain and Portugal in the New World: 1492–1700* (1984).

NOBLE DAVID COOK

TORNEL Y MENDÍVIL, JOSÉ MARÍA (*b.* 1794?; *d.* 11 September 1853), Mexican politician and general. Born in Orizaba, Veracruz, Tornel joined the insurgency in 1813. Captured and sentenced to death, he survived the War of Independence, becoming private secretary to Antonio López de SANTA ANNA (1821) and to President Guadalupe Victoria (1824–1829). In his later career, Tornel occupied many other posts, serving as governor of the Federal District (1833–1834) and as minister of war on several occasions. One of Santa Anna's most devoted supporters, Tornel was always closely associated with him and often acted as his spokesman. A man of great energy, he instituted many reforms in the army and was a prolific author on political issues, a translator of Byron, and a playwright. Fervently interested in education, Tornel promoted the Lancasterian system (involving advanced students as monitors) and was director of the Colegio de Minería from 1843 to 1853.

WILLIAM MARTIN FOWLER, "José María Tornel: Mexican General/Politician (1794–1853) (Ph.D. diss., University of Bristol, 1994).

MICHAEL P. COSTELOE

TORNQUIST, ERNESTO (*b.* 31 December 1842; *d.* 17 June 1908), founder of one of the first and most important industrial investment banks in Latin America. Tornquist played a major part in the financial development of Argentina in the last quarter of the nineteenth century. Born in Buenos Aires into a mercantile family of Swedish origin, he studied in a German-speaking school and entered the family firm of Altgelt, Ferber, and Co. in 1859. In 1874 he became the senior partner in the firm, which was henceforth called Ernesto Tornquist and Co. The history of the company was marked by steady growth over fifty years, leading the way in Buenos Aires in the fields of international and industrial finance. Tornquist and Co. was the agent for BARING BROTHERS in Buenos Aires from the 1880s until 1902, as well as representative for prominent Belgian, German, and French banks. Tornquist personally promoted the establishment of the first sugar refinery in Argentina, established in the city of Rosario in 1887; the largest Argentine meat-packing firm, the Sansinena Company; and several of the first metallurgical and chemical firms in the Argentine capital. He was a close financial adviser to the governments of Julio ROCA, Carlos PELLEGRINI, and other conservative leaders at the turn of the century, participating in most of the important monetary and financial reforms of the time. His firm today is a prominent commercial bank in Buenos Aires.

Ernesto Tornquist & Co., 1874–1924 (1924).

CARLOS MARICHAL

TORO, DAVID (*b.* 24 June 1898; *d.* 25 July 1977), president of Bolivia (1936–1937). Born in Sucre, Toro rose from military cadet to chief of staff during the CHACO WAR. Together with army officer Germán BUSCH he overthrew the civilian president José Luis Tejada SORZANO in May 1936, and Toro became president. Toro initiated a nationalistic government of "state syndicalism" and "military socialism," which included tax and banking reforms and the establishment of syndicates (unions) that all interest groups were expected to join. The possessions of the Standard Oil Company of New Jersey were nationalized and the Bolivian state oil monopoly (Yacimientos Petroliferos Fiscales Bolivianos—YPFB), still an important Bolivian agency, was established. Nearly all other social and economic changes were unsuccessful, but a pivotal accomplishment of the Toro period was a decree granting women total equality in all endeavors. The Toro presidency was the very beginning of the great changes that took place in Bolivia after the Chaco War. In July 1937 Busch took over the presidency in a bloodless coup. As ex-president, Toro remained moderately active in government and civic affairs.

Quién es quién en Bolivia (1942); PORFIRIO DIAZ MACHICAO, *Toro, Busch, Quintanilla, 1936–1940* (1957); CARLOS D. MESA GISBERT, *Presidentes de Bolivia: Entre urnas y fusiles* (1990).

CHARLES W. ARNADE

TORO, FERMÍN (*b.* 14 June 1806; *d.* 23 December 1865), Venezuelan intellectual, politician, and diplomat. Toro entered public life as a functionary in the ministry of finance in 1828. In 1831 he was a representative in Congress. He was appointed by the regime of José Antonio PÁEZ to preside over the commission charged with bestowing funerary honors on Simón Bolívar's remains when they were repatriated to Caracas. He provided an important synthesis of his economic ideas in his *Reflexiones sobre la ley del 10 de abril de 1834* (1845). He was the secretary of Alejo Fortique, Venezuela's minister plenipotentiary to Great Britain (1839–1846), in London (1839–1841) as well as minister plenipotentiary in New Granada and then in Spain, France, and England in 1846–1847.

During the first years of the José Tadeo MONAGAS regime, Toro was minister of finance. But as a representative in Congress, he confronted Monagas after the January 1848 assault on Congress. When Monagas was overthrown in 1858, Toro again became politically active, assuming the posts of minister of finance and minister of foreign affairs under President Julián CASTRO. He was a member of the Valencia Convention in 1858 before retiring from public life and devoting himself to his research in botany, anthropology, and linguistics.

See AUGUSTO MIJARES, *Libertad y justicia social en el pensamiento do Don Fermín Toro* (1947); VIRGILIO TOSTA, *Fermín Toro; Político y sociólogo de la armonía* (1958); JOSÉ ANTONIO DE ARMAS CHITTY, *Fermín Toro y su época* (1966). A selection of Toro's most important writings are in *Fermín Toro: La doctrina conservadora*.

INÉS QUINTERO

TORO ZAMBRANO, MATEO DE (*b.* 20 September 1727; *d.* 26 February 1811), president of the first national government of Chile (1810–1811). One of the great creole magnates of eighteenth-century Chile, and certainly one of the richest, Toro Zambrano played a full part in the public life of the colony, as militia officer, *alcalde* (mayor) and *corregidor* (municipal magistrate) of Santiago, lieutenant to the governor (1768), and as a member of the committee that disposed of the expropriated properties of the Jesuits after their expulsion in 1767 (he acquired one of the largest Jesuit haciendas). King CHARLES III conferred on him the title of Conde de la Conquista in 1770.

The crisis of the Spanish empire after 1808 thrust Toro Zambrano into an unexpected role: in July 1810, following the deposition of the Spanish governor Francisco Antonio García Carrasco (1742–1813), Toro Zambrano became interim governor of the colony. Creole patriots agitating for a national junta persuaded him (partly through his confessor) to agree to a *cabildo abierto* (open town meeting) on 18 September 1810. At this historic assembly a junta was elected with Toro Zambrano as president. He played little part in the work of the new government, and sometimes fell asleep at its meetings. Greatly affected by his wife's death (January 1811), he died soon after.

JAIME EYZAGUIRRE, *El conde de la Conquista* (1951; 2d ed., 1966).

SIMON COLLIER

TORQUEMADA, JUAN DE (*b.* ca. 1562; *d.* 1 January 1624), Franciscan missionary and historian. Passages in Torquemada's major work, *Monarquía indiana* (Indian Monarchy), lead us to believe that he was born in Spain. He was ordained around 1587 and held several important positions in the Franciscan order. Torquemada was the chronicler of the order, a guardian in Santiago de Tlatelolco and Tlaxcala, and provincial of the Holy Gospel. The *Monarquía indiana* comprises observations on the daily life of the colony and descriptions of NEZAHUAL-PILLI's and MOTECUHZOMA's palaces and other archaeological remains, as well as writings on the pre-Hispanic period that built on the work of such Franciscan historians and linguists as Andrés de Olmos, Bernardino de SAHAGÚN, and Jerónimo de Mendieta. Torquemada also consulted Indian codices and maps and the work of the mestizo historians Fernando de Alva Ixtlilxóchitl and Diego Muñoz Camargo; he followed the ethnographic tradition of Olmos and Sahagún of drawing testimonies from Indian informants. This variety of sources has led critics to refer to Torquemada as the "chronicler of chroniclers."

HOWARD FRANCIS CLINE, *Torquemada and His Franciscan Predecessors: Further Notes on Sources and Usages in the Monarquía Indiana* (1969); and JUAN DE TORQUEMADA, *Monarquía indiana*, 7 vols. (1975–1983), esp. vol. 7, which is a collection of studies of Torquemada and the *Monarquía indiana*.

JOSÉ RABASA

TORRE, LISANDRO DE LA (*b.* 6 December 1868; *d.* 5 January 1939), Argentine statesman, political leader, advocate of popularly elected local government. De la Torre was born in Rosario, Sante Fe, to a landowner father and a mother who descended from one of Argentina's oldest families. After finishing secondary school in Rosario, he studied law at the University of Buenos Aires during a time of political ferment, graduating in 1886. In 1888 he published a thesis comparing models of municipal government in the western world, entitled *El régimen municipal*. He participated in the political demonstration at El Parque in 1889, organized by students and reform-minded youths. He joined the Civic Union (soon to become the Unión Cívica Radical [UCR] of Leandro ALEM and Aristóbulo DEL VALLE, in the three aborted revolutions of 1890, 1891, and 1893, undertaken to reform Argentine politics. De la Torre broke with the UCR over political strategy, and fought a duel with Hipólito YRIGOYEN in 1895, after which the two remained lifelong antagonists. In 1908 de la Torre, a successful cattle breeder in Sante Fe, founded the Liga del Sur (League of the South), an agrarian political party, to reform local government. In Argentina's first truly democratic by-elections of 1911, he won a seat in the Sante Fe legislature. In 1914 he founded the Partido Demócrata Progresista (Progressive Democratic Party [PDP]) as an alternative to Yrigoyen's UCR, which in some provinces was gaining on the entrenched oligarchic governments. As presidential candidate for the PDP in the 1916 national elections, de la Torre tried to unite reform-minded conservatives and progressives against Yrigoyen's populist campaign. At the last minute, in a three-way race, de la Torre was abandoned by key conservatives, and Yrigoyen won the election by the narrowest of margins. De la Torre served in the Chamber of Deputies from 1912 to 1916 and from 1922

to 1926, and in the Senate from 1932 to 1937. A spellbinding orator, he fought for land reform, separation of church and state, female suffrage, civil divorce, and for the production of domestic industries. He is best remembered for his passionate defense of Argentine meatpacking plants.

In 1932 de la Torre was defeated in his quest for the presidency as candidate of the Democratic Alliance (PDP and Socialist Party). Defeats suffered in the Senate at the hands of conservatives, the assassination in the Senate chamber of his close political ally Enzo Bordabehere, and the failure of his ranch in the arid western province of La Rioja led de la Torre to despondency. He resigned his seat in the Senate, and ultimately he committed suicide in Buenos Aires. His writings are collected in the seven-volume *Obras* (5th ed., 1952). De la Torre, the uncompromising politician and indefatigable champion of social justice, remains an icon for nationalists and the left alike.

RAÚL LARRA, *Lisandro de la Torre: Vida y drama del solitario de Pinas* (1950); EDGARDO AMARAL, *Anecdotario de Lisandro de la Torre* (1957), *Lisandro de la Torre y la política de la reforma electoral de Sáenz Peña* (1961); SAMUEL YASKY, *Lisandro de la Torre de Cerca: Los momentos culminantes de su vida política* (1969); JUAN M. VIGO, *De la Torre contra todos* (1974); GEORGETTE MAGASSY DORN, "Idealism Versus Reality: The Failure of an Argentine Political Leader, Lisandro de la Torre" (Ph.D. diss., Georgetown University, 1981).

GEORGETTE MAGASSY DORN

See also **Argentina: Political Parties.**

TORRE, MIGUEL DE LA (*d.* 1838), Spanish general. Torre led Spanish troops against Simón BOLÍVAR and revolutionary armies in the wars for Venezuelan and Colombian independence. Following a six-month armistice between General Pablo MORILLO Y MORILLO and Bolívar, the Spanish crown gave Torre command of royalist troops. The two sides fought at the Battle of CARABOBO, in Venezuela on 24 June 1821. The deaths of between 1,000 and 1,500 Spanish soldiers assured Venezuelan and Colombian independence; historians called it the "Colombian Waterloo." Torre fled to Puerto Cabello where he surrendered two years later. He was appointed civil and military governor of Puerto Rico in 1823 and named count of Torrepando.

JOSÉ DOMINIQUE DÍAZ and MIGUEL DE LA TORRE, *Mémoires du Général Morillo* (1826); IRENE NICHOLSON, *The Liberators: A Study of Independence Movements in Spanish America* (1969), pp. 190–193; DONNA KEYSE RUDOLPH, *Historical Dictionary of Venezuela* (1971), p. 111.

CHRISTOPHER T. BOWEN

TORRE TAGLE Y PORTOCARRERO, JOSÉ BERNARDO DE (fourth marqués of Torre Tagle; *b.* 1779; *d.* 1825), president of Peru in 1823. He inherited several royal positions, including a seat on the Lima city council. Elected *alcalde* of Lima (1811–1812), he became a deputy to the Spanish Cortes in 1813. In late 1820, as governor of Trujillo, he announced in favor of José de SAN MARTÍN, who was advocating a monarchy for independent Peru. When Peru's first president, José de la RIVA-AGÜERO, began acting independently of Congress, that body moved to replace him with the very conservative Torre Tagle (1823). Peru was then left with two governments: Riva Agüero's stood for interests in northern Peru, while Torre Tagle's represented Lima. Neither had much support or lasted very long.

Torre Tagle presided over a weak, bankrupt state. When it appeared on the verge of collapse, he committed treason by negotiating secretly with the Spaniards against Simón BOLÍVAR, to whom Torre Tagle had given full control of the army in 1823. Surrendering to the royal army, Torre Tagle presided over the last year of Spanish rule in Peru.

TIMOTHY E. ANNA, *The Fall of the Royal Government in Peru* (1979); PETER BLANCHARD, *Slavery and Abolition in Early Republican Peru* (1992).

VINCENT PELOSO

See also **Wars of Independence.**

TORRE Y HUERTA, CARLOS DE LA (*b.* 15 May 1858; *d.* 1950), Cuban naturalist, educator, writer, and public figure. Born in Matanzas, de la Torre was the son of a professor. He began his studies under his father, who instilled in him a love of science and objective methodology. De la Torre earned his baccalaureate from the Instituto de La Habana, and then moved on to study zoology and mineralogy at the university under the famous scientist Felipe Poey. There young Carlos's enthusiasm for mollusks quickly earned him the nickname Carlos Caracol, or Charles the Snail. In 1879 he discovered a new species of mollusk and earned a master's degree. In 1881 de la Torre earned his doctorate from the University of Madrid and moved to Puerto Rico. For several years he was on tenuous terms with the scientific community in Cuba, but he finally returned in 1892 and served as director of two reviews: *La enciclopedia* and *La revista enciclopédica.* During the CUBAN WAR OF INDEPENDENCE (1895–1898), de la Torre fled to Paris, where he worked closely with naturalists at the Museum of Natural History and across the Channel at the British Museum. In 1900 he returned to Cuba and cofounded the Cuban National Party, on whose platform he was elected to the Havana City Council. De la Torre continued to write on many subjects, including ethnohistory and anthropology in his later years. He received honorary doctorates from Harvard and Jena universities and was considered a pioneering member of the international community of naturalists.

CARLOS DE LA TORRE Y HUERTA, *Clasificación de los animales observados por Colón y los primeros exploradores de Cuba; Distribu-*

ción geográfica de la fauna malacológica terrestre de Cuba; Historia de Cuba; and *Geografía de Cuba* (1955); CARLOS EUGENIO CHARDÓN, *Los naturalistas en la América Latina* (1949).

KAREN RACINE

TORREJÓN Y VELASCO, TOMÁS DE (baptized 23 December 1644; *d.* 23 April 1728), Spanish composer active in Peru. Torrejón y Velasco may have been born in Villarrobledo, Albacete, Spain. He was the son of one of Philip IV's huntsmen and spent his childhood in Fuencarral, becoming a page in the palace of Don Pedro Fernández de Castro, the count of Lemos. Named viceroy of Peru in 1667, the count brought the twenty-three-year-old Torrejón with him to America. From 1667 until 1672 Torrejón worked in Lima's armory as superintendent and later as magistrate and chief justice of Chachapoyas Province. Torrejón's musical career in Lima started on 1 January 1676, when he was named *maestro de capilla* of Lima's cathedral, a position he retained until his death fifty-two years later. Lima was the center of South America's musical life at that time and Torrejón became its leading figure. To celebrate the installation of the second grand organ of the cathedral, eight polychoral *villancicos* composed by Torrejón were performed. His fame spread to Cuzco, Trujillo, and Guatemala, and was enhanced after the premiere of his memorial vespers for Charles II in June 1701. That same year his opera *La púrpura de la rosa,* with a libretto by Pedro Calderón de la Barca, was lavishly premiered at the viceroyal palace on 19 October. It had been commissioned by the new viceroy, the count of Monclova, to celebrate Philip V's eighteenth birthday. As the first operatic work written and produced in the New World, *La púrpura de la rosa* is of great musicological significance. It has a semimythological plot, based on the story of Venus and Adonis but with popular Spanish characters added. The vast collection of Torrejón's religious music is kept in the archives in Lima, Cuzco, and Guatemala. He died in Lima.

ROBERT STEVENSON, *The Music of Peru* (1960), and *Torrejón y Velasco: La púrpura de la rosa* (1976); GÉRARD BÉHAGUE, *Music in Latin America* (1979); *New Grove Dictionary of Music and Musicians,* vol. 19 (1980).

SUSANA SALGADO

TORREÓN, city in southwestern Coahuila, Mexico, on the Nazas and Aguanaval rivers, in the heart of the Comarca Laguna.

In the colonial era, the future site of Torreón was part of the Marquesado of San Miguel de Aguayo, but after Mexican independence the area passed through a number of different owners. In the mid-nineteenth century the area gave rise to a small ranch community, which expanded rapidly with the arrival of the Mexican Central Railroad in 1883. Five years later the International Railroad also passed through Torreón, linking it to Durango and Piedras Negras, and Torreón received villa status in 1893. With the arrival of the Coahuila and Pacific Railroad in 1903, Torreón became the third largest railroad center in Mexico. It was recognized as a city in 1907.

Torreón was strategically important in the Mexican Revolution and formed the geographical core of Francisco MADERO's Antireelectionist movement. On 14–15 May 1911, Torreón was the site of one of the bloodiest massacres in the history of the revolution when forces loyal to Madero occupied the city. In the confusion that followed, there erupted a race riot in which over two hundred fifty Chinese were murdered. On 1 October 1913 Francisco VILLA took the city after two days of fierce fighting against Victoriano HUERTA's Federalist troops. Villa retook the city in early April 1914. Today, Torreón is a large urban and industrial city with a population of 328,086 (1980).

WILLIAM K. MEYERS, "La Comaraca Lagunera: Work, Protest, and Popular Mobilization in North Central Mexico," in *Other Mexicos: Essays on Regional Mexican History, 1876–1911,* edited by Thomas Benjamin and William McNellie (1984), pp. 243–274; ALAN KNIGHT, *The Mexican Revolution,* vol. 1, *Porfirians, Liberals and Peasants* (1986), esp. pp. 207–210, 278–279, 321–322, 424–426.

AARON PAINE MAHR

TORRES, JUAN JOSÉ (*b.* 1921; *d.* 1976), army officer and president of Bolivia (1970–1971). Born in Cochabamba, Torres was a career soldier. He stayed in the armed forces even during the 1952–1964 rule of the Movimiento Nacionalista Revolucionario (MNR) following the Bolivian National Revolution, in spite of the fact that in his youth he had belonged to the Bolivian Socialist Falange (FSB), a fascist-oriented party and bitter enemy of the MNR. Torres was a co-conspirator in the overthrow of MNR leader President Víctor PAZ ESTENSSORO in November 1964, and held important posts in the succeeding military regime. He was in command of the army unit that in 1967 suppressed the guerrilla operation of Ernesto "Che" GUEVARA.

When General Alfredo OVANDO overthrew President Luis Adolfo Siles Salinas in September 1969, General Torres became commander in chief of the armed forces. In that position, he supported the "nationalist" position of Ovando. However, in July 1970 he was forced to resign the post because of pressure from right-wing army leaders. When right-wing officers forced the resignation of President Ovando early in October 1970, General Torres emerged as president, with the support of the leadership of the Central Obrera Boliviana (COB), the national labor confederation. Torres presided over a "nationalist" and "leftist" regime. He cancelled the U.S. Steel concession on the Matilda zinc mine and expelled the Peace Corps from Bolivia.

The COB and leftist parties organized the so-called Popular Assembly, which sought to play the role of the 1917 Russian soviets, but it was not granted any official power by Torres. The COB refused several official invitations from Torres to join his administration. In August 1971, Colonel Hugo BANZER SUÁREZ, former head of the Military College, led a conspiracy that ousted Torres, who fled to Argentina, where he was assassinated in 1976.

GUILLERMO LORA, *A History of the Brazilian Labor Movement* (1977).

ROBERT J. ALEXANDER

See also **Bolivia: Organizations; Bolivia: Political Parties.**

TORRES, LUIS EMETERIO (*b.* 1844; *d.* 1935), governor and military commander. A veteran of the war against the French intervention and postwar political revolts in Sinaloa, Torres used the ties he cultivated with the notables of Álamos (southern Sonora) and with Porfirio DÍAZ (while a federal deputy) to secure leadership of a political circle that rose to power in Sonora in the late 1870s and controlled the state until 1911. Though he was elected governor five times (uniquely retaining alternation during the Porfiriato), his principal associates—Ramón CORRAL and Rafael Izábal—were the administrative and legislative directors. Torres managed political relations within the state and with Mexico City; after 1887 he served as commander of Baja California and then of the entire Northwest military zone. Torres embodied the Porfirista ideal of promoting progress and order: APACHE raids were terminated; YAQUI INDIAN autonomy ended (partly through the use of deportation); economic activity markedly expanded; all political opposition was suppressed.

STUART F. VOSS, "Towns and Enterprise in Northwestern Mexico: A History of Urban Elites in Sonora and Sinaloa, 1830–1910" (Ph.D. diss., Harvard University, 1972); FRANCISCO R. ALMADA, *Diccionario de historia, geografía y biografía de sonorenses* (1983); RAMÓN EDUARDO RUIZ, *The People of Sonora and Yankee Capitalists* (1988).

STUART F. VOSS

TORRES, TORIBIO, early-nineteenth-century Honduran religious painter, known especially for his classical realist portraits. Torres painted many of the bishops of Comayagua as well as many biblical scenes for Honduran churches. Reflecting the predominant style of painters of the early independent period, most of his paintings are serious portraits of leading personages, although he painted few of the political leaders of the independence movement in Honduras.

J. EVARISTO LÓPEZ and LONGINO BECERRA, *Honduras: 40 pintores* (1989).

RALPH LEE WOODWARD, JR.

TORRES BELLO, DIEGO DE (*b.* 1551; *d.* 1638), Jesuit founder and first provincial of the Paraguay missions. Born in Villalpando, Castile, Torres joined the Society of Jesus and in 1581 was sent to work in Peru. He served for a few years as superior of the mission in Juli, near Lake Titicaca, then as superior of the Jesuit colleges in Cuzco, Quito, and Potosí. The Juli mission later served as a model for the Paraguay missions. In 1604 Paraguay and Chile were created as a separate Jesuit province, and Torres Bello was designated the first provincial. He set up his residence in Córdoba, Argentina, where he founded the novitiate as well as a seminary, which later became a university. Determined to protect the Indians from the Spaniards, he won approval for his plan to gather the former into mission towns, or "reductions." The first of these missions was founded in 1609; by the eighteenth century there were thirty. Torres Bello laid out the basic norms for the missions in a list of eighteen recommendations. Proficient in Aymara, Quechua, and Guaraní, he personally oversaw the building of the first missions. He finished his term as provincial in 1615, and spent his latter days working in the colleges of Buenos Aires and Chuquisaca, and in the missions among the Indians. He died in Chuquisaca.

RUBÉN VARGAS UGARTE, *Historia de la Compañía de Jesús en el Perú*, vol. 1 (1963); PHILIP CARAMAN, *The Lost Paradise: The Jesuit Republic in South America*, 2d ed. (1990); SILVIO PALACIOS and ENA ZOFFOLI, *Gloria y tragedia de las misiones guaraníes* (1991).

JEFFREY KLAIBER

See also **Jesuits; Missions.**

TORRES BODET, JAIME (*b.* 17 April 1902; *d.* 15 May 1974), Mexican poet and public figure. Torres Bodet, who published his first book at age sixteen, distinguished himself as a preparatory student and became a protégé of José VASCONCELOS at nineteen. He joined the ATENEO DE LA JUVENTUD in 1918 with other budding intellectual figures, many of whom established the major literary circle known as the "Contemporáneos" in the late 1920s. The prototypical Mexican intellectual of his age, Torres Bodet became a major figure in the public world of international and educational affairs. A professor at the National University, he twice served as secretary of education (1943–1946 and 1958–1964). In foreign affairs, after a long career in the diplomatic service, including posts as ambassador to France and Italy, he became secretary of foreign relations (1946–1948) and secretary general of UNESCO in 1948. Awarded the National Prize for Literature in 1966, he left a monumental four-volume memoir.

JAIME TORRES BODET, *Obras Escogidas* (1961); EMMANUEL CARBALLO, *Jaime Torres Bodet* (1968); SONJA P. KARSEN, *Jaime Torres Bodet* (1971); GUILLERMO SHERIDAN, *Los contemporáneos ayer* (1985).

RODERIC AI CAMP

TORRES GARCÍA, JOAQUÍN (*b.* 25 July 1874; *d.* 8 August 1949), Uruguayan painter and sculptor. Born in Montevideo, Torres García lived in France, Spain, and New York City from 1892 to 1932. He executed a number of murals and the stained-glass windows of the cathedral of Palma de Mallorca. He was a founding member of both the Cercle et Carré in Paris (1930) and the Asociación de Arte Constructivo in Montevideo (1935). Torres García considered himself a realist. Because of his passion for geometry, order, synthesism, construction, and rhythm, Angel Kalenberg spoke of the linguistic quality of Torres García's art, characterizing his creations as ideograms. His work provides an interesting example of pictorial duality, purely plastic elements being sensitively and skillfully fused with the expression of personal feeling. Among his publications are *Structure* (1935), *The Tradition of Abstract Man* (1938), *The Metaphysics of Indo-American Prehistory* (1940), and *Universal Constructivism* (1944).

Museum of Modern Art of Latin America (1985).

AMALIA CORTINA ARAVENA

TORRES RESTREPO, CAMILO (*b.* 2 February 1929; *d.* 15 February 1966), Colombian revolutionary priest. From an upper-class (though not particularly wealthy) Bogotá family, Camilo Torres began the study of law at the Universidad Nacional in Bogotá, but in 1947 abruptly changed his career goals and entered the Roman Catholic seminary. His vocation was not grounded in traditional religiosity; rather, he was attracted to the progressive social Catholicism that was a strong current in postwar Europe and would gain added impetus from the reforms of the Second Vatican Council and from the movement of LIBERATION THEOLOGY. After his 1954 ordination he studied sociology at Louvain, in Belgium; taught sociology at the Universidad Nacional; served as university chaplain; and worked with Colombia's agrarian reform agency and other social programs. Like many Colombian intellectuals of the 1960s, he was influenced by the Cuban Revolution and felt increasingly alienated from his country's political and socioeconomic establishment.

Torres's social activism and willingness to work with Marxists troubled his ecclesiastical superiors, who ordered him to choose between priestly duties and secular concerns. In response he abandoned the active priesthood and in 1965 launched a new leftist coalition known as Frente Unido (United Front). His acknowledged charisma attracted followers, but he felt frustration over the difficulty of organizing a viable movement with any chance of implementing radical reform by peaceful means. He therefore gave up the legal struggle and joined the Ejército de Liberación Nacional (Army of National Liberation), which of all the guerrilla organizations operating in Colombia was the one most closely associated with the Cuban model.

Torres died in the first military engagement in which he took part. Nevertheless, his memory and his writings continued to exert strong influence on Colombian leftists, for many of whom his personal example legitimated the recourse to violent action.

GERMÁN GUZMÁN, *Camilo Torres*, translated by John D. Ring (1969); WALTER J. BRODERICK, *Camilo Torres: A Biography of the Priest-Guerrillero* (1975).

DAVID BUSHNELL

See also **Colombia: Revolutionary Movements.**

TORRES Y PORTUGAL, FERNANDO DE (sixteenth c.), seventh viceroy of Peru. Born in Jaén, Torres y Portugal received the title of conde de Villardompardo in 1576. In 1585 he was appointed VICEROY of Peru, where he served until 1584. His rule was marred by conflict with the INQUISITION over the activities of his son, don Jerónimo de Torres; nephew, don Diego de Portugal; and secretary, Juan Bello. Torres y Portugal also granted a Peruvian ENCOMIENDA to his grandson, don Francisco de Torres y Portugal. During his rule, Torres y Portugal focused on the silver production of POTOSÍ. After Thomas Cavendish ravaged the coast during his viceregency, Torres y Portugal became concerned with the defenses of the Pacific coast. In an effort to protect the realm he ordered the purchase of five galeons, two smaller ships for coastal service, and two galleys, along with fifty-four pieces of artillery. He returned to Spain in 1592.

MANUEL DE MENDIBURU, *Diccionario histórico-biográfico del Perú* (1874–1890).

JOHN F. SCHWALLER

TORRIJOS HERRERA, OMAR (*b.* 13 February 1929; *d.* 31 July 1981), maximum leader and supreme chief of the Panamanian Revolution, chief of state, and commander in chief of the Panamanian National Guard (1968–1981). Born in Santiago de Veraguas, he entered a military academy in El Salvador after attending public schools in Panama.

A career military man, General Omar Torrijos Herrera rose through the ranks of the Panamanian National Guard, joining several other colonels in leading a coup on 11 October 1968 that removed President Arnulfo ARIAS MADRID after only ten days in office. Unsuccessful efforts by his colleagues to secure power left Torrijos as the sole leader of the guard.

Torrijos is most remembered for his successful campaign to establish Panamanian control and sovereignty over the canal, a popular cause in Panama, which represented the fulfillment of a longtime national ambition. The general skillfully orchestrated popular sentiment and focused world opinion through a meeting of the U.N. Security Council in March 1993. The Security Council met in the Legislative Palace in Panama City, very close to the frontier separating the Canal Zone from Panama. The Torrijos–Carter Treaty, signed 7 September 1977, established a gradual transition process, assuring U.S. operation of the canal until 31 December 1999 but guaranteeing Panamanian control of the canal on 1 January 2000, thus ending U.S. jurisdiction over Panama's economic resource. The treaty also eliminated the Canal Zone and its special privileges for U.S. citizens three years hence and brought Panama a dramatic increase in canal revenues.

Torrijos's contribution to Panamanian politics, however, was far more significant, for his revolution changed his nation's political institutions and extended political participation to previously excluded and ignored ethnic groups and social classes. A self-made man of the middle class, he focused on ending the dominance of the elite of Spanish ancestry and on opening the political system to the urban masses of laborers and the middle class, which consisted largely of mulattoes and blacks, groups that had previously been denied even citizenship, much less political participation. In this sense, Torrijos permanently changed the nation's politics by opening the system, increasing participation, and ending segregation—an achievement similar to that of neighboring Costa Rica in the 1948 revolution.

The guard represented the main avenue of advance for these classes, and hence led the way to changes placing them in the political mainstream. The Constitution of 1972, which institutionalized Torrijos's personal control of the state, also expanded the National Assembly to 505 members, theoretically making it more representative of the nation, though all key powers resided in the hands of the maximum leader.

Shifting the nation from import substitution to export-oriented economic growth, Torrijos focused on banking, services, and transportation. The Banking Law of 1970 removed all reserve requirements and all limits on the movement of funds into and out of the country, and allowed establishment of secret accounts while virtually eliminating taxation on bank transactions. These provisions made Panama the "Switzerland of Latin America" overnight, establishing it as an international financial center of convenience and leading to a vast expansion in the banking sector. Construction of new roads, a transisthmian oil pipeline, and a new international airport, as well as new container ports, made the nation a focal point of transportation and transfer that complemented the canal.

Torrijos' reforms included the Labor Code of 1972, which instituted a minimum wage, compulsory arbitration, and the principle of state control of the economy, theoretically establishing the state as the protector of the masses and further weakening the power of the oligarchy. A housing code established the principle of government-subsidized public housing and launched a massive housing and public works construction effort

Oscar Torrijos Herrera shaking hands with U.S. President Jimmy Carter at the signing of the Panama Canal Treaty. JIMMY CARTER LIBRARY.

in the cities. Reaching out to the equally neglected peasant masses, he increased government spending for rural access roads and promoted peasant settlements through land acquisitions to increase grain production. Between 1969 and 1973, some 260 farm settlements were formed. Covering 540,000 acres, most were acquired through expropriation in return for long-term bonds or for payment of overdue back taxes.

A fervent nationalist, Torrijos restored pride to his nation by resisting U.S. pressures and joining the nonaligned movement as part of the resistance to the United States. He led the nation in confronting the age-old nemesis, the UNITED FRUIT COMPANY, regarding taxes and land ownership; opposed the U.S. blockade of Fidel Castro's Cuba; and allowed the use of Panama as a conduit for Cuban arms supplied to the Sandinista rebels in Nicaragua. Yet he also cooperated with the United States in security matters, accepted compromises regarding the canal, sharing responsibilities for its defense, and provided shelter to the exiled Shah of Iran. His willingness to accept gradual change regarding canal jurisdiction ended an era of violent confrontations and enabled the peaceful settlement of a volatile dispute. Torrijos's death in an unexplained airplane crash cut his tenure and revolution short.

WALTER LAFEBER, *The Panama Canal: The Crisis in Historical Perspective* (1979); GEORGE PRIESTLEY, *Military Government and*

Popular Participation in Panama: The Torrijos Regime, 1968–1975 (1986).

KENNETH J. GRIEB

TORTUGA ISLAND, a major Caribbean base for French buccaneering from 1630 to 1700. Tortuga Island, just north of the western tip of Hispaniola (present-day Haiti), was an important strategic location in particular for the activities of seventeenth-century French BUCCANEERS. The island had been a rendezvous for rovers of all nations since the time of Francis DRAKE, and from 1630 on, as TOBACCO production gave way to SUGAR growing, it became the headquarters for French freebooting.

Anthony Hilton, aware of its centrality, first settled the island in 1630, helping to provide a strategic location from which freebooters could safely travel. Considering Tortuga a pirate stronghold, the Spanish attacked and captured it in 1634, causing much destruction and killing many people. By 1640, however, the island had been repopulated by numerous English and French, many of whom had migrated there from Caribbean areas suffering from the tobacco depression.

The English initially gained the upper hand in government, oppressing many of the French on the island. Thus, in 1640 the governor of Saint Christopher, L. de

Poincy, sent a group composed of Huguenots, under the command of M. Le Vasseur, to Tortuga. In August of that year this group entered the island unhindered and ordered the English to leave. Thereafter the island remained in French hands, although the Spanish unsuccessfully attacked it in 1643 and again in 1654.

Tortuga became an international haunt of buccaneers after the massacre of the Providence Company's settlers in 1634. After attaining power, Le Vasseur fortified Tortuga and established himself as semiofficial governor and leader of robbers. As the century progressed, the island continued to grow in importance as a buccaneer stronghold.

Assuming the governorship of French Hispaniola, and thus Tortuga, in 1665, Bertrand d'Ogéron strongly supported the activities of the buccaneers. While aiding these men on Tortuga, he also tried to establish a more respectable and secure settlement on western Hispaniola. The Tortuga buccaneers played an important role in the Anglo-Dutch War of 1672 to 1678, weakening the Dutch. The seven years from 1678 to 1685 also proved to be very active ones for these buccaneers. The successful buccaneers Captain Nicholas Van Horn and Laurens-Cornille Baldran de Graaf attacked numerous Spanish settlements. But in 1697 the Spanish ceded Saint Domingue (Hispaniola) to France, and the governor of the colony, Jean-Baptiste du Casse, persuaded the remaining buccaneers on Tortuga to settle peacefully on Saint Domingue.

The importance of establishing French control over Tortuga cannot be overestimated, for from this beginning sprang the greatest French colony, Saint Domingue, which became the richest and most highly cultivated of the West Indian islands. Ironically, this area, including Tortuga, now forms one of the poorest countries in the hemisphere, modern-day Haiti.

PÈRE P-F-X. CHARLEVOIX, *Histoire de l'Isle Espagnole ou de Saint-Domingue*, 2 vols. (1730–1731); C. H. HARING, *The Buccaneers in the West Indies in the XVII Century* (1910); A. P. NEWTON, *Colonising Activities of the English Puritans* (1914); N. M. CROUSE, *The French Struggle for the West Indies, 1665–1713* (1943); J. H. PARRY, et al., *A Short History of the West Indies*, 4th ed. (1987); M. A. PEÑA BATLLE, *La isla de Tortuga* (1988).

BLAKE D. PATTRIDGE

See also **Piracy.**

TOSAR, HÉCTOR ALBERTO (*b.* 18 July 1923), Uruguayan composer, pianist, and conductor. Born in Montevideo, Tosar began his studies in that city with Wilhelm Kolischer (piano), Tomás Mujica (harmony), and Lamberto Baldi (composition and orchestration). When he was seventeen, his Toccata for orchestra was premiered in Montevideo by maestro Baldi. In 1946 Tosar received a Guggenheim fellowship and went to the United States to study composition with Aaron Copland. With a grant from the French government in 1948 he went to France, where he remained for three years studying under Darius Milhaud, Jean Rivier, and Arthur Honegger (composition), and Eugène Bigot and Jean Fournet (conducting). In 1951 he won the SODRE first composition award for *Oda a Artigas,* a cantata for speaker and orchestra. He also won first prize at the First Inter-American Music Festival (Montevideo) in 1957 for his Divertimento for strings. He composed a Te Deum in 1960 commissioned by the Koussevitsky Foundation.

Tosar was chairman of the composition department at the Puerto Rico Conservatory (1974) and professor (1983–1984) and director of Montevideo's Escuela Universitaria de Música (1985–1987) and Conservatorio Nacional. From 1987 to 1991 he was composer-in-residence at the SODRE. He was also professor of composition and analysis at the Instituto Simón Bolívar in Caracas, and later taught composition at Indiana University (1981–1982). His early works, which combine contrapuntal and harmonic structures in free forms, are dramatic and rarely nationalistic. In his later works Tosar has experimented with jazz rhythms, new forms of instrumentation, as in his aleatoric composition for thirteen instruments, *A-13,* and serial structures. His *Recitativo y variaciones para orquesta* was commissioned by the Fourth Inter-American Music Festival and premiered in Washington, D.C., in 1968. In the 1980s several of his works were premiered in the United States, Mexico, and Venezuela. Tosar has also composed music for the synthesizer.

GÉRARD BÉHAGUE, *Music in Latin America* (1979); *New Grove Dictionary of Music and Musicians*, vol. 19 (1980); SUSANA SALGADO, *Breve historia de la música culta en el Uruguay,* 2d ed. (1980).

SUSANA SALGADO

TOTONACS, a major and historically important ethnic group of east-central Mexico. Inhabiting portions of the high eastern plateau, the rugged Sierra Madre Oriental, and the hilly central coastal plain along the Gulf of Mexico, the Totonacs have successfully adapted to a very wide range of habitats. Their life-styles are accordingly varied but tend to have two basic formats, one that exploits the drier highland environments and the other, the lusher humid lowlands.

The lowland Totonacs were the first indigenous peoples observed closely by the Spaniards when they arrived in 1519 and were induced to join an alliance against their Aztec overlords. Totonac is generally classified, along with closely related Tepehua, as a separate and somewhat enigmatic language family called Totonaca, which may be distantly related to Mayan. Dialectical differences, variously put at three or four, are recognized. Recent census figures (1980)—at best only a rough estimate of the present strength of Totonac culture—indicate a total of 185,836 speakers over the age of five for Totonacapan, the traditional area in the states of Veracruz and Puebla. As a result of increasing acculturation, many Totonacs no longer habitually speak their mother tongue, and growing numbers are moving to urban centers as laborers.

Archaeological evidence suggests that the Totonacs may have been relatively late arrivals on the Gulf Coast and that some ancient cities assumed to have been built by them, such as EL TAJÍN and SANTA LUISA, were actually associated with earlier peoples. Historically, resource-laden Totonacapan has been coveted by many groups. This is reflected today in the interspersed settlements found in some instances with Nahua, Otomí, Tepehua, or Huastec speakers. When Hernan Cortés arrived at the huge Totonac city of Zempoala (CEMPOALA), most of Totonacapan had already been subjugated by the Aztecs. After the Spanish Conquest the Totonacs suffered severe population decline and dispersion occasioned by catastrophic epidemics of European-induced diseases as well as by their resistance to evangelization and colonial policies.

The Totonacs remain subsistence agriculturalists with a traditional Mesoamerican emphasis upon maize, beans, and squash. They raise some livestock and, in the lowlands, occasional cash crops such as vanilla. In the highlands the population is concentrated in small towns whereas in the lowlands it is scattered in villages, hamlets, and house compounds near the fields. COMPADRAZGO, a form of ritual kinship, is an important social bond in both areas. Expansion of the oil industry has led to the destruction of the coastal rain forest, land speculation, and a considerable reduction of traditional Totonac farmland.

Ritual life tends to be more elaborate in the isolated reaches of the mountains. There, some *mayordomías* persist and a greater diversity of dance groups can be found. Among the latter, *huehues*, *negritos*, and *santiaguerros* are common. Popular in both areas are two physically rigorous dances of pre-Columbian origin: the *guaguas* (*quetzalines*) and the *voladores*. Although these were once pan-Mesoamerican rituals, the Totonacs, particularly of the lowlands, consider them to be very much their own and excel at their presentation. Apart from local patron-saint days, the celebration of All Saints' Day (also called Day of the Dead) with elaborate altars and offerings is particularly important to the Totonacs.

The principal ethnographic studies are ISABEL KELLY and ANGEL PALERM, *The Tajín Totonac*, pt. 1 (1952); and ALAIN ICHON, *La religion des Totonaques de la Sierra* (1969). An important early synthesis is WALTER KRICKEBERG, *Die Totonaken* (1918–1925). Recent data on origins, environment, and historical migration can be found in S. JEFFREY K. WILKERSON, *Ethnogenesis of the Huastecs and Totonacs* (1973); "Eastern Mesoamerica from Prehispanic to Colonial Times: A Model of Cultural Continuance," in *Actes du XLIIme Congrès International des Américanistes*, vol. 8 (1976): 41–55; and "Man's Eighty Centuries in Veracruz," *National Geographic Magazine* 158, no. 2 (August 1980): 202–231.

S. JEFFREY K. WILKERSON

See also **Volador Dance.**

TOURISM, the movement of people away from their homes for short periods of time for the purpose of relaxation and recreation. Latin America's beaches, mountains, rain forests, distinctive cultures, archaeological sites, and rich history attract millions of tourists every year. About 85 percent of visitors to Latin America come from the United States, Canada, and Europe. Significant regional variation exists in the extent of tourist development, with Mexico and the Caribbean together accounting for more than 50 percent of Latin American arrivals.

ECONOMIC ASPECTS

Latin America accounts for about 10 percent of tourism's international revenues, estimated to total some U.S.$250 billion annually (1990). The industry provides a source of critically needed foreign exchange, generates substantial employment for low-skilled workers, and creates a market for indigenous craftspeople. Tourism shares characteristics with Latin America's traditional export of primary materials insofar as the industrialized world provides both the capital required to develop the industry and the market that absorbs its goods and services. It requires considerable investment (transportation, communication, water, sanitation, lodging, advertising, and promotion) and is vulnerable to natural disasters (earthquakes, hurricanes), economic slowdown that contracts demand in major markets, and internal disruptions that discourage visitors.

HISTORY

Three identifiable stages characterize the evolution of tourism: (1) the era of the traveler, which lasted until approximately the last half of the nineteenth century; (2) prototourism, from about 1880 to 1940; and (3) modern mass tourism, which emerged after World War II. For a long time, travelers—explorers, adventurers, merchants, scientists, and other individuals—sufficiently motivated by financial gain or by interest in the area's unique qualities, overlooked the hazards of the voyage to Latin America.

Prototourism emerged when railroads and steamships made travel more comfortable, convenient, and safe. Leisured sightseers and people in search of warm climates for health reasons comprised the sojourners in the Caribbean by the turn of the twentieth century, with Jamaica and Cuba as early entrants in the business. Captain Lorenzo D. Baker, U.S. banana merchant, added passenger revenue to his produce profits and inaugurated Jamaica's winter tourist season, a distant forerunner to its thriving post-1960 industry. The close relationship of the United States with Cuba fostered travel to the island.

Mexico enjoyed considerable cross-border tourism in the 1920s, prompted by prohibition in the United States and Ford's relatively inexpensive "Tin Lizzie" as a means of transportation. Cuba took advantage of its proximity to the winter-chilled U.S. eastern seaboard to create Latin America's most successful international vacation destination of the period. Cubans built hotels, country clubs, and casinos, and developed beaches and other attractions enjoyed by affluent Europeans and North Americans. Pan American Airways introduced air travel into Latin American tourism with its Miami–Havana route in 1928. After an extremely profitable but brief seven-year period, Cuba's nascent tourist industry succumbed to worldwide depression and internal political upheaval. Luxury cruise ships also carried thousands of passengers to the Caribbean and Central America before World War II diverted ships from leisure travel to the transport requirements of the military.

Modern mass industrial tourism is a postwar phenomenon. Improvements in air transport facilitated the large-scale movement of people and materials over long distances in a reasonably short time. This made foreign air travel feasible for a critical mass of industrial workers with paid vacation time and disposable income. The United States looked to Latin America for customers to replace Europeans, who were just beginning the process of economic recovery. Even before the war ended, the Roosevelt administration had encouraged hemispheric neighbors to attract tourists as a way of quickly gaining the foreign exchange necessary to buy U.S. consumer products and capital goods for their own industrialization.

Mexico immediately began to lure its share of visitors, taking advantage of the Pan American highway for automobile traffic from the United States and turning Acapulco, a Pacific port frequented by Europeans and North Americans during the war, into a luxury resort reached by plane. The Mexican government recognized tourism as a viable development strategy and, in addition to attracting visitors to archaeological sites and indigenous communities, began in 1970 to build large-scale facilities at Cancún, Ixtapa, the Baja California peninsula, and Oaxaca. By 1990 tourism ranked alongside petroleum as an earner of hard currency. Mexico also joined Belize, Guatemala, Honduras, and El Salvador in a regional project, the Ruta Maya, to exploit the remnants of the ancient Maya civilization for touristic purposes. Andean nations similarly capitalized on Inca cultural heritage and relics to attract visitors.

In the 1950s and 1960s the governments of various Caribbean island nations began to tap the pleasure travel market, building significant industries that currently account for substantial portions of gross domestic product and employment. Cuba rebuilt its industry and dominated the region until the revolution of 1959 and the U.S. embargo kept the tourists away. After thirty years Cuba is competing once again, with tourists mainly from Europe, Latin America, and Canada.

Several South and Central American countries delayed entry in the tourism marketplace but are now promoting the physical and/or cultural qualities most likely to win favor with tourists. An environmental or ecological tourism market, for example, has encouraged Costa Rica, Brazil, Belize, and Ecuador to attract visitors to rain forests and nature preserves. Argentina and Chile advertise skiing facilities to take advantage of the reversal of seasons in the Northern and Southern hemispheres. Guatemala and Panama base tourism in part on the distinctive handicrafts produced by women in their indigenous populations.

CRITICISMS OF TOURISM

As the industry has grown, critics have voiced concerns, including environmental deterioration, disruption of indigenous communities, the dominance of transnational hotel and airline chains in some locations, the maldistribution of profits, the distortion of folkloric traditions, political pressure from governments whose citizens comprise the tourist market, and the economic inequality between tourists and the resident labor force that perpetuates a First World–Third World dichotomy. Such criticism has provoked a reevaluation of policies and practices in tourist destinations but not a rejection of the industry.

JOHN M. BRYDEN, *Tourism and Development: A Case Study of the Commonwealth Caribbean* (1973); FRED P. BOSSELMAN, *In the Wake of the Tourist* (1978), chap. 1; HARRY G. MATTHEWS, *International Tourism: A Political and Social Analysis* (1978); JACQUES ROGOZINSKI, *The Impact of Tourism in the Economy: the Mexican Case* (1980); SHIRLEY B. SEWARD and BERNARD K. SPINRAD, eds., *Tourism in the Caribbean: The Economic Impact* (1982); DENNIS CONWAY, *Tourism and Caribbean Development* (1983); FRANCOIS ASCHER, *Tourism: Transnational Corporations and Cultural Identities* (1985); FELICITY EDWARDS, ed., *Environmentally Sound Tourism Development in the Caribbean* (1988); Bob Shacochis, "In Deepest Gringolandia. Mexico: The Third World as Tourist Theme Park," *Harper's Magazine* 279 (July 1989): 42–50; VALENE L. SMITH, ed. *Hosts and Guests: The Anthropology of Tourism,* 2d ed. (1989).

ROSALIE SCHWARTZ

TOUSSAINT L'OUVERTURE. *See* **L'Ouverture, Toussaint.**

TRABA, MARTA (*b.* 25 January 1930; *d.* 27 November 1983), Argentine-Colombian novelist, art critic, and university professor. Traba earned a degree in literature from the Universidad Nacional de Buenos Aires (1948) and took courses with art critic Jorge Romero Brest. In 1949–1950, she studied art history with Pierre Francastel at the Sorbonne and René Huyghe at L'École du Loure. In Paris she met and married Alberto Zalamea, a Colombian intellectual. She left Europe for Colombia with her family in 1954. In 1958 Traba published her first study on modern art, *El museo vacío.* In 1961 she published an important and pioneering study on Latin American painting, *La pintura nueva en Latinoamérica,* in which she offered a critique of the Mexican muralists and Argentine painting, among other topics, that generated considerable controversy. She taught art history at the Universidad de América and the Universidad de los Andes in Bogotá and became a strong advocate for the creation of the Museum of Modern Art in Bogotá, which was constituted in 1962. She was its director from 1964 to 1967. In 1965 Traba moved the museum to the Universidad Nacional de Bogotá, where she joined the faculty. That year she also published her most important study on Latin American art, *Los cuatro monstruos cardinales*. Although Traba published a book of poems in 1952, *Historia natural de la alegría*, it was not until 1966 that her writing of fiction began in earnest. She received the prestigious Cuban Casa de las Américas prize for her first novel, *Las ceremonias del verano* (1966). *Los laberintos insolados*, another novel, was published in 1967. Both novels explore the possibilities of interior growth and exposure to foreign cultures. *Pasó así* (1968), *La jugada del sexto día* (1970), and *Homérica latina* (1979) followed.

Increasingly, Traba's fiction portrayed political turmoil, repression, persecution, and horror in countries under military regimes (Argentina, Uruguay, and Chile). These are the central themes in *Conversación al sur* (1981; Mothers and Shadows, 1986) and *En cualquier lugar* (1984). *De la mañana a la noche: Cuentos norteamericanos* (1986) and *Casa sin fin* (1988) were published posthumously. In 1969, after divorcing her first husband, Traba married the Uruguayan critic and writer Angel Rama. They lived in Montevideo, Puerto Rico, Caracas, and Washington, D.C., between 1969 and 1982. Traba and Rama were forced to leave the United States in 1982 when the U.S. Department of State denied them resident visas, a decision that generated heated controversy. They set up residence in Paris, France, where they lived until their death in an airplane crash near Madrid.

Marta Traba, edited by Emma Araújo de Vallejo (Bogotá, 1984); Magdalena García Pinto, *Women Writers of Latin America* (1991).

MAGDALENA GARCÍA PINTO

TRADE. *See* **Commercial Policy (Colonial)** and specific countries.

TRADE

Colonial Brazil

Colonial internal trade in Brazil was circumscribed by geographical, transport, financial, and administrative constraints; it was organized in regional systems focused on important plantation zones and their port cities. The export economy was the focus of both the colonial administration and most of the available merchant capital, and it tended to determine the transport routes. Small vessels carried high-bulk commodities along the coast, but the road network was so poor that overland trade was limited to self-transporting livestock and the relatively high-value, low-bulk goods that could

be carried by human porters on mule trains (*tropas*) conducted by *tropeiros*.

Internal trade can be divided into three categories: (1) an extension of the export-import trades in which export commodities were funneled to coastal port cities and imports were distributed from the ports to communities on the coast and in the interior; (2) the internal labor trade in African, Afro-Brazilian, and Amerindian slaves; (3) the trading of commodities and livestock produced in Brazil to supply Brazilian cities and towns, export producers, and mining operations. This discussion will focus on the last category of internal trade. The extent and volume of colonial internal trade can be divided into four periods: pre-1700, 1700–1750, 1750–1808, and 1808–1822.

Before the inception of the MINING INDUSTRY at the end of the seventeenth century, internal exchanges were limited in extent. As the port cities and plantation zones, especially in the Northeast, increasingly experienced shortages of Brazil's staple food of manioc flour (*farinha*), specialized manioc-producing zones emerged within bays and on the coast, for example, at Maragogipe, Jaguaribe, Cairú, and Camamú to supply the Salvador region, and at Una, Porto Calvo, and Alagoas in Pernambuco.

In the Northeast from the 1590s on, livestock ranches were increasingly distanced from their markets in the plantation zones and ports, first along the coast to Paraíba, Rio Grande do Norte, and Sergipe, and then up the São Francisco River valley. Cattle were driven to fair towns on the edge of the plantation districts, to Santo Amaro, for example, which served the region of Salvador. Dried and salted beef (*carne seca*) was also sent from the cattle districts to feed plantation slaves and the urban poor. Similarly, Rio de Janeiro drew its supplies of cattle on the hoof from nearby pastures in its own captaincy. São Paulo, isolated in the first two centuries of colonization, slowly forged trading relationships with other parts of Brazil through commerce in flour, marmalade, and, especially in the first half of the seventeenth century, Amerindian slaves.

Between 1700 and 1750 the discovery of gold and later diamonds in Minas Gerais, Mato Grosso, and Goiás created new transport routes and internal trade networks. Some supplies and livestock intended for the coast were initially diverted to the new mining markets, but during the eighteenth century, cattle ranches extended into the interior near these markets. As the principal export port for gold, the city of Rio de Janeiro took on greater importance and became the focus for the expanded internal trade network of central, southeastern, and southern Brazil.

In order to control contraband, the government forbade the opening of new roads into the interior without permission and set up registers (*registros*) to tax livestock, slaves, and goods by weight as they passed from one captaincy to another. Traffic was further burdened by fees for river crossings (*passagens*). Effective settlement of southern Brazil began in this period, and this region became an important source of mules and cattle on the hoof for other captaincies.

After 1750, gold production began to decline, and coastal export agriculture also experienced a prolonged recession. In the 1790s, however, export production intensified and diversified in traditional plantation zones and expanded into some areas that had previously produced primarily for the internal market. This export resurgence created greater markets for livestock and other commodities, bringing more distant production areas into the internal trade network. As sugarcane replaced cattle in Rio de Janeiro's pastoral areas, southern Minas Gerais became a source of cheese, bacon, and cattle and pigs on the hoof for the Rio market. Beef on the hoof was also drawn from as far away as Rio Grande do Sul and São Paulo (including modern Paraná). A series of droughts in the northeastern interior decimated herds, opening markets for the new *carne seca* industry in Rio Grande do Sul in the late 1780s. Simultaneously, the same captaincy became an important source of wheat for Rio de Janeiro. Rio also began to draw supplies of *farinha* from distant coastal producers such as Santa Catarina in the south and Porto Seguro to the north. As export producers and city dwellers increasingly relied on the market to supply their wants, dried and salted fish, maize, beans, rice, other foodstuffs, and lumber from small coastal communities also found markets in the major cities and plantation zones.

The 1808 arrival of the Portuguese royal family in Rio de Janeiro brought an influx of population, setting off food price inflation and a construction boom. Salvador and other regional export centers also grew because of the expansion and diversification of export production. The government began to pay more attention to the internal economic development of Brazil, and internal trade began to attract merchant capital to a much greater degree than before. In particular, producers and merchants in southern Minas Gerais and Rio Grande do Sul were able to accumulate capital and develop a positive balance of trade by supplying other regions.

At the close of the colonial period, internal trade remained dependent on the export sector as the dynamic force in the economy, and continued to face daunting obstacles. Among the most important were the limited investment in road improvement and expansion, heavy tax burdens on overland trade, and shortage of capital.

CHARLES R. BOXER, *The Golden Age of Brazil* (1962); MARIA THEREZA SCHORER PETRONE, *O Barão de Iguape* (1976); MARIA YEDDA LEITE LINHARES, *História do Abastecimento* (1979); ALCIR LENHARO, *As tropas da moderação* (1979); STUART B. SCHWARTZ, *Sugar Plantations in the Formation of Brazilian Society* (1985), pp. 89–90, 435–436; LESLIE BETHELL, ed., *Colonial Brazil* (1987), pp. 104–110, 113–114, 195–196, 199–200, 303–336.

LARISSA V. BROWN

See also **Commercial Policy: Colonial Brazil; Slave Trade.**

TRADING COMPANIES. *See* **Companies, Chartered.**

TRADING COMPANIES, PORTUGUESE. In the seventeenth and eighteenth centuries the Portuguese crown established several monopoly trading companies to control and stimulate trade between Portugal and Brazil. They included the Brazil Company (Companhia Geral de Estado do Brasil), created in 1649, transformed into a government agency in 1663, and dissolved in 1720; the Maranhão Company (Companhia de Comércio do Estado do Maranhão), 1682–1685; the Grão-Pará and Maranhão Company (Companhia Geral do Grão-Pará e Maranhão), 1755–1777; and the Pernambuco Company (Companhia Geral de Pernambuco e Paraíba), 1759–1777. The fundamental purpose of the Brazil Company was to protect trade with Brazil, while the three other companies were to supply African slave labor and stimulate production and trade in their respective regions.

The Brazil Company The Brazil Company was established on the model of the Dutch and English chartered trading companies to protect Brazilian colonial trade from the depredations of Dutch privateers. The company was required to provide thirty-six warships to convoy merchant fleets between the ports of Lisbon and Oporto in Portugal, and Bahia, Rio de Janeiro, and Recife (after recapture from the Dutch in 1654) in Brazil. In return, the company was given a monopoly over all imports of wine, wheat flour, olive oil, and cod into Brazil for sale at prices it could set itself. Moreover, the company collected taxes on the sugar, tobacco, cotton, hides, and other commodities it transported from Brazil to Portugal. Shares in the company were exempted from confiscation by the INQUISITION or any other court, and much of the capital was raised (under pressure) from New Christian merchants, descendants of Jews required to convert to Catholicism in 1497.

Although the company was somewhat successful in reducing the capture of ships in the Brazil trade, it came under increasing criticism. Some complaints focused on the protection given to New Christian capital, but smaller Portuguese ports and merchants, who were cut out of the Brazil trade, and Brazilian colonists also criticized its operations. Price increases and inadequate supplies of the monopolized staple foods, along with irregularity of the fleets and consequent spoilage of Brazilian commodities, were the major complaints.

In 1658 the monopolies were abolished and the fleet system modified to require only return sailing from Brazil in one annual convoy. The next year company shares were made vulnerable to confiscation by the Inquisition. Shareholders were compensated and the company was incorporated into the government as a royal council by 1663, continuing to provide convoy services in this form until it was dissolved in 1720.

The Maranhão Company The short-lived Maranhão Company, organized in 1682 with a twenty-year charter, was intended to stimulate export-crop production in the sparsely settled northern captaincies by providing African slave labor and regular transport to Portuguese markets. Company abuses of its monopoly privileges combined with resentment of Jesuit activities ignited a revolt by colonists that resulted in the dissolution of the company in 1685.

The Eighteenth-Century Companies In the eighteenth century, two monopoly trading companies were established as part of the Marques de POMBAL's policy to revive and restructure the Portuguese imperial economy. The Grão-Pará and Maranhão Company was designed to stimulate economic development in the still-languishing Brazilian north, while the Pernambuco Company was to revive the economy of that once-prosperous region—in both cases through the introduction of greater supplies of African slave labor, the purchase of traditional and new export crops at good prices, and their transport to Portugal in armed convoys. The companies were also expected to develop colonial markets for Portuguese manufactures. By the 1770s, the Grão-Pará and Maranhão Company was also being used by the crown to expand its military and bureaucratic presence in the Amazon region.

The Maranhão Company was effective in enlarging the supply of African slaves to the north, stimulating greater production of traditional exports, such as cacao, and diversifying export production in Maranhão to include rice and cotton. The Pernambuco Company expanded exports of sugar and hides in Pernambuco, but there was no significant diversification of exports. Both companies provided more regular transport links and funneled large amounts of Portuguese manufactures to colonial markets.

The companies' monopolistic domination of their respective regions' economies produced widespread criticism, especially in Pernambuco. Opponents took advantage of Pombal's fall from power in 1777 to seek the dissolution of the companies that were so associated with his authoritarian rule.

CHARLES R. BOXER, *The Portuguese Seaborne Empire, 1415–1825* (1969); MANUEL NUNES DIAS, *Fomento e mercantilismo: A Companhia Geral do Grão Pará e Maranhão, 1755–1778* (1970); JOSÉ RIBEIRO JÚNIOR, *Colonização e monopólio no nordeste brasileiro: A Companhia Geral de Pernambuco e Paraíba, 1759–1780* (1976); ANTÔNIO CARREIRA, *As companhias pombalinas de Grão-Pará e Maranhão e Pernambuco e Paraíba*, 2d ed. (1983); LESLIE BETHELL, ed., *Colonial Brazil* (1987), pp. 52–53, 264–269, 305–307; BAILEY W. DIFFIE, *A History of Colonial Brazil, 1500–1792* (1987), pp. 249–252, 277–280, 403–411.

LARISSA V. BROWN

See also **Slavery.**

TRANSAMAZON HIGHWAY, the red, earthen two-lane road that crosses Brazil from the east to the west. Constructed in the 1970s, the 3,400-mile-long Transamazônica, or BR-320, begins in João Pessoa and skirts the southern edge of the Amazonian plain. Crossing the Belém–Brasília Highway in northern Goiás, it follows the arch of the Amazon in Pará, cutting through Amazonas. With Peru's failure to build a road that would join BR-320 in Acre, officials in Brazil changed the course of the road from Acre to Benjamin Constant, Amazonas.

Although vehicles use ferries or rafts to cross larger rivers, such as the Tapajós, Xingú, or Madeira, log structures cover smaller ones. Some sections of the Transamazon are compacted earth, others are made of plinthite pebbles; the forest constantly reclaims some portions, and other parts flood during the rainy season.

Transamazônica was created as part of a development project initiated by PIN (Programa de Integracão Nacional), which was announced in June 1970 by President Emílio Garrastazú MÉDICI. The scheme called for the building of the Transamazon Highway as a means of transporting immigrants from the poverty-stricken Northeast to the unpopulated and underdeveloped states of Rondônia, Mato Grosso, and Acre. Six different construction companies contracted labor and brought in supplies, while crews began working on 200-mile sections in 1971. The workers left behind the permanent construction camps they built, which contained housing, electricity, schools, health centers, and post offices that served as frontier posts for immigrants. The Brazilian government reserved 6 miles on either side of the Transamazon as settlement sites for those participating in the program. BR-320 was officially opened in December 1973, but the last stretch of highway had not been completed by 1991.

NIGEL J. H. SMITH, *Rainforest Corridors: The Transamazon Colonization Scheme* (1982); THOMAS E. SKIDMORE, *The Politics of Military Rule in Brazil, 1964–1985* (1988); BEN BOX, ed., *1990 South American Handbook,* 66th ed. (1990); ANDREW REVKIN, *The Burning Season* (1990).

CAROLYN JOSTOCK

TREINTA Y TRES (33) ORIENTALES, group of patriots of the BANDA ORIENTAL (i.e., Uruguay) who in 1825 initiated the final struggle against Brazilian rule. They were led by Juan Antonio LAVALLEJA, a former collaborator of the Uruguayan independence leader José Gervasio ARTIGAS, who had already led one unsuccessful uprising. Lavalleja took refuge in Argentina, where he gathered other disaffected Uruguayans into a liberation movement and courted Argentine private assistance.

On 19 April 1825 Lavalleja made landing on the Uruguayan coast at La Agraciada, near Colonia. Though his group became known as the "Thirty-three Orientals," several of them were Argentine and one was a French volunteer. They quickly expanded their beachhead, obtaining recruits and supplies. At the end of April, Lavalleja was joined by Fructuoso RIVERA, another former lieutenant of Artigas who had lately been serving the Brazilians and had a wide network of followers in

Juramento de los treinta y tres orientales by Juan M. Blanes. Oil on canvas, 1875–1877. Reproduced from Eduardo de Salterain y Herrera, *Blanes: El hombre, su obra y la época* (Montevideo, 1950). MUSEO HISTÓRICO NACIONAL, MONTEVIDEO.

the Uruguayan interior. Initial successes, together with the decision of the insurgents to seek incorporation into the UNITED PROVINCES OF THE RÍO DE LA PLATA, led the authorities at Buenos Aires to give them open support. The result was the Argentine-Brazilian war of 1825–1828, into which the struggle of the Treinta y Tres was subsumed.

JOHN STREET, *Artigas and the Emancipation of Uruguay* (1959); ALFREDO CASTELLANOS, *La Cisplatina, la independencia y la república caudillesca* (1974).

DAVID BUSHNELL

TREJOS FERNÁNDEZ, JOSÉ JOAQUÍN (*b.* 18 April 1916), president of Costa Rica (1966–1970), professor, dean, and vice rector of the University of Costa Rica.

José Joaquín Trejos Fernández came to national prominence only after being nominated as a presidential candidate in 1965 when the former presidents and political adversaries Rafael Ángel CALDERÓN GUARDIA (1940–1944) and Otilio ULATE BLANCO (1949–1953) joined their forces in opposition to the ever more dominant National Liberation Party (PLN). Trejos, although a Calderonist, had little prior political experience but was widely known and respected as a professional of great integrity and rectitude.

After his surprise victory, Trejos's administration distinguished itself in several areas. Among its most notable accomplishments were the sustained growth in the gross national product and the development of the infrastructure on the Atlantic coast with the construction of a highway to Puerto Limon and new wharfage facilities for the port, and the extension of the Tortuguero Canal.

JOSÉ JOAQUÍN TREJOS FERNÁNDEZ, *Reflexiones sobre la educación* (1963); CHARLES D. AMERINGER, *Don Pepe* (1978); and HAROLD D. NELSON, ed., *Costa Rica: A Country Study* (1983).

JOHN PATRICK BELL

See also **Costa Rica: Political Parties.**

TRESGUERRAS, FRANCISCO EDUARDO DE (*b.* 13 October 1759; *d.* 3 August 1833), Mexican painter and architect. In contrast to most well-known artists of his time, Tresguerras pursued his career not in Mexico City but in QUERÉTARO, Celaya, and SAN LUIS POTOSÍ. He dedicated himself to painting, music, architecture, engraving, and writing in turn, and can be considered a particularly interesting example of the self-conscious and confident eighteenth-century New World artist. His most famous creation is the church of Nuestra Señora del Carmen in Celaya, with a single tower over the entrance (1802–1807). In painting and drawing his style is rococo, but in architecture he is neoclassical. Although Tresguerras sought recognition from the ACADEMIA DE SAN CARLOS, he seems never to have been accepted by the Mexico City art establishment.

The best source is still FRANCISCO EDUARDO TRESGUERRAS, *Ocios literarios*, edited by Francisco de la Maza (1962), his collected works. See also MANUEL TOUSSAINT, *Colonial Art in Mexico* (1967).

CLARA BARGELLINI

TRIANA, JOSÉ (*b.* 4 January 1931) Cuban playwright, was born in Hatüey, Camagüey. He returned to Cuba when Fidel Castro came to power in order to support the building of a new society. His early plays captured the nuances and the traditions of the humble classes. The violence inherent in the society is reflected in plays that explore struggles for power, sometimes in mythical terms (*Medea en el espejo*, 1960) or godlike terms (*El general mayor hablará de teogonía*, 1960). These early plays established the bases for his ludic experiments that resonated of Antonin Artaud or Jean Genet. When his masterpiece, *La noche de los asesinos* (1966), won the coveted Casa de las Américas Prize in 1965, it earned him both international recognition and eventually the enmity of the Castro regime. The allusions to generational conflict within a destabilized society attributed to Fulgencio Batista were veiled to obscure a more virulent criticism of the Revolution itself. Triana was not allowed to publish or to present plays again in Cuba.

Triana sought asylum in Paris in 1980 and resumed his theatrical activities. *Worlds Apart*, performed in English by the Royal Shakespeare Company in 1986, was the translation of *Palabras comunes*, itself an adaptation of his earlier *Diálogo para mujeres*. Set in Cuba at the turn of the century, this semihistorical play examines the hypocrisy in sexual and racial attitudes in the Cuban society of the time as a metaphor for the years of the Castro Revolution. *Revolico en el Campo de Marte* (1971) is a verse play with folkloric touches; *Ceremonial de guerra* (1968–1973) is another historical play set in 1895 during the struggle for Cuban independence. In this case the metaphor serves for a society that has lost its direction in its search for truth. Triana's latest play is a monologue, *Cruzando el puente* (1991), in which an abused and abusive character "crosses the bridge" into a world of madness.

Triana is clearly one of the most accomplished playwrights of his generation in terms of dramatic technique and his commitment to a theater that engages important political and social issues with human interest. He manipulates elements of Cuban folklore and culture, even in exile, with great dexterity to achieve one of the most elusive and difficult features of the theater—plays of local interest that transcend their time and space to speak to international audiences.

FRANK DAUSTER, "The Game of Chance: The Theater of José Triana," in *Dramatists in Revolt: The New Latin American Theater*, edited by Leon F. Lyday and George W. Woodyard (1976): 167–189; ROMÁN V DE LA CAMPA, *José Triana: Ritualización de la sociedad cubana* (1979); ISABEL ALVAREZ-BORLAND and DAVID GEORGE, "*La noche de los asesinos*: Text, Staging, and Audience," *Latin American Theatre Review* 20; no. 1 (Fall 1986): 37–48; DIANA TAYLOR, "Theatre and Revolution: José Triana," in *Theatre of Crisis: Drama and Politics in Latin America* (1991): 64–95.

GEORGE WOODYARD

TRIBUNAL DE CUENTAS. On 24 August 1605 PHILIP III ordered establishment of a *tribunal de cuentas* (tribunal of accounts) in Bogotá, Lima, and Mexico City with jurisdiction over New Granada, Peru, and New Spain (Mexico), respectively. Headed by three accountants called *contadores de cuentas* and staffed by a host of lesser bookkeepers and copyists, the *tribunal de cuentas* regulated record-keeping procedures and audited accounts kept by officials of the REAL HACIENDA (royal treasury) in their jurisdiction. In some regions a *contador de cuentas* was required to inspect treasuries (*cajas*) personally to ensure adherence to proper accounting procedures. At the end of an accounting period, all royal treasury officials submitted their ledgers to the tribunal for auditing. The tribunal, in turn, checked the accounts, challenged discrepancies, and then sent the books to the CONTADURÍA of the COUNCIL OF INDIES in Spain.

Although theoretically the tribunal ensured honest, efficient royal record keeping in the Indies, in fact, the system broke down because *tribunal contadores* simply had too much to do and were virtually drowned in a sea of paper that made it impossible for them to keep up. In fact, in the late eighteenth century, some tribunals were more than twenty years behind in completing their audits.

Recopilación de leyes de Reynos de las Indias, 4 vols. (1681; repr. 1973), libro VIII, título I and II; GASPAR DE ESCALONA AGÜERO, *Gazofilacio real del Perú*, 4th ed. (1941).

JOHN JAY TePASKE

TRINIDAD AND TOBAGO, two islands about 7 miles off the coast of Venezuela. Trinidad and Tobago's land area encompasses 1,981 square miles, an area slightly smaller than Delaware. Trinidad and Tobago dispute the maritime boundary with Venezuela in the Gulf of Paria. The nation's climate is tropical, with a rainy season lasting from June to December. The two islands lie outside the usual path of hurricanes and other tropical storms. The terrain is mostly plains, with some hills and low mountains. The distribution of land use is as follows: 14 percent arable land; 17 percent permanent crops; 2 percent meadows and pastures; 44 percent forest and woodland; 23 percent other (total includes 4 percent irrigated). Trinidad and Tobago's natural resources include crude oil, natural gas, and asphalt. Trinidad and Tobago have an annual deforestation rate of 0.4 percent. In 1990 the nation's population was approximately 1.34 million, 64 percent of which live in urban areas. The ethnic divisions are as follows: 43 percent African, 40 percent East Indian, 14 percent mixed, 1 percent European, 1 percent Chinese, 1 percent other.

Columbus, on his third voyage, sighted three mountains on 31 July 1498. Either predetermined or motivated by the symbolic number of mountains, he named the land after the Trinity, hence Trinidad. Tobago, then named Bellaforma, was seen but not visited. As on other Caribbean islands, Columbus met the peaceful Arawak Indians, but the visit was brief, only for refuge and fresh water.

The next contact with Trinidad did not occur until

1510. Spanish vessels intent on trading with the Arawaks landed on Trinidad, but before long they killed a number of Indians and took many others as slaves to Puerto Rico and Santo Domingo. The Spanish monarch was outraged and condemned the action. The Arawak Indians, however, were soon decimated. After the discovery of gold in Peru, Trinidad, like other Caribbean islands, did not hold as much interest for the Spaniards, although there were occasional attempts at colonization. French corsairs and pirates from other nations also used the island as a base.

In 1592, the town of San Josef de Oruña was founded, although only nominally populated. It was not until the late 1700s, however, that immigration was seriously encouraged and solidified with the 1783 Royal Cedula of Colonization. This legislation encouraged slavery for sugar production and provided the impetus for the colony's growth. Spain also encouraged the immigration of non-Spanish Catholics, and many French planters came to Trinidad. In 1783, the *cabildo* was moved to Port of Spain, and a year later the able politician José María Chacon arrived in Trinidad. Under Chacon, the colony saw an increase in the production of pitch and the construction of an observatory. In 1792, Port of Spain became the first town in the New World to be placed accurately on the map.

The French Revolution further increased the number of French in Trinidad, which caused the Spanish governor great difficulty. Problems escalated until 1797, when Admiral Harvey and twelve British armed ships appeared off the coast of Trinidad. Governor Chacon was entertaining Spanish Admiral Apodoca, who upon seeing the British fleet burned his armada rather than face the British in battle. Spanish capitulation humiliated Chacon, and resulted in the island's peaceful transfer of power to the British. The transfer was legally recognized in 1802 with the Peace of Amiens.

Lieutenant Colonel Thomas Picton was placed in charge of the island, but the citizens, other than having to swear allegiance to England, saw little change in legislative affairs. Trinidad was declared an "island of experiment" and denied a legislative assembly in order to curb slaveowners from passing political and economic legislation in their best interests. Picton in fact tried to improve the slaves' conditions by writing a progressive SLAVERY code; however, the code quickly lapsed.

Unlike Trinidad, Tobago was not visited until 1580 and as a result never became a Spanish colony. For two centuries, Tobago was disputed by European powers and, between 1626 and 1802, changed hands twenty-six times. Tobago was important to sailing vessels because of its location along the trade winds and its safe anchorages and watering places. French corsairs often found respite on the island. Tobago was awarded to England by the Treaty of Paris (1763) and was initially associated with Barbados to the east. In 1781, the French seized control of the island and initiated a policy of development and settlement. In 1802, Tobago was once again

returned to British control. Tobago, like other Caribbean islands, suffered economic and political decline throughout the nineteenth century. In 1888, after much protest from Trinidad, the British government made Tobago a ward of Trinidad.

In 1844, following the abolition of slavery in 1834, Trinidad began importing labor from India. These indentured servants were in many ways participants in a new form of slavery. Legislation was confusing, as it aimed to protect the Indians while simultaneously not damaging the plantation economy. Indian immigration further diversified Trinidad's cultural makeup.

In 1904, the British began to take an interest in Trinidad's oil potential, and the resource soon became Trinidad's major export. Foreign ownership and low royalty payments caused Trinidad to see little benefit from the energy industry. The agrarian industry produced little economic gain for the nation. Foreign investment continued to disturb the citizenry.

In 1962, Trinidad and Tobago received independence. Eric Williams served as prime minister until his death in 1981. Social and economic problems persisted and culminated in the February Revolution in 1970. On 26 February, university students gathered and protested Canadian imperialism and racism. Over the next two months, the movement grew, becoming a major black power movement, until martial law was declared on 21 April. Trinidad's political foundations remained intact; however, groups such as the National Joint Action Committee (NJAC) were able to profit from the turmoil. The NJAC's ideology was rooted in anti-imperialism, yet it failed to articulate any fundamental societal changes. It also failed to attract the East Indian citizens who occupied the same socioeconomic status as the African Trinidadians. Years of racial tension prevented any African-Indian unity.

Following a brief economic boom as oil producers in the 1970s, Trinidad and Tobago were forced to diversify their economies. Yet in the late 1980s, they still felt the burdens of oil shortfalls and were forced to enact austerity measures. As in other Caribbean nations, these actions were met with frustration from the lower classes, who saw wages shrink while the economy remained unstable.

GERTRUDE CARMICHAEL, *The History of the West Indian Islands of Trinidad and Tobago, 1498–1900* (1961); ERIC WILLIAMS, *History of the People of Trinidad and Tobago* (1962); RYAN SELWYN, *Race and Nationalism in Trinidad and Tobago* (1972); JAN KNIPPERS BLACK et al., *Area Handbook for Trinidad and Tobago* (1976); BRIDGET BERETON, *A History of Modern Trinidad, 1783–1962* (1981); FRANCES CHAMBERS, *Trinidad and Tobago* (1986); FRANKLIN W. KNIGHT and COLIN A. PALMER, eds., *The Modern Caribbean* (1989); FRANKLIN W. KNIGHT, *The Caribbean: Genesis of a Fragmented Nationalism* (1990).

ALLAN S. R. SUMNALL

See also **British–Latin American Relations; Buccaneers; Petroleum Industry.**

TRINIDAD, PARAGUAY, city of 18,300 inhabitants in the Paraguayan state of Itapúa, not far from the town of Encarnación, some 175 miles southeast of Asunción. It was founded in 1706 as an important Jesuit missionary center. The three-aisle church (no longer existent) was built in 1730 according to the plans of the Italian architect Giovanni Battista Primoli. The facade displays stone carvings by unknown Guaraní artists. Timber, yerba maté, and some vineyards are the mainstays of the agrarian economy.

CLEMENT MC NASPY, *Lost Cities of Paraguay: The Art and Architecture of the Jesuit Reductions, 1607–1767* (1982); FERNANDO MEDINA, *El paraíso demolido: Las reducciones jesuíticas del Paraguay* (Mexico, 1987).

CÉSAR N. CAVIEDES

TRINIDADE ISLAND, a small, uninhabited volcanic island 680 miles off the coast of Espírito Santo. Discovered by Tristão da Cunha for Portugal in the sixteenth century, the island was visited by English astronomer Edmund Halley in 1700 when he explored the South Atlantic as captain of the *Paramour*. The island was reputed to be the site of a fortune in ecclesiastical gold and silver buried by pirates in the nineteenth century. This rumor may have encouraged the 1895 invasion of the island by Great Britain. Britain's justification for its actions was that the island had been unoccupied for more than a century. Upon Brazilian protest and mediation by Dom Carlos I, king of Portugal, Great Britain recognized Brazilian rights to the island in 1896.

E. F. KNIGHT, *Cruise of the "Alerte"* (1929).

SHEILA L. HOOKER

TRINITARIA, LA, Dominican independence movement founded in 1838. La Trinitaria was a secret society organized by Juan Pablo DUARTE, Francisco de Rosario Sánchez, and Ramón MELLA in 1838 to drive out the Haitian occupation of Santo Domingo (1822–1844). The society was organized into three-man cells with a complex series of codes and passwords. Trinitaria ideals included democracy, representative government, and independence. It attracted widespread support from Dominican patriots and within five years had cells in most major centers. Members signed blood oaths of loyalty to the society and to the independence movement. Its meetings were characterized by rituals using religious symbolism. Its success in mobilizing opposition against the Haitian government led to persecution and repression. After participating in the overthrow of President Jean-Pierre BOYER, the new president, Charles Hérard, exiled the society's leaders.

Once the Haitian occupation ended, Trinitaria leaders were marginalized from the new government by the country's new military leaders. Although it was prevented from attaining power, the ideals and symbol of La Trinitaria remained an inspiration and guiding force for future social movements that wanted to rid the Dominican Republic of repressive domestic governments and foreign intervention.

SELDEN RODMAN, *Quisqueya: A History of the Dominican Republic* (1964); HOWARD J. WIARDA, *The Dominican Republic: Nation in Transition* (1969); IAN BELL, *The Dominican Republic* (1981); HOWARD J. WIARDA and M. J. KRYZANEK, *The Dominican Republic: A Caribbean Crucible* (1982).

HEATHER K. THIESSEN

TRIPLE ALLIANCE. *See* **War of the Triple Alliance.**

TRISTAN, FLORA (*b.* 7 April 1803; *d.* 14 November 1844), French social critic and utopian socialist who left important writings on mid-nineteenth-century Europe and Peru. In 1833–1834, fleeing a disastrous marriage, the Paris-born Tristan sought the support of her deceased father's family in Peru, the aristocratic Tristans. Unable to convince them that she was a legitimate member of the family, she traveled extensively in the midst of a civil war. Her travels culminated in the insightful 1838 travelogue *Pérégrinations d'une paria*. Her subsequent publications in Europe dealt with such major issues as living conditions in London, feminism, and socialism. Her intellectual and political activities continued until her death in Bordeaux. The painter Paul Gauguin was her grandson.

FLORA TRISTAN, *Peregrinations of a Pariah, 1833–34*, translated by Jean Hawkes (1987); MARY LOUISE PRATT, *Imperial Eyes: Travel Writing and Transculturation* (1992), esp. pp. 155–171; DORIS BEIK and PAUL BEIK, eds. and trans., *Flora Tristan, Utopian Feminist: Her Travel Diaries and Personal Crusade* (1993).

CHARLES F. WALKER

TRONCOSO DE LA CONCHA, MANUEL DE JESÚS (*b.* 3 April 1878; *d.* 30 May 1955), Dominican lawyer, university professor, and president (1940–1942). A native of Santo Domingo, Troncoso de la Concha received a licentiate in law from the University of Santo Domingo in 1899 and taught civil law there. From 1911 until his death in 1955, he held many important government positions, such as minister of justice, interior and police; development and communication; and war and naval affairs. During the era of Rafael Trujillo (1930–1961), he served as vice president (1938–1942). After the death of Jacinto B. Peynado in 1940, Troncoso de la Concha also became the nominal head of state. (In reality, Trujillo continued to run the Dominican Republic.)

Of his historical works, the most important is *Genesis de la Ocupación Norteamericana de Santo Domingo*, in which he analyzed the political and economic motives for the U.S. occupation of the Dominican Republic. Another one of his important historical writings is *La Ocu-*

pación de Santo Domingo por Haití (1942), in which he made the unorthodox assertion that the Dominican population actually welcomed the Haitian occupation. Among his literary works, the *Narraciones Dominicanas* (1953) occupies a leading position. He died in Santo Domingo.

R. EMILIO JIMÉNEZ, ed., *Manuel de Jesús Troncoso de la Concha*, 5th ed. (1960).

KAI P. SCHOENHALS

TROPICAL DISEASES. *See* **Diseases.**

TROPICALISMO, a Brazilian arts and music movement also known as *tropicália*, which lasted roughly from 1967 to 1969. Its participants were inspired in part by poet Oswald de ANDRADE's 1928 "Manifesto antropofágico" (Cannibalistic Manifesto), in which he expressed the idea of artistic cannibalism, defined as the "cultural devouring of imported techniques to reelaborate them with autonomy." By imaginatively and ironically mixing foreign and Brazilian culture, rock and samba, the folkloric and the urban, the erudite and the kitsch, the *tropicalistas* hoped to foster new ideas and perceptions about both Brazilian reality and foreign cultural influences (such as rock and roll) that were becoming part of that environment.

Tropicalismo manifested itself in the theater in productions such as José Celso Martínez Correa's 1967 staging of de Andrade's *O rei da vela*, and in the plastic arts through the work of artists like Hélio Oiticica (whose 1967 ambient artwork "Tropicália" gave the movement its name). The leading proponents of *tropicalismo* in the area of music were Gilberto GIL, Caetano VELOSO, Tom Zé, Gal Costa, Nara Leão, Torquato Neto, Os Mutantes, Capinam, and conductors Júlio Medaglia and Rogério Duprat. Together, they released "Tropicália" (1968), an album that was a collective musical manifesto. Seminal *tropicalismo* songs include Gil's "Domingo no parque" (Sunday in the Park), and Gil Neto's "Geléia geral" (General Jelly), and Veloso's "Alegria alegria" (Joy, Joy). Musically, such compositions fused Brazilian folk styles, rock, and modern electronic music, and were credited with greatly expanding experimentation in Brazilian popular music.

ANA MARIA BAHIANA, *Nada será como antes* (1980); CHARLES PERRONE, *Masters of Contemporary Brazilian Song: MPB 1965–1985* (1989); CHRIS MC GOWAN and RICARDO PESSANHA, *The Brazilian Sound: Samba, Bossa Nova, and the Popular Music of Brazil* (1991).

CHRIS MCGOWAN

TROPICALISTA SCHOOL OF MEDICINE (BAHIA), an informal "school" formed by a dozen physicians in Bahia (1860–1890) that made discoveries in parasitology and contributed to ongoing debates on beriberi, leprosy, tuberculosis, dracontiasis, and other tropical disorders. The Tropicalistas started as an outsider movement critiquing the Bahian Medical School for outdated teaching and Brazilian doctors for lack of original investigation into Brazilian disorders. The three founders were foreigners. Otto Wucherer (1820–1875), a German and arguably the most important member, discovered the existence of hookworm (*Ancylostoma*) in Brazil in 1865. He was the first person to describe the embryonic filaria (*Wucheria bancrofti*) in 1866, known today as the cause of filariasis. The Scotsman John L. Paterson (1820–1882) introduced Lister's method of antisepsis to Bahian physicians and organized fortnightly meetings for physicians to discuss their cases and keep abreast of medical advances. The meetings led to the birth of the "school." Paterson also proposed the creation of the journal *Gazeta Médica da Bahia*. The Portuguese founder was José Francisco da Silva Lima (1826–1910), who wrote about beriberi in Bahia, was the first to describe the disorder ainhum (a disease affecting the toes), and provided the perseverance needed to make the *Gazeta Médica da Bahia* one of the most successful medical journals in nineteenth-century Latin America. The Tropicalistas initiated one of the most innovative medical episodes in nineteenth-century Brazil.

ANTONIO CALDAS CONI, *A escola tropicalista bahiana* (1952); JULYAN G. PEARD, "The Tropicalista School of Medicine of Bahia, 1860–1889" (Ph.D. diss., Columbia University, 1990), and "Tropical Medicine in Nineteenth-Century Brazil: The Case of the 'Escola Tropicalista Bahiana,' 1860–1890," in *Warm Climates and Western Medicine: The Emergence of Tropical Medicine, 1500–1900*, edited by David Arnold (forthcoming).

JULYAN G. PEARD

TROTSKY, LEON (*b.* 26 October 1879; *d.* 21 August 1940), Russian revolutionary. Trotsky, originally named Lev Davidovitch Bronstein, was born to a Jewish family in Yanovka, Ukraine. With Nikolai Lenin, he led the Russian Revolution of October 1917; later he guided the Red Army and created the concept of "permanent revolution."

Following Lenin's death, Trotsky's opposition to Stalin resulted in his exile to Turkey, France, and Norway. In January 1937 he came to Mexico at the invitation of President Lázaro CÁRDENAS and lived for a time at the home of Diego RIVERA and Frida KAHLO. Throughout his stay in Mexico, prominent labor leaders such as Valentín CAMPA and Vicente LOMBARDO TOLEDANO protested his presence in their country. On 24 May 1940 the famous muralist David Alfaro SIQUEIROS led an attack on Trotsky's house, but although some 200 shots were fired and one guard was abducted and murdered, Trotsky and his family were unharmed. On 20 August 1940 Ramón Mercader, a Catalan assassin working for the Soviet secret police, attacked Trotsky in his home in Coyoacán. He died the next day.

ISAAC DEUTSCHER, *The Prophet Outcast* (1963), and JEAN VAN HEIJENOORT, *With Trotsky in Exile: From Prinkipo to Coyoacán* (1978).

BARBARA A. TENENBAUM

TRUJILLO, a district, province, and department (now called "LaLibertad") in Peru, with a capital of the same name. The capital was one of the first European towns (*villas*) established after the Spanish invaded Peru. In 1534, Diego de ALMAGRO laid it out in a fertile coastal river valley, very near the old CHIMÚ capital of CHAN CHAN. He named the settlement after the Spanish homeland of his partner, Francisco PIZARRO. The latter returned to officially found the town in March 1535. Throughout the sixteenth century, the city remained the seat of political and economic power of the Peruvian viceroyalty in the north, being the principal residence of *encomienda*-holding families. It quickly became an important stopover on the overland route south to Lima, the city of the kings. Wheat, sugarcane, and some silver produced in the hinterland provided the basis for a thriving import-export trade.

The city's early predominance did not go unchallenged in the following years. In 1563, another Spanish town, the *villa* of Santiago de Miraflores, was built in the valley of Saña. Despite energetic protests to the central authorities, Trujillo lost some of its most prominent citizens, part of its wide territorial jurisdiction, and a proportion of the MITA (rotating, draft Indian laborers), who were reassigned to serve the Spanish founders of the city, which became known as Saña. In 1609 Trujillo became the seat of a bishopric. Its religious hegemony, however, was threatened about a decade later by an earthquake that made the bishop move his headquarters north to LAMBAYEQUE. A reluctant bishop was ordered by superiors back to Trujillo, and enticed to move with subventions from the government to rebuild his church. Finally, the constant threat of pirates forced the city to enclose itself inside thick defensive walls before the end of the seventeenth century.

Throughout colonial times, Trujillo nonetheless remained an important coastal center of agricultural production and, in the late eighteenth century, of MINING. In the 1780s, it became an intendancy, which restored its control over much of its original territorial jurisdiction.

During the nineteenth century, Trujillo was often the scene of political struggles. It was José Bernardo de Tagle y Portocarrero TORRE TAGLE, the intendant of Trujillo, who joined the cause for independence under José de SAN MARTÍN, giving the movement an important and early boost. Shortly thereafter, in 1823, the city became the scene of rivalry between José Mariano de la RIVA AGÜERO Y OSMA, Peru's first president, and Torre Tagle, who with the help of General Antonio José de SUCRE, established a rival government. Simón BOLÍVAR, the noted Spanish American liberator, used the city as a temporary administrative center for his authoritarian regime in 1824. During these years the Department of Trujillo was renamed the Department of La Libertad, a name it retains. Trujillo was also the locale of a short-lived revolt during the presidential term of José Rufino ECHENIQUE, and later it was pillaged by the invading Chileans during the WAR OF THE PACIFIC (1879–1883).

In the twentieth century, Trujillo became famous as the birthplace of Víctor Raúl HAYA DE LA TORRE, founder of the political party Alianza Popular Revolucionaria Americana (APRA). The consolidation of some sixty-five agricultural estates into three giant agro-industrial complexes after World War I caused massive discontent among the landed class and the city's commercial interests. These segments of society and the organized sugar plantation workers made Trujillo the solid center of APRA. In the 1930s, after Luis M. SÁNCHEZ CERRO was elected and then shot by an APRA sympathizer, the rank-and-file Apristas revolted. The military, called in to repress the rebellion, rounded up men with bruises on their trigger fingers and shoulders, indicating that they had fired weapons; marched them to the ruins of Chan Chan; and summarily shot them. This became known as the "Trujillo massacre" and marked the beginning of a legacy of hatred between APRA and the military, which was not finally overcome until Alan García won the presidential elections and was allowed to take office in 1985.

Today the city fathers have preserved Trujillo's colonial air, evoking tradition, ceremonialism, and conservatism in the architecture of the city center, especially around its central plaza and main commercial street, with their renovated CASONAS (great houses), which provide the visitor and Trujillanos alike with reminders of its rich history.

MIGUEL FEIJOO DE SOSA, *Relación descriptiva de la ciudad, y provincia de Trujillo del Perú* (1763; repr. 2 vols., 1984); FREDERICK B. PIKE, *The Modern History of Peru* (1967); RUBÉN VARGAS UGARTE, *Historia general del Perú* (1971), esp. vols. 1–3, 5–6, 9–10; PETER F. KLARÉN, *Modernization, Dislocation, and Aprismo: Origins of the Peruvian Aprista Party, 1870–1932* (1973); DAVID P. WERLICH, *Peru: A Short History* (1978).

SUSAN E. RAMÍREZ

See also **Peru: Political Parties—Peruvian Aprista Party.**

TRUJILLO, GUILLERMO (*b.* 1927), Panamanian artist. Trujillo completed a degree in architecture in Panama in 1953 and continued his studies in Spain at the San Fernando Academy, the Moncloa School of Ceramics, and the Escuela Superior de Arquitectura. From 1959 to 1988, he was a professor in the School of Architecture at the University of Panama.

Trujillo is an accomplished painter, sculptor, ceramist, printmaker, and draftsman, with a personal style and iconography rooted in the indigenous cultures and traditions of Panama. Initially he was influenced by Spanish informalism and considered part of the Latin American neofigurative movement, and his paintings cover a wide range, from social satires such as *Los Comisionados* (1964) to landscapes and semi-abstractions based on botanical or archaeological themes, like *Paisaje No. 3* (1972).

MÓNICA KUPFER, *A Panamanian Artist, Guillermo Trujillo: The Formative Years* (M.A. thesis, Tulane University, 1983); P. PRADOS, *El Paraíso Perdido de Guillermo Trujillo* (1990); *Guillermo Trujillo: Retrospectiva* (catalogue from the Museo de Arte Contemporáneo, Panama, 1993).

MONICA E. KUPFER

TRUJILLO, JULIÁN (*b.* 28 January 1828; *d.* 18 July 1883), president of Colombia (1878–1880). Born into the Popayán gentry, he attended the university there, receiving his law doctorate in 1849. Trujillo fought in the civil wars of 1854 and 1859–1863 in the army of General Tomás Cipriano de MOSQUERA, becoming a colonel in 1861 and a general in 1863. He was noted for his courage, and his military prowess in defeating the Antioquian Conservatives in 1877 brought him the presidency. Trujillo's term was marred by a deteriorating economy and deepening dissention among the ruling Liberals. In his quest for an accommodation with the church and the Conservatives, Trujillo was thwarted by the Radical Liberal Congress. His developmental policies were regionally oriented. He contracted for a canal across Panama and negotiated with Francisco Javier CISNEROS for a railway from the Pacific to the Cauca Valley. A transitional figure holding moderate Liberal views, Trujillo was caught between the Radicals and Rafael NÚÑEZ's Nationalists, toward whom he leaned. He served as general in chief of the army in 1881 and was elected a senator in 1882. He died in Bogotá.

HELEN DELPAR, *Red Against Blue* (1981), pp. 121–123; HERNÁN HORNA, *Transport Modernization and Entrepreneurship in Nineteenth Century Colombia* (1992), pp. 83–86.

J. LEÓN HELGUERA

See also **Parra, Aquileo.**

TRUJILLO, MANUEL (*b.* 1846; *d.* 1945), Paraguayan naval officer and memorialist. Born in Asunción, Trujillo entered the armed forces at an early age, joining in the military buildup ordered by President Francisco Solano LÓPEZ in the early 1860s. He was stationed at the state shipyard and arsenal, working under the direction of British engineers hired by the government to help construct a Paraguayan navy.

During the WAR OF THE TRIPLE ALLIANCE (1864–1870), Trujillo fought in half a dozen battles, from the seizure of the port of CORRIENTES (April 1865) to the fall of Angostura (December 1868). He served aboard several Paraguayan steamers, including the *Yporá* and the *Igurey,* and thus was in a good position to observe naval tactics after the disastrous experience at Riachuelo in June 1865.

Trujillo published a brief account of his war experiences, *Gestas guerreras,* in 1911. Owner of a general store in later life, he was much in demand at veterans' conventions as one of the oldest survivors of the conflict.

E. A. M. LAING, "Naval Operations in the War of the Triple Alliance, 1864–70," in *Mariner's Mirror* 54 (1968): 253–280.

THOMAS L. WHIGHAM

TRUJILLO MOLINA, RAFAEL LEÓNIDAS (*b.* 24 October 1891; *d.* 30 May 1961), military officer and ruler of the Dominican Republic (1930–1961). In 1918 Trujillo, a native of San Cristóbal who had been a telegraph operator and security guard, joined the National Guard that had been established by the U.S. occupation forces in the Dominican Republic. His obedience, discipline, and organizational talents, as well as his enthusiastic participation in the suppression of a guerrilla movement in the eastern part of the country, endeared him to the occupiers, who promoted him rapidly. In 1924, when the National Guard was transformed into the Dominican National Police, Trujillo became its chief officer. When the National Police became the National Armed Forces in 1928, Trujillo emerged as its commander in chief. By using his power as military chief in the maneuverings of Dominican politics, Trujillo became president by 1930.

THE ESTABLISHMENT OF SUPREME POWER (1930–1940) During the next decade, Trujillo established the most totalitarian control over his people that any Latin American country had theretofore experienced. All political parties, newspapers, radio stations, trade unions, and private associations that did not agree with him ceased to exist. Persistent opponents were bribed, jailed, murdered, or driven into exile. In order to "whiten" (*blanquear*) his country, Trujillo ordered the massacre of all Haitians in the Dominican Republic. In October 1937, an estimated 25,000 Haitians were slain by his agents. After the completion of this slaughter, the Dominican ruler encouraged the immigration of European Jews and refugees from the Spanish Civil War, as well as Japanese and Hungarians after 1956.

During the first decade of his rule, Trujillo converted much of the Dominican Republic into his private fief by acquiring immense landholdings and monopolies over the export-import trade. Primarily in order to increase his personal fortune (estimated by 1960 to have been U.S.$800 million), Trujillo modernized his country by the introduction of agricultural machinery, new industrial plants, and a paved road system. Impressed by the modernity, cleanliness, and stability of his country, foreign journalists and politicians heaped praise on the Dominican dictator, who launched a campaign of self-glorification. Santo Domingo became Ciudad Trujillo, and Pico Duarte, the highest mountain in the Caribbean (10,500 feet) was renamed Monte Trujillo. The province

273

in which he had been born was named for his father, José Trujillo Valdez, and a western province became known as El Benefactor, a title the dictator had bestowed on himself.

After having himself fraudulently reelected in 1934 for another four years, Trujillo began in 1938 the practice of installing puppet presidents whom he could control from behind the scenes. The first of these presidents was a professor of law, Jacinto B. Peynardo, one of whose first actions was to appoint Trujillo's nine-year-old son, Rafael Trujillo Martínez (Ramfis), brigadier general. Upon Peynado's death in 1940, Manuel de Jesús TRONCOSO DE LA CONCHA became president of the Dominican Republic.

By means of various austerity measures, Trujillo succeeded in making regular payments on the Dominican Republic's debt to the United States, which pleased U.S. President Franklin D. Roosevelt so much that he invited Trujillo and his family for a White House visit in 1939. One year later, the Trujillo–Hull Treaty went into effect, ending the collection of Dominican customs duties by the United States. Trujillo hailed the closing of this humiliating chapter in Dominican history as his personal triumph and erected a monument commemorating the treaty along Santo Domingo's waterfront, where it still stands.

WORLD WAR II AND THE COLD WAR (1940–1955)
When the United States became involved in World War II, the Dominican Republic was one of the first Latin American countries to declare war on the Axis. The conflict proved to be a great boon for the export of Dominican coffee, cocoa, tobacco, and sugar. When it became clear by 1944 that the democracies would triumph over the fascist powers, Trujillo thought it wise to create a "political opening" by permitting the organization of a number of opposition parties. The Dominican ruler used the start of the cold war in 1947 to put an end to this experiment by arresting, torturing, and killing the leaders of the opposition that he had allowed to emerge only three years before. Trujillo portrayed himself as the staunchest anticommunist leader of Latin America and in 1955 convoked a Fair of Peace and Brotherhood of the Free World that cost the then astronomical sum of U.S.$50 million. The fair, which was only sparsely attended by foreign dignitaries, represented the apogee of Trujillo's power.

SANCTIONS, DECLINE, AND DEATH (1956–1961)
After the twenty-fifth anniversary of his rule in 1955, Trujillo was beset by both external and internal challenges. The era of dictators in Latin America seemed to draw to a close. In 1955, Juan Perón was toppled in Argentina. Two years later, Gustavo Rojas Pinilla fled Colombia, and in 1958 Marcos Pérez Jiménez was overthrown in Venezuela. By 1959 Trujillo was the unwilling host to Fulgencio Batista, who had fled to Santo Domingo when the triumphant guerrillas of Fidel Castro entered the Cuban capital on 1 January of that year. Venezuela's new president, Rómulo Betancourt, and Fidel Castro of Cuba assisted in the launching of an anti-Trujillo expedition by Dominican exiles on 14 June 1959.

Left to right: Joaquín Balaguer, Rafael Leónidas Trujillo, and Hector B. Trujillo. ORGANIZATION OF AMERICAN STATES.

The revolutionaries, who returned to their native land by both air drops and coastal landings, were either killed or captured. Although this expedition met with disaster, it inspired some domestic enemies of Trujillo's to form a secret Castroite organization called the Fourteenth of June Movement, which was led by the charismatic lawyer, Manolo Tavarez.

When Trujillo retaliated by bombing Rómulo Betancourt's car, injuring the Venezuelan president and killing a number of his advisers, the Organization of American States imposed severe economic sanctions in 1960 on the Dominican Republic. The administration of Dwight D. Eisenhower, already displeased over Trujillo's 1956 kidnapping and murder of Columbia University instructor Jesús de GALÍNDEZ, dealt a crippling blow to the dictator by imposing a special excise tax on Dominican sugar. Domestically, Trujillo aroused a wave of opposition from all segments of society, including the Roman Catholic hierarchy, when it was learned that his secret police had waylaid, raped, and then murdered the three young daughters (Patria, Minerva, and Maria Teresa Mirabel) of a prominent merchant. When a desperate Trujillo dispatched agents to Communist eastern Europe to seek help against the United States, the CIA sent arms to opposition elements in Santo Domingo; they attacked and killed Trujillo on the night of 30 May 1961. Thus the aging dictator was removed after an iron rule of thirty-one years, but the legacy of his reign loomed over his nation for decades to come.

ARTURO R. ESPAILLAT, *Trujillo: The Last Caesar* (1963); ROBERT D. CRASSWELLER, *Trujillo: The Life and Times of a Caribbean Dictator* (1966); G. POPE ATKINS and LARMAN C. WILSON, *The United States and the Trujillo Regime* (1972); JESÚS DE GALÍNDEZ, *The Era of Trujillo: Dominican Dictator* (1973); BERNARD DIEDERICH, *Trujillo: The Death of the Goat* (1978); JOSÉ RAFAEL VARGAS, *Trujillo: El final de una tiranía* (1985); BERNARDO VEGA, *Unos desafectos y otros en desgracia: Sufrimientos bajo la dictadura de Trujillo* (1986), *La vida cotidiana dominicana a través del archivo particular del generalísimo* (1986), *Los Trujillo se escriben* (1987), *Trujillo y Haiti* (1988), *Nazismo, fascismo, y falangismo en la República Dominicana*, 2d ed. (1989), and *Eisenhower y Trujillo* (1991).

KAI P. SCHOENHALS

TSUCHIYA, TILSA (*b.* 1932; *d.* 23 September 1984), Peruvian painter. Tsuchiya, a native of Supe, created in her paintings a personal mythology inspired in part by her country's Chavín, Nazca, and Inca cultures. She studied at the National School of the Fine Arts in Lima (1954–1959) and at the workshops of Fernando de SZYSZLO, Carlos Quisquez Asin, Manuel Zapata Orihuela, and Ricardo Grau. From 1960 to 1964 she studied painting and engraving at the École des Beaux Arts in Paris. Her artistic training in Peru and France exposed her to diverse styles of painting: muralism, indigenism, abstract expressionism, and surrealism. She represented Peru at the XV BIENAL DE SÃO PAULO (1979). Her work has been exhibited throughout Europe, Latin America, and the United States. She died in Lima.

HOLLIDAY T. DAY and HOLLISTER STURGES, *Art of the Fantastic* (1987), DAWN ADES, *Art in Latin America: The Modern Era, 1820–1980* (1989); ORIANA BADDELEY and VALERIE FRASER, *Drawing the Line: Art and Cultural Identity in Contemporary Latin America* (1989).

MIRIAM BASILIO

TUCUMÁN, province of northwestern Argentina with 1,134,309 inhabitants (1989). The city of San Miguel de Tucumán (1989 population 498,580) was founded in 1565 at the foothills of the Nevado del Aconquija by Captain Diego de Villarroel of Peru to facilitate the transit between Upper Peru and the territories on the Río de la Plata and Cuyo. Its establishment on the Sali River, north of the original foundation, occurred in 1685, when the town was already a significant stopover and supply center for mule trains traveling between CHARCAS (Alto Peru) and the interior of the RÍO DE LA PLATA. The colonial economy hinged also on sugarcane cultivation, citrus fruits, pastures, maize, and tobacco and allowed the development of a landed aristocracy quite different from that of Córdoba and Buenos Aires. Its patriarchal origin explains the remarkable ascendancy of this interior province in the events leading to the independence of the UNITED PROVINCES OF THE RÍO DE LA PLATA, the

San Marco de Tucumán cathedral, 1951. ORGANIZATION OF AMERICAN STATES.

fact that the first Argentine congress opened in Tucumán in 1816, and the role that José de SAN MARTÍN, a native of the province, played in the emancipation of southernmost South America. However, the regionalistic strife that followed independence worked against Tucumán as other regional centers near the littoral acquired greater political power.

During republican times Tucumán was somewhat spared from the inflow of foreign immigrants and retained its Spanish colonial flavor and predominantly agrarian structure. It was only during the twentieth century that industrialization began, attracting sugar-processing plants, chemical establishments, distilleries, a cement factory, textile mills, and several furniture-manufacturing enterprises. The National University of Tucumán (founded in 1914) and a well-regarded natural history museum exert great cultural influence on the whole northwestern region of Argentina. However, the decline of the SUGAR INDUSTRY that began in the area after World War II unleashed a lasting depression in the region's agrarian economy, which industrialization and an agricultural renewal stemming from the irrigation works at the Cadillal Dam have been unable to relieve. The socioeconomic problems of the region are compounded by the high migration rate of peasants from depressed rural areas of Argentina's northwest and from Bolivia.

ARMANDO BAZÁN, *Historia del noroeste argentino* (Buenos Aires, 1986); and CARLOS PÁEZ DE LA TORRE, *Historia de Tucumán* (Buenos Aires, 1987).

CÉSAR N. CAVIEDES

TUCUMÁN CONGRESS, held from 1816 to 1820, was the first assembly to discuss a new constitution. In late 1815, delegates from the Río de la Plata region were called to meet in the interior city of Tucumán. Convening in March 1816, the congress declared independence on July 9 and elected the first supreme director, Juan Martín de PUEYRREDÓN, in an effort to centralize political authority. Buenos Aires used the occasion to try to assert its control over the territory, but its centralizing ambitions faced the provincial federalist opposition led by José ARTIGAS, and the country degenerated into civil war between centralists and federalists. A Portuguese invasion of Montevideo and the Banda Oriental defeated Artigas; the federalist opposition passed to caudillo leaders of Santa Fe and Entre Ríos. Asserting unilateral control over riverine trade and export-import commerce, Pueyrredón made a final effort to establish control that led to the first, highly centralized constitution of the UNITED PROVINCES OF THE RÍO DE LA PLATA in April 1819. The constitution did not embrace republican ideas, and would surely have led to a monarchist state. The combined forces of the provinces forced Pueyrredón to resign in June 1819. The congress dissolved in February 1820.

DAVID BUSHNELL, *Reform and Reaction in the Platine Provinces, 1810–1852* (1983), esp. pp. 16–18; DAVID ROCK, *Argentina, 1516–1982: From Spanish Colonization to the Falklands War* (1985; rev. ed. 1987), esp. pp. 92–93.

JEREMY ADELMAN

TÚCUME, also known as El Purgatorio, the largest late pre-Hispanic (ca. 1000–1532) site in the LAMBAYEQUE Valley on Peru's north coast. The site is built around and atop a steep hill rising from the coastal plain. A monumental sector composed of eleven large adobe pyramid complexes and associated structures lies on the north and northwest sides of the hill; smaller structures, workshops, and cemeteries are on the other sides.

Because the Peruvian coast is a desert, crops can be grown only through irrigation from the rivers that descend from the highlands. Thus it is Túcume's location on a major pre-Hispanic canal that accounts for much of the site's importance.

Túcume probably began about 1000, as the capital of an independent polity, after the fall of nearby BATÁN GRANDE; later, it fell to three successive waves of foreign conquerors. First, around 1350, the CHIMÚ Empire took over the Lambayeque region, moving north from its capital at CHAN CHAN in the MOCHE Valley. The Chimú were followed in the 1470s by the INCAS, who came from CUZCO, in Peru's southern highlands. Finally, the Spanish conquistadores arrived in 1532 and soon controlled the entire north coast of Peru. Within twenty years, Túcume was in ruins and the surviving population had moved to a nearby village.

The largest and most complex occupation was under the Incas. At this time, structures were built all over the hill, making it look like the largest HUACA (shrine, mound) in the pre-Hispanic world. During the same period the local Túcume people comprised the bulk of the population. As in much of their empire, the Incas apparently used the local elites to help govern conquered provinces.

Scientific research at Túcume began around the turn of the twentieth century, but until recently no large-scale excavations had been carried out at the site. From 1988 to 1994, a major research effort was organized by Thor Heyerdahl, led by Daniel H. Sandweiss and Alfredo Narváez, and funded by the Kon-Tiki Museum in Oslo, Norway, and private donors. In addition to the data on the Inca occupation, emerging results show that Túcume was involved in maritime activities, probably including long-distance exchange.

A general review of the site and the results of recent research is in THOR HEYERDAHL, DANIEL H. SANDWEISS, and ALFREDO NARVÁEZ, *The Pyramids of Túcume* (1995). PAUL KOSOK provides excellent photographs and data on the pre-Hispanic canal systems at Túcume and related sites in *Life, Land, and Water in Ancient Peru* (1965), pp. 147–179. CHRISTOPHER B. DONNAN reviews pottery, chronology, and mythology in late pre-Hispanic Lambayeque in ''An Assessment of the Validity of the Naymlap Dynasty,'' in *The Northern Dynasties: Kingship and Statecraft in Chimor* edited by Michael E. Moseley and Alana Cordy-Collins, (1990), pp. 243–274. In the same volume IZUMI SHIMADA places the Lambayeque region in a deeper chronological framework in his "Cultural Continuities and Discontinuities on the Northern North Coast of Peru, Middle-Late Horizons," pp. 279–392.

DANIEL H. SANDWEISS

TUGWELL, REXFORD GUY (*b*. 10 July 1891; *d*. 21 July 1979), governor of Puerto Rico (1941–1946). In 1932, Tugwell became one of the original members of Franklin ROOSEVELT's brain trust. He later served as the assistant secretary of agriculture, the director of the Resettlement Administration, chairman of the city planning commission of New York, and chancellor at the University of Puerto Rico. Republicans and big sugar businesses opposed his appointment to the governorship.

Tugwell favored home rule for Puerto Rico and continued economic development through such institutions as the Development Company, the Development Bank, and the Water Resources Authority. He served as the last federally appointed governor of Puerto Rico.

REXFORD G. TUGWELL, *The Stricken Land: The Story of Puerto Rico* (1947); ENRIQUE LUGO-SILVA, *The Tugwell Administration in Puerto Rico, 1941–1946* (1955); CHARLES T. GOODSELL, *Administration of a Revolution: Executive Reform in Puerto Rico Under Governor Tugwell, 1941–1946* (1965).

CHRISTOPHER T. BOWEN

TULA, the capital of the TOLTECS, central Mexico's dominant civilization in the Early Postclassic period (A.D. 900–1250). The NAHUATL name is Tollan (Place of the Reeds). Aztec legends recorded in the colonial period describe Tula and its builders in glowing terms; archaeologists have verified some of these claims but others are obvious exaggerations.

Located on a ridge overlooking a verdant river valley in Hidalgo, Tula dates back to the eighth century. By 1100 it was a city of at least 35,000 inhabitants, covering almost 6 square miles. Tula Grande, the city's main civic and religious precinct, included temples, ball courts (playing fields), and colonnaded halls surrounding a large open plaza. The buildings were adorned with carved friezes, ornaments, and numerous freestanding stone sculptures, including the famous recumbent CHACMOOL figures. Pyramid B, known as the Temple of QUETZALCOATL, featured friezes composed of carved and stuccoed panels on all sides, and *atlantes*, gigantic stone sculptures depicting Toltec warriors, supported the temple roof.

Thousands of densely packed but well-constructed houses filled the city. Most had foundation platforms, stone and adobe walls, flat roofs, compacted earth or stucco floors, and subterranean storm drains. They com-

Butterfly Warriors, Tula. Reproduced from Andre Emmerich, *Art Before Columbus* (1963). PHOTO BY LEE BOLTIN.

monly occur in groups of three or four ranged around interior courtyards. Poorer families presumably occupied less substantial wattle and daub houses with thatched roofs.

Some of Tula's inhabitants cultivated lands outside the city, but many worked as artisans. Their products included utilitarian objects consumed by everyone in Toltec society and luxury goods reserved for the elite and for export. Pottery vessels, figurines, textiles, cutting tools and scrapers made from obsidian, and jewelry are just a few of the craft products for which archaeological evidence exists.

The reasons for Tula's demise are not clear. Aztec legends attribute it to drought, famine, and civil unrest, but archaeologists have not been able to verify these accounts. After a century of abandonment, Tula was reoccupied by people of Aztec affiliation who ransacked the ruins in search of sculptures, buried offerings, and other treasures. Ironically, they left an archaeological site so impoverished that a few twentieth-century scholars refused to accept it as the Toltec capital described in the legends!

RICHARD A. DIEHL, *Tula: The Toltec Capital of Ancient Mexico* (1983); DAN M. HEALAN, JANET M. KERLEY, and GEORGE J. BEY III, "Excavation and Preliminary Analysis of an Obsidian Workshop in Tula, Hidalgo, Mexico," in *Journal of Field Archaeology* 10, no. 2 (1983): 127–145; ALBA GUADALUPE MASTACHE, ANA MARIA CRESPO, ROBERT H. COBEAN, and DAN M. HEALAN, *Estudios sobre la antigua ciudad de Tula* (1983); BEATRÍZ DE LA FUENTE, SILVIA TREJO, and NELLY GUTIÉRREZ SOLANA, *Escultura en Piedra de Tula* (1989); DAN M. HEALAN, ed., *Tula of the Toltecs: Excavations and Surveys* (1989).

RICHARD A. DIEHL

See also **Archaeology; Mesoamerica.**

TULUM, a small but significant Late Postclassic (A.D. 1250–1500) trading and religious center located on the east coast of the Yucatán Peninsula in Quintana Roo, Mexico. It was the most important member of a network of coastal sites, including Tancah, Xelhá, and the island of Cozumel, on a seaborne trade route along the Caribbean coast to Honduras.

The site commands a dramatic setting on a cliff overlooking the Caribbean Sea. It is protected on its three sides by a wall 2,640 feet long and almost seven feet high. The major structures of the site lie in the center of a rectangular enclosure 1,254 feet long. The Castle, the smaller Temple of the Diving God, the Temple of the Initial Series, and the Temple of the Frescoes are the most important buildings. There are also structures in the corners of the walls and along the enclosure. Compared with Classic buildings, the structures at Tulum are small and poorly built.

Polychrome murals and stucco reliefs decorate the interior and exterior walls of the buildings. The paintings are of ritual themes; many are multitiered works showing gods in scenes of ceremonial action. Those of the Temple of the Frescoes and the Temple of the Diving God are the best preserved. The Mixtec style of the paintings is similar to that of the coastal site of Santa Rita Corozal, Belize, which supports the idea that there was cultural contact along the coast. Stucco relief decoration occurs on the corners and niches of buildings. One important motif, a bee god with wings, portrayed in a frontal, diving position, occurs in several locations. The keeping of honey bees is a present-day Yucatán industry, and honey was probably an export in the past.

SAMUEL KIRLAND LOTHROP, *Tulum: An Archaeological Study of the East Coast of the Yucatán,* Carnegie Institution of Washington Publication 335 (1924); DONALD ROBERTSON, "The Tulum Murals: The International Style of the Late Postclassic," in *Verhandlungen des 38, Internationalen Amerikanistenkongresses,* vol. 2 (1970), pp. 77–88; and ARTHUR G. MILLER, *On the Edge of the Sea: Mural Painting at Tancah-Tulum, Quintana Roo, Mexico* (1982).

EUGENIA J. ROBINSON

See also **Mesoamerica; Mixtecs.**

TUMBES, northernmost Peruvian city. Located on the Pacific coast near the Ecuadorian border, at an elevation of 450 feet, Tumbes is an important regional center. It was the site of a significant pre-Columbian fortress, one of the first to be described by Spanish explorers. Its size and beauty suggested to Pedro de Candía and Alonso de Molina, the first European witnesses, the potential wealth of the Inca peoples to the south. The fortress, along with a temple of the sun decorated with gold and silver and a house of the virgins, dominated the site. Agustín de Zárate, who arrived in the early 1540s, reported it was "one of the finest sights in the country until the Indians of Puna Island destroyed it." Diego de ALMAGRO was made "commander" of the fortress of Tumbes, and Hernando de LUQUE was appointed its first bishop.

At the northernmost part of the Peruvian desert, Tumbes receives sufficient annual rainfall to support scrub vegetation, and the Tumbes River provides irrigation water. In the early seventeenth century, Antonio Vázquez de Espinosa, who traveled the Americas and wrote an extensive geographical treatise, described the area as highly productive. Today, corn is planted for local consumption, and tobacco, rice, and cotton are cultivated. Cattle and goats are raised, and fish are caught. Petroleum was found at nearby Zorritos in 1864, but production levels never matched those of PIURA.

NOBLE DAVID COOK, *Demographic Collapse: Indian Peru, 1520–1620* (1981); ANTONIO VÁZQUEZ DE ESPINOSA, *Compendio y descripción de las indias occidentales* (1948).

NOBLE DAVID COOK

TUNGA (*b.* 8 February 1952), Brazilian artist. Born in Palmares, Pernambuco, Antônio José de Barros Carvalho e Mello Mourão received a B.A. in architecture from the Universidade Santa Ursula, Rio de Janeiro, in 1974. He is a leading member of a generation of Brazilian artists, including Waltercio Caldas, Cildo Meireles, and José RESENDE, who emerged in the early 1970s; they and others founded the journals *Malasartes* in 1975 and *A parte do fogo* in 1980. Inspired by Marcel Duchamp, René Magritte, and the Brazilian neo-concrete artist Lygia CLARK, among others, Tunga creates unsettling installations, sculptures, and films. His installations often feature magnetized objects. Recurring motifs in his work include Siamese twins joined by the hair, lizards consuming each other's heads, and tori—indicative of his interest in topology. By problematizing the concept of binary opposition through the use of magnetism and such motifs, Tunga offers a critique of Western rationalism and the authoritarian institutions it has fostered. He lives in Rio de Janeiro and Paris.

Tunga: "Lezarts"/Cildo Meireles: "Through" (1989); GUY BRETT, "Tunga," in his *Transcontinental: Nine Latin American Artists,* edited by Elizabeth A. Macgregor (1990), pp. 48–55; PAULO HERKENHOFF, "The Theme of Crisis in Contemporary Latin

American Art,'' in *Latin American Artists of the Twentieth Century* (1993), pp. 134–143.

JOHN ALAN FARMER

TUNJA, a town in northeastern Colombia, 81 miles northeast of Bogotá, 1990 estimated population 250,000. This highland town was founded by the conquistador Gonzalo Suárez Rendón in 1539 on the site of the Chibcha settlement of Hunza, and was declared a city in 1541. During the colonial period, Tunja was a small but important urban center in a largely deurbanized region; by 1610 its population included over seventy *encomienda* holders and was divided into three parishes. Tunja was a relatively minor participant in the COMUNERO REVOLT of 1781 and in the struggle for independence, but one of the key patriot victories of the War of Independence was won at the battle of BOYACÁ, southeast of the town, on 7 August 1819. The decay of the highland agricultural and artisanal economy over the 1800s plunged Tunja into a long period of stagnation, despite its political role as capital of the department of Boyacá (1821–1832), province of Tunja (1832–1857), state of Boyacá (1858–1885), and department of Boyacá (1886–present). A Conservative Party bastion since the mid-nineteenth century, the town was long the scourge of Liberal publicists for the dominant role of the Catholic church in local affairs. Much of the town's colonial architecture, both civil and religious, is well preserved.

RAMÓN C. CORREA, ed., *Historia de Tunja*, vol. 1 (1944).

RICHARD J. STOLLER

TÚPAC AMARU (*b*. ca. 1554; *d*. 1572), Inca emperor during early colonial period (1571–1572). Túpac Amaru, the third son of MANCO INCA, reigned briefly as emperor of the Inca rump state in the last Inca capital of VILCA-BAMBA, in the *montaña* region of eastern Peru. He was crowned in 1571; the next year the Spanish took the city of Vilcabamba, and Túpac Amaru and his family were captured. Taken to Cuzco, he was condemned to death and executed in the main plaza before a huge crowd of Indians. He was the last of the Inca emperors, and his death extinguished the dynasty. He has remained, nevertheless, a potent symbol of resistance and rebellion in Peru even to the present day. His name has been used by various left-wing guerrilla groups.

BURR CARTWRIGHT BRUNDAGE, *The Lords of Cuzco: A History and Description of the Inca People in Their Final Days* (1967); JOHN HEMMING, *Conquest of the Incas* (1970).

GORDON F. MCEWAN

See also **Incas.**

TÚPAC AMARU (José Gabriel Condorcanqui) (*b.* March 1738; *d.* 18 May 1781), the most famous leader and martyr of the Great Andean Rebellion of 1780–1783.

Born in Surimana, Canas y Canchis (Tinta), José Gabriel was the son of Miguel Condorcanqui and Rosa Noguera and a descendant of Inca TÚPAC AMARU, executed by Viceroy Francisco de TOLEDO in 1572. Orphaned in 1750, José Gabriel was raised by an aunt and uncle. As heir to the *cacicazgo* (chieftainship) of Tungasuca, Pampamarca, and Surimana, he attended Cuzco's San Francisco de Borja school. In 1760 he married Micaela Bastidas Puyucahua, and they had three sons: Hipólito, Mariano, and Fernando.

At age twenty-five José Gabriel claimed the *cacicazgo* and also became a successful teamster on the route linking Cuzco to Potosí. His travels made him aware of mounting dissatisfaction with colonial rule. The *repartos* (distributions of merchandise), whereby *corregidores* (provincial governors) forced Indians to purchase costly, unwanted goods, caused great discontent. Indians also resented the abusive MITA (draft labor) for the mines of POTOSÍ. The government's failure to correct the corruption and abuse of the colonial system proved increasingly galling to José Gabriel. Empowered by other caciques from Tinta, he spent 1777 and part of the following year in Lima, attempting to secure the province's exemption from the *mita*. When Visitador José Antonio de Areche rejected his suit, the cacique considered traveling to Spain to press his case. Meanwhile, he unsuccessfully petitioned the government to recognize him as the marquis of Oropesa, the vacant title that belonged to the heir of the original Incas.

Frustrated at each turn, he returned to Tinta in mid-1778, encouraged by influential friends in Lima to act against the illegality and abuse that the regime allowed to flourish. During the following two years, he conspired and planned. Sporadic local revolts independently erupted throughout the Andes. Areche's policies heightened tensions. He established new customhouses to col-

Portrait of Tupac Amaru II; detail from Peruvian 500-inti note.

lect higher taxes and intended to force mestizos to pay tribute. Dissatisfaction extended beyond the Indian population to include many creoles and mestizos.

On 4 November 1780, José Gabriel, taking the name Túpac Amaru, struck, arresting Antonio de Arriaga, the *corregidor* of Tinta. A convenient target, Arriaga had openly feuded with local clergy and had been excommunicated by the bishop of Cuzco, Juan Manuel Moscoso y Peralta. Túpac Amaru transported Arriaga to Tungasuca, where he tried Arriaga for corruption and abuse of the *repartos* and hanged him on 10 November. As the news spread, both rebels and royalists gathered forces. Many caciques of Tinta joined Túpac Amaru, whose relatives provided most of the movement's leadership. Building support, Túpac Amaru decreed the emancipation of slaves on 16 November. At Sangarara two days later, the rebels defeated a force sent out from Cuzco. Nonetheless, the mounting violence in the wake of Sangarara caused many creoles and mestizos to withdraw their support for the rebellion.

In early December, Túpac Amaru captured Lampa and Azángaro, and his influence threatened both southern and Upper Peru. Viceroy Augustín de JÁUREGUI and Areche mobilized reinforcements and supplies for the defense of Cuzco. News of their imminent arrival brought Túpac Amaru's forces north from Callao to attack Cuzco. With 40,000 to 60,000 troops, he besieged Cuzco from 2 to 9 January 1781. Aid from royalist caciques helped prevent Cuzco's fall, and Túpac Amaru retreated. Defeated in Tinta, he was betrayed and captured in Langui on 6 April 1781. While the rebellion continued, his captors took him to Cuzco for interrogation and trial. On 18 May he witnessed the torture and execution of his wife and other captive family members and then was pulled apart by four horses.

Although the Great Andean Rebellion comprised more than Túpac Amaru's revolt, other insurgents looked to his leadership. For many Indians his ancestry allowed him to carry the banner of Inca legitimacy, and his violent protest against Spanish colonialism won broad sympathy. Yet his rebellion failed owing to the massive mobilization carried out by the government, his inability to win lasting support from mestizos and creoles, and opposition from many caciques.

DANIEL VALCARCEL, *La rebelión de Túpac Amaru* (1947); LILLIAN ESTELLE FISHER, *The Last Inca Revolt, 1780–1783* (1966); BOLESLAO LEWIN, *La rebelíon de Túpac Amaru y los orígenes de la Independencia Hispanoamérica* (1967); ALBERTO FLORES GALINDO, ed., *Túpac Amaru II—1780* (1976); COMISIÓN NACIONAL DEL BICENTENARIO DE LA REBELIÓN EMANCIPADORA DE TÚPAC AMARU, *Actas del Coloquio International: "Túpac Amaru y su tiempo"* (1980); JOSÉ ANTONIO DEL BUSTO DUTHURBURU, *José Gabriel Túpac Amaru antes de su rebelión* (1981); SCARLETT O'PHELAN GODOY, *Rebellions and Revolts in Eighteenth-Century Peru and Upper Peru* (1985); and STEVE J. STERN, ed., *Resistance, Rebellion, and Consciousness in the Andean Peasant World, 18th to 20th Centuries* (1987), pp. 94–139.

KENDALL W. BROWN

TÚPAC CATARI (JULIÁN APAZA) (*b.* ca. 1750; *d.* 14 November 1781), leader of an AYMARA insurrection in 1781, which laid siege to La Paz for six months. A commoner born in Ayoayo, Sicasica, Julián Apaza was orphaned at age twelve. He worked in the mines, traded coca leaves and cloth, and married Bartolina Sisa, with whom he had three children. Contemporaries described him as lighter in complexion than most Aymaras and of medium height.

Apaza first came to public notice in early 1781, when insurrection convulsed the provinces of Sicasica, Yungas, and Pacajes. Spanish officials mistakenly blamed the turmoil on TÚPAC AMARU, who rebelled in November 1780 near Cuzco. Ambitious, charismatic, and messianic, Apaza quickly rose to command the Aymara rebels north of La Paz. Speaking only Aymara, he combined Christian and native rhetoric and claimed to receive messages from God through a small silver box he carried. On some occasions he dressed like the Inca, at others like a Spanish official. He also changed his name to Túpac Catari, associating himself with the great indigenous leaders Túpac Amaru and Tomás Catari. Lacking any traditional claim to leadership, he proclaimed himself viceroy, saying he had received authority from Túpac Amaru.

Túpac Catari's greatest undertaking was the siege of La Paz, which began on 14 March 1781. With an army numbering from 10,000 to 40,000, he controlled access to the city and brutally killed those captured while trying to escape. On 18 July, General Ignacio Flores's army temporarily broke the siege but then had to withdraw. Thereupon Túpac Catari joined his forces with those of Andrés Túpac Amaru and again besieged La Paz. Unable to breach the defenses, they dammed the Choqueyapu River above La Paz to unleash a destructive flood on the city. The approach of another royal column under José de Resequín saved La Paz. Túpac Catari may have lost 5,000 at La Paz, while the besieged suffered two or three times more deaths, many from starvation and disease.

Túpac Catari withdrew toward the north, rejecting offers of pardon. At Peñas on 9 November, Tomás Inga Lipe, a former ally, betrayed him, and he was taken into government hands. Quickly interrogated and condemned, on 14 November he was tied to four horses and cruelly torn apart.

Lack of artillery handicapped Túpac Catari at La Paz, and rivalry between the Aymaras and Quechuas prevented successful integration of the rebel movements, although they occasionally cooperated. Túpac Catari declared his intention of driving the Spanish from Peru, but he also talked of liberating the Aymaras from Inca oppression.

The best study is MARÍA EUGENIA DEL VALLE DE SILES, *Historia de la rebelíon de Túpac Catari, 1781–1782* (1900). Also valuable are M. RIGOBERTO PAREDES, *Túpac Catari: Apuntes biográficos* (1897, 1973); ALIPIO VALENCIA VEGA, *Julián Tupaj Katari, caudillo de la liberación india* (1950); LILLIAN ESTELLE FISHER, *The Last*

Inca Revolt, 1780–1783 (1966); BOLESLAO LEWIN, *La rebelión de Túpac Amaru y los orígenes de la independencia de Hispanoamérica,* 3d ed. (1967), esp. pp. 509–526; MARCELO GRONDÍN, *Tupaj Katari y la rebelión campesina de 1781–1783* (1975); and JORGE FLORES OCHOA and ABRAHAM VALENCIA, *Rebeliones indígenas quechuas y aymaras* (1980).

KENDALL W. BROWN

TUPAMAROS. *See* **Uruguay: Political Parties: National Liberation Movement.**

TUPI, a linguistic trunk composed of seven distinct language branches, among which the TUPI-GUARANI family is by far the most widespread. Tupi speakers were the principal indigenous inhabitants of early colonial Brazil, occupying much of the coast between the Río de la Plata and the mouth of the Amazon. While the early literature pointed out the cultural and linguistic unity of these peoples, it also emphasized their fragmented political relations, portraying indigenous Brazil as a patchwork of shifting alliances and animosities. Specific ethnic denominations emerged within this context, and colonial sources divided the coastal Tupi into diverse subgroups, including the Tupinikin, TUPINAMBÁ, Tememinó, Tupiná, Amoipira, Caeté, POTIGUAR, and Tobajara.

Though these larger tribal agglomerations emerged clearly in the context of warfare, the semisedentary agrarian village remained the basic unit of Tupi social and political organization. Composed of four to eight communal *malocas* (lodges), sixteenth-century Tupi villages varied greatly in size and population, ranging from around 100 to over 1,000 inhabitants. Soil exhaustion, growing scarcity of game or fish, political factionalism, or the emergence of a charismatic new leader contributed to the constant fragmentation and subsequent regeneration of villages.

Each village had a headman, often the founder of the community, whose prestige rested on oratorical skills and prowess as a warrior, but whose authority was limited mainly to the military sphere. Shamans also wielded considerable authority in daily life, while the occasional presence of wandering prophets also played

European view of Tupi men in their natural and civilized state. Reproduced from Claude d'Abbeville, *Histoire de la mission des pères capuchins en l'isle de Maragnan* (Paris, 1614). COURTESY OF THE JOHN CARTER BROWN LIBRARY AT BROWN UNIVERSITY.

an important role in Tupi-Guarani spiritual affairs. Warfare, motivated by constant vendettas between indigenous factions, was a central element in Tupi society and history. The main objective was to obtain prisoners in order to avenge past wrongs, as enemy captives were sacrificed and subsequently eaten in an elaborate ritual ceremony.

During the sixteenth century, the coastal Tupi faced a series of new challenges that ultimately led to their defeat and near extinction. The Portuguese conquest, initially carried out through the intricate mechanism of intertribal relations, eventually found more effective allies in the fatal triad of disease, slavery, and confinement to missions. However, even facing such formidable odds, Tupi peoples reached into their past and developed new forms of resistance. Local groups joined warrior forces to form "confederations," traditional leaders organized violent uprisings against colonists and Jesuit missionaries, and messianic leaders inspired migrations in retreat from areas of Portuguese influence. Nonetheless, the combined effects of colonial oppression, epidemic disease, and migration resulted in the depopulation of the coast by the first half of the seventeenth century. While a few, small groups remain on the coast, several Tupi societies continue to flourish to this day in central Brazil and the Amazon.

In spite of the relatively rapid decline of coastal Tupi populations, their impact on the formation of Brazilian society and culture was great. Peasant populations throughout Brazil, in many cases the result of Tupi-Portuguese miscegenation, preserved indigenous agricultural techniques and crops along with customs and folk beliefs. In the nineteenth century, romantic and naturalist literature and art adopted Tupi symbols, while nationalists such as Couto de Magalhães and Emperor Dom Pedro II actively promoted the use of *nhengatú* (vulgar Tupi) as a national language. In the twentieth century, the modernist generation of 1922 evoked the Tupi past, particularly in the creative use of cannibalism as a metaphor for Brazilian culture.

On Tupi languages, ARYON DALL'IGNA RODRIGUES, *Línguas brasileiras* (1986), is an excellent starting point. The coastal Tupi are described and analyzed exhaustively in two seminal works of Brazilian anthropology by FLORESTAN FERNANDES, *A organização social dos Tupinambá* (1948) and *A função social da guerra na sociedade Tupinambá* (1951). Two recent studies introduce new perspectives on Tupi culture: MANUELA CARNEIRO DA CUNHA, ed., *História dos índios no Brasil* (1992); and EDUARDO VIVEIROS DE CASTRO, *From the Enemy's Point of View* (1992). A general account of the conquest may be found in JOHN HEMMING, *Red Gold* (1978). STUART SCHWARTZ, *Sugar Plantations in the Formation of Brazilian Society* (1985), provides an excellent discussion of the decline of native societies in sixteenth-century Bahia. WARREN DEAN covers the southern coast in "Indigenous Populations of the São Paulo—Rio de Janeiro Coast: Trade, Aldeamento, Slavery, and Extinction," in *Revista de História* 117 (1984). On the Tupi in literature, see DAVID MILLER DRIVER, *The Indian in Brazilian Literature* (1942).

JOHN M. MONTEIRO

TUPI-GUARANI, one of the most widespread families of South American Indian languages. It encompasses more than forty languages spoken in Brazil, Paraguay, Argentina, Bolivia, Peru, French Guiana, Venezuela, and Colombia. According to the classification of Aryon D. Rodrigues, the Tupi-Guarani family is made up of the following languages: Amanaye, Anambe, Apiaka, Araweté, Asurini do Tocantins (Akwáwa), Asurini do Xingu, Ava (Canoeiro), Chiriguano, Emerillon, Guaja, Guajajára, Guarani Antigo, Guarani Paraguaio, Guarawo (Guarayu), Guayaki (Arhe), Hora (Jora), Izoceño (Chane), Kaiwa (Kayova, Pãi), Kamayura, Kayabi, Kokáma, Kokamiga (Cocamilla), Lingua Geral Amazônica (Nheengatu), Lingua Geral Paulista (Tupi Austral), Mbia (Guarani), Nandeva (Txiripa), Omágua, Parakanã, Parintintin, Siriono, Surui (Mujetire), Takunyape, Tapiete, Tapirape, Tembe, Tupi-Kawahib (Tupi do Machado, Pawate, Wiraféd), Tupinamba, Turiwára, Uruba, Wayami, Wayampipuku, and Xeta (Serra dos Dourados).

The most widely spoken Tupi-Guarani language is Paraguayan Tupi, with 3 million speakers, followed by Chiriguano, Ava, and Bolivian Guarani, which is spoken by 50,000 people in Bolivia. Twenty-one Tupi-Guarani languages are spoken in Brazil by 33,000 Indians. The most popular of them, numbering 7,000 each, are the Tenetehára (Guajajára and Tembe) in the states of Maranhão and Pará, and the Kaiwa in the state of Mato Grosso do Sul. Kaiwa is also spoken by 8,000 people in Paraguay, where it is known as Pãi or Pãi-Tavyterã.

The great geographical diffusion of the Tupi-Guarani languages is proof of earlier migrations, which continued after the beginning of European colonization in Brazil and Spanish America. The Guarani-Mbia continued to migrate, having moved from southwestern Brazil, through northeastern Argentina and eastern Paraguay, until they reached the Atlantic coast. For almost five centuries they migrated up the coast to Brazil's Northeast. They occupied most of the eastern coast of Brazil when the Portuguese colonizers met them in the early sixteenth century. The migrations probably had religious and mythical motivation; according to Guarani-Mbia mythology, the "land without evil" was supposed to be across the big sea. As a consequence of the migrations, Guarani-Mbia is the most geographically widespread of the languages and is spoken in Paraguay, Argentina, and in Brazil from Espíritu Santo to Rio Grande do Sul. In colonial South America two of the languages were extensively documented. Father José de ANCHIETA made the first grammatical description of Tupinamba, published in 1595, and also produced a number of poems and plays in the language. Around 1625 the missionaries Alonso de Aragona and Antonio Ruiz da Montoya prepared two grammars of Guarani. The latter also published a catechism and two dictionaries.

CHARLOTTE EMMERICH

TUPINAMBÁ, Tupi-speaking peoples of coastal Brazil. While colonial sources specifically identify the Tupinambá with Rio de Janeiro, Bahia, and Maranhão, modern ethnologists employ the term to designate all the coastal TUPI. Expert warriors, the Tupinambá engaged in constant combat with other Tupi groups, each taking captives who were submitted to lengthy rituals culminating in sacrifice and cannibalism.

Tupinambá warfare, as a fundamental aspect of intervillage relations, in turn provided one of the keys to the European conquest of the coastal region. Initially, local groups forged alliances with Portuguese and French interests in order to gain the upper hand against traditional enemies. But the Europeans were interested mainly in slaves, which distorted the traditional goals of warfare and moved the Tupinambá to resist colonial rule. The Tupinambá's refusal to abandon ritual sacrifice and cannibalism led the Portuguese to launch brutal military campaigns in Bahia and Rio de Janeiro, especially during Mem de SÁ's tenure as captain-general (1557–1572). This policy resulted in the enslavement of many and the confinement of others in Jesuit missions (reducões).

Following their military defeat, which was exacerbated by epidemic disease, several Tupinambá groups embarked on long migrations, led by charismatic prophets. The majority settled on the northern coast of Maranhão and in the middle Amazon Valley, while one small contingent reached Spanish Peru. Another prophetic resistance movement, known as the *Santidade,* flourished closer to Bahia during the second half of the sixteenth century. By the mid-seventeenth century, the coastal Tupinambá no longer existed as an independent indigenous society.

STUART SCHWARTZ provides cogent summaries of Tupinambá society and history, with particular emphasis on Bahia, in *Early Latin America* (1983) and *Sugar Plantations in the Formation of Brazilian Society* (1985). Tupinambá relations with the Europeans receive detailed treatment in JOHN HEMMING, *Red Gold* (1978). The classic Brazilian work remains FLORESTAN FERNANDES, *Organização social dos Tupinambá* (1948).

JOHN M. MONTEIRO

See also **Slavery.**

TURBAY, GABRIEL (*b.* 28 January 1901; *d.* 17 November 1946), Colombian Liberal leader. Of Syrian-Lebanese descent, he was trained in medicine at the Universidad Nacional in Bogotá, but devoted little time to its practice. He attracted attention during the 1920s as a member of a circle of young socialist intellectuals. After the Liberal Party's return to power in 1930, he occupied a series of responsible government positions, and in 1946 he was the official Liberal candidate for president, opposing the dissident Liberal Jorge Eliécer GAITÁN and Conservative Mariano OSPINA PÉREZ. The latter won as a result of the

Liberals' division. Turbay then left Colombia for a European tour; he died suddenly in Paris.

AGUSTÍN RODRÍGUEZ GARAVITO, *Gabriel Turbay, un solitario de la grandeza,* 2d ed. (1966); HERBERT BRAUN, *The Assassination of Gaitán: Public Life and Urban Violence in Colombia* (1985); EDUARDO DURÁN GÓMEZ, *Gabriel Turbay, estadista santandereano* (1988).

DAVID BUSHNELL

TURBAY AYALA, JULIO CÉSAR (*b.* 18 June 1916), Colombian Liberal Party politician and president (1978–1982). Turbay was born in Bogotá and received a bachelor's degree from the Escuela Nacional de Comercio. Amid growing public dissatisfaction over the Liberal–Conservative power-sharing arrangement known as the Frente Nacional (National Front), then in its twentieth year, he won the presidential election of 1978, in which only 41 percent of the electorate voted. Antigovernment guerrilla groups subsequently intensified their operations, attempting to assassinate the president in 1978, staging an audacious theft of army weapons in 1979, and holding a score of diplomats hostage in the Dominican embassy in 1980. Turbay responded by stepping up military antiguerrilla operations, which soon produced an outcry against numerous arbitrary arrests and the physical abuse of detainees. Colombia was economically stable under Turbay, and government authority was never seriously threatened by the extralegal armed forces. Yet criticism of the political status quo, which Turbay represented, signaled an impending opening of the Colombian political system.

Since 1982 Turbay has been a senior member of the Liberal Party, leading a group known as the Turbayistas. However, his following is modest at best, owing to the unpopularity of his presidency and to personal shortcomings.

DANIEL PÉCAUT, *Crónica de dos décadas de política colombiana, 1968–1988,* 2d ed. (1989); DAVID BUSHNELL, *The Making of Modern Colombia, a Nation in Spite of Itself* (1993).

JAMES D. HENDERSON

See also **Colombia: Political Parties; Colombia: Revolutionary Movements.**

TURCIOS LIMA, LUIS AGOSTO (*b.* 1941; *d.* 2 October 1966), Guatemalan guerrilla leader. On 13 November 1960, Turcios Lima led young military officers in rebellion against the corrupt government of Miguel YDÍGORAS FUENTES (1958–1963). In the aftermath of a coup that lacked ideological direction, Turcios Lima became an advocate of communist revolution through guerrilla warfare and organized the Rebel Armed Forces (FAR) with fellow officer Marco Antonio YON SOSA in 1962. Although Yon Sosa broke from the Communist Party and the FAR in 1965, Turcios Lima reluctantly accepted its decision to suspend military activity in order to give civilian president Julio César MÉNDEZ MONTENEGRO (1966–1970) an opportunity to bring the reactionary military under control. The military, trained and supplied by the United States, rejected Méndez's reformist policies and launched a brutal campaign against the FAR following the accidental death of Turcios Lima. From the devastating losses suffered in the late 1960s, the rebel leaders of the 1970s concluded that there was no democratic alternative to armed revolution.

SUSANNE JONAS and DAVID TOBIS, eds., *Guatemala* (1974), esp. pp. 176–203; JIM HANDY, *Gift of the Devil: A History of Guatemala* (1984), esp. pp. 230–234.

PAUL J. DOSAL

See also **Guatemala: Revolutionary Movements.**

TUYUTÍ, BATTLE OF, a major engagement of the WAR OF THE TRIPLE ALLIANCE (1864–1870) that took place on 24 May 1866. After the crossing of Argentine and Brazilian forces into Paraguayan territory earlier in the year, the Allied commander, General Bartolomé MITRE, assembled a force of some 35,000 men to drive the Paraguayans from their entrenched positions at the fortress of HUMAITÁ. As these units moved northward through the marshes, the Paraguayans prepared a strong defensive line at Tuyutí, a small area of relatively high ground several miles below the fortress. At the last moment, Marshal Francisco Solano LÓPEZ, the Paraguayan commander, abandoned his defensive strategy in favor of a frontal attack, deploying 22,000 troops, in hopes of catching the Allies off guard. The planned dawn attack never materialized, however, and the Paraguayans were delayed until noon, which gave the Allies time to prepare impressive defenses of their own, especially on their left flank. The resulting carnage was terrible: the Paraguayans lost about 6,000 men and the Allies about 8,000 before the battle subsided at 4 P.M.

The inability of the Paraguayan cavalry to achieve an envelopment of the Allied rear decided the contest in favor of the Allies, whose exhausted forces were unable to capitalize on their victory. López managed to continue active operations around Humaitá for another two years.

CHARLES J. KOLINSKI, *Independence or Death! The Story of the Paraguayan War* (1965); LEANDRO APONTE BENÍTEZ, *Hombres . . . armas . . . y batallas de la epopeya de los siglos* (1971), pp. 181–182.

THOMAS L. WHIGHAM

TZENDAL REBELLION, a major Indian revolt among the Tzeltal, Tzotzil, and Chol Indians of the highlands of Chiapas (1712–1713). Opinions vary as to the causes of the revolt, but most versions agree that the period after 1690, and especially 1700, had been one marked by economic crises, epidemics, and locust plagues in the province. The Indian population was at its demographic nadir, Spanish tribute and labor demands were on the increase, a rapacious generation of civil and clerical leaders was in control in San Cristóbal, the provincial capital, and, under the pressure, divisions began to appear in Indian village society as lesser elites showed discontent not only with their worsened circumstances but also with their own leadership, whom they accused of being unable to defend them.

In the 1690s the *alcaldes mayores* of Chiapas were charged with assessing and collecting the tribute, a task they turned into a monopolistic personal enterprise. To this must be added the activities of Bishop Juan Bauptista Álvarez de Toledo, who set about financing an aggressive program of monumental building in San Cristóbal with a series of money-collecting *visitas* to the countryside.

In 1708 the Chiapan highlands were stirred by the first of a series of Indian cults which the Spanish clergy condemned as heretical. A messianic hermit also disturbed the peace until he was seized and exiled to Mexico. In June 1712 the Virgin Mary appeared to a young girl in Cancuc, and, within weeks, the village had defied attempts to destroy the cult and had summoned over twenty Indian villages to rise up and expel the Spaniards.

Spanish, *pardo,* and loyal Indian militias were unable to contain the revolt, but relief arrived from two sources. From Guatemala came an army led by Governor and Captain-General Toribio de COSSÍO. Another column led by the local *alcalde mayor* advanced from Campeche.

After a series of battles Cancuc was taken and mopping-up operations pacified the other villages. During their brief independence the Cancuc leaders, helped by Sebastián Gómez de la Gloria, an Indian from San Pedro Chenalhó, attempted to establish legitimacy, set up a government, and ordain a new native clergy. The Spanish authorities were seriously alarmed by this, and the defeat of the revolt was so thorough that it left the province devastated and in deeper poverty.

ROBERT WASSERSTROM, "Ethnic Violence and Indigenous Protest: The Tzeltal (Maya) Rebellion of 1712," in *Journal of Latin American Studies* 12 (1980): 1–19; VICTORIA R. BRICKER, *The Indian Christ, the Indian King: The Historical Substrate of Maya Myth and Ritual* (1981), pp. 55–69; KEVIN M. GOSNER, *Soldiers of the Virgin: An Ethnohistorical Analysis of the Tzeltal Revolt of 1712* (1992).

MURDO J. MACLEOD

TZ'UTUJIL (or Zutuhil), a Maya group that lives today in the western Guatemalan highlands in an area south, west, and northwest of Lake Atitlán. Tz'utujil, one of the Quichean Maya languages closely related to Kaqchikel, is spoken by approximately 50,000 people today.

In the Late Postclassic period the Tz'utujil capital was at Chiya' (or Chiaa or Chuitinamit), the ruins of which lie across the bay from Santiago Atitlán. During much of the Late Postclassic period the Tz'utujils were subordinate to the K'ICHE'. They gained independence in the late fifteenth century, but hostilities among the Tz'utujil, K'iche' and KAQCHIKEL resulted in the loss of Tz'utujil territory to both groups.

The Tz'utujils fell under Spanish control in 1525, and by the mid-sixteenth century a new Tz'utujil capital had been established at Santiago Atitlán. Today Santiago Atitlán is the largest and most important Tz'utujil community.

FELIX W. MC BRYDE, *Cultural and Historical Geography of Southwest Guatemala* (1947); SANDRA ORELLANA, *The Tz'utujil Mayas* (1984).

JANINE GASCO

UAXACTUN, a Formative and Classic period MAYA site in northern Petén, Guatemala. It is located between TIKAL and EL MIRADOR, 25 miles north of Tikal, its largest neighbor. Uaxactun, situated between the watersheds for the Gulf of Mexico and those for the Caribbean, participated in the cross-peninsular trade routes. Investigations during the 1930s by the Carnegie Institution of Washington used the relationships between architecture, ceramics, and carved dated inscriptions to establish the first detailed chronology of the Maya area.

The earliest dated inscription is 8.14.10.13.15 (about A.D. 328) from Stela 9; the latest is 10.3.0.0.0 (A.D. 889) on Stela 12. Uaxactun (eight stone) is a modern name based on the cycle-eight date of Stela 9. Although it may have initially been under the sway of El Mirador, in A.D. 358 (8.16.1.0.12) Uaxactun first shows the Tikal emblem glyph (on Stela 5), indicating that by this time it was likely under the control of Tikal.

Excavation of Structure E-VII by removal of rubble from a badly destroyed Classic pyramid uncovered a Late Formative truncated pyramid with stairways on four sides and a complete covering of molded stucco, including large masks beside the stairs. This important structure also formed the western element and viewpoint for a plaza with three carefully aligned pyramids along its eastern edge. Sunrise sightings from the eastern stairway of structure E-VII to one of the three structures on the eastern edge of the plaza permitted accurate determination of the solstices and equinoxes. This initial revelation led to further discoveries of astronomically aligned structures throughout the Maya area.

The site consists of major structures along low ridges surrounded by a dense concentration of house mounds. This concentration indicates that farming methods more intensive than slash-and-burn agriculture were practiced in the area.

SYLVANUS G. MORLEY and GEORGE W. BRAINERD, *The Ancient Maya,* 4th ed. (1983), pp. 293–296; LINDA SCHELE and DAVID FREIDEL, *A Forest of Kings* (1990), esp. pp. 136–164.

WALTER R. T. WITSCHEY

UBICO Y CASTAÑEDA, JORGE (*b.* 10 November 1878; *d.* 14 June 1946), military figure and president of Guatemala (1931–1944). Born in Guatemala City, Ubico was educated at schools in the United States before entering the military academy in Guatemala (1894), where he remained for three years. He entered the military in 1897, and fought in the border war with El Salvador in 1906, attaining the rank of colonel by the age of twenty-eight.

Jorge Ubico y Castañeda, ca. 1939. UPI / BETTMANN.

Ubico served as governor of two states, and, beginning in 1922, as minister of war under President José María ORELLANA until 1926. The regime of General Ubico remains controversial in spite of considerable economic accomplishments, due to his repressive methods and the popularity of the 1944 revolution that overthrew his regime. Coming to power as president by unanimous election during the turbulent years of the Great Depression, Ubico promoted economic stabilization through frugal policies that restricted government spending while imposing law and order through a restrictive and harsh security apparatus.

Ubico's primary legacy to his nation was the establishment of a systematic infrastructure network, which constituted the basis of the modern Guatemalan economy. By constructing the nation's first highway and telegraph networks, he brought about national unity by linking previously remote parts of the republic with the central core. Ubico considered the Petén highway his greatest accomplishment. Though never quite reaching that distant frontier region, this highway extended the first links from the capital into the northern highlands and the Verapaz region in central Guatemala. The caudillo left the nation with 6,330 miles of road, almost five times the amount that existed when he assumed office. Most were dirt roads constructed by hand.

Ubico's extensive public-works projects included the first paved streets in Guatemala City, the capital, with accompanying sewers, and facilities to house government offices. Construction during his tenure included virtually all the ministry buildings, the National Palace,

the Presidential Palace, the legislative building, the Supreme Court building, the post office, and the telegraph office. His efforts extended to a sports stadium, racetrack, public bandstands and parks, public bathhouses, and an aqueduct to bring fresh water to the capital.

Significantly, Ubico's program extended into the nation's smaller cities and remote hamlets. The effort provided virtually all provincial capitals with government buildings, telegraph offices, and military barracks, while extending limited water and electricity service into small towns throughout the nation, following the newly built roads. This marked a clear departure from practices of previous central governments. As a result, the regime and the caudillo enjoyed considerable popularity in the countryside. Construction, however, was done primarily by hand by poorly paid laborers. These efforts promoted economic revival and expansion, while serving to facilitate control from the capital.

Ubico directed a *personalista* regime in which all government actions required his personal approval and all officials took their orders directly from the chief executive. Those in remote regions received authorizations via telegraph. Military officers held key government positions, and his Progressive Party controlled all aspects of government and the legislature, conducting two plebiscites that reelected Ubico without opposition.

Ubico's regime used harsh methods to maintain internal order. Security forces kept a watchful eye on the populace, and political opposition was ruthlessly suppressed. The government controlled the only radio stations and carefully monitored the press. The only facilities to receive external news reports were housed in the National Palace.

Ubico sought to revive agriculture by promoting the cultivation of unused land and to integrate the Indians into the mainstream of the national economy by drawing them from subsistence agriculture into commercial farming. The Vagrancy Law of 1934 abolished debt peonage and substituted a labor obligation to the state, under which all citizens who did not cultivate their own plot of land of a minimum size were considered vagrant unless they were employed for a minimum of 150 days per year. While this constituted the first change in the rural labor system since colonial days, the requirement was long enough to supply labor for the harvesting and planting of export crops. Ubico sought to promote crop diversification, and the highway system enabled an expansion in food production by opening new areas to cultivation and linking once remote regions to the national market.

Ubico sought to promote Guatemalan dominance in Central America, conducting a diplomatic rivalry with his counterpart in El Salvador and seeking to reassert Guatemalan claims to British Honduras (Belize). Ubico maneuvered carefully to influence domestic politics in Nicaragua and Honduras. While his efforts were initially directed toward promoting the rise of the Liberal Party in neighboring nations, he later sought to promote stability in the isthmus through rapprochement with the incumbent regimes of the other Central American countries. Although this was a time-honored policy, it produced rumors of a so-called DICTATORS LEAGUE during the late 1930s and early 1940s. The Belize question also resulted in an acrimonious and protracted dispute with Great Britain.

The advent of World War II proved particularly trying, given the importance of the large German community that constituted a significant part of the Guatemalan economy. Until the mid-1930s most Guatemalan coffee was sold on the Hamburg market. Though attracted by German investment and the strong centrist policies of national socialism, Ubico remained a staunch nationalist, rejecting outside influence. Ubico supported the United States as soon as it became involved in World War II, despite his dispute with England regarding Belize, and he supplied agricultural products, such as QUININE, to the United States to offset the loss of Asian sources.

The Ubico regime was overthrown in 1944 by a revolt led by students, junior military officers, and disgruntled members of the urban middle class who felt his policies favored the landowners. Ubico went into exile to the United States, where he died.

The most comprehensive, documented account is KENNETH J. GRIEB, *Guatemalan Caudillo: The Regime of Jorge Ubico, Guatemala, 1931–1944* (1979). For a contemporary view see CHESTER LLOYD JONES, *Guatemala: Past and Present* (1940). A hostile "inside" account by a former official and later opponent can be found in Carlos Samayoa Chinchilla, *El dictador y yo* (1967). Numerous official government and party publications provide listings of the regime's public-works construction efforts. See also KENNETH J. GRIEB, "The Guatemalan Military and the Revolution of 1944," *The Americas* 32, no. 4 (1976): 524–543.

KENNETH J. GRIEB

UGARTE, MANUEL (*b.* 1878; *d.* 2 December 1951), Argentine diplomat and writer. Born in Buenos Aires, Ugarte as a young man joined the Socialist Party. A prolific writer, he founded the daily *La Patria* and the review *Vida de Hoy* and became a prominent member of progressive literary and journalistic circles in the capital. A passionate anti-imperialist and pan-Hispanist, Ugarte served during Juan D. PERÓN's first presidency as Argentine ambassador to Mexico (1946–1948), Nicaragua (1949), and Cuba (1950). He formulated Pan-Hispanism in opposition to U.S.-backed Pan-Americanism. His diplomatic career was cut short by failing health, however. He died in Nice, France, in 1951, and three years later was buried in La Recoleta cemetery in Buenos Aires. His writings include travel books (*Visiones de España*, 1904), novels (*La venganza del capataz,* 1925), short stories, poems, and political essays (*El porvenir de la América latina*, 1911; *El destino de un continente*, 1923; and *La nación latinoamericana*, 1978).

BENJAMÍN CARRIÓN, *Las creadores de la nueva América . . . Manuel Ugarte . . .* (1928); NORBERTO GALASSO, *Manuel Ugarte*, 2 vols. (1974); BENITO MARIANETTI, *Manuel Ugarte: Un precursor en la lucha emancipadora de América Latina* (1976); RICUARTE SOLER, *Cuatro ensayos de historia: Sobre Panamá y nuestra América* (1983); ALBERTO GUERBEROF, *Izquierda colonial y socialismo criollo* (1985); MARÍA DE LAS NIEVES PINILLOS, *Manuel Ugarte: Biografía, selección de textos y bibliografía* (1989).

RONALD C. NEWTON

UGARTE, MARCELINO (*b.* 1860; *d.* 1929), Argentine provincial politician, one of the last of the old-regime potentates. A product of the Colegio Nacional and the law faculty of the University of Buenos Aires (from which he did not graduate), Ugarte entered Buenos Aires provincial politics in 1888 and rose to governor in 1902. His administration founded schools, built canals and railroads, opened farmlands in the south of the province, and reduced the public debt. In 1913, in the aftermath of the passage of the SÁENZ PEÑA LAW, he became a national senator. His power declined with the growth of Radical strength, however, and he resigned in 1914 to reclaim the provincial governorship. In 1916, balked by political opponents and at odds with President Hipólito YRIGOYEN, he withdrew to private life—a withdrawal hastened by Yrigoyen's intervention in the provincial government.

RONALD C. NEWTON

ULATE BLANCO, OTILIO (*b.* 25 August 1891; *d.* 27 October 1973), president of Costa Rica (1949–1953) and founder of the National Union Party (PUN).

Otilio Ulate Blanco came early to an exciting and sometimes turbulent life of journalism and politics when he left high school at age seventeen following his father's premature death. He worked for and invested in a number of daily newspapers until he became the owner and publisher of the premier Costa Rican newspaper *El Diario de Costa Rica*. He was the founder of *La Hora*.

His long involvement in political affairs came to dominate his life from the time he was chosen (1947) as the presidential candidate of the united opposition parties (made up of the National Unification Party, the Democratic Party, and the Social Democratic Party) to oppose the progovernment candidate, former president Rafael Ángel CALDERÓN GUARDIA (1940–1944). The government's effort to deny Ulate's victory in the 1948 election served as the catalyst for revolution. Ulate was inaugurated in 1949 following eighteen months of de facto government by the Junta Fundadora de la Segunda República headed by José FIGUERES FERRER.

Ulate's administration emphasized fiscal restraint and pacification. He ran unsuccessfully in the presidential election of 1962. In 1965 Ulate allied the PUN with Calderón Guardia's National Republican Party to support what was to be the successful candidacy of José Joaquín TREJOS FERNÁNDEZ (1966–1970).

Although its main subject is Ferrer Figueres, CHARLES D. AMERINGER'S, *Don Pepe* (1978), has much material on Ulate because their political paths crossed on many occasions. OLGA MARTA ULATE, *A la luz de la moral política* (1976), is a collection of writings by and about Otilio Ulate. JOHN PATRICK BELL, *Crisis in Costa Rica* (1971), covers Ulate's prominent political role between 1940 and 1949.

JOHN PATRICK BELL

See also **Costa Rica: Political Parties.**

ULLOA, ANTONIO DE (*b.* 12 January 1716; *d.* 5 July 1795), naval officer, scientist, and royal bureaucrat. Born in Seville, Antonio de Ulloa was educated in his native city and subsequently, like his compatriot Jorge JUAN Y SANTACILIA, at the new Spanish naval academy (Guardia Marina) in Cádiz. In 1734, at eighteen, Ulloa was chosen to accompany Juan and the French expedition going to the Indies to measure the exact length of a degree on the equator. Ulloa spent the next ten years (1735–1744) in South America, first assisting Charles Marie de la Condamine at some thirty-five different locations near Quito, then in Lima advising the viceroy on shoring up the coastal defenses of Peru. The two officers finally left for Spain in October 1744 on separate ships, but not before returning to Quito to make new observations with their own instruments. Reunited in Spain in 1746, Ulloa and Juan wrote *Relación histórica del viaje a la America Meridiónal* (Historical Report on the Voyage to America), a four-volume descriptive account of the various places they had visited in the Indies. They also wrote for crown officials a secret report exposing corruption, inefficiency, fraud, and abuses in the Indies that was published later in England in 1826 as an anti-Spanish tract entitled *Noticias secretas de America* (Secret Information on America).

Ulloa remained in the royal service for the next forty-five years. In the early 1750s he traveled about Europe garnering information on road and canal building and dredging harbors, and seeking to attract skilled artisans to migrate to Spain. In 1757 he assumed the governorship of the mercury mine at HUANCAVELICA in Peru. Although he disliked that post intensely, he increased mercury production a bit, reduced the debt of the mine by 200,000 pesos to 77,000 pesos and exposed fraud in the royal treasuries of Peru, which led to a falling out with Viceroy Manuel de AMAT Y JUNIENT in Lima. Leaving Peru in 1764 to return to Spain, Ulloa found himself sidetracked in Havana by a royal order to go to Spanish LOUISIANA as governor. His tenure in New Orleans from March 1766 until his forced flight on 1 November 1768 was as stormy as his time in Huancavelica, as he once again proved an unpopular, irascible administrator, especially with the French residents.

Back in Spain, Ulloa returned to Cádiz to teach and do research, his true forté.

CHARLES III called him back into the royal service—in the 1770s as a naval commander and in the 1780s as chief of Spanish naval operations—but Ulloa was always more content engaged in experiments in science or applied science: astronomy, navigation, bookbinding, metallurgy, printing inks, engraving, electricity and magnetism, surgical techniques, weaving, and agriculture. A representative figure of the Spanish ENLIGHTENMENT, Ulloa remained intellectually vigorous until his death in 1795, the same year he published the most up-to-date guide in Europe on the latest navigational techniques.

JOHN J. TE PASKE, ed. and trans., *Discourse and Political Reflections on the Kingdoms of Peru . . .* (1978).

JOHN JAY TePASKE

UMAÑA BERNAL, JOSÉ (*b.* 18 December 1899; *d.* 1 August 1982), Colombian poet and politician. A member of the Los Nuevos generation, Umaña studied with the Jesuits and attended law school at the National University. A multifaceted man, he was a professional reporter, collaborating on newspapers and journals. As a man of the theater, he wrote the prize-winning play *El buen amor* (1927) and directed Bogotá's Municipal Theater in the 1930s. As a politician, he served in parliament, became Colombia's consul to Chile (1927), and traveled throughout Europe, the United States, and Latin America. As a poet, Umaña was rooted in Parnassian and Symbolist esthetics. True to his heritage, he maintained an intellectual approach to poetry, adhering to formal precision, musicality, and purity of language. After translating Rainer Maria Rilke's works, his own earlier emphasis on love and sadness became tinged with introspection and concern for his own death. His best poetry collections are: *Décimas de luz y yelo* (1942), *Poesía 1918–1945* (1951), and *Diario de Estoril* (1948).

Diccionario de la literatura latinoamericana: Colombia (1959); LUIS MARÍA SÁNCHEZ LÓPEZ, *Diccionario de escritores colombianos* (1978); FERNANDO CHARRY LARA, *Poesía y poetas colombianos* (1985).

MARÍA A. SALGADO

UMBANDA, a spirit-possession religion practiced by millions of Brazilians, primarily in urban areas. It emerged in the 1920s and 1930s when Brazil was experiencing a measure of political and economic integration at the national level. Umbanda's widespread popularity can be attributed to its focus on helping people deal with a great variety of personal problems and illnesses. Its syncretized cultural elements from Africa, Europe, and precolonial Indo-Brazil also make it attractive.

Umbandists typically hold public spiritist sessions in religious centers located in middle-class and working-class districts twice each week. Inside the Umbanda center are two major areas. Those who have come for spiritual assistance sit in the rear half, with women on one side and men on the other. The front half is devoted to ritual activities and includes an altar covered by a white lace-edged drape. Flowers, a glass of water to draw off evil spiritual fluids from the surroundings, and numerous images of Catholic saints, Old Blacks (spirits of African Brazilians), Caboclos (spirits of Brazilian Indians), and other Brazilian folkloric characters are found on the altar.

The service begins by recognizing Exú, with a special request that this potentially dangerous spirit not disrupt the evening's proceedings. The Umbanda leader, known as "Mother" or "Father," or an assistant, carries a censer filled with burning incense to all parts of the Umbanda center. Individuals use their hands to pull the smoke to their bodies for purification. In the front half of the center, the spirit mediums dressed in white clothing dance in a counterclockwise direction to the polyrhythmic beat of two or three West African drums and other percussion instruments. Using a call-and-response pattern, the leader and mediums acknowledge and praise important deities and spirits of the dead through song. Members of the congregation join in the singing. The leader may offer a brief talk on the importance of charity and of the spiritual works to be performed later that evening. Usually an assistant takes an offering.

Drumming and singing become more intense as spir-

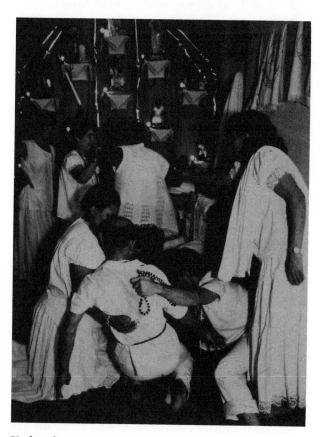

Umbanda ceremony. PULSAR IMAGENS E EDITORA / JUCA MARTINS.

its of the dead begin to possess the mediums, who by this time are frequently in a light state of trance. As possession occurs, the smiling expression of the mediums is transformed into the stern countenance of the Caboclo spirits or into the face of the aged and calm Old Black spirits. Individuals move forward for a consultation about family or job-related difficulties with one of the possessing spirits. Some say they are feeling nervous, tense, or depressed. Others have headaches. The spirits offer practical advice and recommend magical assistance, such as burning a candle to influence a particular spirit. Before returning to a seat in the rear, an individual may be turned around numerous times. Also, the spirit passes the medium's hands over the client's body. Both of these acts help remove the evil spiritual fluids said to be causing the client's personal problems.

Umbanda's activities apparently serve a variety of functions. Camargo argues that Umbanda has a therapeutic function and helps individuals to integrate into urban society. Brown focuses on Umbanda patron-client relations as part of the larger Brazilian political patronage system and notes that Umbandists have elected state deputies from Rio de Janeiro and Pôrto Alegre. Prust regards Umbanda as a place where social networking occurs within a hierarchical social structure in a patron-client relationship. The spirit world is merely an extension of the social hierarchy of the material world and is used to meet one's personal needs. Lerch, taking into account the fact that the majority of Umbanda mediums are women, views Umbanda mediumship as giving women an opportunity to participate with power and authority in the public domain. Superior religious knowledge combined with a medium's personal communication network enables her to distribute material goods, food, and jobs from one client to another according to availability and need.

Da Matta views Umbanda as compensating daily social and political frustrations of the poor by providing opportunities for role reversal, in which a poor individual may act as a spirit medium advising and curing the wealthy. Pressel recognizes the therapeutic and integrative roles of Umbanda and characterizes it as a type of "national folk religion" that helps provide a national identity for some. This identity stems from a mélange of Central African spirits, West African Yoruba deities, Catholic saints, Caboclos, and Old Blacks. Other ethnic and regional characters relating to specific areas of Brazil have been added as Umbanda has spread into more remote parts of the country.

CÂNDIDO PROCÓPIO DE FERREIRA DE CAMARGO, Kardecismo e Umbanda: Uma interpretação sociológica (1961); ESTHER PRESSEL, "Umbanda Trance and Possession in São Paulo, Brazil," in Felicitas D. Goodman, et al., eds., Trance, Healing, and Hallucination (1974), pp. 113–225; PATRICIA B. LERCH, "Spirit Mediums in Umbanda Evangelizada of Porto Alegre, Brazil: Dimensions of Power and Authority," in A World of Women, edited by Erika Bourguignon (1980), pp. 129–159: ROBERTO DA MATTA, "The

Ethnic of Umbanda and the Spirit of Messianism: Reflections on the Brazilian Model," in *Authoritarian Capitalism,* edited by Thomas Bruneau and Philippe Faucher (1981), pp. 239–264; RUSSELL R. PRUST, *Brazilian Umbanda: An Urban Resource Distributional System* (1985); DIANA DE GROAT BROWN, *Umbanda: Religion and Politics in Urban Brazil* (1986).

ESTHER J. PRESSEL

See also **African Brazilian Religions; Syncretism.**

UNANUE, HIPÓLITO (*b.* 13 August 1755; *d.* 15 July 1833), Peruvian physician, academician, and author. Unanue was born in Arica, Peru. He studied medicine at the University of San Marcos and became a doctor in 1786. In 1789 he won the chair of anatomy at San Marcos, initiating a long and illustrious academic career there.

Unanue first achieved recognition as a principal author for the MERCURIO PERUANO, the voice of enlightened Peruvians in the early 1790s. His international reputation, however, rested on *Observaciones sobre el clima de Lima* (1806; revised 1815), in which he outlined and documented his theory that climate was primarily responsible for disease.

Unanue brought eighteenth-century medicine to Peru. Through his efforts, Lima secured first an anatomical amphitheater (1792) and then the San Fernando College of Medicine and Surgery, which began functioning in 1811.

With the coming of independence, Unanue served briefly as a government minister. He died amid the instability of early Republican Peru, his contributions to Peruvian intellectual life largely forgotten.

JOHN E. WOODHAM, "The Influence of Hipólito Unanue on Peruvian Medical Science, 1789–1830: A Reappraisal," in *Hispanic American Historical Review* 50, no. 4 (November 1970): 693–714, and "Hipólito Unanue and the Enlightenment in Peru" (Ph.D. diss., Duke University, 1964).

MARK A. BURKHOLDER

See also **Medicine.**

UNGO, GUILLERMO MANUEL (*b.* 1931; *d.* 28 February 1991), leader of the Democratic Revolutionary Front (FDR) of El Salvador. Son of Guillermo Ungo, the founder of the Christian Democratic Party of El Salvador (PDC), Ungo taught law at the University of Central America (UCA). In 1964 he helped found the National Revolutionary Movement (MNR), which, with the proscription of the left-leaning PAR (Party of Renovating Action) in 1967, became the major social democratic party in the nation. He was chosen by José Napoleón DUARTE to be his vice-presidential running mate when the United National Opposition (UNO) coalition was formed to contest the 1972 presidential elections. After the fraudulent defeat of UNO and the exile

of Duarte by the military in 1972, Ungo remained in the country as head of the MNR and as a law professor at UCA.

With the overthrow of President Carlos Humberto ROMERO on 15 October 1979, Ungo became a member of the First Junta of the Revolution. However, when he resigned in January 1980 because of the junta's inability to control the army, the government collapsed. In 1980 Ungo brought the MNR into the newly formed Democratic Revolutionary Front (FDR) and became its president after the murder of its six leaders on 28 November 1980. When the FDR and the guerrilla alliance, the Farabundo Martí National Liberation Front (FMLN), joined forces in October 1980, Ungo and the other members of the Diplomatic-Political Commission (the civilian leadership of the FDR-FMLN, headquartered in Mexico City) were forced to live in exile. Living alternately in Mexico City and Panama City, Ungo became the major spokesman for the democratic forces supporting the guerrilla insurgency.

Ungo took advantage of the political opening afforded by the plan for settling the insurgency wars in Central America proposed by President Oscar ARIAS SÁNCHEZ of Costa Rica in February 1987 (known as the Arias peace plan) and returned to El Salvador in late 1987 to help found the Democratic Convergence, a coalition of the MNR, the Popular Social Christian Movement (MPSC), and the Social Democratic Party (PSD). He ran as its presidential candidate in the elections of 1989, and received a surprisingly low 3.9 percent of the vote.

ROBERT ARMSTRONG and JANET SHENK, "El Salvador: A Revolution Brews," in *NACLA Report on the Americas* (July–August 1980); JAMES DUNKERLEY, *The Long War: Dictatorship and Revolution in El Salvador* (1982); HILARY MACKENZIE, "Q&A: Guillermo Ungo—Return of an Exile," in *MacLean's,* 4 January 1988, 6–8; PATRICK LACEFIELD, "El Salvador: No Peace in Sight," in *Dissent* (Spring 1990): 154–156.

ROLAND H. EBEL

UNI. *See* **Brazil: Organizations: Union and Indigenous Nations.**

UNICATO, a term that generally refers to Argentine regimes from 1874 to 1916. Specifically, *unicato* denotes the corrupt, one-party system exercised by the Partido Autonomista Nacional with centralized power directed by President Miguel JUÁREZ CELMAN from 1886 to 1890.

Nicolás AVELLANEDA had introduced this practice, and Julio Argentino ROCA maintained it. Under Juárez Celman, the term came into common use because he made it clear that the president should control the government as well as the party. *Unicato* thus referred to one-man rule during Juárez Celman's authoritarian regime. Juárez Celman established the *unicato* because he relied particularly upon Córdoba land speculators who sought quick results. Mortgage bankers, eager for money but lacking adequate reserves, issued *cédula* land bonds. Juárez Celman encouraged many provinces to set up their own banks and to contract foreign loans. With external credit, the banks enriched *unicato* supporters of provincial governments. During the 1890 congressional sessions, Juárez Celman provided 3.9 million pesos for his provincial allies. He never restored the gold standard after Roca suspended it in 1885. Once new paper money issues tripled after 1886, the depreciation of the currency accelerated against the gold standard. The Bank of Córdoba was the most flagrant offender, securing political favors in exchange for loans that frequently were not paid back.

The term *unicato* also represents the unpopularity of the political system and its loss of legitimacy. The arbitrary techniques used to maintain its supporters in power became increasingly unacceptable when the financial and economic system deteriorated at the end of the 1880s. The *unicato* policy of maintaining the same authorities year after year was one of the causes of the 1890 revolt and the formation of the Union Cívica and its radical offshoot. The *unicato* tradition ended with the enactment of the Roque Sáenz Peña law of 1912, which established new voter rolls and introduced the secret ballot and a new system of voting.

JOHN HENRY WILLIAMS, *Argentine International Trade Under Inconvertible Paper Money, 1880–1916* (1920); EFRAÍN BISCHOFF, *Historia de Córdoba, cuatro siglos* (1977); DOUGLAS W. RICHMOND, *Carlos Pellegrini and the Crisis of the Argentine Elites, 1880–1916* (1989).

DOUGLAS W. RICHMOND

See also **Argentina: Political Parties.**

UNIÓN DE ARMAS, Spain's plan to tax its colonies in the Indies to finance Spain's war in seventeenth-century Europe during the reign of King Philip IV. The most ambitious of several taxation plans, it was championed by the king's *valido* (chief minister), the conde-duque de OLIVARES, in 1625. According to the plan, each province of the empire would contribute to the support of a common military reserve. Since the Indies could not easily provide manpower for imperial defense, in 1627 the crown assessed Peru 350,000 ducats and Mexico 250,000 ducats, payable annually from the viceregal treasuries for an initial period of fifteen years.

This plan, a thinly disguised attempt to integrate the fiscal institutions of the empire, prompted much opposition in the Indies. In Mexico the *cabildos* (town councils) of the realm debated the matter until 1632 before registering their reluctant approval. Opposition to the *unión de armas* was even stronger in Peru, where an acceptable compromise plan to raise the revenues—doubling the *alcabala* (sales tax) and the *avería* (fleet tax) and imposing a levy of two *reales* on each bottle of domestic wine—did not emerge until 1638. In the end,

crown revenues from the *unión de armas* raised substantial sums in the Indies but never approached the 600,000 ducats demanded annually by the crown.

The principal work on the *unión de armas* in Spain is J. H. ELLIOTT, *The Count-Duke of Olivares: The Statesman in an Age of Decline* (1986), pp. 244–277. For the Indies, see FRED BRONNER, ''La unión de armas en el Perú: Aspectos políticos-legales,'' in *Anuario de Estudios Americanos* 24 (1967): 1133–1176 and JONATHAN I. ISRAEL, *Race, Class, and Politics in Colonial Mexico, 1610–1670* (1975), pp. 178–180. For a discussion in the context of seventeenth-century fiscal reform see KENNETH J. ANDRIEN, *Crisis and Decline: The Viceroyalty of Peru in the Seventeenth Century* (1985), pp. 133–164.

KENNETH J. ANDRIEN

UNITARIO, an Argentine follower of centralist government during the early independence period. From the outset of independence, patriotic creoles split between federalist and centralist factions—the latter known as unitarists. The original centralist Constitution of 1819 failed to win the support of the littoral provinces, led by the caudillos of Santa Fe and Entre Ríos, whose combined forces invaded and occupied Buenos Aires in 1820, leaving the local populace terrified. Unitarists evolved out of the initial centralist factions, and sought to rebuild the country after the anarchy of 1820 and the loss of territory (Paraguay, Bolivia, and the Banda Oriental effectively split permanently from the United Provinces of the RÍO DE LA PLATA). Their leader was Bernardino RIVADAVIA, a mulatto follower of the doctrines of the English utilitarian Jeremy Bentham. Rivadavia returned from a diplomatic mission in 1821, and became minister of government and foreign affairs for the Buenos Aires governor, Martín Rodríguez. He immediately set about reforming the administration, culminating in the gathering of a constitutional convention in 1824. A draft of a centralizing constitution was presented in January 1825, and was approved a year later. In its wake, Rivadavia was elected the first president of the Republic. His legislation included land reform, the establishment of the Bank of the Province of Buenos Aires, the revamping of the fiscal machinery (and abolition of the hated Spanish tithes and consumer taxes), and securing diplomatic recognition. It was also an era of flourishing culture, with the proliferation of newspapers, theaters, and, perhaps most important, the creation of the University of Buenos Aires in 1821.

Buenos Aires, however, had clearly centralist ambitions, and some of these reforms were unpalatable to other provinces. The constitution was rejected by the provinces, an action stripping Rivadavia and his followers of claims to legitimacy. He was forced to resign on 7 July 1827, and left the region for good. Rivadavia was replaced as governor of the Province of Buenos Aires by Manuel DORREGO, a leader more attuned to the federalist cause. But the unitarists did not abandon their claims and, led by General Juan LAVALLE, sought to retake Buenos Aires by force of arms. They executed Dorrego on 3 December 1828 and renewed the civil war. Order finally came with Juan Manuel de ROSAS's seizure of power (1829–1852). Rosas relied on a hybrid administration combining policies of the unitarists and federalists.

SERGIO BAGÚ, *El plan económico del grupo rivadaviano (1811–1827)* (1966); DAVID BUSHNELL, *Reform and Reaction in the Platine Provinces, 1810–1852* (1983), esp. pp. 20–30.

JEREMY ADELMAN

UNITED FRUIT COMPANY, one of the first and largest multinational corporations in the Western Hemisphere. As the company has diversified production, the name has been changed to AMK, to United Brands, and, as of the early 1990s, Chiquita, Inc. Often called "The Octopus" by Central Americans, United, through its size and power, personified to many Latin Americans the economic imperialism of the United States.

Three men created United Fruit. Ship captain Lorenzo Dow BAKER in 1870 began supplementing his New England trade with bananas from Jamaica. With fruit importer Andrew W. Preston and a number of other partners, he formed the Boston Fruit Company in 1885. The third figure was Minor C. KEITH, who in the same period was building a railroad from Costa Rica's central valley to the Caribbean port of Limón. A heroic and deadly venture, the railroad needed cargo, and Keith began growing and marketing bananas on a large scale to provide the traffic. Most of the fruit went to New

Orleans; when his agent in that city failed, Keith turned to Preston for financial and sales help. The result, in 1899, was the linking of the three men in a New Jersey corporation they called the United Fruit Company; Preston was president and Keith, vice president.

With the formation of United, a haphazard, boom-or-bust operation was turned into a huge, highly efficient element of world trade. Baker's lone steamer was succeeded by the "Great White Fleet" of more than one hundred ships before 1910; Keith's holdings added more than one hundred miles of rail line to the corporation. A public stock subscription of about $11 million in 1900 permitted the acquisition of hundreds of thousands of acres of land throughout Latin America, only a fraction of which was cultivated at any one time.

United grew so fast that it usually absorbed competitors or helped them survive in order to ensure an adequate crop in times of widespread disease. (United even lent money to help STANDARD FRUIT build a railroad in Honduras.) But the banana grows readily, and soon Sam ZEMURRAY's CUYAMEL FRUIT COMPANY began to provide real competition. After a bitter land dispute that also involved the Honduras-Guatemala border, Zemurray sold out for $33 million in United stock. When the Great Depression sent the stock plummeting, Zemurray charged mismanagement, took over the Latin American operations, and restored the company's value.

In time the magnitude of the corporation brought serious troubles. It has often been a target for takeovers;

Tramming Bananas, Corocito Farm. Photo by Eric Steinfeldt. BENSON LATIN AMERICAN COLLECTION, UNIVERSITY OF TEXAS AT AUSTIN.

one president, Eli M. Black, committed suicide, probably because of revelations concerning company bribes of Honduran officials. The company is perhaps best known among Latin Americans for its part in the overthrow of Guatemalan President Jacobo ÁRBENZ in 1954. Árbenz had pushed through a land reform bill that particularly affected United Fruit because it was the nation's greatest landowner. But with the aid of the U.S. government, a rebel faction overthrew Árbenz, the reforms were wiped out, and United got its land back.

Through the years United lost much of its power. No longer is it a major landowner, because financing local growers and contracting for their fruit crop is much less risky economically and politically; specialists took over the cruise business; diversification has meant less reliance upon Latin America for the company's principal income; antitrust actions forced the sale of the Guatemala division to Del Monte, creating a second strong competitor (besides Standard Fruit) at United's expense; and unwillingness to invest heavily in research in the 1960s pushed United behind Standard in banana sales, even though United is still a much larger corporation overall.

CHARLES D. KEPNER, JR., and JAY H. SOOTHILL, *The Banana Empire* (1935); CHARLES MORROW WILSON, *Empire in Green and Gold* (1947); STACY MAY and GALO PLAZA, *The United Fruit Company in Latin America* (1958); WATT STEWART, *Keith and Costa Rica* (1964); THOMAS MC CANN, *An American Company: The Tragedy of United Fruit* (1976); RICHARD H. IMMERMAN, *The CIA in Guatemala* (1982); STEPHEN SCHLESINGER and STEPHEN KINZER, *Bitter Fruit: The Untold Story of the American Coup in Guatemala* (1982); PAUL J. DOSAL, *Doing Business with the Dictators: A Political History of United Fruit in Guatemala, 1899–1944* (1994).

THOMAS L. KARNES

See also **Banana Industry.**

UNITED NATIONS. At the founding conference of the United Nations, which was held in San Francisco in 1945, the Latin American states had two primary concerns: protecting their sovereignty as small powers and protecting the autonomy of their regional system, the INTER-AMERICAN SYSTEM. Since 1933, President Franklin D. Roosevelt's GOOD NEIGHBOR POLICY had facilitated the peaceful settlement of disputes in Latin America through its principle of nonintervention. After World War II, the Latin American states sought to ensure their continued autonomy in regional affairs by taking an active role from the outset in the formation and operation of the new world body that became the United Nations.

Proposals for the creation of the United Nations were first discussed at the Dumbarton Oaks Conference in Washington, D.C., in 1944. The Latin American states had resented their exclusion from this conference and distrusted the five major powers meeting there, who were known to favor the primacy of the international organization over regional bodies. Seeking to work out a united front for protecting their interests at the upcoming San Francisco Conference, representatives of the Latin American states met at the Inter-American Conference on Problems of War and Peace in Mexico City in February–March 1945. The resultant Act of Chapultepec put forward a Latin American pro-regional consensus in its provision calling for collective action against aggressors.

At the San Francisco Conference in April–June 1945, the twenty Latin American states, which constituted two-fifths of the fifty-one attending states, did indeed attain their objective of preserving the autonomy of their regional system. A prime mover in their success was Colombian foreign minister Alberto LLERAS CAMARGO, who chaired the relevant subcommittee. Another important subcommittee member was Senator Arthur Vandenberg, a member of the U.S. Senate Foreign Relations Committee. He was the author of the Vandenberg Amendment, an important provision for Latin America. It became UN Charter Article 51, which provided for the "inherent right of individual or collective self-defense" of states. Of special importance to Latin America was Chapter 8 of the UN Charter, particularly Article 52.1, which states that "nothing in the present Charter precludes the existence of regional arrangements or agencies for dealing with such matters relating to the maintenance of international peace and security as are appropriate for regional action," and Article 53.1, providing that a regional "enforcement action" required "the authorization" of the Security Council.

The unity and influence of the Latin American bloc at the San Francisco Conference worked in Latin America's favor with regard to representation in the UN. Two seats were assigned to Latin America among the six nonpermanent seats in the Security Council (the Big Five—England, France, China, the Soviet Union, and the United States—had permanent seats and the veto) and among the fifteen judges of the main judicial body of the United Nations, the International Court of Justice. The Economic and Social Council (ECOSOC), originally an eighteen-member body, had four seats designated for Latin America. Subsequent enlargements of the council resulted in increases for Latin America: in 1973, when membership reached fifty-four, the region garnered ten seats. The first Latin American UN secretary-general, Javier Pérez de Cuéllar of Peru, was selected over three decades after the founding of the organization, and served from 1982 to 1991.

During the Cold War, the primacy of the ORGANIZATION OF AMERICAN STATES over the United Nations (via Article 52 of the UN Charter) in regional disputes well served the security interests of the United States, which converted the OAS into an anti-Communist alliance against Cuba and the Dominican Republic. When the United States intervened militarily in the Dominican Republic in 1965 and won ex post facto OAS approval of an inter-American peace force to be sent there, some Latin American states turned to the United Nations, seeking its involvement to counter the United States. This event was significant in establishing the legitimacy of the United Nations, in the view of Latin America, as a neutral arbiter in regional disputes.

In the mid-1960s, the Latin American states joined other developing states in forming a caucusing group to bargain more effectively with the developed states on economic issues. They formed the Group of 77 (G-77), a name that referred to the number of developing states in the UN at the time, in order to present a united front before the first meeting of the UN Conference on Trade and Development (UNCTAD I), in Geneva, Switzerland, in 1964. UNCTAD became a permanent organ of the UN General Assembly. In 1974, the G-77 states were successful in passing a General Assembly resolution calling for a New International Economic Order (NIEO) to replace the existing system, which these states believed was dominated by the Western capitalist and former colonial powers. In late 1974, another resolution provided for the Economic Charter on the Rights and Duties of States (CERDS), first proposed by Mexican President Luis ECHEVERRÍA IN 1972.

In April 1982 Argentina attempted to reclaim the Falkland Islands, which the British had controlled since 1833. At the outset of the conflict, most Latin American states were critical of Argentina for violating the nonintervention principle and supported the efforts of the United States, which announced its neutrality, to settle the dispute by serving as a mediator. However, when the United States sided with England, its NATO ally, and maintained that the United Nations, not the OAS, was the proper forum for resolution of the dispute, the Latin American states turned against the United States and supported Argentina in the OAS.

In the 1980s, a major struggle developed between the United States and the Sandinista government of Nicaragua, which came to power after a Sandinista-led popular insurrection overthrew dictator Anastasio SOMOZA in July 1979. The United States resorted to intervention, first covert and then overt, by aiding the CONTRAS, Nicaraguan exiles operating out of neighboring Honduras. Fearing United States military intervention, four Latin American states—Colombia, Mexico, Panama, and Venezuela—formed the Contadora Group, which became the Contadora Process, an effort to negotiate a settlement. (The states involved in the process expanded to include Argentina, Brazil, Peru, and Uruguay in 1985; the Rio Group in 1987 included the eight states' foreign ministers in addition to the secretaries-general of the OAS and the UN.) In 1984, Nicaragua brought a case against the United States before the International Court of Justice (ICJ), accusing it of intervention. In 1986, the ICJ handed down a decision against the United States.

After negotiating a Central American accord, the Central American presidents requested that the UN oversee the accord's implementation. In 1989, the UN Security Council approved the creation of the UN Observer Group in Central America (ONUCA), which, jointly with an OAS body, disarmed the contras and escorted them from Honduras into Nicaragua. At the request of the Nicaraguan government, the UN created the UN Observer Group for the Verification of Elections in Nicaragua (ONUVEN) to oversee the March 1990 elections. In 1990, the UN Security Council approved the creation of the UN Observer Group for El Salvador (ONUSAL), which negotiated a settlement in the civil war in December 1991. The UN also negotiated a settlement in Guatemala between the government and a guerrilla movement in June 1994.

The role of the UN in Latin America with regard to peacemaking and peacekeeping is significant in that it marks a willingness on the part of the Latin American community to risk its autonomy in regional affairs in favor of international monitoring. Though ONUCA acted jointly with the OAS, ONUSAL acted alone, as did the group that achieved settlement in Guatemala in 1994. The UN has also institutionalized, since the 1980s, its election-observer role in Latin America, one that the region has welcomed. Thus, though its relations with the United Nations have been confrontational at times, in the 1990s Latin America had achieved a successful balance between regional autonomy and international cooperation.

JOHN A. HOUSTON, *Latin America in the United Nations* (1956), chaps. 1 and 2; J. LLOYD MECHAM, *The United States and Inter-American Security, 1889–1960* (1961), chaps. 9, 10, and 14; CHARLES G. FENWICK, *The Organization of American States: The Inter-American Regional System* (1963), chap. 12; SAMUEL G. INMAN, *Inter-American Conferences, 1826–1954: History and Problems* (1965), chap. 15; HAROLD E. DAVIS and LARMAN C. WILSON, *Latin American Foreign Policies: An Analysis* (1975), chap. 3; G. POPE ATKINS, *Latin America in the International Political System*, 2d rev. ed. (1989), chaps. 8 and 9; JACK CHILD, *The Central American Peace Process, 1983–1991: Sheathing Swords, Building Confidence* (1992).

LARMAN C. WILSON

See also **Falklands/Malvinas War; Nicaragua: Political Parties; Pan-American Conferences.**

UNITED PROVINCES OF CENTRAL AMERICA. *See* **Central America, United Provinces of.**

UNITED PROVINCES OF THE RÍO DE LA PLATA, an early designation (from 1811 at the latest) for what later became the Argentine Confederation and later still the Argentine Republic. The terminology was suggestive of the United States model and thus of a federative relationship among the provinces that had comprised the Spanish viceroyalty of the same name. In practice, tension between Federalist and Unitarist tendencies thwarted all attempts at formal constitutional organization until 1853, when an enduring Argentine constitution was adopted.

A congress of the United Provinces, meeting at Tucumán, issued Argentina's declaration of independence on 9 July 1816. It did so in the name of the United Provinces of South America, suggesting some doubt as to the precise geographic scope of the union. There were deputies at Tucumán from what is now Bolivia, which had been part of the viceroyalty, though none from Paraguay and Uruguay, which had also belonged to the viceroyalty and whose de facto separation was not yet recognized by Argentine authorities. For most purposes the United Provinces amounted to the territory of present-day Argentina, which alone came under the more or less effective control of the governments that ruled in succession from Buenos Aires following the original May Revolution of 1810.

TULIO HALPERÍN-DONGHI, *Politics, Economics, and Society in Argentina in the Revolutionary Period* (1975), translated by Richard Southern (1975); JOHN LYNCH, *The Spanish American Revolutions, 1808–1826*, 2d ed. (1986), chap. 2.

DAVID BUSHNELL

See also **Argentina: Movements** (for Federalists and Unitarists).

UNITED STATES–LATIN AMERICAN RELATIONS

encompass not only the political relationship between the United States and governments of the continent but also those political, economic, social, and cultural exchanges that often profoundly influence the conduct of diplomacy. Historically, political, economic, and security concerns have dominated U.S. policy toward Latin America. A parallel development has been the evolution of an inter-American system and its capstone institution, the ORGANIZATION OF AMERICAN STATES (OAS, 1948), largely dominated by the United States. In modern times, however, the relationship between the United States and Latin America has become more complicated. Thus, such diverse issues as immigration of Latin Americans into the United States, tourism, the role of U.S. companies in Latin America, and the spread of Protestant evangelicalism among Latin America's indigenous populations have indirectly impacted on the shaping of the "new hemisphere" and its prospects for democracy.

THE FORMATIVE ERA (1776–1830)
The United States won its independence with Spanish assistance, but relations with Spain were uneasy because of U.S.–Spanish conflict in the trans-Appalachian West and the lower Mississippi Valley. After 1803, when Louisiana became U.S. territory, U.S. pressure on Spanish FLORIDA escalated and set the general pattern of U.S. policy toward the Spanish–American WARS OF INDEPENDENCE after 1810.

President Thomas Jefferson (1801–1809) expressed doubts about Haitian independence in 1804, fearing that the antislave revolutionary contagion would spread to the United States. President James Madison (1809–1817) sent agents to several of the new revolutionary camps in

1810. In the War of 1812 (1812–1814), he exploited Spanish defensive weakness by encouraging private Americans to intrude into Spanish Florida. By 1813, U.S. forces had occupied Spanish Florida from the Perdido River to the Mississippi River, and in 1819 the United States acquired the entire Spanish province.

Though many Americans sympathized with the Spanish-American revolutionary struggles, strategic issues dictated a U.S. policy of official neutrality. Nonetheless, revolutionary agents operated in the United States and procured aid and weapons. After 1821 (when Mexico won its independence), U.S. policy, in part inspired by changes in British policy after the Napoleonic Wars (1803–1815), moved toward recognition of the new republics. Both perceived a threat of a Spanish reconquest. The United States began extending formal diplomatic recognition to the new republics, and in December 1823 (in response to a British proposal for a joint statement) President James Monroe (1817–1825) announced what became known as the MONROE DOCTRINE. Its most important principle declared U.S. opposition to further European territorial aggrandizement in Latin America. A second professed the U.S. hope in the future of republican, not monarchical, governments in Latin America (though the United States readily acknowledged the independence of imperial Brazil). The Monroe Doctrine established a unilateral policy. Under the leadership of Simón BOLÍVAR, several of the new republics crafted a defensive hemispheric structure (excluding all save Spain's former colonies) at the PANAMA CONGRESS of 1826, but only GRAN COLOMBIA ratified it.

THE NINETEENTH CENTURY
In the period 1830–1900, U.S. strategic and economic concerns gave priority to the promotion of commerce (especially in the Caribbean), interest in a transisthmian passage, and the "North Americanization" of the Monroe Doctrine in the 1840s. In the 1840s and 1850s, when dissident Cubans and U.S. SLAVE interests fostered revolution in Spanish Cuba, the U.S. government tried to purchase Cuba. The TEXAS REVOLUTION (1835–1836) and the annexation of Texas as a state in 1845, U.S. strategic and economic interests in California, and the vigorous U.S. commercial expansionism in the 1840s brought the MEXICAN WAR (1846–1848) and diplomatic confrontation with rival Great Britain in Central America. In 1846, in a treaty with New Granada (Colombia), the United States guaranteed transit rights across the Isthmus of Panama. In 1850 the United States and Great Britain signed the CLAYTON-BULWER TREATY, providing for a jointly constructed and controlled canal across the Isthmus of Panama. In the 1850s, U.S. attention turned to Nicaragua, where filibusters led by William WALKER (who had reintroduced slavery in Nicaragua) held power until ousted by Central American armies. Fears of U.S. territorial ambitions in Latin America prompted meetings of hemispheric states at Lima in 1847 and Santiago de Chile in 1856.

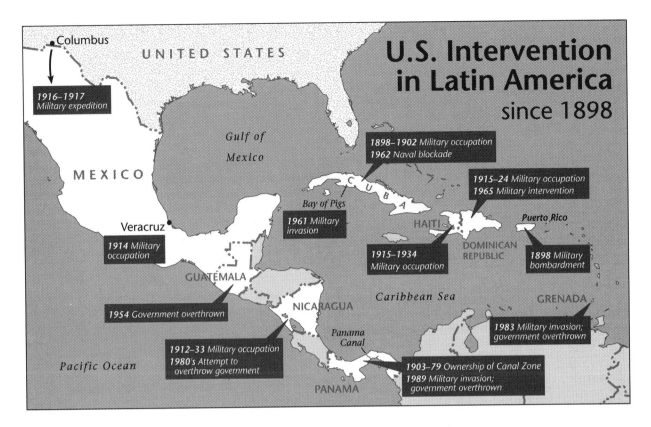

U.S. Intervention in Latin America since 1898

- Columbus — *1916–1917 Military expedition*
- UNITED STATES
- Gulf of Mexico
- MEXICO
- Veracruz — *1914 Military occupation*
- GUATEMALA — *1954 Government overthrown*
- NICARAGUA — *1912–33 Military occupation* / *1980's Attempt to overthrow government*
- Pacific Ocean
- PANAMA — *Panama Canal* / *1903–79 Ownership of Canal Zone* / *1989 Military invasion; government overthrown*
- CUBA — *1898–1902 Military occupation* / *1962 Naval blockade*
- Bay of Pigs — *1961 Military invasion*
- HAITI — *1915–1934 Military occupation*
- DOMINICAN REPUBLIC — *1915–24 Military occupation* / *1965 Military intervention*
- Puerto Rico — *1898 Military bombardment*
- Caribbean Sea
- GRENADA — *1983 Military invasion; government overthrown*

During the U.S. Civil War (1861–1865), the French empire of NAPOLEON III (supported by Mexican conservatives) imposed the monarch MAXIMILIAN in Mexico, precipitating a guerrilla war led by the ousted civilian leader, Benito JUÁREZ. The administration of Abraham Lincoln supported Juárez and after 1864 pressed the French to leave with threats of intervention. Juárez's forces brought down Maximilian's empire in 1867, and U.S. economic interests in Mexico—particularly MINING, ranching, and railroading—increased rapidly from the 1870s. Elsewhere, the United States tried to mediate the war between Cubans and Spaniards that raged from 1868 to 1878. Afterward, U.S. business interests expanded in Cuban SUGAR. The French commenced to dig a canal across Panama, and in 1885 a revolt in Panama prompted U.S. military intervention. In 1881, U.S. Secretary of State James G. BLAINE proposed a Pan-American conference to end the WAR OF THE PACIFIC (1879–1884), between Chile and the allies Bolivia and Peru, and to promote closer commercial ties. Blaine's efforts collapsed under Chilean opposition, but when he again became secretary of state (1889), he hosted such a conference in Washington, D.C.

In the 1890s, heightened U.S. economic and strategic interests brought confrontation with Chile, a war scare with Great Britain in 1895 during the Venezuela–British Guiana boundary dispute (during which Secretary of State Richard Olney boasted that the United States was "practically sovereign" in the Western Hemisphere), and culminated in the Spanish-American War (1898).

Most Americans believed that U.S. intervention was humanitarian, but it actually stemmed from economic and strategic concerns, to prevent the collapse of the Cuban sugar economy and to fulfill a historic U.S. quest to absorb Cuba as U.S. territory.

THE IMPERIAL ERA (1900–1933)

The U.S. victory over Spain in 1898 commenced a tremendous expansion of U.S. power and influence in Latin America, especially in the Caribbean. In 1902, U.S. forces departed Cuba but left in their wake an independent republic beholden to the United States and, by terms of the PLATT AMENDMENT, subject to U.S. intervention. U.S. interests in a canal across the Isthmus of Panama increased. When Nicaraguan leader José Santos ZELAYA refused to yield sovereign rights over a passage across Nicaragua, President Theodore ROOSEVELT (1901–1909), who favored the route across Panama, turned his attention to negotiation of a canal treaty with Colombia. The terms ran afoul of Colombian nationalist sentiment, and the U.S. government threw its support to a successful revolutionary movement by Panamanian dissidents and signed a canal treaty with Panama.

In the 1902–1903 Venezuelan debt crisis, in which Germany, Great Britain, and Italy blockaded the Venezuelan coast, Roosevelt voiced concern over European intervention in the hemisphere. He used the Venezuelan debt imbroglio as justification to meddle in the debt-plagued Dominican Republic and announced the ROOSEVELT COROLLARY to the Monroe Doctrine, where-

298

by the United States upheld the doctrine by intervening in Latin America to "prevent European intervention." Citing the persistent unrest in Cuba, Roosevelt dispatched an army to the island in October 1906. For three years, Americans ruled Cuba. In Central America, the United States supported the isthmian peace treaties of 1907, and Roosevelt's successor, William Howard Taft (1909–1913), pushed U.S. financial intrusion, known as DOLLAR DIPLOMACY, as the means of avoiding the use of troops. However, Taft dispatched a military force to Nicaragua in 1912.

President Woodrow WILSON (1913–1921) condemned "gunboat diplomacy" and dollar diplomacy as imperialism, but his determination to advance U.S. economic interests, preserve U.S. security interests in the face of German operations in the region, and especially to "teach" Latins to "elect good men" transformed him into the biggest interventionist of all U.S. leaders. Though pledging to seek no territorial concessions from Latin American republics, Wilson tried to influence the course of the MEXICAN REVOLUTION (1910–1917), dispatched an occupying force to Veracruz in April 1914, and, following the raid by revolutionary Pancho VILLA on Columbus, New Mexico, in 1916, sent the PERSHING EXPEDITION deep into northern Mexico. In 1915 the Wilson administration launched a nineteen-year de facto military occupation of Haiti, and in 1916 established an eight-year military governance of the Dominican Republic.

U.S. involvement in World War I brought an expansion of U.S. political, and especially economic, involvement throughout Latin America. Latin American intellectual and literary figures decried the North American cultural threat to Latin traditions. The United States emerged in the 1920s as the overwhelmingly dominant economic presence in Latin America and, relying on its economic strength, began to dismantle its empire in the Caribbean, send financial advisers to Latin America, and negotiate more positively with Mexico in PETRO-LEUM disputes brought on by the Mexican constitution of 1917. In late 1926, the United States commenced a large-scale intervention in Nicaragua against the guerrilla army of Augusto César SANDINO that lasted until 1933, when U.S. forces had been largely supplanted by the Nicaraguan national guard under Anastasio SOMOZA GARCÍA.

THE GOOD NEIGHBOR POLICY TO THE CUBAN REVOLUTION

In the 1930s, President Franklin D. ROOSEVELT (1933–1945) professed a new policy toward Latin America based on nonintervention, noninterference, and reciprocity. At the inter-American conference at Montevideo, Uruguay, in 1933, the Roosevelt administration pledged nonintervention, though at the time Roosevelt's emissary to revolutionary Cuba, Sumner WELLES, was effectively charting Cuba's internal political affairs. Roosevelt signed new economic agreements with Latin

American governments in an effort to restore U.S. trade in the hemisphere. After 1935, U.S. concerns over German economic and political influence in Latin America brought efforts to create a hemispheric defense agreement, partially achieved at Lima in 1938. There was a serious crisis with Mexico over that nation's expropriation of foreign petroleum companies in 1938.

From September 1939, when World War II broke out in Europe, the United States intensified its efforts to create an anti-Axis front in Latin America and to subordinate Latin America's U.S.-economies to the U.S. war effort. Though anti-American sentiment remained strong throughout Latin America, especially in Argentina and Mexico, U.S. policy was largely successful. The U.S. obtained defense sites, critical in Brazil, and virtually incorporated the Mexican economy into the U.S. war economy. Latin American rural workers, especially in Mexico, Central America, and the Caribbean, migrated to urban factories. Mexicans worked on U.S. farms, ran the railroads, labored in defense plants, and served in the U.S. military. U.S. economic and political pressures on Southern Cone nations, reluctant to jeopardize their neutrality, intensified, and by the end of the war even defiant Argentina had declared war on Germany. At the Chapúltepec meeting of March 1945, Latin

"The Yankee Peril." Cartoon by Mayol. Reproduced from Albert Shaw, *A Cartoon History of Roosevelt's Career* (New York, 1910).

America opted for a regional security arrangement, though the United States was already shifting to the global trajectory symbolized by the United Nations. The formal culmination of the regional approach was the Inter-American Treaty of Reciprocal Assistance (1947) and the Organization of American States (1948).

In the postwar era, the United States shifted its political and economic concerns to Europe and Asia, and tried to break down hemispheric economic barriers to U.S. exports and private investments. Latin American leaders pressed for increased U.S. public support and protection of their domestic markets, modeled on the U.S. Marshall Plan for war-torn Europe. After the Korean War erupted, the United States emphasized regional and bilateral security agreements and became increasingly concerned about Communist influence in Latin America. In 1954, the CENTRAL INTELLIGENCE AGENCY brought down a non-Communist leftist government in Guatemala; in 1959, following several years of civil strife and a protracted guerrilla struggle, Fidel CASTRO toppled the government of dictator Fulgencio BATISTA in Cuba.

THE CUBAN REVOLUTION TO THE PRESENT

Castro vowed to restructure Cuba along Marxist lines and to de-Americanize the island's political culture. The severity of revolutionary reforms brought a conflict with the United States (where anti-Castro Cubans had fled) culminating in the abortive BAY OF PIGS INVASION of April 1961, President John F. Kennedy's (1961–1963) first hemispheric crisis. U.S. opposition to the CUBAN REVOLUTION inevitably stunted the purpose of the ALLIANCE FOR PROGRESS, a vast and ambitous social and economic reform program commenced early in the decade. By the time of Kennedy's death in November 1963, U.S. security concerns were already overriding its commitments to "peaceful revolution" through democratic means in Latin America. When President Lyndon Johnson (1963–1969) dispatched 20,000 troops to the Dominican Republic in the spring of 1965, on the pretext that the rebellion there would create "another Cuba," Latin Americans were persuaded that Washington's commitment to social justice had dissolved.

But the Alliance for Progress fueled Latin America's economic modernization at the expense of democratic government and social justice for the poor, thus perpetuating the dual society of rich and poor. This was most evident in such countries as Mexico and Brazil, which enjoyed impressive economic growth from the 1950s but where social inequities were severe. By the 1970s, with the U.S. distracted by Vietnam, Latin America appeared to be veering back to authoritarian governments, in Brazil, Argentina, and (with the U.S.-supported coup against socialist Salvador ALLENDE) Chile. Latin American leaders increasingly supported a hemispheric economic agenda diverging from that of the United States and Panama's call for a new canal treaty. President Jimmy Carter (1977–1981) identified with the "North-South" as opposed to the "East-West" vision of Latin America's place in U.S. foreign policy. He signed a canal treaty with Panama, criticized violations of human rights in Latin America, and initially supported the SANDINISTA revolution that brought down Anastasio SOMOZA DEBAYLE in Nicaragua. By the end of his administration, many Americans believed that such reformist approaches to Latin America distracted from the real security risks the United States confronted in the region.

Following his resounding victory in the 1980 election, President Ronald Reagan (1981–1989) committed U.S. efforts to toppling the leftist Sandinista government of Nicaragua and supporting the rightist government of El Salvador in its war against Communist guerrillas. After initally following a neutral line, Reagan sided with the British against Argentina in the FALKLAND ISLANDS conflict of 1982, and in 1983 he dispatched the military to bring down the leftist government in Grenada. Such hard-line policies were accompanied by modest amounts of nonmilitary aid (the most publicized was the Caribbean Basin Initiative of 1983) and expressions of support for democracy and social justice in strife-torn Central America. The 1984 KISSINGER REPORT on the isthmian condition meshed reformist and strategic arguments.

By the late 1980s, it was clear that the U.S. efforts to mold Latin America in its own political and economic image had failed. The U.S.-backed CONTRA rebellion in Nicaragua collapsed under Latin American efforts for a negotiated settlement, and the United States joined Latin America as a debtor nation. Yet, mostly because of internal pressures, authoritarian governments succumbed to democratic regimes, and Latin America strengthened its economic ties with European and Asian nations. Americans increasingly turned to new "security" concerns, especially in regard to the large numbers of undocumented aliens (many from Latin America), a problem addressed in the 1986 Immigration Reform and Control Act, and the social crisis wrought by narcotics trafficking. President George Bush (1989–1993) commenced an ambiguous approach to Latin America. With the Christmas 1989 invasion of Panama, aimed at bringing down dictator Manuel NORIEGA, he revived charges of U.S. imperialism. His proposal for closer economic ties, especially free trade with Mexico, however, promised a new era in the long and often troubled relationship between the United States and Latin America.

The approval of the North American Free Trade Agreement (NAFTA) by the United States Congress in 1993, following a debate riddled with warnings about the loss of jobs to Mexico and loss of control on the U.S.-Mexican border, culminated an economic integration that took its basic character in World War II, when the United States incorporated not only Mexico but all Latin America into its economic system. At the same time, beliefs in hemispheric unity and cultural exchange deepened. Wartime unity proved fragile. North Americans and Latin Americans profoundly disagreed over everything from the role of the state in the economy and U.S. domination to the survival of democracy, human rights, and the cultural impact of intruding North Americans. A half-century later, those hopes and fears persist.

J. LLOYD MECHAM, *A Survey of United States–Latin American Relations* (1965); ALONSO AGUILAR MONTEVERDE, *Pan Americanism from Monroe to the Present: A View from the Other Side,* trans. by Asa Zatz (1969); GORDON CONNELL-SMITH, *The United States and Latin America: An Historical Analysis of Inter-American Relations* (1974); GRAHAM STUART and JAMES L. TIGNER, *Latin America and the United States* (1975); HAROLD E. DAVIS, JOHN J. FINIAN, and F. TAYLOR PECK, *Latin American Diplomatic History: An Introduction* (1977); COLE BLASIER, *The Hovering Giant: United States Response to Revolutionary Change in Latin America* (1985); ABRAHAM F. LOWENTHAL, *Partners in Conflict: The United States and Latin America* (1987); LESTER D. LANGLEY, *America and the Americas: The United States in the Western Hemisphere* (1989); RICHARD M. MORSE, *New World Soundings: Culture and Ideology in the Americas* (1989); DAVID SHAVIT, *The United States in Latin America: A Historical Dictionary* (1992).

LESTER D. LANGLEY

See also **Drugs and Drug Trade; Panama Canal Treaties.**

UNITED STATES—MEXICO BORDER. The U.S.—Mexico BORDERLANDS constitute the region where the United States and Latin America have interacted most intensely. The nature of that relationship involves conflict, accommodation, and interdependence.

THE BOUNDARY AND INTERNATIONAL CONFLICT
International borders are likely to be the scene of conflict due to such basic factors as vague territorial limits, unclear title to natural resources, ethnic rivalries, and restrictions placed on the movement of goods and people across the political line. Where frontier conditions exist, lawlessness is frequently a problem. In remote, sparsely populated areas, the restraints that govern residents of settled regions are at best weak. Underfinanced local governments struggle to exert their ineffective authority over wide expanses of territory. The international line itself represents a powerful escape valve for fugitives from the law. Bigots and racists tend to take advantage of prejudices that run strong in small communities. In short, at the outer edges of nations, oppressors and transgressors of all shades enjoy shields from punishment not available in the heartland. In the history of the U.S.–Mexico border, these and other problems have complicated the relations between the two countries, making life difficult for the area's residents during periods of heightened animosity.

The TEXAS rebellion (1836) and the MEXICAN–AMERICAN WAR (1846–1848) exemplified the border-focused conflict in the first half of the nineteenth century. Disorder and bloodshed continued after the demarcation of the new political line following the signing of the Treaty of GUADALUPE HIDALGO (1848) and the GADSDEN PURCHASE (1853).

One of the greatest sources of strife in the nineteenth century arose from recurring transboundary Indian raids. A provision in the Hidalgo Treaty bound the United States to prevent Indian incursions into Mexico. Unable or unwilling to carry out this requisite, the United States abrogated the stipulation in 1853 with the completion of the Gadsden Purchase. Nevertheless, an understanding remained that each country assumed responsibility for preventing indigenous tribes from using the respective national territories as springboards for transborder forays. As the depredations into the Mexican borderland settlements continued year after year, Mexico bitterly protested the alleged U.S. indifference to the problem.

Problems with slave hunters, smugglers, robbers, cattle thieves, and desperate characters of all shades further increased the tension between the two countries. The general lawlessness characteristic of many Americans living along the border led to violation of Mexico's territorial integrity, including repeated FILIBUSTERING expeditions into several northern states. Mexican border residents suffered plunder, pillage, and murder at the hands of desperadoes and adventurers. Among the many foreigners who sought to establish empires or colonies on Mexican soil, none is better known than William WALKER, whose invasion of Baja California and Sonora in 1853 was short-lived. The U.S. frontier, particularly in Texas, also endured depredations from criminal elements who used the Mexican borderlands as a base of operations. Cattle rustling and smuggling particularly disturbed Texans. Retaliatory raids fomented by Anglo mistreatment of Mexicans, such as Juan Nepomuceno Cortina's exploits in the Brownsville-Matamoros region in the 1850s, fanned racial hatred even more.

Each country accused the other of failing to suppress such disorders, and by the late 1870s relations became strained almost to the breaking point. With the advent of the railroads in the 1880s and the subsequent influx of more civilized elements and influences, however, marauding and raiding activities declined. During the next three decades the frontier experienced relative peace and order.

The MEXICAN REVOLUTION of 1910 introduced a new era of instability when Mexican bandits and revolutionaries raised havoc in the Texas and New Mexico borderlands. For a time, residents in the U.S. border states lived in fear that extremists from the neighboring country, aided by militant Mexican Americans, would attempt to retake lands lost by Mexico in the nineteenth century. The tensions of the decade occasioned several crossings of U.S. troops into Mexican territory, including the unsuccessful chase of Pancho VILLA by General John J. PERSHING in 1916–1917. War between the two countries seemed likely at mid-decade, but the crisis

abated as the violent phase of the Revolution waned and as the United States turned its attention to World War I. Thereafter confrontation over borderland violence ceased as a major diplomatic issue between the two nations.

Pinpointing the precise location of the border became a highly volatile problem in the first years of binational contact, and remained a sore point until very recently. Disagreement over whether the Rio Grande or the Nueces River constituted the actual boundary between Texas and Mexico became the immediate cause of the Mexican-American War. Acrimony continued over this issue because of the inexact identification of the new line of demarcation in the Treaty of Guadalupe Hidalgo. Errors in surveying caused the Mesilla Valley in present-day New Mexico to become a hotly disputed territory until Antonio López de Santa Anna gave in to U.S. pressure and sold the area as part of the GADSDEN PURCHASE in 1853. Changes in the course of the unpredictable and often violent Rio Grande have resulted in boundary disputes as well. The best known of such controversies began in Paso del Norte (now Ciudad Juárez, Chihuahua)/El Paso, Texas, in 1864, when the river suddenly turned southward, resulting in a section of Mexican land known as "EL CHAMIZAL" being annexed by the United States. Mexicans attempted for decades to regain the lost land through arbitration, escalating their efforts during the era of Porfirio Díaz, but the United States would not accept Mexico's claim to the Chamizal.

In 1911 the American government refused to abide by a decision favorable to Mexico rendered by the International Boundary Commission. After decades of stalemate, the two governments finally resolved the issue in 1963 by agreeing to terms essentially worked out in the 1911 arbitration. With the signing in 1970 of a treaty to resolve remaining and future boundary differences, the possibility of serious conflict over border delimitation diminished considerably.

Another problem that has caused bitter controversy pertains to the distribution and use of the water in the rivers that form part of the border region: the Rio Grande, the Colorado River, and the Tijuana River. A century of controversy began in the 1870s when irrigation development reached the U.S. borderlands. Decades of negotiation resulted in two treaties that established terms for the division of waters, one in 1906 and one in 1944. Yet both treaties contained serious flaws. The 1906 pact divided the water of the upper Rio Grande (from its source to Fort Quitman, Texas) but left the apportionment of the waters of the lower Rio Grande, the Colorado, and the Tijuana unresolved. These omissions triggered a generation of agitation. Matters calmed down somewhat in 1944 with the ratification of the second treaty, but the new pact (covering the waters of the Rio Grande below Fort Quitman and of the Colorado and Tijuana rivers) not only overestimated stream flow but also contained ambiguous provisions regarding drought and water quality, thus

302

leaving both Mexican and American farmers dissatisfied with the amount and type of water available for their irrigation projects. These and other problems diminished the effectiveness of the treaty. The excessive salt content of the Colorado River water reaching Mexico, which after 1961 began causing serious damage to thousands of acres of Mexican land, became a particularly troublesome issue. The two countries did not resolve this problem until 1973, when a new binational pact provided for the reduction of salinity through the construction of a desalting plant by the United States, the cooperative rehabilitation and improvement of the impaired lands, and the waiver of previous Mexican claims.

INTERDEPENDENCE IN THE BORDERLANDS

After the delimitation of the boundary in the mid-nineteenth century, new settlements emerged and existing ones grew as migrants arrived from the interiors of Mexico and the United States. A symbiotic relationship evolved between one side of the border and the other, with the United States assuming the role of dominant partner. One immediate effect of the establishment of the new boundary in 1848 was to convert Mexican frontier settlements at the Rio Grande into satellites of the U.S. economy. The competition provided by Anglo merchants who moved into the region devastated many Mexican businesspeople who had no access to capital and manufactured goods, both of which were more readily available to their counterparts across the line. For ordinary *fronterizos*, the major effect of the new border was a higher cost of living, for after 1848 tariffs had to be paid on "foreign" commodities. As a result of economic dislocation, scores of Mexicans migrated to the United States, where living conditions were more favorable.

The Mexican government provided some relief to the border communities by allowing a *zona libre* (free zone) to function in certain border areas beginning in the late 1850s. Under the *zona libre,* Mexican border residents could import foreign products without having to pay the normal duties. That helped to stimulate the economy of the border towns, but the external dependence increased. In 1885 the Porfirio Díaz regime recognized the unique conditions at the frontier and extended the *zona libre* the length of the border. Local trade flourished, ushering in prosperity unseen in previous eras. Yet dependence on the U.S. economy grew deeper because the commercial stimulus was being driven from abroad. Then in 1905, following protests from U.S. merchants hurt by the diversion of commerce to the Mexican side, and pressures from Mexican businesspeople and industrialists in the interior who resented the preferential treatment given borderlanders, the Mexican government eliminated the *zona libre*. In the decades that followed, borderlanders continuously petitioned for the return of free trade but succeeded only in convincing Mexico City to allow duty-free importation at selected parts of the border.

Meanwhile, U.S. capitalists penetrated the economies of the northern Mexican states, in particular Chihuahua and Sonora. By the 1880s American companies had built railroads along important routes that connected central Mexico with El Norte (The North) and with the United States. As the railroads reached rich mining districts and productive agricultural and ranching areas, they came to symbolize U.S. dominance, for they facilitated the export of precious metals and raw materials to the United States. The railroads also transported Mexican workers to U.S. work sites throughout the borderlands.

As owners of Mexican mines, oil fields, farms, ranches, and sundry industries, Americans exerted disproportionate influence in Mexico, engendering resentment among Mexicans. That resentment played a pivotal role in the turmoil that gripped Mexico in the early years of the twentieth century, an unrest that assumed nationwide proportions by 1910, eventually exploding into a full-scale revolution.

After the Revolution, Mexico began the process of political, economic, and social reconstruction, slowly eliminating the conditions that had precipitated internal instability. Modernization and sustained economic growth became strongly institutionalized in the northern states and in the U.S. Southwest. Thus a closer relationship evolved between the two sides of the boundary, shaping the region in ways that differed considerably from earlier periods, when isolation, underdevelopment, and disorder were commonplace.

In 1919, the Volstead Act made it illegal to produce or sell alcohol in the United States, causing the Mexican border cities to become magnets for manufacturers of liquor and operators of bars, nightclubs, casinos, and related establishments. Many U.S. entrepreneurs joined Mexican businesspeople in catering to the demands of a large American clientele eager for alcoholic beverages and entertainment not readily available in the United States. Consequently, cities like Ciudad Juárez and Tijuana acquired reputations as centers of vice and moral abandon.

The onset of the Great Depression temporarily halted the trend toward institutionalized interdependence along the border. Massive unemployment created strong pressures to rid the United States of foreign workers, with Mexicans targeted as a primary group for deportation and "repatriation." Thus in the 1930s approximately 500,000 Mexicans, many of them U.S. citizens, left the United States involuntarily and as repatriates. For the border communities, the returnees presented special challenges because most of them needed basic assistance and transportation to the interior.

The greatest socioeconomic changes in the borderlands have taken place since World War II. At that time the U.S. government began to invest enormous amounts of capital throughout the Southwest in military installations, defense-related industries, and infrastructure projects. The infusion of these external funds stimulated the entire economy, helping to convert the U.S. border

Pioneer assembly plant, Tijuana, Mexico. PHOTO BY DON BARTLETTI / LOS ANGELES TIMES.

region into one of the most dynamic areas in the country. As an extension of the U.S. Southwest, northern Mexico benefited considerably from these trends, as well as from the industrialization policies promoted from Mexico City during the same period. By the late twentieth century El Norte emerged as one of the most modern and prosperous regions within the Mexican republic.

Both sides of the border sported a greatly expanded economy capable of sustaining substantially larger populations. Traditional extractive and agricultural industries were pushed into the background, replaced by manufacturing and high-tech industries that relied heavily on government spending. New forms of industrialization emerged with the establishment of MAQUILADORAS, foreign-owned assembly plants situated on the Mexican side of the border. Urban centers throughout the binational borderlands assumed a new look, evolving from isolated, underdeveloped towns into modern, vibrant metropolises. Some cities achieved national prominence within their respective nations. At the border, communities like Ciudad Juárez–El Paso and Tijuana–San Diego became highly integrated binational centers of great significance for both nation-states.

The post–World War II economic expansion spurred impressive population growth throughout the borderlands. By 1990, 13.2 million people lived in the Mexican border states, compared with 3.8 million three decades earlier; north of the boundary, the population of the border states more than doubled during those years, rising from 19.7 million to 51.9 million. Thus the combined population of the borderlands was 65.1 million by 1990.

J. FRED RIPPY, *The United States and Mexico* (1926); RAÚL A. FERNÁNDEZ, *The United States–Mexico Border: A Politico-Economic Profile* (1977); LINDA B. HALL and DON M. COERVER, *Revolution on the Border: The United States and Mexico, 1910–1920* (1988); OSCAR J. MARTÍNEZ, *Troublesome Border* (1988); RAÚL A. FERNÁNDEZ, *The Mexican-American Border Region: Issues and Trends* (1989); LAWRENCE A. HERZOG, *Where North Meets South: Cities, Space, and Politics on the U.S.–Mexico Border* (1990); OSCAR J. MARTÍNEZ, *Border People: Life and Society in the U.S.–Mexico Borderlands* (1994).

OSCAR J. MARTÍNEZ

UNIVERSIDAD AUTÓNOMA DE SANTO DOMINGO, the oldest university in the Americas, founded by papal bull of Paul III in 1538. Originally called la Universidad de Santo Tomás de Aquino, the University was run by the DOMINICAN order until 1801, when it was closed; it reopened as a lay institution in 1815 and was reorganized in 1914. Dictator Rafael TRUJILLO moved it to University City (the grounds of the unsuccessful World's Fair) in 1955 and later added Autónoma to its name, which was meaningless during his rule.

UASD was a very traditional university in terms of curriculum—mainly law, philosophy, and medicine for a long time—pedagogy, and organization. It was the only university until 1962, when the UNIVERSIDAD CATÓLICA MADRE Y MAESTRA was established in SANTIAGO DE LOS CABALLEROS. After Trujillo was assassinated in 1961, UASD became a hotbed of opposition to Joaquín BALAGUER (then president), who was an alumnus and former rector. Following President Juan BOSCH's overthrow by the military in 1963 and the resultant civil war and U.S. intervention in 1965, the UASD students fought for his return and opposed the United States. During the civil war a group of conservative professors and students left UASD and formed their own university, the Universidad Nacional Pedro Henríquez Ureña. Balaguer's election in 1966 was strongly opposed by UASD students; he retaliated against them by cutting UASD's budget.

The student enrollment was around 60,000 in the early 1990s.

EMILIO RODRÍGUEZ DEMORIZI, *Cronología de la Real y Pontífica Universidad de Santo Domingo, 1538–1970* (1970); and FRANK MOYA PONS, *El pasado dominicano* (1986), chap. 8.

LARMAN C. WILSON

UNIVERSIDAD CATÓLICA MADRE Y MAESTRA, a university founded jointly in 1962 by the business community and the Conference of Dominican Bishops in SANTIAGO DE LOS CABALLEROS, the second largest city and economic center of the Dominican Republic—85 miles northwest of the capital, Santo Domingo. Along with the conservative but progressive elite, a prime mover in UCMM's creation was the bishop of Santiago, Hugo Eduardo Polanco Brito. Although it is a private and secular university, its rector has always been a priest, starting with Bishop Polanco. The university was established to be insulated from national politics, in contrast to the UNIVERSIDAD AUTÓNOMA DE SANTO DOMINGO, and to provide instruction and training in the fields that were needed for the development and modernization of the country. It follows the U.S. university model.

UCMM opened on a limited basis in the academic year 1962–1963 with some seventy students in the faculties of education and philosophy. It remained open during the 1965 civil war and steadily increased in enrollment to around 12,000 in the early 1990s. In its early years UCMM received important foreign assistance, including faculty development, from the U.S. government and several universities, the Ford Foundation, and the British government. While President Joaquín BALAGUER starved the Universidad Autónoma in the capital during his first term (1966–1970) because of its leftist students, he was generous to UCMM, which was not dependent on government funds.

IAN BELL, *The Dominican Republic* (1981); AGRIPINO NÚÑEZ COLLADO, *La UCMM: Un nuevo estilo universitario en la República Dominicana*, 2 vols. (1982); and FRANK MOYA PONS, *El pasado dominicano* (1986), chap. 18.

LARMAN C. WILSON

UNIVERSIDAD CENTRAL DE VENEZUELA, the leading university of Venezuela, founded by royal decree as the Royal and Pontifical University of Caracas on 22 December 1721. It was the only university in the province of Venezuela during colonial days. A defender of the king's law and privilege and keeper of the purity of the Catholic faith, the university provided courses in theology, law, and medicine.

The university's elite and ecclesiastical orientation was modified after independence, when Simón BOLÍVAR promoted its academic renovation with the help of José María VARGAS and José Rafael Revenga. It was named the Central University of Caracas in 1827. The reform was intended to transform the university into a self-supporting scientific and academic center. New courses were created; measures which impeded the entrance of nonwhites were eliminated; costs of the right to a degree were lowered; staff salaries were raised; and courses were taught in Castilian rather than in Latin. Results, however, were mixed: between 1830 and 1899 the university experienced both splendor and decadence both financially and academically.

In the absence of organized political parties during the Juan Vicente GÓMEZ regime, the university became a focus of opposition to the dictator. Gómez responded by shutting down the university from 1912 to 1922, gradually reorganizing each department to his liking. In 1943 the construction of a university city was decreed by President Isaías MEDINA ANGARITA, and the process of scientific and academic modernization was resumed. Gradually, new colleges were established and new areas of specialization were added. In the early 1990s, the university consisted of eleven colleges, thirty-five schools, forty-one research institutes, more than 8,000 professors, and about 70,000 students. In the late twentieth century, it considerably broadened its activities, including the development of postgraduate courses in numerous disciplines.

JUAN DE DIOS MÉNDEZ Y MENDOZA, *Historia de la Universidad Central de Venezuela*, 2 vols. (1911, 1924); and ILDEFONSO LEAL, *Historia de la Universidad Central de Venezuela, 1721–1981* (1981).

INÉS QUINTERO

UNIVERSITIES

Colonial Spanish America

Approximately thirty-one universities functioned in Spanish America between the mid-sixteenth century and the winning of independence. Seven universities were founded in the sixteenth century, thirteen in the seventeenth, nine in the eighteenth, and two after 1800. Nine of these institutions were of major importance because of their public character, size, and location; these were Santo Domingo (founded 1538); Mexico and Lima (both founded in 1551); Charcas in Bolivia (1614); Córdova in Argentina (1621); Guatemala (1676); Havana (1721); Caracas (1723), and Santiago, Chile (1738). The primacy, wealth, and population of Lima and Mexico made their universities institutional models for all the others. Together, the colonial universities graduated an estimated 150,000 persons, of whom perhaps 15 to 20 percent received advanced degrees.

The minor universities, generally smaller, poorer, and more isolated, were really college-universities, dependent in government and operation upon a college run by a religious order, almost always the DOMINICANS or JESUITS. If these institutions were more than two hundred leagues from one of the major universities, they were entitled to confer degrees. The organization of minor institutions followed that of the University of Alcalá, in which a single college was dominant.

The major (public) universities were governed by their faculty and graduates, led by an elected rector within the terms of royal and papal charters. Their statutes were based on those of the University of Salamanca.

All the universities consistently sought, and some secured, the privileges of Salamanca, most notably exemption for graduates from personal taxation and the separate legal jurisdiction for students and faculty called the *fuero académico*. The key feature of major university governance, however, was the Cloister (*Claustro*), an assembly of all graduates holding advanced degrees. This body received and obeyed or protested royal orders, petitioned the crown, managed the money, dealt with the curriculum and the faculty, and conducted ordinary relations with the church and local government. Within the limits set by statutes and enforced royal orders, the Cloister ran the university.

The executive officer of the Cloister was the rector, elected annually by and from its number. The rector called and presided over all Cloister meetings, enforced the statutes and decisions, disciplined faculty and students, inspected pupilages, and presided over examinations and the trial lectures by which professors were chosen. The rector's powers were balanced by those of the *maestrescuela,* who as judge of the schools administered the *fuero académico,* adjudicating disputes or crimes involving students or graduates. He granted degrees in the name of pope and king, presided over the graduation ceremony, and administered the oaths the graduates took.

In contrast, the Alcalá statutes confided governance not to the graduates assembled in cloister, but to the members of a single college, who elected one of their own to serve as rector. This official exercised all the powers of the rector in a large university as well as those of the *maestrescuela.* Management of money and university business was confined to the college; the Cloister had only minor powers over classroom practice and curriculum.

Both the Salamanca- and the Alcalá-style universities had two types of faculty. Junior or temporal chairs were held for four to six years; senior or proprietary posts, once won, were held for life. Both kinds of posts were filled by trial lectures or *oposiciones,* in which contestants, working in isolation, prepared a lesson on a passage from a standard text and then gave and defended it before the students, who selected the winner. From the beginning, these contests were contentious and disorderly and were therefore the subject of progressively more elaborate regulation. Finally, after about 1675, students were excluded from voting; the lessons were heard by juries of experts, and government officials made the final choice.

The *oposición* was only one of the many disputations that were interwoven with classwork. The academic career assumed a knowledge of Latin; the bachelor's degree in arts added to that at least three years' study of logic and natural and moral philosophy. A student could then proceed to one of the major faculties: law, theology, or medicine, all of which required four or five more years of study. In addition to attending classes, students were required to propose and argue increasingly elaborate and difficult theses. The culmination was the licentiate degree, which required three or four years of residence and defense of a number of major "acts" or disputations. Finally, the candidate withstood an examination without limitation of time or number of examiners, followed by a secret vote. The doctorate was entirely ceremonial, expensive, and really only an admission to the corporation of teachers.

The structure of learning that supported the Hispanic worldview at the time most universities were founded was undoubtedly scholastic. But it was a vigorous scholasticism sustained by talented men, suffused by new ideas, and dealing with important questions. Given the limits imposed by their geographic isolation and relative poverty, Hispanic-American universities played a substantial role in the intellectual life of their time.

By the same token, Latin American universities in the eighteenth century shared in the gradually emerging changes in learning. Criticism of the exhausted scholasticism of the eighteenth century gradually spread, as evidenced by, for example, the works of the Spanish philosopher Benito Geronimo Feijóo y Montenegro, but it was to be found also in the Latin texts used in the arts courses.

After the accession of Charles III in 1759, reforms acquired concentration and focus. The proscription of the Jesuits in 1767 removed a powerful institutional rival of many universities, which in many cases inherited Jesuit libraries, buildings, and income. From about 1770 on, new plans of studies were developed in Spain and America that made a larger place for mathematics, Newtonian physics, and modern geography and cosmography. Next, the courses of civil and canon law were changed to emphasize the primacy of the crown over the church and the importance of Spanish rather than Roman and canon law. The theology courses were drastically modified to include critical church history and to strengthen dogmatic rather than speculative scholastic theology. Finally, the education of medical doctors was changed to include modern texts; training in anatomy, chemistry, and botany; and clinical practice.

These changes were, as ever, affected by the precarious and inadequate financing of most institutions.

Neither were they achieved without opposition or controversy. Nevertheless, they produced far-reaching changes in the worldview that paralleled those occurring in Spain at the same time.

The most useful brief introduction is JOHN TATE LANNING, *Academic Culture in the Spanish Colonies* (1940). His *The University in the Kingdom of Guatemala* (1955) and *The Eighteenth-Century Enlightenment in the University of San Carlos de Guatemala* (1956) constitute the most thorough study of a single university. AGUEDA MARÍA RODRÍGUEZ CRUZ, O.P., *Historia de las universidades hispanoamericanas*, 2 vols. (1973), is replete with facts and has useful documentary appendices and an extensive bibliography, unfortunately it is not very analytical. Still more documents are in CÁNDIDO M. AJO GONZÁLEZ DE RAPARIEGOS Y SÁINZ DE ZÚÑIGA, *Historia de las universidades hispánicas: Orígines y desarrollo desde su aparación hasta nuestros días*, 8 vols. (1957–1972). On Lima, see LUIS ANTONIO EGUIGUREN, *La Universidad Nacional Mayor de San Marcos* (1950). On Mexico, see SERGIO MÉNDEZ ARCEO, *La Real y Pontífica Universidad de Mexico* (1952), and ALBERTO MARÍA CARREÑO, *La Real y Pontífica Universidad de México, 1536–1865* (1961). On scholasticism and reform, see O. CARLOS STOETZER, *The Scholastic Roots of the Spanish American Revolution* (1979).

GEORGE M. ADDY

See also **Enlightenment, The; Fueros.**

The Modern Era

The Spanish American university, with its main intellectual and administrative origins in the University of Salamanca in thirteenth-century Spain, was one of the most enduring colonial institutions. Late-eighteenth- and early-nineteenth-century intellectual and political influences jarred the university, but did not alter its social, economic, and political functions.

The WARS OF INDEPENDENCE and the struggles of early nationhood weakened the universities, but most survived, little changed from their colonial past. They had now become national rather than "royal and pontifical" universities, institutions of the state rather than of crown and church. The University of Buenos Aires was one of the earliest (founded 1821) and most important of the new universities. Some of the new universities, such as the University of the Republic of Uruguay (founded 1833), would remain as the only higher education institution of the country during the nineteenth century. Political and economic difficulties hindered the development of the new and old universities. In Mexico, for example, the Royal and Pontifical University (founded 1551) was modified, closed, and reopened several times between 1810 and 1865. A national university was finally reestablished under the guidance of Justo Sierra with the founding of the National University of Mexico in 1910. For those universities that did function, one supposed prevailing influence was the Napoleonic university, with its emphasis on centralization, the development of distinct faculties, and the training of professionals to meet the demands of emerging nation-

states. One of the most famous universities to emerge within this intellectual context was the University of Chile, founded by the Venezuelan intellectual Andrés BELLO. Despite the French influence, the university included some moral and humanistic education along with professional training. The University of Chile, in a manner similar to several other new state universities, also had control over primary and secondary EDUCATION.

For much of Latin America in the nineteenth century, university life was narrowly defined, focusing on jurisprudence and the training of lawyers to promote the interests of the CREOLE elite that emerged after the Wars of Independence, or medicine and the education of physicians. Faculties of law and medicine dominated the university, acting almost as independent fiefdoms rather than as parts of a larger institution. Conflict in the history of the university in the nineteenth century stemmed from competition between liberal and conservative forces. A central issue was the extent of religious influence in education. The dominant trend was toward secular education, controlled by the state. The scholastic education of the past gave way to the training of the social and political elite of the new nations. *Positivism* provided the philosophical basis for efforts to reorganize the university, emphasizing secular, scientific education to achieve the positivist goals of order and progress. Education under the tutelage of positivism was designed to establish the framework for the orderly economic and social development of society.

Brazil was the exception in university education as it was in so much else. During the colonial period, the University of Coimbra in Portugal served the needs of the empire. In Brazil, JESUIT colleges and seminaries served as centers for advanced studies. With independence, a national educational system was created, but not a university. Technical and vocational institutes satisfied the need for higher education until the creation of the first Brazilian university in the twentieth century. The University of Rio de Janeiro, established in 1920, is usually considered the first Brazilian university, but it was not until 1931 that the first Statute of Brazilian Universities (usually requiring that the university consist of the three faculties of law, medicine, and engineering) was passed. The University of São Paulo (established in 1934) was the first university to fulfill the requirements of the statute.

Law and medicine remained the classic subjects of the university, but were gradually accompanied by a growing emphasis on engineering, mathematics, and the chemical and physical sciences. This was a reflection of the positivist and utilitarian emphasis that affected the university in the late nineteenth century. Education as professional training rather than as the formation of character through humanistic inquiry had become dominant. Yet this education was often inadequate, emphasizing more the title that came with university education than the knowledge. While the university experienced changes in the nineteenth century, it had still not shed its image as an institution of the colonial period (though the nineteenth-century organizational influences were pronounced), serving the interest of a narrow elite rather than the needs of the nation.

This institution, its tradition prompting labels such as "medieval," "monastic," and "anachronistic," came under attack in the early twentieth century. The calls for change culminated in the Córdoba Reforms, initiated in June 1918 at the University of Córdoba in Argentina. The demands of the Córdoba Reforms soon became the Magna Carta of Latin American universities, guiding their development in the twentieth century. Most influential have been the demands for university autonomy, including political, administrative, and financial independence; election of university administrators, with the participation of faculty, students, and alumni; open classrooms and free education; improved teaching and control over faculty; a curriculum appropriate for the current needs of society; and university extension programs, designed to make the university an agent of social reform. University autonomy remained one of the most vocal demands of students and faculty in the twentieth century. Though not often recognized during the turmoil of university politics, autonomy was a tradition that the colonial university had inherited from the University of Salamanca. This included the participation of students in the selection of faculty.

Few of these reforms were enacted in their entirety, but they did signal that the university had become a center of political and social activity, aware of its potential for challenging the past and creating the future. In addition to its traditional teaching and research mission, the university now had a "social mission," broadly defined as the commitment to using the resources of the university to create more equitable and just societies.

This has made the Latin American university a very visible political institution, much more so than in the United States or Europe. The expectation that the university would provide the solution to the social and economic woes of Latin America has been a source of inspiration and frustration since 1918. It represents the core of the dilemmas that confronted the university as it tried to reconcile the different emphases of training versus education, humanism versus scientism, and reformism versus conservation of the established order.

While the Córdoba Reforms faced obstacles that minimized their implementation, they did provide the basis for regional cooperation among Latin American universities. International meetings of faculty and students discussed issues and proposed cooperative programs. This regional effort culminated in the First Congress of Latin American Universities, hosted by Guatemala in 1949. This led to the creation of the Union of Latin American Universities (UDUAL), which expressed its goal "of orienting university education to the full development of the human personality" in the Carta de Guatemala. UDUAL continues to function, publishing *Universidades*,

Library, National Autonomous University of Mexico (UNAM), ca. 1985. OWEN FRANKEN / STOCK, BOSTON.

a good source of information on the modern Latin American university.

After World War II, the universities entered a new phase of growth. The physical presence of the university changed with the emergence of the university cities, sprawling modern campuses that did resemble cities. One of the most widely admired new campuses was that of the NATIONAL AUTONOMOUS UNIVERSITY OF MEXICO in Mexico City. The new university city proclaimed the modernity of the university and reinforced the strong centralizing tendency of Latin American politics.

Latin American universities entered a period of unprecedented growth in the 1960s. Increasing social demand for education led to mushrooming enrollments in existing universities and the creation of new ones, public and private. (See the accompanying table.)

The percentage of women enrolled has increased faster than general enrollments. In the 1980s women comprised 58 percent of students in Panama (1985), 57 percent in Uruguay (1987) and Cuba (1988), 51 percent in Brazil (1988), 47 percent in Argentina (1987), and 41 percent in Mexico (1988). In addition to increases in university enrollments, there have been jumps in the number of men and women attending non-university institutes of higher education.

The proliferation of higher education institutions included many private universities. A few private universities continued to exist from earlier periods. Notable among them was the Jesuit Pontifical Javerian Catholic University of Bogotá, founded in 1622. Following World War I these were joined by several new Catholic universities. In addition, there were the "popular universities," at times extensions of national universities, at other times independent efforts to take the knowledge and skills of the university to the rural and urban poor. These new institutions did not compensate for the inability of the nation to satisfy the increasing demographic and social pressures for university education. As a result, private higher educational institutions grew more rapidly, and included secular as well as religious education. In 1980, 35 percent of higher-education students attended private institutions. Because private universities differ from public universities in finance, organization, student background, and often in curriculum, it makes it particularly difficult to generalize about recent changes in university education in Latin America.

Student unrest in the 1960s, more common in the public than in the private university, responded to university-related problems and to broader social issues. Lack of access to the university and the increasing distance between university curriculum and professional opportunities contributed to unrest. The traditional programs of law, medicine, and engineering still dominated. Internally, the university faced the old problems of part-time, unprepared faculty; dominance of the traditional organizational structure of the university, particularly the *cátedra*, the chair of professorship so powerful in university affairs; and the lack of adequate support for teaching and research. Finance was a continual problem that often made university autonomy more rhetorical than real. Competition for state funds increased friction between the university and government. Inadequate planning and uncertain revenues in both state and university hampered the development efforts of the university. With the global recession of the 1970s, financial problems became more severe. At the same time, partly as a response to the unrest of the 1960s, new organizations emerged to challenge traditional university life. Staff and faculty unions in particular have exercised their power to demand better salaries and working conditions.

Externally, the university failed to address the social and economic needs of development. Critics went much further, interpreting the university as an instrument of an oppressive international economic order that depended on the economic and social polarization of Latin American society for its well-being. This was reminiscent of the demands of 1918, but was now couched in Marxist terms with clearly stated revolutionary objectives. The university was seen as training an elite that served the needs of national and international capital. In response there was the call for the "popularization" of the university, to use it as a weapon in the fight for social and economic justice. In addition to simply increasing enrollments, the critics called for linking the university to the working classes, forming alliances with them to create a new bloc in the struggle against oppression.

University Enrollments

Country	Enrollment	
Argentina	755,206	(1987)
Bolivia	106,602	(1989)
Brazil	1,503,560	(1988)
Chile	250,000	(1990)
Colombia	474,000	(1989)
Costa Rica	67,000	(1990)
Cuba	250,600	(1988)
Dominican Republic	123,700	(1985)
Ecuador	190,000	(1989)
El Salvador	80,800	(1989)
Guatemala	51,860	(1986)
Haiti	4,471	(1986)
Honduras	36,000	(1989)
Mexico	1,256,942	(1989)
Nicaragua	26,800	(1987)
Panama	62,143	(1990)
Paraguay	29,400	(1990)
Peru	419,000	(1987)
Uruguay	62,461	(1988)
Venezuela	528,000	(1990)

SOURCE: *South America, Central America, and the Caribbean,* 4th ed. (1993).

The charged political climate of the late 1960s and early 1970s erupted in violence in Latin America. The most renowned conflict occurred in Mexico City on the eve of the 1968 Olympics as students clashed with army and police at the Plaza de la Tres Culturas. University reform was no longer the only issue. Students demanded sweeping reforms that affected the social, political, and economic life of their countries. The reform efforts often clashed with the repressive military regimes then in power, leading to particularly chilling effects on university life in countries such as Argentina, Brazil, and Chile.

An important development within the university in the 1960s was a new emphasis on extension and social-action programs. They had the responsibility for helping to create a new awareness of the social and economic reality of the oppressive conditions of life rather than simply diffusing the dominant culture of the elite. At the same time, they designed and implemented programs to combat illiteracy, malnutrition, and infant mortality. In a word, extension was to become the bridge between university and society, a network of communication that would overcome the chasm that had traditionally separated the university from the society that it supposedly served.

For general introductions to the university, see LUIS-ALBERTO SÁNCHEZ, *La universidad latinoamericana* (1949); DARCY RIBEIRO, *La universidad latinoamericana* (1971); HANNS-ALBERT STEGER, *Las universidades en el desarrollo social de la América Latina* (1974); JOSEPH MAIER and RICHARD W. WEATHERHEAD, eds., *The Latin American University* (1979). Specialized studies include DANIEL C. LEVY, *Higher Education and the State in Latin America* (1986), an analysis of the differences between private and public universities; DONALD J. MABRY, *The Mexican University and the State: Student Conflicts, 1910–1971* (1982), a detailed history of student activism; and IVÁN JAKSIĆ, *Academic Rebels in Chile: The Role of Philosophy in Higher Education and Politics* (1989), a study of the interaction between the history of a discipline, the university, and politics.

JOHN C. SUPER

UNIVERSITY OF THE WEST INDIES, the major university system of the English-speaking Caribbean, formed as the result of a growing need for economic, political, and cultural integration in the region. It has three main campuses, located in Mona, Jamaica; Saint Augustine, Trinidad; and Cave Hill, Barbados. It was established by royal charter in 1948, for 500 to 600 students. Jamaica's main campus serves all of the Caribbean. The Trinidad branch, formally named the Imperial College of Tropical Agriculture, houses the faculties of agriculture and engineering. Until 1962, the university was affiliated with the University of London. Now it is an accredited university offering bachelor's, master's, and doctoral degrees in arts, medicine, natural sciences, and education.

D. A. TURNER, "Science in the 70s: Observations on Science Education in Jamaica," in *Caribbean Quarterly* 20, no. 2 (June 1974): 15–24; ERIC WILLIAMS, "The University in the Caribbean," in *Universities for a Changing World: The Role of the University in the Later Twentieth Century*, edited by Michael D. Stephens et al. (1975).

DARIÉN DAVIS

URABÁ, a gulf in northwestern Colombia and the surrounding region of plains and adjacent hills, lying mainly within the department of ANTIOQUIA. The region was explored in 1501 by Rodrigo de BASTIDAS and Juan de la Cosa, who were impressed by the amount of gold possessed by the native inhabitants. In 1510 Alonso de OJEDA founded San Sebastián, the first Spanish settlement on the mainland of the New World, near the Indian village of Urabá on the eastern shore of the gulf. Conflict with the Indians led to the early abandonment of San Sebastián, and the surviving Spaniards moved across the gulf, where they founded Santa María de la Antigua.

Urabá languished during the remainder of the colonial period, but in the nineteenth century it was the focal point of Antioquia's effort to build a direct outlet to the Caribbean. It was not until 1954 that a road was completed linking MEDELLÍN to Turbo, the largest city on the gulf of Urabá. Afterward the region experienced rapid population growth and became a major producer of bananas and other tropical products. During the 1980s, labor unrest, guerrilla activity, and killings by paramilitary death squads made Urabá one of the most violent areas in Colombia.

JAMES J. PARSONS, *Antioquia's Corridor to the Sea: An Historical Geography of the Settlement of Urabá* (1967).

HELEN DELPAR

URBANIZATION. *See* **Cities and Urbanization.**

URBINA, JOSÉ MARÍA (*b.* March 1808; *d.* 4 September 1891), *jefe supremo* (supreme leader) of Ecuador (1851–1852) and president (1852–1856). Born in Ambato, Urbina attended the Naval School at Guayaquil briefly but left early to participate in military actions (siege of Callao, 1824–1826; Malpelo, 1828; defense of Ecuadorian independence, 1830). Rising rapidly through military ranks, he became aide-de-camp to President Juan José FLORES. On a diplomatic mission to Bogotá for President Vicente ROCAFUERTE, he committed a serious indiscretion and was recalled in 1837. Caught plotting against the government, he was banished but returned in 1839 to enter politics under the tutelage of President Flores. For his political loyalty to Flores, Urbina was rewarded with the governorship of Manabí. In 1845 he joined rebels to topple Flores from power. He was promoted to brigadier general and rose to high posts in the provisional government.

President Vicente Ramón ROCA (1845–1849) named Urbina chief of the general staff, which enormously increased his political and military power. In 1851, Urbina led a revolt and proclaimed himself *jefe supremo*. He would dominate Ecuadorian politics for the rest of the decade.

As *jefe supremo* Urbina abolished slavery and repelled an armed invasion by Flores from Peru. Under a new constitution he was elected president in 1852 and served a four-year term that was characterized by vigorous executive domination, glib assertions of liberal principles, stern control of the press, and the expulsion of the JESUITS. He severed relations with the Vatican, quarreled with Peru over asylum given to Flores and over Ecuador's southern boundary, and sought unsuccessfully to establish a U.S. protectorate over Ecuador.

From 1856 to 1859, Urbina was the *éminence grise* of the Francisco ROBLES administration, which collapsed in 1859 after a Peruvian attack at Guayaquil. Urbina fled into exile, plotted in Peru to regain power in Ecuador, but did not return until 1876. He helped place Ignacio VEINTEMILLA in power, but his influence diminished rapidly thereafter. He died in Guayaquil, forgotten by friends and denounced by liberal leaders.

JOSÉ LE GOUHIR Y RODAS, *Historia de la república del Ecuador*, vol. 1 (1920), pp. 401–539; LUIS ROBALINO DÁVILA, *La reacción anti-floreana* (1967).

MARK J. VAN AKEN

URBINA, LUIS GONZAGA (*b.* 8 February 1864; *d.* 18 November 1934), Mexican journalist and poet. Born in Mexico City, Urbina studied at the National Preparatory School before launching his career as a journalist. He began composing poetry before the age of sixteen. In 1881 he published some of his verses in *La patria ilustrada*. In 1887 he met his mentor, Justo SIERRA MÉNDEZ. Thanks to that friendship, Urbina obtained various government positions as well as posts at periodicals, where he wrote theater criticism and some of the first movie reviews in Mexico. Under Sierra's direction and with the cooperation of Pedro HENRÍQUEZ UREÑA and Nicolás Rangel, Urbina compiled the two volumes of Mexican literature, *Antología del centenario* (1910), produced for the centenary celebrations of that year. Although he is considered a poet of the MODERNISMO movement, Urbina represents the persistence of romanticism with his *vespertinas*, poems that reflect upon love and melancholy. In 1913 he was appointed director of the National Library, but two years later he left Mexico to live first in Cuba and then in Spain.

GERARDO SAENZ, *Luis G. Urbina: Vida y obra* (1961); ALFONSO RANGEL GUERRA, "Cartas de Luis G. Urbina a Alfonso Reyes," in *Nueva Revista de Filología Hispánica* 37, no. 2 (1989); ANGEL MIQUEL, *El nacimiento de una pasion. Luis G. Urbina: Primer cronista mexicano de cine* (1991).

JOHN WALDRON

URDANETA, ANDRÉS DE (*b.* 1508; *d.* 3 June 1568), Spanish navigator and explorer. A native of Villafranca de Oria, Guipúzcoa, Urdaneta served as a page on the circumnavigation of García Jofre de Loaysa in 1525. After being shipwrecked in the Moluccas, he returned to Spain in 1536. Urdaneta journeyed to Guatemala in 1538, and in 1541 he went to New Galicia with Pedro de ALVARADO. He was *corregidor* of the province of Ávalos in 1543, and visitor of that province until 1545. He became a novice in the AUGUSTINIANS in 1552 and was named pilot-missionary to the Philippines under Miguel LÓPEZ DE LEGAZPI in 1559. He sailed from Navidad, Jalisco, in November 1564, reached the Philippines in February 1565, and returned to New Spain 8 October 1565. On his return voyage he established the eastbound route, via Japan and California, to Acapulco that was used by the MANILA GALLEON. Urdaneta retired in 1566 to a monastery in Mexico City, where he died.

MARIANO CUEVAS, *Monje y marino, la vida y los tiempos de Fray Andrés de Urdaneta* (1943); ENRIQUE CÁRDENAS DE LA PEÑA, *Urdaneta y "el tornaviaje"* (1965).

W. MICHAEL MATHES

URDANETA, RAFAEL (*b.* 24 October 1788; *d.* 23 August 1845), Venezuelan independence leader and Colombian president. Born in Maracaibo, Venezuela, Rafael Urdaneta studied in Bogotá and at the start of the independence movement joined the patriots of New Granada. He took part in the first civil conflicts (as a federalist) as well as in the struggle against Spain, serving as Bolívar's second in command in the ADMIRABLE CAMPAIGN (1813). Following the Spanish reconquest of 1815–1816, he was one of those who kept resistance alive in the plains of the Orinoco Basin and later took part in the final liberation of Venezuela.

Urdaneta filled important positions in the government and congress of Gran Colombia. As minister of war in 1828–1829, he was military strongman of Simón BOLÍVAR's final dictatorship. With Bolívar gone, in 1830 he became president-dictator in a last-ditch effort to preserve the power of the Bolivarian party and the unity of Gran Colombia. Forced to step down early in 1831, he returned to Venezuela, where he continued to play a key political role. He was on a diplomatic mission to Spain when he died in Paris.

CARLOS ARBELÁEZ URDANETA, *Biografía del General Rafael Urdaneta, último presidente de la Gran Colombia* (1945); GERHARD MASUR, *Simón Bolívar* (1948; rev. ed. 1969); DANIEL FLORENCIO O'LEARY, *Bolívar and the War of Independence*, edited and translated by Robert F. Mc Nerney, Jr. (1970).

DAVID BUSHNELL
WINFIELD J. BURGGRAAFF

See also **Wars of Independence.**

UREÑA, FELIPE (*d.* after 1773), Mexican sculptor, RE-TABLO master. Ureña was largely responsible for the spreading of *estípite* baroque throughout New Spain, in places very distant from Mexico City. His decoration of the sacristy of the Church of San Francisco in Toluca, dedicated in 1729, is the first native work in the style. Ureña had what must have been a sizable workshop in Mexico City, but he also executed retablos and architectural projects in Guanajuato, Aguascalientes, Durango, Oaxaca, and elsewhere. His most famous work, still extant, is the Jesuit church La Compañía in Guanajuato, on which he labored between 1747 and 1765, with interruptions for other projects. Fragments of his wood sculpture exist in Durango.

CLARA BARGELLINI, *La arquitectura de la plata* (1991), pp. 138–140.

CLARA BARGELLINI

UREÑA DE HENRÍQUEZ, SALOMÉ (*b.* 21 October 1850; *d.* 6 March 1897), Dominican educator and poet. Ureña de Henríquez was born in Santo Domingo. Her father, Nicolás Ureña de Mendoza, was a distinguished politician, lawyer, and poet who provided her with an excellent education. Together with her husband, Francisco HENRÍQUEZ Y CARVAJAL, she implemented important education reforms in the Dominican Republic, stressing the significance of women's education. Ureña de Henríquez was the founder of the Instituto de Señoritas. She was profoundly influenced by the Puerto Rican educator Eugenio María de HOSTOS (1839–1903), who resided in Santo Domingo for over a decade. A fervent liberal, she supported the Blue Party of Gregorio LUPERÓN and opposed presidents Buenaventura BÁEZ and Ulises HEUREAUX. Beset by frequent illness and faced with the civil wars and dictatorships of one of the most turbulent epochs of Dominican history, she never lost faith in the positivist creed of order and progress.

Ureña de Henríquez was regarded as one of the finest Dominican poets and her writings became known throughout Latin America. Her poetry takes up a variety of themes, such as patriotism ("A Quisqueya," "En defensa de la sociedad," "Anacaona"), sentimentality ("La llegada del invierno," "Tristezas," "Horas de angustias," "El ave y el nido"), and social and political reform ("Ruinas," which is regarded as one of her best poems). She was the mother of the educator and literary critic Camila Henríquez Ureña; the writer, teacher, and diplomat Max HENRÍQUEZ UREÑA; and the writer, philosopher, and educator Pedro HENRÍQUEZ UREÑA. She died in Santo Domingo.

SALOMÉ UREÑA DE HENRÍQUEZ, *Poesías completas* (1989). See also DIANE E. MARTÍNEZ, ed., *Spanish American Women Writers* (1990), and *Enciclopedia dominicana*, vol. 7 (1978), pp. 183–185.

KAI P. SCHOENHALS

URETA, ELOY G. (*b.* 1892; *d.* 1965), Peruvian military leader, presidential candidate, and diplomat. Ureta was born in Chiclayo and educated in Chorrillos Military Academy (1909–1913) and the Advanced War School (1922). As brigadier general in 1941, Ureta was in charge of the military operations during the war with Ecuador. He became a popular military figure especially after the victory achieved in the battle of Zarumilla (24 July 1941). He was promoted to division general in 1941. He retired from the army to run unsuccessfully for the presidency in 1945. He was awarded the honorary rank of marshal in 1946. Between 1949 and 1955 he was the Peruvian ambassador to Spain. He died in Madrid.

DANIEL MASTERSON, *Militarism and Politics in Latin America: Peru from Sánchez Cerro to "Sendero Luminoso"* (1991).

ALFONSO W. QUIROZ

URIARTE–BAYARTA AGREEMENT (correctly the Uriarte–Vallarta Agreement), the initial boundary arrangement between Guatemala and Mexico, was signed on 7 December 1877 by Ramón Uriarte, the Guatemalan minister to Mexico, and Ignacio Luis Vallarta, the Mexican foreign minister.

The boundary dispute reflected imprecise frontiers between colonial jurisdictions. Guatemala inherited claims to CHIAPAS and SOCONUSCO from the UNITED PROVINCES OF CENTRAL AMERICA, contending these districts had been part of the Captaincy-General of Central America. Mexico considered these districts to be part of the Captaincy-General of YUCATÁN, which became part of Mexico.

The agreement provided for demarcation of the boundary from the port of Ocos to Mount Izbul (Ixbul). Although never ratified, despite several time-limit extensions, the agreement provided the basis for the treaty of 27 September 1882, which established this line as the boundary between Mexico and Guatemala.

RAMÓN URIARTE, *La convención de 7 de diciembre de 1877: Apuntes para la historia de la cuestión de límites entre Guatemala y México* (1882); GORDON IRELAND, *Boundaries, Possessions and Conflicts in Central and North America and the Caribbean* (1941).

KENNETH J. GRIEB

URIBE, JUAN CAMILO (*b.* 20 February 1941), Colombian artist. Born in Medellín, Uribe is known for his conceptualist and experimental work, which uses popular, religious, and historical icons from Colombian culture. He has participated in group shows since 1968. In 1972 he won first prize at the National Independent Salon, and first prize at the Third Salon of Young Artists in Bogotá, where he had his first solo exhibit three years later at the Galería Oficina. He went to Paris on a grant from the Colombian government in 1977, the same year he represented Colombia at the São Paulo Biennial. His work was shown at the Museum of Contemporary Art in Caracas and at the Primera Bienal del Grabado de América in Maracaibo, Venezuela. Uribe's installation *Arte Telescopio* (1979) featured numerous individual slide viewers hanging from the ceiling throughout the room, documenting bits of his personal life, his exhibits, his friends, and his work.

EDUARDO SERRANO, *Cien años de arte colombiano, 1886–1986* (1986).

BÉLGICA RODRÍGUEZ

URIBE HOLGUÍN, GUILLERMO (*b.* 17 March 1880; *d.* 26 June 1971), Colombian composer. Guillermo Uribe Holguín began the study of music in Bogotá, where he was born, and continued his studies in New York and at the Schola Cantorum in Paris. He conducted, taught, served as director of Colombia's Conservatorio Nacional (1910–1935, 1942–1947), and wrote a work on harmony as well as an autobiography. But he is best known as a composer, generally considered Colombia's greatest. His extensive body of works includes eleven symphonies, concerti and chamber music, numerous piano pieces, and songs. In style and technique he was strongly influenced by French impressionism, and for many years he disdained the use of elements from popular Colombian musical culture. Starting with his second symphony (*Del terruño*) in 1924, however, he turned increasingly to national rhythms and melody in his composing, thus giving qualified expression to musical nationalism.

NICOLAS SLONIMSKY, *Music of Latin America* (1945; 1972), pp. 171–172; ELIANA DUQUE *Guillermo Uribe Holguín y sus "300 trozos en el sentimiento popular"* (1980).

DAVID BUSHNELL

URIBE URIBE, RAFAEL (*b.* 12 April 1859; *d.* 15 October 1914), Colombian political caudillo, one of the leaders of the Liberal Party between 1880 and his assassination in 1914. Born on an estate in Antioquia, Uribe was the son of a wealthy landowner. He was educated at the Colegio del Estado (the present-day University of Antioquia).

Due to the singular nature of Colombian politics, Uribe was a political leader who had to do double duty as a military leader, like many others of his generation, in the all-too-frequent civil wars between Liberals and Conservatives. He participated in the civil wars of 1876, 1885, 1895, and 1899.

A charismatic caudillo, he never reached the presidency of the nation because he attained political leadership when the Liberal Party had been displaced by a coalition dominated by the Conservative Party; this group established a hegemony over the country until 1930. Uribe and the rest of the Liberal leadership had to labor under political persecution and even exile, a situation that eventually led to the most traumatic of civil wars, the War of the Thousand Days (1899–1902).

As an ideological leader, Uribe is reputed to have been instrumental in a major ideological shift of his party after 1904, when, in the short article "Socialismo de Estado," he exhorted the Liberals to move away from laissez-faire economics and espoused state intervention in economic and social welfare. His platform is reminiscent of the measures then being implemented in Uruguay by President José BATLLE Y ORDÓÑEZ (1903–1907), rather than the socialism his enemies accused him of. However, in the Colombia of the 1900s, it was considered subversive to ask the wealthy to pay taxes.

GERARDO MOLINA, *Las ideas liberals en Colombia, 1849–1914* (1970); EDUARDO SANTA, *Rafael Uribe Uribe* (1974); CHARLES W. BERGQUIST, *Coffee and Conflict in Colombia, 1886–1910* (1978); HELEN DELPAR, *Red Against Blue: The Liberal Party in Colombian Politics, 1863–1899* (1979).

JOSÉ ESCORCIA

URIBURU, JOSÉ EVARISTO (*b.* 19 November 1831; *d.* 25 October 1914), Argentine statesman, president of Argentina (1895–1898), and senator (1901–1910). Scion of an aristocratic Salta family, Uriburu was part of the so-called Generation of 1880 and one of the most representative figures in the oligarchic politics of the late nineteenth and early twentieth centuries. A leading member of the elite's political machine, the National Autonomist Party (PAN), Uriburu assumed the presidency of the nation after the sudden resignation of Luis SÁENZ PEÑA. Like his predecessor, Uriburu had to deal with the great 1890 depression and he continued Sáenz Peña's policy of consolidating the national and provincial debts. Though brief, his presidency nonetheless produced a number of notable accomplishments. Uriburu's resolution of the ongoing dispute with the British railroad companies over profit guarantees as well as other measures restored investor confidence and led to a return of British capital. In his diplomatic career, Uriburu was one of the principal mediators of the treaty between Chile and Peru that ended the WAR OF THE PACIFIC.

NATALIO R. BOTANA, *El orden conservador: la política argentina entre 1880 y 1916* (1977); HORACIO J. M. GUIDO, *Secuelas del unicato, 1890–1896* (1977).

JAMES P. BRENNAN

See also **Argentina: Political Parties.**

URIBURU, JOSÉ FÉLIX (*b.* 20 July 1868; *d.* 29 April 1932), leader of the army's first military coup and Argentine president (1930–1932). Born in Salta and a nephew of Argentine President José E. URIBURU, Uriburu initially chose a career in the military rather than politics. Rising through the ranks, he became director of the War College (Escuela Superior de Guerra) in 1907. After serving as a military attaché in Germany and England prior to World War I, he attained the rank of general in 1921.

Under President Marcelo T. de ALVEAR (1922–1928), he served as inspector general of the army (1923–1926). Disaffection with President Hipólito YRIGOYEN's second administration (1928–1930) encouraged conservatives to rebel against the elected government. Although retired from active service, Uriburu led the coup that toppled Yrigoyen on 6 September 1930 and inaugurated Argentina's Infamous Decade.

As provisional president, Uriburu attempted to establish a quasi-fascist regime. His government intervened in the country's universities, censored the national press, and imprisoned or exiled leaders of the political opposition. When the ousted Radical Party swept the April 1931 elections in Buenos Aires Province, his government intensified the repression of political opponents. Dwindling support among conservatives and the military forced him to abandon his plans. His government supervised a second election that gave Agustín P. JUSTO the presidency (1932–1938) and brought the CONCORDANCIA to power.

ROBERT A. POTASH, *The Army and Politics in Argentina, 1928–1945: Yrigoyen to Perón* (1969); MARÍA DOLORES BÉJAR, *Uriburu y Justo: El auge conservador, 1930–1935* (1983), pp. 13–52.

DANIEL LEWIS

URQUIZA, JUSTO JOSÉ DE (*b*. 18 October 1801; *d*. 11 April 1870), Argentine soldier and statesman. Urquiza was born in Talar de Arroyo Largo, Entre Ríos, the son of a merchant and landowner. He studied at the Colegio de San Carlos in Buenos Aires and in 1821 became a lieutenant in the militia. In 1826–1827 he served in the Entre Ríos congress, where he argued for democracy, federalism, and educational improvements; he also persuaded the congress to reject the 1826 Constitution. Urquiza expanded his business activities and became a follower of Ricardo LÓPEZ JORDÁN, who was defeated by a revolution supported by Santa Fe Governor Estanislao López. Urquiza fled to Uruguay, and in 1831 he returned to Entre Ríos to take command of the Army of Observation. In 1837 he was again elected to serve in the provincial congress. In 1838 he was with the Entre Ríos army massed to oppose an attack by Fructuoso RIVERA of Uruguay and Berón de Astrada of Corrientes. The attack was repulsed, thanks largely to Urquiza's cavalry. Urquiza continued fighting interprovincial battles. In 1845 he was named governor of Entre Ríos, a province where the dictator and governor of Buenos Aires, Juan Manuel de ROSAS, had little influence.

Urquiza established a well-equipped militia composed primarily of landowners, and he financed progressive programs in public education. In 1848 he began building the Palacio San José, his residence, and founded the Colegio del Uruguay. Urquiza was reelected governor in 1849, and in 1851 he announced to the provincial governments and the exiles in Montevideo that he would undertake a campaign against

Justo José de Urquiza, 1860. ORGANIZATION OF AMERICAN STATES.

Rosas. To further that goal, he negotiated an alliance with Brazil and Uruguay.

Urquiza opened his campaign by raising the siege of Montevideo by Manuel ORIBE. When his forces crossed into Uruguay, many of Oribe's troops and some from Buenos Aires joined them. Meanwhile, Rosas had declared war on Brazil. Urquiza was to command a combined force of Argentine, Brazilian, and Uruguayan troops. Rosas took no defensive measures to stop Urquiza's advance but assembled his army at Santos Lugares. Rosas was defeated at nearby CASEROS on 3 February 1852 by a superior cavalry. He fled to Buenos Aires, where he and his daughter sought refuge in the home of the British minister and a few days later sailed for England.

Urquiza appointed Vicente López y Planes as interim governor. In May 1852, at a meeting of provincial governors, at San Nicolás de los Arroyos, Urquiza was named temporary director of the Argentine Confederation. Buenos Aires disapproved, however, and in September it seceded from the confederation. All the provinces except Buenos Aires approved the constitution in 1853, Paraná became the capital of the confederation, and Urquiza was elected president (1854–1860). The new government lacked adequate resources to create the institutions that would further national integration and economic development. Several military invasions were launched to bring Buenos Aires into the union, and in 1859 Congress authorized Urquiza, governor of Entre Ríos since 1 May 1860, to use military force to subdue the rebellious province. The armies of the confederation under Urquiza clashed with the Buenos Aires army, led by Bartolomé MITRE, at PAVÓN on 17 September 1861. Urquiza's cavalry won, but the infantry was defeated. Urquiza left the battlefield. Some maintain that he was ill, others that he realized that Buenos Aires could not be defeated, and still others that he was disgusted with the disputes among military and civilian leaders. Urquiza, constitutionally prohibited from succeeding himself, secured the election of José María Dominguez as governor in 1864, and in 1865 he sought—unsuccessfully—to prevent war with Paraguay. Francisco Solano LÓPEZ attacked Corrientes, thus compelling Urquiza to support the unified Argentine government of Mitre.

On 11 April 1870, a group of conspirators assassinated Urquiza at his home. Two of his sons were killed in Concordia, Entre Ríos. Urquiza had amassed a considerable fortune in land, cattle, and meat-salting plants. He and his wife had eleven children, and he legitimized twelve of his natural children.

JACINTO R. YABEN, "Urquiza, J. J. de," in *Biografías argentinas y sudamericanas*, vol. 5 (1940), pp. 964–975; VICENTE CUTOLO, "Urquiza, J. J. de," in *Nuevo diccionario biográfico argentino*, vol. 7 (1985), pp. 444–451; BEATRIZ BOSCH, *Urquiza y su tiempo*, 2d ed. (1980); ALBERTO J. MASRAMÓN, *Urquiza, libertador y fundador* (1982); SUSANA T. P. DE DOMÍNGUEZ SOLER, *Urquiza: Ascendencia vasca y descendencia en el Río de la Plata* (1992). In English see JOSÉ LUIS ROMERO, *A History of Argentine Political Thought* translated by Thomas F. McGann, (1963); JOHN LYNCH, *Argentine Dictator: Juan Manuel de Rosas, 1829–1852* (1981); LESLIE BETHELL, ed., *Argentina Since Independence* (1993), and *Spanish America After Independence, c. 1820–c. 1870* (1987); DAVID BUSHNELL and NEILL MACAULAY, *The Emergence of Latin America in the Nineteenth Century* 2d ed., (1994); JOSEPH T. CRISCENTI, ed., *Sarmiento and His Argentina* (1993).

JOSEPH T. CRISCENTI

URRACÁ (*d.* 1531), Panamanian indigenous leader, one of the most romanticized figures in the country, and a symbol of Panamanian patriotism. For nine years he fought the Spaniards Gaspar de Espinosa and Pedrarias Dávila in what is now Veraguas and Natá. Although he was captured once by the Spaniards, he was able to escape. His encounters with the Spaniards are described in Antonio de HERRERA Y TORDESILLAS's *Historia general de los hechos de los castellanos en las islas y tierra firme del mar océano* (1549–1625).

ERNESTO DE JESÚS CASTILLERO REYES, *Historia de Panamá*, 7th ed. (1962); JORGE CONTE PORRAS, *Diccionario biográfico ilustrado de Panamá*, 2d ed. (1986).

JUAN MANUEL PÉREZ

URREA, JOSÉ DE (*b.* 1797; *d.* August 1849), Mexican general. A fourth-generation frontier military officer,

Urrea was born in the presidio of Tucson. He followed in his father's footsteps: commanding frontier garrisons; fighting insurgents; seconding Agustín de ITURBIDE's plan for independence, but supporting the republicans against the empire. The involvement of both father and son in the rebellion of the Plan of Montaño led to his father's exile and José's dismissal. He reentered the army two years later (1829), rising to the rank of general in 1835 as a protégé of SANTA ANNA. He distinguished himself in opposing the independence of Texas. As military commander of Sonora and Sinaloa, Urrea launched a series of unsuccessful revolts to reestablish the Federal Constitution of 1824, first in that region in 1837, and then nationally in 1839, 1840, and 1841. With Santa Anna's return to power that latter year, Urrea returned to Sonora as governor and commander general (1842–1844). His aggressive policies against the economic interests and political power of centralist sympathizers, and against the autonomy of the YAQUI and Mayo Indians, provoked a civil war in the state that continued for three years, until a new national government forced him to yield his command. He then fought under Santa Anna in the war with the United States (1846). He died in Durango, of cholera.

FRANCISCO R. ALMADA, *Diccionario de historia, geografía y biografía de sonorenses* (1983), pp. 709–712.

STUART F. VOSS

URREA, TERESA (*b.* 1873; *d.* 1906), popular figure among Mexican revolutionaries. A mestiza born in Ocorini, Sinaloa, Mexico, Teresa Urrea began, around 1890, to claim divine guidance and to preach social reform from her father's rancho at Cabora in the southern part of the state of Sonora. Thousands of YAQUI and Mayo Indians, along with mestizos and whites of various social groups, flocked to hear and revere her as la Santa (saint) de Cabora. In 1892, when armed movements in her name began to wrack the region, the government deported her and her father to Nogales, Arizona, where she continued to inspire armed forays into Mexico. As fame for her healings spread, she traveled from New York to California, performing her "miracles." She died at age thirty-two, in Clifton, Arizona. Throughout her "mission" she denied fomenting revolution, although hundreds of rebels died in her name.

WILLIAM CURRY HOLDEN, *Teresita* (1978); PAUL D. VANDERWOOD, "Santa Teresa: Mexico's Joan of Arc," in *The Human Tradition in Latin America: The Nineteenth Century*, by William Beezley and Judith Ewell (1989), pp. 215–232; BRIANDON DOMECQ, *La insólita historia de la Santa de Cabora* (1990).

PAUL J. VANDERWOOD

URRIOLAGOITÍA, MAMERTO (*b.* 5 December 1895; *d.* 4 June 1974), president of Bolivia (1949–1951). Born in Sucre, Urriolagoitía became a lawyer and specialized in international law. From 1919 to 1937, he served as Bolivia's Consul General in Great Britain. At the conclusion of his diplomatic career, he returned to Sucre and won election to Bolivia's Senate in the early 1940s. Urriolagoitía became a leading member of a conservative Republican party coalition (Partido de la Unión Republicana Socialista—PURS). In the election of 1947, the PURS candidate Enrique HERTZOG was elected president and Mamerto Urriolagoitía, vice president. Hertzog resigned in May 1949, a few days after the mid-term election resulted in a vote that favored the middle-class reformist Nationalist Revolutionary Movement (MNR). As president Urriolagoitía repeatedly used military intervention to put down worker uprisings in the mining areas and cities. After the MNR won the May 1951 presidential elections, Urriolagoitía resigned on 16 May 1951. He handed over the government to General Hugo BALLIVIÁN, who, a few days later, abrogated the elections.

HERBERT S. KLEIN, *Parties and Political Change in Bolivia, 1880–1952* (1969), pp. 388–400, and *Bolivia: The Evolution of a Multi-Ethnic Society* (1992), pp. 222, 224.

ERWIN P. GRIESHABER

URRUTIA LLEÓ, MANUEL (*b.* 1901; *d.* 5 July 1981), Cuban lawyer and judge, appointed president after the CUBAN REVOLUTION of 1959 and dismissed six months later by Fidel CASTRO. Born in Las Villas province, Urrutia received a law degree in 1923 from the University of Havana and was appointed municipal judge of Oriente Province in 1928. He was later named the magistrate of the district of Santiago. Urrutia first gained national recognition in 1957, when he ruled for the dismissal of 100 youths charged with rebellion against the Batista dictatorship for their involvement in Castro's 1953 attack on the Moncada barracks. Castro's decision to appoint Urrutia as president was apparently based on the assumption that Urrutia would be a compromise candidate acceptable to both radicals and moderates who supported Batista's overthrow. Yet from his first days in office, Urrutia showed little ability in the art of politics practiced amid a volatile revolutionary movement. After attacking growing Communist influence within the government, Urrutia was forced to resign on 17 July 1959, and public sentiment against him was so great that he had to take refuge in the Venezuelan embassy. Urrutia later fled to the United States, where he became a university professor and organizer of an anti-Castro movement. He wrote *Fidel Castro and Co., Inc: Communist Tyranny in Cuba* (1964), his account of the revolution. Urrutia died in Queens, New York.

RAMÓN EDUARDO RUIZ, *Cuba: The Making of a Revolution* (1970); SAMUEL FARBER, *Revolution and Reaction in Cuba, 1933–1960* (1976); LUIS A. PÉREZ, JR., *Cuba: Between Reform and Revolution* (1988).

MICHAEL POWELSON

URSÚA, PEDRO DE (*b.* ca. 1511–1516; *d.* 1 January 1561), leader of the search for EL DORADO, the "Land of Cinnamon." Born in Navarre, Spain, Ursúa reached Cartagena de Indias on Colombia's coast in 1545. He served as administrator and military leader, pacified the Chitarero and Muso Indians, and founded the cities of Pamplona and Tudela. As *justicia mayor* (municipal deputy) of Santa Marta in the early 1550s, he brought the Tairona Indians under Spanish domination. Subsequently he undertook the task of subduing runaway slaves on the Isthmus of Panama and succeeded in capturing "King" Bayamo, thus ending a threat to intercolonial trade.

The Peruvian viceroy Andrés HURTADO DE MENDOZA, marqués de Cañete, authorized Ursúa's search for El Dorado, reputed to be in the upper Amazon basin. Ursúa collected about 370 Europeans, from 20 to 30 blacks, and from 600 to 2,000 Indian auxiliaries from several Andean cities in February 1559. They constructed several brigantines, flatboats, rafts, and canoes on the upper Huallaga River, setting forth in September 1560. Pedro de Ursúa faced discontent from the start: some were bothered by the presence of his mestiza mistress, Inés de Atienza; others chafed at the hard work and difficult conditions en route downriver. Lope de AGUIRRE was at the head of the mutinous group that assassinated Ursúa as he rested in his hammock near the juncture of the Putumayo and Amazon rivers.

The tale of Aguirre's bloody descent to the Atlantic is one of the most tragic in the era of discovery. Over a hundred of his fellow explorers were killed as Aguirre rebelled against all authority, save that of the sword. Survivors sailed out of the Amazon northwestwardly to the island of Margarita, then headed back toward Peru. Aguirre was finally surrounded by a group of royalists in Venezuela and killed on 27 October 1561.

JOHN HEMMING, *Red Gold: The Conquest of the Brazilian Indians* (1978), pp. 195–197; JOSÉ ANTONIO DEL BUSTO DUTHURBURU, *La pacificación del Perú* (1984), pp. 142–154.

NOBLE DAVID COOK

URUGUAI, VISCONDE DO (Paulino José Soares de Sousa; *b.* 4 October 1807; *d.* 15 July 1866), Brazilian statesman. Born in Paris, Uruguai was a key spokesman for the early Conservative Party and the driving force in the diplomacy leading to the overthrow of Argentina's dictator, Juan Manuel de ROSAS in 1852. Uruguai began his studies at Coimbra and completed them in São Paulo in 1831. His brilliance and character attracted support and early promotion as a magistrate in São Paulo, and then in Rio de Janeiro. His marriage into an established provincial planter clan brought political entrée through his brother-in-law, Joaquim José Rodrigues Tôrres (later Viscount de ITABORAÍ). In 1834, he was elected to the assembly of Rio de Janeiro Province, which in turn elected him a provincial vice president. In 1836, he was appointed president of the province; that same year the province elected him a national deputy. In the chamber of deputies, with Tôrres and Eusébio de QUEIRÓS, Uruguai led the SAQUAREMAS. The latter were the *fluminense* radical reactionaries of the Conservative Party, which had been created in 1837, in an era of reaction, and was directed by Bernardo Pereira de VASCONCELOS, Honório Hermeto Carneiro Leão, and Tôrres. Uruguai's role was that of jurist and orator. He and Vasconcelos formulated the positions that halted the Regency's liberal momentum and shored up the authoritarian centralization that was identified with the monarchy. His son and namesake, known as Paulino, maintained this legacy against the reformism of Uruguai's former protégé, the Viscount do RIO BRANCO, in the 1870s.

Uruguai, increasingly disgusted with politics, was proudest of his role as foreign minister (1849–1853). He earned his title by defending the empire's perennially insecure southern interests from Rosas's Uruguayan ambitions. It was Uruguai, aided in the field by Honório Hermeto Carneiro Leão (later Viscount de PARANÁ) and Viscount do Rio Branco, who secured Uruguay and the Urquiza alliance that defeated Rosas. Subsequently, Uruguai, after accepting a brief diplomatic mission to Europe, began a retreat from politics. Although meeting responsibilities as a senator (1849) and councillor of state (1853), he gradually sought the solace of study. The *Ensaio sôbre direito administrativo* was published in 1862 and *Estudos práticos sobre a administração das provincias do império* was published in 1865.

JOÃO PANDÍA CALÓGERAS, *A política externa do império*, vol. 3 (1933); JOSÉ ANTÔNIO SOARES DE SOUSA, *A vida do visconde do Uruguai* (1944); THOMAS FLORY, *Judge and Jury in Imperial Brazil* (1981); ILMAR ROHLOFF DE MATTOS, *O tempo saquarema* (1987).

JEFFREY D. NEEDELL

URUGUAY. [Coverage begins with a two-part survey of Uruguayan political history. There follow a variety of entries on specialized topics: **Colegiado; Congress of 1825; Constitutions; Electoral System; Geography; Medidas Prontas de Seguridad; Organizations;** (administrative, cultural, economic, labor, etc.); **Plebiscites; Political Parties;** and **Revolutionary Movements.**]

Before 1900

INDIANS AND SPANIARDS
Before its discovery by Spain in 1516, Uruguay was populated by a few thousand indigenous people. To these peoples the European conqueror gave a variety of names: Charrúas, Minuanes, Bohanes, Guenoas, Yaros, Chanáes, and GUARANÍS. Their territories spread beyond Uruguay into what later became neighboring Argentina and Brazil. The dominant and numerically most important race, the Charrúas, were advanced hunters, while the Chanáes in addition practiced a primitive agriculture, which had also been developed more fully by the enclaves of Guaraní settlement. But all were societies fundamentally based on hunting, canoeing, and fishing. A limited quantity of archaeological remains bears witness to the practice of decorating pottery and working stone.

The arrival of the Europeans, and of the cattle and horses they left behind in Uruguay at the beginning of the seventeenth century, changed the demography, customs, and natural environment of the indigenous peoples. Having become skilled horsemen hunting wild cattle, they ended up decimated by smallpox and by persecution by the white men as their culture was inimical to the forms of labor introduced by the Spaniards. Traditionally, 1831 is identified as the year in which the Charrúas disappeared as a population of any importance, wiped out by the soldiers of the first republican government of independent Uruguay. This annihilation did not diminish the importance of indigenous blood as an element in the composition of the rural population, especially the Guaranís, from territories occupied by the JESUIT MISSIONS.

Nonetheless, the so-called extermination of the Indians at Salsipuedes in 1831 established the myth of a European, white Uruguay, which the dominant classes in the country encouraged, all the more as immigration from outside the continent became the basis for Uruguay's population growth.

The BANDA ORIENTAL (literally "Eastern Bank") was the name given by the Spaniards to the territory that became Uruguay. It was a region of late colonization, mainly during the period of Bourbon Spain in the eighteenth century. It was populated for three principal reasons: the quality of its natural grassland and the multiplying numbers of livestock derived from those left by the Spanish discoverers, the advantages of Montevideo as the only natural port on the RÍO DE LA PLATA, and the fact that it was a frontier territory in permanent dispute between the Spanish and Portuguese crowns. This struggle was often the explanation for the foundation of its cities and towns, as was the case, for example, of the first important European settlement, Colonia del Sacramento, founded by Portugal in 1680, and of Montevideo, established by Spain between 1724 and 1730. The lack of a fixed frontier had its effect on the economy, promoting a contraband trade which made a mockery of Spain's commercial monopoly, as well as on society, encouraging horsemanship and the practice of arms.

Natural grassland, and ownerless cattle and horses running free, gave rise to the ESTANCIA (ranch), dedicated to cattle production, and to the dominant figure in rural areas, the *estanciero* (ranchowner). Appearing around 1780–1800 were the first SALADEROS (meat-salting plants), which converted part of the beef production into *tasajo*, hard and lean salt beef, consumed at first only by the slaves of Cuba and Brazil. The *saladeros* were part *estancia* and part industry in Montevideo. Although steam power was adopted in 1832 to render the fat, the production of *tasajo* itself required only the dexterity of the GAUCHO (horseman) to lasso the semiwild cattle, and the skill of the laborers—until 1830 almost all black slaves—who cut the meat in thin strips. The meat was then salted and placed in piles for two or three days, and then laid out in the sun to dry—a process that was, in effect, a manufacture.

Through the port of Montevideo there was a legal trade with Spain and (after 1779) with Buenos Aires as well as an unlawful trade with Portuguese Brazil and with European ships that made "emergency" entries into the harbor. This activity generated sufficient income to maintain the Spanish bureaucracy that governed the Banda Oriental as well as the wealthy traders who formed the municipal body known as the *cabildo,* the imperfect but only school of self-government to which *criollos* had access. The Banda Oriental formed part of the Viceroyalty of the Río de la Plata following its belated creation in 1776, but Montevideo and a large adjacent area were included in it as a governorship.

The population of the Banda Oriental—about 30,000 in 1800, of whom one-third lived in Montevideo—was divided more clearly perhaps on regional and racial bases than in terms of social classes. Montevideo, as the seat of Spanish authority, was stratified by race and class. Merchants, financiers, absentee *estancieros,* and holders of high office formed an upper class that still kept the flavor of its humble origins in Catalonia, the Canaries, or the Basque country. Traders, storekeepers, the military, less exalted officials, and craftsmen, constituted a middle class in embryo. Below all the rest was the black slave population, one-third of the total.

The interior was a rural world in which social distinctions, though real, tended to be blurred or combined with other cultural and economic aspects in such a way as to become very distinctive. The *estancieros* (known as *latifundistas*) who owned large tracts of land had ejected earlier and less wealthy livestock producers who had lacked the same influence with the Spanish authorities. The majority of these great landowners did not have good title to the lands they held. Many had done no

more than begin the process of legal acquisition in Buenos Aires before abandoning it, weary of the slowness of Bourbon bureaucracy as well as its cost, which invariably exceeded the price of the land itself. Others had purchased defined tracts of land from the Spanish crown, but such *estancias* proved to be much greater in size than what had been paid for. As a result the *estancieros* were collectively dependent on the policy of the state, both Spanish at first and independent republican subsequently.

The population of the interior was nomadic and frequently of mixed race. Life was easy, with food consumption consisting almost entirely of meat, which was freely available. Meat production was hugely in excess of a demand limited to the tiny internal market and restricted external markets in Cuba and Brazil. The Banda Oriental, with perhaps 6 million cattle and half a million horses, had the greatest number of both per head of population of any country in the world. The lowest rural laborer—the *gaucho*—was a horseman (even the beggars in Montevideo were mounted), and had an assured supply of food. When one of the leaders of the 1811 revolution was questioned about how he lived, he replied, "When I needed a shirt I worked; when I needed nothing I did not work." For rural laborers, work was optional, not obligatory. The *latifundistas* regarded with disgust an independent labor force that was only compelled to work when the state from time to time took measures against "vagrants."

The situation was not free of tensions. The Spanish authorities did not allow the *estancieros* to sell cattle hides freely to British and Portuguese merchants, and frequently threatened to make them pay for the lands that they occupied unlawfully. They carried out the threat, for example, in August 1810, just months before the outbreak of the revolution for independence in February 1811. Traders and livestock producers were inconvenienced by subjection to the political, judicial, and commercial authorities (Viceroy, Real Audiencia, and

Vista general de Montevideo taken from the New Cemetery. Lithograph by Eugenio Ciceri, based on drawing by Adolfo d'Hastrei, printed by Augusto Bry (Paris). MUSEO HISTÓRICO NACIONAL, MONTEVIDEO, URUGUAY.

Tribunal del Consulado) located in the neighboring, competing, and envied city of Buenos Aires. The gauchos and Indians hated all those measures emanating from the governor of Montevideo, or the *cabildo*, which attempted to limit the volume of contraband trade, or persecute vagrants, or expel small landholders from the territories of the great *estancias*. This last issue had generated enormous resentment. The pioneer settlers had rounded up cattle previously running wild and unclaimed, built ranch houses and cattle pens, and driven off the Portuguese and Indians who had invaded their land. And now that the region had been made habitable, they were turned off the land by those owed favors by governors or viceroys, or by wealthy merchants from Buenos Aires or Montevideo who had bought the land and secured expulsion orders against those settled on it. The whole of Uruguay had been settled in four or five successive waves of pioneer settlers, who then found themselves declared "trespassers" by the colonial authority.

CATTLEMEN AND CAUDILLOS, 1810–1850

All of these resentments, both toward local authorities and toward Spain and Buenos Aires, came to a head in 1811, as a result of the earlier French invasion of the Iberian peninsula and the weakening of the constraints of colonial rule. That year the interior rebelled against Spanish authority emanating from Montevideo. The revolution was led by a *criollo* commander of the loyalist (Spanish) army itself: José Gervasio ARTIGAS. The revolution at first respected the authority of the Junta de Mayo in Buenos Aires, but political, social, and economic differences soon separated *orientales* from *porteños*. In 1813 the April Congress proclaimed the political principles of the revolution: independence from Spain; organization of a single state comprising all the regions of the former Viceroyalty of La Plata, at first as a confederation and subsequently on a federal basis; democracy; and republicanism. Buenos Aires was not to be the capital.

In September 1815 Artigas issued a regulation that distributed the vast wealth of those opposed to the revolution, "bad Europeans and worse Americans," to the least favored in society, especially Indians, freed slaves, and poor *criollos*. Each was to receive a modest (by the standards of the time) *estancia*, with the obligation to build a ranch house and two cattle pens, and to round up the cattle. The enforcement of the regulation was in part delayed by the Portuguese invasion in 1816, but the confiscation of the great *estancias* prior to their redistribution contributed to the hatred that the old upper class of the colonial period began to feel toward Artigas and his followers.

Between 1811 and 1814 the *orientales* fought against Spain and eventually succeeded with help from Buenos Aires in occupying Montevideo. Before then, however, in January 1814, Artigas reached the decision that the objective of the revolution could not be to substitute one despotism for another, Buenos Aires in place of Spain,

and left the army of Buenos Aires to continue the siege of Montevideo alone. The city fell to the *porteños* in June, after which Artigas made war on Buenos Aires, aided by the littoral provinces of the Uruguay and Paraná rivers, Entre Ríos, Corrientes, and Santa Fe, all of which were attracted by the idea of federalism. The struggle then became one between federalists, who were also republicans, and the forces of Buenos Aires, who were royalist as well as centralist. In 1815, with the victory at Guayabos, Artigas succeeded in displacing the *porteños* and restoring Montevideo to the *orientales*, and established his authority throughout the country.

From 1816 until 1820 Artigas confronted the invasion forces of the Portuguese monarchy now established in Rio de Janeiro. In addition to their traditional desire to occupy the old Banda Oriental, long disputed with Spain, the Portuguese now invaded out of fear that the south of Brazil might otherwise be contaminated with republican and federalist principles. The invasion had the blessing of Buenos Aires, and ended in defeat for Artigas in 1820.

With its trade and LIVESTOCK industry in ruins following nine years of continuous revolutionary war, the country was in the hands first of Portugal (1820–1822) and then of Brazil (1822–1825). An important element of the upper class collaborated with the invading forces, who, under the command of an able Portuguese general, Carlos F. Lecor, promised to impose order and to restore the property confiscated by Artigas to its former owners. In 1821 a congress of collaborating *orientales* voted for the incorporation of what was now called the Cisplatine Province into the United Kingdom of Portugal, Brazil, and the Algarve.

Eventually, however, the upper class became disillusioned with the Brazilian authorities, and other social sectors found similar frustrations. Anti-Portuguese sentiments, strong in a population of Spanish origin that had been resisting Portuguese encroachments since the seventeenth century, were quickly rekindled. It became evident that the Portuguese were giving preference to their own in the distribution of lands and in commercial concessions. The cost of maintaining the army of occupation was heavy. Lecor's authoritarian rule did not permit even a semblance of self-government, not even following the introduction of the Brazilian Constitution of 1824.

The second stage of the revolution began in April 1825, when thirty-three *orientales*—the number and nationality of whom was in truth somewhat mythical—invaded the country and within a few months had raised a revolt throughout the interior against the Brazilians, who were thus confined to Montevideo. Following the victories at Rincón and Sarandí, the government of Buenos Aires gave its formal backing to the *orientales*, and at the end of 1825 also entered the war against Brazil. The leader of the *orientales* was now Juan Antonio LAVALLEJA, a rural caudillo, who was soon joined by another, Fructuoso RIVERA. Their objectives were more modest than those of Artigas. Whereas the latter sought federalism and social egalitarianism as well as independence from external control, his two former lieutenants were content to free the Banda Oriental from Brazilian rule, while leaving undecided (perhaps deliberately) the nature of future relations with Buenos Aires as well as any solution to the question of landownership. On 25 August 1825 the House of Representatives of the Provincia Oriental declared first the absolute independence of the country, and then its union with the other provinces.

The war with Brazil came to an end with an indecisive victory at Ituzaingó in February 1827. For some months Britain had been attempting to mediate the conflict through its envoy, Lord Ponsonby. The war had seriously disrupted British trade with Argentina because of the Brazilian blockade of the port of Buenos Aires. In addition, though a secondary consideration, Britain had some interest in encouraging the independence of a small state on the Río de la Plata to prevent Argentine control of both sides. The Río de la Plata gave access to the largest system of navigable rivers in South America, and by "internationalizing" it, Britain could ensure that her trade would not be impeded by a strong Argentina. On 4 October 1828 the Brazilian Empire and the Argentine Confederation ratified a preliminary peace agreement declaring the Cisplatine Province separate from Brazil and an independent state. Thus the birth of independent Uruguay was the combined result, in proportions that national historiography has discussed with great fervor, of British self-interest and the Uruguayan desire for autonomy and opposition to the porteños.

An elected assembly approved the constitution of the new country, officially designated the Estado Oriental del Uruguay, in 1830. A judicial system based on European and North American models appeared to safeguard internal order. The new state was to be a republic, and individual rights were to be guaranteed through the classic separation of powers. The right to vote was denied to the illiterate, laborers, servants, and vagrants, who collectively constituted the majority of the population. In principle, a minority would elect deputies and senators for three and six years, respectively. They in turn, every four years, would name the president of the republic, who could not serve a second term immediately after the first. This was the constitution that ruled the destiny of Uruguay until 1919.

The reality of the country, however, prevailed over this Europeanized legal framework. Until at least 1876, Uruguayan affairs were dominated by civil wars out of which emerged the two parties, Colorados and Blancos, that eventually modernized and survived into the twentieth century. The first constitutional president, Fructuoso Rivera (1830–1834; 1838–1842), faced three uprisings led by the other main rural caudillo, Lavalleja. His successor, Manuel ORIBE (1835–1838), in turn faced two challenges from Rivera. At the battle of Carpintería in

1836, the warring factions for the first time used the devices that would become their traditional forms of identification: white (*blanco*) for the forces of the government, who styled themselves "Defenders of the Law," and at first pale blue (the other main color on the Uruguayan flag) but subsequently red (*colorado*) for Rivera's followers. In his second challenge in 1838, Rivera was successful. This time he was assisted by a squadron of the French, who were anxious to displace Oribe, who had allied himself with Juan Manuel de ROSAS, governor of Buenos Aires. Rivera occupied Montevideo and had himself elected president for a second term in 1839. That same year Rivera declared war on Rosas, who continued to regard Oribe as the legitimate president of Uruguay, and thus began the GUERRA GRANDE. Both the Uruguayan factions now had international support: Rivera was backed by unitarian refugees from Argentina, as well as by the French and British squadrons in the Río de la Plata. The Europeans were fearful that Rosas might annex Uruguay and were also keen to break up his monopoly of shipping on the Paraná River. But with Rosas's support, Oribe now began the siege of Montevideo, which endured for nine years (1843–1851). The conflict was not resolved until the two European nations withdrew their forces and the Brazilian Empire intervened on behalf of a Colorado Montevideo. Oribe (and Rosas) was defeated, but the peace agreement that was signed on 8 October 1851 declared that there were neither victors nor vanquished.

The atmosphere immediately following this conflict was one of reconciliation between the two factions. The destruction of livestock, commerce, and private wealth during the long conflict encouraged unity. But by now factionalism was engrained in the collective memory, and civil conflict soon broke out again. The Blanco president Juan F. Giró (March–October 1852) was overthrown by a mutiny of the mainly Colorado army. The new Colorado leader, the rural caudillo Venancio FLORES, governed as president until 1855. In 1856 the spirit of unity and the desire to forget the resentments of the past brought Gabriel A. Pereyra to power (1856–1860). During his presidency a group within the Colorado Party, called the Conservative Party, raised a rebellion, but its leaders were defeated and executed at Quinteros by government troops. During 1860–1864 President Bernardo P. Berro attempted to continue the policy of unity, but the parties reemerged. In April 1863 Flores invaded the country with the support of the Argentine president, Bartolomé MITRE, and with the eventual collaboration of Brazil. Berro looked for assistance to Paraguay to reestablish, as he described it, an equilibrium in the Río de la Plata region. But following Flores's capture of Paysandú in January 1865, one of his generals ordered the principal Blanco leaders to be shot. Thus did each faction acquire its martyrs, and an emotional force that would ensure permanence for both. During Venancio Flores's dictatorship (1865–1868) Uruguay joined Brazil and Argentina in the WAR OF THE TRIPLE ALLIANCE against Paraguay. In February 1868 Flores, whose regime had awakened old passions, was assassinated; the same day the former Blanco president, Bernardo Berro, also fell victim to an assassin. New martyrs fed the traditions of the parties.

Flores was the first in the long continuous series of Colorado governments that did not end until 1959. He was succeeded by a constitutional president, Lorenzo Batlle (1868–1872), who faced an uprising under the rural Blanco caudillo Timoteo Aparicio. This was known as the Revolution of the Lances, a sufficient comment on the primitive military technology of the period. Measured in terms of its duration (1870–1872) and destructive effect on livestock, it was second only among Uruguay's civil wars to the Guerra Grande. The factions were reconciled at the so-called Peace of April 1872, as a result of which for the first time the Blancos shared in the government of the country with the Colorados through the practice of COPARTICIPACIÓN (coparticipation). Nonetheless disorder persisted until 1876, when Colonel Lorenzo LATORRE seized power.

It was essentially through the series of struggles, and the various events accompanying them, that Blancos and Colorados acquired some degree of political, social, and even regional significance. The different personalities and social connections of Oribe and Rivera, and the greatest of the wars, the Guerra Grande, gave a new form to the opposition of capital city and interior, which had existed since the colonial period. The Colorados identified with besieged Montevideo, with immigrants, and with unobstructed access for European influence. The Blancos, with their roots in the surrounding countryside, took their identity from the rural environment and the great landowners, and were essentially *criollo.*

Yet these differences do not adequately explain the extent of internal chaos in Uruguay in this period. A fuller understanding of the country, as well as an interpretation of its political character, must take into account its economic, social, and cultural structures, and the technology available to a preindustrial state. The three pillars of conservatism in Latin America, the Catholic church, the army, and landed property, were all weak in Uruguay. Within the church there was no Uruguayan hierarchy in 1830, and not until 1878 was the country granted its first bishopric. The junior clergy was few, often foreign, theologically not well trained, and of uncertain moral character. Lacking major properties of its own, the church's influence was confined to the representation of the majority religion of the country's inhabitants. The army was small, and did not have a monopoly of coercive power. The rural worker used horses, the lasso, and the knife in normal activity, and at the whim of his leader became an active revolutionary and rival to the professional soldiery. Landed property dominated the agrarian structure, but was not firmly established. Those in possession during the years of the revolutionary wars fought against the landowners of the colonial period, whose titles were also often less

than perfect. Government had to mediate in these disputes, which often boiled over into battles between Blancos and Colorados. The former in general corresponded to the class of large landowners; the latter more to those who occupied lands, whether large or small, but who lacked legal papers of ownership for them. Hence, instead of the Uruguayan state straightforwardly representing the landowning class, the status of those holding land depended in fact on the political character of the state itself.

Transport and communication facilities remained those of a cattle-raising society. Provided he could change horses en route, a man could ride from Montevideo to San Fructuoso (240 miles) in two days, whereas the regular stagecoach service (which itself only began in 1850) took at least four or five days, even assuming that the rivers and streams were passable and not flooded. Carts carrying hides and wool needed a month for the journey. Cattle were moved to the *saladeros* on the hoof, a task requiring the special skills of the *troperos* (herdsmen). Agriculture, on the other hand, depended entirely on cumbersome and expensive transport by cart, and therefore developed only in the vicinity of the centers of demand. Only the littoral region on the Uruguay River benefited from improved communications, with a three-day steamship service connecting Salto and Montevideo from 1860. Maintaining control of the interior from distant Montevideo with such transport and communication was very difficult. By the time news of a rural uprising reached the capital, the rebellion had taken root. Even the various armies of the government had difficulty in knowing their respective positions and in combining forces, as happened, for example, to the Colorados during the Revolution of the Lances.

THE BIRTH OF MODERN URUGUAY: 1850–1900

The Colorado military governments of Lorenzo Latorre (1876–1880), Francisco Vidal (1880–1882), Máximo Santos (1882–1886) and Máximo TAJES (1886–1890) established centralized power in Uruguay with dominance over the rural caudillos, thus making rural uprisings far more difficult though not yet impossible. There were several reasons why the state and its army could now exercise a monopoly of physical coercion: armaments had become expensive (the Remington repeating rifle and Krupp artillery were now deployed) and required training not available to the gauchos; the introduction of the telegraph and the railway strengthened the power of Montevideo; and developments both in the economy and in society impeded the costly rebellions of the past.

Another factor that contributed to the strengthening of domestic peace was the growth of nationalism, which put an end to the internationalization of the Uruguayan party system based on alliances with Argentine unitarians and federalists and Brazilian factions. The unification of both Argentina and Brazil around Buenos Aires and Rio de Janeiro, respectively, meant that there were fewer appeals from these countries for Uruguayans to take sides in their internal disputes. In this sense, the Revolution of the Lances was the first wholly Uruguayan civil war.

The period of militarism was succeeded by the presidential and authoritarian but civilian governments of Julio HERRERA Y OBES (1890–1894) and Juan Idiarte Borda (1894–1897). These exclusively Colorado regimes, bolstered by electoral manipulation, were countered by two Blanco rebellions led by the rural caudillo Aparicio SARAVIA. His rising in March 1897 led to a Colorado government with Blanco acquiescence, that of Juan Lindolfo CUESTAS (1897–1903). However, following the election of José BATLLE Y ORDÓÑEZ in 1903, Saravia led the last great rural rebellion in 1904. These two revolts differed from their predecessors in that their political manifestos went beyond mere adherence to party tradition. On both occasions the Blancos defended the modern causes of respect for the popular will in elections and proportional representation for the parties in the legislature.

Internal peace and strong central government in Montevideo were accompanied by changes in the demography, economy, society, and culture of the nation. Uruguay in 1830 had barely 70,000 inhabitants. By 1875 the population was 450,000, and by 1900 it had reached a million. This spectacular increase, by a factor of fourteen in 70 years, was unparalleled elsewhere in the Americas. The high birth rate before 1890 (between 40 and 50 per thousand inhabitants) was combined with relatively low mortality (between 20 and 30 per thousand), but even more crucial in the demographic transformation was European immigration. French, Italians, and Spaniards before 1850, Italians and Spaniards thereafter, arrived in five waves of migration during the nineteenth century. Mass immigration to Uruguay occurred relatively early in comparison with that to Argentina, and was huge in proportion to the very small population of 1830. During the half-century after 1840 the population of Montevideo was between 50 and 60 percent foreign, nearly all of whom were from Europe. The national census of 1860 found that 35 percent of Uruguayans were foreign, a proportion declining to 17 percent in 1908.

The Europeans (especially) and the Brazilians had values that were different from those of the *criollos*. They were more enterprising, and more acquisitive. Their interests were protected during internal wars by their consuls, and any losses were invariably compensated by the Uruguayan state, which was vulnerable to external pressure. By the 1870s they had become the principal wealth-owners in both the capital and the interior, with 56 percent of property in Montevideo and 58 percent of interior land. European immigrants were also pioneers in the manufacture of consumer goods, and in 1889 controlled about 80 percent of such establishments.

The economic structure of the country also changed. Sheep farming was added to cattle production on the *estancias* between 1850 and 1870. According to the census of 1852, the sheep flock was no more than 0.8 million, yielding 14 to 18 ounces of wool per head of a quality fit only for making mattresses. In 1868, however, the flock was estimated at 17 million and now yielded 40 ounces of merino wool per head, as a result of the crossbreeding that had begun with livestock imported from France and Germany. In 1884 wool took the place of hides as Uruguay's most important export commodity, and it retained that position until the great expansion of frozen beef in the second decade of the twentieth century. In addition to the unimproved cattle, whose commercial value largely consisted of the hide, the *estanciero* now produced wool, which was sold at good prices in the European market. Sheep farming was also the foundation of a rural middle class: it made use of lower-quality pastures, needed only one-fifth of the land per animal compared with cattle, and required at first an increased labor input.

By the end of the nineteenth century Uruguay thus had economic characteristics that differentiated it from the rest of Latin America. It produced a foodstuff, meat, and provided for two other basic human needs, leather for footwear and wool for clothing. Its export markets were diversified rather than dependent on a single importer: Brazil and Cuba for *tasajo;* France, Germany, and Belgium for wool; and the United Kingdom and United States for hides. Since Europe was importing commodities that it also produced but at higher cost, Uruguay benefited from a high differential rent. Recent estimates of per capita income in the nineteenth century, based on the assumption that per capita exports represented 15 percent of per capita income, suggest that incomes were high in Uruguay during 1870–1900 (US$317 in 1881–1885, for example), comparable to or higher than those in the United States and much higher than those in Brazil. It should also be noted that Britain's policy of free trade—like that of Europe in general—was an essential part of the economic system within which Uruguay sold commodities in Europe that competed with Europe's own agricultural sector. As long as unrestricted trade lasted, until the international economic crisis at the beginning of the 1930s, Uruguay occupied a secure and profitable position within the European imperial systems.

The arrival of the sheep was followed by the enclosure of the *estancias*. Wire fences were erected between 1870 and 1890, as much to ensure exclusive access for a landowner's livestock to his pasture as to allow crossbreeding of the flocks and herds with European pedigree stock. Fencing destroyed the livelihoods of the laborers who previously guarded the livestock, and gave rise to the previously unknown problem of rural poverty and hunger. It was ironic that this technological unemployment should have been the breeding ground for the last civil wars at the turn of the century, since both sheep and wire fencing implied massive investments, which underlined for the *estancieros* the need for internal order. The landowners who were at the forefront of these changes established in 1871 the Asociación Rural to represent their interests and to seek domestic peace at all costs.

Concurrent with these rural developments was the transformation of urban Uruguay. Beginning in 1860 the first foreign capital began to arrive, especially from Britain. Pioneer investments between 1863 and 1865 included Liebig's Extract of Meat factory, the London and River Plate Bank, and the first London loan to the Uruguayan government. In 1884 the sum of British investments was estimated at £6.5 million; by 1900 the total had reached £40 million. British investment in Uruguay was small compared to its total export of capital to the rest of the world, but was very large relative to domestic urban capital. Uruguay was the fifth most important Latin American recipient of British capital, after Argentina, Mexico, Brazil, and Chile; but on a per capita basis, only Argentina received more. The British built the railways—the first line was opened in 1869 and in 1905 there were 1,200 miles of track—as well as the urban infrastructure of Montevideo (water supply, gas, telephones, trams), while increasing the volume of lending to the government and securing a near-monopoly in the local insurance market.

In the case of the railway companies, the British investors secured important concessions from the Uruguayan government, which urgently needed rail transport at any price provided it could be used to put down rural rebellions. Most of the lines benefited from a government dividend guarantee of 7 percent on a fixed capital sum of £5,000 per kilometer of track. The result was a system characterized by curves and gradients, unnecessarily extended by between 5 percent and 10 percent of its length. The state could only intervene in the fixing of railway tariff rates if profits exceeded 12 percent, which, needless to say, they never did. But the railway was an essential tool if the government was to control the interior. When the RÍO NEGRO was spanned by a railway bridge in 1886, the two halves of Uruguay, which invariably had been divided by winter floods, were then united.

Other British companies in Montevideo as well as the railways provoked public hostility with their high tariffs and deficient service. By 1880–1900 the performance of gas, water, railways, and insurance had raised doubts in the minds of the political elite concerning the benefits Uruguay received from foreign investment unsupervised by the state. These sentiments led to the law of 1888, which instituted strict controls on the accounting of the railway companies, and in 1896 to the founding of the first state bank, the Banco de la República Oriental del Uruguay (BROU).

After 1875, population growth and protectionist legislation encouraged the birth of Uruguay's modern manufacturing industry. Small and restricted to the production of consumer goods (foodstuffs, beverages, furniture, textiles, leather), such activities nonetheless gave rise both to capitalists anxious for political stability and to a small proletariat that was hostile to the idea of enlisting in the armies of either the Blancos or the Colorados.

The social structure that resulted from these developments, and at the same time promoted them, was very different from that of the first half of the nineteenth century. Social classes were now more clearly differentiated. Landownership was nonetheless complex since alongside the LATIFUNDIO smaller farm units based on the exploitation of sheep had developed. The 1908 census suggests that farms of between 250 and 6,250 acres, roughly equivalent to the *estancias* of the rural middle class, accounted for 52 percent of total land area, whereas just 1,391 *latifundios* (in excess of 6,250 acres) occupied 43 percent of the land. This distribution was the result of a long historical process that preserved the position of the large landowners, but required them to coexist with an important rural middle class. The wars of independence and subsequent civil conflicts entailed the destruction and theft of livestock and the general disruption of rural production, but they also had another consequence: property rights changed hands rapidly in the nineteenth century. The *latifundio* still existed in 1900, but the *latifundistas* were not the same families as in the colonial period or in the early years of independence. Uruguay's rural upper class had the taint of being nouveau riche, thus diminishing its power and social standing.

At the beginning of the twentieth century the *estancieros* had two monopolies, of land and of cattle, and the value of both was rising with improvements in the *saladero* industry but above all with the establishment in 1905 of the first FRIGORÍFICO (meat-freezing plant) exporting frozen meat to Europe. Rural workers no longer had the choice of vagrancy or employment on the *estancia*: they had to work to feed themselves. Those who were unable to work found themselves left to rot in what were called the *pueblos de ratas* (rat towns), eating food of poor quality in place of their previous meat diet. The modern gaucho was reduced to domestic service or prostitution in the case of the women; general labor, sheepshearing, contraband, or cattle-thieving for the men. It was at this point that internal migration to the cities began. In Montevideo, the idea of a "social question" appeared for the first time. Although upward social mobility was possible, life for workers in industry was hard. A working day of 11 to 15 hours provided the background for anarchist ideology and the foundation of the first trade unions around 1875. The old fear of urban employers of a Blanco uprising was gradually replaced by the new threat of class-based revolution.

There were changes also in the intellectual and cultural environment. The Universidad de la República opened its doors to students of law in 1849, medicine in 1876, and mathematics in 1888. In 1877, the Lorenzo LATORRE government acted on the ideas of José Pedro Varela to reform primary education, devoting resources to its development while making it obligatory and free.

The rate of illiteracy, previously high, began to fall. The need to increase the population's political involvement, and train it more adequately to fit the changing economic structure, lay behind these developments.

At the same time there was a tendency toward social and cultural secularization. In 1861 the Catholic church began to lose its jurisdiction over cemeteries. In 1879 the state took over the registration of marriages (Registros de Estado Civil), though conceding that the religious ceremony should precede the civil. However, in 1885 civil marriage became obligatory and had to take place before the church ceremony. The first divorce law was approved in 1907. In state schools Catholicism continued to be taught, but the hostility of education officials and of many teachers reduced this to rote learning of the catechism with no explanation. Even this vestige of religious education was suppressed in 1909. More significantly, perhaps, university students adopted an eclectic spiritualism in the third quarter of the century, and subsequently moved to POSITIVISM and agnosticism, even to atheism. The Catholic church thus found itself under attack and reacted accordingly, but most of the nation's elite and a good part of the population in general remained hostile to it or regarded it with indifference. According to the 1908 census, among native-born men in Montevideo only 44 percent declared themselves to be Catholics, a few more than the 40 percent who were ''liberal.'' One other sign of modernity was the emergence of a new demographic model. Around 1890 the birth rate began to fall, and the average age of marriage for women rose from twenty to twenty-five. People began to practice artificial birth control even in the face of vigorous denunciation by the clergy. Thus did Uruguay, the first of all Latin American countries to become fully Europeanized, enter the twentieth century.

J. E. PIVEL DEVOTO and ALCIRA RANIERI, Historia de la República Oriental del Uruguay (Montevideo, 1981); JOSÉ PEDRO BARRÁN and B. NAHUM, Historia rural del Uruguay moderno, 7 vols. (Montevideo, 1967–1978); J. A. ODDONE, Economía y sociedad en el Uruguay liberal (Montevideo, 1967); A. VÁZQUEZ ROMERO and W. REYES ABADIO, Crónica general del Uruguay, 3 vols. (Montevideo, 1980–1981); M. H. J. FINCH, A Political Economy of Uruguay Since 1870 (Hong Kong, 1981); GERARDO CAETANO and J. RILLA, Historia contemporánea del Uruguay (Montevideo, 1994).

JOSÉ PEDRO BARRÁN

See also **Treinta y Tres (33) Orientales.**

The Twentieth Century

The history of Uruguay since 1900 contrasts remarkably with the preceding period. Until 1875 civil conflict was the dominant theme. The modernization of Uruguay in the final decades before 1900 involved the creation of a state structure by strong governments capable of suppressing insurrections. The concentration of authority in Montevideo created conditions in which foreign capital could flourish, building an economic infrastructure that further consolidated the new state system. Yet in many respects Uruguay in 1900 still appeared primitive. Economic modernization was still restricted. The division between the main political parties, the Blancos and the Colorados, remained a threat to public order. The electorate was small, and elections were nominal.

By the 1920s, however, Uruguay was transformed. In place of anarchy and conflict, the country developed an institutional structure that was stable, innovative, and democratic. Social policy was adventurous and characterized by egalitarian and humanitarian influences that had few equals elsewhere in the world. The economic structure was developed by new export trades, an enlarged role for the public sector, and an expanding manufacturing industry promoted by the state. In its cultural life Uruguay enjoyed a diversity and richness extraordinary in so small a country. The perception of Uruguay as somewhat exceptional, even utopian, in its middle-class prosperity and stability took root in the 1920s and was widely shared inside and outside the country for much of the next half-century.

A feature of the nineteenth century that survived to the end of the twentieth was the dominance in politics of the Colorado and Blanco (or National) parties. The appearance of a two-party system, however, should not be mistaken for democratic stability, nor the parties regarded as conventional vehicles for interest aggregation and policy formulation. They originated as armed bands competing for control of the territory of Uruguay in the 1830s, and loyalty to them was entrenched long before any sense of nationhood existed. This fact is crucial to understanding the instinctive loyalty that each party still commands. Adaptation to the age of mass politics was only possible through the development of complex electoral legislation in the first half of this century (collectively known as the LEY DE LEMAS) and the system of double simultaneous voting (DSV), by which victory goes to the most voted faction of the most voted party. Each party has therefore developed its own liberal, moderate, and conservative factions, which unite under the party banner rather than with those of similar ideological convictions but with different loyalties. As in the nineteenth century, but now by other means, the party struggle is fundamentally to secure control of executive power. Uruguayans elect administrations rather than governments.

The economic and demographic dominance of Montevideo, paradoxical in a country whose economic welfare has always depended on livestock production, is also a legacy of the nineteenth century. Political pressures, exerted by an urban population rising from one-third of the total in 1900 to one-half in the 1990s, have been reflected in the social and economic policy of the twentieth century. The rural sector has provided livestock products for processing and export, while contributing financially to the development of Montevideo and

the welfare of its population either by taxation or by urban investment of the rural surplus. The urban-rural tension is particularly significant because, although the high level of exports per capita has endowed Uruguayans with one of the highest standards of living of any Latin American country during this century, the rate of growth of rural output and exports over the long period has been very low. In the late 1950s, Uruguay entered a period of secular economic stagnation that focused attention on the causes of poor performance in the livestock sector. For some, the problems of Uruguay in the late decades of the twentieth century are a consequence of a misplaced modernity: state-sponsored welfare prejudicing growth. Others have blamed unenterprising landowners or Uruguay's small size within the international economy. However explained, the deterioration of the economy undermined Uruguay's utopia. By the late decades of the century, the earlier self-confidence was displaced by a debilitating nostalgia for a long-gone golden age.

THE AGE OF BATLLE Y ORDÓÑEZ (1900–1930)

José BATLLE Y ORDÓÑEZ held office twice as president, in 1903–1907 and 1911–1915. No other figure in Uruguayan history has had such a decisive influence on the country's development. Indeed the phrase Batllist Uru-

guay, which in a strict historical sense refers to his political and social accomplishment, also defines an ideology of state-mediated negotiation and redistribution as a means of resolving social conflict that has been dominant through most of the twentieth century. In the belief that it has continued to inspire in the capacity and responsibility of the state to solve the economic and social problems of the citizenry, it has formed a central and enduring part of Uruguay's political culture.

Batlle y Ordóñez himself, a commanding figure who was both a visionary and a politician of great skill, came to the presidency through the ranks of the Colorado Party within a political system that was still oligarchic and largely nonparticipatory. His first major challenge was the uprising led by the Blanco caudillo Aparicio SARAVIA in 1903, a last attempt to stem the incursions of a unified state and commercial landownership into the traditional Uruguay in the north. With modernization, civil wars were even more costly to the developing livestock sector. The overwhelming military defeat dealt Saravia finally freed the sector from that threat, but lasting peace required increased political participation and concessions to the Blanco Party in Montevideo to ensure its supremacy over the caudillo faction of the interior. In 1910 the modern system of double simultaneous voting was introduced to allow a divided party to maintain its cohesiveness by aggregating the votes of its different tendencies.

The background to Batlle's administrations was one of rising prosperity based on the export of rural production. The establishment of the first meat-freezing plant (FRIGORÍFICO) in 1904 ushered in a period of rising export values based on the breeding of high-quality cattle capable of producing beef for freezing and chilling. Whatever the inefficiencies and inequities of a rural structure based in *latifundismo*, the political dangers were too great, and the potential gains at a time of economic expansion too limited, to make agrarian reform a priority. Arable production was encouraged, but efforts to diversify the economy were directed mainly toward Montevideo. The tentative protectionism of the 1880s was strengthened and systematized under Batlle. There were also government initiatives promoting the incorporation of new technology in arable farming and manufacturing. Finally, the participation of the public sector in the economy was extended to include banking, insurance, electricity supply, and basic chemicals.

Batlle's social reformism was even more remarkable. Legislation in defense of labor included the eight-hour day in 1915. Provision for retirement pensions, with low age and service prerequisites, was extended from the public sector to areas of the private sector in 1919. Old-age pensions, proposed in 1914, were finally granted in 1919. But if labor and social-security enactments were the central welfare provisions, the range of liberal, secular, and humanitarian legislation implemented at the time conveys the extent of Batlle's radicalism. Separation of church and state, the right of women to initiate divorce, the abolition of capital punishment and of entertainments involving cruelty to animals, full legal rights for children born out of wedlock, and increased educational provision, were all achieved before 1920.

Batlle was an exceptional leader who consciously attempted to create in Uruguay a model country. At the same time, his idealism was molded to fit the challenges and tensions that Uruguay confronted, and indeed it is arguable that his radicalism had a conservative aim. Although the antagonism of the two traditional parties had in the past been destructive, Batlle had no intention of allowing such loyalties to be displaced by the more dangerous doctrines of class. The Colorados had to champion the cause of the workers if they were to maintain their dominance in Montevideo, but Batlle was no socialist or class warrior. Batlle preferred to demonstrate that the party was better able to secure workers' objectives than were trade unions or left-wing political groups. The obstacle to reform was not capital as such, and much of Batllism promoted the interests of small domestic producers. It was rather the costly, low-quality service provided by British companies in railways and other economic and social structures that gave Batlle a target he could share with all ranks of Uruguayans.

While Batlle's reforms were remarkable mainly for their timing or context, his proposals in 1913 to change

Artigas Monument in Montevideo. STOCK, BOSTON.

the 1830 Constitution were unique. He saw dangers in concentrating executive powers in one person and proposed instead a nine-person collegiate executive (COLEGIADO) that would also consolidate Colorado control of government. The 1918 Constitution dispersed executive authority between a president and the nine members of the National Council of Administration until its overthrow in 1933. The new constitution, even as modified, represented the high-water mark of Batlle's reforms. To overcome Blanco opposition, the doctrine of COPARTICIPACIÓN had to be revived, giving both parties the right to nominate the public posts. The split that resulted within the Colorado Party between Batllists and the conservative wing brought to an end the reformist era. At the start of his administration in 1916, President Feliciano VIERA announced that there would be no further initiatives.

The 1920s was a decade of prosperity and relative quietude. After the frantic activity of the Batlle y Ordóñez administrations, political life settled into a pragmatic pattern of alliances and agreements within and between the parties. Although the end of the First World War sharply cut the level of demand and prices for livestock products, growing demand in Britain for chilled beef kept the economy buoyant. Landowners increasingly complained of the burden of taxes and of the prices the foreign-owned meat-freezing plants paid for cattle. The greater threat to prosperity, however, was that while producers continued to improve the quality of their livestock, they showed no inclination to modernize methods of production or to improve their natural pastures and thus increase the animal-supporting capacity of the land. Within the urban economy, manufacturing industry continued to grow, though largely in the basic consumer industries established before the war; construction activity was also at a high level. During the decade about 200,000 immigrants arrived in Montevideo, with a higher proportion than previously from central Europe, but only a fraction of this number settled.

Late in the 1920s, Batllist reformism resurfaced, with proposals for enlarging the public sector in meat-packing (the Frigorífico Nacional), alcohol and cement production, and the import and refining of oil (Ancap), as well as extensions to the pension program. To secure Blanco support for Ancap, factions of the two parties agreed to the Pact of CHINCHULÍN (Pork-Barrel Pact) in 1931, thereby increasing Blanco participation in state patronage. But by then an era had ended. Batlle y Ordóñez died in 1929, shortly before the full force of the international depression reached the Río de la Plata.

REACTION AND NEO-BATLLISM (1930–1970)

In March 1933, President Gabriel TERRA dispensed with the collegiate executive and organized an authoritarian regime based on conservative Colorado and Blanco factions, which had been excluded from the pork barrel. His coup d'état was presented as a reform of an inefficient constitution, intended to restore probity in public life and halt the growth of the bureaucracy and public sector. The reality was rather different. Although the 1918 Constitution did create an executive that was unwieldy, the origins of the coup are easier to find in the opposition of employers (organized in the Committee of Economic Vigilance) to further social reformism, the traditional mistrust of the British public-utility companies toward the Batllists (in addition to the new fears of the oil companies aroused by the Ancap proposal), and the landowners' need to negotiate a trade deal with Britain that would secure a continuing share of the British beef market. The ambitious Terra, already in office as president since 1931, was an ideal instrument with which to implement this agenda. Besides the 1934 Constitution, which concentrated executive power in his hands, he had the support of an alliance of his own Colorado followers and those of Luis Alberto de HERRERA in the Blanco Party; the independent Blancos and Batllist Colorados were banished to the wilderness.

However, the conservative project of those who backed the coup ran against two obstacles. First, the depression of the export trade, whose value was 40 percent lower in 1932 than in the peak year 1930, was not a consequence of unfavorable policy and therefore reversible. Although the old regime had used trade and exchange controls to limit its impact, any expectation by landowners that controls would be removed and the peso allowed to depreciate ignored the changed circumstances of the 1930s. The curtailed share of the British beef market was permanent; there was no prospect of a significant revival in demand for Uruguay's exports; and manufacturing production for a protected domestic market became increasingly profitable. Relief for the landowners was therefore modest and short-term. Second, many of the characteristics of Batllism, fundamentally the growing dependence of the urban population on state policies and provision, were rooted less in ideology than in the reality of a country whose rural food- and export-producing sector could not employ even the natural increase in the rural population. Hence, in spite of attacks on the fiscal profligacy of the previous regime, public employment grew faster under Terra than it had before 1933. The program of social and labor legislation was interrupted and trade unions severely curbed, but by the late 1930s the urban economy was growing strongly.

By the time Alfredo BALDOMIR, a relatively liberal Terraist, was elected to succeed Terra in 1938, constitutional change again seemed possible. Terra's regime had been illiberal rather than repressive (a "*dictablanda*"), but in basing itself exclusively on two-party factions, the new political order could only be provisional. With urban manufacturing now the dynamic sector, the conditions that had earlier made Batllism possible and even necessary were appearing once more. The international context also encouraged liberalization. Official sympathy with Italian fascism was not matched in the streets, whereas the Republican cause in the Spanish Civil War received massive popular support. The Second World War further isolated the Herrerist Blancos, whose official neutrality masked suspicion of the United States and contrasted with the pro-Allies (and especially pro-U.S.) sentiments of the Colorados. In 1942 the legislature was dissolved in what was termed the *golpe bueno* (good coup); under the new constitution of that year all political groups now operated without restriction.

Although the Batllist Colorados did not return to power immediately, they and organized labor were the principal beneficiaries of the new order. The growth of manufacturing in the late 1930s was checked somewhat by wartime shortages, but the national commitment to industrialization was strengthened. By 1945 almost 100,000 workers were employed in the manufacturing industry, and they were increasingly organized in mass-membership trade unions whose ideological orientations (a source of division and weakness in the labor movement before 1933) mattered less than their negotiating function. This revival of trade unionism also revived the issue of class politics as a challenge to the established parties. The issue, and the way it was resolved, was exemplified by growing public concern about working-class living standards. All parties, and at first even urban employers who wished to see their protected market extended, favored higher real wages. The mechanism to effect this, while maintaining state (i.e., party) control over relations between capital and labor, was the introduction in 1943 of tripartite wages councils. The *consejos de salarios* were the outcome of a corporatist tendency that had been developing in the 1930s and a populism (in place of the paternalism of Batlle y Ordóñez) that recognized the political need to harness rather than deny class consciousness.

The presidency of Juan José AMÉZAGA (1943–1947), the first under the new constitution, was effectively a transitional administration. It was the succession in 1947 of Luis BATLLE that signaled the era of neo-Batllism and national self-esteem. Social-security legislation was extended so that by 1954 all occupations were eligible for a retirement pension, and workers' rights were further protected. Although production in the livestock sector of the economy remained stagnant, the high export prices of the wartime and postwar periods fueled the process of economic diversification through import-substituting industrialization. Traditional export activities supported subsidies to the new dynamic industries and arable agriculture through a multiple exchange-rate system and other controls. The sense of national self-sufficiency (and the size of the public sector) was enhanced by state acquisition in 1948 of the railways and other former British public-utility assets. In all these ways the aims of the first Batllist period were accomplished or extended. But it was above all with the Constitution of 1952, which entirely replaced the office of president with the collegial National Council of Government (NCG), that neo-Batllism reached its high point. Accepted unenthusiastically by the electorate, the new *colegiado* rested on an agreement between Batllist Colorados and their arch-opponent, Luis Alberto de Herrera. For Herrera, facing the prospect of apparently endless exclusion from office, the *colegiado* offered co-participation in government: representation for the minority party in the NCG and on the boards of public-sector enterprises, and thus a share in the patronage.

Midcentury marked the high point of Uruguay's achievement as a nation built on prosperity, innovation, and consensus. The 1952 Constitution lasted until the indecision and delay that marked its history became insupportable; but it was the ending of economic growth in the late 1950s that undermined the *colegiado*, and the ensuing economic stagnation constituted the dominant theme of Uruguay's history thereafter. Restricted to a market of 2.25 million inhabitants, the manufacturing industry's growth phase was brief. Rural-sector export performance was weak in the 1950s as a result of discriminatory policy, rising domestic demand for beef, and above all the persistent failure to develop and incorporate a technology of pasture improvement appropriate to the country's natural conditions. While populist policy stimulated demand and sought to disguise the resulting distortions, the productive base of the economy was increasingly incapable of responding positively. By the end of the 1950s the annual rate of price increases had reached 40 percent, and there were severe balance-of-payments difficulties. In 1959, following recommenda-

tions by an International Monetary Fund (IMF) mission, a stabilization program of exchange and monetary reforms was attempted.

This retreat from interventionism implied a changed political complexion. Luis Batlle was not eligible for a second term as president in 1950, but he was the outstanding figure in the NCG elected in 1954, and the dominance of the Colorado Party continued. In 1958, however, an alliance of traditional Herrerists and the *ruralista* movement of small producers enabled the Blancos to defeat the Colorados for the first time in the twentieth century, and their victory was repeated in 1962. This historic reversal of fortunes for the parties signified little more than disillusion with the Colorados. The invitation to the IMF in 1958 was made more promptly than would have been the case with a Colorado majority, but it proved impossible to maintain the new policy orientation. The other policy initiative of the early 1960s, the creation of the Investment and Economic Development Commission (CIDE) to lay the basis for an economic plan, received general support. In other respects the interval of Blanco dominance implied little change; whichever party held a majority, the effect of the second collegial constitution was to promote the pursuit of short-term political advantage at the expense of long-term policy formulation. The electoral system (DSV and *ley de lemas*), encouraging the division of each party into contending factions, had the same result. As the economic crisis deepened, so the traditional disposition of Uruguayans to seek solutions from the state increased the power of the parties, which alone could open the door to employment in the bureaucracy or accelerate approval of a pension claim. Through the agency of clientelism, the impotence of the parties to halt rising inflation and unemployment had the perverse consequence of strengthening their short-term position.

Although the left-wing parties could make little inroads, with only 9 percent of the total vote in 1962, political debate outside the institutional structure became increasingly radicalized during the 1960s. The Cuban Revolution and the frustration of CIDE's endeavors were two factors emphasizing that there were choices available to the country that the political process could not articulate. Industrial unrest increased, and in 1964 the trade-union movement achieved for the first time a unified central body, the National Assembly of Workers (CNT). But constitutional reform, rather than solutions to the economic crisis, was the main issue in the elections of 1966. They were won by a right-wing faction of the Colorado Party proposing the restoration of the presidency, which (following the death of President Oscar GESTIDO in late 1967) was occupied until 1972 by Jorge PACHECO ARECO.

The four years of Pacheco's rule were a transitional but decisive stage in the downfall of institutional government that culminated in 1973. To the long-run problem of economic decline was added the shock in 1968 of inflation exceeding 100 percent for the first time. Pacheco's response was to increase the representation of private-sector interests in his administration while suppressing dissent through the almost continuous imposition of emergency security measures. A second IMF-sponsored stabilization program was implemented and, in combination with a less orthodox wage and price freeze, was briefly effective in reducing the rate of price increases. Devaluation of the peso increased the incomes of exporters but further reduced the urban real wage. With the legislature incapable of mounting effective opposition, bitter confrontations between workers and students and the government spilled onto the streets.

By 1970, however, the greatest challenge to the authority not merely of the government but of the institutions of the state itself came from a clandestine source, the urban guerrilla National Liberation Movement (MLN-T), or Tupamaros. Though the movement had begun to organize by 1963, it was the oppressive but frequently incompetent practice of state security after 1968 that brought the Tupamaros to national and international notice and strengthened its characteristically middle-class membership. Early operations to secure resources, reveal corruption, and release captives demonstrated wit and intelligence, but the incoherence and alien nature of its revolutionary ideology and the descent into personal violence (kidnappings, executions, and random attacks on military personnel) eroded public support. In 1971 the armed forces took command of antisubversive operations, and during the following year the Tupamaros as a guerrilla movement were totally defeated.

DICTATORSHIP AND DEMOCRACY (SINCE 1970)

The demise of the Tupamaros marked the beginning, not the end, of the threat to Uruguay's democratic institutions. The 1971 elections were won by Pacheco's nominee, Juan María BORDABERRY, who owed his victory (with 23 percent of the votes) over the Blanco leader Wilson FERREIRA ALDUNATE (26 percent) to the DSV system. By 1972, however, the political initiative lay with the military, which had come to regard the political elite of all parties as financially corrupt or tainted with subversion.

The military coup of 1973 occurred in stages. In February, Bordaberry allowed his presidential authority to be countermanded; in June, the legislature was dissolved; and in succeeding months there followed a complete repression not merely of left-wing institutions and their members but indeed of all political and intellectual activity. Pressure groups of all kinds, including those of employers, were silenced. Whereas the use of torture by the security services was first authoritatively denounced in 1970, the violation of human rights now became systematic. Bordaberry was retained until 1976 as a nominal president in a "civilian-military" regime, but effective authority from early 1973 rested with the commanders-in-chief and the military-controlled Council of National Security (COSENA). The ideology of the regime was the defense of the nation against a Marxist threat and the cleansing of its institutions; the armed forces had therefore to devise an acceptable political system to succeed their regime.

Bordaberry's own design for a corporatist state, with Blanco and Colorado parties replaced by nominees and "currents of opinion," resulted in his downfall. The military identified the parties as authentic national institutions, whose multiclass allegiance offered the best defense against a politics based on class. The military's plan, announced in 1976–1977, deprived those who had been politically active in the previous decade of their political rights, and it set out a timetable for political reconstruction leading eventually to a controlled democracy. The first stage would be the preparation by the military of a new constitution, to be approved by the people in a referendum in 1980.

The only area of government in which civilians remained influential after the coup was economic policymaking. An economic plan published by the Colorado government in 1973 spelled out proposals to reshape the economy by promoting market forces and the price mechanism. In modified form the plan was adopted by the military, which shared with economic liberals a lowest common denominator of anti-Marxism, and Alejandro Végh Villegas was appointed in 1974 to superintend its implementation from the Ministry of Economy and Finance. Although he resigned in 1976, as architect of the neoliberal economic model in Uruguay, Végh had considerable significance. Between 1973 and 1980 the economy grew continuously, with nontraditional exports as the leading sector. Control of inflation (which had reached 100 percent once more in 1973) was a major objective but did not receive priority over a restructuring of the economy that saw real wages almost halved during the course of the regime. The greater openness of the economy and optimism among exporters after decades of protectionism were positive achievements, but at the end of 1978 the emphasis on incentives to exporters was abandoned in favor of a stabilization effort through manipulation of a preannounced but overvalued exchange rate. Cheap dollars encouraged a massive inflow of consumer goods. By the early 1980s the economy was once more in decline, and when the experiment with exchange-rate policy was abandoned in 1982, both public and private sectors were burdened by huge external debts. The final years of the military regime were marked by economic decline, inflation, rising debt-service payments, unemployment, and falling real wages, but there were no new initiatives to revitalize the economy.

Although the collapse of the economic model contributed to the downfall of the regime, its political project failed at the first stage. The military's constitution perpetuating its political role was submitted to the electorate in 1980 and was rejected by 57 percent of the electorate. Opposition to the regime, which had until then been private and hazardous, now started to become public and undisguised. In 1982 internal party primaries were held, in which 77 percent of voters supported opposition party factions. Inconclusive talks between military and political leaders on the transfer of power were held in 1983. By the time they resumed in 1984, both parties to the negotiations were anxious that they should succeed, since failure would strengthen the position of the intransigents on either side. The armed forces now seemed less intent on maintaining long-term political influence than on securing a safe passage back to barracks. Their tactics to achieve this centered on weakening the prospects of the radical opposition groups in the elections of November 1984. Hence, the Frente Amplio coalition of left-wing parties (but not its leader, Líber SEREGNI) was rehabilitated, and Ferreira Aldunate, a vociferous critic of the regime, was arrested on his return from exile. As a result, the Blancos were not party to the NAVAL CLUB PACT in August, which set the terms of the transfer and reinstated the 1966 Constitution, but they agreed to respect the election result. In March 1985, Julio María SANGUINETTI was inaugurated as the first democratically accountable president since 1972.

A feature of the restored political system of 1985 was the extent to which it resembled the system overthrown in 1973. Perhaps because reform might have implied disloyalty to the country's institutions and political traditions, there was no inquest into what had gone wrong before 1973. The 1966 Constitution and the voting system were restored intact. The Frente Amplio raised its vote in 1984 to 22 percent, but the traditional parties (and to some extent the old leaderships) continued to

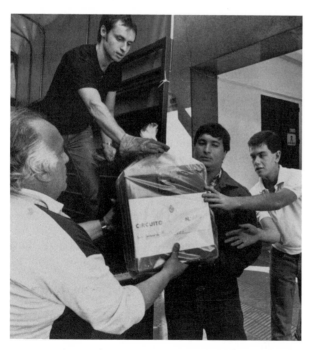

Poll workers in Montevideo during the 1989 elections. REUTERS / BETTMANN.

dominate. Sanguinetti secured a personal vote of 31 percent, more than Gestido or Bordaberry had received, but this gave him neither a personal mandate nor a majority in the legislature.

Sanguinetti's administration, billed as a government of national unity on the strength of ministries granted to minority factions or distinguished individuals, faced two central challenges: to placate the military and to resurrect the economy. The first issue was sharpened by the immediate release of those Tupamaros still in jail and the political rehabilitation of the MLN-T, which joined the Frente Amplio coalition in 1989. Tension increased over the question of an amnesty for human-rights violations committed by military personnel during the regime. At the end of 1986 a law was approved exonerating the armed forces for such offenses; it was challenged in a 1989 referendum, but endorsed by 57 percent of voters. Thereafter, military discontent centered more on issues of pay and pensions, and the fear of further intervention steadily receded.

Amid the euphoria of redemocratization, and with widespread calls for expansionist economic policy to revitalize the economy on the basis of domestic demand, Sanguinetti opted instead for an economic strategy that prioritized export-led growth. The wage and employment benefits were real, if modest, but the gross domestic product grew strongly in 1986–1987. Inflation was curbed but not controlled. The Sanguinetti administration succeeded in consolidating the new democracy, but by 1988 there was a widespread sense that it had been inadequate to secure overdue change and reform.

The mood of frustration was reflected in the 1989 elections, in which a Blanco candidate was elected president for the first time this century. Luis Alberto LACALLE, grandson of Herrera, received only 21 percent of the vote, but this was sufficient to defeat his nearest challenger, Jorge Batlle, son of Luis and great nephew of Batlle y Ordóñez. Less predictably, both leaders, at the head of the largest factions of the two traditional parties, proposed market-oriented economic strategies in which the privatization of state-owned assets and the reform of the social security system were prominent. In 1991 the legislature gave conditional approval to a law permitting the sale of parts of the public sector, but popular opposition forced a referendum in 1992 on the measure, which was rejected by 72 percent of voters. The size of the majority signified a remarkable reaffirmation of faith in the Batllist ideology of state provision.

PHILIP B. TAYLOR, *Government and Politics of Uruguay* (1960); GÖRAN G. LINDAHL, *Uruguay's New Path: A Study in Politics During the First Colegiado, 1919–1933* (1962); MILTON I. VANGER, *José Batlle y Ordóñez of Uruguay: The Creator of His Times, 1902–1907* (1963); JOSÉ PEDRO BARRÁN and BENJAMÍN NAHUM, *Batlle, los Estancieros y el Imperio Británico*, 8 vols. (1979–1987); MILTON I. VANGER, *The Model Country: José Batlle y Ordóñez of Uruguay, 1907–1915* (1980); M. H. J. FINCH, *A Political Economy of Uruguay Since 1870* (1981); GERMÁN D'ELÍA, *El Uruguay neo-batllista, 1946–1958* (1982); ROSA ALONSO ELOY and CARLOS DEMASI, *Uru-*

guay, 1958–1968: Crisis y estancamiento (1986); ANA FREGA, MÓNICA MARONNA, and YVETTE TROCHON, *Baldomir y la restauración democrática, 1938–1946* (1987); MARTIN WEINSTEIN, *Uruguay: Democracy at the Crossroads* (1988); GERARDO CAETANO and RAÚL JACOB, *El nacimiento del terrismo, 1930–1933* (1989); CHARLES GUY GILLESPIE, *Negotiating Democracy: Politicians and Generals in Uruguay* (1991).

HENRY FINCH

URUGUAY: COLEGIADO, the two forms of plural executive system with which Uruguay experimented in the twentieth century. The first *colegiado* (collegial executive) was established with the 1919 Constitution and lasted until the 1933 coup by President Gabriel TERRA. The *colegiado* was proposed by President José BATLLE Y ORDÓÑEZ during his second term as president (1911–1915). He thought that the instability and abuse of power so rampant in Latin American politics could be ameliorated by doing away with a presidential system. His proposal produced an uproar even within his own party, where some of his political rivals saw the project as merely a way for him to perpetuate his dominance of national politics. Batlle's original plan called for a *junta de gobierno*, which would consist of nine members, one to be elected each year after an initial election of all nine.

The split within his own party (the Colorados) and opposition from the Blancos (National Party) led to the election in 1916 of a constitutional convention dominated by Batlle's opponents. After over a year of maneuvering, they reached a compromise: The presidency was not eliminated, but the functions of the office were limited to the conduct of foreign affairs and the preservation of international order and external security. A National Council of Administration was created to deal with all other activities of the state. This council consisted of nine members, with six chosen from the majority party and three from the minority party. The expectation was, therefore, that it would include six Colorados and three Blancos. The president and the council would both be elected by popular vote, with the president serving a four-year term and the council members serving for six years, with two members being elected every two years. The 1919 Constitution thus set a bold experiment into motion.

Elections were very close during the 1920s, but the Colorados controlled the presidency. The inefficiencies of the collegial system were masked by the economic well-being Uruguay enjoyed through its trade with Britain. But the depression of the 1930s brought changes. President Terra found the sharing of power with the council totally inadequate for him to deal effectively with the economic and social emergency brought on by the collapsing world economy. Thus, in 1933, with the support of the Blanco leader Luis Alberto de HERRERA, Terra closed Congress and abolished the National Council of Administration. The 1934 Constitution, written by Terra and Herrera, restored a presidential system and divided the Senate between the political factions of the two coup leaders. Although a fully constitutional presidential system was restored by the 1942 Constitution, it was not until 1952 that Uruguay would again experiment with a collegial executive.

The second *colegiado* was a purely collegial executive system under which Uruguay was governed from 1952 until 1966. It is called the *Colegiado Integral* because, unlike its predecessor under the 1919 Constitution, there was no office of the president to share executive power with the collegial body.

The second *colegiado* fulfilled Batlle y Ordóñez's old dream of a plural executive for Uruguay. The impetus for its adoption came from his conservative sons, César and Lorenzo, who were increasingly overshadowed within the Colorado Party by their dynamic cousin, Luis BATLLE BERRES, who served as president from 1947 to 1951. Batlle Berres was an urban populist whose faction had won an overwhelming victory in the 1950 presidential elections. Devastated by the results, Blanco leader Luis Alberto de HERRERA reversed his long-standing opposition to a collegial executive and joined with pro-*colegiado* Colorados in the call for constitutional reform. Unable to head off a plebiscite, Luis Batlle Berres supported the reform, which was approved with the adoption of the 1952 Constitution.

Under the new charter the executive, now called the National Council of Government, consisted of nine members, with six seats going to the majority party and three to the party receiving the next highest number of votes. Economic decline and stagnation led to a historic first when the Blancos gained control of the *colegiado* in the 1958 elections, their first control of the executive in the twentieth century. Many changes were expected, but given the almost total coparticipation (power sharing) imposed by the 1952 Constitution and the need to sign an International Monetary Fund agreement, policy shifted very little. With continued economic drift, the Blancos retained control of the executive in the very close 1962 elections. During their second term, pressure built for a more efficient state and executive. Once again, constitutional reform was the mechanism. In the midst of a declining economy, growing inflation, and increased social unrest, Uruguay returned to a presidential system with the adoption of the 1966 Constitution.

The second experiment with a collegial executive succumbed, as did the first, to economic decline and the inadequacy of the government's response. On both occasions the *colegiado* was blamed for the problem, but as the mild dictatorship in the 1930s and the increased authoritarianism and descent into military government in the 1970s demonstrated, the problem rested in political leadership, not the *colegiado*.

MILTON VANGER, "Uruguay Introduces Government by Committee," in *American Political Science Review* 48, no. 2 (June 1954): 500–513; PHILIP TAYLOR, JR., *Government and Politics of Uruguay* (1960); GÖRAN LINDAHL, *Uruguay's New Path: A Study in Politics During the First Colegiado* (1962); MARTIN WEINSTEIN, *Uruguay: The Politics of Failure* (1975).

MARTIN WEINSTEIN

URUGUAY: CONGRESS OF 1825, body convoked by the leaders of Uruguay's rebellion against Brazilian rule. The congress opened on 20 August, just four months and one day after Uruguayan exiles, known as the "Thirty-Three Orientals," crossed over from Argentine territory to begin the expulsion of Brazilian forces. It met at the small town of Florida, slightly north of Montevideo (which was under Brazilian occupation and was not represented). On 25 August it declared null and void the incorporation of Uruguay into the Portuguese and subsequently Brazilian monarchies and proclaimed union with Argentina in the UNITED PROVINCES OF THE RÍO DE LA PLATA. It named Juan Antonio LAVALLEJA governor and designated Uruguayan representatives to the congress of the United Provinces.

The Uruguayan congress, which eventually moved to the town of San José, created a first set of governmental institutions and enacted a series of reforms, such as a law of free birth, inspired by the same liberal ideology professed by the dominant UNITARIST faction at Buenos Aires (which after slight delay accepted Uruguayan annexation and took the province under its protection). The congress closed its sessions in July 1826.

JOHN STREET, *Artigas and the Emancipation of Uruguay* (1959), chap. 9; ALFREDO CASTELLANOS, *La Cisplatina, la independencia y la república caudillesca (1820–1838)* (1974).

DAVID BUSHNELL

See also **Uruguay: The Colonial Period and the Nineteenth Century.**

URUGUAY: CONSTITUTIONS. Uruguay has had six constitutions during its existence as a sovereign state: 1830, 1918, 1934, 1942, 1952, and 1966. Nevertheless, its adherence to constitutional democracy—except for eleven and a half years of military rule in the 1970s and 1980s—is remarkable in a region not known for following the norms of elections, civil liberties, and social welfare.

The 1830 Constitution confirmed the independence and juridical sovereignty of Uruguay, officially known as the República Oriental del Uruguay, as established by Brazil and Argentina in a treaty mediated by the English diplomat Lord John Ponsonby. The constitution established a presidential system with the chief executive elected by the General Assembly, or Congress (consisting of the Senate and the Chamber of Deputies) every four years. The president could be reelected after a four-year interim. Comparable to those of his U.S. counterpart, the president's powers included the roles of commander in chief, protector of domestic peace and external security, and architect of the budget. The president governed with a set of ministers, whom he appointed and dismissed at will. Early on, the General Assembly established the right to question (interpellate) the ministers, thus establishing the tradition of a presidential system with an active and influential legislature. The local unit of government was the department, governed by a *jefe político* (executive magistrate), who lived in the principal town of each department and was appointed by the president. During the nineteenth century, the constitution was violated almost as frequently as it was honored. Nevertheless, it remained in force for ninety years, making it the third longest in the history of Latin America.

The 1918 Constitution was the result of a compromise between José BATLLE Y ORDÓÑEZ's vision of a collegial executive and more conservative elements within his own Colorado Party who joined with the Blancos (National Party) in wishing to preserve at least a partially presidential system. This charter was a unique experiment in constitutional law. It created a president who was popularly elected for a four-year term and who would be responsible for foreign affairs and domestic and external security through his control of the armed forces and police. All other executive powers would be in the hands of a National Council of Administration, which consisted of nine members elected by thirds every two years. The 1918 Constitution thus produced a bicephalous executive (*see* URUGUAY: COLEGIADO). The arrangement, coupled with extremely close elections between the Colorado and Blanco parties during the 1920s resulted in a growing stalemate in decision making. With the death of José Batlle in 1929 and the onset of the Great Depression, President Gabriel TERRA found himself increasingly frustrated by the partially collegial executive system. He joined forces with the Blanco leader Luis Alberto de HERRERA in a 1933 coup that in effect dissolved the bold experiment put in place in 1918.

The 1934 Constitution, in effect written by Terra and Herrera, returned Uruguay to a presidential system by eliminating the dual executive. It gave the two factions led by the coup leaders total control of the Senate, with fifteen seats for each. The president (Terra) would rule with a Council of Ministers. Parliamentary approval of ministers meant that in practice three ministers would be given to the minority party, that is, Herrera's faction. In effect, the coparticipation that had been put in place by the 1918 Constitution was renewed, but it was now restricted to the two coup factions. Under the constitution the boards of directors of all government agencies and AUTONOMOUS ENTITIES, which in Uruguay included industrial and commercial corporations, would consist of three to five members who had to be approved by 60 percent of the Senate.

The 1942 Constitution was the product of a "constitutional coup" by President Alfredo BALDOMIR, who closed the General Assembly on 21 February 1942, just before the scheduled elections. On 29 May he presented his constitutional reform proposal to his newly created Council of State, declaring that the new constitution would go into effect if approved in a plebiscite the following November. There was no doubt that it would be approved since it ended the outdated and unpopular features of the 1934 Constitution. The new charter eliminated the arbitrary division of the Senate between the two 1933 coup factions, calling for senators to be elected by strict proportional representation. Ministers would again be appointed by the entire Congress, and the boards of state corporations would be selected with guaranteed minority participation. Essentially, the 1942 Constitution abolished the exclusion of the Terra-Herrera alliance that was codified in the 1934 Constitution.

The 1952 Constitution gave Uruguay its second *colegiado*, this time in the form of a purely collegial executive system. The constitution was the result of an agreement between Batlle's sons, César and Lorenzo, and the great caudillo of the Blancos, Luis Alberto de Herrera, who gave up his long-standing opposition to the colegiado when he saw how poorly his party did in the 1950 presidential election. Former president Luis BATLLE BERRES, whose faction dominated the Colorado Party and controlled the presidency, could not oppose such a powerful combination pushing for constitutional reform.

The constitution created a nine-member executive, or *colegiado*, known as the National Council of Government, with six seats going to the majority party and three to the dominant minority party. The division of patronage between the Colorados and Blancos was assured by a constitutional clause mandating that the boards of directors of all state services and industrial enterprises consist of five members, divided three to two between the two major parties. Thus, the long-standing tradition of coparticipation was fully constitutionalized. The healthy Uruguayan economy of the 1940s and 1950s served to mask the inefficiencies of this system.

The 1966 Constitution, which returned Uruguay to a presidential system by eliminating the *colegiado*, was approved in a plebiscite on 27 November 1966. The new charter lengthened the term of all elected officials to five years and reaffirmed the electoral tradition of having all offices contested at the same time, that is, once every five years. The return to the presidential system was a reaction to Uruguay's growing economic crisis and the malaise that had overcome the Colorados and Blancos. The political elite, faced with increased social unrest, rising inflation, and virtually no economic growth, decided to streamline the government by returning to a presidential system. The new constitution created a Central Bank to help control monetary and fiscal policy and a Social Security Bank to try to rationalize the administration of retirement funds. In an attempt to depoliticize the running of state enterprises, the three to two division in their directorships was eliminated. Maintaining the 60 percent requirement for confirmation as director, however, implied that the two tradi-

tional parties would continue to split the assignments and the patronage that went with them.

The new constitution also contained several articles on land reform and internal order, which reflected the growing insecurity of the political and economic elites. Article 168 specifically gave the president the power to invoke a state of emergency under the *Medidas Prontas de Seguridad* (Prompt Security Measures). These allowed, in effect, a limited form of a STATE OF SIEGE. This power had existed in the previous constitution but only in cases of invasion or internal rebellion. The provision proved crucial to the government of President Jorge PACHECO ARECO (1967–1972), who operated under the *medidas* for all but a few months of his presidency.

In reality, the constitution was suspended under President Juan María BORDABERRY in April 1972 and was ignored by the military during its dictatorship from 27 June 1973 until the restoration of civilian rule in 1985. During this period the General Assembly passed a series of institutional acts that the dictatorship used to circumvent the constitution. The military tried to get its own constitution approved, but the project was defeated in a plebiscite in 1980. The 1967 Constitution was fully restored by president Julio María SANGUINETTI on 1 March 1985.

JUSTINO JIMÉNEZ DE ARECHAGA, *La constitución nacional*, 10 vols. (1949), and *La constitución de 1952*, 4 vols. (1952); HÉCTOR GROS ESPIELL, ed., *Las constituciones del Uruguay* (1956); ALBERTO PÉREZ PÉREZ, *Constitución de la República Oriental del Uruguay*, 2 vols. (1970).

MARTIN WEINSTEIN

URUGUAY: ELECTORAL SYSTEM

DOUBLE SIMULTANEOUS VOTE
The "double simultaneous vote," a crucial element of the Uruguayan electoral and party systems, allows the voter to choose a set of specific candidates within the party of his choice. The practice has been used since 1910, although it has undergone some important constitutional changes. The system is similar to that used in the United States in the primary and general presidential elections, except that the voter simultaneously indicates the party of his preference as well as the candidate of his preference within the party. The candidate with the most votes from the party with the most votes wins. Senators and representatives are elected this way as well.

The practice has contributed to the survival of "catchall" parties with mixed ideologies and class bases, and it has provided a basic mechanism through which differing factions within parties can cohabit and negotiate. On the other hand, the double simultaneous vote has been criticized for promoting intraparty factionalism and transforming parties into mere "vote cooperatives." The Left has called it one of the reasons for the perpetuation of an artificial bipartisan format, which is reinforced by the Ley de Lemas. However, the Left itself uses this electoral mechanism when it embraces the strategy of popular fronts. The double simultaneous vote allows it to present unified electoral fronts while still maintaining original party identities.

LEY DE LEMAS

Ley de Lemas (Law of Party Names), is a key component of the complex Uruguayan electoral process. A complement to the "double simultaneous vote," it regulates the registration and use of party *lemas* (literally "mottoes," it refers to the formal name) and *sublemas* (the names of factions within the parties). A 1925 law defined the notions of *lema* and *sublema,* the criteria for their registration and guidelines for considering them permanent or temporary. This law recognized the traditional political identities of the Blancos and the Colorados and legitimized the practice of the double simultaneous vote for inter- and intraparty competition. A 1934 law stipulated that proprietorship of a party's *lema* belonged to the party *sublema* that had the most legislators, and that this *sublema* could place conditions on or deny the use of the *lema* to others. In 1939 another law was passed that restricted the registration of *lemas* with names similar to existing ones.

The Constitution of 1952 explicitly established a rule that permitted the reunification of the Blanco (National) Party under a single *lema.* The factionalism in this party had resulted in part from the laws of 1934 and 1939. This rule, however, was applicable only to "permanent" *lemas,* thereby preventing different parties on the Left from unifying into popular fronts while still maintaining their original identities. It did not prevent the creation of the FRENTE AMPLIO in 1971, although this coalition's members still had to vote under the slogan of only one of its constituent parties, the Christian Democrats. When this party left the Frente Amplio in 1989, the political system decided to recognize the Frente as a permanent *lema.*

PHILIP B. TAYLOR, "The Electoral System in Uruguay," in *Journal of Politics* 17 (1955): 19–42; ALBERTO PÉREZ PÉREZ, *La ley de lemas* (1971); ALDO SOLARI, "El sistema de partidos y régimen electoral en el Uruguay," in ROLANDO FRANCO, ed., *El sistema electoral uruguayo* (1986); LUIS E. GONZÁLEZ, *Political Structures and Democracy in Uruguay* (1991).

FERNANDO FILGUEIRA

URUGUAY: GEOGRAPHY. Uruguay's official name, the Oriental Republic of Uruguay, reveals that it was once the eastern part of the former UNITED PROVINCES OF THE RÍO DE LA PLATA created in the Viceroyalty of Río de la Plata at the time independence from Spain was declared in 1810. The country stretches between the URUGUAY RIVER in the west and the coast of the Atlantic in the east, and from the Cuareím creek, the Cuchilla de Santa Ana, and the Yaguarón River in the north to the shores of the RÍO DE LA PLATA estuary. The relief features of the country are not greatly defined. The highlands of the country's core are the Plateau of Haedo, with several outreaching ridges (or *cuchillas*), and the Cuchilla Grande, or Central Hills. They never rise above 1,320 feet and divide the country into three distinct plains. To the east extends the low-lying, humid Atlantic coastal plain; to the south the narrower Platine River plains are interrupted by rocky outcrops such as the classic "sighted hill," from which the city of Montevideo took its name; to the west slopes the broad fluvial plain of the Uruguay River, dominated by the valley of the RÍO NEGRO, the main watercourse of central Uruguay, fed and maintained by several streams arising in the Haedo Plateau.

The climate is temperate and humid, with higher summer temperatures and precipitation in the northwest due to continental warming in the Uruguay River basin. In the Río de la Plata estuary, cold winds from Argentine Patagonia can bring winter temperatures down to freezing, but along the Atlantic coastal plains the tempering influence of the sea makes for pleasant winters and mild summers. The vegetation reflects the climate and the topographic conditions: forested areas are scarce and restricted to patches along the major watercourses and to the wetlands that border on southern Brazil, where hardwoods alternate with palm stands. In the southern plains and central hills, shrubs and grassland (PAMPAS) dominate the scenery. These are the regions where most of the cattle ranches and wheat-growing farms are located.

The country is organized into nineteen departments, each of them administered by an *intendente* (governor) directly elected by the people every five years. Population imbalances across the country are reflected in the makeup of the departments: Montevideo, with 1.25 million (1985) inhabitants, contains 42 percent of the Uruguayan population, whereas the department of Flores (in the southwest) has a mere 24,745 people. Sixty-six percent of the population lives in a belt that runs along the Río de la Plata from the department of Maldonado to that of Colonia, encompassing the capital. Correspondingly, approximately 80 percent of the manufacturing establishments, 95 percent of the service industries, and 87 percent of the administrative and cultural institutions are also located in this belt. This concentration of resources and population has worked in favor of cultural homogeneity and has created the best demographic conditions in Latin America. Life expectancy is 71 years, the daily calorie intake is 2,970 per person, infant mortality is a low 23.8 per thousand, and the birthrate is 19.5 per thousand. In the late twentieth century, however, the welfare state became overburdened.

After its separation from the United Provinces of the Río de la Plata in 1828, Uruguay continued with its traditional colonial ranching activities, but along the Río de la Plata, European immigrants embarked on nontraditional agricultural pursuits, creating a dichotomy in the primary activities of the country that has persisted to the present. In republican times, the quality of the cattle improved through better pasturage, and beef became suitable for export. In the central part of the country, large sheep-raising establishments produced wool as a major export commodity. Land dedicated to the production of wheat and flax expanded in the southwestern area of Uruguay, and forage covered all remaining grazing areas. Thus, the bases of the agrarian export economy were established, and the social and political peace that reigned during the rule of José BATLLE Y ORDÓÑEZ (1903–1907 and 1911–1915) fortified the development of the country. While industries of primary products, such as flour mills, packing plants, textile mills, and leather tanneries, became the pillars of the national economy, many manufactured goods as well as gasoline and natural gas had to be imported. For as long as exports equaled imports, Uruguay functioned as a welfare state and strove for modernization, but when the demand for foreign goods increased and exports of traditional items declined in the 1960s and early 1970s, the country fell into a period of unruliness that culminated in the collapse of democracy in 1972.

The classic historical geography of the country is W. H. HUDSON, *The Purple Land* (New York, 1927). Recent works include MARVIN ALISKY, *Uruguay: A Contemporary Survey* (1969); JORGE CHEBATAROFF, *Tierra uruguaya* (Montevideo, 1954); ERNST GRIFFIN, "Testing the Von Thunen Theory in Uruguay," in *The Geographical Review* 63 (1973): 500–516, and "Causal Factors Influencing Agricultural Land Use Patterns in Uruguay," in *Revista Geográfica* (Mexico), 80 (1974): 13–33; JAIME KLACZKO and J. RIAL ROADE, *Uruguay: El país urbano* (Montevideo, 1981); and J. M. G. KLEINPENNING, "Uruguay: The Rise and Fall of a Welfare State Seen Against a Background of Dependency Theory," in *Revista Geográfica* (Mexico), 93 (1981): 101–117.

CÉSAR N. CAVIEDES

See also individual features and regions.

URUGUAY: MEDIDAS PRONTAS DE SEGURIDAD,

a form of emergency rule granted to the executive under Uruguay's 1966 Constitution (Article 118, Section 17). The Prompt Security Measures are a mild form of a STATE OF SIEGE, which permit the president to suspend some civil liberties. The president must act in concert with the appropriate ministers, and Congress can terminate, or nullify the effect of, any measures taken by the president under this power. President Jorge PACHECO ARECO first invoked the *Medidas* on 13 June 1968 while drafting striking bank workers and declaring a freeze on wages and prices. Except for a brief period in 1969, Pacheco used these emergency powers throughout his presidency to deal with strikes and the growing threat from the urban guerrilla movement known as the Tupamaros. As the economic situation deteriorated and social and political tensions rose, the increasingly authoritarian Pacheco found the measures to be his one sure way to take action, and Congress reluctantly acquiesced. Many feel that the abuses carried out under the measures paved the way for Uruguay's descent into dictatorship in 1973.

MARTIN WEINSTEIN, *Uruguay: The Politics of Failure* (1975); M. H. J. FINCH, *A Political Economy of Uruguay Since 1870* (1981).

MARTIN WEINSTEIN

URUGUAY: ORGANIZATIONS

Autonomous Entities
Entes Autónomos

Entes autónomos is the juridical term for the commercial or industrial state enterprises in Uruguay that are the legacy of the welfare-oriented and state-interventionist ideology of the Colorado Party leader José BATLLE Y ORDÓÑEZ. There are some twenty nationalized industrial and commercial activities run by a board of directors selected by the government. Batlle believed that national sovereignty and the general welfare could be protected only by an interventionist state. Thus, beginning in 1912 with electricity, a wide array of state-owned services were created. Over the decades these grew to include the ports, railroads, an official radio broadcasting service, the national airline (PLUNA), the telephone company (ANTEL), sanitation, water, and oceanographic and fishing activities. The most famous and largest of the entities, the National Association for Fuel, Alcohol, and Cement (ANCAP), was created during the depression and proved to be a huge source of jobs and patronage. ANCAP was given a legal monopoly to refine oil and produce alcoholic beverages and cement. Batlle had wanted these activities in state hands, but he died before his goal was realized. Economic crisis, however, prodded the political elite into action.

While the vision that inspired the autonomous entities may have been noble, in practice many of these state corporations became inefficient make-work operations that served as patronage machines for the Blanco and Colorado parties. Control of the entities and of such decentralized services as education, social security, and housing, through such organs as the State Mortgage Bank, Social Security Bank, State Insurance Bank, and the Bank of the Republic, became so important politically that the composition of their boards became the subject of constitutional debate, and formulas were written into several constitutions on how directors were to be assigned.

Louis Lacalle, elected president in 1989, hoped to privatize several of the entities or at least to allow private participation in them. He had a law passed that enabled him to sell the telephone company, but the law was overwhelmingly abrogated in a plebiscite held in

1992. Nevertheless, Lacalle managed to eliminate some of the monopolies currently held by ANCAP and by some of the public banks.

PHILIP B. TAYLOR, JR., *Government and Politics of Uruguay* (1960).

MARTIN WEINSTEIN

Catholic Workers' Circle

The Catholic Workers' Circle (Círculo Católico de Obreros de Montevideo) was founded on 21 June 1885 by Juan O'Neill and Luis Pedro Lenguas, who modeled it on those created by the Spanish bishop José María de Urquinaona y Bidot in the Canary Islands and later in Barcelona. Urquinaona corresponded with O'Neill and Lenguas and explained to them how the circles worked. The Circle of Montevideo, like similar organizations in Spain and Latin America, followed the social teaching of the CATHOLIC CHURCH. The Circle of Montevideo later founded regional centers throughout the country. It had begun with 600 members, and its membership increased quite considerably in later years. The circle was a labor organization designed to protect workers according to the teachings of the church. But it provided more services than a regular labor organization, among them medical services in its own hospital, a legal aid office, and other charitable services. Its membership included employers and conservative professionals as well as workers; hence, it offered more conservative solutions to social problems than those of radical labor. In fact, it was created, like many other Catholic organizations, to provide an alternative to the radical labor ideas that appeared in the late nineteenth and early twentieth centuries.

Círculo Católico de Obreros de Montevideo (1936).

JUAN MANUEL PÉREZ

See also **Catholic Action; Leo XIII, Pope.**

National Workers Convention
Convención National de Trabajadores—CNT

The National Workers Convention is a trade union umbrella organization that developed between 1964 and 1966, when its structure and program were approved. In terms of membership and years of existence, it has been the most successful Uruguayan trade union organization. Its major predecessors were the anarchist Federación Obrera Regional Uruguayana (Uruguayan Regional Labor Federation—FORU), the anarcho-syndicalist Unión Sindical Uruguaya (Uruguayan Union of Syndicates—USU), the Communist Confederación General del Trabajo del Uruguay (General Labor Confederation of Uruguay—CGTU), and the mostly Communist Unión General de Trabajadores (General Labor Union—UGT).

The CNT was established at a time of deepening social and economic problems and resulting demands for land reform, industrial planning, nationalization of key industries and the banking system, and substantial state intervention in housing, education, and social security. Following the 1973 coup d'état, the CNT was forced underground by President Juan María BORDABERRY, but not before it confronted the dictatorship with a general strike that brought about the arrest, imprisonment, and exile of many union leaders.

In 1983 the regime permitted the creation of a coordinating committee, the Plenario Intersindical de Trabajadores (PIT), to prepare for a May Day demonstration. The 1984 congress of the PIT rebaptized the organization as the PIT-CNT, whose main concerns have been the recovery of real wages to predictatorship levels and the legal prosecution of human rights violations. The PIT-CNT has refused to join any of the continental trade union organizations. Its membership in 1992 was estimated at 200,000.

HÉCTOR RODRÍGUEZ, *Nuestros sindicatos, 1865–1965* (1965) and *Unidad sindical y huelga general* (1985); GERMÁN D'ELÍA, *El movimiento sindical* (1969); ALFREDO ERRANDONEA and DANIEL COSTABILE, *Sindicato y sociedad en el Uruguay* (1969); JORGE LUIS LANZARO, *Sindicatos y sistema político: Relaciones corporativas en el Uruguay, 1940–1985* (1986); RUTH BERINS COLLIER and DAVID COLLIER, *Shaping the Political Arena* (1991).

DIETER SCHONEBOHM
FERNANDO FILGUEIRA

Rural Association
Asociación Rural

The guild of Uruguayan landowners was founded in 1871. Although partisan political activity was not inherent in its makeup, it lobbied strongly during the dictatorship of Lorenzo LATORRE and has continued to do so. In 1915 the ranchers were confronted by Batllist social reforms, and from the nucleus of the old Rural Association they created the Federación Rural. While the Association had always defined itself as a nonpolitical and nonpartisan organization, the Federation explicitly assumed a political character and adopted a platform in direct opposition to Batllist policies and reforms. The Asociación Rural was an important representative of the interests of wealthy landowners, but it lost its monopoly and hegemony to the Federación Rural, and as the twentieth century progressed, it increasingly came to represent medium and small rural producers.

JOSÉ PEDRO BARRÁN and BENJAMIN NAHUM, *Historia rural del Uruguay moderno, 1851–1885*, vol. 1 (1967); ENRIQUE MÉNDEZ VIVES, *El Uruguay de la modernización*, vol. 5 (1977).

FERNANDO FILGUEIRA

See also **Batllismo.**

Workers' Interunion Plenary–National Workers' Assembly
Plenario Intersindical de Trabajadores–
Convención Nacional de Trabajadores—
PIT–CNT

Uruguay's union confederation resulted from the merger of the names of the historical Convención Nacional de Trabajadores and the Plenario Intersindical de Trabajadores. The PIT came to public light through the demonstrations of 1 May 1983, and from then on was a fundamental force in the democratic movement, organizing demonstrations and general strikes that helped legitimize the opposition and erode the military regime. Toward the end of the regime in 1984, the PIT was renamed PIT–CNT, confirming its historical roots in the CNT, which had never been questioned. During the first democratic administration, it adopted a profile less radical than the one it had before 1973. While maintaining its radical rhetoric, it became highly conciliatory in practice.

MARTIN WEINSTEIN, *Uruguay: Democracy at the Crossroads* (1988); FERNANDO FILGUEIRA, "El movimiento sindical en la encrucijada: Restauración y transformación democrática," in *Revista Uruguaya de Ciencia Política*, no. 4 (1991): 67–82; CHARLES GILLESPIE, *Negotiating Democracy* (1991).

FERNANDO FILGUEIRA

URUGUAY: PLEBISCITES. There have been four plebiscites (1951, 1966, 1980, 1989) in Uruguay since World War II. The plebiscite of 25 November 1951—the last Sunday in November, which is the traditional date for elections in Uruguay—approved the Constitution of 1952. This Constitution abolished the presidential system and gave Uruguay a collegial executive, known as the COLEGIADO, consisting of nine members. The 27 November 1966 plebiscite marked the abandonment of Uruguay's experiment with the *colegiado* by approving the 1966 Constitution, which returned Uruguay to a presidential system.

The 30 November 1980 plebiscite was an attempt by Uruguay's military government to "constitutionalize" the armed forces' control of the government. Its proposed constitution called for the creation of a National Security Council (COSENA) that would be dominated by the military and exercise a virtual veto power over executive-branch decisions. An interim president would serve for five years. In addition, the constitutional project called for an automatic majority for the winning party in the legislature.

The traditional parties (Blancos and Colorados) were given little or no opportunity to campaign for a "no" vote, and the Left remained banned. The official and progovernment media campaigned for a "yes" vote, arguing that this was the only way to get the military back to the barracks. The military expected to win, just as Augusto PINOCHET had in Chile only a few months ear-

lier, but the proposed constitution was defeated by a 58 to 42 percent vote. This vote was a strategic defeat for the dictatorship. It let average citizens know that they were not alone in the opposition to the seven-year-old dictatorship. The military's defeat in the 1980 plebiscite began a process that led to the November 1984 elections and the restoration of constitutional democracy.

The 16 April 1989 plebiscite was held to determine whether a law granting amnesty to the military would be repealed. The so-called Law on the Expiration of the Punitive Power of the State had been passed in December 1986 to avoid a crisis with the military, which stated that it would not honor subpoenas to testify in civilian trials concerning human-rights abuses during its nearly twelve years in power. Under Uruguay's constitution, any law can be overturned by plebiscite if 25 percent of all eligible voters sign a petition to hold such a referendum. Most observers doubted that the anti-amnesty forces could collect the nearly 550,000 signatures that would be necessary, especially with pleas from the government against the idea and veiled threats from the armed forces. Nevertheless, 635,000 signatures were presented to the Electoral Court, which then took more than a year to verify the signatures, a task that required the last-minute in-person verification of some 20,000 Uruguayans.

During the referendum campaign the Julio María SANGUINETTI government and most politicians in the Blanco and Colorado parties supported a vote to uphold the amnesty law. Most of the Left, the labor unions, church and human-rights groups, and a few centrist politicians supported the repeal of the law. In an outstanding example of democracy in action, the Uruguayan people voted on 16 April 1989. The amnesty law was upheld by 57 to 43 percent. The vote to overturn the amnesty carried in Montevideo, where almost half the population lives, but was quite poor in the much more conservative interior of the country. The vote was seen as a victory for the Sanguinetti administration, but the

Uruguayans check a list to find out where they should cast their votes, Montevideo, 1989. REUTERS / BETTMANN.

337

Colorado Party lost some goodwill in the process, which contributed to its defeat in the November elections.

LUIS E. GONZÁLEZ, "Uruguay, 1980–1981: An Unexpected Opening," in *Latin American Research Review* 18, no. 3 (1983): 63–76; MARTIN WEINSTEIN, "Consolidating Democracy in Uruguay: The Sea Change of the 1989 Elections" (Bildner Center for Western Hemisphere Studies of the Graduate Center of the City University of New York, Working Paper Series, 1990); LAWRENCE WECHSLER, *A Miracle, A Universe: Settling Accounts with Torturers* (1990).

MARTIN WEINSTEIN

URUGUAY: POLITICAL PARTIES

Anticolegialistas

The anticolegialistas were a group of politicians within the Colorado Party of José BATLLE Y ORDÓÑEZ who were opposed to his 1913 proposal for the creation of a *colegiado* (collegial executive system) to replace the president. Under Batlle's proposal a nine-member council would take over the executive function. More conservative than Batlle and led by his former interior minister, Pedro Manini Ríos, the *anticolegialistas*, who called themselves *riveristas*, formed a splinter party in 1916 known as the Riverista Colorado Party.

Although ostensibly opposed to the *colegiado* because they thought it would make for a cumbersome and inefficient executive, the *anticolegialistas* were opposed to many of the liberal reforms and the progressive social agenda pushed by Batlle. When the *anticolegialistas* received a majority in the elections to the 1916 constitutional convention, Batlle was forced to compromise on his proposal. Thus, the 1919 Constitution created a bicephalous executive, with a president who was responsible for foreign affairs and security matters and a nine-member National Council of Administration that was responsible for all other state activities.

PHILIP B. TAYLOR, JR., *Government and Politics of Uruguay* (1960); MILTON VANGER, *The Model Country: José Batlle y Ordóñez of Uruguay, 1907–1915* (1980).

MARTIN WEINSTEIN

See also **Uruguay: Colegiado.**

Blanco Party

The Blanco Party, also known as the Partido Nacional, is one of the two traditional political parties in Uruguay. It came together under Manuel ORIBE, the second president of the country (1835–1838), in his struggles against Fructuoso RIVERA, the country's first president (1830–1835), who represented the Colorados. The Blanco Party represented the more conservative forces of the country. The nineteenth century was plagued with conflicts between these two political parties, which often led to civil war. The first conflict began in 1836, when Rivera rose against Oribe. An agreement was reached by the two

groups after the Blanco revolution of 1897, led by the half-Brazilian gaucho Aparicio SARAVIA. Under the terms of the agreement, the Blancos were given control of six of the nineteen departments and minority representation in Congress.

When José Batlle y Ordóñez became president in 1903, the country was still divided from the civil war, with the Colorados controlling thirteen departments and the Blancos controlling six, acting mostly on their own, with Montevideo unable to reach them and bring them into line with the rest of the country. Both sides were very distrustful of each other. In January 1904, war broke out once again. The Blancos, led by Saravia, fought for eight months, until Saravia himself was killed in battle. After Saravia's death, Blanco resistance collapsed, and an agreement was reached. The Blancos lost control over the six departments. A new electoral law, although endorsing the principle of proportional representation (a major point of the peace agreement after the first Saravia revolution), in fact practically did away with it, leaving the Colorados in complete control of the country.

Following the defeat suffered in the 1904 civil war, the Blanco Party began to reorganize itself into a modern political party and to accentuate its differences with the Colorados. Its main political aims were those of Saravia: the secret ballot and proportional representation. This transformation was accomplished through the leadership of Luis Alberto de Herrera, who controlled the party from 1920 to 1959. But the party was divided, despite Herrera, between the conservative Herreristas and more progressive forces, such as the Unión Blanca Democrática.

In 1958, for the first time in ninety-three years, the Blancos won the national elections, and they did so again in 1962. The first period of Blanco domination (1959–1963) was controlled by the Herreristas, and the second one (1963–1967) was dominated by the UBD faction. Blanco success was the result of a combination of factors, such as economic problems in the country; urban terrorism; accusations of graft, corruption, and incompetence against the Colorados; and the divisions that plagued the Colorados. After the death of Herrera in 1959, Benito Nardone assumed leadership of the party. He was as vigorous as Herrera. Subsequently, the Blancos fared no better than the Colorados. They had to face the economic situation left by the Colorados and instituted an austerity program. As a result of these policies, they antagonized labor. In 1971, the Blanco candidate, Wilson Ferreira Aldunate, received more votes than the Colorado candidate but lost the election because of the complicated *lema* system of voting, which combined primary elections and general elections in one ballot.

BALTASAR L. MEZZERA, *Blancos y Coloradose* (1952); RUSSELL H. FITZGIBBON, *Uruguay: Portrait of a Democracy* (1954); JULIO LIST CLERICETTI, *Historia politica uruguaya, 1938–1972* (1984); GERARDO CAETANO et al., *De la tradición a la crisis: Pasado y presente de nuestro sistema de partidos* (1985).

JUAN MANUEL PÉREZ

Broad Front
Frente Amplio

A coalition of the Uruguayan Left that was formed in March 1971, the Frente Amplio united the country's traditional Left (Communists and Socialists), the Christian Democrats, the new radical Left, and splinters of the traditional parties, such as Alba Roballo and Zelmar MICHELINI, with his List 99 from the Colorado Party, and Enrique ERRO and Francisco Rodríguez Camusso from the Blanco (National) Party. The Frente was the culmination of the strategy of popular fronts that had been embraced by much of the Left in Latin America in the 1970s. In Uruguay, some earlier attempts were the Leftist Freedom Front (Frente Izquierda de Liberación—FIDEL) put forth by the Communist Party and the Popular Union, which united the Socialists and the Blanco splinter group led by Erro. The Frente Amplio arose during a convulsive period in Uruguayan political history that was characterized by crises in the traditional parties, left-wing radicalism in the unions, and the appearance of an urban guerrilla movement. In the elections of 1971, the Frente won 18.3 percent of the vote.

With the coup d'état in 1973, the Frente was outlawed, and its leaders were jailed, persecuted, and sent into exile. Working in secret or from abroad, they developed strategies to oppose the dictatorship, and by the end of the dictatorship the Frente Amplio had become a key negotiator. Legalized once again for the 1984 elections, it won 21.3 percent of the vote. When its more moderate factions—List 99 and the Christian Democrats—were excised, the coalition showed that it had attained its own identity, one that went beyond the groups that composed it. In 1989 it had its first victory in the capital, electing the Socialist Tabaré Vázquez to the municipal administration of Montevideo, and it demonstrated that it remained a significant force nationally, winning 21.2 percent of the overall vote.

CARLOS REAL DE AZÚA, "Política, poder y partidos en el Uruguay de hoy," in LUIS BENVENUTO et al., *Uruguay Hoy* (1971); CARLOS ZUBILLAGA and ROMEO PÉREZ, "Los partidos polítocos, in *El Uruguay de nuestro tiempo* (1983); MIGUEL AGUIRRE, *El Frente Amplio* (1985); GERARDO CAETANO et al., *De la tradición a la crisis: Pasado y presente de nuestro sistema de partidos* (1985); LUIS E. GONZÁLEZ, *Political Structures and Democracy in Uruguay* (1991).

FERNANDO FILGUEIRA

Christian Democratic Party
Partido Democrático Cristiano—PDC

The first Catholic organization to act politically in Uruguay appeared in 1910 under the name Catholic Union. In 1919 it won its first parliamentary seat and declared the founding of the Civic Union. Although it carried little weight electorally (3 to 5 percent) through the twentieth century, it did undergo important transformations in the 1950s and 1960s. In 1962, for example, one of its leaders, Juan Pablo Terra, transformed the Civic Union into the Christian Democratic Party, assuming the fundamental theses of progressive Social Christianity and of Christian Democrats internationally. In 1971 the party joined the FRENTE AMPLIO (FA), aligning itself with the Uruguayan Left. This caused conservatives in the party to split off and found the Union of Radical Christians. The Christian Democratic Party left the FA following the coup d'état of 1973, but rejoined in 1984. Juan Pablo Terra did not agree with the decision to rejoin the FA and distanced himself from the party. After poor returns in the elections of 1985, the party entered a period of crisis and strategic redefinition. The result was another distancing from the FA in order to present itself in the elections of 1989. The Christian Democrats joined another center-left coalition, the New Space, a social-democratic group.

CARLOS REAL DE AZÚA, "Política, poder y partidos en el Uruguay de hoy," in Luis Benvenuto et al., *Uruguay Hoy* (1971); GERARDO CAETANO et al., *De la tradición a la crisis: Pasado y presente de nuestro sistema de partidos* (1985).

FERNANDO LÓPEZ D'ALESSANDRO

Colorado Party

The Colorado Party is one of the two traditional political parties in Uruguay. It developed around the country's first president, Fructuoso RIVERA. The name Colorado, or red, derived from the color of the ribbons the soldiers wore in battle. The Colorado Party found itself in constant struggles with its more conservative opponent, the Blanco Party, for much of the nineteenth century. These struggles often led to civil war.

The Colorado Party has dominated the presidency almost uninterruptedly since independence. Only in the periods 1835–1838 and 1959–1967 were the Colorados not in power. The Colorados have tended to represent the urban middle class, while the conservative Blancos have rural support. And although the Colorados have dominated the presidency, they have had to make occasional concessions to the Blancos in order to govern. The party began to acquire the form of a true political organization under the leadership of José BATLLE Y ORDÓÑEZ, who was elected president in 1903. In his two administrations (1903–1907, 1911–1915), Batlle introduced radical sociopolitical reforms that made Uruguay a model of democracy as well as a model of a welfare state.

The period 1919–1933 was one of high prosperity, and the three Colorado administrations experienced few problems in governing the country, but divisions within the party did appear, particularly over Batlle's reforms. Aside from the Batllistas, which represented the largest faction, others appeared, such as one opposed to the *colegialismo* (a collegial executive for the nation) imposed by Batlle and several that followed individual leaders. The death of Batlle in 1929 accelerated the divisions within the party. Batlle's reforms did not satisfy everyone. Those on the left thought his reforms had not gone far enough, focusing particularly on his failure to subdivide the great estates for the small farmers. On the other hand, the reforms antagonized the conservatives because they required state intervention in the economy. In 1930, the conservative Colorado Gabriel TERRA was elected. He faced strong opposition from within his own party and from the Blancos, but was able to strike a compromise with the Blanco leader Luis Alberto de HERRERA. Still, his position was precarious. In 1933, he established dictatorial rule, abolished Batlle's *colegiado* system, and concentrated the executive power in the presidency. In 1938, the *colegiado* was revived by Alfredo BALDOMIR, and in 1951, during Andrés Martínez Trueba's presidency, a plebiscite approved the *colegiado* as the only executive body.

From the 1940s on, the two main factions within the party have been the Lista 14, representing *colegialistas*, and the Lista 15, representing *presidencialistas*. As a consequence of its internal divisions, the party lost control of the national council from 1959 to 1967. After that time, the Colorados regained the presidency once again, but the 1960s were a period of turmoil, exemplified by the terrorist organization the Tupamaros and by economic problems. In 1966, a major reorganization of the political system abolished the *colegiado* system, and a five-year presidency was established. President Juan María Bordaberry, elected in 1971, dissolved Congress in 1973 under pressure from the army, which had been playing an important role in civilian affairs since it began fighting terrorism. The army removed Bordaberry in 1976 and remained in control until 1984, when the country returned to civilian rule.

BALTASAR L. MEZZERA, *Blancos y Colorados* (1952); RUSSELLL H. FITZGIBBON, *Uruguay: Portrait of a Democracy* (1954); JULIO LISTA CLERICETTI, *Historia política uruguaya, 1938–1972* (1984); GERARDO CAETANO et al., *De la tradición a la crisis: Pasado y presente de nuestro sistema de partidos* (1985).

JUAN MANUEL PÉREZ

Communist Party
Partido Comunista—PC

Founded 18 April 1921 by a majority within the SOCIALIST PARTY, the Uruguayan Communist Party joined the Communist International in 1922. Its first years were characterized by such extreme radicalism that it had to be disciplined by the International. Toward the end of the 1920s, under the leadership of Eugenio GÓMEZ, the party adopted the views of Stalinism. During this period it occupied, along with the rest of the Left, a marginal position in electoral politics, while making some advances in the area of unionism. As part of the de-Stalinization process, Gómez was expelled from the party in 1955 and replaced as its leader by Rodney ARISMENDI. With this change of direction, Uruguayan Communists reevaluated the role of democracy and set their

sights on the creation of popular fronts. Their first such effort was the Leftist Freedom Front (FIDEL) of the 1960s. By the end of the 1960s, Communism was hegemonic in the Left in both the political and union arenas. During this period an armed wing was created as a contingency against a coup d'état.

In 1971 the party was a founding member of the FRENTE AMPLIO, the most important leftist coalition in the history of the country. When the first signs of the impending coup appeared, the Communists supported the military's declarations, which contained shades of progressivism similar to those of VELASCO ALVARADO in Peru. The conservative and authoritarian nature of the June 1973 coup, however, placed the Communists in opposition to the new military regime. From 1973 until the end of the dictatorship, the Communists suffered systematic persecution by the military government. The party was legalized by the democratic government in 1985 and in 1986 it began adjusting to perestroika in the Soviet Union. In 1989, after the best electoral results in its history (about 10 percent of the vote) and Arismendi's death, the Communist Party entered an internal crisis, finally splitting into two factions: the *renovadores* (renovators), which included all of its legislators, and the *históricos* (traditionalists), which retained the majority in the party and therefore its structure.

CARLOS REAL DE AZÚA, ''Política, poder y partidos en el Uruguay de hoy,'' in Luis Benvenuto et al., *Uruguay Hoy* (1971); GERARDO CAETANO et al., *De la tradición a la crisis: Pasado y presente de nuestro sistema de partidos* (1985); FERNANDO LÓPEZ D'ALESSANDRO, *Historia de la Izquierda Uruguaya*, vol. 3, *La fundacíon del Partido Comunista y la división del anarquismo* (1992).

FERNANDO LÓPEZ D'ALESSANDRO

Socialist Party
Partido Socialista—PS

The first guilds and associations with Marxist orientations appeared in Uruguay at the end of the nineteenth century. In 1901, with some support from progressive Masons, they ran in municipal elections and were defeated. In 1904, Emilio FRUGONI attempted to organize the Socialists in support of BATLLISMO and electoral collaboration, but this plan failed. The Socialist Party was formed on 12 December 1910 with the intention of participating in elections, and a seat was finally won.

Uruguayan socialism arose as a radical response to Batllist social reform. This is in part why the majority of the PS formed the Communist Party in 1921. With this split, the Socialists lost their parliamentary representation until 1928, and they developed a more Western and reformist stance under the direction of Frugoni. In the mid-1950s a new generation of militants encouraged an ideological redefinition that radicalized the PS into a revolutionary and anti-imperialist body. In 1962, with factions that had split from the National Party, the Socialists ran in elections as part of the Popular Union, but the attempt failed roundly. Frugoni distanced himself from the party permanently. At the same time, young militants began to develop a clandestine armed wing, which, after its separation from the party, gave rise to the NATIONAL LIBERATION MOVEMENT, or Tupamaros.

The Socialist Party was outlawed in 1967, then legalized again in 1971, when it became a founding member of the FRENTE AMPLIO and won a parliamentary seat. In 1972 it assumed a Marxist-Leninist ideological stance, which it renounced in 1985. The party was outlawed along with the rest of the Left following the 1973 coup d'état, and it remained so until 1984, when it was formally incorporated into the negotiations for the movement toward democracy. In 1989, the successful Frente Amplio candidate for mayor of Montevideo was the Socialist Tabaré Vázquez.

CARLOS REAL DE AZÚA, "Política, poder y partidos en el Uruguay de Hoy," in Luis Benvenuto et al., *Uruguay Hoy* (1971); GERARDO CAETANO et al., *De la tradición a la crisis: Pasado y presente de nuestro sistema de partidos* (1985); FERNANDO LÓPEZ D'ALESSANDRO, *Historia de la Izquierda Uruguaya*, 3 vols. (1988–1992).

FERNANDO LÓPEZ D'ALESSANDRO

See also **Masonic Orders.**

Unity and Reform
Unidad y Reforma—UR

The designation Unity and Reform was taken by the old List 15 of the Batllist faction of the Uruguayan Colorado Party, founded by President Luis BATLLE BERRES between 1952 and 1954. When Batlle Berres died in 1964 his son, Jorge Batlle, assumed the directorship of the faction. But Batlle Berre's death precipitated a crisis over who would lead List 15. During the elections of 1966, List 15 began to designate itself as "Unity and Reform," alluding both to the necessity of overcoming political factionalism and to Batlle's project of reinstating the presidency and doing away with the COLEGIADO. The Colorado Party won the election, and the referendum reinstating the presidency was approved. Paradoxically, the candidate to triumph within the Colorado Party was not Batlle, but rather General Oscar GESTIDO. The descendants of List 15 later abandoned the designation Unity and Reform and adopted the term Radical BATLLISMO.

ANGEL COCCHI, *Nuestros partidos* (1984); MARTIN WEINSTEIN, *Uruguay: Democracy at the Crossroads* (1988).

JOSÉ DE TORRES WILSON

URUGUAY: REVOLUTIONARY MOVEMENTS

National Liberation Movement
Movimiento de Liberación
Nacional—Tupamaros/MLN-T

The MLN-T was a guerrilla movement that came out of concealment in 1967 to become a major political force until its decimation by the military in 1972. The Tupamaros, who took their name from TÚPAC AMARU, a seventeenth-century Inca chieftain who led an unsuccessful rebellion against the Spaniards, were founded in late 1962 by a group of Socialist Party dissidents. Raúl SENDIC, a law student who had organized the sugarcane workers in the northeast, is recognized as the originator of the movement. The founding members spent their first few years training, stealing weapons, and organizing clandestine cells. In 1967, in the midst of some spectacular robberies, they announced their existence with a letter to a leftist newspaper stating that they were willing to use violence to raise political consciousness and ultimately change the political and economic structure of the country.

The writings and propaganda of the Tupamaros were clearly nationalist, socialist, and revolutionary but never offered a coherent economic or political plan. The Tupamaros did not see their movement as capable of directly challenging the military or the government for power. Rather, they sought to incite mass action by pointing out the corruption and inefficiency of the government and its security apparatus. By establishing themselves as a "parallel power" to the government, the Tupamaros hoped to be at the vanguard of a larger revolution.

Recruiting from among the intellectuals, professionals, and unionized workers, the Tupamaros initially developed a Robin Hood image through a series of robberies, exposures of questionable financial transactions by the political elite, and the distribution of food in poor neighborhoods. But this image faded with a series of kidnappings and the assassination of U.S. AID public safety officer Daniel Mitrione. In response to a mass prison escape by more than 100 Tupamaros in 1969, the military was put in charge of antiguerrilla activity. In 1971 the Tupamaros kidnapped British ambassador Geoffrey Jackson and held him as a guarantee that the November 1971 elections would take place. The Tupamaros correctly believed that the leftist coalition known as the FRENTE AMPLIO (Broad Front) could not win these elections, but they suspended their activities until after the elections as a show of support.

On 14 April 1972 the Tupamaros ended their truce with a series of assassinations of police and military officials who they claimed were members of death squads. Some eleven people died that day, and the government received parliamentary approval for the declaration of a state of "internal war." The military was given a blank check and, aided by the defection of a top Tupamaro leader, Hector Amadio Pérez, and the massive use of torture, it destroyed the Tupamaros over the next several months.

Many in Uruguay blame the Tupamaros for the descent into military dictatorship in 1973. There is no question that the Tupamaros exacerbated social conflict and helped politicize the armed forces, but the dictatorship was installed after the Tupamaros were destroyed, and it remained in power almost twelve years.

With the resumption of civilian constitutional government in March 1985, all political prisoners, including the Tupamaro leader who had been held under inhumane conditions, were released. The Tupamaros then announced their intention to organize as a peaceful political party. They publish a newspaper and have a radio program, but have little influence in Uruguayan politics.

For an analysis of the Tupamaros' ideology and recruitment patterns see ARTURO C. PORZECANSKI, *Uruguay's Tupamaros: The Urban Guerrilla* (1973). For an analysis of the theoretical foundations of the movement see ABRAHAM GUILLEN, *Philosophy of the Urban Guerrilla: The Revolutionary Writings of Abraham Guillen*, edited by Donald C. Hodges (1973). For a useful set of interviews and documents see MARIA ESTHER GILIO, *The Tupamaro Guerrillas* (1972).

MARTIN WEINSTEIN

URUGUAY RIVER, stream originating in the central plateau of Río Grande do Sul (Brazil) and following a crescentic course toward the southwest for 960 miles. In its upper reaches the valley is narrow and scarcely populated. South of latitude 28 degrees, the Uruguay valley widens, and settlements become more numerous in Brazilian territory: São Tomé, Itaquí, Uruguaiana. Bella Unión is the first Uruguayan town, and from there to Carmelo, where it empties into the RÍO DE LA PLATA estuary, the river forms the natural boundary between Uruguay and Argentina. For 170 miles, up to PAYSANDÚ, the river is navigable by small ships that transport wool, hides, and grain to Montevideo. On the middle course are located the Uruguayan cities of Salto, Paysandú, and Fray Bentos and the Argentine towns of Paso de Los Libres, Monte Caseros, and Concordia. In Uruguaiana the international highway from Santa Fé/Paraná to Pôrto Alegre (Brazil) crosses the Uruguay River, and at Paso de los Libres the railroad from Ibicuy (Argentina) to Santa Maria (in Rio Grande do Sul) crosses into Brazil. International cooperation between Argentina and Uruguay has resulted in the construction of the hydroelectric plant of Salto Grande, which provides power to both countries.

EDUARDO V. HAEDO, *El río Uruguay* (Montevideo, 1957).

CÉSAR N. CAVIEDES

URVINA JADO, FRANCISCO, from 1902 to 1925 the director of the BANCO COMERCIAL Y AGRÍCOLA, the leading financial institution of Guayaquil—the national commercial center and entrepôt for Ecuador's lucrative cacao bean export trade. Government spending relied heavily on funds borrowed from the Banco Comercial y Agrícola. Critics of this arrangement, such as the sierra (highland) businessman and politician Luis N. Dillon, claimed that the mounting debt gave the bank power to dictate terms to the government. Dillon and others believed that Director Urvina secretly ran Ecuador from behind the scenes. In 1922 Ecuador's monoculture ex-

port economy collapsed. The ensuing crisis led to public disclosure of the bank's unsound currency emissions, which had been largely necessitated by government borrowing. Urvina served as a convenient target for popular anger. Following a coup led by young military officers on 9 July 1925, the government seized the assets of the Banco Comercial y Agrícola, arrested Urvina, and sent him into exile.

The best treatment of fiscal and monetary issues is LINDA ALEXANDER RODRÍGUEZ, *The Search for Public Policy: Regional Politics and Government Finances in Ecuador, 1830–1940* (1985). For the broader political economic context, see OSVALDO HURTADO, *Political Power in Ecuador*, translated by Nick D. Mills, Jr. (1985). Detailed discussion of banking can be found in JULIO ESTRADA YCAZA, *Los bancos del siglo XIX* (1976). The socioeconomic context is analyzed in the path-breaking study by LOIS CRAWFORD DE ROBERTS, *El Ecuador en la época cacaotera* (1980).

RONN F. PINEO

See also **Alfaro Delgado, José Eloy.**

URZAGASTI, JESÚS (*b.* October 1941), Bolivian poet, writer, and journalist. Urzagasti, one of the most important writers in Bolivia today, was born in Gran Chaco Province, in a small cattle-raising town, and emigrated to La Paz as a young man. Having decided to become a writer, he abandoned plans for a career in geology. He now works for *Presencia*, a leading Bolivian newspaper.

Urzagasti's first novel, *Tirinea*, was published in 1969; next was *Cuaderno de Lilino* (1972), a book of prose dedicated to a child. *Yerubia* (1978) is his only book of poetry. *En el país del silencio* (1987), Urzagasti's major novel, deals autobiographically with three decades of historical turmoil viewed through the eyes of a narrator who has maintained a sense of solidarity with society and a perception of man's relationship with nature. *De la ventana al parque* (1992), a shorter novel, explores the possibilities of cultural survival and of communication in a country marked by cultural diversity and by verticality of power.

On Urzagasti's poetry, see BLANCA WIETHÜCHTER, "A propósito de las contraliteraturas," in *Hipótesis*, no. 17 (1983), and in "Poesía boliviana contemporánea," in *Tendencias actuales en la literatura boliviana*, edited by Javier Sanjinés C. (1985). On Urzagasti's narrative, see LUIS H. ANTEZANA, "Del nomadismo: *Tirinea* de Jesús Urzagasti," in his *Ensayos y lecturas* (1986); MIEMBROS DEL TALLER HIPÓTESIS, "Dos novelistas contemporáneos: Jesús Urzagasti y Jaime Sáenz," in *Revista iberoamericana*, no. 134 (1986); MAURICIO SOUZA, "En el país del silencio: Lectura," in *El zorro Antonio*, no. 6 (1989).

ANA REBECA PRADA

USHUAIA, town of 11,029 inhabitants (1980) located in a well-protected bay on the northern shore of the BEAGLE CHANNEL in Argentine TIERRA DEL FUEGO and capital of the homonymous territory. Founded in 1868 by the British missionary Thomas Bridges in his efforts to christianize and protect the Fuegino Indians in their contacts with whalers, seal hunters, and gold prospectors, it was named after the small boat with which Charles Darwin visited the bay in 1832. In 1884 the Argentine government built a village near the mission station, and in 1886 a penal colony was established to supply labor for the exploitation of the adjacent rain forest. Expansion of sheep-raising *estancias* on the flat plains of the island of Tierra del Fuego intensified the functions of Ushuaia as the main Argentine service center of the region. A strong naval detachment was established there in the early 1900s. Ushuaia, the southernmost urban area of Latin America, has been a duty-free port since 1976, enhancing its attraction for tourists who come to enjoy the alpine scenery.

ERNESTO J. FITTE, *Crónicas del Atlántico Sur* (Buenos Aires, 1974); ARNOLDO CANCLINI, *Tomas Bridges: Pionero en Ushuaia* (Buenos Aires, 1980); and E. LUCAS BRIDGES, *Uttermost Part of the Earth: Indians of Tierra del Fuego* (1988).

CÉSAR N. CAVIEDES

USIGLI, RODOLFO (*b.* 17 November 1905; *d.* 18 June 1979), Mexican writer. Born in Mexico City, Usigli was the child of European immigrants. His father died when he was young and his ambitious mother raised four children in the difficult period of the Mexican Revolution. Belonging to the lower-middle-class and suffering from extremely poor vision, Usigli was unable to finish secondary school. In spite of his lack of social status and formal education, however, by the 1940s Usigli emerged as one of the leading innovators in Mexican drama and a major advocate for the establishment of a national theatrical tradition. In his efforts to modernize Mexican dramaturgy, he frequently interpreted the symbols and historical events that contributed to the formation of a Mexican national identity. The plays *El gesticulador* (The Imposter [written 1937, staged 1947]) and *Corona de sombra* (Crown of Shadow [written 1943, staged 1947]) attest to his concern with understanding Mexico's national cultural identity. In addition to his numerous plays, Usigli also published a psychological-detective novel, *Ensayo de un crimen* (Trial Run for a Murder [1944]), which was filmed by Luis BUÑUEL in 1955. Besides being a dramatist, Usigli also worked as a drama historian, university teacher, and diplomat. He died in Mexico City.

AURORA OCAMPO, ed. "Usigli, Rodolfo," in *Diccionario de escritores mexicanos* (1967), pp. 393–395; RAMÓN LAYERA, "Rodolfo Usigli," in *Latin American Writers*, edited by Carlos A. Solé and Maria Isabel Abreu, vol. 3 (1989), pp. 1033–1042.

DANNY J. ANDERSON

USLAR PIETRI, ARTURO (*b.* 16 May 1906), Venezuelan writer and politician born in Caracas. Uslar Pietri epit-

omizes the Latin American writer and intellectual who participates in political life. After obtaining a doctorate in political science (1929), he joined the diplomatic corps and was sent to Paris. He returned to Venezuela in 1934, and taught political economy at the Universidad Central; later he held high positions in several Venezuelan ministries and was a delegate to the League of Nations. After the government fell in 1945, Uslar Pietri went to the United States as an exile and taught at Columbia University. He returned to Venezuela in 1950, reentering political life in 1959 as a senator.

In 1969, Uslar Pietri dedicated himself more to literature and teaching. His essays and fictional works evidence his interest in Venezuela's political and economic problems. Currents of democratic thought run through this concern for the national. The first volume of Uslar Pietri's ample and wide-ranging literary output, *Barrabás y otros relatos*, was published in 1928. Written in a modernist prose style, *Barrabás* introduces elements of vanguardism by developing the inner voices of the characters. His novel *Las lanzas coloradas* (1931) brought him fame and was his most important contribution to Spanish American letters. The novel's plot centers on the violence and chaos in the Venezuelan countryside resulting from the military and ideological confusion during the Wars of Independence. This work is a "novel of the land" or a "novel of national interpretation."

Uslar Pietri's most important short-story collection, *Red* (1936), retains the same vanguardist elements initiated in *Barrabás*, but in this work the author shifts his attention to the vernacular life by using techniques of magical surrealism. Of this collection, "La lluvia" is considered a masterpiece of the genre. Less important works are *El camino de El dorado* (1947), a novel about the conqueror Lope de AGUIRRE; *El laberinto de fortuna: Un retrato en la geografía* (1962), a political work focusing on the epoch of the Juan Vincente GÓMEZ dictatorship (1908–1935). Essay collections include *Letras y hombres de Venezuela* (1948), *De una a otra Venezuela* (1950), *Breve historia de la novela hispanoamericana* (1954), *En busca del Nuevo Mundo* (1969), and *Bolívar Hoy* (1983). Uslar Pietri has also written about theater in *Teatro* (1958), a work in which plays of his appear, and has turned his hand to poetry in *El hombre que voy siendo* (1986).

JOSÉ LUIS VIVAS, *La cuentística de Arturo Uslar Pietri* (1963); DOMINGO MILIANI, *Arturo Uslar Pietri: Renovador del cuento venezolano contemporáneo* (1965); R. M. R. DOUGHERTY, "The Essays of Arturo Uslar Pietri" (Ph.D. diss., University of Illinois, 1971); JOHN S. BRUSHWOOD, *The Spanish American Novel* (1975), pp. 88–91; TERESITA JOSEFINA PARRA, *Visión histórica en la obra de Arturo Uslar Pietri* (1979).

JUAN CARLOS GALEANO

USPALLATA PASS, passage connecting Mendoza in Argentina with Los Andes and Santiago in Chile. Named for the small village of Uspallata in an intermountainous depression some 140 miles west of Mendoza, the rail and motor route to Chile follows the course of the torrential Mendoza River and passes through the villages of Polvaredas and Punta de Vacas before reaching its culmination at Las Cuevas (13,170 feet). An international railway tunnel leads from there to the Chilean side of the Andes. The motor road reaches its highest point (13,860 feet) at the foot of the Christ of the Andes monument.

CÉSAR N. CAVIEDES

USUMACINTA RIVER, a waterway in northwestern Guatemala and southeastern Mexico. Beginning in northern Guatemala, where the Chixoy and La Pasión rivers meet, the Usumacinta flows through a sparsely populated area marking the border between Chiapas, Mexico, and Petén, Guatemala. Surrounded by tropical forest, the river cuts across the rolling limestone plateau of the Petén before entering Tabasco state. In Tabasco the waterway forms an alluvial floodplain and annually inundates large areas, creating numerous lagoons and swamps. Near Frontera, Tabasco, the Usumacinta joins the Grijalva River and flows into the Bay of Campeche. Together, the Usumacinta-Grijalva river system forms Mexico's largest watershed by volume, accounting for nearly half of the country's stream flow.

Historically, the river was a trade artery for the lowland Mayas, yet its modern use has been limited to moving logs and chicle downstream. Efforts to incorporate this peripheral area into modern Mexico have centered upon hydroelectric and flood-control projects. A large dam near Balancán, Tabasco, produces electricity and has enabled the reclamation of agricultural lands and pastures in Tabasco. Further upstream, Mexico and Guatemala have proposed a series of dams along their common border, but the project has been postponed because of costs, the possible flooding of important archaeological sites, and international pressure against developing the largest remaining rain forest in Central America.

DAVID BARKIN and TIMOTHY KING, *Regional Economic Development: The River Basin Approach in Mexico* (1970), esp. pp. 102–107; NANCY M. FARRISS, *Maya Society Under Colonial Rule: The Collective Enterprise of Survival* (1984), pp. 152–154; LARRY ROHTER, "Dam Project Is Seen as a Threat to Maya Sites," *New York Times*, 26 March 1987, sec. 1, p. 13.

MARIE D. PRICE

UTATLAN, capital of the Late Postclassic highland Maya K'iche' polity, also known as K'umarcaaj (its K'iche' name). The site is located approximately one mile west of the town of Santa Cruz del Quiché, department of Quiché, Guatemala. Utatlan proper occupies a relatively inaccessible plateau that can be reached only via a causeway and bridge from the east and a rugged stairway cut into the mountainside from the west. Several nearby plateaus were the sites of the contemporary K'iche' settlements of Chisalin, Ismachi, Resguardo, and

Pakaman. The entire group of settlements is referred to as Greater Utatlan.

Utatlan proper consists of over seventy structures divided into a central civic plaza, three elite residential complexes, and additional courtyard groups. The civic plaza is flanked on the west by a temple dedicated to the deity Tojil and on the east by the Awilix Temple, dedicated to the moon goddess. A long, low structure, thought to be the "council house" or administrative center of the dominant Cawek lineage at the site, bounds the plaza on the north. At the southwest corner of the plaza is an I-shaped ball court. The elite residential complexes were made up of temples, rectangular structures, and large, multi-roomed buildings called palaces.

Considerable information about Utatlan and its residents as well as K'iche' history is available in ethnohistoric documents. According to K'iche' myth, their ancestors migrated to the Guatemalan highlands from the Gulf Coast sometime after 1200. Gradually the K'iche', from their capital at Utatlan, grew to dominate the central highlands and became the most powerful state in the region. During the late 1400s, however, K'iche' power waned as groups like the Kaqchikel and Tz'utujil asserted their independence.

A K'iche' warrior, Tecum, the grandson of the K'iche' ruler, led the battle against the invading Spaniards in 1524 and died in the process. The conquistador Pedro de ALVARADO subsequently burned Utatlan; a new town, Santa Cruz, was established for the surviving inhabitants.

The most notable K'iche' document to survive today is the POPOL VUH, the creation story written sometime in the mid-sixteenth century by members of the K'iche' noble lineages. Perhaps working with older pictorial manuscripts, the authors of the *Popol Vuh* recorded their history. A copy of the manuscript written in the Roman alphabet was seen by a Dominican priest, Francisco XIMÉNEZ, in 1701–1703. XIMÉNEZ copied the text in both K'iche' and with a Spanish translation. His copy of the *Popol Vuh*, now housed at the Newberry Library in Chicago, is the only known extant version.

JOHN W. FOX, *Quiché Conquest* (1978), esp. pp. 16–39; ROBERT M. CARMACK, *The Quiché Mayas of Utatlan* (1981); *Popul Vuh*, translated by Dennis Tedlock (1985).

JANINE GASCO

UXMAL ("thrice built") is a MAYA city located in northwestern Yucatán south of the range of hills known as the Puuc. The site was occupied in the eighth century and reached its maximum florescence between about 850 and 925, shortly after which it, along with many other sites in the Puuc district, was abandoned. Epigraphic research has revealed that Uxmal was governed around 900 by a ruler, "Lord Chac," who took the name of the Yucatecan Maya rain god, and has demonstrated political contacts between Uxmal and Chichén Itzá.

Uxmal's central civic-ceremonial area is defined by a

Workers at Uxmal, Section 1. PEABODY MUSEUM, HARVARD UNIVERSITY.

View of Uxmal, Yucatán. PHOTO BY FRANCO TORRIJOS.

low masonry wall and covers approximately one-half mile north–south by less than one-half mile east–west, with smaller residential structures lying outside. Except for three small Chenes-style buildings, Uxmal's major edifices are superlative examples of Puuc architecture, featuring a construction technology based on lime concrete cores and fine cut-masonry facades. Long, horizontal buildings display complex arrays of precarved stone mosaic elements assembled to form motifs such as step frets, simple and sawtoothed lattices, engaged colonnettes, long-snouted "rain god" masks, and human figures.

Uxmal is known for magnificent edifices such as the Pigeon Group, named for a distinctive openwork roof comb on the structure called the House of Pigeons; the Pyramid of the Magician (or Adivino), a multistage pyramid–temple constructed in five separate campaigns; and the ball court, whose inner platform walls bore feathered serpent sculptures and hieroglyphic rings. Uxmal's most striking architectural monuments are the 328-foot-long range building, or "palace," known as the House of the Governor, perhaps "Lord Chac's" royal residence and administrative center, and the Nunnery Quadrangle, a large compound bordered on four sides by elaborately sculptured, multiroom range buildings set at different levels.

MARTA FONCERRADA DE MOLINA, *La escultura arquitectónica de Uxmal* (1965); H. E. D. POLLOCK, *The Puuc: An Architectural Survey of the Hill Country of Yucatán and Northern Campeche, Mexico* (1980); JEFF KARL KOWALSKI, *The House of the Governor, a Maya Palace at Uxmal, Yucatán, Mexico* (1987).

JEFF KARL KOWALSKI

VACA DE CASTRO, CRISTÓVAL (*b.* ca. 1492; *d.* after 1576), governor of Peru (1541–1544). Born in a small town (Izagre) near León, Spain, Vaca de Castro served as *oidor* (judge) of the Audiencia of Valladolid (1536). Recognizing his administrative abilities, CHARLES I appointed him (September 1540) for a three-year term to investigate Peru's chaotic political situation. Vaca de Castro reached Panama in January 1541, and because of difficult weather decided to travel overland rather than sail. From coastal Buenaventura in present-day Colombia, he proceeded to Cali, where he recuperated for three months from an illness. In Popayán he learned Francisco PIZARRO had been assassinated and Peru was under the control of Diego de ALMAGRO the Younger. Vaca de Castro then moved southward, collecting an army to oust Almagro.

Early in 1542 he left Quito, marched to Piura in northwest Peru, then to Trujillo, back into the highlands, then on to Huamanga. By then Vaca de Castro had the aid of Lima and letters of support from Gonzalo PIZARRO in the south. Almagro had been staying in Cuzco and had been negotiating with royalists. The administration of Peru was settled on 16 September 1542 at the battle of Chupas, one of the bloodiest battles of Peru's civil wars. Almagro fled, but was soon captured. He was executed in Cuzco and buried alongside his father.

Vaca de Castro undertook to defuse Peru's turmoil by removing its cause—the large number of discontented soldiers. He supported three major expeditions: In 1543, Captain Juan de Porcel entered the Bracamoros in northwest Peru; Diego de Rojas began the exploration and settlement of the Tucumán region in present-day northwest Argentina; and Captain Juan Pérez de Vergara initiated the conquest of the Moyobamba and Rupa-Rupa in the upper jungle in 1544. A threat of a newly revived INCA state was lessened when the energetic and highly capable leader MANCO INCA was assassinated by a group of Spaniards the same year.

The arrival of Peru's first viceroy, Blasco NÚÑEZ VELA, brought the end of Vaca de Castro's tenure. The viceroy was welcomed into Lima (15 May 1544) but refused to take advice from the ex-governor. Believing Vaca de Castro to be a member of a conspiracy against him, the new viceroy imprisoned the official and charged him with forcing Indians to work in the mines without salary, authorizing their employment as beasts of burden, and selling ENCOMIENDAS. Before hearings got under way, the viceroy himself was jailed by adherents of Gonzalo Pizarro. Vaca de Castro escaped to Spain, only to face charges there. Caught between the Pizarrist and Almagrist factions at court, he found himself in jail again, in Valladolid, Arévalo, and later Simancas. It was not until 1555 that the court freed and rehabilitated him.

In 1556 he returned to the Council of Castile and in 1559 received back salary. He served on the council until his retirement in 1566. Thereafter, he lived in the convent of San Agustín in Valladolid. After his death, his remains were transferred by order of his second son, Pedro de Castro, Archbishop of Granada, to the Colegiata del Sacro-Monte of Granada.

MANUEL DE MENDIBURU, *Diccionario histórico biográfico del Perú* (1935); JOSÉ ANTONIO DEL BUSTO DUTHURBURU, *Historia general del Perú: Descubrimiento y conquista* (1978).

NOBLE DAVID COOK

VACCARO BROTHERS (Joseph, Luca, and Felix), three Sicilian Americans who, with a son-in-law, Salvador D'Antoni, engaged in the produce business in New Orleans at the close of the nineteenth century. In 1899 a severe freeze destroyed their orange groves, and of necessity they began the importation of bananas from Honduras. Building railroads, wharves, and Honduras's first bank and hospital, Vaccaro Brothers and Company modernized the banana trade and became Honduras's largest investor and exporter before World War I, and second only to the older UNITED FRUIT COMPANY in the international banana trade. The need for capital for research, and expansion to other nations, caused this family company to go public in 1925.

RICHARD H. ROSE, *Utilla: Past and Present* (1904); "The Story of the Standard Fruit and Steamship Company," in *New Orleans Port Record,* October 1947, p. 19; THOMAS L. KARNES, *Tropical Enterprise: The Standard Fruit and Steamship Company in Latin America* (1978).

THOMAS L. KARNES

See also **Banana Industry.**

VALCÁRCEL ARCE, EDGAR (*b.* 4 Dec. 1932), Peruvian composer. He was born in Puno and studied in Lima at the National Conservatory with Andrés SAS and at Hunter College in New York City with Donald Lybbert. With a fellowship from the Torcuato Di Tella Institute, Valcárcel studied in Buenos Aires at the Centro Latinoamericano de Altos Estudios Musicales (1963–1964). He studied there with Alberto GINASTERA, director of the center, and Olivier Messiaen, Luigi Dallapiccola, Gerardo GANDINI, Riccardo Malipiero, and Bruno Maderna. He was in New York City in 1966 with a Guggenheim Foundation fellowship to do graduate work on electronic music under the guidance of Vladimir Ussachevsky and Alcides LANZA. In 1986 he became a professor at the National School of Music in Lima and in 1989 the director of that institution. In 1976 he was a visiting professor of composition at the Faculty of Music, McGill University, Montreal. Valcárcel has received the National Music Prize in 1956 and 1965, the State Choir Prize in 1965, the Composition Prize of the Grand Masonic Lodge in 1971, and the Inocente Carreño Prize, Caracas, in 1981.

His principal works include *Variaciones* for piano (1963); *Espectros* no. 1 for flute, viola, and piano (1964); *Cantata para la noche inmensa* for men's choir and orchestra (1964); *Canto coral a Tupac Amaru* no. 1 for soprano, baritone, chorus, and orchestra (1968); Sonata no. 1 for piano (1965); *Dicotomías* nos. 1 and 2 for piano (1966) and no. 3 for chamber ensemble (1966); *Invención* (1966), electronic sounds; *Fisiones* for chamber ensemble (1967); *Hiwaña uru* for winds, strings, and piano (1967), in memory of Andrés Sas; Piano Concerto (1968); *Canto Coral a Tupac Amaru* no. 2 for chorus and electronic sounds on tape (1968); *Antaras* for flute and electronic sounds (1968); *Checán* no. 1 for flute, oboe, clarinet, bassoon, horn, and piano (1969), no. 2 for orchestra (1970), and no. 3 for nineteen instruments (1971); Sonata no. 2 for piano (1971); *Karabotasat Cutintapata* for orchestra (1977); *Zampoña sónica* for flute and tape (1976); *Retablo* no. 2 (*Flor de Sancayo*) for piano and electronic sounds (1975); *Antimemorias* no. 2 for orchestra (1980); *Checán* no. 4 for choir (1981); *Homenaje a Stravinsky* for two pianos, flute, French horn and percussion (1982); *Andahuaylillas* for organ (1983); *Concierto para guitarra y orquesta* (1984); and *A Theodoro* for soprano and three French horns (1986).

Compositores de America 17 (1971):113–120; JOHN VINTON, ed., *Dictionary of Contemporary Music* (1974), p. 790; GÉRARD BÉHAGUE, *Music in Latin America: An Introduction* (1979), pp. 313–314; *Octavo festival internacional de música contemporánea* (1992), pp. 29, 83, 119–120.

ALCIDES LANZA

VALDÉS, GABRIEL DE LA CONCEPCIÓN (pseud. Plácido; *b.* 18 March 1809; *d.* 26 June 1844), Cuban poet. Plácido, the pseudonym he adopted and through which he became known, was born in Havana, the illegitimate son of a mulatto hairdresser and a Spanish dancer. Shortly after birth he was left at a home for illegitimate childen, but when he was a few months old, he was retrieved by his father's family, who raised him. He received no schooling until the age of ten, and then his education was haphazard, as was his lifelong economic situation (he was occasionally jailed for indebtedness).

Plácido's poetic talent did not earn him money—he worked as a silversmith and a maker of tortoiseshell combs—but it earned him the admiration of the established poets of the day, including José María HEREDIA. His ability to improvise verse on the spot for various occasions spread his fame and created a great demand for his attendance at all manner of social activities. Eventually his popularity came to be his undoing, however, as the Spanish authorities became suspicious of his active social life and arrested him for conspiracy. Although there was then as later no evidence of his participation in any conspiracy, he was shot by a firing squad in Matanzas. Thus martyred, he became a symbol of the cause of independence.

Plácido's poetry incorporates into traditional Spanish lyrical forms tropical imagery and the romantic themes of intense pathos and the urge for freedom. Although Plácido is not considered a poet of the first rank, many of his poems are recited by heart by Cubans of all ages and have come to form part of popular folklore.

FREDERICK S. STIMSON, *Cuba's Romantic Poet: The Story of Plácido* (1964).

ROBERTO VALERO

VALDÉS CASTILLO, GERMÁN. *See* **Tin-Tan.**

VALDÉZ, JUAN, fictitious Colombian coffee grower, created in 1959 by the National Coffee Growers Federation of Colombia for its advertising campaigns in the United States. Valdéz and his donkey have proven remarkably durable in both print and electronic advertising; a stylized logo was introduced in 1981, and mere invocation of his name is considered sufficient in recent campaigns. Valdéz does not figure in Colombian domestic advertising (where individual brands, rather than the federation, are in control), but his name is familiar to Colombians, who consider him a caricature for foreign consumption, albeit a positive one. While the Valdéz image of a grower lovingly scrutinizing each coffee bean is, to put it mildly, idealized—the western Colombian coffee harvest is a fast-paced affair increasingly reliant upon tens of thousands of migrant wage-laborers—it does suggest the continuing predominance of independent small- and medium-sized producers in Colombia, as opposed to the larger agribusiness-style operations that characterize Brazil.

RICHARD J. STOLLER

See also **Coffee Industry; Colombia: Organizations.**

VALDIVIA, LUIS DE (*b.* 1561; *d.* 5 November 1642), Spanish JESUIT who spent much of his life in Chile defending and protecting the rights of Indians. In 1589, shortly after entering the Society of Jesus, Valdivia was assigned to the province of Peru, where he remained until 1593, when he was assigned to Chile. There he dedicated himself to Christianizing and protecting the Indians against the Spaniards, for which he gained many enemies.

Valdivia believed that waging war on the Indians to subjugate and Christianize them was not morally right. The Indians were free beings and had control over their lives; therefore, they should become Christians or crown subjects of their own free will. At the insistence of the viceroy of Peru, the count of Montesclaros, Valdivia went to Spain in 1609 to inform the crown about the conditions in the region and the efforts to pacify it. He was heard by the COUNCIL OF THE INDIES, and after about a year and a half, on 8 December 1610, a royal *cédula* (decree) ordered a change from offensive to defensive methods in the war against the Indians of Chile. In 1611 he went back to Chile, where he gained many more enemies as a result of the new policy. His enemies tried to thwart his efforts by complaining to royal officials and even to the crown. But a *cédula* of 21 November 1615 reiterated the policy. In 1620 Valdivia returned to Spain permanently.

BEATRICE BLUM, "Luis de Valdivia, Defender of the Araucanians," in *Mid-America: An Historical Review* 24, no. 2 (1942): 109–137; JOSÉ ARMANDO DE RAMÓN FOLCH, *El pensamiento político social del Padre Luis de Valdivia* (1961).

JUAN MANUEL PÉREZ

See also **Las Casas, Bartolomé de; Missions.**

VALDIVIA, PEDRO DE (*b.* ca. 1500; *d.* 1553), Spanish conquistador and founder of Chile. Before undertaking the expedition to Chile, Valdivia had already acquired extensive military experience. He entered the army in 1521, participated in the Spanish campaigns in Flanders and Italy, and fought in the battle of Pavia (24 February 1525). He retuned to Spain and married Marina Ortíz de Gaete, a native of Salamanca. The sources available contain conflicting information about this union. Some sources say that he was married before the Italian campaigns, while others say he married after. From 1525, when he was in Milan, to 1535, when he embarked on his voyage to the New World, not much is known about his life.

Valdivia probably sailed for Venezuela in an expedition led by Jerónimo de Alderete. He remained in Venezuela for a year or a year and a half, another period in his life for which there is not too much information. He then went to Peru as a member of an expedition to help Francisco PIZARRO suppress an Indian rebellion led by MANCO CAPAC. His experience in the military served him well, and in 1537, Pizarro named him his aide-de-camp. Valdivia gained a reputation as a brave soldier in the war between Pizarro and Diego de ALMAGRO. He and Gonzalo Pizarro led the infantry against the forces of Almagro in the decisive battle of Salinas on 6 April 1538. As a reward for his services, Francisco Pizarro granted Valdivia an ENCOMIENDA in the valley of La Canela.

Valdivia, however, was a man of adventure, and he asked permission from Pizarro to go to Chile, despite the fact that Almagro had gone before and had come back disappointed because he had not found gold. To finance his expedition, Valdivia sold his lands. In the middle of January 1540, he left for Chile from Cuzco accompanied by twelve Spaniards; one woman, Inés de Suárez (who later became the second of four significant women in Valdivia's life); about one thousand Indians; and a few black slaves. Others joined him as he moved

Portrait of Pedro de Valdivia. ORGANIZATION OF AMERICAN STATES.

on to Chile. Late in 1540, Valdivia reached the Copiapó Valley and called the new land Nueva Extremadura. He moved farther south to Coquimbo and then to the Mapocho Valley, and on 24 February 1541, near the Mapocho River, Valdivia founded Santiago del Nuevo Extremo, present-day Santiago.

The city endured an Indian siege while Valdivia was absent, and the Spaniards suffered many hardships because reinforcements and supplies did not arrive until two years later, in 1543. With more men and supplies, Valdivia continued exploring and in 1544 founded LA SERENA, halfway between the Copiapó Valley and Santiago. In 1545, he went further south to Quilacura, and at the same time, his lieutenants were exploring other areas.

In 1547, Valdivia left for Peru with the intention of getting more supplies and found himself in the middle of a rebellion led by Gonzalo PIZARRO. He sided with the crown's *visitador*, Pedro de Lagasca, and became an important factor in Pizarro's defeat. He returned to Chile on 21 January 1549, after being cleared by Lagasca of accusations leveled against him by his enemies. Once in Chile, Valdivia continued his explorations and founded more cities: Concepción (1550), VALDIVIA (1552), and Villarica (1552). He died in 1553 in a battle against the ARAUCANIANS led by LAUTARO.

Valdivia symbolizes the spirit of the CONQUISTADORES in his desire for adventure and his drive to explore new lands. He resembles, for example, Alvar Núñez CABEZA DE VACA, Vasco Núñez de BALBOA, and Hernando de SOTO: men who were driven more by the spirit of adventure than by the hope of finding gold.

FRANCISCO ESTEVE BARBA, *Descubrimiento y conquista de Chile* (1946); IDA STEVENSON WELDON VERNON, *Pedro de Valdivia: Conquistador of Chile* (1946); JAIME DELGADO, *Pedro de Valdivia* (1987); CARMEN PUMAR MARTÍNEZ, *Pedro de Valdivia: Fundador de Chile* (1988).

JUAN MANUEL PÉREZ

See also **Explorers and Exploration.**

VALDIVIA, CHILE, capital city of the Lake Region in southern Chile (1990 population 113,512), located on the lower Valdivia River. Founded by Pedro de VALDIVIA in 1552 almost in the middle of ARAUCANIAN (MAPUCHE) Indian territory, it was an isolated Spanish enclave in hostile territory during most of the colonial period. In spite of repeated sieges, it was never overrun by the Indians. After independence it was the only part of the Lake Region securely held by the Chileans, and it was chosen as the center of the colonization efforts destined to weaken the southern flank of Araucania. Between 1849 and 1880, numerous German and Swiss families settled in the intermediate depression between the ANDES and the Coastal Range, cleared the forests, and started farming and logging enterprises. German colonists established breweries, lumber industries, leather manufactures, and small shipyards that fostered a period of prosperity during the first half of the twentieth century. From Valdivia colonization efforts spread to Osorno, Frutillar, Río Bueno, and Puerto Varas. When industries began to concentrate in Central Chile, Valdivia stagnated, and the earthquake of May 1960 inflicted serious damage to the decaying city. Recovery has been slow, helped mostly by cultural establishments such as the University of Valdivia.

GABRIEL GUARDA, *La toma de Valdivia* (Santiago, 1970).

CÉSAR N. CAVIEDES

VALDIVIA, ECUADOR, archaeological site in coastal Guayas Province. Valdivia is where the Early Formative VALDIVIA CULTURE was first defined by Ecuadoran Emilio Estrada in the mid-1950s and subsequently investigated by the Smithsonian archaeologists Clifford Evans and Betty Meggers. The site (G-31) is at the mouth of the Valdivia River valley. Cultural refuse of the Valdivia occupation covers some 4.2 acres on the slope and basal portion of a low spur. The deposits are deepest in the basal sector of the site, where a later GUANGALA occupation of smaller size overlies the Valdivia deposits. Deep excavations conducted here in 1961 yielded abundant remains of Valdivia pottery, chipped stone artifacts, fire-modified rock, fish and animal bones, and shell. No visible stratigraphy was recognized during excavation, however, and no archaeological features were identified.

The unique ceramic materials and associated radiocarbon dates recovered at Valdivia allowed the investigators to establish a four-phase ceramic sequence (labeled A through D) thought to reflect slight developmental change through time. At the time, the basal materials were thought to represent the earliest pottery in the New World. Its relative sophistication raised the question of origins and led the investigators to hypothesize a trans-Pacific diffusion of this pottery tradition in the latter half of the third millennium B.C. from the Neolithic Jomon culture of Japan. This argument was subsequently challenged by a number of scholars and was finally laid to rest in the early 1970s by the discovery of ceramics predating phase A both at the Valdivia site itself and at Loma Alta, a village site located on alluvial bottomland some 6 miles up the Valdivia Valley. The latter find constituted another ceramic "phase" in the emerging eight-phase chronology of Betsy Hill.

The littoral location of the site, and its obvious reliance on marine and estuarine subsistence resources, led the investigators to characterize Valdivia culture as generally a semisedentary maritime adaptation of egalitarian fishermen and shellfish gatherers having only a marginal reliance on horticulture. In reality, this characterization pertains only to smaller beachfront sites, such as G-31, which appear to have specialized in the exploitation of littoral resources. Such sites formed one component of a more complex regional settlement system that involved the exchange of maritime resources with inland farming villages for horticultural produce and terrestrial game resources.

In spite of their problematic interpretations of Valdivia culture, the pioneering work of Meggers, Evans, and Estrada at site G-31 stands as a landmark in South American archaeology.

EMILIO ESTRADA, Valdivia: Un sitio arqueológico formativo en la provincia del Guayas, Ecuador (1956); BETTY J. MEGGERS et al., Early Formative Period of Coastal Ecuador: The Valdivia and Machalilla Phases (1965); BETTY J. MEGGERS, Ecuador (1966); HENNING BISCHOF and JULIO VITERI GAMBOA, "Pre-Valdivia Occupations on the Southwest Coast of Ecuador," in American Antiquity 37, no. 4 (1972): 548–551; DONALD W. LATHRAP et al., Ancient Ecuador: Culture, Clay, and Creativity, 3000–300 B.C. (1975); ROBERT A. FELDMAN and MICHAEL E. MOSELEY, "The Northern Andes," in Ancient South Americans, edited by Jesse D. Jennings (1983).

JAMES A. ZEIDLER

See also **Real Alto.**

VALDIVIA CULTURE, the prehistoric culture that occupied the Pacific coastal lowlands of Ecuador during the Early Formative period (3500–1500 B.C.). It was orig-

inally identified as the type site of VALDIVIA in coastal Guayas Province by the Ecuadoran Emilio Estrada, and subsequently investigated by the archaeologists Betty Meggers and Clifford Evans in the early 1960s. Valdivia culture was thought by those scholars to represent an egalitarian, semisedentary littoral adaptation based upon fishing and shellfish gathering, with only rudimentary reliance on horticulture. Its unique ceramic style and "Venus" figurine tradition were originally thought to be the earliest in the New World, and their origins were attributed to diffusionary trans-Pacific voyaging by Neolithic Jomon fishermen from Japan.

More recent research at other important coastal sites, such as San Pablo, REAL ALTO, and Salango, as well as inland sites, such as Loma Alta, Colimes, and San Lorenzo del Mate, has promoted considerable rethinking of the nature of Valdivia culture, its origins, economic base, settlement organization, and cosmological beliefs. The archaeologist Donald Lathrap has forcefully argued that Valdivia represents a "tropical forest culture" having a fundamentally riverine settlement focus whose ultimate origins can be traced to early population dispersals from the Amazon Basin. Newer subsistence data indicate a mixed economy of floodplain horticultural production (based on maize, beans, root crops, cotton, and gourds), hunting, fishing, and the gathering of wild plants and shellfish. Certain coastal settlements, such as the type site, are viewed as sites that specialized in the exploitation of maritime and estuarine resources.

These studies have shed new light on Valdivia chronology and the pace of social change during its 2,000-year time span. An eight-phase ceramic sequence established by Betsy Hill has permitted a more precise delineation of temporal trends in settlement pattern and internal site layout. Large-scale excavations at village sites such as Real Alto and Loma Alta have permitted detailed reconstruction of Valdivia households, community patterning, social organization, and ceremonial behavior, all of which underwent significant changes between phases 1 and 8. As a result, it is now clear that Valdivia represents a dynamic, fully sedentary society of village horticulturalists characterized by progressive demographic growth and an increasing degree of social ranking and status inequality through time. Beginning as early as Middle Valdivia times, long-distance maritime trade with the complex societies of coastal Peru may have provided an impetus for social change leading to greater complexity in the later Valdivia phases.

There is also evidence of a progressive geographic expansion of Valdivia communities to the north and to the south, out of the Guayas Province heartland. Beginning in Middle Valdivia times (phase 3), when settlements appeared on the offshore islands of LA PLATA and PUNÁ, this outward expansion culminated in Terminal Valdivia times (phase 8), when large inland ceremonial centers with satellite communities appeared in the wetter environments to the north and to the south. Both the San Isidro site in northern Manabí and the La Emergenciana site in El Oro represent phase 8 ceremonial centers with monumental public architecture of a magnitude not seen in previous Valdivia phases.

EMILIO ESTRADA, *Valdivia: Un sitio arqueológico formativo en la provincia del Guayas, Ecuador* (1956); BETTY J. MEGGERS, *Ecuador* (1966); BETSY D. HILL, "A New Chronology of the Valdivia Ceramic Complex from the Coastal Zone of Guayas Province, Ecuador," in *Nawpa Pacha* 10–12 (1972–1974): 1–32; DONALD W. LATHRAP et al., *Ancient Ecuador: Culture, Clay, and Creativity, 3000–300 B.C.* (1975); DONALD W. LATHRAP et al., "Real Alto: An Ancient Ceremonial Center," in *Archaeology* 30, no. 1 (1977): 2–13; ROBERT A. FELDMAN and MICHAEL E. MOSELEY, "The Northern Andes," in *Ancient South Americans*, edited by Jesse D. Jennings (1983); JAMES A. ZEIDLER, "Maritime Exchange in the Early Formative Period of Ecuador: Geo-political Origins of Uneven Development," in *Research in Economic Anthropology*, edited by Barry L. Isaac, vol. 13 (1991), pp. 247–268.

JAMES A. ZEIDLER

See also **Real Alto.**

VALENCIA, ANTONIO MARÍA (*b.* 10 November 1902; *d.* 22 July 1952), Colombian composer, pianist, and teacher. Born in Cali, Valencia began his musical studies with his father, cellist and teacher Julio Valencia Belmonte. Later he entered the Bogotá Conservatory (1917–1919) to study piano with Honorio Alarcón. After concert tours in the southern United States, Valencia moved to Paris and enrolled at the Schola Cantorum (1923–1929), where he studied under Vincent d'Indy (composition), Paul Braud (piano), Paul le Flem (counterpoint and fugue), Louis Saint-Requier (harmony and conducting of vocal and instrumental groups), Gabriel Pierné (chamber music) and Manuel de Falla (orchestration). He was offered a professorship, but at the end of his studies he returned to Colombia, where he gave concerts and pursued a career in composition. His early works show an affinity for national music, though his Paris training later led to a concentration on European forms. In his last years, Valencia returned to the melodies and rhythms of his homeland.

Valencia wrote a considerable number of choral religious works demonstrating a solid technique and exceptional use of counterpoint, as, for example, in his Requiem Mass (1943). Among his chamber music works are *Duo en forma de sonata* (1926), for piano and violin; *Emociones caucanas* (1938), for violin, piano, and cello; songs on French texts; and many piano pieces. He composed *Chirimía y bambuco sotareño* (1942) for orchestra and wrote orchestrations and arrangements of French music. Valencia founded the Conservatory and School of Fine Arts of Cali (1933), remaining as its director until his death. He was also director of the Bogotá Conservatory (1937–1938). He died in Cali.

Composers of the Americas, vol. 4 (1958), pp. 105–110; GÉRARD BÉHAGUE, *Music in Latin America* (1979); *New Grove Dictionary of Music and Musicians*, vol. 19 (1980).

SUSANA SALGADO

VALENCIA, GUILLERMO LEÓN (*b.* 27 April 1909; *d.* 4 November 1971), president of Colombia (1962–1966). The son of Guillermo Valencia, a celebrated poet and Conservative political leader, Valencia was born in POPAYÁN and studied law at the University of Cauca. Serving in the senate and in the Conservative Party leadership, he became known as a flamboyant orator and impassioned follower of Conservative chieftain Laureano GÓMEZ (president, 1950–1953), who appointed him ambassador to Spain in 1950. Later he moderated his partisanship and distanced himself from Gómez. He was an outspoken critic of President Gustavo ROJAS PINILLA (1953–1957). An order (1 May 1957) that Valencia be placed under house arrest sparked a wave of civic unrest that ended the Rojas regime nine days later. Valencia was slated to be the first presidential candidate of the Frente Nacional (National Front), but he was blackballed by Gómez. Instead, he became the National Front nominee in 1962, winning 62.1 percent of the vote.

As president, Valencia continued many of the policies of his predecessor, Alberto LLERAS CAMARGO (1958–1962), though he is usually considered a less competent chief executive. During his administration the armed forces smashed communist-influenced "republics" in central and southern Colombia. In 1964, however, surviving militants founded a southern guerrilla bloc that became the forerunner of the Fuerzas Armadas Revolucionarias Colombianas (Colombian Revolutionary Armed Force—FARC). Valencia also confronted economic difficulties, notably a fall in coffee prices, balance of payments problems, depreciation of the *peso*, and inflation. Opposition to a new sales tax led to a threatened general strike in January 1965, which was averted partly because of government concessions. Criticism of the government by Minister of War General Alberto Ruiz Novoa, who harbored political ambitions, heightened tensions until he was removed in January 1965. After retiring from the presidency in 1966, Valencia again served as ambassador to Spain.

JONATHAN HARTLYN, *The Politics of Coalition Rule in Colombia* (1988), esp. pp. 120–124.

HELEN DELPAR

VALENTIM, MESTRE. *See* **Fonseca e Silva, Valentim da.**

VALENZUELA, LUISA (*b.* 26 November 1938), Argentine writer. The daughter of Argentine writer Luisa Mercedes Levinson, Valenzuela was born in Buenos Aires and grew up in Corrientes and Buenos Aires, which provided settings for her later fiction. She began her writing career as a journalist for the newspaper *La Nación* and published her first short story at age seventeen. Between 1956 and 1961 she lived in France, where she wrote her first novel, which was published in 1966. But it was with the publication of *Hay que sonreír* (One Has to Smile, 1966) and a collection of short stories, *Los heréticos* (1967), that she was recognized as a promising young writer. In 1969 she won a Fulbright scholarship to participate in the International Writers Workshop at the University of Iowa, where she wrote *El gato eficaz* (1972), a novel in which language rather than characters is the central concern. Later, she traveled throughout Mexico and became interested in Mexican indigenous cultures. She used some of these experiences in writing the stories in *Donde viven las águilas* (Where Eagles Live, 1983). During 1972 Valenzuela lived in Barcelona, where she wrote *Como en la guerra* (1977). This novel also centers on language and surrealistic experiences.

Returning to Argentina, Valenzuela wrote *Aquí pasan cosas raras* (Strange Things Happen Here, 1975). When she felt that the military government threatened her well-being, she moved to New York City. During her sojourn in the United States, some of her works were translated into English. She was featured in popular magazines like *Time* side-by-side with other well-known Latin American writers, and in 1986 the *Review of Contemporary Fiction*, a scholarly journal published in the United States, dedicated an issue to Valenzuela's fiction. *El libro que no muerde* (1980) and *Cambio de armas* (Other Weapons, 1982) were written during this time. The latter is a collection of five lengthy short stories in which Valenzuela's fiction reaches depth and maturity, where female and male sexuality represents the warped and misunderstood relationship between men and women, who are witness to the disintegration of a reality in which they are victims and victimizers.

In 1983 Valenzuela went back to Argentina, where she published a novel on the political manipulations and sorceries of José López Rega, a picturesque and macabre member of the cabinet of the last Peronist regime, entitled *Cola de lagartija*. Two subsequent novels also deal with Argentina's reality, *Novela negra con argentinos* (Gothic Novel with Argentines, 1990) and *Realidad nacional desde la cama* (National Reality from the Bed, 1990).

SHARON MAGNARELLI, *Reflections/Refractions: Reading Luisa Valenzuela* (1988); VICTORIA GUEST, *Reweaving the Violated Narrative* (1990); JUANAMARÍA CORDONES-COOK, *Poética de transgresión en la novelística de Luisa Valenzuela* (1991).

MAGDALENA GARCÍA PINTO

VALERO, ROBERTO (*b.* 27 May 1955; *d.* 23 September 1994), Cuban writer. Born in the city of Matanzas, Cuba, Valero studied at the University of Havana (1975–1980). In 1980 he joined the approximately 10,800 Cubans who entered the Peruvian Embassy asking for political asylum, and left the island with the MARIEL BOATLIFT. Valero received a Ph.D. in literature from Georgetown University in 1988 and taught both there and at the George Washington University. During his years in Washington he wrote acclaimed books of poetry, such

as *Desde un oscuro ángulo* (From a Dark Corner) in 1981 and *En fin, la noche* (At Last the Night) in 1984. At the time of his death, Valero had published extensively, had gained wide recognition for his poetry, and had been honored with several prestigious literary awards. His highly lyrical work is marked by a search for the spiritual and a preoccupation with death and man's relationship to God. In addition to his poetic output, Valero also published a novel, *Este viento de cuaresma* (This Lenten Wind) a finalist for Spain's Nadal Prize in 1989, and a book of literary criticism, *The Forlorn Humor of Reinaldo Arenas* (1991) for which he received the Letras de Oro award in 1989. Valero's other poetic works include *Dharma* (1985), *Venías* (You Came) (1990), and *No estaré en tu camino* (I Will Not Be in Your Way), a finalist for the Adonais Prize in 1991. He was an editor of the art and literature journal *Mariel*. Valero died in Washington, D.C.

REINALDO ARENAS, "El ángulo se ilumina," in Arenas, *Desde un oscuro ángulo* (n.d., ca. 1982), pp. 7–9; EDUARDO LOLO, "Otra vez el día," in *Círculo: Revista de Cultura* 21 (1992): 133–140.

MARÍA BADÍAS
GEORGETTE MAGASSY DORN

VALLADARES, ARMANDO (*b.* 30 May 1937), Cuban poet and prose writer. Valladares was born in Pinar del Río Province. In 1961, while employed by the revolutionary government on the staff of the Cuban postal service, he was arrested and accused of being a counterrevolutionary. After refusing to participate in the government's "rehabilitation" program, he was subjected to severe beatings, torture, forced labor, and twenty-two years of confinement. While in prison he began to write poetry, which he smuggled out of the country in many ingenious ways. His wife, Martha, fought relentlessly to bring international attention to his case, and when his poetry gained recognition outside of Cuba, he became a symbol of the struggle against human rights abuses in that country. When at last Valladares's case was taken up by Amnesty International, which once made him its prisoner of the year, it attracted worldwide attention, dealing a severe blow to the Cuban government's image abroad.

After his release in 1982, Valladares continued to decry the abuses he saw and suffered while in prison in Cuba, and in 1985 he published a memoir of the ordeal, *Contra toda esperanza* (*Against All Hope*), his best-known work, which became a best-seller. He served for a time as U.S. ambassador for human rights to the United Nations. Direct and unpretentious, his poetry is permeated by genuine anguish and the desire to end cruelty. Other works by Valladares include *El corazón en que vivo* (1980).

BRITT ARENANDER, *Fallet Valladares* (1981).

ROBERTO VALERO

VALLADARES, TOMÁS (*d.* after 1850), Nicaraguan politician. Active in the confusing era of the breakdown of the UNITED PROVINCES OF CENTRAL AMERICA, Valladares served as a senator and then president of the Chamber of Deputies in Nicaragua. He was interim chief of state from 1840 to 1841 and subsequently continued to participate in politics. As one of Nicaragua's leading liberals, Valladares served on a junta with Evaristo Rocha, Patricio Rivas, Hilario Ulloa, and Joaquín Caso in the 1840s and was a lieutenant in the wars against José Rafael CARRERA, which tore apart the isthmus at midcentury.

EDUARDO CÁRDENAS, *20,000 biografías breves* (1963).

KAREN RACINE

VALLADOLID CONSPIRACY (1809), a group that gathered in Valladolid, Michoacán, to discuss political issues. It included military men, clergymen, and lawyers. Discontented with the Spanish colonial regime because of the coup d'état of September 1808, which had ended the possibilities of furthering their autonomist interests, they moved from conversation into conspiracy in September 1809. Following the autonomist proposal presented by the Ayuntamiento of Mexico in 1808, they intended to establish a junta or congress in Valladolid in order to prevent the peninsular Spaniards from turning New Spain over to the French. The conspirators counted upon the support of military units and of some Indian communities, who were promised an exemption from paying tribute. The insurrection, which was to occur on 24 December 1809, was revealed on 21 December. The plotters, among them Captain José María García Obeso and Lieutenant José Mariano Michelena, as well as the Franciscan Friar Vicente de Santa María, were arrested. Although their role in the conspiracy was clearly proved by the authorities, they were not severely punished. This leniency was due, in part, to the conciliatory attitude of the viceroy, Archbishop Francisco Javier de Lizana y Beaumont. Several of the plotters took part in the conspiracy of 1810, which gave rise to the insurgent movement.

LUCAS ALAMÁN, *Historia de Méjio* (1985), vol. 1; JOSÉ MARIANO MICHELENA, ''Verdadero origen de la revolución de 1809,'' in *Documentos históricos,* edited by Genaro García, 2d ed., vol. 1 (1985); and *Diccionario Porrúa de historia, biografía y geografía de México,* 5th ed., vol. 3 (1986), p. 3,070.

VIRGINIA GUEDEA

VALLBONA, RIMA DE (*b.* 15 March 1931), Costa Rican writer. A professor of Spanish at the University of St. Thomas in Houston, Texas, Vallbona obtained her Ph.D. in modern languages from Middlebury College. She also studied in France and Spain. She has received many Costa Rican and international awards for her fiction, which includes the novels *Noche en vela* (1968), *Las sombras que perseguimos* (1983), and *Mundo, demonio y mujer*

(1991); and the collections of short stories *Polvo del camino* (1971), *La salamandra rosada* (1979), *Mujeres y agonías* (1982), *Baraja de soledades* (1983) and *Cosecha de pecadores* (1988). Vallbona has written two scholarly books on her compatriots: *Yolanda Oreamuno* (1972) and *La obra en prosa de Eunice Odio* (1980).

Some of Vallbona's stories have been translated into English and appear in NORA ERRO-PERALTA et al., eds., *Beyond the Border* (1991), and ENRIQUE JARAMILLO LEVI, ed., *When New Flowers Bloomed* (1991).

SUSAN E. CLARK

VALLE, ARISTÓBULO DEL (*b.* 15 March 1845; *d.* 29 January 1896), Argentine politician, journalist, constitutional lawyer, and mentor to reform-minded youth in the 1880s and 1890s. Born in Dolores, Buenos Aires Province, in modest circumstances, he was an early example of the burgeoning Argentine middle class. A veteran of the WAR OF THE TRIPLE ALLIANCE, del Valle wrote for the newspapers *El Nacional* and *La Nación,* and served in the Buenos Aires provincial legislature. Elected to the national Congress in 1872, he was a deputy (1872–1876) and later a senator (1877–1895). He distinguished himself as the Senate's most effective orator and defender of the middle class. He played a leading role in the revolutions of the early 1890s, but when they failed, he worked within the oligarchic government to stave off anarchy. He served for short periods as minister of war, navy, interior, and finance under President Luis SÁENZ PEÑA.

Del Valle is credited as one of the early founders, with Leandro ALEM, of the Unión Cívica Radical. He established the country's first reformist newspaper, *El Argentino,* and taught constitutional law at the University of Buenos Aires, steering a different course from his conservative predecessor José M. ESTRADA. Del Valle's major works include: *Nociones de derecho constitucional* (Aspects of Constitutional Law [1897]), *Cuestión de límites interprovinciales* (Interprovincial Boundary Question [1881]), and *La política económica argentina en la década del 80* (Political Economy of Argentina in the 80s [1955]). De Valle's most influential congressional speeches are gathered in *Discursos selectos* (1922) and *Discursos políticos* (1938). His death at the age of fifty deprived the country of one of its leading reformers and most effective public speakers.

ELVIRA ALDAO DE DÍAZ, *Reminiscencias sobre Aristóbulo del Valle* (1928); JULIO A. CAMINOS, *Tres figuras del noventa* (1948); OLGA N. BORDI DE RAGUCCI, *Aristóbulo del Valle en los orígenes del radicalismo* (1987).

GEORGETTE MAGASSY DORN

See also **Argentina: Political Parties.**

VALLE, JOSÉ CECILIO DEL (*b.* 22 November 1776; *d.* 2 March 1834), Honduran scholar and statesman. Born in

Choluteca, Honduras, Valle moved with his family to newly established Guatemala City in 1789 and matriculated the next year at the University of San Carlos. With the assistance of his teacher, Fray Antonio de LIENDO Y GOICOECHEA (1735–1814), and Pedro Juan de Lara, he received a degree in philosophy in 1794 and continued to study civil and canon law until he was admitted to the bar in 1803. Enthused by the Enlightenment philosophies of his teachers, he began a pursuit of knowledge that eventually gained him acknowledgment as an authority in economics and as the most prominent scholar of Central America.

Valle's talents and diligence led him to a life of politics at an early age. For almost twenty years, he faithfully served the captaincy general of Guatemala in hopes of obtaining a high official post in Spain. During the turbulent era prior to independence, Valle advanced rapidly in local politics and became the leader of the moderate conservatives. He served as the mayor of Guatemala City in 1820. Reluctant to support independence from Spain, he nonetheless assumed leadership of the apparently inevitable movement in the fear that social revolution, rather than political freedom, would become the focus of the turmoil. Indeed, he was largely responsible for the writing of the declaration of independence. He was a member of the provisional junta that took control of the government of CENTRAL AMERICA on 15 September 1821 and annexed the region to Mexico under Agustín de ITURBIDE, who later became (1822) Emperor Agustín I.

Under the empire, he held several official posts. As the representative from the province of Tegucigalpa (Honduras) to the Constituent Congress of Mexico, he served with distinction and rose to become the vice president of the congress. Although Iturbide imprisoned him on false charges of conspiracy, he was exonerated six months later and made secretary of foreign and domestic affairs. After the fall of Iturbide, Valle was appointed secretary of the department of justice and ecclesiastical affairs by the newly formed Mexican Republic.

When Central America decided to seek its own political destiny, Valle returned to Guatemala in January 1824 and was chosen, along with José Manuel de la Cerda and Tomás O'Horan, to be a member of the provisional junta that governed the isthmus until elections for the United Provinces of Central America were held in 1825. In the presidential elections, Valle won a plurality of the electoral votes, but a technicality prevented him from taking office. The federal congress elected instead Manuel José ARCE (1786–1846). Valle responded to the injustice by publishing the *Manifiesto de José del Valle a la nación guatemalteca* (1825), in which he gave an account of the services he had rendered his country and demonstrated the invalidity of Arce's election. During the Arce administration, he represented the department of Guatemala as a deputy to the congress. He ran for the presidency again in 1830 and lost to Francisco MORAZÁN. Finally, Valle was elected president of Central America in 1834, but he became seriously ill on his estate, La Concepción, some 60 miles from Guatemala City, and died en route to his inauguration.

RAMÓN ROSA, *Biografía de don José Cecilio del Valle* (1882); JOSÉ CECILIO DEL VALLE and JORGE DEL VALLE MATHEU, eds., *Obras de José Cecilio del Valle*, 2 vols. (1929–1930); FRANKLIN DALLAS PARKER, *José Cecilio del Valle and the Establishment of the Central American Confederation* (1954); PEDRO TOBAR CRUZ, *Valle: El hombre, el político, el sabio* (1961); LOUIS E. BUMGARTNER, *José del Valle of Central America* (1963); JOSÉ CECILIO DEL VALLE, *Pensamiento vivo de José Cecilio del Valle ... Selección y prólogo de Rafael Heliodoro Valle* (1971); ELVIA CASTAÑEDA DE MACHADO, *Valle en la génesis del panamericanismo* (1977); RAFAEL LEÍVA VIVAS, *Valle: Precursor del sistema interamericano* (1977).

MICHAEL F. FRY

José Cecilio del Valle. ORGANIZATION OF AMERICAN STATES.

VALLE, RAFAEL HELIODORO (*b.* 3 July 1891; *d.* 29 July 1959), Honduran diplomat, professor, journalist, poet, historian, and literary critic. Valle, a descendant of José Cecilio del VALLE, was born in Tegucigalpa but received his higher education in Mexico, where he spent much of his adult life. He served the Honduran government in diplomatic posts in Central America, Mexico, and the United States. As Honduran ambassador in Washington, D.C., in the early 1950s, he was especially active in promoting inter-American cultural affairs. He also was a leading journalist in Mexico, where he served as editor of *El Universal* and *Excelsior* (1921–1925). Later, as a professor at the Universidad Nacional Autónoma de Mexico, he wrote prolifically. Among the works he produced were the six-volume *La anexión de Centro América a México* (1921–1927), *Historia de las ideas contemporáneas en Centro América* (1960), and many other historical books and articles dealing especially with Honduras and Mexico. His journalistic and literary writings won him the María Moors Cabot Prize of the Inter-American Press Association in 1940. Valle died in Mexico.

OSCAR ACOSTA, *Rafael Heliodoro Valle, vida y obra*, 3d ed. (1981).

RALPH LEE WOODWARD, JR.

VALLEJO, CÉSAR (*b.* 16 March 1892; *d.* 15 April 1938), Peruvian poet. Vallejo is Peru's most renowned poet, and his works are remarkable for their striking originality, lexical complexity, and compressed power. They reveal a profound concern for the suffering of others and nostalgia for his Andean childhood. His journalism, dramas, novels, and short stories gloss the major social, political, and cultural movements of the first third of the century and assert the legitimate, if neglected, place of Latin America in contemporary culture and history.

The youngest of eleven children in a middle-class mestizo family, Vallejo entered the University of Trujillo in 1910 to pursue literary studies, but dropped out. He returned in 1913 and received his B.A. in Spanish literature in 1915, at the same time that he began his study of law. He pursued his legal studies until returning to Lima in 1917 as a schoolteacher. After his return, he experienced two ill-fated love affairs, the second one ending shortly before the death of his lover. In 1918 he suffered the loss of his mother, whose memory remained a recurrent theme in his poetry. Falsely accused of participating in political violence in his Andean hometown of Santiago de Chuco in 1920, he was imprisoned for 112 days (6 November 1920–26 February 1921), to which he alluded in his mature poetry as the "gravest moment" of his life.

Seeking wider cultural and intellectual opportunities, Vallejo left Peru for Europe in 1923, spending most of his final fifteen years of life in self-imposed, impoverished exile in France, with periods in Spain and two influential trips to Russia. Expelled from France for leftist political activities in 1931, he joined the Spanish Communist Party in Madrid. He returned to France in 1932. He died in Paris from an unidentified illness.

Vallejo published two books of poetry before leaving Peru: *Los heraldos negros* (1918) and *Trilce* (1922). The first showed signs of an original poetic voice that emerged powerfully in the irrational and hermetic expression of the second work, which shattered all traditions of poetry written in Spanish. *Poemas humanos* (1939) represented the poet at the height of his power to

César Vallejo at Fontainebleau, 1926. ARCHIVO CARETAS, LIMA.

express the plight of the human animal abandoned in an irrational, absurd world where salvation can come only through fraternal self-sacrifice.

Vallejo worked with other writers and intellectuals to further the Republican cause during the Spanish Civil War and visited the war front twice. *España, aparta de mí este cáliz* (1938) was first published by Republican soldiers on the front lines. Although in his last years Vallejo sought to inform Europeans about Peruvian culture, he never returned to Peru.

The best general study in English is JEAN FRANCO, *César Vallejo: The Dialectics of Poetry and Silence* (1976), which offers not always accurate translations of some poems. In the chapter on Vallejo in JAMES HIGGINS, *The Poet in Peru* (1982), his life and work are adequately synopsized, but the poetry quoted is not translated. See also Higgins's more extensive introduction in English preceding the untranslated poems in *César Vallejo: An Anthology of His Poetry* (1970). An acceptable translation of *The Black Heralds* is that of Richard Schaaf and Kathleen Ross (1990). A very free translation by Clayton Eshleman of *Trilce* (1992) nonetheless improves on that of David Smith (1973). The most extensive translation of Vallejo's posthumous poetry, including *Spain, Take This Chalice from Me,* is by Clayton Eshleman and José Rubia Barcia, *César Vallejo: The Complete Posthumous Poetry* (1978). None of Vallejo's drama, prose fiction, or extensive journalistic writing has been translated into English.

KEITH MCDUFFIE

VALLEJO, MARIANO GUADALUPE (*b.* 4 July 1807?; *d.* 18 January 1890), military commander in California. Mariano Vallejo was born in Monterey, son of Ignacio Vallejo, an early settler from Jalisco, and María Antonia Lugo. After joining the Monterey military company at age fifteen, he rose to commandant of the San Francisco presidio by age twenty-four. As military commander and director of colonization of the northern frontier during the 1830s, Vallejo evaluated Russian intentions in CALIFORNIA, established the Sonoma colony and organized the civilian government of San Francisco, and pacified Indian tribes. Vallejo was appointed *jefe militar* (military chief) of the revolutionary government of 1836, but soon disengaged himself from the rebel group. After central Mexican authority was reestablished, he was appointed military commander of California, whose prime concern was encroaching foreign influence.

Considered a friend of Americans, Vallejo was a force for moderation among leading Mexican citizens of California during the period leading up to the U.S. conquest. Vallejo's personal collection of eleven thousand documents of early California, a major source for Hubert Bancroft's *History of California* (1884–1890), now resides in the Bancroft Library of the University of California.

MYRTLE M. MC KITTRICK, *Vallejo, Son of California* (1944); RALPH J. ROSKE, *Everyman's Eden: A History of California* (1968).

E. JEFFREY STANN

VALLENATO. *See* **Cumbia.**

VALLENILLA LANZ, LAUREANO (*b.* 11 October 1870; *d.* 16 November 1936), Venezuelan politician and intellectual. Vallenilla Lanz traveled to Caracas at a very young age to take up engineering, but he did not finish his studies. After a brief stay in Barcelona, Venezuela, he returned to Caracas and mixed with the intellectual circles in the capital. He was a contributor to *El Cojo Ilustrado,* publishing essays on historical themes, which earned him a reputation, to a degree, as an intellectual. Vallenilla Lanz was named Venezuelan consul in Amsterdam in 1904 and remained in Europe for six years. In Paris he attended the Sorbonne and the College de France, which distinctly influenced his orientation toward the positivist trends of the era.

After his return to Venezuela in 1910, Vallenilla Lanz contributed to important periodicals, met President Juan Vicente GÓMEZ, and became active in politics as a member of the intellectual circle close to the president. He performed important public duties and in 1915 became director of *El Nuevo Diario,* the official government mouthpiece. He conducted an important campaign in defense of the regime and in 1919 published *Cesarismo democrático.* In this work, one of his most important, he used positivist theoretical suppositions as a basis for analyzing the Venezuelan past and concluded by justifying the autocrat as a "Gendarme Necesario," or a natural outgrowth of the collective evolution of Venezuelan society. The work generated contrary opinions. It was translated into several languages and became one of the key works of positivist thought in all of Latin America. Vallenilla Lanz was a member of the Academy of History (1918). In 1931 he was appointed minister of Venezuela in Paris.

GERMÁN CARRERA DAMAS, *El concepto de la historia en Laureano Vallenilla Lanz* (1966); FEDERICO BRITO FIGUEROA, *La contribución de Laureano Vallenilla Lanz a la comprensión histórica de Venezuela* (1985); and NIKITA HARWICH VALLENILLA, ed., *Cesarismo democrático y otros textos* (1991).

INÉS QUINTERO

See also **Positivism.**

VALPARAÍSO, major port city of Chile (1990 population 276,756) located 90 miles west of Santiago. Visited for the first time by Juan de Saavedra, a captain of Spanish conquistador Diego de ALMAGRO, in 1536, it was used throughout colonial times as a port for small vessels bound for Callao, Peru. A tortuous road connected the port with Santiago. Despite the garrison that protected the port from pirate attacks, the miserable emplacement was raided at least seven times during the colonial period. Independence brought more prosperity to Valparaíso than to any other Chilean settlement. The expedition to liberate Peru led by José de SAN MARTÍN departed from Valparaíso in 1821. Later the city was chosen by commercial agents from England, France, the United States, and the German states as the port of entry for trade with Chile and other South American countries on the Pacific coast. These activities gave rise to a national bourgeoisie, which, in many instances, married into the landowning aristocracy and foreign merchant families. Most of the elite families in Chile bear foreign names (Edwards, Alessandri, Cousiño, Subercauseaux, or Ross) of families whose patriarchs were bankers and entrepreneurs in town.

In the second half of the nineteenth century, Valparaíso was larger than Santiago and became a center for national and international banks. It was also the port of call for ships bound for Callao, Guayaquil, Panama, Acapulco, California, and British Columbia. Valparaíso was also the departure point for ships carrying wheat to Tahiti and Australia.

The decline of Valparaíso began with the advent of steam navigation, which made it necessary for ships to stop for coal at the mines of the province of Concepción, and was accelerated in 1914 by the opening of the PANAMA CANAL, which relegated Valparaíso to a port "at the end of the world." The port installations were never sufficiently expanded, and a freight port in San Antonio, closer to Santiago, competed with Valparaíso as shipper of fruits and copper. The building of railways and motor roads to Santiago precipitated the decline of Valparaíso as most of the trading firms and consulates moved to the capital city.

The final blow came in the 1960s and 1970s, when most of the middle-class population left the picturesque but crowded city and took up residence in the contiguous sister city of VIÑA DEL MAR. In the early 1980s the latter city, which had been a famed resort, surpassed Valparaíso by more than 30,000 inhabitants, and the trend continues. Today Valparaíso is the site of three universities: University of Valparaíso, Catholic University of Valparaíso, and Technical University "Federico Santa María." It is also Chile's main navy and marine base and the location of El Mercurio, founded in 1827, and reputed to be the oldest existing journal in the Spanish language.

The most complete historical account of the city is BENJAMÍN VICUÑA-MACKENNA, Historia de Valparaíso (Santiago, 1936). See also WILLIAM A. REID, Valparaíso: The South Pacific Emporium (1925). Recent reminiscences are contained in FRANCISCO LE DANTEC, Crónicas del viejo Valparaíso (Valparaíso, 1984).

CÉSAR N. CAVIEDES

VANDOR, AUGUSTO (b. 1920; d. 30 June 1969), Argentine labor leader. During the early 1960s, exiled past-president Juan D. PERÓN charged the head of the Metal Workers' Union, Augusto Vandor, with promoting the conservative tendency of an increasingly fractious Peronist movement. Vandor's control extended beyond his powerful union. From 1962 until his assassination by the Monteneros in 1969, he controlled what was known as the 62 Organizations (or "62"), the dominant wing of the Peronist General Labor Confederation (CGT).

Vandor and Vandorismo came to define four important developments in Argentine labor. First, Vandor's methods of personalist political control were emulated by subsequent labor bosses, including Lorenzo Miguel (Metal Workers) and Jorge Triaca (Plastics Workers). Second, Vandor's leadership of the 62 marked a transformation in the relationship between the Peronist labor movement and the government from intransigent opposition during the 1950s to a more pragmatic blend of negotiation and conflict in the 1960s. Third, Vandorismo characterized the emergence of an authoritarian and sometimes violent tendency in the labor movement as Vandor set about defeating political opponents within the CGT and in the Peronist movement. Fourth, under Vandor the 62 rose to lead the Peronist movement as the only significant legal component of Peronism. The 62 continued to comprise almost all significant trade unions within the labor movement until the takeover of the CGT by the government after the 1976 coup d'état.

OSVALDO CALELLO and DANIEL PARCERO, De Vandor a Ubaldini, 2 vols. (1984); DANIEL JAMES, Resistance and Integration: Peronism and the Argentine Working Class, 1946–1976 (1988); and DANIEL RODRÍGUEZ LAMAS, Radicales, peronistas y el movimiento obrero, 1963–1973, 2 vols. (1989).

DAVID M. K. SHEININ

VANGUARDIA, LA. See under **Coronel Urtecho, José.**

VAQUEIROS, cowboys, from the Portuguese word vaca (cow). Brazilian cowboys have been important figures in the Northeast, the center-west, and in RIO GRANDE DO SUL, where they are called GAÚCHOS. The northeastern SERTÃO (backlands) is a region of frequent drought and thorny CAATINGA (scrub forest). Protectively dressed from head to foot in sturdy leather, including breastplates for their agile horses, vaqueiros of the sertão have been adept at finding water underground. In times of extreme drought, vaqueiros worked as bandits and hired guns or migrated out of the region. The decline of the northeastern ranching industry has made the vaqueiro a rare sight today.

In the open tropical savanna of the central states and RORAIMA, vaqueiros dress simply in cotton clothing and straw hats, and in the past rode barefoot, using a toe stirrup. Their horses are resilient, although until the 1930s in the PANTANAL of MATO GROSSO and on MARAJÓ ISLAND in the Amazon delta, disease regularly decimated mounts, frequently forcing vaqueiros to use tame steers as replacements.

From colonial times, vaqueiros were instrumental in expanding the Brazilian state into its interior. Cattle drives to distant markets lasted weeks or months, frequently crossing piranha-infested rivers. Salaries on ranches often included one calf in four, permitting some vaqueiros to become small ranchers. By the mid-twentieth century the availability of unoccupied land had declined, while the expansion of rail systems and local meat-packing plants modified the ranching economy, forcing the cowboy into wage labor. Nevertheless, modern vaqueiro work habits have changed little from the past.

EDWARD LAROCQUE TINKER, Horsemen of the Americas and the Literature They Inspired, 2d ed. (1967); LÚCIO DE CASTRO SOARES, "Vaqueiro de Marajó," JOSÉ VERÍSSIMO DA COSTA PEREIRA, "Vaqueiro do Rio Branco," MARIA FAGUNDES DE SOUSA DOCA, "Vaqueiro do Nordeste," and ELZA COELHO DE SOUZA, "Boiadeiro," in Tipos e aspectos do Brasil, 10th ed. (1975), pp. 65–66, 68–70, 267–268, 457–458; RICHARD W. SLATTA, Cowboys of the Americas (1990), p. 199.

ROBERT WILCOX

VAQUERÍA, a wild-cattle hunt. Wild cattle by the millions roamed the PAMPA during the colonial era. Although it lacked deposits of precious metals, the Río de la Plata became a wealth-producing region thanks to its huge herds of wild cattle and horses. In *vaquerías*, whether licensed or illegal, gauchos used a hocking blade (*desjarretadera*) to sever the tendon of a cow's hind leg. Then, after crippling hundreds of animals, the riders returned to slaughter and skin them. Once sun-dried, the hides were ready for export. *Vaquerías* gradually depleted the number of animals on the pampa. By the mid-eighteenth century, ESTANCIAS began to replace these wild-cattle hunts as the primary means of exploiting livestock.

EMILIO CONI, *Historia de las vaquerías de Río de la Plata* (1930); MADALINE WALLIS NICHOLS, *The Gaucho* (1968), pp. 22–25; RICHARD W. SLATTA, *Cowboys of the Americas* (1990), pp. 12–14.

RICHARD W. SLATTA

VAQUERO, the working cowhand of Mexico, who began his career on Indian frontier missions during the colonial period. Priests used Indian novices to tend the herds of livestock that populated many mission outposts. These vaqueros became excellent riders and ropers who skillfully made much of their own equipment. Indian and mestizo vaqueros modified Spanish equipment and riding techniques according to the needs imposed by their local conditions. Vaqueros in Baja California, for example, made extensive use of leather clothing to protect themselves from cacti and other thorny plants. In 1832, vaqueros sailed from Spanish California to Hawaii to train Hawaiians in cattle herding. The Hawaiian cowboy is called *paniolo* (from *español*).

During the nineteenth century, the expansion of the United States into the Southwest led to the MEXICAN WAR of 1846, after which some vaqueros went to work on Anglo-American ranches. They taught Anglo cowboys how to handle wild cattle and braid lariats, and imparted much of their folklore and rancing savvy. Vaqueros today, like old-time cowboys, are a vanishing breed.

DAVID DARY, *Cowboy Culture: A Saga of Five Centuries* (1981); RICHARD W. SLATTA, *Cowboys of the Americas* (1990).

RICHARD W. SLATTA

See also **Charro.**

VARAS DE LA BARRA, ANTONIO (*b.* 13 June 1817; *d.* 3 June 1886), Chilean politician. An outstanding figure of his period, Varas was the closest political associate of the Conservative president Manuel MONTT. Eight times a deputy and twice a senator, he served as minister of the interior from 1850 to 1856, in 1860–1861, and again briefly in 1879. Although he fully supported the authoritarian stance of his intimate friend Montt, Varas was an altogether more attractive character. (In his old age he

became quite liberal.) Montt wanted Varas to be his presidential successor in 1861, a prospect that deeply angered the opposition. By accepting the interior ministry again in April 1860, Varas implicitly abandoned all claim to presidential succession. His unselfishness, which won widespread praise, paved the way for the election of the less controversial José Joaquín PÉREZ MOZCAYANO. After 1861, Varas headed the National (or, as it was revealingly nicknamed, Montt-Varista) Party in Congress.

ANTONIO VARAS, *Correspondencia*, 5 vols. (1918–1929).

SIMON COLLIER

See also **Chile: Political Parties.**

VARELA, FELIPE (*b.* 1821; *d.* 4 June 1870), Argentine caudillo. Varela was one of the last great regional chieftains of the Argentine interior provinces during the long process of state formation. Born in Huayacama, Catamarca, he moved to La Rioja, where he participated in the civil wars against Buenos Aires. In due course, he became a close ally of Angel Vicente PEÑALOZA. In 1848 Varela was driven from Argentina to Chile, where he displayed some acumen for business. He became associated with Colonel Tristán Dávila, a local mining magnate, and rose through the ranks of the Chilean military based in Atacama. Ironically, he was promoted to captain in Chile's army for his service in defense of the central government. Varela returned to Argentina in 1855 and became the President Justo URQUIZA's loyal follower. He participated in the prolonged federalist resistance of the provinces against Buenos Aires, aligning with Governor Juan Sáa of San Luís in the bloody civil war against Buenos Aires-backed forces. Still a loyal Urquizista, Varela joined the last-ditch alliance against Buenos Aires that led to the 1862 mass insurrection in La Rioja. Varela displayed his military prowess, trouncing Buenos Aires forces repeatedly, but the federalists could not overcome the odds. Following the defeat and execution of Peñaloza (1863), Varela fled again to Chile in 1865. He returned to Argentina in 1866, but his distaste for Buenos Aires's plans for the country led him to revolt for the last time in 1867. He could not, however, defeat the combined forces of Buenos Aires and its allies, led by the Taboadas of Tucumán. After a series of bloody encounters, he fled to Bolivia and then to Chile, where he died at Náutico, sick and impoverished.

BEATRIZ BOSCH, *Urquiza y su tiempo* (1980); DAVID ROCK, *Argentina, 1516–1982: From Spanish Colonization to the Falklands War* (1985; rev. ed. 1987), esp. pp. 126–127.

JEREMY ADELMAN

VARELA, FLORENCIO (*b.* 23 February 1807; *d.* 20 March 1848), Argentine poet and patriot. Brother of the famous neoclassical, civic poet, Juan Cruz Varela, Florencio wrote his first verses at the age of fifteen in celebration of the decisive battle of AYACUCHO during the WARS OF INDEPENDENCE. Varela studied law at the University of Buenos Aires, graduating in 1827. Following the Argentine revolution of 1828, he fled to Montevideo. In 1830, he published *El día de Mayo* (May Day), a volume containing five poems dedicated to the Uruguayan people. In exile, Varela became a leader of the Unitarian cause against the dictator Juan Manuel de ROSAS. Newspapers supporting Rosas recognized the ardor of Varela's attack, calling him a "savage Unitarian, traitor, and vile slanderer."

In 1841–1842, Varela lived in Río de Janeiro, where he wrote several articles for the *Jornal do Comercio* defending Uruguay against accusations that it had usurped territory from Brazil. While in Río, Varela became friends with Bernardino RIVADAVIA, who furnished Varela with documentary material for a book he was preparing on Argentine history. In 1843, the Uruguayan government sent Varela on an official mission to France and England.

Tireless in his efforts to overthrow Rosas and use the press as a vehicle for shaping public opinion, Varela founded in October 1845 the *Comercio del Plata*, in whose columns he undermined the political and military structure keeping Rosas in power. Varela was also cofounder of a publishing house that brought out works in Spanish translation as well as books by Hispanic-American writers.

LEONCIO GIANELLO, *Florencio Varela* (1948); JUAN ANTONIO SOLARI, *Florencio Varela, el decano de los jóvenes* (1948); RAFAEL ALBERTO ARRIETA, *Historia de la literatura Argentina*, vol. 2 (1958), pp. 149–154, and vol. 6 (1960), pp. 31–32.

MYRON I. LICHTBLAU

See also **Literature.**

VARELA, JOSÉ PEDRO (*b.* 1845, *d.* 1879), Uruguayan educator. Varela's leadership proved essential in the country's development of free, universal, and secular EDUCATION. His early contact with educational theory came from his father, who, in 1846, translated from the French the first book on pedagogy to be published in the Plata region. During a trip to the United States in 1867 Varela met Argentine educator and future president Domingo SARMIENTO, whose writings on public education he admired. Under the influence of Sarmiento and the Bostonian educator Horace Mann, Varela decided to dedicate his life to Uruguayan educational reform.

In 1868 Varela published the first of many articles in the Montevidean press promoting free and universal elementary schooling. He became a lecturer on educational reform at the National University that same year. In 1869 he founded Amigos de la Educación Popular, which played a central role in the dissemination of his ideas. Through his newspaper, *La Paz*, he promoted progressive educational ideas and criticized the govern-

ment of General Lorenzo BATLLE. His most influential writings include *La educación del pueblo* (1874) and *La legislación escolar* (1877). In 1865 the first school with a curriculum designed in accordance with Varela's ideas was founded.

Varela's thinking on education centered on his humanistic beliefs: free and obligatory instruction for all citizens, regardless of sex, race, or social class; the development of a rational and scientific curriculum, as opposed to the traditional, scholastic orientation of the Spanish colony; the central role of the state in training teachers and providing for schools; and the intimate link between educating the populace and the emergence of Uruguay as an independent and prosperous country. The idealistic thrust of his ideas, like those of Sarmiento, was premised on the belief that the individual, empowered through education, would become an agent in the modernization of the region's social and political institutions.

In 1876 Varela was named president of the Comisión de Instrucción Pública, which drafted the important *Ley de educación común* (1877). His death at the age of forty-four did not impede the development of one of the most ambitious and successful systems of public education on the continent, which was based on his ideas.

In addition to his books on education, Varela wrote a volume of lyrical poems, *Ecos perdidos* (1985), which rates among the finest Uruguayan lyrical expressions of the period.

ARTURO ARDAO, "Prologue," in *Obras pedagógicas: La educación del pueblo* by José Pedro Varela (1964).

WILLIAM H. KATRA

VARELA, JUAN CRUZ (*b.* 23 November 1794; *d.* 23 January 1839), Argentine journalist, politician, poet. In 1810 Varela, a native of Buenos Aires, entered the Montserrat seminary in Córdoba to study for the priesthood; he graduated in 1816 but did not take holy orders. Varela instead turned to love poetry, writing "La Elvira" (1817), "Mi pasión" (1817), and "El enojo" (1819) among others. In 1818 he returned to Buenos Aires, where he staunchly supported liberal politics. He was a friend of Bernardino RIVADAVIA, becoming his press spokesman and the secretary of the General Congress of 1826. Varela wrote for *El Centinela* and *El Mensajero Argentino* and supported Rivadavia's reforms. He supported the upstart General Juan Gallo Lavalle against the legitimate governor of Buenos Aires, Manuel Dorrego, who was executed in 1828 with the encouragement of Varela among others. This act only served to fortify the very forces Lavalle sought to defeat, and by 1829 Varela had to abandon Buenos Aires for exile in Montevideo. In Uruguay he continued to write articles and poetry opposing Juan Manuel de ROSAS. Varela lived a spartan life in Montevideo and tried unsuccessfully to return to Buenos Aires. He died in Montevideo.

JUAN MARÍA GUTIÉRREZ, *Juan Cruz Varela: Su vida—sus obras—su época* (1918) and *Los poetas de la revolución* (1941).

NICHOLAS P. CUSHNER

VARELA Y MORALES, FÉLIX (*b.* 20 November 1788; *d.* 25 February 1853), Cuban priest, thinker, and patriot. Orphaned at an early age, Varela was still a child when he moved to Saint Augustine, Florida. (The area had been returned to Spain by Britain in 1783 under the Treaty of Paris.) There he was consigned to the care of his maternal grandfather, the commander of the city's Spanish garrison. He became the pupil of Fr. Michael O'Reilly, then the vicar of East Florida, who eventually became his role model. It was Fr. O'Reilly who influenced his decision to enter the priesthood rather than become a soldier, as his family traditions called for. "I wish to be a soldier of Jesus Christ," Varela said at the time. "I do not wish to kill men, but to save their souls."

Varela began attending the San Carlos Seminary in Havana in 1803 and was ordained in 1811. By that time he had already started to teach philosophy at the seminary, which in those days was also open to lay students. He thus became the mentor of many of the most distinguished Cuban intellectuals of the period; later they recognized their debt to him, stating that "he was who first taught us to think."

As an opponent of decadent scholasticism and one of the first who wrote philosophical textbooks in Spanish rather than Latin, Varela enjoyed the support of the bishop of Havana, José Díaz de Espada y Landa. The bishop asked him to teach a new course at the seminary on the constitution framed by the Spanish CORTES in 1812. Such was the reputation of his lectures that he was elected to represent Cuba in the Cortes in 1821. While serving, Varela made several significant contributions, advocating a more benign rule over the colonies and submitting a proposal for the abolition of slavery within fifteen years. Unfortunately, the restoration of Spanish absolutism in 1823 made it impossible for the Cortes to discuss these proposals. Forced into exile by this turn of events, he shortly arrived in the United States.

Varela settled in New York, where he soon stood out as a man of irreproachable life, a learned and devoted parish priest, an able administrator, and a wise educator and director of souls. Above all, he was known for his work with the sick and the poor especially during the great cholera epidemic of 1832, when his charity sometimes reached heroic dimensions. As one contemporary put it, his name was "one of benediction in the city of New York." For this reason Varela was admired and respected by everyone. First in 1829, on a temporary basis, and then without interruption from 1837 onward, he held the office of vicar general for New York, a post second in importance only to that of bishop. He attended several of the Baltimore Councils as an advisor to American bishops. Varela also played a leading role as a public defender of the Catholic faith in the violent Catholic–Protestant clashes of the period.

Varela's achievements as a priest are as much a part of U.S. ecclesiastical history as they are part of Cuba's history. But although he never made any effort to return to his native land, he always regarded it as his country. Cubans, for their part, rightly regard him as the ideological father of their nationality. When Varela went to Spain as a member of the Cortes, he described himself as "a son of liberty, an American soul." At the time, however, he would have been satisfied with some form of colonial self-government for Cuba. But he soon discovered that most Spanish deputies, including many who enjoyed the reputation of being very liberal, distrusted Spanish Americans and had no faith in their ability to govern themselves. It was then, and most especially after King FERDINAND VII dissolved the Cortes, that he gave up the hope of achieving autonomy for Cuba within the framework of the Spanish monarchy and became the great prophet of Cuban independence.

Varela published his pro-independence articles in the newspaper *El Habanero,* which he founded in the United States. At the time, there were many Cubans who were in favor of Spanish rule, and some of them advocated the annexation of the island to Colombia or Mexico, just as others would support annexation to the United States a few years later. Varela argued against all of these paths. He morally justified rebellion against the oppressive colonial government, saying that it was "inspired by nature and upheld by the sacred laws of self-preservation." As for the idea of Cuba becoming the province of a neighboring state, he wrote: "I am the first to oppose the union of the island to any government. I should wish to see her as much of a political island as she is such in geographical terms."

Ill health eventually led Varela to retire to Saint Augustine, where he died. As a priest, Varela was well ahead of his time; his liberal norms and principles were more in consonance with the orientation of the Second Vatican Council (1962–1965) than with some nineteenth-century Catholic doctrines. As a thinker, he infused new life into philosophical studies in Cuba. As a patriot, he can be justly regarded as the founding father of Cuban nationalism.

JOSEPH and HELEN M. MC CADDEN, *Félix Varela: Torch Bearer from Cuba,* 2d ed. (1984). For a shorter biography, see JOSÉ I. LASAGA, *Cuban Lives: Pages from Cuban History,* translated by Nelson Durán, vol. 1 (1984), pp. 157–180.

JOSÉ M. HERNÁNDEZ

VARGAS, DIEGO DE (*b.* 1643; *d.* 8 April 1704), Spanish governor and recolonizer of New Mexico (1691–1697; 1703–1704). Heir of a proud but indebted noble house in Madrid, Vargas sailed for New Spain in 1673. Appointed by the viceroy, he was commended for his service as ALCALDE MAYOR of Teutila (Oaxaca) (1673–1679) and Tlalpujahua (Michoacán) (1679–1687). In 1688 he was appointed governor of New Mexico, a colony in exile since the PUEBLO REBELLION of 1680, when the Spaniards fled into the El Paso area. Acceding to office in El Paso in 1691, Vargas led a determined, two-stage reconquest. With the aid of PUEBLO INDIAN auxiliaries, he reoccupied the capital at Santa Fe, reimposing Spanish rule and putting down a second revolt in 1696. Confined by his successor in 1697 on charges of misgovernment, Vargas returned to Mexico City, stood trial, and was acquitted. The crown, meanwhile, rewarded him with a noble title of Castile—Marqués de la Nava de Barcinas. Reinstated as governor in 1703, he died the following year at Bernalillo while on a campaign against APACHES.

Although Vargas's final resting place is unknown, a shopping mall, bank, and university dormitory bear his name, and he is the central figure in Santa Fe's annual fiestas.

J. MANUEL ESPINOSA, *Crusaders of the Rio Grande: The Story of Don Diego de Vargas and the Reconquest and Refounding of New Mexico* (1942; repr. 1977); JOHN L. KESSELL et al., eds., *Remote Beyond Compare: Letters of Don Diego de Vargas to His Family from New Spain and New Mexico, 1675–1706* (1989).

JOHN L. KESSELL

VARGAS, GETÚLIO DORNELLES (*b.* 19 April 1883; *d.* 24 August 1954), president of Brazil (1930–1945 and 1951–1954). Vargas was the dominant political personality of Brazil for nearly a quarter century, and his legacy persisted after his death by suicide. He is widely regarded as the prime mover of the nationalistic social and economic changes that have prompted the modernization of Brazil since the 1930s.

BACKGROUND

Vargas's personal and political prowess stemmed largely from his family heritage and his experience in the authoritarian political system in the border state of Rio Grande do Sul. The third of five sons of a regionally prominent family, Vargas was born at São Borja, a small town in western Rio Grande do Sul on Brazil's frontier with Argentina. His parents, General Manoel do Nascimento Vargas and Candida Dornelles Vargas, were from rival clans that regularly took opposite sides in armed political contests. In this situation, young Getúlio learned the patience, tact, and tolerance that became the hallmark of his political style. Initially intent on pursuing a military career, he resigned from the army after five years to study law in Pôrto Alegre.

EARLY POLITICAL CAREER

Vargas first became involved in state politics while a law student, campaigning for the gubernatorial candidate of the Republican Party. For this service, when he graduated in 1907, he was appointed to the district attorney's office in Pôrto Alegre, where he remained for two years. He then returned to São Borja to practice law

and to run successfully for a seat in the state legislature. The only significant function of that body was to approve periodically the governor's budget. Membership in the legislature, however, assured the political future of those who demonstrated unquestioning support of the Republican governor. The Republican Party regime, based loosely on the hierarchical philosophy of POSITIVISM, was a veritable dictatorship in which the governor exercised absolute control over the state administration and party. The perennial governor, BORGES DE MEDEIROS, ruled by decree in all matters except finance, placed maintaining a balanced budget and treasury surplus above building public works and providing social services, and insisted upon personal loyalty from all party officials. In 1912, Vargas learned that even mild criticism of Borges's rule was unacceptable. For such a mistake he was removed from the state legislature and barred from reelection for five years, until he had displayed appropriate contrition and sworn renewed fealty to his party's boss. When he later became political head of the nation, Vargas was never to demand such obeisance from his followers, but he would share Borges's insistence upon keeping the reins of power in his own hands.

Vargas rose to national prominence in the 1920s, a decade of protest and revolts by young military officers (*tenentes*) and disgruntled civilians against corrupt rule by professional politicians in the service of the rural oligarchy. The *tenentes* were eventually defeated—killed, jailed, or exiled by the government—but they remained heroes to much of the press and the urban population. Vargas made no public statements against the young rebels, even though he held increasingly important posts in the established state and national governments. In 1922 he went to Rio de Janeiro as a newly elected congressman and head of his state's congressional delegation. Four years later he was elevated to the cabinet as finance minister of President Washington LUÍS PEREIRA DE SOUSA, and in 1928, following an uncontested election, Vargas succeeded Borges de Medeiros as governor of Rio Grande do Sul. In contrast to Borges's rigidly conservative fiscal management, Vargas secured federal funds for ambitious development projects of value to farmers and urban businessmen. He also abandoned Borges's strict partisanship, promoting a policy of collaboration with the opposition party. In these ways he united Rio Grande do Sul behind his bid for the presidency of Brazil in the March 1930 elections or, if that failed, by revolution.

THE RISE TO POWER

Vargas had no scruples against the use of force for political ends, but preferred to secure his objectives by nonviolent means, if possible. Because no opposition candidate had ever been elected president in Brazil, he first sought to head the administration ticket, but was rebuffed by President Washington Luís. In these circumstances, Vargas authorized his colleagues to make contingency plans for revolution. At the same time he accepted the nomination of the reformist Liberal Alliance, a coalition formed from Republican Party regimes in three states and opposition parties elsewhere. The Vargas campaign was also supported by the *tenentes* and their civilian followers, who were clamoring for political and social change. Despite his popularity in the cities, he was badly defeated by the entrenched rural-based political machines in seventeen of the twenty states.

While Vargas appeared to accept defeat gracefully, he was in fact patiently waiting for the propitious moment to launch a decisive assault on the federal government. That moment came on 3 October 1930, when the revolution broke out simultaneously in Rio Grande do Sul, Minas Gerais, and Paraíba, the states that had backed his presidential campaign. The troops on both sides were primarily regular army units and militarized state police. After three weeks, by which time the rebels were in control of most of the coastal states, the army high command in Rio de Janeiro staged a coup d'état to halt the intraservice war. The military junta ordered a cease-fire, deposed and exiled President Washington Luís, and agreed to transfer power to the rebel leader when he reached the capital. On 3 November Getúlio Vargas was installed as chief of the provisional government for an unspecified term, with no limitations on his authority.

THE VARGAS ERA

Moving quickly to consolidate his position, Vargas suspended the 1891 Constitution, announced the pending reorganization of the judiciary, dismissed the Congress and all the state legislatures, and replaced elected state governors with interventors responsible only to him. In response to widespread expectations for social reform, he created new cabinet ministries for labor and education, and appointed as their heads civilian reformers with strong ties to state Republican Party leaders. With regard to the armed forces, Vargas granted amnesty to the military rebels of the 1920s, authorized their return to active duty in their respective units, and appointed regular officers dedicated to the principles of hierarchy and discipline as war and navy ministers. By these actions Vargas eliminated constitutional checks on the executive power, deprived the once-dominant state parties of any legitimate public functions, and, through the interventors, gained control over political activity at all levels throughout the nation. He was now undisputed dictator of Brazil.

There was no protest, because it was widely agreed that a temporary dictatorship was necessary in order to carry out the aims of the revolution. Vargas's heterogeneous following, however, could not agree on the nature and extent of those aims or the length of time required to attain them. Professional politicians and senior military commanders were willing to accept moderate democratic reforms, but they expected the traditional political system to be restored, essentially intact, within a few months. In contrast, most junior officers and civilian radicals saw Vargas as the providential leader who must remain dictator as long as it might take to secure their goals of order, justice, and honest government for the Brazilian people.

Vargas did not publicly reject either interpretation of his role, but most of his actions tended to favor the radicals. He attempted to placate his conservative allies by making repeated vows to respect the de facto autonomy long enjoyed by state governments, and to hold elections to restore constitutional rule as soon as a thorough revision of the electoral laws could be completed. Eventually, however, he so antagonized the conservatives by ignoring states' rights and refusing to call for immediate elections that the establishment political elites in São Paulo and some of his former supporters in other states tried to overthrow him.

The Constitutionalist Revolution of 1932, which raged for three months before collapsing, was far costlier in lives and treasure than the Revolution of 1930. It was limited chiefly to the state of São Paulo, because elsewhere all interventors and the armed forces remained loyal to the dictatorship. Although Vargas's national popularity remained high, the São Paulo rebels claimed a moral victory, for within a year elections were held for the constituent assembly that wrote the Constitution of 1934. This charter incorporated all reforms enacted by the provisional government, restored full civil rights, and provided for the election of a new congress as well as elected state governors and legislatures. On 17 July 1934, the constituent assembly elected Vargas president of Brazil for a four-year term.

The changes introduced in Brazil under Vargas were expressed in national and often nationalistic terms, but could not fail to reflect the impact of the world economic depression and the struggle between fascism and democracy abroad. The Great Depression cut deeply into Brazil's revenues from agricultural exports and exposed the country's great dependence on foreign sources for industrial products. Vargas dealt pragmatically with these problems, nationalizing much of the nation's rail and sea transportation, setting up advisory councils and official agencies to revive the export economy, and promoting the growth of industry in Brazil by private foreign and domestic firms. These essentially economic policies not only enhanced the regulatory powers of the central government but also contributed to a great increase in the size and importance of the federal bureaucracy, the middle class, and the urban labor force, which then became permanent features of Brazilian society.

Vargas had no firm ideological convictions: he was motivated by love of power and what he saw as Brazil's national interests. These qualities determined his responses to the increasingly bitter rivalry among fascist and antifascist political systems in the Western world. Abroad, the United States and Nazi Germany were vy-

Getúlio Vargas announcing the coup d'état in November 1937. ICONOGRAPHIA.

ing openly for Brazil's support. Within Brazil, neofascist, liberal democratic, and Communist organizations clashed and competed for followers, posing a potential threat to Vargas's rule. Thus, in foreign affairs he pursued a flexible policy seeking advantages for Brazil from both camps. At home, following the abortive Communist-led revolt in November 1935, Vargas relied on his congressional majority to suspend civil rights and strengthen his police powers for most of the remainder of his term. A spurious Communist threat was the avowed justification for the coup d'état of 10 November 1937, which Vargas and the armed forces staged to create the allegedly totalitarian ESTADO NÔVO (New State).

Ostensibly patterned on the European fascist dictatorships, the Estado Nôvo lacked the usual political party, militia, and national police loyal to the dictator. Vargas saw no role for political parties, and he relied upon the army to maintain order. For more than seven years he ruled Brazil without the constraints of Congress or the distractions of parties and elections. His domestic policies continued as before to focus chiefly on the urban population and on the need to strengthen the material and human bases for industrialization. Their fruits were seen in large national electrification and steel manufacturing projects, as well as in the great expansion in public health services and in education at all levels. The major social reforms under the Estado Nôvo were enactment of a minimum wage law and codification of all labor legislation enacted since 1930, which had the effect of bringing urban workers into the political arena as staunch supporters of Vargas.

Despite his apparent identification with fascism and

the pro-German bias of some Brazilian military commanders, Vargas finally decided that Brazil's interests would best be served by a close relationship with the United States. In 1942 Brazil entered World War II as one of the Allied powers, and in 1944 Brazil sent a substantial expeditionary force to fight in the Italian campaign.

The incongruity of waging war against dictatorships in Europe while living under a dictator at home was not lost on the Brazilian people, who pressed for an early return to democracy. During 1945 Vargas abolished censorship, released political prisoners, issued a new electoral law authorizing political parties (two of which he himself organized), and called for the election of a new government in December. Fearing that he was planning another coup d'état, the army, led by officers recently returned from Italy, deposed Vargas on 29 October 1945, without recriminations, and installed an interim civilian regime to preside over the December elections.

Although he did not participate in the campaign, Vargas was elected to the Senate, but chose not to serve or to comment publicly on national issues. Rather, he spent the next five years quietly at his home in São Borja. He returned to politics as the candidate of his Brazilian Labor Party in the 1950 presidential elections. He waged a vociferously populist campaign and won with a large plurality. With the grudging acceptance of the armed forces, he was installed in office on 31 January 1951. However, as a democratically elected president obliged to share power with a bitterly divided Congress, Vargas proved unable to cope with the soaring inflation that eroded his labor following, or with the widespread ultranationalism to which his past policies had contributed. In mid-1954 he was overwhelmed by a wave of public revulsion caused by exposure of gross corruption and criminal activities within his official entourage. When the military withdrew its support and demanded his resignation, he complied on 24 August 1954; later that day he committed suicide. Vargas left a political testament in which he presented his death as a sacrifice on behalf of Brazilian workers.

JOHN W. F. DULLES, *Vargas of Brazil: A Political Biography* (1967), remains the finest biography in English. The leading study by a Brazilian scholar is PAULO BRANDI, *Vargas, da vida para a história* (1983). Other scholarly accounts that cover the entire Vargas era include the succinct review of highlights of his regimes in JOSÉ MARIA BELLO, *A History of Modern Brazil, 1889–1964* (1966), chaps. 23–24; THOMAS E. SKIDMORE, *Politics in Brazil, 1930–1964: An Experiment in Democracy* (1967), which focuses on political events; and JOHN D. WIRTH, *The Politics of Brazilian Development, 1930–1954* (1970), which examines the mechanisms Vargas used to promote industrial development.

Much of the literature about Vargas and his regime consists of detailed works dealing with specific policies or limited time periods. STANLEY E. HILTON is concerned with Brazil's prewar foreign policy in *Brazil and the Great Powers, 1930–1939: The Politics of Trade Rivalry* (1975). Vargas's daughter, ALZIRA VARGAS DO AMARAL PEIXOTO, who served as his private secretary, presents a sympathetic interpretation of her father's political leadership to 1938 in *Getúlio Vargas, meu pai* (1960). ROBERT M. LEVINE, *The Vargas Regime: The Critical Years, 1934–1938* (1970), is a scholarly study of Vargas's response to ideological conflict during the mid-1930s, while KARL LOEWENSTEIN, *Brazil Under Vargas* (1942), provides a contemporary view of Vargas as dictator of the Estado Nôvo. A thorough political analysis of Vargas's final administration is found in MARIA CELINA SOARES D'ARAUJO, *O segundo governo Vargas, 1951–1954: Democracia, partidos e crise política* (1982).

ROLLIE E. POPPINO

VARGAS, JOSÉ MARÍA (*b.* 10 March 1786; *d.* 13 July 1854), physician and president of Venezuela (1834–1836). Born in Puerto de la Guaira, Venezuela, Vargas excelled in his studies in philosophy, theology, and medicine at the Royal Pontifical University in Caracas. He continued his medical studies at the University of Caracas (1808). With the fall of the First Republic, he was taken prisoner and then released in 1813. In 1814, he traveled to Edinburgh and London to pursue his medical education, becoming proficient in anatomy, surgery, chemistry, and botany. He returned to Venezuela in 1825 and by 1827 was appointed rector of the Central University by Simón BOLÍVAR. While serving as the university's rector, Vargas founded the faculties of anatomy, surgery, and chemistry.

In 1834, he reluctantly accepted the nomination for the nation's presidency, which he won. Several months after he became president, the military's LAS REFORMAS REVOLUTION broke out (June 1835). Vargas was taken prisoner and expelled from the country. But José Antonio PÁEZ defeated the "reformists," and Vargas was returned to power in August.

Vargas is fondly remembered for continuing to see patients on a medical basis while serving as president. During his short term, Vargas extended education to all youngsters, founded a national library, and promulgated a new legal code. Citing poor health, he resigned in 1836. Returning to academia, he traveled to New York, where in 1853 he unsuccessfully sought a cure for an eye ailment. He died while in New York.

AUGUSTO MÁRQUEZ CAÑIZALES, *José María Vargas* (1973); FRANCISCO LINARES ALCÁNTARA, *Vargas: Apoteosis del siglo XIX* (1986); BLAS BRUNI CELLI, *La Hora de Vargas* (1986) and *Imagen y huella de José Vargas* (1987).

ALLAN S. R. SUMNALL
INÉS QUINTERO

See also **Medicine.**

VARGAS LLOSA, MARIO (*b.* 28 March 1936), Peruvian writer and politician. Vargas Llosa is Peru's best-known novelist, one of the creators of the so-called boom in Latin American fiction during the 1960s, and one of the most celebrated Latin American writers of the twentieth century. In addition to novels, he has written short stories, plays, essays, and literary, cultural, and political criticism. In 1990 he undertook a short-lived political career as a candidate for the presidency of Peru. He has taught at various universities, including Washington State University, Harvard, Georgetown, the University of Puerto Rico, the University of London, and Cambridge University. Many of his works have been translated into English and numerous other languages.

Born into a middle-class Peruvian family, Vargas Llosa experienced an idyllic childhood in Bolivia and Piura, Peru, where his grandfather held local political office. There followed a difficult adolescence, spent mainly in Lima, where he coped with his parents' separation and with life in the Leoncio Prado Military School in Lima, an experience he wrote about in his first novel, *La ciudad y los perros* (1963; *The Time of the Hero,* 1966). The military school was viewed by the author as a microcosm of Peruvian society, with all its machismo, prejudices, and hypocrisy. After its publication, a thousand copies of the novel were burned on school grounds.

Vargas Llosa became involved in socialist causes as a student at the National University of San Marcos in the 1950s, but he soon grew disillusioned with the official communist aesthetic of social realism. In the late 1950s his short stories began appearing in Peruvian journals and newspapers. One story won him a brief trip to France in 1958, and he subsequently traveled in the Amazonian jungle of Peru. He later won a scholarship to the University of Madrid, where his doctoral thesis on Gabriel GARCÍA MÁRQUEZ became a major critical study of that writer. In 1959 Vargas Llosa moved to Paris, where he worked for the French radio-television network and came to the attention of several prominent Latin American writers, including Jorge Luis BORGES, Alejo CARPENTIER, Miguel Ángel ASTURIAS, Carlos FUENTES, and Julio CORTÁZAR. His self-imposed exile in Europe and the United States ended only in 1974. Since 1990 he has lived in Spain and England; in 1994 he became a Spanish citizen.

Two of Vargas Llosa's most important novels appeared in the 1960s, *La casa verde* (1966; *The Green House,* 1968), and *Conversación en la catedral* (1969; *Conversation in the Cathedral,* 1975), and made him internationally famous. In 1967 he received Venezuela's Rómulo Gallegos prize for *La casa verde.* In his acceptance speech he described the role of Latin American writers as that of maintaining a continuous, never-ending insurrection against ignorance and exploitation. More recent works include *La guerra del fin del mundo* (1981; *The War of the End of the World,* 1984); *Elogio de la madrastra* (1988; *In Praise of the Stepmother,* 1990); and *El pez en el agua: Memorias* (1994; *A Fish in the Water: A Memoir,* 1995). In 1993 Vargas Llosa was awarded Spain's prestigious Cervantes Prize in Literature.

Vargas Llosa's novels may be considered a renewal of the nineteenth-century European realist tradition. Like much of the literature of the boom, they are experimental works. His innovative narrative techniques include

Mario Vargas Llosa campaigning at Calca, 1990. SYGMA.

the structural dispersion of the narrative, the interpenetration of different narrative levels, and the complex juxtaposition of multiple points of view, or dialogic counterpoint (often challenging to the reader because it may involve the presentation of two or more scenes as one). Other innovations include the simultaneous presentation of different temporal sequences (often involving flashbacks or shifts based on analogy); what Vargas Llosa has called the "Chinese boxes" technique, in which narrative elements contain within themselves other narrative elements that reflect the original material; references to popular culture, such as the *telenovela* or soap opera; humor—a rare element in Latin American literature heretofore; the use of slang and taboo language; and the fusion of a "subjective" psychological reality with a carefully realized "objective" observation of reality.

Narrative innovations aside, Vargas Llosa's work follows a perennial Latin American literary tradition that sees cultural and political criticism as an integral part of fiction, although his sensibilities generally prevented him from sliding into a simplistically Manichaean view of reality. His steadily growing interest in the Peruvian and international political situation during the 1970s and 1980s, as well as his exceptional influence as a public figure both inside and outside of Peru, led him to campaign seriously in the 1990 presidential campaign, which he lost to the independent candidate Alberto Fu-

jimori. Vargas Llosa's campaign, supported by a center-right coalition, dramatized his shift from the left-wing political beliefs he had held as a young man to a more conservative libertarian view.

Despite his participation in Peruvian political and cultural life, Vargas Llosa purports not to use the novel as political statement. It is his belief that literature is larger than politics, that it is born of, and indeed feeds upon, the real world, yet it does not simply reflect that world but embodies a "real dissatisfaction" with it. Literature shows us both what we are and what we would like to have been. To put it another way, perhaps, literature supplements, if it does not complete, the human being's capacity for infinite desire.

JOSÉ MIGUEL OVIEDO, *Mario Vargas Llosa: La invención de una realidad* (1970); HELMY F. GIACOMAN, *Homenaje a Mario Vargas Llosa* (1971); DAVID P. GALLAGHER, *Modern Latin American Literature* (1973); EMIR RODRÍQUEZ MONEGAL, *Narradores de esta América*, vol. 2 (1974); JOHN S. BRUSHWOOD, *The Spanish American Novel* (1975); CHARLES ROSSMAN and ALAN WARREN FRIEDMAN, *Mario Vargas Llosa: A Collection of Critical Essays* (1978); JOSÉ MIGUEL OVIEDO, *Mario Vargas Llosa* (1981); DICK GERDES, *Mario Vargas Llosa* (1985); RAYMOND LESLIE WILLIAMS, *Mario Vargas Llosa* (1986); GEORGE R. MC MURRAY, *Spanish American Writing Since 1941: A Critical Survey* (1987).

KEITH MCDUFFIE

See also **Literature; Peru: Political Parties.**

VARNHAGEN, FRANCISCO ADOLFO DE (*b.* 17 February 1816; *d.* 29 June 1878), Brazilian historian and viscount of Porto Seguro (1874). The founder of modern historical writing in Brazil, Varnhagen, however, lived most of his life abroad. The son of a German military officer who had been engaged to supervise the recently created ironworks in Sorocaba (São Paulo), he was raised in Portugal, where his family had been established since Brazilian independence. After first receiving military training to become an engineer, he went on to study paleography and political economy. In 1841, he was granted Brazilian citizenship and, in the following year, he obtained a position in the Brazilian army, where he began his diplomatic career, serving in Portugal (1842–1852), Spain (1852–1858), several Latin-American republics (1859–1868), and Austria (1868–1878). He was a member of the Portuguese Royal Academy of Sciences and of the Brazilian Historical and Geographical Institute.

A product of the intellectual climate of Portuguese romanticism, Varnhagen considered the nation to be the natural framework for historical writing but, at the same time, followed the rules of historical research established by German scholars at the beginning of the century. Probing into the archives of Portugal, Spain, and Brazil, he prepared the work for which he is today chiefly known: the *História geral do Brasil antes da sua separação e independência de Portugal* (1856–1857). He also published a study on the Dutch occupation of Brazil (1871), a second, much altered, edition of the *História geral do Brasil* (1877) and, on his death, left unfinished the *História da independência do Brasil* (1916). His interests also included the history of Brazilian literature and Amerindian cultures and languages. Although deprived of literary craftsmanship and tainted by a very conservative outlook, which marred some of his judgments, his work stands, by virtue of the depth and scope of its scholarship, above all others in nineteenth-century Brazilian historical writing.

J. CAPISTRANO DE ABREU, "Necrológio de Francisco Adolfo de Varnhagen, Visconde de Porto Seguro" (1878), in *Ensaios e estudos (crítica e história), Iᵉ série* (1931), pp. 81–91; FRANCISCO ADOLFO DE VARNHAGEN, *Correspondência ativa*, edited by Clado Ribeiro de Lessa (1961); NILO ODÁLIA (org.), *Grandes scientistas sociais*, vol. 9, *Varnhagen: História* (1979); JOSÉ HONÓRIO RODRIGUES, "Varnhagen: O primeiro mestre da historiografia brasileira (1816–1878)," in *História combatente* (1982), pp. 191–225.

GUILHERME PEREIRA DAS NEVES

VARO, REMEDIOS (*b.* 16 December 1908; *d.* 8 October 1963), Spanish painter. Born in Anglés, a town in Gerona, Catalonia, Remedios Varo was the daughter of an Andalusian hydraulic engineer and a Basque mother. In 1924 she enrolled at the Academy of San Fernando in Madrid. She moved to Barcelona in 1932 and shared a studio with the Catalan artist Esteban Francés. She participated in the Exposición Logicofobista, organized by ADLAN (Amics de les Arts Nous; Friends of the New Art), in 1936. In Barcelona, Varo met the French surrealist poet Benjamín Péret, with whom she traveled to Paris in 1937, and became involved with the activities of the surrealist circle. Fleeing World War II, Varo immigrated to Mexico in 1942; there she met other exiled artists, including Leonara Carrington, Wolfgang Paalen, José and Kati Horna; with Carrington, Varo established close personal and artistic ties. Most of Varo's works were produced during her stay in Mexico, where she remained until her death. Her works display a range of fantastic subjects, some of which are based on her interest in alchemy and the occult.

LUCÍA GARCÍA DE CARPI, *La pintura surrealista española, 1924–1936* (1986); FUNDACIÓN BANCO EXTERIOR (Madrid), *Remedios Varo* (1988); JANET A. KAPLAN, *Unexpected Journeys: The Art and Life of Remedios Varo* (1988); BEATRIZ VARO, *Remedios Varo: En el centro del microcosmos* (1990).

ILONA KATZEW

VARONA Y PERA, ENRIQUE JOSÉ (*b.* 13 April 1849; *d.* 19 November 1933) Cuban philosopher, intellectual, and vice president (1913–1916). A native-born Cuban, Varona earned a Ph.D. from the University of Havana and became a representative from Cuba to the Spanish Cortes, where he strongly supported Cuban autonomy. He called for independence, moved to New York, and joined José MARTÍ's independence movement, editing the revolutionary paper, *La Patria Libre*. After Martí's death, he became Cuba's most influential polemicist. While a member of the cabinet of Governor Leonard WOOD during the U.S. occupation, he directed the reopening and reorganization of the University of Havana. Although serving as vice president under General Mario García MENOCAL, he opposed the president's reelection bid and joined the conservative cause. An opponent of the corruption in post-occupation regimes, he served as a vice president of the National Association of Veterans and Patriots against the government of Alfredo ZAYAS and led students against faculty improprieties at the University of Havana under Zayas and against the repression of opposition by Gerardo MACHADO.

Varona led the POSITIVIST movement in Cuba, blending the teachings of Auguste Comte with those of other European positivists. A fervent nationalist, he died lonely and unsatisfied. However, his voice and his writings served to lead Cubans during the turbulence of the 1920s and 1930s, and his philosophical and political contributions helped forge the reality of Cuban nationhood.

A prolific writer, Varona left a bibliography of 1,880 items. Some of these are still available, though not in English. An examination of his philosophy is available in FRANCISCO ROMERO, "Enrique José Varona," in *Positivism in Latin America, 1850–1900*, edited by Ralph Lee Woodward, Jr. (1971) and

MIGUEL ANGEL CABONELL, *El Varona que yo conocí* (1950). A good though dated biography is ELÍAS JOSÉ ENTRALGO and ROBERTO AGRAMONTE, *Enrique José Varona: Su vida, su obra, y su influencia* (1937).

JACQUELYN BRIGGS KENT

VASCONCELOS, BERNARDO PEREIRA DE (*b.* 27 August 1795; *d.* 1 August 1850), Brazilian statesman. Born in Ouro Preto, Vasconcelos took his degree in Coimbra (1818) and returned to Brazil in 1820, soon beginning a career as a crown magistrate in São Paulo and Maranhão. He began his political career in the first legislature (1826). He achieved prominence in the conflicts of the REGENCY period (1831–1840). He helped lead the opposition to the First Reign's absolutist centralism, a struggle that led to PEDRO I's abdication in 1831. Vasconcelos, a minister in the Regency's first cabinet, also figured importantly in the triumph of liberal moderates and consequent decentralizing reforms, notably the ADDITIONAL ACT of 1834. Later, ambition, social unrest, and secessionism thrust him into opposition to moderate Diogo Antônio FEIJÓ, who was then serving as regent. He sought social order and national unity by identifying the crown's central power with the interests of the propertied classes. After Pedro I's death (1834), Vasconcelos allied the more conservative moderates to the first emperor's reactionary supporters. They formed a parliamentary majority that triumphed with the ascension of Regent Pedro de Araújo Lima (later Marqués de OLINDA) and the birth of the Conservative Party (1837).

This movement, known as the *Regresso* (reaction), pitted itself against the decentralist liberalism Vasconcelos had once championed. In conservative cabinets (1837 and 1839) and the Senate (after 1838), Vasconcelos, with Paulino José Soares de SOUSA (later Viscount do URUGUAI), reversed the earlier reforms. They promoted the Interpretation of the Additional Act (1840), reforms of the Criminal Code, and restoration of the Council of State (1841). The Liberal minority attempted to thwart this Conservative reversal by forcing the early majority of PEDRO II, who then called them to power (1840). However, the Liberals' cabinet soon imploded, and the Conservative march resumed until the early 1850s, despite brief Liberal administrations and revolts. Vasconcelos, as a senator and councillor of state (1841), remained a preeminent conservative chieftain until his untimely death in 1850.

OTÁVIA TARQÜINIO DE SOUSA, *Bernardo Pereira de Vasconcelos e seu tempo* (1937); THOMAS FLORY, *Judge and Jury in Imperial Brazil* (1981); RODERICK BARMAN, *Brazil: The Forging of a Nation, 1798–1852* (1989).

JEFFREY D. NEEDELL

VASCONCELOS CALDERÓN, JOSÉ (*b.* 28 February 1882; *d.* 30 June 1959), Mexican philosopher and politician. Vasconcelos, a multifaceted intellectual and political figure, had a significant impact on intellectual thought in Latin America and on higher education and political behavior in Mexico. Intellectually, his work on the "cosmic race" (1925), which maintained that the mestizo race combined the best of indigenous and European qualities, was a great contribution to the growing literature of the region. His multivolume autobiography (1935–1939) is a classic in acerbic, intellectual literature. During his tenure as education minister in Mexico in the 1920s, he provided an important refuge for many radical students from South America, exposing them to the dynamic undercurrents of Mexico in the postrevolutionary era. At the same time he also attempted to bring art, music, and classical literature to the Mexican masses, fostering a flowering of the arts most notable for its painting, made world-famous by a generation of muralists that included Diego RIVERA, David ALFARO SIQUEIROS, and José Clemente OROZCO. And although he opposed political centralism, Vasconcelos helped to centralize the educational system as it is organized today.

As a moral leader of students and intellectuals, he ran against Pascual ORTIZ RUBIO, the first official party candidate for the presidency of Mexico, in 1929. His campaign was innovative in that it drew many young female activists into politics. Although he abandoned his supporters in defeat, his essays and articles, written in exile but published in *El Universal*, were among the most widely read in Mexico. He remained in Europe until 1940. While many of his supporters, embittered by the experience, rejected politics altogether after his defeat, others joined the government party, hoping to bring about change from within. These activists, among them Adolfo LÓPEZ MATEOS (president 1958–1964), dominated Mexican politics for many years but ignored their original goals.

Vasconcelos was born in Oaxaca, the son of Ignacio Vasconcelos and Carmen Calderón. His grandparents had ties to Porfirio DÍAZ, whom Vasconcelos later opposed. After completing his education at the National Preparatory School and the National University in 1905, he joined the intellectual circle of the ATENEO DE LA JUVENTUD. He became interested in political reform when Francisco I. MADERO began his anti-reelectionist activity against Porfirio Díaz. He served as Madero's confidential agent in Washington, D.C., and became vice president of the Progressive Constitution Party. Although he never taught a single class, he became rector of the National University (1920–1921) and then secretary of public education (1921–1924). While in exile in Europe from 1924 to 1928, he founded *Antorcha* (1924–1925), an intellectual magazine he used to oppose the Calles regime. In later life, he lost touch with his generation and his disciples, becoming an apologist for fascism.

RICHARD B. PHILLIPS, "José Vasconcelos and the Mexican Revolution of 1910" (diss., Stanford University, 1953); GABRIELLA DE BEER, *José Vasconcelos and His World* (1966); JOHN H.

HADDOX, *Vasconcelos of Mexico* (1967); HUGO PINEDA, *José Vasconcelos, político mexicano, 1928–1929* (1975); JOSÉ JOAQUÍN BLANCO, *Se llamaba Vasconcelos* (1977); JOHN SKIRIUS, *José Vasconcelos y la cruzada de 1929* (1978); JOSÉ VASCONCELOS, *Memorias*, 2 vols. (1982–1983).

RODERIC AI CAMP

See also **Mexico: Political Parties; Philosophy.**

VÁSQUEZ, FRANCISCO DE ASÍS (also Vázquez; *b.* 10 October 1647; *d.* 1713) Guatemalan chronicler of FRANCISCAN colonial church history. Vásquez is best known for writing the carefully detailed, *Crónica de la provincia del santísmo nombre de Jesús de Guatemala* in two volumes, the first appearing in 1714, the second one in 1716, edited and printed by the San Franciscan Monastery in Antigua, Guatemala. He is also the author of *Historia del venerable hermano Pedro de José de Bethancourt* and *Historia lauretana*. The latter narrates the vicissitudes of the Virgin of Loreto, who is venerated in the San Francisco Church in Antigua.

As well as being a renowned professor of philosophy and theology, Vásquez was deputy of the Third Order and superior of the Franciscan monasteries of Guatemala and San Salvador. He became the bishop's representative for the province of Nicaragua and held the titles of examiner of curates and confessors, and censor of the Inquisition. He became the chronicler and custodian of the Franciscan province of Guatemala, a position of supreme prominence in the Franciscan order.

AGUSTÍN MENCOS FRANCO, *Literatura guatemalteca en el período de la Colonia* (1967), pp. 33–45; JOSÉ A. MOBIL, *100 Personajes Historicos de Guatemala* (1979), pp. 67–69.

JANE EDDY SWEZEY

VÁSQUEZ, HORACIO (*b.* 1860; *d.* 1936), president of the Dominican Republic (1899, 1902–1903, 1924–1930). Horacio Vásquez came to be recognized as the last president of the Dominican Republic's oligarchic era. He had been very active in plots to overthrow the Dominican dictator Ulises HEUREAUX during the 1890s and ultimately came to power after Heureaux's assassination in 1899. His supporters came to be known as *Horacistas* and soon grew to become a major political party.

Characterized as inept and chaotic and yet as the most democratic of the period, the Vásquez era government was marked by severe political factionalism and increasing U.S. involvement in Dominican affairs. At the same time, the republic experienced accelerated economic growth and the emergence of a wealthy merchant and planter class. This era was most known, however, for the evolution of U.S. involvement, from customs collection to controlling national elections, and finally to outright occupation in 1916. Vásquez played a major role during the 1916–1924 occupation as a member of the negotiating committee that effected the withdrawal of the U.S. Marines. Supported by Washington in his 1924 presidential bid, he came to be seen as a puppet of the U.S. government. This perception and economic hardship brought on by the Great Depression resulted in increasing political factionalism, which led to his ouster in 1930 by the army commander Rafael Leónidas TRUJILLO MOLINA, who symbolized a new era of dictatorship for the Dominican Republic. Vásquez died in exile in the United States.

SELDEN RODMAN, *Quisqueya: A History of the Dominican Republic* (1964); HOWARD J. WIARDA, *The Dominican Republic: Nation in Transition* (1969); IAN BELL, *The Dominican Republic* (1981); HOWARD J. WIARDA and M. J. KRYZANEK, *The Dominican Republic: A Caribbean Crucible* (1982).

HEATHER K. THIESSEN

VÁSQUEZ DE ARCE Y CEBALLOS, GREGORIO (*b.* 9 May 1638; *d.* 1711), Colombia's major colonial painter. Vásquez, a native of Bogotá, studied under Gaspar de Figueroa (1594–1658) and his son Baltasar (1629–1667), both celebrated locally for their canvases. About 1657 Vásquez set up his own studio. With him worked his two children, Feliciana and Bartolomé-Luis, and his brother, Juan Bautista. His patrons were mainly local religious communities. Vásquez's best oeuvre (1680–1705) is religious in theme. Some four hundred paintings are attributed to Vásquez. Many display mediocre composition and perspective and occasional poor figure rendition. These faults have perhaps unfairly been blamed on Vásquez, since there is no agreement regarding the attribution of numerous works.

Vásquez's real forte was drawing. Over one hundred drawings survive, and are truly masterpieces. In 1701, Vásquez was accused of rape and imprisoned for a time. This experience caused him severe economic loss and mental anguish. He died, insane, in Bogotá.

GUILLERMO HERNÁNDEZ DE ALBA, *Gregorio Vásquez de Arce y Ceballoz* (1966); FRANCISCO GIL TOVAR, *La obra de Gregorio Vásquez* (1980).

J. LEÓN HELGUERA

See also **Art.**

VÁZQUEZ DE AYLLÓN, LUCAS (*b.* ca. 1475; *d.* 18 October 1526), judge and leader of an ill-fated colony in La Florida. Vázquez de Ayllón, an official in the Audiencia of Santo Domingo, sponsored two exploratory voyages to the Atlantic coast of La Florida. The earlier one, led by Pedro de Quejo and Francisco Gordillo in 1521, gave rise to the legend of Chicora, a fabled land of riches in the Carolina region.

In 1523 Vázquez de Ayllón was granted a royal charter to establish a colony on the southeast Atlantic coast.

Named San Miguel de Gualdape, the colony of six hundred, including African slaves, lasted only for three months in 1526. Many of the colonists, along with Vázquez de Ayllón, lost their lives. It is believed that the African slaves were abandoned when the colony withdrew. The exact location of the colony has not been established.

HENRY HARRISSE, *Discovery of North America* (1892; repr. 1961), esp. pp. 198–213; PAUL E. HOFFMAN, *A New Andalucia and a Way to the Orient: The American Southeast During the Sixteenth Century* (1990).

JERALD T. MILANICH

VASSOURAS (1994 est. pop. 48,000), a city in the highlands Paraíba Valley in Rio de Janeiro State dedicated to cattle raising and mixed farming. In the nineteenth century, this city's COFFEE production for the foreign market was the highest in the world. The name Vassouras ("broom") derives from a locally grown bush that was used to make brooms. From humble beginnings, Vassouras was settled by migrants from Minas Gerais and by court favorites who were awarded crown grants to settle along the Paraíba River to cultivate coffee. By the time of the census of 1872, the population was over 39,000, half slave and half free.

Vassouras was one of the most prosperous coffee counties in the Paraíba Valley. The neoclassic urban architecture that made its debut in Rio de Janeiro in 1816 was introduced after mid-century in the palatial mansions that successful planter elites constructed on the banks and tributaries of the Paraíba River. Prosperous planter-merchants who diversified their property among rural estates, slaves, commerce, urban real estate, and investments in budding financial institutions were recipients of prestigious nobility titles (baron and viscount) conferred in the imperial court. Vassouras became a frequently visited and popular highlands cultural center with the advent of railroad communication from Rio de Janeiro in the 1870s.

Crises beset the coffee economy in the 1870s, and planters whose investments were restricted to slaves and land faced reversals of fortune as creditors foreclosed on their property. The urban-based abolition movement that contributed to slave unrest and the departure of ex-slaves from the coffee plantations in the aftermath of the 13 May 1888 emancipation decree shattered the mainstays of the commercial plantation system.

Post-emancipation Vassouras never fully recovered from the demise of the slave-based plantation complex. Cattle now graze the hills where coffee trees once flourished. As in other towns in the Paraíba Valley, the barren and eroded hills of Vassouras are grim reminders of the legacy of the coffee boom.

STANLEY J. STEIN, *Vassouras, A Brazilian Coffee County, 1850–1900: The Roles of Planter and Slave in a Plantation Society* (1985); NANCY PRISCILLA SMITH NARO, "Customary Rightholders and Legal Claimants to Land in Rio de Janeiro, Brazil, 1870–1890," in *The Americas* 48, no. 4 (April 1992): 485–517.

NANCY PRISCILLA SMITH NARO

See also **Slavery.**

VATAPA. *See* **Cuisines.**

Vassouras. Rendered by Jacottet after Víctor Frond. Secretario Fazenda, Rio de Janeiro, 1858. COLLECTION OF GILBERTO FERREZ.

VAZ FERREIRA, CARLOS (*b.* 15 October 1872; *d.* 3 January 1958); Uruguayan educator, writer, and philosopher. Trained as an attorney, he became a professor of philosophy at the age of twenty-three and later taught legal philosophy at the University of the Republic, where from 1913 until his death he organized and taught seminars. He held directorships in primary-, secondary-, and university-level education. In 1933, during the coup d'état of Gabriel TERRA, he was rector of the university. Later, he inspired and founded the College of Humanities and Sciences and served as its first dean.

Vaz Ferreira produced most of his writings between the years 1905 and 1910. He published *Los problemas de la libertad* (1907), *Conocimiento y acción* (1908), *Moral para intelectuales* (1908), *El pragmatismo* (1909), and *Lógica viva* (1910). A good part of these are based on notes from his conferences, and his later work undertaken while at the university basically develops these themes and their pedagogical derivations, which are an essential part of all of his work. With Vaz Ferreira, the sharp polemics of the 1870s and 1880s between different schools of philosophy were brought to a close. He initiated a postpositivist neospiritualism that would characterize Uruguayan thought in the first half of the twentieth century.

PEDRO CERUTI CROSA, *Crítica de Vaz Ferreira* (1933); AGUSTÍN ÁLVAREZ VILLABLANCA, *Carlos Vaz Ferreira* (1938); ARTURO ARDAO, *Introducción a Vaz Ferreira* (1961); JESUALDO SOSA, *Vaz Ferreira* (1963); DIANA CASTRO, *Pensamiento y acción en Vaz Ferreira* (1969); *Cuadernos de Marcha* 63–64 (July–August 1972); SARA VAZ FERREIRA DE ECHEVARRÍA, *Carlos Vaz Ferreira* (1984); CARLOS MATO, *Vaz Ferreira* (1991) and *Pensamiento uruguayo*, vol. 1 (1991).

JOSÉ DE TORRES WILSON

VÁZQUEZ DE CORONADO, FRANCISCO (*b.* 1510; *d.* 22 September 1554), Spanish explorer. Vázquez de Coronado was born in Salamanca, second son of nobleman Juan Vázquez de Coronado and Isabel de Lujan. In 1535, he arrived in Mexico with the newly appointed viceroy, Antonio de MENDOZA. As the viceroy's protégé, he was appointed a member of the *cabildo* of Mexico City. A short time after his arrival, Vázquez de Coronado had become an important landowner and had married Beatriz de Estrada, daughter of the royal treasurer, Alonso de Estrada. In 1539, he succeeded to the governorship of Nueva Galicia, due to the imprisonment of his predecessor, Nuño de GUZMÁN. In 1540, Mendoza selected him to lead a massive expedition to explore an unknown area of North America that Fray Marcos de NIZA claimed was CÍBOLA, one of seven cities of untold wealth. The group included over 300 potential conquistadores from Spain, 1,000 Indians, Fray Marcos and five other Franciscans, at least three women, and well over 1,000 pack animals. Vázquez de Coronado's explorers marched from Compostela on the west coast

of Mexico through Sonora, eastern Arizona, New Mexico, and the panhandles of Texas and Oklahoma to the Great Bend of the Arkansas River in central Kansas. The expedition was a disaster; it found no wealth, and Vázquez de Coronado and his party destroyed as many as thirteen Pueblo villages in New Mexico while putting down an indigenous uprising against Spanish maltreatment. However, it was responsible for the European discoveries of the Grand Canyon, the Continental Divide, and the Great Plains as well as the people, flora, and fauna of those regions. Its members influenced the cartography of the area and established a written heritage for northwestern Mexico and the southwestern portion of present-day United States. Vázquez de Coronado lived for another twelve years after the expedition's return in 1542. A broken man, he died in Mexico City and was buried in the Church of Santo Domingo.

HERBERT EUGENE BOLTON, *Coronado on the Turquoise Trail: Knight of Pueblos and Plains*, 4th ed. (1990); STEWART UDALL, *In Coronado's Footsteps* (1991); DAVID J. WEBER, *The Spanish Frontier in North America* (1992).

JOSEPH P. SÁNCHEZ

VEDIA Y MITRE, MARIANO (*b.* 1881; *d.* 19 February 1958) Argentine politician and writer. Born and raised in Buenos Aires, Vedia y Mitre earned a law degree from the University of Buenos Aires. He entered education administration, becoming supervisor of secondary schools (1909–1911) and rector of the Colegio Bernardino Rivadavia (1910–1916). At the same time, from 1908, he was professor of history at the University of Buenos Aires and wrote a series of lesser historical works dealing with nineteenth-century Argentine history. Vedia y Mitre entered municipal politics dramatically in November 1932 when he was made *intendente* (mayor) of Buenos Aires, a position he occupied until February 1938. A controversial administrator, he ran roughshod over the city council, signed many contracts with foreign transport and public works companies, and ruled in an autocratic style befitting the conservative and fraudulent political spirit of the decade.

Vedia y Mitre made his mark by breaking the political logjam blocking Argentina's transportation system. The Buenos Aires Transport Corporation was set up to regulate all public transportation (subways, buses, tramways, and local railways). He resolved a long-standing dispute with electricity companies over service charges, had major soccer stadiums and a riverside bathing zone and promenade built, and widened the celebrated Avenida Corrientes. He crowned his achievements with a massive obelisk, modeled on that in the Place de la Concorde in Paris, built in the center of a construction project for the city's widest avenue to commemorate the four-hundredth anniversary of the founding of Buenos Aires in 1536. Vedia y Mitre oversaw one of the last major public works and construction waves in Buenos

Aires, in an effort to fulfill the Argentine elite's ambitions to inhabit one of the world's great capitals. He died in Montevideo.

DAVID ROCK, *Argentina, 1516–1982: From Spanish Colonization to the Falklands War* (1985; rev. ed. 1987), chap. 6; RICHARD WALTER, *Politics and Urban Growth in Buenos Aires: 1910–1942* (1993), esp. chaps. 9–10.

JEREMY ADELMAN

VEGA, AURELIO DE (*b.* 28 November 1925). Born in Havana, Vega is one of Cuba's most prominent composers of the twentieth century. He received his bachelor's degree in humanities from De La Salle College in Havana in 1944, then went on to complete a doctorate in diplomacy at the University of Havana in 1947. His musical training began with private lessons from Frederick Kramer (1942–1946).

In 1947 Vega was appointed cultural attaché to the Cuban consulate in Los Angeles. There he studied composition with Ernest Toch. Upon his return to Cuba in 1949, Vega became editorial secretary of *Conservatorio*, the official publication of the Havana Municipal Conservatory. The following year he composed *Legend of the Creole Ariel* for piano and cello.

From 1953 to 1959 Vega was dean of the MUSIC department of the University of Oriente in Santiago. In the latter year he returned to Los Angeles. He became professor of music at San Fernando Valley State College (now California State University at Northridge), and has continued to produce a variety of musical works.

Compositores de la América/Composers of the Americas 7 (1961): 98; A. B. RAMSAY, "Aurelio de la Vega: His Life and His Works" (Ph.D. diss., San Fernando Valley State College, 1963); *New Grove Dictionary of Music and Musicians* (1980).

DARIÉN DAVIS

VEGA, JORGE LUIS DE LA (*b.* 27 March 1930; *d.* 26 August 1971), Argentine painter and draftsman. Vega was born in Buenos Aires and studied architecture at the National University. Believing that nonrepresentational art had reached a dead end, he helped to form the New Figuration Group in 1960. In his work Vega depicts violence with a passionate eloquence that stands in marked contrast to the formal refinement of lyrical abstraction and geometrical art. Over the years he had numerous exhibitions in North and South America.

Museum of Modern Art of Latin America (Washington, D.C., 1985); VICENTE GESUALDO, ALDO BIGLIONE, and RODOLFO SANTOS, *Diccionario de artistas plásticos en la Argentina* (1988).

AMALIA CORTINA ARAVENA

VEIGA, EVARISTO FERREIRA DA (*b.* 8 October 1799; *d.* 12 May 1837), Brazilian journalist and politician. Veiga was a newspaper owner, writer, and congressional deputy elected for three consecutive terms to represent the state of Minas Gerais. As a political propagandist he was influential in promoting the cause of Brazil's independence from Portugal, declared by PEDRO I in 1822. Famed for his comment, "We want a constitution, not a revolution," Veiga represented the nationalist interests of Brazil's agro-exporting sector. Once the constitution was promulgated in 1824, Veiga pressed for its execution, arguing that it would be interpreted from a liberal standpoint. Veiga supported independence and the abdication of Pedro I in favor of Pedro's native-born son as measures that would increase the political power of the Brazilian elite and ensure ready access to international markets. His views were propagated through his newspaper *Aurora Fluminense* (1827–1835). Veiga was also the founder of the Sociedade Defensora da Liberdade e da Independéncia Nacional (Society for the Defense of National Liberty and Independence), one of three major political groups during the regency that followed the abdication of Pedro I in favor of six-year-old PEDRO II in 1831. Veiga is held to have been responsible for many of the regents' decisions, most notably the creation of the National Guard as a force that could confront local armies and militias and contain regional unrest.

SUEANN CAULFIELD

VEIGA VALE, JOSÉ JOAQUIM DA (*b.* 1806; *d.* 1874), Brazilian sculptor. Veiga Vale spent most of his adult life in the state of Goiás. Lacking formal artistic training, he early began to experiment with woodcarving. Although born in the nineteenth century, his art appears to have remained virtually unaffected by the then popular neoclassical tradition taught at the Imperial Academy of Fine Arts in Rio de Janeiro. Rather, his carvings display an archaic quality that firmly embeds them in the eighteenth-century baroque tradition. His best-known work, the *Santíssima Trindade*, still holds a place of honor in an important religious procession in Vila Boa de Goiás, Veiga Vale's hometown. His series of carved religious figures, housed today in the Museu de Arte Sacra da Boa Morte in Goiás, gained recognition in 1940, when an exhibition of his works took place in Vila Boa de Goiás.

EDUARDO ETZEL, *O Barroco no Brasil* (1974); *Arte no Brasil*, vol. 1 (1979), pp. 310–311.

CAREN A. MEGHREBLIAN

VEINTEMILLA, JOSÉ IGNACIO DE (also spelled Veintimilla; *b.* 31 July 1828; *d.* 19 July 1908), president of Ecuador (1878–1883). Born in Quito, Veintemilla studied at the Military College and was commissioned second lieutenant in 1847. He rose rapidly through the ranks, partly through involvement in politics, and became brigadier general in 1866. Under President Jerónimo CARRIÓN (1865–1867) he became minister of war.

After narrowly escaping execution by President GARCÍA MORENO in 1869, he fled into exile.

Veintemilla returned from exile in 1875, ostensibly to support the liberal administration of President Antonio BORRERO. However, with support from coastal liberals, he seized power in 1876 and arranged his own election in 1878. His presidency was plagued by great tension and violence between liberals and clerical conservatives, provoked in part by the government's suspension of the ultramontane concordat and by the mysterious poisoning of the archbishop of Quito.

Veintemilla claimed credit for reopening the University of Quito, providing free elementary schools, promoting railroad construction, and maintaining prudent neutrality during the WAR OF THE PACIFIC. He governed arbitrarily and in 1882 sought to perpetuate his rule through dictatorship, but he was forced from office and exiled the next year.

JUAN MURILLO M., *Historia del Ecuador de 1876 a 1888* (1946), esp. pp. 86–286; LUIS ROBALINO DÁVILA, *Borrero y Veintemilla*, 2 vols. (1966); FRANK MACDONALD SPINDLER, *Nineteenth-Century Ecuador. An Historical Introduction* (1987), esp. pp. 98–129.

MARK J. VAN AKEN

VELASCO, JOSÉ MARÍA (*b.* 6 July 1840; *d.* 26 August 1912), Mexican painter. Velasco, a major landscape painter, is the foremost Mexican painter of the nineteenth century. He was the favorite pupil of the Italian landscapist Eugenio Landesio, who taught at the ACADEMIA DE SAN CARLOS between 1855 and 1873. Velasco succeeded him in 1875 and remained on the staff for the rest of his life. In *Excursion in the Environs of Mexico City* (1866), an early work, small figures from different walks of life, against a background of enormous trees and a distant landscape, suggest historical and social commentary. Velasco never ignored the human presence in landscape, but with time that presence became less anecdotal. In 1873 he executed the first of several large canvases titled *Valley of Mexico,* his most famous works.

Although he painted elsewhere in the country (Oaxaca, Veracruz) and produced views of buildings, self-portraits, and portraits, the broad vistas and the clear light of central Mexico were Velasco's favorite subjects. In *The Bridge of Metlac* (1881) he celebrates the modernity of the age of Porfirio DÍAZ by depicting a train moving through a tropical landscape. *Hacienda of Chimalpa* (1893), a vast, simplified landscape in silvery tonalities, is his most important late work.

Although Velasco traveled to international exhibitions where his paintings received prizes (Philadelphia in 1876, Paris in 1889, and Chicago in 1893), his style was hardly affected by these contacts. Velasco had a strong scientific bent, and he executed many drawings and paintings of plants, animals, and archaeological objects and sites for scientific institutions and publications, as well as meticulous studies of rocks and vegetation.

José María Velasco, 1840–1912, catalog of Philadelphia Museum of Art and Brooklyn Museum exhibition (1944); CARLOS PELLICER, *José María Velasco: Pinturas, dibujos, acuarelas* (1970).

CLARA BARGELLINI

VELASCO, JOSÉ MIGUEL DE (*b.* 29 September 1795; *d.* 13 October 1859), president of Bolivia (1829, 1839–1841, 1848). Velasco was born in Sucre. In 1815 he joined the royalist army. After five years of service and promotion to lieutenant colonel, Velasco defected to the Republican cause. He fought under José de San Martín, Simón Bolívar, and Antonio José de Sucre Alcalá, and participated at the battle of AYACUCHO in 1824. After Sucre departed Bolivia in 1828, the new congress elected Andrés de SANTA CRUZ president and Velasco vice president. While Santa Cruz was absent from Bolivia, uprisings by other caudillos led to Velasco's ascension to the presidency in January 1829. Six months later, at the request of Congress, Velasco relinquished the presidency to Santa Cruz. During the latter period of the Peru-Bolivian Confederation, Velasco took advantage of the growing unpopularity of Santa Cruz, whose meddling in Peru had become very expensive for Bolivia. Velasco deposed Santa Cruz in 1839, but he in turn was overthrown by another ambitious general, José BALLIVIÁN, in 1841. Velasco returned to the presidency in 1848 after the populace of Bolivia became disenchanted with Ballivián. Lacking any coherent program and without widespread support in the army, Velasco was overthrown by Manuel Isidoro BELZÚ later the same year.

MOISÉS ASCARRUNZ, *De siglo a siglo, hombres celebres de Bolivia* (1920), pp. 77–79; JULIO DÍAZ ARGUEDAS, *Los generales de Bolivia (rasgos biográficos) 1825–1925* (1929), pp. 63–66.

ERWIN P. GRIESHABER

VELASCO, LUIS DE (*b.* ca. 1511; *d.* 1564), second viceroy of Mexico. Velasco was born in Carrión de los Condes, Palencia, in Spain, into the extended family of the constables of Castile. His early career included service in France and Navarre (viceroy, 1547–1548). In 1549 he was appointed the viceroy of Mexico. He served from his arrival in 1550 until his death. Central to his rule was the implementation of the NEW LAWS, which placed restrictions on the *encomienda.* The discovery of silver mines on the northern frontier caused a need for protection from the nomadic Indians. Velasco helped to define the military policy. He also supported expeditions, specifically to Florida under don Tristán de Luna. His son, don Luis de Velasco (the Younger), daughter, and half-brother married into the creole elite. The latter years of his rule were marred by the visitation of Licentiate Jerónimo de Valderrama and by an upsurge of creole animosity toward Spain due to the implementation of the New Laws.

JAMES S. OLSON, ed., *Historical Dictionary of the Spanish Empire, 1402–1975* (1992), p. 624.

JOHN F. SCHWALLER

VELASCO, LUIS DE ("THE YOUNGER") (*b.* 1538; *d.* 1617), viceroy of Mexico and of Peru. Born in Carrión de los Condes, Palencia, in Spain, Velasco first went to Mexico in 1560 to join his father, who was the second VICEROY. Earlier he had gone with his brother, don Antonio de Velasco, as a member of the party which accompanied PHILIP II to England for his marriage to Queen Mary. In Mexico, Velasco married doña María de Ircio, daughter of a conquistador. In 1565 he assisted in the uncovering of the "Cortes Conspiracy." After returning to Spain in 1585, he served as ambassador to Florence. In 1589 he was appointed viceroy of Mexico, where he served until becoming viceroy of Peru in 1595. In 1604 he retired to his estates in Mexico only to be reappointed viceroy of Mexico in 1607 and eventually president of the COUNCIL OF THE INDIES in Spain in 1611. He was granted the title of marqués de las Salinas del Río Pisuerga in 1609.

Velasco is credited with the successful pacification of the northern Mexican frontier, reorganization of the textile mills, and the initiation of the drainage of the Valley of Mexico. In Peru he reorganized the system of Indian labor, regulated the textile mills, and reorganized the mercury mines of Huancavelica.

MANUEL DE MENDIBURU, *Diccionario histórico-biográfico del Perú* (1874–1890); VICENTE RIVA PALACIO, *México a través de los siglos*, vol. 2 (1939), pp. 447–450, 538–555.

JOHN F. SCHWALLER

VELASCO ALVARADO, JUAN (*b.* 16 June 1910; *d.* 24 December 1977), military officer and president of Peru (1968–1975), leader of a radical nationalist government that introduced a number of reforms and increased state intervention in economic, social, and political affairs. Velasco was born in Piura and entered the army as a private in 1929. In 1930 he was accepted to the officers' military school, from which he graduated first in his class. After serving as army officer in the Peruvian jungle, he continued his military training in the Advanced War School. In 1959 he was promoted to the rank of brigadier general, and in 1962–1963 he was the military attaché in Paris. In 1963 he was promoted to division general and served in Washington, D.C.

In 1968, Velasco and twelve other army officers plotted to oust President Fernando BELAÚNDE TERRY. They allegedly elaborated the PLAN INCA, a blueprint for introducing strategic reforms intended to modernize the country and avoid leftist and social uprisings. Soon after the coup of 3 October 1968, Velasco and his government team initiated a process of nationalization of the petroleum, mining, fishing, and agrarian industries. A vast agrarian reform was implemented, and in 1974 the press was nationalized. With initial popular support, Velasco's popularity had declined considerably by 1975. In 1973 he suffered a stroke that led to the amputation of his left leg. General Francisco MORALES BERMÚDEZ CERRUTI led a 1975 coup that ousted Velasco and prepared for the return of democracy in 1980. Velasco died in Lima.

JUAN VELASCO ALVARADO, *La revolución peruana* (1973); GEORGE PHILIP, *The Rise and Fall of the Peruvian Military Radicals, 1968–1976* (1978); PETER CLEAVES and MARTIN SCURRAH, *Agriculture, Bureaucracy, and Military Government in Peru* (1980).

ALFONSO W. QUIROZ

VELASCO IBARRA, JOSÉ MARÍA (*b.* 19 March 1893; *d.* 30 March 1979), president of Ecuador (1934–1935, 1944–1947, 1952–1956, 1960–1961, 1968–1972). Trained in law at the Central University in Quito, Velasco began his long and remarkable political career at an early age. He was elected to Congress in 1932, became president of the Chamber of Deputies in 1933, and replaced the president of the republic a year later. He attained the presidency five times but was forcibly removed on four occasions. Only his third presidency (1952–1956) was completed in accordance with constitutional provisions.

A spellbinding orator and charismatic figure of the first order, Velasco dominated national politics for nearly five decades. When out of office he was busily planning a return to power, and few prominent public figures were not associated with him at one time or another. A lifelong critic of political parties, Velasco won power through a personal electoral machine, which was dismantled once he left office. Unable to delegate authority, Velasco was a disastrous administrator whose authoritarian proclivities encouraged political unrest.

A widely read intellectual, Velasco had minimal comprehension of economic issues and was inclined toward short-term opportunistic policies. By nature a conservative, Velasco nonetheless put forward a populist image throughout his career. During his 1960 presidential campaign his views were avowedly leftist in character, reflecting the impact of the CUBAN REVOLUTION.

Velasco's fifth and final term, after a narrow victory in 1968, was characteristic of his earlier terms in office. The constitution was eventually suspended, and ultimately the military intervened. Velasco went into exile, returning in 1979 to bury his wife; he died a month later. With his demise, the remaining Velasquista forces disintegrated.

GEORGE I. BLANKSTEN, *Ecuador: Constitutions and Caudillos* (1951); JOHN D. MARTZ, *Ecuador: Conflicting Political Culture and the Quest for Progress* (1972); OSVALDO HURTADO, *Political Power in Ecuador*, translated by Nick D. Mills, Jr. (1980); AGUSTÍN CUEVA, *The Process of Political Domination in Ecuador*, translated by Danielle Salti (1982).

JOHN D. MARTZ

See also **Arosemena Monroy, Carlos Julio.**

VELÁSQUEZ, DIEGO DE (*b.* ca. 1465; *d.* 11/12 May 1524) Spanish explorer, conqueror, and first governor of Cuba (1514–1524). Born in the region of Segovia, in Old Castile, Velásquez left few records of his early life. He won early acclaim fighting with the Spanish forces in Italy and his reputation grew when he traveled to the New World on COLUMBUS's second voyage in 1494. For his active role in the conquest of the natives on Hispaniola, he received land and *encomiendas,* amassing great wealth in agriculture. He served as lieutenant governor before being named to lead the expedition to conquer Cuba. Velásquez and three hundred men sailed for Cuba in 1511 and, upon arrival, founded Baracoa, establishing it as the island's first administrative headquarters. The conquest of the island, renowned for its barbarity, lasted three years and decimated the native population.

In 1515, Velásquez moved the capital to Santiago de Cuba. During his government, the center of Spanish activities in the New World shifted to Cuba and the island prospered under his capable leadership. In his latter years, dissension arose over many of his activities, including the use of Indian labor, leading to his dismissal as governor in 1521, though he regained the position in 1523. He died unexpectedly the next year. His wealth diminished with his losses from investments in exploration expeditions, like those of Francisco HERNÁNDEZ DE CÓRDOBA and of Hernán CORTÉS, yet at his death he was the richest Spaniard in the Americas. He created and organized a profitable and successful colony in Cuba; founded many towns whose names remain today; established a strong Spanish presence in the region, implanting her administration and her culture; and made Cuba a launching point for expeditions throughout the Western Hemisphere.

Little recent work is available on Diego Velásquez or the conquest of Cuba, and less is in English. For detailed accounts on these matters, see RAMIRO GUERRA Y SÁNCHEZ et al., *A History of the Cuban Nation,* vol. 1, translated by Emilio Chomat (1959), or IRENE WRIGHT, *The Early History of Cuba, 1492–1586* (1916; rep. 1970).

JACQUELYN BRIGGS KENT

VELÁSQUEZ, JOSÉ ANTONIO (*b.* 8 February 1906; *d.* 14 February 1983), the first and foremost Honduran primitivist painter. Born in Caridad, department of Valle, Velásquez was a barber by profession, without formal artistic training. He began to paint in 1927, and after working at various places throughout Honduras, he moved in 1930 to the village of San Antonio de Oriente, where in addition to being the barber and telegraph operator, he painted scenes of the village. His unique, primitive paintings, reflect the innocence and tranquility of that Honduran village where he spent the next thirty years of his life.

His paintings were discovered in 1943 by Doctor Wilson POPENOE, director of the Agriculture School at El Zamorano, and his wife. Popenoe hired Velásquez as a barber at his school, but he and his wife encouraged Velásquez to market his paintings in Tegucigalpa. They sold there only at low prices until 1954, when the Popenoes arranged for an exhibition of his work at the Pan American Union in Washington, D.C. This event catapulted Velásquez to international recognition, and in 1955 he was awarded Honduras's most prestigious art award, the Pablo ZELAYA SIERRA National Prize for Art. Among many other honors, he was elected mayor of San Antonio de Oriente. Now famous, he moved in 1961 to Tegucigalpa and in 1971 was the subject of a movie produced by Shirley Temple Black and filmed in San Antonio de Oriente.

J. EVARISTO LÓPEZ and LONGINO BECERRA, *Honduras: 40 pintores* (1989).

RALPH LEE WOODWARD, JR.

VELÁZQUEZ CÁRDENAS DE LEÓN, JOAQUÍN (*b.* 12 June 1732; *d.* 7 March 1786), Mexican lawyer, mathematician, and miner. Velázquez de León was born near Tizicapán (state of Mexico) where his father and uncle were miners. After his father's death he was tutored in native languages by Manuel Asensio. Later he was placed in the care of his uncle, Carlos Celedonia Velázquez de León, vice-rector of the Colegio Seminario de México, who encouraged his nephew to study science and mathematics. In 1765, Velázquez de León became an instructor at the Real y Pontífica Universidad. From 1765 to 1768, Velázquez de León and Juan Lucas de Lassaga (a Spaniard) studied various aspects of mining and mineralogy, especially smelting methods. In 1766 they presented a plan to the Spanish crown for separating gold from silver. After experimenting for two years, however, the plan proved to be flawed.

In the early 1770s, Velázquez de León visited Europe, where he was already known for his astronomical observations and maps. Upon his return he and Lucas de Lassaga published the *Representación que a nombre de la minería de ésta Nueva España* (1774). It portrayed a deteriorating MINING INDUSTRY that should be reorganized to include a guild and a tribunal to give overall direction, a bank to provide credit and loans, and a mining college to teach modern techniques. Its most important finding was that the industry would benefit from miners supplementing their practical knowledge with scientific knowledge. Some reforms were implemented during the next decade, although the college was not launched until after Velázquez de León's death in 1786. How much the reforms contributed to the acceleration in output of silver remains open to debate. As director general of the Mining Tribunal, Velázquez de León was also in charge of technical education and experimentation. He helped to write the new mining code (1783), which tried to bring mining laws into conformity with mining practices, and he participated in the founding of the tribunal's bank.

Walter Howe, *The Mining Guild of New Spain and Its Tribunal General 1770–1821* (1949); Clement G. Motten, *Mexican Silver and the Enlightenment* (1950, 1972); Roberto Moreno, "Apuntes biográficos de Joaquín Velázquez de León—1732–1786," in *Historia mexicana* 25 (Julio–Septiembre 1975): 41–75.

Richard L. Garner

VELÁZQUEZ SÁNCHEZ, FIDEL (*b.* 14 April 1900), Mexican labor leader. Velázquez Sánchez is probably the longest-lived top labor union official in Latin America, having served continuously as secretary general of the Mexican Federation of Labor (CTM) from 1950 to the 1990s. His notoriety comes from his long continuity rather than from any dramatic ideological or structural contributions to the Mexican or Latin American labor movement. Velázquez Sánchez's influence stems from his reputation for being indispensable to the control of numerous affiliated unions and to their acceptance of their status as a co-opted member of the dominant political coalition in Mexico. Because he has been so successful at this task, no president has either wanted to remove him, or has had the political courage to do so. This perception of his power has gained him a measure of autonomy from Mexico's president, making him the only Mexican official to have enjoyed this advantage for so long. Since the 1970s, it has led Velázquez, on occasion, to take stronger, more independent positions for labor vis-à-vis the executive branch, sometimes bringing his vision of politics into conflict with that of the incumbent president. However, because of Mexico's declining economic fortunes during most of the 1970s and 1980s, and the consequent high levels of unemployment, Velázquez has not been able to translate his potential power into much political influence. Although the PRI's perpetuation of electoral fraud in the 1990s had made it more dependent on the support of the CTM as the major member of the labor sector, the number of PRI candidates from that sector continues to decline. Velázquez is considered to be representative of the old-style politicians or "dinosaur" faction in contemporary political life.

Velázquez was born in Villa Nicolás, state of México, the son of poor farmers. He completed primary school while working in the fields. It is likely that Velázquez entered the union movement because his father, Gregorio Velázquez Reyna, was killed defending his farm, and Fidel was wounded in the shoulder during the incident. Velázquez began work as a dairyman in the 1920s, and became a labor activist at that time. He assumed his first union post in 1921 and became secretary general of the Milk Industry Workers Union in 1929. Originally a member of the executive committee of the CTM (1936–1940), he became secretary general of the major federation from 1940 to 1946. He, in collaboration with other labor union leaders, succeeded in wresting control away from Vicente Lombardo Toledano. That success eventually led to his domination of the union

after 1950. In his capacity as secretary general of the CTM, and dean of Mexico's union leaders, Velázquez served as senator from the Federal District (1946–1952 and 1958–1964) and has represented the labor sector on the National Executive Committee of the PRI on several occasions. Many observers speculate about the ability of the CTM to remain united after Velázquez's death.

Kevin J. Middlebrook, "The Political Economy of Mexican Organized Labor, 1940–1978" (diss., University of Michigan, 1982); Virginia López Villegas-Manjárrez, *La CTM vs. las organizaciones obreras* (1983); Ian Roxborough, *Unions and Politics in Mexico: The Case of the Automobile Industry* (1984); George Grayson, *The Mexican Labor Machine: Power, Politics, and Patronage* (1989).

Roderic Ai Camp

See also **Mexico: Political Parties.**

VÉLEZ DE ESCALANTE, SILVESTRE (*b.* ca. 1750; *d.* April 1780), Franciscan missionary and explorer. Born in Santander, Spain, Escalante joined the FRANCISCAN order at age seventeen and served among the PUEBLO INDIANS of New Mexico. In 1776 he accompanied Fray Francisco Atanasio Domínguez in an attempt to find a northwesterly route from New Mexico to Monterey. Although the Domínguez-Escalante expedition failed to open a new road to the Pacific coast, it was the earliest known European exploration of the Four Corners area. Escalante's journal provided the earliest written description of this region. Escalante returned to Santa Fe in 1777 and remained in New Mexico for several more years, serving as a missionary and ecclesiastical official.

Herbert Eugene Bolton, *Pageant in the Wilderness: The Story of the Escalante Expedition to the Interior Basin, 1776* (1951); Eleanor B. Adams and Fray Angélico Chávez, eds. and trans., *The Missions of New Mexico, 1776: A Description by Fray Francisco Atanasio Domínguez, with Other Contemporary Documents* (1956); Fray Angélico Chávez and Ted J. Warner, eds. and trans., *The Domínguez-Escalante Journal* (1976).

Suzanne B. Pasztor

VÉLEZ SARSFIELD, DALMACIO (*b.* 18 February 1800; *d.* 30 March 1875), perhaps the greatest Argentine jurist of the nineteenth century. Vélez Sarsfield was born in the city of Córdoba and studied law at the law faculty of the university there, graduating in 1823. From 1824 to 1827 he was a deputy in the Constituent Congress in Buenos Aires and was briefly one of the first professors of political economy of the period. During the 1830s he practiced law, wrote important juridical works that included *Instituciones reales de España* and *Prontuario de práctica forense*, and was named president of the Academy of Jurisprudence in 1835. In the 1850s Vélez Sarsfield was deputy and senator in the local legislatures of the province of Buenos Aires and an adviser to the provincial government. In 1863 he was named minister of finance of Argentina by President Bartolomé MITRE, and from 1868 to 1873, was minister of the interior under President Domingo SARMIENTO. He is perhaps best known for his work as coauthor, with Eduardo ACEVEDO, of the Commercial Code of Argentina (1857) and as author of the Civil Code (1864).

ABEL CHANETON, *Historia de Vélez Sarsfield* (1969); ABELARDO LEVAGGI, *Dos estudios sobre Vélez Sarsfield* (1988).

CARLOS MARICHAL

VELOSO, CAETANO (*b.* 7 August 1942), Brazilian singer-songwriter. Veloso was the principal figure, along with Gilberto GIL, of TROPICALISMO, a dadaist-like late 1960s Brazilian movement of cultural and musical renovation, which included Torquato Neto, Helio OITICICA, José Carlos Capinam, Tom Zé, Gal Costa, and others. As performer, cultural agitator, and composer of numerous songs, including the 1960s classic "Alegria, alegria" (1967, Happiness, Happiness) and tropicalismo's manifesto "Tropicália" (1968), he and Gil are almost universally credited with redefining the aesthetics of Brazilian popular music through the incorporation of foreign elements such as rock, dismantling existing barriers between popular and "high" culture forms such as concrete poetry, and reelaborating folk forms.

Since his 1972 return to Brazil from England, where he had been forced into exile by the military government in 1969 (probably because he was a prominent proponent of *tropicalismo*), Veloso has continued a prolific career as a singer-songwriter, utilizing genres as diverse as SAMBA, rap, and reggae to produce hybrid compositions with broad popular appeal. "His importance in Brazil," writes Perrone, "can be compared with that of Bob Dylan and John Lennon in the Anglo-American sphere."

AUGUSTO DE CAMPOS et al., *Balanço da bossa e outras bossas,* 2d ed. (1978); GÉRARD BÉHAGUE, "Brazilian Musical Values in the 1960s and 1970s: Popular Urban Music from Bossa Nova to Tropicalia," in *Journal of Popular Culture* 13, no. 3 (1980): 437–452; CHARLES A. PERRONE, *Masters of Contemporary Brazilian Song* (1989).

ROBERT MYERS

See also **Música Popular Brasileira.**

VENEGAS DE SAAVEDRA, FRANCISCO JAVIER (*b.* 1760, *d.* 1838), viceroy of Mexico (1810–1813). Venegas distinguished himself in 1808 as an officer fighting the French in Spain. Named to govern New Granada (Bogotá) by the Spanish regency (of which his uncle was a member), he was instead diverted to serve in Mexico, where he assumed office as viceroy just two days before the outbreak of Father Miguel HIDALGO's rebellion in September 1810. Venegas responded skillfully to the crisis in the colony, confronting and partially containing the military threat from the rapidly growing insurgency, cre-

ating new militia units, imposing a series of wartime revenue measures, instituting an internal security system for the capital and other cities, and abolishing Indian tributes. In attempting to maintain his own authority, Venegas effectively abrogated much of the liberal Spanish Constitution of 1812, though he quarreled with the ultraroyalist faction in the colony. Noted for his personal integrity, Venegas retired in relative poverty to Spain, where he was eventually ennobled (1816). He later served in a series of high political posts.

MANUEL RIVERA CAMBAS, *Los gobernantes de México*, vol. 3 (1964), pp. 287–322; HUGH M. HAMILL, JR., *The Hidalgo Revolt, Prelude to Mexican Independence* (1966); TIMOTHY E. ANNA, *The Fall of the Royal Government in Mexico City* (1978).

ERIC VAN YOUNG

VENEZUELA. [Coverage begins with a two-part survey of Venezuelan political history. There follow a variety of entries on specialized topics: **Constitutions; Immigration; Las Reformas Revolution; Organizations** (cultural, economic, labor, etc.); **Political Parties;** and **Revolutionary Movements.**]

The Colonial Era

Venezuela's historical development during the colonial period took place in six subregions. During Christopher Columbus's third voyage, when Europeans first set sight on the coast of Venezuela, there was nothing that drew the special attention of the Spanish. None of the areas dominated the other in terms of population or natural resources. During the course of the next three centuries, however, the Coastal Ranges, which stand behind the coast in the central and eastern parts of the country, would come to dominate the others.

Each of the regions has unique characteristics, and in the early sixteenth century there was little to suggest that the area would become a unified country. The Coast Region is a narrow strip along the Caribbean that stretches from Lake Maracaibo in the west to the Orinoco Delta in the east. It is here that foreigners entered the area and attempted to plunder the coastal towns. The Segovia Highlands form a transitional area between the Andes and the Coast Region in the western part of Venezuela. The inhabitants of these highlands, and those of the Andes, which forms a third area, became increasingly dominated by the economic and political elites from the Coastal Ranges.

The other three regions are in the central and eastern parts of the area. There are two Coastal Ranges, one immediately inland from the coast in the center of what became Venezuela and the other in the east. During most of the colonial period the Central Coastal Range would be associated with the province of Caracas and the Eastern Coastal Range with Cumaná. The fifth area is the llanos, a vast plain forming the interior heartland of Venezuela. Finally, Guayana, which lies east of the Orinoco River, had the least impact upon the development of the province. During the course of three hundred years one can detect the emergence of the dominance of the Coastal Ranges over the other five areas, and of the Coastal Range near Caracas over the Coastal Range near Cumaná.

THE PEOPLE

There were differences in the various groups of indigenous peoples who populated Venezuela prior to the arrival of the Spanish. There were stable sedentary farmers in the Central Coastal Range and in the Andes, slash-and-burn agriculturalists in the llanos, and hunters and gatherers along the coast and in the major river valleys.

The ability of the indigenous peoples to retain their culture during the colonial period was directly related to the relative power of the Spanish. Not surprisingly, indigenous peoples were able to thrive and resist domination most effectively outside the area dominated by the Europeans. In the Andes, on the llanos, and in Guayana indigenous peoples were able to live more or less on their own terms. The large numbers of whites and blacks entering the Coastal Ranges, however, spelled the end of indigenous cultural traditions in those areas. In the regions that the Spanish avoided, the indigenous people continued to live undisturbed until the twentieth century. Perhaps 15 to 20 percent of the total population in 1800 of approximately 900,000 could be classified as Indian.

Africans came to Venezuela as slaves from the Caribbean Islands, from Colombia, and some directly from Africa. Most came during the last half of the eighteenth century with the opening of free trade as part of the BOURBON REFORMS. Slaves could be found in all parts of Venezuela and were utilized in a wide variety of occupations. At the end of the colonial period approximately 10 percent of the population of colonial Venezuela were African slaves.

The other primary racial group was the Spanish. As in other colonies there was a division into those born in Spain and those born in America. Two other distinct groups were important in the social development of Venezuela. The Canary Islanders, who were associated with agriculture, lived near Valencia and identified themselves as a separate ethnic group. The Basques, who came in large numbers during the monopoly of the CARACAS COMPANY in the eighteenth century, were successful in obtaining power and wealth during the late colonial period. All whites, including those born in America and Iberia, represented perhaps 20 percent of the total population at the end of the colonial period.

By the end of the colonial period the majority of the people living in Venezuela were of mixed-race background (PARDOS). They formed by far the largest ethnic group, perhaps just over one-half of the total population. They dominated the population of the Coastal Ranges at the end of the colonial era and would become an important component of the forces fighting to over-throw the Spanish during the Wars of Independence in the second decade of the nineteenth century.

Venezuela's population was sparse during the colonial period. Although pressures increased at the end of the eighteenth century, for the most part subsistence was not a problem. The majority of the people lived on the agriculture of manioc, maize, and beans, which was supplemented by the abundant supply of meat from the llanos.

THE LABOR SYSTEM

Venezuela's labor system developed in response to, and as a part of, the Caribbean sphere, which was initially the object of gold and slave raids. For a short time in the 1520s pearls were gathered off the coast, but this source of wealth was quickly exhausted. Lacking a great indigenous civilization and significant mineral wealth, Venezuela's labor system would develop much differently than elsewhere on the continent.

Before the arrival of the Spanish, the indigenous population is estimated to have been perhaps fifty thousand along the coast and in the coastal valleys. Others lived in the inland valleys. The Venezuelan indigenous population fell by 50 to 75 percent during the first century after the Conquest.

The conquest and settlement of Venezuela spread from the extremes in the east and west toward the center. From Cumaná in the east and Coro in the west, the conquest and settlement converged at Caracas by the last quarter of the sixteenth century. The early search for profits from slave raiding, gold extraction, and pearl fishing gave way to agricultural development. The production of wheat and cacao caused the colonists to turn to the ENCOMIENDA system. This development proceeded slowly from the central valleys (Caracas, Valencia, and Barquisimeto) to the outlying areas. In the latter, Indian slavery persisted until the seventeenth century. Encomiendas in Venezuela entailed predominately personal service rather than tribute collecting until the end of the seventeenth century.

In the coastal regions encomienda labor gave way to African slave labor by the third decade of the seventeenth century, especially in the cacao plantation economy. With the exception of the mission areas and the far south, Indians in Venezuela maintained the old pattern of subsistence agriculture. Cacao replaced wheat as the principal source of export earnings. The cacao tree was indigenous to Venezuela, and originally the beans were shipped exclusively to Mexico. The market greatly increased when Europeans began to acquire a taste for the product. Caracas emerged as the dominant area of Venezuela because of its role in controlling the production of both wheat and cacao.

CONQUEST AND COLONIZATION

Most of the earliest exploration of what is today Venezuela was a result of the search for slaves to serve the Spanish settlers on Cuba and Hispaniola. This activity did little to establish a permanent Spanish presence in Venezuela. It did, however, provide the Spanish with enough information to cause them to seek other sources of wealth that would provide more permanent settlements.

The Spanish were attracted initially to the islands of Cubagua and Margarita because of the rich pearl beds, which proved to be a source of considerable income for the colonists and the crown in the 1520s and 1530s. The beds quickly played out, although the Spanish had by then established towns on Margarita Island and on the mainland at Cumaná and Barcelona.

The first Hispanic settlement in the vicinity of Caracas was established by settlers from Margarita Island. In 1558 Francisco FAJARDO and a few Margariteños settled near the future port of La Guaira. The settlers spent a year trading along the coast, but were driven off by local Indians. Undaunted, Fajardo returned the next year with reinforcements from Margarita Island. This time he divided the indigenous people into encomiendas, the first to be created along the Venezuelan coast. The settlers from Margarita Island had pushed near to the site of what became Caracas. The formal establishment of the town was accomplished by settlers who pushed eastward from the colony's other Hispanic center in Coro.

Serious exploration and settlement of western Venezuela came in 1528, when CHARLES I granted the WELSER banking house the administration of Venezuela in repayment for the bank's support in the religious wars of the sixteenth century. Governor Ambrosio Alfínger and Nicolas FEDERMANN led the early expeditions, which were followed for the next two decades by many others. Driven by their desire to find EL DORADO, the German explorers found little else of interest. After two decades the Germans could claim that they had founded Coro and Maracaibo, increased geographic knowledge, and intensified Indian hostility. Nominally the Welser possession lasted until 1556, but the Spanish effectively regained control in the late 1540s.

From the base at Coro, the Spanish established a string of successful settlements. These towns indicated that the colony had matured from the era of simple exploitation under the Welser grant. The establishment of the towns of El Tocuyo (1545), Barquisimeto (1552), Valencia (1556), and Caracas (1567) brought to an end the first phase of the colonial period, which was characterized by the establishment of encomiendas.

The growth of towns during the first two-thirds of the sixteenth century was a very slow process. Prior to the mid-century the Spanish founded four towns, which served as stations for the pearl fisheries and as slaving stations. Two were successful: Cumaná (founded 1520) and Coro (founded 1527). Paría was abandoned after only a short time and a hurricane struck the fourth, New Cádiz. Fourteen towns were founded during the third quarter of the century. The second wave of community building occurred in the interior valleys as opposed to the earlier development on the coast. These newer sites shared with earlier communities the fact that they were hampered by Indian raids and the lack of an adequate labor base.

Caracas served as a base for the further exploration of the colony, which was not secured, however, until smallpox greatly reduced Indian resistance in 1580. The indigenous population declined by perhaps two-thirds in the immediate Caracas valley, from perhaps 30,000 to 10,000, because of the epidemic. The elimination of the indigenous peoples as a serious threat to Caracas and the surrounding area allowed the colony to develop in a much more stable climate.

The period from the last quarter of the sixteenth century to the establishment of the captaincy general in the 1770s was an era of slow, almost imperceptible change. The overriding theme of the period was the establishment of Caracas as the dominant economic, social, and political power of the area today known as Venezuela. At the opening of this period Venezuela was a collection of independent geographic regions tied to New Granada, the Caribbean, or Spain. Caracas itself was just one of a number of towns surrounded by a limited geographic area that interacted much more with a distant part of the empire than with another region of what would become Venezuela.

THE COLONIAL ECONOMY

The colonial Venezuelan economy was diversified, producing agricultural products for internal and external markets. In the seventeenth century cacao, wheat, tobacco, and hides dominated external trade. Other products included cotton, indigo, gold, and copper. These products were exported primarily to Mexico and Spain, with the largest volume of trade in the seventeenth century being the cacao and wheat going to Mexico. The funds obtained from external trade went largely to purchase African black slaves and manufactured products from Europe.

There was also a sizable internal trade within the three major economic zones of what would eventually become Venezuela: the central valleys surrounding Caracas, the eastern periphery focusing upon Cumaná and the interior plains, and the western periphery reaching from the Andes to Coro and Maracaibo. At the beginning of the mature colonial period these three areas had little contact with one another. There was a great deal of intraregional trade, but very little interregional trade. There was nothing inevitable about Caracas's eventual domination over the other areas. The Spanish colonial system, which during the eighteenth century called for increasing centralization, was itself responsible for the eventual emergence of Caracas as the dominant city and province.

By the end of the sixteenth century caraqueños were selling wheat to Cartagena, where it was used to supply the Spanish fleet, thus bringing the city's residents into the world trading system. In the 1620s Caracas residents discovered that cacao beans could be sold profitably to

Indians in Mexico. In 1622 Mexican imports of Venezuelan cacao were about 6,960 pounds annually, but during the period from 1620 to 1650 they averaged about 133,400 pounds a year, and from 1651 to 1700, 748,200 pounds. This caused an expansion of the area under cultivation from the coastal valleys to the fertile valleys of the Tuy River and its tributary streams. In the 1720s the success of the cacao trade attracted the attention of the Spanish crown, leading to the establishment of the Real Compañía Guipuzcoana de Caracas or Caracas Company.

The Caracas Company was a mercantile enterprise chartered to control trade between Venezuela and Spain from 1728 to 1784. It was formed in Spain in 1728 by José de PATIÑO. The company was given the exclusive right to control the cacao trade between Venezuela and Spain. In return for this monopoly, the Caracas Company agreed to suppress the contraband trade, defend the Venezuelan coast, stimulate regional production of cacao, and provide slaves to the colony.

The Caracas Company was a mixed success. The first four decades of its existence were marked by expansion and profit. The production and legal exportation of cacao increased significantly during the decades, from 2.5 million pounds per year in the 1720s to over 6 million pounds annually in the early 1760s. This expansion in cacao production and trade, however, did little to enhance the overall condition of the colony. The planters elected to increase production in order to counteract the lower prices paid by the Caracas Company for cacao. This pushed the expansion of the plantation system, a classic case of growth without development. The efforts to halt contraband activities were not totally successful. Finally, the Caracas Company was unable to supply the colony with sufficient numbers of black slaves or European goods. These problems, the Bourbon Reforms, and the wars that disrupted trading patterns caused the company's fortunes to decline, and the crown terminated the Caracas Company's charter in 1784.

The Caracas Company's most enduring legacy was that it ensured the primacy of Caracas over the remainder of the captaincy general. By expanding the economic sphere of the capital, both in terms of area and power, the activities of the Caracas Company preceded the political centralization of the colony later in the century.

MISSIONARY ACTIVITY

The establishment of the Caracas Company was just one example of the crown's increased emphasis on the colony after years of neglect. By the middle of the eighteenth century the crown also moved to increase its control over church and government. The FRANCISCANS, CAPUCHINS, DOMINICANS, JESUITS, and AUGUSTINIANS were active in Venezuela during the colonial period. The Franciscans were active from the early years in the colony, eventually establishing themselves in the central area in and around Caracas. In Venezuela the Franciscans are best remembered for their influence on culture and on education. The order contributed substantially to the rise of the dominance of Caracas since it selected the city as the location of its activities in the colony. The location of the center of learning in the colony in Caracas further enhanced the city as the primary settlement in the colony. The separate group of Franciscans were active as missionaries in the Píratu area of eastern Venezuela.

On a much larger scale, the Capuchin order formed part of the Great Mission Arc stretching from Paraguay to the Andes. The two major areas of missionary penetration were in the llanos, established by the Capuchin Franciscans in the last half of the seventeenth century, and in the interior south of Cumaná, established around 1650. The Capuchins were extraordinarily active, founding over 150 towns.

The Dominicans, Augustinians, and Jesuits also contributed to the colony's spiritual development. Each had much less of an influence than the Franciscans and the Capuchins, but nevertheless were part of the missionary activity that enhanced the expansion of European society. By the middle of the eighteenth century the crown moved to control the orders by putting secular clergy in charge of the missions. In 1767 the crown expelled the Jesuits from the colonies and confiscated their property.

THE BOURBON REFORMS

The Caracas Company and the Franciscans are but two examples of institutions that assisted in the dominance of Caracas over the outlying provinces. Perhaps even greater emphasis should be placed on a series of actions taken by the Spanish monarchs known collectively as the Bourbon Reforms, which created the CONSULADO, the INTENDANCY, the Caracas Battalion, the AUDIENCIA, and the captaincy general.

In 1776 the crown ordered the creation of the Intendancy of Venezuela, which placed the six provinces of Venezuela (Caracas, Cumaná, Barinas, Mérida de Maracaibo, Guayana, and Trinidad and Margarita) under a single fiscal administrator in Caracas. In effect this made the intendant's approval necessary for any major project involving royal funds.

Political and military authority were centralized in Caracas with the creation of the Captaincy General of Venezuela. This reform, effected in 1777, was to a large extent mandated by defense interests. Since the creation of the Caracas Battalion in the 1750s, the military forces in Caracas had more influence and power than those in the other provinces. In 1771 a thorough reorganization of the militia created a new command structure that allowed the reform to spread throughout the other provinces. The final bureaucratic centralization occurred in 1786 with the creation of the Audiencia of Caracas. Prior to this date appeals to a legal tribunal had to go to Santo Domingo or Bogotá. This not only eliminated a great deal of expense and time, but reinforced the dominance of Caracas over the other provinces.

During the last quarter of the eighteenth century these reforms helped create the conditions for an expansion of commerce and production. The intendant became an active participant in economic expansion, a new role for the Spanish monarchy. Trade was liberalized, including the legalization of the trade for many articles formerly available only as contraband. A *consulado* linking merchants and planters from all over Venezuela into a powerful representative group was formed in the 1780s. In 1789 the crown allowed Venezuela at least partial "free trade." Expeditions to the Antilles were allowed in order to trade agricultural products for slaves, and the crown even began to approve of trade with allies and neutral nations during the repeated wars with Great Britain.

Other institutional changes added to the prominence of Caracas. In 1725 the Seminary of Caracas was upgraded to the Real y Pontífica Universidad de Caracas. A Colegio de Abogados was established in the 1780s. In 1804 the crown created the Archbishopric of Venezuela, which brought the bishops of Mérida de Maracaibo and Guyana-Cumaná under the power of the Caracas seat.

TOWARD INDEPENDENCE

Venezuela was a beneficiary of the Bourbon economic policies. This was especially true in the export sector, which depended upon SLAVERY and tenancy. Several minor uprisings in the two decades prior to 1810 indicated that there were tensions. In 1795 slaves and free laborers seized a number of plantations in the area near Coro before being ruthlessly suppressed. Two years later royal officials discovered a plot led by local creole military officers and supported by representatives of all classes. The most dangerous plot may have been that of Francisco de MIRANDA, who made two unsuccessful efforts to liberate Venezuela in 1806.

On 19 April 1810 the *cabildo* in Caracas deposed the captain-general and the audiencia. The leaders appointed a junta made up of moderate autonomists and revolutionary nationalists. With both groups composed of members of the elite, there was widespread agreement on economic issues. The junta reduced taxes and established free trade. Property qualifications kept most of the population from participating in the political process. Congress convened in March 1811, replaced the junta with a three-person executive, declared independence on 5 July, and wrote a federalist constitution. The two most important leaders were Francisco de Miranda and Simón BOLÍVAR, neither of whom were revolutionaries in the sense of wanting to improve the lot of the majority of the Venezuelan people.

The new republican government was unpopular and was criticized by both radicals and conservatives. The First Republic had a short life. In 1812, after a calamitous earthquake that was taken as an omen by the people, royalist forces persuaded Miranda to capitulate. He did so with the understanding that the lives and property of the republicans would be protected. Bolívar was

outraged at Miranda's seemingly treasonous activity and arranged for the latter's arrest by the Spanish. Miranda was sent to Spain, where he died four years later. The stage was set for the long struggle for independence under the leadership of Bolívar.

In 1813 Bolívar returned to fight in Venezuela with a new political philosophy. Instead of democracy and federalism, as represented in the 1811 Constitution, Bolívar called for centralization and a more independent military after the fall of the First Republic. Despite some successes, Bolívar and his republican forces were repeatedly defeated by royalist forces. His most difficult opposition came from José Tomás BOVES, a royalist caudillo who had organized the *llaneros* of southern Venezuela into a cavalry.

In 1815 Ferdinand VII sent General Pablo MORILLO to northern South America to pacify Venezuela. Morillo, who replaced General Juan Manuel de Cajigal as captain-general, allied himself with the wealthy planter class that had called for the break with Spain in 1811. The lack of efficient bureaucracy forced Morillo to confiscate property to supply his army of pacification. Relying on terror and the military prowess of his experienced corps, Morillo conquered Venezuela and most of New Granada.

The harsh policies of Morillo resulted in a realignment of social forces in the struggle for the expulsion of the royalists. The creole elites saw clearly that independence from Spain and from tyrants such as Morillo was necessary to maintain their own power and status. Two groups that had formerly fought for the royalists, the *llaneros* and the blacks, joined forces with Bolívar and the elites, creating an alliance between the socially conservative elite and the lower classes. The Venezuelan *llaneros* were led by José Antonio PÁEZ, a brilliant military leader and future Venezuelan president. A national congress meeting in Angostura in 1819 named Bolívar president.

The Congress of ANGOSTURA called for the creation of the Republic of Colombia (oftentimes called GRAN COLOMBIA), which would unify Venezuela, New Granada, and the still-to-be liberated Ecuador. A constituent assembly met in 1821 to write a new constitution, giving the centralist executive wide-ranging powers. Bolívar, with the title of provisional president of Colombia, began his conquest of northern South America.

It soon became clear that the final chapter in the war between Spain and Venezuela would be settled by force of arms. The patriot victory at the battle of BOYACÁ in August 1819 caused Morillo to see that the end was at hand. After the liberal rebellion in Spain in 1820, he was ordered to negotiate with the patriots on the basis of the Constitution of 1812. In November 1820 representatives of Bolívar and Morillo signed a six-month armistice.

The Battle of CARABOBO is considered to be the final major military engagement of the War for Independence in Venezuela. On the morning of 24 June 1821 the patriots, under the command of Bolívar, faced royalist troops under the leadership of General Miguel de la TORRE, who had taken command of the Spanish forces after the departure of Morillo the previous year. Bolívar's forces were joined at Carabobo by the *llaneros* of José Antonio Páez. The patriot force outnumbered the royalists, and half of the royalist force was captured, the rest fleeing to the fort at Puerto Cabello. The patriots also gained important munitions, including artillery pieces and a large amount of ammunition. Bolívar entered Caracas less than a week later. He organized a government at Cúcuta on the border of New Granada and Venezuela, marking the beginning of Venezuelan national reconstruction.

FRANCISCO DE PONS, *Travels in Parts of South America During the years 1801, 1802, 1803, and 1804* (1806); JAMES BIGGS, *The History of Don Francisco de Miranda's Attempt to Effect a Revolution in South America* (1910); ALEXANDER VON HUMBOLT and AIME BOAPLAND, *Personal Narrative of Travels to the Equinoctial Regions of the New Continent, During the years 1799–1804* (1818); L. DUARTE LEVEL, *Historia patria* (1911); BARTOLOMÉ TAVERA ACOSTA, *Historia de Carúpano* (1930); ROLAND D. HUSSEY, *The Caracas Company, 1780–1784: A Study in the History of Spanish Monopolistic Trade* (1934); HECTOR GARCÍA CHUECOS, *Estudios de historia colonial venezolana* (1937–1938); JOSÉ ANTONIO DE SANGRONIZ Y CASTRO, *Familias coloniales de Venezuela* (1943); HECTOR GARCÍA CHUECOS, *La capitanía general de Venezuela: Apuntes para una exposición del derecho político colonial venezolano* (1945); DEMETRIO RAMOS PÉREZ, *El tratado de limites de 1750 y expedición de Iturriaga el Orinoco* (1946); EDUARDO ARCILA FRIAS, *Economía colonial de Venezuela* (1946); ENRIQUE BERNARDO NÚÑEZ, *La ciudad de los techos rojos: Calles y esquinas de Caracas* (1947–1948); FRANCISCO JAVIER YANES, *Historia de la Provincia de Cumaná* (1949); CASTRO FULENCIO LÓPEZ, *Juan Bautista Picornell y la conspiración de Gaul y España* (1955); HECTOR GARCÍA CHUECOS, *Siglo dieciocho venezolano* (1956); EDUARDO ARCILA FARIAS, comp., *El Real Consulado de Caracas* (1957); CARACCIOLO PARRA PÉREZ, *Historia de la Primera República de Venezuela* (1959); FEDERICO BRITO FIGUEROA, *La estructura económica de Venezuela colonial* (1964); J. A. DE ARMAS CHITTY, *Guayana: Su tierra y su historia* (1964); GRAZIANO GASPARINI, *La arquitectura colonial en Venezuela* (1965); JERÓNIMO MARTÍNEZ-MENDOZA, *Venezuela colonial* (1965); EDUARDO ARCILA FRIAS, *El régimen de la encomienda en Venezuela* (1966); MERCEDES M. ÁLVAREZ, *Temas para la historia del comercio colonial* (1966); CARLOS ITARRIZA GUILLÉN, *Algunas familia caraqueñas* (1967); MERCEDES M. ÁLVAREZ, *El tribunal del Real Consulado de Caracas* (1967); RAUL TOMÁS LÓPEZ RIVERO, *Fortificaciones de Maracaibo: Siglos XVII y XVIII* (1968); JOSÉ SUCRE REYES, *La capitanía general de Venezuela* (1969); JURT NAGEL VON JESS, *Algunas familias maracaiberas* (1969); GERMÁN CARRERA DAMAS, *La crisis de la sociedad colonial* (1971); SANTIAGO GERARDO SUÁREZ, *Marina, milicia y ejército en la colonia* (1971); JESSE A. NOEL, *Trinidad, provincia de Venezuela: Historia de la administracion española de Trinidad* (1972); CARLOS ITARRIZA GUILLÉN, *Algunas familias de Cumaná* (1973); ROBERT SEMPLE, "Bosquejo del estado actual de Caracas incluyendo un viaje por La Victoria y Valencia hasta Puerto Cabello, 1810–1811," in *Tres Testigos Europeos de la Primera República* (1974); JOHN V. LOMBARDI, *People and Places in Colonial Venezuela* (1976); J. L. SALCEDO BASTARDO, *Historia fundamental de Venezuela* (1977); ALLAN J. KUETHE, *Military Reform and Society in New Granada, 1773–1808* (1971); JOHN V. LOMBARDI, *Venezuela: The Search for Order, the Dream of Progress* (1982); JAMES LOCKHART and STUART B. SCHWARTZ, *Early Latin America: A History of Colonial Spanish America and Brazil* (1983); ROBERT J. FERRY, *The Colonial Elite of Early Caracas* (1989).

GARY MILLER

See also **Slavery, Indian; Venezuela: Constitutions.**

Venezuela Since 1830

THE INDEPENDENCE PERIOD: 1808–1830

Venezuela's insertion into the world economy came through a sequence of events that followed in general design the pattern of all of the Spanish American republics born at the beginning of the nineteenth century. As elsewhere, various uprisings, protests, and incidents throughout the latter years of the eighteenth century and the first few years of the nineteenth, marked Venezuela as a society uneasy about its future and dissatisfied with its political, economic, and social relationships. Much can be made of these indications of unrest, from the enthusiasm of young intellectuals for the writings of various French and Spanish Enlightenment authors to the abortive revolution sponsored by Francisco de MIRANDA during his ill-fated invasion of the Venezuelan coast at Coro in 1806. Slave rebellions and uprisings related to race and class conflict also preoccupied Venezuelans of the period. While these incidents clearly indicated a state of unrest, the impetus for major change came, as it always had, from Spain.

In 1808 the Napoleonic invasion of Spain precipitated the abdication of CHARLES IV in favor of his son FERDINAND VII. Ferdinand fell into the hands of Napoleon's troops who, holding him captive, placed Joseph BONAPARTE on the Spanish throne. These events led to the creation in Spain of a Supreme Central Junta dedicated to the restoration of the legitimate monarch Ferdinand VII and committed to the government of Spain in the name of the captive king. In the face of advancing Napoleonic forces, the junta moved to Seville and then to Cadiz. Finally, in 1809, the Spanish junta dissolved in favor of a Regency Council.

The news of these events produced a constitutional crisis in Caracas as well as elsewhere in Spanish America. In response, on 19 April 1810, the Caracas *cabildo* held an open session to assert its right to govern the Captaincy General of Venezuela. It removed the French-imposed captain-general and organized the Junta Conservadora de los Derechos de Fernando VII. This action formally marks the beginning of the independence movement in Venezuela, although for the participants, the determination of actual independence would not come for over a decade. In retrospect, this tentative assertion of local control led directly to a full declaration of independence and the successful construction of an independent republic. For those involved in the events of 1810–1820, these decades appeared turbulent and uncertain.

Who knew, in 1810, whether NAPOLEON would send his armies to America to wreak vengeance on the colonials who refused to accept his designated king? Who knew whether Ferdinand VII would return to the throne as an absolutist monarch and send his troops to America to wreak vengeance on those colonials who had ousted his royal officials in favor of a junta or a French pretender? Faced with this uncertain future, the colonials followed the Spanish peninsular model, hoping that the formula of a junta to conserve the rights of Ferdinand VII would protect them from charges of treason should the restoration of the Spanish king come quickly.

Events, of course, often moved faster than the participants could anticipate, and by 1811 the Venezuelan patriots, as those pursuing independence called themselves, succeeded in convening a general congress of the United Provinces of Venezuela that declared the country independent of Spain on 5 July 1811. The congress, recognizing the extensive European military experience of one of its most famous native sons, Francisco de Miranda, placed the country's defense in his hands. Spain, again, intervened, and when the Spanish Cortes of Cadiz approved a liberal constitution in March and restored Ferdinand VII to the throne, the Venezuelan patriots lost ground and Miranda surrendered to the Spanish captain, Domingo Monteverde, in July of 1812.

Whatever the events in Spain that reinforced the success of Spanish rule, the Venezuelan experiment in independent self-government proved a dismal failure. Called the Patria Boba, or infant republic, the Venezuelans proved better at the theory than at the practice of government. A weak executive and a timid congress were unable to mobilize the necessary resources. Miranda had better credentials as a European general than as a Latin American military chieftain, and even when he finally received dictatorial powers, he could not rally the masses. Coro, the former capital of Venezuela, along with Maracaibo and Guayana, refused to join Caracas in the independence effort, fragmenting the united American front necessary to liberate Venezuela. Young radicals such as Simón BOLÍVAR had too little experience at the time to provide the local leadership the republic needed. So, the first effort at independence failed, and Venezuela remained in the hands of loyal Spanish forces.

Even though defeated in Caracas and elsewhere in Venezuela, the patriots refused to give up, and Bolívar and his colleagues reentered the fight from Colombia by way of Cartagena and then up the Magdalena into the Andes, from where they launched a lightning campaign north along the Andes in what has come to be known as the Campaña Admirable (ADMIRABLE CAMPAIGN). The Mérida town council recognized the force of this patriot chieftain and awarded Bolívar the title of Liberator in June of 1813, a title he kept above all others.

In the rapid advance on Caracas, Bolívar issued a decree of WAR TO THE DEATH against Spanish rule. Much discussed by contemporaries and historians, this decree declared everyone in America who had been born in Spain an enemy unless they worked actively for independence, and everyone born in America a friend even if they worked for Spain. Regarded by some as a barbaric example of republican excess, others recognized this decree as a wartime effort to create a national identity for a country as yet unsure of itself. In search of adherents, desperate for recruits and supporters, the decree of War to the Death served to polarize the population around the independence campaign. The Campaña Admirable succeeded quickly, and in August Bolívar entered Caracas, where his title of Liberator was confirmed.

The short-lived triumph collapsed at the hands of the Spanish loyalist commander, a native Venezuelan named José Tomás BOVES. Out in the llanos south of Caracas he declared his own war to the death against the patriots and succeeded in mobilizing the plainsmen cavalry against them. Little inclined to fight for the interests of the urban elite represented by the patriots of Bolívar's class, the llaneros at Boves's direction fought fiercely on behalf of the king. By mid-July 1814, Bolívar and his colleagues found themselves on the run, and on 16 July, Boves entered Caracas triumphant in the name of the king. Bolívar fled Venezuela for Cartagena in September and with the irony of historical fate, Boves, now triumphant, died from wounds received in battle. His royalist cause appeared secure nonetheless, for by 1815 a Spanish army of some 10,000 men under Pablo MORILLO, an able Spanish captain, arrived in Venezuela. This marked the end of the Second Republic in the nomenclature of Venezuelan independence historiography.

In the Caribbean, the Venezuelan patriots in exile continued planning and developing their agenda for independence. One of the most celebrated documents of the period, Bolívar's so-called Jamaica Letter, offered a political philosophy for the independence of Venezuela designed to attract the attention of British and other European sympathizers. By 1816, Bolívar had found a strong American supporter in President Alexandre PÉTION of Haiti, who sponsored his failed attempt to invade Venezuela in 1815 and then his successful invasion farther east at Barcelona in 1817. From there, Bolívar marched toward Angostura, where he joined forces with other independence CAUDILLOS maintaining a successful guerrilla presence in Guayana. He joined Manuel Piar in the successful siege of Angostura (1817). Moving quickly to establish a republican presence and institutionalize the military efforts into a government initiative, Bolívar established a newspaper in 1818, the *Correo de Orinoco,* and convened the second national congress in 1819 in Angostura, which elected him president of Venezuela.

Drawing on this base of support, Bolívar organized an army and crossed the Andes into Colombia where, in August of 1819, he defeated the royalist army at BOYACÁ outside of Bogotá. This action effectively liberated New Granada (now Colombia). The congress then created the Republic of Colombia from the provinces of Ecuador, New Granada, and Venezuela and elected Bolívar president. This assertion of authority, of course, required a military campaign to actually liberate central and western Venezuela, still held by the royalists.

Once again, events in Spain influenced the development of Venezuelan affairs. In 1820, the Spanish Liberals succeeded in forcing Ferdinand VII to accept their CONSTITUTION OF 1812, a document that curbed his absolutist powers. As part of the Liberal success, Pablo Morillo in Venezuela received orders to negotiate with the patriots, leading to an armistice. The patriots, seeing an opportunity, broke the truce after two months, and in January captured Maracaibo. While a congress of Cúcuta continued the task of forming a republic for Colombia, complete with its own liberal constitution, the military effort led by Bolívar and made possible in Venezuela by the armies of Santiago MARIÑO and José Antonio Páez finally defeated the main royalist army in Venezuela at the second battle of CARABOBO (June 1821).

Over the next few years, Bolívar and the Venezuelan and Colombian armies continued to defeat various royalist strongholds. In 1822, the United States recognized the Republic of Colombia, and later in that year Bolívar held a famous Guayaquil meeting with Agustín de SAN MARTÍN, the liberator of Argentina and Chile. This meeting apparently convinced San Martín to leave control of Ecuador and Peru to Bolívar's Colombian forces. The patriots captured Puerto Cabello, Venezuela, in November 1823, concluding the military phase of the Venezuelan independence movement.

Between 1824 and 1829 Venezuela and the rest of greater Colombia remained preoccupied with the problems of inventing a country. The notion of GRAN COLOMBIA, a brilliant concept drawn from Bolívar's clear recognition of the weakness of individual Spanish American jurisdictions and based on the models of the Spanish colonial period, could not withstand the interests of the local elites. The centrifugal forces splintering Spanish America into independent republics based on the colonial jurisdiction of the audiencias overcame even the charismatic leadership of as effective a general and statesman as Simón Bolívar. By 1829, the task of keeping greater Colombia together exceeded Bolívar's capabilities. In Venezuela, José Antonio Páez led the separatists. Building on the resentment against a government as remote and unconnected to Caracas as was Bogotá's, Páez supported a separatist rebellion in 1829 and led Venezuela out of Gran Colombia, marking the state's emergence as a separate and independent republic.

THE CONSERVATIVE OLIGARCHY: 1830–1847

The years from 1830 through the 1870s fall into two major periods named by Venezuelan historiography as the Conservative Oligarchy (1830–1847) and the Liberal Oligarchy (1848–1865). During this time, Venezuela passed through the transition required to become a full participant in the expanding world economy, especially

View of downtown Caracas. STOCK, BOSTON.

the segment dominated by northern Europe (England, Germany, and France), and later on including the United States. Venezuela's economic and political development depended almost entirely on exporting primary agricultural products into this world market.

Although these years saw considerable controversy and various rebellions, changes in the terms of trade and rules of economic life generated the greatest tensions within Venezuela. Driven by world markets for its various commodities, principally coffee and cacao, Venezuelans often found their plans for political and economic development abruptly derailed or substantially diverted by events outside their borders. A bitter controversy over an 1834 law that favored the rights of creditors over the rights of debtors permitted a glimpse into the changes affecting Venezuelan affairs. Formerly, most credit in Venezuela, and especially agricultural credit, came from long-term loans provided by the church with low interest. Independence brought an influx of European capital, delivered in the form of short-term commercial loans with relatively high interest rates.

The 10 April 1834 law made it easier for creditors to foreclose on Venezuelans caught without funds in the short time frames of these loans. When the price of coffee or chocolate declined in Europe, the optimistic estimates of Venezuelan landowners collapsed and they would default on their loans. Used to longer term relationships, Venezuelan planters found the adjustment to short-term, high-interest-rate loans difficult, and they looked to the political process to protect them. Issues of this nature helped polarize Venezuelan politics between a group calling itself Conservative, whose political philosophy appeared to be primarily liberal in its favor of free trade and minimal government restrictions, and a group called Liberal, which looked to the rural landowners for its support and championed policies that appeared to recall Spanish colonial values.

The ideological and programmatic content of these parties may have had less to do with their cohesion than their personalist ties. Liberals tended to draw on the strength of the military heroes of independence and especially those associated with the Bolivarian faction. The Conservatives tended to cluster around individuals who had rejected Bolívar's Gran Colombia and had either encouraged Venezuelan separatism or had not participated much in the independence epic itself.

The Conservatives had as their champion José Antonio Páez, the hero of independence whose vision for Venezuela never lost its focus in pursuit of grand designs. This great llanero warrior turned out to be a careful, canny, and effective caudillo, and as long as his personal strength remained intact, he kept the Conservatives in power. Although labeled Conservative, Páez's regimes had their difficulties with the church until 1832, when the archbishop of Caracas and the bishop of Mérida returned from their exile and swore to uphold the state. In 1833 Congress accepted a solution to the question of patronage and then abolished the tithe. In 1834 Congress granted freedom of worship to all citizens. These changes did not satisfy the church and in 1836 the archbishop of Venezuela, Ramón Ignacio Méndez, refused to recognize civil jurisdiction and the state exiled him.

Throughout this period, Páez governed either directly or through intermediaries, emerging from retirement to put down this or that rebellion or to guarantee the continuation of policies and individuals that met with his approval. The sequence of administrations began with the first administration of Páez (1831–1835). Then, at the request of the civilians in Congress, Páez ceded power to Venezuela's first civilian president, José María VARGAS, an intellectual with no military or significant political experience and no participation in independence wars.

As soon as Vargas took office he found himself at war with the pro-Bolívar separatists from eastern Venezuela led by General Santiago Mariño. This Revolution of the Reforms, as it was called, had a mixed set of objectives, but in addition to resentments over the reduced influence of the independence Bolivarian heroes, the *reformistas* had a separatist agenda that would have set up eastern Venezuela as a republic, perhaps under the leadership of Mariño. Páez, called out of retirement, defeated the rebels, but prevented the government from imposing severe penalties for their actions. Vargas, unable to insist on punishment for the rebellion's leaders, resigned in favor of Vice President Andrés Narvarte (1836–1837) and then Vice President Carlos SOUBLETTE (1837–1839), who completed his term in close collaboration with Páez.

These years saw continued growth of the economy, with a prospering cacao industry and a boom in the coffee sector, but at the same time Soublette had to suppress various uprisings, notably a popular revolt led by Ezequiel Zamora. In 1847, Páez, thinking his fellow general José Tadeo MONAGAS suitably loyal to the Conservative cause but nonetheless a representative of the eastern caudillos, allowed him to become president for the 1847–1851 period. Within a year, however, Monagas had given amnesty to Liberals convicted of treason and conspiracy and the Conservatives withdrew their support from the government. A subsequent popular revolt in 1848 gave Monagas an opportunity to dissolve the Congress, and a Páez effort to overthrow Monagas and return the country to the Conservatives failed. This marked the beginning of what Venezuelans call the Liberal Oligarchy.

THE LIBERAL OLIGARCHY AND THE FEDERAL WARS
The next national election brought José Gregorio MONAGAS to the presidency (1851–1855), continuing the policies of his brother. Congress passed the first mining code in 1854, followed by a revision in 1855 that reaffirmed the Spanish rule that subsoil rights belong to the nation and not to private owners of the surface land. Also in 1854, José Gregorio Monagas signed the law abolishing slavery in Venezuela. In 1855, José Tadeo returned to the presidency. His second term saw the beginnings of modernization in Venezuela, with the installation of a telegraph line between Caracas and the port of La Guaira. A new constitution in 1857 strengthened the powers of the presidency at the expense of the powers of the states. A rebellion against Monagas for his abuses of power forced him to resign the presidency in 1858.

The end of the Monagas era of the Liberal Oligarchy signaled the end of the first era of independent government in Venezuela. The country had succeeded in defining its national territory, establishing a functioning government that could handle the task of linking Venezuela into the Atlantic export economy, and enhancing its colonial agricultural structures sufficiently to continue to provide increased quantities of coffee and stable amounts of cacao to that market. Venezuela did not resolve the question of legitimate political power, failing to find a mechanism that could manage and transfer power. Unable to rely on constitutional legitimacy, the country continued to depend on caudillos backed by force to maintain the authority of its governments.

While effective for short periods in times of prosperity, this system had too little popular support to survive hardship or contentious disputes over the disposition of the benefits of power. The resulting political and military instability, enhanced by considerable social instability, led to a sequence of uprisings that eventually ended the Páez era and plunged the country into a five-year destructive cycle of rebellion and civil war called the Federal Wars (1859–1863).

Ostensibly fought over the question of central versus state authority and power, the Federal Wars represented a dispute over the management of the country's foreign commerce and trade. A provisional government of General Julián CASTRO sponsored a constitutional convention in Valencia that produced the Constitution of 1858, designed to reconcile federalist and centralist ideas about the relative authority of states and the central government. The Federalists, unwilling to accept this compromise, went to war in 1859 under the leadership of General Ezequiel Zamora against the administration of Dr. Manuel Felipe Tovar, who had been named president for the 1859–1861 period.

Zamora won a major victory in this war in 1859, but in 1860 an assassin killed him and the government's troops defeated the Federalist forces at Coplé, ending this period of Federalist rebellion. Tovar's administration gave way to the administration of Dr. Pedro Gual in 1861; Gual presided for less than a year when General José Antonio Páez returned once again to lead the Centralists. The Caracas merchants supported Páez's presidency, hoping for stability, but by 1863 the Centralists lost the Federalist Wars, and the Treaty of Coche signified the end of the Páez era.

In time-honored fashion, a new constituent assembly met from late 1863 to mid-1864 to establish the priorities of the triumphant Federalist forces and draft a new constitution. This group elected General Juan C. FALCÓN, the victorious leader of the Federalists, as provisional president, with General Antonio GUZMÁN BLANCO as vice-president.

THE FEDERALISTS AND THE REGIMES OF ANTONIO
GUZMÁN BLANCO AND CIPRIANO CASTRO: 1864–1908
Between 1864 and 1870, Venezuela experimented with the governmental structure established in the 1864 constitution. A newly federalized Caracas welcomed the leadership of General Falcón, first as provisional president from 1863–1865 and then as president for the period 1865–1868. The Federalists suffered economic difficulties and constant political and military disturbances in the various states. Finally, Liberals and Conservatives joined together in a coalition to overthrow the Federalist government. General José Tadeo Monagas returned to lead this revolution and Falcón resigned into exile in 1868. For two years the coalition of Liberals and Conservatives tried to control the states from the central government within the boundaries of the Constitution of 1864, but this effort generally failed.

General Antonio Guzmán Blanco, a Federalist vice-president under Falcón, organized a Liberal Union opposition to the coalition, and in 1870, supported by elements of all parties, Guzmán Blanco occupied the capital, ending the experiment with a decentralized federalist government.

Between 1870 and 1908 Venezuela experienced considerable economic and political progress with a more or less strong, stable central government. Much of the transportation and communications infrastructure was modernized. Similar to the positivist movements in Mexico, Argentina, and elsewhere in Spanish America, the Venezuelans in this *Guzmanato*, as it was called, placed a strong emphasis on positivist values of effective hard work, conservative social values, strong support for order and progress, and little concern for the underclasses. Committed to the pursuit of a Venezuela tightly coupled to Europe and to a lesser extent North America, these leaders organized their country to be responsive to the economic, social, and intellectual interests of the leading overseas countries of France, England, Germany, and the United States.

Guzmán Blanco, the first Venezuelan strongman with no ties to the independence generation, displayed a ruthless effectiveness. His administrations, textbook liberal regimes, made education free and obligatory and reduced the power and prerogatives of the church to the extent that he exiled Archbishop Silvestre Güevara y Lira in 1870, closed the seminaries, and gave the university jurisdiction over religious studies. He later established civil marriages and a civil registry of births and deaths (1873) and closed convents and other religious communities. A rebellion in 1872 against his government not only resulted in the defeat of the rebels but the unprecedented execution of the rebel leaders. A final uprising against Guzmán Blanco in 1874–1875 involving Generals León Colina and José Ignacio Pulido also failed, marking the end of major resistance until Guzmán Blanco chose to leave power near the end of the nineteenth century.

Even though Antonio Guzmán Blanco remained the most powerful force behind the government during this generation, he often acted through presidential surrogates. From 1877–1878 General Francisco LINARES ALCÁNTARA served as his hand-picked successor. Linares Alcántara turned against Guzmán Blanco and a counterrevolution in 1879 led by Generals Gregorio Cedeño and Joaquín CRESPO restored Guzmán Blanco to power as the Supreme Director of the Republic.

Guzmán Blanco's second major period of direct government, 1879–1884, known in Venezuelan historiography as the *Quinquenio*, represented a period of economic change and prosperity with considerable railroad and telegraph construction and a renovation of public works in Caracas and other major cities. As did other Spanish American states at the time, Venezuela modernized at least the surface elements of its society to more closely match European models. It invested heavily in infrastructure to make the colonial export economy compete effectively in world markets with such commodities as coffee. Guzmán Blanco consolidated political and economic power in the central government in Caracas with a reduction in the number of states and the assignment of presidential elections to a Federal Council (Constitution of 1881).

In the 1884–1886 period, Guzmán Blanco turned over the presidency to General Joaquín Crespo, whose two-year term ended with the reelection of Guzmán Blanco for a third administration, known as the *Aclamación*. This period proved to be the least successful of the Guzmán Blanco presidencies, either because changing circumstances no longer matched his style or, more likely, because the accumulated resentments against his repressive political tactics made it impossible for him to govern.

Guzmán Blanco's success in negotiating large foreign loans for Venezuela had made him rich, and in his later years he became an expatriate in his own country. He spent such a large portion of his time in Europe that he clearly lost the personal commitment to local Venezuelan affairs so necessary for the control of a fractious and still highly personalist government apparatus. He was elected president again in 1886, but faced with substantial opposition, he turned over the government to General Hermógenes López, president of the Federal Council, and returned to Europe for good (1888).

Elected as the first civilian president since 1834, Dr. Juan Pablo RÓJAS PAÚL disassociated himself from Guzmán Blanco, but his short term (1888–1890) provided only a transition to the administration of Raimundo ANDUEZA PALACIO (1890–1892). Andueza tried to hold on to the presidency for a second term by dismissing Congress and calling a constituent assembly in 1892, but General Joaquín Crespo led what he called the Legalist Revolution and took control of the government for a second time (1892–1898).

Crespo continued the constitutional reform movement and a national assembly returned the country to a constitution similar to that of 1864. The Crespo administration also revived the Guayana boundary dispute with Great Britain that led to an arbitration demanded by U.S. President Grover Cleveland.

Serious economic crisis in 1895 paralyzed commerce and produced a mass action of Caracas workers and artisans protesting the lack of jobs. As happened elsewhere in Spanish America, the economic difficulties encouraged European-inspired workers' parties. Venezuela's Popular Party appeared in these years, dedicated to improving the education of workers and the creation of cooperatives.

General Ignacio Andrade's short administration (1898–1899) continued with additional constitutional reforms that reestablished the states as they were in the 1864 constitution and gave the president the right to name provisional presidents of each state. Venezuela lost the arbitration hearing with Great Britain over the Guayana boundary dispute, and President Andrade's administration fell to the so-called Liberating Revolution, which brought General Cipriano CASTRO into power.

Cipriano Castro's tenure (1899–1908) marks the transition from Guzmán Blanco's nineteenth-century administration to the modern bureaucratic authoritarian regimes of twentieth-century Venezuela. His ascendancy also asserted the strength of the Andean region in Venezuelan political life. Recognizing that Caracas and its sophisticated bureaucratic apparatus had the skills and the knowledge required to connect Venezuela into the Atlantic trading world, the Andean ascendancy showed that the Caraqueño elite did not have the political tools needed to manage a poorly integrated national governing system that barely organized the country sufficiently to produce the goods Venezuela traded. So the transaction between Caracas and its hinterland used the Andinos' authority of force to manage the countryside and used the Caraqueño elites' technical sophistication to manage world markets, credit, trade, and diplomacy. This bargain began with Cipriano Castro but did not reach its full development until the subsequent regime of Juan Vicente GÓMEZ.

The two presidencies of Cipriano Castro (1899–1905 and 1905–1909) were dominated by internal dissension, international conflict, and a growing recognition that hydrocarbon deposits would become an ever larger part of the Venezuelan export business. A revolution led by General Manuel Antonio Matos in 1901–1903, supported by international interests, attempted to oust Castro, but failed. Castro then refused to pay European creditors, which resulted in a blockade of the Venezuelan coast by English, German, and Italian ships. This crisis, resolved in 1903 by the Washington Protocol, required Venezuela to allocate 30 percent of its customs receipts to pay the European claims and represented a considerable loss of prestige for Venezuela. The growing importance of hydrocarbons in the Venezuelan economy led to a 1904 mining code and then a 1905 law that permitted hydrocarbon concessions for periods of up to fifty years. A regulation the subsequent year reaffirmed the right of the president to grant and administer these hydrocarbon concessions without intervention by the congress.

Cipriano Castro proved to be a poor national leader and a petty tyrant. As his support declined along with his health, he relied more and more on his vice president, General Juan Vicente Gómez, an Andean colleague who had accompanied him on the campaigns of prior years. Gómez, recognizing the declining health and effectiveness of Castro, encouraged him to go to Europe for a cure. Once Castro was safely out of the way, Gómez deposed him at the end of 1908 and took over the presidency.

FROM JUAN VICENTE GÓMEZ TO MARCOS PÉREZ JIMÉNEZ: 1908–1958

The era of Juan Vicente Gómez inaugurated the contemporary history of Venezuela. During the generation of his control (1908–1935), Venezuela became one of the world's foremost exporters of petroleum products.

Based on the substantial revenues generated from this export, Gómez modernized and controlled Venezuela, transforming it from an agricultural into a petroleum export economy. He also transformed the political process. Gómez took advantage of improvements in transportation and communications, seen first during the years of Cipriano Castro but institutionalized during the Gómez regime. With a telegraph in every hamlet and village in Venezuela, the central government knew within minutes or hours about any hostile political activities. With the improvements in roads and railroads, the central government moved troops around the republic with much more efficiency.

No longer could a rural caudillo gather his friends and neighbors, issue a call to arms, and begin a march on Caracas. At the first sign of such activity, reported in detail to the capital on the telegraph run by the state, Gómez mobilized his local supporters and federal troops to quash the incipient revolution. The means of violence, guns and ammunition, became something of a government monopoly. Where earlier caudillos could count on the household armament of every Venezuelan to provide at least the basic military matériel for an uprising, by the end of the nineteenth century, the growing sophistication and expense of rifles, cannon, Gatling guns, and other armaments made them largely inaccessible to individuals. Revolution became a process of subverting government military detachments or of seeking foreign support to launch a rebellion. All of this Gómez used to his advantage to keep his regime free from serious challenge for most of his years in office.

The Gómez period began with a provisional presidency (1908–1910) and a new constitution that led to his first official presidency (1910–1914). When his term concluded, he provoked a political crisis over his intention to seek another term, suspended constitutional guarantees, and imprisoned his opposition. Using loyal place holders to run the details of government, Gómez granted José GIL FORTOUL presidential powers in 1913 and Victorino Márquez Bustillos in 1914. In 1915 a compliant Congress reelected Gómez for the 1915–1922 period, but Gómez retained Márquez Bustillos as provisional president for the entire period.

These early decades of the Gómez era saw the beginning of the petroleum boom that was to remake the political and economic destiny of the country. A subsidiary of the Royal Dutch Shell company (Caribbean Petroleum Company) began commercial operations in Venezuela with the Zumaque-I oil well in the Mene Grande field of the Lake Maracaibo Basin, beginning the full-scale exploitation of petroleum. Petroleum exploration expanded with the construction of pipelines from the Mene Grande field to Venezuela's first oil refinery in San Lorenzo and with the first significant exports of petroleum into the world market.

Throughout this early period, Gómez's regime contended with a variety of plots and attempted revolts, but his government suppressed them all and imprisoned, tortured, or killed various conspirators. Venezuela continued to revise its laws on hydrocarbons, reaffirming its ownership of the subsoil rights as well as the government's right to concede concessions for exploration and exploitation of petroleum. Venezuela passed its first hydrocarbons law in 1920, and in 1921 Gómez permitted foreign oil companies to participate in the drafting of new legislation even more favorable to them.

In 1922, the ever-agreeable Congress reelected Gómez for the period 1922–1929. Continuous changes in the hydrocarbons law in 1922 improved conditions for foreign oil companies. This law, which also had largely unenforced benefits legislated for workers, remained mostly in force for over two decades, with minor alterations in 1925 and 1928. Gómez also created the Venezuelan Petroleum Company (CVP) to serve as the government's vehicle for awarding concessions. American oil companies began buying these concessions from the CVP in 1924. The accelerating pace of oil expansion produced not only great wealth for Venezuela and selected Venezuelans, but it also generated a labor movement and the first labor protest against the high cost of living in 1925 in the Bolívar fields. Government troops suppressed the strike. While the government approved the first labor law permitting unions and recognizing accident compensation, death benefits, and a nine-hour work day, this law did not take effect until the end of the Gómez era in 1935. By 1926, Venezuela had completed its transformation into an oil export economy, with the value of petroleum exceeding coffee.

Not all Venezuelans approved of the caudillo's dictatorial regime or the selectivity of petroleum prosperity. A student protest in 1928 led to the arrest of student leaders, sympathy strikes, and riots. Student leaders joined with young military officers in a failed effort to provoke a barracks revolt. Gómez retaliated by closing the Central University and the Military Academy. Many among these early revolutionaries later became the principal leaders of the post-Gómez democratic regimes and regarded the 1928 strike as a formative experience.

In 1929, making what was true in practice true in law, Congress appointed Gómez chief of the army and appointed Juan Bautista Pérez president of the republic. Gómez, living in Maracay as had become his tradition, continued to run the government. The Juan Bautista Pérez administration (1929–1931) suppressed various antigovernment revolts while the country's petroleum exports grew until Venezuela became the world's largest oil exporter in 1929. Dissatisfied with Pérez, Congress in 1931 asked for his resignation, reformed the constitution once again, and then reelected Gómez as president.

In this term (1931–1935), Gómez had his minister of foreign relations, Itriago Chacín, occupy the presidency. Reflecting the influence of international politics on domestic affairs, Venezuelans founded a Communist Party in 1931, although the government refused to make it legal. In December of 1935, Juan Vicente Gómez died of natural causes, ending his regime and unleashing a difficult two-decade transition period from caudillo government to democratic reforms.

General Eleazar LÓPEZ CONTRERAS (minister of war and marine) had the task of containing the forces unleashed by the death of Gómez. Elected president for the period 1936–1941, López encountered a host of new political parties that immediately joined in opposition to the government. A widespread strike in 1936 failed to force the government to adopt democratic reforms, and a variety of leftist parties, including the precursor to Democratic Action, joined together in the National Democratic Party (PDN). The government refused to recognize this party because of its leftist orientation.

Continued turmoil produced an oil workers' strike in 1936–1937, supported by the PDN, that forced López to grant a wage increase, although he dissolved the union and exiled its political leaders. A new hydrocarbons law for the first time appeared to give more control of the petroleum resources to the state, and the government chartered the Venezuelan Central Bank in 1939. Lopez also enacted a social security law.

General Isaías MEDINA ANGARITA (1941–1945) served as López's hand-picked successor. Democratic Action (AD), Venezuela's dominant political party after 1958, was formed and gained government recognition under Medina. In 1942, continuing the modernization of Venezuela's social and economic legislation, the government passed the country's first income tax law. A 1943 hydrocarbons law established the first nationalistic petroleum legislation that placed the country's interests first. To counter the growing strength of AD, the government supported the creation of the Venezuelan Democratic Party (PDV). Increased political freedom and discussion spawned other organizations, including a politically powerful and enduring Federation of Chambers of Commerce and Industry (Fedecámaras).

In 1945, this political reformism produced a constitutional change that retained an indirect system for the election of the president, instituted the direct election of congressional deputies, and ended restrictions on Communist activities. An agrarian reform law, a popular and contentious issue in many other Spanish American countries at about the same period, promised to distribute government land to peasants. These reforms and the gradual opening of the political process, including the grant of legal status to the Communist Party (PCV), failed to forestall revolt, and in October 1945, AD and the Patriotic Military Union (a group of young military officers) succeeded in overthrowing the government of Medina.

Although the period 1945–1948, known as the *trienio* junta, offered a dramatic promise for democratic reform, the leaders of the civilian-military council could not maintain their reform movement. The seven-man council led by Rómulo BETANCOURT recognized two major parties, the Democratic Republican Union (URD) in 1945 and the Committee for Political Organization and Independent Election (COPEI), or Social Christian Party, in 1946; these groups played a major role in the subsequent development of Venezuela's democratic tradition. URD came from the perspective of left-of-center reformism and COPEI from a solidly Christian Democratic tradition.

The council approved a new oil company earnings tax designed to gain a true fifty-fifty split between government and private companies in oil profits, and approved a new election law that allowed direct election of the president and of delegates to a national constituent assembly. Along with other reform activities, the oil workers founded a union in 1946 (Fedepetrol), and in the elections for the National Constituent Assembly, Betancourt's party, AD, won a majority. This assembly took over the government from the council and succeeded in suppressing an army revolt. The subsequent elections brought Rómula GALLEGOS, the famous Venezuelan author, to office as the first popularly elected civilian president in Venezuelan history.

Gallegos entered office in 1948 with high intellectual and cultural prestige, and his administration moved quickly to implement a variety of radical reform measures, including an agrarian reform law that would expropriate private property with compensation and an income tax on companies guaranteeing the government 50 percent of the profit on petroleum exports. Military officers, concerned with the radical nature of these reforms, met with Gallegos in November of 1948, and soon thereafter a military coup deposed him, ending the democratic experiment.

For the next decade, Venezuela operated under the control of various military officers or coalitions of officers. For the 1948–1952 period, a junta headed by three officers, Carlos DELGADO CHALBAUD, Marcos PÉREZ JIMÉNEZ, and Luis Felipe Llovera Páez managed the country. They exiled Gallegos, dissolved Democratic Action, suppressed strikes, disbanded the AD-dominated Confederation of Venezuelan Workers (CTV), outlawed the Communist Party, and suspended classes at the Central University of Venezuela. Dissension in the ranks of the military produced the assassination of junta president Delgado Chalbaud in 1950.

Conservative forces organized the Independent Electoral Front (FEI) to support the candidacy of Pérez Jiménez for president. When the elections of 1952 gave the victory to the URD party, Pérez Jiménez voided the results, sent URD leaders into exile, and had the armed forces designate him provisional president. Between 1952 and 1958 Pérez Jiménez served as president, naming his brand of authoritarian rule the New National Ideal. This ideal relied, as did many similar Spanish American authoritarian regimes at that time, on extensive public works to generate employment and heavy doses of political repression to maintain the authority of the government and resist radical or reformist initiatives.

The National Constituent Assembly, recognizing the

inevitable, named Pérez Jiménez president officially for the 1953–1958 term and approved a new constitution. Two new universities appeared, in part to supplant the radical traditions of the closed Central University of Venezuela. The Universidad Católica Andrés Bello and the Universidad Santa María were to have high academic standards and no political activity. In 1956, the Pérez Jiménez government, responding to its foreign supporters, granted new oil concessions after a lapse of just over a decade. The repressive nature of the Pérez Jiménez regime became so extreme that the archbishop of Caracas, Monsignor Rafael Arias Blanco, issued a pastoral letter in 1957 criticizing labor conditions, and a clandestine Movement for National Liberation (MLN) appeared under the leadership of military officers plotting to overthrow the dictator. Pérez Jiménez, turning to a classic tactic of authoritarian rulers, staged a plebiscite on his presidency for the 1958–1963 period. In response, on 23 January 1958, the air force led a rebellion against the dictator supported by popular uprisings and a gen-

eral strike. Pérez Jiménez left the country for exile in Miami.

THE DEMOCRATIC GOVERNMENTS OF AD
AND COPEI: 1958–1994

The fall of Pérez Jiménez in 1958 ended the cycle of authoritarian, military regimes begun with Juan Vicente Gómez in 1908. The fifty years of military-sponsored rule left unresolved the issue of legitimacy in Venezuelan political life. No government since independence had survived economic difficulty or political stress without the support of military force, and many of the changes in political power had come only when the military could be persuaded to intervene. Venezuela's democratic era, which began in 1958, marked a radical departure from its political traditions, less because the military ceased to be important than because the civilian leadership found ways to keep the military focused on the maintenance of civilian government rather than the assumption of political power. This change came only at the cost of a difficult struggle, and while in retrospect we can see that the democratic tradition owes its founding to the ouster of Pérez Jiménez, the stability of this tradition appeared much in doubt during the early years.

In January 1958, a junta of military officers and civilian leaders led by Rear Admiral Wolfgang LARRAZÁBAL assumed control of the country, and Venezuela's political exiles returned to begin reconstituting the political parties that had operated in exile or clandestinely in the country. In the turbulent months of 1958, the principal political parties, AD, COPEI, and URD agreed in the Pact of Punto Fijo to support the winner of the presidential election and, whatever the electoral outcome, to support a coalition government. In the November election, AD and its candidate Rómulo Betancourt won the presidency with a 49 percent plurality. Before Betancourt took office, the government increased its share of petroleum profits to over 60 percent.

The 1959–1964 administration of Rómulo Betancourt produced a dramatic sequence of events that challenged the stability and viability of democratic government and generated a series of social and political reforms that continue to shape Venezuela. Juan Pablo Pérez Alfonso, named minister of mines and hydrocarbons, became the Venezuelan government's chief architect of an international petroleum policy through OPEC in collaboration with other world producers. The government passed a new and more effective agrarian reform law in 1960.

Throughout the Betancourt regime, many factions on the left and right attempted to overthrow the government or eliminate the president. An assassination attempt in June 1960 failed, although Betancourt was wounded and the government charged the Dominican Republic's dictator, General Rafael TRUJILLO, with the attempt and sought sanctions from the Organization of American States (OAS). From the left, the government was challenged by the Movement of the Revolutionary Left (MIR), the first of several fragments from the AD party. The coalition government lost URD's support in November 1960 and the MIR and the Communist Party of Venezuela (PCV) began a campaign against the government.

Within this turmoil, the government moved quickly to push an activist economic agenda with the construction of Ciudad Guayana, a center in eastern Venezuela along the Orinoco designed by an urban planning team made up of United States educators. OPEC met in Caracas, further establishing Venezuela's leading role in this organization. In 1961, Congress took control of the granting of oil concessions away from the presidency.

By 1962, the moderate reformist tendencies of AD appeared too timid to many, and dissidents from various factions moved into opposition, resulting in several armed rebellions, some involving the military. The government suspended the activities of the PCV and the MIR and splinter groups, principal among them the Armed Forces of National Liberation (FALN), began a

guerrilla war against the government to disrupt the 1963 elections. These groups operated in a manner similar to other revolutionary groups in Spanish America, many inspired by the example of the Cuban revolution and all sharing a radical ideology, the rhetoric of which was international but the programs of which addressed local concerns and issues.

Venezuela broke relations with Cuba in 1963 when an arms cache that proved to have originated there was found on a deserted beach. The Venezuelans sought OAS sanctions. In spite of threats of major violence, the 1963 elections took place on schedule, and Raúl LEONI, AD's candidate, became president with 32 percent of the vote.

The Leoni presidency (1964–1969) continued the programs established by the Betancourt regime, although Leoni maintained a somewhat lower political profile. His government struggled to construct a working majority and various coalitions failed to endure throughout his period. The government succeeded in gaining OAS sanctions against Cuba for its sponsorship of revolution in Venezuela. Continued guerrilla activity led to suspensions of constitutional guarantees, but none of the efforts to overthrow the government succeeded. Venezuela became more active in hemispheric affairs with its participation in the LATIN AMERICAN FREE TRADE ASSOCIATION (LAFTA), and was successful in getting an accord with Great Britain that recognized its position on the Guayana boundary dispute (1965). It participated in the Punta del Este conference on Latin American economic integration in 1967, and agreed in the same year to form a regional ANDEAN COMMON MARKET with Colombia, Chile, Ecuador, and Peru.

Indicative of the growing effectiveness of national institutions, in 1968 the supreme Court of Justice convicted the former dictator Marcos Pérez Jiménez of corruption in office. The Leoni years, less violent than his predecessors but still turbulent, ended with the transfer of power to the opposition Christian Democratic Party (COPEI) with the election of Dr. Rafael CALDERA for the 1969–1974 period with 27 percent of the vote.

Caldera, with a weak mandate, had difficulty with his program in the legislature as AD refused to participate in a coalition, creating a stalemate. Caldera lifted the ban on the Communist Party but eliminated the autonomy of the university. OPEC met again in Caracas, and a new income tax law continued increasing the Venezuelan share of oil company profits. Splinter political parties continued to form, including the Movement to Socialism (MAS), which emerged out of the PCV in 1971. Expanding the growing government control of Venezuelan oil, Congress passed a Hydrocarbons Reversion Law in 1971 that prepared for government control of existing concessions when their terms expired. The government nationalized the natural gas industry in the same year. In 1973 Venezuela formally joined the ANDEAN PACT, bringing its economy into closer collaboration with others in its region.

Carlos Andrés PÉREZ, AD's candidate, won the election of 1973 with a 49 percent share, reversing the decline in winning pluralities and representing another peaceful transition of power from one party to another in Venezuela's new democratic tradition. The first Pérez administration (1974–1979) saw a great increase in government intervention in the economy and an increase in economic prosperity, based mostly on the growth of petroleum revenues. Pérez's government nationalized the iron industry in 1974, and the steel and petroleum industries in 1975. This ambitious program of change produced its detractors and in the 1978 elections, Luis HERRERA CAMPÍNS, the COPEI candidate, won the presidency with 46 percent of the vote, yet another peaceful change of governing parties.

Herrera Campíns (1979–1984) struggled with economic difficulties as the oil boom and the extravagant expansion of Venezuela based on the revenues derived from petroleum appeared to come to an end. Although COPEI had strong political support at the beginning of this period, the economic decline of Venezuela brought about by the decline in the world price for petroleum and the general crisis of international debt provided the most serious challenges. Venezuela worked with OPEC to try to freeze the price of petroleum in 1981, but this effort failed and the government found itself with an inflation rate of 8 percent (high for Venezuela) and an unemployment rate of at least 8 percent. The Venezuela oil company became part of a controversy over its management, and the government, in search of new sources of revenue in 1982, launched a program to develop the tar sand belt north of the Orinoco, a long-term project that would require high oil prices to be profitable.

Faced with rumors of an imminent devaluation of the bolívar, Venezuela's reserves declined due to large amounts of capital flight from the country, and the government took control of dollar accounts of state businesses. Inflation in 1982 reached 8.3 percent, and about $5 billion apparently fled the country due to speculation against the bolívar. By 1983 about 70 percent of the exterior debt of Venezuela, calculated at about $30 billion, came due, and in February the government introduced a new system of controls on foreign exchange to stop capital flight, froze prices for sixty days, and stopped paying interest on the national debt.

While the economic news during the Herrera Campíns period went from bad to worse, diplomatic and political activity also continued apace. Congress declared former president Pérez responsible for the inflated price of a refrigerator ship that exceeded its cost by some $10 million, and this conviction served as a symbol of the widespread corruption and profiteering that characterized the Venezuelan boom of the late 1970s. Venezuela lost one of its most prominent founders of the democratic era when Rómulo Betancourt died in 1981 at the age of seventy-three. On the diplomatic scene, the dispute between Venezuela and Guyana revived when the truce between the two countries ended in 1982. Elsewhere in the hemisphere, Venezuela sided, diplomatically and verbally, with Argentina in the FALKLANDS/MALVINAS WAR with Great Britain.

Clearly, the increased economic uncertainty and Venezuela's unaccustomed inflation and currency instability contributed greatly to the defeat of COPEI and the election of Jaime LUSINCHI of AD as president for the 1984–1989 period with a large margin of 57 percent and control of Congress. The Lusinchi regime continued to cope with economic difficulties derived from the decline in the world price of oil and the general international economic difficulties of world trade. It introduced a variety of austerity measures with the hope that growth would restore the country to its traditional stability and prosperity. However, inflation continued to rise and reached an unheard-of 20 percent in the Lusinchi period. The government made an agreement with its principal international bankers on a refinancing plan and resisted the approach of the International Monetary Fund involving major changes in the country's economic structure.

In search of a prosperous past, Venezuelans turned once again to Carlos Andrés Pérez (1990–1994) to help them resolve the Venezuelan version of the Latin American economic readjustment crisis. In his first incarnation, Pérez had spent freely and nationalized liberally, but with the changing times, his policies changed also. Imposing strong austerity measures, his regime promptly triggered a violent street riot for four days beginning on 27 February 1989 that almost toppled his presidency and left many dead and much property destruction. Even the fury of the populace could not deter the necessary readjustments demanded by the world market and especially by the continued low price of oil. Pérez continued carefully but systematically to privatize the economy, returning as much of the public sector as possible into private hands, opened up Venezuelan opportunities to foreign investment, and reduced the high subsidies paid for a wide range of consumer goods.

Although this policy produced considerable improvement in economic statistics (inflation at 80 percent in 1989 fell to around 30 percent by 1994 and the country's growth rate in the early 1990s exceeded most other Latin American countries), too many Venezuelans found themselves worse off than a decade earlier, with over 40 percent of the population living in poverty, perhaps half of these in extreme poverty by some calculations. The continued drumbeat of inflation and unemployment, accompanied by rising resentment against perceived profiteering in high places, including the presidency, led Congress to bring corruption charges against the president. In May, Carlos Andrés Pérez stepped down to answer the charges and Congress appointed noted historian Ramón J. Velásquez to serve out the rest of the term (1993–1994).

THE POST-PETROLEUM ECONOMY, FROM VELÁSQUEZ TO CALDERA

Velásquez, relieved of at least the controversy over corruption, proceeded with the privatization plans, the economic reforms, and especially with the imposition of a value-added tax to address a growing government deficit. Implemented against great public protest and with much controversy and speculation, the tax continued to dominate political and popular discourse throughout the period of the presidential campaigns. With the economy stagnating at an expected growth rate of only 2 or 3 percent, the country struggling with continued capital flight, and inflation sticking stubbornly to around 30 percent, the December 1993 electoral battle focused on issues of the economy but turned on the personal qualities of the candidates. The old political parties of AD and COPEI, both seriously weakened by internal strife and splintering factions, and in AD's case by the fall from grace of former president Carlos Andrés Pérez, ran weaker campaigns against upstart parties and coalitions.

The winning party, led by disaffected COPEI founder and former president Dr. Rafael Caldera, combined a heterogeneous group of left-of-center, Christian Democrats, and conservative or reformist splinter groups into a coalition called the Convergencia. Trading on the magic of Caldera's name, his reputation for personal honesty, and the echoes of the prosperous and dynamic period of his previous presidency, the Convergencia argued for a new approach, different from the Pérez austerity, more just in its distribution of the pain of economic readjustment, and free from the corruption of past regimes. Caldera's coalition won the election with about 30 percent of the vote, with about 40 percent of the electorate abstaining (a new high), ending the era of two-party government that had prevailed from 1959 to 1994.

Although most of the historiography on Venezuela appears in Spanish, a number of English-language publications provide a good introduction. For the large sweep of Venezuelan history see JOHN V. LOMBARDI, *Venezuela: The Search for Order, The Dream of Progress* (1982) and for good general history focused on the twentieth century see JUDITH EWELL, *Venezuela: A Century of Change* (1984) and the chapters by various authors in JOHN D. MARTZ and DAVID J. MYERS, eds., *Venezuela: The Democratic Experience* (1986).

An excellent perspective on the colonial history of Venezuela appears in ROBERT J. FERRY, *The Colonial Elite of Early Caracas: Formation and Crisis, 1567–1767* (1989), while ROBERT L. GILMORE, *Caudillism and Militarism in Venezuela, 1810–1910* (1964) provides a clear look at nineteenth-century themes. No reference to Venezuela's history can ignore the life and times of Simón Bolívar, and AUGUSTO MIJARES, *The Liberator* (1983), provides a Venezuelan perspective on that great independence hero.

Oil and politics dominate the recent history of Venezuela. On petroleum see FRANKLIN TUGWELL, *The Politics of Oil in Venezuela* (1975), LAURA RANDALL, *The Political Economy of Venezuelan Oil* (1987), and ANIBAL R. MARTINEZ, *Venezuelan Oil* (1989), and on the economy see ROBERT LORING ALLEN, *Venezuelan Economic Development: a Politico-Economic Analysis* (1977). ENRIQUE A. BALOYRA and JOHN D. MARTZ, *Political Attitudes in Venezuela* (1979), and DANIEL H. LEVINE, *Conflict and Political Change in Venezuela* (1973) provide a broader perspective.

A glimpse into the two major democratic political parties and the political life of their leaders is in ROBERT J. ALEXANDER, *Rómulo Betancourt and the Transformation of Venezuela* (1982), and DONALD L. HERMAN, *Christian Democracy in Venezuela* (1980). Given the significance of the military in Venezuela's affairs from Gómez on, WINFIELD J. BURGGRAAFF, *The Venezuelan Armed Forces in Politics, 1935–1959* (1972) offers a sound analysis. The often countervailing forces of labor and peasants appear in STEVE ELLNER, *Organized Labor in Venezuela, 1958–1991* (1993), and JOHN DUNCAN POWELL, *The Political Mobilization of the Venezuelan Peasant* (1971).

Now dated but still useful is Lombardi et al., *Venezuelan History: A Comprehensive Working Bibliography* (1977). The best general source on all topics in Venezuelan history remains MANUEL PÉREZ VILA, ed., a *Diccionario de historia de Venezuela* (1988), a multi-authored three-volume encyclopedia that also includes excellent bibliographical notes.

JOHN V. LOMBARDI

See also **Pan-American Conferences.**

VENEZUELA: CONGRESSES OF 1811, 1830, AND 1864, the congresses in which the principal political transformations of nineteenth-century Venezuela occurred. Venezuela's first Constituent Congress, convened in 1811, declared independence on 5 July and went on to ratify the first constitution of a Latin American republic. The Congress was comprised of representatives from the seven provinces that adhered to the 19 April 1810 pronouncement of the *cabildo* of Caracas, which marked the beginning of Venezuela's independence movement. These representatives set up the chief governing authority of the republic. They elected men to the executive and judiciary; they also normalized and organized all the judicial, political, fiscal, and economic operating mechanisms of the newly established republic. The Congress was the scene of the most important debates of the era. Because of the devastating March 1812 earthquake, and the social crisis it provoked, the Congress approved the concession of extraordinary powers to the executive and effectively suspended its own activities. The fall of the republic and the flare-up of war prevented any further sessions from taking place.

The Constituent Congress of Venezuela convened in Valencia from 6 May to 14 October 1830 to sanction the dissolution of GRAN COLOMBIA and the establishment of Venezuela as an independent republic. Its members ratified a constitution organizing the republic under a central-federal system that lasted twenty-seven years. Under the electoral system they established, eligibility for office was limited and the right to vote was based on economic factors such as landownership and income level. Elections were held on 25 March 1831, and José

Antonio PÁEZ was proclaimed president. The new republic's chief executive began to fix the bases of the nation along liberal lines.

After the FEDERAL WAR (1859–1863), a Constituent Congress met from December 1863 to April 1864. It ratified the 1864 Constitution, which established a federal system that it technically maintained into the 1990s. The Congress of 1864 also approved an electoral system of universal male suffrage, administrative decentralization, and provincial autonomy. The name "Republic of Venezuela" was replaced by the name "United States of Venezuela."

PABLO RUGGERI PARRA, *Historia política y constitucional de Venezuela*, 2 vols. (1949); JOSÉ GIL FORTOUL, *Historia constitucional de Venezuela*, 4th ed., 3 vols. (1953–1954); CONGRESO CONSTITUYENTE 1930, VENEZUELA, *Actas del Congreso Constituyente de 1830*, 3 vols. (1979–1982); and MANUEL PÉREZ VILA, ed., *Actas de los congresos del ciclo Bolivariano: Congreso Constituyente de 1811–1812*, 2 vols. (1983).

INÉS QUINTERO

VENEZUELA: CONSTITUTIONS As of the early 1990s, Venezuela has had twenty-six constitutions since 1811, the most recent promulgated in 1961. Why this apparent surfeit of constitutions for a country that was dominated by caudillos and military elites throughout much of its independent history? Owing to chronic instability, virtually every new regime sought to declare its independence from predecessor regimes by writing a new constitution. In the Spanish American tradition, instead of adding amendments or changing specific provisions, an entirely new constitution was enacted, even if very little of substance was actually changed. In the nineteenth century two of the main changes made dealt with, first, the balance between centralism and federalism and, second, expansion or retraction of the suffrage. One feature of Venezuela's constitutional history has remained constant, however: Venezuelan government is essentially presidentialist. Even the most recent and most democratic constitution—that of 1961—provides for a powerful chief executive who can assume extraordinary powers.

The first constitution of the new Republic of Gran Colombia, inspired by the U.S. Constitution and the French Declaration of the Rights of Man, was written in 1811 and clearly reflects the thinking of an educated oligarchy. It provided for a weak central government and placed literacy requirements on suffrage and property-holding requirements on officeholding. The Angostura Constitution of 1819, reflecting the reaction against excessive federalism, strengthened the power of the executive and central authority. In 1830, after breaking away from Gran Colombia, Venezuela promulgated its own constitution, which reflected a compromise between unitary and federalist government. Between 1830 and 1900 eight constitutions were written, again reflect-

ing slight changes in the balance of power between the federal government and the states.

Venezuela's symbolic reverence for federalism is seen most strikingly in the 1864 Constitution, which expressed an extreme form of regionalism and localism. This exaggerated federalism was counteracted in 1881, when a constitution enacted by the dictator Antonio GUZMÁN BLANCO reduced the number of states from twenty to nine in order to shrink the number of powerful state caudillos who aspired to national power. It also replaced direct suffrage with indirect suffrage. In 1909 the twenty states were restored and have remained until the present day.

Under the dictatorship of General Juan Vicente GÓMEZ (1908–1935), seven constitutions were written, and, like so many previous constitutions, they were honored more in the breach than in the observance. Indeed, student wags referred to the course in constitutional law at the Central University as mythology. One interesting aspect of Gómez's later constitutions—after oil was discovered—was a move from economic liberalism toward the limitation of the right to private property in order to conserve natural resources.

The overthrow of General Gómez led to a politically more liberal regime, which was reflected in the Constitution of 1936. It shortened the presidential term from seven to five years, guaranteed certain individual rights, and made cabinet ministers responsible to Congress. However, it left intact the indirect election of the president and outlawed communism. The 1947 Constitution, which was in effect only briefly, was drafted by a constituent assembly controlled by the social democratic Democratic Action (Acción Democrática). The most politically and socially liberal constitution in Venezuela's history up to that time, it provided for the direct and secret vote for president and Congress, and explicitly guaranteed the rights of workers and peasants.

After ten years of military dictatorship (1948–1958), the architects of the new democratic system framed a constitution that called for a strong central government but expressed due concern for individual liberties and for social justice. The Constitution of 1961, promulgated during the presidential term of Rómulo BETANCOURT, was designed not only to ensure popular democratic government but also to create a modern welfare state that would seek a more equitable distribution of the national wealth. These principles are reflected in lengthy sections that enumerate a host of political, economic, and social rights. The Constitution of 1961 provides for twenty states, two federal territories, and a federal district. All governors are appointed by the president, an indication that a country that still pays lip service to federalism is in reality a centralist republic. Although it specifies three independent and equal branches of government, numerous provisions underscore the powerful role of the president and the executive branch. They authorize the president to declare a state of emergency and to suspend or curtail certain constitutional guarantees in the wake of internal disorder or external conflict. The president, however, cannot succeed himself and cannot run as a candidate for ten years after he leaves office. The document provides for a bicameral Congress and a Supreme Court whose justices are elected by Congress for nine-year terms.

In practice, the 1961 Constitution—the longest lived of any Venezuelan constitution—generally worked well for many years. But the deterioration in the functioning of the post-1958 democratic system during the 1980s and early 1990s has led to calls for constitutional reform.

RUSSELL H. FITZGIBBON, ed., *The Constitutions of the Americas* (1948); AMERICAN UNIVERSITY, FOREIGN AREAS STUDY DIVISION, *Area Handbook of Venezuela* (1964); JOSÉ GIL FORTOUL, *Historia constitucional de Venezuela*, 3 vols. 5th ed. (1967); GERALD E. FITZGERALD, ed., *The Constitutions of Latin America* (1968); R. LYNN KELLEY, "Venezuelan Constitutional Forms and Realities," in John D. Martz and David J. Myers, eds., *Venezuela: The Democratic Experience* (1977), pp. 27–46.

WINFIELD J. BURGGRAAFF

VENEZUELA: IMMIGRATION. Upon establishing an independent nation in 1830, Venezuelans instituted a policy of populating their nation with European immigrants. Immigration laws of 1831, 1837, and 1840 authorized the national government to subsidize the relocation of European agricultural workers to Venezuela. But despite efforts to recruit immigrants throughout Europe, few came. Between 1832 and 1845, only 12,610 persons immigrated to Venezuela. The majority of these came from the Canary Islands, a traditional source of Venezuelan immigrants.

During the second half of the nineteenth century, Venezuelan governments continued to try, without success, to attract white European immigrants. In part, they desired laborers for the rural areas, but increasingly they sought immigrants to "whiten" the multiracial populace. The desire to whiten the population not only led to an increased demand for European immigrants but also contributed to legislation that excluded nonwhites from immigrating to Venezuela. In 1855, the National Congress defeated a proposal to pay contractors to bring Chinese workers to Venezuela. On 20 July 1891, a new immigration code prohibited the immigration of blacks and Asians.

The new code failed to achieve its desired results for two reasons. First, whites did not flock to Venezuela. Second, blacks from the Antilles did come, either illegally or by obtaining temporary work permits. By 1898, some 5,000 to 7,000 blacks had entered the Guayana and Orinoco regions from nearby Trinidad and British Guiana. East Indians fled to eastern Venezuela to escape from indentured servitude in nearby Trinidad.

During the administration of Juan Vicente GÓMEZ (1908–1935), attempts to encourage massive immigration from Europe met with little success. Corruption and poor economic conditions in Venezuela before the

petroleum boom meant that the opportunities for social mobility found in other countries, such as the United States, Argentina, and Brazil, did not exist. Gómez further complicated matters by his distrust of foreigners, especially non-Catholic, non-Spanish-speaking individuals, whose culture and intentions he did not understand. His xenophobia, and that of his followers, offset any immigration his administration sponsored.

On 15 September 1938, a presidential decree established the Technical Institute of Immigration and Colonization as a department of the Ministry of Agriculture and Livestock. Its primary objectives included implementation of a rural development program, the settlement of immigrants in rural districts, and the "ethnic improvement of the country's population."

A large influx of immigrants began only after World War II. Between 1941 and 1961, immigration increased markedly; the foreign-born population grew from 49,928 to 526,188. Since the 1940s, Colombians accounted for the largest percentage of foreign population, although between 1950 and 1961 Spaniards and Italians made up the largest portion of immigrants. The latter two groups moved mostly to urban centers, where they had considerable success as merchants, contractors, and business leaders.

In 1966 the restrictions on nonwhite immigration ended, but by that time whites dominated the economy. As in other parts of Latin America, Spanish and Italian immigrants and their descendants controlled important sectors of the economy, especially the construction industries, export-import enterprises, and small businesses.

European immigration has slowed since the 1960s. However, population movements from Chile, Peru, and Ecuador, as well as from Santo Domingo and Colombia, have increased as illegal aliens have flocked to Venezuela.

ELIZABETH YABOUR DE CALDERA, *La población de Venezuela: Un análisis demográfico* (1967); CHEN-YI CHEN and MICHEL PICOUET, *Dinámica de la población: Caso de Venezuela* (1979); SUSAN BERGLUND-THOMPSON, "The 'Musiues' in Venezuela: Immigration Goals and Reality, 1936–1961" (Ph.D. diss., University of Massachusetts, 1980); SUSAN BERGLUND, "Las bases sociales y económicas de las leyes de inmigración venezolanas: 1831–1935," in *Boletín de la Academia Nacional de la Historia* 64, no. 260 (1982): 951–962, and ". . . Y los ultimos serán los primeros. La inmigración masiva en Venezuela, 1945–1961," in *Población y mano de obra en América Latina*, compiled by Nicolás Sánchez Albornoz (1985); ERMILA TROCONIS DE VERACOECHEA, *El proceso de la inmigración en Venezuela* (1986); JUAN ALMECIJA B., "El crecimiento demográfico venezolano, 1936–1971," in *Boletín de la Academia Nacional de la Historia* 71, no. 281 (1988): 131–148.

WINTHROP R. WRIGHT

See also **Immigration.**

VENEZUELA: LAS REFORMAS REVOLUTION, a Venezuelan militarist movement in 1835 against the government of Dr. José María VARGAS (1835–1836). The consensus attained with the creation of the republic in 1830 began to disintegrate as a result of political tensions dividing the ruling elite. With the privileges they had won during the years of the War for Independence progressively waning, the members of the military viewed the candidacy of Santiago MARIÑO in the elections of 1834 with the hope of regaining their power. Mariño's defeat at the polls and the victory of Vargas caused further political disintegration, which resulted in the armed uprising of an important group of military men. All active members of the Liberating Army, these included Santiago Mariño, Pedro Briceño Méndez, Diego Ibarra, and Pedro Carujo, among many others.

The revolution broke out in Maracaibo and Caracas in June and July 1835. The revolutionaries drove Vargas from power in July and proposed the return to military rule, the establishment of a federal system, the installation of Catholicism as the state religion, and the taking over of public offices by men who had made independence possible. However, the movement was suffocated militarily by José Antonio PÁEZ, and its instigators were expelled from the country. Vargas returned as president in August 1835.

CARACCIOLO PARRA-PÉREZ, *Mariño y las guerras civiles*, 3 vols. (1958–1960); ROBERT L. GILMORE, *Caudillism and Militarism in Venezuela, 1810–1910* (1964); CATALINA BANKO, *Poder político y conflictos sociales en la República Oligárquica, 1830–1848* (1986); and MANUEL PÉREZ VILA, *La Revolución de las Reformas* (1984).

INÉS QUINTERO

VENEZUELA: ORGANIZATIONS

Economic Society of the Friends of the Country
Sociedad Económica de Amigos del País

The Economic Society of the Friends of the Country was an institution to promote the economic and educational progress of Venezuelan society. The society was inspired by similar organizations that arose in Europe in the middle of the eighteenth century. It was created by the Organic Law of Public Education of 18 March 1826 and finally organized in 1829. It consisted of a representative group of notables from diverse professions and of various political orientations. Their object was to diagnose Venezuelan society and take steps that would promote progress in the recently formed republic.

The society's primary areas of concern were agriculture, commerce, the arts and crafts, and public instruction. It created a commission to examine each of these areas. The society put out documents expressing views about the organization of the state, judicial codes, and economic liberalism. It designed various studies gauging the problems and deficiencies in Venezuela and often laid out the solutions that its members felt should be implemented. The society engaged in intensive activities from its beginnings in 1829, and many of them are recorded in the periodical published by the institution

itself, *Memorias de la Sociedad Económica de Amigos del País*. From the outbreak of LAS REFORMAS REVOLUTION in 1835, it was in a partially dismantled state until its final extinction in 1847.

RAMÓN HERNÁNDEZ RON, *La Sociedad Económica de Amigos del País* (1943); and SOCIEDAD ECONÓMICA DE AMIGOS DEL PAÍS, CARACAS, *Memorias y estudios, 1829–1839*, 2 vols. (1958).

INÉS QUINTERO

Federation of Students of Venezuela
Federacíon de Estudiantes de Venezuela—FEV

The Federacíon de Estudiantes was a Venezuelan student organization opposed to the government of Juan Vicente GÓMEZ (1908–1929, 1931–1935). The General Association of Students was established in 1909, and on various occasions it participated in protests against the government. As a result the university was closed several times and the unity among its academicians destroyed. When the university reopened in 1925, the General Association of Students was reborn with the new name Federation of Students of Venezuela (Federación de Estudiantes de Venezuela—FEV).

In 1928, FEV sponsored the week of the student, a festival that turned into an antigovernment demonstration. As a result FEV organizers were imprisoned or exiled but their actions had gained great popularity and became Venezuela's first urban mass movement. Exiled FEV leaders formed several political parties, two of which had lasting significance—the Partido Revolucionario Venezolano (PRV) and the Agrupación Revolucionaria de Izquierda (ARDI). The FEV was dissolved until 1935, but with the death of Gómez in that year, it reappeared as one of the organizations leading the protests of 1936.

E. LÓPEZ CONTRERAS, *Proceso político social, 1928–1936* (1955); MARÍA DE LOURDES ACEDO DE SUCRE and CARMEN MARGARITA NONES MENDOZA, *La generación venezolana de 1928* (1967); JOAQUÍN GABALDÓN MÁRQUEZ, *Memoria y cuento de la generación del vientiocho* (1978); ARTURO SOSA and ELOI LEGRAND, *Del garibaldismo estudiantil a la izquierda criolla: Los orígenes marxistas del proyecto de A.D. (1928–1935)* (1981).

INÉS QUINTERO

Patriotic Society of Caracas
Sociedad Patriótica de Caracas

The Patriotic Society of Caracas was a Venezuelan pro-independence organization. After the *cabildo* of Caracas ousted the Spanish governor on 19 April 1810 and later formed the Junta Conservadora de los Derechos de Fernando VII, the Patriotic Society was formed in Caracas the following August with the purpose of propagandizing on behalf of the emancipation process. The society was inspired by similar clubs in revolutionary France. Francisco de MIRANDA and Simón BOLÍVAR took the lead in organizing and promoting it. Antonio Muñoz

Tebar, Vicente Salias, Francisco Espejo, Miguel Peña, and others also participated. Its fundamental objective was to achieve independence and the establishment of a democratic republic in Venezuela. Its voice was the periodical *El Patriota Venezolano*.

The society attained a high degree of popularity in the first half of 1811 due to the radical positions its members expressed in favor of declaring independence once and for all in Venezuela. Branches were formed in Valencia, Puerto Cabello, Barcelona, and Barinas. With the fall of the First Republic in 1812, the society dissolved and was never re-formed.

ANDRÉS F. PONTE, *La Revolución de Caracas y sus próceres* (1960); and P. MICHAEL MC KINLEY, *Pre-Revolutionary Caracas: Politics, Economy, and Society, 1777–1811* (1985).

INÉS QUINTERO

VENEZUELA: POLITICAL PARTIES

Communist Party
Partido Comunista de Venezuela

Communist ideas began to be heard in Venezuela during the administration of Juan Vicente GÓMEZ. In 1926 a group from the opposition, including Gustavo MACHADO and Salvador de la Plaza, organized in Mexico the Communist-oriented Venezuelan Revolutionary Party. Later, revolutionary ideas gained popularity among those sent to prison as a result of the antigovernment student activity of 1928. It was not until 1 May 1931, however, that the first manifesto of the Communist Party was circulated, and that year is believed to be the year the Venezuelan section of the Communist International was founded. Despite disagreements and internal factionalism, it survived as an illegal party until 1941, when the government of Isaías MEDINA ANGARITA legalized it. After the revolution of 18 October 1945, the party participated in Venezuelan elections, winning 3.6 percent of the vote for a constituent assembly in 1946. It was outlawed again by the military government of Marcos PÉREZ JIMÉNEZ in 1950 but was legalized once again in 1958, when democracy was reinstated.

Inspired by the guerrilla movements developing in Latin America during the 1960s, the party promoted armed struggle against the government of Rómulo BETANCOURT. With the guerrillas defeated, the party resumed legal operations and went through various splits, the most important of these involving the rise of the Movement to Socialism in 1973. Twenty years later it remained a small minority party, winning about 1 percent of the vote. Its program supported the installation of a socialist system based on the principles of Marxism and the class struggle.

JUAN BAUTISTA FUENMAYOR, *1928–1948: Veinte años de política* (1968); ROBERT J. ALEXANDER, *The Communist Party of Venezuela* (1969); FERNANDO KEY SÁNCHEZ, *Fundación de Partido Comunista de Venezuela*, 2d ed. (1984); and MANUEL CABALLERO, *Entre Gó-*

mez y Stalin: La sección venezolana de la Internacional Comunista, 2d ed. (1989).

INÉS QUINTERO

Conservative Party
Partido Conservador

The Conservative Party was founded in the 1840s as the pro-government party during the administration of José Antonio PÁEZ. With the establishment of the republic in 1830, the elite forged a consensus concerning the political system to be adopted for Venezuela. Nevertheless, during the next five years disagreements arose, resulting in a split into two opposing political factions competing for power.

The group in power and centered around Páez came to be called the Conservative Party by the rival faction, the Liberals, and this is the name that has been used in Venezuelan historiography. Its composition was diverse, consisting of businessmen, landowners, and intellectuals, but the party's economic policies tended primarily to favor the business sector. The Conservatives remained dominant until 1847, when they were displaced as a result of the political turnabout undertaken by President José Tadeo MONAGAS. They took part in his overthrow in 1858 and confronted the Liberals during the FEDERAL WAR (1859–1863). The Conservatives subsequently lost political influence, however, and the period of Liberal dominance began. The Conservative Party never returned to office.

ROBERT L. GILMORE, *Caudillism and Militarism in Venezuela, 1810–1910* (1964); CATALINA BANKO, *Poder político y conflictos sociales en la República Oligárquica, 1830–1848* (1986); and ELÍAS PINO ITURRIETA, *El pensamiento conservador venezolano del siglo XIX: Antología* (1992).

INÉS QUINTERO

Democratic Action
Acción Democrática—AD

Democratic Action is one of Venezuela's two major political parties and an important force in building and strengthening the modern democratic system. Its origins date back to the so-called Generation of '28, when a group of university students organized massive protests against the long-standing dictatorship of Juan Vicente GÓMEZ. Driven into exile, these young activists returned in 1936 following Gómez's death and founded the Venezuelan Organization (ORVE). They continued the struggle for democratic pluralism and on 13 September 1941 officially established AD. The new party gradually built grass-roots support while fighting for direct elections.

Faced with official barriers to competitive elections, AD, together with junior military officers, launched a successful uprising on 18 October 1945. During the next three years AD introduced far-reaching reforms, first under the provisional presidency of Rómulo BETAN-COURT and then under the elected administration of Rómulo GALLEGOS, an eminent writer and educator. Gallegos was toppled by the military in late 1948. For the next decade AD was harassed and persecuted by the dictatorship of Marcos PÉREZ JIMÉNEZ. In 1958, following an uprising that ousted the dictatorship, AD collaborated with rival parties to create the democracy that has endured ever since.

Rómulo Betancourt was elected to a five-year term and survived despite assassination attempts from the Right and the guerrilla insurgency of Castroites. He was succeeded in 1964 by his fellow *adeco* (member of Acción Democrática) Raúl LEONI. Five years later AD lost the presidency to Rafael CALDERA of the Social Christian COPEI Party as a result of a debilitating party division. In 1974, AD recaptured power with the victory of Carlos Andrés PÉREZ, a onetime protégé of Betancourt. The party lost to COPEI in 1979, regained the presidency with Jaime LUSINCHI in 1984, and retained it in 1989 in the person of Pérez. He was the first modern president to win a second term after the constitutionally mandated two terms out of office.

Along with COPEI, AD has dominated national politics and has maintained an extensive organizational structure. Ideologically it is a member of the Socialist International and is regarded as the most influential Latin American member. Pérez has been a recognized leader of democratic forces in the Americas, and AD intends to maintain its prominence. At the same time, the party works to retain its organizational vigor, which is reflected in part by control over the national labor movement. The moderate reformism of AD, combined with permanent allegiance from many citizens, has assured its continuing importance in the formulation and implementation of public policy in contemporary Venezuela.

ROBERT J. ALEXANDER, *The Venezuelan Democratic Revolution* (1964); JOHN D. MARTZ, *Acción Democrática: Evolution of a Modern Political Party in Venezuela* (1966); RÓMULO BETANCOURT, *Venezuela: Oil and Politics*, translated by Everett Baumann (1979); ROBERT J. ALEXANDER, *Rómulo Betancourt and the Transformation of Venezuela* (1982); DAVID J. MYERS, "The Venezuelan Party System: Regime Maintenance Under Stress," in *Venezuela: The Democratic Experience*, edited by John D. Martz and David J. Myers, rev. ed. (1986); JOHN D. MARTZ, "Venezuela," in *Latin America and Caribbean Contemporary Record*, vol. 6, edited by Abraham F. Lowenthal (1989).

JOHN D. MARTZ

Liberal Party
Partido Liberal

The Liberal Party arose in Venezuela in 1840 to oppose the government of José Antonio PÁEZ. Its formation resulted from the breakup of the consensus among the ruling elite that had been the foundation for the republic's establishment in 1830.

In the pages of *El Venezolano*, the Liberal Party's mouthpiece, an intense campaign was waged in defense of political pluralism, freedom of the press, and the existence of parties as a mechanism for settling political differences. In the area of economics, party members expressed fierce opposition to the Conservative government's measures because they favored the business sector. Like the Conservative Party, the Liberal Party was composed of groups with diverse orientations and interests; however, its stress was upon promoting agriculture and defending the interests of landowners.

The Liberals initially backed the first government of José Tadeo MONAGAS, then later participated in the March Revolution of 1858, in which they allied with the Conservatives in removing Monagas from power. Seeing their political participation limited under the government that arose out of this revolution, the Liberals distanced themselves from the regime. They mounted a new revolution which quickly spread throughout the country and initiated the FEDERAL WAR (1859–1863).

During the period of great political instability after the war, the Liberals came to power. Finally in 1870, with the triumph of the April Revolution led by Antonio GUZMÁN BLANCO, the period of Liberal Party dominance, which would last until the end of the century, began. By the end of Cipriano CASTRO's regime in 1908, however, the party was virtually defunct.

ELÍAS PINO ITURRIETA, *Las ideas de los primeros venezolanos* (1987); and INÉS QUINTERO, *Pensamiento liberal del siglo XIX: Antología* (1992).

INÉS QUINTERO

Movement to Socialism
Movimiento al Socialismo—MAS

At a session of the central committee of the Venezuelan Communist Party in 1969, there arose a series of differences that led in 1970 to the split of twenty-two of its members who left to form the MAS on 19 January 1971. The dissidents sought to promote a nondogmatic Marxism. They did not desire unconditional alignment with the Soviet Union, especially after the 1968 Soviet invasion of Czechoslovakia. They also rejected the idea that socialism could be imported mechanically from one country to another, since each country has its own experiences and reality. The MAS criticized the bureaucratization, excessive centralism, and monolithic nature of the Communist Party, which they felt impeded debate and the exercise of democracy. The program of the MAS postulated the construction of a democracy that was socialist, pluralist, participatory, and self-managing. It called for the elimination of state or political monopolies, a substantial improvement in the living conditions of Venezuelans, and reforms of the education and electoral systems, all under the slogan of attaining "Venezuelan socialism."

The creation of the MAS represented an important

attempt at renovating Venezuelan political thought. Since its foundation, it has participated in all electoral processes, establishing itself as the third strongest political force in the country. Nevertheless, its electoral representation has never surpassed 10 percent. It has managed to maintain significant representation in the national Congress, municipal councils, and state legislatures, but does not appear to be a viable contender for power.

No work detailing the political course of the MAS has been published. The following books, written by participants in the process, provide information on the creation and evolution of the party. TEODORO PETKOFF, ¿Socialismo para Venezuela? (1970); ELEAZAR DÍAZ RANGEL, ¿Cómo se dividió el PCV? (1971); TEODORO PETKOFF, Proceso a la izquierda (1976); MOISÉS MOLEIRO, La izquierda y su proceso (1977); POMPEYO MÁRQUEZ, Una polémica necesaria (1978); JOSÉ VICENTE RANGEL, Venezuela y Socialismo (1978). See also STEVE ELLNER, Venezuela's Movimiento al Socialismo: From Guerrilla Defeat to Innovative Politics (1988).

INÉS QUINTERO

Social Christian COPEI Party
Partido Social Cristiano COPEI
COPEI Party

The Committee for the Organization of Independent Electoral Politics (Comité de Organización Política Electoral Independiente—COPEI) was established after World War II as a Christian Democratic political party. Founded in 1946, COPEI, together with Acción Democrática (AD), was one of the two principal political parties in Venezuela in the second half of the twentieth century.

In 1934 the Christian Democratic movement was established internationally at the Congress of Catholic Youth in Rome. The young Venezuelan Rafael CALDERA RODRÍGUEZ, one of COPEI's founders, participated in this event. Back home, he and other Catholic young people later founded the National Student Union (UNE) in 1936, separating themselves from the Federation of Venezuelan Students, which defended the process of educational secularization. Later, the UNE founded the Electoral Action organization in order to participate in the municipal elections of 1938. In 1942 this organization merged with the Nationalist Action Movement and called itself Acción Nacional (National Action), finally taking the name by which it is still known, COPEI, in 1946.

Over the next half century, the party participated in every national electoral process in Venezuela and achieved steady growth. After the overthrow of the Marcos PÉREZ JIMÉNEZ regime in 1958, the party formed an alliance with the Democratic Action Party and the Democratic Republican Union in order to bring about a government of national unity that would guarantee the preservation of democracy. At that time it had about 15 percent of the vote. In 1968 Caldera Rodríguez, the party's principal national figure, won the presidential elec-

tions and COPEI achieved power for the first time, significantly increasing its share of the vote. In 1978 the party scored another victory with the election of its candidate, Dr. Luis HERRERA CAMPINS, as president of the republic. In the mid-1990s COPEI remained the second national party. The party had some triumphs in regional elections; several state governors were elected from its ranks; and in the mid-1990s it was represented significantly—although it was not the majority party—in Congress.

With a Christian socialist orientation, the party's basic doctrines follow the general principles of the Christian Democratic International, to which it belonged. Its members defended the democratic system, civil and political liberties, a program of social benefits, individual freedoms, and the incentive of private property.

RAFAEL CALDERA, Especificidad de la democracia cristiana Rafael Caldera, 2d ed. (1973); JOSÉ ELÍAS RIERA OVIEDO, Los socialcristianos en Venezuela (1977); DONALD HERMAN, Christian Democracy in Venezuela (1980); and GUILLERMO LUQUE, De la Acción Católica al Partido Copei, 1933–1946 (1986).

INÉS QUINTERO

VENEZUELA: REVOLUTIONARY MOVEMENTS

Armed Forces of National Liberation
Fuerzas Armadas de liberación
Nacional—FALN

The FALN was a pro-Cuban Marxist-Leninist guerrilla army that began operations in Venezuela in 1962. Its membership included groups opposed to the government of President Rómulo BETANCOURT: dissident military officers, radical members of the Venezuelan Communist Party, and leaders of the Movement of the Revolutionary Left (Movimiento de Izquierda Revolucionaria—MIR), a breakaway splinter faction of Betancourt's ruling Democratic Action Party (Acción Democrática—AD).

Following his election in 1958, Betancourt faced bitter opposition from several factions. By 1960, some leftists had organized the MIR. Two years later, radicals from the Communist Party, such as Douglas Bravo and Teodoro Petkoff, set up the FALN to undertake a Cuban-inspired struggle against the legitimate Venezuelan government. At that time, the leaders of the newly founded FALN advocated a long, campesino war against the government rather than a coup. They were joined in 1962 by Américo Martín and by the reactionary Lieutenant Colonel Juan de Díos Moncada Vidal, who became one of the FALN's guerrilla commanders.

During 1962, the FALN launched an urban and rural guerrilla war. The following year, it tried to disrupt the elections to force a military coup. But it did not succeed, and some 90 percent of the electorate went to the polls.

On assuming office in 1964, Raúl LEONI declared a state of emergency. He invoked censorship, closed schools, arrested demonstrators, lifted congressional immunity, and suspended the writ of habeas corpus. He rounded up leaders of the Communist Party, including members of the National Congress, and isolated the FALN from its urban supporters. A strong military campaign further reduced guerrilla forces. Leoni also used the police to eliminate FALN sympathizers.

Forced to the countryside, the FALN fought in isolated districts. It never mounted a popular war there, however; as one woman later wrote of her life as a guerrilla, "nothing has occurred here." Without popular support the FALN faltered. Even continued assistance and encouragement from Cuba could not keep the FALN struggle alive.

During its existence, the FALN attracted women to its ranks. One, Arelia Laya, served as a commander in Lara. Students also joined the FALN as "weekend warriors," but their sporadic involvement proved ineffectual and their participation steadily declined.

By 1967, the Communist Party withdrew its support of the FALN. In 1968, newly elected President Rafael CALDERA offered amnesty to any guerrilla who voluntarily surrendered. Most of the FALN leaders accepted this offer and, like Martín and Petkoff, turned their attention to legitimate political movements. Bravo and some MIR factions continued the struggle for a few more years.

RICHARD GOTT, *Guerrilla Movements in Latin America* (1971); ANGELA ZAGO, *Aquí no ha pasado nada* (1972); DAVID BLANK, *Politics in Venezuela* (1973); TEODORO PETKOFF, *Razón pasión del socialismo: El tema socialista en Venezuela* (1973); RAYMOND ESTEP, *Guerrilla Warfare in Latin America, 1963–1975* (1975); ALFREDO PEÑA, *Conversaciones con Américo Martín* (1978) and *Conversaciones con Douglas Bravo* (1978); JUDITH EWELL, *Venezuela: A Century of Change* (1984).

WINTHROP R. WRIGHT

VERA CRUZ, ALONSO DE LA (also Veracruz or Gutiérrez de Veracruz; *b.* ca. 1507; *d.* 1584), Augustinian friar and distinguished philosopher, theologian, and educator in early colonial Mexico. Born in Caspueñas, Toledo, Spain, he studied grammar, literature, and rhetoric at the University of Alcalá. Afterward he pursued philosophy and theology at the University of Salamanca, where he was a pupil of the famous Dominican Francisco de Vitoria. He traveled to Mexico in 1536 at the invitation of Francisco de la Cruz and took the Augustinian habit in 1537. The long, varied list of Vera Cruz's accomplishments includes serving as missionary to the Tarasacan Indians, whose language he mastered; teaching in the Augustinian *colegio* in Michoacán, where he established one of the earliest New World libraries; founding the monasteries of Cuitzeo, Yuririapúndaro, Cupándaro, and Charo in Michoacán; and founding the College of San Pablo in Mexico City in 1575 and endowing it with a fine collection of books that he had transported from Spain in sixty boxes. In 1553, Vera Cruz was appointed first rector and professor of Scripture and Thomistic theology at the newly established University of Mexico. A preeminent orator and classic writer in the Spanish language, Vera Cruz was an eloquent voice of Scholastic theology in Mexico and has been called the "father of Mexican philosophy." He died in Mexico City.

ARTHUR ENNIS, *Fray Alonso de la Vera Cruz, O.S.A. (1507–1584): A Study of His Life and His Contribution to the Religious and Intellectual Affairs of Early Mexico* (1957); ERNEST J. BURRUS, ed., *The Writings of Alonso de la Vera Cruz*, 5 vols. (1967–1975); O. CARLOS STOETZER, *The Scholastic Roots of the Spanish American Revolution* (1979).

J. DAVID DRESSING

VERACRUZ (CITY). The principal seaport of Mexico is located 265 miles southeast of Mexico City on the Gulf Coast. This city has been Mexico's major center of foreign commerce and primary source of commercial revenue since the Spanish conquest.

On Good Friday, 22 April 1519, Hernán CORTÉS landed his Spanish expedition on the small island of SAN JUAN DE ULÚA, near the present city of Veracruz, and established the first base of operations for his conquest of the Aztec civilization. The Spaniards found the coastal plain inhabited by Totonac Indians, who had established their administrative center at Zempoala, 25 miles to the north. The first settlement, which Cortés named Villa Rica de la Vera Cruz, was established several miles to the north, where ships could anchor more easily. The Spanish conquistador immediately appointed town councilmen, who in turn named him captain of the expedition with full military authority. Veracruz thus became the first municipality in the Spanish colony of NEW SPAIN (Mexico).

In 1599 the Spanish viceroy ordered the settlement of Veracruz to be moved next to the port itself so the storehouses and treasury would be adjacent to the ships. During the colonial period Veracruz flourished as the only official Gulf port of New Spain and the major link between the colony and Cádiz (Spain). Its customhouses provided the primary source of revenue for colonial government. Needless to say, its wealth attracted numerous foreign privateers. John HAWKINS and Sir Francis DRAKE plundered the town in 1568, while the French corsairs left the town, with its 6,000 inhabitants, in ruins in 1683. These foreign incursions prompted the Spaniards to build massive fortifications, which culminated with the erection of the Fortress of Santiago and the island fortress San Juan de Ulúa to protect the harbor.

Throughout the nineteenth century, the city of Veracruz continued to remain Mexico's window to the world and the "treasury of the republic," but these attributes took on new meaning as rival political factions battled for control of its revenues. Although Veracruz and its environs could boast a population of only 14,340 at the time of independence in 1821, its commercial importance was second only to that of Mexico City. By midcentury at least three-quarters of Mexico's exports and imports passed through the port. Every major British, French, and German commercial house in Mexico City maintained a branch office in Veracruz. Travelers described the city's population as dominated by Africans and mulattoes. Despite the frightening reports of yellow fever epidemics, ravaging hurricanes (*nortes*), and the lack of potable drinking water, Veracruz was still considered a tempting financial prize to Europeans. The French ordered the occupation of the port in 1838 to secure the repayment of defaulted French loans. In 1847 the U.S. forces under General Winfield Scott opted for an amphibious landing to the south of the city so as to launch a devastating bombardment of the city from the rear. When the French intervened again in 1861, they seized Veracruz's customhouses to cover Mexico's outstanding debts.

Liberal as well as Conservative rebel leaders were no less eager to fill their coffers with Veracruz revenues and to launch their revolts from a port that provided a perfect escape should their rebellions fail. *Veracruzano* Antonio López de SANTA ANNA announced his rebellion against Emperor Agustín ITURBIDE there in 1823. Liberal leader Benito JUÁREZ found refuge from the merciless attacks of the Conservative armies long enough to establish his capital there between 1858 to 1860.

Veracruz was decimated by these continual occupations and sieges, but it underwent an astounding revival in the late nineteenth century. President Porfirio DÍAZ set about to increase foreign trade by encouraging foreign investors to modernize docks, dikes, and wharves and construct a potable water system. The completion of two railroad lines to the capital vastly improved living conditions and contributed to a dramatic rise in its population from 16,000 in 1877 to 53,000 in 1910.

During the Revolution of 1910, Veracruz once again played a critical role as a major source of income for the central government as well as for rival revolutionary factions. The United States likewise recognized its strategic importance when it seized the customhouses in April 1914 to cripple the government of Victoriano HUERTA. Venustiano Carranza's forces took possession of the port immediately after the U.S. occupation and made it their capital from November 1914 until August 1915, while repelling the armies of Francisco "Pancho" VILLA and Emiliano ZAPATA. During his stay in Veracruz, Carranza issued important decrees concerning agrarian and labor reforms which won him the much-needed support of the Mexican lower classes. The city emerged as a key center of organized labor during the Revolution as longshoremen, railroad workers, tradesmen, and tenants formed militant anarchist and anarcho-syndicalist unions.

Veracruz port facilities have undergone several rehabilitation programs since 1940 to improve unloading equipment and warehouse facilities and to reconstruct the waterfront. By 1990 the city and metropolitan area had grown into a prosperous commercial and industrial center with over 1 million inhabitants. Its shipments include such items as petroleum, fruits, molasses, rum, coffee, tobacco, and chicle. As a manufacturing center, it

Panoramic view of the city of Veracruz, 1846. ENRIQUE SEGARRA T., VERACRUZ, MEXICO.

produces chemicals, cement, flour, tobacco products, soap, candles, liquor, tiles, footwear, and chocolate. Despite its hot, muggy climate, its slow pace of life attracts tourists for its picturesque colonial Plaza of the Constitution, abundant seafood, and vivacious *jarocho* (Veracrucian) music. The song "La Bamba" has probably brought more fame to this city than its beaches. Its inhabitants also take pride in its renowned Mardi Gras celebration, the largest in Mexico.

MANUEL B. TRENS, *Historia de la H. Ciudad de Veracruz y de su ayuntamiento* (1955); ROBERT QUIRK, *An Affair of Honor* (1962); CARMEN BLÁZQUEZ DOMÍNGUEZ, *Veracruz liberal, 1858–1860* (1986); BERTA ULLOA, *Veracruz, capital de la nación, 1914–1915* (1986); ALFRED H. SIEMENS, *Between the Summit and the Sea* (1990); MICHAEL C. MEYER and WILLIAM L. SHERMAN, *The Course of Mexican History*, 4th ed. (1991).

HEATHER FOWLER-SALAMINI

VERACRUZ (STATE). The eleventh largest Mexican state (28,114 sq. mi.) and the third most populous (6,940,544 inhabitants in 1990), Veracruz stretches for some 400 miles along the Gulf of Mexico and comprises three broad physiographical and cultural regions.

Northern Veracruz stretches from the Río Tamesí in the north to the Sierra de Chiconquiaco in the south, and rises from sea level to elevations as high as 9,000 feet in the Sierra Madre Oriental. Most of the region is lowland, with a climate ranging from hot and humid to hot and subhumid, with a summer wet season. During the pre-Hispanic period, OLMEC influence at such places as Santa LUISA (ca. 1150 B.C.) gave way to interaction with highland cultures and a refocusing of settlement at the centers of El TAJÍN (ca. A.D. 400–900) and Castillo de Teayo (founded ca. A.D. 850). Cattle ranches spread throughout the lowlands during the colonial period, after warfare and disease had virtually exterminated the native population, a pattern persisting until the twentieth-century development of petroleum resources stimulated immigration. The foothills around Papantla harbor most of the state's remaining native peoples.

Central Veracruz stretches south from the Sierra de Chiconquiaco to the Río Blanco, and rises from sea level to peaks as high as 18,405 feet in the neovolcanic axis, resulting in a dramatic altitudinal zonation of vegetation from savanna to pine-oak forest. The climate ranges from hot and subhumid with an intense winter dry season in the lowlands to temperate and humid at higher elevations, and permits a wide range of crops. During the pre-Hispanic period, Remojadas (ca. A.D. 300–900) and CEMPOALA (founded ca. A.D. 1200) were major centers.

In 1519 the Spaniards under Hernán CORTÉS landed here and allied themselves with the TOTONACS before going on to conquer the Aztecs. By 1600 the crown had established Veracruz at its present location as the official port of New Spain. Jalapa, now the state capital, hosted the annual merchant fair. The region had become a vital transportation corridor between Spain and New Spain. The rapid demise of the Indian population stimulated the establishment of livestock in the lowlands and sugarcane on the more humid slopes around Jalapa and Orizaba, where African slaves resisted and established refuge communities. Control of the region continued to play a key role in the struggle for power in Republican Mexico: by Antonio López de SANTA ANNA (1833–1855), by the United States (1847–1848, 1914), by Benito JUÁREZ's Liberals (1858–1861), and by the French (1862–1867). Turn-of-the-century migration to the growing textile mills of Orizaba provided a proletarian base for the subsequent popular revolution.

Southern Veracruz stretches from the Río Blanco in the north to the Río Tonalá in the south, and rises from sea level to elevations as high as 5,413 feet in the Sierra de los Tuxtlas. Much of the region is tropical lowland with a hot, humid climate. During the pre-Hispanic period it was the heartland of the prototypical Olmec, established at such centers as SAN LORENZO (ca. 1200–900 B.C.) and La Venta (ca. 900–400 B.C.), just south of the Río Tonalá in Tabasco. Subsequently the region became a resource hinterland for highland cultures, a pattern the Spaniards continued by establishing livestock ranches and sugar plantations. Only with the control of lowland diseases, the discovery of petroleum, and the construction of drainage and irrigation projects in the twentieth century has the region's population increased dramatically.

MANUEL B. TRENS, *Historia de Veracruz*, 6 vols. (1947–1950); THOMAS T. POLEMAN, *The Papaloapan Project* (1964); JOSÉ GARCÍA PAYÓN, "Archaeology of Central Veracruz," in *Handbook of Middle American Indians*, vol. 11, edited by Gordon F. Ekholm and Ignacio Bernal (1971); PETER GERHARD, *A Guide to the Historical Geography of New Spain* (1972); ARTURO GÓMEZ-POMPA, "Ecology of the Vegetation of Veracruz," in *Vegetation and Vegetational History of Northern Latin America*, edited by Alan Graham (1973); HEATHER FOWLER SALAMINI, *Agrarian Radicalism in Veracruz, 1920–38* (1978); MICHAEL D. COE and RICHARD A. DIEHL, *In the Land of the Olmec*, 2 vols. (1980); JORGE L. TAMAYO, *Geografía moderna de México*, 9th ed., rev. (1987); ALFRED H. SIEMENS, *Between the Summit and the Sea* (1990); PATRICK J. CARROLL, *Blacks in Colonial Veracruz* (1991).

ANDREW SLUYTER

VERACRUZ, OCCUPATION OF, the April 1914 seizure of Veracruz, Mexico, by U.S. troops to prevent delivery of a shipment of arms to the regime of General Victoriano HUERTA, whose government President Woodrow WILSON had declined to recognize. Although the landing on 21 April was justified as a response to the Tampico incident a week earlier, when Mexican soldiers arrested a group of U.S. sailors, the selection of Veracruz rather than Tampico as the site of the landing was due to the arms shipment.

U.S. Marines and Navy personnel sought to seize only the customs house and dock area, but resistance by Mexican troops and the local populace, which shocked public opinion and policy makers in the United States,

Marines of the U. S. Navy pose in arcade of the Plaza de Armas in Veracruz, April 1914. ARCHIVO GENERAL DE LA NACIÓN, MÉXICO.

resulted in the occupation of the entire city. The military operation was undertaken on short notice, with little planning and a small force. Had Mexican federal troops offered more organized resistance, the landing would have proven very costly. The Revolutionaries condemned the occupation but refused Huerta's request to join forces against the U.S. invaders. While many expected U.S. troops to launch a full-scale military intervention, they occupied only Veracruz.

Veracruz remained occupied for seven months, a factor that contributed to the fall of the Huerta regime but did not fully deny him access to arms shipments from abroad. Efforts to mediate through the NIAGARA FALLS CONFERENCE proved unsuccessful. The episode produced considerable strain between the Wilson administration and the Revolutionaries because of Venustiano CARRANZA's refusal to negotiate with the United States or to offer any guarantees for the citizens of Veracruz. His stance delayed the evacuation of the port by several months.

U.S. troops withdrew in November 1914, in effect turning the port and vast quantities of war material over to Carranza in time to support his efforts in a new conflict with General Francisco ("Pancho") VILLA.

ROBERT E. QUIRK, *An Affair of Honor: Woodrow Wilson and the Occupation of Veracruz* (1962); KENNETH J. GRIEB, *The United States and Huerta* (1969); JOHN M. HART, *Revolutionary Mexico* (1987).

KENNETH J. GRIEB

VERAPAZ, a mountainous district in central Guatemala, divided since 1877 into two departments, Alta Verapaz and Baja Verapaz.

Alta Verapaz covers 3,354 square miles and has a population of 390,000 (1985); its chief agricultural products are COFFEE and cardamom. The capital is Cobán. Baja Verapaz covers 1,206 square miles and has a population of 150,000 (1985); its chief agricultural products are corn, beans, sugarcane, and citrus. The capital is Salamá. Ethnically, the population of Verapaz is mainly Kekchí and Pokonchí Indian.

Sharply folded mountains have isolated the Verapaz from cultural, religious, and political changes to the north and south. The inhabitants of the region, which the Kekchí called Tezulutlán, repulsed conquest with such ferocity in 1530 that the Spaniards named it the "Land of War." But Fray Bartolomé de LAS CASAS saw in this area an opportunity to put into practice his precept of a peaceful conquest and conversion of the Indians. Around 1542, Dominicans entered the region and began missionary work by establishing *reducciones*, with Cobán as the principal mission center. The crown declared the area the exclusive domain of the Dominican order and forbade Spanish settlement there. By the end of the decade, most of the area, now renamed Verapaz (Land of True Peace), was under Dominican control and nominally Christian.

Dominican control continued, albeit somewhat diminished, until the early part of the nineteenth century. In defiance of royal orders, LADINOS (non-Indian Guatemalans) settled in the Baja Verapaz in the colonial period, and their influx accelerated after independence. Difficulty of communication kept the Alta Verapaz isolated until mid-century.

About 1860, Ladino and foreign merchants, especially Germans, moved into the Verapaz. In the Alta Verapaz, settlers acquired large estates, formerly Indian communal lands, on which Indians remained as servile laborers. The new owners transformed the Verapaz into a leading coffee department.

The commercialization of the coffee industry came about largely through the efforts of a small group of Germans who controlled production, processing, and distribution. They provided capital resources, marketing connections, entrepreneurial skills, and a capitalist approach to investment and profit. Germans initiated transportation improvements and built a railroad to connect with a water route to the Caribbean port of Livingston, which reinforced the department's economic separation from the rest of Guatemala. German hegemony continued until World War II, when the Guatemalan government expropriated and then nationalized most German-owned properties.

The construction of a paved highway between Cobán and Guatemala City in the early 1970s linked the Verapaz more closely to the rest of the country and brought economic and social changes. The opening of roads, however primitive, into areas previously accessible only by muleback, stimulated commerce and attracted immigrants from other parts of Guatemala. This influx of non-Kekchí/Pokonchí will doubtless alter the character of the Indian population.

Evangelical groups have been active throughout the area, and a significant minority of the population now belongs to various Protestant sects. The Verapaz was the scene of considerable guerrilla activity in the early 1980s, which resulted, in part, in an increased national military presence in the area.

JOSÉ VICTOR MEJÍA, *Geografía descriptiva de la República de Guatemala* (1922); GUILLERMO NÁÑEZ FALCÓN, "German Contributions to the Economic Development of the Alta Vera Paz" (M.A. thesis, Tulane University, 1961); ARDEN R. KING, *Cobán and the Verapaz* (1974); FRANCIS GALL, comp., *Diccionario geográfico de Guatemala*, 4 vols. (1976); KARL THEODOR SAPPER, *The Verapaz in the Sixteenth and Seventeenth Centuries,* translated by Theodore E. Gutman (1985).

GUILLERMO NÁÑEZ FALCÓN

VERGARA, MARTA (*b.* 1898; *d.* after 1948), leader of the Chilean women's movement, founding member of the Comité Pro Derecho de las Mujeres (1933) and, with other members of the Asociación de Mujeres Universitarias, of the Movimiento Pro Emancipación de la Mujer Chilena (MEMCH) (1935). Vergara edited the MEMCH journal, *La Mujer Nueva.* Her political sympathies were with the Chilean left and the Chilean Communist Party, though she was not a party member. Vergara lived and traveled abroad much of her life and was connected to the international diplomatic and intellectual communities. From 1941 to 1948, she lived in Washington, D.C., where she served as Chilean representative to the Inter-American Commission of Women.

MARTA VERGARA, *Memorias de una mujer irreverente* (1961).

CORINNE ANTEZANA-PERNET

See also **Feminism and Feminist Organizations.**

VERGARA ECHEVEREZ, JOSÉ FRANCISCO (*b.* 10 October 1833; *d.* 15 February 1889), late-nineteenth-century Chilean statesman. A prominent politician, Vergara, the son of an army officer, was educated as an engineer. While holding public office, including a ministerial portfolio, he was particularly recognized for his service during the WAR OF THE PACIFIC. Beginning his career as a nursemaid for an indecisive and perhaps senescent general, Vergara, a colonel of a National Guard cavalry unit, first served in the Tarapacá campaign. Landing with the troops at Pisagua, he fought at San Francisco and participated in the ill-fated attack on Tarapacá.

Although Vergara resigned from active military service, he continued to advise the army's general staff, often suggesting well-conceived plans which, unfortunately, the military commander rejected. Vergara subsequently held the post of minister of the interior in the Domingo SANTA MARÍA government. Although he was a brilliant and dedicated administrator, he failed to win the Conservative Party's nomination for the 1886 presidential campaign. Upon retiring to his farm in what is now Viña del Mar, he unexpectedly died.

JOSÉ FRANCISCO VERGARA, "Memorias," in *Guerra del Pacífico: Memorias de José F. Vergara y diario de campaña de Diego Dublé Almeida,* edited by FRANCISCO RUZ TRUJILLO (1979); WILLIAM F. SATER, *Chile and the War of the Pacific* (1986), pp. 21, 23, 27, 32–34, 37–38, 47–51, 54–56, 182–185.

WILLIAM F. SATER

VERÍSSIMO, ÉRICO (*b.* 17 December 1905; *d.* 1975), Brazilian novelist. Born in Cruz Alta, Rio Grande do Sul, Veríssimo belonged nonetheless to the later modernist novelists of Brazil, who at first preferred the *novela,* a short novel emphasizing one character and limited space and time. One of his first such fictional efforts, *Clarissa,* was an immediate success. The youthful Veríssimo was fascinated by the plastic arts, but he left painting with colors for painting with words. Counterpoint, flashbacks, montage, simultaneity, telescoping, diary, and documentary are only a few of the devices he used in his broad, cosmopolitan view of the world. Veríssimo wrote in the first person and expressed details so convincingly that the reader readily becomes absorbed in the characters; yet psychological development and philosophy are subordinate to the story.

Veríssimo's humanistic and ideological themes were often conveyed by symbols and portrayed in characters. Music is often found in his works as allusions and symphonic structures, for instance, in *Música ao longe* (1935). Dialogue, used sparingly in his early novels, becomes increasingly important in his great multivolume work, *O tempo e o vento.*

Veríssimo quickly developed the novel as his preferred genre. He was the first in Brazil to make effective use of the point-counterpoint novel. He focused on urban life and immediately became a best-selling novelist, the first writer in Brazil to live by the pen. Other novels,

Caminhos cruzados (1935), *Um lugar ao sol* (1936), *Olhai os lírios do campo* (1938), and *O resto é silêncio* (1943), followed in rapid succession, each a result of Veríssimo's continuing experimentation in his medium.

In *O tempo e o vento*, Veríssimo gives his broad, penetrating view of the history of his home state. On a wide panoramic screen developed in three volumes (the third of which has three parts), Veríssimo chronicles the vicissitudes of two families. He presents in human and symbolic terms the rise of Rio Grande do Sul from the mythical past and its history from the founding of its society in the middle of the eighteenth century to the dictatorship of Getúlio VARGAS in the first half of the twentieth. The principal subject of this great work is the evolution of the urban middle class, along with all the inherent issues, both in the state and in the nation. Volume 1, *O continente*, appeared in 1949 and volume 2, *O retrato*, in 1951; the first two books of volume 3, *O arquipélago*, were published in 1961, and the third, the following year.

GUILHERMINO CÉSAR, "O romance social de Érico Veríssimo," in *O contador de histórias: Quarenta anos da vida literária de Érico Veríssimo*, compiled by Flávio Loureiro Chaves (1972); REGINA ZILBERMAN, *A Literatura no Rio Grande do Sul* (1982).

RICHARD A. MAZZARA

See also **Literature: Brazil.**

VERNET, LOUIS (*b.* 1792; *d.* 1871), first governor of the Islas Malvinas (FALKLAND ISLANDS) under the authority of Buenos Aires (1829–1831). Vernet was a central figure in the incidents that led to the establishment of continuous British possession of the islands. He was born in France but he had lived in Hamburg and the United States before coming to Buenos Aires in 1817. In 1826 he set up a cattle business on the islands that provisioned passing ships with fresh and salted beef before they rounded Cape Horn. His presence and activities were challenged by seal hunters (mainly from the United States), so in 1829 the Buenos Aires government appointed him governor and gave him exclusive control of fishing and hunting in the area, an act that was protested by the British. In 1831, after several warnings against unlawful hunting, Vernet seized the *Harriet*, a U.S. sealing vessel, and took it to Buenos Aires. George W. Slacum, the U.S. consul in Buenos Aires, reacted strongly, called Vernet a pirate, and demanded payment for damages. The U.S. Navy corvette *Lexington* was in the Río de la Plata at the time, and at Slacum's instigation its captain, Silas Duncan, sailed to the islands in late 1831, destroyed Vernet's settlement, and declared the islands *res nullis* (property of no one). A little over a year later the British expelled the remaining Argentines and began their century and a half of continuous occupation of the islands.

MARY CAWKELL, *The Falkland Story 1592–1982* (1983); EUGENIO A. L. RAVENAL, *Las Islas de la Discordia, el asunto de las Malvinas* (1983); LOWELL S. GUSTAFSON, *The Sovereignty Dispute over the Falkland (Malvinas) Islands* (1988).

JACK CHILD

See also **Falklands/Malvinas War.**

VERRUGA. *See* **Diseases.**

VÉRTIZ Y SALCEDO, JUAN JOSÉ DE (*b.* 11 July 1719; *d.* 1799), governor of Buenos Aires (1770–1777), viceroy of Río de la Plata (1778–1784). Born in Mérida, Yucatán, while his father was serving as governor, Vértiz was trained as a military man in Spain and later participated in the Italian campaigns. He arrived in Río de la Plata as governor in 1770. Although he was forced to step aside during the brief viceroyalty in CEVALLOS, he soon succeeded him. As second viceroy of Río de la Plata, Vértiz was the true architect of viceregal government in the Río de la Plata. While governor and later viceroy, Vértiz was a very successful leader: he implemented a series of far-reaching reforms, including the creation of the intendency system; free trade; improvement of public services, education, and welfare; geographical exploration; construction of forts; and agricultural experimentation. Vértiz returned to Spain in 1784.

JOSÉ TORRE REVELLO, *Juan José de Vértiz y Salcedo: Gobernador y virrey de Buenos Aires* (1932); ENRIQUE UDAONDO, *Diccionario biográfico colonial argentino* (1945), pp. 937–939.

SUSAN M. SOCOLOW

VESCO, ROBERT LEE (*b.* 4 Dec. 1935), U.S. financial manipulator and white-collar thief. Born into a lower-class Detroit neighborhood to immigrant parents, Vesco achieved wealth with his International Controls Corporation (ICC). An investigation of ICC's takeover of International Overseas Services (IOS) by the U.S. Securities and Exchange Commission in the early 1970s led to a protracted hearing in 1973 that revealed many of Vesco's questionable financial activities. These ventures included $250,000 in illegal contributions to President Richard Nixon's 1972 reelection campaign, for which Vesco was indicted twice. Vesco, in the meantime, transferred his operations to the Bahamas and to Costa Rica, where he had cultivated a close relationship with José FIGUERES. While remaining in Costa Rica, he evaded U.S. extradition attempts but eventually became the source of such a political scandal there that he was forced to retire to the Bahamas after the Costa Rican government refused his request for citizenship in 1978. Seeking again to evade U.S. extradition, he filed for political asylum in the Bahamas in 1980. When the Bahamas, under intense U.S. pressure refused, Vesco found refuge in Antigua in 1981, promising to invest heavily in that newly independent island. In 1982, however, U.S. pressure forced that government to renounce Vesco, who then fled to Costa Rica

405

and in 1983 to Nicaragua, where Tomás BORGE arranged asylum for him in Cuba.

ANTHONY HERZOG, *Vesco, From Wall Street to Castro's Cuba: The Rise, Fall, and Exile of the King of White Collar Crime* (1987).

RALPH LEE WOODWARD, JR.

VESPUCCI, AMERIGO (*b.* 18 March 1454; *d.* 22 February 1512), Florentine navigator and cosmographer. Vespucci came from a merchant family engaged in the trade of wine, silk, and woolens as well as in other commercial and banking interests. He was very well educated by his uncle Guido Antonio and traveled with him to Paris as a secretary on a diplomatic mission during 1481–1483. In 1489 he went briefly to Seville to examine the accounts of Florentine agents. He returned to Spain in 1492 and in a letter to Italy in December referred to himself as a Florentine merchant resident there. Vespucci was clearly aware of the return of COLUMBUS from the "Indies" and of the preparations for the great second fleet.

Vespucci joined an expedition of four ships that left Cádiz on 10 May 1497. Its purpose was to test the theories of Columbus, especially the physical configuration of CUBA. The leadership of the expedition is unclear, but Vespucci kept a record and may have acted as a navigator. From the Canaries they entered the Caribbean between Puerto Rico and the Virgin Islands, and sailed westward to Costa Rica. It is likely they continued north along the Mexican Gulf coast and the southern United States and sailed around Florida as far north as Chesapeake Bay. Vespucci provides the only account of this voyage, tracing the outlines of a northern continental mass in a report to Piero Soderini in 1504. The group returned to Cádiz on 15 October 1498.

The next year Vespucci joined another fleet of three or four ships that included Juan de la Cosa and Alonso de Hojeda. They left Cádiz 16 May 1499, touched the African coast, the Canaries, and Cape Verdes, and split up. Amerigo's ship went south, landing on Cape St. Vincent in Brazil on 27 June 1499, ten months before Pedro Alvares CABRAL's discovery. Returning to Seville, he received letters from Italian merchant friends in Lisbon with an invitation from King MANUEL I to explore under Portugal's flag.

In May 1501, with orders to explore from Cape St. Agustín southward, Vespucci left Lisbon to examine lands mentioned by Cabral. The group passed the Canaries and stopped at Dakar, on the African coast, where they met Cabral's fleet returning from India. They touched Brazil and sailed to the south. When the land seemed to aim westward, Gonzalo Coehlo, the commander of the expedition, resigned, and Amerigo Vespucci assumed leadership, obviously to avoid problems regarding the division between Portuguese and Spanish spheres of influence as established by the Treaty of TORDESILLAS. In the search for a southwest passage to the Orient, they touched what became Montevideo, and passed the La Plata estuary (Río Jordán). They contin-

Amerigo Vespucci. ORGANIZATION OF AMERICAN STATES.

ued sailing to the south; in the first week of April, approaching the straits later discovered by MAGELLAN, they planted a flag in Patagonia. They returned to Lisbon via Sierra Leone and the Azores, reaching home port in September 1502.

After returning, Vespucci composed letters to Lorenzo di Pier Francesco de'Medici that were ultimately published. These, in somewhat garbled form, announced the discovery of a continent, *Mundus Novus*. Vespucci undertook a fourth voyage in 1503–1504. He left Lisbon on 10 May 1503, passed through the Cape Verdes and Sierra Leone, and reached Bahia on 20 August 1503. The leader of the group was Captain Gonzalo Coelho; Vespucci captained one of the six vessels. They explored to the south of San Vicente and traded for logwood. Vespucci later wrote Soderini in Florence reporting the details of the fourth voyage. Vespucci wished to return to his wife María as well as to his relatives and associates in Seville. Taking leave of Portugal, he returned to Seville in 1505. He journeyed to court, where King Ferdinand naturalized him as a citizen of Castile. In 1508 he joined Juan de la Cosa and Juan DÍAZ DE SOLÍS and was appointed *piloto mayor* (chief pilot) in Burgos on 22 March. This office combined trade, administration, and science. Vespucci headed the University of Mariners and collected and prepared composite maps or master charts on the basis of the most accurate knowledge then available. He died childless in Seville with wife María Cerezo and nephew Giovanni at his side. A variation of his name, America, was included on the new continent of the Martin Waldseemüller map printed on 25 April 1507 in the small printing house in the Monastery of Sainte-Dié in Lorraine.

FREDERICK J. POHL, *Amerigo Vespucci: Pilot Major* (1966); GERMÁN ARCINIEGAS, *Amerigo and the New World* (1978).

NOBLE DAVID COOK

VIAL, PEDRO (*b.* ca. 1746; *d.* 1814), explorer and pathfinder of the Spanish Southwest. A native of Lyons, France, Vial spent his first years in the New World on the Missouri River, working as a gunsmith for various southwestern tribes. As part of the Spanish attempt to protect and strengthen the northern frontier, he was recruited to open three new roads connecting SANTA FE with Spanish outposts to the east. Commissioned by the Spanish governor of Texas, Vial established an overland communication route between SAN ANTONIO and Santa Fe in 1787. Under the auspices of the governor of New Mexico, he opened a second road from Santa Fe to Natchitoches, Louisiana, in 1788. From 1792 to 1793 Vial blazed a third trail from Santa Fe to Saint Louis, traveling what later became the Santa Fe Trail. After these trailblazing excursions, Vial continued to work for the Spanish crown. He was enlisted to help protect Spain's claims to Texas and New Mexico against Anglo-American encroachment, and he led an unsuccessful attempt to intercept the Lewis and Clark expedition of 1804–1806. With his extensive knowledge of the Southwest, including its native tribes and languages, Vial was also a valuable guide and interpreter, serving in this capacity until his death in Santa Fe.

The best account of Vial's pathfinding exploits is NOEL M. LOOMIS and ABRAHAM P. NASATIR, *Pedro Vial and the Roads to Santa Fe* (1967). See also CARLOS E. CASTAÑEDA, *Our Catholic Heritage in Texas*, vol. 5 (1942), pp. 150–170.

SUZANNE B. PASZTOR

VIAMONTE, JUAN JOSÉ (*b.* 9 February 1774; *d.* 31 March 1843), Argentine military officer and governor of Buenos Aires. Born in Buenos Aires, Viamonte began a professional military career in the late colonial period. He opposed the BRITISH INVASIONS of 1806–1807, and after the May Revolution of 1810 he joined the first disastrous expedition of the Argentine patriots to Upper Peru. He later took part in the struggle against Federalist dissidents of the littoral provinces and their Uruguayan protector, José Gervasio ARTIGAS.

Viamonte retired from the military in 1822 but remained active in public life, serving as acting governor of Buenos Aires in 1829, just before the first governorship of Juan Manuel de ROSAS. He became governor again in 1833, but his essential moderation and evenhanded treatment of Rosas's enemies infuriated the latter's supporters, who unleashed a campaign of terrorism. In 1834 Viamonte resigned, paving the way for Rosas to return to office. Increasingly disaffected, he moved in 1840 to Uruguay, where he died in Montevideo.

ARMANDO ALONSO PIÑEIRO, *Historia del general Viamonte y su época* (1959); *Vidas de grandes argentinos*, vol. 3 (1963), pp. 305–312.

DAVID BUSHNELL

VIANA, FRANCISCO JOSÉ DE OLIVEIRA (*b.* 20 June 1883; *d.* 28 March 1951), Brazilian social theorist. Born in Saquarema, Viana was a major figure in the alienated first generation of the Old Republic (1889–1930). Viana was a publicist and jurist whose legacies are the tradition of authoritarian nationalism and the Estado Novo's *trabalhista* (corporativist sindicalist) legislation. Viana, trained at the Faculty of Law in Rio de Janeiro, was influenced by Serzedelo Correia and Sílvio ROMERO. A disciple of Alberto Tôrres in the 1910s, he first gained prestige writing critical essays, which were an established genre in the era's journalism. His greatest work, *Populações meridionais do Brasil* (1920), was followed by other studies on Brazilian society, history, and politics, the best of which were written before 1940.

With the Revolution of 1930, analysis began to give way to application, as Viana served President Getúlio VARGAS as consultant, jurist, and minister. His most notable impact was on constitutional law and corporativist legislation that successfully helped contain and co-opt the political potential of the emerging urban proletariat. His direct influence on the intellectual milieu of the 1920s and 1930s was enormous, especially his analysis of Brazil's social, racial, and political evolution. He asserted that Brazil, hindered by mass degradation, racial inferiority, and tendencies toward disaggregation and clientelism, was historically predisposed toward enlightened, centralized, authoritarian government and endangered by liberalism. Although his ideas derived from European POSITIVIST and corporativist theorists from the 1880s to the 1920s, he remains indirectly influential today. He died in Niterói.

JOÃO BATISTA DE VASCONCELOS TORRES, *Oliveira Viana* (1956); THOMAS E. SKIDMORE, *Black into White* (1974); JARBAS MEDEIROS, *Ideologia autoritária no Brasil* (1978); EVALDO VIEIRA, *Autoritarianismo e corporativismo no Brasil* (1981); JEFFREY D. NEEDELL, "History, Race, and the State in the Thought of Oliveira Viana," in *Hispanic American Historical Review* 75, no. 1 (February 1995): 1–31.

JEFFREY D. NEEDELL

VICARIO FERNÁNDEZ, [MARÍA] LEONA (*b.* 10 April 1789; *d.* 21 August 1842), Mexican insurgent heroine. A rich heiress, Vicario Fernández lived under the care of her uncle, Agustín Fernández de San Salvador. Working in her uncle's law office was Andrés QUINTANA ROO (1787–1851), with whom she was betrothed. After Quintana Roo joined the movement in 1812, she decided to help the insurgents. Affiliated with the secret society, LOS GUADALUPES, she received and distributed insurgent correspondence. She also sent the insurgents money, arms, and weapons, and helped several individuals to join them. She fled in March 1813, when she was discovered in San Antonio Huixquiluean on her way to Tlalpujahua. Her uncle convinced her to return, and she was detained in the College of Belén. Although the authorities prosecuted her, she did not inform on the conspirators. When she was rescued and taken to Oaxaca by the insurgents in April 1813, the authorities confiscated her property. The insurgent Congress granted her a pension that same year. She married Quintana Roo, whom she followed in his travels as deputy of the Congress. They were discovered in 1817 and she was captured in the sierra of Tlatlaya; both accepted amnesty from the royalists. Her remains rest in the Column of Independence.

GENARO GARCÍA, *Leona Vicario, heroína insurgente* (1910); JOSÉ MARÍA MIQUEL I VERGÉS, *Diccionario de insurgentes* (1969), pp.

597–598; *Diccionario Porrúa de historia, biografía y geografía de México*, vol. 3 (1986), p. 3120.

VIRGINIA GUEDEA

VICEROYALTY, VICEROY, the largest territorial unit in the Spanish colonies and its chief executive. The failure of the first AUDIENCIAS to provide stable rule in the New World and the desire to gain control over the new colonies resulted in the Spanish crown's naming viceroys for the newly created viceroyalties (regions) of NEW SPAIN (1535) and PERU (1543). The viceroyalty of New Spain encompassed land from the northern boundary of the province of Panama to what is now the United States and included the Caribbean islands and part of the province of Venezuela. The Philippine Islands ultimately fell under its jurisdiction as well. The viceroyalty of Peru included Panama and all Spanish possessions in

South America, with the exception of a coastal strip of Venezuela. When the crown created the viceroyalties of NEW GRANADA in northern South America and of the RÍO DE LA PLATA (roughly present-day Argentina, Uruguay, Paraguay, and Bolivia) in 1739 and 1776, respectively, it reduced the viceroyalty of Peru to Peru, Charcas, and Chile.

Viceroys were to serve as the monarch's alter ego and, as such, lived in palaces surrounded by retainers. As the chief executive, a viceroy presided over the *audiencia* located in his capital; had ultimate responsibility for the receipt, expenditure, and remission to Spain of tax revenues; served as commander in chief of the military; exercised royal patronage over the church; was charged with the settlement and economic development of his territory; and was responsible for the humane treatment of the native population.

From 1535 to 1808, the crown gave regular appointments to ninety-two men for the posts of viceroy. In the beginning, it named men of impeccable social standing and demonstrated ability. Many viceroys had titles of nobility, claimed military qualifications, and belonged to military orders. When the extension of European conflicts to the New World led the crown to emphasize military ability, especially in the eighteenth century, the social background of viceroys declined. In general, the greater weight given to ability over birth resulted in viceroys who, as a group, served satisfactorily in their posts.

Viceroys were named for a limited tenure, in contrast with *audiencia* ministers. The average tenure in office of seventeenth- and eighteenth-century viceroys in New Spain and Peru was between six and seven years. With only a few exceptions, viceroys were men born and reared in Spain.

The title "viceroy" was also used in Brazil beginning in 1720, but the authority of the office was normally limited to a captaincy-general. Rio de Janeiro replaced Bahia as the viceregal capital in 1763.

CLARENCE H. HARING, *Spanish Empire in America* (1947); DAURIL ALDEN, *Royal Government in Colonial Brazil* (1968); MARK A. BURKHOLDER, "Bureaucrats," in *Cities and Society in Colonial Latin America*, edited by Louisa Schell Hoberman and Susan Migden Socolow (1986).

MARK A. BURKHOLDER

VICOS PROJECT, a controversial experiment in applied anthropology in the 1950s and the 1960s in the department of Ancash, in the north-central Andes of Peru. In 1951, Cornell University–based scholars, under an agreement with Peruvian authorities, rented the publicly owned hacienda of Vicos with the intention of improving the lives of the peasants and conducting research. Storerooms, a school, and a clinic were built; basic medical care was provided; and modern agriculture and marketing techniques were taught. In 1962, the estate was sold to the peasants. Some scholars have questioned the objectives and/or results of the Cornell-

Peru Project. The Vicos experiment influenced the 1969 agrarian reform.

HENRY F. DOBYNS, PAUL L. DOUGHTY, and HAROLD D. LASSWELL, eds., *Peasants, Power, and Applied Social Change* (1971); BARBARA D. LYNCH, *The Vicos Experiment: A Study of the Impacts of the Cornell-Peru Project in a Highland Community* (1982); WILLIAM W. STEIN, "Reflexiones críticas sobre el Proyecto Peru–Cornell," in *Revista del Museo Nacional* (Lima), 48 (1986–1987): 287–316.

CHARLES F. WALKER

VICTORIA, GUADALUPE (*b.* 29 September 1785; *d.* 21 March 1842), Mexican revolutionary leader and president (1824–1829). Born in Tamazula, Durango, under the name Miguel Fernández y Félix, he studied law at the College of San Ildefonso but abandoned his studies in 1811 to join MORELOS's forces, changing his name to Guadalupe Victoria in honor of the Mexican Virgin and for victory. He emerged as one of the major insurgent leaders after Morelos was killed.

Accepting the Plan of IGUALA in 1821, Victoria was soon jailed for his opposition to Emperor ITURBIDE. In 1824 he became Mexico's first president. Although he attempted to consolidate the new government by avoiding excesses and refusing to side with either the ESCOCESES (Scottish rite Masons) or the YORKINOS (York rite Masons), he proved unable to transfer his office peacefully to Manuel GÓMEZ PEDRAZA in 1829. Victoria's administration suffered from lack of funds and an inability to control the radical mass politics that divided the nation. Thereafter, he retired from public life because of chronic illness.

ELMER W. FLACUS, "Guadalupe Victoria: Mexican Patriot and First President" (diss., University of Texas, 1951); ROMEO FLORES CABALLERO, *Counterrevolution: The Role of the Spaniards in the Independence of Mexico* (1974), pp. 47–124; MICHAEL P. COSTELOE, *La Primera República Federal de México, 1824–1835* (1975), pp. 11–216; STANLEY C. GREEN, *The Mexican Republic: The First Decade, 1823–1832* (1987), pp. 41–161; JAIME E. RODRÍGUEZ O., "Mexico's First Foreign Loans," in his *The Independence of Mexico and the Creation of the New Nation* (1989), pp. 215–235.

JAIME E. RODRÍGUEZ O.

VICTORIA, MANUEL (*d.* after 1832), governor of BAJA CALIFORNIA (1829–1831) and Alta California (1831–1832). Lieutenant Colonel Victoria was very unpopular during his brief administration for seeking to abolish the AYUNTAMIENTOS (town councils) in Alta California and to replace the local politicians with military rule. Victoria was overthrown in a revolt of his own troops and immediately recalled to Mexico. His overthrow led to greater autonomy in Alta California.

DAVID J. WEBER, *The Mexican Frontier, 1821–1846: The American Southwest Under Mexico* (1982).

ROBERT H. JACKSON

VICUÑA. *See* **Llama.**

VICUÑA LARRAÍN, FRANCISCO RAMÓN (*b.* 1775?; *d.* 13 January 1849), Chilean Liberal politician. A prominent personality in the congresses and governments of the 1820s, Vicuña Larraín was president of the Senate in 1829 and in that capacity was the first to become acting president of the republic while President Francisco Antonio PINTO (1775–1858) recuperated from an illness (July 1829). In September 1829 an irregularity in the election of the vice president by congress (which selected a Liberal in spite of the fact that a Conservative had won a plurality of votes) provoked the successful Conservative rebellion that over the next few months destroyed the Liberal regime and inaugurated a long period of Conservative hegemony (1830–1857). Vicuña Larraín, who continued as acting president following Pinto's final withdrawal from office, was powerless to stem the tide: on 7 November 1829 a public tumult in Santiago forced him to hand power over to a junta headed by General Ramón FREIRE (1787–1851). With the presidential sash hidden in a hat, Vicuña Larraín withdrew to Valparaíso and from there to Coquimbo, where he was captured when the province fell into Conservative hands. He was the brother of Manuel Vicuña Larraín (1777?–1843), first archbishop of Santiago; father of the Liberal politician Pedro Félix Vicuña Aguirre (1806–1874); and grandfather of the brilliant writer-politician Benjamín VICUÑA MACKENNA (1831–1886).

DIEGO BARRAS ARANA, *Historia general de Chile* (1884–1902), vol. 15.

SIMON COLLIER

VICUÑA MACKENNA, BENJAMIN (*b.* 25 August 1831; *d.* 25 January 1886), Chilean lawyer, politician, and historian. The son of an eccentric intellectual father, Vicuña Mackenna was educated at the University of Chile. He became involved in politics while still a student, achieving the distinction of being jailed by the Manuel MONTT administration for participating in the 1851 revolution. Following that abortive struggle, Vicuña Mackenna traveled abroad, then returned to Chile, only to be exiled a second time. Following the 1861 conclusion of Montt's administration, Vicuña Mackenna successfully ran for the legislature, where he served as both a deputy and a senator.

During Chile's ill-fated war against Spain in the mid-1860s, Vicuña Mackenna traveled to the United States, where he attempted to purchase weapons. In the early 1870s, as the provincial governor of Santiago, he instituted various programs to beautify the city. After Federico ERRÁZURIZ prevented him from receiving the Liberal Party's 1876 nomination for president, Vicuña Mackenna ran as a candidate of the Liberal Democratic Party, an organization he created. Although he campaigned throughout the country, it became clear that the Liberal political machine had rigged the election in favor of Aníbal PINTO. Consequently, Vicuña Mackenna withdrew his nomination, although he continued to serve in the Senate.

An avowed nationalist, Vicuña Mackenna had many firm opinions, which he never hesitated to share, either in the press or the halls of Congress. In addition to his political career, he proved to be an extremely prolific writer. He wrote for numerous newspapers as well as authored dozens of books, many of them valuable monographs, on a variety of economic and historical topics.

LUIS GALDAMES, *A History of Chile* (1941), pp. 166, 315, 320, 353–354, 426; EUGENIO ORREGO VICUÑA, *Vicuña Mackenna, vida y trabajos*, 3d. ed. (1951).

WILLIAM F. SATER

See also **Chile: Political Parties.**

VICÚS, a culture that inhabited the upper Piura Valley on the far north coast of Peru. It is believed that the Vicús culture began at about A.D. 100 and continued until between A.D. 500 and 700. Until very recently, most archaeological materials of this culture were ceramics excavated by grave robbers in search of gold. Early scientific work was restricted to the study of a small number of tombs. The Upper Piura Archaeological Project (1987–1990) worked the area between Cerro Vicús and Loma Negra, excavating public and domestic architecture. A large ceremonial site dating to the Vicús culture was found at Cerro Vicús. This complex features a large trapezoidal structure that has a central ramp and four terrace levels that ascend the central structure.

The public architecture is composed of wooden posts set in rows at about sixteen-inch intervals. They are joined by braided cord and a framework of cane on both sides of the logs. This frame is filled with clay mortar that was pushed into it, leaving finger and cloth impressions in the mud. Vicús domestic architecture is rectangular in shape and is built of logs and perhaps wattle and daub.

Vicús ceramics exhibit influences from the Ecuadorian coast, southern Colombia, and the contemporaneous GALLINAZO and MOCHE cultures of the north coast of Peru. They are best known for their negative, or resist, painted and burnished surfaces as well as vessels of white paint on red clay. A three-phase sequence has been proposed for the Vicús style. White paint on red clay is present throughout the sequence, negative painting is absent during the first phase, and it appears in very scarce quantities during the second phase of the Vicús sequence. The second phase also marks the introduction of modeling techniques that exhibit close ties to the Gallinazo style. A marked presence of Gallinazo-related negative painting and Moche-style artifacts are only present in the last phase.

The relationship between the Vicús, Gallinazo, and

Moche cultures is one of the most pressing areas of archaeological inquiry on the far north coast of Peru. This is because Gallinazo- and Moche-related materials are mixed in the same artifact assemblages, and because it is very difficult to assign the Moche-related materials to a specific temporal phase.

RICHARD L. BURGER, "Current Research: Andean South America," in *American Antiquity* 54, no. 1 (1989): 187–194; and "Current Research: Andean South America," in *American Antiquity* 55, no. 1 (1990): 172–179; PETER KAULICKE, "El Periodo Intermedio Temprano en el Alto Piura: Avances del Proyecto Arqueologico 'Alto Piura' (1987–1990)," in *Bull. Inst. Fr. Etudes Andines* 20, no. 2 (1991): 381–422.

HEIDY P. FOGEL

See also **Archaeology.**

VIDAURRI, SANTIAGO (*b.* 25 July 1808; *d.* 8 July 1867), governor of the state of Nuevo León–Coahuila, Mexico (1855–1865). Born in Lampazos (Nuevo León) near the United States border, Vidaurri was one of the most outstanding leaders of northern Mexico. While secretary of the Nuevo León government in 1855, he rebelled against President Antonio López de SANTA ANNA and became one of the stalwarts of liberalism in the northeast. On 23 May 1855 he occupied Monterrey, the capital of Nuevo León. Two days later he revealed the Plan Restaurador de la Libertad (Plan for the Restoration of Freedom), which announced his support for the republican cause. On orders from the Northern Army, he took possession of Saltillo, the capital of Coahuila, on 23 July 1855. From then until his dismissal by President Benito JUÁREZ, he governed both states, which he formally united on 19 February 1856. His military and political hegemony extended to Tamaulipas, where the border and maritime customhouses proved to be strategic. During his administration, he furnished customhouses on the Río Bravo, instituted the so-called Vidaurri tariff, and maintained strong liberal trade policies. This program won him the support of merchants from Monterrey, other areas of the northeast, and from Texas, and helped him amass substantial resources for supporting armed forces under his control, which he used to defend liberalism and maintain his own regional power.

The Vidaurri era, which coincided with the Civil War in the United States, laid the foundation for the future economic and industrial development of Monterrey. Vidaurri's autocratic behavior and harsh exploitation of the customhouses provoked a crisis with Juárez, which exploded in the beginning of 1864. In order to subdue Vidaurri, Juárez decreed the separation of Nuevo León and Coahuila on 16 February and imposed martial law. In March, Vidaurri abdicated and left the country. Some time later he joined the empire of MAXIMILIAN. He was named *consejero* (adviser), *ministro de hacienda* (chancellor of the exchequer), and commander of one of Maximilian's brigades. Vidaurri was captured in Mexico City

when the French forces were defeated. Porfirio DÍAZ ordered his execution by firing squad.

More information about his personal, political, and military life can be found in ISRAEL CAVAZOS GARZA, *Diccionario biográfico de Nuevo León* (1984). For the impact of Vidaurri's politics on the commercial development of Monterrey, see MARIO CERUTTI, *Economía de guerra y poder regional en el siglo XIX: Gastos militares, aduanas y commerciantes en años de Vidaurri (1855–1864)* (1983).

MARIO CERUTTI

VIDELA, JORGE RAFAEL (*b.* 2 August 1925), military leader and president of Argentina (1976–1981). Born in Mercedes, province of Buenos Aires, he graduated from the Military Academy (COLEGIO MILITAR) in 1944. During his early career he was rewarded with assignments of significant responsibility and educational opportunity. In 1954 he graduated from the Senior War College, and he became the director of the Military Academy in 1971. Two years later Videla was promoted to chief of the General Staff, the number two position in the army. In 1975, General Videla was elevated to commander in chief of the Argentine Army.

These were trying times for Argentina. Juan PERÓN died on 1 July 1974 and his wife, María Estela Martínez de PERÓN, political novice, succeeded him. Urban guerrilla violence increased significantly; kidnappings, assassinations, and car bombings were common. Also, the country was staggering under triple-digit inflation. On 24 March 1976 the Argentine armed forces seized control of the government. General Videla emerged as its leader and was declared president of the republic.

Videla carried out an aggressive war against the guerrillas. He retired in 1981, turning the government over to his handpicked successor, General Roberto VIOLA. Videla and other members of the military juntas that ruled between 1976 and 1982 were tried for excesses committed during what became known as the DIRTY WAR. The defendants were charged with imprisonment without charge, torture, and executions. On 9 December 1985, Videla was convicted and sentenced to life in prison. In December 1990 he was released under a general amnesty.

SUSAN CALVERT and PETER CALVERT, *Argentina: Political Culture of Instability* (1989); MARTIN EDWIN ANDERSEN, *Dossier Secreto* (1993).

ROBERT SCHEINA

VIEIRA, ANTÔNIO (*b.* 6 February 1608; *d.* 18 July 1697), JESUIT missionary, preacher, writer, and diplomat. Born in Lisbon and taken as a child to Bahia, Vieira went to live in that city's Jesuit college at the age of fifteen. Ten years later he delivered his first sermon, to an audience of black slaves at a Bahian sugar mill.

In 1641, Vieira was sent to Lisbon by the viceroy in Bahia to express the support of the Brazilian colony for

King JOÃO IV following the Portuguese Restoration. He soon became the court preacher and a confidant of the king, who dispatched him on a series of diplomatic missions to Amsterdam and Rome. Among the ideas for which he was attacked during the 1640s were proposals to limit the power of the Inquisition, to encourage New Christian merchants to invest in Portuguese commercial enterprises, and to cede Pernambuco to the Dutch, for which he was vilified as "the Judas of Brazil."

Vieira returned to Brazil in 1653 as superior of the Jesuit MISSIONS in the Amazon. Relations between the Jesuits and settlers there were strained by the missionaries' control over the distribution of Indian workers to Europeans. João IV gave Vieira the additional task of curbing the notorious slaving expeditions the Portuguese were conducting in the Amazon. From his base in São Luís do Maranhão, Vieira sought to improve relations between the Jesuits and the settlers while leading a series of highly successful missionary expeditions in the hinterlands. Unable to enforce crown legislation protecting the Indians, Vieira returned briefly to Portugal in 1655 to present his case against the settlers at court. Soon after his arrival in Lisbon, Vieira preached his most famous sermon, the "Sermão da Sexagésima," from the pulpit of the royal chapel. In it he attacked the homiletic conventions of the day and the idleness of the clergy in Portugal, particularly that of the Jesuits' rivals, the DOMINICANS. Sounding one of the central themes of his writings, Vieira argued that work in the overseas missions was the highest service a religious could render to the church.

Tensions with the settlers persisted after Vieira's return to Maranhão. In what proved to be the turning point of his missionary career, rebellious settlers expelled Vieira and his fellow Jesuits from the Amazon in 1661 and sent them back to Lisbon. Vieira gradually abandoned his effort to promote the peaceful incorporation of the Indians into colonial society. During the latter part of his career Vieira worked to protect the Indians by separating them from the settler communities as completely as possible.

While in the Amazon, Vieira wrote *Esperanças de Portugal* (1659), a privately circulated prophetic treatise that was to provide the pretext for his arrest in 1663 by the Inquisition. Vieira for many years criticized the Inquisition on both religious and socioeconomic grounds. He was an equally vigorous critic of the church hierarchy, and with the death of João IV in 1656 he was no longer protected from retribution. Drawing on traditional Jewish messianism and apocalyptic folk beliefs then current in Portugal, Vieira developed—in *Esperanças* and his subsequent defense before the tribunal, as well as in later writings such as *História do futuro*—a millenarian interpretation of Portuguese history that placed evergreater emphasis on the crown and the Jesuits as agents of divine providence. Vieira spent five years in prison and under house arrest. Following his release by the Inquisition in 1668, he had a successful sojourn as a preacher in Rome before returning to Brazil in 1681. During the last years of his life he served again as a Jesuit administrator, edited his sermons for publication, and wrote *Clavis Prophetarum*, a treatise left unfinished at his death. Vieira continues to be considered one of the greatest writers in the Portuguese language and a central figure in the religious and political history of the Luso-Brazilian world.

The standard biography is JOÃO LÚCIO D'AZEVEDO, *História de Antônio Vieira*, 2 vols. (1918–1920). For an excellent survey see CHARLES R. BOXER, *A Great Luso-Brazilian Figure: Padre Antônio Vieira* (1957). Vieira's writings have not been translated into English. Among the most important are the *Sermões*, 16 vols., edited by Augusto Magne, S.J. (1943–1945); *Cartas do Padre Antônio Vieira*, 3 vols., edited by João Lúcio d'Azevedo (1925–1928); *Livro Anteprimeiro da História do Futuro*, 2 vols., edited by José van den Besselaar (1976), which includes an excellent introduction; *Obras Escolhidas*, 12 vols., edited by Hernani Cidade and Antônio Sérgio (1951–1954); and *Defesa Perante o Tribunal do Santo Ofício*, 2 vols., edited by Hernani Cidade (1957).

THOMAS M. COHEN

VIERA, FELICIANO (*b.* 8 November 1872; *d.* 13 November 1927), president of Uruguay (1915–1919). Viera was the son of a veteran colonel of the Colorados who fought in the internal wars of Uruguay. At first a proponent of BATLLISMO, he separated from the main body of this group and gave rise to a splinter faction known as Vierismo. More conservative than José BATLLE and his reformist followers, Viera maintained a popular and charismatic style. After the failure of the Batllist constitutional project at the polls in 1916, Viera became the main force behind a movement to halt the social reforms that had characterized previous periods. In this way, Viera obtained a vote of confidence from the conservatives, which he in fact never betrayed. The political faction his actions had generated lost relevance with his death.

MILTON VANGER, *The Model Country: Batlle of Uruguay* (1980); JOSÉ P. BARRÁN and BENJAMÍN NAHUM, *La derrota del batllismo, 1916* (1987).

FERNANDO FILGUEIRA

VIEIRA, JOSÉ CARLOS DO AMARAL (*b.* 2 March 1952), Brazilian composer and pianist. Amaral Vieira was better known as a pianist until 1984, when an Amaral Vieira Festival featuring an amazing diversity of musical works by the young composer was held in São Paulo. The festival included fourteen concerts during which 157 works by Vieira were performed. When Vieira later announced his intention to record the complete piano works and transcriptions of Franz Liszt, a project that would require seventy compact discs to complete, and it became obvious that no commercial company would undertake this vast project, Vieira established Scorpio, his own recording label. New musical works and vast projects appear to blossom forth from his fertile mind and nimble fingers with incredible rapidity. In a nation in which Heitor VILLA-LOBOS established a tradition of explosive creativity with more than one thousand musical works, Vieira is attempting to surpass his predecessors. Vieira's compositional style in works such as *Elegy, Nocturne and Toccata* (for piano [1980]), and *Variações Fausto* (a set of variations in fantasia form on a theme of Franz Liszt's *Faust Symphony* [1985]) shows his ability to write brilliantly for the piano and his intense involvement with the compositional style of Franz Liszt.

DAVID P. APPLEBY

VIEYTES, HIPÓLITO (*b.* 12 August 1762; *d.* 5 October 1815), journalist and political figure of Argentine independence. Born in San Antonio de Areco, Buenos Aires Province, Vieytes attended the well-known Real Colegio de San Carlos, where he studied law and philosophy. Committed to physiocratic doctrines and to the promotion of useful works, he spread his views by establishing various newspapers, including the *Semanario de Agricultura, Industria y Comercio* in 1802, and collaborated with Manuel BELGRANO on *El Correo de Comercio* in 1810. Many scholars credit Vieytes with the inception of modern journalism in his country. Vieytes served in the capital as police superintendent and representative to the General Constituent Assembly in 1813. Though he is regarded as one of the intellectual authors of the Argentine independence movement, he eventually succumbed to the political instabilities of the time. Vieytes was arrested and exiled in 1815 after the overthrow of Supreme Director Carlos María de ALVEAR. He died in San Fernando shortly thereafter.

ALBERTO REYNA ALMANDOS, *Claros orígenes de la democracia argentina* (1957); ARTURO CAPDEVILA, *Vidas de grandes argentinos*, vol. 3 (1966), pp. 313–317.

FIDEL IGLESIAS

VIGIL, DONACIANO (*b.* 6 September 1802; *d.* 11 August 1877), governor of NEW MEXICO (1847–1848). Vigil was a popular and well-educated native New Mexican. In New Mexico's Revolution of 1837, Vigil was captured at La Cañada by the revolutionists and appointed secretary for the rebel government. While questions were raised about his loyalty, he was later cleared of any misconduct. In the 1830s and 1840s, Vigil served as a member of the departmental assembly, editor of a Spanish newspaper in New Mexico, and military secretary under governor Manuel Armijo. When the United States occupied New Mexico in 1846, General Stephen W. KEARNY appointed him secretary of the territory and

upon the assassination of Charles Bent (*d.* 1847) in Taos, Vigil became governor. An antimilitarist, Vigil proclaimed the first elections in the territory under U.S. rule. Later, he served in the territorial legislature.

RALPH EMERSON TWITCHELL, *The History of the Military Occupation of the Territory of New Mexico from 1846 to 1851* (1909), pp. 207–228; STANLEY CROCCHIOLA, *Giant in Lilliput: The Story of Donaciano Vigil* (1963); JANET LECOMPTE, *Rebellion in Rio Arriba, 1837* (1985), esp. pp. 13–16, 40–61.

AARON PAINE MAHR

VIGIL, FRANCISCO DE PAULA GONZÁLEZ (*b.* 13 September 1792; *d.* 9 June 1875), Peruvian priest, liberal politician, and author. Vigil rose to prominence in the early post-Independence era for his 1832 attack on presidential usurpation of constitutional authority. In 1834 he presided over the liberal National Convention, and in 1836 he helped prevent Bolivian annexation of his native TACNA. From 1845, Vigil served as director of Peru's National Library, writing voluminously on church-state relations and national reform. Influenced by Enlightenment thought, Vigil extolled the virtues of reason, freedom of conscience, republicanism, education, and work. His religious dissertations provoked condemnation by the church for their assertion of the authority of national churches over the Roman Curia.

JORGE BASADRE, "Homenaje: Francisco de Paula González Vigil," in *Textual* 10 (October 1975): 13–23; JEFFREY L. KLAIBER, *Religion and Revolution in Peru, 1824–1976* (1977).

MATTHEW J. O'MEAGHER

See also **Anticlericalism.**

VILA, incorporated township of the Portuguese Empire. The first *vila* in Brazil was established in SÃO VICENTE in 1532. By 1650, only thirty-seven more *vilas* and cities had been founded, seven by the crown and the remainder by local initiative. The *vila* incorporated both secular and ecclesiastical power as the site of the town council and church. Town councils (*câmaras municipais*; SENADOS DA CÂMARA) consisted of elected councilmen, justices of the peace, and the procurator; appointed auxiliary employees. After 1696, a crown magistrate (*juiz de fora*) was added. Town councils exercised broad local powers including taxation, price setting, market supervision, hygiene standards, law enforcement, and public works. During the colonial period, councils overstepped their formal boundaries and even overruled viceroys and governors. Their political and judicial powers were curtailed under the empire in 1828.

CHARLES R. BOXER, *Portuguese Society in the Tropics: The Municipal Councils of Goa, Macao, Bahia, and Luanda, 1510–1800* (1965); A. J. R. RUSSELL-WOOD, "Local Government in Portuguese America: A Study in Cultural Divergence," in *Comparative Studies in Society and History* 16 (March 1974): 187–231;

RICHARD M. MORSE, "Brazil's Urban Development: Colony and Empire," in *From Colony to Nation: Essays on the Independence of Brazil*, edited by A. J. R. Russell-Wood (1975).

JUDY BIEBER FREITAS

VILA RICA. *See* **Ouro Prêto.**

VILAR, MANUEL (b. 15 November 1812; d. 25 November 1860), sculptor. Trained in his native Barcelona and Rome, Vilar was chosen as director of sculpture when the ACADEMIA DE SAN CARLOS in Mexico City was reestablished. He arrived in 1846. Vilar had studied with Pietro Tenerani and was sympathetic to the ideals of the Nazarenes (a group of German painters who sought to revitalize Christian art). He brought to Mexico an important collection of plaster casts acquired in Rome, and worked with the energy of a believer in the redemptive value of art to revive monumental sculpture in Mexico. He produced work with themes that were classical, religious, and secular, as well as portraits. Probably his most ambitious work was a full-size bronze statue of a pre-Columbian hero, *Tlahuicole* (1851). Autographed manuscripts and many documents provide information about his life and career.

SALVADOR MORENO, *El escultor Manuel Vilar* (1969).

CLARA BARGELLINI

VILARIÑO, IDEA (b. 1920), Uruguayan poet and critic. She taught literature in the high school system of Montevideo, where she was born, as did many other women of her generation. She began teaching in 1984 as a humanities faculty member at the University of the Republic in Montevideo. She has written critical studies of the poetry of the Spaniard Antonio Machado, *Grupos simétricos en poesía de Antonio Machado* (1951), and the Uruguayan Julio HERRERA Y REISSIG, *Julio Herrera y Reissig* (1950), as well as many articles on other Spanish poets. She published a thorough study on TANGO lyrics in *Las letras de tango* (1965). Her critical essays have appeared in *Clinamen, Asir, Hiperión, Marcha, Puente, Carte Segrete, Texto Crítico, La Opinión, Revista del Sur,* and *Brecha.* She is also an accomplished translator of Shakespeare into Spanish.

Vilariño's poetic expression is concise, with minimal utilization of rhetorical devices, and expresses a dark world, where the vital elements fail to survive. In form, her poetry is also brief, without much artifice. She has published *La suplicante* (1945), *Cielo, cielo* (1947), *Paraíso perdido* (1949), *Nocturnos* (1955), *Poemas de amor* (1957), *Pobre mundo* (1966), *Treinta poemas* (1967), *Poesía* (1970), and *Segunda antología* and *No* (1980).

JUAN PARRA DEL RIEGO, *Nocturnos, y otros poemas* (1965); SUSANA CRELIS SECCO, *Idea Vilariño: Poesía e identidad* (1990).

MAGDALENA GARCÍA PINTO

VILCABAMBA (Quechua for "Sacred Plain"), the last capital of the Inca rump state after the Spanish conquest. After the capture and execution of the last Inca, Túpac Amaru, by the Spanish, the city was abandoned and its location lost. In the twentieth century the search for Vilcabamba was a principal preoccupation of explorers. Hiram BINGHAM originally identified the ruins at Espíritu Pampa (Quechua for "Spirit Plain" or "Ghost Plain"), in the *montaña* about 100 miles northwest of Cuzco, as Vilcabamba. He later changed his mind and insisted that MACHU PICCHU had been Vilcabamba. In 1964 the American explorer Gene Savoy convincingly demonstrated that Bingham's original identification of Espíritu Pampa as the lost city of Vilcabamba was correct.

JOHN HEMMING, *The Conquest of the Incas* (1970); GENE SAVOY, *Antisuyo* (1970) and *Vilcabamba: Last City of the Incas* (1970).

GORDON F. McEWAN

See also **Incas.**

VILLA, FRANCISCO "PANCHO" (b. 5 June 1878; d. 20 July 1923), Mexican revolutionary, general, governor of Chihuahua (1913–1915). Christened Doroteo Arango, one-time bandit and muleteer, Villa became one of the most important and controversial leaders of the MEXICAN REVOLUTION (1910–1920).

The history of Villa's youth is masked in legend. He was by occupation a hacienda peon, miner, bandit, and merchant. There is a colorful story of his killing a *hacendado* who had raped his sister and his subsequent escape to banditry. Most certainly, according to biographer Friedrich Katz, he was a cattle rustler, which far from branding him an outlaw brought him a degree of popular renown. Villa eventually settled in San Andrés, Chihuahua, a village in the throes of violent protest against taxes imposed by the Chihuahua state government controlled by the TERRAZAS family.

In 1910 Villa joined the revolution led by Francisco I. MADERO in Chihuahua. After Madero's victory in May of 1911, Villa retired to Chihuahua City, using his mustering-out money to begin a meat-packing business. He returned to military duty in 1912 to fight against the counterrevolution of Pascual OROZCO, Jr. His commander, General Victoriano HUERTA, ordered him executed for insubordination, but Madero intervened, sending him to prison, from which he escaped shortly thereafter. Following a few months in exile in the United States, Villa returned to avenge the overthrow and assassination of Madero by Huerta in February 1913. In March 1913 Villa crossed the Rio Grande from Texas with a handful of men. His key lieutenants came from the northern villages that had once been military colonies in the Indian wars of the eighteenth and nineteenth centuries. Toribio Ortega and Porfirio Talamantes, for example, had led their Chihuahuan villages, Cuchillo Parado and Janos, respectively, in protests against land

Francisco "Pancho" Villa. LA FOTOTECA DEL INAH.

expropriations. With his peasant-worker army, Villa conquered Chihuahua in the name of the Constitutionalist movement in 1913.

In control of Chihuahua from late 1913 through 1915, Villa expropriated the estates of the landed oligarchy and used the revenues they produced to finance his army and government. His rule in Chihuahua was an ingenious compromise between the need to satisfy the demands of the revolutionary masses for land reform and the immediate necessity of obtaining funds to win the war first against Huerta and then against his despised rival, Venustiano CARRANZA. He promised to distribute the confiscated properties after the triumph of the Revolution. In the meantime, these estates, some managed by his generals and others by a state agency, supported the widows and orphans of veterans and the starving unemployed of the mining and timber regions of Chihuahua, and provided the necessary funds for supplying the Villista army.

His Division of the North, led by an elite corps, the *dorados*, paved the way to Huerta's defeat. Along the way south from his initial victories in Chihuahua, Villa fought bloody battles, first at Torreón in April and then at Zacatecas in June 1914. His split with Carranza widened, however, and Villa withdrew from the campaign.

It was during the fight against Huerta that Villa first manifested his hatred for Spaniards. In Torreón he rounded them up and shipped them across the U.S. border, in the meantime confiscating their property. Later he would commit additional atrocities against them.

The Constitutionalists defeated Huerta in 1914 but almost immediately split into two factions, one led by Villa and the other by Carranza. One of the crucial issues between the two leaders was Carranza's intention to return the landed estates confiscated by the Villistas to their owners. This would have undercut much of Villa's support by depriving him of the main symbol of reform and the main source of his funds.

When a revolutionary convention met in Aguascalientes in the fall of 1914, Villa, allied with Emiliano ZAPATA, the peasant leader from the state of Morelos, demanded that Carranza abdicate as leader of the Revolution. When Carranza refused, Villa and Zapata declared themselves to be in armed opposition under the provisions of the convention. In November 1914 the Conventionist armies of Villa and Zapata occupied Mexico City. The Constitutionalists were in apparent disarray. The Conventionist alliance between Villa and Zapata dissipated, however, because neither of their regionally based, popular movements could sustain long-term military or political success outside its home area.

In a series of brutal battles in the center of the country in 1915 (Celaya, 6–7 April and 13–16 April; León, throughout May; Aguascalientes, 10 July), however, Villa suffered major defeats at the hands of the Carrancista general Alvaro OBREGÓN SALIDO. Villa's tactics of unrelenting attack were disastrous in the face of Obregón's entrenched troops. Villa's once mighty army disintegrated. The crucial battle took place at León (also called Trinidad), where over thirty-eight days at least five thousand men died.

Villa, though badly defeated and eliminated as a major military force, stayed in the field. His prestige was irretrievably damaged and his allies rapidly defected. In late 1915 he made a desperate effort to establish a foothold in Sonora but failed when Obregón dispatched troops through the United States to reinforce Constitutionalist troops in Agua Prieta. A series of defeats followed, sending Villa back across the Sierra Madre to Chihuahua.

Villa was forced once again to adopt guerrilla tactics. Many of his aides, especially the more respectable former Maderistas, went into exile in the United States. Villa stayed and tormented the national and state governments for four years. This "second wind" of Villismo brought it back to its roots as a local, popular movement based in the sierras of Chihuahua.

In 1916 Villa responded to U.S. recognition of and cooperation with Carranza by viewing Americans with increasing hostility. One of his lieutenants murdered seventeen American engineers at Santa Isabel, Chihuahua, in January. On 8–9 March several hundred Villista raiders crossed the border into Columbus, New Mexico. Although his motives for the attack are much debated, there is some evidence Villa sought to precipitate a military intervention by the United States in order to prevent an agreement with Carranza that would have rendered Mexico a virtual protectorate of the United States.

A force led by U.S. general John J. PERSHING futilely chased Villa from mid-March 1916 until early February 1917, nearly a year. After Pershing's withdrawal, for the next two years Villa periodically occupied Chihuahua's major cities, Ciudad Juárez and Hidalgo de Parral. He was able to raise armies of from one thousand to two thousand men.

Shortly after the 1920 overthrow and murder of Carranza by his own army, led by Alvaro Obregón, the interim president of Mexico, Adolfo DE LA HUERTA, negotiated Villa's amnesty and retirement. As part of the bargain, the general obtained a large hacienda in northern Durango, Canutillo, and a substantial subsidy for himself and a retinue of his troops. In 1923 Villa was assassinated in Hidalgo de Parra, perhaps because the national regime feared he would join de la Huerta, who would rebel some months later.

FRANCISCO R. ALMADA, *Gobernadores del Estado de Chihuahua* (1980), provides the basic biographical data. See also MARTÍN LUIS GUZMÁN, *Memoirs of Pancho Villa*, translated by Virginia H. Taylor (1965); FRIEDRICH KATZ, *The Secret War in Mexico* (1981), "Pancho Villa, Peasant Movements, and Agrarian Reform in Northern Mexico," in *Caudillo and Peasant in the Mexican Revolution*, edited by D. A. Brading (1980), and "Pancho Villa: Reform Governor of Chihuahua," in *Essays on the Mexican Revolution: Revisionist View of the Leaders*, edited by George W. Wolfskill (1979); SILVESTRÉ TERRAZAS, *El verdadero Pancho Villa* (1984).

MARK WASSERMAN

VILLA-LOBOS, HEITOR (*b.* 5 March 1887; *d.* 17 November 1959), Latin America's most famous twentieth-century composer. Born in Rio de Janeiro, Heitor Villa-Lobos was the son of a minor library official and amateur musician, Raul Villa-Lobos, and Noemia Villa-Lobos. The composer's earliest childhood recollections were of

Saturday evenings when friends came to the household for music making. Villa-Lobos's first musical instruction was from his father, who taught him to play the cello and provided him with ear training. When Villa-Lobos was asked if he considered himself to be self-taught, he often replied that he received such a complete musical foundation from his father that further instruction was unnecessary.

In 1899 Raul Villa-Lobos died during a smallpox epidemic, leaving the family in desperate financial circumstances. Noemia Villa-Lobos attempted to provide for the needs of the family by taking in laundry. Although she enrolled Tuhú, as she called young Heitor, in classes that would prepare him for a medical career, he was much more interested in all-night music-making sessions with young improvisers of popular music, the *chorões*. He frequently missed school, and when his mother tearfully objected, he ran away from home to live with an aunt who was more sympathetic to his musical interests and who played Bach preludes and fugues in a manner that never ceased to amaze him.

At eighteen Villa-Lobos traveled in the northern and northeastern parts of Brazil, an area rich in folk traditions. After selling some rare books that had belonged to his father, Villa-Lobos embarked on a journey through Brazil that lasted several years. He was gone such a long time that his mother assumed, not unreasonably, that he had been killed. Although Villa-Lobos frequently cited the period of his travels as one of collecting folk melodies which he subsequently used in his major works, there is little evidence that he made a systematic effort to collect folk materials firsthand. However, he did acquire an extensive knowledge of his

Heitor Villa-Lobos. ORGANIZATION OF AMERICAN STATES.

native country—its folk traditions, customs, and various kinds of musical styles.

Back in Rio de Janeiro by 1911, he began to establish himself as a musician and composer. In 1913 he married Lucilia Guimarães, a pianist and teacher at the National Institute of Music. Limited financial resources necessitated their moving into the small house of the Guimarães family. Villa-Lobos kept the family awake most of the night as he composed, usually beginning after the evening meal and working at the piano throughout the night. By 1915 he had collected a portfolio of works and arranged several concerts, the first of which was held in Nova Friburgo, a town in the state of Rio de Janeiro. By November of the same year he was ready for a complete program of his works in the the capital city of Rio de Janeiro.

The first review of Villa-Lobos's works were mixed. While recognizing a significant original talent, all the critics noted his lack of traditional training and disregard of conventional harmonic and formal principles of writing. In his attempt to find more acceptable expression for some of his musical ideas, Villa-Lobos was supported by his friend Darius Milhaud, who joined the staff of the French embassy in Rio in 1917. Milhaud encouraged Villa-Lobos to find his own way rather than imitate European models. With a recommendation from Arthur Rubinstein, Villa-Lobos secured funds in 1923 for a short trip to Europe, where he presented a few concerts of his music. In 1927 he obtained assistance for a longer stay, and with the help of Rubinstein and several Brazilian musicians in Paris, he performed several works at the Salle Gaveau, in Paris, on 24 October and 5 December 1927. With these performances Heitor Villa-Lobos established himself as a talented and original composer, and soon thereafter received invitations to present his music and conduct orchestras in London, Amsterdam, Vienna, Berlin, Brussels, Madrid, Liège, Lyon, and other European cities.

Villa-Lobos remained in Europe until 1930. With the country in a state of intense political disruption, Villa-Lobos decided to return to Europe to resume his career shortly after his arrival. In the meantime, however, he wrote a memorandum to the state government in São Paulo, expressing his distress at the condition of musical training and proposing a program of universal music education. He was summoned to appear at the governor's palace to defend his proposal. The next years were the busiest of Villa-Lobos's life. He postponed his plans to return to Europe and remained in São Paulo, and later Rio de Janeiro, as organizer and director of a program of choral singing, music education, and mass choral performances intended to instill patriotism. All of these programs were supported by the Getúlio VARGAS government. In 1944 Villa-Lobos visited the United States for the first time and during the final years of his life, he spent several months each year in Paris and New York.

Villa-Lobos wrote a torrent of musical works, variously estimated at two or three thousand, including arrangements and adaptations. Although he is recognized for his incredible fecundity and facility of musical writing, most of his music is unknown and has not been performed internationally, despite worldwide performances during the Villa-Lobos Centennial Celebrations in 1987 and 1988, which gave a broader representation of his life work. His sixteen *Choros* are a microcosm of the riches of Brazilian rhythmic invention and the diversity of its folk music. His *Nonetos*, although frequently referred to as chamber music, call for a gigantic percussion section. His late string quartets, written when the composer was near death, represent some of his finest writing. Individual works such as *Uirapurú* (The Magic Bird) draw their inspiration from various Brazilian myths and show the composer's mastery of orchestration. The best-known work of Villa-Lobos is the aria from *Bachianas brasileiras* no. 5, written in 1938. Because of his use of national and regional materials, he is regarded as a crucial figure in the development of Brazilian musical nationalism. Capturing, and building on, the urban salon music tradition of Ernesto Nazareth, Villa-Lobos molded diverse elements into a musical language that has been internationally recognized as an expression of both individual genius and the spirit of Brazilian music.

STANLEY SADIE, ed., *The New Grove Dictionary of Music and Musicians* (1980); DAVID P. APPLEBY, *The Music of Brazil* (1983); VASCO MARIZ, *Heitor Villa-Lobos: Compositor brasileiro*, 11th ed. (1989).

DAVID P. APPLEBY

VILLACORTA CALDERÓN, JOSÉ ANTONIO (*b.* 1879; *d.* unknown), Guatemalan historian, anthropologist, and bibliographer. Villacorta Calderón is particularly noted for his general histories of Guatemala and his important editorial work. Significantly, he edited the Maya sacred book *Anales de los Cakchiqueles* (1937). He also compiled in his *Bibliografía guatemalteca* (1944) a complete listing of bibliographic information for all the volumes exhibited at a national exposition in honor of the anniversary of printing in Guatemala in 1939. His most famous and widely read work, *Historia de la República de Guatemala* (1960), is a detailed survey of Guatemala, from political independence from Spain to 1885, based on extensive research in secondary and archival sources. Often used as a textbook in schools, the book has been influential in shaping the historical views of countless Guatemalans. Villacorta Calderón was one of the most significant and prestigious of the shapers of academic life in twentieth-century Guatemala.

JOSÉ ANTONIO VILLACORTA CALDERÓN, *Monografía del departamento de Guatemala* (1926); *Bibliografía guatemalteca* (1944); *J. Antonio Villacorta C. en las ciencias y letras americanistas, juzgado por sus contemporáneos* (1949); and *Historia de la República de Guatemala, 1821–1921* (1960).

MICHAEL F. FRY

VILLAGRA, FRANCISCO DE (Villagrán; *b.* 1512?; *d.* 22 June 1563), Spanish conquistador. A soldier with experience in North Africa, Villagra went to America in 1537, and accompanied Pedro de VALDIVIA (1500–1553) on his expedition to Chile in 1540. During Valdivia's absence from the new colony in 1547–1548, he acted as interim governor, and in that capacity ordered the execution of Pedro SANCHO DE HOZ, who had plotted to seize control. In 1549 Valdivia sent him to fetch reinforcements from Peru, a mission he eventually completed after many adventures. Early in 1552, again on Valdivia's instructions, he attempted an overland expedition to the Strait of Magellan by way of the eastern side of the Andes, only to turn back at the Río Negro.

After Valdivia's death (December 1553), Villagra unsuccessfully claimed the governorship of Chile: his forcible seizure of the government was firmly resisted by the *cabildo* (municipal council) of Santiago. He remained an active leader in the warfare against the ARAUCANIANS, bringing about the defeat of the *toqui* (chief) LAUTARO in 1557. It was not until the departure of governor García HURTADO DE MENDOZA (1535–1609) that Villagra finally secured the governorship (1561–1563). On his death it passed to his cousin Pedro de Villagra (1563–1565), a brilliant tactician, who was eventually dismissed by the viceroy of Peru.

SIMON COLLIER

VILLAGRÁ, GASPAR PÉREZ DE (*b.* 1555; *d.* 1620), soldier and chronicler. Born in New Spain, Villagrá was one of the few early creoles to study at the University of Salamanca. After his return to New Spain he was appointed *procurador general* (solicitor general) and captain in Juan de OÑATE's 1596 conquest and colonization expedition to New Mexico, where Villagrá participated in many operations, including the battle of Ácoma (1599). After a visit to Spain, Villagrá published his epic poem *Historia de la Nueva México* (1610), which related the history of the Oñate expedition. Although sometimes marked by hyperbole and heroic vision, Villagrá's *Historia* remains valuable today as an eyewitness account of the conquest of New Mexico.

His literary achievement notwithstanding, shortly afterward he was found guilty of executing two deserters in New Mexico and forcibly bringing dozens of Ácoman women to convents in Spain, for which he was banished from the province for six years and from Mexico City for two years. In 1620, en route from Spain to fill a bureaucratic position in Guatemala, Villagrá died at sea.

RALPH EMERSON TWITCHELL, *Captain Don Gaspar de Villagrá: Author of the First History of the Conquest of New Mexico by the Adelantado Don Juan de Oñate* (1924); GASPAR PÉREZ DE VILLAGRÁ *History of New Mexico,* translated and edited by Gilberto Espinosa (1933).

AARON PAINE MAHR

VILLAGRÁN, JULIÁN AND JOSÉ MARÍA ("EL CHITO"), Mexican insurgents. Julián Villagrán (*b.* 1760; *d.* 21 June 1813), his son Chito (*b.* ca. 1780; *d.* 14 May 1813), and their kinsmen, clients, and allies were in many ways typical of the great creole clans of lower and middling economic position who led the insurgency in the Mexican provinces in the period 1810–1821. Julián was a muleteer, minor landowner, and sometime militia officer; Chito, a delinquent and estate foreman in their native town of Huichapán in central Mexico. Chito joined the rebellion to escape legal charges against him for the murder of a local landowner and town official with whose wife he had been amorously involved; Julián, to protect his son and to pursue vague political and economic goals. Their forces attacked or occupied a number of important provincial towns from late 1810 through mid-1813, including Huichapán, Ixmiquilpán, Zimapán, and Tulancingo. Both refused to acknowledge any higher insurgent authority in their spheres of influence; both rejected royalist pardons; and both were captured and executed in 1813.

ALEJANDRO VILLASEÑOR Y VILLASEÑOR, *Biografías de los héroes y caudillos de la independencia* (1962), vol. 1, pp. 110–118; CHRISTON I. ARCHER, "Banditry and Revolution in New Spain," *Bibliotheca Americana,* 1, no. 2 (1982): 59–89; BRIAN R. HAMNETT, *Roots of Insurgency: Mexican Regions, 1750–1824* (1986).

ERIC VAN YOUNG

See also **Mexico: War of Independence.**

VILLAGRÁN KRAMER, FRANCISCO (*b.* 5 April 1922), vice president of Guatemala (1977–1980). Born in Guatemala City into a Protestant family, Francisco Villagrán earned his law degree at the University of San Carlos in 1951. Active in the October Revolution (1944), he served both Juan José ARÉVALO (1945–1951) and Jacobo ARBENZ (1950–1954) at international conferences. He helped Mario MÉNDEZ MONTENEGRO (1912–1965) found the Partido Revolucionario (PR) in 1957, but broke with the PR to organize the more leftist Revolutionary Unity Party (URD) in 1958.

Considered a radical, he was exiled by the Enrique PERALTA AZURDIA military regime (1963–1966) in 1965. The new constitution drafted that year raised the minimum age for the presidency from thirty-five to forty to specifically bar him from the 1966 elections.

Concerned about growing political polarization and violence, Villagrán returned to the PR in 1978 to become General Romeo LUCAS GARCÍA's (1978–1982) running mate in order to, in his words to a *Washington Post* reporter, "avoid a Custer's last stand in Guatemala." Failing to moderate the repressive character of the regime, he helped organize the Democratic Front Against Repression in 1979. He resigned as vice president in September 1980. He subsequently became a leader in the Christian Democratic Party (DCG), and also worked for the World Bank.

HENRY WELLS, ed., *Guatemala: Election Factbook* (1966); CARLOS C. HAEUSSLER YELA, *Diccionario General de Guatemala*, vol. 3. (1983); FRANCISCO VILLLAGRÁN KRAMER, *Biografía política de Guatemala: Los pactos políticos de 1944 a 1970* (1993).

ROLAND H. EBEL

VILLALBA, JÓVITO (*b.* 23 March 1908), Venezuelan political leader. A native of Nueva Esparta State, Villalba attended the Central University of Venezuela, where he became one of the most prominent members of the student Generation of 1928 as leader of the Venezuelan Students Federation. His eloquent oratory in opposition to the dictatorship of Juan Vicente GÓMEZ resulted in his imprisonment from 1928 to 1934. After 1935 the young lawyer was a founder and leader of influential political organizations. In 1946 he joined a new political party, the Republican Democratic Union (Unión Republicana Democrática—URD), and quickly rose to be its secretary-general, a post he held for decades. In 1952 he ran for president in a military-sponsored election, but his apparent victory over the official candidate was nullified by the military authorities, who promptly deported him. After his return from exile in the United States in 1958, Villalba became a principal architect of the new democratic political system. He headed the URD, served in Congress, and ran unsuccessfully as his party's presidential candidate in 1963 and 1973.

IVÁN CLAUDIO, *Breve historia de URD* (1968); MANUEL VICENTE MAGALLANES, *Los partidos políticos en la evolución histórica venezolana* (1973); ROBERT J. ALEXANDER, ed., *Biographical Dictionary of Latin American and Caribbean Political Leaders* (1988).

· WINFIELD J. BURGGRAAFF

VILLALONGA, JORGE (Conde de la Cueva; *b.* ca. 1665; active late seventeenth and early eighteenth centuries), viceroy of the New Kingdom of Granada (1719–1724). Philip V named Villalonga the first viceroy of the newly established Viceroyalty of New Granada in June 1717. Promoted from his position as governor of the Callao presidio, Villalonga was to effect the political reform program established by Antonio de la PEDROSA Y GUERRERO at the king's behest (1718–1719). Specifically, metropolitan officials expected Villalonga to solidify the Caribbean defenses of New Granada, curb smuggling, quell political infighting, promote economic development and so increase crown revenues, and project royal authority. From his very arrival in Santa Fe in November 1719 with demands for pomp, however, Villalonga provoked much internal opposition to his policies and demeanor. While Villalonga's RESIDENCIA (end-of-tenure review) generally praised him, the king and his ministers judged his rule to be ineffective at best, for in late 1723 they decided to extinguish the viceroyalty and return the colony to *audiencia* rule. Villalonga returned to Spain in 1724 and became minister of war.

The best surveys of Villalonga's rule and the first attempt to establish the Viceroyalty of New Granada are in Spanish and include MARÍA TERESA GARRIDO CONDE, *La primera creación del virreinato de Nueva Granada (1717–1723)* (1965); and SERGIO ELÍAS ORTIZ, *Nuevo Reino de Granada: El virreinato, 1719–1753*, in *Historia extensa de Colombia*, vol. 4 (1970), pp. 29–58.

LANCE R. GRAHN

VILLALPANDO, CRISTÓBAL DE (*b.* ca. 1650; *d.* 20 August 1714), painter. Villalpando is responsible for the most agitated of Mexican colonial baroque paintings; he was also for many years an official of the painters' guild of Mexico City. There is considerable discussion about his training. Suggestions include study with José JUÁREZ, Antonio Rodríguez, and his father-in-law, Diego Mendoza of Puebla. Much is also made of the influence on his work of Baltasar de Echave Rioja. His works are found throughout Mexico and many are of enormous size, decorating vaults and entire walls. His earliest known paintings were for a RETABLO at Huaquechula, Puebla, signed and dated in 1675. Between 1684 and 1686 he executed four huge canvases for the sacristy of the cathedral of Mexico City, and in 1688 he painted the dome of the Capilla de los Reyes of Pueblo Cathedral. Often inventive in their iconography, his compositions recall Peter Paul Rubens and Juan de Valdés Leal. His brilliant coloring is sometimes shrill, and he makes generous use of shadow for dramatic effects. His production is uneven.

FRANCISCO DE LA MAZA, *El pintor Cristóbal de Villalpando* (1964).

CLARA BARGELLINI

VILLANUEVA, CARLOS RAÚL (*b.* 30 May 1900; *d.* October 1976), Venezuelan architect. Villanueva was educated in Paris at the Lycée Condorcet and the school of architecture of the École Nationale des Beaux-Arts, where he studied with Gabriel Héraud. Villanueva's projects were numerous and demonstrated a long-term vision devoted to re-creating the landscape of Caracas. In addition to acting as an architectural consultant to the Worker's Bank of Venezuela, he was a pioneer of urban renewal, planning El Silencio in Caracas, and the low-cost General Rafael Urdaneta housing developments in Maracaibo during the 1940s. Between 1944 and 1957 he designed several buildings for the University of Caracas, among them the library and the medical school. Villanueva is known for his design of "floating structures," which include his crowning achievements: the university's Olympic Stadium (1950) and the Olympic Swimming Pool (1957). Villanueva was the founder and first president of the Venezuelan Society of Architects; he was also a professor of ARCHITECTURE at the Central University of Venezuela.

419

DOROTHEA MOHOLY-NAGY, *Carlos Raúl Villanueva and the Architecture of Venezuela* (1964); RAFAEL PÁEZ, *Los hombres que han hecho Venezuela* (1979).

MICHAEL A. POLUSHIN

VILLARÁN, MANUEL VICENTE (*b.* 11 October 1873; *d.* 21 February 1958), a leading authority on constitutional issues in early-twentieth-century Peru. Villarán was born in Lima. At the age of twenty-three, having received a degree in law, he joined the department of sociology at the University of San Marcos. In 1904 he led the progressive Civilista faction that supported José PARDO Y BARREDA for president. He argued passionately for education, saying that Peru needed well-educated middle and working classes to forge a modern nation. But he also agreed with Javier PRADO Y UGARTECHE that the laziness and mental inertia of the indigenous people were the cause of the country's low level of development. He was minister of justice, religion, and instruction during Augusto LEGUÍA's first government (1908–1910) and helped to bring the first U.S. educators to Peru. In 1918 he wrote a newspaper essay, "Costumbres electorales," decrying the sorry state of political maturity of the Peruvian masses in the nineteenth century. In 1922 he became the rector of San Marcos and held that post until early 1924. Subsequently, he taught law and advised various governments during the 1920s and 1930s. After World War II he lived in virtual obscurity. Villarán's books include *El arbitraje de Washington en la cuestión peruanochilena* (1925), *Bosquejo histórico de la constitución inglesa*, 2d ed. (1935), and *La Universidad de San Marcos de Lima: Los orígenes, 1548–1577* (1938).

JESÚS CHAVARRÍA, *José Carlos Mariátegui and the Rise of Modern Peru, 1890–1930* (1979); STEVE STEIN, *Populism in Peru: The Emergence of the Masses and the Politics of Social Control* (1980).

VINCENT PELOSO

See also **Peru: Political Parties.**

VILLARRICA, capital city of the department of Guairá in south-central Paraguay (not far from the Tebicuary River), with 34,801 inhabitants (1982). Founded in 1570, the small Spanish enclave suffered continued attacks by Paulista raiders from Brazil during colonial times until it was established as a permanent settlement in 1682. It is the center of the YERBA MATÉ industry of Paraguay and an important processor of orange concentrates. After World War I, German colonists moved into the uplands north of Villarrica and formed the agrarian bases of the region with tanning establishments, flour mills, sugar mills, and cotton-threading mills.

HUGO G. FERREIRA, *Geografía del Paraguay* (Asunción, 1975).

CÉSAR N. CAVIEDES

VILLARROEL LÓPEZ, GUALBERTO (*b.* 1908; *d.* 21 July 1946), president of Bolivia (1943–1946). Villarroel was a virtually unknown military officer when he came to power in a coup against the administration of General Enrique PEÑARANDA. An instructor in the reformist military college and a key figure in the secret nationalist military lodge Razón de Patria (the Nation's Right, known as RADEPA), Villarroel allied himself with the leftist-fascist Nationalist Revolutionary Movement (Movimiento Nacionalista Revolucionario—MNR) during the coup.

Under his government, largely dependent upon the MNR for popular support, important mine labor legislation was passed. In 1945 the government organized the First National Indian Congress, during which a thousand Indian leaders met. As a result, *pongueaje*, or free-labor services to the hacienda owners, was abolished, and other reforms were advanced, though the legislation was never enacted.

Despite its attempt at reform, the Villarroel regime brutally suppressed the opposition, executing various opposition leaders after a failed coup in 1944. Villarroel himself went to his death in 1946, when a teacher's strike turned violent. A mob stormed the presidential palace and hanged the president from a lamppost in the adjoining plaza.

The Villarroel regime is noted for its attempts at social reform and for the participation of the MNR, which in 1952 would lead Latin America's second social revolution.

A good summary of the Villarroel period is contained in HERBERT S. KLEIN, *Parties and Political Change in Bolivia, 1880–1952* (1969), pp. 369–382. See also LUIS PEÑALOZA C., *Historia del Movimiento Nacionalista Revolucionario, 1941–1952* (1963), pp. 55–94. A classic historical novel about the president is AUGUSTO CÉSPEDES, *El presidente colgado (Historia boliviana)* (1966).

ERICK D. LANGER

See also **Bolivia: Political Parties.**

VILLAS BÔAS BROTHERS, rights activists who became internationally known during the 1960s and 1970s for their defense of Brazilian Indians. Orlando (*b.* 1914), Cláudio (*b.* 1916), and Leonardo (*b.* 1918; *d.* 1961) Villas Bôas opposed the policy of the Brazilian government, which at that time favored rapid integration of Indians into the national society and economy. They argued strongly that reservations should be protected from outside influences for an indefinite period to protect Indian cultures and ways of life.

The brothers were members of the Roncador-Xingu expedition of 1943 sent to survey unexplored regions of central Brazil. Their experience with unacculturated Indians of the Upper Xingu River Basin convinced them to remain there and devote their lives to the welfare and protection of Indians. In 1954, when a devastating measles epidemic struck the Upper Xingu tribes, the Villas Bôas brothers mobilized the support of the Medical School of São Paulo, which set up a model program of medical assistance for the Indians.

In 1961 the Villas Bôas brothers were instrumental in persuading the Brazilian government to set aside most of the Upper Xingu region (8,800 square miles) as a national park for protection of the Indians and wildlife preservation. The two surviving brothers, Orlando and Cláudio, became the administrators of the Xingu National Park. Anthropologists, journalists, and other visitors were impressed with the well-being and peace in which the Indians of the park lived. In 1967 the Villas Bôas brothers received the Founders' Gold Medal of the Royal Geographical Society and in 1971 they were nominated for the Nobel Peace Prize.

Some supporters of Indian self-determination have criticized the Villas Bôases' administration of the Xingu Park as overly protective and paternalistic. It has also been pointed out that idyllic images of the park disseminated in Brazil and abroad tend to mask the much less favorable conditions under which many Indians in other parts of the country live.

ROBIN HANBURY-TENISON, *A Question of Survival for the Indians of Brazil* (1973); ORLANDO VILLAS BÔAS, *Xingu: The Indians, Their Myths* (1973); SHELTON H. DAVIS, *Victims of the Miracle: Development and the Indians of Brazil* (1977); ADRIAN COWELL, *The Decade of Destruction: The Crusade to Save the Amazon Rain Forest* (1990); ORLANDO VILLAS BÔAS and CLÁUDIO VILLAS BÔAS, *A marcha paro o oeste* (1994).

NANCY M. FLOWERS

See also **Indian Policy, Brazil; Xingu Reserve.**

VILLAURRUTIA, JACOBO DE

VILLAURRUTIA, JACOBO DE (*b.* May 1757; *d.* 23 August 1833), judge and journalist in Central America and Mexico. Jacobo de Villaurrutia López Osorio was born in the city of Santo Domingo on the island of Hispaniola. His father was Antonio Villaurrutia, a native of Mexico; his mother was María Antonieta López de Osorio. In his youth, he moved to Spain, where, as part of the family, he was a page for Francisco LORENZANA, archbishop of Mexico and later cardinal and archbishop of Toledo. Under Lorenzana's protection, Villaurrutia began his studies, completing the equivalent of a master's degree on 14 May 1781, and a doctorate in law four days later from the University of Toledo.

Villaurrutia began a successful career in public administration. On 2 November 1782 he was appointed magistrate and chief justice for Alcalá de Henares, a post he held for five years. In May 1792 he was named judge of the Audiencia of Guatemala, and later became a founder of the Sociedad Económica de Amigos del País (Economic Society of Friends of the Country). The purpose of this organization and similar ones in the Spanish dominions was to promote industry and the arts. They also promulgated the ideas of Spanish intellectuals through JOURNALISM.

Villaurrutia's innovative ideas led to his removal from his post in 1808 and transfer as a criminal court magistrate to Mexico City, where he continued his work in journalism, aided by Carlos María de BUSTAMANTE. His periodical was finally suppressed by Viceroy José de ITURRIGARAY. When problems arose as a result of Napoleon's invasion of Spain, Villaurrutia played an important role in opposing the Spanish authorities in Mexico, for which he was expelled from Mexico in 1814. Upon returning to Spain, he was appointed judge in Barcelona and became dean and internal regent. When Mexican independence was declared in 1821, he resigned and returned to Mexico, where he was appointed regent of the *audiencia* in 1822 and president of the Supreme Court of Justice in 1824. In 1827 he was circuit judge for the Federal District, the state of Mexico, and the territory of Tlaxcala. In November of the same year he was elected minister of the Supreme Court, and in 1831 he became its president. He died of cholera in Mexico City.

MANUEL BERGANZO, *Diccionario de historia y geografía* (1853–1856), and "Biografía de don Jacobo de Villaurrutia," in *Anales de la Sociedad de geografía e historia de Guatemala* 25 (December 1951): 388–396.

OSCAR G. PELÁEZ ALMENGOR

See also **Guatemala: Organizations.**

VILLAURRUTIA, XAVIER

VILLAURRUTIA, XAVIER (*b.* 27 March 1903; *d.* 25 December 1950), Mexican poet, critic, and playwright. Villaurrutia was born and died in Mexico City. He belonged to the generation known as the Contemporaries. With Salvador NOVO, he participated in the review and theatrical group Ulises. He studied drama at Yale (1935–1936) and was one of the first professional writers of his country. He wrote an avant-garde novel (*Dama de corazones*, 1928) and the plays *Parece mentira* (1934), *¿En qué piensas?* (1938), and *La hiedra* (1941). His screenplays include *Vámonos con Pancho Villa* (1934) and *Distinto amanecer* (1943). He translated William Blake, André Gide, and many others and was a critic of literature, film, and the fine arts (*Textos y pretextos*, 1940). The most notable of his work, however, is his brief and rigorous poetry: *Reflejos* (1926), *Nocturnos* (1933), *Décima muerte* (1941), *Canto a la primavera* (1948), and especially *Nostalgia de la muerte* (Buenos Aires, 1938), in which the verbal creativity of the avant-garde is united with classic Spanish lyricism and a reflection on mortality reminiscent of Nahuatl poetry. His works were collected by Alí Chumacero, Luis Mario Schneider, and Miguel Capistrán (*Obras*, 2d ed. 1966). Eliot Weinenberg has translated *Nostalgia for Death* (1992), which includes an essay by Octavio PAZ.

MERLYN H. FORSTER, *Fire and Ice: The Poetry of Xavier Villaurrutia* (1967); EUGENE MORETTA, *The Poetic Achievement of Xavier Villaurrutia* (Cuernavaca, Mexico, 1971); OCTAVIO PAZ, *Xavier Villaurrutia en persona y en obra* (1978).

J. E. PACHECO

See also **Literature: Spanish America.**

VILLAVERDE, CIRILO (*b.* 28 October 1812; *d.* 20 October 1894), Cuban writer. Villaverde was born on a sugar plantation and, as a young writer and lawyer in Havana, he wrote romantic stories and accounts of his travels in his home province, Pinar del Río. Dedicated to freeing Cuba from Spanish control, Villaverde favored annexation by the United States and, to that end, worked as a secretary for General Narciso LÓPEZ. Because of his conspiratorial activities, Villaverde was imprisoned by the Spaniards in 1848. One year later, he escaped to the United States, where he worked as a teacher, married fellow Cuban Emilia Casanova, and continued contributing to Spanish-speaking publications.

Villaverde resided in the United States until 1858, and then again from 1861 until his death. In 1882 he published *Cecilia Valdés*, a novel about Spanish colonialism and SLAVERY in early-nineteenth-century Cuba. It shows how the Cuban oligarchy's push toward modernization of the SUGAR INDUSTRY had dramatic consequences for the slaves, symbolized by the book's eponymous female protagonist. With this novel of manners, more than with any other work, Villaverde secured his place in Cuban literary history.

The best discussion of Villaverde's works is in WILLIAM LUIS, *Literary Bondage* (1990). See also IMELDO ALVAREZ, ed., *Acerca de Cirilo Villaverde* (1982), and REYNALDO GONZÁLEZ, *Contradanzas y latigazos* (1983).

INEKE PHAF

VILLAVICENCIO, Colombian city. The capital of Meta Department, located on the left bank of the Guatiquía River, east of the Cordillera Oriental. It is 1,542 feet above sea level and 76 miles from Bogotá. Villavicencio, which was earlier called Gramalote, was formally established in 1842. Called the "Gateway to the LLANOS," it is, with approximately 190,000 inhabitants, the main urban center of the plains region and a distribution and shipment center for cattle and other plains foodstuffs. Villavicencio has a university known for its program in tropical zoology. The city is served by an airport and is a highway hub. It also is the main public health center for the region.

ENRIQUE ORTEGA RICAURTE, comp., *Villavicencio, 1842–1942* (1943); INSTITUTO GEOGRÁFICO AGUSTÍN CODAZZI, *Diccionario geográfico de Colombia*, vol. 2 (1980), pp. 1778–1779.

J. LEÓN HELGUERA

VILLAZÓN, ELIODORO (*b.* 22 January 1848; *d.* 14 September 1940), president of Bolivia (1909–1913). Born in Sacaba in the department of Cochabamba, Villazón was trained as a lawyer. He entered politics and became deputy from Cochabamba to the Assembly of 1871 when he was only twenty-three years old. At the National Convention of 1880 he caught the attention of Narciso CAMPERO, the recently installed president (1880–1884). Under Campero, Villazón was appointed minister of finance and later financial agent in Europe. After returning from abroad, Villazón joined the Liberal Party and became one of its most loyal members. When the Liberals came to power after the FEDERAL WAR of 1898, Villazón became minister of foreign affairs. In 1909 the leader of the Liberals, Ismael MONTES, who had been president from 1904 to 1908, selected Villazón to be the party's presidential candidate in a special election made necessary by the death of Montes's successor. Elected overwhelmingly, Villazón, as caretaker for Montes, continued government support for railroad construction and successfully negotiated loans with Europeans that led to the formation of the Banco de la Nación.

WILLIAM BELMONT PARKER, *Bolivians of Today*, 2d ed. (1922), pp. 317–320; HERBERT S. KLEIN, *Parties and Political Change in Bolivia, 1880–1952* (1969), pp. 43–44.

ERWIN P. GRIESHABER

VILLEDA MORALES, RAMÓN (*b.* 1908; *d.* 8 October 1971), Honduran president (1957–1963). Villeda Morales studied medicine in Europe and Honduras. Called the "Little Bird" for his small stature and oratorical prowess, he was also known for his cosmopolitan polish, rare in Honduran politicians. He dominated the Liberal Party as chairman and founded the party newspaper, *El Pueblo*. Although he won a plurality in the 1954 presidential election, a subsequent coup deprived him of office.

In 1957 Villeda Morales came to power after a military coup overthrew Julio LOZANO DÍAS. Between the coup and his inauguration, Villeda Morales seems to have participated in a pact of the Blue Water (named after the UNITED FRUIT COMPANY villa where the clandestine pact was apparently devised). He agreed to conform radical agrarian and labor reforms to ALLIANCE FOR PROGRESS ideology in return for ample U.S. aid and Honduran military support. The 1958 labor code brought realistic worker benefits. The 1962 Agrarian Reform Law nationalized, with compensation, undeveloped land for peasants. In response to the 1954 United Fruit strike, peasant organizations were legalized. However, Villeda Morales's close relationship with Serafino Remauldi, a Central Intelligence Agency (CIA) operative and labor representative, assured that an AFL-CIO alliance of peasant and labor organizations dominated labor.

The limited reforms of Villeda Morales nonetheless

brought conservative opposition and charges of Communist infiltration. Afraid that the 1963 Liberal presidential candidate would make good on Villeda Morales's "second republic" rhetoric, military chief Oswaldo LÓPEZ ARELLANO staged a successful coup two months before the election.

Several factors point to CIA involvement in the Arellano coup. Villeda Morales, who had CIA links through Remauldi, piqued the agency by pushing for a more radical successor. This apparently prompted CIA endorsement of Arellano's coup. Also, CIA backing is indicated by the quick commendation of the coup by the U.S. ambassador and the Voice of America, although this support was repudiated by the U.S. State Department.

Arriving in New York in 1971 as Honduran ambassador to the United Nations, Villeda Morales suffered a fatal heart attack. The Honduran Liberal Party continues to invoke the memory of Villeda Morales as a Kennedyesque figure.

PHILIP AGEE, *Inside the Company: A CIA Diary* (1975); ROBERT MAC CAMERON, *Bananas, Labor, and Politics in Honduras, 1954–1963* (1983); JAMES RUDOLPH, ed., *Honduras: A Country Study* (1983).

EDMOND KONRAD

VILLEGAIGNON, NICOLAS DURAND DE (*b.* 1510; *d.* 29 January 1572), French colonizer in Brazil. Born in Provins, Villegaignon was a knight of Malta and nephew of the Grand Master. He served under Emperor Charles V at Algiers and fought the Turks in Hungary and at Tripoli. An experienced seaman, Villegaignon defied the English fleet by escorting Mary Stuart (later called Mary Queen of Scots) to France to marry the dauphin. Villegaignon, a warrior and humanist, anguished over spiritual matters and at one point embraced Calvinism.

As vice-admiral of Brittany, he interested Admiral Gaspard de Coligny in using Brazil, a land already visited by Normans and Bretons, as a sanctuary for Protestant refugees. In November 1555, with three boats manned by Catholics and Protestants, Villegaignon arrived at Guanabara Bay. He fortified a small island as a base for further exploration, naming the colony La France Antarctique. Encouraged by the reformer John Calvin, three hundred Protestants arrived in March 1557. Villegaignon, noted for his generous treatment of the native peoples, was less forgiving to the Protestants, whom he punished harshly for even slight transgressions. He returned to France in 1559, leaving his nephew in charge.

The newly arrived French colonists encountered resistance from the established Portuguese settlers in Brazil. Deemed heretics by the Portuguese, they supported the indigenous peoples against their colonial overlords. With only seventy-four men, the French held out for twenty days until the Portuguese (led by Mem de SÁ) took the island and razed the fort. Survivors fled to the mainland to live among the native people. Villegaignon

finally conceded the colonial rights to Portugal, and he remained in France until his death.

CHARLES ANDRÉ JULIEN, *Les français en Amérique* (1946) and *Les débuts de l'expansion et de la colonisation françaises* (1947); SAMUEL ELIOT MORISON, *The European Discovery of America*, vol. 2 (1974); BRASIL, SERVICO DE DOCUMENTAÇÃO GERAL DA MARIUHA, *Historia naval brasileira*, vol. 1 (1975); MICHEL MOLLAT and JACQUES HABERT, *Giovanni et Girolamo Verrazano, navigateurs de François 1ᵉʳ* (1982); FRANK LESTRINGANT, *Le Huguenot el le sauvage* (1990); and PHILIPPE BONNICHON, *Los navegantes franceses y el descubrimiento de America* (1992).

PHILIPPE BONNICHON

See also **French Colonization in Brazil.**

VILLEGAS, MICAELA. *See* **Perricholi, La.**

VILLEGAS, OSCAR (*b.* 18 March 1943), Mexican playwright. Villegas, a native of Ciudad del Maíz and a graduate of the directing program of the National Institute of Fine Arts, is generally considered to be the most talented playwright of his generation. His inveterate experimentation produces plays rich in interesting techniques, including one, *El señor y la señora* (1969), in which the speeches are not identified by character. His themes are contemporary and sometimes shocking: youth, love, sex, myths, values, and traditions, presented most often in one-act plays. Villegas's two major plays are *Atlántida* (1976), which takes place in a declining society without values, and *Mucho gusto en conocerlo* (1985), which also paints the hypocrisy and perversions that assault human sensibilities. Difficult economic and theatrical conditions in Mexico have hindered productions of Villegas's works; by occupation he is a ceramicist.

GEORGE WOODYARD, "El teatro de Oscar Villegas: Experimentación con la forma," in *Texto Crítico* 4, no. 10 (May–August 1978): 32–41; RONALD D. BURGESS, "The Early Years: Villegas and López," in *The New Dramatists of Mexico* (1967–1985) (1991), pp. 14–29.

GEORGE WOODYARD

VIÑA DEL MAR, Chilean seaside town located approximately 100 miles west of Santiago and adjacent to the port of Valparaíso. Originally a hacienda dating from the colonial period and once the home of prominent Chilean politician José VERGARA, it became a city in 1878. The site of a battle during the 1891 civil war, it is now an affluent suburb of Valparaíso. During the summer, it attracts many to its beaches and casino.

AGUSTÍN EDWARDS, *My Native Land* (1928), pp. 72–73; HAROLD BLAKEMORE, "Chile," in Harold Blakemore and Clifford T. Smith, editors, *Latin America: Geographical Perspectives* (1971), p. 505.

WILLIAM F. SATER

VINCENT, STÉNIO JOSEPH (*b.* 1874; *d.* 1959), president of Haiti (1930–1941). A member of the mulatto elite, Vincent was a lawyer, diplomat, and politician. He served as the mayor of Port-au-Prince and went on several diplomatic missions to Paris, Berlin, and the Hague. Vincent headed both the anti-interventionist Nationalist Party and the Patriotic Union and gained the presidency on the basis of his opposition to the U.S. occupation. Vincent was elected president by the National Assembly in November 1930. Although he entered office committed to the principle of parliamentary government, he based his power on officially controlled plebiscites.

As president, Vincent was widely regarded as partial toward mulattoes. He was particularly suspicious of the *Garde d'Haiti,* a predominantly black national guard organized by the U.S. Marines. As such he built up his own special presidential guard, which kept its weapons in the National Palace. In 1934 Vincent visited the United States and convinced President Franklin D. ROOSEVELT to withdraw the U.S. Marines. Thereafter, Vincent's fervent nationalism abated somewhat. In 1935 Vincent extended his tenure in office by five years. In addition, he declared the Senate "in rebellion to the will of the people" and expelled its members from the chamber. He then made several overtures to improve U.S.-Haitian relations and to attract U.S. tourists, such as offering to amend a law that would have facilitated casino gambling.

Vincent's popularity waned, however, because of his antipathy toward blacks and his weak reaction to the Dominican massacre of Haitians in 1937. In 1941 Vincent decided against having his term in office extended again and instead retired peacefully. He died in Port-au-Prince.

ROLAND I. PERUSSE, *Historical Dictionary of Haiti* (1977); ROBERT J. ALEXANDER, ed., *Biographical Dictionary of Latin America and Caribbean Leaders* (1988); BRENDA GAYLE PLUMMER, *Haiti and the United States: The Psychological Moment* (1992), esp. pp. 133, 141–144, and 154–157.

DOUGLAS R. KEBERLEIN

See also **United States–Latin American Relations.**

VIÑES Y MARTORELL, BENITO (*b.* 19 September 1837; *d.* 23 July 1893), pioneer of hurricane forecasting. A Jesuit priest born in Catalonia, Spain, Viñes was sent to Havana to take charge of the Belén Observatory (Belén was a Jesuit preparatory school), where he carried out his scientific work for the rest of his life. He was well acquainted with all that was then known about HURRICANES, which amounted to very little as far as the signs announcing their coming or their passing were concerned. He devoted his life to finding a way to detect these signs.

Viñes began by studying the movements of the clouds that he called "featherlike cirrostratus." He then combined the data he gathered with information about the relationship between changes in barometric pressure and the paths of hurricanes that had blown through at the same time in previous years. After a while, he found it possible to predict, within certain limits, the path that a hurricane would follow. On 11 September 1875 he was able to make the first accurate hurricane forecast in history. A year later, again in September, the only sea captain who did not heed his warning lost his ship in the Straits of Florida.

In time Viñes was able to establish a network of information sources in the Caribbean. But he never had at his disposal the sophisticated observing tools that are available today, and thus his "laws of the hurricanes" (which also explained the structure of these tropical storms) have been superseded by researchers. This does not mean, however, that the essential validity of his observations has been proved erroneous. On the contrary, according to Dr. Neil L. Frank, director of the U.S. National Hurricane Center, they have been rediscovered and confirmed. Viñes's work is a historical landmark in the field of hurricane forecasting. Viñes died in Havana.

For a short biography of Viñes, see JOSÉ I. LASAGA, *Cuban Lives: Pages from Cuban History* (1988), vol. 2. See also JOSÉ FERNÁNDEZ PARTAGAS, ed., *Memoir of the Homage to Rev. Father Benito Viñes, S.J. in the Centennial of the First Hurricane Forecast* (1975).

JOSÉ M. HERNÁNDEZ

VIOLA, ROBERTO EDUARDO (*b.* 13 October 1924; *d.* 10 October 1994), military leader and president of Argentina (1981). Born in the city of Buenos Aires, he graduated from the Military Academy (COLEGIO MILITAR) in 1944. While a colonel, Viola served as an Argentine representative to the Inter-American Defense Board in Washington, D.C. (1967–1968). In 1975 he was promoted to chief of the General Staff, the number two position in the army. He was deeply involved in the DIRTY WAR (1970–82) against the urban guerrillas. On 31 July 1978 he was promoted to commander in chief of the Argentine Army. In 1981 he succeeded General Jorge VIDELA as the senior member of the military junta and president of the republic. In early November, Viola fell ill. Although he recovered, General Leopoldo GALTIERI politically outmaneuvered him in the ruling military junta and by 29 December had seized the presidency, forcing Viola into retirement. On 9 December 1985 Viola was sentenced to seventeen years in prison for his participation in the Dirty War. In December 1990 he was released under a general amnesty.

OSCAR R. CARDOSO et al., *Falklands—The Secret Plot* (1987); SUSAN CALVERT and PETER CALVERT, *Argentina: Political Culture of Instability* (1989); MARTIN EDWIN ANDERSEN, *Dossier Secreto* (1993).

ROBERT SCHEINA

VIOLENCIA, LA. Between the mid-1940s and the early 1960s Colombia was convulsed by political violence, which according to various estimates claimed between 100,000 and 250,000 lives. This period is known simply as "the Violence," a designation suggesting the inadequacy of any single explanation for the phenomenon; the name also suggests, as the historian Gonzalo Sánchez has noted, the hurricane-like force that made the phenomenon so incomprehensible to its countless victims. While the idiom of the *Violencia* was political—a struggle between affiliates of Colombia's two dominant parties, Liberal and Conservative—in its regional variations and in its consequences, the *Violencia* cannot be understood apart from its social and economic grounding.

Colombia's postindependence history had been characterized by frequent episodes of political violence, but these were clearly bounded and usually elite-led conflicts whose social repercussions were limited. The Liberal election victory of 1930, however, triggered a new modality of endemic partisan violence, centered in the countryside and rarely organized (though sometimes manipulated) by political elites. This violence flared anew with the Conservatives' return to power in 1946, first in "backward" regions like Nariño and Boyacá, then throughout much of the interior. This violence both fed, and was fed by, the growing estrangement between party leaders at the national level, which culminated in late 1949 in the dictatorship of Mariano OSPINA PÉREZ. Ospina's use of viciously sectarian Conservative police (nicknamed *chulavitas*, after the rural subdivision that provided many of them), and the response of lightly organized Liberal guerrillas, raised the level of violence to unprecedented levels by 1949–1950. The uprisings in Bogotá, Cali, Barrancabermeja, and other cities following the assassination of populist Liberal leader Jorge Eliécer GAITÁN in April 1948 also brought the *Violencia* to urban centers, albeit fleetingly.

By 1950–1953 most of rural Colombia, with the notable exception of the Atlantic Coast, was engulfed by the *Violencia*, but its characteristics varied widely. On the vast eastern plains, or llanos, Liberal resistance took on an increasingly redistributive, revolutionary character under Guadalupe Salcedo; this was also true of the movement of Rafael Rangel in the Magdalena River valley of SANTANDER, a region with a long radical tradition. In southern Tolima, Liberal and Communist forces fought the Conservative regime, and not infrequently each other. But throughout much of the country— Boyacá and the Santanders in the northeast, and the coffee-producing regions of northern Tolima, Antioquia, and Caldas—the *Violencia* defied easy social or ideological characterization: Liberal and Conservative

Aftermath of La Violencia. WIDE WORLD.

smallholders, sharecroppers, and laborers fought each other with unbridled ferocity, with no more explicit "program" than their respective party affiliations.

The overthrow of the Conservative dictatorship by the military under General Gustavo ROJAS PINILLA in June 1953 slowed the *Violencia* in some regions, particularly on the llanos, but violence in much of Colombia continued unabated. The military itself was responsible for some of the more grotesque episodes of the mid-1950s, including mass executions and aerial bombardments in Tolima. In 1957 the leaders of the two parties reached an agreement, eventually known as the National Front, which permitted a return to civilian rule in 1958 under a rigid scheme of Liberal-Conservative parity at all levels. This agreement, with its corresponding legitimation of the state's role in "pacification" through both socioeconomic and military strategies, made possible the gradual diminution of the *Violencia* by the early 1960s; just as important, the agreement permitted the effective redefinition of continuing violence as simple delinquency (in the case of *bandolerismo*, the BANDITRY that plagued the western coffee zones until the late 1960s), or as subversion (in the case of the leftist guerrilla groups whose origins lay in the Liberal/Communist split of the early 1950s).

The cumulative effects of the *Violencia* by the early 1960s were enormous, not only in the number of lives lost and properties destroyed. The face of Colombia was transformed as the cities filled with hundreds of thousands of rural migrants: new urban markets and a new urban work force propelled Colombian industrialization as peaceful development never could. Rural property was also transformed, as smallholders were displaced by agribusiness (in Cesar and Valle del Cauca), or by town-dwelling merchants (in Caldas); even where smallholder neighbor fought neighbor, the lack of "structural" change masked profound dislocation, which official policies (such as a Supreme Court decision restoring the properties of those who lost them by force or threat) could not reverse.

The historiography of the *Violencia* has until recently been divided between the empirical and the analytical, each lacking the necessary element of the other, as several writers have noted. Although an understanding of the Manichaean logic of Colombia's political system is accepted as a key element in any understanding of the *Violencia*, secularly political explanations are no longer considered sufficient; however, ambitious socioeconomic explanations that privilege the structural imperatives of industrialization of agrarian capitalism have also lost favor. Instead, analysis has focused on regional and local cases, revealing a diversity of causal factors rooted in, among other things, class structure and political culture. Of attempts at innovative synthesis, those of Daniel Pécaut and Charles Bergquist are particularly noteworthy: the former emphasizes the "hegemonic crisis" of the state as the violently "prepolitical" invades the political realm, while the latter argues for the Hobbesian logic of nominally political violence between socially indistinguishable smallholders.

PAUL H. OQUIST, *Violence, Conflict, and Politics in Colombia* (1980); DANIEL PÉCAUT, *Orden y violencia*, 2 vols. (1987); GONZALO SÁNCHEZ GÓMEZ, " 'La Violencia' in Colombia: New Research, New Questions," translated by Peter Bakewell, in *Hispanic American Historical Review* 65, no. 4 (November 1985): 789–807; CHARLES BERGQUIST, RICARDO PEÑARANDA, and GONZALO SÁNCHEZ, eds., *Violence in Colombia: the Contemporary Crisis in Historical Perspective* (1992).

RICHARD J. STOLLER

See also **Class Structure; Colombia: Political Parties; Colombia: Revolutionary Movements; Gómez Castro, Laureano; Lleras Camargo, Alberto.**

VIRACOCHA, the greatest of the Inca gods. Viracocha created all the other gods, as well as men and animals, and so ruled them all. The deity had no name but only a series of titles most commonly given as Ilya-Tiqsi Viracocha Pachayacachiq, which in Quechua means "Ancient Foundation, Lord, Instructor of the World." The Spanish most commonly referred to him as Viracocha, using one of his titles as a name. Viracocha was usually represented as a man, and the Spanish reported seeing a solid gold standing figure about the size of a ten-year-old boy.

Viracocha was believed to have traveled through the Andes after the creation, performing miracles and teaching people how to live. He finally set off across the Pacific Ocean from a place near Manta in Ecuador, walking on the water. Viracocha was believed to have turned over the administration of his creation to the deities of the Inca pantheon and to the HUACAS (natural spirits).

The term *Viracocha* also came to be applied to Europeans by the natives of the Andes. It is still used today as the common Quechua name for Caucasian foreigners.

JOHN H. ROWE, "Inca Culture at the Time of the Spanish Conquest," in *Handbook of South American Indians*, vol. 2 (1946), pp. 183–330; BURR CARTWRIGHT BRUNDAGE, *The Empire of the Inca* (1963) and *The Lords of Cuzco: A History and Description of the Inca People in their Final Days* (1967); ARTHUR A. DEMAREST, *Viracocha: The Nature and Antiquity of the Andean High God* (1981); GEOFFREY W. CONRAD and ARTHUR A. DEMAREST, *Religion and Empire: The Dynamics of Aztec and Inca Expansionism* (1984).

GORDON F. McEWAN

See also **Incas.**

VIRGIN ISLANDS, an archipelago of small islands and reefs between PUERTO RICO and the LEEWARD ISLANDS. The British Virgin Islands are a crown colony, while the American Virgin Islands—Saint Thomas, Saint Croix, and Saint John—have shared a common Danish history since the seventeenth century. In 1917, the United States acquired the islands to protect the Panama Canal. However, American and West Indian cultures conflict, adding to problems of race, local independence, rivalry between Saint Thomas and Saint Croix, and the tourist economy, a continuation of the Danish free port tradition.

Christopher COLUMBUS discovered the Virgin Islands in 1493, and named them after Saint Ursula and her 10,000 fellow virgin martyrs. Despite Saint Thomas's harbor midway in the Caribbean, possible attack from Spaniards and CARIBS discouraged colonization. Nevertheless, the Danish West India Company established a permanent settlement in 1672.

Since Danes were interested only in slave trading and customs receipts, the original Dutch trading and culture dominated. Capitalism broke down national barriers, and a mixed planter and merchant class developed that was hostile to the Danish metropole. Continuous Danish neutrality made Charlotte Amalie, the port of Saint Thomas, wealthy from auctioning war prizes and selling stores to buccaneers.

After U.S. purchase, the Supreme Court dashed islanders' citizenship hopes by defining the islands as an "unincorporated territory." Both the Navy Department and succeeding civilian governors failed to solve problems of race, local government, and a dependent economy even though the islands were a "laboratory of the New Deal."

During World War II, alien labor and economic dependency on government increased, and blacks and mulattoes filled local bureaucracies. After the war the Virgin Islands became dependent on permanent military facilities. TOURISM started in the 1960s, becoming the latest in a string of boom/bust economies related to the islands' strategic location. A government and private-sector partnership built a tourism image for cruise ships and "shopping bag" tourism. In spite of labor inflow and low unemployment (0.23 percent), extensive moonlighting indicated a low-pay/inflation economy.

The three main islands have different geographies and societies. Saint John, once having one hundred SUGAR plantations, degenerated rapidly after a ferocious slave rebellion in 1733, and has a small population and little influence. Saint Thomas's commercial and cosmopolitan tradition has been augmented by consecutive immigrants: "Cha-Chas" from nearby SAINT BARTHÉLEMY, laborers from Puerto Rico and the other Antilles, and U.S. "Continentals." Saint Croix, bought from France in 1733, has been dominated by Danish sugar planters. By 1954, 40 percent of the island was still owned by twelve families and one foreign corporation. The rivalry between the commercial and planter oligarchies of Saint Thomas and Saint Croix carried over into the relations with the new black middle-class elite.

HENDRIK DE LEEUW, *Crossroads of the Buccaneers* (1937); GORDON K. LEWIS, *The Virgin Islands: A Caribbean Lilliput* (1972).

EDMOND KONRAD

VIRGINIUS AFFAIR, a confrontation that resulted in the summary execution in 1873 of 53 Americans at the hands of Spanish authorities in Cuba. The *Virginius*, a Cuban-owned vessel traveling under the American flag, regularly carried arms to revolutionaries in Cuba. While it was on such a mission in October 1873, a Spanish cruiser captured the *Virginius* and took it to Santiago, where the executions took place. Subsequent negotiations between Washington and Madrid resulted in an $80,000 reparation award to the families of those executed, but the Spanish commander responsible was not punished; he was instead promoted to a higher rank.

CHARLES E. CHAPMAN, *A History of the Cuban Republic: A Study in Hispanic-American Politics* (1927); PHILIP S. FONER, *A History of Cuba and Its Relations with the United States*, vol. 1 (1962); RAMIRO GUERRA Y SÁNCHEZ, *Guerra de los diez años, 1868–1878*, 2 vols. (1972).

THOMAS M. LEONARD

VISCARDO Y GUZMÁN, JUAN PABLO (*b.* 20 June 1748; *d.* February 1798), Peruvian Jesuit. Viscardo was born in Pampacolca (region of Arequipa) into a long-established creole family. He entered the Society of Jesus in 1761 and, although still a novice, was affected by the expulsion of the JESUITS ordered by CHARLES III in 1767. Early the following year Viscardo went to Cádiz, a trip which marked the beginning of an exile that took him to Italy, France, and England, where he died.

Viscardo is best known for his inflammatory "Letter to Spanish Americans," published in French in 1799 and in a Spanish translation in London in 1801. In it, Viscardo cataloged the alleged tyranny of colonial Spanish rule for three centuries and forcefully outlined why the colonies should be independent. Some historians consider him the "first and most important ideological precursor of Hispanic American independence." It has yet to be demonstrated, however, that his "Letter" was a significant stimulus for independence.

RUBÉN VARGAS UGARTE, S.J., *La carta a los españoles americanos de Don Juan Pablo Viscardo y Guzmán*, 2d ed. (1964); D. A. BRADING, *The First America: The Spanish Monarchy, Creole Patriots, and the Liberal State 1492–1867* (1991), pp. 535–540.

MARK A. BURKHOLDER

VISCONTI, ELISEU D'ANGELO (*b.* 1866; *d.* 1944) Brazilian painter. Born in Italy, Visconti came to Brazil as an infant with his family. Although he studied music during his youth, he chose painting over the violin. He took his first art classes at the Liceu de Artes e Ofícios (School of Arts and Crafts) in Rio de Janeiro. Then in 1885 he enrolled in Brazil's Imperial Academy of Fine Arts, where his talents were quickly recognized. During the first artistic competition of the republic, Visconti won a travel award that allowed him to study in Europe. While there, he won prizes and recognition as a student at the École des Beaux Arts in Paris and took classes at the School Guérin, where he studied decorative art under the tutelage of Eugène Grasset.

He returned to Brazil in 1897 and by 1901 had his first individual exhibition, showing eighty-eight works. In 1905, while in Paris, he received a governmental commission from Brazil, the first of many, to execute a panel painting destined for the entrance of the Municipal Theater in Rio de Janeiro. For the foyer, ceiling, and proscenium of the theater, he also did paintings celebrating the arts through allegorical themes.

In 1946 Brazil's National Museum of Fine Arts organized a retrospective of his works that included 285 oil paintings as well as watercolors, drawings, and decorative pieces. Visconti's work is stylistically eclectic with influences drawn from impressionism and realism. He once referred to himself as a "presentist" who produces an art that is constantly changing and modifying.

Arte no Brasil, vol. 2 (1979), pp. 578–587.

CAREN A. MEGHREBLIAN

VISITA, VISITADOR, a special investigation undertaken in the Spanish colonies in response to perceived mismanagement or an emergency.

Visitas were of two types. A specific visita focused on a single official or lesser jurisdiction such as a village or *corregimiento*. A general visita, in contrast, focused on an entire AUDIENCIA district or viceroyalty. In a general visita, a *visitador-general* was sent from Spain to undertake a detailed and often lengthy examination of government and church officials' actions and of conditions within a specified region. Since a *visitador-general* could interrogate anyone he chose and was often sent because of concerns over a viceroy's behavior, relations between him and the viceroy were rarely cordial. While general visitas invariably disrupted the viceroyalty where they took place, few, if any, were clear successes.

First seriously used in the New World in the 1540s, general visitas proved to be very expensive and, consequently, few were undertaken. The best-known late colonial visita was that of New Spain by José de GÁLVEZ from 1765 to 1771. Gálvez took a series of steps to bolster royal revenues, notably by establishing a royal tobacco monopoly that won him acclaim at court. When he subsequently became minister of the Indies in 1776, he sent *visitadores-generales* to New Granada and Peru. Their actions contributed to uprisings against the government in both locations.

CLARENCE H. HARING, *The Spanish Empire in America* (1947), pp. 153–156.

MARK A. BURKHOLDER

VITALINO PEREIRA DOS SANTOS, MESTRE (*b.* 1909; *d.* 1963), Brazilian sculptor. Mestre Vitalino's work was virtually unknown until 1947 when the Pernambucan painter and illustrator Augusto Rodrigues saw his

art and recognized that his miniature clay figurines represented a new popular ceramic tradition for Brazil. The sculptures recount daily life among the inhabitants and their animals in the backlands of Vitalino's home state of Pernambuco. Unlike other popular ceramicists of his time, Vitalino sculpted them with a softness of line and curve, and imbued them with wit and subtle irony. His work was included in the 1948 Exposicão de Arte Popular in Rio de Janeiro. Prior to 1953 Vitalino grouped together and painted his subjects. Later, his compositions focused on single figures, which he left unpainted. He influenced the popular artists Nó Caboclo and Zé Rodriguez. Vitalino's sons continued the tradition popularized by their father.

Arte no Brasil, vol. 2 (1979), esp. pp. 830–831.

CAREN A. MEGHREBLIAN

VITERI Y UNGO, JORGE (*b.* 23 April 1802; *d.* 25 July 1853), bishop of El Salvador and Nicaragua. Born in San Salvador of Spanish parents and educated in Guatemala, Viteri was active in the politics of Central America following the collapse of the federation. A noted orator and a leading adviser to Rafael CARRERA, who was close to the Guatemalan conservative elite, he became a member of the Guatemalan COUNCIL OF STATE in 1840. In 1842 he visited the Vatican, where he secured establishment of a separate diocese of El Salvador, to which Pope Gregory XVI named him the first bishop. Viteri also arranged for appointment of Francisco de Paula GARCÍA PELÁEZ as archbishop of Guatemala.

Viteri was an active force in Salvadoran politics in alliance with General Francisco MALESPÍN, but when Malespín ordered the execution of a priest, Pedro Crespín, in 1845, Viteri excommunicated Malespín. Opposition to Viteri's meddling in politics forced him out of El Salvador in 1846. He went to Nicaragua, where the Vatican formally named him bishop of Nicaragua and Costa Rica on 5 November 1849. He was active in the politics of Nicaragua until his death.

E. AGUILAR, *El . . . los documentos que comprueban la complicidad que el Sr. Obispo Viteri ha tenido en . . . [el trastorno del] orden de este estado el l de noviembre último* (1846); RAMÓN LÓPEZ JIMÉNEZ, *Mitras salvadoreñas* (1960), pp. 47–71; SANTIAGO R. VILANOVA MELÉNDEZ, "Doctor y maestro don Jorge Viteri y Ungo, primero obispo de la diócesis de San Salvador," in *San Salvador y sus hombres* (1967), pp. 109–122; ARTURO TARACENA, "Biografías sintéticas," in *Revista de la Academia guatemalteca de estudios genealógicos, heráldicos e históricos* 7 (1979): 552; RALPH LEE WOODWARD, JR., *Rafael Carrera and the Emergence of the Republic of Guatemala, 1821–1871* (1993).

RALPH LEE WOODWARD, JR.

VITIER, CINTIO (*b.* 25 September 1921), Cuban essayist, poet, and literary critic. The son of prominent Cuban educator Medardo Vitier, Cintio Vitier was born in Key West and spent most of his childhood in Matanzas,

Cuba. In 1935 he moved to Havana, where from 1942 to 1947 he was editor of the literary journal *Clavileño*. Although he received a law degree from the University of Havana, he never entered the profession. During his student years he became part of the literary group that revolved around the magazine *Orígenes*, through which he befriended the founder, José LEZAMA LIMA, as well as the poets Eliseo DIEGO and Fina García Marruz, whom he married in 1947. Between 1947 and 1961 he taught French and compiled key anthologies of Cuban poetry, including *Diez poetas cubanos, 1937–1947* (1948), *Cincuenta años de poesía cubana, 1902–1952* (1952), and *Los grandes románticos cubanos* (1960).

Vitier is best known for his literary analysis. One of his books on this subject, *Lo cubano en la poesía* (1957, repr. 1970), is still considered one of the most sensitive, authoritative works defining the Cuban poetic sensibility.

Vitier has edited critical editions of the complete works of José MARTÍ and, along with Fina García Marruz, is the recognized authority on Martí within the island. (He was director of the José Martí wing of the National Library from 1968 to 1973 and a researcher at the Centro Martiano from 1987 to 1988.) He has edited several literary publications, including *La Nueva Revista Cubana, Anuario Martiano,* and *Revista de la Biblioteca Nacional "José Martí."* Since 1959 he has represented Cuba at numerous international cultural activities. As of the mid-1990s, he was retired and living in Cuba.

BENIGNO SÁNCHEZ-EPPLER, *Habits of Poetry, Habits of Resurrection* (1986), deals with the influence of the Spanish Nobel laureate Juan Ramón Jiménez on the work of Eugenio Florit, José Lezama Lima, and Cintio Vitier. See also ARCADIO DÍAZ QUINONES, *Cintio Vitier: La memoria integradora* (1987).

ROBERTO VALERO

VITÓRIA, capital of the Brazilian state of Espírito Santo since 1823. A port city (1993 population 227,360) Vitória is located on the island of Vitória in the bay of Espírito Santo. Founded in 1535 by Vasco Fernandes Coutinho, the city was originally named Vila de Nossa Senhora da Vitória. On the periphery of the city is Tubarão, Brazil's principal port for iron ore exports. Railways connect Vitória to the mines of Minas Gerais and the city of Rio de Janeiro.

SHEILA L. HOOKER

VITORIA, FRANCISCO DE (*b.* 1486; *d.* 12 August 1546), one of the founders of international law. Francisco de Vitoria, a Dominican friar, was the *prima* (senior) professor of theology at the University of Salamanca (1526–1546). His published works include *De Indis I* (1537/1538) and *De Indis II* or *Dure jure belli* (1538/1539), collections of lectures published posthumously. Vitoria outlined the rights of Spaniards in the New World and

wrestled with the moral questions raised when a government founded on Christian principles imposes its will on pagans. Subscribing to the Thomistic theory that all men (including pagans) are rational beings who belong to a worldwide community based on natural law and a law of nations (*jus gentium*), Vitoria argued that Spaniards should respect the political sovereignty and property rights of the native peoples they found in the Indies. Thus, Spaniards did not have any inherent rights over subjects in the New World based on jurisdiction. War was justified only if natives prevented Spaniards from trading and living with them in peace, practiced cannibalism, refused to allow missionaries to preach, or discouraged conversion to Christianity.

BERNICE HAMILTON, *Political Thought in Sixteenth-Century Spain* (1963), esp. pp. 119–134 and 171–176; J. A. FERNÁNDEZ-SANTAMARÍA, *The State, War, and Peace: Spanish Political Thought in the Renaissance, 1516–1559* (1977), esp. pp. 58–119.

SUZANNE HILES BURKHOLDER

VIVANCO, MANUEL IGNACIO (*b.* 1806; *d.* 1873), conservative Peruvian military CAUDILLO. Born in Lima, the son of a Spanish merchant, Vivanco was educated in the traditional San Carlos school. He joined the independence forces to fight the decisive battles of JUNÍN and AYACUCHO. After Independence Vivanco sided with several military leaders, including Pedro Bermúdez, the conservative Felipe Santiago SALAVERRY, and Agustín GAMARRA, who opposed the PERU-BOLIVIA CONFEDERATION. In 1841, Vivanco campaigned on behalf of his own "regenerating" movement with the undemocratic intent of strong government to end the caudillo struggle.

Especially strong in the southern provinces of Arequipa, Vivanco was able to control power during the multiple military uprisings of the early 1840s. However, in 1844, his archenemy, General Ramón CASTILLA, was able to defeat Vivanco's forces and initiate a gradual reorganization of the Peruvian state. Vivanco continued to oppose Castilla. In the elections of 1850 he ran against Castilla's official candidate, José R. ECHENIQUE. In 1856 he started a revolution against Castilla in Arequipa. During the beleaguered regime of Juan Antonio PEZET, Vivanco was the Peruvian representative who in 1865 signed the popularly repudiated Vivanco-Pareja Treaty that led to the ousting of Pezet and the decline of Vivanco's popularity. He died in Valparaíso, Chile.

JORGE BASADRE, *Historia de la República del Perú*, vol. 3 (1963), pp. 697–707; CELIA WU, *Generals and Diplomats: Great Britain and Peru, 1820–40* (1991).

ALFONSO W. QUIROZ

VIZCAÍNO, SEBASTIÁN (*b.* 1548; *d.* 1623), Spanish explorer and cartographer of the Californias. A native of Estremadura, Vizcaíno was a cavalry commander in the invasion of Portugal in 1580. He went to New Spain in

1583 and became merchant-militia commander at Manila in 1586. He conducted explorations in connection with his pearl-fishing monopoly, in the Gulf of California, from June to November 1596, founding La Paz on 13 September. Vizcaíno was general of an expedition that charted and mapped the Pacific coast of the Californias from 5 May 1602 to 21 February 1603; it also gave place-names from Cabo San Lucas to Cabo Blanco (in present-day Oregon). He was chief magistrate of Tehuantépec in 1604 and opened a supply route from Coatzocoalcos to the Pacific in 1606. After being granted an ENCOMIENDA in the province of Ávalos in 1607, Vizcaíno served as the first European ambassador and cartographer in Japan (March 1611–January 1614). In October–November 1615 Vizcaíno repelled Dutch corsairs led by Joris von Spilbergen in Colima. After serving as chief magistrate of Acapulco (1616), he retired in 1619 to Mexico City, where he died.

W. MICHAEL MATHES, ed., *Californians I: Documentos para la historia de la demarcación comercial de California, 1583–1632* (1965); W. MICHAEL MATHES, *Sebastián Vizcaíno and Spanish Expansion in the Pacific Ocean, 1580–1630* (1968).

W. MICHAEL MATHES

See also **Explorers and Exploration.**

VODUN (VOODOO, VAUDUN). Vodun is a syncretic folk religion that contains elements of African, largely Dahomean, beliefs as well as Catholicism. It is largely associated with Haiti but can be found in various forms throughout the Caribbean and the United States. The name "voodoo" was initially used by the colonists to refer to African dances, but locally it was also a pejorative label of occult rites and dances. The term is derived from the Dahomean word *vodun* meaning "spirit."

Vodun is a loosely organized religion based on the African beliefs of communication with divine spirits through dances, trances, and ultimately possession. There is a concerted effort to maintain a harmonious relationship between the spirits and the believers (*fidèles*). The *loa*, or spirit, is vital. The High God (Bon Dieu) manifests itself through the *loa* in a process called possession or epiphany. Many *loas* are African deities, but some are also indigenous to HAITI. Agarou and Anago are two of the latter. As in many other New World religions, there is a profound respect for and deification of one's ancestors. The actual number of *loas* is infinite. Unlike saints, the *loas* do not have genders. Both good and evil spirits are recognized. In northern Haiti, for example, Lima is an evil *loa*. Each *fidèle* has one special *loa* called the *loa-protecteur*.

Vodun plays an important role in the perpetuation of folk culture and social mores. Children learn about the *loas* through stories with social messages against taboos such as murder, theft, and incest. Similar to the adoration of saints in the rest of Latin America, there are many celebrations or annual feasts for particular *loas*. In

Voodoo Dance. Oil painting by Rosemarie Deruisseau, 1980. Depicts Voodoo dance called Yanvalou. From Betty LaDuke, *Compañeras* (1980). COURTESY OF BETTY LA DUKE.

these feasts, food is offered to the *loa*. Since it is the essence of the offering that is consumed, it may be scattered, buried, or consumed directly by the *loa* during a possession. There are four main participants in the vodun ceremony: the *houngan*, the priest, who is also an important community leader; the priest's assistants, the *badjicans*; the *serviteurs*, those who become possessed; and the *fidèles*, the believers.

It is believed that vodun took on a definite form between 1750 and 1790 and played an important part in the rebellion of the Haitians against the French. It continues to play an important role in the Haitian political milieu.

Classic works on voodoo in Haiti are MELVILLE J. HERSKOVITS, *Life in a Haitian Valley* (1937); ALFRED MÉTRAUX, *Voodoo in Haiti* (1959); HAROLD COURLANDER, *The Drum and the Hoe* (1960). See also GEORGE E. SIMPSON, *Religious Cults of the Caribbean: Trinidad, Jamaica, and Haiti* (1980).

DARIÉN DAVIS

VOLADOR DANCE, a unique and athletic ritual dance of pre-Columbian origin utilizing a high pole. Once practiced by many peoples throughout ancient Mexico and Central America, the dance today is primarily observed by the TOTONACS, and occasionally by neighboring groups, in the Mexican states of Veracruz and Puebla. Its precise origins and significance are obscure, but it apparently reached its apogee with other solar rituals just before the Spanish Conquest. The dance retains many of its ancient characteristics, including steps, action sequence, orientation to the four cardinal points, and flute and drum accompaniment.

There are four, and at times six, dancers, called *voladores* (fliers), plus the musician. Having climbed the pole, as high as 137 feet, the dancers fall off a rotating platform with ropes tied to their waists. As the cords unwrap from the staff, they swirl around it for several minutes before reaching the ground. Except for touristic purposes, the dance is normally performed on local feast days.

Descriptions of the dance as traditionally practiced by the highland Totonacs can be found in ALAIN ICHON, *La religion des Totonaques de la Sierra* (1969); and for the lowland Totonacs in

Voladores of Papantla performing the Volador dance, May 1951. ARCHIVO GENERAL DE LA NACIÓN, MÉXICO.

SALOMÓN PÉREZ DIEGO D'POZA, *Danza de los voladores* (1968). The nature of the dance today is examined in S. JEFFREY K. WILKERSON, "The Flute Calls, Totonac Voladores: Ritual Fliers of Mexico," *The World and I* 6, no. 6 (June 1991): 638–651.

S. JEFFREY K. WILKERSON

VOLCANOES, integral part of the geologic makeup of Mexico, Central America, the Antilles, and the Andean nations of Latin America. In historic times, normally with little variation, about fifty volcanoes are active in any given year in the world. Compared with other natural hazards, volcanic eruptions are less frequent, result in relatively fewer human casualties, and ordinarily produce less economic loss. Nevertheless, several eruptions in Latin American history were remarkable for loss of life. Deadly eruptions after 1600 include Cotopaxi in Ecuador (1741: 2,000 lives lost; 1877: 1,000), Nevado del Ruiz in Colombia (1845: 1,000; 1985: ca. 25,000), Soufrière on Saint Vincent (1902: 1,560), Pelée on Martinique (1902–1905: 29,000), Santa María in Guatemala (1902: 6,000), and El Chichón in Mexico (1982: ca. 2,000). The three 1902 disasters, together with that of 1985, account for 75 percent of all twentieth-century deaths from volcanic activity worldwide.

Latin American historical documents record numerous additional eruptions. Mexico has a volcanic chain along the nineteenth parallel. There, for example, Colima had eruptions of various magnitude in 1576, 1590, 1611–1613, 1749, 1770, 1795, 1806–1808, 1818, 1869, 1885–1886, 1892, 1909, and 1913. Popocatépetl erupted with moderate to large force in 1720; Orizaba, in 1545, 1566, 1569, 1630, and 1687; San Martín, in 1664 and 1793–1794. Only two volcanoes have been born in historic times in North America, both in Mexico: Jorullo in 1759 and PARICUTÍN in 1943.

In Central America, only Honduras has no volcanoes. Elsewhere, moderate to large eruptions include Arenal (Costa Rica, 1500s and 1968–1969), Momotombo (Nicaragua, 1560 and 1609), Pacaya (Guatemala, 1565, 1664, and 1965), Santa Ana (El Salvador, 1576 and 1880), San Miguel (El Salvador, 1586), Masaya (Nicaragua, 1670), San Salvador (El Salvador, 1671), Atitlán (Guatemala, 1827), Turrialba (Costa Rica, 1866), Momotombo (Nicaragua, 1905), Irazú (Costa Rica, 1918 and 1963–1965), Acatenango (Guatemala, 1925), Izalco (El Salvador, 1955 and 1957), Poas (Costa Rica, 1961), Cerro Negro (Nicaragua, 1962, 1968, and 1971), and Rincón de la Vieja (Costa Rica, 1967). The 1835 eruption of Cosigüina in Nicaragua was one of the major volcanic events in recorded history. In addition to that of 1902, Santa María in Guatemala had sizable eruptions in 1922, 1956, and 1976. Guatemala's Fuego is the Central American volcano with the greatest number of moderate to large eruptions, a dozen from the 1580s to the 1970s. El Salvador's Ilopango, which erupted in 1875, also erupted in pre-Columbian times, probably causing shifts in settlement patterns.

In the Antilles, volcanic activity began at much studied Pelée about 13,500 years ago. Notable eruptions occurred in 1851 and 1929–1932, in addition to the 1902–1905 episode. Soufrière (Saint Vincent) erupted in 1718, 1812, 1902–1903, 1971–1972, and 1979. There has been volcanic activity in historic times on Guadeloupe, Saint Kitts, and Dominica as well.

Volcanic activity is fairly common in the Andean nations. In Colombia, Nevado del Ruiz has had twelve eruptive stages in the last 11,000 years; in historic times, notably in 1595, 1845, and 1985. Galeras erupted with moderate to large force in 1535, 1590, 1616, 1717, 1834, 1869, and 1924. Puracé erupted in 1849 and 1885; Doña Juana, in 1899. Ecuador has some of the largest volcanoes in the world. Cotopaxi has had a dozen moderate to large eruptions in historic times, notably those of 1744, 1768, and 1877. Reventador has been just as active, with larger twentieth-century eruptions in 1929, 1936, 1944, 1958, and 1960. Guagua Pichincha (near Quito) erupted in 1566, 1587, 1660, and 1831; Tungurahua, in 1886 and 1918—all with moderate to large explosions. Sangay has been regularly active, especially in the 1730s, 1840s, and 1930s. Ecuador's territory includes the Galápagos with Fernandina, Cerro Azul, and Sierra Negra volcanoes.

Peru's volcanic activity has had moderate force, aside from Huayna Putina's large eruption in 1600. El Misti, Peru's most famous volcano, erupted in 1677, 1784, and 1787; Tutupaca, in 1780 and 1802. Ubinas has erupted with the greatest frequency, a dozen times between 1677 and 1969. Among Latin nations, Chile has the greatest number of active volcanoes, mainly in the less-populated south. In colonial days, Peteroa (1660 and 1762) and Nevados de Chillán (around 1750) erupted. Twentieth-century eruptions have included Puyehue (1921 and 1960), Cerro Azul (also called Quizapu, 1907, 1914, and 1932), and Llaima (1946–1947 and 1957).

Latin America's historic eruptions provide examples of diverse physical hazards: (1) Pyroclastic flows of hot rock fragments mixed with hot gases move rapidly from the volcano, as at El Chichón (1982) and Pelée (1902). (2) Lahars, or mudflows, result from ice/snowmelts or released water impoundments mixed with debris. These submerge adjacent farmland and villages, as at Cotopaxi (1877), Santa María (1902), Irazú (1964–1965), and Nevado del Ruiz (1985). (3) Tephra, or ash falls, make breathing difficult, cover vegetation, and can collapse or bury structures. Eruptions notable for the distance tephra traveled are Cosigüina (1835: 672 miles), Soufrière (1902: 792 miles), and Cerro Azul (1932: 1,776 miles). Some evidence indicates that weathered volcanic soil is especially fertile; research supports the conclusion that volcanic dust contributes to global cooling by blocking sunlight. (4) Lava, or molten rock, erupts relatively nonexplosively and moves slowly. Nevertheless, it can engulf whole villages, as at Parícutin (1943). (5) Sometimes explosions send forth solid projectiles, as at Arenal (1968). (6) Toxic gases can be health hazards (Masaya, 1946). Before the twentieth century, disease and starvation were more significant longer-term results of eruptions.

Volcano News (1979–1986) superseded by *Volcano Quarterly* (1992); PAYSON D. SHEETS and DONALD K. GRAYSON, eds., *Volcanic Activity and Human Ecology* (1979); TOM SIMKIN et al., *Volcanoes of the World* (1981); RUSSELL J. BLONG, *Volcanic Hazards* (1984); CENTRO REGIONAL DE SISMOLOGÍA PARA AMÉRICA DEL SUR, *Riesgo volcánico: Evaluación y mitigación en América Latina* (1989); ROBERT TILLING, ed., *Volcanic Hazards* (1989); DAVID T. LESCINSKY, "Nevado del Ruiz Volcano, Colombia: A Comprehensive Bibliography," in *Journal of Volcanology and Geothermal Research* 42, no. 1–2 (1990): 211–224.

ROBERT H. CLAXTON

VOLIO JIMÉNEZ, JORGE (b. 26 August 1882; d. 20 October 1955), Costa Rican politician. Volio Jiménez was born in Cartago, Costa Rica, to a bourgeois family. From a young age, he held Christian and reformist ideas, in pursuit of which he formed study groups and in 1902 created the daily *La Justicia Social.* In 1903 he went to the University of Lovain in Belgium to study for the priesthood. He was ordained in 1909, at which time he also received a master's degree in philosophy. He then took his Christian-socialist ideas back to his country and worked as priest and professor. In 1911, his fighting spirit took him to Nicaragua, where he participated in the resistance against the U.S. intervention. In 1915, he left the priesthood in order to work as a journalist and professor. Between 1917 and 1919 he fought against the dictatorship of General Federico TINOCO in Costa Rica, whose defeat in the battle of El Jobo led to the reestablishment of a liberal democracy. In 1920 Volio Jiménez received the rank of major general. In 1922 he was elected to Congress and in 1923 he formed the Reformist Party, of which he was a candidate for president.

During the 1920s, Volio Jiménez outlined a reformist ideology that questioned the liberal system and the dominant oligarchy and advocated reforms favoring the working class. His program called for state intervention to obtain agrarian reform, civil rights, tax reform, political democracy, a public university, and protection of the nation's resources. He played an important role in awakening the workers, peasants, and middle class to political participation, and several of his ideas were later put into practice, especially during the 1940s. Owing to his alliance with the liberals, he served as vice president of the republic from 1924 to 1926. In 1932 he participated in a failed coup d'état and later retired from politics. Between 1940 and 1948, he was dean of Philosophy and Letters at the University of Costa Rica. From 1954 until his death in San José, Costa Rica, he served in Congress.

CARLOS ARAYA POCHET, *Historia de los partidos politicos: Liberación nacional* (1968).

JORGE MARIO SALAZAR

Inauguration of steel and iron mill at Volta Redonda, 1946. ICONOGRAPHIA.

VOLTA REDONDA, Brazil's first state-owned steel mill. Located in the town of the same name in the state of Rio de Janeiro, the National Steel Company's (CNS) Volta Redonda is one of Brazil's major import-substituting industrialization projects.

Forewarned of a coming shortage of steel in the late 1930s, the first Getúlio VARGAS administration (1930–1945) began to explore ways to build Latin America's first modern steelworks. At the time, Brazil was consuming some 400,000 tons of steel per year, about two-thirds of it imported. Once World War II started in Europe, the British blockade kept European steel out of Brazil, and U.S. firms were unable to meet Brazil's growing demand. Under nationalist pressure, the Vargas administration proposed to build a state-owned steel corporation. The country had high-grade iron ore and a trained labor force, but it lacked capital and the technology to launch a steel-producing project. Deftly playing off against each other a U.S. fear of Nazi Germany and a German concern for Brazil's alliance with the United States, Vargas was able to call in bids from both. The U.S. proposal, which called for granting $20 million to transfer technology and buy equipment, was better than the German one, although the Brazilian military openly favored an association with Germany, then rising as a continental military power.

The Brazilian government ultimately chose Volta Redonda, an inland town between Rio de Janeiro and São Paulo in the Paraíba Valley, although it considered several seaports where supplies of raw materials and the exporting of steel could be handled more easily. A major concern was the war itself: Brazil feared German submarine attacks on any U.S.-funded project.

The oldest of Brazil's steelworks, CNS has had a series of ups and downs. Not known for efficiency and productivity, it has had a long history of bitter labor relations. In 1990, the Fernando Collor de MELLO government offered up Volta Redonda for privatization, despite vigorous opposition from the steelworkers.

WERNER BAER, *The Development of the Brazilian Steel Industry* (1969); JOHN D. WIRTH, *The Politics of Brazilian Development 1930–1954* (1970).

EUL-SOO PANG

See also **Iron and Steel Industry.**

VON VACANO, ARTURO (*b.* 1938), Bolivian writer and journalist born in La Paz. Except for *El apocalipsis de Antón* (1972), an allegorical novel dealing with the violence and contradictions of a drastically stratified society in a setting marked by native cultural sacredness, the narrative of Von Vacano is highly autobiographical. *Sombra de exilio* (1970) concerns the reaching of adulthood during the Revolution of 1952 and the following years. *Morder el silencio* (1980) continues the experience of the man in *Sombra de exilio* and sets forth the impossibility of a literary vocation in a social context paralyzed by military dictatorship, violence, and the predominance of utilitarian values. All of Von Vacano's narrative strongly criticizes power and is characterized by a sense of blocked social redemption. *Morder el silencio* has been published in English as *Biting Silence* (1987), with the translation by Von Vacano himself. Von Vacano has published short pieces in Bolivian literary magazines and newspapers. Fleeing Bolivia in 1980, he lived as an exile in the United States, working as a writer, editor, and translator for United Press International in New York and Washington, D.C.

For a general view of Bolivian contemporary narrative and Von Vacano's place in it, see LUIS H. ANTEZANA, "La novela en el último cuarto de siglo," in *Tendencias actuales en la literatura boliviana,* edited by Javier Sanjinés C. (1985). See also ANA REBECA PRADA, "Sobre *Morder el silencio* de Arturo Von Vacano," *Revista iberoamericana,* no. 134 (1986): 255–264. For interviews with Von Vacano, see ALFONSO GUMUCIO DAGRÓN in his *Provocaciones* (1977), and *Hipótesis,* no. 7 (1978).

ANA REBECA PRADA

VOODOO. *See* **Vodun.**

WAGLEY, CHARLES WALTER (*b.* 9 November 1913; *d.* 25 November 1991), American anthropologist. Born in Clarksville, Texas, and a graduate of Columbia University (B.A., 1936; Ph.D., 1941), Wagley was a leading scholar of Latin American studies and one of the most prominent anthropologists of his time. He directed Columbia's Institute of Latin American Studies from 1961 to 1969 and was the Franz Boas Professor of Anthropology from 1965 to 1971 at the same institution. In 1971 Wagley moved to the University of Florida at Gainesville, where he became Graduate Research Professor of anthropology and Latin American studies. Wagley is best known for three field studies he carried out in Brazil between 1939 and 1950. His 1939–1940 study among the Amazonian Tapirapé Indians culminated in several articles and the book *Welcome of Tears: The Tapirapé Indians of Central Brazil* (1977), which was published in Portuguese in 1988. Collaborative work among the Tenetehara, carried out in 1941–1942 with his friend and colleague Eduardo Galvão, led to the book *The Tenetehara Indians of Brazil* (1949). The most widely known of Wagley's works, *Amazon Town: A Study of Man in the Tropics* (1953), is based upon fieldwork carried out first in 1948 among farmers and rubber collectors in the town of Itá (a pseudonym) on the banks of the Amazon.

In later years Wagley dedicated himself to writing works on race and class in Brazil, including *Minorities in the New World: Six Case Studies* (1958), with Marvin Harris; *The Latin American Tradition: Essays on the Unity and the Diversity of Latin American Culture* (1968); and *Race and Class in Rural Brazil* (1952), an edited volume based upon the Bahia State–Columbia University Community Study Project directed by Wagley in collaboration with the Brazilian anthropologist Thales de AZEVEDO.

MAXINE L. MARGOLIS and WILLIAM E. CARTER, eds., *Brazil, Anthropological Perspectives: Essays in Honor of Charles Wagley* (1979).

JANET M. CHERNELA

WALCOTT, DEREK (*b.* 23 January 1930), poet, playwright, and painter from Saint Lucia in the Lesser Antilles. Winner of the 1992 Nobel Prize for literature, Walcott was the first native of the Caribbean to win this prestigious award. Given the award for, among other works, his book *Omeros* (1990), an epic poem divided into sixty-four chapters, the academy cited Walcott for his "historical vision, the outcome of a multi-cultural commitment." Walcott has been described as "the best poet the English language has today." Of both African and European ancestry, Walcott describes himself as "the divided child of the wrong color," and much of

Walcott's artistic efforts have concentrated on his own multiethnic heritage.

Born in 1930 in Castries, Saint Lucia, his grandmothers on both sides were descended from slaves, while both of his grandfathers were European. Walcott's parents were both educators, and he grew up amid books and received strong encouragement to pursue his education. Walcott's father died when the younger Walcott was only one year old, and along with his twin brother and sister, Walcott was raised by his mother. His first published work, *25 Poems* (1948), appeared when he was only eighteen years old. He was denied a scholarship to study in England, so in 1950 he went to Jamaica to study on scholarship at the University of the West Indies, where he majored in French, Latin, and Spanish. In 1953 Walcott moved to Trinidad, and in the late 1950s he left there for New York City, where he founded his own repertory company, the Trinidad Theatre Workshop.

The book that first brought Walcott recognition was a collection of his poems entitled *In a Green Night* (1962). In 1986 Walcott won the Los Angeles Times Book Prize for his *Collected Poems* (1986), which includes selections from all his major works, especially *Sea Grapes* (1975), as well as the entire text of *Another Life* (1973) and his autobiography in verse. In 1988 he became the first Commonwealth citizen to be awarded the Queen's Gold Medal for Poetry. In 1991 he was awarded the W. H. Smith Literary Award in Britain. Also a noted playwright, Walcott won an Obie Award in 1971 for his play, *Dream on Monkey Mountain* (1970), which in 1994 was produced in Sweden. But Walcott's expression of the Caribbean experience through poetry was what brought him the Nobel Prize. Most recently, Walcott has worked to produce his play *Odyssey*, a retelling of the Homeric epic using Walcott's store of characters, images, and slang from his own Caribbean background.

Walcott's life has not been devoid of controversy. In 1981, while teaching at Harvard University, a student of Walcott's accused him of sexual harassment. After looking into the charges, the university wrote a letter of reproachment to Boston University, where Walcott had begun teaching.

From the early 1980s, Walcott taught poetry and creative writing at Boston University, while dividing his time between Trinidad and the United States. In 1994 he was working on a stage translation of Homer's *Odyssey* for the Royal Shakespeare Company. Married three times, Walcott had three children by the early 1990s.

IRMA E. GOLDSTRAW, *Derek Walcott: An Annotated Bibliography of His Works* (1984); ROBERT D. HAMNER, *Derek Walcott*, rev. ed. (1993); TODD LORETO, ed., *Derek Walcott: Selected Poems* (1994).

MICHAEL POWELSON

WALKER, WILLIAM (*b.* 8 May 1824; *d.* 12 September 1860). The most famous American FILIBUSTER, Walker conquered Nicaragua in 1855–1856. His various expeditions to Mexico and Central America from 1853 to 1860 fostered anti-Americanism in the region. In particular his impact upon Nicaragua, which suffered extensive property destruction and much loss of life because of his involvement there, was especially profound and lingers to this day. Walker's expeditions interrupted normal transit across Nicaragua's isthmus and embroiled the United States in disputes with Mexico, the countries of Central America, Colombia, and Great Britain.

EARLY LIFE

Walker was born in Nashville, Tennessee, and graduated from the University of Nashville in 1838. He received an M.D. degree from the University of Pennsylvania in 1843 and furthered his medical education in Europe, after which he spent several years in law, journalism, and politics in New Orleans and California. Perhaps curiously, given his later military escapades, surviving documents describe the slightly built Walker as a shy, somewhat effeminate youth. Several scholars have argued that the death in 1849 of Ellen Galt Martin, a deaf mute with whom he had fallen in love, radically transformed Walker's personality and paved the way for his filibustering career.

EXPEDITION TO MEXICO

The self-proclaimed "Colonel" Walker's filibusters began on October 1853, when, aboard the schooner *Caroline,* he departed San Francisco with forty-five followers bound for Mexico's Baja (Lower) California but actually intending the eventual conquest of the Mexican state of Sonora. Walker captured La Paz on 3 November, raised a flag with two stars signifying Lower California and Sonora, proclaimed the creation of the Republic of Lower California, and soon announced himself president. Mexican resistance forced Walker to flee to Ensenada, which he proclaimed his capital. Reinforcements from California arrived there, but Walker experienced supply deficiencies and made the mistake of provoking resistance from Antonio María Melendrez by attacking the ranch of Melendrez's father.

On 18 January 1854, Walker proclaimed the formation of the Republic of Sonora, consisting of the states of Sonora and Lower California. In March, Walker and about one hundred filibusters set out for Sonora. He crossed the Colorado River into Sonora on 4 April but soon returned to Lower California. Harassed by Mexican guerrillas, Walker retreated northward, crossing the U.S. border with his thirty-three remaining followers on 8 May and surrendered to U.S. military authorities. In October, a jury in San Francisco acquitted Walker of violating American neutrality laws. By threatening Mexico with uncompensated territorial losses, however, Walker's expedition may have helped persuade Mexico to cede, in a treaty signed on 30 December 1853, the territory which became known as the GADSDEN Purchase.

EXPEDITIONS TO CENTRAL AMERICA

Though Walker became one of the most despised figures in Central American history, he initially entered Nicaragua's affairs by invitation. Locked in conflict with the Legitimist, or Conservative, ruling party in Nicaragua, that country's Democrats, or Liberals, contracted in 1854 for Walker to bring three hundred filibusters (described as colonists, to avoid flagrantly violating U.S. neutrality statutes) to Nicaragua and occupy 52,000 acres of land. Walker and fifty-seven men calling themselves the Immortals departed San Francisco on 4 May 1855 and arrived in Nicaragua in June. As colonel of *La Falange Americana* (the American phalanx), Walker captured Granada, the Legitimist capital, on 13 October.

In a subsequently negotiated agreement, Walker became commander in chief of the Nicaraguan army under a coalition government. When he came into possession of letters by Minister of War Ponciano Corral, the former Legitimist Army commander, soliciting intervention from other Central American states to oust Walker, he had an excuse to eliminate his most formidable rival by having him executed for treason. From November 1855 to June 1856, Walker ruled Nicaragua through a figurehead, President Patricio RIVAS. Walker received reinforcements, assisted by the Accessory Transit Company, an American enterprise holding a monopoly over isthmian transit across Nicaragua. The weekly English- and Spanish-language publication *El Nicaragüense* testified to Walker's Americanization of the country. To encourage native support, the paper dubbed Walker the Gray-eyed Man, after a Mosquito Indian legend.

In May 1856, the United States recognized Rivas's government. Following Rivas's break with Walker that June, the filibuster was elected president on June 29 in a controlled election. Inaugurated on 12 July, Walker entertained visions of one day ruling all Central America. However, the loss of U.S. recognition, growing U.S. interference with his supply of reinforcements, armed interventions by other Central American states receiving support from Great Britain, the opposition of shipping magnate Cornelius Vanderbilt, and epidemic disease combined to undermine Walker's cause. His reestablishment of slavery in a 22 September decree won him increased favor in the slave states of the American Union, but this move could not save his regime. Forced to evacuate Granada, Walker had the city destroyed.

On 1 May 1857, Walker surrendered to U.S. naval captain Charles H. Davis and subsequently returned to the United States. Still claiming the presidency of Nicaragua, Walker devoted the rest of his life to FILIBUSTERING schemes.

In 1860, landing at Trujillo, Honduras, by way of Ruatán and Cozumel, Walker eventually surrendered to British naval commander Norvell Salmon, who in turn handed him over to Honduran authorities. He was executed at Trujillo by a local firing squad on 12 September 1860.

William Walker as president of Nicaragua, 1856. From *Leslie's Illustrated Weekly Newspaper*, 1856. Reproduced from Frederic Rosengarten, Jr., *Freebooters Must Die* (1976). COURTESY OF HARVARD COLLEGE LIBRARY.

WILLIAM O. SCROGGS, *Filibusters and Financiers: The Story of William Walker and His Associates* (1916); ALBERT Z. CARR, *The World and William Walker* (1963); FREDERIC ROSENGARTEN, JR., *Freebooters Must Die! The Life and Death of William Walker, the Most Notorious Filibuster of the Nineteenth Century* (1976); CHARLES H. BROWN, *Agents of Manifest Destiny: The Lives and Times of the Filibusters* (1980); WILLIAM WALKER, *The War in Nicaragua* (1860; repr. 1985).

ROBERT E. MAY

See also **United States–Latin American Relations.**

WALLACE, PETER (*fl.* 1630s), Scottish buccaneer. According to popular legend, Captain Peter Wallace (Willis) was the first European to harbor inside the barrier reef along the coast of present-day BELIZE. His base of operations was said to be founded in 1638 near the mouth of the Belize River. Wallace captained the *Swallow*, out of Tortuga Island, and Swallow Cay off the coast of Belize City is said to have been named after his ship. His name in Spanish became "Wallix" and later "Valis" or "Ballese" and was used as the name for the settlement at the mouth of the Belize River. Emory King, president of the Belize Historical Society, favors this thesis and notes that recently discovered documents from the Bay Islands refer to the area as "Wallix" or "Wallis."

Other theories suggest that Belize may be of MAYA origin from the word *belix*, meaning "muddy water" or *belakin*, meaning "land that looks toward the sea." It is also possible that the name Belize is derived from the Spanish term *baliza* or the French term *balise*, meaning "lighthouse" or other sea marker indicating dangerous conditions, the mouth of an important river, or the site of previous wrecks. In the eighteenth century, for example, the Spanish referred to a small settlement at the mouth of the Mississippi River as the *belize*.

NARDA DOBSON, *A History of Belize* (1973), esp. pp. 47–52; EMORY KING, *I Spent It All in Belize* (1986), esp. pp. 9–10; TOM BARRY, *Belize: A Country Guide* (1989), p. 1.

BRIAN E. COUTTS

WAR OF FOUR DAYS, a struggle beginning 29 August 1932 in Quito that resulted from the congressional disqualification of president-elect Neptalí BONIFAZ ASCASUBI. Bonifaz, previously the first president of the Banco Central, in 1931 won Ecuador's first free election in nearly forty years. In the inevitable postelection maneuvering, Congress voted to disqualify Bonifaz on the grounds that he had been born on foreign soil. The son of a Peruvian diplomat and Ecuadorian mother, he was born at the Peruvian Embassy in Quito, technically foreign territory. More to the point, however, Bonifaz had until age forty-six listed his citizenship as Peruvian. A bitter military clash over the presidency erupted, with fighting in and around Quito. Four battalions from the Quito garrison supported Bonifaz, defending against attacks from General Ángel Isaac Chiriboga Navarro and Colonel Carlos Salazar. Quito suffered four days and nights of fierce combat during which the city went without light, water, and food. Fighting raged from house to house, with sharp exchanges of artillery fire in residential neighborhoods. The anti-Bonifaz provincial units prevailed by 1 September 1932, but only after at least 200 people had been killed.

DAVID W. SCHODT, *Ecuador: An Andean Enigma* (1987), provides a summary treatment of Ecuadorian political economy. OSVALDO HURTADO's *Political Power in Ecuador*, translated by Nick D. Mills, Jr. (1985), offers an interpretive analysis. JOHN D. MARTZ, *Ecuador: Conflicting Political Culture and the Quest for Progress* (1972), and GEORGE I. BLANKSTEN, *Ecuador: Constitutions and Caudillos* (1964), provide accounts of the political context.

RONN F. PINEO

WAR OF INDEPENDENCE. *See* **Wars of Independence.**

WAR OF JENKINS'S EAR (1739–1748), war between Spain and England over transatlantic trade in the West Indies. The war resulted from the failure of England and Spain to negotiate disputes arising from issues addressed at the Peace of Utrecht (1713–1714), which granted England and, in particular, the South Sea Company, the *asiento* and the right to send a shipload of merchandise to Spanish America every year. In 1738 Captain Robert Jenkins appeared before the House of Commons and claimed that personnel on *guarda costas*, ships commissioned by local governors to search for contraband on English ships, boarded his vessel; in an ensuing dispute, his ear was cut off. After the English capture and destruction of fortifications at Portobelo, Panama, American trade was revitalized through the transition from the fleet system to the use of single ships licensed by the crown, the *registros*, which, through more rapid and frequent service, provided a greater volume of trade between Spain and its colonies. The war ended with the Treaty of Aix-la-Chapelle.

JOHN HORACE PARRY, PHILIP SHERLOCK, and ANTHONY MAINGOT, *A Short History of the West Indies* (1987); JOHN LYNCH, *Bourbon Spain, 1700–1808* (1989).

SUZANNE HILES BURKHOLDER

WAR OF THE MASCATES, a battle between native Brazilian planters and Portuguese immigrant merchants in 1709–1711. The onset of Brazil's so-called Golden Age led to the swarming of Portuguese to the littoral and interior of Brazil. Their arrival triggered anti-Portuguese nativist sentiment in several parts of Portugal's most vital colony. One center of such sentiment was the northeastern sugar-producing captaincy of PERNAMBUCO, where persistent bitter feelings existed between the indebted sugar-planting self-proclaimed aristocrats who controlled the political life of the capital, Olinda, and the merchants and clerks who lived in the port town of Recife. The planters considered the merchants, whom they termed *mascates* (peddlers), their social inferiors and blamed them for their indebtedness. The merchants and their allies resented the pretensions of the planters and their opposition to the incorporation of Recife as an independent town.

A series of clashes between the two groups led to the flight of two governors, a prolonged but ineffective siege of Recife, a surprise uprising by Recife's garrison, an early call for regional independence, and a severe repression undertaken by newly arrived governor Felix José Machado de Mendonça (1711–1715). Although there were surprisingly few casualties, the Pernambucan disturbances produced enduring resentments that would find expression in later revolts, especially those of 1817 and 1824.

C. R. BOXER, *The Golden Age of Brazil, 1695–1750: Growing Pains of a Colonial Society* (1962), chap. 5 and sources cited therein.

DAURIL ALDEN

WAR OF THE PACIFIC (1879–1884), an important conflict arising from a long-standing border dispute which pitted Chile against Bolivia and Peru. For years Bolivia and Chile had both claimed portions of the ATACAMA DESERT. Then, in 1874, after years of bitter argument that threatened to precipitate a war, La Paz and Santiago settled the issue by having Chile relinquish its claims to the southern portion of the desert, in return for which La Paz promised not to increase the taxes on any Chilean corporation operating in the once-disputed territory.

In late 1878, the Bolivian dictator Hilarión DAZA raised the export tax on a Chilean company mining nitrates in the Atacama. When La Paz refused to abrogate this impost, Chile, arguing that the Bolivian tax nullified the 1874 treaty, reoccupied the area it had once claimed. Daza responded by declaring war on Chile, but Santiago did not respond immediately. In April 1879, Chile officially learned that Peru had secretly signed an alliance promising to aid Bolivia if it went to war with Chile. When Peru stated that it would honor this obligation, Chile declared war on Peru and Bolivia.

Daza apparently adopted his truculent policy because his nation needed money and he believed that Santiago, already embroiled in a boundary dispute with Argentina, would not dare risk a two-front war. The Bolivian leader, however, miscalculated. Chile's president, Aníbal PINTO, although initially willing to negotiate, had little choice: domestic political and economic interests demanded that he act or be deposed.

Chile's declaration of war seemed foolhardy, since the combined Peruvian and Bolivian divisions outnumbered Chile's by two to one and Peru's fleet possessed four ironclads—including two topheavy, and therefore unseaworthy, monitors—to Chile's two. In truth, because they all lacked a skilled officer corps, adequate weapons, and a technical infrastructure, none of the belligerents seemed prepared for war.

In order to attack their adversary and supply their troops once they went on the offensive, the two principals, Chile and Peru, first had to win control of the sea-lanes. Although the Chilean navy seemed better prepared, its commander, Admiral Juan WILLIAMS REBOLLEDO, adopted a passive strategy. Instead of attacking the Peruvian fleet at its home base of Callao, Williams blockaded the nitrate port of Iquique. Because this tactic deprived Peru of nitrate revenues, he believed that it would force the Peruvian fleet to attack him. Instead of complying, however, the Peruvian commander, Admiral Miguel GRAU, reinforced Lima's

War of the Pacific
1879–1884

⚔ Land Battle
🛡 Naval Battle
⟋ Present Border

PERU

Lake Titicaca

Moquegua

La Paz

Tacna ⚔

Arica ⚔

Altiplano

BOLIVIA

Lima
Callao ⊕ Chorrillos
● Chilca
Lurín River

Same scale as main map.

Pisagua ⚔ Dolores
Junín ⚔ Tarapácá
Iquique 🛡

Atacama Desert

Lima ⊡ ⟋ Enlarged Areas

La Paz

Pacific Ocean

⊙ Santiago

Atlantic Ocean

100 miles
160 kilometers

Pacific

⚓ Punta Arenas

Pt. Angamos 🛡 CHILE

● Antofagasta

Commander and officials of a Chilean warship. PHOTOGRAPHIC ARCHIVE, UNIVERSIDAD DE CHILE.

southern garrisons and harried Chilean shipping. Finally, stung into action by an angry public, Williams ventured north to attack Callao. When he arrived, he discovered that the Peruvian navy had gone south to Iquique, where it attacked the Chilean wooden ships, the *Esmeralda* and the *Covadonga,* that were blockading Iquique. During the unequal struggle, the Peruvians sank the *Esmeralda* but in the process ran one of their two ironclads, the *Independencia,* aground, leaving Admiral Grau with but one seaworthy ironclad, the *Huascar.* Thus, the battle off Iquique on 21 May 1879 altered the naval balance of power and the course of the war.

Grau, outnumbered, continued to attack Chile's coast. He even sent a vessel south to Punta Arenas to capture ships as they passed through the Strait of Magellan carrying war matériel to Chile. Williams did not respond until Peru's navy seized the Chilean troop transport the *Rimac.* Wounded by the ensuing public outrage, Williams quit. His replacement, Admiral Galvarino Rivera, working in conjunction with civilian officials to refurbish the Chilean fleet, then launched an offensive designed to destroy the *Huascar.* On 8 October 1879, off Point Angamos, Chile's two ironclads, the *Blanco Enca-*

lada and the *Cochrane,* cornered the *Huascar.* Although outnumbered, Grau refused to strike his colors. Within minutes the Chilean gunner straddled the *Huascar* and killed most of its crew, including Grau. The surviving sailors attempted to scuttle the ship, but a Chilean boarding party captured the *Huascar* before it could sink.

Although the Chileans now controlled the sea-lanes, they did not know whether to strike at the Peruvian heartland, as they had in the 1836 WAR of the PERU-BOLIVIA CONFEDERATION, or to nibble away at the edges of their enemies' territory. Given the Chilean government's lack of confidence in its military, it decided to attack the southernmost Peruvian province of Tarapacá. In October 1879 the Chileans landed at Pisagua and Junín. Although Santiago's troops had to make a seaborne assault and scale well-defended bluffs, they subdued the enemy garrisons. After establishing a beachhead, Chilean commander General Erasmo Escala planned to advance inland, severing Iquique's supply lines to the interior of Peru. This tactic, in conjunction with a naval blockade, was designed to effect a Chilean takeover of the nitrate-rich province of Tarapacá.

Neither Peru nor Bolivia had remained passive while

the Chileans were marshaling their forces. General Daza had ponderously marched his improvised, hastily raised army from the *altiplano* to Arica. The plans called for Daza to march his men south to a point where they would link up with a Peruvian army led by General Juan Buendía, who would advance from the south. Once united, the allied force would then supposedly drive the Chileans back into the sea from which they had so ungraciously arrived.

This grandiose operation never occurred as planned. The inept Daza led his ill-prepared and poorly equipped men into the desert, where they quickly succumbed to the heat and lack of supplies. Rather than persevere (not one of Daza's strong points), the Bolivian simply returned to Arica, without informing Buendía of his changed plans. Meanwhile, the Chileans penetrated the interior, capturing the oasis of Dolores.

Fortunately for Chile's Escala, an advance party from his force sighted Buendía's troops as they marched north. Thus aware of the Peruvian advance, the Chileans threw up hasty positions on a small mountain overlooking the coveted water supply. The combined Bolivian-Peruvian force launched their attack late in the afternoon of 19 November 1879. Their futile assaults in the face of determined Chilean opposition collapsed. The allied army fled to the interior.

Before the Chileans captured the province of Tarapacá, one more battle remained. One of Escala's subordinates, who believed the Peruvians to be demoralized, launched an attack on the city of Tarapacá. This audacious plan collapsed because of faulty intelligence and an unexpectedly quick Peruvian response. Although the Chileans lost heavily in that engagement, the remaining Peruvians retreated and within a matter of days Chile had occupied Iquique.

The Chilean military's poor performance in the Tarapacá campaign forced President Aníbal Pinto to act cautiously. He ordered his men to land in the province of Tacna, a strategy which he hoped would force the Peruvians to counterattack. When they did not, Pinto ordered an assault on Moquegua. The Chilean commander, Manuel Baquedano, easily captured the city but had to launch a brutal frontal assault to dislodge the Peruvians from the high ground. Regrettably from the Chilean point of view, this action did not inspire Peruvian commander Admiral Lizardo Montero to counterattack. Thus, Baquedano ordered his men to cross the desert and capture the city of Tacna.

This trek began on 8 April 1880. By early May the Chileans had advanced to within 23 miles of their objective. The allied army had dug in on a promontory commanding the road to Tacna. As before, Baquedano simply overpowered his outmanned enemy. While successful, this tactic proved costly in terms of men; some Chilean units suffered 30 percent casualties. Still, the assault carried Tacna and permitted the Chileans to take the port of Arica in a daring predawn assault. By June, Chile controlled Tacna.

Following an abortive peace conference, the Chileans planned to move on Lima. After the Chilean civilians raised an army of 20,000, Baquedano ordered General José Villagrán to secure a bridgehead at Chilca while Baquedano brought up the main portion of the army by sea. With some mid-campaign personnel changes the attack went as planned, so that by early December 1880 the Chilean army stood poised to attack Lima.

The Peruvian defenses consisted of two lines of hastily built fortifications anchored on low mountains and reinforced by the fleet's remaining monitor. Rather than flanking Lima's defense line, which would have allowed the Chileans to envelop their objective, Baquedano as always ordered a frontal assault. On 13 January 1881 the Chileans forded the Lurín River and, after bloody fighting, broke the enemy's line. Chilean discipline, however, collapsed: rather than pursuing the enemy, many troops looted the city of Chorrillos, allowing the enemy's army to flee to Lima. When an attempt to negotiate the surrender of the Peruvian capital collapsed, the Chileans again attacked, easily vanquishing the remaining defenders dug in along the Surco River. By 17 January, the Chileans had taken Lima.

Regrettably for Chile, peace did not follow. A newly formed Peruvian government proved hesitant to cede Tarapacá as well as Tacna to Chile. Moreover, the remnants of the Peruvian army continued to resist. Facing the possibility of a protracted war, in 1881 and 1882 the Chileans launched punitive expeditions to eradicate Peruvian reistance. The struggle dragged on, however, consuming Chilean treasure and blood. Only in 1883, when the Chilean army had vanquished the forces of Andrés CÁCERES at Huamachaca, did Peru capitulate and sign a peace treaty ceding Tarapacá to Chile and allowing it to occupy Tacna and Arica for ten years. When faced with the possibility of an invasion, Bolivia, which had withdrawn into the *altiplano*, accepted an armistice that gave the Atacama to Chile. By 1884, Chile had increased its size, acquired a monopoly of the world's supply of nitrates, and dominated the Southern Hemisphere's Pacific Coast.

ROBERT N. BOYD, *Chili: Sketches of Chili and the Chilians During the War 1879–1880* (1881); MARIANO FELIPE PAZ-SOLDÁN, *Narración histórica de la guerra de Chile contra Perú y Bolivia* (1884); GONZALO BULNES, *La guerra del Pacífico* (1919); CARLOS DELLEPIANE, *Historia militar del Perú*, vol. 2 (1941); ROBERTO QUEREJAZU CALVO, *Guano, salitre, sangre* (1979); *Historia del ejército de Chile*, vols. 5 and 6 (1981); AUGUSTO PINOCHET, *La guerra del Pacífico* (1984); WILLIAM F. SATER, *Chile and the War of the Pacific* (1986).

WILLIAM F. SATER

WAR OF THE PERU–BOLIVIA CONFEDERATION

(1836–1839), a conflict between Chile and an alliance of Peru and Bolivia. In 1836, the Bolivian leader Andrés SANTA CRUZ created a confederation consisting of his country and PERU. The government in Santiago, displeased by the creation of a more powerful neighbor to the north, soon had reason to fear the confederation when the Santa Cruz government nullified an 1835 treaty that had given Chileans preferential tariff treatment. Peru, anxious to develop its port of CALLAO, also imposed a special tax on goods entering the nation via the Chilean port of VALPARAÍSO. Both measures jeopardized Santiago's economy. Angered by these steps and the fact that a political enemy, General Ramón FREIRE, had used a Peruvian port to launch an expedition hoping to depose the Joaquín PRIETO government, Chile's leader, Diego PORTALES, ordered his fleet to attack Callao, where it seized three Peruvian vessels. Infuriated, Santa Cruz arrested Chile's envoy but almost immediately released him with an apology. Portales seized upon the occasion of this diplomatic gaffe to demand that Santa Cruz apologize for the arrest; pay Chile money it had lent Peru; offer compensation for the abortive Freire expedition; and, finally, not only limit Peruvian naval strength but dissolve the confederation. When Santa Cruz refused, Portales declared war.

Initially, Chile did not fare well. Santa Cruz's troops vanquished the first Chilean expeditionary force soon after it landed in Peru. Santa Cruz's peace terms proved generous: Chile had only to return the three boats it had captured earlier and tacitly recognize the confederation. In return, the confederation would pay part of its debt to Chile and would permit Santiago's army to return home. However, once the Chileans reached home, their government repudiated the agreement and sent another army, under General Manuel BULNES, against the confederation. In early 1839, Bulnes defeated the forces of Santa Cruz, first at the battle of Buin, then on 20 January 1839 at Yungay. The Bolivian leader fled and the confederation collapsed, allowing Chile to control the Pacific Coast for decades.

ROBERT N. BURR, *By Reason or Force: Chile and the Balancing of Power in South America, 1830–1905* (1965), pp. 33–57; *Historia del ejército de Chile* (1981), pp. 189–240.

WILLIAM F. SATER

See also **Peru–Bolivia Confederation.**

WAR OF THE REFORM (MEXICO). *See* **Reform, the.**

WAR OF THE SPANISH SUCCESSION (1701–1713), a conflict between France and Austria (Bourbons and Hapsburgs) for the Spanish throne. After the death of the childless Hapsburg monarch CHARLES II, the principal candidates for the Spanish throne were the Austrian archduke Charles and Philip of Anjou, the grandson of the French monarch Louis XIV. Both were direct descendants of PHILIP IV of Spain through the marriages of his daughters. On his deathbed, Charles II left the throne to Philip of Anjou, but the inheritance was disputable since Philip's grandmother, María Teresa, had re-

nounced her rights to the Spanish throne when she married Louis XIV.

In May 1702, an Austrian, British, and Dutch alliance declared war on France and Spain. With a shortage of troops, arms, and supplies, Spain depended on France to support Philip's claim. Thus, the war on Spanish soil was fought chiefly by foreign troops. The war began with an unsuccessful allied attempt to seize Cádiz in August 1702. This was quickly followed by the destruction of the Franco-Spanish silver fleet in Vigo Bay, resulting in Spain's increased reliance on French shipping for the protection of the fleet system. Although trade between France and the Spanish colonies was officially prohibited, interloping trade thrived under the mask of French protection and during the war France benefited more from Spain's colonies than Spain did.

In 1703 Portugal joined the allies, thus giving England a strategic base for operations. Aided by rebels and insurgents, the allies took Valencia and Catalonia in 1705 and entered Madrid in 1706. However, a decisive Franco-Spanish victory at Almansa in 1707 marked an important turning point in the war. The Treaty of Utrecht (1713) acknowledged PHILIP V as king of Spain and the Indies, gave Charles (now emperor) the Spanish Netherlands and possessions in Italy (thereby dissolving the Burgundian-Hapsburg empire), and made important trading concessions to England (the ASIENTO, or slave trade).

PEDRO VOLTES BOU, *El Archiduque Carlos de Austria, rey de los Catalanes* (1953); JUAN MERCADER RIBA, *El capitans generals* (1957) and *Felipe V y Catalunya* (1968); HENRY KAMEN, *The War of Succession in Spain, 1700–1715* (1969); and ALAN DAVID FRANCIS, *The First Peninsular War, 1702–1713* (1975).

SUZANNE HILES BURKHOLDER

WAR OF THE SUPREMES (1839–1842), a series of regional rebellions in Colombia, during the regime of José Ignacio de MÁRQUEZ. The origins of the rebellions varied, but all shared a resentment of centralist control by Bogotá, and all were led by self-styled *jefes supremos* (supreme chiefs), usually of military extraction. The first revolt, in the southwestern province of Pasto in June 1839, started as a protest against the closure of several small convents; but by mid-1840, under the caudillo José María OBANDO, its goal was the ouster of Márquez, and a federal reorganization. Separate rebellions in the northeastern provinces, Antioquia, and the Atlantic coast (September–October 1840) also sought a vaguely defined "federalism"; rebels in Panama (November 1840) sought outright independence. By late 1840 the government's position seemed hopeless—a top official admitted as much in a famous circular—but crucial victories in October 1840–April 1841 turned the tide, and a combination of mass amnesties and occasional executions pacified the country by early 1842. The war produced a conservative, centralist reaction as seen in the Constitution of 1843; it also accelerated the political polarization that would give rise to the Liberal and Conservative parties by the end of the decade.

GUSTAVO ARBOLEDA, *Historia contemporánea de Colombia*, vol. 1 (1918); ROBERTO M. TISNÉS JIMÉNEZ, *María Martínez de Nisser y la Revolución de los Supremos* (1983).

RICHARD J. STOLLER

See also **Herrán, Pedro de Alcántara; Mosquera, Tomás Cipriano de.**

WAR OF THE THOUSAND DAYS (1899–1902), the last and greatest of Colombia's nineteenth-century civil wars. On 18 October 1899, Liberals in the northeastern department of SANTANDER rose in revolt against the Conservative regime in power since 1886, and warfare soon spread throughout much of the country. The Liberals failed to capitalize on their early victory at Peralonso (15–16 December 1899), permitting the government to retain the initiative throughout the war. At Palonegro (11–25 May 1900), near Bucaramanga, the government routed the Liberals in the largest battle in modern South American history. During the next two years the focus shifted to the central departments of Cundinamarca and Tolima, and conventional warfare gave way to a guerrilla struggle, both sides frequently acting without control from above. By late 1902 the warring factions, and the country, were exhausted; but the Liberals' position was far more desperate, after their failure to win support from Liberal regimes in neighboring countries. In October–November 1902 the largest Liberal armies, in PANAMA and on the Atlantic coast, capitulated in return for amnesty and limited political reforms; Liberal guerrilla holdouts in the interior were then crushed by the government. As many as 100,000 may have died in the conflict, from disease more than from combat wounds; the war also produced, albeit indirectly, Panama's separation from Colombia (under United States auspices) in 1903.

CHARLES W. BERGQUIST, *Coffee and Conflict in Colombia, 1886–1910* (1978).

RICHARD J. STOLLER

WAR OF THE TRIPLE ALLIANCE (Great War, Paraguayan War), the protracted conflict (November 1864–March 1870) in which Paraguay fought to preserve its sovereignty from Argentina, Brazil, and Uruguay.

CAUSES OF THE WAR

Brazil precipitated the conflict by invading Uruguay and interfering in its domestic affairs. In response Paraguayan dictator Francisco Solano LÓPEZ closed the PARAGUAY RIVER to Brazilian traffic, seized a Brazilian steamer, invaded the Brazilian province of MATO GROSSO, and ignored Argentina's denial of permission to cross the Misiones region to attack the province of Rio Grande do Sul in Brazil. The victory of the Colorados, the liberal party in Uruguay, which Brazil supported, along with Argentine anger over Paraguay's invasion of its territory, concern over the growing power of Paraguay, and military attacks on Brazil led to an alliance of Argentina, Brazil, and Uruguay, which declared war against Paraguay on 1 May 1865.

The Paraguayan army carried the war into the Brazilian provinces of MATO GROSSO and RIO GRANDE DO SUL, but Paraguay's success was short-lived. At the battle of Riachuelo on 11 June 1865, the Brazilian navy severely damaged the Paraguayan fleet on the PARANÁ RIVER south of CORRIENTES, limiting it to defensive actions. The Paraguayan armies that had invaded the provinces of Corrientes, Argentina, and Rio Grande do Sul also were soundly defeated. Within six months the allies halted the Paraguayan offensive and thereafter kept the war confined to Paraguay. By January 1866, allied ships had blockaded Paraguay, and in April allied armies crossed the frontier. A Paraguayan victory at Curupaití in September 1866 discouraged further allied offensives, and Paraguayan defenders confined the allied forces of Bartolomé MITRE to the southwest border region.

Paraguayans regard the May 1866 and November 1867 battles of Tuyutí in the HUMAITÁ region as victories, since they slowed allied actions. But the war turned against Paraguay in 1868. In January, Brazilian General Luis Alves de LIMA E SILVA, who later become the duke of Caxias, took command of the allied armies and one month later a Brazilian naval vessel passed the well-fortified complex of Humaitá, ascended the Paraguay River, and bombarded Asunción. The fall of Humaitá left Asunción indefensible, so López shifted the capital first to Luque and then to Piribebuy. The Lomas Valentinas campaigns, which occurred in the Valentine Hills some 20 miles south of Asunción in December 1868, foreshadowed the defeat of Paraguay.

The allies took Asunción and looted it but did not establish a provisional government until 15 August 1869, when both Caacupé, the new site of the Paraguayan arsenal, and Piribebuy had been captured. Brazilian troops under the Conde d'Eu, Gaston Luis Felipe d'Orleans, destroyed the Paraguayan army at Piribebuy in a bloody campaign, after which López fled north with the remnants of his army. The ACOSTA-ÑU confrontation between Brazilian troops and Paraguayan adolescent soldiers on 16 August 1869 led to many more deaths. López continued to wage guerrilla warfare until Brazilian cavalry surprised and killed him on 1 March 1870 at CERRO CORÁ.

From the opening of the war López directed his own armies and then, after the first disasters, assumed field command. His use of brutal measures to continue the war, including the drafting of young boys, his intolerance of disagreement, and the execution, imprisonment, and torture of officers, government officials, and their family members during the last year of the war revealed him to be a desperate, cruel dictator. Yet his fight to defend Paraguay against overwhelming odds made him national hero.

On 20 June 1870, Brazil, Argentina, and Paraguay signed a preliminary accord that ended the war, promised elections within three months, guaranteed nonintervention in Paraguayan politics, and assured free navigation of the Paraná and Paraguay rivers. The last Brazilian troops evacuated Paraguay six years later, but Argentina continued to administer Villa Occidental until 1878, when the arbitration of U.S. President Rutherford B. Hayes resulted in its recognition as Paraguayan territory.

The causes of the war are disputed. Blame has been attributed to Francisco Solano López, Bartolomé MITRE, Dom PEDRO II of Brazil, Uruguayan internal political disturbances, Brazilian national interests, and British intrigue. Most historians today believe the war developed from the efforts of Brazil, Argentina, Uruguay, and Paraguay to preserve political stability and a balance of power in the region.

The war lasted six years, in part because the allies did not marshal sufficient military power. By threatening to dismember Paraguay, they encouraged desperate Paraguayan resistance and López's stubborn persistence. According to allied agreements, Argentina was to contribute 25,000 men, Uruguay 5,000, and Brazil 40,000, but by the beginning of 1865 Brazil and Uruguay were

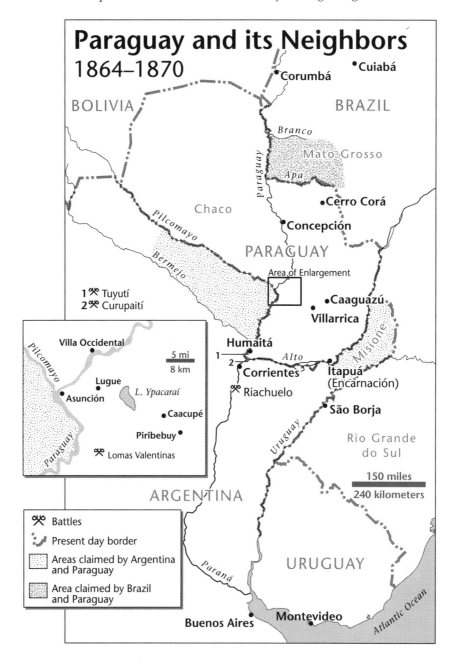

Paraguay and its Neighbors 1864–1870

- CUIABÁ
- Corumbá
- BOLIVIA
- BRAZIL
- Branco
- Mato Grosso
- Paraguay
- Apa
- Chaco
- Pilcomayo
- Bermejo
- Cerro Corá
- Concepción
- PARAGUAY
- Area of Enlargement
- 1 ⚔ Tuyutí
- 2 ⚔ Curupaití
- Caaguazú
- Villarrica
- Misiones
- Villa Occidental
- Lugue
- L. Ypacaraí
- Asunción
- Caacupé
- Piribebuy
- ⚔ Lomas Valentinas
- 5 mi / 8 km
- Humaitá
- 1
- 2
- Alto
- Corrientes
- Itapuá (Encarnación)
- ⚔ Riachuelo
- São Borja
- Rio Grande do Sul
- 150 miles / 240 kilometers
- ARGENTINA
- Paraná
- Uruguay
- ⚔ Battles
- ⋰ Present day border
- ▦ Areas claimed by Argentina and Paraguay
- ▦ Area claimed by Brazil and Paraguay
- URUGUAY
- Buenos Aires
- Montevideo
- Atlantic Ocean

Paraguayan prisoners of war guarded by soldiers of the Triple Alliance, ca. 1866.
BIBLIOTECA NACIONAL DE URUGUAY.

each 20 percent under force, and Argentina sent less than half the promised troops. In August 1867 the allied army had 43,500 troops, of which 36,000 were Brazilians, 6,000 Argentines, and 1,500 Uruguayans. To defend Paraguay, López had 35,305 soldiers and 3,306 officers in 1864 and successfully recruited replacements during the war.

RESULTS OF THE WAR

Despite its defeat Paraguay remained independent, serving as a buffer between Argentina and Brazil, but it paid a high price. The war destroyed a half century of economic development, ended social experimentation that had favored the campesinos, and destroyed a system of modernization based on the country's own resources. Paraguay lost between 8.7 and 18.5 percent of its prewar population—not 50 percent, as is often claimed—38 percent of its prewar territory, including the loss to Argentina of an economically valuable 17,568 square miles in the Misiones area, and all of its heavy and most of its light industry. Foreign influences and dependence on Argentina and Brazil replaced the self-sufficient, nationally directed economy of earlier decades, and a new political instability was reflected in the thirty-two presidents who administered Paraguay between 1870 and 1932.

The war also affected Brazil and Argentina. In Brazil the war created respect for the professional officers associated with the rising urban middle classes. It delayed consideration of internal issues such as slave emancipation. And although the war squandered lives and funds abroad, it increased the size of Brazil's territory. Argen-

tina, the chief beneficiary, obtained territory and destroyed Paraguay's rival power. Argentina invested less capital and fewer lives in the war than the other allies, while its cattle ranchers, farmers, and merchants benefited from the Brazilian military's purchases of Argentine food and supplies. And President Mitre used the war to subdue the interior and increase the power of centralized authority.

A great deal of literature about Paraguay has focused on the causes of the war. PELHAM HORTON BOX, *The Origins of the Paraguayan War* (1930, repr. 1967), blames Francisco Solano López for the war, while F. J. MC LYNN, "The Causes of the War of Triple Alliance: An Interpretation," in *Inter-American Economic Affairs* 33 (Autumn 1979):21–43, faults the policies of Argentina, specifically its president, Bartolomé Mitre; JUAN JOSÉ CRESTO, *La correspondencia que engendró una guerra: Nuevos estudios sobre los orígenes de la guerra con el Paraguay* (1953, repr. 1974) holds the internal political conflicts of Uruguay responsible, and CARLOS PEREYRA, *Francisco Solano López y la guerra del Paraguay* (1953), attributes the war to Brazil. JOSÉ ALFREDO FORNÓS PEÑALBA, "Draft Dodgers, War Resisters, and Turbulent Gauchos: The War of the Triple Alliance Against Paraguay," in *The Americas* 38 (April 1982):463–479, believes foreign interests, particularly those of the British, to be more responsible, whereas EFRAÍM CARDOZO, *Vísperas de la guerra del Paraguay* (1954), argues that efforts to maintain a balance of power in the Río de la Plata region were responsible for the war. DIEGO ABENTE, "The War of the Triple Alliance: Three Explanatory Models," in *Latin American Research Review* 22, no. 2 (1987):47–69, reexamines the evidence with mathematical models and concludes that a modified power transition best explains the origin of the war.

The major revisionist work on the demographics of Paraguay was contributed by VERA BLINN REBER, "The Demographics of Paraguay: A Reinterpretation of the Great War, 1864–1870," in *Hispanic American Historical Review* 68 (May 1988):289–319. The most complete descriptions of the war are found in JUAN BEVERINA, *La guerra del Paraguay*, 5 vols. (1921), and EFRAÍM CARDOZO, *Hace cien años: Crónicas de la guerra de 1864–1870*, 6 vols. (1866–1872). JOHN HOYT WILLIAMS, *The Rise and Fall of the Paraguayan Republic, 1800–1870* (1979):206–226, gives a description of the campaigns and effects of the war, as do two primary sources, GEORGE THOMPSON, *The War in Paraguay* (1869), and ANDREW JAMES KENNEDY, *La Plata, Brazil, and Paraguay During the Present War* (1869). The results of the war are well covered in HARRIS GAYLORD WARREN, *Paraguay and the Triple Alliance: The Postwar Decade, 1869–1878* (1978).

VERA BLINN REBER

"WAR TO THE DEATH," the name given to a speech by Simón BOLÍVAR during the Venezuelan War of Independence. After the fall of the First Republic, the failure of Spanish navy captain Domingo Monteverde to observe the capitulation of 25 July 1812 caused the struggle for independence to take on a progressively more violent nature. Many denunciations were made against cruelties and excesses committed by the royalist troops, as well as against provocations by the republicans. When Bolívar entered Venezuela on 15 June 1813, he delivered in Trujillo what came to be known as his "War to the Death" speech, which ended with the sentence: "Spaniards and Canarios, depend upon it, you will die, even if you are simply neutral, unless you actively espouse the liberation of America. Americans, you will be spared, even when you are culpable" (from Lynch, *The Spanish American Revolutions*, p. 203). The speech is significant in that it spared the Venezuelans who may have supported the royalists. It was Bolívar's aim then to go beyond royalist and republican categories and to make this a war between nations—Spain and America. In this sense, the speech was an affirmation of Americanism.

The war progressed, and prisoners continued to be executed on both sides until 1820. That year brought the signing of the War Regularization Treaty between Bolívar and Pablo MORILLO, commander of the opposing Spanish forces, ending the period of "war to the death."

See CRISTÓBAL MENDOZA, *Guerra a muerte* (1951), and LINO IRIBARREN CELIS, *Glosas para una nueva interpretación de la historia militar de Venezuela durante la Guerra a Muerte, 1814* (1964). On the War of Independence in general, see JOHN LYNCH, *The Spanish American Revolutions, 1808–1826* (1973).

INÉS QUINTERO

WARD, HENRY GEORGE (*b.* 27 February 1797; *d.* 2 August 1860), British diplomat in Mexico. Son of Robert Plumer Ward, a British member of Parliament, Henry Ward entered the diplomatic service immediately after finishing his education at Harrow. Although only twenty-six when British Foreign Secretary Lord Canning appointed him second commissioner to Mexico in 1823, Ward had previously been appointed attaché at the Brit-

ish legation in Stockholm in 1816, at The Hague in 1818, and at Madrid in 1819. His mission was to evaluate the political stability of Mexico's new government. Together with Lionel Hervey and Charles O'GORMAN, he negotiated a trade, friendship, and navigation agreement between Mexico and Britain. In May 1825 he was officially appointed chargé d'affaires and finally succeeded in obtaining ratification by Mexico of a Treaty of Friendship, Commerce, and Navigation between Mexico and Great Britain on 15 March 1826, well before U.S. envoy Joel R. Poinsett, who promoted U.S. interests in Guadalupe Victoria's cabinet, could negotiate a similar treaty. Ward intervened in Mexican politics in favor of the conservative Scottish Rite Masons (ESCOSESES) and against the liberal York Rite Masons. He was influential in the naming of Manuel MIER Y TERÁN as the director of the commission to establish the boundary between Mexico and the United States.

In February 1827 Canning recalled him from Mexico, in part because of his lavish expenditures. He returned to Britain in July 1827 and the following year published his two-volume work *Mexico in 1827*, written to evaluate mining possibilities and to stress the economic advantages of Britain's processing of Mexican raw materials. He went on to become a member of parliament and governor of Ceylon and Madras.

J. FRED RIPPY, *Rivalry of the U.S. and Great Britain over Latin America (1808–1830)* (1929); HENRY MC KENZIE JOHNSTON, *Mission to Mexico* (1992).

CARMEN RAMOS-ESCANDÓN

WARS OF INDEPENDENCE: SOUTH AMERICA. By the end of the eighteenth century, there were increased complaints in colonial South America against Spanish rule: the restrictions on direct trade outside the empire, the discrimination against American natives in appointment to high office, and other grievances real and imaginary. The dynamic economies of Caracas and Buenos Aires were more inconvenienced by Spanish commercial policy than were silver-mining Peru and Upper Peru (modern Bolivia), where economic growth was slower. Likewise, there was awareness of the American Revolution and, among the educated, familiarity with the liberal and democratic political ideas emanating from France and the Anglo-Saxon world. But in the two Perus, for example, the dominant Hispanic minority, its fears of the Indian majority heightened by memory of the TÚPAC AMARU revolt of 1780–1781, was hesitant to set in motion a process of change that it might not be able to control.

Prior to the Napoleonic invasion of Spain and the deposition of the Spanish royal family in 1808, there was little interest in outright independence; indeed there was widespread support for the Spanish Central Junta formed to lead resistance against the French. Some of the colonists would have preferred to set up

Wars of Independence in Spanish America 1810–1825

Battle Site
Viceroyalty of New Spain
Viceroyalty of New Granada
Viceroyalty of Peru
Viceroyalty of Río de la Plata

1 Captaincy General of Cuba
2 Captaincy General of Guatemala
3 Captaincy General of Venezuela
4 Audiencia of Santa Fe
5 Presidency of Quito
6 Presidency of Charcas

autonomous JUNTAS to rule in the king's absence. But the first efforts to create such juntas were thwarted by colonial officials who remained loyal to the Spanish junta. Indeed, the first junta actually set up in America, at Montevideo in September 1808, was an ultraloyalist body whose leaders doubted the fealty to Spain of the French-born acting viceroy of the Río de la Plata, Santiago de LINIERS Y BREMOND.

By contrast, juntas in La Paz in July and Quito in August 1809 were the work of colonists who were determined to take control into their own hands, even though still professing allegiance to Ferdinand VII. In Quito, such professions were perfectly sincere. There the junta was led by members of the local nobility who wished to preserve existing social structures yet were convinced of their own right to a greater voice in political affairs. To exercise regional power in the name of a distant monarch seemed a perfect formula for achieving these objectives. It was not acceptable, however, to the viceroy of Peru, José Fernando ABASCAL, who dispatched forces to Quito as well as to La Paz to suppress the juntas.

REVOLUTIONARY AGITATION

In the first half of 1810 the continuing decline of Spanish fortunes in the war against Napoleon inspired colonial activists to try again. On 19 April leading CREOLES in Caracas established a junta to take the place of the Spanish CAPTAIN-GENERAL of Venezuela, and on 25 May a similar junta emerged in Buenos Aires. Santa Fe de Bogotá followed on 20 July with a junta that initially included the viceroy of New Granada but soon dismissed his services. Santiago de Chile obtained its junta on 18 September, while Quito set up another of its own on 22 September.

447

Peru conspicuously held aloof, but in Upper Peru by the end of the year a revolutionary army sent from Buenos Aires had introduced a new political order.

All the new governments initially pledged allegiance to the captive Ferdinand VII, but they lost no time in asserting their own powers. They dismissed officials suspected of disloyalty and suppressed outright opposition by force. They opened ports to neutral trade, decreed changes in the tax system, and enacted other miscellaneous reforms. At Caracas the new leadership moved quickly to abolish the SLAVE TRADE, though not to disturb the institution of SLAVERY itself.

The more radical supporters of the new governments, such as Mariano MORENO, one of the secretaries of the Buenos Aires junta, used the press and political agitation to prepare Spanish Americans for more sweeping changes, publishing the first Latin American edition of Jean-Jacques Rousseau's *Social Contract.* In Caracas Francisco de MIRANDA joined Simón BOLÍVAR and other revolutionary activists in founding the Sociedad Patriótica to promote public improvements and gain support for independence. The campaign succeeded when on 5 July 1811 Venezuela became the first of the Spanish colonies to declare outright separation from the mother country.

LOYALIST RESISTANCE

Well before the Venezuelan declaration, it had become clear that not everyone was prepared to accept the creation even of juntas ostensibly loyal to Ferdinand. The Buenos Aires junta had to cope with a counterrevolutionary conspiracy only weeks after it seized power, and its forces also met resistance—at first easily overcome—in their occupation of Upper Peru. Nor did Paraguay and Uruguay, both integral parts of the same Viceroyalty of Río de la Plata, accept its claim to rule.

Likewise, outlying Venezuelan provinces such as Maracaibo and Guayana refused to accept the leadership of Caracas and its junta, which proceeded to use force in a not very successful attempt to win their obedience. Guayaquil and Cuenca (in what is now Ecuador) rejected the establishment of the second Quito junta, exactly as they had rejected the first in 1809. The junta of Santa Fe de Bogotá faced the defiance of local juntas in places such as Cartagena that insisted they had as much right as anyone in the colonial capital to exercise the power of deposed royal officials, as well as the defiance of certain areas that wanted to maintain as far as possible the colonial status quo. Peru, moreover, continued to stand apart, despite miscellaneous plotting and a minor uprising (quickly suppressed) in June 1811 at the southern town of Tacna, inspired in part by the presence of Buenos Aires forces nearby in Upper Peru.

One source of opposition to the unfolding new order was the peninsular Spaniards, who included most top colonial bureaucrats and churchmen as well as many of the wealthiest merchants. These by and large opposed any alteration in the formal relationship between America and Spain, preferring to obey whatever rump government continued to hold sway in some part of Spain. However, the Spanish element was nowhere numerous enough to control events unaided, particularly as creole officers and other Spaniards already integrated by marriage and other ties were heavily represented in the military command structure.

Among the creoles some remained distrustful of change. Others were alarmed by the efforts of the Buenos Aires forces invading Upper Peru to enlist support, for tactical reasons, of the Upper Peruvian Indian majority. The Indians, however, distrusted the intentions of the newcomers from the south and generally avoided entanglement. Black slaves and *pardos* (free blacks) in Venezuela looked askance at a revolution led by slave-owning, race-conscious creoles and were often susceptible to the appeals of loyalist opponents—even though the new government had outlawed the slave trade and in its December 1811 republican constitution outlawed discrimination on racial grounds.

The best predictor of alignments for and against the revolution was regional rivalry. It was no accident that Maracaibo and Guayana, whose political subordination to Caracas dated only from 1777 and were still not wholly reconciled to it, refused to follow the orders of the Caracas junta; nor that distant Paraguay, whose mostly mestizo population spoke more Guaraní than Spanish and felt few cultural or other ties with Buenos Aires, failed to accept the revolutionary authorities in the port city as successors to the viceroy. Guayaquil in Ecuador resented the domination of Quito and felt greater attraction, economically and otherwise, to Lima; it therefore collaborated with Peru's loyalist Viceroy Abascal.

Similar divisions of sentiment on regional lines could be seen in Peru itself. Still mindful of past Indian revolts, even reform-minded creoles in Lima generally continued looking for change to come within the imperial system. Yet in the Peruvian highlands resentment of Lima's hegemony was sufficiently intense for groups of disaffected creoles and mestizos to throw support to sporadic Indian uprisings over concrete local abuses, as at Huánuco in 1812. Two years later, creoles and mestizos in Cuzco who resented Lima and chafed under the rule of the local AUDIENCIA launched an uprising and enlisted the support of the Indian leader Mateo García Pumacahua (*see* PUMACAHUA REBELLION), until then a staunch loyalist. The more successful he was in recruiting other Indians, however, the more the original supporters of the rebellion had second thoughts. In the end, all highland uprisings were put down.

The resources at the disposal of the Peruvian viceroy not only proved capable of quelling outbreaks in Lima's Andean hinterland but (as in 1809) effectively defended the legitimist cause in neighboring colonies. Quito autonomists were again bested by forces from Lima—though not until 1812, by which time they had got around to a half-hearted declaration of independence. Peruvian armies supplemented by local levies similarly rolled back, in 1811, the Buenos Aires forces that had occupied Upper Peru the year before; and they repelled new invasions from the same direction in 1813 and 1815. Finally, the viceroy's forces restored Spanish authority in Chile in a campaign of 1813–1814 whose successful conclusion led to an exodus of Chilean patriots seeking refuge on the eastern side of the Andes.

CONFLICT IN THE RÍO DE LA PLATA

Revolutionary authorities in what is now Argentina went through a series of transformations from junta to junta, from first to second triumvirate, and finally a succession of "supreme dictators," in the course of which they enacted measures to limit the power of the church, expand individual liberties, and promote ties with northern Europe, but not formally declaring independence until 1816. They managed to hold the northwestern provinces against counterattacking loyalists from Upper Peru, who in 1812 penetrated as far as Tucumán. Yet after an unsuccessful campaign early in 1811 to bring Paraguay into obedience, they watched as Paraguayans in May 1811 set up their own junta, in practice independent of both Spain and Buenos Aires.

Argentine forces became bogged down in Uruguay in a confusing contest among pro-Spanish loyalists, local Uruguayan patriots, adherents of Buenos Aires, and Portuguese troops sent from neighboring Brazil in the hope of winning a foothold for Portugal in the Río de la Plata. In the short term the victor was the Uruguayan leader José Gervasio ARTIGAS, to whom Buenos Aires forces turned over the city of Montevideo in February 1815, a year after they had wrested it from the Spanish. In 1816 superior forces from Brazil made a clean sweep and annexed the entire area.

WAR IN THE NORTH

Fortunately for those loyal to Spain, Venezuela was closer than the Río de la Plata not just to Spain itself but, more important, to Cuba and Puerto Rico, where colonial rule was not yet seriously challenged. With reinforcements from Puerto Rico as well as Venezuelan recruits, the Spanish commander Domingo de Monteverde in March 1812 launched an offensive against Venezuela's republican government and almost immediately received the fortuitous help of a major earthquake that wreaked havoc on Caracas and other patriot-held centers. Republican morale as well as material resources suffered, but the new regime was already weakened by internal dissension. Appointment of Francisco de Miranda as dictator in April could not stave off defeat. Soon after the patriots' loss of the strategic coastal fortress of Puerto Cabello, Miranda capitulated, on 25 July 1812. Taken prisoner in violation of the surrender terms (when a group of former associates prevented his escape), Miranda was shipped to a Spanish prison, where he died in 1816.

This loss was by no means the end of the fighting in Venezuela. Early in 1813 a group of patriots led by Santiago MARIÑO, who had early taken refuge in Trinidad, began carving out a base of operations in the east, and later in the year Bolívar, who had fled first to Curaçao and then to Cartagena, crossed into Venezuela from the west, with backing from an independent government established in New Granada. After a successful whirlwind campaign, Bolívar reentered Caracas on 6 August; however, he did not restore the 1811 Venezuelan constitution but ruled in effect as military dictator.

Earlier on his way to Caracas Bolívar had issued his decree of "WAR TO THE DEATH" that promised execution for any Spaniard not actively supporting independence. This measure did not initiate but rather formalized the increasing brutality of the war in Venezuela. It was never uniformly applied in practice. However, the harshest phase of the struggle was about to come, as royalist guerrilla leaders exploited not just regional but ethnic and social tensions to build up irregular forces of devastating effectiveness. Especially damaging to the patriot cause were the *llaneros* (plainsmen) of the Orinoco Basin, skilled horsemen of generally mixed race and recently threatened in their way of life by the attempt of creole landowners (for the most part now patriots) to convert the previously open range of the region into large private estates. Recruited by the royalists, they helped chase Bolívar and other revolutionary leaders into exile or hiding once more by the end of 1814.

Bolívar again made his way to New Granada, where since 1810 the revolutionists had contained royalist forces in certain regional enclaves but became enmeshed in their own internecine disputes. The most important of these quarrels pitted Santa Fe de Bogotá, which under the leadership of Antonio NARIÑO aspired to bring together all New Granada under a centralist form of government, against other provinces that wanted a loose federation. Lacking any effective general organization, the provinces of New Granada declared independence in piecemeal fashion—Cartagena as early as 1811 and Santa Fe two years later. But the patriots proved unable to maintain their independence. Nariño was taken captive in mid-1814 while on a campaign against one of the royalist enclaves and shipped to prison in Spain like the Venezuelan Miranda.

The return of Bolívar later that year did not save the situation. Weakened by their disunity, New Granada's patriots were no match for the veteran troops that Spain was able to send to America following the final defeat of Napoleon and the restoration of Ferdinand VII. An expeditionary force led by Pablo MORILLO reached Venezuela in early 1815, after the patriot regime there had collapsed, and proceeded later that year to New Granada. Morillo took Cartagena after a bitter siege in December; a column dispatched to the interior entered Santa Fe in 1816.

THE REVIVAL OF PATRIOT FORTUNES

By mid-1816, the one part of Spanish South America where the revolutionists clearly had the upper hand was present-day Argentina, where formal independence was at last declared on 9 July 1816. Moreover, the first indication of a definitive turning of the tide was the successful crossing of the Andes early in 1817 by a joint army of Argentines and displaced Chilean patriots under the command of Argentina's José de San Martín. Coming out into the Central Valley of Chile, San Martín defeated the royalists in the battle of Chacabuco on 12 February. San Martín suffered one serious defeat before his second major triumph in the battle of Maipú on 5 April 1818. Meanwhile, however, he set up a revolutionary government in Chile, which he entrusted to his Chilean collaborator Bernardo o'Higgins, and that government finally issued Chile's declaration of independence in February 1818.

A few royalist enclaves remained after Maipú, but San Martín could now start preparing for an expedition northward to Peru, which had all along been his ultimate objective. He landed in Peru in September 1820 and consolidated a coastal foothold while hoping for either a general uprising in his favor or a negotiated peace with the Spaniards. Neither one occurred, but the royalists did withdraw their forces to the highlands, allowing San Martín to occupy Lima, where he proclaimed Peruvian independence on 28 July 1821. He organized a government and decreed various liberal reforms but was still avoiding a frontal assault on the royalist armies massed in the Andes when in July 1822 he traveled to Guayaquil to confer with his Venezuelan counterpart, Bolívar.

In the north the fortunes of war had changed even more radically. Bolívar had left New Granada slightly before Morillo restored it to royalist control, spending time in the West Indies. In 1816 he returned to Venezuela, ultimately joining forces with José Páez and other *llaneros*. Bolívar failed to dislodge the royalists from the Venezuelan highlands, but with Páez's help he created a patriot stronghold in the Llanos and in the east, organizing a government at Angostura on the lower Orinoco River.

In mid-1819 Bolívar scored his greatest military triumph by turning westward from the *llanos* to the heart of New Granada, where the royalists faced mounting discontent and a rise in patriot guerrilla activity. Bolívar's army climbed the Andes and on 7 August 1819 won a crucial victory in the battle of Boyacá. After that, resistance quickly collapsed in the central core of the colony, including Santa Fe de Bogotá which Bolívar entered three days after Boyacá.

It took three more years to expel the royalists from all outlying areas of New Granada, but meanwhile Bolívar and Páez liberated Andean Venezuela, where the definitive engagement was fought at Carabobo in June 1821. Panama fell into Bolívar's hands later the same year through a local uprising. Another spontaneous revolt had earlier deposed the royalist authorities at Guayaquil, and Bolívar commissioned his trusted lieutenant Antonio José de Sucre to proceed there to organize a campaign against Quito. Sucre's efforts culminated in victory at Pichincha, 24 May 1822, on the very outskirts of Quito, which sealed the liberation of the Ecuadorian highlands.

In July 1822 Bolívar pressured Guayaquil into joining the Republic of Colombia—formally established by the Congress of Cúcuta of 1821 to comprise all the former Viceroyalty of New Granada. He also conferred with San Martín on what still remained to be done. The details of their discussions remain a matter of controversy, but the upshot is known: San Martín resigned his command in Peru, clearing the way for Bolívar in 1823 to accept a Peruvian invitation to come and take command. Bolívar had the difficult task of combining his Colombian forces with the Chileans and Argentines left behind by San Martín and local recruits; and the Peruvian patriot leader proved fickle. The royalist armies still holding the Peruvian Andes were larger than any he had faced before. Eventually, however, Bolívar mounted a campaign that resulted in Sucre's victory at Ayacucho on 9 December 1824. It was the last major engagement of the war in South America. Royalist resistance in Upper Peru crumbled soon afterward, and the last Spanish fortress in South America, at the Peruvian port of Callao, surrendered in January 1826.

THE IMPACT OF THE INDEPENDENCE STRUGGLE
The Wars of Independence had uneven effects. Venezuela, where population may even have declined slightly, was hardest hit, while Paraguay was affected hardly at all. Agriculture was frequently disrupted and livestock herds decimated by passing armies, but in most cases the recovery of grazing and crop farming needed little more than time and good weather. Mine owners, however, suffered widespread destruction of shafts and equipment, and merchants had seen their working capital diverted to military expenses on both sides of the struggle.

The conflict left the newly independent governments with a burden of domestic and foreign debt, as well as a class of military officers, many of humble background, who were often unwilling to accept a subordinate peacetime role. Others who backed the losing side suffered loss of positions or confiscation of assets, but there was little change in basic social structures. One of the few exceptions was a sharp decline in slavery due to (among other factors) the drafting of slaves for military service in exchange for freedom.

Additional changes flowed not from the nature of the fighting but from the breakdown of imperial controls resulting in expanded contacts with the non-Spanish world and elimination of barriers to trade with countries outside the empire. Foreign ideas and customs likewise found penetration easier, mainly among the educated and more affluent upper social sectors.

The best overview in any language is that contained in the pertinent chapters of John Lynch, *The Spanish-American Revolutions, 1808–1826,* 2d ed. (1986). Valuable monographs on specific regions include Tulio Halperin-Donghi, *Politics, Eco-*

nomics, and Society in Argentina in the Revolutionary Period (1975); SIMON COLLIER, *Ideas and Politics of Chilean Independence, 1808–1833* (1967); TIMOTHY ANNA, *The Fall of the Royal Government in Peru* (1979); STEPHEN K. STOAN, *Pablo Morillo and Venezuela, 1815–1820* (1970); CHARLES W. ARNADE, *The Emergence of the Republic of Bolivia* (1957); and JOHN STREET, *Artigas and the Emancipation of Uruguay* (1959).

DAVID BUSHNELL

WASHBURN, CHARLES AMES (*b.* 1822; *d.* 1889), U.S. diplomat and minister to Paraguay during the WAR OF THE TRIPLE ALLIANCE (1864–1870). A political appointee of Abraham Lincoln (and brother of Elihu Washburne, an important Republican politician), Washburn arrived in Asunción in November 1861. At first he was on good terms with Paraguay's president, Francisco Solano LÓPEZ, but their relationship deteriorated after the war began. In 1867, Washburn offered his services as mediator between Paraguay and the Allies, but his pompous, uncompromising personal style hardly made him the best diplomat for the task.

Rebuffed on all sides, Washburn then publicly took up the role of protector of all foreign residents in Asunción, despite the fact that López had branded many of them as probable spies. These suspicions soon focused on Washburn himself, who was accused of being the ringleader of a massive conspiracy against the government. Although nothing was ever proved, López had scores of people tortured and quite a few executed in an effort to demonstrate the U.S. minister's guilt. Instead of labeling the charge a monstrous fabrication, however, Washburn fed the suspicion by replying in detail to the accusations. He only barely escaped from Paraguay thanks to the timely arrival, in 1868, of a U.S. warship sent to remove him from the country. He later defended his actions at a Senate investigation into Paraguayan affairs and in a vituperative two-volume memoir, *The History of Paraguay* (1871).

HARRIS GAYLORD WARREN, *Paraguay: An Informal History* (1949).

THOMAS L. WHIGHAM

WASHINGTON CONFERENCE (1889). *See* **Pan-American Conferences.**

WASHINGTON TREATIES OF 1907 AND 1923. In 1907 and again in 1922–1923, Washington, D.C., was the site for a Central American international conference. On both occasions the prospect of escalating isthmian conflict prompted interested powers—the United States and Mexico in 1907 and the United States alone in 1922—to bring the Central American nations together in an effort to resolve their outstanding problems. Building on the institutional machinery developed at the 1906 MARBLEHEAD and SAN JOSÉ conferences, the isthmian

delegates at the 1907 Washington Conference produced a series of treaties and conventions designed to promote isthmian peace and stability. The 1907 treaties featured a permanent CENTRAL AMERICAN COURT OF JUSTICE with mandatory jurisdiction and a recognition policy—the TOBAR DOCTRINE—that called for the nonrecognition of Central American governments that came to power by revolutionary means. A subsequent dispute over the Central American Court's ruling on the BRYAN-CHAMORRO TREATY led Nicaragua to denounce the treaties in 1917.

Uncertainty over the continuing status of the agreements and renewed international tension in Central America induced the United States to convene another Central American conference in December 1922. The resultant treaties included a more stringent de jure recognition policy, a Central American Tribunal with nonmandatory jurisdiction, and an arms limitation agreement. Dissatisfaction with the new recognition policy, however, led to the 1932 denunciation of the Washington Treaties by Costa Rica and El Salvador.

DANA G. MUNRO, *Intervention and Dollar Diplomacy in the Caribbean, 1900–1921* (1964), esp. pp. 151–155, and *The United States and the Caribbean Republics, 1921–1933* (1974), esp. pp. 123–126; RICHARD V. SALISBURY, ''Domestic Politics and Foreign Policy: Costa Rica's Stand on Recognition, 1923–1934,'' in *Hispanic American Historical Review* 54, no. 3 (1974): 453–478; THOMAS M. LEONARD, *U.S. Policy and Arms Limitation in Central America: The Washington Conference of 1923* (1982).

RICHARD V. SALISBURY

WATER WITCH INCIDENT. While surveying the PARANÁ RIVER in February 1855, the USS *Water Witch* was fired upon from the Paraguayan fort Itapirú, killing the helmsman and injuring others. The American warship had been sent to survey the RIO DE LA PLATA system, a regular undertaking by warships of the major naval powers. A year earlier, the *Water Witch*'s commanding officer, Lieutenant Thomas Jefferson Page, had been involved in a dispute between Paraguayan president Carlos Antonio LÓPEZ and a U.S. business concern. As a result, Paraguay closed its waterways to foreign warships, but the United States considered the Paraná River an international waterway. In 1858 the United States dispatched a squadron of warships, which included the *Water Witch*, to resolve the issue. While the majority of the squadron remained downriver at Corrientes, Argentina, the *Water Witch* and the *Fulton* proceeded to Asunción, arriving in January 1859. The U.S. commissioner, James B. Rowlin, negotiated an apology, a $10,000 indemnity for the family of the slain helmsman, and a new commercial treaty between Paraguay and the United States.

THOMAS J. PAGE, *La Plata, the Argentine Confederation, and Paraguay* (1859); PABLO MAX YNSFRÁN, *La expedición norteamericana contra el Paraguay, 1858–1859*, 2 vols. (1954–1958).

ROBERT SCHEINA

WATERMELON RIOT (PANAMA RIOT), an incident in Colón, on the isthmus of Panama, the part of New Granada (later Colombia) on 15 April 1856. Under the BIDLACK TREATY of 1846, New Granada granted the United States the "right of way or transit" across Panama in return for a U.S. pledge to guarantee the "perfect neutrality" of the isthmus and maintain uninterrupted transit. With the discovery of gold in California, U.S. investors completed a transisthmian railroad in 1855, increasing the number of travelers passing through Panama.

In the spring of 1856, the refusal of a U.S. citizen to pay a Colón street vendor for a piece of watermelon resulted in an altercation in which a shot was fired. An outraged mob of 600 local residents attacked U.S. citizens wherever they found them, and shots fired by both sides resulted in eighteen North American and two Panamanian deaths and sixteen North American and thirteen Panamanian wounded.

The incident, the first known anti-American riot in Panama, led to a U.S. decision to permanently station warships off the coast. This response, in turn, led to the first U.S. armed intervention in Panama when 160 marines landed at Colón on 19 September 1856 to protect U.S. citizens and preserve order, thereby preventing the outbreak of civil war. A subsequent claims commission awarded U.S. citizens $160,000 in damages for losses resulting from a dispute over a piece of watermelon worth ten cents.

E. TAYLOR PARKS, *Colombia and the United States: 1765–1934* (1935); GRAHAM H. STUART and JAMES L. TIGNER, *Latin America and the United States* (1975); J. FRED RIPPY, *The Capitalists and Colombia* (1976).

KENNETH J. GRIEB

WEAPONS INDUSTRY. The manufacture of armaments is a relatively recent phenomenon in Latin America that has enabled the hemisphere's countries to reduce their dependence on external markets. Latin America's major arms makers are Argentina, Brazil, and Chile. Under military rule, each of these countries built up its own self-sufficient weapons industries to make handguns, rifles, machine guns, hand grenades, armored personnel carriers, combat aircraft, tanks, submarines, patrol boats, missiles, rockets, and sophisticated communications gear. During the cold war the United States and the Soviet Union specialized in high-technology systems, leaving low-tech weaponry to such advanced developing countries as Argentina, Brazil, and Chile. The world was never short of regional wars and authoritarian regimes, particularly in Africa, Latin America, the Middle East, and Asia, which offered expanding markets.

In the early 1980s, the world arms market surpassed $50 billion annually. The U.S. Arms Control and Disarmament Agency has estimated Latin America's share of the world arms market at that time to be less than 10 percent. Brazil alone accounted for between 6 and 8 percent of the world's total, or more than 90 percent of Latin America's exports. Brazil, as the most diversified exporter, annually sold as much as $2 billion worth of aircraft, armored cars, missiles, rocket launchers, and communications equipment. The Middle East was its major buyer. In 1985, Iraq alone spent more than $1 billion to import various systems of Brazilian armament. Argentina now sells rockets, missiles, and low-flying reconnaissance aircraft. Chile's main exports are in the area of explosives, such as mines, cluster bombs, and aircraft bombs. In Argentina, armament manufacturing was a state-owned military enterprise, whereas in Chile and Brazil private firms predominated in the arms business.

The rise of the arms industry in Latin America resulted from a number of factors: sanctions and embargoes imposed by the United States for political and ideological reasons, a desire to attain self-sufficiency, and as a natural outgrowth of successful industrial economies. Argentina began the General Directorate of Military Factories (Fabricaciones Militares), its chief arms maker, during World War II as a way to substitute domestic arms for imports. U.S.-Brazilian fallout during the Jimmy Carter administration, Brazil's industrial capabilities, and growing demands by overseas markets all fueled the arms industry boom. When the United States and Europe refused to sell arms to the PINOCHET regime in Chile (1973–1990), it developed a self-sufficient domestic weapons industry. The military regimes of the Southern Cone countries were able to meet their own internal security needs.

The Brazilian arms industry was built around a thousand private firms and 400 producers of components. In its heyday it was producing an aircraft every twenty hours, an armed personnel carrier every eighteen hours, and 1,000 weapons systems per week. Embraer, the air force's aircraft manufacturer, alone had more than 500 component suppliers. The country's twenty shipyards produced submarines, patrol boats, and tankers, working through some 400 suppliers. After the late 1980s, however, Latin America's arms industry fell on hard times as the cold war ended, the Iraq-Iran war came and went, and newly installed civilian regimes in the developing world cut back on military spending.

HELENA TUOMI and RAIMO VAYRYNEN, *Transnational Corporations, Armaments, and Development* (1982); AUGUSTO VARAS, *Militarization and the International Arms Race in Latin America* (1985); JOSEPH F. CLARE, JR., "Whither the Third World Arms Producers?" in *World Military Expenditures and Arms Transfers 1986* (1986), pp. 23–28; NICOLE BALL, *Security and Economy in the Third World* (1988); MORTON S. MILLER, "Conventional Arms Trade in the Developing World, 1978–1986: Reflections on a Decade," in *World Military Expenditures and Arms Transfers 1987* (1988), pp. 19–24; AUGUSTO VARAS, *La política de las armas en América Latina* (1988); PATRICE FRANKO-JONES, *The Brazilian Defense Industry* (1992).

EUL-SOO PANG

WEFFORT, FRANCISCO CORREIA (*b.* 17 May 1937), one of Brazil's leading political scientists, known for his probing analysis of populism, syndicalism, and the role of leftist- and labor-based political movements in the consolidation of democracy in Brazil and other Latin American nations with a history of authoritarian and corporatist regimes. A 1962 graduate of the University of São Paulo, Weffort has taught in Brazil and abroad. He is a faculty member of the Political Science Department of the University of São Paulo and a founding member of the Center for the Study of Contemporary Culture. Weffort was one of the original founders of the Workers Party (PT), serving as its secretary-general in the early 1980s. In 1995 he became minister of culture under President Fernando Henrique Cardoso.

Weffort's writings include *O populismo na política brasileira* (1978), *Por quê democracia?* (1984), and *PT, um projeto para o Brasil* (1989).

DARYLE WILLIAMS

WEINGÄRTNER, PEDRO (*b.* 1853; *d.* 1929), Brazilian painter. Born in Pôrto Alegre, Weingärtner did not take up painting until he went to Germany in 1879. After four years in Hamburg and Karlsruhe, he moved to Paris, where he studied under the painters Tony Robert-Fleury and Adolphe Bouguereau. In 1885 he received a travel award from the personal coffers of the Brazilian emperor Dom Pedro II that allowed him to continue his artistic training in Italy. Before leaving for Rome, however, he had his first exhibition. The ten paintings he showed were received favorably, and one critic was so impressed with Weingärtner's drawing abilities that he declared him "Brazil's first painter." While in Rome, he executed genre paintings and paintings with themes drawn from classical subject matter. Examples include *Bad Harvest, Jealousies, Bacanal,* and *Cock Fights.* The French press criticized *Cock Fights* when it was shown at the Paris Salon because it was a copy of Jean-Léon Gérôme's painting of the same title. Weingärtner's first GAUCHO paintings were exhibited in 1892. Paintings such as *Late Arrival* and *Tangled Threads* affirmed his talent.

Throughout his later life, Weingärtner spent many years living and painting in Rome. In spite of the winds of modernism, he remained devoted to themes of daily life, classical subject matter, and life among the gauchos in Pôrto Alegre.

Arte no Brasil, vol. 2 (1979), pp. 569–570.

CAREN A. MEGHREBLIAN

WELLES, SUMNER (*b.* 14 October 1892; *d.* 24 September 1961), a career diplomat from the United States who became assistant secretary of state (1933–1937), under secretary of state (1937–1943), and a principal adviser on Latin American affairs to President Franklin D. ROOSEVELT. After several minor assignments, Welles went on a special mission to the Dominican Republic in 1922, where he negotiated the withdrawal of U.S. Marines from the country. Next, Welles directed U.S. policy at the Central American conference (1922–1923), which sought to bring constitutional government and arms limitation to the isthmus. Convinced that the United States should not intervene in Latin American internal affairs, he supported the GOOD NEIGHBOR POLICY of Roosevelt and the subsequent noninterference with Caribbean dictators and Brazil's Getúlio VARGAS in the 1930s. Welles's most noted assignment was to Cuba in 1933, where he determined that U.S. interests were threatened in the political chaos that followed the ouster of President Gerardo Machado. Welles advised his government against recognition of the revolutionary government and called for the stationing of U.S. warships in Cuban waters. His actions made him persona non grata in Cuba and led to his recall in December 1933. From the Buenos Aires conference (1936–1942), Welles labored for Latin American cooperation in the face of the developing war in Europe. Following his resignation in 1943 over policy disputes with Secretary of State Cordell Hull, Welles criticized U.S. policy toward Juan Perón in 1945.

SUMNER WELLES, *The Time for Decision* (1944) and *Where Are We Heading?* (1946); IRWIN F. GELLMAN, *Good Neighbor Diplomacy: United States Policies in Latin America, 1933–1945* (1979).

THOMAS M. LEONARD

WELSER, HOUSE OF, wealthy and influential German banking and commerce house based in Augsburg, which leased from the Spanish crown a large part of western Venezuela from 1528 until 1545. The lease was extended as partial payment of a considerable debt contracted by Charles V with the house of Welser. The agreement granted the Germans administration of that region (then largely unexplored and unsettled) and the right to explore, colonize, and extract whatever wealth they could. In exchange, the Welsers' obligations included the foundation of two towns of 300 *vecinos* each, the construction of three fortifications, and the importation of 50 German miners to the island of La Española (Hispaniola). The representatives of the Welsers mounted numerous expeditions into the Venezuelan interior to extract a return on their investment. Their search for gold and their pillaging alienated both Spaniards and Indians, and eventually convinced the Spanish crown to deny renewal of the lease in 1545 and to completely sever German ties with Venezuela by 1556.

JUAN FRIEDE, *Los Welser en la conquista de Venezuela* (1961); JULES HUMBERT, *La ocupación alemana de Venezuela en el siglo XVI Periódo llamado de los Welser, 1528–1556* (1983).

J. DAVID DRESSING

WEST INDIES FEDERATION. During the long history of British colonialism there were numerous attempts at federating several or all of the English-speaking Caribbean islands. The plans invariably came from a Colonial Office bent on cutting administrative costs. Local residents were seldom consulted, but when they were, they tended to be quite opposed to such schemes. In 1876 there were serious riots in Barbados when "Bajans" learned that the Colonial Office planned to integrate them into a Windward Islands federation. Antifederalist sentiment was especially strong in the larger islands, such as Jamaica and Trinidad, and in the mainland territories of British Guiana and British Honduras. In 1926 the Wood Commission reported that hostility against proposals for a federation was so intense that no realization could be foreseen. A similar finding was rendered by a 1936 commission about a proposed federation linking Trinidad with the Windward and Leeward islands.

The Colonial Office revived federation ideas with even greater vigor after World War II. The war represented a major watershed in West Indian life, a change that appeared to make such a federation a logical and realistic proposition. The most important changes were those which affected the colonial relationship. With its back against the wall, Great Britain ceded the defense of its Caribbean islands to the United States when it traded fourteen islands for forty U.S. destroyers. Additionally, the ability of German U-boats to cut the commercial and navigational lines with the region meant that the United States replaced Great Britain as the area's most important commercial partner.

The war also wrought internal political and social changes. Labor disturbances that spread throughout the region in 1936–1938 spawned powerful trade union movements and political parties based on them. Since these parties uniformly favored decolonization, it was assumed that they would favor it in any particular package the British were willing to offer. This sentiment led to the first conference on a British West Indian Federation in Montego Bay, Jamaica, in 1947. The meeting was successful in setting up a Standing Closer Association Committee, which drafted a federal constitution. The committee presented its report to a conference in London in 1953. Except for British Guiana and British Honduras, the governments of the ten other territories accepted the committee's proposals on federation.

In 1956 a third, and final, conference was held in London. All that remained was the selection of a site for the federal capital. This decision turned out to be more difficult than expected, a clear indication that the federation would not be free of conflict. After much acrimonious interisland bickering, they selected the one island that all the others had originally opposed, Trinidad. Twelve hundred miles of sea now separated Jamaica from its ostensible capital city. In the 1958 federal elections, the federalist party won a slim majority, carried mostly by the vote of the smaller islands. In both Trinidad and Jamaica,

the sitting governments, which supported federation, lost. Since local politics was also very much a part of the election, it is difficult to know where anti-incumbent sentiment left off and antifederation feelings began. Regardless, the vote did not bode well for the future of the federation, as majorities in the two islands that comprised over 80 percent of the land area, 77 percent of the population, and three-quarters of the wealth had voted against it.

Barbados's Sir Grantly Adams was selected as the first federal prime minister. He presided over a federal government with little power and even less funds. With no power to raise its own taxes, it depended on contributions from the different members, assessed in terms of national income. It also received and distributed the grants that still came from the Colonial Development and Welfare Acts. In short, it had just enough to keep up appearances and fund the UNIVERSITY OF THE WEST INDIES and the West India Regiment. This was not a federal government that could overcome the intense insularity of islands so distant geographically and politically from each other. By 1961 that insularity was particularly intense in Jamaica, where Alexander Bustamante and his Jamaican Labour Party forced a referendum on the island's continuance in the federation. Their main complaint was that with the removal of British grants to the smaller islands, the larger islands would have to pick up the tab.

Despite a valiant effort by Norman Manley and his People's National Party to save the federation, the secessionist sentiment won. Following this decision, Trinidad's Eric Williams communicated his intention of following Jamaica's example with the celebrated statement that "nine minus one leaves zero." By 1962 the West Indies Federation was dead. All that is left of the effort are the University of the West Indies and the sentiment that forming an economic union is a more realistic first step toward an eventual political union. At this writing, the region is still struggling to make that first step a firm and convincing one.

FRANLIN W. KNIGHT, *The Caribbean: The Genesis of a Fragmented Nationalism* (1990); PETER CALVERT, *Political and Economic Encyclopaedia of South America and the Caribbean* (1991).

ANTHONY P. MAINGOT

See also **Caribbean Sea: Commonwealth States.**

WEYLER Y NICOLAU, VALERIANO (*b.* 17 September; *d.* 20 October 1930), captain-general of Cuba (1896–1898) who supervised the Spanish war effort to subdue the independence movement on that island. His mission was twofold: to end the Cuban conflict by military means and to restore colonial consensus through political methods. He instituted what would become the model by which colonial powers responded in their colonies: the reconcentration policy.

The reconcentration policy divided Cuba into war

zones. In these zones the entire population was ordered into concentration camps located in the major cities. The Spanish Army then assumed that all those found in these areas were rebels and dealt with them accordingly. The concentration camps were not meant to punish their residents, but Spanish and local officials were not prepared to care for the displaced peasants. Inadequate food supplies and sanitary facilities led to the spread of disease and the death of tens of thousands of the 300,000 inhabitants.

Under General Weyler the royalist army inflicted widespread destruction of life and property. In addition to the reconcentration policy and the attacks on the rebels, the army burned entire villages, homes, fields, and food reserves. They also slaughtered the livestock. Vast stretches of the countryside were reduced to wasteland. The new offensive led by Weyler succeeded in containing the revolutionaries but was unable to defeat them. Weyler's tactics proved to be counterproductive, as the atrocities resulted in more Cubans supporting the revolution and caused a public outcry in the United States and even in Spain. In January 1898 Weyler was replaced and a more conciliatory Spanish policy was adopted.

Enciclopedia universal illustrada, vol. 70 (1958), pp. 153–156; FRANK FREIDEL, *The Splendid Little War* (1958); HUGH THOMAS, *Cuba; or, the Pursuit of Freedom* (1971); LOUIS A. PÉREZ, JR., *Cuba: Between Reform and Revolution* (1958).

DAVID CAREY, JR.

See also **Cuba: War of Independence.**

WHALING. Sixteenth-century accounts of Brazil contain numerous references to whales, although whaling was apparently never undertaken during the century. Several species, including gray, blue, humpback, and sperm whales, migrated to protected points along the Brazilian coast from June to August for breeding purposes, and their presence soon attracted mercantile interest. Around 1602 Biscayan fishermen introduced whaling to the Bay of All Saints at Salvador, Bahia. Simultaneously, the Portuguese crown declared the capture of whales and the preparation of derivatives a royal monopoly. During the rest of the seventeenth century, whaling stations spread from Bahia north to Pernambuco and Paraíba and south to Rio de Janeiro, São Paulo, and Santa Catarina on the basis of regionalized royal grants. In 1743, however, the grants pertaining to operations from Rio de Janeiro to Santa Catarina were incorporated into a single privilege, and by 1765 POMBALINE policy dictated the consolidation of all Brazilian whaling activity into one exclusive grant. This consolidated privilege prevailed until 1801, when the royal monopoly was terminated.

Contrary to the designs of liberal crown policy, rather than attracting fresh entrepreneurial energy to whaling, the suspension of exclusive privilege marked the beginning of a process of stagnation and decline of a once prosperous industry. Few investors were willing to risk their capital in whaling, given that two centuries of particularly predatory practices had greatly depleted the whale populations (females, for example, were lured to whalers by way of the capture of suckling offspring). Likewise, routine refining and preparatory processes had rendered Brazilian whale oil, meat, baleen, and spermaceti inferior in quality and high in price when compared with foreign products. By the mid-nineteenth century, Brazilian whaling had succumbed to European and U.S. competition, although sporadic activity continued into the twentieth century.

An authoritative history of Brazilian whaling is MYRIAM ELLIS, *A baleia no Brasil colonial* (1969). See also CAIO PRADO JÚNIOR, *The Colonial Background of Modern Brazil*, translated by Suzette Macedo (1967), pp. 217–218; and ANDRÉE MANSUY-DINIZ SILVA, "Imperial Re-organization, 1750–1808," in *Colonial Brazil*, edited by Leslie Bethell (1987), pp. 261–269.

DOUGLAS COLE LIBBY

See also **Fishing Industry.**

WHEAT, widely cultivated crop important to Latin America's large-scale agribusiness as well as to small-scale peasant cultivation. Christopher Columbus introduced wheat to the New World in 1493, and the following year the first crops were reaped. The early settlers planted typical Spanish wheats of the day, such as *Triticum vulgare*. Eventually, however, hardier varieties of common wheat (*Triticum aestivum*), used in making bread and pastry, and durum wheat (*Triticum turgidum*), used in making pastas, replaced the original species. Although wheat was grown primarily for domestic use throughout the region, wheat-flour consumption tends to be highest where European influences have predominated, as in Chile and Argentina, whereas in areas where indigenous and African cultures have persevered, maize, rice, and manioc remain the principal sources of starch.

In the late nineteenth and early twentieth centuries, wheat became commercially important in a few Latin American countries. In the 1880s, for example, Argentina started to produce a large enough surplus to become a leading wheat-exporting nation. Seeking farmers to raise alfalfa as cattle feed, the cattle barons of the Argentine pampas attracted European peasants by offering them sharecropping arrangements. To prepare the land for alfalfa, the immigrants grew wheat, which proved a successful crop in its own right. Other major producer nations include Brazil, Chile, Mexico, and Uruguay, but none produces surpluses rivaling Argentina's.

Originally domesticated in the Near East, wheat is not naturally suited to Latin America's tropical climate. It grows best where temperatures are mild and rainfall moderate. This explains the success of wheat cultivation in temperate subtropical regions like the belt of the grassland extending from Rio Grande do Sul in Brazil southwest through Uruguay to Buenos Aires province in Argentina. Depending on seasonal climatic conditions, wheat also does well at high altitudes, such as in the central plateau of Mexico and the highland valleys of Ecuador.

The development of high-yield, rust-resistant wheat varieties has been the focus of considerable scientific investigation in Latin America. Experimental farms established in Argentina and Uruguay before World War I eventually bred durable grains that were well adapted to local climates and mechanical harvesting. In Mexico, a green revolution study initiated in 1943 with Rockefeller Foundation participation yielded a stout, semi-dwarf hybrid that withstood the weight of fertilizers without falling over. These discoveries helped wheat growers around the world.

Despite the fact that the improved varieties and the machines made to harvest them generally were available only to large-scale agribusiness, small-scale peasant agriculture contributed greatly to wheat production in many Latin American countries. Studies conducted in the 1970s showed that peasants produced nearly one-third of the wheat consumed in Mexico and 70 percent in Colombia. In sharp contrast to farming wheat from the air-conditioned cab of a modern combine, these peasant farmers often planted, tended, and harvested by hand. Improving their productivity and conditions continued to be a compelling problem in Latin America, for the region as a whole remained dependent on wheat imports: more than 8.2 million short tons were imported in 1989 alone. Critics of the agribusiness blame this situation on the few powerful brokers that control most of the world wheat trade.

JAMES R. SCOBIE, *Revolution on the Pampas: A Social History of Argentine Wheat, 1860–1910* (1964); RUDOLPH F. PETERSON, *Wheat: Botany, Cultivation, and Utilization* (1965); ROGER BURBACH and PATRICIA FLYNN, *Agribusiness in the Americas* (1980); EMILIANO ORTEGA, "Peasant Agriculture in Latin America," in *CEPAL Review* 16 (April 1982): 75–111; CHARLES B. HEISER, JR., *Seed to Cultivation: The Story of Food*, new ed. (1990), pp. 67–79.

CLIFF WELCH

WHEELOCK ROMÁN, JAIME (*b.* 30 May 1947), Nicaraguan leader and member of the Sandinista National Directorate. Jaime Wheelock was born in Managua. His family owned a large coffee farm in the fertile region of Carazo, near the town of Jinotepe. Wheelock gained firsthand knowledge of large agro-export operations that would influence his politics later in life. He attended the best schools in Managua and traveled abroad frequently.

Wheelock met several Sandinista leaders in the 1960s but did not join the movement until 1969. In 1970 he was accused of killing a National Guardsman and fled to Chile, where he studied politics, sociology, and agri-

cultural law. Considered brilliant by his professors, he has been described by both friends and enemies as vain, materialistic, and intellectually arrogant. During his studies in Germany in 1972 and 1973, Wheelock applied Marxist-Leninist thought to Nicaraguan politics and society. This resulted in his *Imperialismo y dictadura* (1975), a historical survey of coffee farming and agro-export industrialization since the nineteenth century. He identified what he thought was a large rural proletariat exploited by large landowners and banking interests in agriculture. The argument follows Marx's prediction that in the transition from feudalism to capitalism the emerging bourgeoisie would experience internal crisis and the working masses would develop class consciousness. However, this thesis has been sharply criticized by scholars of political and economic development in Nicaragua. Much of the research was based on Wheelock's dogmatic bias for proletarian revolution.

Wheelock published the book in Nicaragua and injected his ideological and theoretical perspective into the Sandinista debate over tactics and strategy. A clash between Wheelock's "Proletarian Tendency" and the prevailing doctrine of prolonged popular war was inevitable. The Proletarians considered the Maoist, voluntarist approach of Carlos FONSECA, Henry RUÍZ, and Tomás BORGE to be a waste of time. This view was borrowed directly from Marx's conclusion that peasants were incapable of self-mobilization and revolt. The internecine struggle of the Sandinista leadership reached a pinnacle with bitter exchanges. Borge threatened Wheelock with physical harm, which caused him to take refuge in the house of a priest. The Proletarians were purged from the guerrilla organization in October 1975.

However, Wheelock pressed forward with his notion of how revolution would come about in Nicaragua. He organized labor strikes among poor barrio dwellers as the national crisis worsened in 1977 and 1978. Wheelock, Luis Carrión, and Carlos Núñez focused their attention on the vast settlements on the outskirts of Managua, where they gained a substantial following. This contributed to the reunification of the Proletarians with the Sandinista directorate in March 1979. Wheelock helped coordinate the final offensive against the SOMOZA regime in urban slums.

Wheelock became minister of agriculture and agrarian reform after the insurrection. He directed the redistribution of land confiscated from Somoza and his associates to peasants. However, Wheelock was an exponent of pragmatic, gradualist policies that were reflected in the 1981 agrarian reform law. He recognized the dangers of encouraging invasions of non-Somocista estates by rapidly distributing land confiscated by decrees 3 and 38, which affected only Somocista properties. Wheelock favored creating large-scale, capital-intensive state farms that would facilitate a centralized economy. This position contradicted that of many officials who wanted to allow peasants to determine agricultural policies. Thus, the proletarian tendency that dominated the Ministry of Agriculture divided along these lines, putting distance between Wheelock and supporters of Luis Carrión and Carlos Núñez.

By 1983 the Sandinista agrarian program was threatened by the influence of counterrevolutionary forces in rural areas. Many peasants in the northeast had not benefited from the government's strategy, and they began to join the contras. Wheelock therefore decided to increase the pace of land distribution. He oversaw the creation of an extensive cooperative system known as the Area of People's Property, which gave more control over planting and harvesting to individual farmers. In 1984 the Ministry of Agriculture handed out titles to over 2 million acres. Furthermore, Wheelock supported the expansion of the National Union of Farmers and Cattlemen, an organization of small and medium producers who accounted for a large percentage of agroexports and basic grains.

A new agrarian reform law was passed in January 1986. Wheelock used some of its provisions to expropriate the property of several large exporters of coffee and cotton, accusing them of sending bank credit out of the country instead of using it for production. The objective was to demonstrate Sandinista resolve to support small private farmers and peasant cooperatives. Nevertheless, the general failure of agrarian reform was one of the contributing factors to the electoral defeat of the regime in February 1990. The Nicaragua Opposition Union and Violeta BARRIOS DE CHAMORRO received majorities in most rural areas. Wheelock has written several articles in the postelection period justifying the actions of the Ministry of Agriculture. He blames aggression from the Reagan administration and decapitalization of the banking system by "unpatriotic" producers for the Sandinistas' inability to secure property rights and, thus, the loyalty of peasants.

As of 1993, Wheelock retains his post on the Sandinista National Directorate. At the party congress in July 1991, the debate over agrarian reform intensified and Wheelock was the target of much criticism. Several social scientists and political figures opened a public dialogue about the plight of the peasant in the Nicaraguan revolution. Wheelock responded in the newspaper *Barricada*, explaining his views about agricultural policy in the 1980s. He also denied the rumor that he controls several properties confiscated from Somocistas. He continues to live in a large farmhouse outside of Managua.

JAMIE WHEELOCK ROMÁN, *Imperialismo y dictadura*, 5th ed. (1980); FORREST COLBURN, *Post-Revolutionary Nicaragua* (1986); GABRIELE INVERNIZZI et al., *Sandinistas: Entrevistas a Humberto Ortega Saavedra, Jaime Wheelock Román y Bayardo Arce Castaño* (1986); ROSE SPALDING, ed., *The Political Economy of Revolutionary Nicaragua* (1987); DENNIS GILBERT, *Sandinistas* (1988); JAIME WHEELOCK, "La verdad sobre la reform agraria," in *Barricada*, 28–30 August 1991.

MARK EVERINGHAM

See also **Nicaragua: Political Parties.**

WHEELWRIGHT, WILLIAM (*b.* 16 March 1798; *d.* 26 September 1873), U.S. transportation entrepreneur. Stranded in Buenos Aires in 1822, Massachusetts-born Wheelwright, a merchant mariner, arrived in 1824 in Chile, where he operated a merchant vessel to Panama. Following a short stay in Ecuador, he returned to Chile, where he founded another maritime company, which operated out of the nation's most important port, VALPARAÍSO. In 1835 the Chilean government awarded Wheelwright a monopoly to operate a shipping company, the Pacific Steam Navigation Company, which sailed between Valparaíso and Panama. Wheelwright purchased two ships, the *Chile* and the *Peru*, which arrived in Chilean waters in 1840. Wheelwright subsequently expanded the service to include not merely Valparaíso but also Chile's northern mining ports of Caldera, Huasco, and Coquimbo as well as Europe. Wheelwright later shifted his emphasis in the transportation industry by helping to build the first rail lines connecting the northern port of Caldera with the mining center of Copiapó. He also constructed a railroad between Santiago and Valparaíso, thereby facilitating Chile's exportation of wheat. This entrepreneur also helped establish telegraph service connecting the capital with Valparaíso. He subsequently left Chile for Argentina, where he again became involved in railroading.

JAY KINSBRUNER, "The Business Activities of William Wheelwright in Chile, 1829–1860" (Ph.D. diss., NYU, 1964) and "Water for Valparaíso: A Case of Entrepreneurial Frustration," in *Journal of Interamerican Studies and World Affairs* 10 (1968): 653–661; ROLAND E. DUNCAN, "William Wheelwright and Early Steam Navigation in the Pacific, 1820–1840," in *The Americas* 32, 2 (1975): 257–281.

WILLIAM F. SATER

WHITE Y LAFITTA, JOSÉ (*b.* 31 December 1835; *d.* 15 March 1918), Cuban violinist and composer. A world-famous black musician, White was born in Matanzas, Cuba. There he met the renowned American composer Louis M. Gottschalk, who in 1855 persuaded White's family to send him to study at the Paris Conservatory. There he worked under the master violinist Jean-Delphin Alard, whom he temporarily replaced at the Conservatory when Alard was away.

White was highly praised by the critics and musicians of his time. He traveled throughout the world, playing for royalty and receiving standing ovations from the most sophisticated audiences. He may have been the first black musician to appear with an American orchestra. At home he sympathized with the Cuban insurgents in the TEN YEARS' WAR (1868–1878) against Spain. He composed a popular piece for violin and orchestra titled "La bella cubana," for which he was expelled from Cuba in 1875 when his playing it in a Havana theater caused a patriotic disturbance. Most of his works, however, are classic compositions. His Violin Concerto was played for the first time in the United States in New York City in 1974.

For a short biography of White, see josé i. lasaga, *Cuban Lives: Pages from Cuban History* (1881; repr. 1968), vol. 2. See also james m. trotter, *Music and Some Highly Musical People* (1878).

José M. Hernández

WHYTEHEAD, WILLIAM KELD (*b.* ca. 1810; *d.* July 1865), British engineer active in Paraguay. When Paraguayan president Carlos Antonio lópez decided to launch a major modernization program for his country in the mid-1850s, he turned to British experts—a natural choice, considering that he had already cemented good relations with Britain thanks to the 1853–1854 visit of his son, Francisco Solano lópez. Thus, the younger López applied to the firm of John and Alfred Blyth of Limehouse, who agreed to supply Paraguay with more than a hundred trained machinists and engineers. To act as engineer in chief, the Blyth brothers selected their most talented man, a Scot named William Keld Whytehead.

Though only in his early thirties, Whytehead had proved himself as an arms designer and arsenal operator in France. He even held several patents for improvements in the steam engine. When he arrived in Asunción in January 1855, Whytehead was given a measure of power unheard of for a foreigner: he directed hundreds of Paraguayan laborers as well as all of his European colleagues. Over the course of a decade in rustic Paraguay, he supervised the construction of a modern arsenal, an iron foundry and industrial smithy, a railroad, new port facilities and government buildings, and a shipyard that, during Whytehead's time, produced a half-dozen steamships. Such tremendous changes in such a short time were rightly regarded as a marvel.

While paying close attention to these projects, Whytehead also had to mediate disputes between the various engineers and the Paraguayan government. For all of this, he received the handsome salary of 600 pounds annually (a sum second only to that of the president) along with many other perquisites. His myriad responsibilities notwithstanding, he still found time to maintain a voluminous correspondence in several languages (including Swedish) and to contribute articles to European technical journals.

The coming of the war of the triple alliance (1864–1870) placed new burdens on Whytehead. He received orders to place all of the state projects on a war footing. Not surprisingly, he began to feel the pressure of overwork. A bachelor, he had no opportunity to find solace in family life, and in the end homesickness, physical exhaustion, and repeated bouts of illness drove him to a state of depression and ultimately suicide.

josefina plá, *The British in Paraguay, 1850–1870* (1976); john hoyt williams, *The Rise and Fall of the Paraguayan Republic, 1800–1870* (1979), pp. 180–190.

Thomas L. Whigham

WILDE, EDUARDO (*b.* 15 June 1844; *d.* 5 September 1913), Argentine statesman, diplomat, and writer. Wilde, born in Tupiza, Bolivia, became a symbol of the liberal "Generación del Ochenta" (Generation of 1880) that came to power with President Julio Argentino roca in 1880. Wilde graduated from the Medical School of the University of Buenos Aires in 1870 and made an outstanding contribution during the yellow fever epidemic that scourged that city in 1871. In 1875 he was appointed professor of forensic medicine and toxicology at the University of Buenos Aires and professor of anatomy at the Colegio Nacional. He became interested in issues of public health and in 1878 published his *Curso de higiene pública*. He served in Congress as a national deputy for Buenos Aires (1874–1876, 1876–1880). President Roca chose him as his minister of justice and education, and it was in that post that Wilde made his mark. In the early 1880s, a series of laws gave the national government jurisdiction over primary education and the Civil Register of Births and Marriages (Office of Vital Statistics), which had been in the hands of the catholic church. After successfully defending the secularizing laws, Wilde remained at the forefront in the ensuing confrontations with militant Catholics, which continued during his service as minister of the interior under President Miguel juárez celman (1886–1889). During this period he returned to his concern with public health, pushing forward a project for the construction of a drainage and sewage system for the city of Buenos Aires that would produce a dramatic improvement in sanitary conditions. In 1898 he was appointed president of the National Department of Health and was later chosen to represent his country in Madrid and Brussels. He published several collections of articles and short stories, such as *Tiempo perdido* (1878) and *La lluvia* (1880).

On Wilde's contributions to public health, see héctor recalde, *La higiene y el trabajo*, 2 vols. (1988); on the conflicts between Catholics and liberals, and the role played by Wilde, see néstor t. auza, *Católicos y liberales en la generación del ochenta* (1975); on Wilde's literary career, see enrique pezzoni, "Eduardo Wilde: Lo natural como distancia," in *La Argentina del ochenta al centenario*, edited by G. Ferrari and E. Gallo (1980).

Eduardo A. Zimmermann

WILLIAMS, ALBERTO (*b.* 23 November 1862; *d.* 17 June 1952), Argentine composer, conductor, pianist, and teacher. Born in Buenos Aires into a family of musicians, Williams's first teacher was Pedro Beck (piano). Later he studied with Nicolás Bassi (harmony) and Luis Bernasconi (piano) at the Escuela de Música in Buenos Aires. While very young he gave piano recitals at the Teatro Colón. Williams published his first piece, the mazurka *Ensueño de juventud*, in 1881. At age twenty he received a government scholarship and went to Paris, where he enrolled at the National Conservatory and studied under Georges Mathias (piano), Auguste Durand (harmony), and Benjamin Godard (counterpoint).

He was also a pupil of César Franck's and Charles de Bériot's in composition. After publishing a number of piano pieces in Paris, he returned in 1889 to Argentina, where he gave recitals and began incorporating into his works tunes, rhythms, and forms derived from native folklore. In Argentina, he became a pioneer of the nationalist style, which began with his *El rancho abandonado* (1890), a piano work. From 1892 on, he promoted nationalism in music, founding performance series such as the Concerts of the Athenaeum, National Library Concerts, Popular Concerts, and the Buenos Aires Conservatory Concerts. He was also active in the field of music education, where he could apply the modern methods he'd learned in Paris. In 1893 he founded the Buenos Aires Conservatory of Music, later renamed the Conservatorio Williams, which he directed until 1941. He conducted in Buenos Aires and Europe, where, in performances of his own work, he led the Berlin Philharmonic in 1900 and gave three concerts in Paris during the 1930 season.

Williams's works can be divided into three periods: the first, marked by a European influence, runs through 1890; the second, for which he is known as the progenitor of Argentine nationalism, covers 1890–1910; and the third, which dates from the publication of his Symphony no. 2 (1910), was nationalist but with an international character. Williams wrote nine symphonies and other orchestral works, chamber music, choral and vocal works, and several piano pieces, as well as several pedagogical and technical books. He died in Buenos Aires.

Composers of the Americas, vol. 2 (1956); RODOLFO ARIZAGA, *Enciclopedia de la música argentina* (1971); GÉRARD BÉHAGUE, *Music in Latin America* (1979); *New Grove Dictionary of Music and Musicians,* vol. 20 (1980).

SUSANA SALGADO

WILLIAMS CALDERÓN, ABRAHAM (*b.* 16 March 1896; *d.* 24 March 1986), Honduran military figure and politician. In 1954, Honduras suffered directly the political results of the coup d'état in Guatemala in the form of a large strike against the UNITED FRUIT COMPANY in the North Coast region. The strike was due in part to the perception of the company as dominating Central American politics. Political unrest, exacerbated by the strike, culminated in a split within the National Party (PNH) when it became clear that the party would nominate former President Tiburcio CARÍAS ANDINO (president 1933–1949), who owed his political career to United Fruit. Former vice president Williams Calderón is known primarily for leading the newly organized National Reformist Movement (MNR) splinter group in the 10 October 1954 presidential election. He lost to Ramón Villeda Morales, who obtained 121,213 votes. The aging Carías Andino received 77,041 votes, and Williams Calderón received 53,041. Despite his poor showing in the polls, Williams Calderón and the MNR

continued to play an active political role. However, with the National Party splintered, the Liberal Party (PLH) won the 1957 elections as well.

LUIS MARIÑAS OTERO, 2d ed., *Honduras* (1983); JAMES A. MORRIS, *Honduras: Caudillo Politics and Military Rulers* (1984).

JEFFREY D. SAMUELS

WILLIAMS REBOLLEDO, JUAN (1826–1910), Chilean naval officer who commanded his country's fleet in 1865 during its difficult struggle against the Spanish navy. The son of an English officer who had helped Chile win its independence and a resourceful officer himself, Williams not only attempted to hold off the Spanish—an impossible task, given the small size of Chile's fleet—but managed to capture one of Madrid's vessels, the *Covadonga.* Williams again served as commander of the Chilean flotilla during the WAR OF THE PACIFIC. By then an old man and perhaps ill, Williams seemed incapable of waging as aggressive a war as he had decades earlier. Obsessed with the idea of winning the Conservative Party's nomination for the 1881 presidential campaign, Williams acted cautiously to avoid any disasters which might wreck his political career. His failure to blockade Callao and his overall incompetence, which resulted in the capture of the *Rimac,* as well as his refusal to cooperate with the Aníbal PINTO government eventually led to his dismissal. As a pro-BALMACEDA officer he refused to join his naval colleagues in launching the 1891 revolution. Williams also worked as a hydrographer, fixing the borders between Chile and Bolivia, and served as the maritime governor of Atacama.

WILLIAM F. SATER, *The Heroic Image in Chile* (1973), pp. 40–42, 46, 49, 65–68, 171–172, and *Chile and the War of the Pacific* (1986), pp. 19–20, 39–41, 59–60, 184.

WILLIAM F. SATER

WILLIMAN, CLAUDIO (*b.* 2 September 1863; *d.* 9 February 1934), president of Uruguay (1907–1911). After graduating with a degree in law in 1888, Williman taught courses in mathematics and physics at the University of the Republic. From 1902 to 1924 he served as rector of the university. He was one of the founders of the College of Mathematics and the School of Commerce, today called the College of Economic Sciences. Between 1904 and 1907, he served as minister of government in the administration of President José BATLLE Y ORDÓÑEZ. After this term, Williman was nominated as a candidate for the presidency by the Colorado Party. He won the election and served from 1907 to 1911.

Williman's administration was characterized by meticulousness and strict control over public spending, and is often considered conservative when compared to that of Batlle y Ordóñez. Throughout the Williman administration, Batlle stayed in Europe with his family, but in 1910 he returned to Uruguay to take up the role of chief of the Colorado Party, and in 1911 he succeeded Williman as president.

BENJAMIN NAHUM, *La época batllista* (1984); WASHINGTON REYES ABADIE and ANDRÉS VÁZQUEZ ROMERO, *Crónica general del Uruguay*, vol. 4 (1984).

JOSÉ DE TORRES WILSON

WILLKA. *See* **Zárate Willka, Pablo.**

WILSON, HENRY LANE (*b.* 3 November 1857; *d.* 22 December 1932), U.S. ambassador to Mexico (5 March 1910–17 July 1913). Born in Crawfordsville, Indiana, Wilson attended public school and studied at Wabash College in Crawfordsville, graduating in 1879. He practiced law in Indiana and Seattle, Washington, until 1897, when he was chosen to represent the United States as minister to Chile and Belgium before serving as ambassador to Mexico (1909–1913). At that time only the U.S. representative in Mexico held the rank of ambassador. Wilson became one of the most controversial envoys to serve in Mexico.

Wilson intensely disliked and was highly critical of President Francisco I. MADERO, who assumed office in November 1911 as the result of a revolution that overthrew the government of General Porfirio DÍAZ. The ambassador disagreed with the aims and conduct of the regime, repeatedly recommending military intervention to restore stability. Wilson also disagreed with the objectives of U.S. President Woodrow WILSON, who took office shortly after Madero's fall and death.

Henry Lane Wilson is best known for his role in the PACT OF THE EMBASSY, which resulted in charges in Mexico that he colluded with General Victoriano HUERTA to overthrow the Madero government and failed to protect the life of Madero. The ambassador felt that his actions were required to end the combat in the capital and protect the lives of American and other foreign residents. He advocated U.S. recognition of the Huerta regime, which he believed offered the best prospect for the restoration of stability in Mexico. President Woodrow Wilson ignored the ambassador in conducting subsequent relations with the Huerta regime, though Ambassador Wilson was not recalled until July 1913. Victoriano Huerta continued as president of Mexico in the face of opposition by President Wilson and a revolution in the north, until he relinquished office on 15 July 1914.

HENRY LANE WILSON, *Diplomatic Episodes in Mexico, Belgium, and Chile* (1927); STANLEY R. ROSS, *Francisco I. Madero: Apostle of Mexican Democracy* (1955); KENNETH J. GRIEB, *The United States and Huerta* (1969); MICHAEL C. MEYER, *Huerta: A Political Portrait* (1972).

KENNETH J. GRIEB

WILSON, WOODROW (*b.* 28 December 1856; *d.* 3 February 1924), president of the United States from 1913 to 1921. An academic-turned-politician who frequently spoke in terms of idealism, Wilson encountered frustrations in the implementation of his policies in Latin America. He disparaged the meddlesome DOLLAR DIPLOMACY of the previous administration of William Howard Taft and expressed confidence in the Latin American nations' capacity for self-government. In response to a mixture of concerns about hemispheric security and political stability, however, Wilson ordered several armed interventions in the region. In 1916, for example, U.S. forces moved into the Dominican Republic, occupied the capital of Santo Domingo, and became embroiled in a frustrating guerrilla war. Wilson also ordered interventions in Cuba and Haiti.

Mexico's unpredictable social revolution posed the greatest hemispheric challenge to Wilson's policies. He attempted to influence events in Mexico with two interventions: the first in the port of Veracruz in 1914 to place pressure on the dictatorial government of Victoriano HUERTA (1913–1914), and the second in northern Mexico in 1916, in pursuit of rebel leader Francisco "Pancho" VILLA, who had raided the border town of Columbus, New Mexico. Neither intervention brought the stable government or hemispheric security Wilson intended. His idealism combined with his use of armed intervention left a legacy of misunderstanding and bad feelings in U.S. relations with Latin America.

ROBERT FREEMAN SMITH, *The United States and Revolutionary Nationalism in Mexico* (1976); MARK GILDERHUS, *Diplomacy and Revolution* (1977) and *Pan-American Visions: Woodrow Wilson in the Western Hemisphere* (1986); BRUCE J. CALDER, *The Impact of Intervention: The Dominican Republic During the U.S. Occupation of 1916–1924* (1984).

JOHN A. BRITTON

See also **United States–Latin American Relations.**

WILSON PLAN (1914), a diplomatic proposal by the Woodrow WILSON administration for a peaceful solution to the civil conflict between political factions in the Dominican Republic and Haiti. Under its provisions, the warring factions would lay down their arms, choose a provisional president (if they could not agree, the U.S. president would select one), and hold a constitutional convention and a peaceful election. Despite the holding of an election for a new president in the Dominican Republic, the political situation in the country further deteriorated, and in 1916 the United States military commenced an eight-year military occupation. In Haiti, the Wilson Plan was virtually unworkable because the president was chosen by the national assembly.

LESTER D. LANGLEY, *The Banana Wars: United States Intervention in the Caribbean, 1898–1934* (1983); DAVID HEALY, *Drive to Hegemony: The United States in the Caribbean, 1898–1917* (1988).

LESTER D. LANGLEY

See also **United States–Latin American Relations.**

WINDWARD ISLANDS. The Windwards consist of GRENADA, SAINT LUCIA, SAINT VINCENT, and the GRENADINE chain. Their name derives from a British administrative division of the Lesser Antilles into "windward" (southern possessions) and "leeward" (northern possessions). Originally settled by the French, they were central to the struggle for the Caribbean. All were ceded to Great Britain between 1763 and 1815. Like the LEEWARDS, their dominant SUGAR economy declined in the nineteenth century. Unlike the Leewards, the lack of a common cultural and governmental tradition, a peasant/middle-class conflict, and a stagnant economy led to a volatile political situation that culminated in the 1979 Grenadan revolution.

Christopher COLUMBUS discovered the Windwards on his second voyage in 1493. Larger in individual area than the Leewards, they are almost entirely of volcanic origin. Coral formation is scarce in their deeper waters, which allowed construction of strategic harbors (Castries on Saint Lucia, Saint George's on Grenada, and Fort-de-France on Martinique). Although classified as neutral CARIB sanctuaries, the Windwards were included in both the 1625 English Carlisle grant and the French grants of 1627 and 1635. In 1764 they became the British "Southern Caribbee Isles," comprising Grenada, Dominica, Saint Vincent, and Tobago. In 1885 Saint Vincent, Grenada, and Saint Lucia were formally listed as the Government of the Windward Islands.

Saint Lucia is between Martinique and Saint Vincent. Local tradition claims shipwrecked Frenchmen discovered the island on 13 December, feast of Saint Alouse. In 1605 Caribs drove off English settlers, but that attempt at settlement became the basis for later British claims. The Caribs signed a treaty with French woodcutters in 1660, but in 1663 Lord Francis Willoughby, British governor of the Antilles, sent one thousand Barbadan settlers to oust the French. Saint Lucia subsequently changed hands twelve more times until 12 April 1782, when George Brydges, Lord Rodney, defeated Admiral François de Grasse in the battle of the SAINTES.

Saint Vincent is 21 miles south of Saint Lucia, and owns Curriacou and the Grenadines, a chain of islets between Saint Vincent and Grenada. It was ceded by France to Britain in the Treaty of Paris (1763). In 1774, after a bloody confrontation, Britain allotted a large area as a Carib sanctuary. Along with Grenada, Saint Vincent rapidly became Anglicized while Saint Lucia and Dominica remained French, both linguistically and culturally.

After the Caribs expelled two hundred English in 1609, the French settled Grenada in 1636. In 1763 Grenada went to Britain under the Treaty of Paris, followed by a bloody SLAVE uprising on the island two years later. In 1795, inspired by the French Revolution, the "brigand" mulatto Julian Fédon, the first nationalist, led a combined French and black revolt.

As on other Antilles islands, the sugar economy declined in the nineteenth century. After emancipation in 1833, former slaves bought the plantations of the departing Anglo-French and created a smallholding economy based on limes, BANANAS, nutmeg, and other agricultural products. However, the new peasantry continued a semifeudal struggle with the new merchant and administrative elite, which was increasingly mulatto or black. In contrast with neighboring Barbados, the social struggle in the Windwards was class-oriented, not race-oriented. It was exacerbated by the continued power of the CATHOLIC CHURCH, a French legacy in all the Windwards.

Eric Gairy was the first truly nationalist leader in the Windwards, bringing Grenada to independence in 1974. His autocratic rule ended in 1979 with Maurice Bishop's People's Revolutionary Government, which promised nationalization of remaining lands and business. The United States, hostile from the beginning, took advantage of Bishop's murder in 1983 to launch an invasion.

ALAN BURNS, *History of the British West Indies* (1965); GORDON LEWIS, *Grenada: The Jewel Despoiled* (1984); FRANKLIN W. KNIGHT and COLIN A. PALMER, *The Modern Caribbean* (1989).

PAT KONRAD

WINE INDUSTRY. An appetite for the fruit of the vine accompanied the Spanish flag and the cross to the Americas. Spanish conquistadores, settlers, and friars preferred wine to the fermented beverages of Amerindians. Reproduction of Iberian secular and religious culture in the New World meant transplantation of viticulture. Sanctification of religious rituals required wine, and missionaries carried vine cultivation and wine production to all corners of the Spanish and Portuguese colonies. Wine was also a staple of the civilized class (*gente decente*), which ensured wine imports, and eventually the establishment of private vineyards and wineries.

Cultivation and fermentation of grapes followed the path of conquest. After Hernán CORTÉS defeated the Aztecs, he ordered his *encomenderos* to plant 1,000 vines for every 100 Amerindians under their care each year for five years. Vineyards and wine production in New Spain centered in Parras, Durango, San Luis de la Paz, and Celaya, north of Mexico City. The first commercial wineries began operation in Parras no later than 1623. By 1779 Franciscan missionaries had carried vine cultivation (*Vitis vinifera*) into California at Mission San Juan Capistrano. Grape cultivation spread throughout the California mission system, and at Mission San Gabriel it grew into a successful business. Under the guidance of Father José Zalvidea, the annual yield at San Gabriel increased between 1806 and 1827, when production reached 400 to 600 barrels of wine and 200 barrels of brandy. These early vineyards produced the Mission grape, known in other regions of the empire as the Criolla or Pais grape.

In South America, Spanish settlers had introduced vine cultivation into the heartland of the Inca Empire by the 1540s. Bartolomeu de Terrazas pioneered viticulture in the Cuzco area, and grapes planted on the eastern slopes of the Andes and near Charcas supported the manufacture of AGUARDIENTE. Neither of these efforts was as successful as the vines introduced by Francisco de Carabantes in the more hospitable desert coastal zone. Vineyards soon blossomed around Lima, Trujillo, and Arequipa. Jesuit estates in the southern coastal region controlled some of the largest and most productive vineyards. Carabantes carried vines to Chile when he was sent by Pedro de Valdivia's expedition in 1548. The vineyard of Diego García de Cáceres produced the first Chilean sacramental wine in 1555. Francisco de Aguirre planted vines in the north near Copiapó, Chile, and his son-in-law Juan Jufré expanded cultivation and carried vines across the Andes to the Cuyo region of Argentina before 1570. Catholic missionaries carried vines into the more remote regions of South America to ensure a steady supply of sacramental wine.

Vines on the east coast of South America came directly from Europe. An expedition by Martim Afonso de SOUSA, captain-general of São Vicente, transported the first vines to Brazil around 1532. Older settlements in Paraguay provided the Jesuit priest Pablo Cedrón with vines for missions in Santiago del Estero in 1557 and later in Córdoba. A Jesuit missionary, Roque GONZÁLEZ DE LA CRUZ, brought vines to the mission of Santa Cruz do Sul in the Portuguese territory of Rio Grande do Sul in 1626.

Cultivation of the vine and production of wine became so successful in the Spanish colonies that wine producers in Spain convinced King PHILIP II to restrict American production. In 1595, the COUNCIL OF THE INDIES imposed limits on wine production and vine cultivation. Philip II's successors repeated the restrictions in 1620, 1628, and 1631. In 1654, the imperial government prohibited new plantations and levied a tax on established vineyards. Despite the crown's attempts to restrict grape vines in its American colonies, *Vitis vinifera* and the Muscat of Alexandria prospered there. Locally produced wine remained an important item in regional trading networks throughout the empire.

Although crown efforts failed to eliminate the colonial wine industry, other factors inhibited its growth. Restricted by regional markets, limited capital, and primitive technology, colonial vintagers operated on a small scale. Vine stocks deteriorated; primitive wine presses and labor-intensive methods of expressing juice, and inadequate storage facilities and temperature controls impeded expansion. When trade restrictions were lifted at the end of the colonial period, European wines—French, Italian, and Spanish—flooded the Latin American market.

Not until the mid-nineteenth century did grape growing and wine production become organized as large-scale commercial enterprises in Latin America. Entrepreneurs introduced new capital and technology, and revitalized the aging vine stock with new varieties. The wine industry became more standardized, centralized,

and lucrative. Private production replaced mission wines, and in some areas all but eliminated foreign competitors.

The Mexican territory of California attracted the first innovators. The change began as the Mexican government started secularizing the missions after 1833. Joseph Chapman and Jean Louis Vignes introduced new vine varieties in the 1830s, but the acknowledged pioneer of the California wine industry was Agoston Haraszthy de Mokesa, who arrived in 1849.

The wine industries of Chile and Argentina profited most from the introduction of new capital, techniques, and varieties of vine. In Chile, Silvestre Ochagavia Errázuriz revitalized wine production by importing new vines and equipment from Europe in 1851, thereby inspiring other growers to modernize their operations. The pioneers of this period included Luis Cousiño, Domingo Concha y Toro, and Manuel Antonio Tocornal Grez. Modern wine production in Argentina started in the western province of Mendoza. Tiburcio Benegas, Emilio Civit, and other prominent landowners used provincial resources and lobbied the national government for aid in modernizing production. New grape varieties and technicians to run the viticulture school were brought from France and Italy. These changes promoted the development of a market for domestic wine.

Government involvement in and regulation of the wine industry increased in Chile and Argentina in the twentieth century. Both countries taxed wine production and supported technical schools to improve yield. In the 1930s the Chilean national government, influenced by prohibitionists, slowed the spread of vineyards by holding maximum production to 60 liters per capita. The military government lifted these restrictions in 1974. The Argentine government drafted comprehensive wine regulatory legislation in 1932 and, in 1959, established the National Institute of Viti-viniculture (INV) in Mendoza. The INV oversees all aspects of the industry. In Chile a private organization of exporters and bottlers fills that role. Wine production increased in Chile from 84 million gallons in 1952 to 160 million gallons in the mid-1980s, when there were 270,000 acres in vines. Argentina has 500,000 (1993) acres planted in vines, and wine is its third largest industry. Argentina is the fourth largest wine producer in the world.

Every country in Latin America makes wine. Two areas besides Chile and Argentina deserve special mention. Mexico successfully revitalized its industry after the Revolution by increasing tariffs and importation restrictions on foreign wines. This encouraged foreign and local investment in vineyards and wineries. In Brazil the state of Rio Grande do Sul has become the most important area of production.

Overall improvements in wine production in Latin America have increased consumption at home and abroad. Argentine and Chilean wines have earned international recognition. Higher quality and lower prices have liberated wine from religious and class restrictions. Today, wine appears on many Latin American tables.

ENRIQUE QUEYRAT, *Los buenos vinos argentinos* (1974); LEON D. ADAMS, *The Wines of America*, 2d ed. (1978); NICHOLAS P. CUSHNER, *Lords of the Land: Sugar, Wine, and Jesuit Estates of Coastal Peru, 1600–1767* (1980); MAURO CÓRTE REAL, *Os Bons Vinhos do Sul* (1981); HARM JAN DE BLIJ, *Wine Regions of the Southern Hemisphere* (1985); OSCAR BUSTOS HERRERA, *El vino chileno* (1985); JOAN E. SUPPLEE, "Provincial Elites and the Economic Transformation of Mendoza, Argentina, 1880–1914" (Ph.D. diss., University of Texas, 1988); THOMAS PINNEY, *A History of Wine in America from the Beginnings to Prohibition* (1989).

JOAN E. SUPPLEE

See also **Alcoholic Beverages.**

WISNER VON MORGENSTERN, FRANZ (*b.* 1800; *d.* 1878), Hungarian military officer active in Paraguay. Coming to South America in 1845 after minor service in the Austrian army, Wisner was contacted by Paraguayan president Carlos Antonio LÓPEZ, who wished to train his rustic battalions in modern European military techniques. For a time, Wisner commanded the tiny state flotilla stationed on the PARAGUAY RIVER. He later headed an expeditionary force that intervened in the Argentine province of Corrientes in 1849. During the 1850s, Wisner gained a trusted position within the Paraguayan hierarchy and played a key role in obtaining the services of British military engineers who supervised the modernizing of the national army, which later effectively resisted the Brazilians and Argentines for six years during the WAR OF THE TRIPLE ALLIANCE (1864–1870).

Wisner, meanwhile, wrote an official biography of the Paraguayan dictator José Gaspar Rodríguez de FRANCIA. He also accepted a commission as chief military engineer on the state railway project, and later at the fortress of HUMAITÁ. Captured at the 1868 battle of Lomas Valentinas (also called Pikysyry), Wisner returned to Paraguay after the war to prepare a major cartographical survey of the country; published in Vienna in 1873, it was easily the best complete map of Paraguay to appear up to that time. In his later years, Wisner, now the patriarch of a large Asunción family, was head of Paraguay's national railroad, and of the Immigration Office.

HARRIS GAYLORD WARREN, *Paraguay and the Triple Alliance: The Postwar Decade, 1869–1878* (1978); CARLOS ZUBIZARRETA, *Cien vidas paraguayas*, 2d ed. (1985).

THOMAS L. WHIGHAM

WOLFF, EGON (*b.* 13 April 1926), Chilean playwright. Wolff is the most staged—both in his own country and abroad—award-honored, and translated of Chilean dramatists; his plays have been performed in thirty countries, translated into twenty languages, and produced as films in Mexico and England. The son of German immigrants, Wolff pursued a parallel career as an engineer, in the manufacture and sale of chemical products. Unlike many artists and intellectuals of his generation, he steered clear of self-serving political posturing. Similarly, his plays are largely devoid of partisan didacticism. He focused instead on the social issues at work in the rapidly changing Chilean society of his day. In terms of form he preferred the fourth-wall theater (in which the proscenium arch represents a "fourth wall" to the audience) and complied with the classical Aristotelian dramatic unities. Stylistically, he favored social and psychological realism, with doses of poetry and humor.

His plays *Mansión de lechuzas* (*Mansion of Owls*, 1958), *Discípulos del miedo* (*Disciples of Fear*, 1958), *Niñamadre* (*A Touch of Blue*, 1960), and his most discussed work *Los invasores* (*The Invaders*, 1963) exemplify his characteristic probing into snobbery, prejudice, and the clash between social classes. He portrays the tension between traditional values—dictated by a crumbling ruling class—and those of the emerging middle class, including the heritage of postwar non-Spanish European immigrants. *El signo de Caín* (*The Sign of Cain*, 1969), *Flores de papel* (*Paper Flowers*, 1970), and *Kindergarten* (1977) explore the concepts of freedom and commitment on an individualistic level. In *Espejismos* (*Mirages*, 1978), *El sobre azul* (*The Blue Envelope*, 1978), *José* (1980), *Álamos en la azotea* (*Poplars on the Roof Terrace*, 1981), *La balsa de la Medusa* (*Medusa's Barge*, 1984), and *Háblame de Laura* (*Tell Me About Laura*, 1986), Wolff deftly and poetically plumbs the depths of personal relationships.

JUAN ANDRÉS PIÑA, "Evolución e involución en las obras de Egon Wolff," in *Mensaje*, no. 269 (1978); KLAUS PORTL, "Wolff's Theater der Angst," in *Revista Iberoamericana*, no. 3 (1979); JACQUELINE EYRING BIXLER, "Language in/as Action in Egon Wolff's *Háblame de Laura*," in *Latin American Theatre Review* 23 (fall 1989): 49–62; ELENA CASTEDO-ELLERMAN, "Egon Wolff," in *Latin American Writers*, edited by Carlos A. Solé and Maria Isabel Abreu, vol. 3 (1989), pp. 1311–1315.

ELENA CASTEDO

WOLFSKILL, WILLIAM (*b.* 20 March 1798; *d.* 3 October 1866), mountain man and California pioneer. Wolfskill was born in Kentucky and moved with his family to Missouri in 1809 under Daniel Boone's (1734–1820) leadership. Wolfskill accompanied William Becknell's (*ca.* 1790–*ca.*1832) second expedition to Santa Fe in 1822 and opened a trading post at Taos, New Mexico. After several years of trapping beaver, he opened the Old Spanish Trail to California in 1831 and settled in Los Angeles. Wolfskill became a pioneer in the cattle, citrus, and wine industries in southern California. He acquired several ranches and became active in community affairs during the Mexican and early American periods. Wolfskill married María Magdalena Lugo in 1841, reared six children, and died in Los Angeles.

LEROY R. HAFEN and ANN W. HAFEN, *The Old Spanish Trail* (1954); IRIS HIGBIE WILSON ENGSTRAND, *William Wolfskill, 1798–1866: Frontier Trapper to California Ranchero* (1965).

IRIS H. W. ENGSTRAND

WOMEN. Every observer soon learns that the term "Latin America" serves more to obscure than to illuminate an understanding of the vast region that lies between the Rio Grande and Tierra del Fuego. Similarly, there is no one Latin American woman: factors of time and place, class, race, ethnicity, age, and marital status, among others, are important considerations whether we are speaking of a Mexican, a Brazilian, a Haitian, or a Guyanese woman. They might not be able to speak to one another since their respective national languages are Spanish, Portuguese, French, and English. Moreover, it is not unlikely that a Guatemalan woman's first language is Maya-K'iche', not Spanish, that a woman of the Andes speaks only Quechua and that a woman of the Amazon speaks only a Tupi dialect. The classic understanding of the peopling of the Americas is built upon the deeply sexual metaphor of the "contact period" in the late fifteenth and early sixteenth centuries, when seafaring European males encountered the indigenous women of Middle, Central, and South America and produced a "new race." The story of MALINCHE/Malintzín (1504?–1528), a Tabascan woman given in tribute to conquistador Hernán Cortés, who through her knowledge of languages subsequently played a pivotal role in the Spanish overthrow of the Aztec regime in central Mexico, became a founding myth of modern Mexico. But this paradigm ignores the presence of French, Spanish, and Portuguese women, who began to arrive as early as 1498, and leaves out women, both free and slave, who came to the Americas from sub-Saharan Africa.

Moreover, since the late nineteenth century the large Latin American nations have received successive waves of immigrants from Europe and Asia. Spaniards, Portuguese, Italians, and Germans settled in significant numbers in Mexico, Argentina, Uruguay, Chile, and southern Brazil. Koreans, Chinese, and Southeast Asians have also immigrated to the Latin American nations; Brazil has the largest population of citizens of Japanese descent of any nation other than the United States. In the past forty years, immigrants from India, Pakistan, Syria, Lebanon, Iran, and Iraq have made their way to South America. Although in some cases the first generation settled in rural areas, the daughters and granddaughters of these European, Asian, and Middle Eastern immigrants now live in Latin American cities as well.

Recent research challenges many long-held preconceptions about the roles women played in colonial society. Distinctions of class, racial heritage, and ethnicity were sharply reinforced by an economy that rested upon various systems of forced labor. Before the contact period, female roles in indigenous societies varied as widely as did the societies themselves: Women were political rulers, priestesses, healers and midwives, agricultural laborers, artisans, market vendors, prostitutes, and slaves. The degree to which the customs of the indigenous peoples were disrupted by colonization was dependent upon the extent of contact.

Family, church, and state were the central institutions that governed colonial life, especially for Iberian and mestiza women. The church largely determined social mores and reinforced the strictures that propertied families placed upon their daughters, for whom marriage or a religious vocation as a nun were the respectable choices. However, the image of the cloistered upper-class Iberian woman must be balanced against examples of women who actively participated in the economy by running large estates and overseeing the complex business affairs of their families. Similarly, the diverse experiences of women of the poorer economic sectors should not be subsumed in blanket assumptions that differentiate their lives from those of their male counterparts only by virtue of their sex.

Women of African descent were present in every region of the Americas. Many slave women worked at field labor on the sugar, tobacco, cotton, and coffee plantations of the Caribbean and mainland. In Brazil, female slaves were found in larger concentrations in urban areas, working in households or earning money for their owners as market women, street vendors, wet nurses, or prostitutes. To the extent that their particular situations allowed them to do so, they kept alive their religious and cultural practices and deeply influenced the formative national cultures in Brazil, the Caribbean, Colombia, and Venezuela.

One of the best-known women of the colonial era is Sor JUANA INÉS DE LA CRUZ (1648 or 1651–1695?), who was born Juana Ramírez de Azbaje and is considered one of the greatest lyric poets in the Spanish language. Because of her particular status, Sor Juana cannot be used as an example of women in colonial Latin America. But perhaps the point is that no woman can be an example, whether she was a domestic slave of Afro-Brazilian heritage in Salvador, Brazil, an Aymara woman of the Bolivian Andes whose male kin were forced to work the silver mines, the mestiza wife of a cattle rancher in northern Mexico, or the illegitimate daughter of a Creole mother, as was Sor Juana.

WOMEN AND NATIONAL FORMATION

Female patriots were vital to the success of the independence movements, and the biographies of these women were used to rouse patriotic fervor; in later years, Latin American women pointed to the loyalty of their predecessors in the effort to gain full citizenship for women.

A central subject for the debate of women's roles in the new nations was the issue of EDUCATION. In the struggle between secular liberal values and religious corporatist politics that marked the nineteenth century, the question of who would educate young women was played out among Catholic female teaching orders, independent dames' schools, and the new public schools.

Women participated fully in the debate that surrounded national definition from the 1890s through the 1920s. Several examples can be cited. In the long guerrilla wars that led to Cuban independence from Spain in 1898, female soldiers known as *mambisas* distinguished themselves in battles against the Spanish troops and became part of the formative myth of the Cuban nation; they were viewed as warriors, patriots, revolutionaries, and the moral center of national sovereignty. Female schoolteachers and factory workers played a crucial role in the politics that led to the MEXICAN REVOLUTION of 1910. Women were at the heart of the great Río Blanco textile workers' strike of 1907. SOLDADERAS, women who fought with the revolutionary troops, became folk heroines. Such organizations as the Hijas de Cuáuhtemoc demanded the resignation of President Porfirio DÍAZ and staged public protests against the regime. In contrast, Carmen Romero Castelló, the president's Creole wife, symbolized the alliance of the regime with the deeply conservative hierarchy of the Catholic church and the Mexican elite's fascination with European styles.

WOMEN'S WORK AND WORKING WOMEN
Teachers and poets, textile workers and microchip assemblers, field hands, culinary artists, vendors, household domestics, nurses, and nuns: the history of women in paid occupations in Latin America has undergone extensive change in the twentieth century. Two antithetical patterns are evident. On the one hand, there is the emergence of the middle-sector working woman—skilled factory workers, teachers, government clerks. While there are great differences in the social and economic statuses of these women, their pay scales, benefits, and relative job security distinguish them as a group from women whose work lies in the unregulated, informal sectors of the economy, which include domestics, market women, vendors, laundresses, prostitutes, and rural laborers.

Factory workers and pieceworkers, drawn from the immigrant or peasant population, were the primary laborers in the textile and tobacco industries after 1900. Women faced great difficulty in organizing to improve their working conditions: the hostility of employers and officials, lack of support from their male coworkers, long working hours, and family demands left scant energy for union work.

Although women had begun entering new fields in urban areas, in 1930 the great majority of them still lived in the country. In Andean America, Paraguay, parts of Brazil, southern Mexico, Guatemala, and Venezuela the population was predominately indigenous. Rural women's work was immensely varied: women carried out mining-related tasks in Potosí; worked communal agricultural plots and ran trade networks in the Peruvian sierra; hulled and sorted spices in the Caribbean; worked the sugar, rubber, and banana plantations of Brazil, Haiti, and Cuba; harvested the wheat and grapes of Chile and Argentina; and did domestic labor on ranches, estates, and plantations. And everywhere women prepared daily meals, cared for children, and maintained their own households in addition to whatever other work they might perform.

CHANGES IN LEGAL AND CIVIL STATUS
Prior to the twentieth century women's civil status was governed by a complex body of statutes rooted in Iberian and ecclesiastical law; in practice, the legal status of most women was determined by their relationship to the male heads of household. Indigenous women living within their traditional communities (Maya, Guajira, Aymara, Guarani) were governed according to the customs of each community. Although elaborate sets of laws governing slave women had evolved by the nineteenth century, individual slave women had little true legal recourse. In all cases, full citizenship was limited to men of property.

The history of female suffrage offers an illustration of the politics involved in seeking redress through legal change. Effective universal suffrage, male or female, did not exist in any Latin American nation until after World War II. Requirements concerning property, type of employment, and residence restricted the vote to certain sectors of the population. Moreover, irregular transitions of power and the suspension of civil liberties, including elections, characterized the political scene in many Latin American nations between 1929, when female suffrage became law in Ecuador, and 1961, when women received the vote in Paraguay. Three periods of enactment may be distinguished (see table 1).

Examination of the list of the first group of states to enact suffrage for women points to the variety of motives that prompted governments to bring women into the national polity. In Mexico, Argentina, Brazil, Colombia, Venezuela, Chile, and Cuba, suffrage resulted from long-fought campaigns on the part of thousands of women and their male allies. In contrast, in Eucador, the political coalition that promulgated the female vote was deeply conservative; it viewed women as loyal to the Catholic church and politically malleable and believed that the female vote would buttress the conservative's political base vis-à-vis challenge from the Socialist Party. Ironically, many members of the political left concurred with the conservative assessment of women's political acumen. In Argentina, Eva María Duarte de PERÓN is often credited with the passage of woman suffrage, but by 1947, Argentine women had waged a half-century-long campaign for the vote; woman suffrage laws had been passed in many other nations of the Western Hemisphere; and commitment to equal political rights was part of the charter of the United Nations, to which Argentina was a signatory. It was a reform whose time had come; what Eva Perón did was to deliver the new female vote for the Peronist Party.

Despite the passage of woman suffrage in every Latin

TABLE 1 Periods of Enactment of Female Suffrage in Latin America

Pre–World War II		World War II		Post–World War II	
Ecuador	1929	El Salvador	1939	Argentina	1947
Brazil	1932	Dominican Republic	1942	Venezuela	1947
Uruguay	1932	Panama	1945	Chile	1949
Cuba	1934	Guatemala	1945	Costa Rica	1949
				Haiti	1950
				Bolivia	1952
				Mexico	1953
				Honduras	1955
				Nicaragua	1955
				Peru	1955
				Colombia	1957
				Paraguay	1961

American country by 1961, suffrage continued to be limited by language and literacy requirements. Rural women were generally excluded. In some countries, such as Guatemala, male suffrage was universal, but female suffrage was restricted to women who could read and speak Spanish; in Peru, Quechua-speaking Peruvians did not receive the franchise until 1980, a restriction that affected the women who stayed in the sierra and maintained the home community to a greater degree than it did the men who migrated out to work or fulfill military service.

THE PERIOD 1959–1989

The CUBAN REVOLUTION triumphed in January 1959; whether Latin American women supported revolutionary activity, favored reform, or were ardent counterrevolutionaries, politics for them as well as for men were permanently altered after 1959.

The 1960 publication in Rio de Janeiro of Carolina Maria de Jesus's *Cuarto de Despejo* (Child of the Dark) is symbolic of the shift in public consciousness. Carolina, who lived in an urban slum, described the daily ordeals she faced collecting and selling rags and paper in order to feed and clothe and educate her children; the book sold 90,000 copies in six months.

Among those committed to change through revolution, women were most active in the urban movements. Young women made up almost half of the "soldiers"—those who carried out bank robberies and kidnappings—of the Tupamaro movement in Montevideo, Uruguay. Among rural guerrilla groups, women were more apt to be seen as *compañeras,* companions of the male revolutionaries. Haydée Tamara Bunke Bider (1937–1967), known as "Tania," was an exception; she was key to Che GUEVARA's effort to establish a revolutionary front in Bolivia and became a martyr to a generation of young women after her death under fire.

LIBERATION THEOLOGY, which emerged from the Latin American Catholic church in the wake of the Second Vatican Council (1965) and the Second Latin American Bishops' Conference (1968), in Medellín, Colombia, did not address the specific needs of women, but women of the church—laywomen, nuns, congregants, and participants in BASE COMMUNITIES—were deeply involved in the church's commitment to "the poorest of the poor." Women were also active in defending traditional ways of life. In Brazil in 1964 and in Chile in 1973, upper- and middle-class women organized street demonstrations to protest the erosion of homemakers' buying power, the spectre of communism, and the threat to the family, and to call for military intervention to "restore order."

In the 1970s, the ideas of the international women's movement spread throughout the continent. In Cuba, where women were organized under the Federación de Mujeres Cubanas (FMC), which explicitly rejected FEMINISM, the issue of women's "double day" was raised at the second National Congress of Cuban Women in 1974. Resolutions were enacted demanding more child-care centers, the acknowledgment that housework is family work and not exclusively "women's" work, and the recognition that children should be raised in a consciously nonsexist way. The platform was influenced to some degree by the international women's movement, but within Cuba it reflected improved female educational levels and the incorporation of women into the work force, phenomena also manifest in the declining national birthrate.

In the nations of Brazil, Uruguay, Paraguay, Argentina, and Chile, the 1970s and early 1980s were marked by the suppression of civil liberties, the ascension of bureaucratic authoritarian military regimes, and a politics of terrorism, including mass arrests, the "disappearing" of political activists, torture, imprisonment, and death squad assassinations. A similar politics of terrorism prevailed in Guatemala and El Salvador and reverberated in the civil war in Nicaragua. Like their male counterparts, women were visible throughout the political spectrum: as victims of political oppression, supporters of incumbent regimes, perpetrators of torture, members of the armed resistance, and those who preferred to close their eyes to the events taking place around them. But the most compelling image to emerge from this era, male or female, is that of *las madres*, the mothers of those who had disappeared in the government's war against terrorism. On April 30, 1977, in Buenos Aires, seven of these women—*las madres*—went to the Plaza de Mayo, the historic center of Argentine government, to stage a silent demonstration on behalf of their disappeared loved ones; four years later, on 1 May 1981, over six thousand Argentines joined them to protest the continued violation of human rights by the military regime. *Las madres* became a metaphor for the thousands of Latin Americans who dared protest through nonviolent means the practice of state terrorism against the populace. In the wake of the crumbling of the military regimes of the mid-1980s, women were successful in bringing women's issues—health care, divorce, domestic violence, political access—into the debates surrounding the redemocratization process.

THE 1990s

By 1990 several trends that indicate dramatic change in the traditional patterns of life for Latin American women converged. First, contemporary Latin American women are overwhelmingly urban: in 1980, only 2 percent of the female labor force in Argentina was described as rural; in Mexico, only 12 percent; in Brazil, which has the highest number of rural women of any major Latin American nation, the figure is 20 percent. Second, the rapid and highly visible entry of middle-class women into the paid labor force—an 83 percent

increase between 1970 and 1990 in all areas of Latin America except the Caribbean—closely resembles the work participation profiles of women in the industrialized West. Driven partly by the harsh inflationary conditions of the 1980s, women's employment outside the home, combined with higher levels of education and greater access to birth control information in urban areas has resulted in a significant drop in the number of children a woman will bear in her lifetime. In Mexico, in 1950, the average birthrate was six children for each woman; in 1990, it was three or less. Birth rates in Cuba, Argentina, Uruguay, and Costa Rica are similar to those of southern European nations. In countries and regions where women are primarily rural and where female literacy remains low, such as Guatemala and Ecuador, high birthrates and high infant mortality rates persist.

The pattern of greater female involvement in the formal labor force exists simultaneously with the growth in concrete numbers of women whose economic status is precarious in the extreme. In 1990, hundreds of thousands of poor women and their families live in and around the megacities of Latin America—São Paulo, Rio de Janeiro, Buenos Aires, Lima-Callao, and Mexico City—and attempt to eke out a daily living in the informal economy. Inflation and government reliance on the ''invisible adjustment,'' a process that rests on the presumed resourcefulness of poor women to support themselves and their children, have seen the deterioration of government support for all social services. Identification of this invisible adjustment shows that a gender understanding has emerged, but the use to which that

Weekly vigil by the families of the victims of repression in front of La Moneda. Santiago, Chile, 1987.
PHOTO BY OSCAR NAVARRO.

understanding has been put—the dismantling of social services—demonstrates that caring for poor, usually ethnically different women and their children is still regarded as an expendable luxury by governments.

The proliferation of multinational corporations seeking cheap labor is also affecting women's employment, notably along Mexico's border with the United States. In the Caribbean, coastal Mexico, Belize, Guatemala, and Costa Rica, the international TOURISM INDUSTRY is a primary and fast-growing employer of female hotel clerks, tourist guides, maids, waitresses, and cooks. Similarly, the picking and packing of agricultural goods for the global market, largely the work of women, puts money directly into the hands of female workers, a practice that is visibly altering traditional male-female and generational relationships in many communities. Increased integration into the global economy is also visible in changing social mores. Latin American women are still largely culturally Catholic, but in practice society is increasingly secular.

The results of two decades of women's political activism are visible in new legislation that expands women's rights in divorce and marriage, in the creation of all-female police stations, and in increased attention to domestic violence against women. In the mid-1980s, several factors converged to bring women into political office in unprecedented numbers. The dynamics of the women's movement mobilized international support for a focus on women. Individuals and local groups of women were increasingly interconnected through global and regional networks. These political trends converged with the high visibility and politicization of women in the politics of redemocratization in Chile, Argentina, Uruguay, Paraguay, and Brazil, and in the internationalized civil wars of Central America. In Mexico, women's heightened political visibility may be seen in the candidate lists and platforms of the 1988 elections; the Partido Revolucionario de los Trabajadores (PRT) called for an end to violence against women, an end to rape, and the right to "voluntary maternity"; the Frente Democrático Nacional promised to create a Secretariat of Women if elected. The majority party, the Partido Revolucionario Institucional (PRI), addressed the issue of sexual molestation and called for the full weight of the law to be brought to bear in prosecuting rape cases. In preparation for the 1988 elections, Venezuelan women organized an umbrella movement, Women Leaders United, under whose auspices rallies, marches, public debates, and TV interviews were held to win support for women candidates. The results were impressive: nineteen women were elected to the House of Deputies, and four were elected to the Senate. In 1989 the women deputies and senators formed a Bicameral Commission for the Rights of Women. Since then, a number of women have won ministerial appointments, and for the first time a woman holds the office of first vice president of the House of Deputies. In Argentina, women have also increased their presence beyond a token. In 1991 women's advocates

succeeded in passing the Ley de Cupos, which set a quota requiring that one-third of all candidates be female. In 1993, thirty-four women were elected to the House. In Nicaragua, Violetta BARRIOS DE CHAMORRO was elected president in the closely monitored elections of 1990.

In 1992, the K'iche' Indian Rigoberta MENCHÚ (b. 1960) was awarded the Nobel Prize for peace for her work on behalf of human rights, notably among the indigenous people of her homeland in northwestern Guatemala. Today Menchú is a highly effective advocate for the rights of indigenous people everywhere.

In the 1990s, women are more highly educated, more urban, and more engaged in activities outside the household (economic, political, and social) than ever before. Modern communications systems, especially radio and television, patterns of migration, and access to transportation have all contributed to an expanded worldview. Throughout Latin America deep political and economic instabilities that threaten efforts to revise gender-based social and cultural attitudes persist. The ostensible gains—political citizenship for women, a focus on the double burden of poor women, greater access to schooling for girls, labor regulations that take women's work into account—are under constant threat of erosion. Women are not coincidental but vital to democracy if it is to prove viable, and they are central to overcoming seemingly implacable social and economic problems. In this effort the importance of collective memory, of bearing witness, of knowing the history of women cannot be underestimated.

JUNE HAHNER, *Women in Latin American History* (1976); ASUNCIÓN LAVRIN, *Latin American Women: Historical Perspectives* (1978); SILVIA MARINA ARROM, *The Women of Mexico City, 1790–1857* (1985); MARIFRAN CARLSON, *FEMINISMO!: The Woman's Movement in Argentina from Its Beginning to Eva Perón* (1988); PATRICIA SEED, *To Love, Honor and Obey in Colonial Mexico: Conflicts over Marriage Choice, 1574–1821* (1988); ELSA CHANEY and MARY GARCÍA CASTRO, *Muchachas No More: Household Workers in Latin America and the Caribbean* (1989); ASUNCIÓN LAVRIN, ed., *Sexuality and Marriage in Colonial Latin America* (1989); MARIETTA MORRISSEY, *Slave Women in the New World: Gender Stratification in the Caribbean* (1989); K. LYNN STONER, *From the House to the Streets: The Cuban Woman's Movement for Legal Reform, 1898–1940* (1989), and *Latinas of the Americas: A Source Book* (1989); ELSA TAMEZ, *Through Her Eyes: Women's Theology from Latin America* (1989); JUNE HAHNER, *Emancipating the Female Sex: The Struggle for Women's Rights in Brazil, 1850–1940* (1990); SUSAN HILL GROSS and MARY HILL ROJAS, *Contemporary Issues for Women in Latin America* (1991); DONNA GUY, *Sex and Danger in Buenos Aires* (1991); FRANCESCA MILLER, *Latin American Women and the Search for Social Justice* (1991); TERESA VALDES and ENRIQUE GOMARIZ, eds., *Mujeres latinoamericanas en cifras: Chile* (1993).

FRANCESCA MILLER

WOMEN IN PARAGUAY According to traditional thought, women have played a more critical role in the history of Paraguay than in other Latin American states—so much so, in fact, that women have assumed the status of patriotic icons. School textbooks portray women as the principal defenders of the nation, as the bravest of the brave in repulsing those who would see Paraguay dismembered and broken. While this image constitutes a historiographical oddity, in reality women have shaped the course of events in Paraguay in some unusual ways.

The GUARANÍ, the dominant Indian group in the Paraguayan region during the pre-Columbian era, set the basic pattern. Semisedentary agriculturalists, they reserved the bulk of labor in the fields for female members of various clans. While men dedicated themselves to hunting and fishing, Guaraní women cultivated maize, beans, manioc root, tobacco, squashes, peanuts, and cotton (also weaving the latter into clothing). They were largely responsible for child-rearing as well.

The arrival of the Spaniards in 1537 did not much affect the lives of Paraguay's women. The Spaniards, seeking a quick route to the silver of Peru, had ascended the Paraguay River carrying only the bare necessities, and no European women accompanied them. Stranded among the Guaraní, they soon took up with Indian women. Regarding the newcomers as members of their extended kin group, the women labored for them just as they labored for Indian men. They bore their children, taught them Guaraní, and helped them forge a colonial order that was only partly Spanish. The first governor, Domingo Martínez de IRALA took several Indian wives and legitimized their offspring.

Very few immigrants entered Paraguay during the colonial period. This fact alone assured that the early pattern of Indian–white relations would retain its influence into the late 1700s. Women still did most of the farm work, though now the earlier Guaraní-based kinship structures had been supplanted by the ENCOMIENDA. The women still raised children who were monolingual in the Indian tongue and who also thought more like Guaraní than like Spaniards, whatever their surnames might happen to be. This socialization process later provided the basis for a rabid nationalism among many Paraguayans, who viewed themselves as being decidedly different from other Latin Americans. National independence, which came in 1811, thus reflected not just political realities but also cultural factors.

Paraguayan women, having prepared the social environment for a sense of cultural separateness, now helped shape the new nation. The dictator Dr. José Gaspar Rodríguez de FRANCIA (1814–1840) forbade marriages between Paraguayans and Spaniards. This reinforced traditional structures governing the role of women while, at the same time, undercutting the influence of such formal, Spanish-based institutions as legally sanctioned marriage and the church. Informal liaisons remained the rule, as did long hours in the field for women. Those hours likely increased during the 1850s and 1860s, when the governments of Carlos Antonio LÓPEZ (1841–1862) and Francisco Solano LÓPEZ (1862–1870) expanded the state military establishment, drafted thousands of men, and left women and children to produce a good portion of the foodstuffs.

The WAR OF THE TRIPLE ALLIANCE (1864–1870) added still further burdens. With all of the men at the front, Paraguayan women supported almost the entire war economy. They donated their jewelry and cash. They worked in hospitals. As the war turned against Paraguay, women volunteered for military service. It is unclear if many actually fought, though observers at the 1869 battle of ACOSTA ÑU reported that the Paraguayan defenders included a considerable number. In that same year, Solano López evacuated the central district and retreated to the northeast, taking with him his now meager army, his Irish mistress, and a multitude of poor women who, malnourished and diseased, nonetheless followed López to the end.

The Paraguayan defeat in 1870 brought new challenges. Brazilian troops occupied Paraguay for six years. With perhaps half the country's population having perished in the conflict, women were said to outnumber men four or five to one. It took a generation to reestablish a proper ratio between the sexes. Throughout this time women struggled as never before to eke out a living on the land and in the towns. Foreign visitors witnessed the toils of female porters, carters, street sweepers, and farm workers. Later writers claimed that this era brought a matriarchal order to Paraguayan society, though this has never been proven conclusively.

The same period did bring some significant changes. In 1869, the first national school for girls was founded in Asunción. Educational opportunities in the capital and elsewhere afforded women career possibilities undreamt of previously. The full ramifications of this change became clear only in the 1900s, when women joined the ranks of recognized educators, poets, and artists.

The twentieth century has not, however, seen a progressive expansion of political influence for Paraguayan women. The various dictatorial regimes as well as the CHACO WAR with Bolivia (1932–1935) and the 1947 Civil War have tended to infuse the political culture of the country with a military spirit that manifestly has limited the participation of women. Women might be scholars, doctors, lawyers, and administrators, but political offices were usually beyond their reach. Only in 1961 did women receive the right to vote, and although some female deputies were elected in the 1960s and 1970s, a full thirty years passed before a Paraguayan president named a woman as minister. Various women's groups and feminist organizations came into being in the 1980s, but overall, as compared with all of its neighbors, Paraguay still has far to go in advancing the interests of its women.

ELMAN R. SERVICE, *Spanish-Guaraní Relations in Early Colonial Paraguay* (1954); OLINDA MASSARE DE KOSTIANOVSKY, *La mujer paraguaya: Su participación en la Guerra Grande* (1970); DOMINGO

M. RIVAROLA, "Apuntes para el estudio de la familia en el Paraguay," *Revista Paraguaya de Sociología* 8, no. 21 (1971): 84–104; GRAZZIELA CORVALÁN and MABEL CENTURIÓN, *Bibliografía sobre estudios de la mujer en el Paraguay* (1986); BARBARA POTTHAST-JUTKEIT, "The Ass of a Mare and Other Scandals: Marriage and Extramarital Relations in Nineteenth-Century Paraguay," *Journal of Family History* 16, no. 3 (1991):215–239.

MARTA FERNÁNDEZ WHIGHAM

WOOD, LEONARD (*b.* 9 October 1860; *d.* 7 August 1927), commander of the First United States Volunteer Cavalry (the "Rough Riders") and U.S. military governor of Cuba (December 1899–May 1902). Born in Winchester, New Hampshire, and an 1884 graduate of Harvard Medical School, Wood became President McKinley's physician in 1895 and established close ties with Theodore Roosevelt. Wood was appointed military commander of both the city and province of Santiago before succeeding John Brooke as governor of Cuba. In 1910 Wood served briefly as a special ambassador to the Argentine Republic. Though Chief of Staff of the Army from 1910 to 1914, he was passed over by Woodrow Wilson to lead the American Expeditionary Force in France in favor of John J. Pershing. Wood was the principal challenger to Warren Harding for the Republican presidential nomination in 1920 and served as governor-general of the Philippines (1921–1927). He died in Boston.

HERMANN HAGEDORN, *Leonard Wood: A Biography*, 2 vols. (1931), is the authorized treatment; and JACK C. LANE, *Armed Progressive: General Leonard Wood* (1978), is the most recent biography. See also DAVID F. HEALY, *The United States in Cuba, 1898–1902: Generals, Politicians, and the Search for Policy* (1963).

LINDA K. SALVUCCI

WOOD. *See* **Lumber Industry.**

WOOL INDUSTRY. As with other commodity-driven Latin American economies based on a single primary sector, Argentine and Uruguayan export-led growth from 1830 to 1900, and the diversification of those nations' economies, was founded on the burgeoning wool industry.

Explorers and traders first brought sheep to the Southern Cone in the sixteenth century. During the colonial period, however, there was no significant wool industry. In the seventeenth and eighteenth centuries, small numbers of the Spanish Merino breed were brought from Spain to Chile and Argentina, but they had little impact on the local sheep stocks. In Argentina the Pampa sheep (descended from the Spanish Churra) and the smaller Criolla produced coarse wool and a finer red wool, respectively. By 1757 the sheep population of Montevideo had reached 71,000, with tens of thousands more in the Río de la Plata region. But it was only after 1810, following a trend in Europe, that Southern Cone ranchers began to take an interest in herd improvement and the quality of wool shorn. Ranchers imported purebred sheep from Germany, Spain, France, the United States, and Australia. They introduced breeding programs and developed fine-wool flocks.

In Argentina, civil war impeded sheep breeding and the emergence of a wool industry until the mid-nineteenth century. In 1822 wool represented only 0.94 percent of total exports from the province of Buenos Aires. By 1851 that figure had risen modestly to over 10 percent. Ranchers bred the Argentine Merino as a larger animal producing medium- to fine-quality wool for export. By 1855 Argentina was exporting 10,000 tons of wool annually, mostly for textile mills in Europe and the United States. In an effort to stimulate wool production, Chile's Sociedad Nacional de Agricultura encouraged the introduction of new methods in animal husbandry. Late nineteenth-century Uruguayan flocks were similar to the European Merinos but produced a high-quality "Montevideo wool type" that enhanced the reputation of the Río de la Plata region's wool exports.

During the mid-1800s, wool production in Argentina and Uruguay determined the integration of the region into the world market. Wool exports grew quickly after 1840 and spurred Argentine and Uruguayan export-led growth. In 1840 Argentina exported less than 2,000 tons of wool. By 1870, 237,000 tons had been shipped overseas (55,000 tons in 1870 alone). From 1875 to 1900, a rapid expansion in the sheep population signaled the emergence of Argentina and Uruguay as world leaders in wool sales. Chile's production lagged behind, while Paraguayan exports were negligible. In Argentina, sheep raising was concentrated chiefly in the provinces of Buenos Aires, Entre Ríos, Corrientes, Santa Fé, and Córdoba (though in the twentieth century, the wool industry expanded to other regions, most notably Patagonia).

Like many Latin American commodity values, wool prices fluctuated quickly. In one case that characterized the relation between wool production on the pampa and world markets, production in Argentina and Uruguay rose with a price increment attributable to the Crimean War and the consequent withdrawal of Russian exports to the European market. But in 1857–1858, with the return of Russian production, prices for Argentine and Uruguayan wool dropped promptly. This pattern of rapid price fluctuations characterized cycles of strong and moderate growth in the wool industry during the late nineteenth century. For the most part, wool-industry profits were high for the *estancieros* (ranchers), the middlemen, and the shipping houses in Buenos Aires and other littoral ports.

Many factors shaped the wool industry during the late-nineteenth-century expansion. At times, labor and land shortages limited expansion. On the other hand, the growth of local credit availability in Buenos Aires and the building of rail lines through many provinces enhanced export opportunities. The export sector was further stimulated by the rise in the international demand for wool as Germany, France, and Belgium followed the British lead into textile industrialization. By 1880 wool represented half the value of Argentine exports; and in 1895 the sheep population in Buenos Aires Province alone reached 84 million, reflecting the leading role wool played in the provincial economy. In the final years of the nineteenth century, however, cereals and meat overtook wool in relative importance to Argentine and Uruguayan sales abroad. Wool did not regain its position of primacy in the Río de la Plata region economy but remained a vital sector of production in the twentieth century.

After 1900 Argentina and Uruguay continued to lead the region in wool production. Chilean exports during the twentieth century have been moderate, while Paraguay has produced little wool. Between 1934 and 1954, Argentina's share of world wool exports ranged from 10 percent to 14 percent. During this period Argentina began large-scale production of wool textiles but, as it had earlier in the century, continued to import large quantities of finished wool goods. In 1937 Argentina imported 2,027 tons of woolen and worsted piece goods, principally from the United Kingdom and Italy. In 1938 the 151,877 tons of wool exported accounted for 11 percent of Argentine exports by value. During the 1930s the principal importers of wool from Argentina were the United Kingdom, Germany, France, the United States, Belgium, and Italy.

By mid-century Argentina's sheep population was the third largest in the world after Australia's and the Soviet Union's. A 1952 census placed the Argentine number at 54 million. The annual consumption of wool by a substantial domestic spinning and weaving industry stood at 60,000 tons. During the 1950s Argentina ranked as the world's fourth largest raw-wool producer, exporting an average 330 million pounds of wool and sheepskins. Chile exported 50 million pounds of wool annually over the same decade, while Paraguay's overseas shipments were negligible. Uruguay ranked fifth in wool exports, with annual shipments of 115 million pounds. Since the 1960s, despite sometimes heavy annual fluctuations, wool exports have remained steady over the long term. Producers have been unable to eliminate foot-and-mouth disease from herds and contend that the industry has been limited in the late twentieth century by a lack of credit and government marketing supports.

BARCLAYS BANK, *Wool* (1960); WERNER VON BERGEN, *Wool Handbook* (1963); COMMONWEALTH ECONOMIC COMMITTEE, *World Trade in Wool and Wool Textiles, 1952–1963* (1965); BANCO GANADERO ARGENTINO, *Temas de economía Argentina: Mercados y precios de la lana* (1969); CARLOS F. DÍAZ ALEJANDRO, *Essays on the Economic History of the Argentine Republic* (1970); *An Illustrated World History of the Sheep and Wool Industry* (1970); ANÍBAL BARRIOS PINTOS, *História de la ganadería en el Uruguay* (1973); MANUEL E. MACCHI, *El ovino en la Argentina* (1974); JONATHAN C. BROWN, *A Socioeconomic History of Argentina, 1776–1860* (1979); VERA BLINN REBER, *British Mercantile Houses in Buenos Aires, 1810–1880* (1979); M. L. RYDER, *Sheep and Man* (1983); HILDA SABATO, *Agrarian Capitalism and the World Market: Buenos Aires in the Pastoral Age, 1840–1890* (1990).

DAVID M. K. SHEININ

See also **Textile Industry.**

WOOSTER, CHARLES WHITING (*b.* 1780; *d.* 1848), officer in the Chilean navy. Born in New Haven, Connecticut, he was the nephew of David Wooster, hero of the Battle of Danbury during the American Revolution. Wooster went to sea at an early age. During the War of 1812 he served on board the U.S. privateer *Saratoga*. Having earned substantial prize money and gained significant influence, he was named captain of the Port of New York after the war. With the death of his young wife he chose to join the fight for independence in Chile.

Investing his entire fortune, Wooster purchased the brigantine *Columbus*, which he outfitted with sixteen guns. He carried a cargo of rifles to Chile, arriving 25 April 1818. Wooster was commissioned into the Chilean navy as a commander and put in charge of the frigate *Lautaro*. The *Lautaro* along with the *San Martín* intercepted a Spanish squadron on 25 October at Talcahuano and captured the frigate *Reina María Isabel*, which was escorting reinforcements for the royalist army in Peru. The following day the Chilean squadron captured the transports one by one. This was a significant victory for the patriots.

When Thomas A. COCHRANE was hired by the Chileans to command their fleet, Wooster resigned rather than serve under the British officer, a former enemy. Between 1818 and 1822 Wooster engaged in commercial pursuits, including whaling. When Cochrane resigned from the Chilean navy, Wooster was recommissioned with the rank of captain and again took command of the *Lautaro*. Between 1822 and 1826 he campaigned against the royalists in Chiloé and southern Peru. In 1829 he was promoted to rear admiral.

Following the capture of Chiloé, the Chilean navy, except for the *Aquiles*, was sold off. In 1829, while Wooster was ashore, the crew mutinied against the selection of Joaquín Vicuña as vice president. At the direction of the Chilean government, Wooster boarded the British frigate *Thesis*, which captured the *Aquiles* and returned it to Chilean control. However, on 8 December Vicuña was driven from the capital and took refuge on the *Aquiles*. The forts at Valparaíso, also in the hands of the rebels, drove the ship out of port. Wooster sailed to Coquimbo, where Vicuña surrendered. These events ended Wooster's career in the navy. Wooster settled in

California, where he had become one of the most powerful property owners in San Francisco.

CLAUDIO COLLADOS NUÑEZ, ed., *El poder naval chileno*, 2 vols. (1985); RODRIGO FUENZALIDA BADE, *Marinos ilustres y destacados del pasado* (1985).

ROBERT SCHEINA

WORLD WAR I, a conflict that presented the nations of Latin America with some difficult choices, as they balanced their need for German investment with distrust of Great Britain and their friendship for the United States. Germany had emerged during the early part of the century as an important new source of investment, offering new capital and alternatives to the traditional reliance on England and France. Most of the nations followed the lead of the U.S. government, however, though there were exceptions. During the period of neutrality, the first Pan-American Financial Conference was held in 1915 to cushion the economic impact of the war.

When the United States entered the conflict during 1917, many Latin American nations followed despite their heightened sensitivities to recent U.S. expansion and hemispheric hegemony. Eight nations declared war on Germany, including Brazil, Cuba, Costa Rica, Guatemala, Haiti, Honduras, Nicaragua, and Panama. Five others broke diplomatic relations, including Bolivia, the Dominican Republic, Ecuador, Peru, and Uruguay, several of which openly announced that they were "neutral in favor of the United States," thus risking retaliation by German submarines. Even nations in the midst of disputes with the United States, such as Mexico, resisted the temptation to support the Germans, despite open proposals such as the ZIMMERMANN TELEGRAM. There were, however, multilateral security arrangements during the neutrality period or during the conflict.

The war and the accompanying Allied blockade of Germany disrupted long-standing trade patterns by impeding commerce with much of Europe, especially when combined with the shift of the European economies to a wartime basis. Latin Americans found themselves cut off from trading partners and sources of investment and capital. The result was increased economic and financial reliance on the United States, refocusing trade northward as well as increasing the importance of interchange with neighboring nations. There were some exceptions, such as raw materials production, which now became more important to the United States. The Chilean NITRATE INDUSTRY boomed during the prewar and war years. These changes in trade patterns laid the basis for stronger financial and economic ties with the United States that persisted after the war. Argentina, Chile, and Mexico remained fully neutral, reflecting ties to Germany, dislike for England, and disputes with the United States.

Eleven Latin American nations participated in the Versailles Conference, with ten signing the treaty and thereby becoming charter members of the LEAGUE OF NATIONS. Six other Latin American nations adhered to the League Covenant, and ultimately all the nations of Latin America became League members, though some later withdrew. Latin America played a significant role in the League and in the establishment of the International Court of Justice and by so doing gained considerable prestige in international diplomacy. Brazil served almost continuously on the League Council during its years of membership, and the court included two justices from the region.

PERCY A. MARTIN, *Latin America and the War* (1925), offers the classic study. See also JOSEPH S. TULCHIN, *The Aftermath of War: World War I and U.S. Policy Toward Latin America* (1971); and MARK T. GILDERHUS, *Pan-American Visions: Woodrow Wilson in the Western Hemisphere, 1913–1921* (1986). Many individual country studies also treat the wartime era.

KENNETH J. GRIEB

WORLD WAR II, an international conflict that, with the exception of Argentina, brought about a sense of inter-American solidarity unknown before. But the Latin American nations did not quickly commit themselves to the Allied cause. Their leaders did not share the concern of the United States with the developing hostilities in Europe and Asia between 1935 and 1938. Rather, they appeared more concerned with reaffirming President Franklin D. Roosevelt's GOOD NEIGHBOR POLICY that had been initiated in 1933. Given these diverse views, Washington found it difficult to obtain Latin America's cooperation on hemispheric defense before 1940. At the Inter-American Conference for the Maintenance of Peace held in Buenos Aires in 1936, Roosevelt and Secretary of State Cordell Hull asked for trade and credit embargoes against the European warring factions. Instead, they received only an innocuous agreement to meet when an emergency arose that affected their common defense. By the time of the Eighth Inter-American Conference of American States in Lima, Peru, in 1938, Austria and Czechoslovakia had fallen to Nazi Germany and China had engaged Japan in a test of survival. Fearing the Western Hemisphere to be in greater danger than in 1936, the U.S. delegation went to Lima seeking a mutual defense pact, but the Latin Americans were not prepared to formulate a plan of action against the Axis powers.

The first collective action to meet the dangers of World War II came at a meeting of foreign ministers in Panama in 1939 following the German invasion of Poland and the outbreak of the European War. The Declaration of Panama proclaimed a safety belt around the Western Hemisphere, extending from 300 to 1,000 miles from the eastern and western coastlines, within which, at least in theory, no belligerent act was to be allowed. After the fall of France in June 1940, the foreign ministers convened a month later in Havana. The subsequent Declaration of Havana decreed that the European colonies in the Western Hemisphere were off limits to the Axis powers and could be occupied by a hemispheric nation pending final settlement of the territory's disposition. Furthermore, any attack upon one hemispheric nation was to be considered an act of aggression against all. By the time of the Havana conference, the United States also had determined its hemispheric military defense policy. A line was drawn at Brazil in order to secure the Caribbean sea routes and the Panama Canal. The Latin American armies would not be raised to the status of a fighting ally, but would act only to meet an external attack until U.S. forces could arrive. Toward that end, agreements placed U.S. military missions in all but Bolivia, to which no mission was ever sent. Subsequently, the Lend-Lease Act of 1941 provided for $400 million in military assistance to Latin America over a three-year period, the bulk of it scheduled to be disbursed in 1943 and later.

Following the Japanese attack on Pearl Harbor on 7 December 1941, Costa Rica, Cuba, the Dominican Republic, El Salvador, Guatemala, Haiti, Honduras, Nicaragua, and Panama immediately declared war on the Axis powers. Meeting at Rio de Janeiro in January 1942, the foreign ministers of all of the Latin American republics recommended that their governments sever diplomatic relations with the Axis nations. Ultimately, Mexico and all of the South American nations did so. Mexico and Brazil declared war on the Axis powers in 1942; Bolivia and Colombia did so in 1943. The ministers at Rio also committed their governments to institute measures to eliminate possible Axis subversion. The most notable measure was the internment and deportation of German, Japanese, and Italian nationals and their descendants to either their homelands or camps in the United States. Unfortunately, many innocent people and political opponents fell victim to the program, and many had their properties confiscated. The Caribbean was the area of the most significant military action. Until late 1942, German U-boats played havoc with Allied shipping in the region. Subsequently, Brazil and Mexico sent troops to the war zones. Throughout the war, Nelson A. Rockefeller's Office of Inter-American Affairs coordinated economic policies. Few Latin American countries benefited from the war because of the loss of European markets. The unimportance of coffee, sugar, and tropical fruits caused severe economic hardship on the Caribbean islands and in Central America. Conversely, the need for Bolivian tin, Chilean copper, and Venezuelan oil brought a measure of prosperity to those nations. Brazil and Mexico also benefited when the United States financed steel mills in those nations. However, no plans for postwar conversion were made, and with Europe in shambles, the Latin Americans did not recover their traditional trading partners after 1945. Allied wartime propaganda also contributed to the demands of the generation of rising expectations. If the Allies were fighting to eliminate tyranny in Asia and Europe, why not put an end to Latin American dictatorships? Political protests along these lines were most evident in Central America near the end of the war.

As postwar planning for the United Nations began to take shape, Washington warned the Latin American states that only those who had declared war on the Axis nations would be eligible for membership in the international organization. The threat prompted Ecuador, Peru, Venezuela, Uruguay, Paraguay, and Chile to declare war in early 1945. Argentina remained reluctant. Argentina's traditional resistance to Washington's dominance of hemispheric affairs was now complicated by its pro-fascist military, which had extended its influence in politics until 1943, when a coup gave it complete control of the government. A large German and Italian immigrant population resided in the nation. Throughout the war, the United States increased the pressure on Argentina. Washington publicly denounced the government for having deserted the Allied cause, froze Argentine gold stocks and tightened shipping regulations, and withheld recognition of President Edelmiro FARRELL from March 1944 to April 1945. When the diplomats convened in Mexico City in early 1945 for the Inter-American Conference on Problems of War and Peace, only Argentina was absent. The gathering's major objective was to strengthen Pan-American solidarity for the upcoming meeting of the United Nations in San Francisco. The resultant ACT OF CHAPULTEPEC contained a proviso stating that the Monroe Doctrine secured the American republics against even an American aggressor, a statement that satisfied Argentina and contributed to its declaration of war against Germany and Japan on 27 March 1945.

HARLEY NOTTER, *Postwar Foreign Policy Preparation, 1939–1945* (1949); JOHN A. HOUSTON, *Latin America in the United Nations* (1956); STETSON CONN and BYRON FAIRCHILD, *Framework of Hemispheric Defense* (1960); STETSON CONN, ROSE C. ENGLEMAN, and BYRON FAIRCHILD, *Guarding the United States and Its Outposts* (1964); ALTON FRYE, *Nazi Germany and the American Hemisphere, 1933–1941* (1967); J. M. ESPINOSA, *Inter-American Beginnings of U.S. Cultural Diplomacy, 1936–1948* (1976); MICHAEL J. FRANCIS, *The Limits of Hegemony: United States Relations with Argentina and Chile during World War II* (1977); GERALD K. HAINES, "Under the Eagle's Wing: The Franklin D. Roosevelt Administration Forges an American Hemisphere," *Diplomatic History* 1 (1977): 373–388; R. A. HUMPHREYS, *Latin America and the Second World War,* 2 vols. (1981–1982); DAVID G. HAGLUND, *Latin America and the Transformation of U.S. Strategic Thought, 1936–1940* (1984).

THOMAS M. LEONARD

See also **Pan-American Conferences.**

WYKE-AYCINENA TREATY (1859), an agreement confirming British rights to Belize. The treaty was signed 30 April 1859 by Pedro de AYCINENA, Guatemalan foreign minister, and Charles Lennox Wyke, British chargé d'affaires and plenipotentiary to Guatemala. The treaty has long been controversial. Article 7, added by the negotiators, ambiguously called for Guatemala and Great Britain to cooperate in erecting a transit way from

Guatemala City to the Atlantic coast "near the settlement of Belize." Disputes over each government's expected contribution prevented the article's fulfillment. An additional convention of 1863 attempted to clarify Article 7, but lapsed because of Guatemala's failure to ratify it. Beyond the road issue, the treaty itself was subject to more fundamental disagreement. Guatemala held that it was a "disguised cession" of territory, possibly violating the CLAYTON-BULWER TREATY of 1850, for which the road was compensation. British governments saw it as a simple boundary agreement, defining the limits of previously held territory. Guatemala continued to contest the validity of the treaty, and thus British rights to Belize, into the late twentieth century.

R. A. HUMPHREYS, *The Diplomatic History of British Honduras, 1638–1901* (1961); WAYNE M. CLEGERN, *British Honduras: Colonial Dead End, 1859–1900* (1967).

RICHARD F. BROWN

WYLD OSPINA, CARLOS (*b.* 19 June 1891; *d.* 17 June 1956), Guatemalan writer and journalist, member of the influential Generation of 1920. Wyld was born in Antigua to wealthy parents, Guillermo Wyld and Soledad Ospina. Largely self-taught, he began to write romantic poetry at an early age. As a novelist he is regarded as a chief exponent of *criollismo*, a literary movement devoted to denouncing social evils and to promoting national regeneration. Among his most notable works in this vein are *El solar de los Gonzaga* (1924; Ancestral Home) and *La gringa* (1935). In his short stories, such as "La tierra de las Nahuyacas" (1933; "The Land of the Nahuyacas"), he was among the first to depict realistically the wretched condition of the Indian majority, thus becoming a precursor of the Indigenista movement.

It was in Mexico that Wyld established himself as a journalist of note, becoming the editor of the paper *El Independiente* (1913–1914). Upon his return to Guatemala, he settled in Quetzaltenango, where he taught literature and worked as the editor of *Diario de Los Altos*. In 1920 he founded, in association with the writer Alberto Vásquez, *El Pueblo*, the organ of the Unionist Party in which he bitterly criticized the Guatemalan dictator Manuel ESTRADA CABRERA. He also founded the cultural magazines *Estudio* (1922) and *Semana* (1939), and from 1922 to 1925 worked as the editor of the prominent newspaper *El Imparcial*. He married Amalia Cheves, a noted poet from Cobán. From 1937 to 1942, he served as deputy in the National Assembly. He died in Quetzaltenango while serving as director of the Bank of the West.

FRANCISCO ALBIZÚREZ PALMA and CATALINA BARRIOS Y BARRIOS, *Historia de la literatura guatemalteca*, vol. 2 (1981), pp. 97–108; CARLOS C. HAEUSSLER YELA, *Diccionario general de Guatemala*, vol. 3 (1983).

JORGE H. GONZÁLEZ

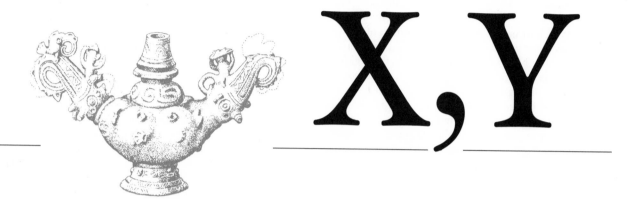

X, Y

XICA DA SILVA. *See* **Silva, Xica da.**

XIMÉNEZ, FRANCISCO (*b.* 28 November 1666; *d.* between 11 May 1729 and mid-1730), a Dominican priest who translated the POPOL VUH, the Maya–K'ICHE' story of creation.

Born in Écija, Andalusia, Ximénez joined the DOMINICAN order in 1688 and was sent to Guatemala to continue his religious studies. He was ordained in 1690. His facility for learning the Indian languages soon became evident, and he was assigned as parish priest in San Juan Sacatepéquez to learn the KAQCHIKEL language. Under the guidance of another friar who knew Kakchikel, he prepared a grammar in that language and went on to master the K'iche' and Tz'utujil languages.

While serving in Chichicastenango from 1701 to 1703, Ximénez found a manuscript of the ancient book of the K'iche' people, the *Popol Vuh*. He translated into Spanish its story of creation and the history of the K'iche' nation. The *Popol Vuh* is now considered the national book of Guatemala.

Later Ximénez founded a hospital for Indians in Rabinal and developed a treatment for rabies. During his stay at Rabinal he also began a careful study of bees. Ximénez became interested in the flora and fauna of Guatemala. His work as a naturalist was recorded in *Historia natural del Reino de Guatemala*. About 1715 he began writing the history of the Dominican order in Guatemala, *Historia de la provincia de San Vicente de Chiapa y Guatemala de la Orden de Predicadores*. His writings were often critical of the Spaniards. He died in the convent of Santo Domingo in Santiago de Guatemala.

JUAN RODRÍGUEZ CABAL, *Apuntes para la vida del . . . Francisco Ximénez* (1935); FRANCISCO XIMÉNEZ, *Historia natural* (1967) and *Historia de la provincia de San Vicente de Chiapa y Guatemala de la Orden de Predicadores* (1971).

DAVID L. JICKLING

XIMENO Y PLANES, RAFAEL. *See* **Jimeno y Planes, Rafael.**

XINGU RESERVE (National Indian Park), a multitribal Indian reserve and national park located in northern Mato Grosso along the XINGU RIVER. The reserve was established in 1961 with two goals in mind: the preservation of flora and fauna for the distant future and the protection of indigenous peoples more immediately. It was created by the Brazilian government on the advice of the VILLAS-BOAS brothers. Within the reserve, non-

Indian settlement, tourism, missionary activity, and commercial enterprise are illegal. The population in 1979 was estimated at 1,800 individuals, representing four language groups: Arawak, CARIB, GÊ, and TUPI. At establishment, the reserve encompassed 13,200 square miles. However, in 1971, after completion of the TRANS-AMAZON HIGHWAY (BR 080), the reserve's boundaries were changed. Approximately 35 percent of the park was detached for commercial development. At the same time, new territory along the Ronuro, Batovi, and Culiseiu rivers increased the total area of the reserve to 18,000 square miles. This new land is poor-quality *campo* (a relatively dry savanna), partially occupied by cattle ranchers and unsuitable for Indian habitation owing to a lack of game. While the operation of the reserve has received world acclaim (the Villas-Boas were nominated for the Nobel Peace Prize), the living conditions of Indians within the reserve have engendered controversy even though they are acknowledged to be better than those of Brazilian Indians in general. The international attention that the Xingu Reserve receives should not obscure endemic Brazilian Indian problems.

ORLANDO VILLAS-BOAS, *Xingu: The Indians, Their Myths* (1973); ROBIN HANBURY-TENISON, *A Question of Survival for the Indians of Brazil* (1973); CARMEN JUNQUEIRA, *The Brazilian Indigenous Problem and Policy* (1973); SHELTON H. DAVIS, *Victims of the Miracle* (1977).

MICHAEL J. BROYLES

See also **Brazil: Geography; Indian Policy.**

XINGU RIVER, a large southern tributary of the AMA-ZON in north-central Brazil; it rises in Mato Grosso, flows north into Pará, then enters the Amazon west of the island of Marajó. The Xingu's total length approaches 1,230 miles, but it is navigable only for the lower 96 miles. Its chief tributary is the Iriri, whose branches flow through Xingu National Park, in northeast Mato Grosso.

In lieu of more efficient alternatives, the Xingu River provided essential access to Brazil's interior for the earliest Catholic missionaries, as well as for Brazilian frontiersmen, traders, and slave raiders. In 1961 the Xingu National Park was created by Orlando and Claudio VILLAS-BÔAS to protect the Amerindians from extermination. The park was enlarged from 8,800 to about 10,400 square miles in 1968, and now includes the TUPI, CARIB, ARAWAK, and GÊ linguistic groups. In 1979 the Villas-Bôas brothers estimated the park's population at 1,800. Non-Indian settlement, missionary activity, commercial exploitation, and tourism are prohibited within the park, but pressure from property developers continues. The controversial TRANSAMAZON HIGHWAY passes through the north section of the park, threatening the Indians' autonomy and isolation, and effectively reducing the park territory by 50 percent. Plans for a Xingu hydroelectric complex threaten more than 9,000 people along the Xingu with resettlement.

ADRIAN COWELL, *The Heart of the Forest* (1961); ORLANDO VILLAS-BÔAS and CLAUDIO VILLAS-BÔAS, "Saving Brazil's Stone Age Tribes from Extinction," in *National Geographic* 134, no. 3 (1968): 424–444, *Xingu: The Indians, Their Myths* (1973), and *Xingu: Tribal Territory* (1979).

CAROLYN E. VIEIRA

See also individual states.

XOCHICALCO, an archaeological site located in the modern state of Morelos, Mexico, that rose to power between A.D. 650 and 700 and was an important political and religious center in central Mexico until A.D. 900. Xochicalco was located in the Aztec tribute province of Cuauhnahuac at the time of the Spanish conquest and was recognized as an important place in native historic traditions.

Xochicalco developed during a period of cultural upheaval and rapid sociopolitical change in central Mexico. The period between 650 and 900 was characterized by the decline of the powerful center of TEOTIHUACÁN, the breakup of its pan-Mesoamerican empire, an increase in militarism, and the emergence of independent, competing city-states within Teotihuacán's former political domain. Xochicalco is representative of all these features. During its maximum development the site covered an area of approximately 1.5 square miles and supported a population of between 10,000 and 15,000 people. Xochicalco is the earliest known fortified city in central Mexico. The site was constructed over a series of low hills, and seven defensive precincts, which were fortified using ramparts, dry moats, and concentric terracing, have been identified.

Most of western Morelos was under Xochicalco's direct political control between 650 and 900. Political power is evident in the scale of monumental architecture, including the construction of central Mexico's first and only paved road system, which linked Xochicalco with outlying sites in the region. Xochicalco engaged in long-distance trade with many areas of MESOAMERICA, including the Gulf Coast, Oaxaca, and the Maya region. The site's many sculpted monuments identify the three earliest named rulers in central Mexico, and the Pyramid of the Plumed Serpents was venerated as a sacred place at the time of the Conquest.

Xochicalco society represents an early expression of the Aztec cultural pattern. This pattern is characterized by military conquest, the formation of tribute empires, internal social stratification based on participation in warfare, and the practice of human sacrifice, which was linked to the religious practice of nourishing the gods through sacrificial ritual.

JAIME LITVAK KING, "Xochicalco en la caída del Clásico, una hipótesis," in *Anales de Antropología* 8 (1970): 102–124; KENNETH HIRTH, "Xochicalco: Urban Growth and State Formation in Central Mexico," in *Science* 225 (1984): 579–586, and "Militarism and Social Organization at Xochicalco, Morelos," in *Meso-*

america After the Decline of Teotihuacán, A.D. 700–900, edited by Richard Diehl and Janet Berlo (1989), pp. 69–81; ROMÁN PIÑA CHÁN, *Xochicalco: El mítico Tamoanchan* (1989).

KENNETH HIRTH

XOCHIMILCO. The name Xochimilco is derived from the Nahuatl words *xochitl* and *milli*, meaning "where the flowers grow" and referring to the rich agricultural productivity that has typified the area since pre-Columbian times. Today, Xochimilco is one of the sixteen *delegaciones* (political subdivisions) of the FEDERAL DISTRICT, but in the twelfth and thirteenth centuries it was the capital of a large and powerful city-state that occupied the southern part of the Valley of Mexico and extended into present-day Morelos. It was defeated by the Aztecs in 1430, at which time its territory was reduced to the southern shore of its namesake lake.

Xochimilco was surrounded by canals and CHINAMPAS (fields reclaimed from the lake marshes by the layering of lake muds and vegetation dug out of the canals) and was described by Hernán CORTÉS as "a pleasant city . . . built on the freshwater lake." Its agricultural lands produced food that was shipped to the Aztec capital as tribute. With a resident POCHTECA, the city also served as a transshipment point for goods coming from the south. These were transferred to canoes, which followed a canal, known as the *acequia real* during the colonial period, directly to TENOCHTITLÁN.

Xochimilco was an intensely loyal part of the Aztec state and fought against Cortés; after its defeat, it was assigned as an *encomienda* to Pedro de ALVARADO. Xochimilco had a population of 20,000 to 25,000 in 1559, when it was designated one of the four colonial *ciudades* in the Valley of Mexico. It maintained a largely Indian population during the colonial period and had few haciendas or other Spanish settlements. Its agricultural products continued to be carried by canoes through a canal into Mexico City as late as the nineteenth century.

Even with the growth of Mexico City in the nineteenth and early twentieth centuries, Xochimilco remained a rural town to the south of the city. By the 1970s, however, the metropolitan suburbs were encroaching on Xochimilco, yet even today about two-thirds of the *delegación* remains in agriculture and forest. Xochimilco's canals no longer lead to Mexico City, but they still link the various *chinampas* and are plied by specially built boats (*trajineras*) that carry thousands of visitors, especially during holidays. Despite the beauty of the area, various changes in land use have prevented recirculation of the water, which has caused a serious deterioration of its quality.

JEFFREY R. PARSONS, KEITH W. KINGTIGH, and SUSAN A. GREGG, *Prehistoric Settlement Patterns in the Southern Valley of Mexico* (1982); MARY G. HODGE, *Aztec City-States* (1984), pp. 81–97; *Atlas de la Ciudad de México* (1987), esp. pp. 320–324.

JOHN J. WINBERRY

XUL SOLAR (Oscar Agustín Alejandro Schulz Solari; *b.* 14 December 1888; *d.* 10 April 1963). Argentine painter and illustrator who also made musical instruments and toys. Xul Solar was born in San Fernando, Buenos Aires Province. He studied engineering and architecture at the University of Buenos Aires. He left school and traveled to Paris, where he studied drawing and painting with Emilio Pettorutti in 1908. His first artistic attempts, in 1917, related to art nouveau forms. The art of Xul Solar possesses an esoteric flavor of deep religious and metaphysical suggestion. In an imaginary space, Xul Solar combines faces, magical elements, and fragmentary objects, treating his material in a schematic, planimetric way with dynamic action and an exceptional refinement of color.

VICENTE GESUALDO, ALDO BIGLIONE, and RODOLFO SANTOS, *Diccionario de artistas plásticos en la Argentina* (1988); MARIO H. GRADOWCZYK, ed., *Xul Solar* (Buenos Aires, 1990).

AMALIA CORTINA ARAVENA

XUXA (*b.* 1963), Brazilian model, actress, singer, and children's television show host. Born Maria da Graça

Xochimilco Lake, 1970. ORGANIZATION OF AMERICAN STATES.

Meneghel in Santa Rosa, Rio Grande do Sul, Brazil, Xuxa (pronounced "shoo-sha") was the highest-paid Brazilian performer even before her children's show "Xou da Xuxa" was picked up by the Fox Network in 1992 for broadcast in the United States. Xuxa first came to public attention in Brazil in 1978 as a model for the national photo magazine *Manchete* (Headline), in which she, a tall blonde, was a striking contrast to most Brazilian models. In 1980 she made further headlines as the girlfriend of soccer star Pelé and by appearing nude in the Brazilian edition of *Playboy* and in films such as *Amor Estranho Amor* by Walter Khoury (1982), which features Xuxa in a sex scene with a young boy. At about this time, the Brazilian press began comparing her with Marilyn Monroe. In 1983 she hosted a children's television show called "Clube da Criança" (Children's Club) for the Manchete Television Network, in which she was presented as a sex symbol, wearing miniskirts and short shorts. As a television personality, she is known for her ingenuousness, spontaneity, and what critics call a permissive approach to children's entertainment. She moved to Brazil's TV Globo in 1986 to obtain broader exposure on a much more widely watched network. The "Xou da Xuxa" show became slicker, and certain trademarks, like Xuxa blowing kisses (*beijinhos*) to the audience increased. As with other Globo stars, her records, concerts, and movies were cross-marketed by Globo television and radio stations. She also began merchandizing a wide variety of products under her name and image. In 1990 production of her show moved to Argentina for the Latin American and Hispanic U.S. markets. Then in 1992, her show was packaged for syndication in English in the United States and was picked up by the Fox Network for early-morning daily broadcast in 1993. For many critics, Xuxa symbolizes a Brazilian ethnic and sexual identity contradiction between a blond ideal and a brown reality.

AMELIA SIMPSON, *Xuxa: The Mega-Marketing of Gender, Race, and Modernity* (1993).

JOSEPH D. STRAUBHAAR

YAGUL, an archaeological site located 23 miles from Oaxaca City and 2 miles from the market town of Tlacolula in the Valley of Oaxaca, Mexico. Yagul was excavated by Ignacio BERNAL, Lorenzo Gamio, and John Paddock during the 1950s and 1960s. Although the site shows evidence of more ancient occupations, most of the excavated and consolidated remains date from the Postclassic period (ca. A.D. 900–1521). The site was occupied at the time of the Spanish conquest, and the people of present-day Tlacolula refer to it as the *pueblo viejo* (old town).

Yagul sits atop a mountainous spur whose peak supports an ancient fortress. On the flanks of the spur was the administrative and ritual center of the ancient city, and on the lands at its base were the houses of common people. Excavations in the center of the city uncovered

the Palace of the Six Patios, a large residence with a floor plan similar to those of the nearby palaces of MITLA. A narrow street ran between the palace and the council hall, whose walls were decorated with *grecas* (mosaics) similar to those of Mitla. A ball court similar to one at MONTE ALBÁN lies near the palace. Also near the palace is Patio 4, a plaza with four mounds around it and an altar at its center. Mound 4E, on the east side, is a temple. In front of it is a large boulder sculpted to resemble a JAGUAR or frog. More than thirty tombs have been excavated at Yagul. Tomb 30 in Patio 4 had panels of false *grecas* decorating it and contained fine Mixteca polychrome pottery vessels. The Yagul excavations served to define the period (ca. A.D. 900–1521) that followed the collapse and general abandonment of Monte Albán and generated a lively controversy concerning proposed MIXTEC conquests of ZAPOTECS in the Valley of Oaxaca during this time.

IGNACIO BERNAL, "The Mixtecs in the Archeology of the Valley of Oaxaca," in *Ancient Oaxaca*, edited by John Paddock (1966), pp. 345–366; CHARLES WICKE, "Tomb 30 at Yagul and the Zaachila Tombs," in *Ancient Oaxaca*, edited by John Paddock (1966), pp. 336–344; IGNACIO BERNAL and LORENZO GAMIO, *Yagul: El palacio de los seis patios* (1974); MARCUS WINTER, *Oaxaca: The Archaeological Record* (1989), pp. 119–121.

MICHAEL D. LIND

YAMANA (also called Yaghanes), maritime inhabitants of the Strait of Magellan and Cape Horn, the so-called nomads of the seas. Their society is thought to have consisted of about 3,500 individuals who lived in a simple social organization recognizing no chiefs or superior authorities. The Yamana believed in Watauinéiwa, a supreme god, invisible and omnipotent, who was accompanied by secondary deities. The Yamana hunted sea mammals, fished, and collected mollusks. They lived in huts made with boughs and tree branches, which they regularly abandoned in search of better hunting. Related prehistorically and linguistically to the ALAKALUF (Kawashkar) to the north, the Yamana occupied the coasts of the BEAGLE CHANNEL and the islands that extend south to Cape HORN. As with the Alakaluf, some argue that the maritime peoples first appeared in these southern waters 5,200 to 6,400 years ago, although others claim a Paleolithic (11,000 B.C.) past.

The material culture, including bone implements, harpoons, and canoes made of tree bark for hunting sea mammals, as well as remains of coastal sites with abundant shell deposits, contrasts with the nearly exclusively terrestrial orientation in the material culture of the SELK'NAM (ONA) to the north and east of the Yamana. Like their neighbors the Alakaluf, the Yamana survived sporadic encounters with European expeditioners in southern waters but were quickly decimated as a result of more intensive encounters with nineteenth-century whalers and early twentieth-century colonists. Today the few Yamana who survive continue to fish but also cultivate small gardens and live in prefabricated houses in the small community of Ukika, near Port Williams, on the north coast of Navarino Island on the southern tip of Chile.

JULIAN H. STEWARD, ed., *Handbook of South American Indians*, vol. 1 (1946), pp. 17–24; RICHARD SHUTLER, JR., ed., *South America: Early Man in the New World* (1983), pp. 37–146; MUSEO CHILENO DE ARTE PRECOLOMBINO, *Hombres del sur: Aonikenk, Selknam, Yamana, Kaweshkar* (1987).

KRISTINE L. JONES
JOSÉ ANTONIO PÉREZ GOLLÁN

YAN. *See* **Prado, João Fernando de Almeida.**

YANACONAS, in the broadest sense of the word, a colonial-era term for indigenous people and their descendants who were separated from their ancestral communities. The specific circumstances under which that separation had occurred and the precise meaning of the term varied considerably throughout the viceroyalty of Peru, but virtually every usage of the term refers to Indians who had been removed—physically, culturally, and economically—from their traditional communities. The Spanish term *yanacona* is thought to derive from the Inca term *yana*, personal servant or retainer whose special duties and altered relationship with other community members had, in turn, altered the *yana's* own relationship with his or her *ayllus* (kin groups). Consistent with their practice of adapting indigenous terms to describe colonial structures that had only a superficial resemblance to traditional practices, the Spaniards first used the term *yanaconas* to describe Indian servants.

When Francisco de TOLEDO Y FIGUEROA reorganized Peru's indigenous communities in the 1570s, he differentiated between *yanaconas de españoles* (of Spaniards), who were in private service to Spaniards, and *yanaconas del rey* (of the king), who, according to Toledo's reasoning, owed allegiance—and therefore taxes and labor service—only to the crown, which could allocate that labor as it saw fit. Toledo conducted a careful census of the *yanacona* population, limiting the number of individuals who could claim either type of *yanacona* status for themselves and their descendants. In the following years, an increasing number of Indians either sought *yanacona* status or had it conferred upon them by employers who secured *licencias de yanaconas* (roughly, *yanacona* permits) from colonial authorities. *Yanaconas* enjoyed certain advantages, including reduced taxes and, most important, protection from the MITA (the state forced-labor system), but *yanaconas*, who participated in a wide range of labor relationships, such as sharecropping, wage labor, and debt peonage, could be brutally exploited by their employers. Although they could not legally be sold into slavery, *yanaconas* were legally tied to the land they worked, and property transfers often included the services of *yanaconas*.

Throughout the colonial period, the increasing number of Indians having—or claiming—*yanacona* status was a constant drain on the state labor system. By the eighteenth century, in some areas of the viceroyalty the number of Indians who were living apart from their home communities—voluntarily or involuntarily, through *yanacona* status or migration or flight—exceeded the number of Indians still living in those communities and trying to fulfill their tax and labor obligations. Various viceroys tried to incorporate the *yanacona* sector into the state labor system, but powerful interests kept most *yanaconas* in the private labor sector. Although the end of colonial rule altered the legal definition of and regulations governing *yanacona* status, the term continued to be applied to Indian laborers.

STEVE J. STERN, *Peru's Indian Peoples and the Challenge of Spanish Conquest: Huamanga to 1640* (1982); KAREN SPALDING, *Huarochirí: An Andean Society Under Inca and Spanish Rule* (1984), esp. pp. 85–88; BROOKE LARSON, *Colonialism and Agrarian Transformation in Bolivia: Cochabamba, 1550–1900* (1988), esp. pp. 82–87; and ANN M. WIGHTMAN, *Indigenous Migration and Social Change: The Forasteros of Cuzco, 1570–1720* (1990), esp. pp. 83–85.

ANN M. WIGHTMAN

See also **Repartimiento; Slavery.**

YANES, FRANCISCO JAVIER (*b.* 12 May 1776; *d.* 17 June 1842), political activist and historian of the Venezuelan independence movement. Yanes was born in Cuba but moved to Venezuela at a very young age. He studied law at the University of Caracas. He was connected with the independence movement from its start. Yanes was a member of the SOCIEDAD PATRIÓTICA DE CARACAS and of the Constituent Congress of 1811; he was also a censor at *El Publicista*, the official publication of the Congress. He left the country at the fall of the First Republic in 1812, returning in 1813. The CONGRESS OF ANGOSTURA designated him a member of the Supreme Court of Justice of Venezuela in 1819 and in 1820 as president of the Court of Almirantazgo.

With the creation of GRAN COLOMBIA, Yanes was appointed a member of the Superior Court of Justice of Venezuela (1821), which was subordinate to the government in Bogotá. He worked on the publication of the periodical *El Observador Caraqueño* (1824–1825) with Cristóbal Mendoza, historian, journalist, and first president of Venezuela (1811), with whom he also collaborated on an important collection of twenty-two volumes of documents concerning Venezuela's emancipation [FRANCISCO JAVIER YANES and CRISTÓBAL MENDOZA, *Colección de documentos relativos a la vida pública del Libertador de Colombia y del Perú, Simón Bolívar*, 22 vols. (1983)]. Yanes was a member of the SOCIEDAD ECONÓMICA DE AMIGOS DEL PAÍS (1829) and of the Constituent Congress of 1830. After 1830 he devoted himself to judicial activities and to his private life. His personal archive can be found in the National Academy of History in Caracas.

No biography of Yanes exists, nor is there any work concerning his intellectual career. However, several renditions of his own works include valuable biographical information: FRANCISCO JAVIER YANES, *Relación documentada de los principales sucesos ocurridos en Venezuela desade que se declaró estado independiente hasta el año de 1821*, 2 vols. (1943); *Compendio de la historia de Venezuela, desde su descubrimiento y conquista hasta que se declaró estado independiente* (1944); and *Manual político del venezolano* (1959).

INÉS QUINTERO

YÁÑEZ SANTOS DELGADILLO, AGUSTÍN (*b.* 4 May 1904; *d.* 17 January 1980), Mexican novelist and public figure. Of the many novels and literary studies Agustín Yáñez produced, he is best remembered for his focus on the regional qualities of his native culture in the small, rural towns of Jalisco, in western Mexico. *Al filo del agua* (*On the Edge of the Storm*), his best-known work in this genre, was first published in 1947 and is considered an outstanding example of a historical novel depicting, in the words of critic John Brushwood, "the reality of Mexico on the edge of the Revolution." Brushwood considers it a turning point in Mexican literature.

Yáñez was born in Guadalajara, Jalisco, the child of modest, extremely religious parents. A law school graduate, he quickly joined the intellectual scene, after first involving himself with the CRISTERO REBELLION, a religious uprising against the government. He moved to Mexico City, where he taught at the National University and served at a number of administrative posts. After holding several minor posts in the federal government, he became governor of his home state (1953–1959). He became a speech writer for President Adolfo LÓPEZ MATEOS, who appointed him assistant secretary of the presidency (1962–1964). In 1964, he became secretary of public education. Unlike many intellectuals, Yáñez did not surround himself with disciples, although he gave his time to intellectual institutions as president of the Seminar of Mexican Culture (1949–1952) and the Mexican Academy of Language (1973–1977).

JOHN S. BRUSHWOOD, *Mexico in Its Novel* (1966); AGUSTÍN YÁÑEZ, *Obras escogidas* (1968); BARBARA GRAHAM, "Social and Stylistic Realities in the Fiction of Agustín Yáñez" (Ph.D. diss., University of Miami, 1969); ALFONSO RANGEL GUERRA, *Agustín Yáñez* (1969); *Mester* 12 (1983), entire issue.

RODERIC AI CAMP

YANOMAMI, the largest unassimilated tribal group in the South American rain forest. Also written as "Yanoama" or "Yanomamö," the term is translated "human being." The Yanomami number perhaps 20,000 and occupy an area covering nearly 30,000 square miles. They are skilled farmers, living in circular communal settlements. Their family of languages, along with several other culture traits, distinguishes them from the CARIB- and Arawak-affiliated peoples that surround them. For example, instead of manioc (*manihot*) the plantain, or cooking banana (*Musa*), is their staple food. The heart of the Yanomami homeland is the isolated, mountainous Parima section of the GUIANA HIGHLANDS. The boundary separating Brazil and Venezuela passes directly through their territory, but very few Yanomami have adopted the national culture of either of these two modern states.

During the colonial period, Spanish and Portuguese expeditions encountered only a few small outlying Yanomami groups, who usually fought them off. Traditional material culture is perishable in this humid environment; except for stone tools and clay vessels, tangible evidence of their past is extremely rare. The Yanomami are probably the same people, however, that have been referred to since the eighteenth century as Waika, Shamatari, Shirishana, or even Guajaribo. The first sustained contact with the Yanomami was not achieved by outsiders until 1947. Since the 1980s, many Yanomami have suffered greatly by encroachments into their territory of Brazilian tin miners and gold prospectors (GARIMPEIROS). In 1991–1992 both Brazil (ca. 23 million acres) and Venezuela (ca. 22 million acres) legally set aside large portions of Yanomami territory as "protected" or "indigenous" areas. The Yanomami have no tribal government of their own.

WILLIAM J. SMOLE, *The Yanoama Indians: A Cultural Geography* (1976); KENNETH GOOD, *Into the Heart: One Man's Pursuit of Love and Knowledge Among the Yanomama* (1991); BRIAN FERGUSON, *Yanomami Warfare: A Political History* (1994).

WILLIAM J. SMOLE

YAQUI INDIANS, an indigenous nation of northwestern Mexico (Sonora) and southwestern United States (Arizona) that has stood out for its long and successful resistance to acculturation and assimilation into Mexican society. Since their "discovery" by Europeans in 1533, the Yaquis have insisted on retaining their own distinctive identity as a separate people and culture, and they have waged numerous wars to prevent the loss of their communities, land, water, and way of life in the Yaqui River Valley. They have steadfastly maintained some form of internal organization and government for more than four hundred years, including the exile barrios outside the Yaqui River Valley in both Sonora and Arizona.

An indigenous people with identity rooted in a land base, the Yaquis were primarily agricultural. During long periods of resistance in the nineteenth and twentieth centuries, however, they were prevented from deriving much of their subsistence from the soil in their contested homeland; thus, many became temporary wage laborers in the haciendas, mines, and railroads of Sonora and Arizona. Nevertheless, unlike other frontier Indian communities, Yaqui participation in the larger

Yaqui Indians taking an oath of submission. Ortiz Station, Sonora, 15 May 1897. ARCHIVO GENERAL DE LA NACIÓN, MÉXICO.

notably its defeat at the battle of TUYUTÍ in May. López was therefore anxious to end the war on honorable terms or, at the very least, to gain time to prepare further defenses. Arrangements were made for a personal interview in the land between the Paraguayan and Brazilian lines. There, López met with the Argentine commander, Bartolomé MITRE. The meeting was a study in contrasts between the splendor of López's uniform and the rough informality of Mitre's attire. Although their conversation was evidently amicable, López was disappointed to find that the Argentines and their Brazilian allies had no intention of giving up the fight while López remained in power in Paraguay. Their efforts frustrated, the two men departed and the war began anew, leading ten days later to a horrendous defeat for the Allies at CURUPAYTY and four more years of fighting.

ADOLFO I. BÁEZ, *Yatayty-Corá: Una conferencia histórica (recuerdo de la guerra del Paraguay)* (1929); CHARLES J. KOLINSKI, *Independence or Death! The Story of the Paraguayan War* (1965).

THOMAS L. WHIGHAM

economy did not result in their permanent assimilation into the larger society. For, even as they worked for wages, they struggled to preserve their autonomous communities—physically, politically, and culturally. This dual characteristic of separatism and partial integration is the source of Yaqui strength and key to their survival as a distinct people and culture up to the present day.

For an interpretive study of Yaqui culture see EDWARD SPICER, *The Yaquis: A Cultural History* (1980). For a narrative history of Yaqui contact and struggle with the outside world see EVELYN HU-DE HART, *Missionaries, Miners, and Indians: Spanish Contact with the Yaqui Nation of Northwestern New Spain, 1533–1820* (1981) and *Yaqui Resistance and Survival: The Struggle for Land and Autonomy, 1821–1910* (1984).

EVELYN HU-DEHART

See also **Indians.**

YATAITY CORÃ, CONFERENCE OF, an abortive peace conference that took place on 12 September 1866 during the WAR OF THE TRIPLE ALLIANCE (1864–1870). The Paraguayan army, led by President Francisco Solano LÓPEZ, had experienced a series of reverses in 1866,

YAXCHILÁN, Maya archaeological site located in Chiapas, Mexico. Renowned for its numerous well-preserved stone monuments beautifully carved with scenes of human figures accompanied by long hieroglyphic texts, Yaxchilán has provided epigraphers with crucial information concerning the history and organization of Classic Maya society. The city's monuments were placed in front of and inside many small temples built atop ridges and terraces that overlook a great U-shaped bend midway along the Usumacinta River, which is now the international border between Mexico and Guatemala.

First brought to public attention in the 1880s through the photographs of two European explorer-archaeologists, Alfred P. Maudslay and Teobert Maler, the Yaxchilán texts have proved critical in deciphering Maya history as told from the point of view of kings. During a period of almost five centuries (A.D. 320–808), the Yaxchilán polity was ruled from its capital by a sequence of *ahaw*, or lords, each of whom oversaw one or more *sahal*, or provincial lords, who governed communities subordinate to the king. While the names of at least fifteen kings are recorded in the texts, the most important of these were Shield Jaguar I (A.D. 647–742) and Bird Jaguar IV (A.D. 709–ca. 770), rulers responsible for building most of Yaxchilán's temples and monuments. The predominant themes of the Yaxchilán inscriptions are warfare and bloodletting, both central activities in the ritual lives of kings. Also recorded in the texts are details of marital and military alliances, ritual practices and religious ideas, and terms for kinship and political office, information that enables archaeologists to reconstruct important aspects of Maya social, political, and religious organization.

A broad historical context for the glyphic information is provided by the excavations of the Mexican archaeologist Robert García Moll, whose preliminary results indicate that Yaxchilán was occupied from the Late Preclassic through the Terminal Classic periods.

ALFRED P. MAUDSLAY, *Biologia Centrali-Americana: Archaeology*, 5 vols. (1889–1902); IAN GRAHAM, *Corpus of Maya Hieroglyphic Inscriptions: Yaxchilán*, vol. 3, parts 1–3 (1977–1988); LINDA SCHELE and DAVID FREIDEL, *A Forest of Kings* (1990), pp. 262–305; CAROLYN E. TATE, *Yaxchilán: The Design of a Maya Ceremonial City* (1992).

KEVIN JOHNSTON

See also **Archaeology; Mayas.**

YBYCUÍ, site of a major foundry and industrial smithy in mid-nineteenth-century Paraguay. Established by President Carlos Antonio LÓPEZ in 1850, as part of a major program of military and state economic expansion, the foundry of Ybycuí (or La Rosada) was well situated to take advantage of local iron deposits and sources of water. It was the only government-sponsored ironworks in South America at the time, and has since become the subject of much scholarly inquiry as a possible example of internally generated industrialization.

Work at the foundry was directed by foreign engineers contracted by López. The labor force was made up of convicts, slaves, some free workers, and, after the beginning of the WAR OF THE TRIPLE ALLIANCE (1864–1870), by prisoners of war. Operations at the foundry were often hampered by technical difficulties. Nonetheless, it did produce a substantial quantity of iron, much of which was for military use (especially for cannonballs and artillery pieces). This made Ybycuí a prime target during the fighting. In May 1869, it was raided by a roving Uruguayan cavalry unit, and a month afterward, Brazilian demolition teams dynamited what was left of the foundry. It was partially restored in the 1960s and now serves as a historical museum.

JOSEFINA PLÁ, *The British in Paraguay, 1850–1870* (1976); THOMAS LYLE WHIGHAM, "The Iron Works of Ybycuí: Paraguayan Industrial Development in the Mid-Nineteenth Century," in *The Americas* 35 (October 1978): 201–218.

THOMAS L. WHIGHAM

YDÍGORAS FUENTES, MIGUEL (*b.* 17 October 1895; *d.* 6 October 1982), president of Guatemala (1958–1963). Born in Pueblo Nuevo, Retalhuleu, to a family of Basque ancestry, Ydígoras pursued a military career, rising to the rank of general. He served as a departmental governor and as the head of the department of highways during the dictatorship of General Jorge UBICO (1931–1944), when he developed a reputation in the countryside as a tough but fair administrator. As a reward for supporting the new junta of the October Revolution (1944), he was named ambassador to Great Britain, where he became impressed by British parliamentary democracy.

In 1950 he ran for the presidency of Guatemala against Jacobo ARBENZ (1950–1954), but was forced into hiding during much of the campaign. Exiled to El Salvador, he helped organize the U.S.-backed insurrection that toppled Arbenz in 1954.

After the assassination of President Carlos CASTILLO ARMAS in July 1957, Ydígoras reorganized his political party, Reconciliación Democrática Nacional, and campaigned for the presidency against Miguel Ortiz Passarelli, the official candidate. When the government declared Ortiz the winner in a disputed election, Ydígoras launched the massive street demonstrations that succeeded in overturning the election. In January 1958 he defeated Colonel José Luis Cruz Salazar in what was considered to be a fair and free election.

The Ydígoras Fuentes regime was a peculiar mixture of populism, economic conservatism, and nationalism. Thus, he strongly supported the creation of the CENTRAL AMERICAN COMMON MARKET and pushed through an industrial incentives law, a law protecting foreign investment, a limited agrarian reform law, and an income-tax law. Ydígoras also permitted substantial personal liberty.

Faced with the threat of Castroite subversion and the need for support from the United States, Ydígoras secretly provided a base for the BAY OF PIGS INVASION. Reaction by nationalist officers led to a military uprising in November 1960 that was put down by loyal army units with U.S. assistance. In 1961 several of the rebellious officers launched the guerrilla movement that has continued into the 1990s.

In March 1962 charges of electoral manipulation, administrative incompetence, and corruption precipitated a student-led protest movement that forced Ydígoras to install a military cabinet in order to retain power. But the military turned against him when he permitted their old nemesis (and also that of the United States), former president Juan José ARÉVALO (1945–1951), to return to Guatemala to contest the 1963 elections. Ydígoras was overthrown on 30 March 1963 in a coup led by his defense minister, General Enrique PERALTA AZURDIA (1963–1966).

Ydígoras lived in exile in Nicaragua, Costa Rica, and El Salvador until the early 1970s, when he returned to Guatemala under an amnesty offered to all ex-presidents living abroad by President Carlos ARANA OSORIO (1970–1974). He commented extensively in the press on Guatemalan affairs. In 1980 he traveled to the Vatican to see fulfilled a goal for which he had worked many years—the beatification of Hermano Pedro de BETHANCOURT.

MIGUEL YDÍGORAS FUENTES, *My War with Communism* (1963); THOMAS MELVILLE AND MARGORIE MELVILLE, *Guatemala—Another Vietnam?* (1971); STEPHEN SCHLESINGER and STEPHEN KINZER, *Bitter Fruit: The Untold Story of the American Coup in Guatemala* (1982, repr. 1983); JAMES DUNKERLEY, *Power in the*

Isthmus: A Political History of Modern Central America (1988), FRANSICO VILLAGRÁN KRAMER, *Biografía política de Guatemala: Los pactos políticos de 1944 a 1970* (1993).

ROLAND H. EBEL

YEGROS, FULGENCIO (*b.* 1780; *d.* 17 July 1821), Paraguayan militiaman and political figure. Born into a well-established and wealthy CREOLE family, Yegros chose a career with the colonial militia at an early age. During the first decade of the nineteenth century, he commanded troops against the Portuguese and their Indian allies. His chief claim to military fame, however, came in 1811, when his cavalry defeated a *porteño* expeditionary force at the battles of PARAGUARÍ and TACUARÍ. The vanquished *porteño* commander, Manuel BELGRANO, invited Yegros to a parley after the conclusion of the fighting, and convinced him to join the patriot cause. Soon thereafter, Yegros joined with other militia leaders in a *cuartelazo* (barracks revolt) against the colonial governor, which led to independence shortly thereafter.

Though ill at ease in the political realm, Yegros joined the junta together with fellow officer Pedro Juan CABALLERO, cleric Francisco Xavier Bogarín, businessman Fernando de la Mora, and a distant relative, José Gaspar de FRANCIA. The latter quickly eclipsed the other members of the junta and began formulating Paraguayan policy without much consulting of his associates. In October 1813 an extraordinary congress assembled in Asunción and replaced the junta with a two-man consular government led by Francia and Yegros. It was clear from the beginning that Francia held all the real power. Yegros's tenure was brief; within a year, Francia abolished the consulate and founded a "supreme dictatorship" that lasted until his death in 1840.

Yegros, who had hoped to retire peacefully to his ranch at Quyquyó, found himself implicated in an antigovernment conspiracy in 1820. Fearing that this might signal the beginning of a revolt, Francia had his old associate arrested, tortured, and finally shot, less than 100 yards from the government house.

LUIS G. BENÍTEZ, *Historia de la cultura en el Paraguay* (1976), p. 97; CARLOS ZUBIZARRETA, *Cien vidas paraguayas*, 2d ed. (1985), pp. 87–92.

THOMAS L. WHIGHAM

YELLOW FEVER. *See* **Diseases.**

YERBA MATÉ, *Ilex paraguariensis*, tea made from the maté plant, a hollylike bush. Pre-Columbian Indians in South America developed a liking for the tea. The GAUCHO and other inhabitants of the Río de la Plata adopted the beverage, which remains very popular. The plant is now cultivated in Paraguay and the northern riverine provinces of Argentina. The highly caffeinic beverage is traditionally served in a pear-shaped gourd (also called a maté). Tea leaves are placed in the gourd and hot water is poured over them. The gourd is passed from person to person, and each sips the hot drink through a metal straw called a *bombilla*. More hot water and leaves are added as needed.

Many folk beliefs and rituals have grown up around the drink. According to a traditional poem, maté served with milk means respect. Sweetened maté indicates friendship; flavored with balm mint, it communicates displeasure. The beverage is most often consumed "straight," with nothing added.

RICHARD W. SLATTA, *Gauchos and the Vanishing Frontier* (1983), pp. 78–79; AMARO VILLANUEVA, *El maté: Arte de cebar* (1960).

RICHARD W. SLATTA

YERMO, GABRIEL DE (*b.* 1757; *d.* 1813), leader of the Mexican coup d'état of 1808. The Sodupe-born Yermo was a rich Spanish merchant and landowner who became the enemy of Viceroy José de ITURRIGARAY (1742–1815) because of financial matters, specifically, the taxes levied on products Yermo imported. Backed by the Audiencia of Mexico, Yermo and 300 armed men apprehended the viceroy and his family on the night of 15 September 1808. By so doing, they successfully prevented the establishment of the governing junta that the *ayuntamiento* (city council) proposed and that Iturrigaray appeared to support. Also detained were several members of the *ayuntamiento* and Fray Melchor de TALAMANTES (1765–1809).

ENRIQUE LAFUENTE FERRARI, *El virrey Iturrigaray y los orígenes de la independencia de Méjico* (1940); *Diccionario Porrúa de historia, biografía y geografía de México*, vol. 3 (1986), p. 3188.

VIRGINIA GUEDEA

YNSFRÁN, EDGAR L. (*b.* 1920; *d.* 1991), Paraguayan politician. When General Alfredo STROESSNER seized power in 1954, he needed competent allies to give his regime a veneer of legitimacy and respectability. In this effort it was natural that he would turn to Edgar L. Ynsfrán, a talented young intellectual who had made a name for himself in Colorado Party circles ever since the 1947 civil war. A protégé of the right-wing former president Juan Natalicio González, Ynsfrán was a lawyer by training. He had already served as a Colorado deputy, police official, and member of the Junta de Gobierno. He was also a much read essayist, an indefatigable worker, and a shrewd party organizer. Most important of all, he was willing to act as Stroessner's agent in political matters.

The general made Ynsfrán his interior minister in the mid-1950s at precisely the time when the democratic opposition—as well as the left-leaning guerrilla groups—were actively seeking the dictator's ouster. Ynsfrán took energetically to combating these threats. Though he gave the impression of being a tranquil, austere scholar, in fact he filled Paraguay's jails with hundreds of political prisoners, many of whom were tortured.

By the mid-1960s, Ynsfrán's repressive apparatus had destroyed nearly all of Stroessner's enemies in the country. The very success of his campaign, however, gave Ynsfrán a measure of power uncomfortably close to that of the president himself. Not wishing to place too much temptation before his minister's eyes, Stroessner abruptly dropped Ynsfrán from the cabinet in 1966. Thereafter the former interior minister devoted himself to business matters and to the building of a magnificent library of Paraguayan books, documents, and memorabilia, much of which was donated to the nation just before his death. In the last two years of his life, he attempted a political comeback, but his unsavory past prevented him from making much headway, even within his own Colorado Party.

EDGAR YNSFRÁN, *Tres discursos* (1956), *passim*; PAUL H. LEWIS, *Paraguay Under Stroessner* (1980), pp. 79–99, 116–134; RIORDAN ROETT and RICHARD S. SACKS, *Paraguay: The Personalist Legacy* (1991), pp. 55–57.

THOMAS L. WHIGHAM

YNSFRÁN, PABLO MAX (*b*. 30 June 1894; *d*. 2 May 1972), Paraguayan educator and historian. Born in Asunción, Ynsfrán received formal training as a diplomat during the 1920s and 1930s, but early on expressed as much interest in the study of history as in the practical application of politics. From 1923 to 1928 he taught philosophy and Roman history at the Colegio Nacional de la Capital (Asunción) at the same time as he served as a congressional deputy.

The CHACO WAR of 1932–1935 found Ynsfrán in Washington, D.C., as Paraguay's chargé d'affaires. There he participated in the 1938 Chaco peace conference and was subsequently chosen to be public works minister by President José Félix ESTIGARRIBIA.

With the start of the Higínio MORÍNIGO dictatorship in 1940, Ynsfrán went into exile in the United States. He became a professor of Latin American history at the University of Texas at Austin, where he remained until his death.

Ynsfrán wrote two finely detailed studies, *The Epic of the Chaco: Marshal Estigarribia's Memoirs of the Chaco War, 1932–1935* (1950), and *La expedición norteamericana contra el Paraguay, 1858–1859* (1954), as well as many articles and polemical pieces.

CHARLES J. KOLINSKI, *Historical Dictionary of Paraguay* (1973), pp. 266–267; JACK RAY THOMAS, *Biographical Dictionary of Latin American Historians and Historiography* (1984), pp. 353–354.

MARTA FERNÁNDEZ WHIGHAM

YON SOSA, MARCO ANTONIO (*b*. 1932; *d*. June 1970), Guatemalan guerrilla leader. On 13 November 1960,

Yon Sosa led a revolt of nationalist army officers against the corrupt government of Miguel YDÍGORAS FUENTES (1958–1963). After a brief exile, he returned to eastern Guatemala as a proponent of radical revolution through guerrilla warfare, and organized the Rebel Armed Forces (FAR) with Luis TURCIOS LIMA and the Communist Party. Yon Sosa broke from the FAR in 1965 over ideological issues, but he continued the guerrilla struggle as leader of the Revolutionary Movement of November 13 (MR-13). An advocate of immediate socialist revolution through general insurrection, Yon Sosa rejected the electoral strategies of the FAR, although the two guerrilla movements forged a tenuous alliance during the devastating counterinsurgency program supported by the United States in the late 1960s. After a confrontation with the army, he fled Mexico, where he was killed by Mexican authorities. The FAR and MR-13 provided the training ground for the rebel leaders of the 1970s.

SUSANNE JONAS and DAVID TOBIS, eds., *Guatemala* (1974), esp. pp. 176–203; JIM HANDY, *Gift of the Devil: A History of Guatemala* (1984), esp. pp. 230–234.

PAUL J. DOSAL

See also **Guatemala: Revolutionary Movements.**

YORKINOS, the York rite Masonic lodges. As Mexican national politics became increasingly polarized in 1825, leading figures such as José Miguel RAMOS ARIZPE, Ignacio Esteva, Manuel GÓMEZ PEDRAZA, Vicente GUERRERO, and Lorenzo de ZAVALA formed Masonic lodges independent of the Scottish ESCOCESES. The U.S. minister Joel R. POINSETT agreed to obtain formal charters from the Grand Masonic Temple in New York, thus formally establishing the York rite lodges or *yorkinos*. Although the *yorkinos* eventually became the "populist" party, initially, the group included many moderates. Within a short time, radicals took control of the lodges, which spread rapidly throughout the nation. In 1827, the discovery of a conspiracy by the Franciscan Joaquín Arenas to return Spain to power resulted in the passage of laws expelling the Spaniards and to state and national electoral victories by radical *yorkinos*. This, in turn, led to an unsuccessful revolt by the *escoceses* and to riots in December 1828 which forced president-elect Gómez Pedraza to flee the country and elevated Guerrero to the presidency. After 1828 the lodges were banned; Mexican Masonry reorganized in 1830 as the *Rito Nacional Mexicano*, but intervened in politics less directly.

LUIS J. ZALCE Y RODRÍGUEZ, *Apuntes para la historia de la masonería en México*, 2 vols. (1950); VIRGINIA GUEDEA, "Las sociedades secretas durante el movimiento de independencia," in *The Independence of Mexico and the Creation of the New Nation*, edited by Jaime E. Rodríguez O. (1989), pp 45–62.

JAIME E. RODRÍGUEZ O.

See also **Masonic Orders.**

YORUBA, a West African people who inhabit southwest Nigeria, the southern Benin Republic (formerly Dahomey), and southern Togo. Known in the Americas by subethnic names such as Yaraba, Oyo, Aku, Nago, Lucumi, Ijesha, Egba, and Ijebu, transatlantic Yoruba-speaking communities and customs have reestablished themselves following dispersal by the slave trade. Yoruba slave exports began in the late 1700s, but the collapse of the Yoruba imperial capital at Oyo circa 1837 and attendant civil wars augmented their slave numbers. This volume was maintained until the abolition of the slave trade in Brazil in 1850. In the British Caribbean, where the slave trade became illegal after 1807, captured Africans were imported as indentured laborers until the 1860s.

Yorubaland's late role as a slave reservoir accounts for the persistence of Yoruba culture in Brazil, Cuba, Trinidad, and Grenada. Cultural manifestations include language use restricted largely to ritual, food preparations and names, folktales and legends, divination methods and accompanying poetry, sacred and secular songs, drum types, and drum rhythms. The most overt cultural domain is religion, centered on natural forces called orishas (ORIXÁS) meaning "saints," or "powers." Each orisha is identified by specific colors, paraphernalia, and chants. Ceremonies are conducted by the self- or family-appointed male or female leader of a religious community, as the religion possesses no overall regulatory body. Yoruba-derived ceremonies are most elaborately articulated in Shango in Recife, CANDOMBLÉ in Bahia, and SANTERÍA of Cuba. Trinidad and Grenada maintain analogous rituals, called Shango or Orisha. Ancestor veneration is a subsidiary aspect of the religion, but is separately enacted in the Saraka in Trinidad and Carriacou (the Grenadines), Etu in Jamaica, and Oku in Guyana.

WILLIAM BASCOM, *The Yoruba of Southwestern Nigeria* (1969), and *Shango in the New World* (1972); GEORGE SIMPSON, *Black Religions in the New World* (1978); SHEILA WALKER, "Everyday and Esoteric Reality in the Afro-Brazilian Candomblé," in *History of Religions* 30, no. 2 (1990): 103–128; and JOSÉ JORGE DE CARVALHO and RITA LAURA SEGATO, *Shango Cult in Recife, Brazil* (1992).

MAUREEN WARNER-LEWIS

YRENDAGÜE, BATTLE OF, a conflict that took place at a small fort in Paraguay near the border with Bolivia during the CHACO WAR (1932–1935). The fighting occurred on 8 December 1934 and secured Paraguay's victory against Bolivia, its landlocked neighbor. Paraguayan General José Félix ESTIGARRIBIA ordered Colonel Eugenio GARAY to occupy Yrendagüe with support from his Eighth Division. The numerically inferior Paraguayan forces marched on foot for about fifty miles to the fort. Once they captured Yrendagüe, the Bolivians lost access to all of the water wells in the area. Water

was extremely scarce in that region of the Chaco, and, as a result, 4,000 Bolivian cavalry troops were forced to surrender and perhaps twice that number died of thirst.

PABLO MAX YNSFRÁN, *The Epics of the Chaco War: Memoirs of General Estigarribia* (1950); DAVID H. ZOOK, *The Conduct of the Chaco War* (1960).

MIGUEL A. GATTI

YRIGOYEN, HIPÓLITO (Irigoyen; *b.* 12 July 1852; *d.* 3 July 1933), president of Argentina (1916–1922, 1928–1930). Controversial, charismatic, and enigmatic, Hipólito Yrigoyen was Argentina's most popular president before Juan Domingo PERÓN. As leader of the Unión Cívica Radical (UCR), or Radical Party, he built a populist organization driven by patronage and run by an efficient urban-based political machine. In 1930 a deteriorating economy, charges of political corruption, and a loss of support by the military sparked a coup that removed Yrigoyen from power.

Born the illegitimate son of a blacksmith in provincial Buenos Aires, Yrigoyen developed a personality that defies easy explanation. Virtually every author or biog-

Hipólito Yrigoyen, ca. 1920. ARCHIVO GENERAL DE LA NACIÓN, BUENOS AIRES; PHOTO BY WITCOMB.

rapher who assumed the task resorted to the term "enigmatic." That he was a remarkable character lies beyond doubt. Over the masses he exercised an extraordinary fascination and displayed a quiet charisma despite poorly developed oratorical abilities. Indeed, except for a single instance in the 1880s, he never made a public speech. Yrigoyen preferred bargains struck in the background and cultivated an air of mystery. His political mission was buried in the moralistic rhetoric of his manifestos; Yrigoyen's philosophy, derived partly from the works of the minor German philosopher Karl Krause, was equally obscure and stressed a mystical belief in a God-given harmony and in moral living. Even in later life, he continued to wear suits of somber shades, lived in modest dwellings in the poorer districts of Buenos Aires, and shunned photographers. Much of this reflects his personal history of political conspiracy.

Yrigoyen's public career began in 1872, when his uncle, Leandro ALEM, secured for him the position of police superintendent in a district of Buenos Aires. The appointment was lost, however, when Yrigoyen was accused of participation in a scheme to rig elections. In 1877 Yrigoyen, together with Alem and Artistóbulo del VALLE, helped to form the short-lived Republican Party, which supported provincial rights and attacked corrupt politics. In 1879 he successfully ran for a seat in Congress and in 1880 was chosen for a high position on the National Council for Education. When his term of office ended in 1882, he bought land and entered the cattle-fattening business.

In 1890 Yrigoyen joined the Unión Cívica and participated in "El Noventa," an armed insurrection that toppled the government of Miguel JUÁREZ CELMAN. Following a struggle over leadership, the party split in 1891 into two factions. One, the Unión Cívica Nacionál, was led by Bartolomé MITRE and the other, the Unión Cívica Radical, was initially guided by Leandro Alem. Yrigoyen worked successfully to wrest control of the UCR from Alem, who committed suicide in 1896. By 1898 Yrigoyen was the acknowledged leader of radicalism. Holding vague populist ideals and driven more by emotion than careful attention to issues, the UCR continued, unsuccessfully, to play at revolution. From the UCR's perspective, illegitimate government legitimized insurrection. In the words of Yrigoyen, on the occasion of the failed uprising of 1905: "Revolutions are an integral part of the moral law of society." According to Manuel GÁLVEZ, his biographer, Yrigoyen realized that he had a mission and destiny that called for the moral and political regeneration of the nation. At any rate, after 1900 he cultivated an air of mystery that he effectively combined with a remarkable behind-the-scenes personal persuasiveness.

Argentina's political scene shifted fundamentally in 1912, when an electoral reform law that provided for universal male suffrage and obligatory and secret voting took effect. Offered a long-awaited political opening, the UCR ran candidates for elected office. In 1916 Yrigoyen won the presidency of Argentina.

Yrigoyen's first term (1916–1922) was marked by contradiction. While the UCR purported to stand for open and honest politics, Yrigoyen did not hesitate to use his executive powers for narrow political ends to "intervene" in provincial elections to assure Radical victories. Yrigoyen's noisy economic nationalism, which targeted foreign capital invested in Argentina, contained more rhetoric than substance and was particularly strident at election time. While the UCR attempted to forge an alliance with organized labor, Yrigoyen readily authorized the use of violence against strikers when they demanded more than Radicals were willing to concede.

Ostensibly a party of the middle class, Yrigoyen's personalist rule, according to Susan and Peter Calvert, "failed to build up a middle-class political philosophy or establish viable institutions for the continued political involvement of newly mobilised groups" (*Argentina: Political Culture and Instability*, p. 97). Lacking programmatic unity, the UCR of Yrigoyen acted pragmatically as it played to the wide range of interests and coalitions that had to be rewarded for their political support. State patronage at a local level took the form of dispersals of free bread, milk, meat, and seed, which wed the electorate to the party. Importantly, the focus of the party's unity became its leader, Yrigoyen. Personalism, patronage, and political loyalty rather than open participation came to typify the years of Radical control.

Yrigoyen's most telling failure was his politicization of the Argentine military. He offended their sense of professionalism when he promoted officers dropped from military service for their participation in the uprising of 1905. He challenged their perceived sense of mission when he used troops to break strikes or to monitor federal interventions in elections; he became deeply involved in the army's inner institutional life. After Yrigoyen won a second term as president in 1928, his meddling in military matters became intolerable, helping to lay the groundwork for the military coup of 1930 that removed him from power.

To military unrest must be added spreading economic dislocation occasioned by world depression. The depression destroyed the ability of the state to grant patronage and undermined the UCR's popular base of support. As the party disintegrated and economic conditions worsened, Yrigoyen lost prestige. He died in 1933 and, in the words of the Calverts, "was accorded the spontaneous tribute of a splendid funeral and became a myth, a symbol of the aspirations of the middle class" (p. 97).

MANUEL GÁLVEZ, *Vida de Hipólito Yrigoyen: El hombre del misterio* (1939); GABRIEL DEL MAZO, *El Radicalismo: Ensayo sobre su historia y doctrina*, vol. 2 (1957); JOSÉ LUIS ROMERO, *A History of Argentine Political Thought* (1963), chap. 8; ROBERT A. POTASH, *The Army and Politics in Argentina, 1928–1945: Yrigoyen to Perón* (1969), chap. 2; PETER H. SMITH, *Argentina and the Failure of Democracy: Conflict Among Political Elites, 1904–1955* (1974), chap. 1; DAVID ROCK, *Politics in Argentina, 1890–1930: The Rise and Fall of Radicalism* (1975); CARL SOLBERG, *Oil and Nationalism in Argentina: A History* (1979), chaps. 2, 3, and 5; SUSAN CALVERT and PETER CALVERT, *Argentina: Political Culture and Instability* (1989), pp. 91–107; TORCUATO S. DI TELLA, *Latin American Politics: A Theoretical Framework* (1990), pp. 125–130.

PAUL B. GOODWIN

See also **Argentina: Political Parties.**

YUCATÁN, a peninsula in southeastern Mexico, including the Mexican states of Yucatán, Campeche, and Quintana Roo, northern Tabasco, northeastern Chiapas, and the northern parts of the modern republics of Guatemala and Belize. The region has been occupied for millennia, most notably by the MAYA, who built their civilization in the area some time after 300 B.C. Europeans arrived on the peninsula during the first decade of the sixteenth century and the Spanish conquistadors conquered the Mayas in 1542, the year in which the Spaniards founded the city of Mérida, the capital of the colonial province and of the modern state of Yucatán. One unfortunate result of contact with Europeans for the Mayas was a substantial demographic decline caused by the introduction of Old World diseases. The Maya population, which had numbered at least 500,000 and perhaps as high as 800,000 in the early sixteenth century, declined to only about 100,000 by the late seventeenth century.

The colonial regime was at first based almost entirely on the Maya peasant community, which produced food and exportable goods, especially cotton textiles, for the Spanish colonists. Spaniards limited their own activities to stock raising on ranches (*estancias*), although in Campeche (the western part of the peninsula) the colonists also organized production of salt and dyewood and established a shipbuilding industry. Politically, the province of Yucatán was ruled by a governor captain-general (*gobernador capitán general*) appointed by the Spanish crown.

In the eighteenth century the Maya population began a demographic recovery, while at the same time the number of non-Indians—Spaniards, mestizos, and mulattoes—also increased substantially. By 1800 the population of the province was over 400,000. Demographic growth resulted in an increased demand for food and other goods, thus leading to the expansion of the landed estates, which produced not only cattle but also maize, sugarcane, rice, and cotton. The economy was also stimulated by commercial and political reforms, including the establishment of the intendancy (chief administrator), which resulted in increased trade with Cuba and the abolition of the REPARTIMIENTO (a peonage system that coerced the Maya into producing cotton textiles).

Yucatán did not participate in the Mexican struggle for independence, but once Mexico became independent in 1821, Yucatán adhered to the rules of the new nation. Disagreements with the Mexican government,

however, led Yucatán's rulers on several occasions to declare the state a sovereign nation. In the decades after independence from Spain those rulers also carried out a program of decolonization and modernization, which, in effect, ended up depriving Maya communities of their traditional lands. As a result, in 1847 the Mayas of the eastern and central parts of the state rose in rebellion and attempted to drive the non-Indians from the peninsula. This CASTE WAR OF YUCATÁN lasted several decades (although most of the violence ended in 1855) and resulted in death and destruction on a massive scale.

In the late nineteenth century, Yucatán—which had been separated from the state of Campeche in 1858—began a recovery based on the export of sisal, or HENEQUEN fiber. Eventually, enormous profits were earned by the large landowners, and Yucatán became the most prosperous state in Mexico. This recovery was accomplished, however, by instituting a rigorous system of debt peonage to force the Mayas to work on the plantations, and, consequently, little of the wealth trickled down to the peasants, who made up the majority of the population.

The conservative regime was so well entrenched that it survived the early years of the MEXICAN REVOLUTION. In 1915, however, the Carranza government, after putting down one last Yucatecan separatist movement, imposed a reformist governor, Salvador ALVARADO (1879–1924), who abolished peonage and permitted labor to organize. By 1918 the socialists, led by Felipe CARRILLO PUERTO (1872–1924), had become the leading political party, and they took power in 1920. Two years later Carrillo Puerto was elected governor. The socialists attempted radical reforms, but their government was overthrown by reactionaries in late 1923; Carrillo Puerto and several of his supporters were executed by firing squad in early 1924. As a result, the Mexican government came to control politics in Yucatán, working through the socialists, who became the basis for the ruling party in the state.

In the 1930s, President Lázaro CÁRDENAS (1895–1970) destroyed the landowning aristocracy in Yucatán by carrying out an agrarian reform. At the same time, however, the henequen industry, which almost ceased to exist by 1990, had begun its long-term decline. Yucatán's economy came to be based mostly on commerce and tourism, with only a minor amount of industry.

ELIGIO ANCONA, *Historia de Yucatán*, 5 vols. (1878–1880); JUAN FRANCISCO MOLINA SOLÍS, *Historia de Yucatán durante la dominación española*, 3 vols. (1904–1913); GILBERT M. JOSEPH, *Revolution from Without: Yucatán, Mexico, and the United States, 1880–1924* (1982); NANCY M. FARRISS, *Maya Society Under Colonial Rule* (1984); ALLEN WELLS, *Yucatán's Gilded Age: Haciendas, Henequen, and International Harvester, 1860–1915* (1985); INGA CLENDINNEN, *Ambivalent Conquests: Maya and Spaniard in Yucatán, 1517–1570* (1987); ROBERT W. PATCH, *Maya and Spaniard in Yucatán, 1648–1812* (1993).

ROBERT W. PATCH

YUNGAS, tropical river valleys of Bolivia that spread northeast to southeast beyond the temperate valleys of the eastern Andean slopes. Here, Amazon winds maintained the humidity necessary for the cultivation of crops not available in the highlands. The pre-Inca AYMARA empire sustained its highland centers by sending MITMAES (colonists) down to the *yungas* to cultivate fruits, maize, and, for highland elite consumption, the stimulant coca. In return, the highlands sent items not produced in the tropical zones, such as meat, potatoes, quinoa, and wool, thus fulfilling their obligations in this Andean system of reciprocity.

With the Spanish conquest and subsequent discovery of silver (see MINING), coca use changed dramatically and was no longer confined to the native elite. Coca consumption now enabled Indians to endure harsh mining activities for protracted periods of time. Production in Cuzco could not meet the increased demand, and the *yungas* of LA PAZ became a major coca zone. Not only did Aymara agricultural migrants continue to replace the nomadic Indians of the region, merchants imported African slaves, who by the early nineteenth century had become a viable Aymara-speaking subgroup in this region. La Paz and its neighboring *yungas* now thrived while other regions experienced economic decline.

Other less accessible *yungas* existed in the provinces of Cochabamba and Santa Cruz. The Chaparé region, northeast of Cochabamba, formerly controlled by the Yuracarés, today produces prodigious amounts of coca. In the colonial period, La Paz merchants intervened and prevented Chaparé competition. The *yungas* of Pocona, which was first settled in 1538 and incorporated into the jurisdiction of MIZQUE before the end of the century, were mass-producing coca by 1557.

Even today, the fertile *yungas* and Oriente regions remain largely underdeveloped despite their year-round growing season. Poor infrastructure, disease (human and plant), pests, floods, and soil erosion discourage serious agricultural activity.

JOSEP M. BARNADAS, *Charcas: Orígenes históricos de una sociedad colonial* (1973), pp. 35, 427; ALBERTO CRESPO R., *Esclavos negros en Bolivia* (1977), pp. 143–146; HERBERT S. KLEIN, *Bolivia: The Evolution of a Multi-Ethnic Society* (1982); MORRIS D. WHITAKER and E. BOYD WENNERGREN, "Bolivia's Agriculture Since 1960: An Assessment and Prognosis," in *Modern-Day Bolivia: Legacy of a Revolution and Prospects for the Future,* edited by Jerry R. Ladman (1982), pp. 238–239; BROOKE LARSON, *Colonialism and Agrarian Transformation in Bolivia: Cochabamba, 1550–1900* (1988), p. 47.

LOLITA GUTIÉRREZ BROCKINGTON

YUNGAY, BATTLE OF, a military action in 1839 that resulted in the destruction of the PERU-BOLIVIA CONFEDERATION, which was headed by Grand Marshal Andrés de SANTA CRUZ and opposed by the Chilean government and a group of Peruvian military leaders. Two military expeditions were sent from Chile to fight the confederation. The first, led by Admiral Manuel BLANCO ENCALADA, was unsuccessful despite the Chilean naval superiority achieved by the end of 1836. However, the second expedition, with a combined force of six thousand men led by General Manuel BULNES and with the participation of Peruvian leaders Agustín GAMARRA, Antonio Gutiérrez de la Fuente, and Ramón CASTILLA, managed to defeat Santa Cruz's forces in the decisive battle of Yungay in the highlands north of Lima. Gamarra's subsequent attempt in 1841 to invade Bolivia led to his defeat and death in the battle of Ingaví.

JORGE BASADRE, *Historia de la República del Peru,* vol. 1 (1963).

ALFONSO W. QUIROZ

See also **War of the Peru-Bolivia Confederation.**

Z

ZAACHILA, an archaeological site located 9 miles south of Oaxaca City, within the present-day village of Zaachila in Oaxaca, Mexico. Zaachila was excavated by Roberto Gallegos in the 1960s. It includes ten visible mounds, one of which, Mound A, was the locus of excavations. Although evidence of older occupations exists at Zaachila, the excavated remains date from the Postclassic period (ca. A.D. 900–1521). Excavations atop Mound A revealed a large residence with rooms arranged around a central patio. Beneath the patio floor were two elaborate tombs with offerings of Mixteca polychrome pottery, onyx vessels, turquoise masks, carved jade, engraved bone, and delicate gold jewelry. The Mixteca polychrome vessels are among the finest ever discovered, and the delicate GOLDWORK rivals that of MONTE ALBÁN Tomb 7. Most remarkable, however, are the stucco reliefs on the walls of Tomb 1. Two owls decorate opposite walls of the antechamber. On the east wall of the main chamber, the stucco figure of a god of death beckons an individual who is identified by the calendrical name Nine Flower. On the west wall, another god of death with a hummingbird above him beckons an individual named Five Flower. Alfonso CASO has identified Five Flower in the painted manuscripts, or CODICES, that detail the genealogies of MIXTEC rulers. He has shown that Five Flower, related to the rulers of the Mixteca Alta center of Yanhuitlán, ruled Zaachila about A.D. 1280. Tomb 1, then, with its rich offering was most likely the final resting place of Five Flower. He and his ancestors and descendants had in all likelihood occupied the residence of Mound A and were among the twenty-three individuals buried in the two tombs beneath its patio floor.

ROBERTO GALLEGOS, "Zaachila: The First Season's Work," *Archaeology* 16, no. 4 (1963): 226–233; ALFONSO CASO, "The Lords of Yanhuitlán," in *Ancient Oaxaca,* edited by John Paddock (1966), pp. 313–335; ROBERTO GALLEGOS, *El Señor 9 Flor en Zaachila* (1978); JOHN PADDOCK, *Lord Five Flower's Family: Rulers of Zaachila and Cuilapán* (1983); MARCUS WINTER, *Oaxaca: The Archaeological Record* (1989), pp. 123–124.

MICHAEL D. LIND

ZACATECAS, a city and a state in north-central Mexico. The name comes from the Zacateco Indians, thought to have built fortifications during the classic period in what is today southern Zacatecas and Aguascalientes to defend central Mexico from the Chichimecs. The city of Nuestra Señora de los Remedios de Zacatecas was founded by Spaniards in 1548. With the discovery of silver at Fresnillo, Sombrerete, and other places, miners, soldiers, merchants, cattle ranchers, missionaries, and royal officials flocked to Zacatecas, which became an important mining region and a major center for expeditions that explored and settled northern New Spain. The province of Zacatecas was part of the Kingdom of NUEVA GALICIA until it became the Intendancy of Zacatecas toward the end of the eighteenth century.

HIDALGO's revolt led large numbers of the wealthiest inhabitants, and even government officials, to abandon Zacatecas. When Hidalgo and his followers passed through Zacatecas in January 1811, after his defeat at Puente de Calderón, he attracted arms and supporters. Battles continued in various parts of Zacatecas throughout 1812 and 1813, and control of the city changed hands several times. With independence and the fall of ITURBIDE, Francisco GARCÍA SALINAS and Valentín GÓMEZ FARÍAS were elected as representatives to the national Congress. In October 1823 the local representatives declared the province the Free and Federated State of Zacatecas. Mining was revived, attracting English capital.

The state and its representatives were important national proponents of liberalism and federalism until the militia of Zacatecas was defeated by national armies under Anastasio BUSTAMANTE in 1832 and Antonio López de SANTA ANNA in 1835. Attacks by Apaches and Comanches increased in the 1840s and remained a serious problem for decades. Victoriano ZAMORA led the liberals supporting the PLAN OF AYUTLA to power in Zacatecas, and Jesús GONZÁLEZ ORTEGA, leading Zacatecan troops, ended the War of the REFORM by defeating the conservatives at San Miguel Calpulalpán (1860). Although French forces occupied Zacatecas in 1864, armed resistance continued throughout the reign of Maximilian.

Trinidad García de la Cadena led an unsuccessful revolt against President Benito Juárez in 1869 and against President Porfirio Díaz in 1886. Despite the growth of mining, agriculture, and technological improvements, the Díaz regime was not popular in Zacatecas. Armed rebellion broke out there in December 1910 with the attempt to arrest supporters of Francisco MADERO. In June 1914, insurgent forces led by Francisco VILLA defeated federal forces holding Zacatecas and destroyed the last of Victoriano HUERTA's army. Violent rebellions associated with the CRISTERO rebellion broke out in 1926 in various parts of the state. Today, Zacatecas is one of the poorest states in Mexico.

ELÍAS AMADOR, *Bosquejo histórico de Zacatecas* (1943); PHILIP WAYNE POWELL, *Soldiers, Indians, and Silver: The Northward Advance of New Spain, 1550–1600* (1952); PETER J. BAKEWELL, *Silver Mining and Society in Colonial Mexico: Zacatecas, 1546–1700* (1971); *Diccionario Porrúa de historia, biografía y geografía de México*, 5th ed. (1986).

D. F. STEVENS

ZACHRISSON, JULIO (*b.* 1930), Panama's foremost printmaker. Zachrisson studied in Panama under Juan Manuel CEDEÑO at the Instituto Nacional de Bellas Artes in Mexico (1953–1959), at the Vanucci Academy in Perugia (1959–1960), and at the San Fernando Academy in Madrid.

Zachrisson's prints, which include etchings, drypoints, woodcuts, and lithographs, are characterized by a unique sense of satire and sociopolitical commentary. The grotesque characters in his fantastic world are drawn from urban Panamanian folklore, Spanish literature, classical mythology, and personal experience. Since the 1970s, he has also painted these subjects in oil on wood or canvas. He now lives in Spain.

MARTA TRABA, *Dos décadas vulnerables en las artes plásticas latinoamericanas, 1950–1970* (1973); ANTONIO GALLEGO, *Historia del grabado en España* (1979); *Zachrisson: obra calcográfica* (catalogue from the Museo Municipal de Bellas Artes, Spain, 1981).

MONICA E. KUPFER

ZACULEU, an archaeological site located in the Huehuetenango Valley of the western Guatemalan highlands, occupied from the Early Classic (ca. A.D. 300) until the arrival of the Spaniards. During the Late Postclassic period, Zaculeu served as the capital of the Mam (Maya) ethnolinguistic group. It sits on an easily defended plateau, protected on three sides by steep cliffs, and may have once had a wall on its fourth side.

Zaculeu was an important center in the Classic period (ca. 300–900). Caches and burials discovered by archaeologists have contained numerous well-crafted goods, such as pyrite plaques and jade carvings.

Many of the structures at Zaculeu were either built or modified during the Late Postclassic period, a period when the population of the settlement is thought to have been substantial. Much of the original residential area presumably lies beneath the modern town of Huehuetenango, so more precise population figures cannot be determined.

The architectural style of the Late Postclassic structures is similar to those at K'iche' and Kaqchikel centers to the east. The arrangement of buildings on the landscape differs, however, presumably reflecting earlier patterns.

Zaculeu and the area it controlled were conquered by the K'iche' sometime between 1425 and 1475, and the K'iche' continued to dominate the area until the arrival of the Spaniards. In 1525 Gonzalo de Alvarado led Spanish forces that conquered the center.

RICHARD B. WOODBURY and AUBREY S. TRIK, *The Ruins of Zaculeu, Guatemala*, 2 vols. (1953); JOHN W. FOX, *Quiché Conquest* (1978), esp. pp. 143–150.

JANINE GASCO

ZAID, GABRIEL (*b.* 14 October 1934), Mexican poet and essayist. Although an engineer by training, Zaid has become one of the Mexican literary establishment's most active members, recognized as a poet, essayist, literary critic, translator, editor, and researcher. He is a member of El Colegio Nacional and the Mexican Language Academy. Zaid won the Xavier Villaurrutia Prize (1972) and the Magda Donato Prize (1986) for his poetry, which has been described as meticulously structured, refined, concise, and as the antithesis of the confessional and exuberant poetry of Jaime Sabines, his contemporary. His literary criticism has concentrated on poetic theory and practice. Besides editing the work of renowned poets, Zaid has promoted the work of young writers in several anthologies. In *Asamblea de poetas jóvenes de México* (1980), he identified a new generation of poets among the ever-increasing numbers who published in small presses and/or literary journals and supplements in the 1970s. As a cultural critic, his books, such as *La economía presidencial* and *De los libros al poder,* and his articles, appearing regularly in *Vuelta,* engage the current political debates.

JOSÉ JOAQUÍN BLANCO, "Gabriel Zaid," in his *Crónica de la poesía mexicana* (1983), pp. 249–255; JULIÁN MEZA, "Autoritarismo presidencial y peticionarismo ciudadano," in *Cuadernos Hispanoamericanos* 448 (1987): 160–164; JULIO ORTEGA, "Una nota sobre *Práctica Mortal* de Gabriel Zaid," in *Lugar de Encuentro,* edited by Norma Klahn and Jesse Fernández (1989), pp. 153–156.

NORMA KLAHN

ZALDÚA, FRANCISCO JAVIER (*b.* 3 December 1821; *d.* 21 December 1882), Colombian president. Born in Bogotá, Francisco Javier Zaldúa was a distinguished professor of law and an active member of the Liberal Party. He served frequently in Congress and in other positions, and presided over the constituent convention of Ríonegro in 1863. In the subsequent division of the party between the more doctrinaire Radicals and the Independents who followed Rafael NÚÑEZ, Zaldúa initially aligned himself with the latter, even though he was essentially a moderate. Thus both factions accepted him as their presidential candidate in 1881. Despite that consensus, however, his term was marked by bitter wrangling with Congress, cut short by his death after less than a year as president.

JAMES WILLIAM PARK, *Rafael Núñez and the Politics of Colombian Regionalism, 1863–1886* (1985), pp. 226–235; IGNACIO ARIZMENDI POSADA, *Presidentes de Colombia 1810–1990* (1989), pp. 163–166.

DAVID BUSHNELL

ZAMBO, the lowest of a series of derogatory names by which Spaniards referred to members of the racially mixed groups called *castas* (castes). While the so-called *castas* could refer to any person of racially mixed origin, Spaniards reserved their most derogatory terms, some of which were zoological, such as "wolf" and "coyote," for those of mixed Indian and black ancestry. These terms originated in the eighteenth century and became

best known through a series of paintings that depicted the various racial mixtures in a variety of settings, showing their dress, food, and family lives. In these paintings *zambo* is the label for the lowest form of racially mixed person. These derogatory terms were rarely used on official records of either a religious or government nature but were usually used as epithets; they are found most frequently in criminal records, which reveal that their use triggered brawls, and in records of civil suits over matters of social status.

NICOLÁS LEÓN, *Last castas del México colonial* (1924); LYLE MC ALISTER, "Social Structure and Social Change in New Spain," in *Hispanic American Historical Review* 43, no. 3 (1963): 349–370; MAGNUS MÖRNER, *Race Mixture in the History of Latin America* (1967); JOHN K. CHANCE, *Race and Class in Colonial Oaxaca* (1978); PATRICIA SEED, "Social Dimensions of Race: Mexico City, 1753," in *Hispanic American Historical Review* 62, no. 4 (1982): 569–606; PATRICIA SEED and PHILIP RUST, "Estate and Class in Colonial Oaxaca Revisited," in *Comparative Studies in Society and History* 25 (1983): 703–709, 721–724; RODNEY ANDERSON, "Race and Social Stratification: A Comparison of Working Class Spaniards, Indians, and Castas in Guadalajara, Mexico, in 1821," in *Hispanic American Historical Review* 68, no. 2 (1988): 209–243; DOUGLAS COPE, *Limits of Racial Domination* (1993).

PATRICIA SEED

ZAMORA, RUBÉN (*b.* 9 November 1942), Salvadoran political leader. Born in Cojutepeque, Zamora received his law degree from the University of El Salvador in 1968; at about the same time, he joined the Christian Democratic Party (PDC). In 1969 he moved to England to pursue graduate studies in political science at the University of Essex. He returned to El Salvador after an army-led reformist coup d'état overthrew the repressive government of General Carlos Humberto ROMERO on 15 October 1979. Zamora was appointed secretary of the presidency (chief of staff) to the newly created civilian-military junta. When conservative army officers blocked political and economic reforms that the junta intended to implement, Zamora and most members of the junta and cabinet resigned on 31 December 1979. The PDC made a pact with the military and joined it in a second junta. Zamora's older brother, Mario, the attorney general for the poor, was assassinated by a death squad in late February 1980. Appalled by the increasing human rights violations and the PDC's insistence on continuing its coalition with the military, Zamora and several other leading Christian Democrats resigned from the party on 9 March. Zamora and his family went into exile in Nicaragua.

In April 1980 Zamora helped found the Democratic Revolutionary Front (FDR), a coalition of political parties, unions, and mass organizations. Together with an influential group of former PDC members, he founded the Popular Social Christian Movement (MPSC) in May 1980, and was its secretary-general until 1993. From January 1981 to December 1986 Zamora served as an MPSC member of the Political-Diplomatic Commission of the

FDR and Farabundo Martí Front for National Liberation (FMLN). In October and November 1984 he returned to El Salvador as a member of the FDR-FMLN negotiating team for the first two meetings between the government and revolutionary organizations.

In November 1987 Zamora returned to El Salvador to help build the MPSC. With Guillermo Manuel UNGO and Enrique Roldán, the leaders of the two social democratic parties, Zamora organized the Democratic Convergence on 27 November 1987, which began to participate in national elections with the 1989 presidential elections. Publicly threatened with death on armed forces radio during the 1989 FMLN offensive, Zamora remained in El Salvador. In 1993 he became the coalition candidate for president of the republic of the Democratic Convergence and the FMLN, which had become a legal political party following the 1992 Salvadoran peace accords that ended the eleven-year civil war. He lost the April 1994 election to ARENA candidate Armando Calderon Sol in a run-off. Zamora continues to live in El Salvador and owns a consulting firm. He has consistently described himself politically as a "social Christian." In practice, this has meant embracing socioeconomic policies that are close to the Social Democrats but are informed by progressive, Roman Catholic theology.

JOSEPH S. TULCHIN and GARY BLAND, eds., *Is There a Transition to Democracy in El Salvador?* (1992); TOMMIE SUE MONTGOMERY, "El Salvador," in *Political Parties of the Americas, 1980s to 1990s,* edited by Charles Ameringer (1992); "Armed Struggle and Popular Resistance in El Salvador: The Struggle for Peace," in *The Latin American Left: From the Fall of Allende to Perestroika* (1993); and *Revolution in El Salvador: From Civil Strife to Civil Peace,* 2d ed. (1995); RICHARD STAHLER-SHOLK, "El Salvador's Negotiated Transition: From Low-Intensity Conflict to Low-Intensity Democracy," in *Journal of Interamerican Studies and World Affairs* 36 (Winter 1994): 1–59.

TOMMIE SUE MONTGOMERY

ZAMORANO, AGUSTÍN JUAN VICENTE (*b.* 1798; *d.* 1842), Spanish military officer in California and printer. A native of Saint Augustine, Florida, Zamorano served as a royalist cadet in the Mexican WARS OF INDEPENDENCE. As a lieutenant of engineers, he went to California with Governor José María ESCHEANDÍA in February 1825. While commandant of the presidio at Monterey (1831–1836), Zamorano ordered (from Boston) the first printing press in California in 1834; the first work printed on it, in the same year, was a set of regulations. Zamorano surveyed the Santa Rosa settlement for Governor José FIGUEROA in 1834, and the following year he printed Figueroa's *Manifesto a la República mejicana,* which concerned colonization. He served as commandant of Loreto in 1839–1840 and was named inspector of Alta California in 1842. He died shortly after his arrival in San Diego.

GEORGE L. HARDING, *Don Agustín V. Zamorano: Statesman, Soldier, Craftsman, and California's First Printer* (1934); CECIL

ALAN HUTCHINSON, *Frontier Settlement in Mexican California* (1969).

W. MICHAEL MATHES

ZANJÓN, PACT OF, the armistice that ended the TEN YEARS' WAR, the first Cuban War of Independence, in 1878. It was made possible by the exhaustion of the Cuban rebels, their failure to expand the struggle to the western half of the island, and the astute policies of the Spanish general Arsenio Martínez Campos. The peace did not provide for the independence of Cuba nor for the abolition of slavery, but it did allow a measure of self-government, the liberation of slaves who had joined the rebel army, and freedom for all rebel leaders who agreed to leave Cuba. Many Cubans criticized and refused to accept these terms, among them the mulatto general Antonio MACEO, who staged the celebrated though futile "Protest of Baraguá" for several months. But even Maceo himself had to leave Cuba eventually, and peace returned to the island for a while.

In spite of the disappointment of Zanjón, Cubans did not give up. The Ten Years' War succeeded in creating a strong nationalistic spirit that very soon manifested itself in further attempts at rebellion against Spain.

HUGH THOMAS, *Cuba; or The Pursuit of Freedom* (1971), chap. 22.

JOSÉ M. HERNÁNDEZ

See also **Cuba: War of Independence.**

ZAPATA, EMILIANO (*b.* ca. 8 August 1879; *d.* 10 April 1919), Mexican revolutionary. Born and raised in the village of Anenecuilco in the small south-central state of Morelos, in 1911 Zapata took up arms against the regime of long-time president Porfirio DÍAZ, and quickly became one of the most prominent leaders of the MEXICAN REVOLUTION (1910–1920). He is most often remembered for voicing rural demands for land and local liberties.

Zapata was the ninth of ten children of a *campesino* (peasant) family. He received little schooling, though he did learn to read and write. During his early years, the centuries-long struggle between Morelian villages and HACIENDAS for land and water was becoming increasingly tense as the haciendas sought to expand. Like other young men raised in this environment, Zapata had trouble with the law from an early age: in 1897 he fled Morelos to avoid arrest for a minor infraction at a fiesta. By 1906 he was helping to defend Anenecuilco's land in the courts, and in 1909 he was elected president of the village council.

Meanwhile, national politics were becoming unsettled. In 1910, after an aborted campaign for the presidency, Francisco MADERO called for a revolution against the dictatorship of Porfirio Díaz. In March 1911 Zapata responded by helping form a small guerrilla band. He soon attained leadership of this group, which grew large enough by May to capture the regional center of Cuautla, Morelos. The taking of Cuautla, only about 50 miles south of Mexico City, was an important factor in forcing Díaz from power.

Zapata soon discovered, however, that the new national leadership was more dedicated to democracy than to land reform. The large landowners of Morelos immediately maneuvered to preserve their power in the state, and it gradually became clear that Madero, a hacienda owner himself, identified with them. Zapata was attacked by the conservative Mexico City press, which began calling him the "Attila of the South" in June for the real and imagined atrocities committed by his followers. Under these circumstances he was reluctant to disarm his forces. After weeks of negotiations, in August 1911 troops were sent against him under the command of General Victoriano HUERTA. Zapata returned to the mountains, now to fight an ostensibly revolutionary regime.

To explain their cause to the nation, Zapata and a local schoolmaster named Otilio Montaño composed the

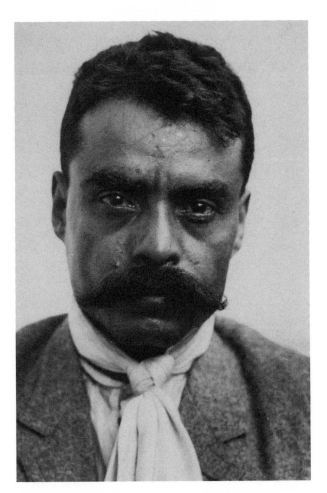

Emiliano Zapata. ARCHIVO HISTÓRICO FOTOGRÁFICO INAH–SEP.

PLAN OF AYALA in November. This document was a remarkable expression of the goals of many of Mexico's peasant rebels. It clarified Zapata's demands for land, calling not only for the return of lands the haciendas had stolen, but for the expropriation of one-third of all hacienda holdings for villages without land titles, and the confiscation of the property of those who opposed Zapata's rebellion. It also insisted on the rule of law and the right of the people to choose their own leaders.

The struggle against Madero lasted until Huerta deposed and assassinated him in a February 1913 coup. Huerta sought to make peace with Zapata, but Zapata did not trust his promises, and the fighting continued. Zapatismo grew as peasants from Morelos, Mexico State, the Federal District, Puebla, Guerrero, and farther afield joined Zapata against the new and in some ways more oppressive regime. As the movement expanded it became more heterogeneous, and it was Zapata's task to discipline it enough to make it a force on the national scene. One measure of his success was that by the summer of 1914 he controlled Morelos and large parts of neighboring states, and threatened Mexico City.

In July 1914 Huerto followed Díaz into exile, and Zapata's forces soon came into contact with the troops of two northern revolutionaries who had also opposed Huerta: Venustiano CARRANZA and Francisco "Pancho" VILLA. Zapata was now confronted with a crucial decision about what kind of alliances, if any, would be most useful to the pursuit of his agenda. Consulting closely with Manuel Palafox, his most prominent intellectual adviser at the time, he eventually sided with the popular Chihuahuan rebel Villa against Carranza, a hacienda owner like Madero who gave little indication that he favored land reform.

By November 1914 the war started again. On 4 December Zapata and Villa met at Xochimilco in the Federal District to firm up their alliance. Two days later they made their official entry into Mexico City, which the Zapatistas had actually occupied in late November. When Zapata captured Puebla on 16 December, it looked as though he and Villa would quickly defeat Carranza, but a series of assassinations in the capital strained relations between the two leaders. Moreover, there was conflict among the urban intellectuals they had put in charge of their national government.

Just before Christmas, Zapata returned to Morelos. With the aid of Palafox, who was minister of agriculture in the new government, he began to carry out the land reform he had promised. In some respects 1915 was a utopian period in Morelos, a time in which Zapata helped the *campesinos* act on their hopes for change in a way that they have seldom been able to do in Mexican history. But internal tensions limited what Zapata could accomplish. Neighboring villages often fought over land and other resources, and differences between Zapatista guerrillas and the civilian population were becoming more evident.

In mid-1915 Villa lost the biggest battles of the revolution to Carrancista general Álvaro OBREGÓN. In early August Zapata's army was driven out of Mexico City, and in the spring of 1916 Carranza's troops invaded Morelos. There was no longer any realistic hope that Zapata might defeat the forces arrayed against him. Some historians contend that this failure was inevitable given the nature of the various revolutionary factions; others have argued that Zapata might have better supported Villa's military effort, or that he might have negotiated a more successful national alliance. In any event, Zapatismo now entered a long decline.

Still Zapata did not give up. With the help of a new chief adviser, Gildardo Magaña, he began to seek alliances with anyone who might help him fight Carranza. But conflict within Zapatismo now reached its highest level, and several prominent leaders defected. The most striking case was that of Otilio Montaño, coauthor of the Plan of Ayala, who was implicated in an uprising against Zapata in May 1917. Zapata ordered Montaño executed to send a message to other would-be traitors, but there was no way to counter the centrifugal forces at work. Zapata's efforts to lure supporters from other revolutionary camps thus became increasingly desperate. Finally, he invited a supposedly disaffected Carrancista colonel named Jesús Guajardo to join him. After exchanging a few letters, on 10 April 1919 Guajardo and Zapata met at a place called Chinameca. With a handful of men Zapata rode through the gate of the hacienda there and Guajardo's troops, assembled as if to give him military honors, shot him dead.

Zapata left a deep mark on Mexican life. Some in Morelos still claim that he is not dead, that a man who looked like him took his place at Chinameca and Zapata is hiding in the mountains until the people need him again. Meanwhile, for both the government of the institutionalized revolution and many of those who have opposed that government over the years, the figure of Zapata has become an enduring symbol of rural Mexico's struggle for justice.

JESÚS SOTELO INCLÁN, *Raíz y razón de Zapata* (1943); JOHN WOMACK, JR., *Zapata and the Mexican Revolution* (1968); ROBERT P. MILLON, *Zapata: The Ideology of a Peasant Revolutionary* (1970); ARTURO WARMAN, *"We Come to Object": The Peasants of Morelos and the National State* (1980); LAURA ESPEJEL, ALICIA OLIVERA, and SALVADOR RUEDA, eds., *Emiliano Zapata: Antología* (1988); SALVADOR RUEDA, "Emiliano Zapata, los signos de un caudillo, biografía de un símbolo," in *Estadistas, caciques y caudillos,* edited by Carlos Martínez Assad (1988), pp. 133–151; ALICIA HERNÁNDEZ CHÁVEZ, *Anenecuilco: Memoria y vida de un pueblo* (1991); SAMUEL BRUNK, "Zapata and the City Boys: In Search of a Piece of the Revolution," in *Hispanic American Historical Review* 73, no. 1 (1993): 33–65; SAMUEL BRUNK, *Revolution and Betrayal in Mexico: A Life of Emiliano Zapata* (1995).

SAMUEL BRUNK

ZAPATA, FELIPE (*b.* 24 May 1838; *d.* 28 July 1902), Colombian Liberal journalist and politician. He was born in Bogotá to a family of the Santander elite and attended the Colegio de Piedecuesta in his home region. He was imprisoned after the Liberals' defeat at Oratorio (1860). As a delegate to the Rionegro Convention (1863), Zapata resisted the extreme federalists and the anticlericals among his colleagues. He was a leading opponent of General Tomás Cipriano de MOSQUERA's increasing authoritarianism, a position revealed in articles published in *La Unión* (March–June 1866) and *El Mensagero* (November 1866–March 1867). In both these Bogotá newspapers, Zapata chipped away at his opponent with calm logic. He later served in several Liberal governments in ministerial roles and was minister plenipotentiary to Great Britain and France in 1874. Zapata did not hesitate to criticize the foibles of his fellow Liberals. He opposed Rafael NÚÑEZ but condemned the Liberal revolutionaries in 1885. He moved to London in that year, becoming a liaison with Francisco Javier CISNEROS and British financiers. He died in London.

RAMÓN ZAPATA, *De los hombres que hicieron historia. Felipe Zapata (El Vidente)* (1971); HELEN DELPAR, *Red Against Blue* (1981), pp. 141–142 and passim.

J. LEÓN HELGUERA

See also **War of the Thousand Days.**

ZAPATISTA ARMY OF NATIONAL LIBERATION. *See* **Mexico: Revolutionary Movements.**

ZAPOTECS, a linguistically related population of indigenous people in the southern Mexican state of OAXACA, of whom there were some 300,000 in the 1990s. Zapotecs have occupied the Oaxaca area since at least 1500 B.C.

The Zapotecs call themselves *bene zaa*, which means either "the native people" or "the cloud people." The term "Zapotec" derives from the NAHUATL *Tzapotecatl*, meaning "people of the *zapote* tree." It was first applied to native inhabitants in Oaxaca by the AZTECS in the fifteenth century.

Present-day Zapotecs are generally divided into four major groups: the Valley Zapotecs, who occupy the fertile Valley of Oaxaca in the center of the state; the sierra or Mountain Zapotecs, occupying the districts of Ixtlán, Villa Alta, and Choapán; the Isthmus Zapotecs, who live on the tropical Isthmus of Tehuantepec; and the Southern Zapotecs of the sierra Miahuatlán region. This distribution corresponds roughly to their location at the time of the Spanish conquest in 1521.

The Zapotec languages (Zapotec and Chatino) belong to Otomanguean, a large linguistic stock that is one of the oldest in MESOAMERICA. It includes a number of other language groups, such as Mixtec, Cuicatec, and Mazatec in Oaxaca, OTOMÍ in the states of Mexico and Hidalgo, and Mangue in Central America, none of which is related to the Mayan or Uto-Aztecan stocks.

Zapotec is a language family or group rather than a single language. The languages within it differ from one another as much as do the modern Romance languages. Scholars disagree about the number of Zapotec languages, some recognizing as few as five while others postulate as many as forty-five.

In pre-Spanish times the Valley Zapotecs had developed one of the earliest writing systems in Mesoamerica (ca. 500 B.C.). Hieroglyphic inscriptions are found in abundance at the ancient Zapotec city of MONTE ALBÁN, now a famous Mexican archaeological site. This metropolis rivaled other Classic Period (ca. 100–900) Mesoamerican cities such as TEOTIHUACÁN in central Mexico, and was built earlier than those in the Maya area. After the fall of Monte Albán around 800, the Zapotecs continued to maintain a distinctive and complex stratified culture at such sites as Zaachila, Mitla, and Yagul in the Valley of Oaxaca and Guiengola near Tehuantepec. The power of Zapotec elites, however, was considerably undermined by invading MIXTECS and Aztecs before the Spanish conquest.

During the Spanish colonial period, Zapotecs were reduced to tribute-paying peasants and today are still predominantly villagers and farmer–artisans. Thus modern Zapotec culture is largely a village culture since Zapotec is, for the most part, spoken only in the home and the village. Modern Zapotec culture is very similar to that of many other parts of rural Mexico and is a complex amalgam of modern Mexican, Spanish colonial, and pre-Hispanic characteristics.

Since the 1970s, many Zapotecs seeking work have migrated to cities in Mexico and to the United States. During this same period, some Valley Zapotec villages, such as Teotitlán del Valle, have specialized in the production of crafts for which they have become nationally and internationally famous. The success of the Teotitlán weavers has brought to the village a renewed pride in its Zapotec heritage that is manifest in the development of programs to preserve Zapotec language and customs. Another town that has shown a particular interest in preserving its Zapotec heritage is Juchitán in the Isthmus region.

The most famous Zapotec is Benito JUÁREZ, born in the sierra village of Guelatao, who was president of Mexico from 1858 to 1872. In recent times, each president of Mexico has made an annual pilgrimage to Oaxaca to celebrate Juárez's birthday, a national holiday.

A general overview of the Zapotecs from earliest times to the present is JOSEPH W. WHITECOTTON, *The Zapotecs* (1984). For the pre-Hispanic period, see KENT V. FLANNERY and JOYCE MARCUS, eds., *The Cloud People* (1983). Good ethnographies of modern Zapotec villages are LYNN STEPHEN, *Zapotec Women* (1991); and LAURA NADER, *Harmony Ideology: Justice and Control in a Zapotec Mountain Village* (1990).

JOSEPH W. WHITECOTTON

ZARACONDEGUI, JULIÁN DE (*d.* 1873), Peruvian merchant. Heavily involved in lending activities in Lima in the 1850s, Zaracondegui had excellent political connec-

tions. By 1860 he had established himself in a variety of enterprises. Owner of a major export-import business in Lima, he was also a member of the Tribunal del Consulado (the merchant regulatory board), a GUANO consignee, a general director of the Banco de Lima, and an officer of the welfare agency called Beneficiencia Pública de Lima. He also served a term in the Chamber of Deputies. In the 1850s Zaracondegui founded a marketing firm to sell Peruvian cotton in Europe, and in 1859 he formed a partnership with the ASPÍLLAGA FAMILY to purchase a cotton plantation in the Saña Valley of the north coast. He put up the necessary cash—the equivalent of $120,000—and the Aspíllagas managed production on the plantation. Soon the cotton failed and the owners turned to sugar, thereafter the main crop in that region.

Zaracondegui's fortunes began to deteriorate after 1870. When one of his partners, Manuel de Argumániz, scandalized Lima by accusing him of undermining the cotton merchandising operation, difficulties befell his other enterprises. The financial crisis of 1873 blindsided many entrepreneurs, Zaracondegui among them, and he committed suicide.

MICHAEL GONZALES, *Plantation Agriculture and Social Control in Northern Peru, 1875–1933* (1985); PAUL GOOTENBERG, *Imagining Development: Economic Ideas in Peru's "Fictitious Prosperity" of Guano, 1840–1880* (1993).

VINCENT PELOSO

ZARAGOZA, IGNACIO (*b.* 1829; *d.* 8 September 1862), Mexican military officer and hero of the battle of PUEBLA (5 May 1862). Born in Bahía de Espíritu Santo, in the Mexican province of Texas, and educated in Matamoros and Monterrey, Zaragoza hoped to pursue a career in business but found his opportunities limited by the devastated condition of the Mexican economy and his status as a mestizo. Zaragoza turned to a traditional occupation in his family—the military. He first joined the militia as a sergeant, and later was accepted into the regular army as a captain in 1853.

Zaragoza supported the PLAN OF AYUTLA in 1854 and spent the rest of his life fighting on the side of the liberals. He fought against Santa Anna's army at Saltillo and in defense of Monterrey. When President Ignacio Comonfort supported the Plan of Tacubaya, Zaragoza organized riflemen in the capital against the conservative forces and in defense of the Constitution of 1857. With Leandro Valle, he led the liberal forces that took Guadalajara from Severo del Castillo and defeated Leonardo Márquez. Zaragoza served as quartermaster under Jesús GONZÁLEZ ORTEGA during the battle of Calpulalpán, where the liberal victory over the conservatives ended the War of the REFORM.

In April 1861 President Benito JUÁREZ named Zaragoza his minister of war, replacing González Ortega, who had resigned in protest of Juárez's policies. Zaragoza held this post until December, when he resigned to take command of the Army of the East, confronting the forces of England, France, and Spain, which had landed in Veracruz that month to force payment of Mexico's foreign debt. After the English and Spanish forces withdrew and the French began their march on Mexico City, Zaragoza lost a battle at Azcultzingo and was forced to retreat. He quickly ordered fortifications built on the small hills of Loreto and Guadalupe that overlooked the city of Puebla. Mexican troops, armed with muskets the British had captured from Napoleon I at Waterloo and had sold to the Mexican government in the 1820s, faced roughly equal numbers of better-equipped and professionally trained French soldiers commanded by General Charles Fernand Latrille, Count of Lorencez. On 5 May 1862, the French made repeated assaults up the slopes of the Cerro de Guadalupe but were beaten back by Zaragoza's army. French casualties numbered roughly one thousand of a force of six thousand. The French retreated to Orizaba to await reinforcements, delaying their invasion of central Mexico for a year and giving Juárez's government time to organize resistance.

The moral and political effects of the victory far outweighed its importance in military terms. Zaragoza's victory over the French at Puebla became a powerful symbol of Mexico's national defiance of foreign interference and the occasion of one of Mexico's most important national holidays, CINCO DE MAYO. Zaragoza died a few months later of typhoid in Puebla.

WALTER V. SCHOLES, *Mexican Politics During the Juárez Regime, 1855–1872* (1957), pp. 70–71, 87–88, 90; GUILLERMO COLIN SÁNCHEZ, *Ignacio Zaragoza: Evocación de un héroe* (1963); JUSTO SIERRA, *Political Evolution of the Mexican People*, translated by Charles Ramsdell (repr. 1969), pp. 293–295, 311–314; RICHARD N. SINKIN, *The Mexican Reform, 1855–1876: A Study in Liberal Nation-Building* (1979), pp. 50, 158, 177; *Diccionario Porrúa de historia, biografía y geografía de México*, 5th ed. (1986).

D. F. STEVENS

See also **French Intervention.**

ZÁRATE WILLKA, PABLO (*d.* 1903), an Aymara Indian from the Bolivian Altiplano who led an Indian uprising that grew out of the Bolivian Civil War (1899). *Willka* is an archaic Aymara word, meaning "greatness" or "eminence," that had previously been used by Indian protest leaders, including Luciano Willka in 1870–1871. We now know that the more important Willka of 1899 was Pablo Zárate, born on an unknown date in Imillaimilla, between Sicasica, La Paz, and Eucaliptus, Oruro.

Zárate, assuming the name *Willka*, originally joined the federalist cause led by José Manuel PANDO, later president of Bolivia, whose main preoccupation was to move the capital from Sucre to La Paz. But Zárate Willka and his Indian contingents soon demanded social changes, including the return of Indian communal lands lost several decades earlier. The uprising turned violent and became extensive. After Zárate Willka's capture in April

1899, the revolt collapsed. He died either while escaping from jail or being transported to another location. However, other versions of his death have some currency.

RAMIRO CONDARCO MORALES, *Zarate, El "Temible" Willka*, 2d enl. ed. (1983), includes lengthy bibliography, pp. 493–504.

CHARLES W. ARNADE

ZARCO, FRANCISCO (*b.* 1829; *d.* 1869), Mexican journalist and politician. Born in Durango's capital, where his father was a minor bureaucrat in the state government and a colonel in the military, Zarco was largely self-educated because his family could not pay for his education. Luis de la Rosa named Zarco to a post in his foreign relations ministry in 1847. Zarco soon turned to journalism, writing political, literary, and biographical articles, some of which earned him the antipathy of President Mariano ARISTA, who had Zarco jailed, and of President Antonio López de SANTA ANNA, who forced him into exile. With the triumph of the Revolution of Ayutla, Zarco was able to return to Mexico and in 1855 was named editor of *El Siglo XIX*, a journal in which he continued to publish until shortly before his death. Representing Durango at the Constituent Congress of 1856–1857, Zarco was elected secretary by acclamation. His history of the congressional debates is a classic work on Mexico's political history. Zarco served as floor manager for the provisions of Constitution, known as the LEY LERDO, that would force the church to sell its real estate. He defended the law as a prudent measure that would save the government from bankruptcy and benefit the clergy as well as the government. Later events pushed Zarco to recommend the confiscation of clerical property on the grounds that the clergy, by supporting the Rebellion of the Polkos in 1847 and the FRENCH INTERVENTION after 1861, had proven to be disloyal to the nation and an "enemy of the people."

At the beginning of the War of the REFORM in 1858, Zarco was arrested by the conservative government but managed to escape. In hiding, he continued to publish for two years, until he was discovered and jailed again. The liberal victory brought his release in December 1860, and the following month, President Benito JUÁREZ asked Zarco to serve as his minister of government and minister of foreign relations. Zarco negotiated a settlement of French claims but resigned when the Mexican congress rejected the proposed treaty.

Zarco remained a supporter of Juárez in congress and his adviser. He continued publishing in Mexico City until May 1863, when the French forces approached, then moved north to San Luis Potosí and later to the United States, where he kept the international community informed about Mexico's struggle for national sovereignty and resistance to monarchy and aristocracy. After the defeat of the Empire, Zarco returned to Mexico and was again elected to the national legislature.

FRANCISCO ZARCO, *Historia del Congreso extraordinario constituyente de 1856–1857*, 5 vols. (1898–1901; repr. 1956); WALTER V.

SCHOLES, *Mexican Politics During the Juárez Regime, 1855–1872* (1957), pp. 6, 60, 69, 92–97, 130–131; RAYMOND CURTIS WHEAT, *Francisco Zarco, el portavoz liberal de la Reforma*, translated by Antonio Castro Leal (1957); RICHARD N. SINKIN, *The Mexican Reform, 1855–1876: A Study in Liberal Nation-Building* (1979), pp. 49, 121, 134, 150–151; *Diccionario Porrúa de historia, biografía y geografía de México*, 5th ed. (1986).

D. F. STEVENS

See also **Anticlericalism.**

ZARUMILLA, BATTLE OF (also known as the battle of Zarumilla-Chacras), 25 July 1941, was fought between Ecuadoran and invading Peruvian troops over disputed border territory in the Ecuadorian coastal province of El Oro. Border skirmishes flared up in 1941 and rapidly escalated into a serious engagement. Ecuadorian President Carlos Alberto ARROYO DEL RÍO nevertheless kept the nation's better units of troops stationed in Quito, choosing to guard his beleaguered presidency against internal enemies. Peru's attack overwhelmed Ecuador's meager defenses. Ecuador suffered some 150 killed and wounded; Peru, about 400. Peru seized El Oro and began to move on the important port city of Guayaquil. As Peru advanced and bombed coastal towns, troops in Guayaquil mutinied. In January 1942 the two nations agreed to the Rio Protocol, whereby Ecuador yielded to demands for 80,000 square miles in exchange for Peru's withdrawal from El Oro. In August 1960 populist Ecuadorian president José María VELASCO IBARRA declared the treaty null and void.

For the most evenhanded treatment of competing boundary claims, see DAVID HARTZLER ZOOK, JR., *Zarumilla–Marañón: The Ecuador–Peru Dispute* (1964). A brief overview can be found in JOHN D. MARTZ, *Ecuador: Conflicting Political Culture and the Quest for Progress* (1972); and GEORGE I. BLANKSTEN, *Ecuador: Constitutions and Caudillos* (1964).

RONN F. PINEO

ZAVALA, JOAQUÍN (b. 30 November 1835; d. 30 November 1906), president of Nicaragua (1879–1883, 1893). Zavala, a native of Managua, continued work on the Pacific Railroad, extended telegraph lines to Las Segovias, favored public education, founded the National Library, and continued the process of secularization by decreasing church influence in both government and education. In addition, he maintained peace in the country.

Zavala, a Conservative, was reelected to the presidency in 1893 when acting President Salvador Machado stepped down in the face of a rebellion led by the Genuines, a splinter group of the Conservative Party, and by Liberals commanded by José Santos ZELAYA. Zavala, however, was an ally and friend of Zelaya's and thought Zelaya could bring modernity to Nicaragua. Nonetheless, Zavala and Zelaya engaged in two battles to determine their country's future. Zavala lost both of these

crucial battles, and his administration quickly fled Managua, leaving the government to Zelaya.

SARA LUISA BARQUERO, *Gobernantes de Nicaragua, 1825–1947* (1945), esp. pp. 139–141; BENJAMIN I. TEPLITZ, "The Political and Economic Foundations of Modernization in Nicaragua: The Administration of José Santos Zelaya, 1893–1909" (Ph.D. diss., Howard University, 1973), esp. pp. 9, 26–30.

SHANNON BELLAMY

ZAVALA, JOSÉ VÍCTOR (b. 1815; d. 1886), Guatemalan military leader. As a young CORREGIDOR, Zavala provided aid that was crucial to José Rafael CARRERA's 1848 return to power. By 1854 Zavala was a core member of Carrera's new government, which also included Zavala in-laws José Najera, Manuel Francisco PAVÓN AYCIENA, and Luís BATRES JUARROS.

Zavala continued his military climb with the successful 1854 siege of Omoa and with the command of Guatemalan troops during the NATIONAL WAR (1856–1857) against William WALKER. Zavala returned to Guatemala as a national hero and proven Carrera ally. His general popularity as a moderate progressive led to public outrage over his loss in the 1869 presidential election. Zavala climaxed his career as commander in chief of the army of Liberal Justo RUFINO BARRIO, who attempted to unify Central America.

JOAQUÍN ZAVALA URTECHO, "Huellas de una familia vasco-centroamericana en cinco siglos," in *Revista de pensamiento conservador de Centroamerica* 24, no. 1 (1970): 140–190; RALPH LEE WOODWARD, *Rafael Carrera and the Emergence of the Republic of Guatemala, 1821–1871* (1993).

EDMOND KONRAD

ZAVALA, LORENZO DE (b. 3 October 1788; d. 15 November 1836), Mexican politician and writer. Born in Mérida, Yucatán, Zavala distinguished himself as a liberal member of the San Juan group in Mérida during the first constitutional period (1810–1814). Incarcerated in 1814, he spent three years in prison. Elected deputy to the restored Spanish Cortes in 1820, Zavala joined other American deputies in favoring home rule. He returned to Mexico in 1822 and was elected to the First Constituent Congress. He sided with Mexico's emperor, Agustín de ITURBIDE, when he dissolved the congress.

After the fall of the monarchy Zavala was elected to Congress once again, this time as a federalist. He joined the *yorkinos* (York Rite Masons) in 1825, becoming a leading radical. In 1827, Zavala was elected governor of the state of Mexico, where he introduced legislation to disentail church property and to break up village lands to encourage private ownership. The following year he joined the revolt of ACORDADA, eventually becoming minister of the treasury in the Vicente GUERRERO administration. In that capacity he had the temerity to levy new taxes in a vain attempt to restore sound fiscal policy. Driven out of office in 1829, Zavala traveled to the

United States and Europe, where he wrote *Ensayo histórico de las revoluciones de Mégico*. He returned to Mexico and to politics in 1832; the following year he was elected to Congress once again. Shortly thereafter, he accepted the post of minister to France, where he remained until 1835.

With the collapse of federalism, Zavala returned to Texas, where he owned vast properties as a result of many years of land speculation. When Texas declared independence, he joined the separatists, becoming the first vice president of that republic. Suffering from poor health, he died in 1836, apparently from pneumonia.

RAYMOND ESTEP, *Lorenzo de Zavala: Profeta del liberalismo mexicano* (1952) and "Lorenzo de Zavala and the Texas Revolution," in *Southwestern Historical Quarterly* 57 (January 1954): 332–335; CHARLES MACUNE, *El estado de México y la federación mexicana* (1978); BARBARA A. TENENBAUM, *The Politics of Penury: Debts and Taxes in Mexico, 1821–1856* (1986).

JAIME E. RODRÍGUEZ O.

ZAVALA, SILVIO (*b.* 7 February, 1909), Mexican historian known for his work on the economic history of sixteenth-century Mexico, the political philosophy of the Spanish Conquest, and the nature of colonial economic institutions. Born in Mérida, Yucatán, he received a doctorate in law from the Universidad Central de Madrid in 1931. Zavala founded and served as director of the *Revista de historia de América* (1938–1965). He was also director of the National History Museum (1946–1954) and president of the Historical Commission of the Pan-American Institute of Geography and History (1947–1965). Zavala founded and was director of the Centro de Estudios Históricos at El Colegio de México (1940–1956) and was president of the college from 1963 to 1966. On the diplomatic front, he represented Mexico as permanent delegate to the United Nations for Education, Science and Culture (1956–1963) and as ambassador to France (1966–1975).

Zavala's scholarly work includes a pioneering study on the nature of the colonial labor systems, *La encomienda indiana* (1935), and one on colonial law, *Las instituciones jurídicas en la conquista de América* (1935). He published eight volumes of documents on labor, *Fuentes para la historia del trabajo en Nueva España* (1939–1946). His work is wide-ranging and includes *Francisco del Paso y Troncoso: Su misión en Europa, 1892–1916* (1938) and other substantial contributions to the study of colonial institutions in Spanish America.

FRANÇOIS CHEVALIER, "Silvio Zavala, primer historiador de la América hispano indígena, el caso del trabajo de la tierra," in *Historia Mexicana* 39, no. 153 (1989): 21–32; SILVIO ZAVALA, "Apreciación sobre el historiador frente a la historia," in *El historiador frente a la historia*, by Horacio Crespo et al. (1992), pp. 47–56.

CARMEN RAMOS-ESCANDÓN

ZAYAS Y ALFONSO, ALFREDO (*b.* 21 September 1861; *d.* 11 April 1934), president of Cuba (1921–1925). An urban leader of the struggle against Spanish domination, Zayas held many offices after independence: president of the Senate (1905), revolutionary leader (1906), and adviser to the occupation authorities during the second U.S. intervention in Cuba (1906–1909). In 1909–1913 he was vice president and in 1921 finally succeeded in ascending to the presidency.

Historians usually focus on the nepotism, graft, and corruption that characterized Zayas's administration and tend to underemphasize his achievements. Nevertheless, despite his mismanagement, Zayas reestablished Cuba's international credit, which had been suffering from a sugar crisis. He succeeded in keeping within certain bounds the interference of U.S. envoy General Enoch CROWDER. And he secured title to the Isle of Pines in 1925 after twenty years of U.S. procrastination. Above all, Zayas recognized that Cuba was undergoing a period of transition and that new social and political forces were emerging in the country. While in office, he had to face increasing student turbulence at the University of Havana, numerous bitter strikes, and even an uprising organized by the Veterans' and Patriots' Association. But Zayas preferred compromise to violence and managed to keep the peace. He always respected the right to dissent. In 1925, unable to secure his own reelection, he ceded the presidency to General Gerardo MACHADO Y MORALES and retired to private life.

A good study on Zayas by Nestor T. Carbonell appears in the PATRONATO RAMON GUITERAS INTERCULTURAL CENTER's *Presidentes de Cuba* (1987), pp. 139–179.

JOSÉ M. HERNÁNDEZ

ZEA AGUILAR, LEOPOLDO (*b.* 30 June 1912), Mexican philosopher and scholar. One of the leading intellectual historians and philosophers in Latin America, Zea obtained undergraduate and graduate degrees from the National Autonomous University of Mexico (UNAM). His distinguished career has included important administrative positions, an impressive publication record, and the mentorship of generations of Latin American students. Among his most celebrated books are: *El apogeo y decadencia del positivismo en Mexico* (1944), *Dos etapas del pensamiento hispanoamericano* (1949), *América en la historia* (1957), and *Filosofía de la historia de América* (1976). He has received numerous academic awards from all over the world and has been instrumental in the development of Latin American intellectual centers and scholarship throughout Latin America.

DAVID MACIEL

ZEBALLOS, ESTANISLAO (*b.* 22 July 1854; *d.* 4 October 1923), Argentine statesman and intellectual. As minister of foreign affairs under presidents Miguel JUÁREZ CELMAN (1888–1890), Carlos PELLEGRINI (1891–1892), and José FIGUEROA ALCORTA (1906–1908), and minister to the U.S. government between 1893 and 1896, Zeballos played a key role in determining Argentine foreign policy during the liberal-conservative era.

Zeballos began his political career as a provincial deputy in Buenos Aires in 1879; he was elected in 1880 and again in 1884 to the National Congress. During his periods as minister of foreign affairs, Zeballos continued the line adopted by the Argentine delegation to the 1889 Pan-American Conference in Washington D.C.: a rejection of any hemispheric economic agreement that could jeopardize Argentine connections with European markets. Also of great consequence for Latin American international relations at the turn of the century was Zeballos's personal feud with José Maria da Silva Paranhos, Barão de RIO BRANCO, a Brazilian diplomat. After 1906, as President Figueroa Alcorta's foreign minister, Zeballos embarked upon an arms race with Brazil which—although Zeballos resigned in 1908—continued until 1914. In 1910, Zeballos became one of the delegates to the fourth Pan-American Conference in Buenos Aires. He was reelected to Congress for the 1912–1916 period and continued to influence public life through his writings on international relations. He wrote frequently for the press, mainly *El Nacional,* which he founded, and *La Prensa.* He also founded and directed a prestigious academic journal, *Revista de Derecho, Historia y Letras.* Professor of international law, he was appointed dean of the University of Buenos Aires Law School in 1910 and 1918. Zeballos was also a founder of the Sociedad Científica Argentina and president of the Sociedad Rural Argentina.

On Zeballos and Argentine foreign policy, see THOMAS F. MC GANN, *Argentina, the United States, and the Inter-American System, 1880–1914* (1957); HAROLD F. PETERSON, *Argentina and the United States* (1964); and ALBERTO CONIL PAZ, "Zeballos y Drago," and GUSTAVO FERRARI, "La Argentina y sus vecinos," both in *La Argentina del ochenta al centenario,* edited by G. Ferrari and E. Gallo (1980).

EDUARDO A. ZIMMERMANN

ZELAYA, JOSÉ SANTOS (*b.* 31 October 1853; *d.* 17 May 1919), president of Nicaragua (1893–1909). Zelaya came to the presidency of Nicaragua in September 1893 by means of a revolution. His presidency was important to Nicaragua from several points of view. Politically, Zelaya's presidency constitutes the only substantial interval of rule by the Liberal Party in Nicaragua's history until the 1930s and the arrival of the Somozas. Liberal rule resulted in several important measures to secularize and modernize Nicaraguan society. Economically, Zelaya presided over a commercial expansion that had considerable effect on Nicaragua's citizens. Internationally, his administration coincided with the period of

José Santos Zelaya, ca. 1906. LATIN AMERICAN LIBRARY, TULANE UNIVERSITY.

Nicaragua's greatest influence on its Central American neighbors.

Although critics often make light of the ideological commitments of Central American political figures, there is no doubt that Zelaya was committed to Liberal reforms. The Constitution of 1893 strengthened municipal government, separated church and state, prohibited convents and monasteries, guaranteed lay education, established a unicameral legislature, and abolished the death penalty. Like other POSITIVIST Latin American leaders, Zelaya was dedicated to bringing economic progress to his country, even by authoritarian methods. He undertook measures to promote export agriculture and granted concessions for the purpose of exploiting natural resources. Railway construction and the building of steamships for use on lakes Managua and Nicaragua received particular attention. Zelaya's zeal for reform, his commitment to economic progress and education, and his youthful cabinet contributed to making Managua an important headquarters for Liberals from northern South America and Central America during his presidency.

Despite democratic procedures outlined in the Constitution of 1893, Zelaya managed elections and ruled as a dictator. He faced approximately fifteen serious efforts by Conservatives to overthrow him. Having modernized and strengthened the Nicaraguan army, Zelaya had little difficulty suppressing his opponents. Unsuccessful rebels were jailed, received amnesty, and often fought again. He was not unusually repressive compared with other Central American presidents of the time.

It was in the field of international affairs that Zelaya made his most significant mark. Sympathetic to the alluring idea of restoring the Central American confederation, he lent his support in 1895 to the creation of the República Mayor, a union of Nicaragua, El Salvador, and Honduras. Although he was an admirer of Justo Rufino BARRIOS, the Guatemalan president who attempted to restore the confederation by force in 1885, Zelaya took no military measures to preserve the union of the three states. When a coup in El Salvador threatened the union, Zelaya counseled nonintervention, and the union collapsed. During the period 1902–1905, he promoted numerous international peace conferences among the Central American states.

Nicaraguan relations with Honduras and Costa Rica, Nicaragua's immediate neighbors, were primarily peaceful in the early years of Zelaya's presidency, although they deteriorated in 1907–1909. Zelaya initiated negotiations resulting in the signing of a treaty that, when it was finally accepted long after Zelaya's presidency, ended a border dispute between Honduras and Nicaragua. The border with Costa Rica, which had been determined by treaty in 1858 but was not marked, also occupied Zelaya's attention. Negotiations with Costa Rica led to the marking of the border in 1898.

Problems with Great Britain and the United States were not so easily resolved. In his first year in office Zelaya determined to recapture Nicaraguan sovereignty over the Miskito Coast, which had been yielded formally by Great Britain over thirty years earlier but which was still subject to British influence over the Miskito Indians. Zelaya sent troops to Bluefields, headquarters for the Miskitos, and expelled the British consul, provoking British wrath and a brief British blockade of the port of Corinto. In the end Zelaya prevailed. A treaty accepting full Nicaraguan sovereignty was signed by Great Britain in 1904. The Miskito Coast was appropriately named the Department of Zelaya in recognition of his bold action.

The United States sided with Nicaragua on the issue of Miskito sovereignty, but other problems steered Nicaraguan relations with the United States on a perilous course. In the late 1890s, when it appeared that engineers preferred a Nicaraguan route for the proposed isthmian canal, negotiations stalled over Zelaya's resistance to Washington's demand for extraterritorial juris-

diction over the canal zone. When canal construction began in 1904 in Panama, the United States closely watched Zelaya, who was rumored to be courting other nations for possible construction of a rival canal. In 1907, when rivalry between Nicaragua and Guatemala spilled over into Honduras and El Salvador, threatening the stability of the Central American isthmus, Washington began to consider Zelaya a meddler and a threat to peace. An incident in 1909 involving the execution of two U.S. mercenaries led to a decision by Washington to support a rebellion against Zelaya. Recognizing that he could not stay in office against the opposition of the United States, Zelaya resigned and went into exile in December 1909.

CHARLES L. STANSIFER, "José Santos Zelaya: A New Look at Nicaragua's 'Liberal' Dictator" in *Revista/Review Interamericana* 7, no. 3 (1977): 468–485, is the principal English-language source on Zelaya. DANA G. MUNRO, *Intervention and Dollar Diplomacy in the Caribbean, 1900–1921* (1964), tracks the relations of the Zelaya administration with the United States, but always taking the point of view of the United States. A dissertation by JOHN E. FINDLING, "The United States and Zelaya: A Study in the Diplomacy of Expediency" (University of Texas, 1971), provides more detail on the relations between the United States and Nicaragua in the Zelaya era than is available in Munro. Neither Munro nor Findling has much to say about domestic issues. Of the Spanish-language sources, JOSÉ DOLORES GÁMEZ, *Remembranza histórica del General J. Santos Zelaya* (1941), and ENRIQUE AQUINO, *La personalidad política del General José Santos Zelaya* (1945) are the best.

CHARLES L. STANSIFER

See also **Nicaragua: Constitutions.**

ZELAYA SIERRA, PABLO (*b.* 1896; *d.* 1933), twentieth-century Honduran painter. Zelaya studied at the Academy of Fine Arts of Costa Rica and subsequently at the San Fernando Academy in Madrid, where he came under the strong influence of Daniel Vásquez Díaz before returning to Honduras. His painting of *Las Monjas* was especially praised and was representative of his paintings while at San Fernando Academy. Although he died young, his neorealist painting made a strong impression in Honduras. His formal style exhibited strong technical perfection, but he often emphasized the figurative rather than the literal. He is credited with applying the Spanish style of Vásquez Díaz to Honduran motifs. His paintings *La muchacha del huacal* and *Dos campesinas* are especially fine examples of this.

J. EVARISTO LÓPEZ and LONGINO BECERRA, *Honduras: 40 pintores* (1989).

RALPH LEE WOODWARD, JR.

ZELEDÓN, BENJAMÍN FRANCISCO (*b.* 4 October 1879; *d.* 4 October 1912), Nicaraguan Liberal general. The Liberal–Conservative coalition formed in the wake of the overthrow of dictator José Santos ZELAYA (1909) proved to be extremely unstable. In July 1912, Minister of War Luis Mena revolted against Conservative President Adolfo DÍAZ. Mena's chief lieutenant, Benjamín Zeledón, followed suit, to protect the coffee interests. Zeledón quickly seized Managua, Granada, and Masaya. Díaz grew increasingly concerned and requested military assistance from U.S. President William Howard Taft, who dispatched a Marine contingent on 4 August 1912. The marines soon numbered 2,700. Mena, outnumbered and overwhelmed, fled the country, leaving the struggle to Zeledón. Both marines and Nicaraguan troops loyal to Díaz pursued Zeledón, who was killed at El Arroyo while attempting to break out of a U.S. encirclement. The victors paraded Zeledón's body on horseback in order to discourage further rebellions.

Doctor General Benjamín F. Zeledón (Managua, 1980); GREGORIO SELSER, *Sandino: General of the Free,* translated by Cedric Belfrage (1981); LESTER D. LANGLEY, *The Banana Wars: United States Intervention in the Caribbean, 1898–1934* (1983); JOHN A. BOOTH, *The End and the Beginning: The Nicaraguan Revolution,* 2d ed. (1985), esp. p. 31; DONALD C. HODGES, *Intellectual Foundations of the Nicaraguan Revolution* (1986).

SHANNON BELLAMY

ZEMPOALA. *See* **Cempoala.**

ZEMURRAY, SAMUEL (*b.* 18 January 1877; *d.* 30 November 1961), Bessarabian immigrant who arrived impoverished in the United States in 1892 and amassed a $30 million fortune in the BANANA INDUSTRY. From 1911, when he financed a revolution in Honduras in order to gain valuable concessions for his CUYAMEL FRUIT COMPANY on the Honduran north coast, until his retirement as president of UNITED FRUIT COMPANY in 1951, he was one of the most powerful North Americans in Central America.

Zemurray began modestly, selling overripe bananas he acquired from United Fruit to upcountry Alabama towns. Later, he acquired a STEAMSHIP to ferry bananas from the north Honduran coast to Gulf coast ports. Cuyamel began as a small company of minor annoyance to United Fruit, but Zemurray (who recognized that knowledge of local conditions was critical in the industry) expanded his business rapidly, especially after the 1911 Honduran revolution. By the 1920s, Cuyamel became more and more a threat to United Fruit's interests, especially in the banana lands along the Honduran-Guatemalan border.

Zemurray anticipated that United would try to absorb Cuyamel, so he secretly began acquiring United stock. In 1929, he accepted United's offer of 300,000 shares of stock for his interest in Cuyamel. With a $30 million account in his ledger, he retired to an estate outside New Orleans and became involved in various philanthropic projects, among them the Middle Amer-

Samuel "the Banana Man" Zemurray. ELIOT ELISOFON, LIFE MAGAZINE / © 1951 TIME INC.

ican Institute at Tulane University. But when the worth of United stock fell to $10 a share during the Great Depression legend has it that Zemurray stormed into United offices, threw his shares on the table, and declared he was taking over. He became managing director of the company in 1933. Zemurray then went back to Central America, fought the Sigatoka disease that was devastating the banana plantations, and in a few years returned United to profitability. He became president of the company in 1938.

THOMAS P. MC CANN, *An American Company* (1976); THOMAS L. KARNES, *Tropical Enterprise* (1978); WALTER LA FEBER, *Inevitable Revolutions: The United States in Central America* (1983).

LESTER D. LANGLEY

See also **United States–Latin American Relations.**

ZENIL, NAHUM BERNABÉ (*b.* 1 January 1947), Mexican painter. Zenil, a native of Chicontepec, Veracruz, graduated from the National Teachers School in 1964 and began to teach primary school. In 1972 he completed studies at the National School of Painting and Sculpture, then continued to teach and paint until the late 1980s, when he dedicated himself to painting full time. Zenil's mixed-media paintings, generally self-portraits done on paper, address social circumstances and traditions in contemporary Mexican society, such as sexual identity, religion, and the family. His paintings are highly personal and autobiographical. Zenil is much influenced by the work of Frida KAHLO and popular painting of the nineteenth century, including the traditional *ex-voto* and *retablo* formats. He often incorporates text into his compositions. Zenil's work is consistently imbued with a profound gay sensibility. His first important exhibitions were held at the Galería de Arte Mexicano, in Mexico City, in 1985. Since that time he has been exhibited and collected internationally.

EDWARD J. SULLIVAN, "Nahum Zenil's 'Auto-Iconography,' " in *Arts Magazine* 63 (November 1988): 86–91, and *Aspects of Contemporary Mexican Painting* (1990), esp. pp. 67–74; LUIS CARLOS EMERICH, *Nahum B. Zenil . . . presente* (1991).

CLAYTON C. KIRKING

ZENO GANDÍA, MANUEL (*b.* 10 January 1855; *d.* 30 January 1930), Puerto Rican writer and politician. Zeno Gandía was born in Arecibo, Puerto Rico, where he attended elementary school. He did undergraduate and graduate work in medicine in Barcelona and Madrid, respectively. During this time he met the Cuban José MARTÍ, with whom he established a friendship that influenced him in literature and politics. Through his novels, newspaper articles, and poetry Zeno Gandía exposed the major social, economic, ethical, and political problems that afflicted Puerto Rico during the nineteenth and early twentieth centuries. In the political arena he fought for Puerto Rican independence from Spain and from the United States. In 1902 Zeno Gandía bought *La Correspondencia*, a newspaper in which he criticized public officials. Because of this criticism he was sued for libel by a U.S. representative, a case he won in the U.S. Supreme Court. In 1904 Zeno Gandía participated in the founding of the Partido de Unión de Puerto Rico, which remained dominant in Puerto Rican politics until the mid-1920s.

Zeno Gandía is considered by many to be Puerto Rico's most important novelist of the nineteenth century, because his works represent the first serious realization of the genre in his country. His novels *La charca* (1894), *Garduña* (1896), *El negocio* (1922), and *Redentores* (1925) were grouped together under the series title of *Crónicas de un mundo enfermo*. In *La charca*, his best-known novel, which richly portrays the rural nineteenth-century Puerto Rican, he expressed all of his theories on naturalism and determinism.

LUZ MARÍA UMPIERRE, *Ideología y novela en Puerto Rico* (1983).

MAYRA FELICIANO

ZEPEDA, ERACLIO (*b.* 24 March 1937), Mexican author. Born in Chiapas, Zepeda was educated at the Universidad Veracruzana, where he also taught. Considered the premier writer and storyteller in Mexico, Zepeda concentrates mostly on the indigenous culture of Chiapas. In 1959, he gained national prominence with the publication of *Benzulul*, a book of indigenous stories. Most of his work is socially oriented, speaking of humanity's basic needs and its relationship to nature. *Asalto nocturno* (1973; Nocturnal Assault) won Mexico's national prize for the best short-story collection in 1974. Also a renowned poet and member of La Espiga Amotinada, Zepeda, with four friends, published the collective work *La espiga amotinada* (1960) and *Ocupación de la palabra* (1965). These anthologies collected the works of a generation of Mexican poets who grounded their poetry in the social reality of the country. Other members of La Espiga Amotinada were Juan Banuelos, Oscar Oliva, Jaime Augusto Shelley, and Jaime Labastida. As a political activist, actor, and popular television personality, Zepeda is a forceful and affirmative figure, having earned worldwide respect and recognition. Other major works are *Andando el tiempo* (1982; Time Marching On), *Relación de travesía* (1985; Cross-Street Story), and *Confrontaciones* (1985; Confrontations).

JOSEPH SOMMERS, "El ciclo de Chiapas: Nueva corriente literaria," *Cuadernos Americanos* 2 (1964): 246–261; BARBARA L. C. BRODMAN, *The Mexican Cult of Death in Myth and Literature* (1976), pp. 76–82; JOSEPH SOMMERS, "Eraclio Zepeda y el oficio de narrar," in *La brújula en el bolsillo* (1982), pp. 14–25; JEANNE C. WALLACE, "Eracillo Zepeda," in *Dictionary of Mexican Literature*, edited by Eladio Cortés (1992).

JEANNE C. WALLACE

ZEPEDA Y ZEPEDA, JUAN DE JESÚS (*b.* 20 November 1808; *d.* 20 April 1885), bishop of Comayagua, Honduras (1861–1885). Zepeda was born in San Antonio de Oriente and ordained a Franciscan priest in 1832. He became Guatemalan auxiliary bishop in 1859 and in 1861 was named bishop of Comayagua, where he soon distinguished himself as a friend of the needy and as a peacemaker. When Liberal President Marco Aurelio SOTO initiated anticlerical legislation in 1879–1880, Zepeda, in poor health, complained but promised not to resist if the state provided funds to partly compensate for the loss of the tithe. Soto evidently complied, but when Luis Bográn Baraona became president in 1883, the church was treated more harshly. Financially weakened, it was unable to carry out even basic programs. Consequently, its role in Honduran society was reduced.

ERNESTO FIALLOS, *Bosquejo biográfico del exmo. y. rmo. mons. Dr. Fray Juan de Jesús Zepeda y Zepeda* (1938); JOSÉ MARÍA TOJEIRA, *Panorama histórico de la iglesia en Honduras* (1986), pp. 138–152.

EDWARD T. BRETT

See also **Anticlericalism.**

ZIMMERMANN TELEGRAM. In January 1917, as WORLD WAR I remained stalemated, Germany decided to resume unrestricted submarine warfare, an action likely to cause the United States to enter the war on the side of the Allies. Seeking a means of immobilizing the United States, Germany seized on the U.S. preoccupation with Mexico.

Accordingly, German Foreign Minister Arthur Zimmerman sent the German minister to Mexico, Heinrich von Eckhardt, a wire for President Venustiano CARRANZA proposing that Mexico form an alliance with Germany against the United States, promising German support for Mexico to "reconquer the lost provinces of Texas, New Mexico, and Arizona," and that Japan be approached to join the alliance. The telegram was intercepted by British intelligence. Publication of the message in March caused outrage in the United States, helping to turn public opinion toward a declaration of war against Germany, which was issued 6 April 1917.

The furor regarding the German proposal obscured the fact that the Mexican Revolutionary Government rejected the idea. The event ultimately served to calm Mexican-American relations, as the United States shifted its focus toward Europe.

BARBARA W. TUCHMAN, *The Zimmerman Telegram* (1958); P. EDWARD HALEY, *Revolution and Intervention: The Diplomacy of Taft and Wilson with Mexico, 1910–1917* (1970).

KENNETH J. GRIEB

ZIPA. *See* Muisca.

ZIPAQUIRÁ, CAPITULATIONS OF. The high-water mark of the COMUNERO REVOLT of New Granada was the gathering in May 1781 of a Comunero army, traditionally said to number 20,000 at Zipaquirá, about 30 miles from Bogotá. The authorities remaining in the capital, in the absence of the viceroy, who was at Cartagena, commissioned Archbishop Antonio CABALLERO Y GÓNGORA to negotiate, hoping above all that the revolutionary army could be prevented from entering the city. With regular forces concentrated on the coast, the archbishop felt compelled to grant most of the Comuneros' demands, including repeal of the new taxes that had triggered the uprising and reduction of others. Among the political concessions was the granting of preference to creoles over peninsular Spaniards in appointments to public office. These "capitulations" were ratified on 8 June by the *junta superior de tribunales* in Bogotá, whereupon the Comunero forces began to disperse. However, once the viceroy heard of the agreement, he formally repudiated it.

JOHN LEDDY PHELAN, *The People and the King: The Comunero Revolution in Colombia, 1781* (1978), chaps. 12–14; MARIO AGUILERA PEÑA, *Los comuneros: Guerra social y lucha anticolonial* (1985).

DAVID BUSHNELL

ZIPOLI, DOMENICO (*b.* 16 or 17 October 1688; *d.* 2 January 1726), Italian organist and composer. Born in Prato, Tuscany, Zipoli commenced musical studies early. At the age of twenty-one, he moved to Naples to study with Alessandro Scarlatti. Later teachers included Lavinio Felice Vannucci and Bernardo Pasquini. Zipoli became choirmaster and organist of the Church of the Jesuits in Rome in 1715. He joined the Society of Jesus in 1716, and the following year traveled to Argentina, where he became choirmaster and organist in the Cathedral of Córdoba. His fame as a composer was established in 1716 with the publication of the *Sonate d'intavolatura,* a collection of keyboard music, the first part for organ and the second for harpsichord. Not much survives of the music he composed while in Argentina, and for many years his contribution to Argentine music was primarily thought to consist of his having brought to it music in the style of Scarlatti and Pasquini. But in 1959, in the Sucre Cathedral archives, a copy made at Potosí in 1784 of one of his masses was discovered. In 1966, the compositions *Tantum Ergo* and *Letania* were found in Beni, Bolivia, by Samuel Claro Valdés. While remembered particularly for his harpsichord works, Zipoli composed sonatas and toccatas for various instruments. He died in Córdoba.

NICOLAS SLONIMSKY, *Music of Latin America* (1945); FRANCISCO CURT LANGE, "La música eclesiástica argentina en el período de la dominación hispánica," in *Revista de estudios musicales* 3 (December 1954); SAMUEL CLARO VALDÉS, "La música de las misiones jesuitas de Moxos," in *Revista musical chilena* 108 (July–September 1969); J. P. FRANZE, "La obra completa para órgano de Domenico Zipoli," in *Buenos Aires musical* 29, no. 46 (July 1974); SAMUEL CLARO VALDÉS, *Oyendo a Chile* (1978); GÉRARD BÉHAGUE, *Music in Latin America: An Introduction* (1979).

SERGIO BARROSO

ZORITA, ALONSO DE (Zurita; *b.* 1511/12; *d.* ca. 1585), judge of the Audiencia of Mexico (1556–1564). Zorita held various legal posts in the Caribbean and South America before reaching New Spain and, after ten years there, returned to Spain. Zorita's early career experiences in the fringe areas influenced the direction he took in Mexico attacking the ENCOMIENDA system and promoting the role of the regular clergy, particularly the FRANCISCANS, in dealings with the indigenous peoples.

Zorita left writings on New Spain's indigenous cultures, Nahua government and tribute systems, the Spanish invasion and post-Conquest Christianization efforts, published partly in his *Breve y sumaria relación de los señores de la Nueva España.* Although portions of his writings are based on earlier (now lost) sources, making them especially valuable, controversy nevertheless exists regarding some of his interpretations of the meaning of terms such as *mayeque* and *calpulli* and his remarks about Nahua nobility and municipal officers.

The most recent biography is RALPH H. VIGIL, *Alonso de Zorita: Royal Judge and Christian Humanist, 1512–1585* (1987).

Skepticism about the reliability of some of Zorita's information comes out, for example, in JAMES LOCKHART, *The Nahuas After the Conquest* (1992), pp. 97, 111, 112, 506, 508.

STEPHANIE WOOD

ZORRILLA DE SAN MARTÍN, JUAN (*b.* 28 December 1855; *d.* 3 November 1931), Uruguayan statesman and poet. Zorrilla de San Martín received his early education in Jesuit schools in Montevideo and in Santa Fe, Argentina. He received his law degree in 1877 from the university in Santiago de Chile. Returning to Montevideo in 1878, he took a position in the federal courts. In 1880, Zorrilla was appointed professor of aesthetics at the National University in Montevideo.

Zorrilla is best known as the author of the epic poem *Tabaré* (1888), an homage to the Charrúa Indians and an exaltation of the fusion of Hispanic and indigenous races. The postromantic verses of *Tabaré* recite the story of Uruguay—its people, its civilization, its spirit, and its aspirations. A dynamic orator, Zorrilla was also one of the most revered public figures in Uruguay: a defender of his country's democratic institutions and the voice of Uruguay in its art and music, its heritage and traditions.

In 1878, Zorrilla founded *El bien público*, a Catholic

José Zorilla de San Martín, ca. 1925. ORGANIZATION OF AMERICAN STATES.

periodical. In 1885, his opposition to President Máximo Santos forced him to resign his position as professor of aesthetics at the National University and take refuge in Argentina, where he joined other Uruguayans in unsuccessful efforts to overthrow Santos.

Zorrilla was elected to Congress by the National Party in 1886. In 1892 he went to Madrid as Uruguayan representative to celebrate the four-hundredth anniversary of Columbus's arrival in the New World, and in 1894 served as Uruguayan ambassador in Paris. In 1899, Zorrilla edited *El Bien*, the new name of the journal he had founded. In recognition of his many years of public service, the National University in 1899 conferred on Zorrilla the title of professor of international law.

Zorrilla's political views apparently clashed with the policies of the liberal government of José BATLLE Y ORDÓÑEZ during the years 1903–1904. Despite this opposition, Zorrilla was appointed treasurer of the Bank of the Republic and was reelected as a government delegate every three years thereafter until his death.

RIMAELVO A. ARDOINO, *La prosa de Juan Zorrilla de San Martín* (1945); ENRIQUE ANDERSON IMBERT, "La originalidad de Zorrilla de San Martín," in *Los grandes libros de Occidente y otros ensayos* (1957), pp. 121–163; DOMINGO L. BORDOLI, *Vida de Juan Zorrilla de San Martín* (1961); CARLOS A. SOLÉ and MARIA ISABEL ABREU, *Latin American Writers*, vol. 1 (1989), pp. 327–331.

MYRON I. LICHTBLAU

See also **Literature.**

ZUBIRÁN ANCHONDO, SALVADOR (*b.* 23 December 1898), Mexican physician, educator, and nutritional expert. A 1923 graduate of the National University, Zubirán was one of an important generation of medical students. A disciple of Gastón Melo, he continued his medical studies at Harvard University, and in 1925 joined the medical faculty at the National University, where he taught for many years. He served as first head of the Child Welfare Department (1937), before becoming assistant secretary of health (1938–1943). Appointed rector of the National University in 1946, he resigned in 1948 after a violent student protest. Following his resignation, he directed programs in nutrition, and his efforts contributed substantially to Mexican knowledge in this field. He served as president of the Mexican Academy of Medicine (1947), and received Mexico's National Prize in Sciences (1968).

Doctor Salvador Zubirán, 50 años de vida profesional (1973).

RODERIC AI CAMP

ZUBIRÍA, JOSÉ ANTONIO LAUREANO DE (*b.* ca. 1780; *d.* after 1845), bishop of Durango, Mexico. Zubiría's pronouncements outlined the canonical justification for bringing the new Mexican church back under episcopal control and curbing aspects of folk piety that

Catholic orthodoxy deemed harmful. Although Zubiría could not enforce his decrees, he laid the foundation for the reforms instituted by the first bishops of Santa Fe under American control.

Many of the criticisms that Zubiría leveled against the churches and Franciscan missions in New Mexico reflected the innovations and improvisations that New Mexicans had adopted since the 1760s, when the Spanish province found itself virtually isolated from the rest of Mexico by COMANCHE, APACHE, and Ute raids. Symbolic of his view of New Mexican religious devotion, Zubiría criticized the crude pictures of the saints that some Franciscan missionaries had painted on animal hides because they had little access to religious art imported from Mexico. The combination of episcopal disapproval and the rise of an indigenous style of SANTOS carved from pine wood and decorated with brightly colored tempera on a coat of gesso led to the loss of most hide paintings from the missions during the Mexican period. Zubiría described even the new devotional art as "ugly images."

Zubiría's denunciation of the Brotherhood of PENITENTES during the 1833 visitation is one of the few descriptions of the confraternity during its formative period. He mentioned that the organization had existed "for a good number of years, but without any authorization or even the knowledge of the bishops." He ordered the clergy in New Mexico to forbid Penitente meetings and ritual, because of "the excesses of very indiscreet corporal punishment which they are accustomed to practice . . . even publicly."

Zubiría's condemnation of the Penitentes had little effect. The church failed in its attempt to exert control over the brotherhood until the reforms of 1851–1852 promulgated by Bishop Jean Baptiste Lamy, first bishop of Santa Fe under the jurisdiction of the United States.

ELIZABETH BOYD, *Popular Arts of Colonial New Mexico* (1974); FRANCES LEON SWADESH, *Los Primeros Pobladores: Hispanic Americans of the Ute Frontier* (1974); MARC SIMMONS, *New Mexico: An Interpretive History* (1977); DAVID J. WEBER, *The Mexican Frontier, 1821–1846: The American Southwest under Mexico* (1982); THOMAS J. STEELE, S.J., and ROWENA A. RIVERA, *Penitente Self-Government: Brotherhoods and Councils, 1797–1947* (1985).

ROSS H. FRANK

ZUBIZARRETA, GERÓNIMO (*b.* 9 October 1880; *d.* 14 May 1952), Paraguayan politician and university professor. Zubizarreta studied and later taught law at the National University in Asunción. After joining the Liberal Party in 1909, he occupied various positions in the party as well as in the Paraguayan Congress. Zubizarreta was highly respected for defending Paraguay's legal position before the CHACO WAR erupted between Paraguay and Bolivia in 1932. In 1937 he headed the Paraguayan delegation at the Buenos Aires Peace Conference but resigned in 1938 after losing in a power struggle with Paraguay's leader of the armed forces, General José Félix ESTIGARRIBIA. He was elected presi-

dent of the Liberal Party in 1946, but he was forced into exile the following year after his arrest under President Higínio MORÍNIGO's regime. He returned to Paraguay in 1951 and remained president of his party until his death.

JULIO CESAR CHAVES, "Géronimo Zubizarreta," in *Cien vida paraguayas* (1961), edited by Carlos Zubizarreta; LESLIE ROUT, *Politics of the Chaco Peace Conference, 1935–39* (1970).

MIGUEL A. GATTI

See also **Paraguay: Political Parties.**

ZULEN, PEDRO S. (*b.* 1889; *d.* 1925) and **DORA MAYER DE ZULEN** (*b.* 1868; *d.* 1957), Peruvian intellectuals and leaders of the INDIGENISMO movement. *Indigenismo* has been one of the most controversial aspects of social reform in modern Peru. Alive since the 1880s in the essays of writers like Ricardo PALMA, Clorinda MATTO DE TURNER, and Manuel GONZÁLEZ PRADA, the movement rests on the idea that the culture of the indigenous Andean population is at the core of the country's culture and should receive its due recognition. Several strategies were developed in the early twentieth century to make this idea a reality. Some of the proponents of *indigenismo* worked directly in the highland center of Cuzco, where under the leadership of men like archaeologist Luis E. Valcárcel, the movement became intertwined with the drive to end the abuse of villagers at the hands of landlords. In Lima early-twentieth-century intellectuals, under the leadership of Pedro Zulen and Dora Mayer, sought to unify urban, sophisticated culture with their Andean roots. To do this they founded the Pro-Indigenous Association in 1909. In a weekly newsletter, *El Deber Pro-Indígena*, they fought for legal relief of Andean misery. Senator Joaquín CAPELO and José Antonio ENCINAS later joined their legal struggle. Soon delegates of the Pro-Indigenous Association throughout the country began reporting in the press and in the association newsletter injustices committed against indigenous people. The association recruited lawyers to defend villagers, and to arouse public opinion it sponsored public debates. The Zulens hoped thus to prod the legislature into passing remedial legislation. After 1919 the government of President Augusto LEGUÍA undermined the effectiveness of the association by absorbing its more important efforts into government programs. Laws, decrees, and resolutions reflecting the influence of the *indigenistas* were passed, but Leguía did not try to enforce them against the opposition of major highland landowners. Many highland villagers thereafter became more aware of their legal rights, and by the mid-1920s the *indigenista* movement had been absorbed into the revolutionary and reformist political movements taking shape in Peru.

EUGENIO CHANG RODRÍGUEZ, *La literatura política de González Prada, Mariátegui, y Haya de la Torre* (1957); THOMAS M. DAVIES, JR., *Indian Integration in Peru: A Half Century of Experience, 1900–*

1948 (1974); JOSÉ TAMAYO HERRERA, *Historia del indigenismo cuzqueño: Siglos xvi–xx* (1980).

VINCENT PELOSO

ZULOAGA, FÉLIX MARÍA (*b.* 1813; *d.* 1898), Mexican military officer and president of Mexico (January 1858– January 1859). Born in Álamos, Sonora, Zuloaga was raised in Chihuahua. He studied for a time in Mexico City but returned to the north, where he began a military career by joining the civic militia of Chihuahua in 1834 and fighting the Apaches and Comanches. He then returned to Mexico City, where he passed the engineering exam in 1838 and received a commission as second lieutenant in an engineering battalion of the regular army. He fought against the separatists in Yucatán, and was raised to the rank of lieutenant colonel in 1841. During the war with the United States, Zuloaga directed the fortifications at Monterrey in 1846 and fought in defense of Mexico City in 1847. After the war he returned to Chihuahua, where he held posts in the city government before returning to the army in 1851. He served as President of the Council of War of the Plaza of Mexico under President SANTA ANNA in 1853. Zuloaga fought against the Revolution of Ayutla in 1854 and was raised to the rank of brigadier general before being taken prisoner by the liberals.

After President Ignacio COMONFORT reintegrated him into the army, Zuloaga fought against a conservative rebellion in Puebla before supporting the Plan of Tacubaya in December 1857. The Plan of Tacubaya backed President Comonfort in the struggle between *puros* and *moderados*, and called for a new congress to write a new constitution "more in harmony with the will of the Nation." At first Comonfort supported the plan; then he organized against it and was deposed by General José de la Parra in January 1858. Benito JUÁREZ, head of the supreme court and next in legal succession to the presidency, assumed that office with the support of the liberals. Zuloaga, however, was elected president by the conservative Council of Representatives of the Departments (22 January 1853). This political clash began the War of the REFORM. By presidential decree, Zuloaga annulled the LEY IGLESIAS, the LEY JUÁREZ, and the LEY LERDO, and reinstated all government employees who had lost their jobs for failing to swear allegiance to the Constitution of 1857. For his part in the execution of Melchor OCAMPO, Zuloaga was declared an outlaw by the liberals. He spent the years of the French Intervention in Cuba but returned to Mexico before his death.

WALTER V. SCHOLES, *Mexican Politics During the Juárez Regime, 1855–1872* (1957), pp. 23, 28–29; *Diccionario Porrúa de historia, biografía y geografía de México*, 5th ed. (1986).

D. F. STEVENS

ZUM FELDE, ALBERTO (*b.* 1889; *d.* 1976), Uruguayan poet, literary critic, and essayist. Alberto Zum Felde was born in Bahía Blanca, Argentina, but his parents moved to Uruguay when he was a young child. He joined the intellectual circle headed by Roberto de las Carreras. His poetry was first published under a pseudonym in *La Razón* and *El Siglo*. In 1908 Zum Felde selected the name Aurelio del Hebrón as his pseudonym and his first book, *Domus aurea* (1908), a collection of sonnets and plays, was published under that name. These modernist sonnets and plays reflect both his talent and the influence that Nietzsche and Ibsen had on his writings.

With the publication of *El huanakauri* (1917), Zum Felde began to distance himself from modernist influences. The book, a didactic poem, argues for the autonomous cultural development of the Americas based upon tradition and historical reality. From 1919 until 1929, he worked as a literary critic for the afternoon edition of the newspaper *El Día* (later called *El Ideal*). He served as secretary, assistant director, and director (1940–1944) of the National Library. During the 1920s he also directed the literary magazine *La Pluma*. One of his notable books, *Proceso histórico del Uruguay* (1919) analyzes the sociopolitical evolution of the country. *Crítica de la literatura uruguaya* (1921) is a collection of weekly articles that were published in 1919–1920 in *El Día*. One of his most important books, *Proceso intelectual del Uruguay y crítica de su literatura* (1930), evaluates intellectual and literary production in the country beginning with the colonial period.

Zum Felde has been credited with the professionalization of literary studies in Uruguay. After his conversion to Catholicism, he published *Cristo y nosotros* (1959) and *Diálogo Cristo-Marx* (1971). Zum Felde was one of nine writers who founded the National Academy of Letters in 1943. In 1957 he won the National Literature Prize, and in 1968 he was awarded Uruguay's Grand Prize for Literature.

FRANCISCO AGUILERA and GEORGETTE M. DORN, *The Archive of Hispanic Literature on Tape* (1974), pp. 511–512; URUGUAY CORTAZZO, *La hermeneutica de Alberto Zum Felde* (1983).

DANUSIA L. MESON

ZUMÁRRAGA, JUAN DE (*b.* ca. 1468; *d.* 3 June 1548), first bishop (1528–1547) and archbishop (1547–1548) of Mexico. Fray Juan de Zumárraga was born in Durango, near Bilbao, Spain; his birthdate is unknown but he was said to have been over eighty at death. Impressed by Zumárraga's campaign against alleged Basque witches, Charles V appointed him bishop of Mexico City. Zumárraga arrived in Mexico in 1528 as bishop-elect and Protector of the Indians. Zumárraga went to Spain in 1532 to report to the emperor; he was consecrated as bishop there in 1534. In 1535 Zumárraga joined forces with Don Antonio de MENDOZA, newly arrived first viceroy, to stabilize colonial rule and promote Indian education and Christianization. In 1536 they founded the Colegio de Santa Cruz, a FRANCISCAN college for indigenous nobles. Zumárraga imported a printing press in

1536 and authored or sponsored a number of imprints, including Erasmian tracts. Zumárraga's thinking, typical of Spanish Franciscans, combined Renaissance humanism with mysticism and militant religious zeal. He conducted inquisitorial proceedings against Indians suspected of religious violations; the trials culminated with the 1539 burning at the stake of Don Carlos Mendoza Ometochtzin, native ruler of Texcoco. In 1547 Zumárraga was named archbishop of a new archdiocese comprising the bishoprics of México, Oaxaca, Michoacán, Tlaxcala, Guatemala, and Chiapas; he died soon after receiving the news.

JOAQUÍN GARCÍA ICAZBALCETA, *Don Fray Juan de Zumárraga: Primer Obispo y Arzobispo de México* (1947); RICHARD E. GREENLEAF, *Zumárraga and the Mexican Inquisition, 1536–1543* (1962); ROBERT RICARD, *The Spiritual Conquest of Mexico* (1966).

LOUISE M. BURKHART

See also **Catholic Church.**

ZUMAYA, MANUEL DE (*b.* ca. 1678; *d.* between 12 March and 6 May 1756), Mexican composer and the first Mexican-born chapelmaster of the cathedral of Mexico City. Zumaya was a choirboy at the cathedral and became a pupil of the chapelmaster, the composer and organist Antonio Salazar. At sixteen he began lessons with the principal organist, José de Ydíaquez. Zumaya was ordained a priest in 1700 and a few years later was appointed one of three organists of the cathedral and polyphony teacher of the choirboys; he served as assistant to and substitute for Salazar. At Salazar's death in 1715, Zumaya was designated his successor as cathedral chapelmaster. To celebrate his twenty-four years at the cathedral, a new great organ was installed, considered the best of its kind in the Americas; its inauguration (15 August 1735) was commemorated with lavish festivities.

As a church composer Zumaya followed the traditional Spanish religious music style, but in some of his *villancicos* and in all his stage works he was strongly influenced by Italian opera. The music of the church at that time was not only for organ; strings and wind instruments accompanied the choirs with embellished melodic lines, strongly resembling operatic arias. In 1708 Zumaya had composed the music for *Don Rodrigo* [*El Rodrigo*], a play performed at the viceroyal palace; the manuscript, however, has been lost. The duke of Linares, the viceroy, made possible the performance of Zumaya's opera *La parténope* at the palace in May 1711. After Tomás de TORREJÓN Y VELASCO's *La púrpura de la rosa*, this opera was the second premiered in the New World and the first written by an American-born composer. In 1739 Zumaya moved to Oaxaca, where he became chapelmaster in 1745. He remained in that position until his death in Oaxaca.

ROBERT STEVENSON, *Music in Mexico* (1952), and "Mexico City Cathedral Music, 1600–1750," *The Americas* 21 (1964): 130; *New Grove Dictionary of Music and Musicians*, vol. 20 (1980).

SUSANA SALGADO

ZUMBI (*b.* 1655?; *d.* 20 November 1695), organizer and leader of the free black republic (QUILOMBO) of PALMARES, in Alagoas state, northeastern Brazil. Little information is available concerning the early life of Zumbi and that which is known is subject to speculation. In 1685 he murdered his uncle Ganga Zumba, who had attempted to live in peace with the Portuguese, and proclaimed himself king of Palmares. He was responsible for the strengthening of a series of fortifications that made Palmares almost invincible to attackers. Zumbi's leadership proved effective in defeating a Portuguese expedition against the *quilombo* in 1686. When the forces of the *bandeirante* Domingos Jorge Velho attacked Palmares in 1691, Zumbi's ambushes and counterattacks devastated them. In 1692 attempts were initiated to surround the *quilombo*, but Zumbi's forces were able to hold out until 1694, when a Luso-Brazilian expedition backed by artillery and reinforcements was finally able to destroy Palmares. Zumbi was decapitated and his head displayed in public in order to prevent any further legends of his immortality, but tradition grew about a heroic suicide in which he threw himself off a cliff rather than surrender and submit to enslavement. The actions of Zumbi forced the Portuguese to change their military strategy with regard to MAROON communities; henceforth, special military units were given the task of finding and destroying potentially dangerous fugitive Maroon settlements. Zumbi is considered an African Brazilian hero; his date of death is commemorated each year.

R. K. KENT, "Palmares: An African State in Brazil," in *Journal of African History* 6 (1965): 161–175; LEDA MARIA DE ALBUQUERQUE, *Zumbi dos Palmares* (1978).

MICHAEL L. JAMES

ZÚÑIGA, IGNACIO, nineteenth-century frontier military officer and politician. Zúñiga rose in the colonial army to command a series of presidio garrisons on Mexico's northwestern frontier, beginning with that of Tucson in 1809. As senator and then deputy in the national congress in the late 1820s, he unsuccessfully opposed the division of the state of Occidente into Sonora and Sinaloa. His 1835 treatise (*Rápida ojeada . . .*) detailed the problems of Sonora and proposed measures to alleviate public insecurities and promote enterprise. He supported the federalist revolts of José de URREA in 1837 and SANTA ANNA in 1841, and served as a federal deputy in 1842.

IGNACIO ZÚÑIGA, *Rápida ojeada al Estado de Sonora, territorios de California y Arizona, 1835* (1835; repr. 1948); STUART F. VOSS,

On the Periphery of Nineteenth Century Mexico: Sonora and Sinaloa, 1810–1877 (1982), pp. 87–91, 102–103; FRANCISCO R. ALMADA, *Diccionario de historia, geografía y biografía sonorenses* (1983), p. 746.

STUART F. VOSS

ZÚÑIGA FIGUEROA, CARLOS (*b.* 1884; *d.* 1964), Honduran neorealist painter. Zúñiga studied during the 1920s at the San Fernando Academy in Madrid, where he received wide acclaim. He returned to Honduras to become one of Central America's leading painters in the following decades. His work was exhibited widely in Central America and the United States. He specialized in realistic portraits of ordinary people, but he also painted many contemporary Honduran leaders of society and politics. His series of historical paintings of Honduras's independence leaders, especially his *Glorification of General Morazán*, received favorable recognition. Toward the end of his life he began to focus his work on those at the bottom of the society—vagabonds, beggars, the mentally ill, and the poor. Unfortunately, a great many of these paintings were destroyed in a 1959 fire.

J. EVARISTO LÓPEZ and LONGINO BECERRA, *Honduras: 40 pintores* (1989).

RALPH LEE WOODWARD, JR.

ZUTUHIL. *See* **Tz'utujil.**

APPENDIX
BIOGRAPHIES IN THE ENCYCLOPEDIA

THE encyclopedia contains biographies of nearly 3,000 persons who have affected the course of Latin American history or culture. The present listing attempts a rough classification of these persons according to occupation or field of activity. The division of human endeavor into twenty-one overlapping fields is necessarily imperfect: many individuals have contributed to several areas, and not all activities are included in our categories. Nevertheless, the editors believe this listing offers a convenient starting point for research on the range of human enterprise in Latin America.

The final category ("Women") merely identifies the 168 female subjects treated herein. Many of them have been neglected in previous compendiums. Although comparable treatments of African and indigenous origin would be of considerable interest, the editors did not attempt such classification on the grounds that the American complex of race mixtures and attitudes is not susceptible to schematic breakdown. For further information the reader is directed to the entries on "Race and Ethnicity" and related topics.

Business, Finance, Trade, and Industry

Aldama y González, Ignacio de
Álvarez, Manuel
Andresote
Antuñano, Estevan de
Aramayo Family
Billinghurst, Guillermo Enrique
Brión, Luis
Bunau-Varilla, Philippe Jean
Camacho Roldán, Salvador
Candamo, Manuel
Escandón, Manuel
Farquhar, Percival
Fernández, Max
Fernandini, Eulogio E.
Ferré Aguayo, Luis Antonio
Hopkins, Edward Augustus
Ibarra, Diego
Ibarra, José de Pineda
Irisarri y Larraín, Juan Bautista

Keith, Minor Cooper
Kinney, Henry L.
Krieger Vasena, Adalberto
Lagos, Ricardo
Le Bretón, Tomás Alberto
Leguía, Augusto Bernardino
Limantour, José Yves
López de Quiroga, Antonio
Ludwig, Daniel Keith
Maluf, Paulo Salim
Marinho, Roberto
Martínez de Hoz, José Alfredo
Mauá, Visconde de
Meiggs, Henry
Menocal, Mario García
Mindlin, José E.
Molina Solís, Olegario
Monte Alto
Mora Porrás, Juan Rafael

Noriega Moreno, Manuel Antonio
Noronha, Fernão de
Orlich Bolmarcich, Francisco José
Ottoni, Teofilo Benedito
Pacheco, Gregorio
Palenque, Carlos
Pardo y Lavalle, Manuel
Parra, Aquileo
Pastrana Borrero, Misael
Patiño, Simón Iturri
Pearson, Weetman Dickinson
Pelé
Piérola, Nicolás de
Pinedo, Federico
Piñol y Sala, José
Porras, José Basilio
Prado, Paulo
Prado y Ugarteche, Javier
Prado y Ugarteche, Manuel

Prat Echaurren, Jorge
Prebisch, Raúl
Quijano, Carlos
Ramos Mejá, Ezequiel
Rengifo Cárdenas, Manuel
Ríos Morales, Juan Antonio
Robles, Marcos Aurelio
Rockefeller, Nelson Aldrich
Romero de Terreros, Pedro
Rosas, Juan Manuel de
Roy, Eugène
Ruíz Tagle Portales, Francisco

Sacasa, Juan Batista
Samper, Agudelo
Sancho de Hoz, Pedro
Santos, Silvio
Sardaneta y Llorente, José Mariano de
Simonsen, Mário Henrique
Terrazas, Luis
Tornquist, Ernesto
Trejos Fernández, José Joaquín
Uribe Uribe, Rafael
Vacarro Brothers

Velázquez Cárdenas de León, Joaquín
Vergara Echeverez, José Francisco
Vernet, Louis
Vesco, Robert Lee
Villanueva, Carlos Raúl
Yermo, Gabriel de
Zamorano, Agustín Juan Vicente
Zaracondegui, Julián de
Zavala, Lorenzo de
Zemurray, Samuel

Cinema, Theater, Television, Sports, and Recreation

Acevedo Hernández, Antonio
Alcoriza, Luis
Álvarez Armellino, Gregorio C.
Amorim, Enrique
Armendáriz, Pedro
Arnaz, Desi
Arriví, Francisco
Arrufat, Antón
Capablanca, José R.
Castro, Juan José
Chocrón, Isaac
Clair, Janete
Clemente Walker, Roberto
Córdova, Arturo de
Cugat, Xavier
Del Río, Dolores
Denevi, Marco
Fernández, Emilio "El Indio"

Figueroa, Gabriel
Galindo, Alejandro
Gambaro, Griselda
García, Sara
Garmendia, Salvador
Gavidia, Francisco Antonio
Gómez-Cruz, Ernesto
Marqués, René
Miranda, Carmen
Monterroso, Augusto
Nalé Roxlo, Conrado
Negrete, Jorge
Pardavé, Joaquín
Pelé
Perricholi, La
Prado y Ugarteche, Mariano Ignacio
Ripstein, Arturo

Rojo, María
Sánchez, Florencio
Santos, Sílvio
Sarduy, Severo
Silva, Orlando
Skármeta, Antonio
Soler, Andrés, Domingo, and Fernando
Steimberg, Alicia
Sumac, Yma
Tin-Tan
Triana, José
Uslar Pietri, Arturo
Valle, Rafael Heliodoro
Wolff, Egon
Xuxa
Zorrilla de San Martín, Juan

Education and Scholarship

Aceval, Benjamín
Acosta, José de
Adem Chahín, José
Adem Chahín, Julián
Alcorta, Diego
Alegre, Francisco Javier
Alemán Valdés, Miguel
Alfaro, Ricardo Joaquín
Alonso, Amado
Alvarado, Lisandro
Álvarez Armellino, Gregorio Conrado
Álvarez Gardeazábal, Gustavo
Amorim, Enrique

Amunátegui Aldunate, Miguel Luis
Anchieta, José de
Anderson Imbert, Enrique
Andreoni, João Antônio
Angelis, Pedro de
Arboleda, Carlos
Argüello, Leonardo
Arosemena, Justo
Arzáns Orsúa y Vela, Bartolomé
Ávila, Julio Enrique
Ayala, Eligio
Ayala, Eusebio
Ayala, José de la Cruz
Ayora Cueva, Isidro

Azara, Félix de
Azevedo, Fernando de
Azevedo, Thales de
Bachiller y Morales, Antonio
Baldorioty de Castro, Ramón
Baptista, Mariano
Baquedano, Manuel
Baquíjano y Carrillo de Córdoba, José de
Baralt, Rafael María
Barbero, Andrés
Barnola, Pedro Pablo
Barreda, Gabino
Barreto de Menezes, Tobias, Jr.

Barros, João de
Barros Arana, Diego
Basadre, Jorge
Bassols, Narciso
Bellegarde, Luis Dantès
Bello, Andrés
Benítez, Jaime
Bermejo, Ildefonso
Bernal y García Pimentel, Ignacio
Bingham, Hiram
Bolaños, Luis de
Bolton, Herbert Eugene
Borges, Jorge Luis
Box, Pelham Horton
Bray, Arturo
Brenner, Anita
Bresser Pereira, Luiz Carlos
Brum, Baltasar
Bunge, Alejandro
Bunge, Carlos Octavio
Bustamante y Rivero, José Luis
Caballero y Rodríguez, José Agustín
Cabrera, Lydia
Calcaño, José Antonio
Caldera Rodríguez, Rafael
Calógeras, João Pandiá
Calvo, Carlos
Campos, Francisco Luiz da Silva
Campos, Roberto (de Oliveira)
Cañas, José Simeón
Cané, Miguel
Capelo, Joaquín
Capistrano de Abreu, João
Cardim, Frei Fernão
Cardoso, Felipe Santiago
Cardoso, Fernando Henrique
Caro, Miguel Antonio
Carrillo Flores, Antonio
Carrillo Flores, Nabor
Caso y Andrade, Alfonso
Caso y Andrade, Antonio
Castañeda, Francisco de Paula
Castillo, Jesús
Castillo Ledón, Amalia
Castro Madriz, José María
Centurión, Carlos R.
Cerezo Arévalo, Marco Vinicio
Cervantes, Vicente
Chávez Sánchez, Ignacio
Clavigero, Francisco Javier
Cobo, Bernabé
Coldazzi, Agustín
Coni, Emilio R.
Constant Botelho de Magalhães,
  Benjamin
Cordero Crespo, Luis
Cornejo, Mariano H.
Corona, Ramón

Correoso, Buenaventura
Corvalán Lepe, Luis
Cosío Villegas, Daniel
Coutinho, José Joaquim da Cunha
  de Azeredo
Couto, José Bernardo
Covarrubias, Miguel
Cuervo, Rufino José
Delfim Neto, Antônio
Deustua, Alejandro O.
Di Tella, Torcuato
Dias, Antônio Gonçalves
Díaz de Guzmán, Ruy
Díaz Soto y Gama, Antonio
Dobles Segreda, Luis
Dobrizhoffer, Martín
Domínguez, Manuel
Drago, Luis María
Durão, José de Santa Rita
Elhuyar, Juan José de
Elhuyar y Zúbice, Fausto de
Encina, Francisco Antonio
Escalada, Asunción
Esquiú, Mamerto
Estimé, Dumarsais
Etchepareborda, Roberto
Facio Brenes, Rodrigo
Falcón, José
Faoro, Raymundo
Feijóo, Benito Jerónimo
Fernandes, Florestan
Fernández Artucio, Hugo
Figueiredo, Afonso Celso de Assis
Figueroa Gajardo, Ana
Figueroa Larraín, Emiliano
Francia, José Gaspar Rodríguez de
Freire, Paulo
Freyre, Gilberto (de Mello)
Frías, Antonio
Frigerio, Rogelio
Frondizi, Risieri
Fuentes, Manuel Atanasio
Fúrlong Cárdiff, Guillermo
Furtado, Celso
Galindo, Juan
Gallegos, Rómulo
Galván Rivera, Mariano
Gamio Martínez, Manuel
Gandavo, Pero de Magalhães
Garay, Blas
García, Genaro
García de Castro, Lope
García Diego y Moreno, Francisco
García Icazbalceta, Joaquín
García Robles, Alfonso
García Salinas, Francisco
Garibay Kintana, Ángel María
Gavidia, Francisco Antonio

Gelly, Juan Andrés
Gil Fortoul, José
Golbery do Couto e Silva
Gómez, Benigno
Gondra, Manuel
González, Joaquín Victor
González, Juan Natalicio
González Casanova, Pablo
González Prada, Manuel
González Suárez, (Manuel María)
  Federico
Gorostiza, Manuel Eduardo de
Gorriti, Juan Ignacio de
Graef Fernández, Carlos
Grau San Martín, Ramón
Groussac, Paul
Guamán Poma de Ayala, Felipe
Guerra y Sánchez, Ramiro
Guevara Arze, Walter
Halperín-Donghi, Tulio
Handelmann, Gottfried Heinrich
Hanke, Lewis Ulysses
Haro Barraza, Guillermo
Henríquez Ureña, Max
Henríquez Ureña, Pedro
Henry the Navigator
Hernández Colón, Rafael
Herrera, Bartolomé
Holanda, Sérgio Buarque de
Hostos y Bonilla, Eugenio María de
Howard, Jennie Eliza
Ianni, Octavio
Ibarguren, Carlos
Incháustegui Cabral, Héctor
Ingenieros, José
Ivaldi, Humberto
Jaguaribe Gomes de Matos, Hélio
James, Cyril Lionel Robert
Jerez, Francisco de
Justo, Juan B.
Kemmerer, Edwin Walter
Koellreutter, Hans Joaquim
Korn, Alejandro
Kumate Rodríguez, Jesús
Labarca Hubertson, Amanda
Landívar, Rafael
Las Casas, Bartolomé de
Lastarria, José Victorino
León-Portilla, Miguel
Léry, Jean de
Lescot, Élie
Letelier Madariaga, Valentín
Lewis, Roberto
Ley, Salvador
Lida, Raimundo
Liendo y Goicoechea, José Antonio
Lima, Alceu Amoroso
Lindo Zelaya, Juan

Liscano Velutini, Juan
Llorente y Lafuente, Anselmo
López, Vicente Fidel
López Michelsen, Alfonso
Lozano, Pedro
Luna Pizarro, Francisco Javier de
Luz y Caballero, José de la
Maldonado, Francisco Severo
Mansilla, Lucio Victorio
Margil de Jesús, Antonio
Marroquín, Francisco
Masferrer, Alberto
Massera, José Pedro
Matienzo, José Nicolás
Maza, Manuel Vicente de
Medina, José Toribio
Mejía del Valle y Llequerica, José Joaquín
Mello, Zélia Maria Cardoso de
Mendes, Gilberto
Méndez Montenegro, Julio César
Mendiburu, Manuel de
Mendieta y Montefur, Carlos
Millas Jiménez, Jorge
Mir, Pedro
Mitre, Bartolomé
Mogrovejo, Toribio Alfonso de
Molina Garmendia, Enrique
Monteiro, Tobias do Rêgo
Montt Torres, Manuel
Moog, Vianna
Mora Porrás, Juan Rafael
Morales Carrión, Arturo
Moreau de Justo, Alicia
Moreno, Fulgencio
Moreno, Mariano
Moscote, José Dolores
Moshinsky Borodianksky, Marcos
Moziño, José Mariano
Munguía, Clemente de Jesús
Mutis, José Celestino
Nabuco de Araújo, Joaquim
Nascimento, Abdias do
Nimuendajú, Curt
Nóbrega, Manuel da
Novo, Salvador
Núñez Vargas, Benjamin
Nusdorffer, Bernardo
O'Gorman, Edmundo
Oliveria, Willy Correia de
Oliveira Lima, Manuel de
Oré, Luis Gerónimo de
Orozco y Berra, Manuel
Ortiz, Fernando
Oviedo y Valdés, Gonzalo Fernández
Pacheco, José Emilio
País, Frank

Palafox y Mendoza, Juan de
Pane, Ignacio Alberto
Pardo y Aliaga, Felipe
Paso y Troncoso, Francisco del
Paterson, William
Paz Soldán Family
Peixoto, Júlio Afrânio
Peláez, Amelia
Pellicer Cámara, Carlos
Pena, Afonso Augusto Moreira
Peralta Azurdia, Enrique
Peralta Barnuevo y Rocha, Pedro de
Pérez Acosta, Juan Francisco
Pérez Aguirre, Luis
Pinheiro, José Feliciano Fernandes
Pinho, José Wanderley de Araújo
Popenoe, Frederick Wilson
Porras Barrenechea, Raúl
Prado, João Fernando de Almeida
Prado, Paulo
Prado da Silva Júnior, Caio
Prescott, William Hickling
Prieto Rodríguez, Sotero
Querino, Manoel Raimundo
Quesada, Ernesto
Quiroga, Vasco de
Rabasa, Emilio
Rama, Angel
Ramírez, José Fernando
Ramírez Vázquez, Pedro
Ramos, Artur
Ramos Mejía, José María
Ramos y Magaña, Samuel
Ravignani, Emilio
Rebouças, André
Restrepo, Carlos Eugenio
Reyes, Rafael
Reyes Ochoa, Alfonso
Ribeiro, Darcy
Ribera y Espinosa, Lázaro de
Riva Agüero y Osma, José de la
Rivarola, Rodolfo
Rocafuerte, Vicente
Rocha, Justiniano José da
Rocha, Manoel Ribeiro
Rocha Pita, Sebastião
Rodrigues, José Honório
Rodrigues, Raimundo Nina
Rodríguez, Simón
Rodríguez Lara, Guillermo
Rodríguez Monegal, Emir
Roig de Leuchsenring, Emilio
Romay y Valdés Chacón, Tomás
Romero, Emilio
Romero, Sílvio
Romero Rubio, Manuel
Rosenblueth, Arturo Stearns
Ruiz de Montoya, Antonio

Saco, José Antonio
Sáenz, Moisés
Sagra, Ramón de la
Salvador, Vicente do
Sánchez, Luis Alberto
Sánchez, Prisciliano
Sánchez de Bustamante y Sirven, Antonio
Sánchez de Tagle, Francisco Manuel
Sandoval Vallarta, Manuel
Santamaría, Haydée
Sarmiento, Domingo Faustino
Sepp, Anton
Serrano, José
Sierra O'Reilly, Justo
Sigüenza y Góngora, Carlos de
Silva Herzog, Jesús
Silva Lisboa, José da
Simonsen, Mário Henrique
Simonsen, Roberto Cochrane
Sodré, Nelson Werneck
Solano, Francisco
Solórzano Pereira, Juan de
Soto Alfaro, Bernardo
Sousa, Gabriel Soares de
Sousa, Otávio Tarquínio de
Southey, Robert
Squier, Ephraim George
Staden, Hans
Stefanich, Juan
Suárez, Marco Fidel
Tallet, José Zacarías
Tamayo, Franz
Tannenbaum, Frank
Taunay, Affonso d'Escragnolle
Tavares Bastos, Aureliano Cândido
Teixeira, Anisio Espinola
Tello, Julio César
Toledo y Figueroa, Francisco de
Torres Bello, Diego de
Torres Bodet, Jaime
Torre y Huerta, Carlos de la
Trejos Fernández, José Joaquín
Tugwell, Rexford Guy
Unanue, Hipólito
Uribe Uribe, Rafael
Uruguai, Visconde do
Valdivia, Luis de
Valencia, Guillermo León
Valle, José Cecilio del
Varela, José Pedro
Varela y Morales, Félix
Varnhagen, Francisco Adolfo de (Visconde de Porto Seguro)
Varona y Pera, Enrique José
Vasconcelos Calderón, José
Vaz Ferreira, Carlos

512

Velázquez Cárdenas de León, Joaquín
Vélez Sarsfield, Dalmacio
Vera Cruz, Alonso de la
Viana, Francisco José de Oliveira
Vieira, Antônio
Vigil, Francisco de Paula González
Villacorta Calderón, José Antonio
Villanueva, Carlos Raúl

Villarán, Manuel Vicente
Vitoria, Francisco de
Wagley, Charles Walter
Weffort, Francisco Correia
Wilde, Eduardo
Ximénez, Francisco
Yáñez Santos Delgadillo, Agustín
Ynsfrán, Pablo Max
Zaldúa, Francisco Javier

Zavala, Joaquín
Zavala, Silvio
Zayas y Alfonso, Alfredo
Zea Aguilar, Leopoldo
Zubirán Achondo, Salvador
Zubiría, José Antonio Laureano de
Zulen, Pedro S. [and] Dora Mayer de Zulen
Zum Felde, Alberto

Exploration and Conquest (including bandeirantes)

Abreu, Diego de
Aguayo, Marqués de
Aguilar, Jerónimo de
Aguilar, Martín de
Aguirre, Lope de
Alarcón, Martín de
Alberni, Pedro de
Almagro, Diego de
Alvarado y Mesía, Pedro de
Álvarez de Pineda, Alonso
Ampíes, Juan de
Andagoya, Pascual de
Anza, Juan Bautista de
Arias de Saavedra, Hernando
Ávila, Pedro Arias de
Balboa, Vasco Núñez de
Bastidas, Rodrigo de
Bazaine, François Achille
Belalcázar, Sebastián de
Bingham, Hiram
Bodega y Quadra, Juan Francisco de la
Bonpland, Aimé Jacques
Borba Gato, Manuel de
Brasseur de Bourbourg, Charles Étienne
Cabeza de Vaca, Alvar Núñez
Cabot, Sebastian
Cabral, Pedro Álvares
Castellanos, Juan de
Cavallón, Juan de
Columbus, Bartholomew
Columbus, Christopher
Columbus, Diego (d. 1515)
Coronado, Juan Vázquez de
Cortés, Hernán
Díaz del Castillo, Bernal
Elcano, Juan Sebastián de
Enciso, Martín Fernández de
Escandón, José de
Espejo, Antonio de
Esteban

Fajardo, Francisco
Féderman, Nicolás
Fernández, Juan
Fernández de Córdoba, Diego
Frémont, John Charles
Galindo, Juan
Gama, Vasco da
Garay, Juan de
Garcés, Francisco Tomás Hermenegildo
García, Aleixo
Girón, Francisco Hernández
González Dávila, Gil
Grijalva, Juan de
Guzmán, Nuño Beltrán de
Henry the Navigator
Heredia y Heredia, José M.
Humboldt, Alexander von
Hurtado de Mendoza, Andrés
Hurtado de Mendoza, García
Ibarra, Diego
Irala, Domingo Martínez de
Jiménez de Quesada, Gonzalo
Juan y Santacilia, Jorge
Kinney, Henry L.
Kino, Eusebio Francisco
La Salle, René-Robert Cavelier, Sieur de
Lasuén, Fermín Francisco de
León, Alonso de
Lepe, Diego de
López, Narciso
López de Legazpi y Gurruchátegui, Miguel
Losada, Diego de
Luna y Arellano, Tristán de
Luque, Hernando de
Magellan, Ferdinand
Malinche
Manso de Velasco, José Antonio
Martínez, Esteban José
Meiggs, Henry

Melgares, Facundo
Mendoza, Pedro de
Menéndez de Avilés, Pedro
Montejo, Francisco de
Narváez, Pánfilo de
Nicuesa, Diego
Niño, Pedro Alonso
Niza, Marcos de
Ojeda, Alonso de
Olid, Cristóbal de
Oña, Pedro de
Oñate, Juan de
Orellana, Francisco de
Oriz de Zárate, Juan and Juana
Pardo, Juan
Pérez, Juan
Pérez de Tolosa, Juan
Pinzón, Martín Alonso
Pinzón, Vicente Yáñez
Pizarro, Francisco
Pizarro, Gonzalo
Pizarro, Hernando
Ponce de León, Juan
Portolá, Gaspar de
Ramalho, João
Reyes, Rafael
Rivera, Pedro de
Rivera y Moncada, Fernando de
Rodríguez Cabrillo, Juan
Rodríguez Freile, Juan
Rondon, Cândido Mariano da Silva
Sarmiento de Gamboa, Pedro
Sedeño, Antonio de
Serra, Junipero
Solís, Juan Díaz de
Soto, Hernando de
Sousa, Martim Afonso de
Staden, Hans
Talamantes, Melchor de
Tavares, Antônio Rapôso
Ulloa, Antonio de
Urdaneta, Andrés de

Ursúa, Pedro de
Valdivia, Pedro de
Vargas, Diego de
Vázquez de Ayllón, Lucas

Velázquez, Diego de
Vélez de Escalante, Silvestre
Vespucci, Amerigo
Vial, Pedro

Villagra, Francisco de
Villagrá, Gaspar Pérez de
Villas Bôas Brothers
Vizcaíno, Sebastián

Journalism (including polemicists)

Acosta, José de
Alamán, Lucas
Alberdi, Juan Bautista
Alencar, José Martiniano de
Alzate y Ramírez, José Antonio de
Amaral, Antônio José Azevedo do
Andrade, Carlos Drummond de
Andreve, Guillermo
Andueza Palacio, Raimundo
Ângelo, Ivan
Antuñano, Estevan de
Arango y Parreño, Francisco de
Arboleda, Julio
Arce Castaño, Bayardo
Arciniegas, Germán
Arguedas, Alcides
Ayala, José de la Cruz
Aycinena Piñol, Juan José de
Azevedo, Fernando de
Báez, Cecilio
Baldorioty de Castro, Ramón
Barreda y Loas, Felipe
Barreiro, Antonio
Barrett, Rafael
Barros Arana, Diego
Barroso, Gustavo Dodt
Beals, Carleton
Bedoya Reyes, Luis
Belaúnde, Víctor Andrés
Beltrán, Pedro
Bergaño y Villegas, Simón
Berges, José
Betances, Ramón Emeterio
Betancourt, Rómulo
Betancourt Cisneros, Gaspar
Blanco, Andrés Eloy
Blanco Acevedo, Eduardo
Blanco Galdós, Hugo
Bocaiúva, Quintino
Brandão, Ignácio de Loyola
Bravo, Mario
Bray, Arturo
Brenner, Anita
Bulnes, Francisco
Bustamante, Carlos María de
Bustamante y Rivero, José Luis
Cabrera Lobato, Luis

Callado, Antônio
Capistrano de Abreu, João
Cárcano, Miguel Ángel
Cárcano, Ramón José
Caro, José Eusebio
Caro, Miguel Antonio
Carpio Nicolle, Jorge
Caso y Andrade, Antonio
Castelli, Juan José
Castro Madriz, José María
Centurión, Carlos R.
Centurión, Juan Crisóstomo
Chamorro Cardenal, Pedro Joaquín
Coelho Neto, Henrique
Coll y Toste, Cayetano
Cooke, John William
Correoso, Buenaventura
Corvalán Lepe, Luis
Cos y Pérez, José María
Cosío Villegas, Daniel
Costa, Hipólito José da
Creydt, Oscar
Cuadra, Pablo Antonio
Cumplido, Ignacio
Cunha, Euclides da
Darío, Rubén
Dávila Espinoza, Carlos Guillermo
Debray, [Jules] Régis
Del Prado, Jorge
Deustua, Alejandro O.
Dickmann, Adolfo
Dickmann, Enrique
Dobles Segreda, Luis
Echeverría, Esteban
Egaña Fabres, Mariano
Escalante, Aníbal
Estrada, José Manuel
Etchepareborda, Roberto
Faoro, Raymundo
Fernández Artucio, Hugo
Fernández Madrid, José
Fernández Retamar, Roberto
Figueiredo, Afonso Celso de
  Assis
Flores Magón, Ricardo
Fortuny, José Manuel
Francia, José Gaspar Rodríguez de

Frondizi, Risieri
Fuentes, Manuel Atanasio
Gainza Paz, Alberto
Gaitan, Jorge Eliécer
Galeano, Eduardo Hughes
Gálvez, Manuel
Gama, Luís
Garay, Blas
Garcilaso de la Vega, El Inca
Garvey, Marcus
Gelly, Juan Andrés
Ghioldi, Américo
Ghioldi, Rodolfo
Gil Fortoul, José
Girri, Alberto
Gómez, Eugenio
Gómez, Juan Gualberto
Gómez Carrillo, Enrique
Gómez Castro, Laureano
González, Florentino
González, Joaquín Víctor
González, Juan Natalicio
Gorostiza, Manuel Eduardo de
Groussac, Paul
Guardia, Ricardo Adolfo de la
Gutiérrez, Gustavo
Gutiérrez, José María
Gutiérrez Estrada, José María
Gutiérrez Nájera, Manuel
Guzmán, Antonio Leocadio
Guzmán, Martín Luis
Haya de la Torre, Víctor Raúl
Henríquez Ureña, Max
Henríquez Ureña, Pedro
Hernández, José
Herrera, Bartolomé
Herrera, Luis Alberto de
Herrera y Obes, Julio
Herzog, Vladimir
Hidalgo, Bartolomé
Hidalgo, Enrique Agustín
Hidalgo y Costilla, Miguel
Holanda, Sérgio Buarque de
Humboldt, Alexander von
Ibarguren, Carlos
Iglesias Pantin, Santiago
Infante, José Miguel

Ingenieros, José
Irisarri y Larraín, Juan Bautista
James, Cyril Lionel Robert
Justo, Juan B.
Krauze, Enrique
Lacerda, Carlos Frederico Werneck de
Larrea, Juan
Las Casas, Bartolomé de
Lastarria, José Victorino
Lida, Raimundo
Lima, Alceu Amoroso
Lima Barreto, Afonso Henriques de
Liscano Velutini, Juan
Lleras Restrepo, Carlos
Lombardo Toledano, Vicente
López Michelsen, Alfonso
López Pumarejo, Alfonso
López Trujillo, Alfonso
López Vallecillos, Italo
López y Fuentes, Gregorio
Lugones, Leopoldo
Luisi, Luisa
Luna Pizarro, Francisco Javier de
Machado, Gustavo
Machado de Assis, Joaquim Maria
Maldonado, Francisco Severo
Mallea, Eduardo
Mañach y Robato, Jorge
Mansilla, Lucio Victorio
Mariátegui, José Carlos
Marinho, Roberto
Martínez Estrada, Ezequiel
Masferrer, Alberto
Massera, José Pedro
Matto de Turner, Clorinda
Mendieta y Montefur, Carlos
Mier Noriega y Guerra, José Servando Teresa de
Milla y Vidaurre, José
Miranda, Francisco de
Miro Quesada Family
Mitre, Bartolomé
Molina, Pedro
Molina Enríquez, Andrés
Monsiváis, Carlos
Montalvo, Juan
Monte Alto
Monteiro, Tobias do Rêgo
Monteiro Lobato, José Bento
Moog, Vianna
Mora, José María Luis
Mora Fernández, Juan
Morales Lemus, José
Moreno, Fulgencio
Moreno, Mariano

Moshinsky Borodianksky, Marcos
Munguía, Clemente de Jesús
Muñoz Marín, Luis
Muñoz Rivera, Luis
Nardone, Benito
Nariño, Antonio
Novás Calvo, Lino
Novo, Salvador
Núñez Moledo, Rafael
Ocampo, Melchor
Ocampo, Victoria
O'Gorman, Edmundo
Olaya Herrera, Enrique
Olmedo, José Joaquín
Ortiz, Fernando
Ospina Rodríguez, Mariano
Otero, Mariano
Ottoni, Teofilo Benedito
Pacheco, José Emilio
Palma, Ricardo
Pardo y Aliaga, Felipe
Paso y Troncoso, Francisco del
Patrocínio, José do
Payno y Flores, Manuel
Paz, Octavio
Paz Soldán Family
Perera, Víctor
Pérez, Carlos Andrés
Pérez Esquivel, Adolfo
Picón Salas, Mariano
Poniatowska, Elena
Porras Barrenechea, Raúl
Posada, José Guadalupe
Prado, João Fernando de Almeida
Prado da Silva Júnior, Caio
Prieto, Guillermo
Puig Casauranc, José Manuel
Quesada, Ernesto
Rama, Angel
Ramírez, Ignacio
Ramírez, José Fernando
Ramos Mejía, José María
Real de Azúa, Carlos
Rebouças, André
Restrepo, Carlos Eugenio
Ribeiro, João Ubaldo
Rio Branco, Barão do
Rio Branco, Visconde do
Rio, João do
Rius
Riva Palacio, Vicente
Roca, Blas
Rocafuerte, Vicente
Rocha, Justiniano José da
Rodó, José Enrique
Rodríguez, Carlos Rafael
Rodríguez, Simón

Rodríguez Cerna, José
Rodríguez Monegal, Emir
Roig de Leuchsenring, Emilio
Rojas, Ricardo
Romay y Valdés Chacón, Tomás
Rubião, Murilo
Saco, José Antonio
Salazar Bondy, Sebastián
Salgado, Plinio
Sánchez, Luis Alberto
Sánchez de Bustamante y Sirven, Antonio
Sanguinetti, Julio María
Santa Cruz y Espejo, Francisco Javier Eugenio de
Santos, Eduardo
Sarmiento, Domingo Faustino
Sarmiento de Gamboa, Pedro
Scalabrini Ortiz, Raúl
Sierra O'Reilly, Justo
Silva Herzog, Jesús
Sodré, Nelson Werneck
Solórzano Pereira, Juan de
Sousa, Otávio Tarqüínio de
Souza, Márcio Gonçalves Bentes
Squier, Ephraim George
Stephens, John Lloyd
Talavera, Natalício
Tallet, José Zacarías
Távara y Andrade, Santiago
Timerman, Jacobo
Torre, Lisandro de la
Torres Bodet, Jaime
Traba, Marta
Tristan, Flora
Trotsky, Leon
Trujillo, Manuel
Turbay Ayala, Julio César
Ugarte, Manuel
Ulate Blanco, Otilio
Urbina, Luis Gonzaga
Valencia, Guillermo León
Valle, Artistóbulo del
Valle, José Cecilio del
Varela, José Pedro
Varela y Morales, Félix
Vargas Llosa, Mario
Varona y Pera, Enrique José
Vasconcelos Calderón, José
Vedia y Mitre, Mariano
Veiga, Evaristo Ferreira da
Villarán, Manuel Vicente
Villaurrutia, Jacobo de
Villeda Morales, Ramón
Walker, William
Wyld Ospina, Carlos
Zapata, Felipe
Zarco, Francisco

Zavala, Lorenzo de
Zavala, Silvio

Zayas y Alfonso, Alfredo
Zeballos, Estanislao

Zulen, Pedro S. [and] Dora Mayer
de Zulen

Labor and Labor Relations (excluding slavery)

Abadía Méndez, Miguel
Aguirre Cerda, Pedro
Alem, Leandro
Allende Gossens, Salvador
Arcos, Santiago
Arismendi, Rodney
Arze, José Antonio
Bilbao Barquín, Francisco
Bravo, Mario
Campa Salazar, Valentín
Cano, María de los Ángeles
Chonchol, Jacques
Collor, Lindolfo
Corral Verdugo, Ramón
Del Prado, Jorge
Eder, Santiago Martín
Fallas Sibaja, Carlos Luis
Flores Magón, Ricardo

Ghioldi, Américo
Ghioldi, Rodolfo
Guervara, Ernesto "Che"
Guiérrez Garbín, Víctor Manuel
Iglesias Pantin, Santiago
Julião Arruda de Paula,
   Francisco
Justo, Juan B.
Lacerda, Maurício Pavia de
Lechín Oquendo, Juan
Lombardo Toledano, Vicente
López, Ambrosio
Machado, Gustavo
Mendes Filho, Francisco "Chico"
   Alves
Molina Solís, Olegario
Monge Álvarez, Luis Alberto
Morones, Luis

Núñez Vargas, Benjamin
Pacheco da Silva, Osvaldo
Palacios, Alfredo L.
Pellacani, Dante
Peña, Lázaro
Prieto Figueroa, Luis Beltrán
Querino, Manoel Raimundo
Recabarren Serrano, Luis Emilio
Riani, Clodsmith
Roca, Blas
Romero Rosa, Ramón
Seoane, Manuel
Siles Zuazo, Hernán
Silva, Lindolfo
Silva, Luis Inácio Lula da
Torre, Lisandro de la
Trotsky, Leon
Velázquez Sánchez, Fidel

Land Ownership (including encomenderos, hacendados, agriculturalists, etc.)

Abasolo, Mariano
Agramonte y Loynaz, Ignacio
Aguayo, Marqués de
Álzaga, Martín de
Arana, Felipe de
Arana, Julio César
Arango y Parreño, Francisco de
Argüello, Santiago
Aspíllaga Family
Austin, Moses
Austin, Stephen Fuller
Aycinena, Juan Fermín de
Bemberg, Otto
Bulnes Prieto, Manuel
Carvajal, Luis de
Cedillo Martínez, Saturnino
Chiari, Rodolfo E.
Chiari Remón, Roberto
   Francisco
Cisneros Betancourt, Salvador

Cortés, Hernán
Cortés, Martín
de León, Martín
Dellepiane, Luis J.
Dieseldorff, Erwin Paul
Egaña Fabres, Mariano
Elías, Domingo
Figueres Ferrer, José
Galindo, Juan
Garay, Juan de
Gildermeister Family
Gómez, Juan Vicente
Guerra, Ramón
Güiraldes, Ricardo
Irala, Domingo Martínez de
Lacalle Herrera, Luis Alberto
Leguía, Augusto Bernardino
López de Quiroga, Antonio
López de Romaña, Eduardo
Machado y Morales, Gerardo

Madero, Francisco Indalecio
Miro Quesada Family
Monte Alto
Mora, Fernando de la
Nicuesa, Diego
Orlich Bolmarcich, Francisco
   José
Paz Soldán Family
Pétion, Alexandre Sabès
Romero, Matías
Rosáins, Juan Nepomuceno
Ruíz Tagle Portales, Francisco
Sousa, Gabriel Soares de
Terrazas, Luis
Toro Zambrano, Mateo de
Torre Tagle, José Bernardo de
   Tagle y Portocarrero
Uribe Uribe, Rafael
Vallejo, Mariano Guadalupe
Zaracondegui, Julián de

Literature, Belles Lettres, and Philosophy

Abadía Méndez, Miguel
Abbad y Lasierra, Íñigo
Abente y Lago, Victorino
Abril, Xavier
Acevedo Díaz, Eduardo Inés
Acevedo Hernández, Antonio
Acosta, José de
Aguiar, Adonias
Aguilera Malta, Demetrio
Aguirre, Nataniel
Agustín, José
Agustini, Delmira
Alamán, Lucas
Albán, Laureano
Alegre, Francisco Javier
Alegría, Ciro
Alegría, Claribel
Alegría, Fernando
Alencar, José Martiniano de
Alexis, Jacques Stéphen
Alfaro, Ricardo Joaquín
Allende, Isabel
Almafuerte
Almeida, José Américo de
Almeida, Manuel Antônio de
Almonte, Juan Nepomuceno
Alonso, Amado
Alonso, Manuel A.
Altamirano, Ignacio Manuel
Alvarado, Lisandro
Alvarado, Salvador
Álvarez Gardeazábal, Gustavo
Alzate y Ramírez, José Antonio de
Amado, Jorge
Ambrogi, Arturo
Amorim, Enrique
Anchieta, José de
Andagoya, Pascual de
Anderson Imbert, Enrique
Andrade, Carlos Drummond de
Andrade, Jorge
Andrade, Mário de
Andrade, Oswald de
Andreve, Guillermo
Ángel, Albalucía
Angelis, Pedro de
Ângelo, Ivan
Appleyard, José Luis
Arboleda, Julio
Arciniegas, Germán
Arcos, Santiago
Arenas, Reinaldo

Arévalo Bermejo, Juan José
Arévalo Martínez, Rafael
Arguedas, Alcides
Arguedas, José María
Argüelles, Hugo
Arias, Arturo
Arias Sánchez, Oscar
Aridjis, Homero
Arlt, Roberto
Arosemena, Justo
Arreola, Juan José
Arriví, Francisco
Arrufat, Antón
Ascasubi, Hilario
Assunção, Leilah
Asturias, Miguel Ángel
Ávila, Julio Enrique
Azar, Héctor
Azcárate y Lezama, Juan Francisco de
Azevedo, Aluísio
Azuela, Mariano
Bachiller y Morales, Antonio
Balbuena, Bernardo de
Ballagas y Cubeñas, Emilio
Balseiro, José Agustín
Bandeira, Manuel Carneiro de Souza
Baquerizo Moreno, Alfredo
Baralt, Rafael María
Barbosa, Domingos Caldas
Barnet, Miguel
Barnola, Pedro Pablo
Barreiro, Antonio
Barreto de Menezes, Tobias, Jr.
Barrios, Eduardo
Barroso, Gustavo Dodt
Basso Maglio, Vicente
Basurto, Luis
Batlle y Ordóñez, José
Batres Montúfar, José
Bedregal de Conitzer, Yolanda
Bélance, René
Bellegarde, Luis Dantès
Belli, Gioconda
Bello, Andrés
Beltrán, Washington
Benedetti, Mario
Benítez, Gregorio
Benítez-Rojo, Antonio
Berenguer, Amanda
Berman, Sabina

Bermejo, Ildefonso
Betances, Ramón Emeterio
Bianco, José
Bilbao Barquín, Francisco
Bioy Casares, Adolfo
Blanco, Andrés Eloy
Blanco Fombona, Rufino
Blest Gana, Alberto
Bombal, María Luisa
Bonifaz Nuño, Rubén
Borge, Tomás
Borges, Jorge Luis
Borno, Joseph Louis E. Antoine François
Bosch Gaviño, Juan
Brañas Guerra, César
Brandão, Ignácio de Loyola
Brannon de Samayoa Chinchilla, Carmen
Brasseur de Bourbourg, Charles Étienne
Brathwaite, Edward Kamau
Brenner, Anita
Brierre, Jean-Fernand
Britto García, Luis
Brull, Mariano
Brunet, Marta
Bryce Echenique, Alfredo
Bulnes, Francisco
Burgos, Julia de
Bustamante, Carlos María de
Caballero y Rodríguez, José Agustín
Caballero Calderón, Eduardo
Cabeza de Vaca, Alvar Núñez
Cabral, Manuel del
Cabrera, Lydia
Cabrera Infante, Guillermo
Cáceres, Esther de
Calcaño, José Antonio
Calderón de la Barca, Fanny
Callado, Antônio
Cambaceres, Eugenio
Camille, Roussan
Camões, Luís Vaz de
Campo, Estanislao del
Campos, Julieta
Campos Cervera, Hérib
Canales, Nemesio Rosario
Candanedo, César
Cané, Miguel
Cantón, Wilberto
Capelo, Joaquín

Cardenal, Ernesto
Cardoza y Aragón, Luis
Caro, José Eusebio
Caro, Miguel Antonio
Carpentier, Alejo
Carranza Fernández, Eduardo
Carrasquilla, Tomás
Carrera Andrade, Jorge
Carrión, Alejandro
Carrión, Manuel Benjamín
Carvajal, Luis de
Casal, Julián del
Casanova y Estrada, Ricardo
Caso y Andrade, Antonio
Castellanos, Juan de
Castellanos, Rosario
Castillo, Jesús
Castillo, Otto René
Castillo y Guevara, Francisca
 Josefa de la Concepción de
Castro Alves, Antônio de
Caviedes, Juan del Valle y
Centurión, Roque Miranda
Cerruto, Óscar
Césaire, Aimé
Céspedes y Quesada, Carlos
 Manuel de
Charry Lara, Fernando
Chauvet, Marie Vieux
Chávez Sánchez, Ignacio
Chimalpahin
Chocano, José Santos
Chumacero, Alí
Cieza de León, Pedro de
Clavigero, Francisco Javier
Cobo, Bernabé
Coelho Neto, Henrique
Coicou, Massillon
Coll y Toste, Cayetano
Colmán, Narciso
Condé, Maryse
Constant Botelho de Magalhães,
 Benjamin
Coronel Urtecho, José
Correa, Julio Myzkowsky
Cortázar, Julio
Cortés, Hernán
Cosío Villegas, Daniel
Costa, Cláudio Manuel da
Couto, José Bernardo
Cruz e Sousa, João da
Cuadra, Pablo Antonio
Cuevas, Mariano
Cunha, Euclides da
Cunha Dotti, Juan
Dalton García, Roque
Darío, Rubén
Debray, [Jules] Régis

Dellepiane, Luis J.
Denevi, Marco
Depestre, René
D'Escoto Brockmann, Miguel
Desnoes, Edmundo Pérez
Dias, Antônio Gonçalves
Dias Gomes, Alfredo
Díaz, José Pedro
Díaz Lozano, Argentina
Díaz Soto y Gama, Antonio
Diego, Eliseo
Diego, José de
Donoso, José
Dragún, Osvaldo
Durán, Diego
Durand, Oswald
Durão, José de Santa Rita
Echeverría, Esteban
Edwards, Agustín
Edwards, Jorge
Edwards Bello, Joaquín
Eguren, José María
Elizondo, Salvador
Encisco, Martín Fernández de
Enríquez de Guzmán, Alonso
Ercilla y Zúñiga, Alonso de
Estrada, José Manuel
Facio Brenes, Rodrigo
Fallas Sibaja, Carlos Luis
Fariña Núñez, Eloy
Féderman, Nicolás
Feijóo, Benito Jerónimo
Fernandes, Millôr
Fernández de Lizardi, José Joaquín
Fernández Madrid, José
Fernández Retamar, Roberto
Figueiredo, Afonso Celso de Assis
Florit, Eugenio
Fortuny, José Manuel
Franco, Rafael
Freire, Paulo
Freyre, Gilberto (de Mello)
Frondizi, Risieri
Fuentes, Carlos
Fuentes y Guzmán, Francisco An-
 tonio de
Funes, Gregorio
Gage, Thomas
Gaitán Durán, Jorge
Galeano, Eduardo Hughes
Galindo, Sergio
Gallego, Laura
Gallegos, Rómulo
Galván, Manuel de Jesús
Gálvez, Manuel
Gama, José Basilio da
Gama, Luís
Gambaro, Griselda

Gamboa Iglesias, Federico
Gaos, José
García, Genaro
García Icazbalceta, Joaquín
García Márquez, Gabriel
García Peláez, Francisco de Paula
Garcilaso de la Vega, El Inca
Garmendia, Salvador
Garro, Elena
Gatón Arce, Freddy
Gavidia, Francisco Antonio
Girri, Alberto
Glantz, Margo
Glissant, Édouard
Goldemberg, Isaac
Gómez, Juan Carlos
Gómez Carrillo, Enrique
Gómez de Avellaneda y Arteaga,
 Gertrudis
Gonzaga, Tomás Antônio
González, Joaquín Victor
González, Juan Natalicio
González, Juan Vicente
González Casanova, Pablo
González León, Adriano
González Martínez, Enrique
González Prada, Manuel
Gorodischer, Angélica
Gorostiza, Manuel Eduardo de
Grimard, Luc
Groussac, Paul
Guarnieri, Gianfrancesco
Gudiño Kieffer, Eduardo
Guerra y Sánchez, Ramiro
Guido, Beatriz
Guillén, Nicolás
Güiraldes, Ricardo
Guirao, Ramón
Gutiérrez González, Gregorio
Gutiérrez Nájera, Manuel
Guzmán, Augusto
Guzmán, Enrique
Guzmán, Martín Luis
Haro Barraza, Guillermo
Henríquez Ureña, Max
Henríquez Ureña, Pedro
Heredia y Heredia, José M.
Hernández, Felisberto
Hernández, José
Hernández, Luisa Josefina
Herrera, Flavio
Herrera y Reissig, Julio
Herrera y Tordesillas, Antonio de
Hidalgo, Bartolomé
Hidalgo, Enrique Agustín
Hippolyte, Dominique
Holguín, Jorge
Hudson, William Henry

Huidobro Fernández, Vicente
Ibáñez, Roberto
Ibáñez, Sara de
Ibarbouro, Juana de
Ibargüengoitia, Jorge
Icaza Coronel, Jorge
Iglesias, José María
Illescas, Carlos
Incháustegui Cabral, Héctor
Isaacs, Jorge
James, Cyril Lionel Robert
Jaramillo Levi, Enrique
Jesus, Carolina Maria de
Juana Inés de la Cruz, Sor
Korn, Alejandro
Krauze, Enrique
Labrador Ruiz, Enrique
Laguerre, Enrique Arturo
Laleau, Léon
Lame, Manuel Quintín
Landa, Diego de
Landívar, Rafael
Larreta, Enrique Rodríguez
Las Casas, Bartolomé de
Leante, César
Leñero, Vicente
Levinson, Luisa Mercedes
Lezama Lima, José
Lida, Raimundo
Liendo y Goicoechea, José Antonio
Lihn, Enrique
Lima, Alceu Amoroso
Lima, Jorge de
Lima Barreto, Afonso Henriques de
Lins, Osman da Costa
Lins do Rego, José
Liscano Velutini, Juan
Lispector, Clarice
Llorens Torres, Luis
López, Willebaldo
López de Cogolludo, Diego
López Portillo, José
López Vallecillos, Italo
López Velarde, Ramón
López y Fuentes, Gregorio
Lorenzana y Buitrón, Francisco
   Antonio de
Lugones, Leopoldo
Luz y Caballero, José de la
Lynch, Benito
Lynch, Marta
Macedo, Joaquim Manuel de
Machado de Assis, Joaquim Maria
Magalhães, Domingos José
   Gonçalves de
Magaña, Sergio
Magdaleno, Mauricio
Maíz, Fidel

Mallea, Eduardo
Mañach y Robato, Jorge
Manzano, Juan Francisco
Marechal, Leopoldo
Marinello, Juan
Markham, Clements Robert
Mármol, José Pedro Crisólogo
Marqués, René
Marroquín, José Manuel
Martínez Estrada, Ezequiel
Martyr, Peter
Masferrer, Alberto
Massera, José Pedro
Matos, Gregório de
Matto de Turner, Clorinda
Meireles, Cecília
Melo Franco, Afonso Arinos de
Melo Neto, João Cabral de
Méndez Ballester, Manuel
Méndez Pereira, Octavio
Milla y Vidaurre, José
Mir, Pedro
Miró, César
Mistral, Gabriela
Mitre, Bartolomé
Molina, Juan Ramón
Molina Bedoya, Felipe
Molinari, Ricardo E.
Montalvo, Juan
Monteiro Lobato, José Bento
Monterroso, Augusto
Montúfar, Lorenzo
Morais, Vinícius de
Morales, Beltrán
Morales, Mario Roberto
Morales Carrión, Arturo
Morejón, Nancy
Moscote, José Dolores
Moshinsky Borodianksky, Marcos
Motecuhzoma II
Motolinía, Toribio de
Munguía, Clemente de Jesús
Muñoz Marín, Luis
Muñoz Rivera, Luis
Mutis, Alvaro
Naipaul, V. S.
Nalé Roxlo, Conrado
Naranjo, Carmen
Nascimento, Abdias do
Neruda, Pablo
Nervo, Amado
Nezahualcoyotl
Novás Calvo, Lino
Novo, Salvador
Núñez Moledo, Rafael
Obaldía, María Olimpia de
Ocampo, Victoria
Odio, Eunice

O'Gorman, Edmundo
O'Leary, Daniel Florencio
Oliveira, Manuel Botelho de
Olmedo, José Joaquín
Onetti, Juan Carlos
Oreamuno, Yolanda
Oribe, Emilio
Orozco, Olga
Orozco y Berra, Manuel
Orphée, Elvira
Ortiz, Fernando
Ortiz de Ayala, Simón Tadeo
Otero, Mariano
Ovando, Nicolás de
Oviedo y Valdés, Gonzalo
   Fernández
Pacheco, José Emilio
Padilla, Heberto
Palacios, Antonia
Palés Matos, Luis
Palma, Ricardo
Pani Arteaga, Alberto J.
Pardo y Aliaga, Felipe
Pareja Diezcanseco, Alfredo
Parra, Nicanor
Parra, Teresa de la
Paso, Fernando del
Paso y Troncoso, Francisco del
Paterson, William
Patrocínio, José do
Payno y Flores, Manuel
Paz, Octavio
Peixoto, Júlio Afrânio
Pellicer Cámara, Carlos
Pena, Luís Carlos Martins
Peralta Barnuevo y Rocha, Pedro de
Perera, Víctor
Peri Rossi, Cristina
Phelps, Anthony
Picón Salas, Mariano
Piñera, Virgilio
Piñon, Nélida
Pita Rodríguez, Félix
Pitol, Sergio
Pizarnik, Alejandra
Plá, Josefina
Pompéia, Raúl
Poniatowska, Elena
Porras Barrenechea, Raúl
Pôrto Alegre, Manuel Araújo
Prado, Pedro
Prescott, William Hickling
Price-Mars, Jean
Prieto, Guillermo
Puga, María Luisa
Puig, Manuel
Puig Casauranc, José Manuel
Queiroz, Dinah Silveira de

Queiroz, Rachel de
Quintana Roo, Andrés
Quiroga, Horacio
Rabasa, Emilio
Rada, Manuel de Jesús
Ramírez, Ignacio
Ramírez, José Fernando
Ramírez Mercado, Sergio
Ramos, Graciliano
Ramos Arizpe, José Miguel
Ramos y Magaña, Samuel
Rego Monteiro, Vicente do
Restrepo, José Manuel
Revueltas, José
Reyes, Alfonso
Reyes, Rafael
Reyes Ochoa, Alfonso
Ribeiro, João Ubaldo
Ribeyro, Julio Ramón
Rio, João do
Riva Agüero y Osma, José de la
Riva Palacio, Vicente
Rivera, José Eustasio
Rivera, Pedro de
Roa Bastos, Augusto
Rodó, José Enrique
Rodrigues, Nelson
Rodríguez-Alcalá, Hugo
Rodríguez Cerna, José
Rodríguez Freile, Juan
Rodríguez Juliá, Edgardo
Roig de Leuchsenring, Emilio
Rojas, Manuel
Rojas, Ricardo
Rokha, Pablo de
Rokha, Winétt de
Romay y Valdés Chacón, Tomás
Romero, Emilio
Romero, Francisco
Romero, José Luis
Romero, José Rubén
Romero, Matías
Romero, Sílvio
Romero Rosa, Ramón
Rosa, João Guimarães
Rosáins, Juan Nepomuceno
Roscio, Juan Germán
Rosenblueth, Arturo Stearns
Roumain, Jacques
Rubião, Murilo
Rueda, Manuel
Ruiz de Alarcón y Mendoza,
    Juan
Rulfo, Juan
Sabat Ercasty, Carlos
Sábato, Ernesto
Sáenz, Jaime
Sagra, Ramón de la

Sahagún, Bernardino de
Sáinz, Gustavo
Salazar Arrué, Salvador Efraín
Salazar Bondy, Sebastián
Salgado, Plinio
Samayoa Chinchilla, Carlos
Samper, José María
Sánchez, Luis Rafael
Sánchez, Prisciliano
Sánchez de Bustamante y Sirven,
    Antonio
Sánchez de Tagle, Francisco
    Manuel
Santa Cruz y Espejo, Francisco
    Javier Eugenio de
Sarduy, Severo
Sarmiento, Domingo Faustino
Sarmiento de Gamboa, Pedro
Sarney, José
Schwarz-Bart, Simone
Scliar, Moacyr
Shimose, Pedro
Sierra, Stella
Sierra Méndez, Justo
Sierra O'Reilly, Justo
Sigüenza y Góngora, Carlos de
Silva, Clara
Silva, José Asunción
Sinán, Rogelio
Skármeta, Antonio
Sologuren, Javier
Solórzano, Carlos
Solórzano Pereira, Juan de
Somers, Armonía
Soriano, Osvaldo
Soto, Pedro Juan
Souza, Márcio Gonçalves Bentes
Squier, Ephraim George
Steimberg, Alicia
Stephens, John Lloyd
Storni, Alfonsina
Suárez, Marco Fidel
Suassuna, Ariano Vilar
Subero, Efraín
Tablada, José Juan
Talamantes, Melchor de
Talavera, Natalício
Tallet, José Zacarías
Tamayo, Franz
Taunay, Alfredo d'Escragnolle,
    Vicomte de
Távara y Andrade, Santiago
Telles, Lygia Fagundes
Tello, Julio César
Thiel, Bernardo Augusto
Toro, Fermín
Torres Bodet, Jaime
Torre y Huerta, Carlos de la

Traba, Marta
Triana, José
Tristan, Flora
Trotsky, Leon
Trujillo, Manuel
Umaña Bernal, José
Unanue, Hipólito
Urbina, Luis Gonzaga
Urzagasti, Jesús
Usigli, Rodolfo
Uslar Pietri, Arturo
Valdés, Gabriel de la Concepción
Valenzuela, Luisa
Valero, Roberto
Vallbona, Rima de
Vallejo, César
Vallenilla Lanz, Laureano
Varela, Florencio
Vargas Llosa, Mario
Varona y Pera, Enrique José
Vasconcelos Calderón, José
Vásquez, Francisco de Asís
Vega, Aurelio de
Vera Cruz, Alonso de la
Veríssimo, Érico
Vespucci, Amerigo
Vial, Pedro
Vieira, Antônio
Vigil, Francisco de Paula
    González
Vilariño, Idea
Villacorta Calderón, José Antonio
Villagrá, Gaspar Pérez de
Villarán, Manuel Vicente
Villaurrutia, Xavier
Villaverde, Cirilo
Villegas, Oscar
Vitier, Cintio
Vizcaíno, Sebastián
Von Vacano, Arturo
Walcott, Derek
Ward, Henry George
Welles, Sumner
Wheelock Román, Jaime
Wyld Ospina, Carlos
Ximénez, Francisco
Yanes, Francisco Javier
Yáñez Santos Delgadillo, Agustín
Ydígoras Fuentes, Miguel
Zaid, Gabriel
Zavala, Lorenzo de
Zavala, Silvio
Zayas y Alfonso, Alfredo
Zea Aguilar, Leopoldo
Zelaya, José Santos
Zeno Gandía, Manuel
Zepeda, Eraclio
Zorita, Alonso de

The Military

Abascal y Souza, José Fernando
Acevedo Díaz, Eduardo Inés
Achá, José María
Acosta, Tomás
Agramonte y Loynaz, Ignacio
Aguayo, Marqués de
Aguilar, Jerónimo de
Aguirre, Juan Francisco de
Alarcón, Martín de
Alberni, Pedro de
Alberto, João
Albuquerque, Antônio Francisco
    de Paula
Aldama y González, Juan de
Alexander, Edward Porter
Alfaro Delgado, José Eloy
Allende, Ignacio
Almazán, Juan Andréu
Almonte, Juan Nepomuceno
Alonso, Mariano Roque
Alvarado, Lisandro
Alvarado, Salvador
Alvarado y Mesía, Pedro de
Álvarez, Juan
Álvarez Armellino, Gregorio
    Conrado
Álvarez Martínez, Gustavo
Amat y Junient, Manuel de
Ampíes, Juan de
Ampudia y Grimarest, Pedro de
Anaya, Pedro María de
Andrade, Gomes Freire de
Andresote
Ángeles, Felipe
Anza, Juan Bautista de
Anzoátegui, José Antonio
Aramburu, Pedro Eugenio
Arana, Francisco J.
Arana Osorio, Carlos
Arbenz Guzmán, Jacobo
Arenales, Juan Antonio Álvarez de
Argüello, Santiago
Arias, Desiderio
Arismendi, Juan Bautista
Arista, Mariano
Armijo, Manuel
Artigas, José Gervasio
Auchmuty, Samuel
Aury, Louis-Michel
Ávila, Pedro Arias de
Ávila Camacho, Manuel
Avilés, Gabriel

Axayacatl
Ayolas, Juan de
Azcuénaga, Miguel de
Balboa, Vasco Núñez de
Balcarce, Mariano
Baldomir, Alfredo
Ballivián, José
Balta, José
Banzere Suárez, Hugo
Barrientos Ortuño, René
Barrios, Justo Rufino
Batista y Zaldívar, Fulgencio
Bazaine, François Achille
Belgrano, Manuel
Belzu, Manuel Isidoro
Beresford, William Carr
Bermúdez, José Francisco
Bermúdez Varela, Enrique
Beruti, Antonio Luis
Bignone, Reynaldo
Blanco, José Félix
Blanco Encalada, Manuel
Blanco Galindo, Carlos
Bodega y Quardra, Juan Francisco
    de la
Bolívar, Simón
Bolognesi, Francisco
Bordaberry, Juan María
Borge, Tomás
Bouchard, Hipólito
Boves, José Tomás
Boyer, Jean-Pierre
Bravo, Leonardo
Bravo, Nicolás
Brión, Luis
Brizuela, Francisco
Brown, William
Bunau-Varilla, Philippe Jean
Busch Becerra, Germán
Bustamante, Anastasio
Bustamante y Guerra, José
Butler, Smedley Darlington
Caamaño Deñó, Francisco
Caamaño y Gómez Cornejo, José
    María Plácido
Caballero, Pedro Juan
Cabañas, José Trinidad
Cáceres, Andrés Avelino
Cajeme
Calfucurá
Calleja del Rey, Félix María
Calles, Plutarco Elías

Camarena, Enrique
Campero, Narciso
Campos, Luis María
Campos, Manuel Jorge
Cañas, José María
Candioti, Francisco Antonio
Cárdenas del Río, Lázaro
Cardozo, Efraím
Carondelet, François-Louis Hector
Carrera, José Miguel
Carrera, José Rafael
Carrión, Jerónimo
Carvalho, Antônio de Albuquerque
    Coelho de
Castañeda Castro, Salvador
Castello Branco, Humberto de
    Alencar
Castilla, Ramón
Castillo Armas, Carlos
Castro, Julián
Castro Jijón, Ramón
Castro Ruz, Fidel
Csatro Ruz, Raúl
Caupolicán
Cazneau, William Leslie
Cedillo Martínez, Saturnino
Cerna, Vicente
Chacón, Lázaro
Chamorro Vargas, Emiliano
Chávez, Mariano
Chirino, José Leonardo
Christmas, Lee
Christophe, Henri
Cienfuegos, Camilo
Cieza de León, Pedro de
Cochrane, Lord Thomas Alexander
Codazzi, Agustín
Comonfort, Ignacio
Constant Botelho de Magalhães,
    Benjamin
Córdoba, José María
Corona, Ramón
Coronado, Juan Vázquez de
Cortés, Hernán
Cortés, Martín
Cos, Martín Perfecto de
Cos y Pérez, José María
Costa e Silva, Artur da
Crespo, Joaquín
Croix, Marqués de
Croix, Teodoro de
Crowder, Enoch Herbert

Cruz, Serapio
Cruz, Vicente
Cuauhtemoc
Cuitlahuac
d'Aubuisson, Roberto
Dávila, Miguel R.
Daza, Hilarión
Debray, [Jules] Régis
Degollado, Santos
Delgado Chalbaud, Carlos
Dessalines, Jean Jacques
Di Tella, Torcuato
Dias, Henrique
Díaz, Félix, Jr.
Díaz, José Eduvigis
Díaz, Porfirio
Dorrego, Manuel
Drake, Francis
Duarte, Juan Pablo
Duarte, Pedro
Dutra, Eurico Gaspar
Echeandía, José María de
Enríquez de Guzmán, Alonso
Enríquez Gallo, Alberto
Escobedo, Mariano
Estigarribia, Antonio de la Cruz
Estrada, José Dolores
Facio Segreda, Gonzalo
Fages, Pedro
Falcón, Juan Crisóstomo
Fallas Sibaja, Carlos Luis
Farrell, Edelmiro
Febres-Cordero Ribadeneyra, León
Fernández de Castro Andrade y
    Portugal, Pedro Antonio
Fernández (Hernández) de
    Córdoba, Francisco
Fernández Oreamuno, Próspero
Ferreira, Benigno
Ferrera, Francisco
Figueiredo, João Baptista de
    Oliveira
Figueroa, José
Filísola, Vicente
Flores, Juan José
Flores, Venancio
Fonseca, Hermes Rodrigues da
Fonseca, Manoel Deodoro da
Fonseca Amador, Carlos
Francia, José Gaspar Rodríguez de
Franco, Guillermo
Frémont, John Charles
Fuentes y Guzmán, Francisco
    Antonio de
Gaínza, Gabino
Galán, Luis Carlos
Galeana, Hermenegildo
Galindo, Juan

Galtieri, Leopoldo Fortunato
Galvarino
Gálvez, Bernardo de
Gálvez, Matías de
Gama, Vasco da
Gamarra, Agustín
Gándara Enríquez, Marcos
Garay, Eugenio
Garcés, Francisco Tomás
    Hermenegildo
García, Calixto
García Conde, Pedro
García y González, Vicente
Garibay, Pedro
Garro, José de
Geffrard, Fabre Nicolas
Geisel, Ernesto
Gelly y Obes, Juan Andrés
Gestido, Oscar Daniel
Girón, Francisco Hernández
Goethals, George Washington
Golbery do Couto e Silva
Gomes, Eduardo
Gómez, José Miguel (d. 1805)
Gómez, José Miguel (d. 1921)
Gómez, Juan Vicente
Gómez Pedraza, Manuel
Gómez y Báez, Máximo
González, Manuel
González, Pablo
González Dávila, Gil
González Ortega, Jesús
Gorostiza, Manuel Eduardo de
Grau, Miguel
Grijalva, Juan de
Guardia Gutiérrez, Tomás
Guardiola, Santos
Güemes, Martín
Guerra, Ramón
Guerrero, Vicente
Guevara, Ernesto "Che"
Gutiérrez, Eulalio
Gutiérrez Brothers
Gutiérrez de Lara, José Bernardo
Guzmán, Nuño Beltrán de
Haro y Tamariz, Antonio de
Hernández, José Manuel
Hernández Martínez, Maximiliano
Herrán, Pedro Alcántara
Herrera, Benjamín
Herrera, José Joaquín Antonio
    Florencio
Herrera, Tomás
Heureaux, Ulises
Holguín, Jorge
Houston, Sam
Huascar
Huerta, Victoriano

Huertas, Esteban
Ibáñez del Campo, Carlos
Ibarra, Juan Felipe
Iglesias, Miguel
Irala, Domingo Martínez de
Iturbide, Agustín de
Itzcoatl
Jerez, Máximo
Jiménez de Quesada, Gonzalo
Julião, Carlos
Justo, José Agustín Pedro
Kearny, Stephen W.
Körner, Emil
La Salle, René-Robert Cavelier,
    Sieur de
Lamadrid, Gregorio Aráoz de
Lanusse, Alejandro Augusto
Laprida, Francisco Narciso de
Laredo Bru, Federico
Larrazábal Ugueto, Wolfgang
Las Heras, Juan Gregorio de
Lavalle, Juan Galo
Lavalleja, Juan Antonio
Leclerc, Charles Victor Emmanuel
Leighton Guzmán, Bernardo
Lemus, José María
León, Alonso de
Levingston, Roberto Marcelo
Leyva Solano, Gabriel
Lima e Silva, Luís Alves de
Linares, José María
Linares Alcántara, Francisco
Lindley López, Nicolás
Lisboa, Joaquim Marques
Lonardi, Eduardo
López, Enrique Solano
López, Estanislao
López, Francisco Solano
López, José Hilario
López, Narciso
López Arellano, Oswaldo
López Contreras, Eleázar
López Jordán, Ricardo
López y Fuentes, Gregorio
Lorenzo Troya, Victoriano
Lott, Henrique Batista Duffles
    Teixeira
L'Ouverture, Toussaint
Lozada, Manuel
Luperón, Gregorio
Maceo, Antonio
MacGregor, Gregor
Machado, Gustavo
Machado y Morales, Gerardo
Madureira, Antônio de Sena
Magloire, Paul Eugène
Majano, Adolfo Arnoldo
Maldonado, Francisco Severo

Malespín, Francisco
Manco Capac
Mandu Ladino
Manning, Thomas Courtland
Mansilla, Lucio Victorio
Manso de Maldonado, Antonio
Manso de Velasco, José Antonio
Mar, José de la
Mariño, Santiago
Márquez, Leonardo
Martínez, Esteban José
Martínez, Juan José
Martínez, Tomás
Matamoros y Guridi, Mariano
Maurits, Johan
Médici, Emílio Garrastazú
Medina Angarita, Isaías
Mejía, Tomás
Mejía Victores, Oscar Humberto
Melgarejo, Mariano
Melgares, Facundo
Melo, Custódio José de
Melo, José María
Mendiburu, Manuel de
Mendieta y Montefur, Carlos
Menéndez de Avilés, Pedro
Menocal, Mario García
Merino Castro, José Toribio
Mier y Terán, Manuel
Mina y Larrea, Javier
Miramón, Miguel
Mitre, Bartolomé
Molina, Arturo Armando
Molina Enríquez, Andrés
Molony, Guy
Monagas, José Gregorio
Moncada, José María
Montalvo y Ambulodi Arriola y
    Casabente Valdespino, Francisco
Monteiro, Pedro Aurélio de Góis
Montes, César
Montes, Ismael
Montt Álvarez, Jorge
Montúfar Montes de Oca, Lorenzo
Mora, Fernando de la
Mora Porrás, Juan Rafael
Morales, Agustín
Morales, Francisco Tomás
Morales Bermúdez Cerruti,
    Francisco
Morales Lemus, José
Morazán, Francisco
Morelos y Pavón, José María
Morgan, Henry
Morillo, Pablo
Mosquera, Tomás Cipriano de
Motecuhzoma I
Motecuhzoma II

Múgica, Francisco José
Muñoz, José Trinidad
Napoleon I
Nariño, Antonio
Narváez, Pánfilo de
Navarro Wolff, Antonio
Neve, Felipe de
Nezahualcoyotl
Nord, Pierre Alexis
Noriega Moreno, Manuel Antonio
Nufio, José Dolores
Núñez Vela, Blasco
O, Genovevo de la
Obando, José María
Obregón Salido, Álvaro
O'Donojú, Juan
Odría, Manuel Apolinario
Ogé, Jacques Vicente
O'Higgins, Ambrosio
O'Higgins, Bernardo
O'Leary, Daniel Florencio
O'Leary, Juan Emiliano
Olid, Cristóbal de
Olivares, Conde-Duque de
Onganía, Juan Carlos
Orbegoso, Luis José de
Ordóñez, José
O'Reilly y McDowell, Alejandro
Orlich Bolmarcich, Francisco José
Orozco, Pascual, Jr.
Ortega Saavedra, Daniel
Ortega Saavedra, Humberto
Ortiz de Zárate, Juan and Juana
Osório, Manuel Luís
Ospina, Pedro Nel
Ovando Candía, Alfredo
Páez, José Antonio
País, Frank
Palacio Fajardo, Manuel
Palafox y Mendoza, Juan de
Pando, José Manuel
Pardo, Juan
Paredes, Mariano
Paredes y Arrillaga, Mariano
Pastora Gómez, Edén
Patiño, José de
Pavón Aycinena, Manuel Francisco
Paz, José María
Paz García, Policarpo
Pedreira, Antonio S.
Peixoto, Floriano Vieira
Peñalosa Briceño, Diego Dionisio de
Peñaloza, Ángel Vicente
Peñaranda del Castillo, Enrique
Peralta Azurdia, Enrique
Péralte, Charlemagne Masséna
Pérez, Albino
Pérez, Juan

Pérez Godoy, Ricardo
Pérez Jiménez, Marcos
Perón, Juan Domingo
Pétion, Alexandre Sabès
Pinochet Ugarte, Augusto
Pizarro, José Alonso
Plaza Gutiérrez, Leonidas
Ponce de León, Juan
Popham, Home Riggs
Porter, David
Portolá, Gaspar de
Prado, Mariano Ignacio
Prats González, Carlos
Prestes, Luís Carlos
Pueyrredón, Honorio
Pueyrredón, Juan Martín de
Ramírez, Francisco
Ramírez, Pedro Pablo
Ramírez Mercado, Sergio
Raousset-Boulbon, Gaston Raul de
Rayón, Ignacio
Reed, Walter
Reeve, Henry M.
Regalado, Tomás
Remón Cantera, José Antonio
Reyes, Rafael
Reyes Ogazón, Bernardo
Riaño y Bárcena, Juan Antonio
Ribas, José Félix
Ricchieri, Pablo
Riego y Núñez, Rafael del
Rigaud, André
Ríos Montt, José Efraín
Riva Palacio, Vicente
Rivera, Pedro de
Rivera Carballo, Julio Adalberto
Rivera y Moncada, Fernando de
Robles, Francisco
Robles, Wenceslao
Roca, Julio Argentino
Rochambeau, Donatien Marie
    Joseph de Vimeur de
Rodríguez, Andrés
Rodríguez Cabrillo, Juan
Rodríguez Erdoiza, Manuel
Rodríguez Lara, Guillermo
Rodríguez Luján, Abelardo
Rodríguez Sandoval, Luis Arsenio
Rojas, Isaac
Rojas Pinilla, Gustavo
Rolón, Raimundo
Romero, Carlos Humberto
Romero Rubio, Manuel
Rosa, Ramón
Rosáins, Juan Nepomuceno
Ruíz, Henry
Ruíz de Apodaca, Juan
Russell, John H.

Sá, Estácio de
Sá, Mem de
Sá e Benavides, Salvador
   Correia de
Salaverry, Felipe Santiago
Salazar, Matías
Saldanha da Gama, Luís
   Felipe da
Salgar, Eustorgio
Salnave, Sylvain
Sam, Tirésias Augustin Simon
Samanez Ocampo, David
San Martín, José Francisco de
Sánchez Cerro, Luis Manuel
Sánchez Hernández, Fidel
Sandino, Augusto César
Santa Anna, Antonio López de
Santa Cruz, Andrés de
Santamaría, Haydée
Santana, Pedro
Santander, Francisco de Paula
Sardá, José
Schneider, René
Scott, Winfield
Sebastian (Sebastião) of
   Portugal
Sedeño, Antonio de
Seguín, Juan Nepomuceno
Sodré, Nelson Werneck
Solís, Juan Díaz de
Somoza Debayle, Anastasio
Somoza García, Anastasio
Sonthonax, Léger Félicité
Soto, Hernando de
Soto Alfaro, Bernardo
Soublette, Carlos
Soulouque, Faustin Élie
Sousa, Martim Afonso de

Sousa, Tomé de
Stroessner, Alfredo
Sucre Alcalá, Antonio José de
Tavares, Antônio Rapôso
Távora, Juárez
Taylor, Zachary
Tejeda Olivares, Adalberto
Thomson Porto Mariño, Manuel
   Tomás
Tinoco Granados, Federico
Tornel y Mendívil, José María
Toro, David
Torre, Miguel de la
Torre Tagle, José Bernardo de
   Tagle y Portocarrero
Torres, Juan José
Torres, Luis Emeterio
Torrijos Herrera, Omar
Trujillo, Julián
Trujillo Molina, Rafael Leónidas
Túpac Amaru
Túpac Catari, Julián Apaza
Turcios Lima, Luis Agosto
Ubico y Castañeda, Jorge
Urbina, José María
Urdaneta, Andrés de
Urdaneta, Rafael
Ureta, Eloy G.
Uribe Uribe, Rafael
Urracá
Urrea, José de
Valdivia, Pedro de
Vallejo, Mariano Guadalupe
Varela, Felipe
Vargas, Diego de
Veintimilla, José Ignacio de
Velasco, José Miguel de
Velasco Alvarado, Juan

Velázquez, Diego de
Venegas de Saavedra, Francisco
   Javier
Vernet, Louis
Vértiz y Salcedo, Juan José de
Vial, Pedro
Victoria, Guadalupe
Victoria, Manuel
Vidaurri, Santiago
Videla, Jorge Rafael
Viera, Feliciano
Villa, Francisco "Pancho"
Villagrá, Gaspar Pérez de
Villagrán, Julián and José María
   ("El Chito")
Villarroel López, Gualberto
Villegaignon, Nicolas Durand de
Viola, Roberto Eduardo
Vivanco, Manuel Ignacio
Walker, William
Weyler y Nicolau, Valeriano
Williams Rebolledo, Juan
Wisner von Morgenstern, Franz
Wood, Leonard
Wooster, Charles Whiting
Ydígoras Fuentes, Miguel
Yegros Fulgencio
Yon Sosa, Marco Antonio
Zamorano, Agustín Juan
   Vicente
Zapata, Emiliano
Zaragoza, Ignacio
Zavala, José Victor
Zelaya, José Santos
Zeledón, Benjamín Francisco
Zuloaga, Félix María
Zumbi
Zúñiga, Ignacio

Monarchs and Royalty (including indigenous leaders)

Agüeybana II
Alvarado Xicotencatl, Leonor
Amélia, Empress
Atahualpa (Juan Santos)
Axayacatl
Bonaparte, Joseph
Cajeme
Calfucurá
Cuauhtemoc
Cuitlahuac
Dessalines, Jean Jacques
Ferdinand II of Aragon
Ferdinand VI of Spain

Ferdinand VII of Spain
Henry the Navigator
Huascar
Huayna Capac
Isabel of Brazil, Princess
Isabella I of Castile
Itzcoatl
João I of Portugal
João II of Portugal
João III of Portugal
João IV of Portugal
João V of Portugal
João VI of Portugal

José I of Portugal
Leopoldina, Empress
Manco Capac
Manco Inca
Manuel I of Portugal
Maria I of Portugal
Maria II of Portugal (Maria da
   Gloria)
Maximilian
Montalvo y Ambulodi Arriola y
   Casabente Valdespino, Francisco
Motecuhzoma I
Motecuhzoma II

Napoleon I
Napoleon III
Nezahualcoyotl
Nezahualpilli
Pedro I of Brazil

Pedro II of Brazil
Philip II of Spain
Philip III of Spain
Philip IV of Spain
Philip V of Spain

Sebastian (Sebastião) of
   Portugal
Teresa Christina, Empress
Túpac Amaru
Zumbi

Music and Dance

Aguirre, Julián
Alcaraz, José Antonio
Aldana, José María
Allende-Sarón, Pedro Humberto
Alomía Robles, Daniel
Alves, Francisco
Amenábar, Juan
Aponte-Ledée, Rafael
Araujo, Juan de
Archila, Andrés
Ardévol, José
Arnaz, Desi
Arrau, Claudio León
Asur, José Vicente
Barroso, Ary
Becerra-Schmidt, Gustavo
Bernal Jiménez, Miguel
Berutti, Arturo
Blanco, Juan
Boero, Felipe
Bolaños, César
Broqua, Alfonso
Brouwer, Leo
Buarque, Chico
Calcaño, José Antonio
Callado Junior, Joaquim Antônio
   da Silva
Campos-Parsi, Héctor
Carlos, Roberto
Carrillo, Julián [Antonio]
Castellanos, Gonzalo
Castillo, Jesús
Castro, Ricardo
Caymmi, Dorival
Ceruti, Roque
Cervantes y Kawanagh, Ignacio
Cervetti, Sergio
Chacrinha
Chávez, Carlos
Cluzeau-Mortet, Luis [Ricardo]
Cordero, Roque
Cotapos Baeza, Acario
Cugat, Xavier
de Jesus, Clementina
Dianda, Hilda
Discépolo, Enrique Santos

Duprat, Rogério
Elizaga, José María
Enríquez, Manuel
Escobar, Luis Antonio
Fabini, [Felix Eduardo]
Fernandez, Oscar Lorenzo
Fernández Hidalgo, Gutierre
Ficher, Jacobo
Franco, Hernando
Gaito, Constantino
Galindo, Blas
Gallet, Luciano
Gandini, Gerardo
Gante, Pedro de
Garcia, José Maurício Nunes
García Caturla, Alejandro
García Morillo, Roberto
Gardel, Carlos
Garrido-Lecca Seminario,
   Celso
Gil, Gilberto
Gilardi, Gilardo
Gilberto, João
Ginastera, Alberto Evaristo
Giribaldi, (Vicente) Tomás E.
Gismonti, Egberto
Goicuría y Cabrera, Domingo
Gomes, Antônio Carlos
Gonzaga, Francisca Hedwiges
Gonzaga, Luiz
González Ávila, Jorge
Guarnieri, M[ozart] Camargo
Gutiérrez de Padilla, Juan
Gutiérrez y Espinosa, Felipe
Halffter, Rodolfo
Hernández Moncado, Eduardo
Holzmann, Rodolfo
Infante, Pedro
Isamitt Alarcón, Carlos
Jara, Víctor
Jobim, Antônio Carlos "Tom"
Kagel, Mauricio Raúl
Koellreutter, Hans Joaquim
Krieger, Edino
Lacerda, Osvaldo
Lamarque Pons, Jaurés

Lanza, Alcides
Lara, Agustín
Lavista, Mario
Lecuona y Casado, Ernesto
Leng, Alfonso
Letelier Valdés, Miguel
Levy, Alexandre
Ley, Salvador
López Buchardo, Carlos
López Capillas, Franciso
Mastrogiovanni, Antonio
Mata, Eduardo
Mendes, Gilberto
Mignone, Francisco
Miranda, Carmen
Mojica, José de Jesús
Moncayo García, José Pablo
Morais, Vinícius de
Morales, Melesio
Nascimento, Milton
Nazareth, Ernesto
Negrete, Jorge
Nepomuceno, Alberto
Nobre, Marlos
Oliveira, Willy Correia de
Orbón, Julián
Orejón y Aparicio, José de
Orellana, Joaquín
Orrego-Salas, Juan Antonio
Ortega del Villar, Aniceto
Paniagua y Vasques, Cenobio
Pardavé, Joaquín
Parra, Violeta
Pasta, Carlos Enrico
Paz, Juan Carlos
Peixe, César Guerra
Peralta, Angela
Pineda-Duque, Roberto
Pinilla, Enrique
Pixinguinha
Ponce, Manuel
Portugal, Marcos Antônio da
   Fonseca
Quintanar, Hector
Revueltas, Silvestre
Riva Palacio, Vicente

Rogatis, Pascual de
Roldán, Amadeo
Rosa, Noel
Rosas, Juventino
Sambucetti, Luís Nicolás
Sandi, Luis
Santoro, Claudio
Sarmientos de León, Jorge
  Alvaro
Sas, Andrés

Sepp, Anton
Serebrier, José
Silva, Francisco Manuel da
Silva, Orlando
Sinhô
Storm, Ricardo
Tauriello, Antonio
Torrejón y Velasco, Tomás de
Tosar, Héctor Alberto
Uribe Holguín, Guillermo

Valcárcel Arce, Edgar
Valencia, Antonio María
Vega, Aurelio de
Veloso, Caetano
Vieira, Amaral
Villa-Lobos, Heitor
White y Lafitta, José
Williams, Alberto
Zipoli, Domenico
Zumaya, Manuel de

Outlawry (including pirates, filibusters, freebooters, privateers, and bandits)

Alvarado Xicotencatl,
  Leonor
Bonnet, Stede
Bonny, Anne
Crabb, Henry A.
Drake, Francis

Hawkins, John
Kinney, Henry L.
Lampião
L'Olonnais, Francis
López, Narciso
Morgan, Henry

Raousset-Boulbon, Gaston
  Raul de
Read, Mary
Sharp, Bartholomew
Walker, William
Wallace, Peter

Political Leaders: The Colonial Era

Abalos, José de
Abascal y Souza, José Fernando
Acosta, Tomás
Alarcón, Martín de
Alberro, Francisco de
Alvarado y Mesía, Pedro de
Álvarez, Manuel
Álzaga, Martín de
Amar y Borbón, Antonio
Amat y Junient, Manuel de
Andrade, Gomes Freire de
Arenales, Juan Antonio Álvarez de
Arias de Saavedra, Hernando
Artigas, José Gervasio
Ávila, Pedro Arias de
Avilés, Gabriel
Aycinena, Juan Fermín de
Aycinena Piñol, Juan José de
Ayolas, Juan de
Azara, Félix de
Azcárate y Lezama, Juan Francisco de
Balboa, Vasco Núñez de
Baldorioty de Castro, Ramón
Barros, João de
Bennett, Marshall

Bobadilla, Francisco de
Borja y Aragón, Francisco de
Boves, José Tomás
Bucareli y Ursúa, Antonio María
Bucareli y Ursúa, Francisco de
  Paula
Caballero y Góngora, Antonio
Cabeza de Vaca, Alvar Núñez
Calchaquí, Juan
Calleja del Rey, Félix María
Camacho Roldán, Salvador
Cañedo, Juan de Dios
Caramurú
Cárdenas, Bernardino de
Carlota
Carondelet, François-Louis
  Hector
Carrera, José Miguel
Carvalho, Antônio de Albuquerque
  Coelho de
Caupolicán
Cavallón, Juan de
Cevallos, Pedro Antonio de
Cisneros, Baltasar Hidalgo de
Coelho, Jorge de Albuquerque
Coelho Pereira, Duarte

Columbus, Bartholomew
Columbus, Diego (d. 1515)
Columbus, Diego (d. 1526)
Coronado, Juan Vázquez de
Cortés, Hernán
Coutinho, José Joaquim da Cunha
  de Azeredo
Croix, Marqués de
Croix, Teodoro de
Cueva, Francisco de la
Cueva de Alvarado, Beatriz
  de la
Cueva Enríquez y Saavedra,
  Baltásar de la
Díaz Vélez, José Miguel
Domínguez, Miguel
Elío, Francisco Javier
Enríquez de Almansa, Martín
Eslava y Lazaga, Sebastián de
Espeleta y Galdeano Dicastillo y
  del Prado, Viceroy
Esquiú, Mamerto
Fages, Pedro
Fagoaga y Lizaur, José María
Fernández de Cabrera, Bobadilla,
  Cerda y Mendoza,

Fernández de Córdoba, Diego

Flores Maldonado Martínez y Bodquín, Manuel Anton

Funes, Gregorio

Gaínza, Gabino

Gálvez, Bernardo de

Gálvez, José de

Gálvez, Matías de

Gama, Vasco da

Garay, Francisco de

García de Castro, Lope

Garibay, Pedro

Garro, José de

Gasca, Pedro de la

Gelves, Marqués de

Gil de Taboada y Lemos, Francisco

Girón, Francisco Hernández

Godoy Cruz, Tomás

Güemes, Martín

Guirior, Manuel

Gutiérrez de Piñeres, Juan Francisco

Guzmán, Nuño Beltrán de

Herrera, Tomás

Huascar

Hurtado de Mendoza, Andrés

Hurtado de Mendoza, García

Iturrigaray, José de

Jáuregui, Agustín de

Kearny, Stephen W.

Ladrón de Guevara, Diego

Lamar, Mirabeau Buonaparte

Las Casas, Bartolomé de

Lasuén, Fermín Francisco de

Lavradio, Marquês do

León, Alonso de

López, Narciso

López de Cerrato, Alonso

López de Cogolludo, Diego

Lorenzana y Buitrón, Francisco Antonio de

Luna y Arellano, Tristán de

Maldonado, Rodrigo de Arias

Manco Inca

Manrique de Zúñiga, Alvaro

Manso de Velasco, José Antonio

Marroquín, Francisco

Martínez, Padre Antonio J.

Maurits, Johan

Mendinueta y Múzquiz, Pedro de

Mendoza, Antonio de

Mendoza Caamaño y Sotomayor, José Antonio de

Mendoza y Luna, Juan Manuel de

Messía de la Cerda, Pedro de

Mompox de Zayas, Fernando

Mon y Velarde, Juan Antonio

Montejo, Francisco de

Morga Sánchez Garay y López, Antonio de

Morgan, Henry

Morillo, Pablo

Moya de Contreras, Pedro

Muñoz Rivera, Luis

Namuncurá, Ceferino

Namuncurá, Manuel

Navarra y Rocaful, Melchor de

Navarro Wolff, Antonio

Neve, Felipe de

Núñez Vela, Blasco

O'Donojú, Juan

Ogé, Jacques Vicente

O'Higgins, Ambrosio

O'Higgins, Bernardo

O'Leary, Juan Emiliano

Olivares, Conde-Duque de

Oliveira, Manuel Botelho de

Oñate, Juan de

O'Reilly y McDowell, Alejandro

Ovando, Nicolás de

Palafox y Mendoza, Juan de

Palou, Francisco

Pardo Leal, Jaime

Parish, Woodbine

Paso, Juan José

Pedrosa y Guerrero, Antonio de la

Peñalosa Briceño, Diego Dionisio de

Pérez de Tolosa, Juan

Pizarro, Francisco

Pizarro, Gonzalo

Pizarro, José Alonso

Ponce de León, Juan

Porras, José Basilio

Portocarrero y Lasso de la Vega, Melchor

Portolá, Gaspar de

Prado y Ugarteche, Jorge

Primo de Verdad y Ramos, Francisco

Quiroga, Vasco de

Rada, Manuel de Jesús

Ramalho, João

Ramírez y Blanco, Alejandro

Ramos Arizpe, José Miguel

Revillagigedo, Conde de

Rivera, Pedro de

Rochambeau, Donatien Marie Joseph de Vimeur de

Roldán, Francisco

Rondeau, José

Rosas, Juan Manuel de

Ruíz de Apodaca, Juan

Sá, Mem de

Sá e Benavides, Salvador Correia de

Saco, José Antonio

Sarmiento de Sotomayor, García

Seguín, Juan José María Erasmo

Seguín, Juan Nepomuceno

Sobremonte, Rafael de

Solís Folch de Cardona, José

Solórzano Pereira, Juan de

Sonthonax, Léger Félicité

Sousa, Martim Afonso de

Sousa, Tomé de

Suárez, Inés de

Talamantes, Melchor de

Toledo y Figueroa, Francisco de

Toledo y Leyva, Pedro de

Torre, Miguel de la

Torres y Portugal, Fernando de

Túpac Amaru

Túpac Amaru (José Gabriel Condorcanqui)

Urdaneta, Andrés de

Ursúa, Pedro de

Vaca de Castro, Cristóval

Valdivia, Pedro de

Velasco, Luis de

Velázquez, Diego de

Venegas de Saavedra, Francisco Javier

Vértiz y Salcedo, Juan José de

Viamonte, Juan José

Vicuña Larraín, Francisco Ramón

Vicuña Mackenna, Benjamin

Villagrá, Gaspar Pérez de

Villalonga, Jorge

Villegaignon, Nicolas Durand de

Weyler y Nicolau, Valeriano

Yegros, Fulgencio

Yermo, Gabriel de

Zapata, Felipe

Zorita, Alonso de

Zumbi

Political Leaders: The National Era

Abadía Méndez, Miguel
Aceval, Benjamín
Acevedo Díaz, Eduardo Inés
Achá, José María
Acosta García, Julio
Agüero Rocha, Fernando
Aguilar Vargas, Cándido
Aguirre Cerda, Pedro
Aguirre y Salinas, Osmín
Alamán, Lucas
Alambert, Zuleika
Alberdi, Juan Bautista
Alberto, João
Albizu Campos, Pedro
Albuquerque, Antônio Francisco
    de Paula
Alem, Leandro
Alemán Valdés, Miguel
Alencar, José Martiniano de
Alessandri Palma, Arturo
Alessandri Rodríguez, Jorge
Alexis, Jacques Stéphen
Alfaro, Ricardo Joaquín
Alfaro Delgado, José Eloy
Alfonsín, Raúl Ricardo
Allende Gossens, Salvador
Almazán, Juan Andréu
Almeida, José Américo de
Alonso, Mariano Roque
Alsina, Adolfo
Alsina, Valentín
Alsogaray, Alvaro
Alvarado, Salvador
Álvarez, Juan
Alvear, Carlos María de
Alvear, Marcelo Torcuato de
Amador Guerrero, Manuel
Amézaga, Juan José de
Amunátegui Aldunate, Miguel Luis
Andrada, Antônio Carlos de and
    Martim Francisco
Andrada, José Bonifácio de
Andrade, Oswald de
Andueza Palacio, Raimundo
Aramburu, Pedro Eugenio
Arana, Felipe de
Arana, Francisco J.
Arana Osorio, Carlos
Aranha, Oswaldo
Araujo, Arturo
Arbenz Guzmán, Jacobo
Arboleda, Julio

Arce, Aniceto
Arce, Manuel José
Arce Castaño, Bayardo
Arévalo Bermejo, Juan José
Argüello, Leonardo
Arias, Desiderio
Arias Calderón, Ricardo
Arias Madrid, Arnulfo
Arias Madrid, Harmodio
Arias Sánchez, Oscar
Arismendi, Juan Bautista
Arista, Mariano
Aristide, Jean-Bertrand
Armijo, Manuel
Arosemena, Florencio Harmodio
Arosemena, Juan Demóstenes
Arosemena, Pablo
Arosemena Gómez, Otto
Arosemena Monroy, Carlos Julio
Arosemena Quinzada, Albacíades
Arrais, Miguel
Arroyo del Río, Carlos Alberto
Arze, José Antonio
Aspíllaga Family
Austin, Stephen Fuller
Avellaneda, Nicolás
Ávila Camacho, Manuel
Ayala, Eligio
Ayala, Eusebio
Aycinena, Mariano de
Aycinena, Pedro de
Aylwin Azócar, Patricio
Ayora Cueva, Isidro
Azcona Hoyo, José Simón
Báez, Buenaventura
Báez, Cecilio
Balaguer, Joaquín
Balbín, Ricardo
Baldomir, Alfredo
Ballivián, José
Balmaceda Fernández, José Manuel
Balta, José
Banzer Suárez, Hugo
Baquerizo Moreno, Alfredo
Barbosa, Francisco Villela
Barbosa y Alcalá, José Celso
Barco Vargas, Virgilio
Bareiro, Cándido
Barrientos Ortuño, René
Barrillas, Manuel Lisandro
Barrios, Gerardo
Barrios, Gonzalo

Barrios de Chamorro, Violeta
Barros, Adhemar de
Barroso, Gustavo Dodt
Barrundia, José Francisco
Barrundia, Juan
Batista, Cícero Romão
Batista y Zaldívar, Fulgencio
Batlle, Lorenzo
Batlle Berres, Luis Conrado
Batlle y Ordóñez, José
Baltres Juarros, Luis
Bazaine, François Achille
Bedoya de Molina, Dolores
Bedoya Reyes, Luis
Béjar, Héctor
Belaúnde, Víctor Andrés
Belaúnde Terry, Fernando
Belgrano, Manuel
Bellegarde, Luis Dantès
Belzu, Manuel Isidoro
Benavides, Oscar Raimundo
Benítez, Jaime
Bernardes, Artur da Silva
Berreta, Tomás
Berrío, Pedro Justo
Berro, Carlos
Bertrand, Francisco
Betancourt, Rómulo
Betancur Cuartas, Belisario
Bignone, Reynaldo
Billinghurst, Guillermo Enrique
Blanco Acevedo, Eduardo
Blanco Galindo, Carlos
Bocaiúva, Quintino
Bolívar, Simón
Bonifaz Ascasubi, Neptalí
Bonilla, Policarpo
Bonilla Chirinos, Manuel
Bordaberry, Juan María
Borge, Tomás
Borges de Medeiros, Antônio
    Augusto
Borja Cevallos, Rodrigo
Borno, Joseph Louis E. Antoine
    François
Borrero y Cortázar, Antonio
Bosch Gaviño, Juan
Boyer, Jean-Pierre
Bramuglia, Juan Atilio
Branco, Manuel Alves
Brás Pereira Gomes, Wenceslau
Bravo, Nicolás

Bray, Arturo
Brizola, Leonel
Brum, Baltasar
Bucaram Elmhalin, Asaad
Bulnes Prieto, Manuel
Bunau-Varilla, Philippe Jean
Busch Becerra, Germán
Bustamante, Anastasio
Bustamante y Rivero, José Luis
Caamaño Deñó, Francisco
Caamaño y Gómez Cornejo, José María Plácido
Caballero, Bernardino
Cabañas, José Trinidad
Cáceres, Andrés Avelino
Cáceres, Ramón
Café Filho, João
Caldera Rodríguez, Rafael
Calderón Fournier, Rafael Ángel
Calderón Guardia, Rafael Ángel
Callejas Romero, Rafael Leonardo
Calles, Plutarco Elías
Calógeras, João Pandiá
Campero, Narciso
Campisteguy, Juan
Campo, Rafael
Cámpora, Héctor José
Campos, Francisco Luiz da Silva
Campos, Roberto (de Oliveira)
Campos Sales, Manuel Ferraz de
Candamo, Manuel
Caneca, Frei Joaquím do Amor Divino
Cañedo, Francisco
Cañedo, Juan de Dios
Cantilo, José Luis
Capelo, Joaquín
Carazo Odio, Rodrigo
Cárcano, Ramón José
Cárdenas del Río, Lázaro
Cárdenas Solorzano, Cuauhtémoc
Cardoso, Fernando Henrique
Cardozo, Efraím
Carías Andino, Tiburcio
Carneiro de Campos, José Joaquim
Caro, Miguel Antonio
Carpio Nicolle, Jorge
Carranza, Venustiano
Carrera, José Rafael
Carrillo Colina, Braulio
Carrillo Puerto, Felipe
Carrión, Jerónimo
Cass, Lewis
Castañeda Castro, Salvador
Castelli, Juan José
Castello Branco, Humberto de Alencar
Castilhos, Júlio de

Castilla, Ramón
Castillo, Ramón S.
Castillo Armas, Carlos
Castillo Ledón, Amalia
Castro, Cipriano
Castro, Julián
Castro Madriz, José María
Castro Pozo, Hildebrando
Castro Ruz, Fidel
Castro Ruz, Raúl
Centurión, Carlos R.
Centurión, Juan Crisóstomo
Cerezo Arévalo, Marco Vinicio
Cerna, Vicente
Céspedes, Carlos Manuel de (the Elder)
Céspedes y Quesada, Carlos Manuel de
Chacón, Lázaro
Chamorro, Fruto
Chamorro Cardenal, Pedro Joaquín
Chamorro Vargas, Emiliano
Chaves, Federico
Chaves, Francisco C.
Chaves, Julio César
Chiari, Rodolfo E.
Chiari Remón, Roberto Francisco
Chibás, Eduardo
Christophe, Henri
Cisneros Betancourt, Salvador
Clouthier del Rincón, Manuel J.
Coll y Toste, Cayetano
Collor, Lindolfo
Collor de Mello, Fernando Affonso
Colosio Murrieta, Luis Donaldo
Colunje, Gil
Comonfort, Ignacio
Concha, José Vicente
Cooke, John William
Cordero Crespo, Luis
Córdova, Jorge
Córdova Rivera, Gonzalo S.
Corral Verdugo, Ramón
Cortés Castro, León
Costa e Silva, Artur da
Cotegipe, Barão de
Creel, Enrique Clay
Crespo, Joaquín
Cristiani, Alfredo
Cruz, Arturo
Cruz, Vicente
Cruz Ucles, Ramón Ernesto
Cuestas, Juan Lindolfo
Dantas, Manuel Pinto de Souza
Dartiguenave, Philippe-Sudré
d'Aubuisson, Roberto
Dávila, Miguel R.
Dávila Espinoza, Carlos Guillermo

Daza, Hilarión
de la Huerta, Adolfo
Decoud, Hector Francisco
Decoud, José Segundo
Del Prado, Jorge
Delfim Neto, Antônio
Delgado, José Matías
Derqui, Santiago
D'Escoto Brockmann, Miguel
Díaz Arosemena, Domingo
Díaz, Adolfo
Díaz, Porfirio
Díaz Ordaz, Gustavo
Dickmann, Enrique
Domínguez, Manuel
Dorrego, Manuel
Dorticós Torrado, Osvaldo
Duarte, Juan Pablo
Duarte Fuentes, José Napoleón
Dueñas, Francisco
Dutra, Eurico Gaspar
Duvalier, François
Duvalier, Jean-Claude
Echenique, José Rufino
Echeverría Álvarez, Luis
Echeverría Bianchi, José Antonio
Egaña Fabres, Mariano
Egaña Risco, Juan
Elías, Domingo
Emparán, Vicente
Enríquez Gallo, Alberto
Errázuriz Echaurren, Federico
Errázuriz Zañartu, Federico
Erro, Enrique
Escobar, Patricio
Espaillat, Ulises Francisco
Espinosa y Espinosa, (Juan) Javier
Esquivel, Manuel Amadeo
Estigarribia, José Félix
Estimé, Dumarsais
Estrada, José María (d. 1856)
Estrada Cabrera, Manuel
Estrada Palma, Tomás
Falcón, Juan Crisóstomo
Faoro, Raymundo
Farrell, Edelmiro
Feijó, Diogo Antônio
Fernandes, Florestan
Fernández Alonso, Sévero
Fernández Crespo, Daniel
Fernández Madrid, José
Fernández Oreamuno, Próspero
Fernández y Medina, Benjamín
Ferré Aguayo, Luis Antonio
Ferreira, Benigno
Ferreira Aldunate, Wilson
Ferrera, Francisco
Figueiredo, Afonso Celso de Assis

Figueiredo, Jackson de
Figueiredo, João Baptista de
  Oliveira
Figueres Ferrer, José
Figueroa Alcorta, José
Filísola, Vicente
Flores, Juan José
Flores, Luis A.
Flores, Venancio
Flôres da Cunha, José Antônio
Flores Jijón, Antonio
Fonseca, Manoel Deodoro da
Fortuny, José Manuel
Francia, José Gaspar Rodríguez de
Franco, Guillermo
Franco, Itamar Augusto Cautiero
Franco, Wellington Moreira
Frei Montalva, Eduardo
Freire Serrano, Ramón
Freyre, Gilberto (de Mello)
Frondizi, Arturo
Fujimori, Alberto Keinya
Gabeira, Fernando Nagle
Gallegos, Rómulo
Galtieri, Leopoldo Fortunato
Galván, Manuel de Jesús
Gálvez, Juan Manuel
Gálvez, Mariano
Gamarra, Agustín
Gamarra, Francisca Zubiaga
  Bernales de (La Mariscala)
Garay, Blas
García Calderón, Francisco
García Godoy, Héctor
García Granados, Miguel
García Meza, Luis
García Moreno, Gabriel
García Pérez, Alan
García Salinas, Francisco
Gaviria Trujillo, César Augusto
Geffrard, Fabre Nicolas
Geisel, Ernesto
Gestido, Oscar Daniel
Gill, Juan Bautista
Girón de León, Andrés de Jesús
Godoi, Juan Silvano
Goethals, George Washington
Golbery do Couto e Silva
Gomes, Eduardo
Gómez, Indalecio
Gómez, José Miguel (d. 1921)
Gómez, Juan Vicente
Gómez, Miguel Mariano
Gómez Castro, Laureano
Gómez Farías, Valentín
Gómez Hurtado, Alvaro
Gómez Morín, Manuel
Gómez Pedraza, Manuel

González, Manuel
González Flores, Alfredo
González Ortega, Jesús
González Videla, Gabriel
González Víquez, Cleto
Grau San Martín, Ramón
Grove Vallejo, Marmaduke
Guardia, Ricardo Adolfo de la
Guardia Gutiérrez, Tomás
Guardia Navarro, Ernesto de la
Guardiola, Santos
Gueiler Tejada, Lidia
Guerra, Ramón
Guerrero, Vicente
Guevara, Ernesto "Che"
Guevara Arze, Walter
Guggiari, José Patricio
Guido, José María
Guimarães, Ulysses Silveira
Gutiérrez, José María
Gutiérrez Brothers
Gutiérrez Garbín, Víctor Manuel
Gutiérrez Guerra, José
Guzmán, Enrique
Guzmán Blanco, Antonio Leocadio
Haya de la Torre, Víctor Raúl
Henríquez, Camilo
Henríquez y Carvajal, Francisco
Hernández, José Manuel
Hernández Colón, Rafael
Hernández Martínez, Maximiliano
Herrán, Pedro Alcántara
Herrera, Benjamín
Herrera, Carlos
Herrera, Dionisio de
Herrera, José Joaquín Antonio
  Florencio
Herrera, Luis Alberto de
Herrera Campins, Luis
Herrera y Obes, Julio
Hertzog Garaizabal, Enrique
Heureaux, Ulises
Holguín, Jorge
Houston, Sam
Huerta, Victoriano
Hurtado Larrea, Osvaldo
Hyppolite, Louis Modestin Florville
Ibáñez del Campo, Carlos
Ibarra, Juan Felipe
Iglesias, Miguel
Iglesias Castro, Rafael
Iglesias Pantin, Santiago
Illia, Arturo Umberto
Infante, José Miguel
Irigoyen, Bernardo de
Irisarri, Antonio José de
Iturbide, Agustín de
Jiménez, Enrique A.

Jiménez Oreamuno, Ricardo
Jovellanos, Salvador
Juárez, Benito
Juárez Celman, Miguel
Julião Arruda de Paula, Francisco
Justo, José Agustín Pedro
Justo, Juan B.
Kinney, Henry L.
Kubitschek, Marcia
Kubitschek de Oliveira, Juscelino
La Serna, José de
Labastida y Dávalos, Pelagio
  Antonio de
Lacalle Herrera, Luis Alberto
Lacerda, Carlos Frederico
  Werneck de
Lacerda, Maurício Pavia de
Lagos, Ricardo
Lanusse, Alejandro Augusto
Laredo Bru, Federico
Larrazábal Ugueto, Wolfgang
Larrea, Juan
Las Heras, Juan Gregorio de
Latorre, Lorenzo
Laugerud García, Eugenio Kjell
Lavalleja, Juan Antonio
Lechín Oquendo, Juan
Leconte, Michel Cincinnatus
Leguía, Augusto Bernardino
Lemus, José María
Lencinas, Carlos Washington
León de la Barra, Francisco
Leoni, Raúl
Lerdo de Tejada, Sebastián
Lescot, Élie
Lesseps, Ferdinand Marie,
  Vicomte de
Levingston, Roberto Marcelo
Lima, Alceu Amoroso
Lima, Pedro de Araújo
Linares, José María
Linares Alcántara, Francisco
Lindo Zelaya, Juan
Liniers y Bremond, Santiago de
Lleras, Lorenzo María
Lleras Camargo, Alberto
Lleras Restrepo, Carlos
Lombardo Toledano, Vicente
Lonardi, Eduardo
López, Carlos Antonio
López, Enrique Solano
López, Estanislao
López, Francisco Solano
López, José Hilario
López, Vicente Fidel
López Arellano, Oswaldo
López Contreras, Eleázar
López de Romaña, Eduardo

López Jordán, Ricardo
López Mateos, Adolfo
López Michelsen, Alfonso
López Portillo, José
López Pumarejo, Alfonso
L'Ouverture, Toussaint
Lozano Díaz, Julio
Lucas García, Fernando Romeo
Luís Pereira de Sousa, Washington
Luna Pizarro, Francisco Javier de
Luperón, Gregorio
Lusinchi, Jaime
Lutz, Bertha Maria Julia
Lynch, Elisa Alicia
Machado, Gustavo
Machado y Morales, Gerardo
Mac-Iver Rodríguez, Enrique
Madero, Francisco Indalecio
Madrazo, Carlos A.
Madrid Hurtado, Miguel de la
Magloire, Paul Eugène
Magoon, Charles Edward
Maldonado, Francisco Severo
Malespín, Francisco
Maluf, Paulo Salim
Manning, Thomas Courtland
Mar, José de la
Mariátegui, José Carlos
Marighela, Carlos
Mariño, Santiago
Márquez, José Ignacio de
Marroquín, José Manuel
Martí, Agustín Farabundo
Martínez, Tomás
Mauá, Visconde de
Maza, Manuel Vicente de
Médici, Emílio Garrastazú
Medina, Hugo
Medina Angarita, Isaías
Mejía Victores, Oscar Humberto
Meléndez Chaverri, Carlos
Meléndez Family
Melgarejo, Mariano
Mella, Julio Antonio
Melo, José María
Menchú Tum, Rigoberta
Méndez Fleitas, Epifanio
Méndez Montenegro, Julio César
Méndez Montenegro, Mario
Méndez Pereira, Octavio
Mendieta, Salvador
Mendieta y Montefur, Carlos
Mendoza, Carlos Antonio
Menem, Carlos Saúl
Menocal, Mario García
Merino Castro, José Toribio
Michelina, Santos
Michelini, Zelmar

Miró Cardona, José
Miro Quesada Family
Mitre, Bartolomé
Molina, Arturo Armando
Molina, Marcelo
Molina, Pedro
Molina Ureña, José Rafael
Monagas, José Gregorio
Monagas, José Tadeo
Moncada, José María
Monge Álvarez, Luis Alberto
Monte Alegre, José da Costa
    Carvalho, Marquís de
Monteagudo, Bernardo de
Montealegre Fernández, José María
Monteiro, Pedro Aurélio de Góis
Montes, Ismael
Montt Torres, Manuel
Montúfar, Lorenzo
Mora Fernández, Juan
Mora Porrás, Juan Rafael
Mora Valverde, Manuel
Morais Barros, Prudente José de
Morales, Agustín
Morales, Eusebio A.
Morales Bermúdez, Remigio
Morales Bermúdez Cerruti,
    Francisco
Morazán, Francisco
Moreira da Costa Ribeiro, Delfim
Morelos y Pavón, José María
Moreno, Mariano
Morínigo, Higínio
Mosquera, Manuel José
Mosquera, Tomás Cipriano de
Mosquera y Arboleda, Joaquín
Muñoz Ledo Lazo de la Vega,
    Porfirio
Muñoz Marín, Luis
Muñoz Rivera, Luis
Murillo Toro, Manuel
Murtinho, Joaquim Duarte
Nabuco de Araújo, Joaquim
Nardone, Benito
Nascimento, Abdias do
Neruda, Pablo
Neves, Tancredo de Almeida
Noboa y Arteta, Diego
Nord, Pierre Alexis
Noriega Moreno, Manuel Antonio
Núñez Moldeo, Rafael
Núñez Vargas, Benjamin
Obando, José María
Obando y Bravo, Miguel
Obregón Salido, Álvaro
Odría, Manuel Apolinario
Oduber Quirós, Daniel
Olañeta, José Joaquín Casimiro

Olaya Herrera, Enrique
Olmedo, José Joaquin
Onganía, Juan Carlos
Orbegoso, Luis José de
Orellana, José María
Oribe, Manuel
Orlich Bolmarcich, Francisco José
Ortega Saavedra, Daniel
Ortega Saavedra, Humberto
Ortiz, Roberto Marcelino
Ortiz Rubio, Pascual
Osório, Manuel Luís
Osorio, Oscar
Ospina, Pedro Nel
Ospina Pérez, Mariano
Ospina Rodríguez, Mariano
Ottoni, Teofilo Benedito
Ovando Candía, Alfredo
Pacheco, Gregorio
Pacheco Areco, Jorge
Pacheco da Silva, Osvaldo
Páez, Federico
Páez, José Antonio
Palacio Fajardo, Manuel
Palacios, Alfredo L.
Palenque, Carlos
Pando, José Manuel
Paraná, Honôrio Hermeto Carneiro
    Leão, Marquês de
Pardo y Barreda, José
Pardo y Lavalle, Manuel
Paredes, Mariano
Paredes y Arrillaga, Mariano
Parra, Aquileo
Pascal-Trouillot, Ertha
Paso, Juan José
Passarinho, Jarbas Gonçalves
Pastora Gómez, Edén
Pastrana Borrero, Misael
Patrón Costas, Robustiano
Pavón Aycinena, Manuel Francisco
Paz, José María
Paz Baraona, Miguel
Paz Estenssoro, Víctor
Paz García, Policarpo
Paz Zamora, Jaime
Peçanha, Nilo Procópio
Pedreira, Antonio S.
Peixoto, Floriano Vieira
Peixoto, Júlio Afrânio
Pellacani, Dante
Pellegrini, Carlos
Pena, Afonso Augusto Moreira
Peña, Manuel Pedro de
Peña Gómez, José Francisco
Peñaloza, Ángel Vicente
Peñaranda del Castillo, Enrique
Peralta Azurdia, Enrique

Pereira, José Clemente
Pérez, Carlos Andrés
Pérez Jiménez, Marcos
Pérez Mascayano, José Joaquín
Pérez Salas, Francisco Antonio
Perón, Juan Domingo
Perón, María Estela Martínez de
Perón, María Eva Duarte de
Pessoa, Epitácio da Silva
Pessoa Cavalcanti de Albuquerque,
  João
Pétion, Alexandre Sabès
Pezet, Juan Antonio
Picado Michalski, Teodoro
Piérola, Nicolás de
Pinedo, Federico
Pinheiro, José Feliciano Fernandes
Pinheiro Machado, José Gomes
Pinho, José Wanderley de Araújo
Pino Suárez, José María
Pinochet Ugarte, Augusto
Pinto Díaz, Francisco Antonio
Pinto Garmendia, Aníbal
Plaza, Victorino de la
Plaza Gutiérrez, Leonidas
Plaza Lasso, Galo
Polk, James Knox
Ponce Enríquez, Camilo
Porras, Belisario
Portes Gil, Emilio
Posadas, Gervasio Antonio de
Prado, Mariano Ignacio
Prado y Ugarteche, Javier
Prado y Ugarteche, Manuel
Prat Echaurren, Jorge
Prestes, Luís Carlos
Prestes de Albuquerque, Julio
Price, George Cadle
Prieto, Guillermo
Prieto Figueroa, Luis Beltrán
Prío Socarrás, Carlos
Puente Uceda, Luis de la
Pueyrredón, Honorio
Pueyrredón, Juan Martín de
Quadros, Jânio da Silva
Queirós Coutinho Matoso da
  Câmara, Eusébio de
Quiñones Molina, Alfonso
Quintana, Manuel
Quintana Roo, Andrés
Quiroga, Juan Facundo
Quiroga Santa Cruz, Marcelo
Ramírez, Francisco
Ramírez, Pedro Pablo
Ramos Mejía, Ezequiel
Regalado, Tomás
Remón Cantera, José Antonio
Restrepo, Carlos Eugenio

Restrepo, José Manuel
Revueltas, José
Reyes, Rafael
Reyes Ogazón, Bernardo
Reyna Barrios, José María
Riani, Clodsmith
Riesco Errázuriz, Germán
Rio Branco, Barão do
Rio Branco, Visconde do
Ríos Montt, José Efraín
Ríos Morales, Juan Antonio
Rivadavia, Bernardino
Rivarola, Cirilo Antonio
Rivas, Patricio
Rivera, Fructuoso
Rivera, Joaquín
Rivera Cabezas, Antonio
Rivera Carballo, Julio Adalberto
Rivera Maestre, Miguel
Rivera Paz, Mariano
Robles, Francisco
Robles, Marcos Aurelio
Roca, Julio Argentino
Roca Rodríguez, Vicente Ramón
Rocha, Dardo
Rocha, Justiniano José da
Rockefeller, Nelson Aldrich
Rodas Alvarado, Modesto
Rodrigues Alves, Francisco de Paula
Rodríguez, Andrés
Rodríguez, Carlos Rafael
Rodríguez Demorizi, Emilio
Rodríguez Lara, Guillermo
Rodríguez Luján, Abelardo
Rojas, Isaac
Rojas, Pedro José
Rojas Paúl, Juan Pablo
Rojas Pinilla, Gustavo
Roldós Aguilera, Jaime
Romero, Carlos Humberto
Romero, Oscar Arnulfo
Romero Barceló, Carlos
Roosevelt, Franklin Delano
Roosevelt, Theodore
Rosa, Ramón
Rosas, Juan Manuel de
Roy, Eugène
Ruiz Cortines, Adolfo
Russell, John H.
Saavedra, Cornelio de
Saavedra Lamas, Carlos
Saavedra Mallea, Juan Bautista
Sacasa, Juan Batista
Sáenz Peña, Luis
Sáenz Peña, Roque
Salamanca, Daniel
Salas, Manuel de
Salaverry, Felipe Santiago

Salazar, Matías
Salgado, Plinio
Salgar, Eustorgio
Salinas de Gortari, Carlos
Salnave, Sylvain
Salomon, Étienne Lysius Félicité
Sam, Jean Villbrun Guillaume
Sam, Tirésias Augustin Simon
Samanez Ocampo, David
Samper Agudelo, Miguel
Sanabria Martínez, Víctor M.
Sánchez, Luis Alberto
Sánchez Cerro, Luis Manuel
Sánchez de Lozada Bustamante,
  Gonzalo
Sánchez Hernández, Fidel
Sánchez Vilella, Roberto
Sandino, Augusto César
Sandoval, José León
Sanfuentes Andonaegui, Juan Luis
Sanguinetti, Julio María
Santa Anna, Antonio López de
Santa Cruz, Andrés de
Santa María González, Domingo
Santana, Pedro
Santos, Eduardo
São Vicente, José Antônio Pimenta
  Bueno, Marquês de
Saraiva, José Antônio
Saravia, Aparicio
Sarmiento, Domingo Faustino
Sarney, José
Schaerer, Eduardo
Schick Gutiérrez, René
Sendic, Raúl
Seoane, Manuel
Seregni, Líber
Serrano Elías, Jorge Antonio
Siles Zuazo, Hernán
Silva, Benedita da
Silva, Lindolfo
Silva, Luis Inácio Lula da
Silva Lisboa, José da
Simon, Antoine
Somoza Debayle, Anastasio
Somoza Debayle, Luis
Somoza García, Anastasio
Soto, Marco Aurelio
Soto Alfaro, Bernardo
Soublette, Carlos
Soulouque, Faustin Élie
Souza, Luiza Erundina de
Stefanich, Juan
Stroessner, Alfredo
Suárez, Marco Fidel
Suazo Córdova, Roberto
Sucre Alcalá, Antonio José de
Tajes, Máximo

Talavera, Manuel
Taunay, Alfredo d'Escragnolle,
  Vicomte de
Tavares Bastos, Aureliano Cândido
Taylor, Zachary
Tejada Sorzano, José Luis
Tejedor, Carlos
Terra, Gabriel
Thompson, George
Tocornal, Joaquín
Tomic, Radomiro
Toro, David
Toro Zambrano, Mateo de
Torre, Lisandro de la
Torre Tagle, José Bernardo de
  Tagle y Portocarrero
Torres, Juan José
Torres, Luis Emeterio
Torrijos Herrera, Omar
Trejos Fernández, José Joaquín
Tronscoso de la Concha, Manuel
  de Jesús
Trujillo, Julián
Trujillo Molina, Rafael Leónidas
Turbay, Gabriel
Turbay Ayala, Julio César
Ubico y Castañeda, Jorge
Ugarte, Marcelino
Ulate Blanco, Otilio
Ungo, Guillermo Manuel
Urbina, José María

Urdaneta, Rafael
Ureta, Eloy G.
Uriburu, José Evaristo
Uriburu, José Félix
Urquiza, Justo José de
Urriolagoitía, Mamerto
Urrutia Lleó, Manuel
Uruguai, Visconde do
Valencia, Guillermo León
Valladares, Tomás
Valle, José Cecilio del
Vallejo, Mariano Guadalupe
Vallenilla Lanz, Laureano
Varas de la Barra, Antonio
Varela, Felipe
Vargas, Getúlio Dornelles
Vargas, José María
Vargas Llosa, Mario
Varona y Pera, Enrique José
Vasconcelos, Bernardo
  Pereira de
Vásquez, Horacio
Veiga, Evaristo Ferreira da
Veintimilla, José Ignacio de
Velasco, José Miguel de
Velasco Alvarado, Juan
Velasco Ibarra, José María
Velázquez Sánchez, Fidel
Victoria, Guadalupe
Victoria, Manuel
Videla, Jorge Rafael

Viera, Feliciano
Vieytes, Hipólito
Vigil, Donaciano
Villa, Francisco "Pancho"
Villagrán Kramer, Francisco
Villalba, Jóvito
Villarroel López, Gualberto
Villazón, Eliodoro
Villeda Morales, Ramón
Vincent, Sténio Joseph
Viola, Roberto Eduardo
Viteri y Ungo, Jorge
Vivanco, Manuel Ignacio
Volio Jiménez, Jorge
Walker, William
Weffort, Francisco Correia
Williams Calderón, Abraham
Williman, Claudio
Wilson, Woodrow
Wolfskill, William
Ydígoras Fuentes, Miguel
Ynsfrán, Edgar L.
Yrigoyen, Hipólito
Zaldúa, Francisco Javier
Zavala, Lorenzo de
Zayas y Alfonso, Alfredo
Zeballos, Estanislao
Zelaya, José Santos
Zubizarreta, Gerónimo
Zuloaga, Félix María
Zúñiga, Ignacio

Public Administration, Civil Service, and Diplomacy

Acosta García, Julio
Aguilar Vargas, Cándido
Albán, Laureano
Alberdi, Juan Bautista
Alberto, João
Albuquerque, Antônio Francisco
  de Paula
Alcorta, Diego
Alfaro, Ricardo Joaquín
Almonte, Juan Nepomuceno
Altamirano, Ignacio Manuel
Alvarado, Salvador
Amador, Manuel E.
Andrade, Carlos Drummond de
Andrade, Gomes Freire de
Andueza Palacio, Raimundo
Angelis, Pedro de
Arana, Felipe de
Arana Osorio, Carlos
Arango y Parreño, Francisco de

Arciniegas, Germán
Arévalo Bermejo, Juan José
Arévalo Martínez, Rafael
Arguedas, Alcides
Argüello, Leonardo
Argüello, Santiago
Arias Sánchez, Oscar
Armijo, Manuel
Arosemena, Justo
Arriaga, Ponciano
Austin, Stephen Fuller
Azcuénaga, Miguel de
Balcarce, Mariano
Baptista, Mariano
Baquíjano y Carrillo de Córdoba,
  José de
Barbosa, Francisco Villela
Barbosa de Oliveira, Rui
Barreda y Laos, Felipe
Barreiro, Antonio

Barrios, Gonzalo
Barros, João de
Barroso, Gustavo Dodt
Barrundia, José Francisco
Barrundia, Juan
Bassols, Narciso
Batres Juarros, Luis
Bedoya Reyes, Luis
Benítez, Jaime
Berges, José
Bernardes, Artur da Silva
Betancourt, Rómulo
Blaine, James Gillespie
Blanco, José Félix
Bonifaz Ascasubi, Neptalí
Borba Gato, Manuel de
Borge, Tomás
Borges, Jorge Luis
Borno, Joseph Louis E. Antoine
  François

Borrero y Cortázar, Antonio
Braden, Spruille
Bunau-Varilla, Philippe Jean
Cabeza de Vaca, Alvar Núñez
Caldera Rodríguez, Rafael
Calderón Fournier, Rafael Ángel
Calderón Guardia, Rafael Ángel
Callejas Romero, Rafael Leonardo
Calógeras, João Pandiá
Calvo, Carlos
Camarena, Enrique
Campero, Narciso
Campo, Rafael
Campomanes, Pedro Rodríguez,
    Conde de
Campos, Francisco Luiz da Silva
Campos, Roberto (de Oliveira)
Campos Sales, Manuel Ferraz de
Cañas, José Simeón
Cañedo, Juan de Dios
Canning, George
Carazo Odio, Rodrigo
Carbo y Noboa, Pedro José
Cárcano, Miguel Ángel
Cárdenas Solorzano, Cuauhtémoc
Carneiro de Campos, José
    Joaquim
Caro, José Eusebio
Caro, Miguel Antonio
Carondelet, François-Louis Hector
Carrillo Colina, Braulio
Carrillo Flores, Antonio
Carrillo Flores, Nabor
Carvalho, Antônio de Albuquerque
    Coelho de
Caso y Andrade, Alfonso
Castañeda Castro, Salvador
Castillo Ledón, Amalia
Castro Madriz, José María
Castro Ruz, Raúl
Cazneau, William Leslie
Cedillo Martínez, Saturnino
Chamorro Vargas, Emiliano
Chatfield, Frederick
Chávez, Mariano
Chonchol, Jacques
Christmas, Lee
Clay, Henry
Cobos, Francisco de los
Coelho, Jorge de Albuquerque
Coelho Pereira, Duarte
Coll y Toste, Cayetano
Collor, Lindolfo
Colosio Murrieta, Luis Donaldo
Colunje, Gil
Concha, José Vicente
Constant Botelho de Magalhães,
    Benjamin

Córdova Rivera, Gonzalo S.
Corona, Ramón
Cortés Castro, León
Costa, Hipólito José da
Cotegipe, Barão de
Coutinho, Rodrigo Domingos
    Antonio de Sousa
Couto, José Bernardo
Creel, Enrique Clay
Crowder, Enoch Herbert
Cruz, Arturo
Dantas, Manuel Pinto de Souza
de la Huerta, Adolfo
Del Monte, Domingo
Delfim Neto, Antônio
Delgado Chalbaud, Carlos
D'Escoto Brockmann, Miguel
Díaz, Félix, Jr.
Díaz Vélez, José Miguel
Dobles Segreda, Luis
Domínguez, Miguel
Dorticós Torrado, Osvaldo
Drago, Luis María
Dulles, John Foster
Durán, Fray Narciso
Dutra, Eurico Gaspar
Echeandía, José María de
Echeverría Álvarez, Luis
Emparán, Vicente
Encinas, José Antonio
Ensenada, Cenón de Somodevilla,
    Marqués de la
Escalante, Aníbal
Escobedo, Mariano
Estimé, Dumarsais
Fabela Alfaro, Isidro
Facio Brenes, Rodrigo
Facio Segreda, Gonzalo
Falcón, José
Fallas Sibaja, Carlos Luis
Feijó, Diogo Antônio
Fernández, Max
Ferré Aguayo, Luis Antonio
Ferrera, Francisco
Figueroa, José
Figueroa Larraín, Emiliano
Finlay, Carlos Juan
Floridablanca, Conde de
Fonseca, Juan Rodríguez de
Forbes, John Murray
Forbes, William Cameron
Fuentes, Carlos
Fuentes, Manuel Atanasio
Gallegos, Rómulo
Galván Rivera, Mariano
Gálvez, José de
Gamboa Iglesias, Federico
Gamio Martínez, Manuel

García Calderón, Francisco
García Godoy, Héctor
García Robles, Alfonso
García Salinas, Francisco
Garrido Canabal, Tomás
Gastão d'Orléans
Gelly, Juan Andrés
Gelly y Obes, Juan Andrés
Goethals, George Washington
Golbery do Couto e Silva
Gomes, Eduardo
Gómez, Indalecio
Gómez, José Valentín
Gómez, Juan Gualberto
Gómez, Miguel Mariano
Gómez Pedraza, Manuel
Gondra, Manuel
Gonzaga, Tomás Antônio
González, Abraham
González, Florentino
González, Manuel
González Ortega, Jesús
Gorostiza, Manuel Eduardo de
Gorostiza Acalá, José
Graef Fernández, Carlos
Guardia, Ricardo Adolfo de la
Guevara, Ernesto "Che"
Gutiérrez, Eulalio
Gutiérrez Estrada, José María
Gutiérrez Garbín, Victor Manuel
Guzmán, Antonio Leocadio
Haro Barraza, Guillermo
Haro y Tamariz, Antonio de
Hawkins, John
Hernández, José
Hernández Colón, Rafael
Herrán, Pedro Alcántara
Herrera Campins, Luis
Herrera Lane, Felipe
Holguín, Jorge
Hull, Cordell
Iglesias, José María
Jiménez, Enrique A.
Juan y Santacilia, Jorge
Kubitschek, Marcia
Kubitschek de Oliveira, Juscelino
Kumate Rodríguez, Jesús
Larrazábal Ugueto, Wolfgang
Lavalle Urbina, María
Lavradio, Marquês do
Le Bretón, Tomás Alberto
Lencinas, Carlos Washington
León de la Barra, Francisco
Leoni, Raúl
Lerdo de Tejada, Miguel
Lerdo de Tejada, Sebastián
Lescot, Élie
Letelier de Solar, Orlando

Lewis, Roberto
Lima, Alceu Amoroso
Lima, Pedro de Araújo
Limantour, José Yves
Lisboa, Joaquim Marques
Lleras, Lorenzo María
Lleras Camargo, Alberto
Lleras Restrepo, Carlos
López, Vicente Fidel
López Arellano, Oswaldo
López Mateos, Adolfo
López Michelsen, Alfonso
López Portillo, José
López Rega, José
Lott, Henrique Batista Duffles
    Teixeira
Lutzenberger, José
Machado, Gustavo
Machado de Assis, Joaquim Maria
Machado y Morales, Gerardo
Madrazo, Carlos A.
Madrid Hurtado, Miguel de la
Magalhães, Domingos José
    Gonçalves de
Maluf, Paulo Salim
Mann, Thomas Clifton
Mansilla, Lucio Victorio
Manso de Maldonado, Antonio
Mariño, Santiago
Márquez, José Ignacio de
Martyr, Peter
Masferrer, Alberto
Maurits, Johan
Médici, Emílio Garrastazú
Mello, Zélia Maria Cardoso de
Melo, Leopoldo
Melo e Castro, Martinho de
Melo Franco, Afonso Arinos de
Melo Franco, Afrânio de
Melo Neto, João Cabral de
Méndez Pereira, Octavio
Mendiburu, Manuel de
Mendieta, Salvador
Mendieta y Montefur, Carlos
Mendoza, Antonio de
Michelina, Santos
Mindlin, José E.
Miró Cardona, José
Mistral, Gabriela
Molina, Marcelo
Molina Bedoya, Felipe
Molina Enríquez, Andrés
Monge Álvarez, Luis Alberto
Monte Alegre, José da Costa Car-
    valho, Marquís de
Monteagudo, Bernardo de
Montealegre Fernández, José María
Monteiro, Pedro Aurélio de Góis

Monteiro, Tobias do Rêgo
Montt Torres, Manuel
Montúfar, Lorenzo
Montúfar Montes de Oca, Lorenzo
Moog, Vianna
Mora, José María Luis
Mora Otero, José Antonio
Mora Porrás, Juan Rafael
Mora Valverde, Manuel
Morales Carrión, Arturo
Morales Lemus, José
Moreno, Fulgencio
Morones, Luis
Morrow, Dwight Whitney
Moshinsky Borodianksky, Marcos
Mosquera, Tomás Cipriano de
Mosquera y Arboleda, Joaquín
Moya de Contreras, Pedro
Múgica, Francisco José
Muñoz Ledo Lazo de la Vega,
    Porfirio
Murillo Toro, Manuel
Murtinho, Joaquim Duarte
Nabuco de Araújo, Joaquim
Naón, Rómulo S.
Neves, Tancredo de Almeida
Novo, Salvador
Núñez Moledo, Rafael
Ocampo, Melchor
Oduber Quirós, Daniel
Olaya Herrera, Enrique
Olivares, Conde-Duque de
Oliveira Lima, Manuel de
Orfila, Washington Alejandro José
    Luis
Orlich Bolmarchich, Francisco José
Orozco y Berra, Manuel
Ortiz, Fernando
Ortiz de Ayala, Simón Tadeo
Ortiz Mena, Antonio
Osório, Manuel Luís
Ospina, Pedro Nel
Ospina Pérez, Mariano
Otero, Mariano
Padilla Peñalosa, Ezequiel
Páez, Federico
Páez, José Antonio
Palacio Fajardo, Manuel
Pani Arteaga, Alberto J.
Paraná, Honôrio Hermeto Carneiro
    Leão, Marquês de
Pareja Diezcanseco, Alfredo
Parra, Aquileo
Passarinho, Jarbas Gonçalves
Pastrana Borrero, Misael
Paterson, William
Patiño, José de
Patiño, Simón Iturri

Payno y Flores, Manuel
Paz, Octavio
Paz Soldán Family
Pearson, Weetman Dickinson
Peçanha, Nilo Procópio
Peixoto, Júlio Afrânio
Pellacani, Dante
Pellegrini, Carlos
Pellicer Cámara, Carlos
Pena, Afonso Augusto Moreira
Pena, Luís Carlos Martins
Peña Gómez, José Francisco
Peña y Peña, Manuel de la
Peralta Azurdia, Enrique
Pereira, José Clemente
Pérez, Albino
Pérez, Carlos Andrés
Pérez Jiménez, Marcos
Pérez Mascayano, José Joaquín
Pessoa, Epitácio da Silva
Pessoa Cavalcanti de Albuquerque,
    João
Picado Michalski, Teodoro
Pinedo, Federico
Pinheiro, José Feliciano Fernandes
Pinho, José Wanderley de Araújo
Piñol y Sala, José
Plaza Gutiérrez, Leonidas
Plaza Lasso, Galo
Poinsett, Joel Roberts
Pombal, Marquês de (Sebastião
    José de Carvalho e Melo)
Porras, Belisario
Porter, David
Portes Gil, Emilio
Prebisch, Raúl
Prieto, Guillermo
Prieto Figueroa, Luis Beltrán
Puig Casauranc, José Manuel
Queirós Coutinho Matoso da
    Câmara, Eusébio de
Queiroz, Dinah Silveira de
Quiñones Molina, Alfonso
Quintana Roo, Andrés
Quintero, Ángel
Rabasa, Emilio
Ramírez, Ignacio
Ramírez, José Fernando
Ramírez Vázquez, Pedro
Ramírez y Blanco, Alejandro
Ramos Arizpe, José Miguel
Ramos Mejía, Ezequiel
Ramos y Magaña, Samuel
Rayón, Ignacio
Reed, Walter
Rejón, Manuel Crescencio
Rengifo Cárdenas, Manuel
Restrepo, Carlos Eugenio

Reyes, Rafael
Reyes Ochoa, Alfonso
Reyes Ogazón, Bernardo
Ribeiro, Darcy
Rio Branco, Barão do
Rio Branco, Visconde do
Rivarola, Rodolfo
Robles, Marcos Aurelio
Roca, Blas
Roca Rodríguez, Vicente Ramón
Rockefeller, Nelson Aldrich
Rodney, Caesar Augustus
Rodríguez, Carlos Rafael
Rodríguez Demorizi, Emilio
Rodríguez Erdoiza, Manuel
Rodríguez Luján, Abelardo
Rojas, Pedro José
Rojas Paúl, Juan Pablo
Rojas Urtuguren, José
   Antonio de
Romero, Matías
Romero Barceló, Carlos
Romero Rubio, Manuel
Rondon, Cândido Mariano da
   Silva
Rosáins, Juan Nepomuceno
Roscio, Juan Germán
Rubí, Marqués de
Rubião, Murilo
Ruiz Cortines, Adolfo
Ruiz de Alarcón y Mendoza,
   Juan
Sá, Mem de
Sá e Benavides, Salvador
   Correia de
Saavedra Lamas, Carlos
Saco, José Antonio
Sáenz, Moisés
Sáenz Garza, Aaron
Salgar, Eustorgio
Salinas de Gortari, Carlos
Sánchez, Prisciliano

Sánchez de Bustamante y Sirven,
   Antonio
Sánchez de Tagle, Francisco
   Manuel
Sánchez Hernández, Fidel
Sánchez Vilella, Roberto
Sandoval Vallarta, Manuel
Santamaría, Haydée
Santos, Eduardo
São Vicente, José Antônio Pimenta
   Bueno, Marquês de
Schaerer, Eduardo
Schick Gutiérrez, René
Scliar, Moacyr
Seguín, Juan José María Erasmo
Sierra Méndez, Justo
Sierra O'Reilly, Justo
Silva Herzog, Jesús
Simonsen, Mário Henrique
Soto Alfaro, Bernardo
Soublette, Carlos
Sousa, Otávio Tarqüínio de
Squier, Ephraim George
Stephens, John Lloyd
Suárez, Marco Fidel
Távara y Andrade, Santiago
Teixeira, Anisio Espinola
Tinoco Granados, Federico
Tocornal, Joaquín
Toro, Fermín
Torres, Luis Emeterio
Torres Bodet, Jaime
Tronscoso de la Concha, Manuel
   de Jesús
Trujillo, Julián
Tugwell, Rexford Guy
Turbay, Gabriel
Ugarte, Manuel
Urbina, José María
Urbina, Luis Gonzaga
Uribe Uribe, Rafael
Urrea, José de

Urrutia Lleó, Manuel
Uruguai, Visconde do
Urvina Jado, Francisco
Valle, Artistóbulo del
Valle, José Cecilio del
Varas de la Barra, Antonio
Vargas, Getúlio Dornelles
Varnhagen, Francisco Adolfo de
   (Visconde de Porto Seguro)
Vasconcelos Calderón, José
Vázquez de Ayllón, Lucas
Velázquez Sánchez, Fidel
Vélez Sarsfield, Dalmacio
Vidaurri, Santiago
Vieira, Antônio
Villanueva, Carlos Raúl
Villas Bôas Brothers
Villaurrutia, Jacobo de
Villeda Morales, Ramón
Vincent, Sténio Joseph
Volio Jiménez, Jorge
Ward, Henry George
Washburn, Charles Ames
Welles, Sumner
Wheelock Román, Jaime
Wilde, Eduardo
Wilson, Henry Lane
Wood, Leonard
Yáñez Santos Delgadillo,
   Agustín
Ynsfrán, Pablo Max
Zaldúa, Francisco Javier
Zamora, Rubén
Zaragoza, Ignacio
Zarco, Francisco
Zavala, Joaquín
Zavala, Lorenzo de
Zavala, Silvio
Zayas y Alfonso, Alfredo
Zeballos, Estanislao
Zubirán Achondo, Salvador
Zubizarreta, Gerónimo

Religion (including saints, shamans, missionaries, and clerical leaders)

Abad y Queipo, Manuel
Abbad y Lasierra, Íñigo
Acosta, José de
Alegre, Francisco Javier
Alexander VI, Pope
Anchieta, José de
Andreoni, João Antônio
Antequera y Castro, José de
Aparecida, Nossa Senhora da

Aristide, Jean-Bertrand
Arns, Paulo Evaristo
Balbuena, Bernardo de
Batista, Cícero Romão
Bazán, Juan Gregorio
Beltrán, Luis
Beltrán, Luis (Saint)
Benavides, Alonso de
Bethancourt, Pedro de San José de

Blanco, José Félix
Boff, Leonardo
Bolaños, Luis de
Bonfim, Nosso Senhor do
Brasseur de Bourbourg, Charles
   Étienne
Caballero y Góngora, Antonio
Câmara, Hélder
Cañas, José Simeón

Caneca, Frei Joaquím do Amor Divino
Cardenal, Ernesto
Cárdenas, Bernardino de
Cardim, Frei Fernão
Carney, James "Guadalupe"
Casaldáliga, Pedro
Casanova y Estrada, Ricardo
Casáus y Torres, Ramón
Castañeda, Francisco de Paula
Castillo y Guevara, Francisca Josefa de la Concepción de
Claver, Pedro
Clavigero, Francisco Javier
Cobo, Bernabé
Conselheiro, Antônio
Cortés de Madariaga, José
Cos y Pérez, José María
Coutinho, José Joaquim da Cunha de Azeredo
Cuadra, Pablo Antonio
Cuevas, Mariano
Delgado, José Matías
Díaz de Guzmán, Ruy
Dobrizhoffer, Martín
Donovan, Jean
Durán, Diego
Durán, Fray Narciso
Durão, José de Santa Rita
Errázuriz Valdivieso, Crescente
Esquiú, Mamerto
Feijóo, Benito Jerónimo
Figueiredo, Jackson de
Fonseca, Juan Rodríguez de
Fresno Larraín, Juan Francisco
Frías, Antonio
Funes, Gregorio
Fúrlong Cárdiff, Guillermo
Gage, Thomas
Gallo Goyenechea, Pedro León
Gante, Pedro de
Garcés, Francisco Tomás Hermenegildo
García, Diego
García Diego y Moreno, Francisco
García Peláez, Francisco de Paula
Gasca, Pedro de la
Girón de León, Andrés de Jesús
Godoy, Manuel
Gómez, José Valentín
González de Santa Cruz, Roque
González Suárez, (Manuel María) Federico
Gorriti, Juan Ignacio de

Gutiérrez, Gustavo
Henríquez, Camilo
Herrán y Zaldúa, Antonio Saturnino
Herrera, Bartolomé
Hidalgo y Costilla, Miguel
Jerez, Francisco de
Juan Diego
Juana Inés de la Cruz, Sor
Kino, Eusebio Francisco
Labastida y Dávalos, Pelagio Antonio de
Landa, Diego de
Landázuri Ricketts, Juan
Landívar, Rafael
Las Casas, Bartolomé de
Lasuén, Fermín Francisco de
Leo XIII, Pope
Liendo y Goicoechea, José Antonio
Lima, Alceu Amoroso
Llorente y Lafuente, Anselmo
López de Cogolludo, Diego
López Trujillo, Alfonso
Lorenzana y Buitrón, Francisco Antonio de
Lozano, Pedro
Luna Pizarro, Francisco Javier de
Luque, Hernando de
Maldonado, Francisco Severo
Maldonado, Rodrigo de Arias
Margil de Jesús, Antonio
Marroquín, Francisco
Martínez, Padre Antonio J.
Martyr, Peter
Matamoros y Guridi, Mariano
Melville, Thomas and Margarita
Menininha do Gantois, Mãe
Mier Noriega y Guerra, José Servando Teresa de
Mogrovejo, Toribio Alfonso de
Montesinos, Antonio de
Mora, José María Luis
Mora y del Río, José
Morelos y Pavón, José María
Mosquera, Manuel José
Motolinía, Toribio de
Moya de Contreras, Pedro
Munguía, Clemente de Jesús
Niza, Marcos de
Nóbrega, Manuel da
Núñez Vargas, Benjamín
Nusdorffer, Bernardo

Obando y Bravo, Miguel
Oré, Luis Gerónimo de
Oro, Justo Santa María de
Palafox y Mendoza, Juan de
Palou, Francisco
Pérez Aguirre, Luis
Piñol y Aycinena, Bernardo
Porres, Martín de
Quiroga, Vasco de
Rada, Manuel de Jesús
Ramos Arizpe, José Miguel
Rivera Damas, Arturo
Rocha, Manoel Ribeiro
Romero, Oscar Arnulfo
Rosa de Lima
Rossell y Arellano, Mariano
Ruiz de Montoya, Antonio
Sahagún, Bernardino de
Sales, Eugênio de Araújo
Salvador, Vicente do
Sanabria Martínez, Víctor M.
Sepp, Anton
Serra, Junipero
Serrano, José
Silva Henríquez, Raúl
Solano, Francisco
Solís Folch de Cardona, José
Subirana, Manuel de Jesús
Talamantes, Melchor de
Thiel, Bernardo Augusto
Torquemada, Juan de
Torres Bello, Diego de
Torres Restrepo, Camilo
Urdaneta, Andrés de
Urrea, Teresa
Valdivia, Luis de
Varela y Morales, Félix
Vásquez, Francisco de Asís
Vélez de Escalante, Silvestre
Vera Cruz, Alonso de la
Vieira, Antônio
Vigil, Francisco de Paula González
Viñes y Martorell, Benito
Viscardo y Guzmán, Juan Pablo
Viteri y Ungo, Jorge
Vitoria, Francisco de
Ximénez, Francisco
Zepeda y Zepeda, Juan de Jesús
Zubiría, José Antonio Laureano de
Zumárraga, Juan de

Revolutionary Leadership (including guerrillas)

Abasolo, Mariano
Agramonte y Loynaz, Ignacio
Agüeybana II
Albizu Campos, Pedro
Aldama y González, Ignacio de
Aldama y González, Juan de
Alem, Leandro
Alfaro Delgado, José Eloy
Alfaro Siqueiros, David
Allende, Ignacio
Allende Gossens, Salvador
Alvarado, Salvador
Andresote
Anzoátegui, José Antonio
Aramburu, Pedro Eugenio
Arce Castaño, Bayardo
Arcos, Santiago
Arias Madrid, Harmodio
Arismendi, Juan Bautista
Arismendi, Rodney
Atahaulpa
Ávila, Alonso de
Azcárate y Lezama, Juan
  Francisco de
Barrett, Rafael
Barrios, Gonzalo
Barrios, Justo Rufino
Barrundia, José Francisco
Bedoya de Molina, Dolores
Bello, Andrés
Berbeo, Juan Francisco
Bermúdez, José Francisco
Bertoni, Moisés
Bilbao Barquín, Francisco
Blanco Galdós, Hugo
Bobo, Rosalvo
Bolívar, Simón
Borge, Tomás
Bravo, Leonardo
Brión, Luis
Caamaño Deñó, Francisco
Caballero, Pedro Juan
Caldas, Francisco José de
Campos, Luis María
Campos, Manuel Jorge
Candioti, Francisco Antonio
Canek, Jacinto
Carlés, Manuel
Carranza, Venustiano
Castro, Julián
Castro Ruz, Fidel
Castro Ruz, Raúl

Céspedes, Carlos Manuel de (the
  Elder)
Chibás, Eduardo
Chirino, José Leonardo
Cienfuegos, Camilo
Cisneros Betancourt, Salvador
Contreras Brothers
Cortés de Madariaga, José
Cos y Pérez, José María
Creydt, Oscar
Cruz, Serapio
de la Huerta, Adolfo
Debray, [Jules] Régis
Delgado, José Matías
D'Escoto Brockmann, Miguel
Dessalines, Jean Jacques
Díaz Soto y Gama, Antonio
Domínguez, Miguel
Dorticós Torrado, Osvaldo
Duarte, Juan Pablo
Echeverría Bianchi, José Antonio
Erro, Enrique
Escalante, Aníbal
Estrada Palma, Tomás
Facio Segreda, Gonzalo
Falcón, Juan Crisóstomo
Febres-Cordero Ribadeneyra, León
Fernández Madrid, José
Flores, Juan José
Flores Magón, Ricardo
Fonseca Amador, Carlos
Freire Serrano, Ramón
Gabeira, Fernando Nagle
Galeana, Hermenegildo
Gallo Goyenechea, Pedro León
Gálvez, Mariano
Gamarra, Agustín
García, Calixto
García Granados, Miguel
Garibaldi, Giuseppe
Godoi, Juan Silvano
Godoy Cruz, Tomás
Gómez, Eugenio
Gómez, José Miguel (d. 1805)
Gómez, José Miguel (d. 1921)
Gómez, José Valentín
José y Báez, Máximo
González, Abraham
González, Pablo
González Prada, Manuel
Grove Vallejo, Marmaduke
Guerrero, Vicente

Guevara, Ernesto "Che"
Gutiérrez, Eulalio
Gutiérrez Brothers
Gutiérrez de Lara, José Bernardo
Guzmán, Martín Luis
Hernández, José Manuel
Herrera, Tomás
Hidalgo y Costilla, Miguel
Hostos y Bonilla, Eugenio María de
Houston, Sam
James, Cyril Lionel Robert
Jauretche, Arturo M.
Justo, Juan B.
La Serna, José de
Laprida, Francisco Narciso de
Laredo Bru, Federico
Larrazábal Ugueto, Wolfgang
Lautaro
Leyva Solano, Gabriel
López, Narciso
López Trujillo, Alfonso
López y Fuentes, Gregorio
L'Ouverture, Toussaint
Maceo, Antonio
Machado, Gustavo
Machado y Morales, Gerardo
Madero, Francisco Indalecio
Mandu Ladino
Marighela, Carlos
Mariño, Santiago
Martí, Agustín Farabundo
Martínez, Juan José
Matamoros y Guridi, Mariano
Mayorga, Silvio
Mella, Julio Antonio
Mella, Ramón Matías
Melo, José María
Mendieta y Montefur, Carlos
Menocal, Mario García
Mina y Larrea, Javier
Miranda, Francisco de
Miró Cardona, José
Molina, Pedro
Molina Ureña, José Rafael
Monagas, José Gregorio
Monagas, José Tadeo
Monteagudo, Bernardo de
Montes, César
Montt Álvarez, Jorge
Montúfar y Larrea, Juan Pío de
Morales Lemus, José
Morelos y Pavón, José María

Morínigo, Higínio
Múgica, Francisco José
Nariño, Antonio
Navarro Wolff, Antonio
Nufio, José Dolores
O, Genovevo de la
Obregón Salido, Álvaro
Oduber Quirós, Daniel
Olañeta, José Joaquín Casimiro
Orozco, Pascual, Jr.
Ortega Saavedra, Daniel
Ortega Saavedra, Humberto
Ortiz de Ayala, Simón Tadeo
Ortiz de Domínguez, Josefa
Padilla Peñalosa, Ezequiel
Páez, José Antonio
País, Frank
Palacio Fajardo, Manuel
Pani Arteaga, Alberto J.
Pastora Gómez, Edén
Peimbert, Margarita
Peña, Antonia
Peña, Lázaro
Péralte, Charlemagne Masséna
Pérez Salas, Francisco Antonio
Piérola, Nicolás de
Pinto Díaz, Francisco Antonio
Portes Gil, Emilio
Prestes, Luís Carlos
Prieto Figueroa, Luis Beltrán

Puente Uceda, Luis de la
Quintana Roo, Andrés
Ramírez Mercado, Sergio
Rayón, Ignacio
Recabarren Serrano, Luis Emilio
Rejón, Manuel Crescencio
Reyes Ogazón, Bernardo
Ribas, José Félix
Riego y Núñez, Rafael del
Rigaud, André
Roca, Blas
Rodríguez, Carlos Rafael
Rosáins, Juan Nepomuceno
Roscio, Juan Germán
Ruíz, Henry
Ruiz, Tomás
Ruiz Cortines, Adolfo
San Martín, José Francisco de
Sánchez, Prisciliano
Sandino, Augusto César
Santa Cruz y Espejo, Francisco
  Javier Eugenio de
Santamaría, Haydée
Saravia, Aparicio
Sardaneta y Llorente, José
  Mariano de
Sendic, Raúl
Seregni, Líber
Siles Zuazo, Hernán
Silva Xavier, Joaquim José da

Sucre Alcalá, Antonio José de
Tallet, José Zacarías
Tejeda Olivares, Adalberto
Torres Restrepo, Camilo
Trotsky, Leon
Túpac Amaru (José Gabriel
  Condorcanqui)
Turcios Lima, Luis Agosto
Urracá
Urrea, José de
Urrutia Lleó, Manuel
Varona y Pera, Enrique José
Vasconcelos Calderón, José
Velasco Alvarado, Juan
Vicario Fernández, [María] Leona
Victoria, Guadalupe
Vidaurri, Santiago
Villa, Francisco "Pancho"
Villagrán, Julián and José María
  ("El Chito")
Villagrán Kramer, Francisco
Wheelock Román, Jaime
Yanes, Francisco Javier
Yon Sosa, Marco Antonio
Zamora, Rubén
Zapata, Emiliano
Zaragoza, Ignacio
Zárate Willka, Pablo
Zayas y Alfonso, Alfredo
Zeledón, Benjamín Francisco

Science and Medicine

Adem Chahín, José
Adem Chahín, Julián
Alcorta, Diego
Alexis, Jacques Stéphen
Almonte, Juan Nepomuceno
Alonso, Manuel A.
Alzate y Ramírez, José Antonio de
Amador Guerrero, Manuel
Ameghino, Florentino
Ávila, Julio Enrique
Azara, Félix de
Barbero, Andrés
Barbosa y Alcalá, José Celso
Bertoni, Moisés
Betances, Ramón Emeterio
Bunge, Alejandro
Bunge, Augusto
Caldas, Francisco José de
Calderón Guardia, Rafael Ángel
Carrillo Flores, Nabor
Cervantes, Vicente

Chagas, Carlos Ribeiro Justiniano
Clavigero, Francisco Javier
Codazzi, Agustín
Coni, Gabriela Laperrière de
Cordero Crespo, Luis
Cruz, Oswaldo Gonçalves
Dobrizhoffer, Martín
Duvalier, François
Elhuyar, Juan José de
Elhuyar y Zúbice, Fausto de
Finlay, Carlos Juan
Frías, Antonio
Fuentes, Manuel Atanasio
García, Diego
García Conde, Pedro
González de Santa Cruz, Roque
Graef Fernández, Carlos
Grau San Martín, Ramón
Haro Barraza, Guillermo
Hernández, Francisco
Houssay, Bernardo A.

Kubitschek de Oliveira, Juscelino
Kumate Rodríguez, Jesús
Leloir, Luis F.
Liendo y Goicoechea, José Antonio
Longinos Martínez, José
Magalhães, Domingos José
  Gonçalves de
Malaspina, Alessandro
Mejía del Valle y Llequerica, José
  Joaquín
Mendinueta y Múzquiz, Pedro de
Messía de la Cerda, Pedro de
Montealegre Fernández, José María
Moreau de Justo, Alicia
Moshinsky Borodiansky, Marcos
Moziño, José Mariano
Murtinho, Joaquim Duarte
Mutis, José Celestino
Nezahualcoyotl
Niza, Marcos de
Nusdorffer, Bernardo

Paterson, William
Peixoto, Júlio Afrânio
Peralta Barnuevo y Rocha, Pedro de
Popenoe, Frederick Wilson
Prieto Rodríguez, Sotero
Ramos, Artur
Ramos Mejía, José María
Rawson, Guillermo
Reed, Walter
Rodrigues, Raimundo Nina

Romay y Valdés Chacón, Tomás
Romero, Emilio
Rosenblueth, Arturo Stearns
Ruiz de Montoya, Antonio
Sandoval Vallarta, Manuel
Santa Cruz y Espejo, Francisco Javier Eugenio de
Scliar, Moacyr
Stephens, John Lloyd
Torres Bello, Diego de

Torre y Huerta, Carlos de la
Unanue, Hipólito
Vargas, José María
Velasco, José María
Velázquez Cárdenas de León, Joaquín
Villeda Morales, Ramón
Viñes y Martorell, Benito
Wilde, Eduardo
Zubirán Achondo, Salvador

Social Protest and Reform

Abad y Queipo, Manuel
Albizu Campos, Pedro
Alem, Leandro
Allende Gossens, Salvador
Alvarado, Salvador
Arguedas, José María
Arismendi, Rodney
Arriaga, Ponciano
Arze, José Antonio
Atahualpa
Bachiller y Morales, Antonio
Barrios, Justo Rufino
Bassols, Narciso
Beals, Carleton
Benedetti, Mario
Betances, Ramón Emeterio
Betancourt Cisneros, Gaspar
Bilbao Barquín, Francisco
Bonilla, Policarpo
Bonilla Chirinos, Manuel
Bravo, Mario
Caballero y Rodríguez, José Agustín
Calderón Guardia, Rafael Ángel
Campa Salazar, Valentín
Cañas, José Simeón
Caneca, Frei Joaquím do Amor Divino
Canek, Jacinto
Carlés, Manuel
Carrillo Puerto, Felipe
Casaldáliga, Pedro
Castro Alves, Antônio de
Castro Pozo, Hildebrando
Castro Ruz, Fidel
Caupolicán
Chibás, Eduardo
Chonchol, Jacques
Cisneros Betancourt, Salvador
Clouthier del Rincón, Manuel J.
Coni, Emilio R.
Coni, Gabriela Laperrière de

Conselheiro, Antônio
Corona, Ramón
Degollado, Santos
Del Prado, Jorge
Díaz Soto y Gama, Antonio
Donovan, Jean
Dorticós Torrado, Osvaldo
Escalante, Aníbal
Escobedo, Mariano
Estrada Palma, Tomás
Fernández Oreamuno, Próspero
Figueres Ferrer, José
Flores Magón, Ricardo
Fonseca Amador, Carlos
Fresno Larraín, Juan Francisco
Frugoni, Emilio
Gabeira, Fernando Nagle
Gaitan, Jorge Eliécer
Galán, Luis Carlos
Galeano, Eduardo Hughes
Gallo Goyenechea, Pedro León
Gama, Luís
Gamarra, Francisca Zubiaga Bernales de (La Mariscala)
García Granados, Miguel
García Salinas, Francisco
Garrido Canabal, Tomás
Garvey, Marcus
Ghioldi, Américo
Ghioldi, Rodolfo
Gómez, Juan Gualberto
Gómez Farías, Valentín
Gonzaga, Tomás Antônio
González, Pablo
González Víquez, Cleto
Grau San Martín, Ramón
Guevara, Ernesto "Che"
Gutiérrez Estrada, José María
Gutiérrez Garbín, Víctor Manuel
Guzmán, Antonio Leocadio
Haro y Tamariz, Antonio de

Haya de la Torre, Víctor Raúl
Hertzog Garaizabal, Enrique
Hidalgo y Costilla, Miguel
Iglesias, José María
Iglesias Pantin, Santiago
James, Cyril Lionel Robert
Jara, Víctor
Jauretche, Arturo M.
Juárez, Benito
Julião Arruda de Paula, Francisco
Justo, Juan B.
Kahlo, Frida
Labarca Hubertson, Amanda
Landázuri Ricketts, Juan
Las Casas, Bartolomé de
Lerdo de Tejada, Miguel
Letelier de Solar, Orlando
Leyva Solano, Gabriel
Lima, Alceu Amoroso
Lima Barreto, Afonso Henriques de
Lleras Restrepo, Carlos
Lombardo Toledano, Vicente
López, Ambrosio
López, José Hilario
López Pumarejo, Alfonso
L'Ouverture, Toussaint
Lozada, Manuel
Luisi, Luisa
Lutz, Bertha Maria Julia
Lutzenberger, José
Luz y Caballero, José de la
Madero, Francisco Indalecio
Madrazo, Carlos A.
Magoon, Charles Edward
Maldonado, Francisco Severo
Mariátegui, José Carlos
Martí, Agustín Farabundo
Medeiros da Fonseca, Romy Martins
Mejía, Tomás
Mejía del Valle y Llequerica, José Joaquín

Mella, Julio Antonio
Mier Noriega y Guerra, José
  Servando Teresa de
Miramón, Miguel
Miró Cardona, José
Molina Enríquez, Andrés
Mon y Velarde, Juan Antonio
Mora, José María Luis
Mora Valverde, Manuel
Morales Lemus, José
Moreau de Justo, Alicia
Morelos y Pavón, José María
Múgica, Francisco José
Muñoz Ledo Lazo de la Vega,
  Porfirio
Muñoz Marín, Luis
Nabuco de Araújo, Joaquim
Nascimento, Abdias do
Neruda, Pablo
O, Genovevo de la
Ocampo, Melchor
Orozco, José Clemente
Ortega Saavedra, Daniel
Ortega Saavedra, Humberto
Ortiz de Ayala, Simón Tadeo
Ortiz de Domínguez, Josefa
Osorio, Oscar
Otero, Mariano
Palacios, Alfredo L.
Pani Arteaga, Alberto J.
Paso, Fernando del
Patrocínio, José do
Paz Estenssoro, Víctor
Peimbert, Margarita
Peña, Antonia
Peña, Lázaro
Péralte, Charlemagne Masséna
Pérez Esquivel, Adolfo
Piérola, Nicolás de

Poblete Poblete de Espinosa, Olga
Portes Gil, Emilio
Prieto, Guillermo
Primo de Verdad y Ramos,
  Francisco
Prío Socarrás, Carlos
Puente Uceda, Luis de la
Quintana Roo, Andrés
Quiroga, Vasco de
Rabasa, Emilio
Ramírez, Ignacio
Ramírez, José Fernando
Rayón, Ignacio
Rebouças, André
Recabarren Serrano, Luis Emilio
Rejón, Manuel Crescencio
Revueltas, José
Reyes Ogazón, Bernardo
Riaño y Bárcena, Juan Antonio
Riego y Núñez, Rafael del
Rius
Riva Palacio, Vicente
Rivera, Diego
Roca, Blas
Rodríguez, Carlos Rafael
Rodríguez de Velasco y Osorio
  Barba, María Ignacia
Rodríguez Luján, Abelardo
Roig de Leuchsenring, Emilio
Romero, Oscar Arnulfo
Rosáins, Juan Nepomuceno
Roumain, Jacques
Ruiz, Tomás
Ruiz Cortines, Adolfo
Sábato, Ernesto
Sáenz de Thorne, Manuela
Salavarrieta, Policarpa
Sanabria Martínez, Víctor M.
Sánchez, Prisciliano

Sánchez Cerro, Luis Manuel
Sandino, Augusto César
Sardaneta y Llorente, José
  Mariano de
Seoane, Manuel
Sierra Méndez, Justo
Siles Zuazo, Hernán
Silva Henríquez, Raúl
Tejeda Olivares, Adalberto
Torres, Luis Emeterio
Torres Restrepo, Camilo
Torre y Huerta, Carlos de la
Tristan, Flora
Trotsky, Leon
Ulate Blanco, Otilio
Urrea, Teresa
Valladares, Armando
Vallejo, César
Vandor, Augusto
Vasconcelos Calderón, José
Velázquez Sánchez, Fidel
Vergara, Marta
Vicario Fernández, [María]
  Leona
Vieira, Antônio
Vigil, Francisco de Paula González
Villa, Francisco "Pancho"
Villalba, Jóvito
Viscardo y Guzmán, Juan Pablo
Volio Jiménez, Jorge
Wood, Leonard
Wyld Ospina, Carlos
Yon Sosa, Marco Antonio
Zamora, Rubén
Zapata, Emiliano
Zarco, Francisco
Zavala, Lorenzo de
Zulen, Pedro S. [and] Dora Mayer
  de Zulen

Technology and Invention

Adem Chahín, Julián
Alvear, Marcelo Torcuato de
Arnaz, Desi
Belly, Félix
Bunau-Varilla, Philippe Jean
Cisneros, Francisco Javier
Codazzi, Agustín
Cos y Pérez, José María
Elhuyar, Juan José de
Elhuyar y Zúbice, Fausto de
Enciso, Martín Fernández de
Escandón, Antonio

Galindo, Juan
Goethals, George Washington
Graef Fernández, Carlos
Humboldt, Alexander von
Keith, Minor Cooper
Lesseps, Ferdinand Marie,
  Vicomte de
Magoon, Charles Edward
Matienzo, Benjamín
Orozco y Berra, Manuel
Pani Arteaga, Alberto J.
Pearson, Weetman Dickinson

Porras, Diego
Pueyrredón, Prilidiano
Ramírez Vázquez, Pedro
Rebouças, André
Reed, Walter
Riaño y Bárcena, Juan Antonio
Rivera, Pedro de
Rivera Maestre, Miguel
Santos-Dumont, Alberto
Squier, Ephraim George
Velázquez Cárdenas de León,
  Joaquín

Vergara Echeverez, José Francisco
Vieytes, Hipólito

Wheelwright, William
Whytehead, William

Wisner von Morgenstern,
Franz

The Visual Arts (including architecture)

Acosta León, Ángel
Aizenberg, Roberto
Aleijadinho
Alfaro Siqueiros, David
Almeida Júnior, José Ferraz de
Alonso, Raúl
Alvarado, Antonio
Álvarez Bravo, Lola
Álvarez Bravo, Manuel
Amador, Manuel E.
Amaral, Tarsila do
Americo de Figuereido e Melo,
  Pedro
Antúnez, Nemesio
Apolinar
Arango, Débora
Arboleda, Carlos
Arciniega, Claudio de
Arden Quin, Carmelo
Arrieta, José Agustín
Arrieta, Pedro de
Atl, Dr.
Baca Flor, Carlos
Balbás, Jerónimo de
Barradas, Rafael
Barragán Morfin, Luis
Basaldúa, Hector
Berni, Antonio
Bicalho Oswald, Henrique Carlos
Bigaud, Wilson
Blanes, Juan Manuel
Bonpland, Aimé Jacques
Borges, Jacobo
Botero, Fernando
Bravo, Claudio
Brecheret, Vítor
Burle Marx, Roberto
Bustos, Hermenegildo
Cabrera, Miguel
Camargo, Sergio de
Camnitzer, Luis
Cantú, Federico
Carballo, Aída
Cárdenas Arroyo, Santiago
Carreño, Mario
Casasola, Agustín
Castro, José Gil de
Cavalcanti, Newton
Cerezo Arévalo, Marco Vinicio

Chambi, Martín
Chávez Morado, José
Chong Neto, Manuel
Clark, Lygia
Clavé, Pelegrín
Codesido, Julia
Concha, Andrés de la
Cordero, Juan
Coronel, Pedro
Correa, Juan
Costa, Lúcio
Covarrubias, Miguel
Cruz Diez, Carlos
Cuevas, José Luis
Cúneo Perinetti, José
Daríe, Sandu
Davidovsky, Mario
Debret, Jean-Baptiste
Deira, Ernesto
di Cavalcanti, Emiliano
Díaz, Gonzalo
Diomede, Miguel
Dittborn, Eugenio
Duarte, Augusto Rodrigues
Dutary, Alberto
Echave Orio, Baltasar de
Eckhout, Albert
Egas, Camilo Alejandro
Egerton, Daniel Thomas
Ender, Thomas
Enríquez, Carlos
Espinosa, José María
Estrada José María (d. ca. 1862)
Euceda, Maximiliano
Felguérez, Manuel
Fernandes, Millôr
Ferrer, Rafael
Ferrez, Marc
Fierro Rimac, Francisco
Figari, Pedro
Figueroa, Pedro José
Fonseca, Gonzalo
Fonseca e Silva, Valentim da
Fontana, Lucio
Forner, Raquel
Fredricks, Charles DeForest
Frisch, A.
Gahona, Gabriel Vicente
Galán, Julio

Gamarra, José
Garay, Carlos
Garay, Epifanio
Gay, Claudio
Gego
Gerzso, Gunther
Gil, Jerónimo Antonio
Gironella, Alberto
Goeritz, Mathias
Gómez, Benigno
González, Beatriz
González, Carlos
González Camarena, Jorge
González Goyri, Roberto
Grandjean de Montigny, Auguste
  Henri Victor
Grau, Enrique
Grilo, Sarah
Grippo, Víctor
Guayasamín, Oswaldo
Guerrero, Xavier
Guerrero y Torres, Francisco
Herrán, Saturnino
Herrerabarría, Adriano
Homar, Lorenzo
Hyppolite, Hector
Iturbide, Graciela
Ivaldi, Humberto
Izquierdo, María
Jaar, Alfredo
Jimeno y Planes, Rafael
Joaquim, Leandro
Juárez, José
Juárez, Luis
Julião, Carlos
Kahlo, Frida
Kosice, Gyula
Lam y Castilla, Wifredo
Landaluze, Víctor Patricio de
Laplante, Eduardo
Laso, Francisco
Leal, Fernando
Lewis, Roberto
Liautaud, Georges
Linares, Pedro
Linati, Claudio
López de Arteaga, Sebastián
Lozza, Raúl
Macció, Rómulo

Mac Entyre, Eduardo
Malfatti, Anita Catarina
Marisol
Martorell, Antonio
Matta Echaurren, Roberto Sebastián Antonio
Meireles de Lima, Vítor
Mele, Juan N.
Mérida, Carlos
Minujin, Marta
Modotti, Tina
Montenegro y Nervo, Roberto
Montes de Oca, Confucio
Morales, Armando
Nascimento, Abdias do
Nebel, Carlos
Niemeyer Soares Filho, Oscar
Noé, Luis Felipe
Obin, Philomé
Obregón, Alejandro
Obregón, José
O'Gorman, Juan
O'Higgins, Pablo
Oiticica, Hélio
Oliviera, Geraldo Teles de
Orozco, José Clemente
Ortiz, Rafael Montáñez
Otero, Alejandro
Pacheco, María Luisa
Pape, Lygia
Parra, Félix
Peláez, Amelia
Pereyns, Simon
Pettoruti, Emilio
Pingret, Édouard Henri Théophile

Pinto, Joaquín
Ponce de León, Fidelio
Porter, Liliana
Portillo, Efraín
Portinari, Cândido Torquato
Pôrto Alegre, Manuel Araújo
Portocarrero, René
Posada, José Guadalupe
Post, Frans Jansz
Prado, Vasco
Pueyrredón, Prilidiano
Quinquela Martín, Benito
Quirós, Cesáreo Bernaldo de
Ramírez Villamizar, Eduardo
Rego Monteiro, Vicente do
Reverón, Armando
Rius
Rivera, Diego
Rodríguez, Lorenzo
Rodríguez Juárez, Juan
Rojo, Viente
Rueda, Manuel
Ruelas, Julio
Rugendas, Johann Moritz
Ruiz, Antonio
Sabogal, José
Salazar Arrué, Salvador Efraín
Salgado, Sebastião
Santa María, Andrés de
Schendel, Mira
Segall, Lasar
Sigaud, Eugenio de Proença
Silva, José Antonio da
Sinclair, Alfredo
Sojo, Felipe

Soldi, Raúl
Soriano, Juan
Soto, Jesús Rafael
Szyszlo, Fernando de
Tábara, Enrique
Tamarón y Romeral, Pedro
Tamayo, Rufino
Toledo, Francisco
Tolsá, Manuel
Torres, Toribio
Torres García, Joaquín
Tresguerras, Francisco Eduardo de
Trujillo, Guillermo
Tsuchiya, Tilsa
Ureña, Felipe
Uribe, Juan Camilo
Varo, Remedios
Vásquez de Arce y Ceballos, Gregorio
Vega, Jorge Luis de la
Veiga Vale, José Joaquim da
Velasco, José María
Velásquez, José Antonio
Vilar, Manuel
Villalpando, Cristóbal de
Villanueva, Carlos Raúl
Visconti, Eliseu d'Angelo
Vitalino Pereira dos Santos, Mestre
Weingärtner, Pedro
Xul Solar
Zachrisson, Julio
Zelaya Sierra, Pablo
Zenil, Nahum Bernabé
Zúñiga Figueroa, Carlos

Women

Aguilar, Rosario Fiallos de
Agustini, Delmira
Alambert, Zuleika
Alegría, Claribel
Allende, Isabel
Amaral, Tarsila do
Amélia, Empress
Ángel, Albalucía
Arango, Débora
Assunção, Leliah
Barrios de Chamorro, Violeta
Bedoya de Molina, Dolores
Bedregal de Conitzer, Yolanda
Belli, Gioconda
Beltrán, Manuela
Berenguer, Amanda

Berman, Sabina
Bombal, María Luisa
Bonny, Anne
Brannon de Samayoa Chinchilla, Carmen
Brenner, Anita
Brunet, Marta
Burgos, Julia de
Cabrera, Lydia
Cáceres, Esther de
Calderón de la Barca, Fanny
Campos, Julieta
Cano, María de los Ángeles
Carballo, Aída
Castellanos, Rosario
Castillo Ledón, Amalia

Castillo y Guevara, Francisca Josefa de la Concepción de
Clair, Janete
Clark, Lygia
Codesido, Julia
Condé, Maryse
Coni, Gabriela Laperrière de
Cueva de Alvarado, Beatriz de la
de Jesus, Clementina
Del Río, Dolores
Dianda, Hilda
Díaz Lozano, Argentina
Espín de Castro, Vilma
Félix, María
Figueroa Gajardo, Ana
Gallego, Laura

543

Gamarra, Francisca Zubiaga Bernales de (La Mariscala)
Gambaro, Griselda
García, Sara
Garro, Elena
Gego
Glantz, Margo
Gómez de Avellaneda y Arteaga, Gertrudis
Gonzaga, Francisca Hedwiges
González, Beatriz
Gorodischer, Angélica
Grilo, Sarah
Gueiler Tejada, Lidia
Guido, Beatriz
Hernández, Luisa Josefina
Howard, Jennie Eliza
Ibáñez, Sara de
Ibarbourou, Juana de
Isabel of Brazil, Princess
Isabella I of Castile
Iturbide, Graciela
Izquierdo, María
Jesus, Carolina Maria de
Juana Inés de la Cruz, Sor
Kahlo, Frida
Kosice, Gyula
Kubitschek, Marcia
Labarca Hubertson, Amanda
Lavalle Urbina, María
Leopoldina, Empress
Levinson, Luisa Mercedes
Lispector, Clarice
Luisi, Luisa
Luisi, Paulina
Lutz, Bertha Maria Julia
Lynch, Elisa Alicia
Lynch, Marta
Malfatti, Anita Catarina
Malinche
Maria I of Portugal
Maria II of Portugal (Maria da Gloria)

Marisol
Matto de Turner, Clorinda
Medeiros da Fonseca, Romy Martins
Meireles, Cecília
Menchú Tum, Rigoberta
Menininha do Gantois, Mãe
Minujin, Marta
Miranda, Carmen
Mistral, Gabriela
Modotti, Tina
Moreau de Justo, Alicia
Morejón, Nancy
Naranjo, Carmen
Obaldía, María Olimpia de
Ocampo, Victoria
Odio, Eunice
O'Gorman, Camila
Oreamuno, Yolanda
Orozco, Olga
Orphée, Elvira
Ortiz de Domínguez, Josefa
Pacheco, María Luisa
Palacios, Antonia
Pape, Lygia
Parra, Teresa de la
Parra, Violeta
Pascal-Trouillot, Ertha
Peimbert, Margarita
Peláez, Amelia
Peña, Antonia
Peralta, Angela
Peri Rossi, Cristina
Perón, María Estela Martínez de
Perón, María Eva Duarte de
Perricholi, La
Piñon, Nélida
Pizarnik, Alejandra
Plá, Josefina
Poblete Poblete de Espinosa, Olga
Poniatowska, Elena
Porter, Liliana
Puga, María Luisa

Queiroz, Dinah Silveira de
Queiroz, Rachel de
Read, Mary
Rodríguez de Velasco y Osorio Barba, María Ignacia
Rojo, María
Rokha, Winétt de
Román de Núñez, Soledad
Rosa de Lima
Rosas de Terrero, Manuela
Sáenz de Thorne, Manuela
Salavarrieta, Policarpa
Sánchez de Thompson, María
Sánchez Manduley, Celia
Santamaría, Haydée
Santos, Marquesa de
Schendel, Mira
Sierra, Stella
Silva, Benedita da
Silva, Clara
Silva, Xica da
Somers, Armonía
Souza, Luiza Erundina de
Steimberg, Alicia
Storni, Alfonsina
Suárez, Inés de
Sumac, Yma
Tejeda, Leonor de
Telles, Lygia Fagundes
Teresa Christina, Empress
Traba, Marta
Tristan, Flora
Tsuchiya, Tilsa
Ureña de Henríquez, Salomé
Valenzuela, Luisa
Vallbona, Rima de
Varo, Remedios
Vergara, Marta
Vicario Fernández, [María] Leona
Vilariño, Idea
Xuxa
Zulen, Pedro S. [and] Dora Mayer de Zulen

CONTRIBUTORS

MARIA ISABEL ABREU
Georgetown University
Bandeira, Manuel Carneiro de
Souza; Bilac, Olavo; Castro Alves,
Antônio de; Dias, Antônio
Gonçalves; Machado de Assis,
Joaquim Maria

ESTHER ACEVEDO
*Dirección de Estudios
Históricos—Instituto Nacional de
Antropología e Historia (México)*
Arrieta, José Agustín; Bustos,
Hermenegildo; Egerton, Daniel
Thomas; Estrada, José María;
Gahona, Gabriel Vicente; Linati,
Claudio; Nebel, Carlos; Obregón,
José; Parra, Félix; Pingret, Édouard
Henri Théophile; Sojo, Felipe

VÍCTOR ACUÑA
Universidad de Costa Rica
Fortuny, José Manuel; Garvey,
Marcus

CHUCK ADAMS
University of Florida
Fishing Industry

R. E. W. ADAMS
University of Texas at San Antonio
Becan; Río Azul

GEORGE M. ADDY
Brigham Young University
Enlightenment, The; Gálvez, José
de; San Carlos de Guatemala,
University of; Universities:
Colonial Spanish America

JEREMY ADELMAN
Princeton University
Alcorta, Diego; Argentina:
Federalist Pacts (1831, 1852);
Argentina: Sociedad de la
Beneficiencia; British Invasions, Río

JEREMY ADELMAN
(cont.)
de la Plata; Cantilo, José Luis;
Cárcano, Ramón José; Chacra;
Martínez de Hoz, José Alfredo;
Porteño; Río de la Plata, Vice-
royalty of; Sáenz Peña, Luis;
Tucumán Congress; Unitario;
Varela, Felipe; Vedia y Mitre,
Mariano

JORGE AGUILAR MORA
*University of Maryland at College
Park*
Azuela, Mariano; Leñero, Vicente;
Revueltas, José; Rulfo, Juan

ADOLFO AGUILAR ZINSER
Diputado Federal, PRD México
Asylum

RICHARD E. AHLBORN
Smithsonian Institution
Santo, Santa

DAURIL ALDEN
University of Washington
Andrade, Gomes Freire de;
Andreoni, João Antônio;
Babylonian Captivity; Beckman
Revolt; Caramurú; Explorers and
Exploration: Brazil; João IV of
Portugal; Lavradio, Marquês do;
Maranhão, Estado do; Sá, Estácio
de; War of the Mascates

ROBERT J. ALEXANDER
*Rutgers, The State University of New
Jersey*
Barrientos Ortuño, René; Bolivia:
Organizations: Bolivian State
Petroleum Corporation (YPFB),
Bolivian Workers Central (COB),
Syndical Federation of Bolivian
Mineworkers (FSTMB); Bolivia:
Political Parties, Bolivian
Communist Party (PCB); Catavi

ROBERT J. ALEXANDER
(cont.)
Massacre; Communism; García
Meza, Luis; Ovando Candía,
Alfredo; Torres, Juan José

JUDITH ALLEN
Madison, Wisconsin
Brazil: National Guard; Dias,
Henrique; Palmares; Pernambucan
Revolution (1817); Quilombo;
Sabinada Revolt

MARÍA DEL CARMEN ALMODOVAR
Universidad de Havana
Echeverría Bianchi, José Antonio;
Miró Cardona, José

JANAÍNA AMADO
Universidade de Brasília
Amazon Region

CHARLES D. AMERINGER
Pennsylvania State University
Caribbean Legion; Costa Rica:
Second Republic; Fernández
Oreamuno, Próspero; Figueres
Ferrer, José; González Flores,
Alfredo; Monge Álvarez, Luis
Alberto; Orlich Bolmarchich,
Francisco José

DANNY J. ANDERSON
University of Kansas
Altamirano, Ignacio Manuel; Arre-
ola, Juan José; Ateneo de la Juven-
tud; Fernández de Lizardi, José
Joaquín; Galindo, Sergio; Gutiérrez
Nájera, Manuel; Magdaleno, Mauri-
cio; Nervo, Amado; Pitol, Sergio;
Puga, María Luisa; Romero, José
Rubén; Usigli, Rodolfo

THOMAS P. ANDERSON
El Salvador: National Republican
Alliance (ARENA); Matanza

CONTRIBUTORS

ANTHONY P. ANDREWS
New College of the University of South Florida
Salt Trade: Mesoamerica

NORWOOD ANDREWS, JR.
Texas Tech University
Durão, José de Santa Rita; Gama, José Basilio da; Oliveira, Manuel Botelho de; Pena, Luís Carlos

PATRICIA ANDREWS
Regalado, Tomás

KENNETH J. ANDRIEN
Ohio State University
Arbitristas; Armada del Mar del Sur; Ecuador: Conquest Through Independence; Galeones; Morga Sánchez Garay y López, Antonio de; Quito, Audiencia (Presidency) of; Quito Revolt of 1765; Unión de Armas

ALEJANDRO ANREUS
Jersey City Museum
Art: The Twentieth Century; Cantú, Federico; Leal, Fernando

CORINNE ANTEZANA-PERNET
University of California, Irvine
Chile: Feminine Party, Movimiento Pro-Emancipación de la Mujer Chilena; Figueroa Gajardo, Ana; Poblete Poblete de Espinosa, Olga; Vergara, Marta

DAVID P. APPLEBY
Eastern Illinois University
Callado Junior, Joaquim Antônio da Silva; Fernandez, Oscar Lorenzo; Gallet, Luciano; Garcia, José Maurício Nunes; Gismonti, Egberto; Gomes, Antônio Carlos; Gonzaga, Francisca Hedwiges; Guarnieri, M[ozart] Camargo; Koellreutter, Hans Joaquim; Krieger, Edino; Lacerda, Osvaldo; Levy, Alexandre; Mendes, Gilberto; Mignone, Francisco; Nazareth, Ernesto; Nepomuceno, Alberto; Nobre, Marlos; Oliveira, Willy Correia de; Peixe, César Guerra; Portugal, Marcos Antônio da Fonseca; Santoro, Claudio; Silva, Francisco Manuel da; Vieira, Amaral; Villa-Lobos, Heitor

ORLANDO R. ARAGONA
Cisplatine Province; Cisplatine War; Laguna, Santa Catarina; Olinda; São Francisco River

JOSEPH L. ARBENA
Clemson University
Clemente Walker, Roberto; Fangio, Juan Manuel; Pelé; Sports

CHRISTON ARCHER
University of Calgary
Aldama y González, Juan de; Alhóndiga; Allende, Ignacio; Bucareli y Ursúa, Antonio María; Calleja del Rey, Félix María; Córdoba, Treaty of (1821); Cuautla, Siege of; Forts and Fortifications: Spanish America; Hidalgo y Costilla, Miguel; Matamoros y Guridi, Mariano; Mexico: War of Independence; Militias: Colonial Spanish America; Plan of Iguala; Riaño y Bárcena, Juan Antonio; Ruíz de Apodaca, Juan; Three Guarantees, Army of the

ARTURO ARIAS
San Francisco State University
Alegría, Claribel; Asturias, Miguel Ángel; Castillo, Otto René; Illescas, Carlos; Monterroso, Augusto; Samayoa Chinchilla, Carlos

CHARLES W. ARNADE
University of South Florida
Achá, José María; Blanco Galindo, Carlos; Bolivia: Agrarian Reform; Bolivia: Constitución Vitalicia; Bolivia: Party of the Revolutionary Left (PIR); Busch Becerra, Germán; Cholo; Cochabamba; Córdova, Jorge; Hertzog Garaizabel, Enrique; Olañeta, José Joaquín Casimiro; Peñaranda del Castillo, Enrique; Peru-Bolivia Confederation; Republiquetas; Saavedra Mallea, Juan Bautista; Tejada Sorzano, José Luis; Toro, David; Zárate Willka, P.

LINDA ARNOLD
Virginia Polytechnic Institute
Judicial Systems: Spanish America

ASTRID ARRARÁ
Princeton University
Sendic, Raúl

G. POPE ATKINS
Institute of Latin American Studies, University of Texas at Austin
Pan-American Conferences: Washington Conference (1889)

PATRICIA AUFDERHEIDE
The American University
Cinema

JO ANN FAGOT AVIEL
San Francisco State University
Arab–Latin American Relations

MIRIAM AYRES
New York University
Lima Barreto, Afonso Henriques de

MARÍA BADÍAS
Georgetown University
Valero, Roberto

JAMES A. BAER
Northern Virginia Community College
Bramuglia, Juan Atilio; Campos, Manuel Jorge; Colegio Nacional de Buenos Aires; Recoleta, La

JOHN BAILEY
Georgetown University
Madrazo, Carlos A.

JOAN BAK
University of Richmond
Brazil: Revolutions: Federalist Revolt of 1893; Farroupilha Revolt; Pinheiro Machado, José Gomes; Pôrto Alegre; Rio Grande do Sul

GEORGE BAKER
Mexico Energy Intelligence, Oakland, California
Petróleos Mexicanos (Pemex); Petroleum Industry

PETER BAKEWELL
Emory University
Banco de San Carlos (Potosí); Bolivia: The Colonial Period; Charcas, Audiencia of; López de Quiroga, Antonio; Mining: Colonial Spanish America; Potosí; Toledo y Figueroa, Francisco de

DANIEL BALDERSTON
Tulane University
Borges, Jorge Luis

CLARA BARGELLINI
Instituto de Investigaciones Estéticas, Universidad Nacional Autónoma de México
Academia de San Carlos; Arciniega, Claudio de; Arrieta, Pedro de; Art: The Colonial Era; Balbás, Jerónimo de; Cabrera, Miguel; Churrigueresque; Clavé, Pelegrín; Concha, Andrés de la; Cordero, Juan; Correa, Juan; Echave Orio, Baltasar de; Gil, Jerónimo Antonio; Guadalupe, Basilica of; Guerrero y Torres, Francisco; Jimeno y Planes, Rafael; Juárez, José; Juárez, Luis; López de Arteaga, Sebastían; Pellicer Cámara, Carlos; Pereyns, Simon; Rodríguez, Lorenzo; Rodríguez Juárez, Juan; Tamarón y Romeral, Pedro; Tolsá, Manuel; Tresguerras, Francisco Eduardo de; Ureña, Felipe; Velasco, José María; Vilar, Manuel; Villalpando, Cristóbal de

B. J. BARICKMAN
University of Arizona
Alves Branco Tariff; Salvador; Tobacco Industry

RODERICK J. BARMAN
University of British Columbia
Andrada, Antônio
Carlos Ribeiro de and Martim Francisco Ribeiro de; Andrada, José Bonifácio de; Capistrano de Abreu, João; Conciliação; Exaltados; Feijó, Diogo Antônio; Gastão d'Orléans; Itaboraí, Visconde de; Pedro II of Brazil; Teresa Christina, Empress

MONICA BARNES
Cornell University
Irrigation

ALWYN BARR
Texas Tech University
Cos, Martín Perfecto de; Texas Revolution

JOSÉ PEDRO BARRÁN
Universidad de la República Oriental del Uruguay
Uruguay: The Colonial Period and the Nineteenth Century

JOEL BARROMI
Ministry of Foreign Affairs, Israel
Israeli–Latin American Relations

SERGIO BARROSO
IREME Music Studio
Cotapos Baeza, Acario; Garrido-Lecca Seminario, Celso; Isamitt Alarcón, Carlos; Lanza, Alcides; Letelier Valdés, Miguel; Zipoli, Domenico

MIRIAM BASILIO
Institute of Fine Arts, New York University
Ferrer, Rafael; Homar, Lorenzo; Martorell, Antonio; Ortiz, Rafael Montáñez; Tsuchiya, Tilsa

RUDY BAUSS
Austin Community College and Park College
Goa and Portuguese Asia; Portuguese Trade and International Relations

PETER M. BEATTIE
Michigan State University
Copacabana Fort, Revolt of; Fonseca, Hermes Rodrigues da; Military Question of the 1880s; Santa Cruz, Fortaleza de

WILLIAM H. BEEZLEY
Texas Christian University
Chiles; Fiestas

BRIAN C. BELANGER
Saint Anselm College
Capuchin Friars; Carmelites; Franciscans; García Icazbalceta, Joaquín; Paso y Troncoso, Francisco del

JOHN PATRICK BELL
Indiana University–Purdue University at Fort Wayne
Arias Sánchez, Oscar; Calderón Fournier, Rafael Ángel; Carazo Odio, Rodrigo; Cartago; Cortés Castro, León; Costa Rica; Costa Rica: National Liberation Party; Echandi Jiménez, Mario; Facio Segreda, Gonzalo; Meléndez Chaverri, Carlos; Mora Valverde, Manuel; Núñez Vargas, Benjamín; Oduber Quirós, Daniel; Picado Michalski, Teodoro; San José, Costa Rica; Sanabria Martínez, Víctor M.; Trejos Fernández, José Joaquín; Ulate Blanco, Otilio

SHANNON BELLAMY
Tulane University
Agüero Rocha, Fernando; Chamorro, Fruto; Chamorro Vargas, Emiliano; Dawson Agreement; Díaz, Adolfo; Guzmán, Enrique; Martínez, Tomás; Moncada, José María; Tipitapa Agreements; Zavala, Joaquín; Zeledón, Benjamín Francisco

ADÁN BENAVIDES, JR.
University of Texas at Austin
Alarcón, Martín de

RAÚL BENAVIDES
University of Texas at Austin
Cuba: Geography

CARMEN BENITO-VESSELS
University of Maryland at College Park
Hernández, Francisco

THOMAS BENJAMIN
Central Michigan University
San Cristóbal de las Casas

ELIZABETH BENSON
Institute of Andean Studies, Berkeley, California
Jaguar

GUY BENSUSAN
Northern Arizona University
Ballet Folklórico de México; Bolero; Corrido; Lara, Agustín; Mariachi; Marimba

FATIMA BERCHT
El Museo del Barrio, New York
Grau, Enrique; Guayasamín, Os.

FRANCES F. BERDAN
California State University, San Bernardino
Garibay Kintana, Ángel María; León-Portilla, Miguel

SUSAN BERGLUND
Universidad Central de Venezuela
Caracas

EMILIE BERGMANN
University of California, Berkeley
Lida, Raimundo

LEOPOLDO M. BERNUCCI
University of Colorado at Boulder
Cunha, Euclides da

CHARLES R. BERRY
Wright State University
Comonfort, Ignacio; Márquez, Leonardo; McLane–Ocampo Treaty (1859)

SUSAN K. BESSE
City College of the City University of New York
Brazil: Civil Code

MELISSA H. BIRCH
University of Virginia
Itaipú Hydroelectric Project

ELBA D. BIRMINGHAM-POKORNY
Southern Arkansas University
Candanedo, César; Jaramillo Levi, Enrique; Obaldía, María Olimpia de; Sierra, Stella; Sinán, Rogelio

JOSIAH BLACKMORE
University of Toronto
Camões, Luís Vaz de

COLE BLASIER
Georgetown University
Soviet–Latin American Relations

PHILIPPE BONNICHON
University of Paris–Sorbonne
French Colonization in Brazil; Villegaignon, Nicolas Durand de

DAIN BORGES
University of California, San Diego
Azevedo, Fernando de; Fernandes, Florestan; Freyre Gilberto (de Mello); Moog, Vianna; Peixoto, Júlio Afrânio; Querino, Manoel Raimundo; Ramos, Artur; Rodrigues, Raimundo Nina

NATALIO BOTANA
Universidad de San Andrés, Buenos Aires
Mitre, Bartolomé

VIRGINIA M. BOUVIER
University of Maryland at College Park
Castellanos, Rosario

CHRISTOPHER T. BOWEN
Tulane University
Montserrat; Pedreira, Antonio S.; Romero Barceló, Carlos; Torre, Miguel de la; Tugwell, Rexford Guy

ROSEMARY BRANA-SHUTE
College of Charleston and University of Charleston
French Guiana; French West Indies; Grenadines; Martinique and Guadeloupe

JEFFREY T. BRANNON
University of Texas at El Paso
Mexico: Nacional Financiera (NAFIN)

MARISABEL BRÁS
Puerto Rico: Political Parties: Overview

JOHN F. BRATZEL
Michigan State University
Military Dictatorships, 1821–1945

HERBERT BRAUN
University of Virginia
Gaitan, Jorge Eliécer

TAMARA BRAY
Wayne State University
Cerro Narrío; Cochasquí; Cotocollao; Ingapirca; La Plata; Tomebamba

WALTER V. BREM, JR.
Bancroft Library, University of California, Berkeley
Campos Sales, Manuel Ferraz de

JAMES BRENNAN
Georgetown University
Alsogaray, Alvaro; Alvear, Marcelo Torcuato de; Argentina: PP: Intransigent Radicals; Balbín, Ricardo; Córdoba, University of; Cordobazo, El; Ghioldi, Rodolfo; Illia, Arturo Umberto; Jauretche, Arturo M.; López Rega, José; Rojas Isaac; Uriburu, José Evaristo

EDWARD BRETT
La Roche College
Carney, James "Guadalupe"; Casanova y Estrada, Ricardo;

EDWARD BRETT
(cont.)
Donovan, Jean; Llorente y Lafuente, Anselmo; Maryknoll Order; Melville, Thomas and Margarita; Rivera Damas, Arturo; Subirana, Manuel de Jesús; Zepeda y Zepeda, Juan de Jesús

JOHN BRITTON
Francis Marion University
Beals, Carleton; Brenner, Anita; Bucareli Conferences; Cristero Rebellion; Mexico: Mexican Regional Labor Confederation (CROM); Mora y del Río, José; Morones, Luis; Morrow, Dwight Whitney; Petroleum Expropriation of 1938 (Mexico); Puig Casauranc, José Manuel; Sáenz Garza, Aaron; Sinarquismo; Tannenbaum, Frank; Wilson, Woodrow

LOLITA GUTIÉRREZ BROCKINGTON
North Carolina Central University
Mizque; Mojos Region; Oriente (Bolivia); Santa Cruz; Tarija; Yungas

KENDALL W. BROWN
Brigham Young University
Arequipa; Arica; Armendáriz, José de; Atahualpa (Juan Santos); Chayanta, Revolt of (1777–1781); Elhuyar, Juan José de; Elhuyar y Zúbice, Fausto de; Huancavelica; Manso de Velasco, José Antonio; Mining: Colonial Spanish America; Mita; Moquegua; Oruro; Peru: From the Conquest Through Independence; Quinto Real; Real Cuerpo de Minería; Túpac Amaru (José Gabriel Condorcanqui); Túpac Catari, Julián Apaza

LARISSA BROWN
Trade: Colonial Brazil; Trading Companies, Portuguese

RICHMOND F. BROWN
University of South Alabama
Aycinena, Juan Fermín de; Aycinena, Mariano de; Aycinena, Pedro de; Aycinena Piñol, Juan José de; Clayton–Bulwer Treaty (1850); Piñol y Sala, José; Wyke–Aycinena Treaty (1859)

MICHAEL J. BROYLES
University of Western Ontario
Brazil: Amnesty Act (1979); Brazil: Superintendency for the Development of Amazonia (SUDAM); Christie Affair; Marajó Island; Ponta Porã (Federal Territory); Tapajós River; Xingu Reserve

MAURICE P. BRUNGARDT
Loyola University, New Orleans
Belalcázar, Sebastián de; Beltrán, Luis (Saint); Claver, Pedro; Féderman, Nicolás; Guiana Highlands; Jiménez de Quesada, Gonzalo; Liberalism

SAMUEL BRUNK
University of Nebraska–Lincoln
Ángeles, Felipe; O, Genovevo de la; Plan of Ayala; Zapata, Emiliano

STEPHEN B. BRUSH
University of California, Davis
Potato

HILARY BURGER
Harvard University
Cabot, Sebastian; Elcano, Juan Sebastián de; Forbes, John Murray; Gutiérrez, José María; Holy Alliance

RICHARD L. BURGER
Yale University
Chavín de Huántar; Cupisnique Culture; Garagay; Kotosh; South America: Pre-Columbian History: Andean Region; Tello, Julio César

WINFIELD J. BURGGRAAFF
University of Missouri–Columbia
Barrios, Gonzalo; Crespo, Joaquín; Delgado Chalbaud, Carlos; Dominican Republic: Constitutions; Falcón, Juan Crisóstomo; Hernández, José Manuel; Herrera Campins, Luis; Llanos (Venezuela); Lusinchi, Jaime; Machado, Gustavo; Mariño, Santiago; Prieto Figueroa, Luis Beltrán; Urdaneta, Rafael; Venezuela: Constitutions; Villalba, Jóvito

MARCUS B. BURKE
Hispanic Society of America
Art: The Nineteenth Century

MICHAEL E. BURKE
Villanova University
Medicine: Colonial

LOUISE M. BURKHART
State University of New York at Albany
Axayacatl; Coatlicue; Cuitlahuac; Huitzilopochtli; Itzcoatl; Motecuhzoma I; Nezahualcoyotl; Nezahualpilli; Tenochtitlán; Tezcatlipoca; Zumárraga, Juan de

MARK A. BURKHOLDER
University of Missouri–St. Louis
Acuerdo; Adelantado; Alcalde; Alcalde Mayor; Alguacil Mayor; Audiencia; Baquíjano y Carrillo de Córdoba, José de; Burgos, Laws of; Cabildo, Cabildo Abierto; Captain-General: Spanish America; Cédula; Cobos, Francisco de los; Conquistadores; Corregidor; Council of the Indies; Criminal Justice; Gazeta de Lima; Gazetas; Humboldt, Alexander von; Juzgado General de Indios; Mercurio Peruano; Minister of the Indies; New Laws of 1542; Oidor; Peralta Barnuevo y Rocha, Pedro de; Pesquisa, Pesquisador; Prescott, William Hickling; Recopilación de Leyes de las Indias; Regidor; Residencia; San Marcos, University of; Sepúlveda, Juan Ginés de; Solórzano Pereira, Juan de; Spanish Empire; Unanue, Hipólito; Viceroyalty, Viceroy; Viscardo y Guzmán, Juan Pablo; Visita

SUZANNE HILES BURKHOLDER
University of Missouri–St. Louis
Afrancesado; Alexander VI, Pope; Aragon; Basel, Treaty of (1795); Campomanes, Pedro Rodríguez, Conde de; Castile; Cateau-Cambrésis, Treaty of (1559); Charles I of Spain; Charles II of Spain; Charles III of Spain; Charles VI of Spain; Ensenada, Cenón de Somodevilla, Marqués de la; Feijóo, Benito Jerónimo; Ferdinand II of Aragon; Ferdinand VI of Spain; Ferdinand VII of Spain; Floridablanca, Conde de; Fontainebleau, Treaty of (1807); Fueros; Godoy, Manuel; Granada, Spain; Isabella I of Castile; London, Treaty of (1604); Madrid, Treaty of (1670); Madrid, Treaty of (1750); Mesta; Military Orders: Spain; Napoleon I; Olivares,

SUZANNE HILES BURKHOLDER
(cont.)
Conde-Duque de; Patiño, José de; Philip II of Spain; Philip III of Spain; Philip IV of Spain; Philip V of Spain; Riego y Núñez, Rafael del; San Ildefonso, Treaty of; Santiago de Compostela; Seven Years' War; Siete Partidas; Spain; Vitoria, Francisco de; War of Jenkins's Ear; War of the Spanish Succession

E. BRADFORD BURNS
University of California, Los Angeles
Nationalism

AMY TURNER BUSHNELL
College of Charleston
Florida; Florida, East; Guale; Saint Augustine

DAVID BUSHNELL
University of Florida
Amar y Borbón, Antonio; Ameghino, Florentino; Angostura, Congress of; Arenales, Juan Antonio Álvarez de; Argentina: The Nineteenth Century; Argentina: Constitutions; Argentina: Movements: Federalists, Unitarists; Argentina: Liga Federal, Liga Litoral, Liga Unitaria; Argentina: National Autonomist Party; Argentine Confederation; Balcarce, Mariano; Barranca Yaco; Belgrano, Manuel; Beruti, Antonio Luis; Bolívar, Simón; Bouchard, Hipólito; Boyacá, Battle of; Caaguazú, Battle of; Caro, Miguel Antonio; Cartagena Manifesto; Castelli, Juan José; Cochrane, Lord Thomas Alexander; Cúcuta, Congress of; Cuervo, Rufino José; Derqui, Santiago; Díaz Vélez, José Miguel; Dorrego, Manuel; Esquiú, Mamerto; Federalism; Fernández Madrid, José; Gelly y Obes, Juan Andrés; Gran Colombia; Granaderos a Caballo; Guerra Grande; Laprida, Francisco Narciso de; Lavalle, Juan Galo; López, Vicente Fidel; Maza, Manuel Vicente de; Montalvo y Ambulodi Arriola y Casabente Valdespino, Francisco; Nariño, Antonio; New Granada, United Provinces; Ospina Rodríguez, Mariano; Pavón, Battle

549

DAVID BUSHNELL
(cont.)
of; Pueyrredón, Prilidiano; Rawson, Guillermo; Restrepo, José Manuel; Rodríguez, Simón; Sáenz de Thorne, Manuela; Salavarrieta, Policarpa; San Lorenzo, Battle of; Santander, Francisco de Paula; Sardá, José; Torres Restrepo, Camilo; Treinta y Tres (33) Orientales; Turbay, Gabriel; United Provinces of the Río de la Plata; Urdaneta, Rafael; Uribe Holguín, Guillermo; Uruguay: Congress of 1825; Viamonte, Juan José; Wars of Independence: South America; Zaldúa, Francisco Javier; Zipaquirá, Capitulations of

KIM D. BUTLER
Rutgers University
African-Brazilian Cultural and Political Organizations; African-Brazilian Emigration to Africa; Candomblé; Capitão do Mato; Menininha do Gantois, Mãe; Orixás

WES SCHWEMMER CADY
University of Southwestern Louisiana
Belgian Colonization Company

GERARDO CAETANO
Universidad de la República, Montevideo; Centro Latinoamericano de Economía Humana
Batlle, Lorenzo; Batlle y Ordóñez, José

BRUCE CALDER
University of Illinois at Chicago
Conference of Latin American Bishops (CELAM)

ROSARIO CAMBRIA
Baldwin-Wallace College
Bullfighting

RODERIC AI CAMP
Tulane University
Adem Chahín, José; Adem Chahín, Julián; Aguilar Vargas, Cándido; Alemán Valdés, Miguel; Almazán, Juan Andréu; Álvarez, Luis Héctor; Ávila Camacho, Manuel; Azcárraga Milmo, Emilio; Bassols, Narciso; Cabrera Lobato, Luis; Camarilla;

RODERIC AI CAMP
(cont.)
Campa Salazar, Valentín; Cárdenas Solorzano, Cuauhtémoc; Carrillo Flores, Antonio; Carrillo Flores, Nabor; Caso y Andrade, Alfonso; Caso y Andrade, Antonio; Castillo Ledón, Amalia; Cedillo Martínez, Saturnino; Chávez Sánchez, Ignacio; Clouthier del Rincón, Manuel J.; Colosio Murrieta, Luis Donaldo; Corral Verdugo, Ramón; Cosío Villegas, Daniel; de la Huerta, Adolfo; Díaz Ordaz, Gustavo; Díaz Soto y Gama, Antonio; Echeverría Álvarez, Luis; Elizondo, Salvador; Fabela Alfaro, Isidro; Gamboa Iglesias, Federico; Gamio Martínez, Manuel; García Robles, Alfonso; Garrido Canabal, Tomás; Garza Sada Family; Gómez Morín, Manuel; Gorostiza Acalá, José; Graef Fernández, Carlos; Gutiérrez, Eulalio; Guzmán, Martín Luis; Haro Barraza, Guillermo; Krauze, Enrique; Kumate Rodríguez, Jesús; Lavalle Urbina, María; Lombardo Toledano, Vicente; López Mateos, Adolfo; López Portillo, José; Madrid Hurtado, Miguel de la; Mexico: Organizations: Federation of Mexican Labor (CTM), National Peasant Federation (CNC); Mexico: Political Parties: Democratic Revolutionary Party (PRD), Mexico: Institutional Revolutionary Party (PRI), Mexico: National Action Party (PAN), Mexico: National Revolutionary Party (PNR), Mexico: Party of the Mexican Revolution (PRM); Mexico: Zapatista Army of National Liberation; Moshinsky Borodianksky, Marcos; Múgica, Francisco José; Muñoz Ledo Lazo de la Vega, Porfirio; Ortiz Mena, Antonio; Ortiz Rubio, Pascual; Padilla Peñalosa, Ezequiel; Pan-American Conferences: Mexico City Conference (1945); Pani Arteaga, Alberto J.; Pino Suárez, José María; Porfiriato; Portes Gil, Emilio; Prieto Rodríguez, Sotero; Ramírez Vázquez, Pedro; Ramos y Magaña, Samuel; Reyes Ochoa, Alfonso; Reyes Ogazón, Bernardo; Rodríguez Luján, Abelardo; Romero Rubio, Manuel; Rosenblueth, Arturo Stearns; Ruiz Cortines,

RODERIC AI CAMP
(cont.)
Adolfo; Salinas de Gortari, Carlos; Sandoval Vallarta, Manuel; Silva Herzog, Jesús; Torres Bodet, Jaime; Vasconcelos Calderón, José; Velázquez Sánchez, Fidel; Yáñez Santos Delgadillo, Agustín; Zubirán Achondo, Salvador

MÁRCIA ELISA DE CAMPOS GRAF
Universidade Federal do Paraná
Curitiba; Paraná, Brazil

DAVID CAREY, JR.
Tulane University
Castro, Julián; Cuba: War of Independence; Esquipulas II; Gómez, Miguel Mariano; Grito de Baire; Hernández Colón, Rafael; Spanish-American War; Teller Amendment; Weyler Y Nicolau, Valeriano

JOHN B. CARLSON
Center for Archaeoastronomy, University of Maryland at College Park
Astronomy

CHARLES CARRERAS
Ramapo College of New Jersey
Forbes, William Cameron; Guzmán Blanco, Antonio Leocadio; Pan-American Conferences: Caracas Conference (1954); Rockefeller, Nelson Aldrich

THOMAS E. CASE
San Diego State University
Centurión, Roque Miranda; Rodríguez-Alcalá, Hugo

ELENA CASTEDO
Wolff, Egon

FERNANDO CASTRO
Instituto de Investigaciones Filosóficas, Universidad de Lima
Chambi, Martín; Photography: The Twentieth Century; Salgado, Sebastião

SUEANN CAULFIELD
University of Michigan
Carioca; Guanabara Bay; Guanabara State; Paraíba River; Teixeira, Anisio Espinola; Veiga, Evaristo Ferreira da

CÉSAR N. CAVIEDES
University of Florida
Acaray River; Aconcagua; Andes; Antofagasta; Argentina: Geography; Artigas; Atacama Desert; Bahía Blanca; Banda Oriental; Bariloche; Barracas; Belén; Bío-bío; Caaguazú; Canelones; Catamarca; Chile: Geography; Chiloé; Christ of the Andes; Chubut; Ciudad del Este; Colonia; Colorado River; Comodoro Rivadavia; Concepción, Chile; Córdoba; Corrientes; Cuyo; Dawson Island; Durazno; Encarnación; Entre Ríos; Flores; Fray Bentos; Guairá Falls; Horn, Cape; Humboldt Current; Jujuy; La Serena; Llanquihue; Luján; Magallanes; Maipo River; Maldonado; Mapocho River; Mar del Plata; Maule; Mercedes; Misiones; Montevideo; Negro, Río; Neuquén; Norte Chico; Norte Grande; Osorno; Paraguay: Geography; Paraguay River; Paraná, Argentina; Paraná River; Patagonia; Paysandú; Pilcomayo River; Punta Arenas; Punta del Este; Río de la Plata; Rosario; Salado River; Salta; Salto; San Juan, Argentina; San Luis; San Rafael; Santa Fe, Argentina; Santiago, Chile; Tarapacá; Tebicuary River; Temuco; Tierra del Fuego; Trinidad, Paraguay; Tucumán; Uruguay: Geography; Uruguay River; Ushuaia; Uspallata Pass; Valdivia, Chile; Valparaíso; Villarrica

JOSÉ CERNA-BAZÁN
University of Texas at Austin
Abril, Xavier

MARIO CERUTTI
Universidad Autónoma de Nuevo León
Vidaurri, Santiago

BILLY JAYNES CHANDLER
Texas A & M University–Kingsville
Lampião

EUGENIO CHANG-RODRÍGUEZ
Queens College and Graduate School, City University of New York
González Prada, Manuel; Mariátegui, José Carlos; Salazar Bondy, Sebastián; Sánchez, Luis Alberto

RAQUEL CHANG-RODRÍGUEZ
City College of the City University of New York
Guaman Poma de Ayala, Felipe

ARLEN F. CHASE
University of Central Florida
Caracol

DIANE Z. CHASE
University of Central Florida
Caracol

FRANCIE CHASSEN-LÓPEZ
University of Kentucky
Oaxaca: The City; Oaxaca: The State

JOHN CHASTEEN
University of North Carolina at Chapel Hill
Saravia, Aparicio

KAREN L. MOHR CHÁVEZ
Central Michigan University
Pucará

JANET M. CHERNELA
Florida International University
Wagley, Charles Walter

JACK CHILD
The American University
Antarctica; Beagle Channel Dispute; Falkland Islands (Malvinas); Falklands/Malvinas War; Magellan, Strait of; Vernet, Louis

MARGARET CHOWNING
University of California Berkeley
Janitzio; Michoacán; Pátzcuaro, Lake

MARY A. CLARK
Tulane University
Kissinger Commission

SUSAN E. CLARK
Odio, Eunice; Oreamuno, Yolanda; Vallbona, Rima de

ROBERT H. CLAXTON
West Georgia College
Earthquakes; El Niño; Volcanoes

LAWRENCE A. CLAYTON
University of Alabama
Callao; Grace, W. R., and Company; Guayaquil: Shipbuilding Industry

WAYNE M. CLEGERN
Colorado State University
Cerna, Vicente

CARROL F. COATES
State University of New York at Binghamton
Bélance, René; Brierre, Jean-Fernand; Camille, Roussan; Chauvet, Marie Vieux; Coicou, Massillon; Condé, Maryse; Depestre, René; Durand, Oswald; Glissant, Édouard; Grimard, Luc; Hippolyte, Dominique; Laleau, Léon; Marcelin Brothers; Phelps, Anthony; Price-Mars, Jean; Schwarz-Bart, Simone

ELIZABETH A. COBBS
University of San Diego
Barbosa de Oliveira, Rui; Melo Franco, Afonso Arinos de; Melo Franco, Afrânio de

JAMES COCHRANE†
Tulane University
Central American Common Market (CACM); Economic Integration; Organization of Central American States (ODECA)

DON COERVER
Texas Christian University
González, Manuel; Iglesias, José María; Plan of La Noria; Plan of Tuxtepec

JOHN COHASSEY
Congada; Fado; Jongo; Miranda, Carmen; Modinha

ISAAC COHEN
Economic Commission on Latin America and the Caribbean
Economic Commission for Latin America and the Caribbean (ECLAC)

THOMAS M. COHEN
Catholic University of America
Portugal: Restoration of 1640; Vieira, Antônio

CONTRIBUTORS

WILLIAM S. COKER
University of West Florida
Florida, Spanish West; Mobile, Battle of; Panton, Leslie, and Company; Pensacola; Pensacola, Battle of

SIMON COLLIER
Vanderbilt University
Amunátegui Aldunate, Miguel Luis; Araucana, La; Arcos, Santiago; Bello, Andrés; Bilbao Barquín, Francisco; Blanco Encalada, Manuel; Blest Gana, Alberto; Bulnes Prieto, Manuel; Carrera, José Miguel; Caupolicán; Chile: Foundations Through Independence Period; Chile: Society of Equality; Chile: Liberal-Conservative Fusion; Egaña Fabres, Mariano; Egaña Risco, Juan; Estanco, Estanquero; Freire Serrano, Ramón; Gallo Goyenechea, Pedro León; Galvarino; Gardel, Carlos; Henríquez, Camilo; Hurtado de Mendoza, García; Infante, José Miguel; Irisarri, Antonio José de; Jara, Víctor; Las Heras, Juan Gregorio de; Lastarria, José Victorino; Lautaro; Letelier Madariaga, Valentín; Lunfardo; Medina, José Toribio; Milonga; Montt Torres, Manuel; Music: Popular Music and Dance; O'Higgins, Bernardo; Oña, Pedro de; Ordóñez, José; Parra, Violeta; Patria Nueva; Patria Vieja; Pelucones; Pérez Mascayano, José Joaquín; Pérez Salas, Francisco Antonio; Pinto Díaz, Francisco Antonio; Pipiolos; Positivism; Prat Echaurren, Jorge; Prieto Vial, Joaquín; Rengifo Cárdenas, Manuel; Ríos Morales, Juan Antonio; Rodríguez Erdoiza, Manuel; Rojas Urtuguren, José Antonio de; Ruíz Tagle Portales, Francisco; Sacristan, Question of the; Salas, Manuel de; Sancho de Hoz, Pedro; Sanfuentes Andonaegui, Juan Luis; Suárez, Inés de; Tango, The; Tocornal, Joaquín; Toqui; Toro Zambrano, Mateo de; Varas de la Barra, Antonio; Vicuña Larraín, Francisco Ramón; Villagra, Francisco de

MICHAEL L. CONNIFF
Auburn University
Adelantado of the South Sea; Amazon River; Amazonas; Arrais, Miguel; Barros, Adhemar de; Belém; Brizola, Leonel; Goulart, João Belchior Marques; Hay–Herrán Treaty (1903); Hay–Pauncefote Treaties (1901); Hull–Alfaro Treaty (1936); Lesseps, Ferdinand Marie, Vicomte de; Madeira-Mamoré Railroad; Panama; Panama: Constitutions; Panama: Democratic Revolutionary Party (PRD); Panama Canal; Panama Canal Company; Panama Canal Treaties of 1977; Pará (Grão Pará); Quadros, Jânio da Silva; Távora, Juárez; Tenentismo

ROBERT EDGAR CONRAD
Gama, Luís; Patrocínio, José do; Rebouças, André; Slave Trade, Abolition of: Brazil

ANNABELLE CONROY
University of Pittsburgh, Center for Latin American Studies
Bolivia: Constitutions; Bolivia: Political Parties: Overview, Democratic Popular Unity

CHRISTEL K. CONVERSE
Argentina: United Officers Group (GOU); Castillo, Ramón S.; Chile: Junta del Gobierno; Chuquicamata Mine; García, Diego; Jockey Club; Larrea, Juan

ANITA G. COOK
Catholic University of America
Huari; Huarpa; Nasca Lines; Paracas; Paracas Peninsular Sites

NOBLE DAVID COOK
Florida International University
Aguirre, Lope de; Almagro, Diego de; Atahualpa; Bobadilla, Francisco de; Capitulations of Santa Fe; Cieza de León, Pedro de; Enríquez de Guzmán, Alonso; García de Castro, Lope; Garcilaso de la Vega, El Inca; Gasca, Pedro de la; Girón, Francisco Hernández; Huascar; Ica; Lepe, Diego de; Line of Demarcation; Núñez Vela, Blasco; Oré, Luis Gerónimo de; Orellana, Francisco de; Ovando, Nicolás de;

NOBLE DAVID COOK
(cont.)
Oviedo y Valdés, Gonzalo Fernández; Pinzón, Martín Alonso; Pinzón, Vicente Yáñez; Pizarro, Francisco; Pizarro, Gonzalo; Pizarro, Hernando; Porras Barrenechea, Raúl; Porres, Martín de; Requerimiento; Rosa de Lima; Solís, Juan Díaz de; Tordesillas, Treaty of (1494); Tumbes; Ursúa, Pedro de; Vaca de Castro, Cristóval; Vespucci, Amerigo

JERRY W. COONEY
University of Louisville
Bray, Arturo; Carrera del Paraguay; Ordenanza de Intendentes; Ribera y Espinosa, Lázaro de

R. DOUGLAS COPE
Brown University
Abad y Queipo, Manuel; Alzate y Ramírez, José Antonio de; Ávila, Alonso de; Balbuena, Bernardo de; Carvajal, Luis de; Cervantes, Vicente; Desagüe; Gante, Pedro de; Garay, Francisco de; Gelves, Marqués de; León, Alonso de; Palafox y Mendoza, Juan de; Parián; Peninsular; Revillagigedo, Conde de; Sigüenza y Góngora, Carlos de

LUIS CORREA-DÍAZ
Catholic University of America
Heiremans, Luis Alberto

AMALIA CORTINA ARAVENA
Aizenberg, Roberto; Alonso, Raúl; Basaldúa, Hector; Berni, Antonio; Carballo, Aída; Diomede, Miguel; Figari, Pedro; Fontana, Lucio; Forner, Raquel; Grilo, Sarah; Kosice, Gyula; Lozza, Raúl; Mele, Juan N.; Minujin, Marta; Quinquela Martín, Benito; Quirós, Cesáreo Bernaldo de; Soldi, Raúl; Torres García, Joaquín; Vega, Jorge Luis de la; Xul Solar

ROLANDO COSTA PICAZO
Universidad de Buenos Aires
Ocampo, Victoria; Sur

552

MICHAEL P. COSTELOE
University of Bristol
Bases Orgánicas; Gómez Pedraza, Manuel; Herrera, José Joaquín Antonio Florencio; Mexico: Centralism; Mexico: Constitutions: Siete Leyes (1836); Paredes y Arrillaga, Mariano; Pastry War; Tornel y Mendívil, José María

BRIAN E. COUTTS
Western Kentucky University
Belize; Belmopan; Esquivel, Manuel Amadeo; Navarro, Martín Antonio (Félix); New Orleans; O'Reilly y McDowell, Alejandro; Price, George Cadle; Wallace, Peter

EDITH COUTURIER
National Endowment for the Humanities
Avio; Obras Pías; Partido; Romero de Terreros, Pedro

MARGARET E. CRAHAN
Hunter College, City University of New York
Chile: Vicariate of Solidarity; Errázuriz Valdivieso, Crescente; Fresno Larraín, Juan Francisco; Human Rights; Pérez Esquivel, Adolfo; Service for Peace and Justice (SERPAJ); Silva Henríquez, Raúl

A. CAROLINA CASTILLO CRIMM
Sam Houston State University
De León, Martín

JOSEPH T. CRISCENTI
Boston College
Alsina, Adolfo; Alsina, Valentín; Caseros, Battle of; Cepeda, Battles of; Garibaldi, Giuseppe; Ibarra, Juan Felipe; López, Estanislao; López Jordán, Ricardo; Peñaloza, Ángel Vicente; Quesada, Ernesto; Ravignani, Emilio; San Martin, José Francisco de; San Nicolás, Acuerdo de (1852); Urquiza, Justo José de

JOHN CROCITTI
University of Miami
Baldorioty de Castro, Ramón; Bonny, Anne; Ferré Aguayo, Luis Antonio; Read, Mary

LARRY N. CROOK
University of Florida
Baião; Banda de Pífanos; Ciranda; Frevo; Gonzaga, Luiz; Maracatu

RAÚL CUCALÓN
U.S. Army Defense Language Institute
Condor; Iguana; Monkey; Puma; Tapir

LIGHT TOWNSEND CUMMINS
Austin College
Baton Rouge, Battle of

ROGER L. CUNNIFF
San Diego State University
Drought Region (Brazil); Pernambuco; Recife

NICHOLAS P. CUSHNER
State University of New York, Empire State College
Abreu, Diego de; Angelis, Pedro de; Argentina: The Colonial Period; Bazán, Juan Gregorio; Bonpland, Aimé Jacques; Bucareli y Ursúa, Francisco de Paula; Castañeda, Francisco de Paula; Colombres, José Eusebio; Díaz de Guzmán, Ruy; Frías, Antonio; Funes, Gregorio; Gómez, José Valentín; Jesuits; Lozano, Pedro; Nusdorffer, Bernardo; Oro, Justo Santa María de; Philippines; Ruiz de Montoya, Antonio; Serrano, José; Solano, Francisco; Varela, Juan Cruz

RICHARD E. DAGGETT
University of Massachusetts
Archaeology

MARY L. DANIEL
University of Wisconsin–Madison
Rosa, João Guimarães

RAMON E. DAUBON
United States Agency for International Development
Inter-American Foundation (IAF)

WILLIAM DAVIDSON
Louisiana State University
Bahía, Islas de

DARIÉN DAVIS
Middlebury College
Bahamas, Commonwealth of the; Barbados; Bimini; Borno, Joseph

DARIÉN DAVIS
(cont.)
Louis E. Antoine François; Casa de las Américas; Dartiguenave, Philippe-Sudré; Heredia y Heredia, José M.; Nord, Pierre Alexis; Ogé, Jacques Vicente; Pétion, Alexandre Sabès; Soulouque, Faustin Élie; Tallet, José Zacarías; University of the West Indies; Vega, Aurelio de; Vodun, Voodoo, Vaudun

SONNY DAVIS
Texas A&M University at Kingsville
Brazil: National Security Doctrine; Brazil: Organizations: Superior Military Tribunal; Brazil: Political Parties: National Renovating Alliance (ARENA); Death Squads; Figueiredo, João Baptista de Oliveira; Herzog, Vladimir

SANTIAGO DAYDÍ-TOLSON
University of Wisconsin–Milwaukee
Bombal, María Luisa; Edwards Bello, Joaquín; Ercilla y Zúñiga, Alonso de; Parra, Nicanor

GABRIELLA DE BEER
City College of the City University of New York
Aridjis, Homero

RENÉ DE LA PEDRAJA
Canisius College
Colombia: Organizations: Confederation of Colombian Workers (CTC), Unified Central of Workers (CUT), Union of Colombian Workers (UTC)

JESÚS F. DE LA TEJA
Southwest Texas State University
Aguayo, Marqués de; Fredonia, Republic of; Gutiérrez de Lara, José Bernardo; Margil de Jesús, Antonio; San Antonio; Seguín, Juan José María Erasmo; Sequín, Juan Nepomuceno; Texas

DALILA DE SOUSA
Spelman College
Race and Ethnicity: Brazil

WARREN DEAN†
New York University
Brazil: 1808–1889; Forests; Rubber

553

SUSAN DEANS-SMITH
University of Texas at Austin
Tobacco Monopoly

WARREN DEBOER
Queens College, City University of New York
South America: Pre-Columbian History: Amazonia

ALLAN FIGUEROA DECK, S.J.
Loyola Marymount University
Alegre, Francisco Javier; Martínez, Antonio J.

MIRIAM DeCOSTA-WILLIS
University of Maryland at Baltimore County
Morejón, Nancy

SUSAN DEEDS
Northern Arizona University
Bent's Fort; Gadsden Purchase; Nueva Vizcaya; Provincias Internas

ANGELA B. DELLEPIANE
City College and Graduate Center, City University of New York
Ascasubi, Hilario; Bioy Casares, Adolfo; Campo, Estanislao del; Cortázar, Julio; Gambaro, Griselda; Gauchesca Literature; Gorodischer, Angélica; Güiraldes, Ricardo; Hernández, José; Hidalgo, Bartolomé; Lynch, Benito; Martín Fierro; Puig, Manuel; Sábato, Ernesto

JOSEPHINE DeLORENZO
Orbigny, Alcide Dessalines d'

HELEN DELPAR
University of Alabama
Antioquia; Barranquilla; Bogotá, Santa Fe de; Bogotazo; Castillo y Guevara, Francisca Josefa de la Concepción de; Chocó; Colombia: Great Banana Strike; Colombia: Political Parties: National Popular Alliance (ANAPO), Radical Olympus; Concordat of 1887; Cumbia; Cundinamarca; Díaz Castro, Eugenio; Gutiérrez González, Gregorio; Herrera, Benjamín; Holguín, Jorge; Leticia Dispute; Llanos (Colombia); Magdalena River; Medellín; Ospina, Pedro Nel; Pan-American

HELEN DELPAR
(cont.)
Conferences: Bogotá Conference (1948); Popayán; Román de Núñez, Soledad; Suárez, Marco Fidel; Urabá; Valencia, Guillermo León

ROBERTA M. DELSON
United States Merchant Marine Academy
Atlantic Islands, Migrants from; Pôrto Seguro

ARTHUR DEMAREST
Vanderbilt University
Dos Pilas; Petexbatún

DAVID DENSLOW
University of Florida
Furtado, Celso

SANDRA McGEE DEUTSCH
University of Texas at El Paso
Argentina: Argentine Civic Legion (LCA); Argentina: Argentine Patriotic League (LPA); Carlés, Manuel

JOSEPH DI BONA
Duke University
Education

TODD A. DIACON
University of Tennessee, Knoxville
Contestado Rebellion; Farquhar, Percival

JESÚS DÍAZ CABALLERO
University of Pittsburgh
Bryce Echenique, Alfredo

JOHN P. DICKENSON
University of Liverpool
Brazil: Geography; Environment and Climate

BERNADETTE DICKERSON
Oakland University
Carimbó; Côco; Maculelê

RICHARD DIEHL
University of Alabama
Toltecs; Tula

THOMAS DODD
United States Embassy, Montevideo, Uruguay
Boundary Disputes: Overview

DALISIA MARTINS DOLES
Universidade Federal de Goiás
Bóia-Fria; Mutirão

RONALD DOLKART
California State University, Bakersfield
Mojica, José de Jesús; Peralta, Angela

CHRISTOPHER B. DONNAN
University of California, Los Angeles
Chotuna

WILLIAM DONOVAN
Loyola College
Conselho da Fazenda; Junta do Comércio; Las Casas, Bartolomé de; Lisbon Earthquake; Provedor Mor da Fazenda; Salt Trade: Brazil

GEORGETTE MAGASSY DORN
Library of Congress
Anderson Imbert, Enrique; Argentina: Progressive Democratic Party; Benítez, Jaime; Dobles Segreda, Luis; Esperanza Colony; Groussac, Paul; Hanke, Lewis Ulysses; Herrera y Reissig, Julio; Howard, Jennie Eliza; Labarca Hubertson, Amanda; Monserrat, Colegio de; Moreau de Justo, Alicia; Quiroga, Horacio; Ruiz de Alarcón y Mendoza, Juan; Salesians; Sánchez, Florencio; Sarmiento, Domingo Faustino; Torre, Lisandro de la; Valero, Roberto; Valle, Artistóbulo del; Valle, Rafael Heliodoro

PAUL J. DOSAL
University of South Florida
Arana, Francisco J.; Dependency Theory; Guatemala: Terrorist Organizations: Mano Blanca, Ojo por Ojo; Industrialization; Turcios Lima, Luis Agosto; Yon Sosa, Marco Antonio

MICHAEL DOUDOROFF
University of Kansas
Blanco, Andrés Eloy; Chumacero, Alí; González Martínez, Enrique; Liscano Velutini, Juan; Subero, Efraín

JAMES DOW
Oakland University
Cannibalism;
Curandero/Curandeiro; Indians

PAUL W. DRAKE
University of California, San Diego
Kemmerer, Edwin Walter

J. DAVID DRESSING
Tulane University
Albuquerque; America; Bonaparte, Joseph; Chicago Boys; Chile: Grupo Cruzat-Larraín; Cortés, Martín; Fúrlong Cárdiff, Guillermo; Gorriti, Juan Ignacio de; Guatemala Company; Herrera Lane, Felipe; Ladino; Latin America; Leloir, Luis F.; L'Olonnais, Francis; Luisi, Luisa; Primo de Verdad y Ramos, Francisco; Rio Grande; Rodney, Caesar Augustus; Vera Cruz, Alonso de la; Welser, House of

JOHN DUDLEY
Tulane University
ABC Countries; Arrau, Claudio León; Atlantic Charter; Auchmuty, Samuel; Beresford, William Carr; Canning, George; Hirsch, Maurice von; Hudson, William Henry; Latin American Free Trade Association (LAFTA); Magellan, Ferdinand; Pan-American Conferences: Punta del Este Meeting (1962); Parish, Woodbine; Popham, Home Riggs; Southern Cone

JOHN W. F. DULLES
University of Texas at Austin
Brazil: Revolutions: Constitutionalist Revolt (São Paulo); Café Filho, João; Lacerda, Carlos Frederico Werneck de; Lacerda, Maurício Pavia de; Prestes, Luís Carlos; Prestes Column

FRANCIS A. DUTRA
University of California, Santa Barbara
Albuquerque, Matias de; Barros, João de; Cabral, Pedro Álvares; Carvalho, Antônio de Albuquerque Coelho de; Coelho, Jorge de Albuquerque; Coelho Pereira, Duarte; Dutch in Colonial Brazil; Eckhout, Albert; Gama, Vasco da; Manuel I of Portugal; Maria I of Portugal;

FRANCIS A. DUTRA
(cont.)
Maria II of Portugal (Maria da Gloria); Maurits, Johan; Melo e Castro, Martinho de; Military Orders: Portugal; Overseas Council (Portugal); Portuguese Empire; Portuguese Overseas Administration; Post, Frans Jansz; Sá e Benavides, Salvador Correia de

DANIEL DWYER
Siena College Friary
Sánchez Manduley, Celia; Santamaría, Haydée

ANANI DZIDZIENYO
Brown University
African–Latin American Relations

MARSHALL C. EAKIN
Vanderbilt University
Belo Horizonte; Brazil: Revolutions: Revolution of 1964; Golbery do Couto e Silva; Minas Gerais; Mining: Colonial Brazil; Monteiro, Pedro Aurélio de Góis; Ouro Prêto

PETER G. EARLE
University of Pennsylvania
Ariel; Arielismo; Rodó, José Enrique

ROLAND H. EBEL
Tulane University
Arana Osorio, Carlos; Arbenz Guzmán, Jacobo; Arévalo Bermejo, Juan José; Castillo Armas, Carlos; Cerezo Arévalo, Marco Vinicio; Continuismo; Guatemala: Revolutionary Action Party (PAR); Lemus, José María; Méndez Montenegro, Julio César; Méndez Montenegro, Mario; Osorio, Oscar; Peralta Azurdia, Enrique; Romero, Carlos Humberto; Sánchez Hernández, Fidel; Ungo, Guillermo Manuel; Villagrán Kramer, Francisco; Ydígoras Fuentes, Miguel

MUNRO S. EDMONSON
Tulane University
Calendars, Pre-Columbian; Mayan Ethnohistory; Popol Vuh

MARTHA EGAN
Art: Folk Art

EVERETT EGGINTON
University of Louisville
Literacy

JOHN ELIAS
Fordham University
Freire, Paulo

DAVID ELTIS
Queen's University, Ontario; W. E. B. Du Bois Institute, Harvard University
Slave Trade, Abolition of: Spanish America

CHARLOTTE EMMERICH
Museu Nacional, Universidade Federal do Rio de Janeiro
Nambikwára; Sambaqui; Tanga; Tupi-Guarani

NORA C. ENGLAND
University of Iowa
Mam; Poqomam

IRIS H. W. ENGSTRAND
University of San Diego
Argüello, Santiago; Crabb, Henry A.; Longinos Martínez, José; Malaspina, Alejandro; Moziño, José Mariano; Rodríguez Cabrillo, Juan; Serra, Junipero; Wolfskill, William

EVAN C. ENGWALL
University of Illinois at Urbana-Champaign
Chorrera

ARTHUR J. ENNIS, O.S.A.†
Villanova University, Augustinian Historical Institute
Augustinians

J. A. EPPLE
University of Oregon
Acevedo Hernández, Antonio; Alegría, Fernando; Brunet, Marta; Prado, Pedro

JOSÉ D. EPSTEIN
The American University
Inter-American Development Bank (IDB)

JOSÉ ESCORCIA
Universidad de Cali
Cali; Cauca Valley; Codazzi, Agustín; González, Florentino; López Pumarejo, Alfonso; Uribe Uribe, Rafael

MARK EVERINGHAM
University of Wisconsin–Green Bay
Arce Castaño, Bayardo; Borge, Tomás; Contadora; Cruz, Arturo; Fonseca Amador, Carlos; Mayorga, Silvio; Nicaragua: Constitutions; Nicaragua: Sandinista National Liberation Front (FSLN); Ortega Saavedra, Daniel; Ortega Saavedra, Humberto; Ramírez Mercado, Sergio; Ruíz, Henry; Sandino, Augusto César; Wheelock Román, Jaime

JUDITH EWELL
College of William and Mary
Picón Salas, Mariano

MARK FALCOFF
American Enterprise Institute for Public Policy Research
Argentina: The Twentieth Century; Frei Montalva, Eduardo; Menem, Carlos Saúl

MINDI J. FARBER DE ANDA
Energetics, Inc., Washington, D.C.
Electrification; Energy

JOHN ALAN FARMER
Museum of Contemporary Art, Los Angeles
Díaz, Gonzalo; Dittborn, Eugenio; Grupo de CAYC; Porter, Liliana; Tunga

ROBERT FELDMAN
The Field Museum
Aspero

MAYRA FELICIANO
University of South Carolina
Soto, Pedro Juan; Zeno Gandía, Manuel

MANUEL FERNÁNDEZ
University of Southern California
Musical Instruments

MARTA FERNÁNDEZ WHIGHAM
Universidad Nacional de Asunción, Paraguay
Academia de la Lengua y Cultura Guaraní; Barrios, Agustín; Benítez, Gregorio; Campos Cervera, Hérib; Cardozo, Efraím; Escalada, Asunción; Franco, Rafael; Garay, Eugenio; Lynch, Elisa Alicia; Plá, Josefina; Women in Paraguay; Ynsfrán, Pablo Max

ELIZABETH FERRER
The Americas Society
Álvarez Bravo, Lola; Iturbide, Graciela; O'Higgins, Pablo; Taller de Gráfica Popular (TGP)

THOMAS FIEHRER
The Plantation Society
Carondelet, François-Louis Hector

CARLOS FILGUEIRA
Centro de Informaciones e Estudios de Uruguay, Universidad de la República, Montevideo
Real de Azúa, Carlos

FERNANDO FILGUEIRA
Northwestern University
Ateneo del Uruguay; Brum, Baltasar; Cuestas, Juan Lindolfo; Herrerismo; Latorre, Lorenzo; Naval Club, Pact of the; Seregni, Líber; Uruguay: Electoral System; Uruguay: Organizations: National Workers Convention, Rural Association, Workers' Interunion Plenary (PIT-CNT); Uruguay: Broad Front; Viera, Feliciano

HENRY FINCH
University of Liverpool
Chinchulín, Pact of; Coparticipación; Marcha; Ruralismo; Uruguay

KENNETH V. FINNEY
North Carolina Wesleyan College
Bonilla, Policarpo; Bonilla Chirinos, Manuel; Cruz Ucles, Ramón Ernesto; Fonseca, Gulf of; Honduras; Olancho; Paz Baraona, Miguel; Tegucigalpa

JOHN R. FISHER
University of Liverpool
Abascal y Souza, José Fernando; Almojarifazgo; Amat y Junient, Manuel de; Avería; Avilés, Gabriel; Casa de Contratación; Caviedes, Juan del Valle y; Commercial Policy: Colonial Spanish America; Croix, Teodoro de; Fleet System (Flota): Colonial Spanish America; Gil de Taboada y Lemos, Francisco; Guirior, Manuel; Jáuregui, Agustín de; Ladrón de Guevara, Diego; O'Higgins, Ambrosio; Proyectistas

MICHAEL FLEET
Marquette University
Chile: Political Parties: Christian Democratic Party (PDC), Movement of National Unity (MUN), Popular Action Unitary Movement (MAPU); Lagos, Ricardo; Leighton Guzmán, Bernardo; Mercurio, El

SARA FLEMING
Amador Guerrero, Manuel; Aponte-Ledée, Rafael; Caamaño Deñó, Francisco; Cáceres, Ramón; Coronado, Juan Vázquez de; Gómez y Báez, Máximo; Guardia, Ricardo Adolfo de la; Guardia Navarro, Ernesto de la; Mérida, Carlos; Muñoz Marín, Luis; Muñoz Rivera, Luis; Olid, Cristóbal de; Remón Cantera, José Antonio; Rivera, Joaquín

NANCY M. FLOWERS
Hunter College, City University of New York
Brazil: Organizations: Conselho Indigenista Missionário (CIMI); Indian Policy, Brazil; Villas Bôas Brothers

HEIDY P. FOGEL†
Yale University
Gallinazo; Gallinazo Group Site; Vicús

CARMENZA OLAYA FONSTAD
Bunker Hill Community College
Medicinal Plants; Spices and Herbs

MERLIN H. FORSTER
Brigham Young University
Henríquez Ureña, Pedro; Literature: Spanish America

DAVID WILLIAM FOSTER
Arizona State University
Almafuerte; Alonso, Amado; Arlt, Roberto; Asociación de Mayo; Bianco, José; Denevi, Marco; Discépolo, Enrique Santos; Estrada, José Manuel; Girri, Alberto; Gudiño Kieffer, Eduardo; Guido, Beatriz; Larreta, Enrique Rodríguez; Levinson, Luisa Mercedes; Lynch, Marta; Mansilla, Lucio Victorio; Molinari, Ricardo E.; Nalé Roxlo, Conrado; Soriano, Osvaldo

WILLIAM R. FOWLER
Vanderbilt University
Lambityeco; Maya, the;
Mesoamerica: Pre-Columbian
History

HEATHER FOWLER-SALAMINI
Bradley University
Tejeda Olivares, Adalberto;
Veracruz (City)

JENNIFER FOX
Cantoria

MARTHA PALEY FRANCESCATO
George Mason University
Fuentes, Carlos

ROSS H. FRANK
University of California, San Diego
Álvarez, Manuel; Barreiro,
Antonio; Chávez, Mariano;
Melgares, Facundo; Penitentes;
Pueblo Rebellion; Zubiría, José
Antonio Laureano de

JUDY BIEBER FREITAS
University of New Mexico
Albuquerque, Antônio Francisco de
Paula; Casa da Torre; Marginal,
Marginalidade; Município,
Município Neutro; Parentela; Vila

JOHN D. FRENCH
Duke University
Brazil: General Labor Command
(CGT); Pacheco da Silva, Osvaldo;
Pellacani, Dante; Riani, Clodsmith

WILLIAM FRENCH
University of British Columbia
Chihuahua

MICHAEL FRY
Fort Lewis College
Esquipulas; Gaínza, Gabino;
Gálvez, Mariano; Mita, Guatemala;
Molina, Pedro; Tamayo, Franz;
Valle, José Cecilio del; Villacorta
Calderón, José Antonio

PETER FURST
*University Museum, University of
Pennslyvania*
Huichols

JUAN CARLOS GALEANO
Florida State University
Carranza Fernández, Eduardo;
Charry Lara, Fernando; Mañach y
Robato, Jorge; Naranjo, Carmen;
Uslar Pietri, Arturo

EDUARDO A. GAMARRA
Florida International University
Banzer Suárez, Hugo; Bolivia: Polit-
ical Parties: Bolivian Socialist Fa-
lange (FSB), Movement of the
Revolutionary Left (MIR), Nation-
alist Democratic Action (ADN),
Nationalist Revolutionary Move-
ment (MNR), Patriotic Agreement
(AP); Comibol; Fernández, Max;
Gueiler Tejada, Lidia; Guevara
Arze, Walter; Lechín Oquendo,
Juan; Palenque, Carlos; Paz Estens-
soro, Víctor; Paz Zamora, Jaime;
Sánchez de Lozada Bustamante,
Gonzalo; Siles Zuazo, Hernán

PAUL GANSTER
*Institute for Regional Studies, San
Diego State University*
Bracero; Camarena, Enrique; Cinco
de Mayo; Maquiladoras

MARIO T. GARCÍA
*University of California, Santa
Barbara*
Chicanos

LEONARDO GARCÍA PABÓN
University of Oregon
Aguirre, Nataniel; Arzáns Orsúa y
Vela, Bartolomé; Bedregal de
Conitzer, Yolanda; Guzmán,
Augusto; Santa Cruz Pachacuti
Yamqui Salcamaygua, Joan de

MAGDALENA GARCÍA PINTO
University of Missouri–Columbia
Agustini, Delmira; Allende, Isabel;
Berenguer, Amanda; Ibarbourou,
Juana de; Mármol, José Pedro
Crisólogo; Matto de Turner, Clo-
rinda; O'Gorman, Camila; Orozco,
Olga; Orphée, Elvira; Parra, Teresa
de la; Peri Rossi, Cristina; Pizarnik,
Alejandra; Silva, Clara; Somers, Ar-
monía; Steimberg, Alicia; Storni,
Alfonsina; Traba, Marta; Valen-
zuela, Luisa; Vilariño, Idea

LAURA GARCÍA-MORENO
Georgetown University
Sáinz, Gustavo

LYDIA M. GARNER
Southwest Texas State University
Additional Act of 1834; Bragança,
House of; Brazil: Council of State;
Brazil: The Empire (First), The
Empire (Second), The Regency;
Brazil: Revolutions: Liberal
Revolution of 1842; Isabel of Brazil,
Princess; Lima, Pedro de Araújo;
Moderative Power

PAUL GARNER
University of Wales
Tehuantepec, Isthmus of

RICHARD L. GARNER
Pennsylvania State University
Velázquez Cárdenas de León,
Joaquín

THOMAS GAROFALO
Paraguay: Colorado Party; Rio
Branco Institute

VIRGINIA GARRARD-BURNETT
*Institute of Latin American Studies,
University of Texas at Austin*
Central American Mission (CAM);
Cochineal; Darién; Heredia; Indigo;
Laugerud García, Eugenio Kjell;
Lucas García, Fernando Romeo;
Mejía Victores, Oscar Humberto;
Mennonites; Moravian Church;
Protestantism; Ríos Montt, José
Efraín; San Cristóbal de las Casas

MARTA GARSD
*Lincoln University College, Buenos
Aires; Supreme Court of Justice,
Republic of Argentina*
Antúnez, Nemesio; Baca Flor, Car-
los; Barradas, Rafael; Blanes, Juan
Manuel; Bravo, Claudio; Cam-
nitzer, Luis; Carreño, Mario; Cas-
tro, José Gil de; Codesido, Julia;
Cúneo Perinetti, José; Deira,
Ernesto; Egas, Camilo Alejandro;
Enríquez, Carlos; Fierro Rimac,
Francisco; Gamarra, José; Gay,
Claudio; González, Carlos; Gonzá-
lez Goyri, Roberto; Grippo, Víctor;
Jaar, Alfredo; Landaluze, Víctor
Patricio de; Laso, Francisco; Macció,
Rómulo; Morales, Armando; Noé,
Luis Felipe; Pacheco, María Luisa;
Pettoruti, Emilio; Pinto, Joaquín;
Portocarrero, René; Szyszlo,
Fernando de; Tábara, Enrique

JANINE GASCO
Institute of Archaeology, University of California, Los Angeles
Dzibilchaltún; Iximché; Malinalco; Mixco Viejo; Palenque; Soconusco; Tz'utujil; Utatlán; Zaculeu

ALBERT GASTMANN
Trinity College
Aruba; Curaçao; Suriname and the Dutch in the Caribbean

MIGUEL A. GATTI
Catholic University of America
Ayala, Eusebio; Báez, Cecilio; López, Enrique Solano; Paraguay: League of Independent Youth; Paraguay: Febrerista Party; Talavera, Manuel; Yrendagüe, Battle of; Zubizarreta, Gerónimo

JUDITH GENTLEMAN
Horton Social Science Center, University of New Hampshire
Mexico: Since 1910

DICK GERDES
University of New Mexico
Aguilera Malta, Demetrio; Ángel, Albalucía; Carrasquilla, Tomás; Carrera Andrade, Jorge; Eguren, José María; Icaza Coronel, Jorge; Miró, César; Ribeyro, Julio Ramón

JOAN GERO
University of South Carolina
Recuay

PAULA S. GIBBS
Tulane University
Cayman Islands

STEVEN S. GILLICK
Gonzaga University
Belly, Félix; Chicle Industry; Confederación de Trabajadores de América Latina (CTAL); Cuba: Federatior of Cuban Workers (CTC); Danish West Indies; Guatemala: Guatemalan Labor Party (PGT); Guevara, Ernesto "Che"; International Railways of Central America (IRCA, FICA); Ley, Salvador; Rodríguez Cerna, José; Sarmientos de León, Jorge Alvaro; Stephens, John Lloyd

JOHN GLEDSON
University of Liverpool
Taunay, Alfredo d'Escragnolle, Vicomte de

THOMAS F. GLICK
Boston University
Science

HORACIO GNEMMI
Universidad Nacional de Córdoba
Architecture: Architecture to 1900

CEDOMIL GOIC
University of Michigan
Donoso, José; Huidobro Fernández, Vicente; Lihn, Enrique; Mistral, Gabriela; Rojas, Manuel; Rokha, Pablo de; Rokha, Winétt de; Skármeta, Antonio

MICHAEL GOLD-BISS
St. Cloud University
Inter-American Organizations; Inter-American System

SHIFRA M. GOLDMAN
Latin American Center, University of California, Los Angeles
Alfaro Siqueiros, David; Cuevas, José Luis; González Camarena, Jorge; Guerrero, Xavier; Izquierdo, María; O'Gorman, Juan; Toledo, Francisco

ELIANA MARIA REA GOLDSCHMIDT
Azevedo, Thales de; Ianni, Octavio; Lagôa Santa; Pedra Furada; Prado da Silva Júnior, Caio; Ribeiro, Darcy; Rocha, Manoel Ribeiro; Romero, Sílvio; Sacramento, Colônia do

ANN GONZÁLEZ
University of North Carolina at Charlotte
Aguilar, Rosario Fiallos de; Albán, Laureano; Arias, Arturo; Belli, Gioconda; Díaz Lozano, Argentina; Molina, Juan Ramón; Morales, Beltrán; Morales, Mario Roberto

JORGE H. GONZÁLEZ
Tulane University
Chiapas; Ibarra, José de Pineda; Los Altos; Molina, Marcelo; Molina Bedoya, Felipe; Quetzaltenango; Wyld Ospina, Carlos

NANCIE L. GONZÁLEZ
University of Maryland
Caribs

FERNANDO GONZÁLEZ DAVISON
Instituto de Investigaciones Políticas y Sociales, Universidad de San Carlos de Guatemala
Carpio Nicolle, Jorge; Central American Parliament; Gómez Carrillo, Enrique; Guatemala: Constitutions; Landívar, Rafael; Liberal Party (Central America); Quetzal

LOUIS W. GOODMAN
The American University
Armed Forces

PAUL B. GOODWIN, JR.
University of Connecticut
Alem, Leandro; Argentina: Organizations: General Labor Confederation (CGT), Yacimientos Petrolíferos Fiscales (YPF); Argentina: Political Parties: Antipersonalist Radical Civil Union, Democratic Union (UD), Radical Party (UCR); Cooke, John William; Dellepiane, Luis J.; Descamisados; Di Tella, Torcuato; Gainza Paz, Alberto; Railroads; Yrigoyen Hipólito

PAUL GOOTENBERG
State University of New York at Stony Brook
Guano Industry

DAVID B. GRACY II
University of Texas at Austin
Austin, Moses; Austin, Stephen Fuller

LAURA GRAHAM
University of Iowa
Brazil: Organizations: Indian Protection Service (IPS), National Indian Foundation (FUNAI), Union of Indigenous Nations (UNI); Gê; Nimuendajú, Curt; Pacification; Rondon, Cândido Mariano da Silva

SANDRA LAUDERDALE GRAHAM
University of Texas at Austin
Casa Grande; Favela; Free Birth Law; Golden Law; Queirós Law; Senzala; Sexagenarian Law

LANCE R. GRAHN
Marquette University
Cartagena; Contraband; El Dorado; Eslava y Lazaga, Sebastián de; Manso de Maldonado, Antonio; Messía de la Cerda, Pedro de; Pedrosa y Guerrero, Antonio de la; Pizarro, José Alonso; Riohacha; Santa Marta; Solís Folch de Cardona, José; Villalonga, Jorge

ROGER GRAVIL
University of Natal, South Africa
Alfonsín, Raúl Ricardo; Aramburu, Pedro Eugenio; Argentina: United Officers Group (GOU); British in Argentina; Cámpora, Héctor José; Lanusse, Alejandro Augusto; Levingston, Roberto Marcelo; Lonardi, Eduardo; Onganía, Juan Carlos; Ottawa Agreement (1932); Roca–Runciman Pact (1933)

MICHAEL R. GREEN
Texas State Archives
Houston, Sam; Lamar, Mirabeau Buonaparte; San Jacinto, Battle of

STANLEY GREEN
Laredo State University
Sánchez, Prisciliano

ANNE GREENE
Bellegarde, Luis Dantès; Péralte, Charlemagne Masséna; Rochambeau, Donatien Marie Joseph de Vimeur de; Sonthonax, Léger Félicité

GERALD MICHAEL GREENFIELD
University of Wisconsin–Parkside
Agreste; Retirante

KAREN M. GREINER
Esmeraldas

KENNETH J. GRIEB
University of Wisconsin–Oshkosh
Aguirre y Salinas, Osmín; Decena Trágica; Dictators League; Eisenhower-Remón Treaty (1955); Hernández Martínez, Maximiliano; Niagara Falls Conference; Noriega Moreno, Manuel Antonio; Orozco, Pascual, Jr.; Pact of the Embassy; Panama Canal: Flag Riots; Panama Canal Tolls Question; Pearson, Weetman Dickinson; Pershing

KENNETH J. GRIEB
(cont.)
Expedition; Quiñones Molina, Alfonso; Russell, John H.; Torrijos Herrera, Omar; Ubico y Castañeda, Jorge; Uriarte–Bayarta Agreement; Veracruz, Occupation of; Watermelon Riot (Panama Riot); Wilson, Henry Lane; World War I; Zimmermann Telegram

TERENCE GRIEDER
University of Texas at Austin
La Galgada

ERWIN P. GRIESHABER
Mankato State University
Belzu, Manuel Isidoro; Campero, Narciso; Daza, Hilarión; La Paz; Morales, Agustín; Urriolagoitía, Mamerto; Velasco, José Miguel de; Villazón, Eliodoro

JO ANN GRIFFIN
Goldwork, Pre-Columbian

WILLIAM J. GRIFFITH
University of Kansas
Abbottsville; Eastern Coast of Central America Commercial and Agricultural Company; Galindo, Juan; Morazán, Francisco

RICHARD GRISWOLD DEL CASTILLO
San Diego State University
Armijo, Manuel; Californios; Gringo; Guadalupe Hidalgo, Treaty of (1848); Kearny, Stephen W.; Polk, James Knox; Taylor, Zachary

PETER GUARDINO
Indiana University
Álvarez, Juan; Guerrero

LOWELL GUDMUNDSON
Mount Holyoke College
Carrillo Colina, Braulio; Cavallón, Juan de; Costa Rica: Constitutions; Facio Brenes, Rodrigo; Fallas Sibaja, Carlos Luis; Guanacaste; Guardia Gutiérrez, Tomás; Montealegre Fernández, José María; Mora Fernández, Juan; Mora Porrás, Juan Rafael; Thiel, Bernardo Augusto; Tinoco Granados, Federico

VIRGINIA GUEDEA
Instituto Mora, Mexico City
Abasolo, Mariano; Academia Literaria de Querétaro; Aldama y González, Ignacio de; Azcárate y Lezama, Juan Francisco de; Bravo, Leonardo; Caballeros Racionales, Sociedad de; Chilpancingo, Congress of; Cos y Pérez, José María; Domínguez, Miguel; Fagoaga y Lizaur, José María; Galeana, Hermenegildo; Galván Rivera, Mariano; Guadalupes, Los; Iturrigaray, José de; Mexico: Constitution of Apatzingán (1814); Mexico: Wars and Revolutions: Coup d'État of 1808; Mina y Larrea, Javier; Morelos y Pavón, José María; Ortiz de Domínguez, Josefa; Peimbert, Margarita; Peña, Antonia; Rayón, Ignacio; Rodríguez de Velasco y Osorio Barba, María Ignacia; Rosáins, Juan Nepomuceno; Sánchez de Tagle, Francisco Manuel; Sanjuanistas; Sardaneta y Llorente, José Mariano de; Talamantes, Melchor de; Valladolid Conspiracy; Vicario Fernández, [María] Leona; Yermo, Gabriel de

MAGDALENA GUTIÉRREZ
University of Illinois–Chicago
Lavalleja, Juan Antonio

DONNA J. GUY
University of Arizona
Argentina: Civil Code; Argentina: Commercial Code; Children; Compadrito; Coni, Emilio R.; Coni, Gabriela Laperrière de; Le Bretón, Tomás Alberto; Linseed

STEPHEN HABER
Stanford University
Banco de Avío; Textile Industry

DAVID T. HABERLY
University of Virginia
Almeida, Manuel Antônio de; Azevedo, Aluísio; Macedo, Joaquim Manuel de; Rio, João do

JUNE E. HAHNER
State University of New York at Albany
Alambert, Zuleika; Fonseca, Manoel Deodoro da; Lutz, Bertha Maria Julia; Peixoto, Floriano Vieira

CHARLES HALE
University of Iowa
Bulnes, Francisco; Sierra Méndez, Justo

LINDA B. HALL
University of New Mexico
Aguascalientes, Convention of; Atl, Dr.

HUGH M. HAMILL
University of Connecticut
Caudillismo, Caudillo

BRIAN HAMNETT
University of Essex
Assembly of Notables; Bazaine, François Achille; Escobedo, Mariano; French Intervention (Mexico); Jecker Bonds; Labastida y Dávalos, Pelagio Antonio de; Lozada, Manuel; Maximilian; Miramón, Miguel; Munguía, Clemente de Jesús; Napoleon III; Orozco y Berra, Manuel; Puebla, Battle and Siege of; Ramírez, José Fernando; Riva Palacio, Vicente

HOWARD HANDELMAN
University of Wisconsin–Milwaukee
Military Dictatorships: Since 1945

MICHAEL HANDELSMAN
University of Tennessee, Knoxville
Carrión, Alejandro; Carrión, Manuel Benjamin

CARL A. HANSON
Trinity University
Portugal

JOHN MASON HART
University of Houston
Casa del Obrero Mundial

ROBERT HASKETT
University of Oregon
Altepetl; Calpulli; Cuauhtemoc; Doce, Los; Guzmán, Nuño Beltrán de; Marquesado del Valle de Oaxaca; Mixtón War; Nahuas; Nahuatl; Pachuca; Parral; Pipiltín; Pochteca; San Luis Potosí; Taxco; Tlatoani; Tlaxilacalli

TIMOTHY P. HAWKINS
Tulane University
Antigua

EVELYN J. HAWTHORNE
Howard University
Brathwaite, Edward Kamau

ROBERT A. HAYES
Texas Tech University
Brazil: The Regency; Cayenne, Brazilian Invasion of; Confederation of the Equator; Lima e Silva, Luís Alves de; Lisboa, Joaquim Marques; Madureira, Antônio de Sena; Melo Custódio José de; Saldanha da Gama, Luís Felipe da

SAMUEL K. HEATH
Southern Methodist University
Cuzco School of Painting

J. LEÓN HELGUERA
Vanderbilt University
Abadía Méndez, Miguel; Álvarez Gardeazábal, Gustavo; Arboleda, Julio; Banco de la República (Colombia); Berrío, Pedro Justo; Camacho Roldán, Salvador; Cano, María de los Ángeles; Caro, José Eusebio; Castellanos, Juan de; Chiquinquirá; Cisneros, Francisco Javier; Córdoba, José María; Gómez Castro, Laureano; Herrán, Pedro Alcántara; Herrán y Zaldúa, Antonio Saturnino; López, José Hilario; Marroquin, José Manuel; Mosquera, Manuel José; Mosquera, Tomás Cipriano de; Mosquera y Arboleda, Joaquín; Navarro Wolff, Antonio; Obando, José María; Pardo Leal, Jaime; Pasto; Pastrana Borrero, Misael; Restrepo, Carlos Eugenio; Rodríguez Freile, Juan; Salgar, Eustorgio; Samper, José María; Sumapaz, Republic of; Trujillo, Julián; Vásquez de Arce y Ceballos, Gregorio; Villavicencio; Zapata, Felipe

MARY W. HELMS
University of North Carolina at Greensboro
Miskito Indians

JOHN HEMMING
Royal Geographical Society, London
Missions: Brazil

JAMES D. HENDERSON
University of South Carolina–Coastal Carolina College
Concha, José Vicente; Conservative Parties; Gómez Hurtado, Alvaro; Turbay Ayala, Julio César

PETER V. N. HENDERSON
Winona State University
León de la Barra, Francisco

RICK HENDRICKS
University of New Mexico
Espejo, Antonio de; Esteban; Niza, Marcos de; Presidio

JOSÉ MANUEL HERNÁNDEZ
Georgetown University
Agramonte y Loynaz, Ignacio; Alberdi, Juan Bautista; Bachiller y Morales, Antonio; Betancourt Cisneros, Gaspar; Caballero y Rodríguez, José Agustin; Capablanca, José Raúl; Cervantes y Kawanagh, Ignacio; Cisneros Betancourt, Salvador; Cuba: Political Movements, Nineteenth Century; Cuba; Autonomist Party; Cuba: Cuban People's Party (Ortodoxos); Cuba: Revolutions: Revolution of 1933; García, Calixto; García y González, Vicente; Goicuría y Cabrera, Domingo; Gómez, Juan Gualberto; Guerra y Sánchez, Ramiro; Laredo Bru, Federico; Lecuona y Casado, Ernesto; Luz y Caballero, José de la; Maceo, Antonio; Machado y Morales, Gerardo; Maine, U.S.S., Sinking of the; Martí y Pérez, José Julián; Mendieta y Montefur, Carlos; Morales Lemus, José; Peña, Lázaro; Reeve, Henry M.; Roig de Leuchsenring, Emilio; Romay y Valdés Chacón, Tomás; Sánchez de Bustamante y Sirven, Antonio; Varela y Morales, Félix; Viñes y Martorell, Benito; White y Lafitta, José; Zanjón, Pact of; Zayas y Alfonso, Alfredo

OMAR HERNÁNDEZ
University of Texas at Austin
Censorship

MARÍA HERRERA-SOBEK
University of California, Irvine
Canción Ranchera

DAVID J. HESS
Colgate University
Spiritism

FREDERIC HICKS
University of Louisville
Flowery Wars

KATHLEEN JOAN HIGGINS
University of Iowa
Léry, Jean de; Manumission

DAVID HIGGS
University of Toronto
Coutinho, Rodrigo Domingos Antonio de Sousa; Inquisition: Brazil

ROBERT M. HILL II
University of Texas at San Antonio
Brasseur de Bourbourg, Charles Étienne

STEPHEN E. HILL
Saint Lucia; Saint Vincent

ROBERT HIMMERICH Y VALENCIA
University of New Mexico
Genízaro; López de Legazpi y Gurruchátegui, Miguel; Niños Héroes; Peña y Peña, Manuel de la

STEVEN J. HIRSCH
George Washington University
Andean Pact; Llama; Puno; Southern Peru Copper Corporation

KENNETH HIRTH
Pennsylvania State University
Chalcatzingo; Cuicuilco; Xochicalco

LOUISA S. HOBERMAN
University of Texas at Austin
Caldas, Francisco José de

PAUL E. HOFFMAN
Louisiana State University
Louisiana; Santo Domingo, Audiencia of

THOMAS H. HOLLOWAY
Cornell University
Capoeira; Coffee Industry; Immigration

SHEILA HOOKER
University of Michigan
Azores; Brazil: Party of Brazilian Social Democracy (PSDB); Burle

SHEILA HOOKER
(cont.)
Marx, Roberto; Butantã Institute; Canary Islands; Cinchona; Corcovado; Espírito Santo; Madeira Islands; Mazambo; Nova Friburgo; Petrópolis; Reinóis; Rhea; Serra do Mar; Sloth; Sumac, Yma; Tietê River; Trinidade Island; Vitória

JOEL HOROWITZ
Saint Bonaventure University
Argentina: American Industrial Society for Machinery (SIAM); Argentina: Argentine Trade Promotion Institute (IAPI); Plaza, Victorino de la; Ramírez, Pedro Pablo

EVELYN HU-DEHART
University of Colorado at Boulder
Asians in Latin America; Yaqui Indians

KATHERINE CLARK HUDGENS
Museum and Schools Information Exchange
Matta Echaurren, Roberto Sebastián Antonio; Posada, José Guadalupe

REGINA IGEL
University of Maryland at College Park
Brandão, Ignácio de Loyola; Piñon, Nélida; Ribeiro, João Ubaldo; Rubião, Murilo; Scliar, Moacyr

FIDEL IGLESIAS
University of Florida
Beltrán, Luis; Godoy Cruz, Tomás; Lamadrid, Gregorio Aráoz de; Paso, Juan José; Posadas, Gervasio Antonio de; Rondeau, José; Sarratea, Manuel de; Tejedor, Carlos; Vieytes, Hipólito

FE IGLESIAS GARCÍA
Instituto de Historia, Havana, Cuba
Cuba: The Colonial Era (1492–1898); Cuba: The Republic (1898–1959)

RICHARD H. IMMERMAN
Temple University
Central Intelligence Agency (CIA)

MARÍA INÉS DE TORRES
Acevedo Díaz, Eduardo Inés; Quijano, Carlos

ESTELA IRIZARRY
Georgetown University
Arriví, Francisco; Burgos, Julia de; Canales, Nemesio Rosario; Diego, José de; Gallego, Laura; Laguerre, Enrique Arturo; Llorens Torres, Luis; Marqués, René; Méndez Ballester, Manuel

ESTELLE JACKSON
Barragán Morfin, Luis

K. DAVID JACKSON
Yale University
Andrade, Oswald de; Concretism

ROBERT H. JACKSON
Texas Southern University
Bear Flag Revolt; California; Chumash Indians; Durán, Fray Narciso; Echeandía, José María de; Figueroa, José; Fort Ross; García Diego y Moreno, Francisco; Lasuén, Fermín Francisco de; New Spain, Colonization of the Northern Frontier; Palou, Francisco; Rivera, Pedro de; Victoria, Manuel

IVAN JAKSIĆ
University of Notre Dame
Chile: Federation of Chilean Students (FECH); Halperín-Donghi, Tulio; Masonic Orders; Millas Jiménez, Jorge; Molina Garmendia, Enrique; Philosophy

DILMUS D. JAMES
University of Texas at El Paso
Technology

MICHAEL L. JAMES
Rutgers, The State University of New Jersey
Batista, Cicero Romão; Brazil: Development Superintendency of the Northeast (SUDENE); Gomes, Eduardo; Marighela, Carlos; Zumbi

LAURA JARNAGIN
Colorado School of Mines
Brazil: Brazilian Institute of the Environment and Renewable Natural; Brazil: National Institute of Colonization and Agrarian Reform; Earth Summit, Rio de Janeiro (1992); Environmental Movements; Lutzenberger, José

SHELLY JARRETT BROMBERG
University of Texas at Austin
Benítez-Rojo, Antonio; Britto García, Luis; Cardoza y Aragón, Luis

DAVID L. JICKLING
Centro de Investigaciones Regionales de Mesoamérica (CIRMA)
Alvarado Xicotencatl, Leonor; Bethancourt, Pedro de San José de; Bethlehemites; Castillo, Jesús; Chinandega; D'Escoto Brockmann, Miguel; García Granados, Miguel; Granada, Nicaragua; Herrera, Flavio; Hidalgo, Enrique Agustín; Institute of Nutrition of Central America and Panama (INCAP); León; López Arellano, Oswaldo; Maldonado, Rodrigo de Arias; Managua; Peace Corps; Rodas Alvarado, Modesto; Ximénez, Francisco

OLGA JIMÉNEZ DE WAGENHEIM
Rutgers, The State University of New Jersey, Newark
Abbad y Lasierra, Íñigo; Agüeybana II; Betances, Ramón Emeterio; Coll y Toste, Cayetano; Grito de Lares; Morales Carrión, Arturo; Operation Bootstrap

H. B. JOHNSON
University of Virginia
Commercial Policy: Colonial Brazil; Factor; Fleet System: Colonial Brazil

LYMAN L. JOHNSON
University of North Carolina at Charlotte
Guilds (Gremios)

RANDAL JOHNSON
University of California, Los Angeles
Aguiar, Adonias; Amado, Jorge; Andrade, Mário de; Cinema Novo; Ramos, Graciliano

KEVIN JOHNSTON
Pennsylvania State University
Seibal; Yaxchilán

JANICE L. W. JOLLY
Copper Industry

KRISTINE L. JONES
Pontífica Universidad Católica Madre y Maestra, Santo Domingo

KRISTINE L. JONES
(cont.)
Alakaluf; Araucanians; Calfucurá; Charqui; Diaguitas; Hornero Bird; Huincas; Malones; Mapuches; Namuncurá, Ceferino; Namuncurá, Manuel; Patagones; Pehuenches; Querandíes; Ranqueles; Roto; Selk'nams; Tehuelches; Yamana

GILBERT M. JOSEPH
Yale University
Alvarado, Salvador; Carrillo Puerto, Felipe; Caste War of Yucatán

CAROLYN JOSTOCK
Acre; Amapá; Brazilnut Industry; Cashew Industry; Education: Pre-Columbian Education; Guaraná Industry; Ludwig, Daniel Keith; Madeira River; Mendes Filho, Francisco "Chico" Alves; Negro, Rio; Rondônia; Roraima; Rubber Gatherers' Unions; Santarém; Seringal; Seringueiros; Transamazon Highway

GLORIA ELISABETH KAISER
Iniciativa Cultural Austro-Brasiliera
Ender, Thomas

KAREN KAMPWIRTH
Knox College
Barrios de Chamorro, Violeta; Chamorro Cardenal, Pedro Joaquín

DEBORAH KANTER
Albion College
Mexico State

MARY KARASCH
Oakland University
Amaranth; Angola; Guiné, Guinea; Manioc; Mina; Slavery: Brazil

THOMAS L. KARNES
Arizona State University
Central America, United Provinces of; Standard Fruit and Steamship Company; United Fruit Company; Vacarro Brothers

WILLIAM H. KATRA
University of Wisconsin–La Crosse
Amorim, Enrique; Appleyard, José Luis; Artigas, José Gervasio; Basso Maglio, Vicente; Beltrán, Washington; Benedetti, Mario; Blandengues; Cáceres, Esther de; Candioti, Fran-

WILLIAM H. KATRA
(cont.)
cisco Antonio; Cunha Dotti, Juan; Díaz, José Pedro; Frugoni, Emilio; Galeano, Eduardo Hughes; Gómez, Juan Carlos; Hernández, Felisberto; Ibáñez, Roberto; Ibáñez, Sara de; Massera, José Pedro; Oribe, Emilio; Sabat Ercasty, Carlos; Varela, José Pedro

ILONA KATZEW
Institute of Fine Arts, New York University
Contemporáneos, Los; Felguérez, Manuel; Rojo, Vicente; Ruelas, Julio; Varo, Remedios

DOUGLAS R. KEBERLEIN
Tulane University
Jiménez Oreamuno, Ricardo; Montes, César; Vincent, Sténio Joseph

PETER KELLER
Bowers Museum of Cultural Art
Gems and Gemstones

SUSAN KELLOGG
University of Houston
Cortés, Hernán; Motecuhzoma II

JACQUELYN BRIGGS KENT
State University of New York at Cortland
Arango y Parreño, Francisco de; Arnaz, Desi; Campos-Parsi, Héctor; Cuba: Club Femenino; Cugat, Xavier; Hostos y Bonilla, Eugenio María de; Intendancy System; Lam y Castilla, Wifredo; Ortiz, Fernando; Puerto Rico; Ramírez y Blanco, Alejandro; Roldán, Amadeo; Varona y Pera, Enrique José; Velázquez, Diego de

JOHN L. KESSELL
University of New Mexico
Anza, Juan Bautista de; Benavides, Alonso de; Bolton, Herbert Eugene; Borderlands, The; Kino, Eusebio Francisco; New Mexico; Oñate, Juan de; Vargas, Diego de

JOHN E. KICZA
Washington State University
Aguilar, Jerónimo de; Cempoala; Croix, Marqués de; Grijalva, Juan de; New Spain, Viceroyalty of; Noche Triste

JAMES PATRICK KIERNAN
Organization of American States
Gaviria Trujillo, César Augusto; Organization of American States (OAS); Pan-American Conferences: Havana Conference (1928), Havana Meeting (1940), Panama Meeting (1939); Pan-American Highway; Panama Congress of 1826; Paraty

THOMAS W. KILLION
National Museum of Natural History, Smithsonian Institution
Cobá; Matacapán; Sayil

A. DOUGLAS KINCAID
Latin American and Caribbean Center, Florida International University
Class Structure in Modern Latin America

NICOLE R. KING
University of Maryland at College Park
James, Cyril Lionel Robert

KENNETH F. KIPLE
Bowling Green State University
Diseases

CLAYTON KIRKING
Phoenix Art Museum
Coronel, Pedro; Galán, Julio; Soriano, Juan; Zenil, Nahum Bernabé

WADE A. KIT
Wake Forest University
Arévalo Martinez, Rafael; Barrillas, Manuel Lisandro; Céspedes, Carlos Manuel de (the Elder); Céspedes y Quesada, Carlos Manuel de; Chacón, Lázaro; Chalchuapa, Battle of; Crowder, Enoch Herbert; Estrada Cabrera, Manuel; Guatemala: Unionist Party; Herrera, Carlos; Herrera, Tomás; Orellana, Joaquín; Orellana, José María; Prensa, La (de Nicaragua); Reyna Barrios, José María; Sugar Industry

ROGER A. KITTLESON
Northwestern University
Borba Gato, Manuel de; Caramuru; Dantas, Manuel Pinto de Souza; Figueiredo, Afonso Celso de Assis; Osório, Manuel Luís; Saraiva, José Antônio; Silva Lisboa, José da

NORMA KLAHN
University of California, Santa Cruz
Bonifaz Nuño, Rubén; Campos, Julieta; Glantz, Margo; Zaid, Gabriel

JEFFREY KLAIBER, S. J.
Catholic University of Peru
Anticlericalism; Catholic Action; Catholic Church: The Modern Period; El Señor de los Milagros; El Señor de los Temblores; González de Santa Cruz, Roque; Jerez, Francisco de; La Serna, José de; Leo XIII, Pope; López Trujillo, Alfonso; Luján, Virgin of; Mogrovejo, Toribio Alfonso de; Torres Bello, Diego de

PETER F. KLARÉN
George Washington University
Ayacucho, Battle of; Blanco Galdós, Hugo; Centromín; Cerro de Pasco Corporation; Costa (Peru); Empresa Petrolera Fiscal; Gamarra, Francisca Zubiaga Bernales de (La Mariscala); Gibbs and Sons, Antony; International Petroleum Company (IPC); Junín, Battle of; Marshals of Ayacucho; Pardo y Aliaga, Felipe; Peru: Peruvian Aprista Party (PAP/APRA); Perupetro; Pescaperú; Salomón–Lozano Treaty (1922); Selva (Peru)

IGNACIO KLICH
University of Westminster
Islam; Middle Easterners

ALAN KNIGHT
Latin American Centre, Oxford University
Cárdenas del Rio, Lázaro; Carranza, Venustiano; Plan of Guadalupe

ROBERT J. KNOWLTON
University of Wisconsin–Stevens Point
Mexico: Wars and Revolutions: The Reform; Plan of Ayutla

JERRY KNUDSON
Temple University
Journalism

EDMOND KONRAD
Tulane University
Chadbourne Plan; Cuba: Revolutionary Movements:

EDMOND KONRAD
(cont.)
Twenty-Sixth of July Movement; Debray, [Jules] Régis; Guerrilla Movements; Leeward Islands; Pérez, Carlos Andrés; Saint Barthélemy; Sierra Maestra; Villeda Morales, Ramón; Virgin Islands; Windward Islands; Zavala, José Victor

JEFF KARL KOWALSKI
Northern Illinois University
Chacmools; Mayapan; Uxmal

MATT KRYSTAL
Tulane University
Chilam Balam

ALLAN J. KUETHE
Texas Tech University
Beltrán, Manuela; Bourbon Reforms; Caballero y Góngora, Antonio; Espeleta y Galdeano Dicastillo y del Prado, Viceroy Manuel A; Flores Maldonado Martínez y Bodquín, Manuel Antonio; Free Trade Act; Gutiérrez de Piñeres, Juan Francisco; Havana; Mendinueta y Múzquiz, Pedro de; Mon y Velarde, Juan Antonio; New Granada, Viceroyalty of

GARY G. KUHN
University of Wisconsin–La Crosse
Ruiz, Tomás

MONICA E. KUPFER
Alvarado, Antonio; Amador, Manuel E.; Arboleda, Carlos; Cedeño, Juan Manuel; Chong Neto, Manuel; Dutary, Alberto; Herrerabarría, Adriano; Ivaldi, Humberto; Lewis, Roberto; Sinclair, Alfredo; Trujillo, Guillermo; Zachrisson, Julio

ELIZABETH KUZNESOF
University of Kansas
Domestic Service; Family; Marriage and Divorce; Population: Brazil

DAVID LAFRANCE
Oregon State University
Cholula; Creelman Interview; Díaz, Félix, Jr.; Effective Suffrage, No

DAVID LAFRANCE
(cont.)
Reelection; González, Pablo; Huerta, Victoriano; Madero, Francisco Indalecio; Puebla (City); Puebla (State); Río Blanco Strike

CARL HENRIK LANGEBAEK R.
University of Pittsburgh
Calima; Colombia: Pacific Coast; Muisca; San Agustín

ERIK D. LANGER
Carnegie Mellon University
Arce, Aniceto; Arze, José Antonio; Ballivián, José; Baptista, Mariano; Belzu, Manuel Isidoro; Bolivia: Bolivia Since 1825; Bolivia: Political Parties: Conservative Party, Liberal Party, Republican Party; Chayanta, Revolt of (1927); Chiriguanos; Federalist War (1898–1899); Fernández Alonso, Sévero; Gutiérrez Guerra, José; Linares, José María; Melgarejo, Mariano; Montes, Ismael; Pacheco, Gregorio; Pando, José Manuel; Patiño, Simón Iturri; Quiroga Santa Cruz, Marcelo; Santa Cruz, Andrés de; Sucre; Tin Industry; Villarroel López, Gualberto

LESTER LANGLEY
University of Georgia
Big Stick Policy; Bryan–Chamorro Treaty (1914); Christmas, Lee; Clark Memorandum; Good Neighbor Policy; Hay–Bunau-Varilla Treaty (1903); Magoon, Charles Edward; Molony, Guy; Roosevelt, Theodore; Roosevelt Corollary; Taft Agreement (1904); Tela Railroad; United States–Latin American Relations; Wilson Plan; Zemurray, Samuel

ALCIDES LANZA
McGill University
Alcaraz, José Antonio; Allende-Sarón, Pedro Humberto; Becerra-Schmidt, Gustavo; Blanco, Juan; Bolaños, César; Brouwer, Leo; Cervetti, Sergio; Cordero, Roque; Davidovsky, Mario; Dianda, Hilda; Gandini, Gerardo; García Morillo, Roberto; Kagel, Mauricio Raúl; Orrego-Salas, Juan Antonio; Paz, Juan Carlos; Pinilla, Enrique; Tauriello, Antonio; Valcárcel Arce, Edgar

GEORGE M. LAUDERBAUGH
Troy State University, Montgomery, Alabama
Galápagos Islands

MARY LOU LECOMPTE
University of Texas at Austin
Charreada; Charro

THOMAS M. LEONARD
University of North Florida
Alfaro, Ricardo Joaquín; Alliance for Progress; Bluefields; Butler, Smedley Darlington; Caribbean Basin Initiative; Cazneau, William Leslie; Clay, Henry; Contras; Cuyamel Fruit Company; Dulles, John Foster; Finlay, Carlos Juan; Goethals, George Washington; Guantánamo Bay; Hickenlooper Amendment; Mann, Thomas Clifton; Monroe Doctrine; Nicaragua: Maritime Canal Company of Nicaragua; No-Transfer Resolution; Ostend Manifesto; Platt Amendment; Reed, Walter; Soto Alfaro, Bernardo; Spooner Act; Virginius Affair; Welles, Sumner; World War II

MADELINE BARBARA LEONS
Towson State University
Shuar

JEFFREY LESSER
Connecticut College
Aranha, Oswaldo; Brazil: Political Parties: Integralist Action, Liberal Alliance; Cohen Plan; Estado Novo

ROBERT M. LEVINE
University of Miami
Conselheiro, Antônio; Ferrez, Marc; Fredricks, Charles DeForest; Frisch, A.; Jesus, Carolina Maria de; Photography: The Nineteenth Century

DANIEL C. LEVY
State University of New York at Albany
National Autonomous University of Mexico (UNAM)

LINDA LEWIN
University of California, Berkeley
João Pessoa; Paraíba

DANIEL LEWIS
San Bernardino Valley College
Argentina: Organizations: Argentine Rural Society; Argentina: Political Parties: Personalist Radical Civic Union, Youth Organization of the Radical Party (FORJA); Bunge, Carlos Octavio; Cárcano, Miguel Ángel; Casa Rosada; Círculo Militar; Concordancia; Farrell, Edelmiro; Frondizi, Arturo; Frondizi, Risieri; Gómez, Indalecio; González, Joaquín Víctor; Guido, José María; Irigoyen, Bernardo de; Justo, José Agustín Pedro; Ortiz, Roberto Marcelino; Quintana, Manuel; Saavedra Lamas, Carlos; Uriburu, José Félix

PAUL H. LEWIS
Tulane University
Argentina: Justicialist Party; Perón, Juan Domingo; Stroessner, Alfredo

HE LI
Merrimack College
Chinese–Latin American Relations

DOUGLAS COLE LIBBY
Universidade Federal de Minas Gerais
Brazil: Organizations: Brazilian Bar Association (OAB); Brazil: Political Parties: Brazilian Democratic Movement Party (PMDB); Brotherhoods; Silk Industry and Trade; Whaling

MYRON LICHTBLAU
Syracuse University
Cané, Miguel; Echeverría, Esteban; Gálvez, Manuel; Lugones, Leopoldo; Mallea, Eduardo; Rojas, Ricardo; Varela, Florencio; Zorrilla de San Martín, Juan

OLAVO BRASIL DE LIMA JÚNIOR
Universidade Federal de Minas Gerais
Brazil: Brazilian Bar Association (OAB), Brazilian Democratic Movement Party (PMDB)

MICHAEL D. LIND
Bernal y García Pimentel, Ignacio; Cholula (Pre-Columbian); Dainzú; Yagul; Zaachila

RICHARD LINDLEY
Austin Community College
Jalisco

HÉCTOR LINDO-FUENTES
Fordham University
Cristiani, Alfredo; Dávila, Miguel
R.; San Salvador; Sonsonate

JUDITH LISANSKY
World Bank
Caboclo

PEGGY K. LISS
Washington, D.C.
Fonseca, Juan Rodríguez de

SHELDON B. LISS†
University of Akron
Chamizal Conflict; Cuba Since 1959

TODD LITTLE-SIEBOLD
Lewis and Clark College
Arias, Desiderio; Barbosa y Alcalá,
José Celso; Bay of Pigs Invasion;
Colono; Corn Islands; Cuartelazo;
Delgado, José Matías; Dominica;
Roca, Blas

EULALIA MARIA LAHMEYER LOBO
Brazil Since 1889

JAMES LOCKHART
University of California, Los Angeles
Chimalpahin

WILLIAM LOFSTROM
United States Department of State
Sucre Alcalá, Antonio José de

JOHN V. LOMBARDI
University of Florida
Venezuela Since 1830

MARY LUCIANA LOMBARDI
*Institute for Historical Study, San
Francisco and Santa Cruz*
Amaral, Tarsila do; Malfatti, Anita
Catarina; Modern Art Week

GAYLE WAGGONER LOPES
United States Department of State
Bumba-Meu-Boi; Hammock;
Jangada; Maranhão; São Luís

MARY ANGÉLICA LOPES
University of South Carolina
Queiroz, Dinah Silveira de; Telles,
Lygia Fagundes

FERNANDO LÓPEZ D'ALESSANDRO
*Instituto de Estudios Sociales,
Montevideo*
Uruguay: Political Parties:
Christian Democratic Party (PDC),
Communist Party, Socialist Party

BRIAN LORDAN
Explorers and Exploration: Spanish
America

JOSEPH L. LOVE
*University of Illinois at
Urbana-Champaign*
Borges de Medeiros, Antônio
Augusto; Cardoso, Fernando Henrique; Castilhos, Júlio de; Chibata,
Revolt of the; Collor, Lindolfo;
Faoro, Raymundo; Política dos
Governadores; Salvacionismo

W. GEORGE LOVELL
Queen's University, Ontario
Caribbean Sea; Castilla del Oro;
Cuchumatanes; Hispaniola;
Mesoamerica

SARAH M. LOWE
*Graduate School and University
Center, City University of New York*
Modotti, Tina

CATHERINE LUGAR
Currency (Brazil); Dutch West
India Company; Erário Régio; João
V of Portugal; José I of Portugal;
Ordenações do Reino (Afonsinas,
Filipinas, Manuelinas); Rice
Industry

WILLIAM LUIS
Vanderbilt University
Ballagas y Cubeñas, Emilio;
Del Monte, Domingo; Guillén,
Nicolás; Manzano, Juan
Francisco

LESLEY R. LUSTER
Bauxite Industry; João I of
Portugal; João II of Portugal; João
III of Portugal; League of Nations;
Methuen, Treaty of (1703);
Pan-American Conferences:
Rio Conference (1942), Rio
Conference (1947), Rio
Conference (1954); Petrópolis,
Treaty of (1903); Rio Treaty

LESLEY R. LUSTER
(cont.)
(1947); San Ildefonso, Treaty of
(1777); Strangford Treaties
(1810)

CHRISTOPHER H. LUTZ
*Plumsock Mesoamerican
Studies/CIRMA*
Antigua (La Antigua Guatemala);
K'iche'

JOHN LYNCH
*Institute of Latin American Studies,
University of London*
Alvear, Carlos María de; Arana,
Felipe de; Paz, José María;
Quiroga, Juan Facundo; Ramírez,
Francisco; Rivadavia, Bernardino;
Rosas, Juan Manuel de; Saavedra,
Cornelio de

EUGENE LYON
Flagler College
Menéndez de Avilés, Pedro; Santa
Elena

PATRICIA J. LYON
Ica, Pre-Columbian

NEILL MACAULAY
University of Florida
Amélia, Empress; Caneca, Frei
Joaquím do Amor Divino; Carlota;
Handelmann, Gottfried Heinrich;
Holanda, Sérgio Buarque de;
Leopoldina, Empress; Pedro I of
Brazil; Prado, Paulo; Rodrigues,
José Honório

DAVID MACIEL
University of New Mexico
Alcoriza, Luis; Álvarez Bravo,
Manuel; Armendáriz, Pedro;
Aztlán; Cantinflas; Casals, Felipe;
Córdova, Arturo de; Del Rio,
Dolores; Félix, María; Fernández,
Emilio "El Indio"; Figueroa,
Gabriel; Galindo, Alejandro;
García, Sara; Gómez-Cruz, Ernesto;
González Casanova, Pablo;
Hermosillo, Jaime-Humberto;
Infante, Pedro; Leduc, Paul; López
y Fuentes, Gregorio; Monsiváis,
Carlos; Negrete, Jorge; Pardavé,
Joaquín; Pocho; Ripstein, Arturo;

DAVID MACIEL
(cont.)
Rojo, María; Soler, Andrés,
Domingo, and Fernando; Tin-Tan;
Zea Aguilar, Leopoldo

COLIN MACLACHLAN
Tulane University
Acordada; Mexico: The Colonial
Period

MURDO J. MACLEOD
University of Florida
Alvarado y Mesía, Pedro de; Cacao
Industry; Cacique, Caciquismo;
Cacos; Cueva, Francisco de la;
Cueva de Alvarado, Beatriz de la;
Geffrard, Fabre Nicolas; Haiti;
Indigenismo; López de Cerrato,
Alonso; Salomon, Étienne Lysius
Félicité; Tecún-Umán; Tzendal
Rebellion

RICHARD S. MACNEISH
Andover Foundation for
Archaeological Research
Calakmul; Casas Grandes; Comal-
calco; Tehuacán; Tlapacoya; Toniná

LORI MADDEN
Shippensburg University
Graça Aranha, José Pereira da;
Queiroz, Rachel de

AARON PAINE MAHR
University of New Mexico
Celaya, Battles of; Comanches;
Escandón, José de; García Conde,
Pedro; Ibarra, Diego; Navajos;
Rubí, Marqués de; Sante Fe, New
Mexico; Torreón; Vigil, Donaciano;
Villagrá, Gaspar Pérez de

ANTHONY P. MAINGOT
Florida International University
Caribbean Common Market
(CARIFTA and CARICOM); West
Indies Federation

SCOTT MAINWARING
University of Notre Dame
Arns, Paulo Evaristo; Boff, Leo-
nardo; Brazil: Organizations: Na-
tional Conference of Brazilian
Bishops (CNBB), Pastoral Land
Commission (CPT); Brazil: Political
Parties: Popular Action (AP); Câ-
mara, Hélder; Passarinho, Jarbas
Gonçalves; Sales, Eugênio de
Araújo

HAMILTON BOTELHO MALHANO
Museu Nacional, Universidade Federal
do Rio de Janeiro
Maloca

PEDRO MALIGO
Michigan State University
Indianismo; Lins, Osman da Costa;
Souza, Márcio Gonçalves Bentes

WILLIAM MALTBY
University of Missouri–Saint Louis
Black Legend

MARKOS J. MAMALAKIS
University of Wisconsin–Milwaukee
Economic Development; Economic
Development, Theories of; Foreign
Trade; Income Distribution; Infor-
mal Economy; Privatization; Public
Sector and Taxation; Service Sector

PATRICK J. MANEY
Tulane University
Hull, Cordell; Roosevelt, Franklin
Delano

LUIGI MANZETTI
Southern Methodist University
Mercosur

LISA MARIĆ
Chemonics International
Alves, Francisco; Pixinguinha;
Rosa, Noel; Silva, Orlando; Sinhô

CARLOS MARICHAL
El Colegio de México
Banco de Londres y México; Banco
de San Carlos (Spain); Banking;
Baring Brothers; Bemberg, Otto;
Casado, Carlos; Castellanos,
Aarón González; Foreign Debt;
Tornquist, Ernesto; Vélez Sarsfield,
Dalmacio

ROBERTO MÁRQUEZ
Mount Holyoke College
Alexis, Jacques Stéphen;
Alonso, Manuel A.; Barnet,
Miguel; Mir, Pedro; Palés
Matos, Luis; Rodríguez Juliá,
Edgardo; Romero Rosa, Ramón;
Roumain, Jacques; Sánchez, Luis
Rafael

CHERYL ENGLISH MARTIN
University of Texas at El Paso
Cuernavaca; Morelos

OSCAR J. MARTÍNEZ
University of Arizona
United States–Mexico Border

TERESITA MARTÍNEZ-VERGNE
Macalester College
Albizu Campos, Pedro

HEITOR MARTINS
Costa, Cláudio Manuel da

WILSON MARTINS
New York University
Lima, Alceu Amoroso

JOHN D. MARTZ
Pennsylvania State University
Arosemena Gómez, Otto;
Arosemena Monroy, Carlos Julio;
Betancourt, Rómulo; Borja
Cevallos, Rodrigo; Colombia:
Constitutions: Overview; Colombia:
Political Parties: Overview,
Conservative Party, Liberal Party;
Ecuador: Constitutions; Ecuador:
Political Parties: Overview,
Conservative Party, Radical Liberal
Party (PLR); Peru: Constitutions;
Peru: Political Parties: Overview;
Plaza Lasso, Galo; Ponce Enríquez,
Camilo; Rodríguez Lara,
Guillermo; Velasco Ibarra, José
María; Venezuela: Democratic
Action (AD)

DANIEL M. MASTERSON
United States Naval Academy
Gondra, Manuel; Gondra Treaty
(1923); Japanese–Latin American
Relations; Military Dictatorships:
1821–1945

SUSAN N. MASUOKA
University of California, Los Angeles:
Fowler Museum
Linares, Pedro

RAY MATHENY
Brigham Young University
Edzná

W. MICHAEL MATHES
University of San Francisco
Aguilar, Martín de; Bodega y
Quadra, Juan Francisco de la;
Lorenzana y Buitrón, Francisco
Antonio de; Martínez, Esteban José;
Neve, Felipe de; Portolá, Gaspar

W. MICHAEL MATHES
(cont.)
de; Rada, Manuel de Jesús; Rivera y Moncada, Fernando de; Soldados de Cuera; Urdaneta, Andrés de; Vizcaíno, Sebastián; Zamorano, Agustín Juan Vicente

KENNETH R. MAXWELL
Council on Foreign Relations, New York
Brazil: Independence Movements; Pombal, Marquês de (Sebastião José de Carvalho e Melo)

JUDITH M. MAXWELL IXQ'ANIL
Tulane University
Annals of the Cakchiquels; Kaqchikel

RACHEL A. MAY
University of Washington, Tacoma
Agriculture; Campesino; Cotton; Fruit Industry; Girón de León, Andrés de Jesús; Gutiérrez Garbín, Víctor Manuel

ROBERT E. MAY
Purdue University
Filibustering; Kinney, Henry L.; López, Narciso; Walker, William

RICHARD A. MAZZARA†
Oakland University
Andrade, Jorge; Auto, Auto Sacramental; Cordel, Literature of the; Dias Gomes, Alfredo; Lispector, Clarice; Literature: Brazil; Modernism: Brazil; Portuguese Language; Suassuna, Ariano Vilar; Veríssimo, Érico

TOMÉ N. MBUIA-JOÃO
Voice of America, Washington, D.C.
Henry the Navigator; Sebastian (Sebastião) of Portugal

ROBERT MCCAA
University of Minnesota
Population: Spanish America

FRANK D. MCCANN, JR.
University of New Hampshire
Aleijadinho; Calógeras, João Pandiá; Canudos Campaign

WILLIAM MCCARTHY
University of North Carolina at Wilmington
Manila Galleon

DAVID MCCREERY
Georgia State University
Debt Peonage; Mandamiento; Montúfar, Lorenzo

ARCHIE P. MCDONALD
Stephen F. Austin State University
Nacogdoches

KEITH MCDUFFIE
University of Pittsburgh
Alegría, Ciro; Arguedas, José María; Neruda, Pablo; Paz, Octavio; Tablada, José Juan; Vallejo, César; Vargas Llosa, Mario

GORDON F. MCEWAN
Denver Art Museum
Apurímac; Ayllu; Chan Chan; Chancay; Chavín; Chimú; Huaca; Huayna Capac; Illapa; Incas; Inti; Machu Picchu; Mamacocha; Mamaquilla; Manco Capac; Manco Inca; Mitmaes; Moche; Nasca; Ollantaytambo; Orejones; Pachacamac; Pachacuti; Pachamama; Quipu; Sacsahuaman; Tahuantinsuyu; Túpac Amaru; Vilcabamba; Viracocha

ANTHONY MCFARLANE
University of Warwick
Bogotá, Santa Fe de: The Audiencia; Colombia: From the Conquest Through Independence

CHRIS MCGOWAN
Billboard Magazine
Barroso, Ary; Bossa Nova; Carlos, Roberto; Caymmi, Dorival; de Jesus, Clementina; Gilberto, João; Jobim, Antônio Carlos "Tom"; Lambada; Nascimento, Milton; Samba; Samba Schools; Tropicalismo

SUE DAWN MCGRADY
Tulane University
Baker, Lorenzo Dow; Bustamante y Guerra, José; Caledonia; Gage, Thomas; Kuna (Cuna); Martyr, Peter; Rivera Maestre, Miguel; Textiles, Indigenous

JILL LESLIE MCKEEVER-FURST
Moore College of Art and Design
Codices

GEORGE R. MCMURRAY
Colorado State University
García Márquez, Gabriel

JOHN MCNEILL
Georgetown University
French–Latin American Relations

DONALD E. MCVICKER
North Central College, Naperville, Illinois
Maize

TERESA MEADE
Union College
Barroso, Gustavo Dodt

CAREN A. MEGHREBLIAN
Art Institute of Seattle
Almeida Júnior, José Ferraz de; Americo de Figueiredo e Melo, Pedro; Bicalho Oswald, Henrique Carlos; Bienal de São Paulo; Brecheret, Vítor; Camargo, Sergio de; Cavalcanti, Newton; Clark, Lygia; di Cavalcanti, Emiliano; Duarte, Augusto Rodrigues; Fonseca e Silva, Valentim da; French Artistic Mission; Joaquim, Leandro; Julião, Carlos; Meireles de Lima, Vítor; Niemeyer Soares Filho, Oscar; Oiticica, Hélio; Oliviera, Geraldo Teles de; Pape, Lygia; Pôrto Alegre, Manuel Araújo; Prado, Vasco; Rego Monteiro, Vicente do; Schendel, Mira; Sigaud, Eugenio de Proença; Silva, José Antonio da; Veiga Vale, José Joaquim da; Visconti, Eliseu d'Angelo; Vitalino Pereira dos Santos, Mestre; Weingärtner, Pedro

JOSÉ CARLOS SEBE BOM MEIHY
Universidade de São Paulo
Carnival

WILBUR E. MENERAY
Tulane University
Gálvez, Matías de

M. NOEL MENEZES, RSM
Sisters of Mercy, Guyana
Guyana; Missionaries of Charity

DANUSIA L. MESON
Eichelbaum, Samuel; Marechal, Leopoldo; Timerman, Jacobo; Zum Felde, Alberto

ALIDA C. METCALF
Trinity University
Agregado; Bandeiras; Degredado; Entrada; Mameluco; Resgate; São Vicente

JOAN E. MEZNAR
Westmont College
Brazil: Republican Party (PR); Brazil: Revolts of 1923–1924; Constant Botelho de Magalhães, Benjamin; Itu, Convention of; Prestes de Albuquerque, Julio

JERALD MILANICH
Florida Museum of Natural History
Álvarez de Pineda, Alonso; Apalachee; Calusa; Luna y Arellano, Tristán de; Narváez, Pánfilo de; Pardo, Juan; Ponce de León, Juan; Tequesta; Timucua; Vázquez de Ayllón, Lucas

MARY JO MILES
Portinari, Cândido Torquato; Rugendas, Johann Moritz; Santos; Segall, Lasar; Southey, Robert; Staden, Hans

FRANCESCA MILLER
University of California, Davis–Washington Center
Asociación Cristiana Femenina (YWCA); Boundary Disputes: Brazil; Chile: Movimiento Pro-Emancipación de la Mujer Chilena; Feminism and Feminist Organizations; Inter-American Congress of Women; Linha Dura; Luisi, Paulina; Poblete Poblete de Espinosa, Olga; Rodrigues Alves, Francisco de Paula; Rosas de Terrero, Manuela; Santos-Dumont, Alberto; Women

GARY M. MILLER
Central Michigan University
Carabobo, Battle of; Caracas Company; Miranda, Francisco de; Morillo, Pablo; Venezuela: The Colonial Era

HUBERT J. MILLER
University of Texas–Pan American
Piñol y Aycinena, Bernardo; Rossell y Arellano, Mariano

JOSEPH C. MILLER
University of Virginia
Slave Trade

MARY ELLEN MILLER
Yale University
Art: Pre-Columbian Art of Mesoamerica

MICHAEL MITCHELL
Arizona State University
Nascimento, Abdias do

JOHN D. MONAGHAN
Vanderbilt University
Maya, the

JOHN M. MONTEIRO
Universidade Estadual de Campinas (UNICAMP)
Diretório dos Índios; Monções; Potiguar; Ramalho, João; Sertanista; Slavery: Indian Slavery and Forced Labor; Tamoio; Tapuia; Tavares, Antônio Rapôso; Tupi; Tupinambá

TOMMIE SUE MONTGOMERY
University of Miami
Christian Base Communities; Zamora, Rubén

JERRY D. MOORE
California State University, Domínguez Hills
Cajamarca, Pre-Columbian

MARILYN M. MOORS
Frostburg State University
Menchú Tum, Rigoberta

WALTRAUD QUEISER MORALES
University of Central Florida
Aramayo Family; Hochschild, Mauricio; Salamanca, Daniel

MAGNUS MÖRNER
University of Stockholm
Race and Ethnicity: Spanish America

CRAIG MORRIS
American Museum of Natural History
Chincha; La Centinela

BARBARA MUJICA
Georgetown University
Barrios, Eduardo; Edwards, Agustín; Edwards, Jorge; Garro, Elena; Onetti, Juan Carlos

JOSEPH E. MULLIGAN
Society of Jesus, Nicaragua
Obando y Bravo, Miguel

PATRICIA MULVEY
Bluefield State College
Aldeias; Anchieta, José de; Brazil: Viceroys of; Capitão Mor; Captain-General: Brazil; Captaincy System; Comarca; Compadresco; Donatários; Junta, Brazil; Misericórdia, Santa Casa da; Nóbrega, Manuel da; Senado da Câmara; Sousa, Tomé de

JOSEPH M. MURPHY
Georgetown University
African–Latin American Religions: Overview; Santería

PAMELA MURRAY
University of Alabama
Boyer, Jean-Pierre; Colombia: Organizations: National Association of Industrialists, National Federation of Coffee Growers, National School of Mines of Medellín; Coltejer; Ecopetrol; El Cerrejón; Estimé, Dumarsais; Foraker Act; García Godoy, Héctor; Leconte, Michel Cincinnatus; Leoni, Raúl; Lescot, Élie; Magloire, Paul Eugène; Muzo Emerald Concession; Panama Railroad; Paz del Río; Salnave, Sylvain; Sam, Jean Villbrun Guillaume

ROBERT MYERS
Yale University
Choro, Chorinho; Gil, Gilberto; Lundu; Maxixe; Veloso, Caetano

CAROLE A. MYSCOFSKI
Illinois Wesleyan University
Messianic Movements: Brazil; Sebastianismo

SILVIA NAGY
Catholic University of America
Shimose, Pedro

GUILLERMO NÁÑEZ FALCÓN
Tulane University, Latin American Library
Dieseldorff, Erwin Paul; Verapaz

NANCY PRISCILLA SMITH NARO
Universidade Federal Fluminense
Colono; Engenho; Fazenda, Fazendeiro; International Coffee Agreement; Land Law of 1850

NANCY PRISCILLA SMITH NARO
(cont.)
(Brazil); Land Tenure: Brazil;
Lavrador de Cana; Mauá,
Visconde de; Praieira Revolt;
Sesmaria; Taubaté Convention;
Vassouras

MARYSA NAVARRO
Dartmouth College
Perón, María Estela Martínez de;
Perón, María Eva Duarte de

JOYCE E. NAYLON
Tulane University
Naipaul, V. S.; Paz García,
Policarpo; Taínos

ROBERT A. NAYLOR
Fairleigh Dickinson University
Bennett, Marshall; British–Latin
American Relations; Lumber
Industry; MacGregor, Gregor;
Mosquito Coast; Poyais

MURIEL NAZZARI
Indiana University
Dowry

JEFFREY D. NEEDELL
University of Florida
Amaral, Antônio José Azevedo do;
Brazil: Liberal Movements; Brazil:
Political Parties: Conservative
Party, Liberal Party, Moderados;
Brazilian Academy of Letters; Insti-
tuto Histórico e Geográfico
Brasileiro; Jacobinism; Monte Ale-
gre, José da Costa Carvalho, Mar-
quís de; Monteiro, Tobias do Rêgo;
Nabuco de Araújo, Joaquim; Ot-
toni, Teofilo Benedito; Paraná,
Honôrio Hermeto Carneiro Leão,
Marquês de; Pinho, José Wanderley
de Araújo; Queirós Coutinho Ma-
toso da Câmara, Eusébio de; Rio
Branco, Barão do; Rio Branco, Vis-
conde do; Rio de Janeiro: The City;
Rocha, Justiniano José da; São Vicente, José Antônio Pimenta Bueno,
Marquês de; Sousa, Otávio Tarqüínio de; Uruguai, Visconde do; Vasconcelos, Bernardo Pereira de;
Viana, Francisco José de Oliveira

BEN A. NELSON
*State University of New York at
Buffalo*
La Quemada

GUILHERME NEVES
Colégios (Brazil); Coutinho, José
Joaquim da Cunha de Azeredo;
Mesa da Consciência e Ordens;
Oliveira Lima, Manuel de;
Padroado Real; Varnhagen,
Francisco Adolfo de (Visconde de
Porto Seguro)

LÚCIA M. BASTOS P. NEVES
*Universidade do Estado do Rio de
Janeiro*
Bacharéis; Barbosa, Francisco
Villela; Colégios (Brazil); Cortes,
Portuguese; Costa, Hipólito José
da; Juntas Portuguesas; Pereira,
José Clemente; Pinheiro, José
Feliciano Fernandes

RONALD C. NEWTON
Simon Fraser University
Blue Book; Braden, Spruille;
Dirty War; Fascism; Frigerio,
Rogelio; German–Latin American
Relations; Germans in Latin
America; Houssay, Bernardo A.;
Matienzo, Benjamin; Monto-
neros; Nazis; Patrón Costas,
Robustiano; Pinedo, Federico;
Rocha, Dardo; Ugarte, Manuel;
Ugarte, Marcelino

WESLEY PHILLIPS NEWTON
Auburn University
Aviation

H. B. NICHOLSON
*University of California, Los
Angeles*
Aztec Calendar Stone; Aztecs;
Quetzalcoatl

THOMAS NIEHAUS
University of the South
Liberation Theology

FREDERICK M. NUNN
Portland State University
Grove Vallejo, Marmaduke; Ibáñez
del Campo, Carlos; Körner, Emil;
Pinochet Ugarte, Augusto

MATTHEW O'MEAGHER
Duke University
Gutiérrez, Gustavo; Landázuri
Ricketts, Juan; Vigil, Francisco de
Paula González

LESLIE S. OFFUTT
Vassar College
Nuevo León

AMY A. OLIVER
The American University
Gaos, José

WILLIAM I. OLIVER
University of California, Berkeley
Hernández, Luisa Josefina; Novo,
Salvador

OTTO OLIVERA
Tulane University
Novás Calvo, Lino; Orbón, Julian

REBECCA J. OROZCO
Izabal

CARL OSTHAUS
Oakland University
Confederates in Brazil and Mexico

THOMAS O. OTT
University of North Alabama
Bobo, Rosalvo; Christophe, Henri;
Citadelle La Ferrière; Dessalines,
Jean Jacques; Élite (Haiti);
Hyppolite, Louis Modestin
Florville; Leclerc, Charles Victor
Emmanuel; L'Ouverture, Toussaint;
Simon, Antoine

KENNETH N. OWENS
*California State University,
Sacramento*
Frémont, John Charles

BRIAN OWENSBY
University of Virginia
Flôres da Cunha, José Antônio;
Paulistas, Paulistanos; Prado, João
Fernando de Almeida; São Paulo
(City); São Paulo (State); Sodré,
Nelson Werneck

AUGUSTO OYUELA-CAYCEDO
University of Calgary
Amazon Basin, Archaeology;
Magdalena Valley; Puerto
Hormiga; Tairona

JOSÉ EMILIO PACHECO
*University of Maryland at College
Park*
Chapultepec, Bosque de; La
Ciudadela; López Velarde, Ramón;
San Juan de Ulúa; Villaurrutia,
Xavier

LUIS PALACÍN
Universidade Federal de Goiás
Araguaia River; Goiás; Tocantins; Tocantins River

COLIN A. PALMER
Graduate School and University Center, City University of New York
Africans in Hispanic America; Slavery: Spanish America

DAVID SCOTT PALMER
Boston University
Ayacucho; Fujimori, Alberto Keinya; García Pérez, Alan; Iquitos; Pérez Godoy, Ricardo; Peru: Organizations: Civil Guard, National Social Mobilization Support System (Sinamos); Peru: Political Parties: Movement of the Revolutionary Left (MIR), National Alliance of Peru, National Democratic Front, Popular Action (AP); Peru: Shining Path

EUL-SOO PANG
Colorado School of Mines
Branco, Manuel Alves; Carneiro de Campos, José Joaquim; Companhia Vale do Rio Doce; Coronel, Coronelismo; Cotegipe, Barão de; Eletrobrás; Engineering; Iron and Steel Industry; Mining: Modern; Patronage; Petrobrás; Santos, Marquesa de; State Corporations; Volta Redonda; Weapons Industry

ROBERT L. PAQUETTE
Hamilton College
La Escalera, Conspiracy of; Slave Revolts: Spanish America

JAMES WILLIAM PARK
San Diego Community College
Núñez Moledo, Rafael

DAVID S. PARKER
Queen's University, Ontario
Oncenio; Peru: Union Club

ROBERT L. PARKER
University of Miami School of Music
Aldana, José María; Castro, Ricardo; Chávez, Carlos; Elizaga, José María; Enríquez, Manuel; Franco, Hernando; Galindo, Blas; Gante, Pedro de; Gutiérrez de Padilla, Juan; Halffter, Rodolfo;

ROBERT L. PARKER
(cont.)
Hernández Moncado, Eduardo; Lavista, Mario; Mata, Eduardo; Ponce, Manuel; Quintanar, Héctor; Revueltas, Silvestre; Rosas, Juventino; Sandi, Luis

LEE A. PARSONS
Jay K. Kislack Foundation
Ball Game, Pre-Columbian

GRETE PASCH
University Francisco Marroquín, Guatemala
Computer Industry

SUZANNE PASZTOR
University of Wisconsin–LaCrosse
Coahuila; Garcés, Francisco Tomás Hermenegildo; Peñalosa Briceño, Diego Dionisio de; Pérez, Albino; Pueblo Indians; Quivira; Vélez de Escalante, Silvestre; Vial, Pedro

DAPHNE PATAI
University of Massachusetts
Silva, Benedita da; Souza, Luiza Erundina de

ROBERT W. PATCH
University of California, Riverside
Canek, Jacinto; Henequen Industry; Landa, Diego de; López de Cogolludo, Diego; Montejo, Francisco de; Sierra O'Reilly, Justo; Yucatán

BLAKE D. PATTRIDGE
Tulane University
Buccaneers and Freebooters; Drake, Francis; Enciso, Martín Fernández de; Hawkins, John; Morgan, Henry; Paterson, William; Portobelo; Saint Christopher (Saint Kitts); Sharp, Bartholomew; Tortuga Island

ANNE PAUL
Institute of Andean Studies, University of California, Berkeley
Art: Pre-Columbian Art of South America

JULYAN G. PEARD
San Francisco State University
Medicine: The Modern Era; Tropicalista School of Medicine (Bahia)

DEBORAH M. PEARSALL
University of Missouri–Columbia
El Paraíso

OSCAR G. PALÁEZ ALMENGOR
Universidad de San Carlos de Guatemala
Bergaño y Villegas, Simón; Calcaño, José Antonio; Castro Madriz, José María; Central America: Independence of; Gazeta de Guatemala; Guatemala City; Sánchez Vilella, Roberto; Villaurrutia, Jacobo de

VINCENT PELOSO
Howard University
Aguardiente de Pisco; Arana, Julio César; Aspíllaga Family; Backus and Johnston; Balta, José; Basadre, Jorge; Candamo, Manuel; Capelo, Joaquín; Castro Pozo, Hildebrando; Chinese Labor (Peru); Cornejo, Mariano H.; Echenique, José Rufino; Elías, Domingo; Encinas, José Antonio; Fernandini, Eulogio; García Calderón, Francisco; Gildemeister Family; Gutiérrez Brothers; Herrera, Bartolomé; López de Romaña, Eduardo; Luna Pizarro, Francisco Javier de; Mendiburu, Manuel de; Pardo y Barreda, José; Pardo y Lavalle, Manuel; Paz Soldán Family; Peru Since Independence; Peru: Organizations: Institute of Peruvian Studies (IEP), National Agrarian Society; Peru: Political Parties: Civilista Party; Piérola, Nicolás de; Pisco; Prado, Mariano Ignacio; Prado y Ugarteche, Javier; Prado y Ugarteche, Jorge; Prado y Ugarteche, Manuel; Prado y Ugarteche, Mariano Ignacio; Sabogal, José; Távara y Andrade, Santiago; Torre Tagle, José Bernardo de Tagle y Portocarrero; Villarán, Manuel Vicente; Zaracondegui, Julián de; Zulen, Pedro S. and Dora Mayer de Zulen

JUAN MANUEL PÉREZ
Library of Congress
Andreve, Guillermo; Arias Calderón, Ricardo; Arias de Saavedra, Hernando; Arias Madrid, Arnulfo; Arias Madrid, Harmodio;

JUAN MANUEL PÉREZ
(cont.)
Arosemena, Florencio Harmodio; Arosemena, Juan Demóstenes; Arosemena, Justo; Arosemena, Pablo; Arosemena Quinzada, Albacíades; Avalos, Pact of (1820); Batllismo; Calvo, Carlos; Chiari, Rodolfo E.; Chiari Remón, Roberto Francisco; Colunje, Gil; Correoso, Buenaventura; Coto War; Díaz Arosemena, Domingo; Drago Doctrine; Emphyteusis, Law of; Figueroa Alcorta, José; Graf Spee; Huertas, Esteban; Irala, Domingo Martínez de; Lautaro, Logia de; Lorenzo Troya, Victoriano; Martínez Estrada, Ezequiel; Méndez Pereira, Octavio; Mendoza, Carlos Antonio; Monteagudo, Bernardo de; Morales, Eusebio A.; Moreno, Mariano; Moscote, José Dolores; Oribe, Manuel; Ortiz de Zárate, Juan and Juana; Panama: Community Action; Panama: Tenants' Revolt; Panama City; Porras, Belisario; Pueyrredón, Juan Martín de; República de Tule; Rivera, Fructuoso; Sáenz Peña, Roque; Sáenz Peña Law; Semana Trágica; Urracá; Uruguay: Organizations: Catholic Workers' Circle; Uruguay: Political Parties: Blanco Party, Colorado Party; Valdivia, Luis de; Valdivia, Pedro de

JOSÉ PÉREZ DE ARCE
Museo Chileno de Arte Precolombino
Music: Pre-Columbian Music of South America

JOSÉ ANTONIO PÉREZ GOLLÁN
Museo Etnográfico, Universidad de Buenos Aires
Algarrobo; Calchaquí, Juan; Comenchingones; Omaguaca; Yamana

CHARLES A. PERRONE
University of Florida
Barbosa, Domingos Caldas; Buarque, Chico; Cruz e Sousa, João da; Lima, Jorge de; Matos, Gregório de; Meireles, Cecília; Melo Neto, João Cabral de; Morais, Vinícius de; Música Popular Brasileira (MPB)

VERÓNICA PESANTES-VALLEJO
University of Chicago
Quito School of Sculpture

PATRICIA PESSAR
Yale University
Emigration

INEKE PHAF
University of Maryland at College Park
Césaire, Aimé; Négritude; Villaverde, Cirilo

WILLIAM D. PHILLIPS, JR.
University of Minnesota–Twin Cities
Columbus, Christopher

RONN F. PINEO
Towson State University
Andagoya, Pascual de; Banco Comercial y Agrícola (Ecuador); Baquerizo Moreno, Alfredo; Bonifaz Ascasubi, Neptalí; Borrero y Cortázar, Antonio; Caamaño y Gómez Cornejo, José María Plácido; Cañari; Carbo y Noboa, Pedro José; Carrión, Jerónimo; Costa (Ecuador); Ecuador: Organizations: Ecuadorian Confederation of Class-based Organizations (CEDOC), Workers Confederation of Ecuador (CTE); Ecuador: Political Parties: Concentration of Popular Forces (CFP), Democratic Alliance (ADE), Democratic Left (ID); Ecuador-Peru Boundary Disputes; Espinosa y Espinosa, (Juan) Javier; González Suárez, (Manuel María) Federico; Guayaquil; Guayaquil: General Strike of 1922; Guayaquil, Group of; Guayaquil, Republic of; Guayaquil-Quito Railway; Huasipungo; Mejía del Valle y Llequerica, José Joaquín; Montúfar y Larrea, Juan Pío de; Noboa y Arteta, Diego; Oriente (Ecuador); Otavalo; Public Health; Quito; Riobamba; Robles, Francisco; Roca Rodríguez, Vicente Ramón; Selva (Ecuador); Sierra (Ecuador); Urvina Jado, Francisco; War of Four Days; Zarumilla, Battle of

JANET M. PLZAK
Automobile Industry

GUIDO A. PODESTÁ
University of Wisconsin–Madison
Goldemberg, Isaac

JOHN POHL
Fowler Museum, UCLA
Mitla; Mixtecs

MICHAEL A. POLL
Abertura; Amazon Pact (1978); Brazil: National Security Law; Distensão; Institutional Acts

MICHAEL A. POLUSHIN
Tulane University
Cuban Missile Crisis; Guirao, Ramón; Jiménez, Enrique A.; Lozano Díaz, Julio; Niño, Pedro Alonso; Sedeño, Antonio de; Villanueva, Carlos Raúl

CHERYL POMEROY
Salt Trade: Andean Region

STAFFORD POOLE, C.M.
Vincentian Studies Institute
Chichimecs; Enríquez de Almansa, Martín; Guadalupe, Virgin of; Juan Diego; Moya de Contreras, Pedro; Syncretism

ROLAND E. POPPINO
University of California, Davis
Vargas, Getúlio Dornelles

MICHAEL POWELSON
Columbia University
Agrarian Reform; Castro Ruz, Fidel; Castro Ruz, Raúl; Cuba: Constitutions; Cuba: Organizations: Democratic Socialist Coalition; Cuba: Political Parties: Communist Party; Cuba: Revolutions: Cuban Revolution; Escalante, Aníbal; Fuentes y Guzmán, Francisco Antonio de; Galván, Manuel de Jesús; Guatemala: Economic Society of Guatemala; Liendo y Goicoechea, José Antonio; Mariel Boatlift; Mella, Julio Antonio; Mella, Ramón Matías; País, Frank; Saco, José Antonio; Urrutia Lleó, Manuel; Walcott, Derek

SHELIA AND THOMAS POZORSKI
University of Texas–Pan American
Caballo Muerto; Pampa de las Llamas-Moxeke; Sechin Alto

ANA REBECA PRADA
Urzagasti, Jesús; Von Vacano, Arturo

ESTHER J. PRESSEL
Colorado State University
African–Latin American Religions:
Brazil; Aparecida, Nossa Senhora
da; Bonfim, Nosso Senhor do;
Buddhism; Umbanda

MARIE D. PRICE
George Washington University
Chapala, Lake; Lerma River; Sierra
Madre; Usumacinta River

CARLOS ALBERTO PRIMO BRAGA
The Johns Hopkins University
Bresser Pereira, Luiz Carlos

ELOISE QUIÑONES KEBER
*Graduate School and University
Center, City University of New
York*
Azcapotzalco; Templo Mayor;
Tetzcoco; Tlaloc; Tlatelolco

INÉS QUINTERO
Universidad Central de Venezuela
Abalos, José de; Admirable
Campaign; Alberro, Francisco de;
Alvarado, Lisandro; Ampíes, Juan
de; Andresote; Andueza Palacio,
Raimundo; Anzoátegui, José
Antonio; Arismendi, Juan Bautista;
Baralt, Rafael María; Barnola,
Pedro Pablo; Bermúdez, José
Francisco; Blanco, José Félix;
Bloqueo de 1902, El; Boves, José
Tomás; Caracas, Audiencia of;
Chirino, José Leonardo; Compañía
Guipuzcoana; Cortés de
Madariaga, José; Cosiata, La (1826);
Cubagua; Emparán, Vicente;
Fajardo, Francisco; Federal War
(Venezuela, 1859–1863); Gil
Fortoul, José; González, Juan
Vicente; Guerra, Ramón; Junta
Suprema de Caracas; La
Libertadora Revolution; Linares
Alcántara, Francisco; Losada, Diego
de; Mariño, Santiago; Michelina,
Santos; Morales, Francisco Tomás;
Ojeda, Alonso de; O'Leary, Daniel
Florencio; Páez, José Antonio;
Palacio Fajardo, Manuel; Palacios,
Antonia; Pérez de Tolosa, Juan;
Quintero, Ángel; Real Consulado
de Caracas; Ribas, José Félix;
Rojas, Pedro José; Roscio, Juan
Germán; Salazar, Matías; Toro,
Fermín; Universidad Central de

INÉS QUINTERO
(cont.)
Venezuela; Vallenilla Lanz,
Laureano; Vargas, José María;
Venezuela: Congresses of 1811,
1830, and 1864; Venezuela: Las
Reformas Revolution; Venezuela:
Organizations: Economic Society of
the Friends of the Country,
Federation of Students of
Venezuela (FEV), Patriotic Society
of Caracas; Venezuela: Political
Parties: Communist Party,
Conservative Party, Liberal Party,
Movement to Socialism (MAS),
Social Christian COPEI Party;
"War to the Death"; Yanes,
Francisco Javier

JACINTO QUIRARTE
University of Texas at San Antonio
Goeritz, Mathias; Herrán,
Saturnino; Rivera, Diego; Ruiz,
Antonio

ALFONSO W. QUIROZ
*Baruch College and Graduate School,
City University of New York*
Amauta; Ancash; Andean Pact;
Barreda y Laos, Felipe; Bedoya
Reyes, Luis; Béjar, Héctor; Be-
laúnde, Víctor Andrés; Belaúnde
Terry, Fernando; Beltrán, Pedro;
Benavides, Oscar Raimundo; Billing-
hurst, Guillermo Enrique; Bingham,
Hiram; Bolognesi, Francisco; Busta-
mante y Rivero, José Luis; Cáceres,
Andrés Avelino; Cartavio; Castilla,
Ramón; Center for Advanced Mili-
tary Studies (CAEM); Deustua,
Alejandro O.; Flores, Luis; Gama-
rra, Agustín; Garmendia, Francisco;
González Prada Popular Universi-
ties; Grau, Miguel; Haya de la
Torre, Víctor Raúl; Huancayo; Huá-
nuco; La Brea y Pariñas; La Oroya;
Leguía, Augusto Bernardino; Lima;
Lima Conference (1847–1848);
Lindley López, Nicolás; Loreto;
Mar, José de la; Marañón River;
Miro Quesada Family; Montaña;
Morales Bermúdez, Remigio; Mo-
rales Bermúdez Cerruti, Francisco;
Odría, Manuel Apolinario; Orbe-
goso, Luis José de; Peru: Organiza-
tions: Confederation of Peruvian
Workers (CTP), Confederation of
Workers of the Peruvian Revolu-

ALFONSO W. QUIROZ
(cont.)
tion (CTRP), General Confedera-
tion of Peruvian Workers (CGTP),
National Club; Peru: Revolutionary
Movements: Army of National Lib-
eration (ELN); Pezet, Juan Antonio;
Plan Inca; Puente Uceda, Luis de la;
Rímac River; Samanez Ocampo,
David; Sánchez Cerro, Luis Man-
uel; Seoane, Manuel; Sierra (Peru);
Talambo Affair; Tarma; Ureta, Eloy
G.; Velasco Alvarado, Juan; Viv-
anco, Manuel Ignacio; Yungay,
Battle of

W. DIRK RAAT
*State University of New York at
Fredonia*
Flores Magón, Ricardo; Revoltosos

JOSÉ RABASSA
University of Michigan
Cabeza de Vaca, Alvar Núñez; Díaz
del Castillo, Bernal; Malinche;
Seven Cities of Cíbola; Soto, Her-
nando de; Torquemada, Juan de

KAREN RACINE
Tulane University
Acosta, Tomás; Acosta García,
Julio; Acosta León, Ángel; Araujo,
Arturo; Arciniegas, Germán; Ar-
güello, Leonardo; Azcona Hoyo,
José Simón; Barrios, Gerardo;
Bigaud, Wilson; Brannon de Sa-
mayoa Chinchilla, Carmen; Cas-
tañeda Castro, Salvador;
Castellanos, Gonzalo; Cienfuegos,
Camilo; Darié, Sandu; Dutch–Latin
American Relations; El Salvador:
Constitutions; Estrada, José Do-
lores; Estrada Palma, Tomás;
González Dávila, Gil; Grau San
Martín, Ramón; Güegüence; He-
rrera y Tordesillas, Antonio de;
Hyppolite, Hector; Jerez, Máximo;
Laplante, Eduardo; Liautaud,
Georges; Martí, Agustín
Farabundo; Masferrer, Alberto; Me-
léndez Family; Mendieta, Salvador;
Molina, Arturo Armando; Obin,
Philomé; Peláez, Amelia; Ponce de
León, Fidelio; Prío Socarrás, Carlos;
Rivas, Patricio; Rojas Paúl, Juan
Pablo; Romero, Oscar Arnulfo;
Sagra, Ramón de la; Sosúa; Torre y
Huerta, Carlos de la; Valladares,
Tomás

CYNTHIA RADDING
University of Illinois at Urbana-Champaign
Pimería Alta; Sonora

SUSAN E. RAMÍREZ
DePaul University
Caballería; Cajamarca; Callejón de Huaylas; Encomienda; Hacienda; Huaraz; Lambayeque; Mayorazgo; Missions: Spanish America; Piura; Trujillo

DONALD RAMOS
Cleveland State University
African Brazilians: Color Terminology; Emboaba; Inconfidência dos Alfaiates; Inconfidência Mineira; Pardo; Silva, Xica da; Silva Xavier, Joaquim J. da

MARÍA DEL ROSARIO RAMOS GONZÁLEZ
Johns Hopkins University
Puerto Rico: Geography

CARMEN RAMOS-ESCANDÓN
Occidental College
García, Genaro; Mexico: Constitution of 1857; Mexico: Constitution of 1917; Nueva Galicia; Nuevo Santander; O'Gorman, Edmundo; Provincial Deputation; Regeneración; Tamaulipas; Ward, Henry George; Zavala, Silvio

LAURA R. RANDALL
Hunter College, City University of New York
Foreign Investment

JOANNE RAPPAPORT
University of Maryland, Baltimore County
Colombia: Colombian Indigenist Institute; Colombia: Colombian Institute for Agrarian Reform (INCORA); Lame, Manuel Quintín; Quimbaya; Resguardo

JANE M. RAUSCH
University of Massachusetts at Amherst
Casanare

LUIS REBAZA-SORALUZ
University of London
Sologuren, Javier

VERA BLINN REBER
Shippensburg University
Asunción; Bermejo River; Box, Pelham Horton; Concepción, Paraguay; Francia, José Gaspar Rodríguez de; López, Carlos Antonio; López, Francisco Solano; Paraguay: The Nineteenth Century; War of the Triple Alliance

F. KENT REILLY III
Southwest Texas State University
La Venta; Olmecs; San Lorenzo

DENNIS REINHARTZ
University of Texas of Arlington
Cartography

JOÃO JOSÉ REIS
Universidade Federal da Bahia
Slave Revolts: Brazil

JULIA BECKER RICHARDS
Centro de Investigaciones Regionales de Mesoamérica (CIRMA)
Mayan Alphabet and Orthography

DOUGLAS RICHMOND
University of Texas at Arlington
Argentina: National Autonomous Party; Avellaneda, Nicolás; Juárez Celman, Miguel; Pellegrini, Carlos; Roca, Julio A. Unicato

EUGENE RIDINGS
Santa Cruz, California
Taunay, Affonso d'Escragnolle; Tavares Bastos, Aureliano Cândido

EDWARD A. RIEDINGER
Ohio State University
Kubitschek, Marcia; Kubitschek de Oliveira, Juscelino

JOEL RIPPINGER
Marmion Abbey, Aurora, Illinois
Benedictines

JAMES W. ROBB
George Washington University
Reyes, Alfonso

MARTHA BARTON ROBERTSON†
Tulane University, Latin American Library
Retablos and Ex-Votos

EUGENIA J. ROBINSON
Tulane University
Chiapa de Corzo; El Baúl; Izapa; La Democracia; Monte Alto; Topoxté; Tulum

MIGUEL ANGEL ROCA
Universidad Nacional de Córdoba
Architecture: Modern

BÉLGICA RODRÍGUEZ
Apolinar; Borges, Jacobo; Botero, Fernando; Cárdenas Arroyo, Santiago; Chávez Morado, José; Cruz Diez, Carlos; Espinosa, José María; Figueroa, Pedro José; Garay, Epifanio; Gerzso, Gunther; Gironella, Alberto; Obregón, Alejandro; Otero, Alejandro; Reverón, Armando; Santa María, Andrés de; Soto, Jesús Rafael; Tamayo, Rufino; Uribe, Juan Camilo

CELSO RODRÍGUEZ
Organization of American States
Etchepareborda, Roberto; Lencinas, Carlos Washington; Melo, Leopoldo; Mendoza; Orfila, Washington Alejandro José Luis; Prebisch, Raúl

LEOPOLDO F. RODRÍGUEZ
Organization of American States
Pan-American Institute of Geography and History

LINDA A. RODRÍGUEZ
Latin American Center, University of California, Los Angeles
Alfaro Delgado, José Eloy; Arroyo del Rio, Carlos Alberto; Ayora Cueva, Isidro; Bucaram Elmhalin, Asaad; Castro Jijón, Ramón; Córdova Rivera, Gonzalo S.; Ecuador: Since 1830; Ecuador: Geography; Ecuador: Revolution of 1895; Ecuador: Revolution of 1925; Enríquez Gallo, Alberto; Febres-Cordero Ribadeneyra, León; Flores Jijón, Antonio; Franco, Guillermo; Gándara Enríquez, Marcos; Hurtado Larrea, Osvaldo; Olmedo, José Joaquin; Páez, Federico; Plaza Gutiérrez, Leonidas; Quito School of Art; Roldós Aguilera, Jaime

MARIO RODRÍGUEZ
University of Southern California
American Revolution, Influence of;
Chatfield, Frederick

JAIME E. RODRÍGUEZ O.
University of California, Irvine
Acordada, Revolt of; Alamán,
Lucas; Bravo, Nicolás; Bustamante,
Anastasio; Bustamante, Carlos
María de; Cañedo, Juan de Dios;
Couto, José Bernardo; Escoceses;
Guayaquil Conference; Guerrero,
Vicente; Iturbide, Agustín de;
Martínez, Juan José; Mexico:
Constitution of 1824; Mexico:
Revolt of 1832; Mier Noriega y
Guerra, José Servando Teresa de;
Mier y Terán, Manuel; Mora, José
María Luis; O'Donojú, Juan; Ortiz
de Ayala, Simón Tadeo; Pichincha,
Battle of; Plan of Casa Mata; Quito
Revolt of 1809; Ramos Arizpe, José
Miguel; Rocafuerte, Vicente;
Rodríguez Sandoval, Luis Arsenio;
Victoria, Guadalupe; Yorkinos;
Zavala, Lorenzo de

MATTHIAS RÖHRIG ASSUNÇÃO
University of Essex
Balaiada; Barreto de Menezes,
Tobias, Jr.; Cabanagem; Tambor de
Mina

CHARLES E. RONAN S.J.
Loyola University, Chicago
Clavigero, Francisco Javier

ANNA CURTENIUS ROOSEVELT
The Field Museum
Marajoara; Santarém Culture;
Taperinha

KEITH S. ROSENN
University of Miami School of Law
Brazil: Constitutions; Brazil:
Electoral Reform Legislation;
Judicial Systems: Brazil

KATHLEEN ROSS
New York University
Acosta, José de; Cobo, Bernabé;
Sarmiento de Gamboa, Pedro

IDA ELY RUBIN
The Americas Foundation
Mac Entyre, Eduardo; Ramírez
Villamizar, Eduardo

A. J. R. RUSSELL-WOOD
The Johns Hopkins University
Brazil: The Colonial Era, 1500–1808

GEORGINA SABAT-RIVERS
Juana Inés de la Cruz, Sor

JAMES SCHOFIELD SAEGER
Lehigh University
Abipón Indians; Antequera y
Castro, José de; Bolaños, Luis de;
Cárdenas, Bernardino de; Chaco
Region; Comunero Revolt
(Paraguay, 1730–1735); Guarani
Indians; Mbayá Indians; Missions:
Jesuit Missions (Reducciones);
Mocobí Indians; Paraguay: The
Colonial Period; Payaguá Indians

ELIZABETH SALAS
University of Washington
Soldaderas

JORGE MARIO SALAZAR MORA
Universidad de Costa Rica
Calderón Guardia, Rafael Ángel;
González Víquez, Cleto; Volio
Jiménez, Jorge

MARÍA A. SALGADO
*University of North Carolina at
Chapel Hill*
Balseiro, José Agustín; Cabrera,
Lydia; Cuadra, Pablo Antonio;
Darío, Rubén; Silva, José Asunción;
Umaña Bernal, José

SUSANA SALGADO
Library of Congress
Aguirre, Julián; Alomía Robles,
Daniel; Amenábar, Juan; Araujo,
Juan de; Ardévol, José; Asuar, José
Vicente; Bernal Jiménez, Miguel;
Berutti, Arturo; Boero, Felipe;
Broqua, Alfonso; Carrillo, Julián
[Antonio]; Castro, Juan José;
Ceruti, Roque; Cluzeau-Mortet,
Luis [Ricardo]; Duprat, Rogério;
Escobar, Luis Antonio; Estrada,
Carlos; Fabini, [Felix Eduardo];
Fernández Hidalgo, Gutierre;
Ficher, Jacobo; Gaito, Constantino;
García Caturla, Alejandro; Gilardi,
Gilardo; Ginastera, Alberto
Evaristo; Giribaldi, (Vicente)
Tomás E.; González Ávila, Jorge;
Gutiérrez y Espinosa, Felipe;
Holzmann, Rodolfo; Lamarque

SUSANA SALGADO
(cont.)
Pons, Jaurés; Leng, Alfonso; López
Buchardo, Carlos; López Capillas,
Francisco; Mastrogiovanni,
Antonio; Moncayo García, José
Pablo; Morales, Melesio; Music: Art
Music; Orejón y Aparicio, José de;
Ortega del Villar, Aniceto;
Paniagua y Vasques, Cenobio;
Pasta, Carlos Enrico;
Pineda-Duque, Roberto; Rogatis,
Pascual de; Sambucetti, Luís
Nicolás; Sas, Andrés; Serebrier,
José; Storm, Ricardo; Teatro Colón;
Teatro Solís; Torrejón y Velasco,
Tomás de; Tosar, Héctor Alberto;
Valencia, Antonio María; Williams,
Alberto; Zumaya, Manuel de

RICHARD V. SALISBURY
Western Kentucky University
Central American Court of Justice;
Estrada Doctrine; Iglesias Castro,
Rafael; Knox-Castrillo Treaty
(1911); Marblehead Pact (1906);
Pan-Americanism; San José
Conference of 1906; Tobar
Doctrine; Washington Treaties of
1907 and 1923

LINDA K. SALVUCCI
Trinity University
Adams-Onís Treaty (1819); El
Morro Castle; Havana Company;
Santiago de Cuba; Wood, Leonard

BALBINA SAMANIEGO
University of Salamanca
Chocano, José Santos

CONSUELO NOVAIS SAMPAIO
Universidade Federal da Bahia
Bahia

KATHRYN SAMPECK
Tulane University
Altun Ha; Cara Sucia; Cerén;
Cerros; Cihuatán; San Andrés;
Tazumal

JEFFREY D. SAMUELS
Goucher College
Álvarez Martínez, Gustavo;
Amapala, Treaties of (1895, 1907);
Cabañas, José Trinidad;
Comayagua; Gracias; Guardiola,
Santos; Herrera, Dionisio de;

JEFFREY D. SAMUELS
(cont.)
Honduras: Constitutions;
Honduras Company; Lindo Zelaya,
Juan; Nacaome; Rosa, Ramón; Soto,
Marco Aurelio; Williams Calderón,
Abraham

JOSEPH P. SÁNCHEZ
Spanish Colonial Research Center,
National Park Service
Alberni, Pedro de; Catalonian
Volunteers; Fages, Pedro; Mexico:
Mexican-American War; Pacific
Northwest; Pérez, Juan; Vázquez
de Coronado, Francisco

DANIEL H. SANDWEISS
Carnegie Museum
Túcume

JAVIER SANJINÉS C.
Duke University
Cerruto, Óscar; Sáenz, Jaime

WILLIAM SATER
California State University, Long
Beach
Alessandri Palma, Arturo;
Alessandri Rodríguez, Jorge;
Ancón, Treaty of (1883); Aylwin
Azócar, Patricio; Balmaceda
Fernández, José Manuel; Baltimore
Incident; Barros Arana, Diego;
Blaine, James Gillespie; Callampas;
Cancha Rayada, Battle of;
Chacabuco, Battle of; Chile: The
Nineteenth Century; Chile:
Constitutions; Chile: Organizations:
Chilean Nitrate Company
(COSACH), Corporation of
Agrarian Reform (CORA),
Development Corporation
(CORFO), Federation of Chilean
Workers (FOCH); Chile:
Parliamentary Regime; Chile:
Political Parties: Christian Left,
Communist Party, Concentración
Nacional, Conservative Party,
Democratic Party, Liberal Party,
Movement of the Revolutionary
Left, National Party, National
Phalanx, Popular Action Front,
Popular Front, Popular Unity,
Radical Party, Socialist Party;
Chile: Revolutions of 1851 and
1859; Chile: Revolution of 1891;
Chile: Socialist Republic of 100

WILLIAM SATER
(cont.)
Days; Chile: War with Spain;
Chonchol, Jacques; Conventillo;
Corvalán Lepe, Luis; Cuerpo de
Carabineros; Dávila Espinoza,
Carlos Guillermo; Easter Island;
Encina, Francisco Antonio;
Errázuriz Echaurren, Federico;
Errázuriz Zañartu, Federico;
Figueroa Larraín, Emiliano;
González Videla, Gabriel; Gran
Minería; Inquilinaje; Lima, Treaty
of (1929); Lircay, Battle of;
Mac-Iver Rodríguez, Enrique;
March of the Empty Pots; May
Pacts (1902); Meiggs, Henry;
Moneda Palace; Montt Álvarez,
Jorge; Nitrate Industry; Papudo,
Battle of; Pinto Garmendia, Aníbal;
Portales Palazuelos, Diego José
Pedro Víctor; Prats González,
Carlos; Rancagua, Battle of;
Recabarren Serrano, Luis Emilio;
Riesco Errázuriz, Germán; Ross
Santa María, Gustavo; Santa María
González, Domingo; Schneider,
René; Semana Roja; Tacna-Arica
Dispute; Tomic, Radomiro;
Vergara Echeverez, José Francisco;
Vicuña Mackenna, Benjamín;
Viña del Mar; War of the Pacific;
War of the Peru-Bolivia
Confederation; Wheelwright,
William; Williams Rebolledo,
Juan

GEORGE SCHADE
University of Texas at Austin
Cambaceres, Eugenio

ROBERT SCHEINA
Industrial College of the Armed
Forces
Baquedano, Manuel; Bignone,
Reynaldo; Buena Vista, Battle of,
Campos, Luis María; Cerdo Gordo,
Battle of; Chaco War; Colegio
Militar (Argentina); Galtieri,
Leopoldo Fortunato; Krieger
Vasena, Adalberto; Maipú, Battle
of; Merino Castro, José Toribio;
Ricchieri, Pablo; Rolón, Raimundo;
Thomson Porto Mariño, Manuel
Tomás; Videla, Jorge Rafael;
Viola, Roberto Eduardo; Water
Witch Incident; Wooster, Charles
Whiting

GUILLERMO SCHMIDHUBER
Centro de Estudios Literarios,
Universidad de Guadalajara
Azar, Héctor; Berman, Sabina;
Ibargüengoitia, Jorge; López,
Wilebaldo; Magaña, Sergio

KAI P. SCHOENHALS
Kenyon College
Báez, Buenaventura; Balaguer,
Joaquín; Bosch Gaviño, Juan;
Cabral, Manuel del; Dominican
Republic; Dominican Republic:
Dominican Revolutionary Party
(PRD); Dominican Revolt (1965);
Grenada; Henríquez Ureña, Max;
Heureaux, Ulises; New Jewel
Movement; Quisqueya; Samaná
Bay; San Domingo Improvement
Company; Santana, Pedro; Santo
Domingo; Tronscoso de la Concha,
Manuel de Jesús; Trujillo Molina,
Rafael Leónidas; Ureña de
Henríquez, Salomé

DIETER SCHONEBOHM
Universidad de la República Instituto
Goethe, Montevideo, Uruguay
Bordaberry, Juan María;
Campisteguy, Juan; Erro, Enrique;
Fernández Artucio, Hugo; Gómez,
Eugenio; Uruguay: National
Workers Convention

THOMAS SCHOONOVER
University of Southwestern Louisiana
Bidlack Treaty (Treaty of New
Granada, 1846); Bunau-Varilla,
Philippe Jean; Dollar Diplomacy;
Greytown (San Juan del Norte);
Hamburg-America Line; Hise-Selva
Treaty (1849); Imperialism; Keith,
Minor Cooper; Kosmos Line;
Manning, Thomas Courtland;
Pacific Mail Steamship Navigation
Company (PMSS); Romero, Matías

MONICA SCHULER
Wayne State University
Maroons (Cimarrónes)

KIRSTEN C. SCHULTZ
New York University
Rio de Janeiro: Province and State

JOHN F. SCHWALLER
University of Montana
Borja y Aragón, Francisco de;
Capellanía; Catholic Church: The

JOHN F. SCHWALLER
(cont.)
Colonial Period; Cofradía; Congregación; Consolidación, Law of; Diezmo; Dominicans; Fernández de Córdoba, Diego; Inquisition: Spanish America; Manrique de Zúñiga, Alvaro; Mercedarians; Patronato Real; Torres y Portugal, Fernando de; Velasco, Luis de; Velasco, Luis de ("the Younger")

ROSALIE SCHWARTZ
San Diego State University
Tourism

STUART B. SCHWARTZ
University of Minnesota–Twin Cities
Hurricanes

CARL E. SCHWARZ
Amparo, Writ of

REBECCA J. SCOTT
University of Michigan
Slavery: Abolition

DARIO SCUKA
Institute for International Affairs, Ltd.
Gasohol Industry

PATRICIA SEED
Rice University
Caste and Class Structure in Colonial Spanish America; Castizo; Compadrazgo; Hidalgo; Mestizo; Zambo

DANIEL J. SEGEL
Militias: Colonial Brazil

CATALINA SEGOVIA-CASE
University of San Diego
Abente y Lago, Victorino; Correa, Julio Myzkowsky; González, Juan Natalicio

PHILIPPE L. SEILER
Tulane University
Bonnet, Stede; Companies, Chartered; Filísola, Vicente; Louisiana Revolt of 1768; Nicuesa, Diego; Rigaud, André; Saintes, Battle of the; Santa Cruz y Espejo, Francisco Javier Eugenio de

MARTHA L. SEMPOWSKI
Rochester Museum and Science Center
Teotihuacán

STANLEY F. SHADLE
College Misericordia
Molina Enríquez, Andrés

DAVID M. K. SHEININ
Trent University
Naón, Rómulo S.; Pueyrredón, Honorio; Vandor, Augusto; Wool Industry

CARA SHELLY
Oakland University
Alagoas; Aracaju; Asiento; Brazilian Highlands; Brazilwood; Caatinga; Ceará; Fernando de Noronha; Fortaleza; Juazeiro do Norte; Maceió; Natal; Piauí; Recôncavo; Rio Grande do Norte; Sergipe; Sertão, Sertanejo; Teresina

WILLIAM L. SHERMAN
University of Nebraska–Lincoln
Audiencia de los Confines; Ávila, Pedro Arias de; Balboa, Vasco Núñez de; Bastidas, Rodrigo de; Columbus, Bartholomew; Columbus Diego (d. 1515); Columbus, Diego (d. 1526); Contreras Brothers; Roldán, Francisco

IZUMI SHIMADA
Southern Illinois University
Batán Grande; Sicán

CARL SHIRLEY
University of South Carolina
Cantón, Wiberto

ALEX SHOUMATOFF
Brasília; Costa, Lúcio

NICOLAS SHUMWAY
University of Texas at Austin
Rodríguez Monegal, Emir; Scalabrini Ortiz, Raúl

EDUARDO SILVA
Fundação Casa de Rui Barbosa, Rio de Janeiro
Bocaiúva, Quintino

MARIA BEATRIZ NIZZA DA SILVA
Universidade Portucalense Infante D. Henrique, Porto, Portugal
Academias; Cardim, Frei Fernão; Coimbra, University of; Debret, Jean-Baptiste; Diálogos das

MARIA BEATRIZ NIZZA DA SILVA
(cont.)
Grandezas do Brasil; Gandavo, Pero de Magalhães; Grandjean de Montigny, Auguste Henri Victor; João VI of Portugal; Pombaline Reforms; Portuguese in Latin America; Rocha Pita, Sebastião; Sá, Mem de; Salvador, Vicente do; Sousa, Gabriel Soares de; Sousa, Martim Afonso de

HAROLD DANA SIMS
University of Pittsburgh
Arenas Conspiracy; Mexico: Expulsion of the Spaniards

WILLIAM SKUBAN
University of California, Davis
Iglesias, Miguel; Tacna

RICHARD W. SLATTA
North Carolina State University
Asado; Banditry; Baquiano; Boleadoras; Bota de Potro; Ceibo; Chiripá; Churrasco; Cielito; Conquest of the Desert; Domador; Estancia; Facón; Frigoríficos; Fundo; Gaucho; Güemes, Martín; Hides Industry; Latifundia; Livestock; Mazorca; Meat Industry; Montonera; Ombú; Pampa; Pato; Payador; Quebrancho Colorado; Saladero; Vaquería; Vaquero; Yerba Maté

ANDREW SLUYTER
Pennsylvania State University
Veracruz (State)

RUSSELL SMITH
Washburn University
Campos, Roberto (de Oliveira); Delfim Neto, Antônio; Simonsen, Mário Henrique

WILLIAM J. SMOLE
University of Pittsburgh
Casiquiare Canal; Yanomami

SUSAN M. SOCOLOW
Emory University
Álzaga, Martín de; Azara, Félix de; Azcuénaga, Miguel de; Cevallos, Pedro Antonio de; Cisneros, Baltasar Hidalgo de; Elío, Francisco Javier; Garay, Juan de; Liniers y Bremond, Santiago de; Mendoza,

SUSAN M. SOCOLOW
(cont.)
Pedro de; Sánchez de Thompson, María; Sobremonte, Rafael de; Tejeda, Leonor de; Vértiz y Salcedo, Juan José de

ETEL SOLINGEN
University of California, Irvine
Nuclear Industry; Nuclebrás

SAÚL SOSNOWSKI
University of Maryland at College Park
Gerchunoff, Alberto; Jews; Rama, Angel; Roa Bastos, Augusto

DAVID SOWELL
Juniata College
Arango, Débora; Barrancabermeja; Buenaventura; Cauca River; Colombia: Since Independence; Colombia: Democratic Society of Artisans; Colombia: Union Society of Artisans; Eder, Santiago Martín; Gólgotas; Independent Republics (Colombia); Lleras, Lorenzo María; López, Ambrosio; Melo, José María; Samper Agudelo, Miguel; Siete de Marzo

HOBART A. SPALDING
Brooklyn College and Graduate School, City University of New York
Anarchism and Anarchosyndicalism; Labor Movements

D. M. SPEARS
Tulane University
American Atlantic and Pacific Ship Canal Company; Anguilla; Barbuda; Bermúdez Varela, Enrique; Cuba: Committees for the Defense of the Revolution (CDR); Nicaragua: Sandinista Defense Committees

JEREMY STAHL
University of Florida
Highways; Salt Trade: Río de la Plata

DIANE STANLEY
Centro de Investigaciones Regionales de Mesoamérica (CIRMA)
Boston Fruit Company; Puerto Barrios

E. JEFFREY STANN
American Association for the Advancement of Science
Larkin, Thomas; Porter, David; Vallejo, Mariano Guadalupe

CHARLES L. STANSIFER
University of Kansas
Squier, Ephraim George; Zelaya, José Santos

CYNTHIA STEELE
University of Washington
Agustín, José; Paso, Fernando del; Poniatowska, Elena

JUDITH GLUCK STEINBERG
Museum of American Folk Art
González, Beatriz

NANCY LEYS STEPAN
Columbia University
Chagas, Carlos Ribeiro Justiniano; Cruz, Oswaldo Gonçalves; Oswaldo Cruz Institute

IRWIN STERN
Columbia University
Almeida, José Américo de; Andrade, Carlos Drummond de; Chico Anísio; Gonzaga, Tomás Antônio; Guarnieri, Gianfrancesco; Magalhães, Domingos José Gonçalves de; Rodrigues, Nelson

D. F. STEVENS
Drexel University
Almonte, Juan Nepomuceno; Ampudia y Grimarest, Pedro de; Anaya, Pedro María de; Arista, Mariano; Arriaga, Ponciano; Buñuel, Luis; Cuevas, Mariano; Degollado, Santos; Díaz, Porfirio; García Salinas, Francisco; Gómez Farías, Valentín; González Ortega, Jesús; Gorostiza, Manuel Eduardo de; Gutiérrez Estrada, José María; Haro y Tamariz, Antonio de; Juárez, Benito; Lerdo de Tejada, Miguel; Lerdo de Tejada, Sebastián; Ley Iglesias; Ley Juárez; Ley Lerdo; Maldonado, Francisco Severo; Mejía, Tomás; Moderados (Mexico); Ocampo, Melchor; Otero, Mariano; Poinsett, Joel Roberts; Prieto, Guillermo; Puros; Ramírez, Ignacio; Rejón, Manuel Crescencio; Scott, Winfield; Zacatecas;

D. F. STEVENS
(cont.)
Zaragoza, Ignacio; Zarco, Francisco; Zuloaga, Félix María

O. CARLOS STOETZER
Fordham University
Krausismo

RICHARD J. STOLLER
Dickinson College
Barco Vargas, Virgilio; Berbeo, Juan Francisco; Betancur Cuartas, Belisario; Colombia: Constitution of 1863; Colombia: Political Parties: National Front; Colombia: Revolutionary Movements: Army of National Liberation (ELN), Army of Popular Liberation (EPL), M-19, Revolutionary Armed Forces of Colombia (FARC); Comunero Revolt (New Granada); Galán, Luis Carlos; Gamonalismo; Lleras Camargo, Alberto; Lleras Restrepo, Carlos; López Michelsen, Alfonso; Márquez, José Ignacio de; Murillo Toro, Manuel; Olaya Herrera, Enrique; Ospina Pérez, Mariano; Parra, Aquileo; Reyes, Rafael; Rojas Pinilla, Gustavo; San Gil; Santos, Eduardo; Socorro; Tunja; Valdéz, Juan; Violencia, La; War of the Supremes; War of the Thousand Days

K. LYNN STONER
Arizona State University
Cuba: Federation of Cuban Women (FMC); Espín de Castro, Vilma; Gender and Sexuality

KAREN E. STOTHERT
University of Texas at San Antonio
Guangala; Las Vegas; Puná Island

JOSEPH STRAUBHAAR
Brigham Young University
Chacrinha; Clair, Janete; Computer Industry; Marinho, Roberto; Radio and Television; Santos, Sílvio; Telenovelas; Xuxa

GEORGE B. STUART
National Geographic Society
Cacaxtla

MANUEL SUÁREZ-MIER
Banco de México
North American Free Trade Agreement (NAFTA)

CONTRIBUTORS

J. DAVID SUÁREZ-TORRES
Georgetown University
Isaacs, Jorge; Rivera, José Eustasio

JAIME SUCHLICKI
University of Miami
Batista y Zaldívar, Fulgencio; Chibás, Eduardo; Cuba: ABC Party; Cuba: Authentic Party (PA); Dorticós Torrado, Osvaldo

WILLIAM SUMMERHILL
University of California, Los Angeles
Alberto, João; Brazil: Advanced Institute of Brazilian Studies (ISEB); Brazil: National Students Union (UNE); Queremistas

ALLAN S. R. SUMNALL
Tulane University
Cuban American Sugar Company; Cuban Intervention in Africa; Gómez, José Miguel (d. 1921); Iglesias Pantin, Santiago; Jamaica; Menocal, Mario García; Rodríguez, Carlos Rafael; San Juan, Puerto Rico; Trinidad and Tobago; Vargas, José María

JOHN C. SUPER
West Virginia University
Alcoholic Beverages; Chincha Islands; Cuisines; Cuzco; Education: Nonformal; Humboldt Current; Nutrition; Querétaro (City); Querétaro (State); Quinine; Titicaca, Lake; Universities: The Modern Era

JOAN E. SUPPLEE
Baylor University
Wine Industry

JANE EDDY SWEZEY
Centro de Investigaciones Regionales de Mesoamérica (CIRMA)
Porras, Diego; Vásquez, Francisco de Asís

PETER A. SZOK
Tulane University
Bertrand, Francisco

LEWIS A. TAMBS
Arizona State University
Brazil: Escola Superior da Guerra (ESG); Brazilian Expeditionary Force (FEB); Castello Branco,

LEWIS A. TAMBS
(cont.)
Humberto de Alencar; Geisel, Ernesto; Lott, Henrique Batista Duffles Teixeira; Sorbonne Group

ARTURO TARACENA ARRIOLA
Universidad de Costa Rica
Batres Juarros, Luis; Batres Montúfar, José; Bedoya de Molina, Dolores; Montúfar Montes de Oca, Lorenzo

CHARLES TATUM
University of Arizona
Rius

BARBARA A. TENENBAUM
Library of Congress
Agiotista; Cumplido, Ignacio; Escandón, Antonio; Escandón, Manuel; Mexico 1810–1910; Montenegro y Nervo, Roberto; Payno y Flores, Manuel; Plan of Agua Prieta; Pronunciamiento; Rabassa, Emilio; Trotsky, Leon

JOHN JAY TePASKE
Duke University
Alcabalas; Bulas Cuadragesimales; Bulas de Santa Cruzada; Coinage (Colonial Spanish America); Composición; Contaduría; Fernández de Cabrera, Bobadilla, Cerda y Mendoza, Luis Gerónimo; Fernández de Castro Andrade y Portugal, Pedro Antonio; Gobernador; Juan y Santacilia, Jorge; Media Anata; Mendoza Caamaño y Sotomayor, José Antonio de; Mesada Eclesiástica; Montepíos; Mutis, José Celestino; Papel Sellado; Perricholi, La; Protomedicato; Real Hacienda; Toledo y Leyva, Pedro de; Tribunal de Cuentas; Ulloa, Antonio de

HEATHER THIESSEN
Tulane University
Belén Conspiracy; Cass, Lewis; Central American Defense Council (CONDECA); Closed Corporate Peasant Community (CCPC); Cortes of Cádiz; Cumaná; Duarte, Juan Pablo; Henríquez y Carvajal, Francisco; Ingenios; Jíbaro; Junta: Spanish America; Livingston Codes; Luque, Hernando de;

HEATHER THIESSEN
(cont.)
Molina Ureña, José Rafael; Montesinos, Antonio de; National Endowment for Democracy (NED); Nicaragua; Pastora Gómez, Edén; Peña Gómez, José Francisco; Puerto Rico: Popular Democratic Party (PPD); Sacasa, Juan Batista; Schick Gutiérrez, René; Somoza Debayle, Anastasio; Somoza Debayle, Luis; Somoza García, Anastasio; Spain: Constitution of 1812; State of Siege; Trinitaria, La; Vásquez, Horacio

JACK RAY THOMAS
Bowling Green State University
Arguedas, Alcides; Markham, Clements Robert; Palma, Ricardo; Pareja Diezcanseco, Alfredo; Riva Agüero y Osma, José de la; Romero, Emilio

GUY P. C. THOMSON
University of Warwick
Obraje; Textile Industry: Colonial

JOHN THORNTON
Millersville University
Africa, Portuguese; Cape Verde Islands; São Tomé

MARK THURNER
University of Florida
Atusparia Revolt

DALE W. TOMICH
State University of New York at Binghamton
Plantations

STEVEN TOPIK
University of California, Irvine
Banco de Brasil; Coffee, Valorization of (Brazil); Encilhamento

JUAN CARLOS TORCHIA ESTRADA
Organization of American States
Korn, Alejandro; Romero, Francisco; Romero, José Luis

JOSÉ DE TORRES WILSON
University of Pittsburgh
Álvarez Armellino, Gregorio Conrado; Amézaga, Juan José de; Arismendi, Rodney; Arroyo Asencio; Berreta, Tomás; Berro,

JOSÉ DE TORRES WILSON
(cont.)
Carlos; Blanco Acevedo, Eduardo; Boiso-Lanza Pact (1973); Caballeros Orientales; Cardoso, Felipe Santiago; Carpintería, Battle of; Changador; Cisplatine Congress; Congress of April 1813; Fernández Crespo, Daniel; Fernández y Medina, Benjamin; Flores, Venancio; Garro, José de; Gestido, Oscar Daniel; Grito de Asencio; Herrera y Obes, Julio; Ituzaingó, Battle of; Mora Otero, José Antonio; Orientales; Pérez Aguirre, Luis; Tajes, Máximo; Uruguay: Unity and Reform; Vaz Ferreira, Carlos; Williman, Claudio

SILVIO TORRES-SAILLANT
Dominican Studies Center, City College of New York
Gatón Arce, Freddy; Incháustegui Cabral Héctor; Rueda, Manuel

CAMILLA TOWNSEND
Colgate University
Cuenca; Soroche

MICHEL-ROLPH TROUILLOT
The Johns Hopkins University
Sam, Tirésias Augustin Simon; Tonton Macoutes

JAVIER URCID
Smithsonian Institution
Monte Albán

ROBERTO VALERO†
George Washington University
Arenas, Reinaldo; Arrufat, Antón; Benítez-Rojo, Antonio; Brull, Mariano; Cabrera Infante, Guillermo; Carpentier, Alejo; Casal, Julián del; Desnoes, Edmundo Pérez; Diego, Eliseo; Fernández Retamar, Roberto; Florit, Eugenio; Gómez de Avellaneda y Arteaga, Gertrudis; Labrador Ruiz, Enrique; Leante, César; Lezama Lima, José; Marinello, Juan; Padilla, Heberto; Piñera, Virgilio; Pita Rodríguez, Félix; Sarduy, Severo; Valdés, Gabriel de la Concepción; Valladares, Armando; Vitier, Cintio

MARK J. VAN AKEN
California State University, Hayward
Cordero Crespo, Luis; Flores, Juan José; García Moreno, Gabriel; Montalvo, Juan; Urbina, José María; Veintimilla, José Ignacio de

NANCY E. VAN DEUSEN
University of Illinois at Urbana-Champaign
Muckers' Rebellion

ERIC VAN YOUNG
University of California, San Diego
Ejidos; Garibay, Pedro; Mescala, Island of; Venegas de Saavedra, Francisco Javier; Villagrán, Julián and José María ("El Chito")

PAUL J. VANDERWOOD
San Diego State University
Messianic Movements: Spanish America; Rurales; Tomochic Rebellion; Urrea, Teresa

MARY KAY VAUGHAN
University of Illinois at Chicago
Antuñano, Estevan de; Barreda, Gabino; Casasola, Agustín; China Poblana; Científicos; Kahlo, Frida; Orozco, José Clemente; Sáenz, Moisés

HUGO VERANI
University of California, Davis
Pacheo, José Emilio

JOHN VERANO
Tulane University
Sipán

GARY M. VESSELS
Georgetown University
Ângelo, Ivan; Assunção, Leilah; Callado, Antônio; Fernandes, Millôr

CAROLYN E. VIEIRA
Campo Grande; Casaldáliga, Pedro; Cuiabá; Florianópolis; Iguaçú; Iguaçu Falls; Mato Grosso; Mato Grosso do Sul; Pantanal; Paraná-Paraguay River Basin; Santa Catarina; Xingu River

ROSÂNGELA MARIA VIEIRA
Howard University
Alencar, José Martiniano de; Coelho Neto, Henrique; Monteiro Lobato, José Bento; Pompéia, Raúl

JON S. VINCENT
University of Kansas
Lins do Rego, José

STUART F. VOSS
State University of New York at Plattsburgh
Apaches; Arizona; Cajeme; Calderón de la Barca, Fanny; Calles, Plutarco Elías; Cananea; Cañedo, Francisco; Corona, Ramón; Leyva Solano, Gabriel; Mazatlán; Obregón Salido, Álvaro; Plan of San Luis Potosí; Raousset-Boulbon, Gaston Raul de; Sinaloa; Torres, Luis Emeterio; Urrea, José de; Zúñiga, Ignacio

MARIA LUISE WAGNER
Georgetown University
Bolivia: Organizations: Federation of Bolivian University Students; Bolivia: Political Parties: Constitutionalist Party; Drugs and Drug Trade; Sayaña

JOHN WALDRON
University of California, Irvine
Urbina, Luis Gonzaga

KATHY WALDRON
Larrazábal Ugueto, Wolfgang

CHARLES F. WALKER
University of California, Davis
Chucuito; Del Prado, Jorge; Pumacahua Rebellion; Rumi Maqui Revolt; Salaverry, Felipe Santiago; Tristan, Flora; Vicos Project

JEANNE C. WALLACE
Rutgers, The State University of New Jersey, Camden
Argüelles, Hugo; Zepeda, Eraclio

RICHARD J. WALTER
Washington University
Argentina: Independent Socialist Party; Argentina: Socialist Party; Argentina: University Reform; Bravo, Mario; Buenos Aires; Dickmann, Adolfo; Dickmann, Enrique; Ghioldi, Américo; Ingenieros, José; Justo, Juan B.; Palacios, Alfredo L.

CONTRIBUTORS

PETER M. WARD
University of Texas at Austin
Cities and Urbanization; Mexico City; Netzahualcóyotl; Tepito

MAUREEN WARNER-LEWIS
University of the West Indies, Jamaica–Mona Campus
Yoruba

J. BENEDICT WARREN
University of Maryland
Tarascans

RICHARD WARREN
St. Joseph's University
Lépero; Quintana Roo, Andrés; Santa Anna, Antonio López de

MARK WASSERMAN
Rutgers, The State University of New Jersey
Creel, Enrique Clay; González, Abraham; Limantour, José Yves; Mexico: Mexican Revolution; Terrazas, Luis; Villa, Francisco "Pancho"

DAVID J. WEBER
Southern Methodist University
Alamo, Battle of the

STEPHEN WEBRE
Louisiana Tech University
D'Aubuisson, Roberto; Duarte Fuentes, José Napoleón; Dueñas, Francisco; El Salvador: Nationalist Democratic Organization (ORDEN); El Salvador: Political Parties: Farabundo Martí National Liberation Front (FMLN), National Conciliation Party (PCN); Football War; Guatemala, Audiencia of; Majano, Adolfo Arnoldo; Marroquín, Francisco; Rivera Carballo, Julio Adalberto

ROBERT S. WEDDLE
Cartography: The Spanish Borderlands; La Salle, René-Robert Cavelier, Sieur de

BARBARA WEINSTEIN
State University of New York at Stony Brook
Manaus; Simonsen, Roberto Cochrane

MARTIN WEINSTEIN
William Paterson College of New Jersey
Baldomir, Alfredo; Batlle Berres, Luis Conrado; Día, El; Ferreira Aldunate, Wilson; Herrera, Luis Alberto de; Lacalle Herrera, Luis Alberto; Medina, Hugo; Michelini, Zelmar; Nardone, Benito; Pacheco Areco, Jorge; Sanguinetti, Julio María; Terra, Gabriel; Uruguay: Colegiado; Uruguay: Constitutions; Uruguay: Medidas Prontas de Seguridad; Uruguay: Organizations: Autonomous Entities; Uruguay: Plebiscites; Uruguay: Political Parties: Anticolegialistas; Uruguay: Revolutionary Movements: National Liberation Movement (MLN–T)

W. MICHAEL WEIS
Illinois Wesleyan University
Brazil: Getúlio Vargas Foundation

CLIFF WELCH
Grand Valley State University
Beans; Brazil: Organizations: Agrarian Front (FA), Democratic Rural Union (UDR), Peasant Leagues, Superintendency of Agrarian Reform (SUPRA), Union of Farmers and Agricultural Laborers of Brazil (ULT); Extractive Reserves; Julião Arruda de Paula, Francisco; Noronha, Fernão de; Silva, Lindolfo; Soybeans; Wheat

JOHN H. WELCH
Lehman Brothers, Inc.
Brazil: National Bank for Economic Development (BNDE); Brazil: National Housing Bank (BNH); Inflation; Murtinho, Joaquim Duarte

ALLEN WELLS
Bowdoin College
Mérida; Molina Solís, Olegario

THOMAS L. WHIGHAM
University of Georgia
Acá Carayá Cavalry; Aceval, Benjamin; Acosta Ñu, Battle of; Aguirre, Juan Francisco de; Alonso, Mariano Roque; Arroyo Grande,

THOMAS L. WHIGHAM
(cont.)
Battle of; Ayala, Eligio; Ayala, José de la Cruz; Ayolas, Juan de; Barbero, Andrés; Bareiro, Cándido; Barrett, Rafael; Berges, José; Bermejo, Ildefonso; Bertoni, Moisés; Brizuela, Francisco; Caballero, Bernardino; Caballero, Pedro Juan; Centurión, Carlos R.; Centurión, Juan Crisóstomo; Cerro Corá, Battle of; Chaco Region; Chaves, Federico; Chaves, Francisco C.; Chaves, Julio César; Colmán, Narciso; Creydt, Oscar; Curupayty, Battle of; Decoud, Hector Francisco; Decoud, José Segundo; Díaz, José Eduvigis; Dobrizhoffer, Martín; Domínguez, Manuel; Duarte, Pedro; Escobar, Patricio; Estigarribia, Antonio de la Cruz; Estigarribia, José Félix; Falcón, José; Fariña Núñez, Eloy; Ferreira, Benigno; Garay, Blas; García, Aleixo; Gelly, Juan Andrés; Gill, Juan Bautista; Godoi, Juan Silvano; Guarani War; Guggiari, José Patricio; Hopkins, Edward Augustus; Humaitá; Immigration, Paraguay; Jovellanos, Salvador; Maíz, Fidel; Méndez Fleitas, Epifanio; Mompox de Zayas, Fernando; Mora, Fernando de la; Moreno, Fulgencio; Morínigo, Higínio; Nueva Burdeos, Colony of; O'Leary, Juan Emiliano; Pane, Ignacio Alberto; Paraguarí, Battle of; Paraguay: The Twentieth Century; Paraguay: Constitutions; Paraguay: Organizations: Asociación Paraguaya del Indígena, Confederación Paraguaya de Trabajadores (CPT); Paraguay: Political Parties: Liberal Party; Peña, Manuel Pedro de; Pérez Acosta, Juan Francisco; Rivarola, Cirilo Antonio; Robles, Wenceslao; Rodríguez, Andrés; Samudio, Juan A.; Schaerer, Eduardo; Sepp, Anton; Stefanich, Juan; Tacuarí, Battle of; Talavera, Natalício; Thompson, George; Trujillo, Manuel; Tuyutí, Battle of; Washburn, Charles Ames; Whytehead, William; Wisner von Morgenstern, Franz; Yataity Corá, Conference of; Ybycuí; Yegros, Fulgencio; Ynsfrán, Edgar L.

580

DAVID E. WHISNANT
University of North Carolina at Chapel Hill
Cardenal, Ernesto; Coronel Urtecho, José

JOSEPH W. WHITECOTTON
University of Oklahoma
Zapotecs

IÊDA SIQUEIRA WIARDA
Library of Congress
Bernardes, Artur da Silva; Campos, Francisco Luiz da Silva; Collor de Mello, Fernando Affonso; Dutra, Eurico Gaspar; Franco, Itamar; Maluf, Paulo Salim; Medeiros da Fonseca, Romy Martins; Mello, Zélia Maria Cardosa de; Mindlin, José E.; Neves, Tancredo de Almeida; Pena, Afonso A. M.; Salgado, Plinio; Sarney, José; Silva, Luis Inácio Lula da

ANN M. WIGHTMAN
Wesleyan University
Altiplano; Cueva Enríquez y Saavedra, Baltásar de la; Forasteros; Hurtado de Mendoza, Andrés; Mendoza y Luna, J. M. de; Navarra y Rocaful, Melchor de; Patria Chica; Portocarrero y Lasso de la Vega, Melchor; Repartimiento; Repartimiento de Mercancías; Sarmiento de Sotomayor, García; Yanaconas

ROBERT WILCOX
Northern Kentucky University
Cangaceiro; Cerrado; Garimpo; Gaúcho; Gold Rushes, Brazil; Jagunço; Vaqueiros

S. JEFFREY K. WILKERSON
Institute for Cultural Ecology of the Tropics
El Tajín; Huasteca, The; Lacandon Forest; Santa Luisa; Totonacs; Volador Dance

J. ROSS WILKINSON
Brazil: Economic Miracle (1968–1974); Casa da Suplicação; Costa e Silva, Artur da; Desembargadores; Figueiredo, Jackson de; Letrados; Luso-Brazilian; Mandu Ladino; Médici, Emílio Garrastazú; Ouvidores; Relações

W. MARVIN WILL
University of Tulsa
Caribbean Antilles; Caribbean Sea: Commonwealth States

ADRIANA WILLIAMS
Covarrubias, Miguel

DARYLE WILLIAMS
University of Maryland at College Park
Brás Pereira Gomes, Wenceslau; Brazil: New Republic; Brazil: Political Parties: Brazilian Democratic Movement (MDB), National Democratic Union of Brazil (UDN); Franco, Wellington Moreira; Gabeira, Fernando Nagle; Guimarães, Ulysses Silveira; Jaguaribe Gomes de Matos, Hélio; Luís Pereira de Sousa, Washington; Morais Barros, Prudente José de; Moreira da Costa Ribeiro, Delfim; Peçanha, Nilo Procópio; Pessoa, Epitácio da Silva; Pessoa Cavalcanti de Albuquerque, João; Positivist Church of Brazil; Weffort, Francisco Correia

RAYMOND LESLIE WILLIAMS
University of Colorado at Boulder
Caballero Calderón, Eduardo; Gaitán Durán, Jorge; Garmendia, Salvador; González León, Adriano; Mutis, Alvaro

LARMAN C. WILSON
The American University
Calvo Doctrine; Drago, Luis María; Duvalier, François; Duvalier, Jean-Claude; Espaillat, Ulises Francisco; Galíndez, Jesús de; Haiti: Constitutions; Law of the Sea; Luperón, Gregorio; Pan-American Conferences: Buenos Aires Conference (1936), Montevideo Conference (1933); Pascal-Trouillot, Ertha; Port-au-Prince; Rodríguez Demorizi, Emilio; Roy, Eugène; Santiago de los Caballeros; United Nations; Universidad Autónoma de Santo Domingo; Universidad Católica Madre y Maestra

JOHN J. WINBERRY
University of South Carolina
Acapulco; Baja California; Bajío; Balsas River; Coatzacoalcos River; Guadalajara; Mexico: Federal District; Mexico, Gulf of; Monterrey; Pánuco River; Papaloapan River; Paricutín; Xochimilco

WALTER R. T. WITSCHEY
Science Museum of Virginia and Virginia Commonwealth University
Abaj Takalik; Altar de Sacrificios; Bonampak; Chichén Itzá; Copán; El Mirador; Kaminaljuyú; Nuclear America; Quelepa; Quirigua; Tayasal; Tikal; Uaxactún

JOEL WOLFE
Williams College
Brazil: Organizations: Brazilian Labor Confederation (COB); Brazil: Political Parties: Communist Party (PCB), Labor Party (PTB), Workers Party (PT); Brazil: Revolutions: Communist Revolts of 1935; Factory Commissions, Brazil

JOSEPH R. WOLIN
Columbia University
Arden Quin, Carmelo; Fonseca, Gonzalo; Gego; Grupo Madí and Asociación Arte Concreto-Invención

STEPHANIE WOOD
University of Oregon
Anáhuac; Arriero; Chalma; Chinampas; Durán, Diego; Fundo Legal; Guanajuato; Macehualli; Mendoza, Antonio de; Motolinía, Toribio de; Naboría; Otomí; Quiroga, Vasco de; Relaciones Geográficas; Sahagún, Bernardino de; Tlaxcala; Zorita, Alonso de

LAURA L. WOODWARD
Centro de Investigaciones Regionales de Mesoamérica (CIRMA)
Lacandones; Lenca; Maximón; Pipiles

RALPH LEE WOODWARD, JR.
Tulane University
Alexander, Edward Porter; Ambrogi, Arturo; Arada, Battle of; Arce, Manuel José; Archila,

RALPH LEE WOODWARD, JR.
(cont.)

Andrés; Aristide, Jean-Bertrand; Aury, Louis-Michel; Ávila, Julio Enrique; Banana Industry; Barrios, Justo Rufino; Barrundia, José Francisco; Barrundia, Juan; Brañas Guerra, César; Brión, Luis; Brown, William; Callejas Romero, Rafael Leonardo; Campo, Rafael; Cañas, José María; Cañas, José Simeón; Carías Andino, Tiburcio; Carrera, José Rafael; Casáus y Torres, Ramón; Central America; Central America: Constitution of 1824; Ciudad Trujillo; Coatepeque, Battle of; Consulado; Creole; Cruz, Serapio; Cruz, Vicente; Dalton García, Roque; Dance of the Millions; El Salvador; Esquilaches; Estrada, José María (d. 1856); Estrada, Juan José; Euceda, Maximiliano; Fernández, Juan; Fernández (Hernández) de Córdoba, Francisco; Ferrera, Francisco; Finca; Gálvez, Bernardo de; Gálvez, Juan Manuel; Garay, Carlos; García Peláez, Francisco de Paula; Gavidia, Francisco Antonio; Gómez, Benigno; Gómez, José Miguel (d. 1805); Grito de Yara; Guadalupe, Convenio de; Guatemala; Guatemala: National Guatemalan Revolutionary Unity (URNG); Hernández (Fernández) de Córdoba, Francisco; Honduras: National Party (PNH); Irisarri y Larraín, Juan Bautista; Jefe Político; Juan Fernández Islands; López Vallecillos, Italo; Malespín, Francisco; Milla y Vidaurre, José; Montes de Oca, Confucio; Muñoz, José Trinidad; National War; Nicarao; Nufio, José Dolores; Paredes, Mariano; Pavón Aycinena, Manuel Francisco; Perera, Víctor;

RALPH LEE WOODWARD, JR.
(cont.)

Pérez Jiménez, Marcos; Piracy; Popenoe, Frederick Wilson; Porras, José Basilio; Portillo, Efraín; Providencia; Rinconcito, Treaty of (1838); Rivera Cabezas, Antonio; Rivera Paz, Mariano; Robles, Marcos Aurelio; Salazar Arrué, Salvador Efraín; San Andrés Island; Sandoval, José León; Serrano Elías, Jorge Antonio; Skinner, George Ure; Suazo Córdova, Roberto; Ten Years' War; Torres, Toribio; Velásquez, José Antonio; Vesco, Robert Lee; Viteri y Ungo, Jorge; Zelaya Sierra, Pablo; Zúñiga Figueroa, Carlos

GEORGE WOODYARD
University of Kansas

Basurto, Luis; Carballido, Emilio; Chocrón, Isaac; Díaz, Jorge; Dragún, Osvaldo; González de Eslava, Fernán; Solórzano, Carlos; Theater; Triana, José; Villegas, Oscar

THOMAS C. WRIGHT
University of Nevada, Las Vegas

Aguirre Cerda, Pedro; Allende Gossens, Salvador; Chile: The Twentieth Century; Chile: Sociedad Nacional de Agricultura (SNA); Letelier de Solar, Orlando

WINTHROP R. WRIGHT
University of Maryland at College Park

Blanco Fombona, Rufino; Caldera Rodríguez, Rafael; Castro, Cipriano; Ciudad Bolívar; Gallegos, Rómulo; Gómez, Juan Vicente; Guzmán, Antonio Leocadio; López Contreras, Eleázar; Maracaibo;

WINTHROP R. WRIGHT
(cont.)

Margarita; Marisol; Medina Angarita, Isaías; Monagas, José Gregorio; Monagas, José Tadeo; Orinoco River; Soublette, Carlos; Venezuela: Immigration; Venezuela: Armed Forces of National Liberation (FALN)

LAWRENCE A. YATES

Counterinsurgency

JORDAN M. YOUNG
Pace University

Brazil: Revolution of 1930

JAMES ZEIDLER
University of Illinois at Urbana-Champaign

Atacames; Bahía; Jama-Coaque; Manteño; Real Alto; Valdivia, Ecuador; Valdivia Culture

ANTONIO ZEPEDA

Music: Pre-Columbian Music of Mesoamerica

EDUARDO A. ZIMMERMAN
Universidad de San Andrés, Argentina

Argentina: Federation of Argentine Workers (FOA); Bunge, Alejandro; Bunge, Augusto; Ibarguren, Carlos; Matienzo, José Nicolás; Ramos Mejía, Ezequiel; Ramos Mejía, José María; Rivarola, Rodolfo; Wilde, Eduardo; Zeballos, Estanislao

ANN L. ZULAWSKI
Smith College

Aymara; Tiwanaku

CLARENCE ZUVEKAS, JR.
United States Agency for International Development

Agency for International Development (AID)

INDEX

Numbers in **boldface** refer to the main entry on the subject. Pages with illustrations, tables, or graphs are cited in *italics*.

A

Abad y Queipo, Manuel, **1:1a–b**
Abadía Méndez, Miguel, **1:1b–2b**; 2:208a
Abaj Takalik, **1:2a–b**, 194a; 3:553b
Abal Medina, Juan Manuel, 1:226b
Abalos, José de, **1:2b**, 88a; 2:237b
Abandoned children, 2:97a, 97b, 98b
    Brazilian death squads, 2:358a; 4:523b
Abascal y Souza, José Fernando, **1:2b–3a**; 2:101b; 4:363a
Abasolo, Mariano, **1:3a**, 6b; 4:55a
Abbad y Lasierra, Íñigo, **1:3a–b**
Abbeville, Claude d', 5:*281a*, *281b*
Abbottsville (Guatemala), **1:3b**
ABC countries, **1:3b–4a**
ABC Party (Cuba), 2:322b–323a, 328b, 329a; 3:484b
ABC Treaty of 1915, **1:3b**, 4a
Abela, Eduardo, 1:508b
Abente y Labo, Victorino, **1:4a**
Aberdeen Act (1845), 4:504b
Abertura (Brazil), **1:4a–b**, 443a; 2:611b; 3:46a, 69b, 426b
Abipón Indians, **1:4b–5a**; 2:389b; 3:266a
Abolition of slavery. *See* Slave trade, abolition of; Slavery: abolition
Abreu, Diego de, **1:5b**
Abreu, João Capistrano, 2:373b
Abril, Xavier, **1:5b–6a**
Abularach, Rodolfo, 1:210b
Acá Carayá Cavalry, **1:6a**
Academia de la Lengua y Cultura Guaraní, **1:6a**; 2:60b
Academia de San Carlos, **1:6b**, 133a, 200b, 202a; 2:175b–176a; 3:59b
Academia Literaria de Querétaro (1810), **1:6b–7a**, 59b; 2:393a; 4:38a, 246b
Academias, **1:7a**, 202a–b
Academy of Christian Humanism 3:222b
Academy of Letters. *See* Brazilian Academy of Letters
Acamapichtli, 1:256b
Ação Integralista Brasileira (AIB). *See* Integralist Action
Ação Popular (AP; Brazil). *See* Popular Action
Acapulco (Mexico), **1:7a–b**; 3:140b, 141a
    fortification, 2:605a
    Manila Galleon trade fairs, 1:7b; 3:507b–508a
Acaray River, **1:8a**

Acción Communal. *See* Community Action
Acción Democrática (AD; Venezuela). *See* Democratic Action
Acción Democrática Nacionalista (ADN). *See* Nationalist Democratic Action
Acción Nacional (Venezuela). *See* National Action
Acción Popular (AP). *See* Popular Action
Accounting systems
    Inca, 4:513a
    Spanish Empire, 2:256a–b; 4:541b, 542b–543a
Aceval, Benjamín, **1:8a**
Acevedo Díaz, Eduardo Inés, **1:8a–b**
Acevedo Hernández, Antonio, **1:8b**
Achá, José María, **1:9a**; 3:573a
Acheson, Dean, 1:404b
Achiote, 5:169b
Aconcagua, **1:9a–b**, 95b
Aconcagua River, 1:9b
Acordada, **1:9b–10a**; 2:298b–299a
Acordada, revolt of (1828), **1:10a**; 3:141a; 4:8b
Acosta, José de, **1:10a–b**
Acosta, José Julián, 1:3b
Acosta, Mariano, 1:67b
Acosta, Tomás, **1:10b**
Acosta García, Julio, **1:10b**
Acosta León, Ángel, **1:10b–11a**
Acosta Ñu, Battle of (1869), **1:11a**; 5:443b
Acre (Brazil), **1:11a–b**, 398a, 399b; 4:563a, 590a, 616a; 5:266b
Action for National Liberation (ALN; Brazil), 3:143a, 525a
ACU. *See* Agrupación Católuca Universitaria
Acuerdo, **1:11b**
Acuerdo Patriótico (AP). *See* Patriotic Agreement
Aculco, Battle of (1810), **1:60a**, 517a; 3:193b; 4:38a
Acuña, Cristóbal de, 2:523a
AD. *See* Democratic Action
Adams, Grantley, 1:288b; 5:454b
Adams, John Quincy, 1:11b, 12a; 4:97a, 194a
Adams–Onís Treaty (1819), **1:11b–12a**, 587b; 2:581b, 582a
Adán, Martín, 1:81b
Additional Act of 1834 (Brazil), **1:12a**, 460b; 2:194a
ADE. *See* Democratic Alliance
Adelantado, 1:12a–b
Adelantado of the South Sea, **1:12b**

Adem Chahín, José, **1:12b–13a**
Adem Chahín, Julián, **1:13a**
Admirable Campaign (1813), **1:13a**; 4:558a; 5:383a, 383b
Adonias Filho. *See* Aguiar, Adonias
Adoption laws, 2:97b
Adrian VI, Pope, 2:28b; 4:52b
Adultery, 2:300a; 3:532b
Advanced Institute of Brazilian Studies (ISEB), **1:443b–444a**
AFL–CIO. *See* American Federation of Labor–Congress of Industrial Organizations
Afrancesado, **1:13b**
Africa
    African–Brazilian return to, 1:15b–16a, 17a
    "Back to Africa" movement, 3:37a–b
    coffee production, 2:190b
    Cuban intervention in. *See* Cuban intervention in Africa
    Guiné or Guinea as terms for, 3:150b
    négritude, 4:171a–b
    slave trade, 5:122a–127a
    Spanish possessions, 5:168b–169a
    see also Arab–Latin American relations; Middle Easterners; *individual countries*
Africa, Portuguese, **1:13a–14b**, 15a; 4:451a–b, 452a
    Cape Verde Islands, 1:540a–b
    Henry the Navigator, 1:584a; 3:180b
    Madeira Islands, 3:486a–b
    map, 4:452a–b
    Minas, 4:56b–57a
    São Tomé, 5:70a–b
    see also Angola
African-Brazilian cultural and political organizations, **1:14b–15b**; 4:162b–163a
African-Brazilian emigration to Africa, **1:15b–16a**, 17a
African-Brazilian identity, 1:542a; 2:175b, 557b, 622a–623a; 3:474b
    Carnival, 1:569b
    color terminology. *See* African Brazilians: color terminology *below*
    Lusotropicalism, 2:623a; 4:521b–522a, 523a, 527a
    maculelê (warrior dance), 3:486a
    Minas, 4:56b–57a
    music, 4:143b–144b, 149a–b

F

L

M

O

Q

R

W

X, Y

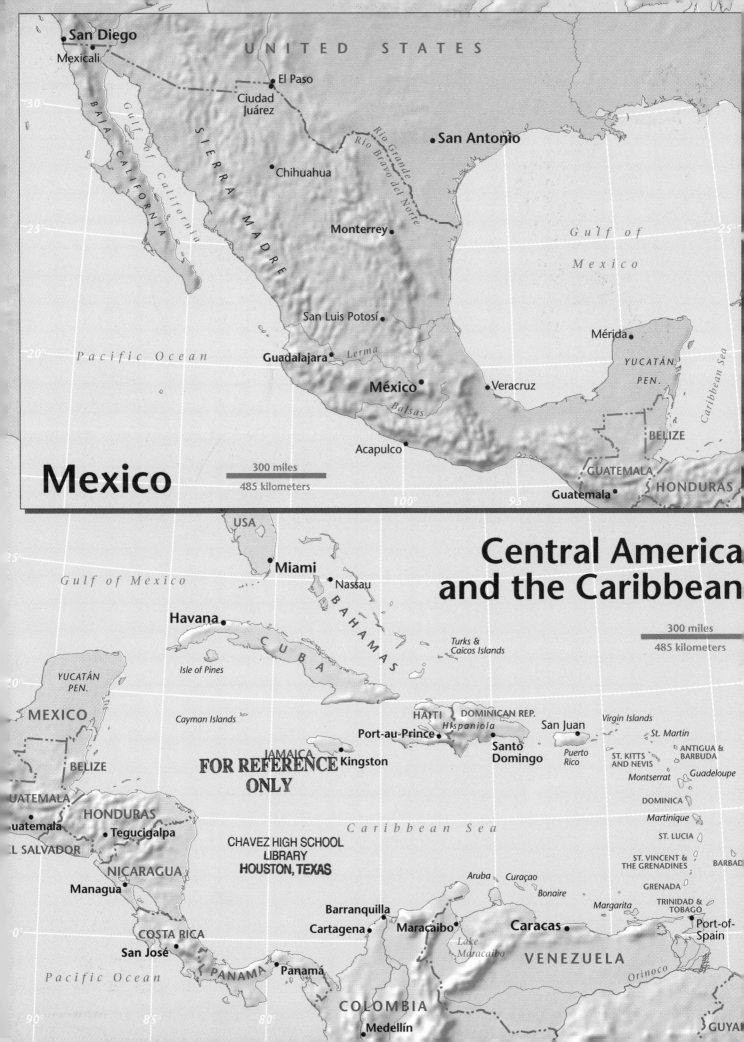

Mexico

San Diego
Mexicali
UNITED STATES
El Paso
Ciudad Juárez
San Antonio
Chihuahua
30
SIERRA MADRE
BAJA CALIFORNIA
Gulf of California
Rio Grande
Rio Bravo del Norte
Monterrey
Gulf of Mexico
25
25
San Luis Potosí
Mérida
YUCATÁN PEN.
Pacific Ocean
20
Guadalajara
Lerma
Caribbean Sea
México
Veracruz
Balsas
BELIZE
Acapulco
300 miles
GUATEMALA
485 kilometers
HONDURAS
Guatemala
100
95

Central America and the Caribbean

USA
Gulf of Mexico
Miami
25
Nassau
BAHAMAS
Havana
CUBA
300 miles
485 kilometers
Isle of Pines
Turks & Caicos Islands
YUCATÁN PEN.
20
Cayman Islands
DOMINICAN REP.
Virgin Islands
MEXICO
HAITI
San Juan
St. Martin
Hispaniola
ANTIGUA & BARBUDA
BELIZE
FOR REFERENCE
JAMAICA
Port-au-Prince
Santo Domingo
Puerto Rico
ST. KITTS AND NEVIS
UATEMALA
ONLY
Kingston
Montserrat
Guadeloupe
uatemala
DOMINICA
HONDURAS
Martinique
L SALVADOR
Tegucigalpa
Caribbean Sea
ST. LUCIA
CHAVEZ HIGH SCHOOL
LIBRARY
HOUSTON, TEXAS
ST. VINCENT & THE GRENADINES
NICARAGUA
BARBAD
Aruba
Curaçao
GRENADA
Managua
Bonaire
Margarita
TRINIDAD & TOBAGO
Barranquilla
Port-of-Spain
Cartagena
Maracaibo
Caracas
0
Lake Maracaibo
VENEZUELA
COSTA RICA
San José
PANAMA
Panamá
Orinoco
Pacific Ocean
COLOMBIA
GUY
90
85
80
Medellín